Alex Geisinger
acgeis@wm.edu
221-7747
office 207

Secured Credit:
A Systems Approach

Secured Credit:
A Systems Approach

Third Edition
Revised Article 9

Lynn M. LoPucki
Security Pacific Bank Professor of Law
UCLA Law School

Elizabeth Warren
Leo E. Gottlieb Professor of Law
Harvard University

ASPEN LAW & BUSINESS
A Division of Aspen Publishers, Inc.
Gaithersburg   New York

Permissions
Aspen Law & Business
1185 Avenue of the Americas
New York, NY 10036

Printed in the United States of America

2 3 4 5 6 7 8 9 0

Library of Congress Cataloging-in-Publication Data

LoPucki, Lynn M.
    Secured credit: a systems approach / Lynn M. LoPucki, Eliza-
    beth Warren. — 3rd ed.
        p.   cm.
    Includes index.
    ISBN 0-7355-1409-7
    1. Debtor and creditor — United States — Cases. 2. Security
    (Law) — United States — Cases. 3. Bankruptcy — United
    States — Cases. I. Warren, Elizabeth.   II. Title.
    KF1501.A7L65 2000
    346.7307'4 — dc21   00–035555

About Aspen Law & Business, Legal Education Division

With a dedication to preserving and strengthening the long-standing tradition of publishing excellence in legal education, Aspen Law & Business continues to provide the highest quality teaching and learning resources for today's law school community. Careful development, meticulous editing, and an unmatched responsiveness to the evolving needs of today's discerning educators combine in the creation of our outstanding casebooks, coursebooks, textbooks, and study aids.

Aspen Law & Business
A Division of Aspen Publishers, Inc.
A Wolters Kluwer Company
www.aspenpublishers.com

For Walter O. Weyrauch

— L.M.L.

For Amelia Warren and Alexander Warren, who remind me
forcefully to consider the student's perspective

— E.W.

Summary of Contents

Contents   *xiii*
Acknowledgments   *xxix*
Introduction   *xxxi*

Part One
The Creditor-Debtor Relationship   1

Chapter 1. Creditors' Remedies Under State Law   3

Assignment 1: Remedies of Unsecured Creditors Under
State Law   3

Assignment 2: Security and Foreclosure   24

Assignment 3: Repossession of Collateral   43

Assignment 4: Judicial Sale and Deficiency   68

Assignment 5: Article 9 Sale and Deficiency   91

Chapter 2. Creditors' Remedies In Bankruptcy   109

Assignment 6: Bankruptcy and the Automatic Stay   109

Assignment 7: The Treatment of Secured Creditors in
Bankruptcy   132

Chapter 3. Creation of Security Interests   155

Assignment 8: Formalities for Attachment   155

Assignment 9: What Collateral and Obligations Are
Covered?   177

Assignment 10: Proceeds, Products, and Other
Value-Tracing Concepts   192

Assignment 11: Tracing Collateral Value During
Bankruptcy   210

Assignment 12: The Legal Limits on What May Be
Collateral   225

Chapter 4. Default: The Gateway to Remedies   247

Assignment 13: Default, Acceleration, and Cure Under
State Law   247

Assignment 14:   Default, Acceleration, and Cure Under
                 Bankruptcy Law   271

Chapter 5.   The Prototypical Secured Transaction   285

Assignment 15:   The Prototypical Secured Transaction   285

Part Two
The Creditor-Third Party Relationship   309

Chapter 6.   Perfection   311

Assignment 16:   The Personal Property Filing Systems   311

Assignment 17:   Article 9 Financing Statements: The
                 Debtor's Name   333

Assignment 18:   Article 9 Financing Statements: Other
                 Information   354

Assignment 19:   Exceptions to the Article 9 Filing
                 Requirement   370

Assignment 20:   The Land and Fixtures Recording
                 Systems   390

Assignment 21:   Characterizing Collateral for the Purpose
                 of Perfection   408

Chapter 7.   Maintaining Perfection   427

Assignment 22:   Maintaining Perfection Through Lapse
                 and Bankruptcy   427

Assignment 23:   Maintaining Perfection Through Changes
                 of Name, Identity, and Use   444

Assignment 24:   Maintaining Perfection Through
                 Relocation of Collateral or Debtor   459

Assignment 25:   Maintaining Perfection in Certificate of
                 Title Systems   473

Chapter 8.   Priority   493

Assignment 26:   The Concept of Priority: State Law   493

Assignment 27:   The Concept of Priority: Bankruptcy Law   508

Chapter 9.   Competitions for Collateral   527

Assignment 28:   Lien Creditors Against Secured Creditors: The Basics   527

Assignment 29:   Lien Creditors Against Secured Creditors: Future Advances   536

Assignment 30:   Trustees in Bankruptcy Against Secured Creditors: The Strong Arm Clause   552

Assignment 31:   Trustees in Bankruptcy Against Secured Creditors: Preferences   575

Assignment 32:   Secured Creditors Against Secured Creditors: The Basics   589

Assignment 33:   Secured Creditors Against Secured Creditors: Land and Fixtures   608

Assignment 34:   Competitions Involving Cross-Collateralization and Marshaling Assets   631

Assignment 35:   Sellers Against Secured Creditors   652

Assignment 36:   Buyers Against Secured Creditors   673

Assignment 37:   Statutory Lien Creditors Against Secured Creditors   693

Assignment 38:   Competitions Involving Federal Tax Liens: The Basics   718

Assignment 39:   Competitions Involving Federal Tax Liens: Advanced Problems   736

Assignment 40:   Why Secured Credit?   754

Table of Cases   777
Table of Statutes   783
Index   789

Table of Contents

Acknowledgments   *xxix*
Introduction   *xxxi*

Part One
The Creditor-Debtor Relationship   1
Chapter 1.   Creditors' Remedies Under State Law   3

Assignment 1:   Remedies of Unsecured Creditors Under
                State Law   3

A.   Who Is an Unsecured Creditor?   3
B.   How Do Unsecured Creditors Compel Payment?   5
     Vitale v. Hotel California, Inc.   6
C.   Limitations on Compelling Payment   15
     Wisconsin Statutes Annotated   17
D.   Is the Law Serious About Collecting Unsecured
     Debts?   19
Problem Set 1   20

Assignment 2:   Security and Foreclosure   24

A.   The Nature of Security   24
     The Invention of Security: A Pseudo History   27
     Basile v. Erhal Holding Corp.   30
B.   Foreclosure Procedure   33
     1.   Judicial Foreclosure   33
          Wisconsin Statutes Annotated   36
     2.   Power of Sale Foreclosure   38
     3.   U.C.C. Foreclosure by Sale   39
Problem Set 2   39

Assignment 3:   Repossession of Collateral   43

A.   The Importance of Possession Pending Foreclosure   43
B.   The Right to Possession Pending Foreclosure —
     Real Property   44
     1.   The Debtor's Right to Possession During
          Foreclosure   44
     2.   Appointment of a Receiver   45
          California Code of Civil Procedure   46
          Illinois Mortgage Foreclosure Law   47
     3.   Assignments of Rents   47
C.   The Right to Possession Pending Foreclosure —
     Personal Property   47

	Del's Big Saver Foods, Inc. v. Carpenter Cook, Inc.	*49*
D.	The Article 9 Right to Self-Help Repossession	54
E.	The Limits of Self-Help: Breach of the Peace	55
	Salisbury Livestock Co. v. Colorado Central Credit Union	*55*
F.	Self-Help Against Accounts as Collateral	61
Problem Set 3		63

Assignment 4: Judicial Sale and Deficiency   68

A.	Strict Foreclosure	68
B.	Foreclosure Sale Procedure	69
C.	Problems with Foreclosure Sale Procedure	71
	Armstrong v. Csurilla	*71*
	1. Advertising	76
	Wisconsin Statutes Annotated	*77*
	Figure 1. Notice of Foreclosure Sales	78
	2. Inspection	77
	3. Title and Condition	79
	Marino v. United Bank of Illinois, N.A.	*79*
	4. Hostile Situation	82
	5. The Statutory Right to Redeem	83
D.	Antideficiency Statutes	84
	California Code of Civil Procedure	*84*
E.	Credit Bidding at Judicial Sales	85
F.	Judicial Sale Procedure: A Functional Analysis	87
Problem Set 4		88

Assignment 5: Article 9 Sale and Deficiency   91

A.	Strict Foreclosure Under Article 9	91
B.	Sale Procedure Under Article 9	92
C.	Problems with Article 9 Sale Procedure	94
	1. Failure to Sell the Collateral	94
	2. The Requirement of Notice of Sale	95
	Federal Deposit Insurance Corp. v. Lanier	*95*
	3. The Requirement of a Commercially Reasonable Sale	97
	Chavers v. Frazier	*98*
D.	Article 9 Sale Procedure: A Functional Analysis	104
Problem Set 5		105

Chapter 2. Creditors' Remedies in Bankruptcy   **109**

Assignment 6: Bankruptcy and the Automatic Stay   109

A.	The Federal Bankruptcy System	109
B.	Filing a Bankruptcy Case	111
C.	Stopping Creditors' Collection Activities	114

D.   Lifting the Stay for Secured Creditors   116
     In re Craddock-Terry Shoe Corp.   *120*
E.   Strategic Uses of Stay Litigation   127
Problem Set 6   129

Assignment 7:   The Treatment of Secured Creditors in
                Bankruptcy   132

A.   The Vocabulary of Bankruptcy Claims   132
B.   The Claims Process   134
C.   Calculating the Amount of an Unsecured Claim   137
D.   Payments on Unsecured Claims   139
E.   Calculating the Amount of a Secured Claim   140
F.   Selling the Collateral   142
G.   Who Pays the Expenses of Sale by the Trustee?   143
H.   Chapters 11 and 13 Reorganizations   145
I.   Valuing Future Payments   147
     In re E.I. Parks No. 1 Ltd. Partnership   *148*
Problem Set 7   152

Chapter 3.   Creation of Security Interests   **155**

Assignment 8:   Formalities for Attachment   155

A.   A Prototypical Secured Transaction   155
     Fisherman's Pier: A Prototypical Secured Transaction   *156*
B.   Formalities for Article 9 Security Interests   159
     1.   Possession or Writing   159
          In re Ace Lumber Supply, Inc.   *160*
     2.   Value Has Been Given   170
     3.   The Debtor Has Rights in the Collateral   171
C.   Formalities for Real Estate Mortgages   172
     Ohio Revised Code Ann.   *173*
Problem Set 8   173

Assignment 9:   What Collateral and Obligations Are
                Covered?   177

A.   Interpreting Security Agreements   177
     1.   Debtor Against Creditor   177
     2.   Creditor Against Third Party   178
     3.   Interpreting Descriptions of Collateral   178
B.   Sufficiency of Description: Article 9 Security
     Agreements   179
     In re Carlos   *179*
     In re Ziluck   *182*
C.   Describing After-Acquired Property   183
     Stoumbos v. Kilimnik   *185*

D.   Sufficiency of Description: Real Estate Mortgages   187
E.   What Obligations Are Secured?   188
Problem Set 9   189

Assignment 10:   Proceeds, Products, and Other
                  Value-Tracing Concepts   192

A.   Proceeds   193
    1.   Definition   193
    2.   Termination of Security Interest in the
        Collateral After Authorized Disposition   195
    3.   Continuation of Security Interest in the
        Collateral After Unauthorized Disposition   196
        Illinois Revised Statutes   *198*
        New York Penal Law   *198*
    4.   Limitations on the Secured Creditor's Ability
        to Trace Collateral   200
        In re Oriental Rug Warehouse Club, Inc.   *202*
B.   Other Value-Tracing Concepts   205
C.   Non-Value-Tracing Concepts   206
Problem Set 10   207

Assignment 11:   Tracing Collateral Value During
                  Bankruptcy   210

A.   Distinguishing Proceeds from After-Acquired
    Property   210
    In re Delbridge   *212*
    In re Hotel Sierra Vista Limited Partnership   *217*
B.   "Cash Collateral" in Bankruptcy   220
Problem Set 11   222

Assignment 12:   The Legal Limits on What May Be
                  Collateral   225

A.   Property That Cannot Be Collateral   226
    1.   Property of a Personal Nature   226
        Federal Trade Commission, Trade Regulation Rules   *228*
    2.   Future Income of Individuals   230
    3.   Pension Rights   231
        In re Green   *232*
        Assignment or Alienation of Plan Benefits   *235*
B.   Future Property as Collateral   236
C.   Valuable Nonproperty as Collateral   236
    In re SRJ Enterprises, Inc.   *238*
D.   Defeating the Limits on What May Be Collateral   243
Problem Set 12   244

Chapter 4.   Default: The Gateway to Remedies   247

Assignment 13:   Default, Acceleration, and Cure Under
                 State Law   247

A.   Default   247
     Standard Default Provisions   *248*
B.   When Is Payment Due?   249
     1.   Installment Loans   249
     2.   Single Payment Loans   250
     3.   Lines of Credit   250
C.   Acceleration and Cure   252
     1.   Acceleration   252
     2.   Limits on the Enforceability of Acceleration
          Clauses   253
          *J.R. Hale Contracting Co. v. United New Mexico
          Bank at Albuquerque*   *253*
     3.   The Debtor's Right to Cure   258
          Old Republic Insurance Co. v. Lee   *259*
          Reinstatement   *260*
D.   The Enforceability of Payment Terms   260
     *Kham & Nate's Shoes No. 2, Inc. v. First Bank of
     Whiting*   *262*
E.   Procedures After Default   265
     Figure 2.   The Spider Ad   266
Problem Set 13   267

Assignment 14:   Default, Acceleration, and Cure Under
                 Bankruptcy Law   271

A.   Stage 1: Protection of the Defaulting Debtor
     Pending Reorganization   271
B.   Stage 2: Reinstatement and Cure   272
     1.   Modification Distinguished from
          Reinstatement and Cure   273
     2.   Reinstatement and Cure Under Chapter 11   274
     3.   Reinstatement and Cure Under Chapter 13   275
     4.   When Is It Too Late to File Bankruptcy to
          Reinstate and Cure?   277
          In re DeSeno   *277*
C.   Binding Lenders in the Absence of a Fixed
     Schedule for Repayment   281
Problem Set 14   282

Chapter 5.   The Prototypical Secured Transaction   285

Assignment 15:   The Prototypical Secured Transaction   285

A.   The Parties   286
B.   Deutsche Approves Bonnie's Loan   286
C.   Deutsche and Bonnie's Document the Loan   287
     1.   Security Agreement and Statement of
          Transaction   287
          Figure 3.   Statement of Transaction   297
     2.   The Financing Statement   297
     3.   The Personal Guarantee   297
          Figure 4.   U.C.C.-1 Financing Statement   298
D.   Bonnie's Buys Some Boats   299
     1.   The Floorplan Agreement   299
     2.   The Buy   302
E.   Bonnie's Sells a Boat   303
F.   Monitoring the Existence of the Collateral   303
Problem Set 15   305

Part Two
The Creditor-Third Party Relationship   309

Chapter 6.   Perfection   311

Assignment 16:   The Personal Property Filing Systems   311

A.   Competition for the Secured Creditor's Collateral   311
B.   What Is Priority?   312
     Peerless Packing Co. v. Malone & Hyde, Inc.   *314*
C.   How Do Creditors Get Priority?   316
D.   The Theory of the Filing System   318
E.   The Multiplicity of Filing Systems   320
     *National Peregrine, Inc. v. Capitol Federal Savings and
         Loan Association of Denver (In re Peregrine
         Entertainment, Ltd.)*   *321*
F.   Methods and Costs of Searching   328
Problem Set 16   330

Assignment 17:   Article 9 Financing Statements: The
                 Debtor's Name   333

A.   The Components of a Filing System   333
     1.   Financing Statements   334
     2.   The Index   335
     3.   Search Systems   337
B.   Correct Names for Use on Financing Statements   339
     1.   Individual Names   339

2.	Corporate Names	340
3.	Partnership Names	341
4.	Trade Names	342
5.	The Entity Problem	343

C. Errors in the Debtors' Names on Financing
Statements 343
*Transamerica Commercial Finance Corp. v. General
Electric Capital Corp. (In re Wardcorp, Inc.)* 345
D. The Future of Article 9 Filing and Searching 350
Problem Set 17 351

Assignment 18: Article 9 Financing Statements: Other
Information 354

A. Introduction 354
B. Filing Office Errors in Acceptance or Rejection 355
1. Wrongly Accepted Filings 355
2. Wrongly Rejected Filings 356
C. Filer Errors in Properly Accepted Filings 356
1. Information Only Necessary to Qualify for
Filing 357
2. Required Information 358
*Deutsche Credit Corp. v. Lowe (In re The
Torgerson Co.)* 361
D. Authorization to File a Financing Statement 364
Problem Set 18 366

Assignment 19: Exceptions to the Article 9 Filing
Requirement 370

A. Collateral in the Possession of the Secured Party 370
1. The Possession-Gives-Notice Theory 370
2. What Is Possession? 372
3. Possession as a Means of Perfection 374
B. Collateral in the Control of the Secured Party 376
C. Purchase-Money Security Interests in Consumer
Goods 378
1. Purchase-Money Security Interest (PMSI) 378
2. Consumer Goods 379
*Gallatin National Bank v. Lockovich (In re
Lockovich)* 380
D. Security Interests Not Governed by Article 9 or
Another Filing Statute 383
*Bluxome Street Associates v. Fireman's Fund Insurance
Co.* 384
E. What Became of the Notice Requirement? 386

Problem Set 19   387

Assignment 20: The Land and Fixtures Recording
                Systems   390

A. Real Property Recording Systems   390
B. What Is Recorded?   392
C. Fixtures   393
    1. What Is a "Fixture"?   394
    2. How Does a Secured Creditor Perfect in
       Fixtures?   395
       In re Cliff's Ridge Skiing Corp.   *395*
    3. Perfecting in the Fixtures of a Transmitting
       Utility   402
D. Personal Property Interests in Real Property   402
Problem Set 20   403

Assignment 21: Characterizing Collateral for the
                Purpose of Perfection   408

A. Determining the Proper Place of Filing   408
    1. Personal Property Distinguished from Real
       Property   409
    2. Inventory Distinguished from Equipment   409
    3. Farm Products Distinguished from Inventory   410
B. Determining the Proper Method of Perfection   411
    1. Instruments Distinguished from General
       Intangibles   411
       In re Latin Investment Corp.   *411*
    2. True Leases Distinguished from Leases
       Intended as Security   415
    3. Realty Paper   416
    4. Chattel Paper and Instruments Distinguished
       from Accounts   416
C. Multiple Items of Collateral   418
    In re Leasing Consultants, Inc.   *418*
Problem Set 21   423

Chapter 7. Maintaining Perfection   427

Assignment 22: Maintaining Perfection Through Lapse
                and Bankruptcy   427

A. Removing Filings from the Public Record   427
    1. Satisfaction   427
       Arizona Revised Statutes Annotated   *429*

	Florida Statutes Annotated	429
	2. Release	430
	3. Article 9 Termination and Release	431
B.	"Self-Clearing" and Continuation in the Article 9 Filing System	432
	Worthen Bank & Trust Co., N.A. v. Hilyard Drilling Co., Inc. (In re Hilyard Drilling Co., Inc.)	435
C.	The Effect of Bankruptcy on Lapse and Continuation	440
	Problem Set 22	440

Assignment 23: Maintaining Perfection Through Changes of Name, Identity, and Use — 444

A.	Changes in the Debtor's Name	445
B.	Changes Affecting the Description of Collateral	448
C.	Exchange of the Collateral	449
	1. Barter Transactions	449
	National Bank of Alaska v. Erickson (In re Seaway Express Corp.)	452
	2. Collateral to Cash Proceeds to Noncash Proceeds	454
	3. Collateral to Cash Proceeds (No New Property)	455
	Problem Set 23	456

Assignment 24: Maintaining Perfection Through Relocation of Debtor or Collateral — 459

A.	State-based Filing in a National Economy	459
B.	Initial Perfection	460
	1. At the Location of the Debtor	460
	Lynn LoPucki, Why the Debtor's State of Incorporation Should Be the Proper Place for Article 9 Filing: A Systems Analysis	462
	2. At the Location of the Collateral	464
C.	Relocation of the Debtor	465
D.	Nation-based Filing in a World Economy	467
	Problem Set 24	470

Assignment 25: Maintaining Perfection in Certificate of Title Systems — 473

	Figure 5. Sample Certificate of Title (Front)	474
	New Zealand Law Commission, Motor Vehicle Title Systems in the USA and Canada	475
	Figure 6. Sample Certificate of Title (Back)	475

A.   Perfection in a Certificate of Title System   479
B.   Accessions and Removals   481
C.   In What State Should a Motor Vehicle Be Titled?   483
D.   Motor Vehicle Registration   485
         Figure 7.   Sample Vehicle Registration   485
E.   Maintaining Perfection on Interstate Movement of
     Collateral   486
     1.   How It Is Supposed to Work   486
     2.   Some Things That Can Go Wrong   486
     3.   Movement of Goods Between Non-Certificate
          and Certificate Jurisdictions   488
Problem Set 25   489

Chapter 8.   Priority   493

Assignment 26:   The Concept of Priority: State Law   493

A.   Priority in Foreclosure   493
B.   Reconciling Inconsistent Priorities   497
     Bank Leumi Trust Co. of New York v. Liggett   *498*
C.   The Right to Possession Between Lien Holders   501
     The Grocers Supply Co. v. Intercity Investment
          Properties, Inc.   *501*
     Frierson v. United Farm Agency, Inc.   *504*
Problem Set 26   505

Assignment 27:   The Concept of Priority: Bankruptcy
                     Law   508

A.   Bankruptcy Sale Procedure   509
     In re Oneida Lake Development, Inc.   *511*
B.   The Power to Grant Senior Liens   515
     In re 495 Central Park Avenue Corp.   *518*
C.   Protection of Subordinate Creditors   523
Problem Set 27   524

Chapter 9.   Competitions for Collateral   527

Assignment 28:   Lien Creditors Against Secured
                     Creditors: The Basics   527

A.   How Creditors Become "Lien Creditors"   527
     Judgment Liens on Real and Personal Property   528
B.   Priority Among Lien Creditors   529
     Priority Among Execution Creditors   529

C. Priority Between Lien Creditors and Secured
    Creditors   531
D. Purchase-Money Priority   532
Problem Set 28   533

Assignment 29: Lien Creditors Against Secured
                Creditors: Future Advances   536

A. Priority of Future Advances: Personal Property   536
B. Priority of Nonadvances: Personal Property   538
    Uni Imports, Inc. v. Exchange National
      Bank of Chicago   *538*
C. The Priority of Future Advances and Nonadvances:
    Real Property   543
    Shutze v. Credithrift of America, Inc.   *544*
Problem Set 29   549

Assignment 30: Trustees in Bankruptcy Against Secured
                Creditors: The Strong Arm Clause   552

A. The Purpose of Bankruptcy Code §544(a)   552
B. The Text of Bankruptcy Code §544(a)   553
    1. The Judicial Lien Creditor of §544(a)(1)   554
        Lien on Motor Vehicle for Damages   *554*
    2. The Creditor with an Execution Returned
        Unsatisfied   555
    3. The Bona Fide Purchaser of Real Property   556
        Midlantic National Bank v. Bridge   *556*
C. The Implementation of Bankruptcy Code §544(a)   562
    1. Exercise of Bankruptcy Code §544(a)
        Discretion by Chapter 7 Trustees   562
    2. Exercise of §544(a) Discretion by Chapter 11
        Debtors in Possession   564
D. Recognition of Grace Periods   565
E. Resistance to Bankruptcy Code §544(a)   566
    James J. White, Revising Article 9 to Reduce Wasteful
      Litigation   *566*
Problem Set 30   571

Assignment 31: Trustees in Bankruptcy Against Secured
                Creditors: Preferences   575

A. Priority Among Unsecured Creditors   575
    1. Priority Under State Law: A Review   575
    2. Priority Under Bankruptcy Law: A Review   576
    3. Reconciling the State and Bankruptcy Policies   576

B.   What Security Interests Can Be Avoided as
Preferential?   577
   1. Generally   577
   2. When Does the "Transfer" of a Security
      Interest Occur?   579
   3. The §547(c)(5) Exception for Accounts
      Receivable and Inventory   581
   4. Relation-Back Rules   582
      Fidelity Financial Services, Inc. v. Fink   583
C.   Strategic Implications of Preference Avoidance   584
Problem Set 31   586

Assignment 32: Secured Creditors Against Secured
                 Creditors: The Basics   589

A.   The Basic Rule: First to File or Perfect   589
B.   Priority of Future Advances   592
C.   Priority in After-Acquired Property   593
D.   Priority of Purchase-Money Security Interests   596
   1. Purchase-Money Security Interests Generally   596
   2. Purchase-Money Security Interests in
      Inventory   598
E.   Purchase-Money Priority in Proceeds   600
F.   Priority in Commingled Collateral   601
Problem Set 32   602

Assignment 33: Secured Creditors Against Secured
                 Creditors: Land and Fixtures   608

A.   Mortgage Against Mortgage   608
   1. Recording Statutes: The Rules of Priority   609
      Race Statute   610
      Notice Statute   610
      Notice-Race Statute   611
   2. Who Is a Good Faith Purchaser for Value?   612
   3. Purchase-Money Mortgages   612
      Purchase-Money Mortgages   613
      Purchase-Money Mortgages   613
B.   Judgment Liens Against Mortgages   613
C.   Construction Liens Against Construction
Mortgages   614
   1. A Prototypical Construction Financing
      Transaction   615
   2. Who Is Entitled to a Construction Lien?   618
      New York Lien Law   618
   3. Priority of Construction Liens   619
      In re Skyline Properties, Inc.   619

      Ketchum, Konkel, Barrett, Nickel & Austin v.
         Heritage Mountain Development Co.   620
  D.   The Priority of Article 9 Fixture Filings   624
     1.   Priority in Fixtures Incorporated During
        Construction   624
     2.   Priority in Fixtures Incorporated Without
        Construction   625
  E.   Priority in Real Property Based on Personal
     Property Filing   626
  Problem Set 33   627

Assignment 34:   Competitions Involving
                Cross-Collateralization and Marshaling
                Assets   631

  A.   Cross-Collateralization Provisions in Security
     Agreements   631
  B.   The Secured Creditor's Right to Choose Its Remedy   633
     1.   Debtor-Enforceable Limits on the Secured
        Creditor's Right to Choose Its Remedy   634
     2.   Release of Collateral   635
  C.   Marshaling Assets   637
     1.   Marshaling as a Limit on the Secured
        Creditor's Choice   638
        In re Robert E. Derecktor of Rhode
          Island, Inc.   638
     2.   Equitable Assignment as an Alternative to
        Marshaling   643
     3.   Can Unsecured Creditors Marshal?   644
     4.   Marshaling Against Property Owned by Third
        Parties   644
  D.   The Effect of Cross-Collateralization on
     Purchase-Money Status   646
  Problem Set 34   648

Assignment 35:   Sellers Against Secured Creditors   652

  A.   Limits of the After-Acquired Property Clause   652
     1.   Rules Governing Title to Personal Property   653
     2.   Rules Governing Security Interests in Personal
        Property   654
     3.   The Filing System as an Exception to *Nemo*
        Dat   656
  B.   Suppliers Against Inventory-Secured Lenders   656
  C.   Sellers' Weapons Against the After-Acquired
     Property Clause   658
     1.   Purchase-Money Security Interests   658

2.	Retention of Title	658
3.	Consignment	659
4.	The Seller's U.C.C. §2-702 Right of Reclamation	660
	In re M. Paolella & Sons, Inc.	*661*
5.	Express or Implied Agreement with the Secured Creditor	665
6.	Equitable Subordination	665
	In re M. Paolella & Sons, Inc.	*666*
7.	Unjust Enrichment	668
Problem Set 35		670

Assignment 36:   Buyers Against Secured Creditors   **673**

A.	Introduction	673
B.	Buyers of Real Property	674
C.	Buyers of Personal Property	675
	1. The Authorized Disposition Exception: U.C.C. §9-315(a)(1)	676
	2. The Buyer-in-the-Ordinary-Course Exception: U.C.C. §9-320(a)	677
	Daniel v. Bank of Hayward	*680*
	3. The Buyer-Not-in-the-Ordinary-Course Exception: U.C.C. §§9-323(d) and (e) and 9-317(b)	686
	4. The Consumer-to-Consumer-Sale Exception: U.C.C. §9-320(b)	687
Problem Set 36		688

Assignment 37:   Statutory Lien Creditors Against Secured Creditors   **693**

A.	The Variety of Statutory Liens in Personal Property	693
	1. Artisans' Liens	694
	Personal Property Lien for Services, Manufacture, or Repair	*694*
	2. Garage Keepers' Liens	695
	Garage Keeper's Lien	*695*
	3. Attorneys' Charging and Retaining Liens	696
	Attorneys' Lien	*696*
	4. Hospital Liens	697
	Hospital Lien	*697*
	5. Landlord's Lien	697
	Landlord's Lien	*698*
	6. Dry Cleaners' and Launderers' Liens	698
	Dry Cleaners' and Launderers' Lien	*698*
	7. Agricultural Liens	699

	Royal Foods Co. v. L.R. Holdings, Inc.	*701*
B.	Statutory Liens in Bankruptcy	704
C.	The Priority of Statutory Liens	706
	Myzer v. Emark Corporation	*708*
D.	Statutory Liens as a Challenge to the First-in-Time Rule	710
E.	Secured Creditor Responses to Statutory Lien Priority	711
	Cleanup and Removal of Hazardous Substances	713
	Problem Set 37	714
	Mechanic's Liens	715
	Wis. Stat. Ann. (West 1994)	*715*

Assignment 38: Competitions Involving Federal Tax Liens: The Basics — 718

A.	The Creation and Perfection of Federal Tax Liens	720
	1. Creation	720
	2. Perfection	720
	New York Lien Law	*721*
	3. Remedies for Enforcement	723
	4. Maintaining Perfection of a Tax Lien	723
	United States v. LMS Holding Co.	*724*
B.	Competitions Involving Federal Tax Liens	727
	1. Security Interest	728
	2. Purchaser	728
	Mayer-Dupree v. Internal Revenue Service	*729*
	3. Judgment Lien Creditor	730
	United States v. McDermott	*730*
	Problem Set 38	733

Assignment 39: Competitions Involving Federal Tax Liens: Advanced Problems — 736

A.	The Strange Metaphysics of the Internal Revenue Code	736
B.	Protection of Those Who Lend After the Tax Lien Is Filed	738
	1. The General Provision Regarding Future Advances, I.R.C. §6323(d)	738
	2. Commercial Transactions Financing Agreements	739
	3. Real Property Construction or Improvement Financing	741
	4. Obligatory Disbursement Agreements	741
	5. Statutory Liens	742
	6. Purchase-Money Security Interests	742

First Interstate Bank of Utah, N.A. v. Internal
    Revenue Service   743
C.   Nonadvances   749
Problem Set 39   750

Assignment 40:   Why Secured Credit?   754

    Thomas H. Jackson and Anthony Kronman, Secured
        Financing and Priorities Among Creditors   754
    Robert E. Scott, A Relational Theory of Secured
        Financing   755
    Steven L. Harris and Charles W. Mooney, Jr., A
        Property Based Theory of Security Interests: Taking
        Debtor's Choices Seriously   758
    Lynn M. LoPucki, The Unsecured Creditor's Bargain   760
    Donald B. Dowart, Memorandum: Priorities of
        Maritime Lien and Preferred Ship Mortgages   763
    Elizabeth Warren, Article 9 Set Aside for Unsecured
        Creditors   764
    Elizabeth Warren, Making Policy with Imperfect
        Information: The Article 9 Full Priority Debates   766
    Lynn LoPucki, The Death of Liability   768
    Ronald J. Mann, The Role of Secured Credit in
        Small-Business Lending   771
Problem Set 40   774

Table of Cases   777
Table of Statutes   783
Index   789

Acknowledgments

We are deeply indebted to Jay L. Westbrook, University of Texas School of Law, for his intellectual contributions to this book. Jay deserves credit as a codeveloper of what we here call "the systems approach." Many of our colleagues contributed to this edition by making comments on earlier editions. They include:

Allan Axelrod, Rutgers-Newark Center for Law & Justice
John D. Ayer, University of California at Davis Law School
Roger Bernhardt, Golden Gate University School of Law
Beth Buckley, SUNY Buffalo School of Law
Amy C. Bushaw, Lewis & Clark, Northwestern School of Law
Kathryn R. Heidt, University of Pittsburgh Law School
Margaret Howard, Vanderbilt University School of Law
Daniel L. Keating, Washington University
Charles Lincoln Knapp, New York University School of Law
Ronald J. Mann, Washington University School of Law
Bruce Markell, University of Nevada, Las Vegas School of Law
F. Stephen Knippenberg, University of Oklahoma Law Center
Steven L. Sepinuck, Gonzaga University School of Law
Paul M. Shupack, Yeshiva University, Cardozo School of Law
Catherine Tinker, University of South Dakota School of Law
G. Ray Warner, University of Missouri-Kansas City School of Law
William J. Woodard, Jr., Temple University School of Law

We are indebted to them, their students, and our own students at the University of Pennsylvania, Harvard, Washington University, the University of Wisconsin, Cornell, and UCLA both for improving the book and for putting up with our errors, both substantive and typographical.

Numerous people who work in the secured credit system were kind enough to answer our questions about the system and otherwise provide information. They include Naran U. Burchinow, General Counsel for Deutsche Financial Services; Carl Ernst, President of UCC Filing Guide, Inc.; Jerry Grossman, at Heller, Erhman, White, and McAuliffe, San Francisco, California; and Ed Hand, UCC Filing and Search Services, Tallahassee, Florida. Joanne Margherita and Karen Mathews served as desktop publishers and manuscript organizers. Barbara Smith, Bill Cobb, Cathy Stites, and Heather Suve provided valuable assistance with research. While our work was in progress, Peter Benvenutti's bankruptcy department at Heller, Ehrman, White, and McAuliffe sheltered one of the authors from the dark, bitter cold of two Wisconsin winters under the rubric "Scholar-in-Residence" and made available the resources of the firm.

The following have granted permission to reprint:

The New York Times for permission to reprint portions of David Margolick, At the Bar, A Maine Lobsterman's Justice, N.Y. Times, Sept. 17, 1993.

North American Syndicate for special permission to reprint the Dunagin's People cartoon that appears in Assignment 35.

The Virginia Law Review for permission to reprint portions of Lynn M. LoPucki, The Unsecured Creditor's Bargain, 80 Va. L. Rev. 1887 (1994).

James J. White and the Loyola of Los Angeles Law Review for permission to reprint portions of James J. White, Revising Article 9 to Reduce Wasteful Litigation, 26 Loy. L.A. L. Rev. 823 (1993).

Deutsche Financial Services for permission to reprint portions of the Security Agreement and Floorplan Agreement that appear in Assignment 15.

Matthew Bender & Co. for permission to reprint the security agreement default provisions from Howard Ruda, Asset-Based Financing.

Anthony B. Kronman, Fred B. Rothman & Company, and the Yale Law Journal for permission to reprint portions of Thomas H. Jackson and Anthony Kronman, Secured Financing and Priorities Among Creditors, 88 Yale L.J.1143, 1147-1148 (1979).

Robert E. Scott and the Columbia Law Review for permission to reprint portions of Robert E. Scott, A Relational Theory of Secured Financing, 86 Colum. L. Rev. 901, 904-911 (1986).

Steven L. Harris, Charles W. Mooney, Jr., Fred B. Rothman & Company and the Virginia Law Review for permission to reprint portions of Steven L. Harris and Charles W. Mooney, Jr., A Property-Based Theory of Security Interests: Taking Debtor's Choices Seriously, 80 Va. L. Rev. 2021, 2021-2023, 2047-2053 (1994).

Donald B. Dowart for permission to reprint Donald B. Dowart, Memorandum: Priorities of Maritime Lien and Preferred Ship Mortgages, Feb. 9, 1993.

The Cornell Law Review for permission to reprint Elizabeth Warren, Making Policy with Imperfect Information: The Article 9 Full Priority Debates, 81 Cornell L. Rev. 1373 (1997).

Fred B. Rothman & Company and the Yale Law Journal for permission to reprint portions of Lynn M. LoPucki, The Death of Liability, 106 Yale L.J. 1 (1996).

Ronald J. Mann and the Georgetown Law Journal for permission to reprint portions of Ronald J. Mann, The Role of Secured Credit in Small-Business Lending, 86 Geo. L.J. 1 (1997).

Introduction

In the movie Wall Street, the neophyte stock broker is concerned that what Gordon Gekko proposes is insider trading. Gekko responds, "Either you're *inside*, or you're *outside*." That is the way it is with credit. Either you're *secured* or you're *unsecured*.

You may already have some sense of the difference. We usually describe secured loans by reference to the collateral. We talk about home loans, car loans, inventory loans, and farm crop loans, to mention just a few. Among the credit extensions usually made on an unsecured basis are credit cards, bonds issued by large companies, student loans, loans between friends, trade credit (a business's purchase of inventory on credit), and the loans by commercial banks and insurance companies to the largest companies.

Credit is secured by property of the debtor when the debtor and creditor have so agreed in an authenticated record. We speak of the secured creditor as having a lien against the property that serves as collateral. The lien, we say, secures the repayment of the debt. The significance of being secured is that secured creditors have a special set of collection rights. Principal among those rights are remedies not available to unsecured creditors and an entitlement to priority over other creditors in the collateral. Priority is the right to have the value of the collateral applied to the creditor's own debt when the value of the collateral is insufficient to pay everyone.

Part One of this book deals with the relationship between the debtor and the secured creditor. In Assignment 1, we explain the remedies available to unsecured creditors against their debtors so the reader will have a baseline from which to understand the additional remedies available only to secured creditors. In Assignments 2 through 5, we explain the remedies available to secured creditors against their debtors in the absence of bankruptcy. In Assignments 6 and 7, we explain how filing bankruptcy immediately interrupts, and ultimately alters, those remedies.

In Assignment 8, we describe how easy it is for debtors to create security interests in their property. Provided that the creditor gives consideration sufficient to support a simple contract, its debtor need only authenticate a record containing a one-sentence grant to render that creditor secured. In Assignments 9 through 12, we explain the reach of the security interest thus created: what collateral it covers and what debts it secures. Assignments 13 and 14 deal with the secured creditor's right to "accelerate" payments of installment debt, such as home mortgages or car loans, when the debtor is in default. Part One concludes with Assignment 15, which describes a prototype secured transaction and gives the reader the opportunity to bring together what he or she has learned in that Part.

Part Two of this book deals with competitions between secured creditors and a variety of third parties who may claim the collateral. For their priority in the collateral to be effective against other competitors, the law requires that most kinds of secured creditors "perfect" their security interests by giving advanced public notice of their existence. Assignments 16 through 21 explain how secured creditors give that notice — principally through filings in public records systems, which their competitors are expected to search. In Assignments 22 through 25, we explain what the holder of a perfected security interest must do to maintain that perfection as circumstances change.

Assignments 26 and 27 explain what it means to have priority — first under state law and then in bankruptcy. Assignments 28 through 39 deal with the issue of who has priority over whom. In those chapters we discuss the various kinds of competitors for collateral, one at a time. Those competitors include other secured creditors, the holders of judicially created liens, bankruptcy trustees, persons who sold the collateral to the debtor, persons who have bought the collateral from the debtor, federal tax liens, and other kinds of statutory liens. Assignment 40 brings together all the reader has learned to evaluate the secured credit system.

We have written this book with an attitude. Legal education has a way of taking simple things and making them seem complex. In this book we have made every effort to do the opposite — to make this complex, technical subject as simple as possible. This is a course for second- and third-year students who have already mastered reading cases. The threshold intellectual task here is to read statutes; the ultimate intellectual task is to see how law functions together with other elements as a law-related system. Someone who masters that task can see law with new eyes — can see better who law helps, who it hurts, what implications it has for planning and transactional work, and how it can be manipulated, for better or for worse, to produce unexpected outcomes.

To make the whole more understandable, we have throughout this book regarded secured credit as a system, with subsystems that work together to accomplish the system's principal goal. That goal is to facilitate lending and, by so doing, to encourage desirable economic activity. To the extent the system succeeds in doing that, it does so in two ways. First, it provides secured creditors with a coercive remedy — repossession and resale of collateral — that does not destroy too much of the value of the collateral in the process. The existence of a coercive remedy encourages debtors to pay voluntarily. The principal subsystems that work to provide this remedy are:

1.   *Procedures for creating security interests.* This subsystem consists of laws, forms, and (dare we say it?) rituals used by debtors and their creditors to elevate claims to secured status.

2. *Rules authorizing self-help repossession.* U.C.C. §9-609 and case law construing its predecessor establish a right, available only to creditors with secured status, to repossess their collateral and procedures by which to attempt to do so.
3. *State remedies system.* State governments provide systems by which government officials declare foreclosures, repossess collateral, and sell the collateral for the benefit of secured creditors. All of this is accomplished pursuant to judicial orders and procedures established by law.
4. *Bankruptcy system.* The federal government provides a bankruptcy system in which bankruptcy judges, bankruptcy trustees, and other officials assure the preservation of secured creditors' collateral while the debtor continues to use the collateral or the bankruptcy officials liquidate it. While these bankruptcy procedures overlap and duplicate those of the older state remedies system, they are less rigid and therefore more effective than those of the state remedies system.

The second manner in which the secured credit system facilitates lending is by letting lenders know before they lend what priority or rights in the collateral they will have against third parties in the event of default. Here, three subsystems are at work:

1. *Public record systems.* Federal, state, and local governments operate thousands of public record systems in which various kinds of secured parties are required to "file" or "record" their interests in order to perfect them. The records in these systems are indexed by public officials and then searched by later lenders who seek to discover the security interests, if any, that will have priority over the ones they themselves plan to take.
2. *Rules of priority.* State law, including Article 9 of the Uniform Commercial Code and thousands of statutory lien laws, contains rules intended to govern priority in competitions between particular kinds of claimants to collateral. Federal law provides additional rules of priority in the areas of bankruptcy, taxation, patents, trademarks, copyrights, admiralty, and others. These rules are interpreted, reconciled, and enforced in state, federal, and bankruptcy courts and, of course, in private negotiations between competing parties.
3. *Bankruptcy lien avoidance.* Secured creditors frequently fail to satisfy the complex technical requirements to perfect their interests. These failures result in relatively few challenges by competing creditors. Bankruptcy law fills the gap by appointing a person to serve as "trustee" in the bankruptcy case, arming that person with the rights of a hypothetical aggrieved lien creditor and providing incentives for the trustee to challenge any security interest that may be vulnerable. From a systems perspective, the effect is to greatly increase the level of enforce-

ment and contentiousness in the system. That in turn increases the incentives of secured creditors to comply with the technicalities of the system, as well as providing jobs for lawyers.

As may already be apparent, the systems approach we employ in this book looks at more than just law. Law is one of many elements that together constitute the secured credit system. To teach the law without teaching the system in which it is embedded would deprive the law of much of its meaning and make it more difficult to understand. But to teach the whole system requires discussion of institutions, people, and things that are not "law." Among them are sheriffs, bankruptcy trustees, filing systems, security agreements, financing statements, search companies, Vehicle Identification Numbers, closing practices, collateral repurchase agreements, and a variety of other commercial and legal practices. Together with law from a variety of sources, these things constitute the system we know as secured credit and the subject of this course. If you would like to know more about the systems approach, see Lynn M. LoPucki, The Systems Approach to Law, 82 Cornell L. Rev. 469 (1997).

Much of the law governing secured transactions is in Article 9 of the Uniform Commercial Code. That article was revised in 1998 and the revisions become effective in July 2001. Former Article 9 will continue to affect the rights of some litigations for several years and problems of transition are inevitable. Many of the basic concepts are the same in both versions. We have chosen to focus almost exclusively on the revised text — and the enduring concepts that are now renumbered. While experienced Article 9 mavens will pride themselves in knowing the details of both versions, the new text will probably govern the vast bulk of Article 9 practice for this generation of law students while the largely repealed text of former Article 9 will slip quickly into the past.

We have tried to include in each assignment all of the information the reader will need to answer the problems at the end. The problems in a set are presented roughly in the order of their difficulty. (In a few of the assignments, there are more problems than necessary. Your teacher will instruct you which to omit.) The most difficult problems often are in a practice setting. Many of them are sufficiently complex to challenge even lawyers who have been practicing commercial law for many years. Our assumption is that each member of the class, working alone or perhaps with one or two others, will find a satisfying solution before class. In class, students will present and discuss a variety of solutions and then attempt to settle on one or two that seem best. The process is not unlike that followed in most large law firms when several lawyers get together for a brainstorming session to formulate strategy for a particular case. Like most lawyers, we think that such sessions are the most challenging plus the most intellectually exciting and fun parts of the practice of commercial law.

Secured Credit:
A Systems Approach

Part One
The Creditor-Debtor Relationship

Chapter 1. Creditors' Remedies Under State Law

Assignment 1: Remedies of Unsecured Creditors Under State Law

Much of law is about liability and the determination of damages. But winning a money judgment for a breach of contract, a tort, a treble damage antitrust suit, or some other kind of case may be only the beginning of the story. One of the authors of this book worked hard on the liability issues of her first trial (a rousing traffic accident in Rockaway, New Jersey, in 1977). At the conclusion of the trial, the judge awarded her client full damages — $147.58. The defendants left the courtroom sullen and unhappy. The plaintiffs were ebullient. But once the courtroom had cleared and smiles and handshakes had been exchanged all around, the client paused and, with evident embarrassment, asked the truly critical question: "Uh, how do we get paid?" A long, painful silence followed. The clever coauthor-to-be did not have the faintest idea. Because the defendants did not whip out their checkbooks and pay up, it seemed that still more legal process might be required.

Liability may be hotly disputed and parties may litigate vigorously, as they did in the Rockaway car accident. Or liability may be undisputed, as often happens when a debtor borrows money and is simply unable to repay. Either way, if no payment follows, the party owed an obligation may find that even after judgment has become "final," there can be a long and sometimes tortuous process ahead before any money changes hands.

A. Who Is an Unsecured Creditor?

The legal concepts of *debtor* and *creditor* apply to a wide variety of human relationships. Perhaps the archetypical debtor-creditor relationship is that between lender and borrower of money. But the legal categories of debtor and creditor are much broader. Anyone owed a legal obligation that can be reduced to a money judgment is a creditor of the party owing the obligation. At the instant one car slid into another, the victim of the Rockaway car accident became a creditor.

Similarly, the company with a valid patent infringement claim, the consumer with a defective product still covered by a warranty, and the child who is the beneficiary of a noncustodial parent's court-imposed support obligation are all creditors. The obligations owed to them can be reduced to money obligations of the company that infringed the patent, the manufacturer or seller of the goods, or the noncustodial parent. "Creditor" embraces a variety of characters in a multitude of circumstances.

Many debtor-creditor relationships are entered into voluntarily, as when a creditor has lent money to a debtor. But many are involuntary. The soon-to-be debtor's first contact with the soon-to-be creditor may be when their cars occupy the same space in the road simultaneously, as in the Rockaway dispute. The parties may meet on a happy occasion, such as the cash purchase of a product covered by a warranty; until the product fails they may not even realize that they are not just buyer and seller, but also debtor and creditor. Or a party may be wary about the credit relationship — a child's representative may be acutely aware of the depressing statistics on support compliance — but the party may have neither the knowledge nor the leverage to negotiate in advance for the collection rights the party will need for swift collection in the event of default.

Unless a creditor contracts with the debtor for secured status or is granted it by statute, the creditor will be *unsecured*. Unsecured creditors are the *general creditors* or *ordinary creditors* that populate state collection proceedings. They include creditors who contracted for unsecured status, but also creditors such as the tort victims mentioned above, who got their creditor status in circumstances that do not permit prior negotiations. They also include incautious creditors, uninformed creditors, and creditors who were unable for any number of reasons to negotiate for security. If the unsecured creditor has already obtained a court judgment to establish liability, the creditor is a *judgment creditor*, but the mere grant of a judgment does not alter the creditor's unsecured status.

In this assignment, we examine the legal remedies available to unsecured creditors. These remedies are available to all creditors. They are the minimum collection rights guaranteed to anyone owed an obligation that can be reduced to a money judgment. In later assignments, we will use these remedies as a baseline for comparing and understanding the enhanced collection rights that secured creditors enjoy.

Nothing in this discussion should be taken to imply that debtors seldom pay their unsecured debts. The likelihood of repayment is an empirical question. In fact, evidence suggests that voluntary payment occurs in the overwhelming majority of cases. Even when debtors would like to escape their obligations, their unsecured creditors typically can muster enough leverage, legal and otherwise, to compel repayment. But these are not the situations most attorneys are likely to encounter in their practices. Unsecured creditors bring lawyers into the tough cases, when the debtors are likely to be resistant and the availability of assets is uncertain. The lawyer who seeks to collect on a judgment on an unsecured debt usually faces a stiff challenge.

B.   How Do Unsecured Creditors Compel Payment?

The unsecured creditor's path to payment is narrow. Not only does the law provide procedures for the collection of unsecured debts, it regulates or bars outright many alternatives. Among the remedies prohibited to unsecured creditors is self-help seizure of the debtor's property. (This rule does not prevent the creditor from "setting off" a debt owing to its debtor against a debt owing from its debtor; it merely prohibits the creditor from seizing property for the purpose of creating such a setoff.) In most instances, a prohibited seizure of a debtor's property will constitute the tort of conversion.

> Conversion is the wrongful exercise of dominion and control over another's property in denial of or inconsistent with his rights. Exercising dominion or control over another's property in denial of, or inconsistent with, his rights constitutes conversion. A plaintiff need not establish that the defendant acted with a wrongful intent. The intent required is not necessarily a matter of conscious wrongdoing. It is rather an intent to exercise a dominion or control over the goods which is in fact inconsistent with the plaintiff's rights. Winkle Chevy-Olds-Pontiac, Inc. v. Condon, 830 S.W.2d 740 (Tex. App. 1992).

Additionally, the creditor that wrongfully takes possession of property of the debtor may be charged with larceny, even though the value of the property taken is less than the amount owed. Finally, though the creditor has the right to demand payment from the debtor, if it does so in an unreasonable manner, it may incur liability for wrongful collection practices. The creditor is entitled to coerce payment of the debt only through the judicial processes specified by the state. Although these processes are fundamentally the same in all states, there are differences in the language used to describe the processes and the myriad ways they are implemented. These differences in language and method of implementation can make it difficult to see the common system structure. In this assignment we try to focus on that common system structure.

The following case tells a story of a person who never intended a debtor-creditor relationship, but was pulled into one anyway. His attorney obtained a court judgment establishing liability, and then spent countless hours trying to collect. We include the case not so much for its exposition of the law governing execution, levy, and the obscure remedy of amercement as for what it shows about the system by which execution is made. The story of Jeffrey Israelow's tenacious pursuit of $6,317 conveys something of the enormity of the unsecured creditor's task when facing a recalcitrant debtor.

The basis for the plaintiff's judgment against Hotel California is only briefly alluded to in the first footnote of the case. The judgment was only a milestone on a long, torturous route to collection. The opinion is something of a catalog of the kinds of problems that plaintiffs encounter in attempting to collect an unsecured judgment against a recalcitrant debtor. What is extraordinary about this case is that the court did something about these problems and published a lengthy opinion. Read it for what it tells you about the collection process, not for legal or procedural detail.

Vitale v. Hotel California, Inc.

446 A.2d 880 (N.J. Super. Ct. Law 1982)

STALLER, J.S.C.

Plaintiff David J. Vitale, Jr. brings this motion pursuant to N.J.S.A. 40A:9-109 to amerce, that is, hold liable the Sheriff of Monmouth County, William Lanzaro, for failing to execute a writ based on a judgment against defendant Hotel California, Inc. (California). [A]mercement of a sheriff has not been the topic of any reported decision in New Jersey since 1907, and [has been] infrequently reported elsewhere.

The chronology of events is as follows: Vitale obtained a final judgment against California in the amount of $6,317 plus costs on August 12, 1980,[2] and thereafter learned that California held the liquor license for "The Fast Lane," a bar featuring "punk rock" entertainers, located in Asbury Park, New Jersey. A writ of execution issued on June 23, 1981, and on July 9 the sheriff received the writ along with a cover letter from plaintiff instructing him to levy upon all monies and personal property at The Fast Lane. A check to cover the sheriff's costs up to $50 was enclosed.

Then began plaintiff's travail with the sheriff's office which gave rise to this proceeding. On July 27 the office indicated to plaintiff's attorney, Jeffrey K. Israelow, that a levy was not possible since the bar was only open

2. In the principal action, Vitale v. Hotel California, Inc., plaintiff obtained a default judgment based on the claim that defendant's wrongful refusal to verify that plaintiff was an employee of defendant at the time of an automobile accident deprived him of income continuation benefits under an insurance policy.

late in the evening, from about 10 P.M. to 2 A.M., and that the writ would be returned unsatisfied. Israelow thereupon advised a deputy sheriff that it was absolutely necessary to proceed to make the levy during the open hours.

The writ was turned over to a deputy sheriff by the name of Guinan whom Israelow persuaded to make the levy during those late weekend hours when the bar was primarily open for business. Guinan reported to Israelow that he went to The Fast Lane on July 31 accompanied by an Asbury Park police officer, identified himself and announced his purpose at the door, but was denied access by the bar's "bouncers." Fearing that violence might ensue, the officers left. Lanzaro confirmed this fact by a letter dated August 3 in which he asked plaintiff for further instructions. Israelow then advised Guinan to make the levy and arrest anyone interfering with execution, pursuant to the officer's authority under N.J.S.A. 2C:29-1 and other statutes. After conferring with his superiors, Guinan informed Israelow that a court order would be necessary to gain access to the establishment!

On August 5, on plaintiff's application reciting the above facts, this court ordered that the sheriff be permitted access to the bar and to arrest anyone who interfered with the levy to show cause before the court why such person should not be held in contempt of the order. Israelow immediately transmitted the order to the sheriff's office with a letter instructing him to levy first upon the cash registers or places where cash might be held and advising him to be accompanied by sufficient personnel to effectuate any arrests that might become necessary. Guinan then went to the bar on the weekend of August 8, but found it had closed early. After speaking with Israelow he again went on the morning of August 15 and was able to seize $714 in cash and other personal property. Guinan reported back to Israelow the same day and indicated his belief that additional money may have been secreted before he was able to levy upon it. When Israelow instructed Guinan to make further levies until the writ was satisfied, Guinan told Israelow that he would have to consult with his superiors before taking further action.

On or about August 17 or 18 Israelow again instructed the sheriff's office to make successive levies and then was informed of the sheriff's contention that only one levy need be made under a writ of execution. After telephoning but not getting through to Lanzaro, Israelow forwarded him a letter dated August 19 and a mailgram dated August 20, again requesting the additional levies. Lanzaro telephoned Israelow on August 21 to tell him that he would consult with Monmouth County counsel, Richard O'Connor. Later that day, O'Connor's office informed Israelow that the sheriff had been instructed not to make any additional levies under the writ.

Unable to reach O'Connor by phone, Israelow wrote a letter to him on August 24 detailing plaintiff's position and threatening to seek amercement. On August 31 Israelow made good the threat by filing this motion.

The hearing on the motion was continued several times until January 14, 1982 at the request of the parties who were trying to negotiate a solution.

The sheriff does not refute the facts outlined above but maintains that it is unreasonable to expect any sheriff to command his officers or deputies "to go forth on an unknown number of occasions, at an unreasonable hour, to seize proceeds of an establishment such as The Fast Lane." The sheriff suggests that plaintiff pursue other "reasonable, speedy and inexpensive measures" to satisfy the judgment, to wit, obtaining an order that defendant pay over proceeds of the operation, conducting proceedings to determine where the proceeds are deposited, or locating and seizing other assets of the judgment debtor.

At argument Israelow described his difficulty in collecting the judgment debt: The personal property levied on at The Fast Lane on August 15 was verified as belonging to the landlord of the establishment. Upon this discovery, that California was only a tenant, a scheduled sheriff's sale was necessarily canceled. Also, California's president made a complete disclosure of assets after she had been arrested on an order to show cause, but an attempted levy on the corporate bank account was unsuccessful because the account was overdrawn.

The sheriff further argues that upon seizure of money on August 15 the writ of execution was satisfied and should have been returned, although no return in fact was ever made within the three-month life of the writ. Lack of proof as to loss or damage to plaintiff resulting from the sheriff's [in]action is also raised as a defense. Lastly, the sheriff maintains that the pleading is deficient for failure to specifically state the basis for amercement.

Three basic, interrelated questions are presented for resolution. (1) Are successive levies possible under one writ of execution? (2) When may a sheriff refuse to levy as instructed by a plaintiff, on the basis that the request is unreasonable or onerous? (3) Was the conduct of Sheriff Lanzaro and his office in respect to the writ such as to subject him to amercement?

Before proceeding to answer the first question, a brief overview of execution procedure would be beneficial. A successful plaintiff who obtains a judgment against a defendant may cause the personal property of the defendant/judgment debtor to be seized and sold and the proceeds applied to the judgment and costs by way of execution. N.J.S.A. 2A:17-1 et seq. To do this, plaintiff obtains a writ of execution, directing the sheriff to levy and make a return within three months after the date of issuance. A "return" is the physical return of the original writ to the court clerk, indorsed with the executing officer's brief description of what was done. In addition, the officer must file a verified statement of when and how much money was collected and the balance due on execution fees or costs. N.J.S.A. 2A:17-9.

The writ must be promptly executed upon and returned, N.J.S.A. 2A:15-20. The writ may be returned before the return date if, notwithstanding diligent effort, the judgment cannot be satisfied any further. Once an execution has been returned, a sheriff cannot thereafter levy upon any property under the writ. Nor can a valid levy be made after the return date. Successive executions upon the same judgment are possible. N.J.S.A. 2A:17-3. Therefore, if the first seizure is insufficient, the creditor may seek an alias writ for levy upon other goods. Thereafter, the plaintiff may seek an unlimited number of pluries writs until the judgment is satisfied. The proceeds from the sheriff's sale of seized property are paid to the judgment creditor or to his or her attorney or to the court clerk. N.J.S.A. 2A:18-26.

Throughout the process plaintiff plays a crucial role. Plaintiff must prepare the writ, have it entered by the court clerk and see that it is delivered to the sheriff with instructions as to levying. If necessary, plaintiff should conduct discovery to locate and identify property to be levied upon. Complementary to plaintiff's responsibility is the sheriff's duty to execute the writ according to the plaintiff's instructions. The writ is in the "exclusive control" of the judgment creditor; the sheriff must follow the creditor's reasonable instructions regarding the time and manner of making the levy and must abide by special instructions to make an immediate levy, if practicable, when plaintiff demonstrates necessity.

I.   SUCCESSIVE LEVIES UNDER ONE WRIT

The first question presented, whether successive levies can be made under one writ, can be simply answered — "yes." The rule that further levies under one writ are authorized under the same writ before the return day if the initial levy does not satisfy the judgment is recognized universally. . . .

If property levied on is not sufficient to satisfy the execution, a return should not be made without a showing that attempting another levy would be fruitless. That is not to say that Sheriff Lanzaro would have been exposed to potential liability for returning the writ after seizure of money on August 15. Arguably, the sheriff might have returned the execution with "so much money as collected." N.J.S.A. 2A:17-15. Had the sheriff in fact returned the writ, plaintiff could then have obtained an alias writ, expecting that more money would be available to be seized at The Fast Lane during the remainder of the summer season. Since an alias writ should not issue before the original execution is returned, and may be voidable as irregular if prematurely issued, plaintiff was under no duty to seek an alias writ, the original writ not having been returned.

[T]he clear import of the communications from Lanzaro's office to Israelow was that plaintiff's request was unreasonable despite plaintiff's preparedness to pay any associated costs or pursue any necessary procedural course. That objection remained, notwithstanding any possible issuance of an alias writ, which properly could not have issued while the original writ was outstanding.

II.   REASONABLENESS OF REQUESTED LEVIES

That brings us to the second question, whether the sheriff rightly refused to honor an unreasonable request to levy. The particular elements of the request perceived as unreasonable must be reviewed.

The sheriff first objects to the "unknown number of occasions" that he and his deputies would have to go forth to attempt levy in order to comply with plaintiff's wishes. Since there is no limit to the number of executions that conceivably could issue within 20 years after a judgment was entered until the judgment is satisfied, there is technically no limit to the number of times that a sheriff might be required to levy. Nevertheless, practical, operational considerations of a sheriff's office impose an obligation on a plaintiff not to request inordinately frequent and numerous levies. The one successful levy netting $714 on August 15 can be used to project what was entailed by plaintiff's request for levies on successive weekend nights. By extrapolation, the sheriff might have had to levy approximately nine times in the space of one to two months to comply with the request. This many potential levies under one judgment may be unusual but is not in itself unreasonable and, under the circumstances, was not excessive since the bar was basically a summer operation. Furthermore, seizure of several hundred dollars at one time demonstrated the effectiveness of this mode of levying.

There was also some indication of irregularity in the days of the week that The Fast Lane was open for business. Sheriff's counsel acknowledged, however, that local newspaper advertisements for The Fast Lane could be consulted to remove uncertainty about operating hours. Plaintiff, moreover, expressed a willingness to facilitate the execution in any way, and no doubt would have relayed the necessary information if lack thereof had actually presented a stumbling block.

The objection as to the unreasonably late hour requested for the levy cannot be sustained either. The bar was open for business, mostly on weekends, from about 10 P.M. to 2 A.M. Israelow directed that service be made during those hours; the sheriff avers that the instruction was to levy at 2 A.M. Whatever the precise instruction was, levy was to be made at some time during those nighttime hours — levying at 2 A.M. would probably find the cash registers near their fullest and thus minimize the number of additional levies required. Levy under a writ of execution may be made at any hour of the day; there is no issue of privacy here that might dictate otherwise. The Fast Lane's late open hours impelled the late-at-night levy. Like police officers, sheriffs and their deputies may be obliged to work at times of the day and week when the rest of the populace sleep or recreate.

The threat of violence engendered by attempting the levy goes to the heart of the sheriff's objections. "[T]o seize proceeds of an establishment *such as The Fast Lane*" uncamouflages what may have been the most unappetizing aspect of the requested levy. (Emphasis supplied.) On July 31, fearing violence, the deputy sheriff and an Asbury Park police officer allowed themselves to be turned away by bouncers at the door. At that juncture, at the sheriff's instigation and upon plaintiff's application, this court ordered, under what it considered as its inherent powers, that anyone interfering with the execution be arrested and brought before the court to show good cause. Armed with the order, the sheriff successfully levied on August 15. Nevertheless, the refusal to make further levies implies that a conscious decision may have been made to risk amercement rather than further confrontations at the bar.

When is physical force appropriate in making a levy? The general rule is that:

> [an] officer may force an entry into any enclosure except the dwelling house of the judgment debtor in order to levy a fieri facias on the debtor's goods and even in the case of the debtor's home, when the officer is once inside, he may break open inner doors or trunks to come at the goods. . . .

[A]ccording to Lanzaro's recital, on July 31 The Fast Lane bouncers did in fact obstruct the officer from "performing an official function by means of intimidation," N.J.S.A. 2C:29-1, giving the officers probable cause to arrest them. Their resistance to the lawful process might have been a basis for criminal conviction. Although the officers did not believe themselves to be in a position to use physical force, they apparently did not summon back-up help to effectuate the levy or make arrests incidental thereto.

Are sheriffs' deputies to be faulted for not using physical force in a nonemergency situation? The nature of law is to physically force people, if need be, to do things or refrain from doing things that they would be free to do or not do in the "natural state"; the hope is that the benefit to society will more than compensate for the loss of individual freedom. Sheriff's officers act as the physical extension of the power of the court, and thus, of the law and the will of the people. Necessarily, then, the privilege of such civil service occasionally demands risking bodily harm to oneself. Only in this way will the lawless be kept from becoming the de facto law makers. Philosophy aside, the record is barren of facts showing any imminent harm to the sheriff's officers on July 31 other than the vague averment that attempting to carry out the levy may have triggered a violent reaction. I find this unembellished defense insufficient to justify not making the levy.

III. AMERCEMENT

Consequently, by concluding that the sheriff failed to abide by plaintiff's proper requests to levy, I reach the question of amercement.

By proceeding in amercement, a judgment creditor may hold a sheriff liable for failing to properly execute against a judgment debtor.

If a sheriff or acting sheriff fails to perform any duty imposed upon him by law in respect to writs of execution resulting in loss or damage to the judgment creditor, he shall be subject to amercement in the amount of such loss and damage to and for the use of the judgment creditor. Such amercement may be made by the court having jurisdiction of the judgment and proceedings for the enforcement thereof in an action or proceeding for amercement or in the nature of an amercement brought for the purpose. The court may proceed in a summary manner or otherwise. The delinquent sheriff or acting sheriff shall also be subject to attachment or punishment for contempt. . . .

Amercement has been defined as "a pecuniary penalty in the nature of a fine, imposed upon a person for some fault or misconduct, he being 'in mercy' for his offense," Black's Law Dictionary 107 (4th ed. 1957), and is derived from the Anglo-French "amercier." Webster's Third New International Dictionary 68 (1971). Traditionally, "amercement" has been used to describe a fine imposed on officers of the court for failing to turn over money or, more particularly, for a sheriff's neglect to levy upon or turn over proceeds of an execution. . . .

Whether or not statutory interpretation favors a liberalized remedy, plaintiff still bears the burden of proof on this motion. Since a public officer such as a sheriff is presumed to have acted properly, plaintiff must clearly establish some default of duty. . . .

The sheriff suggests that plaintiff should have pursued other more reasonable means to satisfy the judgment but points to no failure of plaintiff to satisfy any statutory prerequisites to the requested levies. By comparison, had plaintiff sought to execute against real property, he would have had to first attempt, in good faith, to locate personal property of the debtor and levy upon it. N.J.S.A. 2A:17-1. Discovery proceedings to ascertain personal assets should be conducted before real estate is levied upon. In Spiegel, Inc. v. Taylor, 148 N.J. Super, 79, 84 (Cty. D. Ct. 1977), plaintiff sought an order to allow a constable to enter the debtors' homes for the purpose of making an inventory and levy. The court, referring to the First Amendment right of privacy, citing Griswold v. Connecticut, 381 U.S. 479 (1968), was unwilling to permit "fishing expeditions" which could frighten the inhabitants of the home and possibly endanger the constable where less drastic means such as discovery proceedings or an investigation would suffice.

Plaintiff Vitale has done all that was necessary with respect to the execution herein. . . . The money in The Fast Lane cash registers was subject to levy, N.J.S.A. 2A:17-15, and plaintiff could properly ask the sheriff to enter the bar to seize it. In light of the plaintiff's persistent efforts to negotiate a solution with both the sheriff and judgment debtor, and the unsuccessful levy on the bank account after discovery was conducted of the debtor-corporation's president, the demand upon the sheriff appears all the more reasonable.

The final issue is whether plaintiff has demonstrated a loss. Plaintiff must show that the officer's conduct has deprived him of a "substantial benefit to which he was entitled" under the writ, that but for the officer's conduct, he would have received such benefit through the execution. Plaintiff is not bound to prove the value of the property subject to levy because "[i]t would be highly inconvenient and unjust to require an innocent plaintiff to prove the value of the goods which had been in the sheriff's power but which, through his neglect, may have been eloigned beyond the reach of plaintiff's investigation." White v. Rockafellar, 45 N.J.L. 299 (Sup. Ct. 1833). Based on the findings that the execution was in the hands of the sheriff on July 9, 1981 and that only one levy was actually made on August 15 although the bar was open most weekend nights through the summer and is now closed for the winter, I conclude that plaintiff was denied the benefit of the writ and that the consequential loss amounts to the judgment debt of $6,317 less any amounts heretofore collected. The speculation that The Fast Lane will operate again this summer is not cognizable in mitigation of the amercement but would suggest that the sheriff pursue whatever civil remedy may be available against the judgment debtor for indemnification.

The difficult, distasteful aspects of executing writs demand that sheriffs be dealt with fairly, with an eye to the practicalities of their job. My reluctance to amerce a sheriff beset with such unpleasant tasks is only overcome by the convincing proof that Sheriff Lanzaro owed and breached a duty to plaintiff to make the successive levies as requested. In short, by invoking the remedy of amercement, I choose to satisfy plaintiff's debt where the sheriff has not.

In describing its ruling as a choice to "satisfy" plaintiff's debt, the court exaggerates only slightly. The sheriff will almost certainly write a check to Mr. Vitale. (If you have considered the possibility that the sheriff might not do so, you already have caught the spirit of our subject.) If the sheriff chooses to return to The Fast Lane, the next time it will be to collect for the sheriff's own account.

Vitale shows the highly technical nature of the legal process for collection of a judgment. The steps may be many. At any one of them, the judgment creditor may make a mistake or be frustrated by the mistakes of others. Even the creditor who makes no mistakes, encounters no legal anomalies, and enjoys the full cooperation of officials, may find the path difficult. Mr. Vitale was an employee at The Fast Lane before he became its creditor. He may have known its legal structure (a corporation named Hotel California, Inc. doing business under the trade name "The Fast Lane") and probably had some idea what assets the corporation had. Many creditors will start with far less information.

Even the information known to Mr. Vitale proved inadequate at several points. Recall that earlier in Mr. Vitale's collection efforts, California's president had been arrested on an order to show cause. She was apparently released only after she had made a complete disclosure of assets, including the existence of a bank account. But before Mr. Vitale could get the sheriff to levy on the bank account, the debtor evidently withdrew the money. Also recall that Vitale levied on the personal property in The Fast Lane, probably assuming the property (tables, chairs, and sound equipment) belonged to the judgment debtor. Vitale began the steps necessary to schedule a sheriff's sale, only to discover that the property belonged to the landlord. If the landlord and the judgment debtor were corporate cousins, kissing cousins, or some other kin or conspirators, Vitale *may* have had legal grounds to challenge the separate ownership. But that challenge itself would have increased the expense of collection and perhaps also slowed collection. Notice also that the court's opinion mentions earlier collection attempts only incidentally to the decision at hand; Vitale may have made other efforts to collect this debt. Moreover, note that while The Fast Lane was no ordinary business, it at least had a regular trade in a stable location and generated hard cash on a daily basis. Had the debtor been mobile or able to hide its assets the plaintiff's task might have been much harder.

The *Vitale* case illustrates the power of the judgment creditor ultimately to coerce payment. In *Vitale*, the coercion was through the remedy of levy under writ of execution. Other remedies are available as well. For example, if a third party is in possession of property of the debtor or owes money to the debtor, the creditor can cause the sheriff to serve a writ of garnishment on the third party. The effect of the writ is to require the third party to pay the judgment creditor rather than the debtor. Garnishment and other remedies of unsecured creditors are covered in more detail in the debtor-creditor course.

One side note on the *Vitale* case: We find ourselves speculating on how many attorney hours (and consequent fees) went into this little collection story to net $6,317. Law is not free — a point that may be driven home with more force in collection law than almost anywhere else.

C.   Limitations on Compelling Payment

Vitale also illustrates a number of procedural and practical limitations on the exercise of the judgment creditor's power. For example, the court notes the obligation of the judgment creditor to use discovery to locate assets, which serves as a reminder both of the creditor's right to demand information (backed up by the threat of civil contempt charges and jail) and that the sheriff will only act on clear directions about what to get and where to get it. The sheriff says, in effect, "Figure it out and tell me; then I'll get on out there and do something." The risk of error is even greater than is apparent from the court's opinion in *Vitale*. If the property seized turns out to be that of a third party, the judgment creditor may be liable for any damages caused to the third party. Worse yet, the wrongful exercise of dominion and control over the property of another constitutes the tort of conversion. The third party can refuse to accept return of the property and instead recover its value from the judgment creditor. Even if the judgment creditor is willing to take the risk of a wrongful execution, the *Vitale* court points out creditors have no right to conduct "fishing expeditions" simply by showing up at the debtor's place of business with a cooperative law enforcement officer.

While a judgment creditor has the right to obtain information about the judgment debtor's assets through discovery, the process can be long and painful. The judgment creditor must find the judgment debtor and force him or her to sit for examination. The judgment debtor may be less than forthcoming in discovery. Debtors may not keep their assets in predictable forms. As a result, questions about assets must be carefully framed. Any attorney more than a few years in practice can tell stories about carefully caged answers and tiny verbal loopholes that permitted determined debtors to continue to conceal their assets without crossing the line to criminal fraud or provable perjury. Our favorite story is of a defendant who was asked about cash assets in his bank account (none), his stock market accounts (none), his home (none), his car (none), his office (none), and so on. After the plaintiff had given up on discovering cash, the defendant revealed to a friend that he sat through the entire deposition with more than $10,000 in cash in his pocket. While we can think of a number of ways to frame the question to reveal that fact, we note that the attorney conducting the deposition was a good attorney who was not quite as careful as the defendant — an observation that worries us every time we enter a deposition.

Even if the judgment creditor discovers the location of the assets, the assets may not remain stationary. The debtor compelled to reveal their location may move them before the judgment creditor can get the sheriff to respond. Recall that the money in The Fast Lane's checking account disappeared just one step ahead of the sheriff. Debtors who plan a little more in advance can transfer title to others, move assets out of the jurisdiction, or consume them. All states have adopted laws authorizing the courts to void debtors' "fraudulent transfers" in actions brought by creditors. The study of these laws is beyond the scope of this book. For now it is enough to know that use of these laws is expensive and the laws themselves are relatively ineffective. If, for example, a debtor sells its property to a bona fide purchaser for value and disperses the proceeds in numerous transactions, that value is probably beyond the creditors' reach.

A creditor who has filed suit against the debtor to collect an unsecured debt may be eligible for a "provisional remedy" even before obtaining a judgment. If, for example, the debtor is fraudulently disposing of its property during the lawsuit, the creditor may have the right to an immediate "attachment" of whatever property the debtor still has. But access to this remedy is sharply limited by the constitutional requirements of due process and, in most states, by statutory prerequisites to issuance of a prejudgment writ of attachment.

When debtors refuse to answer questions during discovery, they can be subject to contempt sanctions. If they lie, they can be charged with perjury. But, in fact, few creditors consider it worth it to pursue these remedies and many prosecutors are reluctant to employ them against debtors anyway.

To employ any of the remedies discussed here, creditors typically face many of the information and control problems previously discussed. And the practical problems of finding the debtor or the debtor's property can be overwhelming. When the debtor disappears and the creditor discovers that the assets it has been chasing were the subject of a wire transfer of money to a corporation in the Bahamas, that is probably the end of the game.

Even if the debtor does not deliberately attempt to defeat the creditor's collection effort, the creditor's task may be complex. The creditor may obtain a judgment and begin enforcement procedures only to discover that the debtor has moved to another state. Because a money judgment can be enforced only in the state where rendered, the creditor must establish the judgment in the destination state before invoking the enforcement procedures of that state. If the debtor moves out of the United States, the creditor's task may be even more difficult.

Until the sheriff arrives to levy on a debtor's assets, the debtor can continue to transact business. Without violating any law, the debtor may lose the assets in business operations, exchange them for other assets of reasonably equivalent value, or apply them to the payment of other bona fide debts. It is not fraudulent for a debtor to pay one of its creditors, even if the effect is to leave nothing for others, so long as the debtor does not make the payment for the purpose of defrauding the others. Such a payment is referred to as a *preference.* Absent the filing of a bankruptcy case, once such a payment is made, it is irreversible.

Exemption statutes may provide yet another impediment to collection of the judgment debt. These statutes, which exist in all 50 states, prevent the sheriff from seizing certain property under a writ of execution. The property is said to be *exempt* from the remedies available to unsecured creditors.

The content of the statutes vary from state to state, but many of the recurring themes are present in the Wisconsin statutes that follow.

Wisconsin Statutes Annotated

(West 1994)

§815.18   PROPERTY EXEMPT FROM EXECUTION

(1) This section shall be construed to secure its full benefit to debtors and to advance the humane purpose of preserving to debtors and their dependents the means of obtaining a livelihood, the enjoyment of property necessary to sustain life and the opportunity to avoid becoming public charges.

(2) In this section:

(c) "Debtor" means an individual. "Debtor" does not include an association, corporation, partnership, cooperative or political body. . . .

(e) "Depository account" means [an] account maintained with a bank, credit union, insurance company, savings bank, . . . or like organization.

(f) "Equipment" means goods used or bought for use primarily in a business, including farming and a profession. . . .

(h) "Exempt" means free from any lien obtained by judicial proceedings and is not liable to seizure or sale on execution or on any provisional or final process issued from any court, or any proceedings in aid of court process. . . .

(3) The debtor's interest in or right to receive the following property is exempt. . . .

(a) *Provisions for burial.* Cemetery lots, aboveground burial facilities, burial monuments, tombstones, coffins or other articles for the burial of the dead owned by the debtor and intended for the burial of the debtor or the debtor's family.

(b) *Business and farm property.* Equipment, inventory, farm products and professional books used in the business of the debtor or the business of a dependent of the debtor, not to exceed $7,500 in aggregate value. . . .

(d) *Consumer goods*. Household goods and furnishings, wearing apparel, keepsakes, jewelry and other articles of personal adornment, appliances, books, musical instruments, firearms, sporting goods, animals or other tangible personal property held primarily for the personal, family or household use of the debtor or a dependent of the debtor, not to exceed $5,000 in aggregate value. . . .

(g) *Motor vehicles*. Motor vehicles not to exceed $1,200 in aggregate value. Any unused amount of the aggregate value from paragraph (d) may be added to this exemption to increase the aggregate exempt value of motor vehicles under this paragraph.

(h) *Net income*. Seventy-five percent of the debtor's net income for each one week pay period. The benefits of this exemption are limited to the extent reasonably necessary for the support of the debtor and the debtor's dependents, but to not less than 30 times the greater of the state or federal minimum wage. . . .

(k) *Depository accounts*. Depository accounts in the aggregate value of $1,000. . . .

(6)(a) A debtor shall affirmatively claim an exemption or select specific property in which to claim an exemption. The debtor may make the claim at the time of seizure of property or within a reasonable time after the seizure, but shall make the claim prior to the disposition of the property by sale or by court order. . . . The debtor or a person acting on the debtor's behalf shall make any required affirmative claim, either orally or in writing, to the creditor, the creditor's attorney or the officer seeking to impose a lien by court action upon the property in which the exemption is claimed. A debtor waives his or her exemption rights by failing to follow the procedure under this paragraph. A contractual waiver of exemption rights by any debtor before judgment on the claim is void. . . .

(9) In the case of property that is partially exempt, the debtor or any person acting on the debtor's behalf is entitled to claim the exempt portion of property. The exempt portion claimed shall be set apart for the debtor . . . and the nonexempt portion shall be subject to a creditor's claim. If partially exempt property is indivisible, the property may be sold and the exempt value of the property paid to the debtor. . . .

(12) No property otherwise exempt may be claimed as exempt in any proceeding brought by any person to recover the whole or part of the purchase price of the property or against the claim or interest of a holder of a security interest . . . mortgage or any consensual or statutory lien.

§815.20 HOMESTEAD EXEMPTION DEFINITION

(1) An exempt homestead as defined in §990.01(14) selected by a resident owner and occupied by him or her shall be exempt from execu-

tion, from the lien of every judgment and from liability for the debts of the owner to the amount of $40,000, except mortgages, laborers', mechanics' and purchase money liens and taxes and except as otherwise provided.

§990.01

(14) "Exempt homestead" means the dwelling, including a building, condominium, mobile home, house trailer or cooperative, and so much of the land surrounding it as is reasonably necessary for its use as a home, but not less than 0.25 acre, if available, and not exceeding 40 acres, within the limitation as to value under §815.20. . . .

A few states recognize homestead exemptions without dollar limitation, with the result that houses and the surrounding real estate worth millions of dollars can qualify. Some recognize no homestead exemption at all. Most, like Wisconsin, recognize a homestead exemption, but impose a dollar limit.

Both state and federal law protect debtors' wages. Federal statutes provide that a minimum of 75 percent of debtors' earnings from personal services will generally be exempt in all states. 15 U.S.C.A. §1671. Some states exempt a greater percentage of earnings from personal services, and a few, including Florida (for the head of a household only), Texas, and Pennsylvania, exempt all earnings from personal services. State and federal laws exempt most pensions and retirement accounts.

In short, exemption laws prevent creditors from taking many of the most valuable and easy-to-locate assets that debtors own. Such laws also protect individual debtors, in part by keeping households intact and preventing some debtors from becoming charges of the state. The course on debtors' and creditors' rights examines exemption laws in more detail.

D. Is the Law Serious About Collecting Unsecured Debts?

The law governing the enforcement of unsecured legal obligations affects a wide spectrum of rights. In contract law, tort law, antitrust law, and a long list of other areas, rights and liabilities are enforced only through the imposition of civil liability in the form of unsecured money judgments. Yet, as we have seen in this assignment, the mechanisms for the enforcement of civil judgments for money damages are not always effective.

Legal mechanisms are available for the enforcement of obligations that the law takes seriously. Courts can order those subject to their jurisdiction to meet their legal obligations and imprison them if they refuse to comply. The law authorizes courts to do so in regard to many obligations, including the obligation to pay alimony or child support, the obligation to respect the property of others by not trespassing or stealing, and the obligation to perform under a contract to sell real property. But they do not include judgments for personal injuries, the wages of working people, or the breaches of most kinds of contracts. The availability of effective remedies to enforce particular rights reflects to some degree the relative values society places on those rights. Whether enforcement of a particular right is civil or criminal, monetary or equitable, summary or with great delay, is an important measure of the right itself. It is not surprising to observe that criminal remedies are reserved for violation of rights we hold more dear than mere money obligations. It may be somewhat more surprising, however, to discover that some civil creditors have collection rights superior to those of others. Thus, the study of the mechanisms for the enforcement of debt, both unsecured and secured, can provide insight into the social values reflected in law.

Problem Set 1

1.1.   A year ago, the local Fun Furniture Outlet was having a liquidation sale. Lisa Charney wanted to buy some redwood lawn furniture but didn't have the cash. Her friend and neighbor, Jeffrey Reed, lent $1,000 to Lisa. Jeff and Lisa were good friends, and Lisa said she would pay him back in a couple of months. When she did not, Jeff's reminders became increasingly acrimonious. Now Lisa and Jeff haven't spoken for two months, and she still hasn't paid anything.

Jeff is a journeyman electrician whose union has legal insurance entitling Jeff to four hours of consultation a year with your firm. Jeff came in today, showed you Lisa's signed "I.O.U." for the loan, and asked if he could just go over and take the lawn furniture Lisa had purchased with his money. The furniture is out in the backyard, and he says it looks really nice. Jeff is sure it is worth less than the amount Lisa owes him, but he says he'd be satisfied if he got it. What do you tell him?

1.2.   The following debt collection story appeared in David Margolick's *New York Times* column, "At the Bar":

Jonesport, Me. . . .

Earlier this summer Bert S. Look, whose family has been catching crustaceans out of this sleepy fishing village on the eastern end of the Maine coast since 1910, was the picture of frustration. For months, he has since explained, a local seafood wholesaler named John Kostandin had owed him nearly $30,000, and he was powerless to make him pay. The usual legal remedies, he believed, were worthless.

"I could have gone through nine million district attorneys and nine million lawyers and I wouldn't have gotten anything," Mr. Look said. "I was willing to try anything nonviolent." So, in the best tradition of Maine lobstermen, who cut the lines on the traps of their disreputable competitors, he resorted to self-help. Actually, he had one helper: a self-styled professional prankster known only as "Deep Homard." (Homard is French for lobster.)

In June, Homard, posing as a friend of [horror novelist Stephen King], called Mr. Kostandin. He said that the novelist, who lives nearby in Bangor, needed three-and-a-half tons of lobsters for his annual lobster bake. Of course, the lobsters would end up with Mr. Look rather than Mr. King; at slightly more than $4 a pound, they would neatly cover Mr. Kostandin's tab to Mr. Look. . . .

Apparently enticed by meeting Mr. King — and the prospect of catering future King shindigs — Mr. Kostandin, accompanied by his wife and 78 crates of live lobsters, drove to Dysert's Truck Stop in Hermon, where they were told, Mr. King would meet them. Told there that the novelist had been detained, Mr. Kostandin left the lobsters behind and headed, via a limousine provided by Mr. Look, for a purported rendezvous with the author at the Panda Garden, a Chinese restaurant in Bangor. By the time he deduced that he had been had, Mr. Look had the lobsters, which he promptly sold.

David Margolick, At the Bar, N.Y. Times, Sept. 17, 1993, at B8 col. 1. Mr. Look got only $19,000 for the lobsters. He comes to you for legal representation in collecting the rest. Your first call was to Stephen King. Although the conversation was very scary, it is clear that King doesn't want to be involved. What do we do next?

1.3.   Karen Benning is a successful dentist who was approached last year to lend money to a day care center that wanted to expand. She checked into the center thoroughly and saw that they had a good location, a friendly staff, few outstanding debts, and reasonable profit projections. They had substantial capital assets, including an elaborate network of teaching computers and child-sized exercise equipment. She made a $10,000 loan to the owner, Ted Knopf, repayable in quarterly installments over five years, at prime plus five points.

The center has not missed a quarterly payment. But Benning has heard some very bad reports from a friend who used to have a child in the center, so she renewed her investigations. Benning sees that the center has moved to a new, more "upscale" location that was far more expensive. Their prices are higher, forcing out more than a third of their old customers. Because the new location is farther away from public transportation, many of their old employees have left. Many of the new employees are temps, resulting in high turnover rates and low employee morale. The person now in charge is the brother of the owner, a foul-tempered man who barks orders and frightens the children. Knopf sold the best of the computers and exercise equipment to finance the move and to pay himself and his brother during the start-up phase at the new location. The business is much deeper in debt and is behind on rent and utility payments. Benning is unsure whether the business will even survive, much less whether it will pay her.

Benning consults you for help. She feels sure the business could make a profit if it were properly run. She has heard that the old manager Knopf fired to make room for the brother would be pleased to return. Benning wants to be repaid in full and she is worried. What do you advise?

1.4.   Six months have passed since the preceding problem. The day care center has folded and you have obtained a default judgment against its owner, Ted Knopf, for more than $12,000 in past due interest and principal on Benning's loan. Benning wants to know when she will be paid. What do *you* need to know to answer her question? What are the possible sources of that information? If Knopf doesn't pay the judgment, how will you collect it? What do you think of Benning's suggestion that you send the sheriff to levy on the day care center equipment?

1.5.   Assume now that Knopf is living in Wisconsin. During his deposition, Knopf testifies that he owns the following property, all free and clear of any liens or security interests:

a.   A four-year-old Toyota automobile worth $6,000
b.   A house that he recently inherited from his mother, estimated to be worth about $35,000
c.   The equipment from the day care center, which has a resale value of about $10,000
d.   A bank account with a current balance of $2,265.92

What can the sheriff take from him to satisfy your judgment? Is there any hurry in getting the sheriff to do that? Can you move fast enough?

1.6. During a deposition in aid of execution, you, as Benning's lawyer, asked Knopf whether anyone owed him (Knopf) any money. Knopf hesitated briefly in a way that made you suspicious, and then answered "Not that I can remember." You'd like to jog his memory, or maybe even set up a perjury charge, by following up with some questions that suggest specific kinds of debts that might be owing to him. What questions might you ask? If he does remember a debt, such as a bank account, how and when will you pursue that asset further?

Assignment 2: Security and Foreclosure

A. The Nature of Security

The law provides for enforcement of money obligations. But, as should be apparent from Assignment 1, the legal remedies of unsecured creditors are cumbersome, expensive, and problematic in terms of what they will yield. The financial institutions that make car loans, home loans, and most business loans can and do insist on having a set of collection rights considerably more effective than the baseline set of collection rights discussed in the preceding assignment.

This more effective set of collection rights is known as a *lien*. The Bankruptcy Code, which is the ultimate arbiter of the rights of debtors and creditors when one of the parties petitions for bankruptcy, accurately describes a lien as "a charge against or an interest in property to secure payment of a debt or performance of an obligation." Bankr. Code §101 (definition of "lien"). Thus, a lien is a relationship between particular property (the *collateral*) and a particular debt or obligation. The general nature of the relationship is that if the debt is not paid when due, the creditor can compel the application of the value of the collateral to payment of the debt. The process by which the creditor does this is called *foreclosure*.

The most common form of lien is the *security interest*. Used in its broadest sense, that term encompasses any lien created by contract between debtor and creditor. It includes real estate mortgages and deeds of trust as well as the security interests in personal property created under Article 9 of the Uniform Commercial Code. See Bankr. Code §101 (definitions of "security agreement," "security interest," and "lien"; Internal Revenue Code §6323(h)(1)).

Although security interests will be our primary focus in the remainder of this book, you will also encounter two types of nonconsensual liens: (1) liens granted by statute, such as mechanic's liens (*statutory liens*) and (2) liens obtained by unsecured creditors through judicial process (*judicial liens*).

In Part One of this book, we discuss security interests in the simplest situations — that is, where only the interests of a debtor and a single creditor are involved. We look first at the remedies available to a secured creditor, and then we turn to what a creditor must do to become secured. Later, in Part Two, we will take up the question of priorities — the relative rights of creditors competing for the same collateral.

What property will serve as collateral for a security interest depends on custom and the needs of the particular parties. When a car dealer lends the money to purchase a car, the car will usually be the collateral. When a business borrows, it might grant a security interest in its equipment, its inventory, its accounts receivable or any or all other property it may own. Virtually anything recognized as property can serve as collateral. (Spouses and children won't work, but your dog or your parakeet will.) The usefulness of property as collateral will ultimately depend on (1) how much value the creditor can extract from it after default (will it bring anything at resale?), and (2) how much leverage the creditor can derive from the creditor's ability to deprive the debtor of the property (how much will the debtor be willing and able to pay to keep it?).

The agreement that creates the security interest may impose obligations on the debtor that apply even in the absence of default. (For the curious, there is an example of a security agreement in Assignment 15 of this book. Peek now or save it for later.) The security interest itself has effect only in the event of the debtor's default. The default may be a failure to pay the debt or a failure to comply with some other provision of the security agreement. Because the rights of the holder of a security interest are principally rights that take effect after default, a security interest can be described as a right in property that is contingent on nonpayment of a debt. That is, the right to enforce the debt against the property that serves as collateral is contingent upon the occurrence of a default. The typical methods of enforcement lead to a sale of the collateral and payment of as much of the debt as possible from the proceeds of sale.

The recognition of enhanced collection rights for secured creditors necessarily diminishes the effectiveness of the collection rights of general unsecured creditors. For example, if Creditor A has a security interest in the debtor's car that exceeds the entire value of the car, the value of the car will not be available to satisfy unsecured Creditor B's execution. The ease with which a debtor can grant security interests virtually assures that by the time a debtor is in serious financial difficulty, an unsecured creditor will have difficulty finding property to sell to satisfy its debt. In essence, unsecured creditors get only what is left after provisions have been made for secured creditors. In contested cases, that is usually nothing. Having security, or lacking it, is a key attribute of the relationship between debtors and their creditors.

Considering the disadvantages inherent in being an unsecured creditor, one might wonder why anyone assumes that role. Some creditors may prefer unsecured status because they are compensated by receiving a higher rate of interest. (This is the standard explanation given by economists who study credit.) Others, such as the victim of a car accident or an employee with an action for wrongful discharge, do not choose the role of unsecured creditor; they are thrown into it without the opportunity to negotiate. Some unsecured creditors agree to a contract that leaves them unsecured without realizing that fact or without recognizing its importance. For example, if you have ever prepaid rent on an apartment or paid for an airline ticket (even if you charged it to your credit card), you agreed to accept unsecured status in the event the landlord did not provide the apartment or the airline did not provide the flight. More than a few people have discovered their unsecured status when an airline stopped flying or a landlord went broke.

Others may understand the implications of assuming unsecured status, but be constrained by business custom and practice from seeking secured status. Consider, for example, the law student who accepts a job with a large law firm. Along with the job, the student accepts the status of an unsecured creditor for wages, accrued benefits, and other obligations. To request security for those obligations would be an egregious social error. The problem is not just that the law student lacks bargaining leverage; the inability to negotiate for security applies even to the law student who is in great demand, and the inability persists even if the student were willing to accept a much lower salary. In fact, even if the law firm *wanted* to accede to a job applicant's demand for security, to do so probably would breach the firm's contracts with its bank lenders. Who gets security is as much a matter of established custom as of economics.

Why does the law permit a debtor to grant one creditor collection rights superior to those of another? There are a number of competing economic explanations for this harsh economic inequality, as well as some explanations rooted in custom and long-standing business practice. We think the principal reason is the tremendous complexity the law would have encountered if it had attempted to ban security. Were security banned, debtors temporarily short of cash still would have been able to sell their property to get the cash they needed. They still would have been able to buy it back later when they had the cash. At the same time, debtors would have been unable to grant a lesser right — a right in the buyer/secured creditor to keep the property contingent on the debtor's nonpayment of a debt. The following story is just for fun, but it illustrates that there is little difference between failing to buy back property one previously sold and failure to pay a secured debt. As you read the story, think about how the chancellor should have decided the cases brought before him if he had wished to prohibit the use of property as security and how future lenders and borrowers might have reacted to those decisions.

The Invention of Security: A Pseudo History

The place is medieval England. The time is in the early, particularly dark part of the Dark Ages. Existing legal concepts include the ownership of property, the ability to transfer it, and the ability to contract for such transfers.

Debord is the owner of Blackacre and is in need of a loan. His neighbor, Creech, is willing to make the $100 loan, but wants to be *certain* he* will be repaid. Debord and Creech intend to create what we today call a security interest, but our story opens long before the courts recognized such a device.

To maximize the likelihood that the courts would give effect to their intention without a recognized legal device, Creech and Debord expressed their deal using legal concepts that were familiar to the courts. Their deal had three parts:

True intent of Debord and Creech	*Legal form they adopted*
1. Debord grants Creech a security interest in Blackacre	1. Debord sells and deeds Blackacre to Creech
2. Creech lends $100 to Debord	2. Creech pays $100 purchase price for Blackacre
3. Debord agrees to repay the loan with $10 interest, on March 1	3. Creech grants Debord an option to purchase Blackacre from Creech on March 1 for $110

Because Blackacre was worth $500, once this transaction was in place Creech could be "secure" in the knowledge that the loan would almost certainly be repaid. Even if it were not, he would have something even more valuable, the ownership of Blackacre. Assuming he repaid the loan on time, it cost Debord nothing to provide Creech with this security. The result was to enable the two of them to get together on a loan that might otherwise not have been made.

The first time they made this deal, matters went smoothly. Debord repaid the loan on time and Creech reconveyed Blackacre. But the second time they did it, Debord was late with the payment. When he tendered the money on March 15, Creech refused to take it and refused to

*At that time in history, only men were allowed to engage in these transactions.

reconvey Blackacre. "You breached the deal, and I'm keeping the land," he said with some delight. The law governing the form in which they had put their transaction was on Creech's side. "Time was of the essence" in an option contract, and if the buyer did not pay the purchase price at the agreed time, the buyer lost the right to purchase.

With no remedy at law, Debord went to the chancellor for "equity." He explained the true intention of the deal he had made with Creech and the position Creech was now taking. He emphasized that unless the chancellor granted relief, his $500 property would be forfeited for failure to repay a $100 loan. Although the documents supported Creech's position, the chancellor granted relief. Reciting the maxims (maxims were very big in the Dark Ages) that "Equity abhors a forfeiture" and "Equity looks to substance over form," he ordered that Debord could "redeem" Blackacre by repaying the loan with interest and compensating Creech for any damages sustained by the delay. Debord did so, and never did business with Creech again.

Despite Creech's loss before the chancellor, his experience with secured lending to this point had not been all that bad. True, the Chancellor had dashed his dream of picking up Blackacre for $100. In Debord v. Creech the chancellor had established that even slow-paying debtors had an equitable right to redeem their property. But the chancellor had conditioned this "equity of redemption" on payment in full, including Creech's attorneys' fees. Security worked.

Creech continued to make loans and continued to put them in the form of a "deed absolute" combined with an option to purchase. Inevitably, he ran into a problem. Davenport, another of Creech's borrowers, failed to repay a loan secured by Greenacre. Months passed. Creech had possession of Greenacre and wanted to spruce it up and sell it to another buyer. But what if Davenport later exercised his equity of redemption? How long did Creech have to wait for his title to Greenacre to be clear of the equity of redemption? Creech asked his lawyer. "No way to know," the lawyer said, "short of asking the chancellor." The lawyer prepared a petition asking the chancellor to "foreclose" Davenport's equity of redemption. That petition was the first mortgage foreclosure.

When Creech and his lawyer went before the chancellor, Davenport was there. Davenport made the usual arguments about forfeiture and told the same old stories about how he was just about to come up with the money to redeem. By today's standards, the chancellor was a bleeding-heart liberal. He gave Davenport a continuance, reset the hearing for a date two months away, and expressed his hope that Davenport would redeem before then. Knowing the chancellor, Creech's lawyer feared a string of continuances unless he could persuade the chancellor that Creech's interests were in greater jeopardy than Davenport's.

At the continued hearing, Creech's lawyer presented expert testimony that the value of Greenacre was no greater than the amount of the loan.

Even if the chancellor cut off the equity of redemption today, Creech would take a loss. Davenport had no "equity" in Greenacre to protect, said Creech's lawyer, picking up the language the court of equity used to refer to the amount by which the value of the property exceeded the amount of the loans against it. Because of the accruing interest, the lawyer continued, Creech's potential loss grew greater with every passing day. After Creech's lawyer had finished his presentation, Davenport, in a voice choked with emotion, spoke of his many happy years on Greenacre, the little knoll where his dog was buried, and his expert appraisals showing that Greenacre was worth "at least five times" the amount owing on the loan.

The chancellor reflected on the issues and concluded that where the equities now lay depended on the value of Greenacre. Despite his generally liberal beliefs, the chancellor, a very early Renaissance man, was also a staunch believer in the marketplace. Based on that belief, he devised what he considered a very clever, "market-based" solution. The issue of value would be resolved by offering Greenacre for sale. To assure that the sale was fair and open, the chancellor would have a notice posted in the town square, and the sheriff would conduct a sale of Greenacre on the courthouse steps. The highest bidder would get the land free of Davenport's right to redeem. As the chancellor put it, the sale would "cut off the equitable right of redemption." The proceeds from the sale would be used first to repay Creech's loan, thus assuring that Creech would recover whatever value there was in the property, up to the amount of the loan. If the property brought less than the amount owing to Creech, Creech would have to bring his action for the *deficiency* on the law side. If the property brought more, the *surplus* would go to Davenport on the equity side. Because Davenport would get the market value of the property less the amount he owed on the debt, he would suffer no forfeiture.

The sale was held, and Creech v. Davenport was entered in the Year Book. Unfortunately, the amount of the sale price was not recorded. The entries were, however, sufficient to show that the remedies of the parties to a secured transaction had assumed the form they would retain for a millennium.

This story makes several important points about security and foreclosure. First, it illustrates that parties who wish to do so can easily construct the security relationship using the everyday conventions of sale and option to purchase. (Indeed, it might be difficult to permit a debtor like Debord to transfer ownership of property yet prohibit him from transferring mere collection rights relating to the same property.) If the chancellor had refused to recognize the special nature of the sale from Debord to Creech, the sale and option to repurchase would have been valid. Debord could still have entered into this "secured" transaction, but he would not have been protected against forfeiture. To *prevent* these transactions would have required both the chancellor's recognition of the special nature of this sale and some more aggressive action such as, for example, forfeiting the *creditor's* interest.

Second, the story shows that in the hands of clever parties, or their clever lawyers, existing legal forms can be employed in ways unanticipated by the lawmakers. Using nothing but existing concepts of sale and option, Creech and Debord invented security. Such resourcefulness in structuring transactions is common in commercial law. As the lawyers invent new devices, the courts must consider whether to recognize and give effect to them, or whether to deny recognition and wrestle with the consequences. In making their decisions about whether to recognize new devices, courts are often constrained by the practicalities of enforcing the rules they think most desirable from a policy standpoint. Thus the judges are not entirely in control; lawyers play an active role in shaping the law.

Third, in determining which transactions are in the nature of security and must be foreclosed, one cannot rely on the documents. A transaction is in the nature of security if the effect is to provide one party with an interest in the property of another, which interest is contingent upon the nonpayment of a debt. Even if the only document in existence is a deed absolute, the relationship created may be a mortgage. It is truly the substance of what is going on that matters, not the form.

The lesson to be learned from Creech v. Debord is subtle and complex. Real estate foreclosure is time-consuming and expensive. Lawyers and their clients naturally wish to avoid it when possible. The irony is that if the intent of the contract between the parties is to relieve a secured creditor of the necessity to foreclose, the attempt will fail. Regardless of the form in which the parties choose to cast their deal, the law will recast it as a mortgage. The concept is not an easy one to grasp. As is illustrated in the following case, commercial lawyers frequently embarrass themselves by making deals that run afoul of the "intended as security" doctrine.

Basile v. Erhal Holding Corp.

538 N.Y.S.2d 831 (N.Y. App. Div. 1989)

JUDGES: Mollen, P.J., Thompson, Rubin and Spatt, J.J., concur. . . .

In 1982, the plaintiff, the owner of property located at 244 Morris Avenue in Peekskill, mortgaged the property to the Erhal Holding Corp.

(hereinafter Erhal) in return for a loan at an alleged usurious rate. The plaintiff instituted this action, inter alia, to declare the mortgage null and void on the ground of usury. On June 2, 1986, and June 6, 1986, while the matter was awaiting trial, the parties entered into a stipulation of settlement in open court whereby the plaintiff agreed to execute a mortgage to Erhal in the sum of $101,303.59 together with a deed "in lieu of foreclosure" which would not be recorded by Erhal as long as the plaintiff fulfilled her obligations under the terms and conditions of the mortgage. The mortgage provided, inter alia, that the plaintiff would pay monthly interest payments on the mortgage amount at a rate of 12% per annum for a one-year period; at the end of that period, the entire balance was to become due. The mortgage agreement also included the following provision; "The mortgagor herein has simultaneously executed a deed in lieu of foreclosure which may be recorded by the mortgagee for any default herein."

During the settlement colloquy, the trial court questioned the plaintiff regarding her understanding of the terms of the settlement. At that time, the plaintiff indicated that she understood that if she violated the terms of the mortgage agreement, Erhal could record the deed and become the owner of the subject premises.

The plaintiff subsequently defaulted in several mortgage payments and failed to pay the real estate taxes and fire insurance premiums for the demised premises as provided for in the mortgage agreement. As a result of the plaintiff's default, Erhal recorded the deed in lieu of foreclosure in December 1986. Thereafter, Erhal moved, by order to show cause, for an order declaring that the plaintiff's right of redemption with respect to the property was waived when the mortgage and deed in lieu of foreclosure were executed in June 1986. The plaintiff cross-moved, inter alia, for an order directing Erhal to accept a check in the sum of $101,303.59 plus interest tendered by the plaintiff and to deliver to the plaintiff a satisfaction of mortgage and a deed for the premises, free and clear of all encumbrances.

The Supreme Court granted Erhal's motion and declared that "the plaintiff no longer has any right of redemption of the subject property." The plaintiff's cross motion was denied.

We conclude that the Supreme Court erred in declaring that the plaintiff waived her right of redemption in the demised premises. A deed conveying real property, although absolute on its face, will be considered to be a mortgage when the instrument is executed as security for a debt. The purpose behind this rule was explained in Peugh v. Davis (96 U.S. 332, 336-337):

> It is an established doctrine that a court of equity will treat a deed, absolute in form, as a mortgage, when it is executed as a security for a loan of money. That court looks beyond the terms of the instrument to the real

> transaction; and when that is shown to be one of security, and not of sale, it will give effect to the actual contract of the parties. . . . It is also an estab-lished doctrine that an equity of redemption is inseparably connected with a mortgage; that is to say, so long as the instrument is one of security, the borrower has in a court of equity a right to redeem the property upon pay-ment of the loan. This right cannot be waived or abandoned by any stipu-lation of the parties made at the time, even if embodied in the mortgage. This is a doctrine from which a court of equity never deviates (see also Maher v. Alma Realty Co., 70 A.D.2d 931 ["plaintiffs cannot waive their right of redemption even by stipulation in open court"]).

In this case, it is clear that the deed in lieu of foreclosure executed by the plaintiff with the $101,303.59 mortgage was not intended as an absolute conveyance or sale of the property by the plaintiff but rather was intended to be security for the plaintiff's $101,303.59 debt to Erhal. As such, the deed constituted a mortgage and the attempted waiver of the plaintiff's right of redemption in the property in the in-court stipulation of settlement as well as the mortgage agreement was ineffective. Erhal's sole remedy is to institute an action in foreclosure. The plaintiff will have a right to redeem the property at any time prior to the actual sale of the premises by tendering to Erhal the principal and interest due on the mortgage.

The "intended as security" doctrine applies to personal property transactions as well as those involving real property. U.C.C. §9-109(a)(1) provides that Article 9 applies to "any transaction, regardless of its form, that creates a security interest in personal prop-erty. . . ." Comment 2 to that section elaborates: "When a security interest is created, this Article applies regardless of the form of the transaction or the name that parties have given to it." For example, assume that Smyrna wants to sell her Buick Skylark to Brodsky. Brod-sky wants to take delivery of the car now and pay for it in monthly payments over the course of a year. Smyrna doesn't mind receiving her payments over the course of the year, but neither does she want to be troubled with the formalities of secured credit. Smyrna and Brodsky strike the following deal: Smyrna agrees to sell her car to Brodsky one year from today. The agreement is contingent on Brod-sky's paying the purchase price in equal monthly payments over the year. Until Brodsky has finished paying, Smyrna will remain the owner of the Skylark and keep the title in her name. So long as he is current on his payments, Brodsky will have the right to use it. Once he finishes paying, Smyrna will transfer title to him.

Smyrna and Brodsky may think they have invented an ingenious substitute for security. They have not. What they have done is to reinvent security — just as the lawyers and parties in *Basile* did. Article 9 will apply to the transaction. U.C.C. §9-109(a)(1). For the purpose of applying the rules in Article 9, Brodsky is the owner of the Skylark, Smyrna is a secured party, and the contract they have entered into is a security agreement. If Brodsky and Smyrna fail to comply with the Article 9 rules governing their transaction, they will suffer the consequences.

B. Foreclosure Procedure

The procedures for real estate foreclosure differ widely from state to state and with the type of collateral involved. Article 9 provides a uniform procedure for personal property foreclosure that can be very quick and easy, but it also permits secured parties to use judicial foreclosure methods if they prefer.

As you read the following material, be sure to distinguish the foreclosure of a security interest from the taking of possession of collateral. Foreclosure is a process that operates on the ownership of collateral. It transfers ownership from the debtor to the purchaser at the foreclosure sale and cuts off the debtor's right to redeem the collateral. This change in ownership is typically accompanied by a transfer of possession. But the transfer of possession can occur before, during, or after foreclosure. In some cases, it may not occur at all. For example, the secured creditor may foreclose against collateral, purchase it at the foreclosure sale, and lease it back to the debtor who has been in possession all along. Assignment 3 of this book discusses the secured creditor's right to possession and the means by which the secured creditor can get it. Foreclosure operates on ownership, not possession.

1. Judicial Foreclosure

A foreclosure process is referred to as *judicial* if it is accomplished by the entry of a court order. Procedures by which secured creditors can sue for such orders are available in every state. In a judicial foreclosure, a creditor holding a mortgage or security interest typically files a civil action against the debtor. In the complaint, the creditor details the terms of the loan and the nature of the default, and requests that the equity of redemption be "foreclosed." The complaint is served on the debtor and any subordinate lien holders, who then have a period of time (usually 20 days) in which to raise defenses.

Only in rare cases will the debtor have a defense that would preclude foreclosure altogether. But a debtor who seeks a delay can often find some technical defect in the complaint (such as an erroneous calculation of interest) that will at least require amendment and at most require that the case be placed on a trial calendar that is months or years long. Only when such issues have been resolved and the plaintiff has established that it is entitled to foreclose will the court enter a *final judgment of foreclosure.*

Typically, as part of the judgment, the court will set a date for the foreclosure sale. In the large majority of jurisdictions, the method of sale is specified by statute. The statute usually requires that the county sheriff or the clerk of the court conduct the sale. The procedures specified in the statute may be supplemented by the terms of the final judgment. In most jurisdictions, the sales are held at a particular time of day (usually around mid-day) in a particular place (often immediately outside the main door of the courthouse).

The statute typically requires that the sale be advertised beforehand by the person who will conduct it. The advertising may be by posting notices in some public place or by placing one or more advertisements in a newspaper of general circulation. The period for advertising ranges from as little as a week in some jurisdictions to six weeks or more in others. Because the advertising cannot commence until the final judgment has been entered, the advertising period adds to the minimum time in which foreclosure can be accomplished.

On the date fixed for the sale, the sheriff or clerk conducts an auction. Bids are usually announced orally. In most procedures, the highest bidder must immediately pay the entire purchase price to the sheriff or clerk. In some states, the creditor can pay a part of the bid and return with the remainder of the money in an agreed upon time (typically a day or two). Upon receipt of the money, the sheriff or clerk certifies that person to be the highest bidder.

Under the procedures of most jurisdictions, a foreclosure sale must be *confirmed* by the court. That is, after the auction is held, parties to the mortgage foreclosure case have some period of time in which they can object to the manner in which it was actually conducted. Typical objections are that the sale was not advertised strictly in accord with the final judgment and the applicable statutes, the auction was not held in precisely the location advertised, someone (real or hypothetical) was prevented from attending the sale or bidding, some arrangement between interested parties "chilled" the bidding, or the highest bid was grossly inadequate. In some jurisdictions there will be a confirmation hearing even if no objections have been filed; in others, the court will enter the order after the time for filing objections has expired. The process of confirming the sale also adds to the minimum time in which foreclosure can be accomplished.

After the confirmation order has been entered and the time for appeal has expired, the sheriff or clerk disburses the sale proceeds. If the amount is greater than that owed to the foreclosing creditor, the "surplus" is distributed first to the holders of junior liens or mortgages and then to the debtor. If, as is far more common, the amount realized from the sale is less than the amount owed the foreclosing creditor, the foreclosing creditor can request a judgment for the *deficiency*. If, for example, the property sold for $25,000 but the creditor was owed $40,000, the creditor could sue for a $15,000 deficiency. In many jurisdictions, antideficiency laws prohibit the granting of deficiency judgments in particular kinds of cases or give the court discretion to deny them. (Discussed in Assignment 4.)

Ordinarily, the debtor will remain in possession of the mortgaged premises until the sale has been confirmed by the court. The purchaser is then entitled to possession. If the debtor will not surrender the premises, the purchaser is entitled to a *writ of assistance*, which in some states is known as a *writ of possession*. The writ of assistance directs the sheriff to remove the debtor from the premises and put the purchaser in possession. The process is much like that for a levy under a writ of execution.

The large majority of foreclosures are unopposed, and the debtors often abandon the premises before the sheriff comes to remove them. But a substantial minority of debtors resist at some or all stages of the proceedings. To avoid the foreclosure, they may raise a number of defenses. They may object to the sale, sometimes on the basis of irregularities they themselves played a part in causing. They may appeal the courts' rulings. They may refuse to surrender the premises after they are sold. Usually, their purpose is to delay the proceedings until they can get the money necessary to redeem the property or reinstate the mortgage. Sometimes they simply try to stay in the property as long as they can, with no further plan in mind.

Farm Credit of St. Paul v. Stedman, 449 N.W.2d 562 (N.D. 1989), illustrates both the determination and the effectiveness with which debtors may resist foreclosure. The Stedmans mortgaged their 2,500-acre farm in Foster County to Federal Land Bank of Saint Paul for a $525,000 loan. After the Stedmans defaulted on their loan payments, the Federal Land Bank foreclosed the mortgage. The foreclosure judgment was entered in June 1984. Through the filing of bankruptcy cases, the Stedmans delayed the sheriff's sale until some time in 1988. At that time, the sheriff sold the farm to the Farm Credit Bank of St. Paul. The Stedmans refused to vacate the farm, forcing the Bank to sue to evict them. The Stedmans did not defend the eviction case and the court entered a default judgment of eviction on December 15, 1988. After the default judgment was entered, the Stedmans swung back into action. Representing themselves after the resignation of their attorney, they raised several frivolous defenses to the eviction. The judgment was amended slightly on January 17, 1989. On March 8, the Bank moved for a writ of assistance to get possession, and the trial court set a hearing on the motion for March 28. Before the hearing could be held, the Stedmans appealed from the amended judgment of eviction.

Following their appeal, the Stedmans filed a flurry of documents seeking to stay the judgment of eviction. When both the trial court and the Supreme Court of North Dakota denied relief, the Stedmans obtained further delay by filing another bankruptcy case.

With the bankruptcy case disposed of, the Stedmans argued four issues before the Supreme Court of North Dakota. Among them was the claim that the writ of assistance issued by the trial court to enforce the eviction judgment violated the Fourth Amendment to the U.S. Constitution, which prohibits unreasonable searches and seizures. In its opinion, the Supreme Court of North Dakota pointed out that the writ of assistance used for searches in colonial days and which were outlawed by the Fourth Amendment had nothing in common with the writs of assistance used to enforce judgments of eviction except the name.

On December 20, 1989, five years and six months after the trial court entered judgment of foreclosure and five days before Christmas, the Supreme Court of North Dakota affirmed the judgment of eviction. That would seem to exhaust the Stedmans' defenses and pave the way for the sheriff to physically remove them from the farm property, but with debtors as determined as the Stedmans, we wonder even about that.

Statutes in some states mandate delays or waiting periods in addition to those the debtor can gain by defending the action. Consider, for example, the following Wisconsin statutes:

Wisconsin Statutes Annotated

(West 1994)

§846.10   FORECLOSURE. . . .

(2) No sale involving a one- to four-family residence that is owner-occupied at the commencement of the foreclosure action, a farm, a church or a tax-exempt nonprofit charitable organization may be held until the expiration of 12 months from the date when judgment is entered, except a sale under §846.101. . . . Sales under foreclosure of mortgages given by any railroad corporation may be made immediately after the rendition of the judgment.

§846.101   FORECLOSURE WITHOUT DEFICIENCY;
20-ACRE PARCELS

(1) If the mortgagor has agreed in writing at the time of the execution of the mortgage to the provisions of this section, and the foreclosure action involves a one- to four-family residence that is owner-occupied at the commencement of the action, a farm, a church or a tax-exempt charitable organization, the plaintiff in a foreclosure action of a mortgage on real estate of 20 acres or less . . . may elect by express allegation in the complaint to waive judgment for any deficiency which may remain due to the plaintiff after sale of the mortgaged premises against every party who is personally liable for the debt secured by the mortgage, and to consent that the mortgagor, unless he or she abandons the property, may remain in possession of the mortgaged property and be entitled to all rents, issues and profits therefrom to the date of confirmation of the sale by the court.

(2) When plaintiff so elects, judgment shall be entered as provided in this chapter, except that no judgment for deficiency may be ordered therein nor separately rendered against any party who is personally liable for the debt secured by the mortgage and the sale of such mortgaged premises shall be made upon the expiration of 6 months from the date when such judgment is entered. . . .

The existence of statutes such as these demonstrates that the delay in the procedure for judicial foreclosure is not entirely inadvertent. Particularly in farming regions of the United States, there is a strong populist tradition in which the image of the foreclosing lender is that of the cold, calculating bank seeking a windfall through the debtor's default, while the image of the defending debtor is that of the victim struggling to keep a home and often a means of livelihood. Although it would be easy to make mortgage foreclosure more efficient, for those who make the laws in many states, the perceived fairness of the system is of greater concern.

With the cooperation of the debtor after default, a secured creditor may be able to avoid the necessity to foreclose. If there are no other liens or interests in the collateral, the debtor can simply transfer the property to the creditor by means of a *deed in lieu of foreclosure.* Such a deed does not "clog the equity of redemption" if it immediately extinguishes the mortgage and the underlying mortgage debt. Creditors sometimes persuade the debtor to grant a deed in lieu of foreclosure by persuading the debtor that it is better to lose the house now and have no further liability than to lose the house later and be liable for a deficiency. In some cases, creditors persuade debtors to surrender the property by paying the debtors an additional sum of money — in effect, purchasing the debtors' equity of redemption.

2.   Power of Sale Foreclosure

About 25 states permit the mortgage lender and borrower to opt for a quicker, simpler method of foreclosure against real property. They do so by including in the security agreement a *power of sale*. In some of these states, the security agreement will be in the traditional form of a *mortgage*; in others, including California, it will be in the form of a *deed of trust*. The deed of trust states in essence that the collateral will be held in trust by the creditor or a third party such as a bank or title company. The borrower agrees that in the event of default, the trustee can sell the property and pay the loan from the proceeds of sale. Because the purpose of this arrangement is to secure payment of the loan, the law regards it not as an actual trust but as simply another form of security interest.

Foreclosure is still necessary when the creditor has a power of sale, but it can be accomplished through a procedure that does not include filing a lawsuit. For example, under California law, upon default under a mortgage or deed of trust containing a power of sale, the creditor can record in the public records a notice setting forth the nature of the debtor's default and the creditor's election to sell the property. If the debtor does not cure the default within 90 days, the creditor can set a time and place for sale, advertise it for 20 days, and then sell the property at auction. Pursuant to the power of sale contained in the deed of trust, the trustee conveys title to the purchaser at auction. The sale forecloses the debtor's right to redeem.

The primary purpose for permitting power of sale as an alternative means of foreclosure is to avoid the expense and delay of litigation. But even a power-of-sale foreclosure may end up in court. If the debtor refuses to surrender possession after the sale, the purchaser must sue for it. The cause of action may be for unlawful detainer, ejectment, or eviction. The debtor who has defenses to the foreclosure can defend that action or bring the debtor's own action to enjoin the sale or, if it has already been held, to set it aside. In some states the debtor can also bring a tort action for *wrongful sale*. In some states the secured creditor can sue for a deficiency judgment after the sale has been held, but others prohibit deficiency judgments when the foreclosure is by power of sale.

3. U.C.C. Foreclosure by Sale

The process by which a secured creditor forecloses a security interest in personal property is much simpler than the corresponding process for real property. The difference results largely from historical accident. The law and traditions of real estate foreclosure developed at an earlier time, when the lending of money was considered not quite so respectable as it is today. Restrictions placed on real estate foreclosure during that era have survived, but those restrictions were not extended to the later-developing process of personal property foreclosure.

The differences in procedures for real and personal property foreclosure may also reflect underlying assumptions about what really hurts: Some may feel that the loss of a home or family farm tears the social fabric in a way that repossession of a car does not. The law may reflect an assumption that greater value, social stability, and future wealth are tied up in the ownership of real property. Whether those assumptions are true today is questionable, but the legal differences persist.

Article 9 of the Uniform Commercial Code governs the foreclosure of security interests in personal property. It provides that after default, the secured party may sell, lease, license, or otherwise dispose of any or all of the collateral. U.C.C. §9-610(a). That sale or disposition itself forecloses the debtor's right to redeem the property. U.C.C. §9-623. It extinguishes the creditor's security interest in the collateral and transfers to the purchaser all of the debtor's rights in the collateral. U.C.C. §9-617(a). Alternatively, if the creditor so chooses, it may foreclose by any available judicial procedure. U.C.C. §9-601(a).

Problem Set 2

2.1. In a parallel universe, you are again pursuing Ted Knopf from Problem 1.6 in Wisconsin to recover Karen Benning's $10,000. This time, however, Benning had the foresight to get Knopf to sign a security agreement taking the following property as security. As in Problem 1.6, Knopf owns the property free and clear of any liens or security interests other than Benning's. Which of the following items can Benning reach through foreclosure of her security interest?

   a. A four-year-old Toyota automobile worth $6,000.
   b. A house that Knopf recently inherited from his mother, estimated to be worth about $35,000.
   c. Knopf still owns the equipment from the day care center, which has a resale value of about $10,000.

d. A bank account containing $2,265.92.

See Wisconsin Statutes §815.18, §815.20, and §990.01(14), reproduced in Assignment 1.

2.2. Bonnie Brezhnez runs a used-car lot in a low-income neighborhood. Even with cheap prices and low payments, she ends up repossessing a lot of cars. To ease the administrative burden, Bonnie plans to begin leasing the cars rather than selling them. That is, on a car she currently would sell for $5,000, no money down, with interest at 18 percent per annum, the payments would be $180.77 for three years. Instead, Bonnie proposes to lease the same car for $180.77 per month and offer the lessee an option to buy the car at the end of that period for $10. The lease will provide that, on default, Bonnie has the right to terminate the lease and the option to buy. "If a lessee defaults, I'll just repossess the car and put it back on the lot instead of having to go through all that Article 9 rigamarole," Bonnie says. What advice do you give Bonnie about this plan? U.C.C. §9-109(a)(1), Comment 2 to §9-109, and U.C.C. §1-201(37).

2.3. The statutes of the state in which you are practicing authorize foreclosure against real property only by judicial process. Your firm is on retainer for the asset recovery department of Enterprise State Bank, and your case load includes more than a dozen foreclosures that are now in process for ESB. The cases are averaging about a year in the courts, producing substantial fees for the firm and good billables for you. Last week, Hiri Mashimoto, your contact at the bank, sent you yet another file, a residential foreclosure against John and Linda O'Hurley. You wrote the usual letter detailing the defaults under the mortgage documents and exercising the bank's right to accelerate.

a. Much to your surprise, Linda O'Hurley came to see you today. She explained that about a year ago her husband was diagnosed as having cancer, and that he has been undergoing both chemical and radiation therapy. Given the level of the family's noninsured medical expenses and his reduced workload, the O'Hurleys realize that they can no longer afford the house. She says the house is still worth more than the balance owing on the loan, but her efforts to sell it in a slow market have been unsuccessful. She and her husband are willing to turn the house over to the bank, but they don't want to be sued or to have "a foreclosure on their record." O'Hurley said she is not represented by an attorney, but she would like you to draw up the necessary papers.

The O'Hurley offer sounds fine to Mashimoto, but he wants to know if there are any "legal problems." Are there? Rule 4.3 of the ABA Model Rules of Professional Conduct provides:

In dealing on behalf of a client with a person who is not represented by counsel, a lawyer shall not state or imply that the lawyer is disinterested. When the lawyer knows or reasonably should know that the unrepresented person misunderstands the lawyer's role in the matter, the lawyer shall make reasonable efforts to correct the misunderstanding.

b. What if the O'Hurleys execute the deed today, with an understanding that you will give it back to them if they make up the back payments within 60 days, but that otherwise you will record it?

2.4. Your discussions of the O'Hurley plans got Mr. Mashimoto thinking about other ways to escape the delay and expense of foreclosure. He is back in your office today with an idea for "getting around this foreclosure thing." He proposes that when the bank makes a real estate loan, the bank will require that the borrower sign an irrevocable power of attorney authorizing another bank (the borrower can select the "trustee bank" from an approved list) to execute and deliver a deed in lieu of foreclosure in the event that (1) the debtor is in default under the mortgage and (2) the default continues for a period of 90 days. Mr. Mashimoto realizes that the trustee bank won't sign the deed if the debtor contests the default in any way, and he would still have to foreclose in such case. But he hopes that "at least this will eliminate the expense and delay in the clear cases." Will it?

2.5. Mr. Mashimoto has yet another idea. Many of the bank's commercial loans are made to corporate debtors. He proposes that at the time such a loan is made, in addition to the mortgage against the real estate owned by the corporation, the bank take a security interest in the stock of the corporation and take possession of the share certificates. If there is a default, the bank will foreclose on the stock by conducting a sale pursuant to U.C.C. §§9-610(a), (b), and (c), and 9-604(a)(1). In that sale, the bank can buy the stock for a modest price. The bank will then elect its own employees as directors of the corporation, and the employees as directors will cause the corporation to execute a deed in lieu of foreclosure on the defaulted mortgage. You know that all of this can be done under the corporation law of the state, and someone else in your firm will tend to the securities law issues, but will it work from the debtor-creditor angle? U.C.C. §§9-610(a), (b), and (c), 9-623.

2.6. You are on the staff of state Senator Candy Rowsey. Rowsey sees herself as an activist reformer, and she is concerned about the high cost and excessive litigation involved in mortgage foreclosure. The state currently permits only judicial foreclosure, and the statute has no mandatory waiting periods. But debtors struggling to save their homes or businesses often raise petty issues in the hopes of obtaining delays, much like what happened in the *Stedman* case.

Because Rowsey gets her campaign money from the banks and her votes from the farmers, she doesn't want to do anything that will harm either interest, but she is appalled at the waste of money and judicial effort as the parties fight over issues of no real importance. She wants you to come up with something that will be neutral in its effect but more efficient. Any ideas?

Assignment 3: Repossession of Collateral

A. The Importance of Possession Pending Foreclosure

As we discussed in Assignment 2, the period of time from the debtor's default until the debtor's equity of redemption has been irrevocably foreclosed may be as little as a few days or as much as several years. Who will have possession of the property during that time? The answer is complex.

The secured creditor has a number of reasons to want possession pending foreclosure. First, a debtor whose rights in the property are about to be extinguished through foreclosure may have little incentive to preserve and maintain the property. An angry, frustrated debtor who will be judgment-proof after the foreclosure may even decide to destroy it. Collateral is often in poor condition by the time it is repossessed. A quicker recovery will tend to preserve its value. Second, the use of the collateral between the time the right to foreclose accrues and the time it becomes final may have substantial economic value. If the debtor can continue to live in the mortgaged house without making the mortgage payments, for example, the secured creditor will likely lose that value forever. A fight over possession may be a fight over the economic use of the property during the interim period. Third, if the debtor is in possession of the property in the period leading up to the sale, it may be difficult or impossible for prospective purchasers to evaluate the property, thereby depressing the resale price. This problem may be exacerbated if the debtor is uncooperative.

Debtors have a very different view of the equities. They are, after all, being ousted from possession of property they own. They may not yet have had their day in court. Foreclosure is a legal safeguard that exists in part to protect debtors from wrongful repossession. Even though the vast majority of debtors are in default when foreclosure proceedings are filed against them, some are not. If the latter are ousted from possession during the case, a very real loss is imposed on them. Imagine the plight of a family that is evicted from its home or a business that loses the use of its production machinery. The losses may be significant and sometimes irreparable.

Moreover, the creditor who can make a credible threat to dispossess the debtor — even if only temporarily — has extraordinary leverage over the debtor. The creditor can use that leverage to force other changes in the debtor-creditor relationship, to raise the rate of interest, demand additional collateral, or even to require waiver of a cause of action against the creditor for its breach of the loan agreement.

This kind of leverage can flow in the other direction as well. The debtor who can credibly threaten to retain possession of the collateral for a long time, to run up the cost of repossession, or to reduce the value of the collateral before the creditor can gain possession, may be able to take advantage of the creditor in post-default negotiations.

The ability to gain or retain possession during foreclosure can have a value far in excess of the use value of the property during the period in question. The holder of the enforceable right to possession pending foreclosure can terminate the debtor's business or permit it to continue, can control access to the property while bidders are preparing for the foreclosure sale, or can cut off the cash flow that enables the debtor to continue to resist foreclosure.

Many security agreements provide that the creditor has the right to possession immediately upon default, but such a provision is only the starting point for legal analysis. Whether courts will enforce such a provision depends on the circumstances. Even if the secured creditor obtains the *right* to possession from such a provision, the jurisdiction may require that the secured creditor follow particular procedures to obtain that possession. Because the rules for possession of real estate and personal property differ sharply, we discuss them separately.

B. The Right to Possession Pending Foreclosure — Real Property

1. The Debtor's Right to Possession During Foreclosure

The general rule is that mortgagees never become entitled to possession of mortgaged real property in their capacity as mortgagees. The debtor remains owner of the property and is entitled to possession of it until the court forecloses the debtor's equity of redemption and the sale is held. Only the purchaser at the foreclosure sale (who may, of course, be the mortgagee) is entitled to dispossess the debtor.

The remedies by which purchasers at foreclosure sales obtain possession vary from state to state. In some jurisdictions, the purchaser must file an action for eviction or ejectment and obtain a court order for removal. In others, the court can issue a writ of possession or writ of assistance on motion by the purchaser. In either event, the purchaser can probably have the sheriff on the scene with uniform and gun in no more than 10 to 20 days after the purchase.

2. Appointment of a Receiver

While a foreclosure case is pending, any interested party can apply for the appointment of a *receiver* to preserve the value of the collateral. To illustrate, assume that the collateral is an apartment building. Although some of the apartments are occupied by rent-paying tenants, the total rents have been insufficient to enable the debtor to make its mortgage payment. The debtor-landlord has fallen behind in its mortgage payments, and the mortgagee has filed a complaint for foreclosure. The debtor currently sees no way it can redeem the property, but also knows that foreclosure will take several months. The debtor continues to collect the rents from the existing tenants, but does not pay anything to the mortgagee. It spends no money on necessary maintenance for the apartment building. Tenants begin to complain about the appearance of the property and its poor state of repair. Some move out, further reducing the flow of rents and impairing the value of the collateral. In circumstances such as these, the court may grant temporary relief to the mortgagee in the form of the appointment of a receiver.

The receiver will be an officer of the court with fiduciary obligations to all who have an interest in the property. He or she will have the right to collect the rents and use the money to maintain the building, as well as the authority to rent them out as necessary. Typically, the receiver will retain any rents collected in excess of the amounts necessary to maintain the property, pending the outcome of the mortgage foreclosure action.

On the facts of this illustration, appointment of the receiver will cut off temporarily the debtor's cash flow from the collateral until the judgment of foreclosure cuts it off permanently. The mortgagee does not get access to the cash flow directly, but the cash flow will be used in part to maintain the value of the collateral — in effect giving the mortgagee the benefit of it.

A foreclosing mortgagee does not always succeed in winning the appointment of a receiver. Courts rarely appoint receivers unless the terms of the mortgages provide for such appointments. Even when the mortgages so provide, appointment is an equitable remedy that remains in the sound discretion of the court. The creditor must show that under the circumstances of the particular case its remedy at law (foreclosure alone) is inadequate. That usually will be true only when the value of the property is inadequate to satisfy the mortgage debt and the mortgagor is insolvent so that any deficiency judgment will be uncollectible. Only in rare and extreme circumstances do the courts appoint receivers to take possession of owner-occupied residential real estate; a defaulting debtor can nearly always count on retaining possession of the family homestead while the debtor struggles to save it from foreclosure. Receivers are appointed to take possession of owner-occupied commercial real estate somewhat more often, but the courts are understandably reluctant to dispossess a debtor who is operating its business from the mortgaged premises.

As the *Stedman* case in Assignment 2 illustrated, entry of judgment in favor of the mortgagee is not necessarily the end of a mortgage foreclosure case. After entry of the judgment, debtors may appeal, challenge the procedure by which the property was sold, or exercise their rights to redeem. But during this period, the court is likely to be more receptive to the mortgagee's request for the appointment of a receiver. For example, in Norwest Bank of Des Moines, N.A. v. Bruett, 432 N.W.2d 711 (Iowa Ct. App. 1988), the court took the unusual step of appointing a receiver to take possession of the farm that served as collateral from the debtors who personally occupied it. The court made the appointment after it entered judgment, but during the one-year redemption period provided under Iowa law. The applicable statute provided that "The debtor may redeem real property at any time within one year from the day of sale, and will, in the meantime, be entitled to the possession thereof. . . . " The court determined, however, that debtors could waive this right to possession and that the Bruetts had done so by a provision in the mortgage. The effect was that the Bruetts retained their right to redeem their farm, but lost possession of the farm in the meantime.

Many states have statutes governing the appointment of receivers in mortgage foreclosure cases. Typically these statutes mention a few of the factors of concern to the courts in determining whether to appoint a receiver, but do not prohibit consideration of other factors. The factors mentioned in these two statutes are typical of the statutes generally.

California Code of Civil Procedure

Cal. Civ. Proc. Code §564(b) (West Supp. 1994)

[A] receiver may be appointed by the court in which an action or proceeding is pending, or by a judge thereof, in the following cases: . . .
    2. In an action by a secured lender for the foreclosure of the deed of trust or mortgage and sale of the property, where it appears that the property is in danger of being lost, removed, or materially injured, or

that the condition of the mortgage has not been performed, and that the property is probably insufficient to discharge the deed of trust or mortgage debt.

Illinois Mortgage Foreclosure Law

Ill. Rev. Stat. ch. 110, para. 15-1701(b)(2) (1991)

[In cases involving nonresidential real property,] if (i) the mortgagee is so authorized by the terms of the mortgage or other written instrument, and (ii) the court is satisfied that there is a reasonable probability that the mortgagee will prevail on a final hearing of the cause, the mortgagee shall upon request be placed in possession of the real estate, except that if the mortgagor shall object and show good cause, the court shall allow the mortgagor to remain in possession.

The receiver typically takes possession of the collateral during the foreclosure case and delivers possession directly to the purchaser at the foreclosure sale.

3. Assignments of Rents

If the parties contemplate that the debtor will rent the collateral to others during the term of the mortgage, the mortgage is likely to include a provision by which the debtor assigns the rents from the property to the mortgagee as additional security. The provision gives the mortgagee the right to collect the rents directly from the tenants in the event of default under the mortgage. Because collecting the rents from mortgaged property that has been rented to third parties, like appointing a receiver, is functionally the equivalent of taking possession, some courts are reluctant to give effect to the assignment of rents clause. But other courts hold that a mortgagee who declares a default, notifies the tenants to pay the rent to it, and proceeds to collect the rent without foreclosing, acts within its rights.

C. The Right to Possession Pending Foreclosure — Personal Property

Article 9 of the Uniform Commercial Code governs nearly all security interests in personal property. On the issue of possession pending for foreclosure, it favors the secured creditor in the strongest terms. Unless otherwise agreed, U.C.C. §9-609 gives the secured party the right to take possession immediately on default. The secured party need not involve courts or public officials if the secured party can get possession without a breach of the peace. But if the debtor resists repossession, the secured party must obtain a court order for possession and have the sheriff take possession from the debtor. The easiest way to obtain such an order is by filing an action for replevin.

The replevin action is a direct descendant of the common law "writ of replevin" commonly used to recover possession of wandering cattle and other tangible personal property. Generally speaking, any party entitled to possession of tangible personal property is entitled to the writ. The writ directs the sheriff to take possession of the property from the defendant and give it to the plaintiff. By far the most common users of replevin today are secured creditors entitled to possession of collateral pursuant to U.C.C. §9-609.

To obtain the remedy, the secured creditor files a civil action against the debtor. Immediately upon filing, the creditor can move for an order granting immediate possession pending the outcome of the case. Typically, the plaintiff can obtain a hearing on the motion in no more than about 10 to 20 days. In most states, the plaintiff must give notice of the hearing to the debtor, but in some, the hearing can be held and the writ of replevin issued before the debtor is even aware that the case has been filed. If the secured creditor establishes at the hearing that it is likely to prevail in the action, the court issues the writ of replevin. Issuance of the writ is usually conditioned on the creditor's posting a bond to protect the debtor in the event that the debtor ultimately prevails in the replevin action. The debtor can regain possession by posting a similar bond, but if the debtor is in financial difficulty (as is usually the case in a replevin action), the debtor will probably be unable to do so. Once the writ has been issued and possession of the collateral transferred to the secured creditor, most debtors have no reason to defend the replevin action. Judgment is entered by default. The effect is that after default, a secured creditor usually can obtain possession of collateral that is tangible personal property through judicial procedure within two or three weeks. The creditor can then complete the foreclosure by selling the collateral in a commercially reasonable manner. U.C.C. §9-610.

In the following case, the secured creditor, with the help of the Wisconsin legislature and the state court trial judge, explored the limits of this powerful remedy.

Del's Big Saver Foods, Inc. v.
Carpenter Cook, Inc.

603 F. Supp. 1071 (W.D. Wis. 1985)

CRABB, CHIEF JUDGE. . . .

FACTS

Before December of 1983, plaintiffs Burdell and Janice Robish owned and operated Del's Big Saver Foods, Inc., a retail grocery store. In July of 1983, in order to finance their business, the plaintiffs individually and as officers of their incorporated store, signed a note and security agreement, giving defendant Carpenter Cook Company, a subsidiary of defendant Farm House Foods Corporation, a security interest in "[a]ll furniture, equipment, now owned or hereafter acquired by the [b]orrower, together with all inventory [and] the proceeds from the sale thereof."

On December 6, 1983, the defendant law firm of Doyle, Ladd & Philips, P.C. filed a complaint in the Circuit Court of Vilas County, Wisconsin on behalf of defendant Carpenter Cook, alleging among other things that Burdell and Janis Robish had repeatedly defaulted on their note, that Carpenter Cook had a security interest in some of the Robishes' property, and that pursuant to [UCC §9-609], Carpenter Cook was entitled to possession of the property. Along with the complaint, defendant Carpenter Cook submitted an affidavit in support of its motion for possession of the secured property. In the affidavit, Philip Strohl, an officer of Carpenter Cook, stated that the Robishes had defaulted repeatedly on their loan and had breached other covenants of the security agreement. Strohl asserted that the collateral would deteriorate in the hands of the Robishes. Also, Strohl stated the value of the collateral and its location. Defendant Cook submitted to the court a $100,000 indemnity bond issued by defendant United States Fidelity & Guaranty Company.

On December 6, 1983, the day the complaint was filed in the Vilas County court, the state trial judge issued an order granting defendant Carpenter Cook immediate possession of the collateral, the right to operate the Robishes' store as a going concern, and the right to use the proceeds from the sale of the collateral "in the operation of the store." That same day, defendant Strohl, as agent for defendant Carpenter Cook, with the aid of the defendant law firm, obtained certification of the order from the deputy clerk of the Circuit Court of Vilas County. Members of the defendant law firm then proceeded to plaintiffs' store claiming that if plaintiffs did not turn over possession of the store, the county sheriff would be summoned pursuant to the court order to serve the documents and remove the plaintiffs bodily. In response to these demands, plaintiffs turned over the premises to defendant Carpenter Cook.

Plaintiffs had no notice of defendant Carpenter Cook's intent to take possession of the store, or of the court proceedings to gain possession, until the order was presented to them on December 6, 1983. Plaintiffs would not have relinquished possession of the store but for the court order signed by the circuit judge.

OPINION . . .

In sum, plaintiffs have alleged two causes of action: (1) that in concert with defendants Carpenter Cook (through its agent Strohl) and Doyle, Ladd and Philips, the state trial judge applied Wisconsin's repossession procedures in violation of Plaintiffs' due process rights; and (2) that these same defendants intentionally damaged plaintiffs' business reputation in violation of state law. . . .

Plaintiffs Claim Under 42 U.S.C. §1983

Before a plaintiff can prevail on a claim brought pursuant to 42 U.S.C. §1983, he must prove (1) that the defendant has deprived him of a right secured by the Constitution or the laws of the United States; and (2) that the defendant has deprived him of this right under color of state law.

A.   Deprivation of a Constitutional Right

Plaintiffs contend that the state judge's application of [UCC §9-609] to them deprived them of their Fourteenth Amendment right to due process because their property was taken without notice or an opportunity to contest the possession. Plaintiffs cite the line of Supreme Court cases beginning with Sniadach v. Family Finance Corp., 395 U.S. 337 (1969), and culminating in North Georgia Finishing, Inc. v. Di-Chem, Inc., 419 U.S. 601 (1975), for the proposition that it is a denial of due process for a creditor to repossess property upon ex parte application to a court without giving the debtor notice or an opportunity to contest the taking. Not surprisingly, the defendants cite those same cases to support their claim that plaintiffs in this case have not been denied their constitutional rights.

1.   Due Process Precedent

Sniadach arose out of a challenge to a Wisconsin statute permitting a creditor to freeze the debtor's wages upon application to the clerk of the state court without affording the debtor notice or an opportunity to be heard. The United States Supreme Court ruled that in the context of wages a debtor's property may not be taken without notice and a prior hearing. Sniadach v. Family Finance Corp., 395 U.S. at 340-342.

In Fuentes v. Shevin, 407 U.S. 67 (1972), the Court reviewed a state procedure under which a creditor could obtain a prejudgment writ of replevin through a summary process of ex parte application to a court clerk, upon the posting of a bond for double the value of the property to be seized. The Supreme Court held that these state replevin procedures were unconstitutional because they deprived the debtor of notice and an opportunity to be heard before his property was seized. Id. at 96. The Court explained that even though the debtor had access to certain post-deprivation remedies, those remedies were only "another factor to weigh in determining the appropriate form of hearing, [and were] not decisive of the basic right to a prior hearing of some kind." Id. at 86.

In Mitchell v. W.T. Grant Co., 416 U.S. 600 (1974), the Court retreated from its position in Fuentes. In Mitchell, the Court was reviewing provisions of the Louisiana Code of Civil Procedure that made available to a lien holder a writ of sequestration to forestall waste or alienation of the encumbered property. Although the writ was obtainable on the creditor's ex parte application, without notice to the debtor for an opportunity for a hearing, the writ would issue only upon a detailed affidavit by the creditor and only upon a judge's authorization after the creditor had filed a sufficient bond. The debtor could seek immediate dissolution of the writ, which had to be ordered unless the creditor proved the grounds for issuance (existence of the debt, lien, and delinquency), failing which the court could order return of the property and assess damages in the debt-or's favor. The Court found that the Louisiana procedures satisfied the requirements of the due process clause despite the fact that they permitted an ex parte deprivation of property: the statutory scheme decreased the likelihood of an erroneous prehearing deprivation because the creditor had to present detailed factual allegations to a judicial officer before a sequestration order could be issued, Id. at 616-617, and statutory procedures did not effect a final deprivation of property because the debtor had an immediate right to a post-seizure hearing. Id. at 609-610. From this, the Court concluded that because the statute provided certain pre-deprivation procedures designed to reduce erroneous deprivations, and because the deprivation was only temporary, the Louisiana procedures effected a constitutional accommodation of the interests of debtors and creditors. Id. at 607.

Finally, in North Georgia Finishing, Inc. v. Di-Chem, Inc., 419 U.S. at 601, the Supreme Court examined a Georgia statutory scheme that permitted a creditor to obtain a writ of garnishment issued by a court clerk on an affidavit containing only conclusory allegations and that permitted the debtor to dissolve the garnishment only by filing a bond with the court. The Court held that the garnishment of the debtor's bank account was unconstitutional because there were no predeprivation protections as in Mitchell, and because the debtor was not entitled to an immediate hearing after seizure to dissolve the writ. Id. at 607.

From these cases, I conclude that in creditor repossession or garnishment cases, the due process clause requires either (1) that the debtor be provided a hearing before his property is taken, or (2) that the debtor be provided certain preseizure procedural safeguards, coupled with a prompt post-deprivation hearing before final judgment. Those preseizure safeguards need not include a hearing, but must include a deprivation order issuable only by a judicial officer based upon detailed factual allegations provided by the party seeking possession.

In this case, since I must accept as true plaintiffs' allegation that they did not receive a hearing prior to the seizure of their property, I can grant defendants' motion for summary judgment only if I am satisfied that plaintiffs had the benefit of the requisite predeprivation procedures and the right to a post-deprivation hearing pending final judgment.

2. Wisconsin Procedures

The plaintiffs base their claim on what they contend is the state judge's unconstitutional application of [UCC §9-609]. That section, . . . gives a secured creditor the right to take possession of a defaulting debtor's secured property. It provides that "[i]n taking possession a secured party may proceed without judicial process if this can be done without breach of the peace or may proceed *by action*." (Emphasis added.) Since the defendants Carpenter Cook, Philip Strohl, and Doyle, Ladd & Philips resorted to the courts to seize plaintiffs' property, they proceeded "by action." Plaintiffs' claim is that the state judge misapplied the "by action" method of repossession by permitting a deprivation which fell short of plaintiffs' right to due process.

The text of the UCC and the Official Comments to [§9-609] fail to provide any guidance to the meaning of "by action." However, the courts and commentators agree that "by action" refers to the applicable state's replevin procedures.

It appears that the 1977 revisions of the Wisconsin replevin procedures were drafted specifically in response to the Supreme Court's holdings in *Mitchell* and *North Georgia Finishing*. The preseizure requirements set out in those cases are satisfied by the provision in the Wisconsin replevin procedures that an order directing a return of the property may be issued only by a judge or other judicial officer and only after the creditor has submitted a verified complaint or affidavit containing several detailed allegations specified in the statute. Also, the replevin statutes provide that at any time the debtor may request a hearing before the judge for vacation or modification of the possession order "for any sufficient cause."

Wis. Stat. §810.05. Moreover, the statutes make it clear that the ex parte seizures merely provide for delivery before final judgment.[3]

3. Application of [UCC §9-609] and Chapter 810

The undisputed facts of the seizure in this case reveal that the state court judge did not deprive plaintiffs of their constitutional rights. Carpenter Cook's state court affidavit and complaint incorporated by exhibit into the Robishes' complaint in this case establish that defendants complied with Wis. Stats. §810.02. Thus plaintiffs cannot contend that the judge abridged their preseizure rights. Also, because the judge merely granted an order for possession, rather than entering a final judgment, plaintiffs had an opportunity to seek an immediate post-seizure hearing. Whether plaintiffs exercised their right to a hearing is irrelevant to this discussion. The due process clause guarantees only the "right to an *opportunity* to be heard [and thus] no hearing need be held unless the [debtor], having received notice of his opportunity, takes advantage of it." Fuentes v. Shevin, 407 U.S. at 92 n.29 (emphasis in original). Because the judge complied with the plaintiffs' preseizure procedural rights and did not deny them a post-seizure hearing, plaintiffs cannot prevail on their claim that their due process rights were violated.

ORDER

IT IS ORDERED that defendants' motion to dismiss this case is GRANTED.

In the constitutional rhetoric of this opinion it is easy to miss the harsh reality of what the courts did to the Robishes. Creditor Carpenter Cook filed a replevin action alleging that the Robishes were behind on their payments. The complaint contained no allegations of fraud or special circumstances to warrant what then occurred. No one notified the Robishes of the filing of the case, and they had no opportunity to respond to the allegations made against them. Instead, the court discussed the matter with Carpenter Cook's lawyers and then ordered the sheriff to take the Robishes' business from them and give it to Carpenter Cook. The Robishes learned what was happening only when Carpenter Cook's lawyers arrived and presented them with the order. The entire proceeding occurred in a single day. The court nevertheless held that the Robishes had been afforded due

3. The plaintiff in a replevin action may claim the delivery of the property *prior to final judgment* in a manner provided in this chapter. (Emphasis added.)

process. *Del's Big Saver Foods* is not a bizarre aberration; it is merely the logical extension of what occurs in routine replevin cases every day.

D.   The Article 9 Right to Self-Help Repossession

The creditors discussed in the preceding sections of this assignment probably would have liked to avoid the hassle and expense of working through courts and sheriffs to obtain possession of their collateral. But they probably had no choice. Use of available judicial procedures is often mandatory.

The principal exception is that a creditor with an Article 9 security interest in tangible, personal property can bypass the courts and the sheriff and do its own work. The creditor's reason for doing so is usually to save time, effort, and money. The right to "self-help repossession" is derived from U.C.C. §9-609. That section provides that after default a secured party may take possession of the collateral.

Security agreements typically require that the debtor surrender possession upon default, and some debtors actually do just that. A debtor who is behind on payments on his car loan may simply drive the car to the bank and hand over the keys. But most debtors do not surrender so easily. They ignore the bank's demands for possession and keep on driving. Some try to get together enough money to make up the back payments in the hope that they can renew their relationship with the bank. Others plan to deal with the problem when necessary by filing bankruptcy. Still others simply try to get as much use out of the car as they can before it is taken from them. Probably most debtors have no plan at all — they just wait to see what tomorrow brings. The secured creditor who wants the car from any of these debtors must take the initiative.

The secured creditor can file a lawsuit against the debtor, obtain judicial recognition of its right to possession, and send the sheriff out to take the car. But the secured creditor can move even faster without judicial process. For example, if the car buyer is behind on the payments and the car is parked in a public place, unlocked, with the keys in it, the secured creditor is in business. The agent of the secured creditor, unlike the agent of its unsecured counterpart, is entitled to hop in and drive the car away.

Finding the car with the keys is a neat story, but repossession is seldom so easy. In many cases, the secured creditor will have difficulty locating its collateral. The car may be kept on private property, inside a fence, or in a locked garage. The car itself may be locked or inoperable. And the neighbors may want to know what somebody skulking in the back lot with a picklock is up to.

A small, somewhat disreputable industry specializes in solving these kinds of problems for secured lenders. For a few hundred dollars, these collection or repossession agencies will find an item of collateral, take it from the debtor, and turn it over to the secured creditor. Much can go wrong in the process. Repossessors may invade the property of third parties in search of their collateral or they may repossess the wrong goods. Debtors may defend their possession with harsh words, fists, or guns. The courts generally hold the duty to refrain from breach of the peace during repossession nondelegable, making the secured creditors liable for the consequences of illegal repossessions by their independent contractors. E.g., Robinson v. Citicorp National Services, Inc., 921 S.W.2d 52 (Mo. App. 1996) (holding secured creditor potentially liable for debtor's death by heart attack during a wrongful repossession).

U.C.C. §9-609(a)(2) gives the creditor the option to leave "equipment" temporarily in the possession of the debtor but render it unusable. In the ordinary application of that provision, the collateral is a large piece of equipment, such as a combine or threshing machine, for which removal to a warehouse would be slow and costly. The creditor might remove key parts from the engine so that the equipment could not be used pending sale.

E.   The Limits of Self-Help: Breach of the Peace

A secured creditor is entitled to repossess collateral. This is not a license to engage in any behavior necessary to get it. The U.C.C. permits self-help repossession only if the secured creditor can repossess without breach of the peace. U.C.C. §9-609(b)(2). Not surprisingly, most lawsuits involving a creditor's self-help repossession — and much planning advice about self-help — turn on what constitutes a breach of the peace.

Salisbury Livestock Co.
v. Colorado Central Credit Union

793 P.2d 470 (Wyo. 1990)

GOLDEN, J.

[Colorado Central Credit Union (Colorado Central) loaned money to George Salisbury III (young Salisbury). The loans were secured by young

Salisbury's motor vehicles. Young Salisbury defaulted and Colorado Central sent a team of repossessors after the motor vehicles. The repossessors took some of the motor vehicles from a ranch owned by Salisbury Livestock Company (Salisbury Livestock), a family corporation run by young Salisbury's father, George Salisbury, Jr. The repossessors took the vehicles from an outdoor area adjacent to the ranch house, just after dawn. They gave no advance notice to Salisbury Livestock and encountered no opposition to the repossession. When Salisbury Livestock discovered what had happened, it sued Colorado Central for wrongful repossession and trespass.]

Our review convinces us that Salisbury Livestock is entitled to have a jury decide the merits of its argument. There is no real disagreement as to whether a trespass occurred.[1] The crux of this dispute is whether the entry to repossess was privileged either by the self-help statute or by consent. From our review of the evidence in a light favorable to Salisbury Livestock, we conclude that a reasonable jury could find that it was not. . . .

[U.C.C. §9-609] does not define breach of the peace, and there is no definition offered elsewhere in the Wyoming statutes that address rights of secured parties.[3] In our review of decisions from other jurisdictions we find no consistently applied definition, but agree with the analysis of the Utah Supreme Court in Cottam v. Heppner, 777 P.2d 468, 472 (Utah 1989), that, "[c]ourts have struggled in determining when a creditor's trespass onto a debtor's property rises to the level of a breach of the peace. The two primary factors considered in making this determination are the potential for immediate violence and the nature of the premises intruded upon." These factors are interrelated in that the potential for violence increases as the creditor's trespass comes closer to a dwelling,[4] and we will focus our analysis on them. It is necessary to evaluate the facts of each case to determine whether a breach of the peace has occurred.

We agree with the trial court that the Restatement (Second) of Torts §198 reasonableness requirement provides appropriate criteria for evaluating whether a creditor's entry has breached the peace. If, as here, there

---

1. A trespass against real property is simply defined as, "consist[ing] of an interference with the possessor's interest in excluding others from the land." Restatement (Second) of Torts §163 (1965). In its ruling on the motion for a directed verdict the district court said, "I don't think that there's any doubt under any law that [the entry to repossess] was a trespass, because there was an intentional entering of the land of another."

3. Wyoming's criminal breach of the peace statute, W.S. 6-6-102(a) (June 1988 Repl.), reads, "[a] person commits breach of the peace if he disturbs the peace of a community or its inhabitants by using threatening, abusive or obscene language or violent actions with knowledge or probable cause to believe he will disturb the peace." Restatement (Second) of Torts §116 is more useful in arriving at what constitutes a civil breach of the peace: "A breach of the peace is a public offense done by violence, or one causing or likely to cause an immediate disturbance of public order." We note that, although actual violence is not required to find a breach of the peace, a disturbance or violence must be reasonably likely, and not merely a remote possibility.

4. Decisions elsewhere have established a general rule that a creditor's entry into a residence without permission is a breach of the peace. J. White & R. Summers, Handbook of the Law Under the Uniform Commercial Code 26-6 (2d ed. 1980).

was no confrontation and the timing and manner, including notice or lack of notice, are found reasonable, the entry is privileged. If the jury should find that the manner or timing of this entry was unreasonable because it may have triggered a breach of the peace, it in effect finds the entry a breach of the peace and unprivileged. We foresee the possibility that a rational jury could reach the conclusion that this entry was unreasonable.

As asserted by Salisbury Livestock, one specific inquiry is whether, as discussed in Comment *d*, §198, a demand for the property is required. [Demand is unnecessary] if such demand would be futile, but there must be a determination whether demand would have been futile in these circumstances. Young Salisbury had not responded to Colorado Central's demands for payment, but Salisbury Livestock, on whose property the vehicles were found, was not given an opportunity to deliver the pledged vehicles to Colorado Central or its representatives. Notice is not an express requirement of the statute, but is a common law element which helps to determine the reasonableness of the repossessors' actions. . . .

Neither of the *Cottam* factors, nor the Restatement reasonableness analysis, requires or suggests that a trespass is necessarily a breach of the peace. Property owners may be entirely unaware of a trespass, so that there is no potential for immediate violence. Likewise, a peaceful, inadvertent trespass on lands remote from any home or improvements is unlikely to provoke violence. Therefore, we do not agree with Salisbury Livestock's contention that a trespass without more is a breach of the peace. A trespass breaches the peace only if certain types of premises are invaded, or immediate violence is likely.

However, we cannot agree with Colorado Central's assertion that there can be no finding of a breach of the peace because there was no confrontation. Confrontation or violence is not necessary to finding a breach of the peace. The possibility of immediate violence is sufficient. Two elements of this case create questions which we believe might lead reasonable jurors to a conclusion at odds with the trial court's directed verdict. First, this was an entry onto the premises of a third party not privy to the loan agreement. Particularly if there was no knowledge of young Salisbury's consent to repossession, this could trigger a breach of the peace. The few reported cases involving repossession from third party properties suggest that such entry is acceptable. However, these cases do not address third party residential property. When entry onto third party property is coupled with the second unusual element, the location and the setting of this repossession, the possibility of a different verdict becomes more apparent.

We have not located any cases addressing a creditor's entry into the secluded ranchyard of an isolated ranch where the vehicles sought are not even visible from a public place. The few cases involve urban or suburban driveways, urban parking lots, or business premises. We believe that the location and setting of this entry to repossess is sufficiently distinct, and the privacy expectations of rural residents sufficiently different, that a jury should weigh the reasonableness of this entry, or whether the peace may have been breached by a real possibility of imminent violence, or even by mere entry into these premises: the area next to the residence in a secluded ranchyard.

Not surprisingly, there is considerable dispute over precisely what kind of facts constitute a breach of the peace. The best way to get a sense of what kind of behavior is prohibited, what kind is permitted, and where the gray areas lie, is to read a lot of cases. We recognize the limits on law students' time, however, so we offer a potpourri of reported cases, each involving an allegation of breach of the peace. Cases holding there was a breach of the peace:

1. The creditor took a uniformed police officer to the debtor's home on a repossession attempt. With the police officer present, the debtor verbally consented to the repossession. The police officer was there to prevent anticipated violence. The court concluded that a breach of the peace had occurred, stating that "the fact that the deputy did not say anything is not significant. [To hold otherwise] would set a precedent by involving local law enforcement in self-help repossessions, and would create the very volatile situations the statute was designed to prevent." In re Walker v. Walthall, 588 P.2d 863 (Ariz. Ct. App. 1978).

2. The first time the repossessor attempted to take a heavy duty rotary mower from the debtor's home, the debtor ordered him off the premises. Almost a month later, the repossessor came back with two more men. The debtor was not home, but the debtor's son told the men they should not take the mower and "protested" its removal. But "surrounded" by the three, he did nothing further to stop them because he "was afraid of being beaten." The court held that he had done enough to render the continued repossession illegal, stating that "when [the secured creditor's] agents were physically confronted by [the debtor's] representative, disregarded his request to desist their efforts at repossession and refused to depart from the private premises upon which the collateral was kept, they committed a breach of the peace within the meaning of [U.C.C. §9-609], lost the protective application of that section, and thereafter stood as would any other person who unlawfully refuses to depart from the land of another." Morris v. First National Bank & Trust Co. of Ravenna, Ohio, 7 U.C.C. 131 (Ohio 1970).

3. To repossess a bulldozer, the repossessors cut a chain used to lock a fence. Because that was done after the end of the work day, it left plaintiff's heavy equipment storage area containing approximately $350,000 worth of equipment unsecured and unprotected. Citing a case in which the repossessor's having broken a window to unlock a door to a debtor's residence and repossess a piano was a breach of the peace, the court held that cutting the chain was improper. Laurel Coal Co. v. Walter E. Heller & Co., Inc., 539 F. Supp. 1006 (W.D. Pa. 1982).

Cases holding there was not a breach of the peace:

4. The debtor's complaint for wrongful repossession alleged that the repossessor followed him to Big Stone Gap, Virginia, where he was staying with his daughter. About 2:00 A.M., the repossessor entered plaintiff's truck, started it, raced the engine, and "barrel[ed] out of the lot and down the street." The debtor said he and his daughter "did not know what was happening and were in fear." The court held that the complaint failed to state a cause of action. The court considered the "stealthy manner" in which the repossession was effected as "calculated to avoid a breach of the peace because the prospect of a confrontation with the plaintiff was less at 2 A.M. than it would have been in the daylight hours or in the early evening." Even though the repossession may have violated some traffic ordinance, it was not "an incitement to violence or to break the peace." That the repossessor was an off-duty deputy sheriff also did not matter, because the plaintiff did not know that while the repossession was in progress. Wallace v. Chrysler Credit Corp., 743 F. Supp. 1228 (W.D. Va. 1990).

5. Two repossessors used a wrecker to repossess a woman's automobile from her driveway. Awakened by the noise, she ran outside to stop them and "hollered at them" as they were driving away. The two men stopped. They told her they were repossessing the car. She explained that she had been attempting to bring the past payments up to date and informed the men that the car contained personal items belonging to a third person. The men "stepped between her and the car" when she attempted to retrieve them, gave her the personal items, and drove off with her car "without further complaint from [her]." She admitted that the men were polite throughout the encounter and did not make any threats toward her or do anything that caused her to fear any physical harm. The court held the repossession legal and reversed the verdict that had been returned in her favor. The dissent noted that plaintiff was a

single parent living with her two small children and observed that "facing the wrecking crew in the dead of night, [plaintiff] did everything she could to stop them short of introducing physical force." Williams v. Ford Motor Credit Co., 674 F.2d 717 (8th Cir. 1982).

6. On the secured creditor's first attempt to repossess her car, the debtor successfully ordered the repossessor off the premises. The debtor claimed that she had a gun in the house and would use it if he came back. She later called the repossessor's office and threatened that "if she caught anyone on her property again trying to take her car, [she] would leave him laying right where [she] saw him." Thirty days later, the intrepid repossessor took the car from the debtor's driveway, awakening her with the sound of "burning rubber." No confrontation occurred. The debtor did not know the car was being taken until the repossessor had safely departed with it. The court held that despite the "potential for violence" the debtor had previously communicated, the repossession had not breached the peace. Wade v. Ford Motor Credit Co., 668 P.2d 183 (Kan. Ct. App. 1983).

7. The collateral was inventory and equipment located in the debtor's business premises. The repossessor "obtained the services of a locksmith who enabled him to gain entry onto the premises, whereupon he changed the locks on the doors." The court held this repossession not to be a breach of the peace because the security agreement signed by the debtor provided that, in the event of default, the secured creditor could enter the premises to repossess the collateral. Global Casting, Etc. v. Daley-Hodkin Corp., 432 N.Y.S.2d 453 (N.Y. Sup. Ct. 1980).

8. The two truck rigs that served as collateral were in the possession of a truck equipment dealer. The repossessor obtained possession of the rigs by fraudulently misrepresenting to the truck equipment dealer that the debtor had given him permission to repossess. The court ruled that the misrepresentation was not a breach of the peace because it did not "support a potential for immediate violence." K.B. Oil Co. v. Ford Motor Credit Co., Inc., 811 F.2d 310 (6th Cir. 1987).

9. The secured creditor, Shari Rainwater, was admitted to the offices of the debtor, Rx Medical Services Corporation, by an employee she knew. Over the objection of that employee, she removed collateral consisting of the debtor's computer hardware, software, computer records, and business paper from the offices. The court held her actions did not breach the peace because Rainwater "used no force or threats of force to take the [collateral]." The court stated that consent of the debtor to

repossession was not necessary; all that was needed was consent to her presence in the office, which had been given. Rainwater v. Rx Medical Services Corp., 30 U.C.C. Rep. Serv. 2d 983 (E.D. Cal. 1995).

While the cases regarding breach of the peace are not all consistent and changes in factual nuance can often lead to changes in outcomes, each of these cases represents the view of a majority of courts that have addressed the particular point.

F.   Self-Help Against Accounts as Collateral

Many businesses sell their products or services on credit. For example, it is common for manufacturers of home audio equipment to give their dealers 30 days to pay for merchandise shipped to them. While the debt is outstanding, it is an "account payable" of the dealer-debtor and an "account receivable" of the creditor-manufacturer (APs and ARs, in the accounting lingo). Article 9 defines "account receivable" as simply an "account." U.C.C. §9-102(a)(2). Although each separate account may be small and remain outstanding for only a short period of time, a business that sells on credit will typically have many of them. In the aggregate, the accounts of such a business may have substantial value over a long time. At any given time, a manufacturer of audio equipment, for example, might be owed tens of thousands of dollars by its dealers. When the manufacturer wants to borrow money for its operations, a creditor looking for security might see the accounts as adequate collateral — if it could find a way to reach those accounts cheaply and quickly in the event of default.

One of the objectives of the drafters of Article 9 was to facilitate secured transactions in which the debtors' accounts could serve as collateral. Today, debtors routinely borrow against their accounts. Several arrangements are common, depending on the amount of control that the secured creditor is willing to cede to the debtor while the debtor is not in default. Here are some frequently used alternatives:

1.   The secured creditor may give the debtor virtually complete freedom to collect the accounts and to use the proceeds in its business.
2.   The secured creditor may agree to let the debtor collect the accounts, but require the debtor immediately to apply a specified portion of them to the loan. Under this kind of arrangement the debtor will expect the lender to make additional

loans, usually referred to as "future advances," secured by new accounts as they arise. The result may be a rapid cycle of borrowing, repaying, and reborrowing.

3. The secured creditor may arrange with the debtor that the account debtors will pay directly to the secured creditor. With the permission of the debtor, the secured creditor will notify the account debtors to pay directly to it. This procedure may also involve a rapid cycle of borrowing, repaying, and reborrowing to keep the debtor in business.

4. The secured creditor may vary the arrangements described in the preceding paragraph by requiring the debtor to direct its account debtors to make their payments to a post office box that is under the control of the secured creditor. This arrangement is sometimes referred to as a *lockbox* to signify that the debtor cannot reach the money coming in from its own accounts. The principal reason for using a lockbox rather than direct payment to the secured creditor is to avoid letting the account debtors know that the accounts have been used as collateral.

The bank in our example that lends money to an audio manufacturer secured by an interest in the manufacturer's accounts might use any of these arrangements.

In the event of default, U.C.C. §§9-607 and 9-406(a) provide a self-help remedy to the party holding a security interest in accounts. Under §9-607, the secured creditor who knows the identity of the account debtors can simply send them written notices to pay directly to the secured creditor. Although the express provisions of Article 9 stop short of saying that the account debtor must follow the instructions of the creditor, that is the practical effect.

For example, in Marine National Bank v. Airco, Inc., 389 F. Supp. 231 (W.D. Pa. 1975), Midland National Bank made loans to Craneways that were secured by various collateral of Craneways, including its accounts receivable. In June of 1971, Craneways' president notified the Bank that it had a contract with Airco to reconstruct a crane. Once the work was complete, Airco owed Craneways $23,000.

On July 19, 1971, the Bank sent, and Airco acknowledged receiving, a registered letter notifying Airco that the Bank held a security agreement covering all of Craneways' accounts receivable. The letter demanded that Airco pay any sums due Craneways to the Bank.

In August 1971, Craneways delivered the crane. Airco then paid $18,000 of the balance owing to Craneways. Craneways endorsed the check to the IRS to pay its taxes. In the Bank's lawsuit against Airco, the court entered judgment in favor of the Bank for $13,000, the remaining amount Craneways owed to the Bank.

Marine National demonstrates how powerful the self-help remedy against accounts can be. The Bank was able to recover its collateral — the account — even though that required the account debtor, Airco, to pay more than it owed. Airco theoretically had the right to recover its first payment from Craneways, but by the time Marine National sued Airco, Craneways was out of business and the debt was uncollectible.

In some respects, accounts make good collateral. The self-help remedy is easy to employ and accounts are by their nature readily converted to cash. But there are serious practical problems that render them less than ideal as collateral. A secured creditor's exercise of its right to notify account debtors can have devastating effects. Account debtors are motivated to pay their debts in part by their desire to keep doing business with the debtor and in part by the fear of legal action. To continue our earlier example, absent notice from the bank, the audio dealers generally continue to pay the manufacturer because they know that if they don't, the manufacturer will stop shipping audio equipment to them and may bring suit against them.

If, however, the manufacturer's bank has taken over the account, both motives may be undermined. The takeover signals to the dealers that the bank has lost confidence in the manufacturer's ability to meet its obligations and may suggest that the manufacturer will soon be out of business. The dealers may decide to withhold payment of the accounts in order to protect themselves against the manufacturer's future failure to provide service or honor warranties. Knowing that debtors in financial difficulty lack credibility, dealers may be more likely to complain about the manufacturer's products or to question the manufacturer's accounting. Worse yet, the dealers may realize that if the manufacturer's business fails, it may be difficult for either the manufacturer or the bank to sue them on the unpaid account. The bank financing the manufacturer may not have the information necessary to prove the account obligation to a judge or jury and the failed debtor may be unwilling to assist. As a result, the accounts can be expensive to collect or may become completely uncollectible.

Problem Set 3

3.1. Look back at Problem 1.1. Now assume that Jeffrey produced a second paper at your meeting with him. He explained that he had gone to an office supply store and picked up a form titled "Personal Property Security Agreement" and he had Lisa sign it. You look it over and decide it is a perfectly enforceable security agreement designating the lawn furniture as collateral. Does your advice change? U.C.C. §§9-102(72) and (73), 9-609.

3.2. Faye Maretka is the head of the collections department at
Commercial Finance, a valued, long-time client of your firm. CF frequently has occasion to repossess equipment from building construction sites in several states. CF's usual practice is to obtain judicial
process and then have the sheriff do the actual repossession. When
the judicial process is too slow or the sheriff too inflexible, Maretka
hires local repo people to effect a self-help repossession. To make sure
they act responsibly and effectively, she personally goes with them
and "calls the shots." CF can't afford to bring counsel along every
time they repossess property, so Maretka has asked you to work out
some guidelines on "how far she can go" in attempting a repossession.

Maretka explains the circumstances she usually encounters: The
borrower typically is a general contractor or a subcontractor who is
responsible for some specific aspect of construction, such as excava-
tion or the concrete work. The general contractor deals with the
owner and provides safety and security for the site. Larger sites are
fenced; some, but not all, have guards on the premises during the
night. Some equipment is left on the construction site overnight,
while the rest is typically under heavier security at the debtor's place
of business. Some of the repossession targets are motor vehicles, but
most are heavy equipment such as bulldozers or power generators
that must be carried by truck.

Outline your advice to Maretka. Focus on the situation where the
collateral is a bulldozer owned by a subcontractor, the site is owned
by a developer, and fences and security are provided by the general
contractor. Consider each of these three situations:

 a. Sites where there is neither a guard nor a fence,
 b. Sites where there is a fence but no guard, and
 c. Sites where there is a guard.
 d. As CF's regular counsel, you should also consider whether
     there is anything that should be in CF's security agreements
     about repossession that might make Maretka's job easier.

See U.C.C. §§9-609, 9-201, 9-602(6), 9-603.

3.3. Salvatore Ferragamo is the sole owner of Ferragamo Construction Company. Your firm has worked with Sal for 16 years, doing
all the legal work for his company from incorporation through the
negotiation of its insurance contracts. Terrible weather and late deliveries by suppliers have put the company behind in its work schedule
and consequently in what it can collect from its customers. The company has missed its third monthly payment to ITT Finance, which
provides financing secured by Ferragamo's equipment. Sal says he
needs just a week or two of uninterrupted operations to turn the corner financially.

This morning Sal received a letter by registered mail from ITT declaring the loan in default and directing him to assemble the collateral and make it available to ITT for repossession. Even though his security agreement with ITT provides that he will do precisely that, Sal has decided not to. Instead, he wants to know what he can do, short of bankruptcy, to resist repossession. If the ITT people come for the equipment, how should he handle the situation? What if they bring the sheriff with them? If the ITT people don't bring the sheriff, should Sal call the sheriff? Can he hide the equipment where the repo people won't be able to find it? U.C.C. §9-609. Assume that the state has a statute identical to Wisconsin Statute §943.25: "Whoever . . . conceals any personal property in which he knows another has a security interest . . . is guilty of a Class E felony."

Rule 1.2 of the ABA Model Rules of Professional Conduct provides in part:

> (d) A lawyer shall not counsel a client to engage, or assist a client, in conduct that the lawyer knows is criminal or fraudulent, but a lawyer may discuss the legal consequences of any proposed course of conduct with a client and may counsel or assist a client to make a good faith effort to determine the validity, scope, meaning or application of the law.

3.4. If ITT's lawyers gave ITT the same advice you gave Commercial Finance in Problem 3.2, would they be able to repossess Sal's equipment through self-help? In other words, if both the debtor and the creditor have the best legal advice regarding self-help repossession and follow it carefully, who "wins"?

3.5. Deare Distributors sells farming equipment to retail farming supply stores. Firstbank and Deare have a working arrangement under which Firstbank lends an amount equal to 60 percent of Deare's accounts receivable. When Deare makes a sale, it sends a copy of the invoice to Firstbank. The bank deposits an amount equal to 60 percent of the invoice to Deare's bank account. When the supply store pays the invoice, Deare is required to apply 60 percent of the proceeds to repay the loan immediately.

Deare has requested that Firstbank's interest in the accounts not be made known to the account debtors "because it might make them nervous." Firstbank is considering honoring that request in the absence of default, but it consults with you to ask about the risks of this arrangement. You want to consider why Deare might cheat and how it could do so. Is there any way to discover such cheating without contacting Deare's customers?

3.6. A year after the preceding problem, Firstbank is back with additional questions. Deare ultimately defaulted on the loan, and four months ago Firstbank notified the account debtors to pay Firstbank directly.

a.   Horne's Feed and Seed, one of Deare's account debtors, claims that it paid Deare in full last month and refuses to pay Firstbank. Can Firstbank collect from Horne's? U.C.C. §9-406(a).

b.   Another account debtor, Wilson's Farming Goods, has refused to pay anything, claiming that although they received $42,000 in equipment, they have untended warranty claims amounting to $19,000. What can Firstbank collect from Wilson's? U.C.C. §9-404(a).

3.7.   You have been counsel for Ronald Silber, the owner of Sound Emporium, for several years. Silber tells you that the business is experiencing some temporary cash-flow problems and he would like your advice on how to deal with them. You elicit the following list of problems:

a.   The business owes Southern Savings about $260,000 against the business premises, which are worth about $300,000. The mortgage is at 9 percent, and payments are $2,091 a month. Silber is two payments in arrears, and a third one is due next week. He received a notice from Southern's lawyers stating that if the payments are not brought up to date within ten days, Southern will foreclose.

b.   The business owes about $90,000 to Citizen's Bank. The loan is secured by the trade fixtures and equipment of the business. The loan is at 11 percent per year and the quarterly interest payment in the amount of $2,575 is 45 days past due. The loan officer says it must be brought current or "legal action will be taken."

c.   The utility bill is almost two months past due. The total amount owing for the two-month period is about $1,200. Silber has received the standard form notice that unless payment has been made within ten days, utility service will be cut off.

d.   Two suppliers are hounding Silber to pay invoices that are now more than 120 days old. Silber owes each about $20,000. One supplier has a security interest in the inventory it sold to Sound Emporium; the other does not. Both suppliers have hired local attorneys and are threatening immediate legal action. Silber says he can purchase similar inventory elsewhere for cash.

There are several other creditors, but none are really pushing for immediate payment. Silber wants desperately to keep the doors open because he thinks that in four to six months he can turn the business around. But over the next two or three months, he will have only about $4,000 a month to devote to the payments listed above. Silber says bankruptcy is "absolutely out of the question," and, from the way he says it, you know he means it (at least for now). Instead, he wants your opinion on how to allocate the money among these creditors and he also wants to know "what they can do if they don't get paid." What are your questions for Silber? What do you need to know about the law of your state? Based on what you now know and assuming your state's law is in accord with the majority, what's your advice? See U.C.C. §9-609.

Model Rules of Professional Conduct, Rule 3.2: Expediting Litigation — A Lawyer shall make reasonable efforts to expedite litigation consistent with the interest of the client.

Official Comment: Dilatory practices bring the administration of justice into disrepute. Delay should not be indulged in merely for the convenience of the advocates, or for the purpose of frustrating an opposing party's attempt to obtain rightful redress or repose. It is not a justification that similar conduct is often tolerated by the bench and bar. The question is whether a competent lawyer acting in good faith would regard the course of action as having *some substantial purpose other than delay*. Realizing financial or other benefit from otherwise improper delay in litigation is not a legitimate interest of the client.

In light of these provisions, can you counsel Silber at all?

3.8.   Your firm represents Stanley Zabriskie and Zabriskie Autos. When Zabriskie sells a car, he arranges financing. The loans are made by a separate financing company. When the buyer defaults, Zabriskie usually has to buy the loan back from the finance company and enforce it himself. (This procedure is known as *recourse financing*.) After a default and repurchase, Zabriskie typically refers the matter to Auto Repossessors (AR). If AR can get possession of the car peacefully, Zabriskie pays them $300; if not, Zabriskie refers the matter to Tyler & Yin (T & Y), a law firm that specializes in small collection cases. T & Y will file an action for replevin and, as permitted under local law, obtain the writ of possession without prior notice to the debtor. Provided that the debtor does not defend the replevin action, they charge a flat $600 for the case; otherwise they charge on an hourly basis.

Five months ago, Zabriskie Autos sold a car to Sandra Evans. Evans made the first two payments, then missed the next three. On the few occasions that Stanley Zabriskie has been able to contact her, she has complained about the quality of the car, the representations the salesperson made to her, and the financing Zabriskie obtained for her. Stanley Zabriskie thinks her complaints are just an excuse to keep him from repossessing, but when you press him, he admits there may be some truth to her claims. He'd like to "run this one through the regular procedure." As corporate counsel, what's your advice? U.C.C. §9-609.

3.9.   Your client, Mel Farr, sells used cars to customers with bad credit. After encountering all kinds of problems with repossessions he thinks he has found a technical solution to the problem. He plans to equip each automobile with a computerized device that will allow the car to start only if the driver correctly enters a new code each week. Farr will give each driver the code only upon receipt of the driver's weekly payment. Is this device legal? U.C.C. §§9-102(33), 9-602, 9 609(a)(2). Should it be?

Assignment 4: Judicial Sale and Deficiency

After a judgment has been entered in a judicial foreclosure, the collateral is sold in a public sale. As we suggested in the Pseudo History in Assignment 2, the purpose of the sale was, at least initially, to determine the value of the property. Like law and economics professors today, the Ancients believed that the price a thing could bring at a public sale was the best measure of its value. If that value was in excess of the lien against the collateral, the surplus could be returned to the debtor after payment of the secured debt. If the value was less than the secured debt, the value could be applied against the debt and the debtor could be held liable for the resulting deficiency.

As we also suggested in the Pseudo History, the requirement that collateral be exposed to public sale as part of the foreclosure process generally cannot be varied by contract. Even if the mortgage specifically provides for the secured creditor to become the owner of the collateral in the event of default and foreclosure, the public sale must still be held. Without the sale, the possibility always remains that the creditor has picked up the property at too great a bargain, or, to reverse the focus and put it in the language of the courts, the debtor has suffered a forfeiture. Recall that foreclosures are in equity, and "equity," the maxim goes, "abhors a forfeiture."

As you read this assignment, keep in mind that Article 9 security interests can be foreclosed judicially, see U.C.C. §9-601(a)(1), but seldom are. Assignment 5 discusses the sale procedure commonly employed in nonjudicial foreclosure under U.C.C. §§9-610(a), (b).

A. Strict Foreclosure

Notwithstanding the tradition of a foreclosure sale, some foreclosure procedures or situations do not require a sale of the collateral. They are typically referred to as *strict foreclosures*. Probably the most common is the foreclosure of a *contract for deed*, or *installment land contract*, which is a contract for the sale of real property that provides for the payment of the purchase price in installments over many years, with the deed to be delivered only after the last installment has been paid. A contract for deed has long been recognized as a security device. If the purchaser does not make timely payments, the seller must foreclose through court process. But the large majority of states do not require that the foreclosure conclude with a sale of the property. Instead, if the debtor does not pay the full purchase price in accord with the contract or at least by the end of a statutory *grace period*, the debtor's interest in the property is forfeited and the court confirms that title remains with the seller.

Contracts for deed are used primarily in sales of real estate of relatively small value on small down payments. Their strict foreclosure occasionally forfeits a substantial equity that a buyer has built up over several years, a result that has prompted serious policy concerns and some protective litigation. However, the level of their use is not sufficient to warrant detailed coverage in this book. Throughout the remainder of this assignment, we focus on the typical foreclosure procedures that require public sale of the collateral.

B. Foreclosure Sale Procedure

In most states, statutes specify the manner in which a foreclosure sale must be held. A typical statute might provide that all foreclosure sales within the county are to be held by auction sale on the steps of the courthouse between the hours of 10:00 A.M. and 2:00 P.M. on the first and third Tuesdays of the month, with the property going to the highest bidder for cash. Judicial foreclosure sales are nearly always conducted by a public official, usually the sheriff, the clerk of the court, or a court commissioner. Anyone may bid at the sale. For reasons that will become apparent in the next section, the creditor who brings the foreclosure case is typically the highest bidder at the sale.

The court that orders a foreclosure sale may have discretion to determine some aspects of the manner in which the sale is held, such as the period of advertising, the manner in which bidders identify themselves, and the minimum increments for bidding. When the last bid is made, the officer conducting the sale identifies the highest bidder. Typically, that bidder must immediately make a deposit of a portion of the purchase price in cash or by cashier's check. Under most procedures the balance of the purchase price must be paid within a few hours or days. If the high bidder does not make good on its bid, the applicable procedure may require either that the property then be sold to the second highest bidder or that a new sale be scheduled. The high bidder who did not perform may forfeit its deposit and may also be liable in contract for damages.

In most foreclosure procedures, the court must review the circumstances under which the sale was held and *confirm* the sale before the sale can be consummated. The debtor, or other parties in interest, may object to the sale on the grounds that the officer did not conduct the sale in accord with the law or the judgment of foreclosure, or that the sale price was inadequate. If the court does not confirm the sale, it will schedule a resale. If it confirms the sale, the officer who conducted the sale will execute a deed conveying the property to the purchaser.

Once a sale has been confirmed, the official disburses the sale proceeds. The money goes first to reimburse the foreclosing creditor for the expenses of sale. Next, the proceeds are distributed to the foreclosing creditor up to the amount of the debt secured by the foreclosed lien. Assuming there are no other liens, any remaining surplus goes to the debtor. If the proceeds of sale are insufficient to pay the full amount of the debt secured by the foreclosed lien, the foreclosing creditor may ask the court to enter a judgment for the deficiency. The circumstances under which courts grant deficiency judgments are discussed in section D, below. If the deficiency judgment is granted, the foreclosing creditor can collect it in the same manner as any other judgment on an unsecured debt.

While the foreclosure is in progress, the mortgage debtor has the right to redeem the property from the mortgage by paying the full amount due under the mortgage, including interest and attorneys' fees. This *common law* right to redeem is typically cut off (*foreclosed*, in the legal parlance) as of the time of the sale. In more than half the states, the debtor also has a *statutory* right to redeem the collateral from the buyer after the sale. Statutory rights to redeem range in length from about six months to three years, with one year being the most common period. Except when the court appoints a receiver, the debtor usually remains in possession during the statutory period for redemption. Redemption is accomplished by paying the purchaser the amount the purchaser paid at the sale. Under some procedures, the redemption price will also include interest on the sale price and other expenses incurred by the purchaser in connection with the sale. But the redemption price typically does not include the purchaser's costs of maintaining or improving the property during the period, if any, it was in the purchaser's possession.

Statutory rights of redemption are freely transferrable. As a consequence, debtors who cannot afford to exercise their rights of redemption can sell those rights to others who can exercise them. The greater the discount at which a debtor's property is sold in the judicial sale, the greater is the value of the right to redeem it. The debtor can recapture some of that discount by selling the right to redeem. When the buyer of a statutory right to redeem exercises it after the sale, the auction purchaser loses both the property and the benefit of the purchase. Some courts hold that the redeeming assignee takes the property free and clear of the lien causing the sale and all subordinate liens. The rule makes the price of statutory redemption the price paid at the sale. Others hold that the redeeming assignee takes the property subject to the lien causing the sale, and all subordinate liens. The latter rule makes the price of statutory redemption the same as the price of common law redemption. The redeemer must pay the entire debt.

C. Problems with Foreclosure Sale Procedure

When property is sold at a foreclosure sale, the debtor is often shocked by how little it brings. Sometimes the debtor is sufficiently outraged to bring a lawsuit asking the court to set aside the sale because of the inadequate sale price. In the following case, the debtors asked the court to set aside a foreclosure sale that left them with a large deficiency judgment. The court recognized that the debtors' property was sold for less than its fair market value, but also recognized that usually happens in foreclosure sales.

Armstrong v. Csurilla

817 P.2d 1221 (N.M. 1991)

MONTGOMERY, J.

When property subject to a mortgage or other lien is sold in foreclosure proceedings, the buyer is usually the mortgagee or other lien creditor and the price for which the property is "bought in" is sometimes significantly less than the property's fair market value. This can result in considerable unfairness to the debtor, the owner of the property, who may wind up both losing the property (and any attendant equity) and becoming subject to an onerous deficiency judgment, while the creditor may realize a substantial profit on ultimate disposition of the property and collect the deficiency from the debtor's other assets, if any. This problem can lead to abuse, an abuse which has been well documented and the subject of various attempts at legislative or judicial correction or amelioration.[1]

1. See . . . Washburn, The Judicial and Legislative Response to Price Inadequacy in Mortgage Foreclosure Sales, 53 S. Cal. L. Rev. 843 (1980). The Uniform Land Transactions Act (ULTA) — which, however, has not yet been adopted by any state — contains several provisions designed to prevent double recovery by creditors, protect debtors from the hard-

In this case the debtors, whose property became subject to a judgment lien after their default under two contracts by which they had purchased the property, . . . seek to set aside the foreclosure sale by relying on the equitable doctrine that permits a court to invalidate a judicial sale when the price is so low as to "shock the conscience" of the court. We hold that . . . the debtors, having been afforded opportunities to protect themselves from the consequences of an inadequate price and to provide evidence that the price was inadequate, cannot now avail themselves of that equitable doctrine. . . . We hold that the trial court did not err in the proceedings that led ultimately to confirmation of the sale of the debtors' property, and we affirm its judgment.

I

The case has a simple factual history and a more complicated procedural one. The debtors, William and Josephine Csurilla, entered into two contracts to purchase the real property at issue from Calvin and Dorothy Armstrong on April 5, 1987. The contracts were more or less standard, long-term real estate contracts, prepared by the Csurillas' attorney. The two contracts covered adjacent parcels of land and improvements in Quemado, New Mexico. One covered a gasoline service station, with associated pumps, inventory, and a storage building (the "station contract"); the other covered an adjoining residential dwelling and garage-carport (the "house contract"). One well serves both the house and the service station; electrical, sewer and plumbing lines run through one property to the other; and the garage-carport and storage building share a common wall. The trial court found that the parties used two separate contracts for tax purposes and the convenience of the Csurillas and for no other reason.

The purchase price under the station contract was $156,594, with $1,000 paid down and the balance payable in monthly installments of $1,122.31 commencing April 1, 1987. The station property included approximately $28,600 in inventory. The purchase price for the house property was $75,000, on which $1,000 was paid down, another $52,000 credited by virtue of an exchange of property owned by the Csurillas in Lake Havasu, Arizona, and the deferred balance of $22,000 payable $194.42 per month. Thus, the total purchase price for the two properties was $231,594, and the total monthly debt service was $1,316.73.

Three months after signing the contracts, the Csurillas defaulted under the station contract. They continued making payments on the house

---

ships of deficiency judgments and inadequately priced sales, and bring judicial sales into closer conformity with commercially reasonable, free-market transactions. See U.L.T.A. §§3-501 to 3-513, 13 U.L.A. 599-622 (1977).

contract and did not relinquish possession of either property. They continued to operate the station for a few months but closed it in November 1987. Mr. Armstrong retook possession of the station in September 1988, when the court appointed him as receiver to protect the property. By that time, the property had deteriorated significantly in value; much of the inventory was depleted, and the station was in generally poor condition. It never reopened as a service station.

[The court held that default under the service station contract constituted a default under both contracts and entered a judgment of foreclosure against both properties.] The . . . judicial sale then took place in December 1989, with the Armstrongs buying in both properties for [a total of] $90,000. . . . The Csurillas objected to confirmation of the sale. . . . The court conducted a hearing, received opinion testimony (but no appraisal) as to the value of the property, found that the sale was fair and regular in all respects, and entered an order confirming it. The order also granted the Csurillas a one-month period in which to redeem the property . . . and awarded the Armstrongs a deficiency judgment of $125,037. The Csurillas then . . . took the present appeal to this Court. . . .

V

What protection, then, does a judgment debtor have from the potentially abusive practice described at the beginning of this opinion — sale for an inadequate price, followed by imposition of an onerous deficiency judgment? To answer this question we turn to the Csurillas' final contention — that the price bid by the Armstrongs for the combined house and station property, $90,000, was so low that it should "shock the conscience of the court."

In Las Vegas Railway & Power Co. v. Trust Co. of St. Louis County, 15 N.M. 634, 110 P. 856 (1910), we said:

> It is perfectly well settled that a judicial sale will not be set aside for inadequacy of price unless it be so gross as to shock the conscience, or unless there be additional circumstances which would make it inequitable to allow the sale to stand. . . .
>
> While mere inadequacy of price has rarely been held sufficient in itself to justify setting aside a judicial sale of property, courts are not slow to seize upon other circumstances impeaching the fairness of the transaction, as a cause for vacating it. . . .

From these various formulations, we discern two instances in which equity will intervene to set aside a judicial sale where the price, compared with the value of the property sold, is inadequate. The first is when the

disparity is so great as to shock the court's conscience. While "mere inadequacy" will seldom be sufficient to justify vacating the sale, simply stating that rule obviously connotes some situations in which mere
inadequacy, if sufficiently gross, will warrant the court's intervention.

The second instance in which the sale may be vacated on the ground
of price inadequacy is when, in addition to the inadequate price, there
are circumstances which would make it inequitable to allow the sale to
stand. We need not attempt to catalogue the kinds of "additional circumstances" contemplated by this branch of the rule, because the Csurillas
do not invoke it and contend only that the price for their property was so
grossly inadequate that the court's conscience should have been shocked
and the sale set aside on that ground alone.

When will the disparity between price and value be so great that a
court will be justified in setting aside a judicial sale, either because the
inadequate price, by itself, is so low as to shock the court's conscience or
because the inadequacy, while not so great, is combined with other circumstances resulting in unfairness to the debtor? Obviously, if only the
inadequate price is relied on to invoke the court's equitable discretion,
the inadequacy must be very great — gross — as compared with the
inadequacy that will be sufficient when other, unfairness-producing circumstances are present. In *Las Vegas Railway*, the purchase price
amounted to between 54% and 65% of the property's value and was
held so inadequate as to warrant setting the sale aside, but other
circumstances — two parties interested in the sale were prevented from
bidding — were present. Other cases provide examples of situations in
which courts have found prices bid at judicial sales inadequate under
various circumstances. See, e.g., Chew v. Acacia Mut. Life Ins. Co., 165
Colo. 43, 437 P.2d 339 (1968) (en banc) (69% of appraised value
shocked the court's conscience); Straus v. Anderson, 366 Ill. 426, 9
N.E.2d 205 (1937) (sale for 23% of value would shock average individual); Home Owners' Loan Corp. v. Braxtan, 220 Ind. 587, 44 N.E.2d
989 (1942) (17% of value set aside); Suring State Bank v. Giese, 210 Wis.
489, 246 N.W. 556 (1933) (bid of 20%-60% of property's value set
aside). Professor Washburn, in Washburn, supra note 1, at 866, observes:
"There is general agreement at the extremes as to what constitutes gross
inadequacy. Sale prices less than ten percent of value are generally held
grossly inadequate, whereas those above forty percent are held not
grossly inadequate."[15]

The midpoint of Professor Washburn's range is 25%. We decline to
adopt any fixed numerical percentage as establishing a price-value disparity that in every case will be so great as to shock the court's con-

---

15. Professor Washburn also notes that the debtor faces a heavy task in convincing a
court that a foreclosure sale price is inadequate, since "the court's inquiry into the adequacy
of the foreclosure sale price is limited by two well-established principles: valuation of foreclosed property occurs at the date of the foreclosure sale, and the sale price is conclusive of
the property's value." Id. at 858.

science. The answer to the question necessarily resides in the sound discretion of the trial court, and there are too many subtle variations in the facts of this kind of case to make it feasible to lay down a fixed rule as to when a court's conscience should or should not be shocked.

The policy . . . reflected in Section 39-5-5 — that sheriff's execution sales for less than two-thirds of the appraised value of the property should not be permitted — is perhaps instructive here. However, . . . there are significant differences between a sheriff's sale under a writ of execution and a judicially supervised sale under a court-ordered foreclosure. Where the inadequate price does not fall into the "shock the conscience" range (25% plus or minus 15%, for example), it may still be so inadequate (if less than two-thirds of the appraised value, for example) as to call for judicial invalidation of the sale if other circumstances, leading to unfairness, are present. We do not hold that in every case where the price falls below two-thirds of the fair market value, that price should be held inadequate as a matter of law, or that in every case where the price falls into the 10-40% range (or, conceivably, less) the inadequacy should shock the judicial conscience. We hold only that prices in these ranges call for special scrutiny by the court to be sure that, in the first case, additional circumstances do not produce an inequitable result and, in the second case, the grossly inadequate price is not confirmed absent good reasons why it should be.

In the present case, the purchase price for the combined properties was $90,000. The Csurillas complain that this was only about 39% of the property's value — assuming that its value was the amount they paid for it. There, however, is a major problem for the Csurillas' position in this case. They do not know; the court below did not know; we do not know — no one knows what the actual value of the property was at the time of the judicial sale.

We do know that included with the station property under the station contract was approximately $28,600 in inventory, much of which had been dissipated at the time of the sale. We also know that when the station contract was executed, the service station was operating and apparently making money; by the time of the sale, it had long since been closed and, according to the trial court, some or all of its "going concern" value was gone. In addition, as the court also found when the partial summary judgment was entered in September 1988, the station property had a fair market value "far less" than the amount of that judgment, the property having deteriorated significantly during the Csurillas' ownership. For all of these reasons, it seems likely (although we cannot be sure — no one can) that the sale price approached or exceeded 50% of the property's value. . . .

While the Csurillas claimed that the price was inadequate and now complain generally that consummation of the sale results in great unfairness to them, they do not contend that there was any impropriety in the conduct of the sale itself.[16] And they did not prove, or offer to prove, the extent, if any, to which the price fell short of the property's value. They did not, in other words, meet their burden to give the trial court sufficient information to enable it to exercise its discretion in passing upon the adequacy or inadequacy of the price and, if inadequate, whether the price was so low as to shock the court's conscience. They did not, despite the court's observation in September 1988 that they had not provided evidence of value and despite their own stipulation (when the first sale was set aside by agreement) that they could have the property appraised before the next sale, proceed with an appraisal or otherwise adduce evidence as to the fair market value of the property at the time of the sale. . . .

The order confirming the sale and granting a deficiency judgment is accordingly affirmed.

IT IS SO ORDERED.

A number of aspects of foreclosure sale procedure contribute to its failure to bring reasonable prices for the property that is sold. (1) The sales are poorly advertised. (2) Prospective buyers are given little opportunity to inspect the property before the bidding, but they must accept the property "as is." (3) The rule of caveat emptor applies with regard to the state of the title. (4) The sale often takes place in a hostile environment making it difficult for the prospective bidder to get information about the property. (5) The buyer may be unable to use the property until the statutory redemption period expires.

1. Advertising

An owner who wants to sell property usually advertises for buyers. If the property is a house, for example, the owner may hire a real estate broker to find buyers or will, at the very least, run an ad in a newspaper. The owner will try to describe the house in a way that will both encourage readers to respond and help them decide whether the house is suitable to their needs. Owners who want to sell their property advertise in a manner calculated to attract potential buyers.

The way a foreclosure sale is advertised may be fixed by statute or the judgment of foreclosure. The following procedure is typical:

---

16. Any such impropriety would be the kind of "additional circumstance" that, in combination with an inadequate price, might result in unfairness and so warrant setting the sale aside.

Wisconsin Statutes Annotated

(West 1994)

§815.31   NOTICE OF SALE OF REALTY; MANNER; ADJOURNMENT

(1) The time and place of holding any sale of real estate on execution shall be publicly advertised by posting a written notice describing the real estate to be sold with reasonable certainty in 3 public places in the town or municipality where such real estate is to be sold at least 3 weeks prior to the date of sale; and also in 3 public places of the town or municipality in which the real estate is situated, if it is not in the town or municipality where the sale is to be held.

(2) A copy of the notice of sale shall be printed each week for 6 successive weeks in a newspaper of the county prior to the date of sale.

The officer conducting the sale is rarely concerned with the price the sale will bring. Because debtors sometimes attempt to have sales set aside on the basis that they were not conducted strictly in accord with formal legal requirements, the officer's primary concern is usually to comply with those requirements. The result is sale notices like those in Figure 1, which were published in a Milwaukee legal newspaper.

The sheriffs, lawyers, or parties who place legal notices often select newspapers of limited circulation because the cost of running the ad is lower. Major newspapers segregate legal notices from the advertisements placed by owners and realtors. Either way, the legal notices rarely attract buyers interested in owning the property. To the extent they bring in bidders at all, the bidders are usually professional bargain hunters who plan to resell the property at a profit.

2. Inspection

As we discussed in Assignment 3, under most foreclosure sale procedures the debtor is entitled to remain in possession of the property until after the sale is held. The mortgage contract usually grants the foreclosing creditor the right to inspect the collateral in preparation for bidding at the sale. Such a provision ordinarily will be specifically enforced. Others who wish to bid at the sale can observe the property from adjacent public places, but they have no right to enter in order to inspect.

of Section 8, in Township 7 North, Range 22 East, in the City of Milwaukee, County of Milwaukee, State of Wisconsin, and more commonly known as 1006 West Nash Street.

TERMS OF SALE: 10% CASH, MONEY ORDER OR CERTIFIED CHECK. BALANCE DUE AT TIME OF CONFIRMATION.

Dated at Milwaukee, May 8, 1992.

RICHARD E. ARTISON,
Sheriff of Milwaukee County, Wis.
MACHULAK, HUTCHINSON, ROBERTSON, DWYER & O'DESS, S.C.,
Plaintiff's Attorneys.

The above property is located at 1006 W. Nash St., City of Milwaukee, Wis.

92-4915/5-8-15-22-29-6-5-12

SHERIFF'S SALE

No. 499   Case No. 92-CV-002350

STATE OF WISCONSIN – CIRCUIT COURT – CIVIL DIVISION – MILWAUKEE COUNTY.

Associates Financial Services Company of Wisconsin, Inc., a domestic corporation, Plaintiff, vs Patricia Harmon, Defendant.

By virtue of a Judgment of Foreclosure made in the above entitled action on the 9th day of March, 1992, I will sell at public auction in the 3rd Floor Assembly Room of the Courthouse Annex, 907 N. 10th St., in the City of Milwaukee, Milwaukee County, Wisconsin, on the

22nd DAY OF JUNE, 1992,

at 10:00 o'clock a.m., all of the following described mortgaged premises to-wit:

That part of the Southeast 1/4 of Section 25, in Township 8 North, Range 21 East, in the City of Milwaukee, County of Milwaukee, State of Wisconsin, which is bounded and described as follows: Commencing at a point in the center line of North Teutonia Avenue, said point being 2184.11 feet Southeasterly, measured along said center line, from the point of intersection of said center line with the North line of said 1/4 Section; thence Northwesterly along center line of North Teutonia Avenue 91.90 feet; thence East on a line parallel to the North line of said 1/4 Section 485.64 feet; thence South at right angles to the above described line 91 feet; thence Westerly, parallel to the North line and along the North line of C.S.M. #1255 extended East, to the point of beginning. Except that portion as described in Document No. 3708863.

TERMS OF SALE: 10% down in cash at sale; the balance due within 10 days of confirmation.

Dated at Milwaukee, May 8, 1992.

RICHARD E. ARTISON,
Sheriff of Milwaukee County, Wis.
STUPAR & SCHUSTER, S.C.,
Plaintiff's Attorneys.

The above property is located at 5666 N. Teutonia Ave., City of Milwaukee, Wis.

92-4921/5-8-15-22-29-6-5-12

By virtue of a Judgment of Foreclosure made in the above entitled action on the 18th day of March, 1991, in the amount of $50,253.86, I will sell at public auction in the 3rd Floor Assembly Room of the Courthouse Annex, 907 N. 10th St., in the City of Milwaukee, Milwaukee County, Wisconsin, on the

22nd DAY OF JUNE, 1992,

at 10:00 o'clock a.m., all of the following described mortgaged premises to-wit:

Lot 9, in Block 4 except the East 10 feet thereof, in Jesse Stone Addition, being a Subdivision of Lots 1, 2, 3, 4, 6, 7, 8, 9 and 10 in Block 1 and Lots 1, 2, 6, 7, 8, 9 and 10, Block 2 of the Subdivision into 1 acre Lots of the North 40 acres of the Northeast 1/4 of Section 14, Town 7 North, Range 21 East, in the City of Milwaukee, County of Milwaukee, State of Wisconsin.

TERMS: 10% of successful bid must be paid to Sheriff at sale in cash or by certified check. Balance to be paid upon confirmation.

Dated at Milwaukee, May 8, 1992.

RICHARD E. ARTISON,
Sheriff of Milwaukee County, Wis.
GRAY & END,
Plaintiff's Attorneys.

The above property is located at 3008 N. 47th St., City of Milwaukee, Wis.

92-4928/5-8-15-22-29-6-5-12

SHERIFF'S SALE

No. 513   Case No. 91-CV-011384

STATE OF WISCONSIN – CIRCUIT COURT – CIVIL DIVISION – MILWAUKEE COUNTY.

Lomas Mortgage USA, Inc. f/k/a The Lomas & Nettleton Company, Plaintiff, vs Paula E. Love, et al, Defendants.

By virtue of a Judgment of Foreclosure made in the above entitled action on the 13th day of December, 1991, in the amount of $36,789.22, I will sell at public auction in the 3rd Floor Assembly Room of the Courthouse Annex, 907 N. 10th St., in the City of Milwaukee, Milwaukee County, Wisconsin, on the

22nd DAY OF JUNE, 1992,

at 10:00 o'clock a.m., all of the following described mortgaged premises to-wit:

Lot 23, in Block 16, in the Third Continuation of Boulevard Park, in the South West 1/4 of Section 13, in Township 7 North, Range 21 East, in the City of Milwaukee, County of Milwaukee and State of Wisconsin.

TERMS: 10% of successful bid must be paid to Sheriff at sale in cash or by certified check. Balance to be paid upon confirmation.

Dated at Milwaukee, May 8, 1992.

RICHARD E. ARTISON,
Sheriff of Milwaukee County, Wis.
GRAY & END,
Plaintiff's Attorneys.

The above property is located at 2638-2640 N. 40th St., City of Milwaukee, Wis.

92-4929/5-8-15-22-29-6-5-12

SHERIFF'S SALE

No. 410   Case No. 91-CV-013722

STATE OF WISCONSIN – CIRCUIT COURT – CIVIL DIVISION – MILWAUKEE COUNTY.

St. Francis Bank, FSB, f/k/a St. Francis Savings & Loan Association, a Wisconsin corporation, Plaintiff, vs Michael J. Birlem and Judy A. Huttner n/k/a Judith A. Birlem, his wife, Great Lakes Higher Education Corp., f/k/a Wisconsin Higher Education Corp. and State of Wisconsin, Defendants.

By virtue of a Judgment of Foreclosure made in the above entitled action on the 16th day of December, 1991, I will sell at public auction in the 3rd Floor Assembly Room of the Courthouse Annex, 907 N. 10th St., in the City of Milwaukee, Milwaukee County, Wisconsin, on the

22nd DAY OF JUNE, 1992,

at 10:00 o'clock a.m., all of the following described mortgaged premises to-wit:

Lot 21, in Block 2, in Tehan Subdivision, being a Subdivision of a part of the South East 1/4 of Section 20, Township 6 North, Range 22 East, in the City of Milwaukee, County of Milwaukee and State of Wisconsin. Tax Key No. 595-0649-0.

Dated at Milwaukee, May 8, 1992.

RICHARD E. ARTISON,
Sheriff of Milwaukee County, Wis.
DOUBLE & DOUBLE,
Plaintiff's Attorneys.

The above property is located at 312 W. Van Norman Ave., City of Milwaukee, Wis.

92-4913/5-8-15-22-29-6-5-12

SHERIFF'S SALE

No. 492   Case No. 91-CV-016502

STATE OF WISCONSIN – CIRCUIT COURT – CIVIL DIVISION – MILWAUKEE COUNTY.

Federal Home Loan Mortgage Corp., Plaintiff, vs Alice M. Sowka, a single person, and Balcor Realty Partners, Inc., Defendants.

By virtue of a Judgment of Foreclosure made in the above entitled action on the 16th day of March, 1992, I will sell at public auction in the 3rd Floor Assembly Room of the Courthouse Annex, 907 N. 10th St., in the City of Milwaukee, Milwaukee County, Wisconsin, on the

22nd DAY OF JUNE, 1992,

at 10:00 o'clock a.m., all of the following described mortgaged premises to-wit:

Parcel 2 of Certified Survey Map No. 3132, being in Section 16, in Township 7 North, Range 22 East, in the City of Milwaukee, County of Milwaukee and State of Wisconsin.

Dated at Milwaukee, May 8, 1992.

RICHARD E. ARTISON,
Sheriff of Milwaukee County, Wis.
ROBERT L. HERSH,
Plaintiff's Attorney.

The above property is located at 2523 N. Dousman St., City of Milwaukee, Wis.

92-4918/5-8-15-22-29-6-5-12

Figure 1.   Notice of Foreclosure Sales

Again, such conditions are unlikely to attract buyers who want the property for their own use. What prospective home buyer would like to purchase a house without knowing the floor plan, the condition of the walls and floors, or the functioning of the heating and plumbing? Again, only professionals who plan to find a bargain and resell for a large profit are likely to be interested.

3. *Title and Condition*

Judicial sales are one of the few situations in which the rule of caveat. emptor still applies. As the case that follows illustrates, buyers take subject to any defects in the title that they could have discovered through a search of the public records or an inspection of the property. Mr. Marino might have had a reasonable chance in an action against the seller in an ordinary private sale, but he discovered that in a judicial foreclosure sale he was without remedy.

Marino v. United Bank of Illinois, N.A.

484 N.E.2d 935 (Ill. App. Ct. 1985)

SCHNAKE, J.

Lawrence Marino, plaintiff, successfully bid at a sheriff's sale which took place on November 22, 1983. The property was being sold after United Bank of Illinois filed a complaint to foreclose a mortgage executed by Kenneth and Elizabeth Vosberg on January 9, 1981. After purchasing the property plaintiff attempted, in the instant action, to vacate the sale and to have his purchase money returned, on the basis of misrepresentations alleged to have been made by Linda Kream, an attorney who was sent to bid at the sale as representative of Theodore Liebovich, the attorney for the mortgagee. On May 30, 1984, the trial court ordered the sale vacated. However, on defendant's motion to reconsider, the trial court reversed its earlier order and confirmed the sale. Plaintiff Marino appeals from that order.

On November 22, 1983, the sheriff's sale of the property was held. According to plaintiff, Lawrence Marino, he intended to find out about the property and then make a decision as to whether to bid. He did not examine the records of the Winnebago County recorder's office to check the title, nor did he consult an attorney prior to submitting a bid. He attempted to obtain information through talking with Deputy Sheriff Claytor before the sale. Plaintiff asked Claytor about liens and encumbrances on the property, and Claytor told him that there was a mortgage of $8,800, $2,000 in attorney fees, $2,100 in taxes owed, and other miscellaneous liens, the total of which amounted to $14,327. Claytor told plaintiff to check with Liebovich, the attorney who was handling the case. Plaintiff then talked with attorney Linda Kream, who told him that she was attending the sale in place of Liebovich. According to plaintiff, he asked Linda Kream whether there were any encumbrances on the property. Before replying, Kream looked through a file and replied, "Well there's none that I can see," and then said, "This isn't my case, so I wouldn't know." Kream indicated to Marino that it was Liebovich's case, but that he was not available that day.

Linda Kream testified that she was an associate attorney with the firm of Liebovich and Gaziano and that Liebovich had asked her to appear at the sale and bid on behalf of the United Bank of Illinois. She had a foreclosure file and a cashier's check in an amount over $13,000. Kream testified that she was unfamiliar with the file as she had not been handling the case. Before the sale, plaintiff approached her and asked her how much she was going to bid. After telling him, plaintiff indicated that he would bid $1 more. Kream testified that plaintiff then asked her if there were any liens ahead of the bank's, and that she replied that it was not her case, so she would only know what was contained in the file. Plaintiff asked if she would look through the file, and she did. She then told plaintiff that there did not appear to be any other liens, but that she was not sure and she would not want him to rely on that. On cross-examination, Kream indicated that there was a title policy in file, but that she did not examine it.

Plaintiff successfully bid $13,541 for the property and the court approved the sale on December 12, 1983. On April 6, 1984, plaintiff sought to vacate the sale, alleging that Kream had informed him that no other liens or encumbrances existed on the property, and that he relied on her statement and thereafter purchased the property. He further asserted that he had since been joined as a defendant in an action by First Federal Savings and Loan of Rockford, and that it was at that time that he first became aware of liens and encumbrances superior to his interest. Marino's complaint alleged that United Bank of Illinois had a duty to join all parties with liens on the property, and asked that the sale be vacated and his money returned.

In response, United Bank of Illinois contended that plaintiff was not entitled to set aside the sale unless he could show fraud or misrepresentation, there were no statements made to induce plaintiff to purchase the property, and that plaintiff could not reasonably have relied on any statements that were made. In an affidavit, Kream stated that at the time of the sheriff's sale, she did not have knowledge of the liens which were listed in plaintiff's motion to vacate.

The court found no fraud, but ordered the sale vacated because of Marino's reliance on Kream's unintentional misrepresentation. The court ordered United Bank of Illinois to reimburse Marino for the amount of money it received from the sale. United Bank of Illinois moved for reconsideration, alleging that Marino failed to prove that an assertion of fact was made to him on which he was entitled to reply, that plaintiff failed to prove the existence of the liens, and that there was no cause of action for an unintentional misrepresentation. The court granted defendant's motion to reconsider, vacated its prior order, and confirmed the sheriff's sale of November 22, 1983. Notice of appeal was timely filed.

Generally the doctrine of caveat emptor applies to judicial sales, and the risk of a mistake or defect of title is to be borne by the purchaser unless there is fraud, misrepresentation, or mistake of fact. In this case, plaintiff Marino alleges that because there was a misrepresentation by Kream, equity requires that the sale be vacated.

To establish fraudulent misrepresentation, plaintiff must show a false statement of material fact made by defendant, defendant's knowledge or belief that the statement was false, defendant's intent to induce plaintiff to act, an action by plaintiff in justifiable reliance on that statement, and damage to plaintiff resulting from such reliance. These elements must be proved for a charge of fraud, whether in a suit at law or in equity.

Examining these elements, it is clear that plaintiff failed to prove a fraudulent misrepresentation by attorney Kream. To begin with, plaintiff failed to prove a false statement of material fact. Matters of fact are to be distinguished from expressions of opinion, which cannot form the basis of an action of fraud. A representation is one of opinion rather than fact if it only expresses the speaker's belief, without certainty, as to the existence of a fact. By both plaintiff's and Kream's account, Kream indicated that from the information in the file there did not appear to be any liens or encumbrances, but she expressly told plaintiff that she was not sure of that fact because it was not her case. Her statement would appear to be an opinion since it was only her belief, stated without certainty, as to the existence of a fact. In his brief, plaintiff argues that due to Kream's status as an attorney, she can be said to have held herself out to have "special knowledge" such that there was an implied assertion of fact. In view of her expressed disclaimer of knowledge of any facts of the case, plaintiff's argument is not persuasive.

There was also no evidence that the statement made was known to be false, and the lack of certainty expressed by Kream would not support a finding that she made the statement with the intent to induce plaintiff to act. In determining whether there was justified reliance, it is necessary to consider all of the facts in plaintiff's actual knowledge as well as those which he could have discovered by the exercise of ordinary prudence. While a person may rely on a statement without investigation if the party making the statement creates a false sense of security or blocks further inquiry, it must be determined whether the facts were such as to put a reasonable man on inquiry. In this case, the lack of certainty of Kream's statement was sufficient to put a reasonable person on inquiry, and plaintiff was not justified in relying on that statement without taking appropriate steps to check the title. . . .

Plaintiff contends that it was incumbent upon defendant to search for liens and encumbrances and join all parties having subsequent liens, and that, in foreclosure, the mortgagee should search for intervening transfers or liens and should join record owners as parties defendant. However, in Baldi v. Chicago Title & Trust Co. (1983), 13 Ill. App. 3d 29, 31-33, 446 N.E.2d 1205, 1207-1208, the court rejected an argument that a junior mortgagee should be a necessary party to a foreclosure of a senior encumbrance. While defendant could have joined those parties with subsequent liens on the property, it had no duty to do so.

The judgment of the circuit court of Winnebago County is therefore affirmed.

The court notes that there are "liens and encumbrances" on the property that the bank's foreclosure did not extinguish. Neither their nature, nor the precise reason that the foreclosure did not extinguish them, matters. Whatever the liens are, Marino takes subject to them because he is a purchaser at a foreclosure sale. As the court makes clear, finding out what liens survive foreclosure is the responsibility of the foreclosure sale bidder. Caveat emptor!

The risks to a bidder at a judicial sale extend beyond the state of the title. In Horicon State Bank v. Kant Lumber Co., Inc., 478 N.W.2d 26 (Wis. Ct. App. 1991), the bank foreclosed its mortgage against property owned by the lumber company. In preparation for the sale, the bank hired an appraiser who examined the property and appraised it as worth $6,000. The bank was the only bidder at the sale. It bid $10,000 to be sure the court would confirm the sale. When the bank attempted to resell the property, it discovered that the property was environmentally contaminated and that clean-up costs would be from $5,000 to $13,500 and perhaps more. On the bank's application, the court refused to set aside the sale, saying that the bank's appraiser should have seen evidence of the pollution when the appraiser inspected the property and "the bank should have had the [environmental] evaluation made before the sale." The court concluded "[We] will not intervene if an overbid at a sheriff's sale results from the bidder's ignorance."

As *Marino* and *Horicon* illustrate, a person who would like to bid at a sale may have to incur substantial expense in preparation. Yet many of the judicial sales that are advertised never take place. The debtor finds the money to redeem the property, makes peace with the foreclosing creditor, or files bankruptcy. Persons who have spent time and money preparing to bid at those sales simply lose their investments.

4. Hostile Situation

To make an intelligent purchase of a parcel of real estate, particularly if it includes a building, the buyer must know a good deal about it. Most sales of real property occur between willing buyers and sellers. The buyers get most of the information they need by refusing to purchase unless the seller furnishes it. Because sellers want to sell, they are usually willing to furnish the needed information, as well as to cooperate in providing access to the property, past records, and so on.

Many foreclosure sales, on the other hand, take place in a hostile environment. Often there is no one with either a motive or an obligation to furnish information to prospective purchasers. In fact, a debtor's strategy for retaining its property often calls for preventing third parties from obtaining the information they need to bid. Foreclosing creditors may not be able to furnish information because they do not themselves have access to it. In many cases, the creditors prefer to purchase the property themselves at the judicial sale, evaluate it, and then resell it. As a result, the price at the first sale is of little consequence to them. They are satisfied with a low-price sale, followed by another sale for an amount approaching a market price.

The officer who conducts the sale is rarely a good source of information, either. Typically the officer has no obligation or incentive to furnish information, but the officer may have liability for furnishing incorrect information. As a result, it is not surprising that most have little to say about the condition of the property or the terms of the sale.

Often the debtor's best strategy is to provoke some procedural irregularity in the sale and litigate over it as a means of obtaining delay. For example, the debtor may encourage judgment-proof friends or relatives to make the highest bid at the sale and then not pay the purchase price. The high bidder at a judicial sale must consider the possibility that it will become entangled in litigation over the validity of the sale. Finally, there is always the possibility that after the bidding is concluded, but before the buyer can be put into possession, the debtor will destroy the property.

5. The Statutory Right to Redeem

As we noted above, a debtor who has the right to redeem the property after sale usually also remains entitled to possession. The high bidder at the sale may have to wait months or even years for possession. Even if the bidder can obtain possession, if the right to redeem is later exercised, the bidder may be unable to recover money spent to preserve or improve the property during the bidder's time of possession. That may discourage the successful bidder from making improvements necessary to return the property to productive use until the statutory redemption period runs. That in turn may reduce the amounts that bidders are willing to pay for property at a judicial sale.

With all these problems, it is hardly surprising that there are few bidders at most judicial sales and that, except for credit bids by foreclosing creditors, the bidding usually stops far short of the market value of the property.

D. Antideficiency Statutes

Foreclosure sales rarely yield the "market value" of the property — the amount it would bring in a sale by a willing buyer to a willing seller, neither of whom was under compulsion. Instead, they yield prices that reflect the adverse conditions under which they are held.

Legislatures have responded to the problem by enacting *antideficiency statutes*. These statutes either prohibit the court from granting deficiency judgments in particular circumstances, give the court the discretion to refuse to grant them, or limit the amount of the deficiencies to be granted. Notice that this approach addresses only one aspect of the problem created by inadequate sale prices: the possibility of a deficiency judgment. It does not address the plight of the debtor who has a substantial equity in property but loses it through a forced sale of the property for an inadequate price.

The most common type of antideficiency statute credits the debtor for the fair market value of the property even if the property brings a lower price at the foreclosure sale. For example, assume that the debtor owed $100,000 on the mortgage, the market value of the property was $80,000, but the sheriff sold it for $45,000 at the foreclosure sale. Without an antideficiency statute, the deficiency judgment would be for $55,000. With the type of antideficiency statute discussed here, the deficiency judgment would be for only $20,000. Other common types of antideficiency statutes prohibit deficiency judgments on purchase money mortgages or vest the court with discretion to deny deficiency judgments where they would be inequitable.

California has a particularly rich scheme of antideficiency statutes. The following provisions of the California Code of Civil Procedure are just a few of them, but they illustrate the variety of approaches that are possible.

California Code of Civil Procedure
Cal. Civ. Proc. Code (West Supp. 1994)

§580a.   DEFICIENCY JUDGMENTS

[The statute applies whenever a money judgment is sought for the balance due upon an obligation for the payment of which a deed of trust or mortgage with power of sale upon real property or any interest therein was given as security, following the exercise of the power of sale in such deed of trust or mortgage.] . . . Before rendering any judgment the court shall find the fair market value of the real property, or interest therein sold, at the time of sale. The court may render judgment for not more than the amount by which the entire amount of the indebtedness due at the time of sale exceeded the fair market value of the real property or interest therein sold at the time of sale with interest thereon from the date of the sale; provided, however, that in no event shall the amount of the judgment, exclusive of interest after the date of sale, exceed the difference between the amount for which the property was sold and the entire amount of the indebtedness secured by the deed of trust or mortgage. . . .

§580b.   CONDITIONS UNDER WHICH DEFICIENCY JUDGMENT FORBIDDEN

No deficiency judgment shall lie in any event after a sale of real property . . . under a deed of trust or mortgage given to the vendor to secure payment of the balance of the purchase price of that real property . . . or under a deed of trust or mortgage on a dwelling for not more than four families given to a lender to secure repayment of a loan which was in fact used to pay all or part of the purchase price of that dwelling occupied, entirely or in part, by the purchaser. . . .

§580d.   RENDITION OF DEFICIENCY JUDGMENT AFTER FORECLOSURE UNDER POWER OF SALE FORBIDDEN; EXCEPTIONS

No judgment shall be rendered for any deficiency upon a note secured by a deed of trust or mortgage upon real property or an estate for years therein hereafter executed in any case in which the real property or estate for years therein has been sold by the mortgagee or trustee under power of sale contained in the mortgage or deed of trust. . . .

E.   Credit Bidding at Judicial Sales

The creditor who forces the sale is permitted to bid at it and will usually do so. The procedural shortcomings that discourage strangers from bidding at judicial sales have considerably less effect on a secured creditor who forces the sale. That creditor will know of the sale even though it is poorly advertised, may be familiar with the title and condition of the property already, and may have an enforceable contractual right to inspect it.

The creditor who forces the sale has yet another important advantage. Recall that whatever is paid for the property over and above the expenses of sale, up to the amount of the secured debt, goes to the creditor who forced the sale. Whatever that creditor pays the sheriff for the property, up to the amount of the secured debt, the sheriff will pay back to the creditor as soon as the sale is confirmed. In recognition of this fact, foreclosure sale procedures generally allow the creditor a shortcut. The creditor need not pay the money to the sheriff, merely to get it back a few days later. Instead, the creditor can bid on credit up to the amount of the debt. Such a bid is referred to as a *credit bid*. Recall also that the amount paid for the property at the judicial sale is credited against the debt. When the secured creditor buys the collateral by a credit bid, an equal amount of the debt is canceled. In effect, the creditor buys the collateral for all or part of the secured debt. The creditor is then free to resell the collateral. If the resale is for more than the secured creditor paid at the judicial sale, the creditor earns a profit (or obtains a windfall, depending on how you choose to look at it).

Once the creditor's collateral has been sold at a judicial sale, the balance of the debt is often uncollectible. An antideficiency statute may bar the creditor from obtaining a deficiency. Even if the creditor gets a judgment, the creditor may be unable to collect because the debtor is bankrupt or judgment-proof. In such cases, the creditor loses nothing by bidding the full amount of its debt at the foreclosure sale, even if the bid is far in excess of the value of the collateral.

Assume that a creditor has forced a sale of collateral and knows that it will not be able to collect a deficiency. Such a creditor has little reason not to bid the full amount of its debt. The reason may be clearer from an example. Assume that the debtor owes the creditor $1 million, secured by collateral worth $200,000. If the creditor buys the property for $200,000 at the foreclosure sale, its total recovery on the debt will be the $200,000 it obtains from resale of the property. If, instead, the creditor bids $1 million at the sale, the outcome would be the same. The creditor need not pay the $1 million purchase price to the sheriff; the creditor is entitled to a credit for the amount of its bid. In this scenario too, the creditor's total recovery on the debt is the $200,000 it obtains from resale.

The creditor who makes a high credit bid gains several advantages. The creditor minimizes the likelihood that the sale will be set aside for inadequacy of price. The creditor also minimizes the likelihood that the debtor will exercise its statutory right to redeem the property. Most statutory redemption is for the amount of the sale price. If the debtor in our example wanted to redeem its $200,000 property, the debtor would have to pay $1 million — a highly unlikely event. The foreclosing creditor who is willing to credit bid the entire amount of its secured debt need not incur the expense of evaluating the collateral prior to the sale. If the creditor is outbid, the creditor will recover the full amount of the secured debt; if it is not outbid, it will have the property to inspect, evaluate, improve, and resell at its leisure.

A creditor who buys its collateral at the sale always runs some risk that the sale will be set aside or the property redeemed. Notwithstanding that risk, the creditor-purchaser is completely free to seek a profit on resale. That profit on resale will belong to the creditor, not the debtor.

In fact, purchase by the foreclosing creditor for later resale is by far the dominant pattern in mortgage foreclosures. A recent study of mortgage foreclosures in one county in New York revealed that the mortgagee purchased the property by credit bid in 77 percent of all cases. Eighty-five percent of the creditor-purchasers resold the property within four to five years, and a large majority of the resales took place in the first two years. Of the third parties who purchased at foreclosure sales, about two-thirds resold the property within four to five years. Weschsler, Through the Looking Glass: Foreclosure by Sale as De Facto Strict Foreclosure — An Empirical Study of Mortgage Foreclosure and Subsequent Resale, 70 Cornell L. Rev. 850 (1985).

In effect, this means that the mortgage foreclosure process, in its most common manifestation, is a two-sale process: The first sale, the judicial one, is not so much a real exposure of the collateral to the market as a symbolic formality that cuts off the debtor's right to redeem or at least starts the redemption period running. The resale for market price that will return the property to productive use occurs some time later. Notice what happens to the debtor's equity in the property when the first sale is for only the amount of the foreclosed lien. The buyer at the first sale (usually the lien holder) gets the property for the amount of the lien and resells it for a price approaching market value, thereby capturing the debtor's equity.

F. Judicial Sale Procedure: A Functional Analysis

As we noted at the beginning of this assignment, some commentators see the judicial sale process as intended to value the collateral. By fixing a value for the collateral, the process determines the amount of the deficiency judgment or, if the debtor has an equity in the property, it insures that the equity will not be forfeited. But if that is the intent, the process does not accomplish it. Except in those cases in which foreclosing creditors credit bid the amounts of their debts, the bids at foreclosure and other judicial sales bring only a fraction of the value of the property sold. While credit bids are often near or even in excess of the market value of the property sold, they are hardly a sign that the process is working. To the contrary, the purpose of a credit bid is usually to avoid reliance on the judicial sale process.

Although the judicial sale process does a poor job of valuing the collateral, it has important side effects that some see as its virtue. If the debtor has an equity in the property, a judicial sale threatens to forfeit it. Some commentators suggest that this motivates knowledgeable debtors to liquidate their property before that occurs. If the debtor owes more than the property is likely to bring at the sale, forced sale at an inadequate price may threaten to result in a deficiency judgment in an excessive amount. That in turn motivates knowledgeable debtors to attempt to come to terms with the foreclosing creditor. It would be wrong, however, to conclude that these side effects render the grossly inefficient procedures for foreclosure sale either elegant or efficient. Threatening to blow the property to bits would accomplish as much, and the explosives might be less expensive.

Problem Set 4

4.1.   You represent Commercial Bank with regard to an upcoming judicial foreclosure sale. The balance owing on the mortgage is $53,231. Commercial estimates that the house is worth between $40,000 and $45,000. Under the law of your state, Commercial will not be able to obtain a judgment for any deficiency remaining after the sale. Commercial wants to know how much they should bid at the sale. Consider these possibilities as you map out your strategy:

a.   Commercial is the only bidder present at the sale. For what amount should they buy the property?

b.   A third party has bid $53,232. Should Commercial go higher?

c.   A third party has bid $44,000. Should Commercial go higher?

4.2.   As part of your firm's pro bono program, you represent Sallie Hudson. Sallie fell three payments behind on her mortgage. First Savings, the mortgage lender, accelerated, filed for foreclosure, and obtained a judgment. The foreclosure sale is set for a date four weeks from now. The judgment is for $53,232. Sallie would like to keep the house, but her finances are generally shaky, and she doesn't have the money to redeem it. She is wondering whether she should be doing anything in preparation for the sale? Assume you are in a jurisdiction where the grant of a deficiency is within the discretion of the court, based on the equities of the case. In this situation, the practical effect is that neither you nor First Savings can be certain whether the court will grant a deficiency judgment.

a. If the house has a fair market value of $40,000 to $45,000, what is your answer?

b. If the house has a fair market value of $70,000, what is your answer?

c. Sallie's brother-in-law deals in real estate and has the financial ability to buy this house. He is willing to do so and let Sallie keep living in it. How does that change your answers to a and b?

4.3. In a parallel universe in which you've never met Sallie Hudson, you are interested in buying a house. The neighborhood you like best is Spring Green. In scanning the legal notices this morning, you saw that a house in Spring Green is scheduled for a judicial foreclosure sale in four weeks. The notice shows that First Savings and Loan is plaintiff in the foreclosure case, Sallie Hudson is the defendant, and the case number is 96-263. The notice does not indicate the balance owing on the mortgage. It does give the address and legal description of the property and the name of the creditor's attorney, Jason Kovan. You'd like to try to buy this house, particularly if you can get a bargain on it. What information will you need to formulate a bid? Where will you get it? Will Hudson be willing to help? Kovan? First Savings? The sheriff who will conduct the sale?

4.4. You represent American Insurance Company. They have asked you to prepare a "bidding strategy" for an upcoming foreclosure sale. American holds the first mortgage, in the amount of $20 million, against an apartment building that is under construction and unoccupied. They estimate that the building is worth about $18 million as is. The debtor is a corporation that owns no other assets, but payment of the loan has been guaranteed by four wealthy individuals who are the owners of the corporation. So long as there are no problems with the foreclosure sale, American anticipates that they probably will be able to recover any deficiency from the four guarantors. The law of your state provides for no statutory right to redeem. In planning your strategy, consider the following possibilities:

a. American is the only bidder present at the sale. For what amount should they buy the property?

b. A lawyer representing a corporation you have never heard of appears at the sale and bids $20 million. You doubt that the mysterious bidder actually has $20 million, but under the law of your state, the successful bidder who makes a $1,000 deposit will have four hours to increase the deposit to one-third of the bid price. The officer conducting the sale tells you that if the bidder does not increase the deposit within that time, the court probably will reschedule the sale for a date about a month from now. Should American bid higher?

c.   Under the law of your state, if the high bidder at a public sale fails to purchase the property, the officer conducting the sale must sell to the second highest bidder. Does this change your initial bidding strategy? What if there are two strangers at your sale, and one bids $12 million and the second immediately bids $25 million. What should you do?

4.5.   You received a call from Paul Tosci, a senior lending officer for Seal Rock Bank. The Bank has been approached by a shopping center developer, Margo Marshak, who would like a $2.5 million standby commitment to enable her to bid on a shopping center that is to be sold at a judicial foreclosure sale. On the basis of recent sales of roughly comparable shopping centers, Tosci estimates the value of this one to be $5.1 million. He explains that Marshak will pay a $25,000 nonrefundable fee for the Bank's legally binding commitment to lend $2.5 million against the shopping center in the event that the developer wins the bid. The Bank will also earn the market rate of interest on the loan if the Bank is called on to make it. Marshak will provide title insurance at her own expense and invest at least $500,000 of her own money in the shopping center. What advice do you give Tosci? Is this likely to be good business for Seal Rock? What problems do you foresee? Would you feel better about the deal if (1) Marshak was the one who originally developed the shopping center and her brother-in-law is the debtor being foreclosed against, or (2) Marshak is an outsider with no prior ties to the shopping center?

4.6.   You continue in your job as chief legislative aide to state representative Candy Rowsey. A recent state supreme court decision has ruled that creditors can recover deficiency judgments from their debtors following any kind of foreclosure sale. Several newspaper editorials have decried this result, focusing on hapless homeowners caught in a real estate market downturn. Representative Rowsey chairs the judiciary committee, and she wants a recommendation from you on whether she should propose legislation to restrict deficiency judgments. Give her an outline of your point of view, including the kinds of restrictions you would choose if some proposal to limit deficiency judgments went forward.

Assignment 5: Article 9 Sale and Deficiency

Sales under Article 9 of the Uniform Commercial Code serve essentially the same purposes as judicial sales. They determine the value of the collateral and convert that value into cash. If the debtor has equity in the collateral, conversion to cash makes it possible for the secured creditor to deduct the amount owing from the proceeds of sale and send the remainder to the debtor. If the sale is for less than the amount of the debt, that determination of value provides the basis for a court to later decide what portion of the debt has been paid and what portion remains owing.

As with real property foreclosures, the requirement that the collateral be offered for sale as part of the personal property foreclosure process cannot be waived or varied in the initial lending contract. U.C.C. §§9-602(10), 9-620. For example, a provision in a car loan agreement that, in the event of default and repossession, the secured creditor can retain the car in satisfaction of the debt is unenforceable. The sale is an essential feature of the foreclosure process, and the debtor has a right to have the collateral sold regardless of the contractual language.

A. Strict Foreclosure Under Article 9

After a default has occurred, the debtor can consent to the secured party retaining the collateral in full or in *partial satisfaction* of the obligation it secures. "Partial satisfaction" means that the debtor receives credit against the debt in some amount but continues to owe the remainder. While a right to consent probably sounds harmless enough, in most instances the consent will not be real. U.C.C. §620(c)(2) implies consent if the secured party sends the debtor a proposal for retention of the collateral in full satisfaction of the debt and does not receive a notification of objection to the proposal within 20 days. An oral objection is insufficient. Debtors who do nothing, perhaps because they are confused by the procedures, are deemed to have consented.

This right to consent is subject to three conditions. First, there must be no objection from others holding liens against the collateral.

See U.C.C. §9-620(a)(2). Second, if the collateral is consumer goods, the debtor can consent, in writing or by silence, to strict foreclosure only after repossession. U.C.C. §9-620(a). Third, strict foreclosure is not permitted if the debtor has paid 60 percent of the cash price of consumer goods purchased on credit or 60 percent of the loan against other consumer goods. Once again, the debtor may waive this right after default, but this kind of waiver requires a writing. U.C.C. §§9-620(a)(4) and (e), 9-624(b).

The third exception is directed against the unscrupulous practice of forfeiting debtors' equities in property when the debtors have nearly completed payment. If the debtor has paid 60 percent of the cash price or original loan amount, the likelihood that the debtor has an equity in the property is high. U.C.C. §9-620(e) was drafted to protect debtors against loss of such equities. What is perhaps more remarkable about the provision is its narrowness: It provides no protection to consumers who have paid less than 60 percent and no protection to nonconsumers, regardless of how much the nonconsumers have paid. The implicit assumptions seem to be that consumers who have paid less than 60 percent don't have an equity, and anyone other than a consumer will be sophisticated enough to protect its equity by making the objection described in U.C.C. §9-620(c).

B.   Sale Procedure Under Article 9

When Article 9 applies, U.C.C. §9-610 governs the procedure for sale of the collateral. The most important difference from the judicial sale procedure studied in the previous assignment is that the secured creditor, not a public official, conducts the sale and distributes the sale proceeds. U.C.C. §9-610 gives the creditor broad latitude to determine the method and timing of the sale. Depending on the circumstances, the creditor may be able to sell the property by auction, by setting a fixed price and finding a buyer who will pay that price, or by negotiating with interested parties.

This does not mean a foreclosing creditor can sell the collateral however it pleases. The foreclosing creditor has a duty to the debtor to choose a procedure for sale that is commercially reasonable. In fact, "every aspect of the disposition, including the method, manner, time, place and terms must be commercially reasonable." U.C.C. §9-610(b). To a much greater degree than most judicial sale procedures, the U.C.C. sale procedure is directed at getting a good price for the collateral. Under many judicial sale procedures, for example, shares of stock in Microsoft would have to be sold at a sheriff's sale after foreclosure; under the provisions of Article 9, they can be sold easily and quickly through NASDAQ.

Section 9-611(c)(1) also requires that the creditor give the debtor prior notice of the sale. The purpose of notice is to enable the debtor to observe the sale, participate in it, or otherwise protect its rights. One thing the debtor might do, if it learns of the sale in time, is seek out additional persons to bid.

U.C.C. §9-623 incorporates the common law right to redeem. Under its provisions, redemption is accomplished by paying the full amount of the debt, including the secured creditors' attorneys' fees and expenses of sale. As we explored in Assignment 4, judicial sales are often subject to an additional, statutory right to redeem that continues after the sale. No additional statutory right to redeem exists after an Article 9 sale. At the moment the creditor enters into a contract for disposition of the collateral, it is too late for the debtor to redeem it.

The debtor's right to set aside a defective or irregular sale is more constricted under the U.C.C. than under most judicial sale procedures. If the only defect in the sale is that it was commercially unreasonable, the debtor is likely to be left with merely the right to sue the creditor for damages. (If, however, the collateral is consumer goods, the debtor has the right to recover a statutory penalty. U.C.C. §9-625(c)(2).) But the dispute remains between the debtor and the creditor. The good faith purchaser at a U.C.C. sale can buy with confidence that it will not lose its bargain because the sale is set aside. See U.C.C. §9-617(b).

Sales under Article 9 are governed by these procedures even if the creditor obtained possession of the collateral by filing a replevin case rather than using a U.C.C. self-help remedy. The court that granted the judgment of replevin does not supervise the sale process or confirm the sale after it has occurred. Again, the U.C.C. provisions simplify the sale procedure by eliminating protections for the dispossessed debtor.

When collateral is sold for an insufficient price, the injury to the debtor may come in either of two forms. Where the debtor has an equity in the collateral, the insufficient price may forfeit all or part of this equity. In fact, few debtors sue for such a loss. First, few debtors have any equity to lose. For example, the balance owing on a car loan often exceeds the resale value of the car during the early part of the loan repayment period (when debtors are most likely to default). Second, the debtor who has lost an equity may not have the financial resources necessary to bring suit. Third, even if the debtor can afford to bring suit, it may not be worth it. The cost of the suit may exceed the amount that could be recovered.

The second type of injury to debtors from an insufficient sale price is the entry of a deficiency judgment in an amount larger than is appropriate. Litigation over deficiencies is more common than litigation over a debtor's loss of equity. One reason is that the deficiency litigation is initiated by the creditors, who can usually better afford it, both because they are in better financial condition and because they tend to be repeat players who can make this kind of litigation part of their business routine. Nonetheless, important disincentives to suing for deficiencies exist, especially against debtors who resist. The U.C.C. standard of a "commercially reasonable sale" is so vague that such a debtor can nearly always find something to complain about. By investing a relatively small amount to defend the creditor's action for a deficiency, the debtor can put the creditor to substantial legal expense. If the debtor shows any inclination to resist, the creditor will find it difficult to justify the expense of continuing. Even creditors who win deficiency judgments seldom collect them.

Debtors commonly defend actions for deficiency judgments by asserting that the creditor retained the collateral instead of conducting a sale, that the creditor did not give proper notice of the sale, or that the creditor conducted the sale in a manner that was not commercially reasonable. Each of these defenses is considered below.

C.   Problems with Article 9 Sale Procedure

1.   Failure to Sell the Collateral

U.C.C. §9-610(a) provides that a secured party *may* sell the collateral after default. But there is no specific provision that the secured party *must* sell the collateral after default and no time fixed within which any sale must occur. A secured party who obtains possession of the collateral after default may prefer to keep it and use it. For example, suppose a farmer sold equipment to a neighbor and then had to repossess it. The farmer may then prefer to keep it and use it rather than sell it again. A secured creditor who plans to sell the collateral if necessary may want to keep it temporarily while waiting to see if the repossession itself spurs the debtor or a guarantor to come up with the money. In some cases a secured party might be unable to sell the collateral because a law or regulation prohibits resale or because the collateral has been destroyed or become worthless (for example, a secured party might repossess alcoholic beverages but not have a license to sell them). Finally, a secured party who intends to sell repossessed collateral may simply procrastinate.

While the secured party has possession of the collateral, it may decline in value. That alone entitles the debtor to no remedy. But if the secured creditor's delay in selling is commercially unreasonable, the secured creditor's deficiency will be limited to the amount that would have been left owing if the sale had been commercially reasonable. See U.C.C. §9-626(a).

2.   The Requirement of Notice of Sale

U.C.C. §9-611 requires that the secured party send notice to the debtor, guarantors, and some lienors. To identify the lienors, the secured party may have to conduct a search of the public records. The failure to give this notice does not invalidate the sale, U.C.C. §9-617, but it is a defect that can have the effect of reducing the amount of the deficiency the secured party can recover. The Code operates on the presumption that the debtor should have had notice so that it could observe the sale and perhaps come up with potential buyers. In the following case, the FDIC finds itself defending the sale procedures followed by a bank it has taken over. Citations to revised Article 9 are in brackets. Some of the quotes don't match the cited sections perfectly because the quoted language is from former Article 9, but, nonetheless, the key points of law remain the same.

Federal Deposit Insurance Corp. v. Lanier

926 F.2d 462 (5th Cir. 1991)

JERRY E. SMITH, CIRCUIT JUDGE. . . .

The sole restraints on a seller disposing of collateral pursuant to [U.C.C. §9-610(b)] is that the disposition be commercially reasonable and that the creditor give the debtor proper notice. Before a creditor can sell the collateral underlying a secured loan, [U.C.C. §9-611(b)] requires that the creditor give the debtor "reasonable notification of the time after which any private sale or other intended disposition is to be made." The purpose of this notification is to give the debtor an opportunity to discharge the debt, arrange for a friendly purchaser, or to oversee the sale to see that it is conducted in a commercially reasonable manner. Under Texas law, a guarantor also is entitled to notice.

The guarantors challenge the notice given in this case. The notice sent by the bank provided,

> [The Bank] will sell the [property] at either a public or private sale ten (10) days after the date of this communication. The Bank fully intends to give reasonable notice of such sale, but circumstances attendant to the property are such that the value of the property threatens to decline speedily, therefore the sale may take place immediately.
>
> Proceeds from such sale shall be applied as provided by [U.C.C. §9-615(a)]. There may be a deficiency due and owing the Bank on the debt after the application of the proceeds.

[T]he guarantors assert that their notice was defective because the letter sent to them did not state whether the disposition of the collateral would be by public or private sale and because the sale took place four months, rather than ten days, after the letter was sent. . . . We reject each of these contentions and hold that the guarantors received adequate notice under [U.C.C. §9-613].

Although the goods were sold at a private sale, the bank's letter did not indicate the type of sale at which the goods would be sold. This was not a fatal defect. We follow the lead of the Texas courts in rejecting this as a reason to declare the notice inadequate. As one such court has stated,

> We are aware of decisions by courts in other states that have held that the notice of intent to sell or otherwise dispose of collateral must state whether the sale is to be private or public. However, [U.C.C. §9-613(1)(E)] does not so require. We hold the evidence was sufficient to establish the [collateral] was sold by private sale. As such, the Notice of Intent to Sell did not need to state the time and place of sale.

Hall v. Crocker Equip. Leasing, Inc., 737 S.W.2d 1, 3 (Tex.App. — Houston (14th Dist. 1987), writ denied). Because the notice sent by the bank was adequate to "inform reasonable business persons" that their property would be sold within ten days or more, Siboney Corp. v. Chicago Pneumatic Tool Co., 572 S.W.2d 4, 6 (Tex.Civ.App. — Houston (1st Dist. 1978), writ ref'd n.r.e.), the notice was sufficient to allow the bank to proceed with its planned sale of the goods. The notice is not defective simply because it does not specifically state that the goods would be sold privately.[1]

The guarantors also argue that their notice was invalid because the sale took place four months, rather than ten days, after the letter was sent. This argument ignores the different treatment that Texas law affords creditors who proceed by private rather than public sale. While [U.C.C. §9-613(1)(E)] provides that a secured creditor must provide both the time and place of any public sale, to allow the debtor the chance to show up at the public sale, the requirements for a private sale are less stringent. For a private sale, the creditor only need provide notice "of the time *after which* any private sale or other intended disposition is to be made." (emphasis added). The commentary to [U.C.C. §9-612] provides that " 'reasonable notification' is not defined in this Article; at a *minimum* it must be sent in such time that persons entitled to receive it will have sufficient time to take appropriate steps to protect their interests by taking part in the sale or other disposition if they so desire." [Comment 2] (emphasis added).

---

1. Our analysis is premised upon the final sale's being private, for [U.C.C. §9-613(1)(E)] specifically provides that a secured creditor must provide both the time and place of any public sale.

"[N]o period is set within which the disposition must be made." Id. The clear intent of the code and the commentary is to avoid sales that occur too soon after notice is sent, giving the debtor insufficient time to participate in the sale.[2]

Although it is possible that a sale conducted much later than the time indicated would become stale, we agree with the leading commentators and cases that "generally allow substantial lapses of time between original notice and subsequent private sales." 2 J. White & R. Summers, supra, §27-12 at 606 (citing cases allowing private sales occurring as much as sixteen months after notice sent); see also id. §27-14 at 611 ("A number of cases appear to allow secured creditors a substantial period in which to sell the goods after an initial notice to the debtor."). We believe that a Texas court would find that the sale of collateral four months after notification of the debtor was not so untimely as to mandate a finding that the creditor was required to renotify the debtor of the planned disposition. . . .

The wide latitude afforded the creditor here serves as a reminder for debtors who receive notification of sales. The burden, at least according to this court, seems to shift to the debtor to find out about the sale if the debtor really has any interest in what happens subsequently. Of course, it may be a fair inference from the facts that the debtor did not have any interest — until the creditor came after the debtor for a deficiency judgment. At that point the debtor and the debtor's counsel were very interested in every aspect of the sale that might provide a defense to the creditor's action.

3. *The Requirement of a Commercially Reasonable Sale*

The provision of U.C.C. §9-610(b) requiring that "[e]very aspect of a disposition of collateral, including the method, manner, time, place, and other terms, must be commercially reasonable" is deliberately vague. The purpose is to bring the knowledge and ingenuity of the secured party to bear in determining a reasonable way to dispose of the particular kind of collateral. The underlying assumption is that what methods, manners, times, or places are reasonable will differ with the type of collateral, and perhaps with other circumstances. Procedures that are reasonable to dispose of a few hundred dollars worth of office furniture may not be reasonable for disposing of mil-

---

2. This also is the intent of the security agreement in this case, which provides for a minimum notice of five days.

lions of dollars worth of laboratory equipment. In each case, the secured creditor should discover a reasonable method of disposition and use it. Ordinarily that will be a method that reasonable owners of the particular type of property would use when their own money is at stake.

In most cases in which the commercial reasonableness of a sale is challenged, a close factual inquiry is required. In the following case the debtor had filed for bankruptcy, so the bankruptcy court heard the case without a jury, according to bankruptcy procedures. But the applicable law was the Tennessee version of the U.C.C.

Chavers v. Frazier

93 B.R. 366 (Bankr. M.D. Tenn. 1989)

HONORABLE GEORGE C. Paine, II, BANKRUPTCY JUDGE.

[Mr. and Mrs. Chavers repossessed a Lear jet from the Frazier group and sold it. When the Chavers sought a deficiency judgment in an amount in excess of $400,000, the Frazier group defended on the ground that the sale had not been held in a commercially reasonable manner.]

In order to make the determination of commercial reasonableness, we must look to the facts and circumstances of the sale. Following repossession of the aircraft and the transfer of rights to the Chavers, the Lear jet was sold at a public sale. The aircraft, which sold to Frank Frazier's group for $850,000.00 in March, 1985, was sold in April, 1986 for $415,000.00. Although failure to procure the best price for collateral does not in and of itself make a sale commercially unreasonable, [U.C.C. §9-627(a)], and reasonableness is primarily assessed by the procedures employed, "a sufficient resale price is the logical focus of the protection given debtors. . . . " Smith v. Daniels, 634 S.W.2d 276, 278 (Tenn.App. 1982). The great disparity between the purchase price and the sale price of the collateral approximately one (1) year later raises the issue of whether the total circumstances demonstrate that the Chavers took all steps considered reasonable by prevailing practices to insure that the sale of the Lear jet would bring a fair price. After reviewing the circumstances of the sale and the relevant legal factors, the Court determines that the Chavers have not met their burden for the following reasons.

Procedures employed to sell small jet aircraft are matters particularly within the knowledge of a small group of persons who are experts in the highly technical endeavor. The Chavers offered the testimony of two (2) experts, and [the Frazier group] offered a third expert, Mr. Charles Mulle. After considering both the demeanor and the relative qualifications of these experts, the Court finds that Mr. Mulle was by far the pre-eminent expert. Mr. Mulle was a graduate of Riddle Aeronautic Institute where he received a Bachelor of Science Degree in Aeronautic sciences with a minor in aviation management. Prior to attending Riddle Aeronautic Institute, he served in Army aviation for four (4) years and assisted in the testing projects for certain military aircraft. He has served as a Canadian bush pilot, a corporate pilot, and since 1975 has been employed full time in the commercial aircraft leasing sales and management area. Since 1981 he has been the principal owner of Business Aircraft Leasing, Inc., a company which is solely involved in the buying, selling and leasing of corporate and commercial aircraft. In addition, Mr. Mulle had specific knowledge of the aircraft at issue in this case from the date it was initially ordered from the manufacturer. He had been responsible for leasing the aircraft and had subsequently sold the aircraft to [the Frazier group]. One of the Chavers' expert witnesses agreed that Mr. Mulle was a competent and knowledgeable person in the field of aircraft sales and procedures. The other expert witness offered by the Chavers advised the Court that he respected Mr. Mulle's opinion and looked to him for information and advice. Mr. Mulle's experience was far in excess of that of the Chavers' experts. Based on his experience, candor and qualifications, the Court finds Mr. Mulle highly credible and uniquely qualified to assist the Court in its determination. The Chavers' expert, who actually assisted them in devising a plan for the sale, testified that he had never conducted a retail sale of jet aircraft prior to the transaction in question.

The value of the aircraft at the time of its sale to [the Frazier group] was approximately $825,000.00 to $850,000.00, as established by the testimony of the banker who initially granted the loan to [the Frazier group]. Mr. Mulle testified that the value was in that range and may have contained a premium of approximately $25,000.00 to $50,000.00 because the initial sale was one hundred percent (100%) financed.

1.   THE HASTY SALE WAS NOT REASONABLE

The plaintiffs gained possession of the aircraft on May 2, 1986 and sold it at public auction on June 3, 1986. The Court finds the plaintiffs acted with unreasonable haste in their efforts to sell the aircraft. . . .

The collateral at issue is a jet aircraft with a highly specialized and limited market. Under the circumstances of this case, the Court finds that the time permitted to advertise and market the plane to this select group of potential buyers was grossly inadequate. The Chavers could not satisfactorily explain their actions in April and May of 1986, but the following is clear from the record. First, the Chavers['] . . . principal advisor, who also testified at trial, was extremely inexperienced in the commercial sale of jet aircraft. The plaintiffs were aware that Mr. Mulle had worked on the aircraft previously and that he was available to assist them in the sale of

the aircraft, yet neither the Chavers nor their advisors sought Mr. Mulle
out for advice or aid. The plaintiffs' advisor knew of the proposed repossession on April 23, 1986 and that the custody of the aircraft would pass
to the Chavers on May 2, 1986, but made no immediate recommenda-
tions as to the means of disposing of the aircraft. After "investigating
options" for at least two (2) weeks, he and the Chavers made the initial
decision to sell the aircraft at auction approximately three (3) weeks prior
to the actual sale. All advertising for the sale was done from May 20,
1986 to May 29, 1986 and terminated within five (5) days of the sale.

The other expert witnesses, including the Chavers' own expert,
believed greater time was needed to explore and reach the potential
market. The Chavers' other expert witness testified that six (6) months to
one (1) year was needed for the fair and proper sale of such an aircraft.
Mr. Mulle considered ninety (90) days to be an appropriate, although
minimum, time frame to judge the market and to make commercially
reasonable efforts.

Regardless of the specific time requirements, which this Court does not
determine, it is clear to the Court that the time requirement . . . agreed
to between the Bank and the Chavers was, in itself, unreasonable. The
Court further finds that the Chavers sold an expensive and sophisticated
jet aircraft in [an] unreasonably brief time . . . and that this hasty sale
was a significant cause of the low sale price. . . .

2. THE ADVERTISING WAS NOT ADEQUATE

The Court considered substantial testimony concerning the adequacy
of the advertising and further determines that the advertising was wholly
inadequate for a commercially reasonable sale. Advertisements ran briefly
in the *Wall Street Journal* and a trade publication known as *Trade-A-Plane*.
The advertisements were described by Mr. Mulle as telegraphing a distress sale during "a brief flurry of advertising." Even one of the Chavers'
experts felt that the use of the "as-is" phrase in the text of the advertising suggested a distress sale.

Mr. Mulle described a reasonable advertising protocol as follows. He
testified first that advertisements in the *Wall Street Journal* and *Trade-A-Plane* should be positive and run for an appropriate length of time. The
Chavers' advertisements ran briefly and suggested a distress sale. He also
testified that the potential market for jet aircraft was concentrated in corporations and professional aircraft brokers throughout the country. From
this pool of qualified buyers the most likely prospects should have been
determined; the particular needs of a buyer should have been addressed
in a formal sales effort, including if necessary, taking the aircraft for a
buyer to view. While the Chavers provided some information to those
who responded to their advertisements, such information was described

by Mr. Mulle as "laughable" and indicative of an amateur effort to sell the aircraft. The sales packet provided by the Chavers' advisor to potential buyers did not include a log book summary or copy of the log book, which even the Chavers' advisor admitted was important information to a potential buyer and would reflect the high degree of maintenance required by the Federal Aviation Authority for commercial and charter work.

3. A "DISTRESS SALE" AUCTION WAS NOT REASONABLE

The method of sale is also an important factor. Under these circumstances, the Court finds that an initial effort to contact the fairly limited pool of qualified commercial buyers would have been in keeping with prevailing responsible practice, and not immediate resort to the public sale option, which in the words of even the Chavers' experts, is ordinarily a "last resort" method of sale. The Court finds the use of a public auction, under these circumstances, was not reasonable. It could be expected to draw only those it did — experienced wholesale aircraft dealers in an already small potential market looking for a distress type "deal." Potential retail buyers who would normally have concerns about the aircraft that could be addressed in the normal course of business were not identified and could not be reasonably presumed to attend an auction advertised in this manner within this time frame. This method of sale, while always a possibility, under these facts immediately telegraphed the message that this was a "fire sale." Under these circumstances, there was no reason initially to conduct such a distress disposal of the aircraft, and the Court finds it commercially unreasonable to have done so.

4. AIRCRAFT MAINTENANCE WAS NOT PROPERLY ADDRESSED PRIOR TO THE SALE

A great deal of attention focused on the need for a "hot section inspection" on the aircraft. According to the rules and regulations of the Federal Aviation Authority, jet engines have to be inspected and, if necessary, overhauled. Estimates of the cost of performing this service were varied. From the testimony, it appears to the Court that the Chavers did not even consider whether this work should be accomplished and borne as a cost prior to sale, and if so, what effect it would have on resale value. The Court finds that under the circumstances, and in light of the condition of this particular airplane, a hot section inspection was an important and necessary step to prepare the plane for sale and failure of the Chavers to undertake the inspection seriously lessened their ability to obtain a fair price for the aircraft. The Chavers also failed to investigate paint options, possible financing options and a procedure for either undertaking or "capping" the hot section charges, which process likely would have allowed for recoupment of these charges upon sale. The failure to reasonably prepare the aircraft for sale, in the determination of this Court, constitutes a commercially unreasonable manner of sale.

5.   THE PURCHASE PRICE WAS NOT REASONABLE

The final factor is the purchase price obtained at the sale. Although this factor is not, by itself, determinative, it is a factor to consider. The proof in this case showed that even though the plane sold for $415,000.00, it was insured at that time for $700,000.00, as testified to by the bank officers. Even the Chavers' expert, Mr. Bunyan, was "surprised" that the plane sold for $415,000.00. Mr. Chavers testified that he thought the value of the plane was in the neighborhood of $700,000.00 when it was returned to him. Mr. Mulle testified that it was ludicrous to think that the fair market value of the plane could decrease by approximately one-half of its sale value a year earlier. . . . [Because the Chavers had not introduced evidence from which the court could determine the fair market value of the Lear jet at the time of the sale, the court declined to enter a deficiency judgment.]

Article 9 cases like *Chavers* show the stark contrast to judicial sale cases. The *Chavers* court says that 60 days was a grossly inadequate time for advertising and marketing the aircraft, but judicial sale procedures rarely allow that much time, even for complex collateral worth millions of dollars. The *Chavers* court is disappointed in advertising that ran only briefly in the *Wall Street Journal* and *Trade-A-Plane*, but under judicial sale procedures, the ads for this aircraft might have run in the legal notices column of a local newspaper. The *Chavers* court says that a "distress auction" was not reasonable, yet nearly every judicial sale is precisely that. The *Chavers* court complains about the maintenance of the aircraft, but in a judicial sale, the aircraft could have been sold in exactly the condition in which it was repossessed. Last, notice that the *Chavers* court sets aside a sale for almost 60 percent of the fair market value of the collateral, a price that would easily have passed muster in most judicial sale procedures.

If the secured party fails to give notice of sale or to conduct the sale in a commercially reasonable manner, there is a rebuttable presumption that the value of the collateral was at least equal to the amount of the debt. As a result, the secured creditor can recover a deficiency only by rebutting the presumption. It does that by proving that the collateral was worth some amount less than the amount of the debt. In that event, the secured creditor is entitled to a deficiency in an amount equal to the amount by which the debt exceeds the value of the collateral. Notice that the overall effect is that the court must determine the value of the collateral. See U.C.C. §§9-626(a)(3) and (4).

To illustrate, assume that Paul owes Carson $25,000, and that when Paul defaults, Carson repossesses the fixtures that were subject to Carson's security agreement. The fixtures were worth $12,000, but Carson sells them in a commercially unreasonable manner and receives only $8,000. Carson sues for the deficiency. Provided that Carson carries his burden of proving that the collateral was worth only $12,000, Carson can recover a $13,000 deficiency judgment.

This approach represents a change in revised Article 9 from earlier law, which left the question of a deficiency solely to the courts. But revised Article 9 carves out an exception for consumer contracts, leaving the case law to resolve the consequences of a failure to abide by the requirements imposed on an Article 9 sale. §9-626(b). Interestingly, the jurisdictions are split as to the appropriate remedy for failure to give notice of sale or failure to conduct the sale in a commercially reasonable manner. The majority hold that there is a rebuttable presumption that the value of the collateral was at least equal to the amount of the debt, with the consequence that, if the consumer debtor objects, the court ends up determining what the sale price should have been. A substantial minority hold that any significant irregularity in the sale procedure is sufficient to deny the deficiency altogether — a view that relieves the court of the necessity to guess what the price would have been absent the defect. This means, of course, that the treatment of consumer cases will vary from jurisdiction to jurisdiction.

To illustrate the difference between these views, assume that Consumer Paul owes Carson $25,000, and that when Paul defaults, Carson repossesses the fixtures that were subject to Carson's security agreement. The fixtures were worth $12,000, but Carson sells them in a commercially unreasonable manner and recovers only $8,000. Carson then sues Paul for the $17,000 deficiency. In a jurisdiction that followed the minority rule, the court would not grant a deficiency judgment. In a court that followed the rebuttable presumption rule, the court would begin with a presumption that the collateral was worth the full amount of the debt, $25,000, and no deficiency judgment should be granted. But if Carson proved that the value of the collateral was in fact $12,000, Carson still could recover a $13,000 deficiency judgment.

D.   Article 9 Sale Procedure:
A Functional Analysis

The Article 9 sale procedure may seem like a case of the vampire guarding the blood bank. It is the debtor's property that is being sold. Because Article 9 preserves both the debtor's right to the surplus and the creditor's right to a deficiency, it is the debtor who directly suffers the effects of a poorly conducted sale that brings a low price. The creditor may seem to have no incentive to seek a fair price for the collateral. Yet the secured creditor is given virtually complete control over the manner of sale.

Proponents of the Article 9 sale procedure argue that the requirement of a "commercially reasonable sale," backed by the threat to deny some portion of the deficiency, gives incentives to repossessing secured creditors to encourage bidding and seek a market price for the goods. We doubt it.

The threat to deny a deficiency could be a powerful motivator, at least where the expected deficiency was substantial and the likelihood of collecting it from the debtor high. But the threat in revised Article 9 is only to reduce the amount of the deficiency to what it would have been had the secured creditor complied with Article 9.

The secured creditor that knows it won't be able to collect any deficiency because its debtor is insolvent or bankrupt will want to sell the collateral for the highest net price it can get, because that may be all it collects on the loan. But the secured creditor that expects to collect the deficiency from the debtor or the guarantor has little or no incentive to get a good price at the sale. It expects to get its money either way.

In fact, revised Article 9 seems to give secured creditors the incentive to shoot for a double recovery by purchasing the collateral at sale for less than its value, collecting the deficiency from the debtor or guarantor, and then reselling the collateral in a commercially reasonable sale — for its own account. If the debtor understands what is happening and defends the action for deficiency, the court should limit the deficiency to what the creditor would have lost in a commercially reasonable sale, and that will thwart the secured creditor's attempt to overreach. But in many cases, the debtor won't figure it out and defend. Given that the secured creditor loses nothing in the former cases and gains something in the latter cases by trying, it seems to make sense for secured creditors to try.

The secured creditor will have similarly little incentive to preserve a relatively small equity the debtor may have in the collateral. If the creditor is successful in preserving it, the creditor must pay the surplus over to the debtor anyway. If the creditor is unsuccessful in preserving it, it is unlikely the debtor will be able to bring and win a lawsuit for the damages. Again, the creditor may choose to bid in at a poorly advertised sale and take its chances.

Ultimately, these kinds of speculations are incapable of discovering the true level of effectiveness of the Article 9 sale system. What is needed is empirical evidence on the frequency with which the different fact patterns present themselves. How often do debtors have equity in repossessed collateral? How common is it for creditors to buy at Article 9 sales? How likely are debtors to defend against the entry of deficiency judgments? Unfortunately, little of this kind of evidence is available.

Problem Set 5

5.1.   The bank repossessed Maxwell's silver Mercedes and sent him notification that the bank would sell it in a private sale "after ten days from this notice." The balance owing on the loan, including principal, interest, attorneys' fees and expenses of sale is $10,000.

a.   If the fair market value of the car is $8,000, but it sells for $7,000 in a commercially reasonable sale, what is the proper amount for the court to award as a deficiency? U.C.C. §§9-615(d) and 9-626(a)(3) and (b).

b.   How much would Maxwell have to pay to redeem the car? U.C.C. §9-623.

c.   If Maxwell has enough money to redeem the car, would you recommend that he do so or that he purchase another car just like it for $8,000?

d.   At Maxwell's prompting, a friend of his offers $8,000 for the car. The bank refuses the offer because they follow a policy of selling all the cars they repossess through auto auctions. The friend can't go to the auction, because it is only open to dealers. At the auction, the car sells for $7,000. Now how much should the deficiency be? U.C.C. §§9-626, 9-627.

5.2.   Your firm represents Wewoka State Bank, which recently repossessed and sold the inventory and equipment of an auto parts store. The debt secured by the collateral was in the principal amount of $57,345, plus interest to the date of the sale in the amount of $3,541. The security agreement provides that in the event of default, the debtor will pay the bank's reasonable attorneys' fees incurred in collecting the debt. Your fees are in the amount of $3,000 for replevy of the collateral and $650 for preparing for sale; you intend to charge an additional $350 for your opinion on distribution of the proceeds of sale. The bank also spent $1,500 preserving the collateral while it was in their possession and an additional $750 advertising the sale.

The debtor has numerous other creditors, none of whom has a lien or security interest against the inventory and equipment. One of those creditors, Auto Parts Depot, heard about the auction and sent the bank a letter demanding that the $4,200 owing to them be paid out of the proceeds of sale. (If you need to know what the security agreement says to answer these questions, use the security agreement in Assignment 15, below.)

a.   The highest bid at the auction was $47,136. That money is now in your possession. To whom should you pay it? (That is, indicate to whom you would make the checks out, and in what amounts.) How much is the deficiency? See U.C.C. §§9-615(a), 9-203(b).

b.   If the highest bid at the auction had been $75,000, to whom should you pay the money? Is the bank either required or permitted to pay Auto Parts Depot from the proceeds?

5.3.   East Bank does a steady business in the repossession of automobiles. They sell the automobiles through a "dealers-only" auction. Over the years they have had numerous problems with the sending of notice of sale to the debtors whose cars are being sold. Notices have been sent in improper form or with typographical errors or have been returned because the debtor has changed addresses. Debtors have occasionally challenged the length of notice (East Bank gives five days' notice, but tries to send it at least ten days before the sale). The ten-day delay runs up the storage costs on the automobiles and the bank gets stuck for most of them in the end. The people at the bank think the notice requirement is rather silly anyway, given that the debtors can't get into the auto auction.

East Bank would like you to look into whether there is any way to dispense with the notice requirement. They are sure that none of their borrowers would object to a waiver contained in the security agreement, even if it were specifically pointed out to them. Does East Bank have to send these notices? See U.C.C. §§9-602(7) and 9-603(a) and §§9-611, 9-612, 9-613 and 9-614.

5.4.   Your client, Grizzly Bear Bank, is on a run of bad luck. The Bank recently repossessed what should have been a $345,000 helicopter, only to find that the engine and all of the electronics had been removed by the debtor (in violation of the security agreement), leaving a hull with no resale value. The amount of the debt is currently $345,000. Fortunately, the debt is personally guaranteed by four wealthy individuals.

a.   Grizzly would like to know if it is all right to throw the hull away. If not, what is the Bank supposed to do with it? See U.C.C. §§9-610(a), 9-620, 9-626, and Comment 4 to §9-610.

b.   Assume that Grizzly throws the hull away and the guarantors later prove that if Grizzly had spent $245,000 to install electronics in the hull it would have been able to sell the helicopter for $345,000.

To what deficiency judgment is Grizzly entitled? U.C.C. §§9-102(64), 9-626(a)(3).

5.5. Your client, Pedro Perez-Ortiz, bought a store from Lamp Fair, Inc. for $50,000 down and a promissory note in the amount of $277,000. Pedro couldn't make the payments on the debt, so he gave Lamp Fair the keys. Lamp Fair resumed operation of the store and sent Pedro a bill for $131,000, which the company said was the excess of what Pedro owed after crediting him for the value of the store. Pedro refused to pay, and Lamp Fair has now sued him for the $131,000. When you told Lamp Fair's lawyer that Lamp Fair couldn't sue for a deficiency without selling the store first, she snapped "where does it say that in Article 9?" U.C.C. §§9-610(a), 9-620, 9-626.

5.6. You represent the Chavers, who have repossessed another Lear jet similar to the one they previously repossessed from the Frazier group. In this case, however, the debtor is insolvent; even if a deficiency judgment is entered, it will be uncollectible. The Chavers estimate that the jet is worth about $800,000. The debt is about $850,000. The Chavers would like to avoid the expenses of sale (after the opinion in *Chavers*, Mr. Mulle has raised his rates) and just keep the jet for their personal use.

a. What should they do? U.C.C. §§9-610, 9-611, 9-620, 9-621.

b. What if the debtor objects to their retention of the collateral and they simply ignore the objection? See U.C.C. §§9-619, 9-622. Will they have a title problem if they later decide to sell or encumber the plane? Uniform Motor Vehicle Certificate of Title Act §16(b). Model Rules of Professional Conduct Rule 1.16 provides: "[A] lawyer shall not represent a client or, where representation has commenced, shall withdraw from the representation of a client if: (1) the representation will result in violation of the rules of professional conduct or other law."

c. What if the Chavers simply announce that they have sold the jet to themselves for $800,000? U.C.C. §9-617.

Chapter 2. Creditors' Remedies in Bankruptcy

Assignment 6: Bankruptcy and the Automatic Stay

A. The Federal Bankruptcy System

The preceding assignments focused on the rights of debtors and creditors in the state law collection system. In those assignments we explored the limited rights of ordinary creditors to force their debtors to repay and the enhanced rights of secured creditors in that regard. We also probed the strategic advantages of both debtors and creditors in any struggle over the payment of outstanding obligations. That would have concluded the story, but for the fact that there is a federal collection system.

Because there is, state courts sometimes are not the final arbiters of the rights of parties. If a debtor is in financial difficulty, either the debtor or the creditors may be able to move the matter to a federal bankruptcy forum. Only a small fraction of all debtors fail to pay their debts and thereby become vulnerable to the state collection system. But of those who do, a substantial portion consider bankruptcy the preferable means of dealing with their unpaid obligations.

The bankruptcy system differs from the state collection system in many respects. The state collection system permits creditors to pursue collection over very long periods of time, while the bankruptcy system imposes a relatively quick, efficient resolution of the debtor's financial problems. In order to achieve that faster resolution, the bankruptcy system offers permanent forgiveness of debt (referred to as *discharge*) or rescheduling of repayment (referred to as *extension* or *debt adjustment*). The laws permitting debts to be discharged or extended are complex, and generalizations are difficult. However, when the bankruptcy system works as intended, debtors who qualify for bankruptcy relief emerge with less debt or with debts due on different repayment schedules and their creditors as a group collect at least as much as they could have in the absence of bankruptcy if the debtor had been uncooperative.

The Constitution gives Congress the power to establish "uniform laws on the subject of Bankruptcies throughout the United States." U.S. Const. art. I, §8. Most of the bankruptcy laws currently in force are collected in Title 11 of the U.S. Code and referred to as the Bankruptcy Reform Act of 1978, or, for the bankruptcy cognoscenti, simply as "the Code."*

Under the supremacy doctrine, federal bankruptcy law supersedes state collection law. This means that when a debtor is in bankruptcy, a new set of collection laws govern. In fact, bankruptcy law incorporates many aspects of state collection law and allows them to continue to apply. Nonetheless, it is critical to understand that once a bankruptcy process has begun, federal law — not state law — is the ultimate arbiter of the rights of the parties.

While only a small percentage of all debt is ultimately resolved in bankruptcy, the bankruptcy system has an important impact on debtor-creditor relationships. Two decades ago debtors and creditors bargained in the shadow of their collection rights under state law, including the Uniform Commercial Code. Bankruptcy law had little influence because the likelihood either party would resort to it was vanishingly small. Today, a sufficiently large number of debtors find their way into the bankruptcy courts so that sophisticated lenders bargain with their borrowers primarily in the shadow of bankruptcy law instead. While it would be an exaggeration to say that they expect their debtors to file for bankruptcy, they realize that if a debt is not paid on time, bankruptcy is a real possibility. They may plan to pursue their remedies under state law if their debtors should default, but they understand that their right to do so can be preempted at any time if the debtor files for bankruptcy. For that reason, they structure their relationships with the possibility of bankruptcy in mind. Through their impact on business planning, bankruptcy laws affect the collection system even more than the number of actual bankruptcy filings would suggest.

It is not possible to teach the entire bankruptcy system in a course on secured credit, and we do not attempt to do so here. Nonetheless, it is not possible to understand the secured credit system without understanding the role that bankruptcy plays in it. In this assignment we give a brief overview of bankruptcy and discuss how a bankruptcy filing can stop all the collection actions you studied in prior assignments. In Assignment 7 we explore how creditors collect on a claim in bankruptcy and how much they can expect to receive. In both assignments, pay close attention to the sharp differences in the rights of secured and unsecured creditors.

---

*Reference to "the Code" sometimes offers an opportunity for friendly competition among commercial lawyers as to the identity of the true bearer of the title "the Code." Tax mavens refer to the Internal Revenue Code as "the Code," commercial law generalists refer to the U.C.C. as "the Code," and debtor-creditor specialists refer to the federal bankruptcy statute as "the Code." The whole area is such barren ground for jokes that no one seems inclined to fix the problem and remove this tiny source of humor.

B.   Filing a Bankruptcy Case

A bankruptcy case can be initiated by either a debtor or its creditors, but statistics published by the Administrative Office of the U.S. Courts show that well over 99 percent are initiated by the debtor. The proportion of filings initiated by creditors is considerably higher in business cases, but may be declining in recent years. In a 1983 study, Professor Lynn LoPucki found that 6 percent of a group of small business reorganization cases were initiated by creditors; in a 1994 study, Professors Warren and Westbrook found that only about 3 percent were. Professors LoPucki and Whitford found that 14 percent of the largest bankruptcy reorganization cases (publicly traded companies with more than $100 million in assets) were initiated by creditors in the early 1980s. But a later study by Professor LoPucki shows that the rate was substantially zero for the period 1994-1998. The "voluntary-ness" of a voluntary petition may also vary dramatically: Many debtors walk the plank to the bankruptcy clerk's office with the creditors' swords at their backs, with the creditors having made clear what they will do unless the debtor files. In this assignment we focus on the typical debtor who files a petition with the bankruptcy court — even if that debtor is only a few steps ahead of the creditors.

The debtor may be a business or an individual, and the debtor may choose to file under Chapter 7 (liquidation), Chapter 11 (reorganization, typically for businesses), Chapter 12 (reorganization only for owners of family farms), or Chapter 13 (reorganization only for individuals). The debtor fills out a number of forms, usually with the assistance of an attorney, disclosing a great deal about the debtor's assets, income, debts, and financial history. The debtor pays a filing fee ($170 in Chapter 7, $155 in Chapter 13, $200 in Chapter 12, and $800 in Chapter 11), and the forms are filed (usually by a runner from the attorney's office) with the clerk of the bankruptcy court.

Upon receiving the forms, the bankruptcy clerk stamps the front page with the date and time of filing. At that instant, two things happen: A bankruptcy estate, which consists of all the property of the debtor, is automatically created; and a stay against any collection activities is automatically imposed. Bankr. Code §§362(a), 541(a). Both events occur by operation of law without any additional action by the court.

Because the debtor's property is now a part of a bankruptcy estate, the debtor is not supposed to pay prepetition debts, nor is any prepetition creditor supposed to collect anything from this estate until the case is resolved. From this moment forward, the payments and collections are to be handled according to the procedures imposed by bankruptcy law.

Who is in control after the bankruptcy is filed? In the liquidation cases filed under Chapter 7, the U.S. Trustee appoints (or, in a few cases, the creditors elect) a trustee to administer the estate. In the reorganization and debt adjustment cases filed under Chapters 11, 12, and 13, the debtors are left in control of their own estates, to administer them in accord with bankruptcy law. Trustees are appointed in cases under Chapters 12 and 13, but they do not take possession of the property of the estate. Instead, they examine the debtors, review their repayment plans, receive payments from the debtors after their plans are confirmed by the court, distribute the money they receive to the appropriate creditors, and collect their fees. The debtor continues to work and manage the property much as before the filing. In a Chapter 11 case the debtor's management usually remains in possession of the property of the estate as "debtor in possession" (DIP) and operates the business. If, however, the court determines that the DIP is not running the estate effectively, it may order the appointment or election of a trustee to replace current management. Bankr. Code §1104(a). Such appointments or elections rarely occur before the court has decided to convert the case to Chapter 7.

The bankruptcy case may be resolved through liquidation, reorganization, or some combination of the two. In a Chapter 7 liquidation case, the Chapter 7 trustee liquidates all of the property of the estate. To liquidate property is to convert it into cash — usually by selling it. The trustee makes distributions to unsecured creditors only in money.

The property available for liquidation differs depending on whether the debtor is an individual or a corporation. If the debtor in Chapter 7 is an individual (bankruptcy parlance for a human being), the debtor will be entitled to exempt certain property from the estate. Every Chapter 7 debtor is entitled to keep the property of the bankruptcy estate that would have been exempt from creditors' remedies on a judgment under state law. Bankr. Code §522(b). Thus, the debtor living in a state that would not permit a judgment creditor to claim the debtor's household goods can keep those same household goods if the debtor declares bankruptcy. In addition, in some states, debtors have the option to exempt the property listed in Bankruptcy Code §522(d) instead of the property exempt from execution under state law. Bankr. Code §522(b). Debtors in a low exemption state, such as Pennsylvania, can usually exempt more property under Bankruptcy Code §522(d) than they can under the state exemption laws. Corporations are not entitled to exemptions under either state or bankruptcy law. In a Chapter 7 case all corporate assets are either abandoned or liquidated.

Following liquidation of the nonexempt property of a Chapter 7 estate, the trustee distributes the money pro rata to the general creditors. Bankr. Code §704. If the debtor is an individual, the debtor is then discharged from all remaining debts. If the debtor is a corporation, it has been stripped of all assets. At the end of the liquidation case, the corporate Chapter 7 debtor is a corporate shell that has no assets but still owes all its debts. Bankr. Code §727(a)(1).

Reorganization cases proceed differently. The debtor proposes a plan to pay its creditors all or part of the debts owing to them from currently available assets or future income. If the case is under Chapter 13, the debtor files a proposed budget, with a plan to devote all "disposable income" to the repayment of debt for a period of at least three years. Bankr. Code §1325(b). The plan must also promise to pay creditors at least as much as they would have received in a Chapter 7 liquidation. Bankr. Code §1325(a)(5). The Chapter 13 trustee examines the budget and appears at the court hearing to consider the confirmation of the debtor's plan. Bankr. Code §1302. If the plan is confirmed, the trustee receives the payments from the debtor and distributes them pro rata to the general creditors over the life of the plan. The plan lasts from three to five years, and the debtor is discharged from most remaining debt when the last payment is made. Bankr. Code §1328. A Chapter 12 bankruptcy follows the same basic pattern for cases involving family farms.

The Chapter 11 reorganization is similar to a Chapter 13 debt adjustment, with some key differences. The plan that a debtor in possession proposes in a case under Chapter 11 can provide for payments over any length of time. Some extend for 20 or 30 years, but most plans pay unsecured creditors over a period of about 5 to 7 years. As with a Chapter 13 plan, a Chapter 11 plan must promise creditors at least as much as they would have received in a Chapter 7 liquidation. Bankr. Code §1129(a)(7).

In some respects, the role of the trustee in a liquidating bankruptcy is similar to the role of the sheriff in a state collection action. The trustee finds property, sells it for cash, and distributes the cash to creditors. The difference, of course, is that the trustee has broad control over all the debtor's property and acts on behalf of all the creditors.

Reorganization bankruptcy performs a very different role. In essence, the law encourages and sometimes compels the creditors to accept a modification of the debtor's obligations to them. The purpose is to reduce those obligations sufficiently so that the debtor can meet them, thereby encouraging the debtor to pay what it can rather than nothing at all. For individuals, this means retaining their property and paying from future income. For corporations and other artificial entities, this means continuing operations and paying surviving obligations over time.

All bankruptcies, whether liquidation, reorganization, or some combination of the two, are designed to resolve the claims against the debtor, make some provision for repayment, and discharge the debts that will not be paid.

C. Stopping Creditors' Collection Activities

Once the debtor has filed for bankruptcy, unsecured creditors (*general creditors*, in bankruptcy parlance) can file their claims and have disputes regarding them resolved in the bankruptcy case, but they have few other specific rights as the case moves toward resolution. If the debtor violates the provisions of the Bankruptcy Code, the creditor or the trustee may complain in court. Barring that, there is little that an individual unsecured creditor can do. For unsecured creditors, bankruptcy is a collective — and largely passive — proceeding.

Creditors benefit from some aspects of this collective action. They reduce their costs of collection, confident both that the trustee will act on their behalf and that no other creditors will move ahead of them by seizing the debtor's assets. They can also count on a streamlined process to liquidate the debtor's assets or to collect from the debtor's future income with costs minimized and shared among all the creditors. The creditor who would do little at state law may be better off participating in an automatic collection device for a relatively low cost.

Aggressive creditors, on the other hand, are generally worse off in bankruptcy than they would have been under state collection law. Bankruptcy dissipates the individual creditor's leverage because, to the extent unsecured creditors are permitted to act during the bankruptcy case, it is for the collective gain. The aggressive creditor can no longer enjoy the exclusive benefits of its own diligence in pursuit of assets or its cleverness in seizing property others might have overlooked. Benefits are shared pro rata with all other unsecured creditors.

In the absence of bankruptcy, an aggressive unsecured creditor can disrupt the debtor's business, employment, and financial affairs by seizing assets. The leverage generated by these activities can sometimes be so great that the debtor will do whatever is necessary to pay the debt, even if sale of its assets would yield nothing for the aggressive creditor. Once bankruptcy is filed, the unsecured creditor cannot generate much leverage at all. And at the end of the bankruptcy process, the creditor's claims may be discharged entirely, eliminating any right to collect from the debtor.

Bankruptcy courts take stay violations seriously. They usually hold deliberate violators in contempt of court and impose a fine sufficient to make them regret their transgressions. In some circumstances, a party injured by the stay violation can sue for damages. See Bankr. Code §362(h). Actions taken in violation of the stay are either void or voidable, and many courts impose on even the innocent violator of the stay the obligation to undo the violation by returning property or correcting public records. As a result, few lawyers or parties deliberately violate the automatic stay.

The reasons for the creation of the estate and imposition of the automatic stay are both practical and theoretical. By stopping all payments and collections, bankruptcy provides an opportunity to account for all the assets in the estate and all the charges against the estate. In a sense, the automatic stay locks up the estate temporarily so that an accurate count and an orderly distribution can be made. The stay also gives the debtor breathing room either to make an orderly liquidation of assets or to construct a plan of reorganization. Imposing a stay halts ongoing litigation in the state system and substitutes what is often a more abbreviated and efficient set of bankruptcy procedures for resolving disputes over outstanding debts. Perhaps most critical from the point of view of the general creditor, the stay freezes the relative rights of creditors as of the moment of the bankruptcy filing. The race of diligence fostered by state procedures is over; creditors can take no additional action to improve their own chances of recovery at the expense of others. Instead, all further actions by unsecured creditors against the debtor must be collective actions taken on behalf of *all* the creditors. The stay illustrates, and other Code provisions reinforce, that for general, unsecured creditors, bankruptcy is a collective proceeding.

The language of the Bankruptcy Code fixing the scope of the automatic stay is broad. It provides a stay "applicable to all entities" against "any act" to collect a prepetition debt. Bankr. Code §362(a). The stay protects the debtor personally as well as the property of the estate. The stay applies both to direct collection attempts (e.g., levying against the debtor's property), as well as more indirect attempts (e.g., initiating a lawsuit to establish the debtor's liability on a debt as a prerequisite to eventual collection).

While the stay is broad, it is not unlimited. Only actions to collect prefiling obligations are stayed. The Bankruptcy Code does not halt criminal proceedings against the debtor. If the debtor is under criminal indictment, for example, filing a bankruptcy petition will not stay the trial. Bankr. Code §362(b)(1). (This is not a surprising provision, lest every criminal defendant make a quick stop at the bankruptcy desk on the way to trial.) Similarly, a debtor might file for bankruptcy and receive immediate relief from the government's attempts to collect fines and penalties for past violations of government regulations, but the debtor will still be subject to actions to abate continuing violations. Bankr. Code §362(b)(4). (Again, it is not a big surprise that airlines must follow FAA safety restrictions and oil drillers must comply with pollution regulations, even if they are flying or drilling after they have filed for Chapter 11.)

With regard to unsecured creditors, the automatic stay generally remains in effect until the conclusion of the bankruptcy case. See Bankr. Code §362(c). Unsecured creditors rarely have grounds to lift the stay; they must rely on the operation of the bankruptcy process to collect the debts owed to them. In effect, unsecured creditors are on board for the ride through bankruptcy. They can monitor the process to make certain the rules are followed, or they can rely on the bankruptcy trustee or debtor in possession, but they have only collective rights and they must await disposition of the case to get any money. An unsecured creditor's best course is usually to file a proof of claim, hope for the best, and expect the worst.

D. Lifting the Stay for Secured Creditors

For secured creditors the consequences of bankruptcy are significantly different. While bankruptcy alters the secured creditors' rights in many respects, the bankruptcy system recognizes their most important state-created rights and gives these creditors much better treatment. Bankruptcy may delay enforcement of some of those rights and certain collection actions are barred even by secured creditors, but bankruptcy still promises secured creditors eventual access to either their collateral or to property or money of equivalent value. In most cases bankruptcy gives neither the secured creditor nor the unsecured creditor the right to full payment of the outstanding debt, but in all cases bankruptcy gives the secured creditor the right to be paid at least the value of its collateral.

Because each secured creditor is usually secured by different collateral, the interests of two secured creditors are not likely to be precisely the same. For example, the holder of an over secured first mortgage on the debtor's home may suffer only minor inconvenience from the automatic stay, while the holder of a second security interest in accounts receivable may stand to lose everything unless automatic stay issues are dealt with promptly and skillfully. To assure that their individual rights are protected, bankruptcy procedure permits each secured creditor the right to participate individually in the bankruptcy case rather than forcing on them the collective treatment forced on the unsecured creditors. Secured creditors, each claiming different collateral or different priority in the same collateral, stand in sharp contrast to unsecured creditors who share pro rata in whatever is available after provisions have been made for the payment to secured creditors of the value of their collateral.

Bankruptcy procedure affords secured creditors a number of ways in which they can monitor their collateral and participate individually in the bankruptcy case. Both their greater substantive rights and the fact of their participation give them greater ability to influence the course of the bankruptcy case.

When a bankruptcy case is filed, the collection actions of a secured creditor, like those of an unsecured creditor, are immediately interrupted. But for the secured creditor, imposition of the automatic stay is often only the beginning of a new game. The secured creditor retains its lien and may be able to get the stay lifted and continue with its nonbankruptcy collection efforts.

The grounds for lifting the stay are set forth in Bankruptcy Code §362(d). To summarize, the court must always lift the stay if the trustee or debtor does not provide the creditor with adequate protection. But even if the trustee or debtor provides adequate protection, the court must nevertheless lift the stay if (1) there is no equity in the collateral that the trustee or debtor might realize for unsecured creditors and (2) the collateral is not necessary to an effective reorganization. (The third basis for lifting the stay applies only to a narrow range of "single asset real estate" cases, which we won't discuss here.) This complex combination of requirements may seem a jumble at first, but it sorts out rather sensibly once one understands two reasons why the bankruptcy system might want to commandeer a secured creditor's collateral against the secured creditor's will.

The first is that the collateral may be worth more than the debt secured by it and the estate's equity in it may be available to the debtor and other creditors only through bankruptcy procedure. For example, if Dubchek files under Chapter 7 owing $3,000 to Cicero and the debt is secured by a nonexempt Buick Skylark worth $4,000, the estate has a $1,000 equity in it. If the stay is left in place, the trustee can sell the Skylark for $4,000 and pay the secured creditor $3,000, leaving $1,000 (less the expenses of sale) to pay unsecured creditors. The fear apparently motivating bankruptcy policy in this regard is that if the stay is lifted, Cicero will foreclose and the Skylark will be sold for less than its value, leaving little or nothing for the unsecured creditors. That is, bankruptcy policy is based on the realization that state sale procedures often are ineffective. Even if the Skylark were sold for its full value under nonbankruptcy law, the net proceeds after payment of the secured creditor and the expenses of sale would have been turned over to the debtor, not the unsecured creditors. The unsecured creditors might have had a difficult time reaching them through garnishment or execution.

The second reason for commandeering a secured creditor's collateral is to enable the debtor to reorganize — that is, to remain in business or keep a job, make money, and pay some of the debts. For example, if Dubchek had no equity in the Skylark, but could not continue her profitable Donut Delivery Service without it, the Skylark might be "necessary to an effective reorganization." Bankr. Code §362(b)(2). Without it, Dubchek might have no income and be unable to pay anything to unsecured creditors. (On the other hand, if Dubchek had two cars and the Donut Delivery Service could carry on just as well with either one, retention of the Skylark would not be necessary for an effective reorganization.) In the remainder of our discussion of the stay, we will refer to these two reasons for retaining collateral — that the debtor has an equity in it or that it is necessary to an effective reorganization — as *bankruptcy purposes*. To be entitled to retain the secured creditor's collateral, the debtor or trustee must show at a minimum that its retention of the collateral serves a bankruptcy purpose. In the absence of such justification, the secured creditor can demand that the stay be lifted.

To appreciate fully the importance of these bankruptcy purposes, it is critical to realize how much more effective the bankruptcy system can sometimes be in realizing the full value of the debtor's assets or income earning potential. In re 26 Trumbull Street, 77 B.R. 374 (Bankr. D. Conn. 1987), provides an excellent example. Before bankruptcy, the debtor closed the restaurant it had been operating in leased premises. The bankruptcy estate contained two items of property: the restaurant equipment and the restaurant's interest in its lease. The parties agreed that if the restaurant equipment were removed from the leased premises, the equipment would have been worth only $21,500, but sold together with the lease, it was worth $90,000. The case did not explain why the difference was so great. Most likely, it was because the equipment was suited for use with the leased premises. It fit the space and might even have been damaged through removal. In place, the equipment and lease constituted a restaurant; removed, the equipment was a difficult marketing problem. Nevertheless, if a creditor with a debt of $21,500 (or less) that was secured by the equipment could have repossessed the equipment and sold it separate from the lease for $21,500, the secured creditor would have had little reason not to do so immediately. The estate — and the other creditors — would have lost the additional $68,500 value. Only by leaving the stay in effect could the bankruptcy court assure that would not happen.

Even if the estate's retention of the collateral would serve a bankruptcy purpose, that alone is not sufficient to defeat a secured creditor's motion to lift the stay. The debtor also must protect the secured creditor against loss as a result of the delay in foreclosure that is caused by the stay. Bankr. Code §362(d)(1). The debtor must furnish *adequate protection*, a term of art defined only by example in Bankruptcy Code §361. Generally speaking, a secured creditor's interest is adequately protected when provisions that the court considers adequate have been made to protect the secured creditor from loss as a result of a decline in the value of the secured creditor's collateral during the time the creditor is immobilized by the automatic stay. If the debtor cannot provide what the court considers adequate protection, the court must lift the stay and allow the creditor to foreclose.

To continue with our earlier example, assume that Dubchek owes $5,000 to Cicero and that the Skylark is worth $4,000 when the automatic stay is imposed. Based on these numbers, Dubchek has no equity in the Skylark. But assume further that retention of the Skylark is necessary to Dubchek's reorganization. The court should not lift the stay pursuant to Bankruptcy Code §362(d)(2) because the property is necessary for an effective reorganization. But Cicero is not through. Cicero can move to lift the stay for lack of adequate protection pursuant to Bankruptcy Code §362(d)(1). Under these circumstances, Dubchek must furnish adequate protection against postfiling decline in the value of the car or lose it.

The bankruptcy court decides what constitutes adequate protection. Based on experience with the depreciation of similar automobiles, the parties may show that the decline in the value of the Skylark will be about $1,200 during the year Dubchek will be in bankruptcy, so the value of the car will go from $4,000 to $2,800. If this $1,200 decline in fact occurs, the resulting loss imposed on Cicero would be a result of the delay imposed by the automatic stay. That is, were it not for the automatic stay, Cicero could foreclose now and recover $4,000. If the stay prevents Cicero from foreclosing for a year and the value of the collateral drops to $2,800, Cicero might recover only $2,800, losing the additional $1,200 he would have enjoyed in an early foreclosure. The bankruptcy court will require Dubchek to protect Cicero against this anticipated $1,200 loss.

Cicero's adequate protection may come in any of several forms. Dubchek might pay Cicero $100 each month as the car declines in value. Or Dubchek might grant Cicero an additional lien against property worth at least $1,200. There are few limits on the form the protection must take, so long as it is "adequate" in the eyes of the bankruptcy judge. But if Dubchek does not furnish adequate protection to Cicero, Cicero will be entitled to have the stay lifted and Dubchek's potentially profitable Donut Delivery Service will be history.

Notice that if the car in the preceding example had been worth $10,000, Cicero would have been in no real danger of loss from ordinary depreciation. Even if the value of the car had fallen to $7,000 during bankruptcy, it would have remained easily sufficient to cover the balance on the loan, plus accruing interest and attorneys' fees. Such an excess of collateral value over loan amount is referred to in bankruptcy parlance as a *cushion of equity*. The bankruptcy courts recognize that a cushion of equity of sufficient size may alone adequately protect a secured creditor against loss. If such a cushion already provides adequate protection to the secured creditor, the secured creditor has no right to additional protection in the form of periodic payments or additional collateral.

Exactly how large the cushion of equity must be to provide protection depends on the circumstances. Key circumstances include (1) the nature of the factors that might change the value of the collateral, (2) the volatility of the market in which the creditor might have to sell it, and (3) the rate at which the secured debt is likely to increase in amount. Of course, the apparent size of the cushion of equity depends on the value the court assigns to the collateral. The question of how large a cushion exists often becomes intertwined with the question of how large a cushion is necessary, giving the court considerable flexibility to do what it thinks best.

While secured creditors are entitled to adequate protection against loss from a decline in the value of their collateral, they are not entitled to protection against other losses resulting from imposition of the automatic stay. To illustrate, assume that the Skylark is worth $4,000, Cicero's lien against it is in the same amount, and that the value of the Skylark is not expected to decline during the one-year bankruptcy. On these facts, Dubchek need do nothing to provide adequate protection even though Cicero will lose the time value of his $4,000 in this scenario. But for the stay, Cicero could have invested his $4,000 and earned interest during the year. With the money stuck in a bankruptcy case, he could not.

In the following case, the Craddock-Terry Shoe Corporation was attempting to reorganize in Chapter 11. Two of its secured creditors, Lincoln and Westinghouse, sought to lift the stay, raising issues under both prongs of Bankruptcy Code §362(d). The court addressed whether the stay should be lifted under either, providing us with a look at how the two sections are used in tandem by many undersecured creditors. In order to decide any of the legal issues, however, the court first had to resolve the threshold question of the value of the property. If the court had assigned the property a different value, the outcome might have been different as well.

In re Craddock-Terry Shoe Corp.

98 B.R. 250 (Bankr. W.D. Va. 1988)

WILLIAM E. ANDERSON, UNITED STATES BANKRUPTCY JUDGE

The plaintiffs, Lincoln National Life Insurance Company ("Lincoln") and Westinghouse Credit Corporation ("Westinghouse"), have moved the Court to lift the automatic stay imposed by section 362(a) of the Bankruptcy Code, 11 U.S.C. §362(a), or in the alternative, to provide Lincoln and Westinghouse adequate protection for certain collateral in which they have a security interest. The collateral at issue is the customer mailing lists, catalogues, and certain trademarks of Hill Brothers, a division of Craddock-Terry Shoe Corporation ("Craddock-Terry"), the debtor.

BACKGROUND FACTS

On April 30, 1986, the plaintiffs, Lincoln and Westinghouse, loaned the debtor, Craddock-Terry, $9,000,000. As security for that loan, Lincoln and Westinghouse obtained a security interest in the mailing list, customer list, catalogues and four trademarks ("the collateral") of Hill Brothers, a mail-order division of Craddock-Terry. Debtor's Chapter 11 petition was filed on October 21, 1987. Craddock-Terry has shut down all its operations, except for Hill Brothers.

As of the petition date, debtor owed Lincoln and Westinghouse $9,587,812.50. The debtor does not dispute that Lincoln and Westinghouse have a valid and perfected lien on the mailing list, customer list, catalogues and trademarks of Hill Brothers. The collateral is worth less than the amount owed Lincoln and Westinghouse. In fact, the debtor had on the petition date, and still has, no equity in the collateral.

On January 5, 1988, Lincoln and Westinghouse obtained a court order authorizing a Bankruptcy Rule 2004 examination of the debtor. The examination and document production was conducted during January. Concerned that the value of their collateral appeared to be seriously declining, Lincoln and Westinghouse originally filed their motion for relief from stay on March 1, 1988. Certain procedural defects with regard to the filing of the motion existed on that date, but were cured on March 22, 1988. The hearing on the motion, originally scheduled for April 21, 1988, was continued to May 4, 1988, and final arguments were heard on May 10, 1988.

The evidence introduced at the hearing indicates that, during the Chapter 11 case, Hill Brothers has experienced a serious cash flow problem which has reduced the number of orders which can be filled (the fill rate), cut in half the number of spring catalogues planned to be mailed, and reduced the rate at which new names are added to the Hill Brothers mailing list. In addition, returns of merchandise have increased. These factors have resulted in a serious decline in the value of the collateral.

The plaintiffs presented evidence that on the date debtor's petition was filed, before the adverse impact of the cash flow problems and the list management problems, the value of the mailing list in place and in use at Hill Brothers, was $8.7 million, but that its value on April 30, 1988 was $5.7 million. Their expert at trial had used the same valuation method as that used by an accounting firm whose earlier appraisal the debtor had used to obtain the loans. He testified that he had used a method appropriate for valuing a mailing list in use by a company, known as the discounted cash flow method. The resulting value is the value to the business which is using the list. A mailing list is carefully built up over the years, by adding names each year, and developing an active list of persons who like and buy the particular product of the company. Its value in place to the company using it is necessarily much greater than to an outside buyer or renter.

The debtor presented its own expert testimony from an individual heavily involved in the direct marketing industry. The debtor's expert stated that the fair market value of the list, if sold to other companies, was $700,000 on the petition date and $330,000 as of the hearing date. He utilized a model containing twelve factors from which he calculated the value of the list. These factors included expected revenues and expenses, customer attrition, rental income, comparison to outside lists, and customer affinity for the debtor's product. . . .

DISCUSSION

Bankruptcy Code section 362(d) provides relief from the stay imposed by section 362(a) in either of two circumstances. The stay will be lifted "for cause, including the lack of adequate protection of an interest in property of [a] party in interest." 11 U.S.C. §362(d)(1). The stay will also be lifted "with respect to a stay of an act against property under subsection (a) of this section, if (A) the debtor does not have an equity in such property; and (B) such property is not necessary to an effective reorganization." 11 U.S.C. §362(d)(2). Lincoln and Westinghouse have asserted that they are entitled to relief under either part of section 362(d). The debtor claims to the contrary that its mailing list is vital to its reorganization and that it has offered adequate protection for any decline in the collateral's value. The court will consider sections 362(d)(1) and 362(d)(2) in reverse order.

I. SECTION 362(d)(2)

Neither party disputes that Craddock-Terry has no equity in the collateral. The debt secured by the collateral is greater than $9,000,000, and although the parties have widely divergent views of the value of the collateral for purposes of this motion, each places a lower value on it than the amount of the debt. "Equity" is defined as the amount by which the value of the collateral exceeds the debt it secures. Thus, the debtor has no equity in the collateral and the first requirement of section 362(d)(2) is met.

Each party also agrees that if the debtor can possibly reorganize, this collateral is essential to its survival. Lincoln and Westinghouse claim, however, that even if the debtor retains and uses the collateral, no effective reorganization is possible. In short, Lincoln and Westinghouse have no faith in the debtor's proposed plan for reorganization or its proposed business plan. They point to reduced catalog mailings and the reduced fill rate for customers' orders since the initiation of bankruptcy proceedings, both of which have caused the decline in value of the mailing list and, therefore, of the business itself.

The debtor, on the other hand, while admitting that its fill rate and catalog mailings have decreased, introduced evidence that the intrinsic value of the mailing list has not been irreparably harmed. The debtor's expert testified that an infusion of capital appropriately applied to the mailing list could revive the list's value, and that he had in fact seen this occur in a similar situation. The debtor's own representative testified that approximately $4,000,000 would be available to the debtor from the recent sale of the bulk of the company's assets to The Old Time Gospel Hour and to T/W Properties. He further testified that $900,000 of this influx of cash was designated for revitalization of the mailing list, and thereby, the company.

Since the filing of the debtor's petition the general theme of this reorganization has been to sell most of the company's assets and use the proceeds to reorganize the company's Hill Brothers division into a viable entity. The debtor has finally reached the point where it will have capital with which to effect those plans. The law is clear that a court "should not precipitously sound the death knell for a debtor by prematurely determining that the debtor's prospects for economic revival are poor." In re Shockley Forest Indus., Inc., 5 B.R. 160 (Bankr. M.D. Tenn. 1980). The evidence before the court as yet gives no basis for a conclusion that this reorganization is no longer in prospect, and therefore the court finds that the collateral at issue here is necessary to an effective reorganization. Consequently, the automatic stay will not be lifted pursuant to section 362(d)(2).

II. Section 362(d)(1)

Lincoln and Westinghouse are entitled to relief from the stay, however, if the debtor cannot satisfy section 362(d)(1) by providing adequate protection for the interest of Lincoln and Westinghouse in the collateral. The debtor has offered replacement liens in all its assets, which it claims will provide adequate protection either from the date of the motion or, if necessary, from the date of the petition. The parties agree that the value of the collateral has declined since the date the petition was filed and also since the date the motion was filed. They disagree as to the amount of decline in value and as to the date from which adequate protection is necessary.

The major focus of the parties during the hearing on this motion and in their final arguments was on the proper value to assign to the collateral at the various stages herein. The Bankruptcy Code provides no specific guidance as to the standard to be used to value property for purposes of providing creditors adequate protection with respect to section 362(d). Section 361 establishes three non-exclusive methods of providing adequate protection of a creditor's interest in property, but specifies no means for valuing that interest. Section 506(a) states that the value of a creditor's interest in the estate's interest in property "shall be determined in light of the purpose of the valuation and of the proposed disposition or use of such property, and in conjunction with any hearing on such disposition or use or on a plan affecting such creditor's interest," 11 U.S.C. §506(a), but gives no other insight into how such value should be determined.

Consequently courts have looked to the legislative history behind these two sections to find reasonable and proper methods of valuation. The legislative history of section 506(a) establishes that valuation methods should not be rigid:

> "value" does not necessarily contemplate forced sale or liquidation value of collateral; nor does it always imply a full going concern value. Courts will have to determine value on a case-by-case basis, taking into account the facts of each case and the competing interests in the case.

H.R.Rep. No. 95-595, 95th Cong., 1st Sess. 356 (1977). . . .

In order to determine the most commercially reasonable disposition practicable, the court must follow the directive of section 506 and consider the purpose of the valuation. The purpose of adequate protection "as stated in the legislative history [of section 361] is to insure that the secured creditor receives in value essentially what he bargained for." In re Ram Mfg., Inc., 32 B.R. 969, 971 (Bankr. E.D. Pa. 1983). Therefore "adequate protection for a secured creditor means that the creditor must receive the same *measure* of protection in bankruptcy that he could have had outside of bankruptcy although the *type* of protection may differ from the bargain initially struck between the parties." Id. at 972. (quoting In re Winslow Center Assoc., 32 B.R. 685, 688 (Bankr. E.D. Pa. 1983)) (emphasis in original). In other words, the value of the interest of Lincoln and Westinghouse in the collateral is equivalent to what they could have recovered through foreclosure, had the debtor defaulted but not filed its petition for Chapter 11 relief. The benefit initially bargained for, and to be protected under sections 361 and 362, was the value obtainable from the most commercially reasonable disposition of the collateral within the context of foreclosure proceedings. . . .

A customer list, as an asset, is a strange hybrid. Although actually represented by a physical asset (the list), its worth is basically as an intangible. The utility of the list results both from Craddock-Terry's established reputation and service, and from the inclination of the particular consumers on the list to purchase shoes, of the kind and quality which Craddock-Terry sells, from Craddock-Terry. The testimony indicated that the value of the list is far greater to Craddock-Terry than to anyone else. The debtor's expert testified that even competitors in the shoe business would not value the list as highly as Craddock-Terry for various reasons, including the fact that crossover with their own lists could be as high as fifty percent.

The debtor did introduce evidence of the value of the list if sold through an arms length transaction. The debtor's expert testified that this was not a "fire-sale" value, but indeed the fair market value. He used a model which is widely used in the direct marketing industry to determine mailing list values for third parties. His analysis took into account a variety of factors including not only list maintenance expenses and revenues, but also customer attrition, customer affinity for Craddock-Terry, and replacement cost, among others. His appraisal indicated that the collateral had a fair market value of not more than $700,000 as of the petition date, not more than $500,000 as of February 1988, and not more than $330,000 as of the hearing date. The Court finds this evidence to be credible and, as to the value of the collateral, the only evidence of the most commercially reasonable disposition practicable in these circumstances.

Since there is no dispute that the debtor has no equity in the collateral or that its value has declined during these proceedings, the debtor must provide adequate protection to Lincoln and Westinghouse. The final question presented in this case is the date from which adequate protection is required. Lincoln and Westinghouse argue that they should be protected from the decrease in value of the property resulting from the stay in its entirety, and therefore from the date of the petition. The debtor contends that relief should only cover the period of decline following the date these creditors filed their motion for relief.

The debtor, citing In re Grieves, 81 B.R. 912 (Bankr. N.D. Ind. 1987), contends that to allow a creditor adequate protection from the commencement of the case, even though the creditor does not formally request such protection until some months later, would place an undue burden on the debtor by forcing it to make back payments for an arrearage which the debtor didn't know was accruing. The debtor also claims that such a rule would encourage secured creditors to "sit on their rights" rather than acting to preserve their security. These arguments are not persuasive.

To the contrary, to adopt the rule which the debtor suggests would be even more harmful to the purposes of bankruptcy law. Such a requirement would force creditors to rush to the courthouse as soon as they learn of a debtor's petition in order to ensure that they obtain adequate protection from as early a date as possible. The resulting litigation would likely be prodigious, and certainly would interrupt the expected "breathing space" which debtors normally enjoy after a petition is filed. Surely a debtor in possession will do all it can to preserve the value of all property of the estate whether encumbered or not. Such a requirement, even absent a formal motion by a secured creditor, and even from the commencement of the case, is consonant with bankruptcy policies. . . .

The Court finds that Lincoln and Westinghouse are entitled to adequate protection for all decline in the value of the collateral since the petition date. The value of the collateral on that date, for the purposes of this motion, was $700,000. The debtor has offered replacement liens in all its remaining assets, which its representative testified are worth in excess of $2,000,000 (not including $7,000,000 in accounts receivable). Therefore the automatic stay imposed by 11 U.S.C. §362(a) will remain in effect, and this court will enter an order directing the debtor to execute a security agreement, all necessary financing statements, and any other supporting documents necessary to perfect a valid security interest in remaining assets in which the estate has an aggregate equity of no less than $700,000, in favor of Lincoln and Westinghouse, to secure the same indebtedness secured by the collateral at issue here.

On the face of this opinion, it appears that Lincoln and Westinghouse lost. They moved to lift the stay, and the court refused. But lifting the stay may not have been their real objective. Before the hearing Lincoln and Westinghouse had a security interest in a customer list that was admittedly declining in value. By persuading the court that they were not adequately protected by their existing collateral, they forced the debtor to a choice — let the stay be lifted or provide additional protection. Predictably, Craddock-Terry came up with additional protection. After the hearing, Lincoln and Westinghouse still had the customer list as collateral, but they also had a security interest in other estate assets. The additional collateral satisfied the court that the total value of Lincoln and Westinghouse's collateral would not fall below the $700,000 value it had at the time Craddock-Terry filed bankruptcy.

It is also instructive to notice the effect of the court's decision on unsecured creditors. If the court had simply lifted the stay, without making an award of adequate protection, Lincoln and Westinghouse would have had the customer list and sold it for what they could. The additional $700,000 of assets would have remained unencumbered. If the business had then liquidated, as it most likely would without its customer list, the $700,000 would have been among the assets available to unsecured creditors. Once the award was made, however, those assets became the collateral of Lincoln and Westinghouse. If the reorganization later failed, Lincoln and Westinghouse would be satisfied first from that collateral, perhaps leaving considerably less for the unsecured creditors.

Because the value of the secured creditor's collateral may be in jeopardy, motions to lift the stay receive high priority on the bankruptcy court's calendar. Bankruptcy Code §362(e) provides that the stay is automatically terminated unless, within 30 days after a secured creditor moves to lift it, the court enters an order continuing it in effect. Thus, while the stay is imposed automatically, its continuation is not automatic. More important, this provision demonstrates Congress's intent that stalling tactics on the part of the debtor should not cause the secured creditor to lose value.

Notice that the protection awarded by the court in *Craddock-Terry* was retroactive to the date of the filing of the petition. Most courts make the protection retroactive only to the date of the filing of the motion for adequate protection; a few refuse to make it retroactive at all. Under the latter two views it will be particularly important for a secured creditor who needs adequate protection against ongoing depreciation to make the motion as early as possible.

Not surprisingly, motions to lift the automatic stay constitute a substantial part of the work of the bankruptcy court, particularly in reorganization cases. In an empirical study of Chapter 11 cases, Professor Charles Shafer found that the single most-frequently instituted motion in reorganization cases was a motion to lift the stay. Professor Shafer found, however, that most of the motions did not result in litigation; 87 percent were settled before the court rendered its decision. Charles Shafer, Determining Whether Property Is Necessary for an Effective Reorganization: A Proposal for the Use of Empirical Research, 1990 Ann. Surv. Bankr. L. 79 (Callahan 1990). In liquidation cases there is somewhat less emphasis on getting the stay lifted, because the process is usually much quicker and the secured creditor is about to reach the property anyway. But even in liquidation cases, the traffic is substantial.

Secured creditors can move to lift the stay at any time. Even if a prior motion to lift the stay in the same case was denied, the secured creditor can try again if the circumstances have changed. Secured creditors are most likely to try again when it appears the debtor is settling in for a long stay in bankruptcy.

E. Strategic Uses of Stay Litigation

The effect of an order lifting or modifying the automatic stay differs greatly depending on the nature of the collateral and importance of the collateral to the debtor's business or life. An order lifting the stay to permit repossession of a speedboat the debtor rarely uses may do nothing more than help the debtor get its financial affairs in order. But an order lifting the stay to permit repossession of assets necessary to the operation of the debtor's business may signal the end of that business. For example, had the stay been lifted in the *Craddock-Terry* case, Lincoln and Westinghouse could have repossessed and sold the customer lists. Without its customer lists, Craddock-Terry probably would have been unable to continue its mail-order shoe business. In opposing the motion to lift the stay, Craddock-Terry probably was fighting for its survival.

Yet it does not necessarily follow that if Lincoln and Westinghouse had won the motion they would have taken the lists. Negotiation and negotiated solutions permeate the American legal system, particularly in the commercial law area. One can do more with legal rights than simply enforce them. They constitute the working capital for playing in the great American game of "let's make a deal."

The reorganization of McLouth Steel Company, one of the cases studied by Professors LoPucki and Whitford in their empirical study of large Chapter 11 cases, offers an illustration. McLouth's financing was provided by a group of six banks and four insurance companies. Their $166 million loan was secured by all of the company's assets, primarily steel plants located in Michigan. When McLouth filed for bankruptcy reorganization in the mid-1980s, the secured creditors quickly moved to lift the automatic stay. The cash flow from the steel plants was insufficient to provide adequate protection through periodic payments, and McLouth had no equity in the collateral. The parties realized that if the motion were heard by the court, relief from the stay almost certainly would be granted.

Before the hearing, the parties reached a settlement. The secured creditors agreed not to press their motion or to take possession of the steel mills. McLouth could continue to operate. In return, McLouth agreed to seek buyers for its assets and apply the proceeds of sale to pay down the secured debt. If the assets were not sold by a fixed date, which was then only a few months away, the "drop-dead" provision of the settlement agreement would take effect. Under that provision, the mills would be closed, the stay would be lifted, and the secured creditors would take possession. Probably neither the debtor nor the secured creditors believed that a sale could be completed before the drop-dead date.

As the drop-dead date approached, McLouth had not yet found a buyer for the mills. The creditors expressed their lack of confidence in McLouth's chief executive officer and he obliged by promptly resigning. The creditors extended the drop-dead date for 90 days. When the new drop-dead date arrived, McLouth was in negotiations with a potential buyer, Tang Industries. Again, the secured creditors forbore their right to take possession of the mills, and instead gave McLouth additional time to pursue the possibility of sale. About a year after the filing of the reorganization case, McLouth concluded a sale to Tang and the automatic stay became moot.

What was going on? The secured creditors' acknowledged ability to lift the stay gave them tremendous leverage over the debtor — enough that the secured creditors were virtually in control of the company. At the same time, the secured creditors realized that it was not in their interest to take possession of the mills. Closing the mills would have greatly reduced their sale value. Continuing to operate the mills after foreclosure would potentially have exposed the creditors to a variety of regulatory problems, the most important of which were probably banking and environmental regulations. So long as McLouth did what it was told, there was little to gain by taking possession and much potential trouble to be avoided by not doing so. As a result of this delicate balance of considerations, McLouth's formal legal structure (secured creditors holding claims against a debtor protected by the automatic stay) did not match the true business relationship (secured creditors virtually in control of the company).

McLouth is a good illustration of the strategic use of stay litigation because it is such an extreme example. In most cases, the degree of control a creditor can achieve by means of a threat to lift the stay and repossess the assets is considerably less. But to realize that secured creditors have such means to influence reorganizing debtors is important to understanding the full extent of the enhanced collection rights that secured creditors have in, as well as out, of bankruptcy.

Problem Set 6

6.1. You have been counsel to DataServe, a computer software and servicing company, for over six years. As you were reviewing other legal matters with the CFO, Mandy Elkins, she mentioned that client bankruptcies were costing them some real money. She said that 12 of their clients were currently in bankruptcy and that none of these clients were making any payments on their outstanding accounts, even though DataServe billed them each month. She said they were not accepting any new orders from the nonpayers, but she thought maybe they should do some "serious collection efforts with these guys." What do you tell her? See Bankr. Code §§362(a), 501(a), 502(b) (disregarding the exceptions in §502(b)).

6.2. You have been working for Kansas Savings to collect a $1.2 million loan from Jayhawk Enterprises. The defaulted loan is secured by grain-processing equipment worth $1.5 million, so you haven't been too worried about collection. Your attempts at self-help repossession have been stymied, however, so you have obtained a judgment. You and the sheriff are off this morning to seize the collateral. When you arrive at Jayhawk, the sheriff shows the appropriate writ and announces that he is here to take the grain-processing equipment. Jayhawk's president says you are too late; Jayhawk filed for bankruptcy earlier this morning. Can you go forward with the repo? Bankr. Code §§362(a), 541(a)(1). Can the sheriff? Bankr. Code §101 (definition of "entity").

6.3.   You are the senior in-house counsel for BankWest, a commercial bank in northern California. This morning you received a file referred by a loan officer in one of the Sacramento branches. The case involves the bankruptcy of Prime Cuts, a small restaurant chain that filed for Chapter 11 last week owing BankWest $250,000. According to the file, the loan is secured by the property of one of the restaurants. That restaurant is worth no more than $250,000 and probably less. While some of the other Prime Cut locations have brought in good business, this one was in a weaker location and had few customers. Prime Cuts had closed it just before they filed the bankruptcy petition. The loan officer recommends "we foreclose as soon as possible and take our hit on this one." Can we do that? See Bankr. Code §362(a), (c), and (e).

6.4.   Another of the BankWest files you received is that of Sprouts Up, a Riverside chain of fast-food health-food stores. They too have filed under Chapter 11. Sprouts Up owes $210,000 and has missed four payments. BankWest has begun foreclosure proceedings on the mortgage it holds on the building where the corporate headquarters are located. The building is in a good area, and it is appraised at about $600,000 fair market value. Even at a sheriff's sale you are confident that there would be bidding in excess of your outstanding mortgage. The loan officer anticipates an "agonizingly long reorganization while the corporate officers fight among themselves." She wants the bank to get out as quickly as possible so the bank can loan this money elsewhere. What is your advice? See Bankr. Code §§362(a), (d).

6.5.   The same afternoon that you received the Sprouts Up case, you also get the file for Paradise Boat Leasing. Three years ago, BankWest financed Paradise's purchase of a 65-foot yacht. The yacht rents with crew by the day or the week from a port in the Virgin Islands. Although Paradise is in financial trouble, the yacht loan seems generally in pretty good shape. The value of the yacht is about $350,000, the amount of BankWest's loan is $175,000, and Paradise is current on its payments. Just before Paradise filed under Chapter 11 of the Bankruptcy Code, BankWest got notice that the insurance had been canceled. Under the security agreement it is Paradise's responsibility to keep the yacht insured and its failure to do so constitutes a default.

The security agreement further provides that in the event of default, BankWest can purchase insurance and add the cost to the secured debt and/or take possession of the yacht. BankWest tried to get another policy, but nobody seems to want to insure a boat that belongs to a bankrupt. What do you do now? See 11 U.S.C. §§362(a), (d).

6.6.   Your firm does some debtor's work as well, and you are working on Hill Farms Industries, a food processing company that filed for Chapter 11 three months ago. When you arrived at work this morning your secretary gave you phone messages from two irate creditors of the company. How do you plan to deal with each? Bankr. Code §§361, 362(a), (c), and (e).

a.   The first caller was the attorney for Watson Investment, a company from which Hill Farms borrowed $126,000 unsecured. He was upset that Hill Farms is now six months behind on the loan with no plans to make any payments until it gets a plan confirmed.

b.   The second call was from the attorney for Macklin Mortgage. Macklin has a security interest in Hill Farms sterilization equipment to secure a $50,000 debt Hill Farms owes Macklin. She is upset because she just received an appraisal showing the equipment, which was appraised at $50,000 as of the commencement of the case, is now worth only about $40,000.

Assignment 7: The Treatment of Secured Creditors in Bankruptcy

Bankruptcy not only stops collecting creditors in their tracks, it may also change the amount of money those creditors are entitled to collect. In this assignment we explore how a creditor collects from a bankrupt debtor, focusing once again on important differences between the treatment of unsecured and secured creditors.

A. The Vocabulary of Bankruptcy Claims

To understand the treatment of secured creditors in bankruptcy, it helps to begin with a clear understanding of the terms used and the concepts to which they refer. Unfortunately, nonbankruptcy law uses some of the same terms to describe concepts that are similar but nonetheless different. To minimize confusion, we point out the differences where they are important.

Under both bankruptcy and nonbankruptcy law, a *debt* is a sum of money owing. The amount owing typically fluctuates as interest accrues, attorneys' fees and other collection expenses are incurred, and payments are made. The amount of a debt is determined under nonbankruptcy law, typically by application of contract law, tort law, antitrust law, or some other substantive law that determines the rights and liabilities of disputing parties. When the word "debt" is used in bankruptcy, the reference is nearly always to the debt, in whatever amount, as it exists under nonbankruptcy law.

Debts can be *discharged* in bankruptcy. A discharged debt still exists, but the discharge permanently enjoins the creditor from attempting to collect it. See Bankr. Code §524(a)(2). For all practical purposes, once a debt is discharged, the debtor does not owe it.

Both secured and unsecured debts can be discharged. In either case, the discharged debt would be described as *nonrecourse*, meaning that it cannot be enforced against the debtor. A nonrecourse unsecured debt is merely an artifact of legal metaphysics: It is not connected to anything and has no known consequence. The same is not true for a nonrecourse secured debt.

Although no one owes the nonrecourse secured debt, the failure to pay such a debt can have important consequences. If the lien has not been removed during the bankruptcy case, it continues to encumber the collateral afterward. If the underlying debt is not paid, the creditor can foreclose on the property after bankruptcy. The foreclosure sale will transfer ownership of the collateral to the purchaser, and the proceeds of sale will be applied to pay the nonrecourse debt. If those proceeds are sufficient to satisfy the nonrecourse debt, the debt will be paid in full and any excess will be distributed to junior lien holders or the owner; if they are insufficient to satisfy the discharged nonrecourse debt, the secured creditor cannot obtain a deficiency judgment against the debtor because the debtor no longer owes the debt.

Under Article 9 of the Uniform Commercial Code, the special collection rights of a personal property secured creditor are referred to as a *security interest*. The special collection rights of a previously unsecured creditor who has levied against property of the debtor are referred to as a *lien*. See, e.g., U.C.C. §9-102(a)(52), defining *lien creditor*. The special collection rights of a creditor consensually secured by an interest in real estate are typically referred to as a *mortgage*. U.C.C. §9-102(a)(55). In some states, those rights might be in the form of a *deed of trust*, a device that, despite its difference in form, has much the same effect as a mortgage.

The Bankruptcy Code, §101(51), like the Internal Revenue Code, §6323(h)(1), groups Article 9 security interests together with real estate mortgages and deeds of trust under the term *security interest*. The Bankruptcy Code then lumps security interests together with all other secured statuses, including judicial and statutory liens, under the term *lien*. Bankr. Code §101(37). Thus, an Article 9 security interest, a real estate mortgage, a deed of trust, and the rights of a lien creditor are all liens within the contemplation of the Bankruptcy Code.

A creditor's *claim* in bankruptcy is, in essence, the amount of the debt owed to the creditor under nonbankruptcy law at the time the bankruptcy case is filed. Bankr. Code §§101(5) and (12). Notice that the amount of the claim is the amount actually owed. In this respect, the word *claim* does not have its ordinary meaning when used in bankruptcy. Absent bankruptcy, to say that a party "claims" something implies that the claim may not be correct; the same implication does not inhere in the use of "claim" in bankruptcy.

Only claims that are *allowed* are eligible to share in the distributions made in the bankruptcy case. Bankruptcy Code §502(b) contains a list of the kinds of claims that are not allowed, but the exceptions are not relevant for our purposes. Because the difference between a claim and an allowed claim is so slight, bankruptcy lawyers often speak of "claims" when they mean "allowed claims." We often do the same.

Because the amount of the debt and the amount of the corresponding claim are determined under different rules, they can diverge as the bankruptcy case continues. In determining the creditor's rights in the bankruptcy case, it is usually the amount of the *claim* that is important. In determining the creditor's rights in a non-bankruptcy forum after the stay has been lifted or the bankruptcy case dismissed, it is usually the amount of the *debt* that is important. So, for example, a secured creditor may not be able to expand its *claim* as time passes while the debtor is in bankruptcy, but the amount of the *debt* may continue to climb as a result of the accrual of interest. If the case should be dismissed from bankruptcy without a discharge for the debtor, the creditor might reassert its collection rights at state law. In such a case, the creditor would seek payment of the debt, including all the interest due from the inception of the loan, rather than simply the claim that would have been allowed in the bankruptcy case.

B. The Claims Process

How much creditors are paid from a bankruptcy estate depends on how much the various creditors are owed, the creditors' relative priorities in the estate, and the value available with which to pay them. How the bankruptcy system determines these three variables and combines them to yield a set of distributions for a particular case is the subject of the remainder of this assignment.

To guide you through it, we provide this quick overview. Through a claims process, the bankruptcy system determines the Bankruptcy Code §502 amounts of all creditors' claims — that is, the amounts those creditors were owed under nonbankruptcy law as of the date of bankruptcy. Some claims are permitted to grow through the accrual of interest and collection costs during the bankruptcy case while others are not. The system separates the claims into classes based on the priorities to which they are entitled and other factors. In a Chapter 7 case, the amounts available for distribution are determined by actually selling the assets. In a Chapter 11 case, the value of property that will be distributed under the plan is determined through negotiations or by the court. The proceeds are then matched to the amounts of the claims and their relative priorities to determine the distributions that will be made to each claimant.

Absent bankruptcy, in order to establish the amount owed to it an unsecured creditor has to bring a lawsuit, usually in state court, alleging the facts that establish the underlying liability as well as the amount owed. Even a secured creditor that is unable to gain possession by self-help must bring an action in court. If the debtor contests the action, the secured creditor must prove the existence of the debt and the amount owing.

Once a bankruptcy has been filed, the automatic stay bars creditors from taking those steps. Bankruptcy substitutes a much cheaper, easier system for a creditor to establish its claim. The creditor simply files a one-page form called a *proof of claim*, describing the debt and stating that it remains outstanding. Bankr. Code §501(a). If the claim is based on a written contract or other document, the contract or document must be attached. If no one objects to the claim, the claim is deemed "allowed" in the bankruptcy process. Bankr. Code §502(a). In Chapter 11 cases, the process is even easier. The debtor must file a list of its creditors with the amounts owing to each. If the debtor schedules the debt correctly and does not dispute it, the creditor need not even file a proof of claim. Bankr. Code §1111(a).

Under nonbankruptcy procedures, debtors often have a substantial incentive to dispute collection claims. Absent a dispute, a creditor can obtain a quick judgment and enforce it by seizing the debtor's assets. If the debtor disputes all or part of the debt, the creditor typically has no remedy until the dispute is resolved. In the meantime, the debtor can remain in business and continue to use its assets. It should not be surprising that in the absence of bankruptcy, many debts are disputed on the flimsiest of grounds.

In bankruptcy, however, a determination that the debt is owed does not lead to seizure of the debtor's assets. Whether the debtor retains possession of the property does not turn on whether the money is owed. Thus the principal incentive for the debtor to raise disputes is eliminated. In addition, most of the disputes that are raised in a bankruptcy proceeding are easier to resolve because the parties realize that the estate will pay only a small percentage of whatever is ultimately determined to be owed. If the debtor will pay only ten cents on the dollar of allowed claims, a dispute over whether the debtor owed the creditor $10,000 at the time the petition was filed is actually a dispute over $1,000. Neither side will be as inclined to fight it. For both these reasons, objections to claims in bankruptcy cases are relatively rare. Most claims are simply filed by the creditors and deemed allowed by operation of law.

Claims against the estate are accelerated as a consequence of the bankruptcy filing. Bankr. Code §502(b)(1). If, for example, the debtor owes the creditor $10,000 payable in monthly installments of $1,000 each month over the next ten months and only one payment is currently due, the claim in bankruptcy is the total amount owed, not just the current payment. The creditor will file a claim for $10,000, the full, accelerated debt. And the whole debt, not just the payments currently due, will be resolved during the bankruptcy case.

If a claim is disputed, bankruptcy law provides for a quicker resolution of the dispute than is generally available under state law. While complex disputes may be subject to a full-scale trial after both sides have had an opportunity for discovery, probably most objections to claims are resolved in a single evidentiary hearing. If the ultimate resolution of a claim threatens to delay the bankruptcy case or distribution, the bankruptcy court can estimate the amount of a claim, allow it in the estimated amount, and proceed. Bankr. Code §502(c). In either a hearing on an objection to a claim or in a claims estimation proceeding, a creditor might show, for example, that it had sold the debtor equipment, the agreed price of the equipment, and the payments received by the time of the filing. The debtor might then bring in evidence that the equipment had failed to operate as promised, giving the debtor a contract law right to set off damages against the amount owed. The debtor might claim that nothing is owed or that a reduced sum is appropriate. If the debtor outside bankruptcy had a legal defense to payment, the bankruptcy estate will have the same defense. Bankr. Code §558. But if the bankruptcy court determines that the full amount is owed, the claim will be allowed in full. The court would typically consider the evidence proffered (often by affidavit) and rule on the amount of the claim.

Different creditors may have different bases for their claims. A department store, for example, might have a claim for the charges made by a debtor and not yet paid. An employee might have a claim for past wages. A tort victim might have a claim for injuries. Taxing authorities might have claims for back taxes due. Utilities may have claims for unpaid services. Landlords may have claims for unpaid rents, and hospitals may have claims for services provided that were never paid. Sellers of goods may have claims for the purchase price of goods sold to the debtor. Buyers of goods may have warranty claims against their sellers. Some creditors may even have claims for events that have not yet occurred (e.g., a potential claim against a debtor's guarantor when the debtor is not yet in default), or claims that are not yet fixed in amount (e.g., claims for personal injuries that have not yet been heard by a jury). The list is as long and varied as the number of ways one can become obligated to pay money. Unless the holders of these claims had obtained liens before the filing of the bankruptcy case, their claims will all be unsecured in the bankruptcy case and the amounts owed will be determined through the routine claims procedure. Bankruptcy law gives some groups of unsecured creditors priority over others, see Bankr. Code §507(a), but of the unsecured creditors listed in this paragraph, all but the taxing authorities and the employee would share pro rata with each other.

The procedure for claims estimation is itself remarkable. In re Apex Oil Co., 92 B.R. 843 (Bankr. E.D. Mo. 1988), illustrates the point: A $1.4 billion dispute between the debtor oil company and the U.S. Department of Energy had gone on for years, with no resolution in sight. Within a short time after the debtor filed bankruptcy, the bankruptcy court established procedures for resolving the dispute and scheduled two days of court hearings on the amount of the claim. The parties quickly settled the claim, and the company, which had been spending enormous resources on trying to resolve this dispute, returned to its primary business functions. Such accelerated procedures are necessary for achieving the rapid resolution of financial problems that bankruptcy contemplates. Of course, it should also be apparent that as procedures are abbreviated and parties are hurried toward a compromise, some rough justice may be dispensed along the way.

C. Calculating the Amount of an Unsecured Claim

Most debts listed (*scheduled*, in the parlance of bankruptcy) in a bankruptcy case are undisputed. The debtor owes the money and has no defense. Even so, calculating the amounts in which the various claims should be allowed and from that the amounts appropriate for distribution on each can require considerable knowledge of bankruptcy law.

The amount of an unsecured claim in bankruptcy is essentially the amount owed on the debt under nonbankruptcy law as of the moment the bankruptcy petition is filed. Bankr. Code §502(b). If the creditor's contract with the debtor provides for the debtor to pay the attorneys' fees of the creditor or to reimburse the creditor for other fees, those amounts are included in the Bankruptcy Code §502(b) amount of the claim, provided that they were incurred prior to the time the bankruptcy case was filed. Bankr. Code §502(b)(1).

The amount of the unsecured claim does not grow with the accrual of interest during the bankruptcy case. This conclusion is derived from the restriction that an unsecured creditor's claim may not include "unmatured interest." Bankr. Code §502(b)(2). The reason for disallowing postpetition interest lies in the collective nature of bankruptcy. To understand it, consider that in the vast majority of bankruptcy cases, estate assets will be sufficient to pay only a portion of the claims. As of the moment of the filing of the petition, each unsecured creditor is entitled to a pro rata share of a fixed pool of assets.

To allow interest to accrue on the claims between the filing of the case and the ultimate distribution would not increase the value of the pool. If unsecured creditors were allowed to accrue interest on their claims at the rates specified in their contracts, the only effect would be to shift some of the recovery from low interest creditors to high interest creditors. While some might argue that is the bargain initially struck among the creditors, that is not the policy reflected in the Bankruptcy Code. Instead, for the purposes of accruing postpetition interest, all the unsecured creditors are equal, even if their initial contracts were different. In addition to principled reasons such as preservation of equality among creditors, there are more practical reasons to insist on similar postpetition treatment among the creditors. To give creditors differential rates of interest after the bankruptcy filing would create differences among them that might even undermine the collective proceeding. For example, a creditor who was accruing interest at 21 percent, while another was accruing no interest, might not work nearly so hard nor compromise nearly so readily to conclude the bankruptcy case.

Traditionally, the courts have declined to permit unsecured creditors to include postpetition attorneys' fees in the amounts of their claims. Some recent cases, however, have permitted inclusion of postpetition attorneys' fees in cases where the contract between creditor and debtor provided for their payment.

To illustrate the calculation of the amount of an unsecured claim, assume that Maggie purchased computer paper from John on June 1 at an agreed price of $5,000 payable in three months at 12 percent interest, and that Maggie filed for bankruptcy on September 1. John would file a claim for $5,150 ($5,000 principal and $150 accrued interest). If Maggie filed bankruptcy on July 15 instead, the claim would be for $5,075 ($5,000 plus $75 accrued interest). If Maggie made no payments but delayed filing until the following June 1, John would have to consult the contract and applicable contract law to determine the amount of his claim: If his contract entitled him to accrue interest after default at the same contract rate, he would have a claim for $5,600; if the contract provided for a higher rate of interest after the default (sometimes referred to as a *default rate*) on September 1, as many contracts do, he could claim that higher amount. In addition, if John spent $1,000 in collection costs before the bankruptcy filing, and the contract provided for reimbursement of these costs, he could add that amount to his claim. But John could not claim any amount he would not be entitled to under nonbankruptcy law as of the moment of filing, with the possible exception for attorneys' fees mentioned in the preceding paragraph.

If the estate had sufficient assets to pay 10 percent of the claims against it, John's claim of $5,600 (June 1 filing) would yield a check for $560. The remaining $5,040 would be uncollectible. Absent extraordinary circumstances, the bankruptcy court would discharge Maggie from liability for it. If the claim were larger, including $1,000 in prefiling collection costs and another $500 in default interest, John's claim would grow to $7,100, and his actual recovery would rise to $710.

D.   Payments on Unsecured Claims

How much do unsecured creditors typically receive in a bankruptcy? There have been only a handful of careful empirical studies of the bankruptcy system. In one of the most detailed studies focusing on repayments to creditors in consumer bankruptcies in a single district, Professor Michael J. Herbert and Mr. Dominic E. Pacitti documented repayments to general, unsecured creditors. Their conclusion paints a grim picture for the general creditors listed in Chapter 7 cases:

> During the study period, a total of 4,892 cases were closed in the bankruptcy court. Of these, 4,723 were closed under Chapter 7, 167 under Chapter 13 and 2 under Chapter 11. In percentage terms, 96.55% of the cases were closed under Chapter 7, 3.41% under Chapter 13 and .04% under Chapter 11.
>
> Of the 4,723 Chapter 7 cases, there were 4,515 in which no assets were distributed, and, as noted above, there were 208 cases in which at least some assets were distributed. In percentage terms, 95.6% of the Chapter 7 cases were cases in which nothing was distributed. Of all the cases closed during the study period, 92.3% were no asset Chapter 7 proceedings and 4.25% were Chapter 7 proceedings in which some assets were distributed.

Herbert & Pacitti, Down and Out in Richmond, Virginia: The Distribution of Assets in Chapter 7 Bankruptcy Proceedings Closed During 1984-87, 22 U. Rich. L. Rev. 303, 311 (1988). Persistence of these low payouts was recently confirmed in a study by the U.S. General Accounting Office of distributions in the 1.2 million Chapter 7 bankruptcy cases closed in statistical years 1991 and 1992. The GAO found that about 5 percent (56,994) of those cases generated some receipts for distribution to professionals and creditors, a total of about $2 billion. Money reached the hands of unsecured creditors in only about 3 percent of the Chapter 7 cases.

Not all bankruptcies yield so little. Debtors in Chapter 13 cases frequently promise to repay 100 percent of their outstanding debts. In a multidistrict study of debtors in bankruptcy, the researchers discovered great variation by district, but, overall, 41 percent of the Chapter 13 debtors promised full repayment, and another 21 percent promised to repay more than half their outstanding debts. Teresa Sullivan, Elizabeth Warren, & Jay Lawrence Westbrook, The Persistence of Local Legal Culture: Twenty Years of Evidence from the Federal Bankruptcy Courts, 17 Harv. J.L. & Pub. Poly. 801 (1994). Of course, this means only that the debtors promised to pay, not that the creditors actually got the money — an important distinction in the debtor-creditor biz. In a recent study of the largest Chapter 11 cases, promised payments were also high. Professors LoPucki and Whitford found that plans provided 100 percent repayment of allowed claims in more than one-quarter of the cases. In most instances these were not just paper recoveries. The distributions were made in stocks, bonds, and promissory notes that the creditors could immediately sell for cash. Lynn M. LoPucki & William C. Whitford, Bargaining Over Equity's Share in the Bankruptcy Reorganization of Large, Publicly Held Companies, 139 U. Pa. L. Rev. 125 (1990).

The data from these studies lead to two conclusions, both of which must be kept in mind when evaluating the prospects for recovery in a particular case. First, the fate of most unsecured creditors in bankruptcy is not a happy one. The vast majority face discharge of all or a substantial portion of their outstanding debt with no payment or, at best, nominal payment. Second, there are many cases in which unsecured creditors manage a substantial or even a full recovery. Sophisticated unsecured creditors know that the average recoveries from bankruptcy cases are minuscule because the value of the debtors' assets are small. But they also know that in the cases of debtors with substantial assets, an allowed claim can sometimes yield substantial dividends.

E.   Calculating the Amount of a Secured Claim

Calculating the amount of a creditor's secured claim begins with a determination of the amount owing under nonbankruptcy law, as indicated in Bankruptcy Code §502. This step is the same for a claim secured by a lien as for an unsecured claim.

The next step is to bifurcate the claim as required under Bankruptcy Code §506(a). That section provides that the claim of a secured creditor can be a *secured claim* only to the extent of the value of the collateral. The remainder of the creditor's claim is an *unsecured claim*. Bankr. Code §506(a). If the value of the collateral is less than the Bankruptcy Code §502 amount of the secured creditor's claim, the effect will be to divide the secured creditor's claim into two claims: One will be a secured claim in an amount equal to the value of the collateral, and the other will be an unsecured claim for the deficiency.

To illustrate this bifurcation of claims, consider an example. If Bonnie Kraemer owes First National Bank $40,000 secured by a boat worth $50,000, First National has a $40,000 allowed secured claim. If the boat were worth only $35,000, First National would have a $35,000 secured claim and a $5,000 unsecured claim. Kraemer's unsecured claim would be treated just like any other unsecured claim. The treatment of her secured claim is the primary subject of the remainder of this chapter.

The next step in determining the amount of the secured claim is to determine whether the creditor is entitled to accrue postpetition interest, attorneys' fees, or costs on its claim. As we saw in section C, unsecured creditors cannot accrue such postpetition charges, even if they were entitled to these charges under their contract and under nonbankruptcy law. Bankruptcy Code §506(b) entitles the holder of a secured claim to accrue postfiling interest, attorneys' fees, and costs on its claim when three conditions are met: (1) attorneys' fees and costs must be "reasonable"; (2) payment of the attorneys' fees and costs by the debtor must be "provided for under the agreement under which [the] claim arose"; (3) interest, attorneys' fees, and costs can be accrued only to the extent that the value of the collateral exceeds the amount of the claim secured by it. (Bankruptcy lawyers and judges refer to such a claim as being *over secured*.)

Therefore, to continue with the example, if Bonnie Kraemer's debt of $40,000 is secured by a boat worth $50,000 at the time the bankruptcy case is filed, the claim could grow as interest, attorneys' fees, and other costs accrued during the bankruptcy case, up to an additional $10,000. The entire secured claim could not exceed the value of the collateral, $50,000. If, on the other hand, the collateral were worth only $35,000, First National's $40,000 claim would be bifurcated into a secured claim of $35,000 and an unsecured claim of $5,000, and neither claim would be permitted to grow. (Bankruptcy lawyers and judges would refer to the $40,000 claim as *undersecured*.) Keep in mind that these rules that prevent interest, attorneys' fees, and costs from accruing on a *claim* do not prevent them from accruing on the underlying *debt*.

The ability of over secured creditors to recover interest, attorneys' fees, and costs accrued during bankruptcy as part of their claims minimizes the injury bankruptcy inflicts on them. The data collected in Teresa Sullivan, Elizabeth Warren, & Jay Lawrence Westbrook, As We Forgive Our Debtors 306-311 (1989), documents that in consumer bankruptcies the secured creditors' claims were often fully secured.

Secured creditors may be unable to repossess their collateral or terminate their relationship with the debtor, as we saw in the last assignment, and they may have new payment terms imposed on them, as we will see below. Unlike their unsecured counterparts, however, they can typically look forward to substantial repayment.

F.   Selling the Collateral

As we discussed in the preceding Assignment, a primary purpose of Chapter 7 of the Bankruptcy Code is to maximize the recovery of the creditors by maximizing the sale price of the debtors' property. As we saw in Assignment 4, judicial sale procedures are often grossly ineffective in that regard. Chapter 7 provides a sale procedure that is generally much more effective. Under the supervision of the bankruptcy court, the Chapter 7 trustee sells the property in whatever manner the trustee thinks will maximize the net proceeds. The broader leeway given to the trustee permits alternative forms of sale, such as going-out-of-business sales at the business sites, sales in already established markets, or sales through brokers, to name just a few.

When the trustee liquidates the property of the estate, the trustee ordinarily sells only the debtor's equity in property subject to a security interest, because that is all the estate has succeeded to under Bankruptcy Code §541(a). The trustee does that by making the sale "subject to" the secured creditor's lien. For example, if Bonnie Kraemer's boat were worth $50,000 and the only lien against it was the $40,000 security interest of First National Bank, the trustee would sell the estate's interest for $10,000. The buyer would take the boat subject to the bank's $40,000 lien and the trustee would distribute the $10,000 purchase price to the unsecured creditors, as set forth in Bankruptcy Code §726(a).

The sale in this example would terminate the automatic stay with regard to the boat. Bankr. Code §362(c)(1). The bankruptcy case might continue, but the boat would no longer be part of it. First National Bank would be free to foreclose its lien, just as if there had not been a bankruptcy. As a practical matter, foreclosure probably would not be necessary. The buyer probably bought with full knowledge of First National's lien and its ability to foreclose it, and had already set aside $40,000 to pay First National.

If the boat were worth $35,000 instead of $50,000, the debtor's interest (bare ownership) would have become property of the estate. But that interest would have been of inconsequential value to the estate: The trustee would have a difficult time finding a responsible buyer for a $35,000 boat that was subject to a $40,000 lien. In fact, ownership of such a boat probably would have been a financial burden on the trustee, for to fulfill its minimal obligation to the secured creditor it would have had to incur storage expenses. Section 554(a) of the Bankruptcy Code authorizes the trustee to *abandon* property of the estate that is burdensome or of inconsequential value to the estate. When a trustee abandons property, it ceases to be property of the estate and ownership reverts to the debtor. Abandonment, like sale, terminates the automatic stay. If the debt has not been paid, once the property has been abandoned, the secured creditor can foreclose without further interference from the bankruptcy court.

One other disposition of collateral is common in Chapter 7. Under some circumstances, the trustee can sell the collateral "free and clear of liens." Bankr. Code §363(f). For example, assume again that Bonnie Kraemer's boat was worth only $35,000, but the circumstances were such that the trustee was entitled to sell it free and clear of liens. The trustee presumably would sell it for $35,000 in cash. The sale would transfer First National's lien from the boat to the proceeds of sale. The amount of First National's secured claim would then be limited not by the value of the boat, *approximately* $35,000, but by the value of the proceeds, *exactly* $35,000. A secured creditor may also see a trustee's greater flexibility in conducting a sale as likely to yield more money on liquidation and may ask the trustee to conduct the sale.

If the sale of the boat free and clear of liens brought $50,000 instead, First National's entire claim would be secured. The trustee would pay $40,000 to First National and $10,000 would remain in the estate. The circumstances under which a trustee can sell collateral free and clear of liens are considered in greater detail in Assignment 27 of this book.

G. Who Pays the Expenses of Sale by the Trustee?

The preceding example makes little mention of the expenses that would have been incurred by the trustee in storing or selling the boat. Yet some expenses will be incurred almost any time a trustee sells property. Initially, the trustee will incur them, by, for example, contracting for the services of a real estate broker. When the trustee sells property subject to a security interest, can these expenses be passed along to the secured creditor by deducting them from the secured creditor's proceeds of sale? Or must the estate bear the expenses? In some situations, the resolution of this issue will be critical. Consider, for example, a house that probably can be sold for $100,000, but only through a real estate broker who will charge a $6,000 fee. If the mortgage against this house is $92,000, the estate's interest might be worth anywhere from $2,000 to $8,000, depending on who must bear the expenses of sale.

Resolution of this issue is found in Bankruptcy Code §506(c), which authorizes a trustee who has incurred "reasonable, necessary costs and expenses of preserving, or disposing of" property securing an allowed secured claim to recover them from the property. That language is ambiguous, however, as to whether the trustee deducts the costs and expenses from the secured creditor's share of the proceeds, from the debtor's share of the proceeds, or from some combination of the two. The ambiguity is at least partially resolved by the language limiting the trustee's right to deduct from the proceeds "to the extent of any benefit to [the secured creditor.]" That is, absent benefit to the secured creditor from the trustee's expenditures, the trustee cannot deduct anything from the proceeds of sale.

Some ambiguity remains: "benefit" in comparison to what? Selling through a broker instead of selling without a broker? Paying for a security service instead of letting the property be destroyed by vandals? If this were the comparison, trustees would virtually always be able to charge their costs and expenses to the collateral. In In re The Wine Boutique, Inc., the court answered the "In comparison to what?" question in a manner that would favor secured creditors. In that case, the debtor in possession hired a real estate broker to sell its liquor store. The agent sold the store for $338,000, which all agreed was a fair price. Twin City State Bank held a lien against the store for an amount in excess of $338,000. The trustee nevertheless sought to deduct the $21,000 fee it paid the broker from the proceeds of sale before turning them over to Twin City. Having identified the issue as whether Twin City "benefitted from the sale," the Court answered the question in the affirmative — and stuck Twin City with the costs:

> [In bankruptcy] Twin City did not have to foreclose on the property and incur the financial burdens, and time burdens, that are usually associated with such action. Instead, Twin City was freed from these problems by virtue of the broker's prompt disposition of the property. Further, had *Twin City lifted the stay and taken possession of the realty and the personalty, it would have had to sell same and pay its broker a commission also.* [Emphasis added.]

Notice the comparison employed by the court to answer the "benefit" question. The court compares what actually happened with what would have happened if the stay had been lifted and the secured creditor had dealt with the problem on its own.

Apply this reasoning to the hypothetical in which the trustee incurs $6,000 of selling expense to sell property subject to a $92,000 lien for a gross price of $100,000. Can the trustee recover the $6,000 expenditure from the $92,000 of proceeds otherwise destined for the secured creditor? Applying the analysis from *Wine Boutique*, the answer is probably no, because the secured creditor probably did not benefit from the trustee's expenditure of the brokerage fee. Had the secured creditor lifted the stay and taken possession of the realty in this example, it would most likely have had to sell same and pay its broker a commission as well. But unlike *Wine Boutique*, the loss here would not have come to rest on the secured creditor: The secured creditor almost certainly would have had the contract right to add the amount of the commission to the amount of the secured debt. In contrast to *Wine Boutique*, there is an equity in the property in this hypothetical. As a result, the secured creditor will be able to recover the commission, along with any other expenditures it may have to make in connection with the property, from the property. The secured creditor does not "benefit" from the trustee's costs and expenses because even if the secured creditor incurred those expenses itself, it would have been reimbursed for them in the foreclosure process.

The result is that a trustee's sale of an *undersecured* creditor's collateral will ordinarily benefit that creditor and be deducted from its recovery. But the trustee's sale of property when the debt is sufficiently *over secured* will not. The actual outcome often depends on a complex analysis of what would have happened if the stay had been lifted and the secured creditor had been permitted to liquidate the collateral.

H. Chapters 11 and 13 Reorganizations

In reorganization cases, the debtor typically seeks to keep the property that is subject to a security interest and to continue using it. The property may be anything from a car or boat in a Chapter 13 to millions of dollars' worth of factory equipment or a hotel or office building in a Chapter 11. In many of these cases, the debtor also seeks to reduce the amount of the secured debt and accompanying lien, to reschedule payment over a longer period of time, or to do both. These things can be accomplished over the objection of the secured creditor, if at all, only through confirmation of a Chapter 11 plan or a Chapter 13 plan by the bankruptcy court.

The confirmation of a Chapter 11 plan discharges the old secured debts and payment schedules and substitutes new ones. Bankr. Code

§1141(d)(1)(A). The plan must specify that the creditor retain its lien under Bankruptcy Code §1129(b)(2)(A)(i)(I), but after confirmation, the lien secures only the new debt. The confirmation of a plan to which the creditor has not agreed is graphically referred to by bankruptcy lawyers and judges as a *cramdown*. Chapter 13 also authorizes cramdown. Procedure under Chapter 13 is materially different in that the discharge occurs only after the debtor completes all the payments under the plan. Bankr. Code §1328(a). But once the debtor completes the plan payments, the secured debts will be similarly stripped down to the value of the collateral by entry of the discharge.

Debtors and their secured creditors often agree on the treatment to be accorded the secured creditors under plans, but the negotiations take place in the shadow of what the court would do in the absence of agreement. The terms agreed upon are usually just the parties' best estimate of what the court would impose. For that reason, we examine the statutory standards for cramdown with an eye to determining the minimum repayment the court will consider "fair and equitable," which is the amount the plan proponent will therefore be entitled to cram down. The minimums are basically the same under both Chapter 11 and Chapter 13. Compare Bankruptcy Code §1129(b)(2)(A) with Bankruptcy Code §1325(a)(5). They are most clearly stated in the latter section. Under that section, unless the secured creditor accepts (agrees to its treatment under) the plan, the debtor must either:

1. surrender the collateral to the secured creditor in satisfaction of the secured claim or
2. distribute to the creditor, on account of the secured claim, property with a value as of the effective date of the plan that is not less than the amount of the allowed secured claim.

The first alternative is pretty clear and is one most debtors want to avoid. The second requires some explanation. It essentially establishes a three-step process for testing the adequacy of the proposed distribution to a secured creditor. The first step is to determine the amount of the allowed secured claim. The second is to determine the value of the proposed distribution. The final step is to determine that the latter is at least as great as the former.

Although the secured claim must be paid in full, the payment promised under the plan need not be immediate or in cash. The debtor need only promise the creditor property that has a value at least as great as the amount of the secured claim. Theoretically, the property handed over might be an automobile or an elephant. But nearly always the property is a promise of future payments. The payments are usually regular monthly, quarterly, or annual payments (although an occasional case may provide for a balloon payment at some specified time in the future). A Chapter 13 debtor, for example, might propose to pay $100 per month for three years on her car loan. Alternatively, a debtor might propose irregular payments that reflect the odd times when the debtor expects to have cash available. A farmer, for example, might propose to pay $3,000 of the secured claim on the effective date of the plan and the balance in a lump sum when the debtor sells the wheat crop next August.

I.   Valuing Future Payments

It is not sufficient that the payments total the *amount* of the allowed secured claim. They must have a *value* as of the effective date of the plan of that amount. (The "effective date of the plan" is nowhere defined in the Bankruptcy Code, but it is generally understood to be a date, specified in the plan, about 10 to 30 days after confirmation.) Of course, a payment of $1,000 made on the effective date of the plan has a value of $1,000 as of that date. But a promissory note, delivered on the effective date of the plan, promising to pay $1,000, without interest, one year after the effective date, will have a value lower than $1,000.

This concept is generally known as the *time value of money*. To illustrate the concept, assume that the market rate of interest is 10 percent. In the market in which that rate was fixed, some parties (lenders) are agreeing to pay $100 now in return for the agreement of other parties (borrowers) to pay back $110 one year later. If both lenders and borrowers are acting voluntarily (in some sense at least), this market is telling us that $100 now is the equivalent in value of $110 a year from now.

It follows that the amount of money that must be paid at some later time to have a present value of $X as of the effective date of the plan is $X plus interest at the market rate from the effective date of the plan to the date of payment. So, for example, if a creditor's allowed secured claim is $100, any plan that proposes to pay the creditor at least $100 plus interest at the market rate from the effective date of the plan to the date of payment will meet the "value" requirement. The promise of future payments will have a *present value* as of the effective date of the plan, of at least $100.

In establishing a market rate of interest, the participants in a market consider a number of factors. They estimate the effects of inflation and the likelihood that $100 paid back in a year will not purchase as much as would $100 today. They also consider the risk that this particular borrower or borrowers of this type will not repay the loan or will not repay it in full. The greater the parties' assessments of both inflation and risk, the higher the charge for the use of the creditor's money and the higher the interest rate for the loan.

The term *market rate of interest* is necessarily ambiguous. At any given time, money is being borrowed and lent at many different rates of interest in many different "markets." For example, a bank may be borrowing money from the Federal Reserve at 6.5 percent and paying interest on short-term deposits at 7 percent and long-term deposits at 8 percent, while at the same time it is lending money on home loans at 8.5 percent, on commercial loans at rates from 9 percent to 12 percent, and charging 19% on outstanding credit card balances. If there is such a thing as a market rate of interest, each of these rates must represent a different market. To which market should the court look to fulfill the objectives of the Bankruptcy Code provisions regarding cramdown? In the following case, the court faced precisely that question.

In re E.I. Parks No. 1 Ltd. Partnership

122 B.R. 549 (Bankr. W.D. Ark. 1990)

JAMES G. MIXON, UNITED STATES BANKRUPTCY JUDGE.

[The debtor owned and operated a mobile home park, called the Northern Hills Park, in Arkansas. The Court determined the market value of Northern Hills Park to be $700,000.00, an amount that was exactly equal to the mortgage debt outstanding at the time of the bankruptcy filing. The parties did not dispute this value. The mortgage holder, Shady Grove, objected to the debtor's amended plan because the plan did not propose to pay the market rate of interest on its claim.]

CLAIM OF SHADY GROVE

Shady Grove's claim is stated in the plan to be "approximately $700,000.00" and the value of its collateral, Northern Hills Park, has been determined to be $700,000.00; therefore, Shady Grove holds a fully secured claim in the amount of $700,000.00. 11 U.S.C. §506(a). The plan proposes [to satisfy] Shady Grove's secured claim by giving Shady Grove a Modified Northern Hills Note [which will be] amortized over a thirty (30) year period, due and payable in ten (10) years. Principal and interest will be paid in monthly installments. [The plan provides:]

> Unless the Court orders that another interest rate be applied, the Modified Northern Hills Note shall bear interest at a rate equal to the rate on thirty

(30) year government securities as published in the *Wall Street Journal* on the first business day following the Effective Date of the Plan plus two percent (2%) as a risk factor; provided, however, unless otherwise agreed by Debtor or ordered by the Court, said interest rate shall not exceed ten and one-half percent (10.5%). . . . Shady Grove Associates shall retain all valid liens until its claim is satisfied in full. The remainder of the balance of the Northern Hills Note shall be discharged. . . .

Shady Grove objects to the plan because the interest rate proposed to be paid does not allow Shady Grove to receive the present value of its secured claim.

The treatment of a secured claim of a creditor that votes to reject a plan is governed by the cramdown provisions found in 11 U.S.C. §1129(b)(2)(A)(i)(II). . . . If, as here, the plan proposes to pay a secured creditor in installments, the present value of the future stream of payments must equal the amount of the creditor's secured claim.

The phrase "present value" is described in Collier on Bankruptcy as:

> a term of art for an almost self-evident proposition: a dollar in hand today is worth more than a dollar to be received a day, a month or a year hence. Part of the "present value" concept may be expressed by a corollary proposition: a dollar in hand today is worth exactly the same as (1) a dollar to be received a day, a month or a year hence plus (2) the rate of interest which the dollar would earn if invested at an appropriate interest rate.

5 Collier on Bankruptcy para. 1129.03[4][F][i] (15th ed. 1990). For the present value of the future stream of payments to equal the amount of the secured claim, interest at an appropriate discount rate must be added to the payments.

Many courts, including the Eighth Circuit Court of Appeals, have approved the following guidelines for determining the appropriate rate:

> The appropriate discount rate must be determined on the basis of the rate of interest which is reasonable in light of the risks involved. Thus, in determining the discount rate, the court must consider the prevailing market rate for a loan of a term equal to the payout period, with due consideration for the quality of the security and the risk of subsequent default.

Although it is clear that the discount rate should reflect the "prevailing market rate of interest," determining how that rate should be calculated is not so clear. The complexity stems, in part, from the fact that the market rate of interest can refer to more than one market, e.g., the rate paid to an investor or the rate charged by a commercial lender. An infinite variety of factors influence what parties to a transaction may agree is the market rate of interest.

In three different cases, the Eighth Circuit Court of Appeals has considered how to determine the appropriate market rate of interest, but the

Court has not adopted a specific method. In the first case, Prudential Ins. Co. v. Monnier (In re Monnier Bros.), 755 F.2d 1336 (8th Cir. 1985), the Court of Appeals approved the prepetition contract rate as the appropriate market rate of interest. The Court of Appeals observed that the contract rate had been established by the parties only twenty months before the plan was confirmed; the contract had a payout term equal to the plan; and the contract involved identical security. Id. at 1339. The Court of Appeals indicated that the determination of the appropriate market rate of interest was factual stating, "lacking any evidence correlating other rates with the 'coerced loan' contemplated by the plan, the district court did not err in reinstating the contract rate of interest." Id.

In the second case, United States v. Neal Pharmacal Co., 789 F.2d 1283 (8th Cir. 1986), the Eighth Circuit Court of Appeals did not approve a specific market rate of interest but disapproved an interest rate based solely on the creditor's cost of borrowing money. The Court of Appeals observed that other factors to be considered in arriving at the appropriate market rate of interest included: the length of the payment period, the existence of collateral, and the risk of nonpayment. Id. at 1286.

In the third and most recent decision, United States v. Doud, 869 F.2d 1144 (8th Cir. 1989), the Eighth Circuit Court of Appeals approved a market rate of interest based on the yield for treasury bonds, plus a 2% upward adjustment to account for the overall risk involved. In *Doud*, the Court of Appeals noted that *Monnier Bros.* set "broader standard relating to components of an appropriate interest rate, which should consist of a risk-free rate, plus additional interest to compensate a creditor for risks posed by the plan." Id. at 1146. The Court of Appeals emphasized that determination of the proper market rate of interest in a particular case is a factual inquiry and can only be determined after consideration is given to all the elements involved in computing the appropriate interest rate. Id.

Both the debtor and the objecting creditors cite the Eighth Circuit Court of Appeals cases as support for their positions. Shady Grove argues that the market rate of interest should be determined based upon a hypothetical coerced loan by a commercial lender to the debtor.

Shady Grove offered the expert testimony of Donald Robert Tuller, a banker with twenty-seven years of experience, in support of this argument. Tuller testified that his bank would not loan anyone a 100% loan on a thirty-year amortization payable in ten years. He said that if his bank had to make a coerced loan, the best rate and best terms his bank would offer would be a fifteen-year loan at 12% per annum with annual adjustments to the interest rate to account for market fluctuations. He also stated that the 12% rate anticipated a 3% to 4% "spread" for profit and overhead expense. He said that he considers loans secured by mobile home parks to be high risk loans.

Utilizing a hypothetical coerced loan as a governing analogy overlooks some important dissimilarities to the chapter 11 cramdown process. For example, the hypothetical coerced loan necessarily includes a factor for profit, a factor most courts have rejected for purposes of calculating the market rate of interest to be applied in a bankruptcy case. In addition, many lenders would decline to make any loan secured by collateral equal to 100% of the amount of the loan, especially to a debtor in chapter 11. When asked what rate they would charge for a hypothetical coerced loan, lenders invariably state that rate charged would be the maximum allowed by law. Calculating market rate of interest solely from the viewpoint of a coerced loan tends to jeopardize the success of a chapter 11 plan and defeat the rehabilitative purposes of bankruptcy reorganization.

. . . Since many of the factors relevant to a chapter 11 cramdown are significantly different from the factors that would determine the market rate of interest in a loan transaction, whether coerced or at arms' length, calculating the market rate of interest solely from the viewpoint of a hypothetical coerced lender is inappropriate.

The debtor argues that the appropriate market rate should be calculated by selecting a risk-free rate based on government securities and adding a risk factor. This method has been specifically approved by the Eighth Circuit Court of Appeals in *Doud*. Several bankruptcy courts within the Eighth Circuit have adopted this approach.

The Eighth Circuit Court of Appeals stated that the elements to be considered in arriving at the appropriate market rate of interest include the term of the payout period, the quality of the security and the risk of subsequent default. The debtor offered evidence which touched on each of these factors through the expert testimony of Michael Pyron. [Based on rates currently being paid by the U.S. government on treasury obligations] Pyron concluded that an appropriate risk-free rate was 8.1% to 8.3% for real estate such as that involved here.

Pyron then noted the quality of the security and analyzed the risk factors involved with the debtor. He noted as positive risk factors that: the collateral is real property located in an area with a strong economic base, the neighborhood has active new construction and residential properties, the property values in the area are appreciating, and employment opportunities are available nearby for the residents. The negative factors he noted included: the slope of the property, the flood zone problems, the "degeneration" of the pool, and lower than anticipated occupancy levels. Pyron concluded that an appropriate risk factor, considering the above elements, was 2%, resulting in an appropriate market rate of interest of 10.1% to 10.3%.

. . . Shady Grove's secured status, therefore, is not likely to deteriorate significantly over any portion of the payout period of the plan even if payments under a confirmed plan are not made. The debtor's operating expenses have made it difficult for the debtor to make debt service payments and this problem is compounded by the lack of working capital necessary to make needed capital improvements. The quality of the debtor's management is not as good as it could be because of antipathy between the debtor's general partners and management. However, if the debtor defaults in any proposed plan payment on debt service, the creditor has available its state law remedies of foreclosure. Based on the evidence presented in this case, the creditor's risk of loss upon default does not appear to be exceptionally high.

The Court agrees with the debtor's calculation of the market rate of interest using a risk-free rate plus a risk factor. The debtor's plan proposes a maximum interest rate of 10.5% to be paid on the secured claim of Shady Grove, and the debtor has calculated its cash flow projections based on a 10.5% interest rate. Under the facts in this case, 10.5% constitutes the appropriate market rate of interest to be applied to the payments on Shady Grove's secured claim.

Compared with the unsecured creditors, Shady Grove did pretty well. But compared with its original deal with Parks, Shady Grove did rather poorly. E.I. Parks defaulted under its old contract, but still managed to keep the property. Now it is paying a lower rate of interest.

Problem Set 7

7.1. You are still counsel to DataServe (see Problem 6.1). CFO Mandy Elkins wants you to go over the calculation of a claim so that they can file one correctly when a debtor files for bankruptcy. Mandy has picked out one of the outstanding debts — $30,000 worth of repair work done for Argossy, Inc. The contract provides for interest at 18 percent for all accounts, beginning at billing. The market rate of interest is 12 percent. The work was done on February 15 and the bill was sent to Argossy on March 15. Argossy never paid, and it filed for bankruptcy on September 15. The bankruptcy case is still pending on December 15, when you consult with Elkins. You also note that you spent two hours working on the case in August, for which you billed DataServe $400, but the contract between Argossy and DataServe says nothing about who will pay collection costs. How much is the claim in the Argossy case? Explain to Elkins how you arrived at the calculation. Bankr. Code §502(b).

7.2 Several months after the meeting in Problem 7.1, Elkins called you to say that she just received the trustee's Final Report and

Account showing that after payment of the expenses of administration and the other priority debt, there will be $59,575 available for distribution to general unsecured creditors in the Chapter 7 case. Unsecured claims (including DataServe's) total $1,191,500. She wants to know what that means for DataServe.

7.3   Another of your firm's most active clients is Commercial Investors, a consortium of private investors that places high-risk loans with small businesses. Today Andrea Wu, the Vice-President for the Workouts department, asks you to file a proof of claim against Speedo Printing, a small company that filed for Chapter 11 three months ago. According to CI's records, at the time Speedo filed it owed CI $340,000 plus six months of interest at 12 percent per year. The loan was secured by an interest in Speedo's printing equipment, which was appraised a couple of months ago at $400,000.

a.   Assuming that collateral value holds up in bankruptcy court, how much is CI's claim? Bankr. Code §§502, 506.

b.   If the court also used a 12 percent interest rate for the pending bankruptcy, how much should CI expect to be paid under a plan of reorganization that is confirmed today? Bankr. Code §1129(b)(2)(A)(II).

c.   How much should CI expect to be paid if the reorganization plan is not confirmed for another year?

7.4   Wu is back in your office about a week later. She had the property reappraised, and it seems that the fair market value is more like $325,000. (The earlier appraisal was wrong.) She has also learned that the debtor estimates that there will be sufficient assets to pay the unsecured creditors about 10 percent of their outstanding claims.

a.   Describe CI's claim now. Bankr. Code §§502, 506.

b.   What should CI expect to be paid under a plan of reorganization?

c.   Does it matter to CI whether the plan is confirmed today or a year from today?

7.5.   Another week passes and Wu is back again. At your request, she had been searching her records for a copy of the security agreement. She has finally come to the conclusion that no security agreement was ever signed.

a.   Now what is the nature of CI's claim? Bankr. Code §§502, 506.

b.   If the 10 percent payout for unsecured creditors persists, what should CI expect under a plan of reorganization? See Bankr. Code §§726(a).

7.6.   As a member of the U.S. Panel of Trustees, you have been appointed to serve as trustee in a number of Chapter 7 cases. One of them is the case of Tonia Perez, whose summer house is in the estate. The summer house is encumbered by a mortgage to First Capital. The amount currently owing on the mortgage is $85,000, which includes interest accrued to date at the contract rate of 10 percent per annum. You talked with the real estate broker you ordinarily use in such cases. She told you that she thought she could get $100,000 for the summer house. But the market is slow, and she estimates that there is only about a 50 percent chance that the sale would take place in the next six months. As usual, she would discount her commission from the 7 percent that most brokers charge to the 6 percent she charges you. She estimates your share of the other costs of sale and the prorations at $1,000.

    a.   If you are able to sell this house in exactly six months, how much money will the sale produce for the estate? Bankr. Code §541(a)(1).

    b.   How does that amount vary if you sell at an earlier or later time? Is trying to sell the house the right thing to do? See §§506(b) and (c).

    c.   Can First Capital prevent you from trying to sell? Bankr. Code §554(b).

    7.7.   Martin O'Keefe recently filed under Chapter 7, and you were appointed trustee. After you approved O'Keefe' exemptions, abandoned property that would be worthless to the estate, gathered and liquidated the remaining nonexempt property, and made allowance for payment of your own fees, you have the following:

Proceeds from sale of Piper aircraft	$214,000
Proceeds from sale of coin collection	26,000
Proceeds from turnover of cash in bank account	2,200
Total	$242,200

O'Keefe has only one secured creditor, Friendly Credit, who is owed $150,000 against the Piper aircraft.

    a.   If O'Keefe owes $300,000 to other creditors, all unsecured, what distributions do you make? What is the percentage paid to the unsecured creditors?

    b.   If Friendly Credit's security interest had been in the coin collection instead of the Piper aircraft, what would your distributions have been? What would the percentage paid to the unsecured creditors have been?

Chapter 3.   Creation of Security Interests

Assignment 8:   Formalities for Attachment

In Part One of this book, we focus on the relationship between the debtor and the creditor. In earlier assignments we compared the collection rights of secured creditors with their unsecured counterparts, both under state law rules and in federal bankruptcy. We observed the limited collection rights available to unsecured creditors and the more expansive rights given to secured creditors. In all these assignments we observed that a secured creditor is usually in a better position to collect than an unsecured creditor, although either creditor may face substantial uncertainty if the debtor resists.

In this assignment we turn to the question of how someone becomes a secured creditor. As in earlier assignments, our focus continues to be on security interests created under Article 9 and, for comparison purposes, on mortgages and deeds of trust created under real estate law.

Creditors taking a security interest either under Article 9 or real estate law have one key feature in common: They obtain their status by contract with the debtor. Article 9 secured creditors or real estate mortgagees are, by definition, consensual creditors. That is, they have enhanced collection rights because, at an earlier time in the relationship, their debtors consented to them. In this assignment we explore that agreement between debtor and creditor and how it is regulated by the Uniform Commercial Code or state mortgage laws.

A.   A Prototypical Secured Transaction

Most security interests are created as part of a transaction in which money is lent or property is sold. When a bank lends money to a corporation, for example, it may insist, as a condition of the loan, that the corporation grant it a security interest in some or all of the corporation's assets. Similarly, an automobile dealer who sells on credit will nearly always require the buyer to give a security interest in the automobile purchased.

The law governing security interests is easier to understand when it is placed in the context of the business transactions in which security interests are created. The story that follows describes an ordinary secured transaction: a debtor who borrows money from a bank to start a business.

Fisherman's Pier: A Prototypical Secured Transaction

Pablo Escobar has been in the restaurant management business for several years. Among the eating places he has managed is Fisherman's Pier, which is owned by Stella Parker. Stella recently decided to sell Fisherman's Pier and retire. When Pablo heard the news, he went to talk to her about buying the place. In a series of meetings, Pablo and Stella worked out the terms of sale. Stella would sell Fisherman's Pier, including the kitchen equipment, furniture, fixtures, furnishings, building lease, and goodwill to Pablo for $100,000 in cash.

Pablo did not have $100,000, but he had family and friends lined up to invest in his venture. He could raise enough money to provide working capital for the business, of which about $40,000 could be applied toward the purchase price. The rest would have to be borrowed. Pablo retained attorney Ellen Bartell to draft an "Agreement for Purchase and Sale," which he and Stella signed. The agreement was contingent on Pablo's getting a $60,000 bank loan to complete the purchase. That is, if Pablo could not get the loan, neither party would be bound by the contract.

Pablo made an appointment to see Mark Sun in the Commercial Loan Department of First National Bank. In their first meeting, they talked about the weather, the restaurant business, Pablo's experience, the Agreement for Purchase and Sale, and some of the key terms on which First National makes commercial loans. Before Pablo left, Sun gave him a copy of the bank's Loan Application form.

The application form asked for essentially four kinds of information. The first was personal information about Pablo. What was his date of birth? His social security number? Where had he lived during what periods of time? Was he married? The second was information about his financial condition. What did he own? What debts did he owe? What had his income been over the past several years? The form required that he attach copies of his income tax returns for the past two years. The third was information about his credit history. From whom had he borrowed money in the past? What credit cards did he have? Had he ever filed for bankruptcy? Been foreclosed against? The last part of the form was a description of the collateral he could offer for the loan. Pablo completed the application in a couple of days and returned it to Sun. Sun told Pablo that it "looked like everything was in order" and he thought there would be no problems with the loan. Sun said he would get back to Pablo within about a week.

Sun ordered a credit check on Pablo from a credit reporting agency, personally called three of Pablo's credit references, and scheduled Pablo's application for a meeting of the bank's loan committee. Both the report and the references were good. Sun presented the loan application to the committee and it was approved, contingent on an appraisal of the restaurant at a value of at least $100,000. The bank's appraiser visited the restaurant, looked at the equipment, measured the square footage of the building, checked the business receipts for the past year, collected information on some comparable sales, and appraised the restaurant as having a "market value" of $100,000.

Sun then called Pablo and told him the good news. The loan had been approved and Morton Friedman, the bank's lawyer, would "handle the closing." The lawyers scheduled the loan closing for a date about three weeks away and began preparing the documents and gathering the information they would need.

At the bank's request, Pablo signed a financing statement on the form set forth in U.C.C. §9-521. Friedman sent the financing statement to the Secretary of State for filing in the U.C.C. filing system. The financing statement would provide public notice of the bank's security interest in Fisherman's Pier. Friedman also ordered a search of the U.C.C. filing system for other financing statements filed against Stella Parker or Fisherman's Pier. The bank wanted a security interest in the assets prior to all others; only through such a search would Friedman know whether there were already other security interests against them. The search results showed only one financing statement other than First National's. It was in favor of Valley State Bank, who had lent money to Stella using the restaurant as collateral. Friedman wrote to Valley State Bank, advising them that Stella was selling the restaurant and requesting that Valley State advise him of the exact amount necessary to pay off the loan. He also asked that they prepare a security interest "termination statement" for filing in the U.C.C. records.

The closing was held as scheduled at Ellen Bartell's office. Pablo signed a promissory note for $60,000 and the preprinted form Security Agreement used by First National for most of their small commercial loans (a copy of a security agreement appears in Assignment 15). Stella delivered a bill of sale for the restaurant property, an assignment of her rights under the lease, and the keys to the restaurant. Friedman delivered First National Bank's check to an employee from Valley State Bank. The check was for $38,839, the exact balance outstanding on the Valley State loan, with interest computed up to the day of the closing. The Valley State employee gave Friedman the signed Termination Statement. Friedman delivered a check for the balance of the $60,000 loan (after deducting the expenses, including Friedman's attorneys' fees) to Stella. Pablo paid the balance of the purchase price with a cashier's check he obtained that morning with money from his investors and from his own savings. At that point Stella had her $100,000 sale price, less the amount paid Valley State. Pablo had his restaurant, subject to a $60,000 security interest in favor of First National. First National had Pablo's promissory note for $60,000, secured by a first security interest in the assets of the restaurant. First National could be reasonably confident that if the loan was not paid when due, it would have the right to take possession of the restaurant and sell it to satisfy the outstanding debt. The parties all shook hands and agreed among themselves that the closing was complete.

Secured transactions vary in detail and complexity. As the hundreds of published cases each year attest, some are less than orderly. Nonetheless, the transaction described here is typical of many commercial credit transactions.

Two aspects of the Fisherman's Pier story require some additional explanation. First, as you were reading the story you may have wondered what would have happened if one of the checks or documents had been missing. Most closings are conducted on the implicit understanding that unless all of the contemplated checks and documents are exchanged, none that are exchanged should be taken from the room or be of any effect. If one or more are missing, the parties will select one member of the group to hold the checks and documents currently available until all the contemplated checks and documents are available. Only then is the escrow agent authorized to deliver any of them and only then do they take effect.

Second, while the bank in this story obtained and filed a financing statement, it is important to realize that this step was not necessary to create a security interest enforceable against Pablo. U.C.C. §9-203(b). That a security interest is *enforceable* against the debtor Pablo means that, in the event of default, the secured party can foreclose on the collateral. By contrast, for a security interest to have priority over some other creditors, such as another secured party who lends against the same collateral, the creditor must *perfect* the interest by having the debtor authenticate a financing statement and filing that statement in the public records. (The subject of priority is reserved for Part Two of this book. We mention the financing statement here only because nearly all creditors who create a security interest choose to take the additional step of perfecting it against third parties. Not to mention it would have made the story unrealistic.)

As parties create security interests, they themselves sometimes confuse the formalities necessary to create a security interest with those necessary to perfect it. As you read the following section about the formalities necessary to create a security interest, the reasons for this confusion should become clearer.

B.   Formalities for Article 9 Security Interests

U.C.C. §9-203(b) lists three formalities required for the creation of a security interest enforceable against the debtor: (1) Either the collateral must be in the possession of the secured creditor or the debtor must have "authenticated a security agreement which contains a description of the collateral"; (2) value must have been given; (3) the debtor must have rights in the collateral. Only when all three of these requirements have been met does the security interest *attach* to the collateral and become enforceable against the debtor. U.C.C. §§9-203(a) and (b).

1.   Possession or Writing

Article 9 ratifies two different kinds of security agreements. Most agreements are in writing, but the secured creditor may create a security agreement without a writing if the creditor takes possession of the goods pursuant to an oral agreement to create a security interest.

Perhaps the most familiar example of a security agreement made effective by possession occurs in pawnshops. In a typical pawn, the debtor comes in with an item of some value. (In B-movies of the 1930s and 1940s, a down-and-out musician brings in his instrument to signify that he has reached the end of the line both financially and spiritually. This usually happens in the opening scene, before he meets the woman who saves his life, and so on. It is usually drizzling rain when he approaches the pawnshop.) The pawnshop offers to lend some amount against the goods, typically for 30 days. It holds the goods for the agreed period, during which time the debtor (if fortunes reverse quickly) can come in to pay off the loan and reclaim the collateral. If the debtor does not redeem the property by paying the loan, the pawnbroker sells the collateral and keeps the proceeds of sale.

While pawnshops and pawnbrokers have a long and colorful history, most commercial finance is not based on a creditor's possession of the collateral. Most debtors who borrow against their property want to keep the property while they repay the loan. Those who incur debt to buy a home, an automobile, or production machinery typically are unwilling to defer possession until the debt is paid. Most of the time their creditors really don't want possession anyway. Although commercial financiers realize that they would be more secure if they took possession of the pigs or packing emulsion against which they lend, the added safety is in most cases insufficient to justify the added expense. Even more important, in a commercial context most debtors use the collateral to produce the income to pay the loan. To accommodate them, lenders have devised methods (referred to as *field warehousing*) for taking possession of collateral while at the same time allowing debtors to use it. But even these methods add expense and complexity that most lenders consider unwarranted in most situations. Hence, the most common arrangement is to rely on a written security arrangement and leave the debtor in possession of the collateral.

The prototypical secured transaction is based on a writing. The debtor signs a document called a *security agreement*, which contains a description of the collateral, a description of the obligations secured, and provisions defining default, specifying the rights of the secured creditor on default, requiring that the debtor care for the collateral and keep it insured, and imposing other obligations on the debtor. (Recall that an example of such an agreement appears in Assignment 15.) When the debtor has signed such an agreement, the U.C.C. §9-203(b)(3)(A) requirement of an authenticated security agreement is fulfilled. See U.C.C. §9-102(a)(7).

Although the requirement is simple, in a surprising number of cases the parties fail to satisfy it. Either no security agreement is authenticated by the debtor or the one that is authenticated has no description of the collateral. When that occurs, the secured creditor often attempts to rely on other documents that, although not intended as a security agreement, nevertheless meet the skeletal requirements of U.C.C. §9-203(b)(3). In these cases, the courts are often asked to decide what is the minimum statement that will suffice.

In the following case, the debtor signed a financing statement to be filed in the public records to put other creditors on notice, but the parties did not otherwise document the transaction. When the debtor later filed for bankruptcy, the secured creditor needed to prove that it had a valid security interest in order to have an allowed secured claim.

In re Ace Lumber Supply, Inc.

105 B.R. 964 (Bankr. D. Mont. 1989)

JOHN L. PETERSON, UNITED STATES BANKRUPTCY JUDGE.
At Butte in said District this 4th day of October, 1989.

In this Chapter 7 case, the Trustee has filed objections to the motion of Minot Builders Supply for relief from the automatic stay under §362 of the Code. The basis for the objections is that Minot is not a secured creditor as alleged in the motion. The issue raised by the parties involves whether the Debtor executed a security agreement in favor of Minot to entitle Minot to perfect a security interest in Debtor's inventory, accounts receivable and equipment. . . .

The facts show the Debtor pre-petition operated a retail building supply business and purchased a number of products at wholesale from Minot. By April, 1988, the Debtor's account with Minot was about $160,000.00 and was in default. On April 26, 1988, a telephone conversation took place between two representatives of Minot and Debtor's president, which discussed the delinquent account and future credit purchases between the parties. A copy of the financial statement of the Debtor was reviewed by the parties and Richard Winje, vice president of Minot, took notes of the telephone conversation which reflect a series of numbers about Debtor's financial affairs. The parties decided the Debtor would pay cash on delivery for all future purchases and attempt to pay on the delinquent account in the ensuing two to three weeks.

On May 25, 1988, another three-way conversation between representatives of both companies took place. Taylor, the Debtor's president, was in the office of Minot's credit manager, who arranged a telephone call with Winje in Minot, North Dakota. Again, Winje took personal notes about the delinquent obligation. Taylor agreed, and the notes of Winje reflect, that the Debtor would pay $35,000.00 per month, with interest at 1% over prime, on the delinquent balance, a cash discount would be granted on new purchases if payment was timely made, the current purchases would be limited to $10,000.00 per month, and both the delinquent account and current purchases would be secured by Debtor's inventory, accounts receivable and equipment. . . . Minot's credit manager prepared a U.C.C.-1 financing statement, which was signed by Taylor. A copy was sent to Winje, who signed on behalf of Minot and the U.C.C.-1 financing statement was then sent to the Montana Secretary of State office, where it was filed on June 2, 1988. Subsequent to the agreement, one payment of $35,000.00 was made on the account by the Debtor, but no other payments were made. The agreed payment schedule was modified in November, 1988, but by the date of the bankruptcy petition on May 1, 1989, the Debtor was indebted to Minot in the sum of $162,031.00. Minot was scheduled as a secured creditor in the Debtor's Schedules. Other than the U.C.C.-1 financing statement, no other documents have been signed by the Debtor. All parties believed the execution of the U.C.C.-1 financing statement was sufficient to satisfy the Montana Uniform Commercial Code in order to create a valid security interest by Minot in Debtor's assets.

Based on these facts, Minot asserts in its Motion for Relief from the Automatic Stay that it has a valid security interest in the Debtor's assets described in the U.C.C.-1 financing statement. The Trustee contests such assertion on the basis that [U.C.C. §9-203(b)] requires a security agreement authenticated by the Debtor, and that execution of the U.C.C.-1 financing statement does not satisfy the requirement of [U.C.C. §9-203(b)].

Montana has adopted the provisions of the Uniform Commercial Code regarding perfection of security interests in property. As is pertinent to the present case, [U.C.C. §9-203(b)] states:

> . . . , a security agreement is not enforceable against the debtor or third parties with respect to the collateral and does not attach unless:
>   (a) . . . the debtor has [authenticated] a security agreement [that provides] a description of the collateral. . . ."

In order to perfect the security agreement and interest in the collateral against the Debtor and third parties, such as the Trustee in this case, [U.C.C. §9-310(a)] requires in most instances, a financing statement to be filed with the Secretary of State. [U.C.C. §9-501]. The formal requisites of a financing statement are detailed in [U.C.C. §9-502].

In discussing the requisites of a security agreement required under U.C.C. §9-203(b), the Official Code Comment reflects:

> 1. Subsection (1) states three basic prerequisites to the existence of a security interest: agreement, value and collateral. In addition, the agreement must be in writing unless the collateral is in possession of the secured party. When all of these elements exist, the security agreement becomes enforceable between the parties and is said to "attach." Perfection of a security agreement (see Section [9-308(a)]) will in many cases depend on the additional step of filing a financing statement (see Section [9-310(a)]) or possession of the collateral (Sections [9-312(a), (b) and 9-313(a)]). . . .
>
> 3. One purpose of the formal requisites stated in subsection [U.C.C. §9-203(b)(3)] is evidentiary. The requirement of a written record minimizes the possibility of future disputes as to the terms of a security agreement and as to what property stands as collateral for the obligation secured. . . .
>
> 5. The formal requisite of a writing stated in this section is not only a condition to enforceability of a security interest against third parties, it is in the nature of a Statute of Frauds. Unless the secured party is in possession of the collateral, his security interest, absent a writing which satisfies paragraph [U.C.C. §9-203(b)(3)], is not enforceable even against the debtor, and cannot be made so on any theory of equitable mortgage or the like. If he has advanced money, he is of course a creditor, and, like any creditor, is entitled after judgment to appropriate process to enforce his claim against his debtor's assets; he will not, however, have against his debtor the rights given a secured party by Part 5 of this Article on Default. The theory of equitable mortgage, insofar as it has operated to allow creditors to enforce informal security agreements against debtors, may well have developed as

a necessary escape from the elaborate requirements of execution, acknowledgment and the like which the nineteenth century chattel mortgage acts vainly relied on as a deterrent to fraud.

Since this Article reduces formal requisites to a minimum, the doctrine is no longer necessary or useful. More harm than good would result from allowing creditors to establish a secured status by parol evidence after they have neglected the simple formality of obtaining [an authenticated] writing. [Anderson, Uniform Commercial Code, vol. 8, §9-203:1, pp.660-661 (3d ed.)]

Anderson, supra, §9-203:18, p.670, further states:

When the secured transaction is nonpossessory, the security agreement must be in writing . . . The requirement of a written security agreement is in the nature of a statute of frauds . . . When a written security agreement is required but there is none, the creditor does not have a security interest in the collateral and can not enforce an oral agreement that he have such an interest as against the debtor or third parties.

The facts here show no formal security agreement was signed by the Debtor. What was signed by the Debtor was a standard U.C.C.-1 financing statement, attached to this Order. The creditor contends such suffices as a security agreement, citing In re Amex-Protein Development Corporation, 504 F.2d 1056 (9th Cir. 1974). In that case, a promissory note was signed by the debtor which included language that the note "is secured by a security interest in subject personal property as per invoices." A financing statement signed by the debtor was also filed on record describing items of personal property. There was no issue in the case that the parties intended, as they did in the present case, to create a security interest in the property described in the financing statement. Thus, two documents were signed, a promissory note and a financing statement. Under these facts, the Ninth Circuit Court of Appeals, adopting the district court holding, stated:

NINTH

The Court [Evans v. Everett, 183 S.E.2d 109 (1971)] found that since a security agreement could serve as a financing statement, there would be no sound reason why the converse should not be true. The court held that the financing agreement before it qualified as a security agreement. . . .

Accordingly, the promissory note herein qualifies as a security agreement which by its terms "creates or provides for" a security interest.

Yet, Matter of Bollinger Corp., 614 F.2d 924, 927 (3d Cir. 1980), discussing the holding of *Amex-Protein Development Corp.*, supra, states *Amex* "concluded that as long as the financing statement contains a description of the collateral signed by the debtor, the financing statement may serve as the security agreement and the formal requirements of Section 9-203(b) are met." The Third Circuit continued:

THIRD

Some courts have declined to follow the Ninth Circuit's liberal rule allowing the financing statement alone to stand as the security agreement, but have permitted the financing statement, when read in conjunction with other documents executed by the parties, to satisfy the requirements of Section [9-203(b)(3)(A)].

The Third Circuit adopted the so-called "composite document" rule by reading the promissory note, financing statement and correspondence between the parties together.

When the parties have neglected to sign a separate security agreement, it would appear that the better and more practiced view is to look at the transaction as a whole in order to determine if there is a writing, or writings, signed by the debtor describing the collateral which demonstrates an intent to create a security interest in collateral. [Id. at 928.]

The Court concluded the "minimum formal requirements of Section [9-203(b)(3)(A)] were met by the financing statement and the promissory note, and the course of dealings between the parties indicates the intent to create a security interest."

I do not read the holding of *Amex-Protein* under the facts of that case as allowing a security interest to attach where the only document signed by the debtor was the financing statement. Indeed, *Amex* specifically set the issue as: "Did the Promissory Note Create or Provide for a Security Interest?" and held that when the note was read with the financing statement a security interest was created. Moreover, according to Bollinger, "although a standard form financing statement by itself cannot be considered a security agreement, an adequate agreement can be found when a financing agreement is considered together with other documents." Id. at 927.

I conclude that under Montana law the composite document rule is available to provide evidentiary support to create a security interest in collateral. That rule, however, does not allow only a financing statement signed by the debtor to satisfy [U.C.C. §9-203(b)(3)(A)]. In this regard, I find a major distinction between *Amex-Protein* and the facts in the case sub judice. Other than the financing statement signed by the Debtor, the only other writing presented by the creditor were handwritten telephone notes attached to this Order. The combination of the financing agreement and the telephone notes do not satisfy the requirements of Article 9 in that none of them contain any language creating a security interest in the collateral. As *Amex-Protein* states:

While there are no magic words which create a security interest there *must be language in the instrument* which "leads to the logical conclusion that it was the intention of the parties that a security interest be created." [Id. at 1059. (Emphasis supplied.)]

Further, In re Owensboro Canning Co., Inc., 82 B.R. 450, 453-454 (W.D. Ky. 1988), interpreting identical Uniform Commercial Code sections under §9-203(b)3)(A) and §9-102(73) holds:

> Giving due consideration in tandem to [§§9-203(b)(3)(A) and 9-102(73)] of the Code, White and Summers contend that the question of whether a security agreement is established calls for two independent inquiries which may be stated as follows: The court must first resolve, as a question of law, whether the language embodied in the writing objectively indicates that the parties may have intended to create or provide for a security agreement. [citations omitted]. If the language crosses this objective threshold [citations omitted], that is, if the writing evidences a possible secured transaction and thus satisfies the statute of frauds requirement, then the fact-finder must inquire whether the parties actually intended to create a security interest. [citations omitted]. Parol evidence is admissible to inform the latter [citations omitted], but not the former, inquiry.

objective + subjective [handwritten marginal annotation]

White & Summers, supra.

Other courts have followed the same test. In re Zurliene, 97 B.R. 460, 464 (Bankr. S.D. Ill. 1989), states:

> While this court agrees with Community [creditor] that no specific words of grant are necessary in order to create a security agreement, it also believes that, in the absence of a separate written security agreement there must be some language to reflect the parties desire to grant a security interest, in the documents surrounding the transaction, in order to establish the existence of a security agreement under UCC §9-203. . . .

Applying the above law, I conclude there simply is no language in the only written instrument signed by the Debtor in this case (the financing statement) which embodies any intent to create a security agreement. There are no promissory notes, invoices or written correspondence which grant, create or "objectively indicates the parties intended to create a security interest." I hold as a matter of law the U.C.C.-1 financing statement standing alone is insufficient under [U.C.C. §9-203(b)(3)(A)] to create a security interest in the Debtor's assets. The objections of the Trustee are thus well taken.

IT IS ORDERED the Motion for Relief From the Automatic Stay filed by Minot Builders Supply Association is denied.

In *Ace Lumber Supply*, the court recognized the composite document rule, but still refused to read Winje's notes together with the financing statement, presumably because those notes were not authenticated by the debtor. In a later case, Longtree, Ltd. v. Resource

Control Intl., 755 P.2d 195 (Wyo. 1988), the court applied the composite document rule to include a document that not only was not authenticated by the debtor, but was not even in existence at the time the security agreement was signed. In *Longtree*, debtor RCI agreed to purchase logs and granted a security interest in the logs to the seller, Pacific Star. The purchase agreement described certain logs as the subject of the agreement, but expressly recognized that the agreement was "subject to revision from time to time." Later, the parties revised the agreement to include other logs, but the revision was not authenticated by the debtor. The court nevertheless employed the composite document rule to read the original agreement together with the revision. The court quoted from 8 Hawkland, Uniform Commercial Code Series §9-110:04 (1986):

> One question that has arisen is the extent to which more than one document may qualify as a security agreement, when one document contains the debtor's signature (and perhaps a description of some collateral) and another document contains a description of additional collateral. The majority rule appears to be that so long as the documents express some internal connection with one another, they may be read together for purposes of including the collateral described in the second document within the security agreement's umbrella. This, or even a more liberal application of the statute of frauds function of the security agreement is certainly in keeping with the liberality evidenced by section [9-108(a)]. Some courts, however, would probably require more than mere internal consistency or connection, instead demanding that there be a reference within one document to the other.

As for the Statute of Frauds function to be served by the writing, the court said that the language of the original agreement indicated that it did not purport to be a complete expression of the parties' agreement, but expressly contemplated future revisions. The revisions were consistent additional terms to the agreement and were therefore admissible. Some might conclude that *Longtree* is inconsistent with *Ace Lumber Supply*, while others might find a way to reconcile the two. In any case, it should be clear that, although the requirement is simple, case outcomes are not readily predictable at the margins.

Ace Lumber Supply illustrates the consequence of failing to obtain a signed security agreement: The creditor has no security interest and is therefore an unsecured creditor. When the parties intended to create a security agreement and thought they had succeeded, as they did in *Ace Lumber Supply*, the remedy is surprisingly harsh. Of course, for those who remember covering the Statute of Frauds in first-year contract law, the remedy of nonenforcement even in the face of clear intent of the parties should be familiar.

A number of justifications have been put forward for the requirement of an authenticated security agreement — so many and from so many different directions, in fact, as to cast doubt on whether the requirement can be justified. Not surprisingly, the rationales closely track those offered for the Statute of Frauds, and they raise many of the same issues.

1. *Preventing fraud.* Comment 3 to U.C.C. §9-203 explains that the requirement of a writing in Article 9 is "in the nature of a Statute of Frauds." That, however, hardly adds to its luster. As some leading commentators recently put it, "[t]he statute of frauds is a much despised statute that has fallen into disrepute in the United States, is the laughing stock of Article 2 and has been repealed in England." Speidel, White & Summers, Secured Transactions 89 (West 1987).

   The modern theory is that courts should be skeptical about agreements that are not in writing. If the parties are engaged in an honest transaction, they can memorialize their transaction with at least a minimal writing. On the other hand, to refuse flatly to enforce unwritten agreements, particularly when their existence is not even in dispute, may facilitate more fraud than it prevents.

   The applicability of the Statute of Frauds in the Article 9 context raises an interesting conceptual problem. In the Article 2 context, the fraud supposedly to be prevented is by one party to the contract against the other. In the Article 9 context, however, the fraud to be prevented might be either (1) a creditor falsely claiming the debtor granted it a security interest orally, or (2) the debtor and creditor together falsely claiming that they orally agreed to create a security interest in a situation where a third party will be the only one injured. The debtor, for example, may have filed for bankruptcy by the time the dispute arises (as was the case in *Ace Lumber*) and the secured creditor may be battling the trustee for the collateral, while the debtor sits out the argument. Some courts think that it makes more sense to require documentary evidence in the latter context than in the former, because in the former case, the person defrauded was a party to the alleged agreement and so would know whether it was made at the time or invented afterward. If a third party stood to end up with the collateral in the absence of a valid security interest, that party probably would have no direct knowledge of the transaction and no source of information about it except the writing. If the law did not even require that a writing be created, the defrauded person would be at the mercy of the contracting parties.

2. *Minimizing litigation.* If the security agreement and the description of collateral are in writing, there will be less chance

that the debtor and the creditor will differ as to whether a security interest was granted and, if so, what property was to serve as collateral. That in turn will reduce the number of litigated cases. It also assures that the only agreements enforced will be those intended by the parties, thus minimizing the possibility that a party who did not grant security will be held to have done so.

3. *Cautioning debtors.* The theory here is that many people make oral promises without reflecting on their consequences, but do not make written commitments so lightly. Requiring that the promise of security be in writing to be enforceable will result in debtors making better decisions about whether security agreements are in their interest.

4. *Channeling transactions.* By refusing to enforce oral security agreements, the law encourages the parties to put them in writing. Subscribers to this "channeling" justification usually believe that the parties ought to do that anyway because it is sound business practice, and that the law ought to reinforce such good business practices. (No, this view is not related to the channeling work done by Shirley MacLaine.)

   These last three justifications focus on the good that might come from requiring a writing generally. The cases also reveal many situations in which the requirement of a writing seems to have caused considerable harm. Not everyone is aware that a written security agreement is necessary. Among those who do know of the requirement, some will attempt to comply with it and fail. In both situations, creditors will lose valuable property interests, perhaps even where no one was harmed by the lack of a writing. Sophisticated creditors have no difficulty complying with the requirement, while occasional creditors fall victim to it. A writing requirement produces some neat, satisfying uniformity, but it may come at a high price in particular cases.

5. *Discouraging secured credit.* Secured creditors are typically banks and insurance companies, the most sophisticated financial institutions in the economy. As secured creditors they invoke a legal device that gives them collection advantages not universally shared. When they do so imperfectly, by failing to obtain a security agreement in writing, for example, some observers believe it is fair to pull them down to the level of the unsecured folks they were trying to best.

   The argument has emotional appeal, relying as it does on a kind of populist, David-against-the-corporate-Goliath ethos.

But it is seldom the sophisticated creditor that forfeits an interest in collateral by failing to document it. More commonly, it is the unsophisticated trade creditors and other commercial equivalents of widows and orphans who make the mistakes. Finally, it is worth noting that for every commentator who asserts that "public policy" seeks to discourage secured credit, there are at least two who assert that public policy seeks to encourage it.

The competing policy — that written security agreements should *not* be required in every case — is expressed in the doctrine of equitable mortgages. Under that doctrine, the courts can enforce oral security agreements where to do so would be "equitable." The doctrine has been specifically repudiated in both the text of, and the comments to, U.C.C. §9-203(b)(3). The Code is clear: Widows and orphans who want the special collection rights of the Article 9 secured creditor must jump through the hoops like everyone else.

Cases in which the security agreement did not contain a description of the collateral at the time it was authenticated by the debtor have divided the courts. For example, in In re Hewn, 20 U.C.C. 2d 745 (Bankr. W.D. Wis. 1976), the debtors signed the security agreement while it was blank and contained no description of the collateral. The secured creditor filled in the description of collateral and sent it to the debtors. The debtors received it without comment. Later, the debtors filed bankruptcy. At the request of the trustee, the court held the security interest unenforceable. The court concluded that the U.C.C., as "adopted by Wisconsin, does not allow a secured creditor to complete the security agreement or the financing statement, whether authorized or not, after the debtor has signed the instruments." In re Couch, 5 U.C.C. 255 (M.D. Ga. 1968), comes to a similar conclusion.

In two similar cases, however, the security agreements also contained no description of collateral when they were authenticated by the debtors, but the courts reached the opposite result. In re Blundell, 25 U.C.C. 571 (D. Kan. 1978); In re Allen, 395 F. Supp. 150 (E.D. Ill. 1975). The secured creditors in both cases filled in the descriptions afterwards, in accordance with the intention of the debtors. The courts in *Blundell* and *Allen* upheld the security agreements, commenting that the "sequence of events is immaterial" so long as the resulting document meets the statutory requirements.

It is useful to look closely at U.C.C. §9-203(b)(3)(A) to see what it says about the fill-in-the-blanks-later problem. Does that provision require that the description of collateral be in the agreement at the time the agreement is authenticated? Statutory interpretation often requires close reading.

2.   Value Has Been Given

A security interest is not enforceable until "value has been given." The drafters of the U.C.C. defined "value" in §1-201(44) so broadly that the requirement is virtually always met in a commercial transaction. As a result, it is difficult to discern any policy reason for the inclusion of the *value* requirement in U.C.C. §9-203(b)(1). Although the section does not say who must give value, the assumption seems to be that it is the creditor.

In most security agreements the debtors assume numerous obligations (pay the debt, keep the collateral insured, notify the creditor of any change of address, etc.), raising no question about whether the debtor's promises constitute value. But the secured creditor may assume few or no obligations. In fact, some forms of security agreements do not even have a place for the secured party's signature. Nevertheless, the creditor typically will have lent money, sold property to the debtor on credit, or promised to do one or the other in reliance on the debtor's grant or promise of a security interest. After all, that's usually why the debtor signed the agreement. It is true that a debtor might sign a security agreement with neither a loan nor the promise of a loan. But in that case, the debtor does not need a "no value given" defense. If the creditor hasn't made a loan, the debtor's defense to any collection effort — whether or not a security interest exists — is that the debtor doesn't owe anything to the creditor.

The definition of "value" used in Article 9 not only encompasses all forms of consideration that would support an ordinary contract, it even includes one form of consideration that does not pass muster in common law contracts: past consideration. U.C.C. §1-201(44)(b) provides that "a person gives value for rights (the security interest) if he acquires them . . . (b) as security for . . . a pre-existing debt." This means that even in situations where the debtor grants a security interest to secure an already outstanding debt and the creditor neither gives nor promises anything new in return, the creditor has given value under the Code definitions.

It is worth noting the ease with which an unsecured debt can become a secured debt at any time in the debtor-creditor relationship. While the typical transaction includes the grant of security at the time the debt is incurred, a significant portion of commercial transactions involve credit relationships that start out unsecured and become secured at some time during the course of the business dealings. Some trade creditors ordinarily extend credit on an unsecured basis, as Minot Builders Supply was doing in *Ace Lumber Supply*, but insist on a security agreement if the debtor does not pay within a reasonable time. Or a creditor may have a judgment stemming from a tort action or contract breach, but recognize that the pursuit of state collection remedies might be expensive. The creditor might agree to take payment of the outstanding obligation over time, secured by an interest in some property of the debtor. The Code provides the parties with an easy, enforceable mechanism to change the debtor-creditor relationship to include a security interest.

A situation in which the secured creditor did not give value at all is unlikely to lead to litigation for the simple reason that the secured creditor won't be injured by whatever happened. Nonetheless, the value requirement has not become entirely irrelevant to commercial transactions. For reasons we explain in later chapters, it may matter *when* the secured creditor gave value because only then did the security interest attach. A delay in giving value can sometimes lead to surprising results.

3. The Debtor Has Rights in the Collateral

It may seem to go without saying that a person cannot grant a security interest in someone else's property. Despite that, and the fact that the drafters of Article 9 were not getting paid by the word, they chose to address the matter anyway, in U.C.C. §9-203(b)(2).

The courts have read at least three significant subtexts into this rule. First, they read it to mean that if the debtor owns a limited interest in property and grants a security interest in the property, the security interest will generally attach to only that limited interest. See Comment 6 to U.C.C. §9-203. For example, Wilson Leasing owns machinery and leases it to Darby Construction. Darby grants a security interest in the machinery to CreditLine Investors. CreditLine will have a security interest only in what Darby owns, which is a leasehold. CreditLine will not have a security interest in the machinery. (Of course, CreditLine may have a cause of action against Darby for breach of covenants in the security agreement, and Darby may also have violated its agreement with Wilson Leasing as well.) To lend more dignity to this simple rule that a debtor can't grant a security interest in someone else's property, lawyers sometimes translate it into Latin (*nemo dat non habet*) and then back into old English (He who hath not, cannot give). In oral argument or negotiations, the effect is much more powerful than saying it in ordinary English.

Parties sometimes deliberately create security interests in property in which the debtor has something less than outright ownership. The debtor may, for example, be the lessee under a favorable long-term lease of real property. The right to occupy an apartment that today would rent for $1,000 a month, but to pay only the $440-a-month rent specified in the lease you signed five years ago, before the neighborhood was "hot," may be a valuable right indeed, particularly if many years remain on the lease term. The lessee's rights under such a lease may be a valuable asset. The lessee can grant a security interest in the lease, and if the debtor-lessee defaults under the secured loan, the secured creditor can foreclose on the lessee's rights under the lease. Similarly, a debtor may have no more than a contract to purchase property, but if the contract is favorable and enforceable, the debtor may have significant value. If it does, someone may be willing to lend against it. Once again, Article 9 is written expansively to encompass the creation of security interests in nearly anything that has value, if the parties choose to create them.

The second subtext the courts read into the rule may seem virtually a contradiction of the first. Some "owners" who acquired their rights in property by fraud have the power to transfer to bona fide purchasers ownership rights they themselves do not have. See U.C.C. §2-403. In the same analytic vein, such "owners" can also grant security interests in the rights they do not have. The subject is subtle, complex, and peripheral to an understanding of the basic concepts of security, so we do not address it until nearly the end of this book. For now, it is safe to ignore it.

The third subtext the courts read into the rule relates to the *time* at which the security interest becomes enforceable. For example, assume that Alice owns Blackwidget. The debtor, Harris, grants to Credit Corporation a security interest in Blackwidget. At this instant, CC's security interest is not enforceable because Harris has no rights in the collateral. If Harris later purchases Blackwidget from Alice, CC's security interest becomes enforceable at the precise instant Harris first acquires rights in the property. In later assignments, it will become clear why parties want their security interests to arise at the instant their debtors acquire the collateral. For now, we note that this provision makes that possible.

C. Formalities for Real Estate Mortgages

Like virtually every other aspect of real estate law, the formalities for the creation of real estate mortgages enforceable against the debtor differ from state to state. Most states require that the mortgage be in writing and signed by the debtor in the presence of one or more witnesses. Some, as in the Ohio statute that follows, require acknowledgment — essentially notarization — as well, although most require that step only as a prerequisite to recording the mortgage.

Ohio Revised Code Ann.

(Baldwin 1994)

§5301.01   ACKNOWLEDGMENT OF DEEDS, MORTGAGES, LAND CONTRACTS, AND LEASES

A deed, mortgage, land contract . . . or lease of any interest in real property must be signed by the grantor, mortgagor, vendor, or lessor, and such signing must be acknowledged by the grantor, mortgagor, vendor, or lessor in the presence of two witnesses, who shall attest the signing and subscribe their names to the attestation. Such signing must be acknowledged by the grantor, mortgagor, vendor, or lessor before a judge of a court of record in this state or a clerk thereof, a county auditor, county engineer, notary public, mayor, or county court judge, who shall certify the acknowledgment and subscribe his name to the certificate of such acknowledgment.

While real estate law generally requires more formality to create an enforceable security interest than does Article 9, real estate law is probably also more flexible in dealing with extreme cases. For example, in Wolf v. Schumacher, 477 N.W.2d 827 (N.D. 1991), the court found that an oral mortgage was excepted from the Statute of Frauds on the basis of partial performance. Had the case been governed by the U.C.C., it is unlikely that the security agreement would have been upheld. Notwithstanding an occasional case that saves a careless creditor, real estate practice is known for its obsessive adherence to the details of conveyancing, and the field abounds with stories of millions of dollars that were lost because someone failed to execute some particular paper in the agreed ritualized form. This part of law practice is not a good place for free spirits who are happier working out approaches that are "probably just as good."

Problem Set 8

8.1.   You are working as a law clerk for Judge Heather Clifford. Judge Clifford has given you the exhibits from a recently completed bench trial and asked you "whether they meet the authenticated security agreement requirement of U.C.C. §9-203(b)(3)(A)." The first is a promissory note for $50,000 that was signed by the debtor but not the secured party. The note recites that it is "secured by collateral described in a security agreement bearing the same date as this note."

The second is a financing statement signed by both parties that describes the collateral as "all of the inventory and equipment of [the debtor's] business." The third is a letter from the debtor's attorney to the creditor that states, "Enclosed are the promissory note and financing statement which give you a security interest in my client's inventory and equipment." No other writings were introduced. What do you tell the judge? Is this a question that can be answered from the documents alone, or do you need to read the testimony? U.C.C. §9-102(7).

8.2. You recently joined the legal department at First National Bank and work under the direct supervision of Morton Friedman. To begin your training, Friedman takes you to the Pablo Escobar closing (see pages 156-158). While you are driving back to the bank from the closing, Friedman asks you at precisely what point in time First National Bank's security interest attached to the Fisherman's Pier restaurant. What do you tell him? See U.C.C. §§1-201(44), 9-203(b)(3)(A), 2-501(1).

8.3 When you arrived at the Pablo Escobar closing, you pulled from your file the security agreement you had prepared. The description of collateral read: "The restaurant equipment described on the attached list." No list was attached. Ellen Bartell had promised to bring the list of equipment to the closing so it could be attached, but by the time you arrived at the closing, both of you had forgotten. Without realizing the error, the parties signed the security agreement without the list attached. The closing was completed and the loan proceeds were disbursed. Did the bank, at that moment, have a security interest enforceable against Pablo?

a. Two weeks later, Ellen Bartell remembered the list. She mailed it to Friedman with a letter of apology. When he received it, he immediately stapled it to the security agreement. He then asked you whether you thought the agreement was enforceable. What should your reply have been?

b. Would it have made any difference if Bartell had discovered the omission two years later and the parties did the same thing?

c. What if she discovered it after Pablo filed for bankruptcy and the parties did the same thing? See Bankr. Code §362(a)(4) and (5).

8.4. Early in your second year of solo practice, things seem to have gotten out of control. Although the work is incredibly interesting and you're making really good money, there never seems to be enough time to get everything done. Several months ago, you represented Mestre Equipment on a deal for Mestre to sell earthmoving equipment (essentially, a bulldozer) to Winfield Construction Company. At the closing, Mestre took $80,000 of the purchase price in the form of a promissory note secured by an interest in the bulldozer. A few weeks ago, Winfield filed for bankruptcy. Today, the trustee called and asked that you forward a copy of the security agreement.

When you checked the file, you noted that the financing statement on file with the Secretary of State describes the collateral as a "bulldozer," but the description of the collateral in the security agreement is simply blank. You noted the sick, breathless feeling that seemed to come from the pit of your stomach, but, since you began practicing law, you had learned to recognize as an adrenaline-induced palpitation of the heart. By rummaging around in the file you were able to jog your memory as to what had happened. Ed Mestre had promised you a description of the bulldozer a few days before the closing, but he hadn't sent it. At the closing, you had explained to the president of Winfield that the description of the bulldozer was forthcoming. He signed the security agreement with the description blank and orally authorized you to fill it in when you got the description. Mestre sent you the description a few weeks later when you were especially busy. You stuck the description in the file, meaning to come back to it later, but it slipped your mind.

Your first thought was self-loathing. How could *you*, who always had it together better than your law school classmates, have committed malpractice? Your thoughts turned darker yet when you realized that even if Mestre got most of his $80,000 out of your tight-fisted malpractice carrier (more likely, he'd net about $30,000 to $40,000 after his attorneys' fees — after all, he too was negligent, right?), you were going to be humiliated in the process, he was never going to trust you again, and you would probably never be able to pay even the balance of his loss. Eventually, you settle down to think about what really mattered. What do you do now?

Assume that your state has adopted the Model Rules of Professional Conduct. Those rules provide in relevant part:

Rule 1.4

(b) A lawyer shall explain a matter to the extent reasonably necessary to permit the client to make informed decisions regarding the representation.

Rule 1.6

(a) A lawyer shall not reveal information relating to representation of a client unless the client consents after consultation, except for disclosures that are impliedly necessary to carry out the representation, and except as stated in paragraph (b).

(b) A lawyer may reveal such information to the extent the lawyer reasonably believes it necessary: (1) to prevent the client from committing a criminal act that the lawyer believes is likely to result in imminent death or substantial bodily harm.

Rule 1.16

(b) . . . [A] lawyer may withdraw from representing a client if withdrawal can be accomplished without material adverse effect on the interests of the client, or if:

(1) the client persists in a course of action involving the lawyer's services that the lawyer reasonably believes is criminal or fraudulent; . . .

(3) the client insists upon pursuing an objective that the lawyer considers repugnant or imprudent . . .

Rule 3.3

(a)(2) A lawyer shall not knowingly fail to disclose a material fact to a tribunal when disclosure is necessary to avoid assisting a criminal or fraudulent act by the client.

Rule 4.1

. . . [A] lawyer shall not knowingly make a false statement of material fact . . . to a third person.*

Rule 8.4

A lawyer shall not engage in conduct involving dishonesty, fraud, deceit or misrepresentation.

Terminology

"Fraud" or "fraudulent" denotes conduct having a purpose to deceive and not merely negligent misrepresentation or failure to apprise another of relevant information.

So what do you do?

8.5. Assume that in the previous problem you finally turned the matter over to the client and withdrew. About five months later, you arrived at the bankruptcy court early for a scheduled hearing in another case and decided to listen in on the case then before the court. By coincidence, it was the trustee's case against Mestre Equipment. Mestre's new lawyer, Harold Silver, was examining Ed Mestre, the company president, on direct. Mestre testified that the signature on the security agreement was his own, that the agreement was "genuine" and that it expressed the agreement between the parties. Mestre was not asked, and did not say, when the description of collateral was filled in. Silver offered the agreement in evidence. The trustee did not object and the court admitted it. What do you do now?

---

*The comment to Rule 4.1 provides that a lawyer generally has no affirmative duty to inform an opposing party of relevant facts.—Eds.

Assignment 9: What Collateral and Obligations Are Covered?

A security interest is, in essence, the right to apply the value of the collateral to the holder's debt. It follows that the value of a security interest can be no greater than the value of the collateral covered by it. Legally, a security interest in a toothpick is very much the same thing as a security interest in a cruise ship, but the former is unlikely to be worth as much as the latter.

In this assignment, we begin with the legal principles that govern the interpretation of security agreements generally. Next we apply those principles to the interpretation of the security agreement description of the collateral. From the previous assignment, you know that every security agreement contains a description of the collateral. Each also contains a description of the obligations secured. These descriptions determine what will be covered (unless they conflict with some specific provision of law). In this assignment we will consider the possibility that a description will be so vague or indefinite that it will be legally insufficient. We discuss the circumstances that determine whether property acquired after the agreement is signed is included in descriptions and briefly describe the law governing descriptions of collateral in real estate mortgages. We close with a brief discussion of the law governing what obligations are secured.

As you read, keep in mind that in most secured transactions there will be at least two descriptions of collateral: one in the security agreement that is the contract between the parties and one in the financing statement that will be filed in the public records. In keeping with our focus in Part One of this book on the relationship between the debtor and the creditor, we examine only the security agreement description here. The financing statement description serves different functions. These are addressed in Assignment 18.

A. Interpreting Security Agreements

1. Debtor Against Creditor

A security agreement is, among other things, a contract between debtor and creditor. U.C.C. §9-102(a)(73). The rules that govern the interpretation of contracts generally apply to security agreements as well. See U.C.C. §§9-201(a), 1-201(3), and 1-205. Generally, the court will try to determine the intention of the parties as objectively expressed in the written security agreement. Where the agreement is ambiguous, parol evidence may be introduced; where the writing results from mutual mistake, the security agreement can be reformed. For example, in State Bank of La Crosse v. Elsen, 421 N.W.2d 116 (Wis. Ct. App. 1988), the bank agreed to lend the debtors $15,000, secured by a mortgage against their house. The bank sent the mortgage to the debtors for their signatures along with a cover letter indicating that the mortgage would secure only the $15,000 loan. But the mortgage itself, which both debtors signed, provided clearly that it secured *all* obligations the debtors owed to the bank. One such obligation was the debtors' previously unsecured guarantee of a $44,000 loan the bank had made to the debtors' son. When the debtors' son defaulted on the $44,000 loan, the bank attempted to foreclose against the debtor's house. The court denied foreclosure and instead reformed the mortgage so that it secured only the $15,000 loan. The guarantee remained unsecured, in accord with the agreement of the parties.

2. Creditor Against Third Party

Although a security agreement is a contract between the debtor and creditor, in most circumstances, it binds third parties as well. See U.C.C. §9-201(a). This should strike you as remarkable. We know of no other law that gives *A* and *B* the right to enter into an agreement that is binding on *C*. The effect of this provision is often that the secured party takes collateral that the other creditors were counting on for collection. Not surprisingly, when the courts are called upon to construe the meaning of security agreements in cases involving such a third party, the courts are likely to interpret them more literally than in accord with the intention of the debtor and secured party. That applies also to the provisions of a security agreement that state what collateral is covered by the agreement.

3. Interpreting Descriptions of Collateral

Article 9 defines many types of collateral, including "accounts" (U.C.C. §9-102(a)(2)), "equipment" (U.C.C. §9-102(a)(33)), "inventory" (U.C.C. §9-102(a)(48)), "instruments" (U.C.C. §9-102(a)(47)), "consumer goods" (U.C.C. §9-102(a)(23)), and "general intangibles"

(U.C.C. §9-102(a)(42)). Some of the definitions are not in accord with the common meanings of the defined terms. When parties use one of these terms in a security agreement, the courts usually (but not always) give the term its Article 9 rather than its common meaning. We think the courts are often wrong in doing so; the results can easily be contrary to the intention of parties who were not even aware of the Article 9 definitions of the words they were using. For example, the grant of a security interest in all of the debtor's *accounts* might be intended to include bank accounts, but U.C.C. §9-102(a)(2) defines "accounts" in such a manner that bank accounts are not included. Similarly, U.C.C. §9-102(a)(33) defines "equipment" much more broadly than does the common usage of that term. Only a person who has read the definition would be likely to guess that racehorses might be included in the term. See In re Bob Schwermer & Assoc., Inc., 27 B.R. 304 (Bankr. N.D. Ill. 1983). The owner of a restaurant could easily sign a security agreement with boilerplate language granting a security interest in its "general intangibles" without realizing that its liquor license would be included. See, e.g., In re Genuario, 10 U.C.C.2d 978 (Bankr. R.I. 1989) (grant of a security interest in debtor's "general intangibles" includes liquor license). We believe the better view is that words used in a security agreement, like words used in any other agreement, should be assigned the meaning that the parties intended in using them. The definitions of those same words under Article 9 are only one indication of what the parties might have intended by using them.

B.   Sufficiency of Description: Article 9 Security Agreements

The primary function of the description of collateral in a security agreement is to enable interested parties to identify the collateral. Those parties certainly include the debtor and creditor. They may also include other creditors disadvantaged by the grant of security, trustees in bankruptcy, or courts that must decide cases brought by any of them. To identify the collateral means to determine that a particular item of property is or is not included. In the following case, the court required an unusually high level of precision in describing collateral.

In re Carlos

215 B.R. 52 (Bankr. C.D. Cal. 1997)

Samuel L. Bufford, United States Bankruptcy Judge.

II.   RELEVANT FACTS

[D]ebtors used their Sears charge card to purchase a washing machine for $449.99 on the day after Thanksgiving in 1995, and a 19-inch television and a VCR for $499.76 on March 17, 1997. The debtors filed their bankruptcy case on June 2, 1997.

Sears claims a valid security interest in the merchandise here at issue. The only evidence that Sears has submitted in support of this claim is a statement at the bottom of each of the sales slips which says, "PURCHASED UNDER MY SEARSCHARGE AGREEMENT, INCORPORATED BY REFERENCE, I GRANT SEARS A SECURITY INTEREST IN THIS MERCHANDISE UNTIL PAID, UNLESS PROHIBITED BY LAW" (capitalized in original). Sears has not provided any evidence of the Searscharge agreement.

III.   LEGAL ANALYSIS

In general, the validity of a security interest in goods is determined under California law by reference to Division 9 of the California Commercial Code, which is California's version of Article 9 of the Uniform Commercial Code. For a valid security interest in consumer goods, Sears must meet these requirements in addition to those set forth in the California Civil Code. Sears has the burden of proof to show that it has a valid security interest.

Under both the Uniform Commercial Code and the California version thereof, a valid security interest in personal property requires that (1) either (a) the debtor has signed a security agreement which contains a description of the collateral, or (b) the secured party has possession of the property pursuant to agreement, (2) value has been given, and (3) the debtor has rights in the collateral. [U.C.C. § 9-203]. A description of collateral is sufficient if it reasonably identifies the collateral.

In this case there is no question that the second and third elements are satisfied. In addition, the charge slips are sufficient as signed security agreements.

The main issue governing the validity of Sears' security interest in this case is whether the charge slip contains an adequate description of the collateral. Only one of the sales slips is adequate in this respect. The first, dated 11/24/95, involves merchandise described as "Washer, W." The second involves merchandise described as "TV F19240G"[1] and "VCR, HRVP63".

Collateral must be described in one of two ways — by type or by item. The sufficiency of a description of collateral turns on whether the description adequately describes the type of assets or the individual items.

A description of assets by type is sufficient if it reasonably identifies what is described. Such a description is sufficient if the collateral is exclusively used for the described purpose or can only be classified as the type of collateral described.

Individual items are sufficiently specified if the description meets a two-part test. First, if the collateral is such that the debtor may own other similar items (regardless of whether the debtor in fact has more than one), the description must enable a third party to distinguish the collateral from other property. Alternatively, if the debtor is not likely to own more than one such item, a more general description is sufficient.

The court adopts a community standard in determining whether a debtor may own other similar items to those listed on a charge slip. For consumer purchases, a person is likely to own more than one item of a particular type (such as a refrigerator, a baseball glove or a pair of socks) if an ordinary consumer in the community would have more than one item of this type. While the debtors in this case may be in an economic status where multiple ownership of such goods is unlikely, the court has been provided no evidence on this issue. Furthermore, the court finds it impractical to discriminate between economic classes on this issue: there should be single rule applicable to all debtors, absent unusual circumstances.

In this case, the court finds that a debtor in the Central District of California is only likely to own one washing machine. Thus the description on the Sears charge slip is sufficient for California Commercial Code purposes to create a valid security interest in the washing machine.

On the other hand, many families in the Central District of California have more than one television or VCR. The court finds that the descriptions in the charge slips for the television and the VCR are insufficient for California Commercial Code purposes to create a security interest in these items.

Whether a description enables "interested parties" to identify collateral depends on who the interested parties are, what information

---

1. While the charge slips also have a code following the identity of each of these items, neither Sears nor the debtors have provided any meaning for these codes. Because Sears bears the burden of showing that it holds a valid security interest in these items, the court disregards these codes.

they start with, and what obligations can be placed on them to gather additional information. For example, in In re Schmidt, 1987 U.S. Dist. LEXIS (W.D. Okla. 1987), the security agreement described the collateral as "crops . . . growing on the real estate described by ASCS Farm Serial Numbers . . . J-528, J-552, J-557 & J-572." People dealing in agricultural finance would generally know what these numbers mean and how they could use them to look up the descriptions of the land in other records. The parcels described by the ASCS numbers included both land not farmed by the Schmidts and land farmed by them. The court held the description adequate.

Other courts, particularly bankruptcy courts in cases involving consumer goods, have been less tolerant of descriptions that require additional inquiry to enable a stranger to the transaction to identify the specific goods that serve as collateral.

In re Ziluck

127 B.R. 285 (Bankr. S.D. Fla. 1991)

A. JAY CRISTOL, UNITED STATES BANKRUPTCY JUDGE . . .

The debtors filed for relief under Chapter 7 of the Bankruptcy Code on December 26, 1990 and listed their debt to Tandy in the amount of $3,204.70. Tandy claims a security interest in the consumer goods whose purchase gave rise to the debt and thereby seeks to recover possession of said goods. . . .

. . . The issue is whether the security interest has attached and thereby become perfected under [U.C.C. §9-308(a)].

[U.C.C. §9-203(b)(3)(A)] provides in part that a security interest is not enforceable against the debtor or third parties with respect to the collateral and does not attach unless the debtor has signed a security agreement which contains a description of the collateral. In order for a description of collateral in a security agreement to be sufficient it must "make possible the identification of the items in which a security interest is claimed." American Restaurant Supply Co. v. Wilson, 371 So. 2d 489, 490 (1st DCA 1979). See also In re S & J Holding Corp., Shazamm Enterprises Ltd., 42 Bankr. 249 (S.D. Fla. 1984). The description of the collateral in a security agreement must be more specific than that required in a financing statement. The "security agreement should describe the collateral with details sufficient for third parties to be able to reasonably identify the particular assets covered." American Restaurant, supra, at page 490.

"The cases interpreting the 'reasonably identified' provision have been fairly strict. Language such as 'all property of the undersigned of every name and nature whatsoever' and 'all other personal property' is clearly too broad." *In re S & J Holding,* supra, at page 250. The security agreement in this case, attached as Exhibit A to Tandy's Application, provides in paragraph 12 that a security interest is retained "in all merchandise charged to your Account." This description does not reasonably identify the goods on which the security interest is claimed. The description does not provide any details which would enable a third party to identify the assets which are covered by the security agreement.

The only conclusion possible is that the security agreement fails to comply with [U.C.C. §9-203(b)(3)(A)] since it does not contain a description of the collateral, as that requirement has been interpreted by the courts. Hence, the security interest does not attach to the consumer goods. . . . The Motion of Tandy Credit Corp. is denied.

Judge Cristol mixes two explanations for his holding in this short opinion. One is that a third party working only with this description could not identify the collateral. Recall, however, that was true of the crops in *Schmidt.* The court there was not bothered. On appeal, the district court made short work of Judge Cristol's explanation, and reversed:

[UCC §9-108(a)] provides that "any description of personal property . . . is sufficient whether or not it is specific if it reasonably identifies what is described." The Court believes that the language in paragraph 12 of the security agreement, "we retain a security interest under the Uniform Commercial Code in all merchandise charged to your account," reasonably identifies the property subject to the security interest namely any property purchased with the subject credit card. Accordingly, the Court finds that the security agreement contains a sufficient description of the collateral as required by [UCC §9-203(b)(3)(A)]. In re Ziluck, 139 Bankr. 44 (S.D. Fla. 1992).

Judge Cristol's second explanation is essentially that the description includes too much property. After *Ziluck,* Article 9 was amended to state that "A description of collateral as 'all the debtor's assets' or 'all the debtor's personal property' or using words of similar import does not reasonably identify collateral." U.C.C. §9-108(c). The drafters chose not to state their reasons for adopting this provision. Based on prior case law, the probable reason was that the drafters feared that use of such descriptions would make it too easy to grant a security interest in all of one's property without realizing one was doing so. There is no indication that the provision was intended or will be interpreted to prevent a debtor from giving a security interest in all of the debtor's assets by describing them individually or by categories.

C.   Describing After-Acquired Property

After-acquired property is a term used to refer to property that a debtor acquires after the security interest is created. Recall our discussion back in Assignment 3 about accounts as possible collateral. We talked about how an audio home equipment manufacturer might give its dealers 30 days to pay, and that the "accounts receivable" might be valuable to a creditor of the manufacturer as collateral. But there is an interesting hitch in using the accounts as collateral: The accounts that exist on any given day will disappear as they are paid off. The collateral existing on the day of the loan transaction may shrink considerably in 30 days and nearly disappear in 60 or 90. If the manufacturer remains in the same business and operates on the same terms, more accounts will be generated during that time. The overall value of the debtor's accounts may remain steady. The accounts that are generated after the security agreement is signed are "after-acquired property" — that is, they are acquired by the debtor after the debtor signed the security agreement. Having them as collateral is crucial to the position of the accounts-secured lender. Both debtors and secured creditors may want them to serve as collateral.

Under some of the laws that preceded Article 9, it was impossible to grant a security interest in after-acquired property. If the parties wanted after-acquired property to secure an obligation between them, they had to execute a security agreement each time the debtor acquired additional property. At the time, that was a staggering inconvenience with collateral such as accounts. The drafters of Article 9 addressed the problem by validating provisions in security agreements that extend the description of collateral to after-acquired property. U.C.C. §9-204(a). Such descriptions commonly include the words "after-acquired property," but descriptions can use other words and, as is discussed in the case below, the inclusion of after-acquired property can even be implied in compelling circumstances.

After-acquired property clauses remain in common use, but with computerization of the American economy, the necessity for them is declining. A computer can be programmed to grant a security interest in each account as it is created. As In re Carlos illustrated, some department stores include a security agreement on the receipt for each credit purchase. Similarly, there is no reason why the record of the sale of a case of toothpaste from a distributor to a retail drugstore cannot contain the grant of a security interest. But in the latter illustration, the individual grant of a security interest offers no obvious advantage over an after-acquired property clause and so seems unlikely to replace it.

In the following case, the court discusses the differing views on the necessity for a specific provision in the secured agreement as a prerequisite to claiming after-acquired collateral as security.

Stoumbos v. Kilimnik

988 F.2d 949 (9th Cir. 1993)

FLETCHER, CIRCUIT JUDGE:

[On May 1, 1982, Kilimnik sold a business to AAM, retaining a security interest. The description of collateral was obscure and scattered through several documents, but the court held it to be the equivalent of "inventory and equipment." The security agreement did use "after acquired" language with respect to accounts receivable. When the buyer defaulted in October 1985, Kilimnik seized all of the inventory and equipment then in the possession of the buyer, including inventory and equipment acquired by the buyer after May 1, 1982. The buyer filed bankruptcy and the trustee, Stoumbos, sued Kilimnik for return of the after-acquired inventory and equipment.]

Kilimnik, however, argues that, where a creditor acquires a security interest in equipment and inventory, the court should find that this interest automatically extends to after-acquired inventory and equipment. There is substantial support for the proposition that, where a financing statement or security agreement provides for a security interest in "all inventory" (or uses similar broad language), the document incorporates after-acquired inventory. The rationale is that inventory is constantly turning over, and no creditor could reasonably agree to be secured by an asset that would vanish in a short time in the normal course of business. The position that no express language is required is described as the "majority" view, American Family Marketing, 92 Bankr. at 953, or the "modern trend." Sims Office Supply, 83 Bankr. at 72. There is, however, contrary authority, which reasons that "the [U.C.C.] contemplates that a security agreement should clearly spell out any claims to after acquired collateral." Covey v. First Nat'l Bank (In re Balcain Equip. Co., Inc.), 80 Bankr. 461, 462 (Bankr. C.D. Ill. 1987).

No Washington or Ninth Circuit cases appear to be directly on point. We conclude that we need not decide whether to adopt the "majority" view in this case since the Purchase Agreement does not contain the usual language granting a security interest in "all inventory" or "inventory," but only in the items specifically described in paragraph 1 as "inventory . . . on hand at May 1, 1982."

In addition, the rationale of the "automatic" security interest cases does not apply to after-acquired equipment. Those cases discuss cyclically depleted and replenished assets such as inventory or accounts receivable. Unlike inventory, equipment is not normally subject to frequent turnover.

We are aware that the financing statement mentions after-acquired equipment, suggesting that the parties intended Kilimnik's security interest would extend this far. Yet we must look to the entire circumstances under which the purchase agreement was made to ascertain its meaning. Under Washington law, a contract is interpreted by reference to many contextual factors, including the subject matter of the transaction, the subsequent conduct of the parties and the reasonableness of their interpretations.

The trustee here advances the more reasonable interpretation: Kilimnik took a kind of "purchase money" interest in the equipment he sold to AAM, but he did not get the additional security of a blanket interest in all equipment the company ever acquired after the sale. The subject matter of the transaction also supports this conclusion.

Kilimnik would not have had a clear reason to want after-acquired equipment covered by the purchase agreement. As we have seen, equipment, unlike inventory, is not normally subject to frequent turnover. Even if limited to the equipment on hand at the time of the sale, his interest would have been secure.

In summary, we conclude that Kilimnik's security interest was limited to equipment and inventory owned by AAM on May 1, 1982. . . .

The preceding case illustrates the typical use of after-acquired property clauses: to enable the security interest to "float" on collateral, the precise components of which are constantly changing but which as a whole remains relatively stable in identity and value, much like the accounts example we used to introduce this idea.

While after-acquired property clauses are most frequently used with regard to inventory and accounts receivable, they are also employed in other contexts. After-acquired property clauses are not unusual when creditors take interests in broad categories of collateral such as equipment, farm products, or general intangibles. With regard to each, a particular debtor is likely to be disposing of some items and acquiring others over time, so that it makes more sense to think of the collateral as the category rather than as the individual items within it at any given time. After-acquired property clauses make it possible for the parties to a long-term financing relationship to do that. Such a security interest is also sometimes referred to as a *floating lien*.

Lending contracts often link the total value of the collateral, including after-acquired collateral, to the total amount of the loan. A bank, for example, may agree to lend 65 percent of the purchase price of all inventory owned by the debtor. When inventory is sold, the debtor must pay down the loan; when new inventory arrives, the bank advances a portion of the purchase price. But after-acquired property clauses are not always linked to agreements to make additional loans. Under some arrangements, additional acquisitions of collateral covered by the after-acquired property clause are simply a windfall to the creditor. Perhaps for this reason, after-acquired property clauses become ineffective upon the filing of a bankruptcy case. Bankr. Code §552(a). We explore this subject in more detail in Assignment 11.

D.   Sufficiency of Description: Real Estate Mortgages

While the rules regarding descriptions of collateral in real estate mortgages are controlled by a separate body of law, they are remarkably similar to the rules under Article 9. The description in a mortgage must describe the land sufficiently to identify it. But the description may refer to separate documents, such as maps or plats for that purpose. A description may be so vague as to render the mortgage void. But if the description is merely ambiguous, parol evidence may be used to explain its meaning. Broad descriptions such as "all grantor's property in the county" are generally good as between the mortgagor and mortgagee. (Real estate lawyers refer to these as "Mother Hubbard clauses," presumably because the cupboard will be bare when the next creditor arrives.)

The physical nature of real estate makes it easier to identify than many kinds of personal property. While older descriptions of land, particularly in the northeastern United States, may describe it by reference to "monuments" such as trees, rocks, and streams that are later difficult to identify or less than permanent, in most parts of the United States, descriptions are by reference to maps or plats that are ultimately located by reference to monuments (iron stakes) placed by government survey. The stakes are carefully maintained as reference points for surveyors. As a result, a well-written description of real property can identify it with virtually no uncertainty.

In real estate practice, the debtor executes a separate mortgage document each time the debtor adds land to the secured creditor's collateral. Real estate law recognizes a doctrine of *after-acquired title* that applies to mortgages and permits an earlier mortgage document to convey a security interest in land later acquired by the mortgagor. See United Oklahoma Bank v. Moss, 793 P.2d 1359 (Okla. 1990). But, in contrast to the situation with respect to personal property, where after-acquired property clauses are common, there seems to be little need for the doctrine with respect to real estate transactions and correspondingly little use.

Permanent buildings and other structures permanently affixed to land (known as *fixtures*) become part of the real estate. They are automatically included in a description that refers only to the land. The rule applies whether they are affixed to the real estate before or after the mortgage is executed. Thus, in a sense, every real estate mortgage automatically reaches "after affixed" property. In later assignments we will discuss property affixed to real estate in greater detail.

E.   What Obligations Are Secured?

The general rules regarding interpretation of security agreements apply to provisions specifying what obligations are secured. Virtually any obligation can be secured if the parties make their intention clear. In Pawtucket Institution for Savings v. Gagnon, 475 A.2d 1028 (R.I. 1984), the mortgage secured a promise by the debtor to build a building. That is, if the debtor did not build the building, the debtor would owe a debt for the resulting damages and the mortgage against already existing real property would secure it. In indicating what obligations are secured, no particular form is required. If the security agreement states that it secures a certain debt in the amount of $25,000 and such a debt exists, it is secured. A security interest can also secure a debt that does not yet exist but which the parties contemplate will come into existence in the future. If the future obligation will come into existence as the result of an additional extension of credit by the secured creditor, it is referred to as a *future advance*. U.C.C. §9-204(c) provides that "A security agreement may provide that collateral secures . . . future advances. . . ."

Debtors often execute agreements that purport to secure every obligation to the secured creditor of any kind that may come into existence in the future. If the creditor later lends additional money, a security agreement with such a future-advance clause will assure that the subsequent loan is secured from its inception. Such provisions are often referred to as dragnet clauses. They are valid when contained in Article 9 security agreements. For an example of a very simple, straightforward dragnet clause, see paragraph 3 of the Deutsche Financial Services "Agreement for Wholesale Financing" in Assignment 15.

Future-advance clauses can be included in real estate mortgages. The typical construction mortgage, under which the lender agrees to make advances each time construction reaches designated stages of completion, is an example. There are, however, some limitations on the use of future-advance clauses in real estate mortgages. First, some states "disfavor" the use of dragnet clauses by demanding strict proof that the later advance is one that was in the contemplation of the parties at the time they executed the real estate mortgage. In those states the mortgagee will want to describe the future debt as specifically as possible at the time the mortgage is granted and refer to the mortgage in the documentation for the future debt when it is incurred. Second, some states require that a recorded mortgage indicate a maximum amount of indebtedness to be secured; the mortgage cannot effectively secure more than the amount indicated in it. For example, a $75,000 home mortgage in such a state might recite that it secures a loan in the initial amount of $75,000, that future advances are contemplated, but the mortgage will not secure obligations exceeding $90,000. See, e.g., Fla. stat. ch. 697.04 (1994). Finally, in some states real property cannot secure obligations not reducible to money. Fluctuating accounts, contingent debts, or promises to build a building as referred to above do not fall into that category. Any of them could be reduced to a specific dollar amount at the time of foreclosure. But an obligation to provide future support for a living person might be much more difficult to value and as a result not considered a proper subject of security.

Security agreements and mortgages usually provide that, in the event of default, the debtor will pay the creditor's attorneys' fees and other expenses of collection. They authorize the creditor to add these amounts to the secured indebtedness. These provisions are considered valid and effective in both personal property and real estate security agreements, and, as you have already seen in Assignment 7, in bankruptcy. In recent years, courts have begun to refer to them as "nonadvance" provisions, because the creditor does not advance the amount secured by them to the debtor. Interest that accrues on a secured obligation is also included in the nonadvance category. Between debtor and secured creditor, provisions securing nonadvances are of equal validity and effect with those securing advances.

Problem Set 9

9.1.   Robert and Mary Gillam have come to see you about their financial problems. For the past seven years, they have made their living farming. When they started, they borrowed $35,000 from the First National Bank of Frenville and granted a security interest in "crops growing on the debtor's farm in Osprey County, about 14 miles from Tilanook" and most of their farm equipment. (The location information is correct and the debtors own only a single farm.) The Gillams have paid that loan down to $19,000. It is now the middle of the growing season and the Gillams don't have enough cash to get them through the harvest. They would like to borrow against their current crop, but First National won't lend them any more money. The second lender they approached, Production Credit

Association (PCA), told them that the current crop was unacceptable as collateral because "First National already has it, and we don't make crop loans in second position." This upset the Gillams, because they had assumed that their current crop was not covered by First National's security interest.

    a. Who is right on the point of law?

    b. What should the Gillams do? U.C.C. §§9-108(a), (b), 9-203(b)(3)(A), 9-204.

    9.2. The Gillams are also raising sheep on the property. They sell the wool and sometimes the cuddly little lambs themselves. (You've heard of lamb chops, right?) They would like your written opinion that the sheep are not covered by First Bank's security interest. With the opinion letter, they say that PCA will make a loan against the sheep. Can you give it?

    9.3. Richard Cohen, a client of your firm, asked Sandra Bernhard, the partner for whom you work, for an opinion on a "situation" in which he is involved. Because it is a very small matter, Bernhard has asked you to look into it, tell her what the arguments will be on each side, and evaluate them. You have learned that Cohen lent $30,000 to Aircraft Video Marketing, Inc. (AVMI) four years ago and entered into a security agreement that listed the collateral as "All of Debtor's equipment, including replacement parts, additions, repairs, and accessories incorporated therein or affixed thereto. Without limitation the term 'equipment' includes all items used in recording, processing, playing back, or broadcasting moving or still pictures, by whatever process." AVMI owned certain video equipment at the time the security agreement was signed and acquired additional video equipment of a similar nature later. Like the original equipment, the additional equipment was used in AVMI's business for playing back motion pictures. When AVMI defaulted, another creditor of AVMI's, First National Bank of Omaha, claimed the equipment. After Cohen established that his security interest predated First National's, they dropped their claim to the original equipment. But they continue to claim the equipment AVMI bought later, saying that it is not covered by the terms of Cohen's security agreement. What's your assessment?

    9.4. You are practicing with a small firm in St. Louis that does all the legal work for Walter's Department Store (Walter's). Walter's practice has been to take a security interest in everything that a credit card holder purchases on his or her account. While they do not repossess clothing or other items without resale value, they do repossess many kinds of appliances and household goods. They make the decision after default. Prior to Judge Cristol's opinion in *Ziluck*, they thought they obtained the right to do such repossessions by the following language in the application for a Walter's credit card: ". . . and cardholder grants Walter's a security interest in all items purchased on the account." The reversal of *Ziluck* on appeal is comforting, but Susie McNeil, Walter's credit manager, is worried nonetheless. "If one court can do it, so can another. How do we know that some Court of Appeals isn't going to go the same way as Judge Cristol?" One reason McNeil is looking for greater certainty is that Walter's may need to borrow against its accounts. Can you think of a way for Walter's to take security interests that would be good even under Judge Cristol's reasoning? U.C.C. §§9-203(b)(3)(A), 9-102(23), 9-108(e).

9.5.   Shortly after your conference with Susie McNeil, you met with Sharon Hammacher, general counsel for the Sun Bank chain. Sharon, a close friend from law school, has been considerably more successful than you, and tries to steer business your way when she can. Sharon is redrafting the standard documents the bank uses in routine commercial lending. After several cases in which loan officers have failed at the simple task of checking a few boxes on the security agreement to indicate the collateral covered, Sharon has an idea: The Bank's form security agreement should provide that the Bank takes a security interest in absolutely everything the debtor has, and then the loan officer and the debtor should check boxes to indicate what is *not* included. That way, any omissions will cut against the debtor, not the Bank. Sharon wants to know what you think of her idea. She would also like your suggestions on how to word the omnibus clause. What do you tell her? U.C.C. §9-108(c).

9.6.   As a matter of policy, why should a description that says "all the debtor's property" be invalid?

9.7.   a. In 1997, your firm represented Ed Mestre in the closing of a working capital loan from Firstbank. In that transaction, Ed gave Firstbank a security interest in his "accounts." When Ed recently sold a piece of real estate, the buyer refused to pay Ed the proceeds of sale without a release from Firstbank. Ed doesn't want to go to Firstbank for this release because the relationship is bad, so he has come to you. "I had no idea that the proceeds owing from a sale of real estate were an account," Ed tells you.

Having done your research, you realize that proceeds from the sale of real property were not "accounts" when the agreement was signed in 1997; they only became accounts upon the adoption of revised Article 9. Did the expansion in the Article 9 definition of "accounts" expand the scope of Firstbank's security interest?

b.   If so, does your firm need to do anything about the hundreds of security agreements covering "accounts" it prepared while former Article 9 was in force?

c.   If not, how do you handle this problem with Firstbank?

Assignment 10: Proceeds, Products, and Other Value-Tracing Concepts

In the previous assignment, you learned that when a debtor and creditor contract for a security interest, they must describe the collateral. Once they have done so, they typically put the documents away. They are likely to refer to the documents again only when some difficulty arises in their relationship, by which time it is often too late to make changes.

In the meantime, items of collateral may go through transformations that take them outside the description of collateral in the security agreement. Oil may become plastic, and then plastic shipping containers. Individual cattle in a herd may die, but only after they have produced an even larger number of offspring. Inventory that serves as collateral may be sold on credit. The account debtors who purchased the inventory may pay their accounts with checks, and the debtor may deposit those checks into a bank account.

When a debtor and creditor anticipate such transformations, they usually choose to have the security interest continue in the collateral as it changes form or, if the debtor disposes of it to a third party, to have the security interest attach to whatever the debtor receives in return.

The source of this preference lies in the nature of the secured creditor's relationship to the collateral. Secured creditors look to collateral for repayment. Although they care about the form their collateral takes, they care more about what it is worth. When the debtor transforms the value of an item of collateral to some other type of asset, the secured creditor usually wants and expects the security interest to follow. Were it otherwise, a debtor could unilaterally deprive the creditor of the value of its security interest.

At the time the parties negotiate the security agreement, the debtor generally is willing to permit the security interest to follow the value because the debtor too is typically thinking in terms of value. By giving its secured creditor an interest that "floats" from one item to another as the value is transferred, transformations in value become less threatening to the secured creditor. Where security interests follow value, secured creditors have less reason to object to such transformations. As a result, debtors find it easier to persuade creditors to grant them freedom to make transformations when necessary.

One way to assure that a security interest will follow the value is to include express language in the description of the collateral in the security agreement that covers all forms the value is likely to take. For example, a bank that lends against inventory can easily anticipate that the inventory will be sold, resulting in accounts, negotiable instruments, or money. If the description of collateral is "inventory, accounts, instruments, money, and bank accounts," transformation of the value from one of these forms of collateral to another will not reduce the value of the bank's security. Similarly, if the parties contemplate the possibility that the collateral will be destroyed by accident but the loss will be insured, they can provide that any payment from an insurance company for loss of the inventory also will serve as collateral.

As you might imagine, secured creditors cannot always anticipate the transformations their collateral might undergo or the nature of the property for which it may be exchanged. An alternative might be to encumber all of the debtor's property. But that may unduly restrict a debtor. Consider, for example, the debtor who is financing not the entire business, but only a single piece of equipment. If that debtor grants a security interest in the equipment and every other form that value might later take, the debtor might not be able to obtain inventory financing or other equipment financing. And all the secured creditors would want a first claim on the debtor's accounts, instruments, money, and bank accounts.

A more practical solution is to employ what we call *value-tracing concepts* — terms of art that indicate that in certain kinds of transformations of the collateral the security interest should follow the value in prescribed ways.

The value-tracing concepts most commonly employed are *proceeds, products, rents, profits,* and *offspring.* Debtors and creditors use these terms of art in security agreements and legislatures use them in statutes. In theory, each of these terms identifies a particular set of tracing rules, although, as is usual in law, neither the parties that use the terms, nor the courts that interpret them, always agree on what the rules are. We begin with the most important of these concepts.

A. Proceeds

1. Definition

Read the definition of "proceeds" in U.C.C. §9-102(a)(64). Under this definition, a security interest will follow the value of collateral through some transformations but not others. If the debtor sells the collateral, the security interest will attach to the price paid, whether it is in the form of an account, a promissory note, or cash.

Under former Article 9, there was a split of authority as to whether rent received for the use of collateral was proceeds of the collateral. The argument for inclusion of rent in proceeds was strengthened with the addition of U.C.C. §9-102(a)(64)(C), including "rights arising out of collateral" as proceeds.

Note, however, that the rules are overly generous to the secured creditor in an important sense. The secured creditor is able to claim all of the proceeds of a sale or rental, even though a substantial part of that value does not flow from the collateral, but is instead contributed by the debtor. Consider, for example, the case of a bank that finances the inventory of a furniture store. The store buys an item of furniture wholesale for $500 and sells it retail for $1,000. To generate the $1,000 in proceeds the bank will claim when the item is sold, the debtor store must maintain a place of business, advertise, provide a salesperson to assist the customer, and make delivery. In the typical case, the value of proceeds exceeds the value of the collateral that can be traced into them.

When the parties have done a poor job of expressing their desire that the security interest follow the value of the collateral, some courts are quick to infer it, even if the inference does violence to the definition of the terms used. For example, in McLemore, Trustee v. Mid-South Agri-Chemical Corp., 41 B.R. 369 (Bankr. M.D. Tenn. 1984), one creditor's security agreement provided an interest in the debtor's "corn crop" and "proceeds" of the corn crop and another's provided an interest in "all crops, annual and perennial, and other plant products now planted, growing or grown, or which are hereafter planted or otherwise become growing crops or other plan products" and "proceeds" from these crops. Later, the debtor joined the PIK Diversion Program, a government subsidy program in which the debtor contracted with the U.S. government not to grow crops on the property. The debtor received a substantial cash payment for *not* growing crops on the land identified. The court held that the PIK payments were proceeds of the crops that were never planted. The court reconciled its decision with the definition in U.C.C. §9-102(a)(64) by stating that "Participation in the PIK program 'disposes' of the debtor's corn crops by precluding their cultivation." But to talk of disposing of something that never came into existence is to engage in a legal fiction. The *McLemore* court focused on the economic equivalence of the crops and the payments; the existence of one precluded the existence of the other. While the court did not talk of value tracing, that is what it was doing. We should note that not all courts have taken this route with regard to PIK payments. Some have stuck with the plain meaning of U.C.C. §9-102(a)(64) and found the payments not to be proceeds of the crop. But the *McLemore* case is important as an illustration of the impetus in some courts to translate the limited definition of "proceeds" into a concept of economic equivalence.

"Proceeds" are "collateral" within the definition of the latter term in U.C.C. §9-102(a)(12). As a result, when proceeds are disposed of or rights arise out of them, whatever is received is "proceeds." Thus the proceeds of proceeds are proceeds. To illustrate, assume ZBank has a security interest in the inventory of Billie's Toy Shop. Billie's Toy Shop sells some toys to Marjorie Venutti and Venutti writes a check for the $250 purchase price. We already know that the check is proceeds. Now assume that Billie's Toy Shop deposits the check to its bank account and the check is collected. The money in the account is now proceeds of the toys because it was received in exchange for proceeds of the toys. If Billie's Toy Shop uses the money to buy more toys, the new toys will be the proceeds of the old toys.

Even without using the concept of proceeds or tracing the value from the old toys into the new ones, the new toys would be subject to ZBank's security interest as "after-acquired property." See *Stoumbos v. Kilimnik*, in Assignment 9. The concepts of proceeds and after acquired property frequently overlap, but the former is a value-tracing concept, while the latter is not. We will say more about this later.

Even if the security agreement makes no mention of proceeds, a security interest automatically covers them. The rule derives from U.C.C. §§9-203(f) and 9-315(a). To illustrate, assume the ZBank's security agreement with Billie's Toy Shop describes the collateral as "inventory," but does not mention the proceeds of inventory. ZBank's security interest nevertheless extends to the proceeds of sales of inventory.

2. *Termination of Security Interest in the Collateral After Authorized Disposition*

Secured creditors sometimes authorize their debtors to dispose of the collateral free of the security interest. This authorization might be contained in the security agreement, as when the inventory lender to a department store agrees that the store can sell inventory to customers. Alternatively, this authorization might be expressed by the secured creditor at some later time, as when the bank that financed an automobile approves the owner's plan to sell it. Finally, this authorization might be implied from the circumstances or conduct of the parties, as when the security agreement between an inventory lender and a department store is silent on the matter of sale of collateral or where the bank that financed a herd of cattle knows that the debtor has been selling cattle from the herd to buyers who do not think they are taking subject to a security interest and the bank has not objected to the sales. In any of these instances, U.C.C. §9-315(a)(1) gives effect to the authorization: The buyer takes free of the security interest and the secured creditor can look only to the debtor and the proceeds.

3. *Continuation of Security Interest in the Collateral After Unauthorized Disposition*

In some secured financing arrangements, the parties contemplate that the debtor will sell the collateral only pursuant to further arrangements. For example, the security agreement may require that the secured creditor authorize sales to particular customers. This arrangement is often used in the financing of expensive items of collateral. For example, the bank that finances an airplane dealer may require that the dealer obtain authorization each time it sells an airplane. When the dealer finds a buyer for one of its planes, it makes the contract contingent on the approval of its financing bank and forwards the contract to the bank. One reason for such an arrangement is to allow the bank to pass on the nature and adequacy of the consideration the dealer will receive from the sale. Another is to alert the bank that the consideration is about to be paid, so the bank can be involved in determining what portion should be applied to the secured debt and what portion should remain with the dealer.

The language of many security agreements prohibits sale of the collateral. For example, the following provision appears in the Wisconsin Bankers Association standard form for a Motor Vehicle Consumer Security Agreement: "[The debtor] shall . . . not sell, lease or otherwise dispose of [the automobile] except as specifically authorized in this Agreement or in writing by the Seller." The Agreement does not authorize any sales by the debtor. Of course, such a clause does not mean that the buyer cannot sell the car at all. A security interest is only a contingent right to the collateral in the event that the debtor does not pay the secured obligation. When the debtor pays, the security interest terminates and the debtor is free to sell. The true meaning of such a clause is that the debtor must pay the debt in full to have the right to sell the collateral.

To understand how this might work in practice, assume that Arthur Dent purchased a Ford Prefect with financing from ZBank, under a security agreement that contained the provision set forth in the preceding paragraph and did not otherwise authorize sale. Arthur owes $12,000 against the car, and wants to sell it to Trillian McWilliams for $10,000. If Arthur has $12,000 in cash, he can pay ZBank, terminate its lien, and then sell the car.

Similarly, if Arthur has $2,000 and Trillian is willing to pay in advance, Arthur can do the same. But it would be foolish for a person in Trillian's position to do so. If Arthur got Trillian's money, but for some reason could not (or did not) deliver the car, Trillian might be only an unsecured creditor of Arthur's. Just as ZBank won't give up its security interest until it gets its money, Trillian should not give up her money until she gets clear title to the car.

The solution is to arrange for a simultaneous exchange of the security interest, the car, and the money. Arthur, Trillian, and ZBank will agree that someone will be escrowee or trustee for the transaction. In this example, the parties are likely to select ZBank. (Even with the nasty things some banks have done in recent decades, most people still trust banks more than they trust each other.) ZBank will wear two hats in the transaction: that of secured party and that of trustee or escrowee. Arthur and Trillian will pay their money to ZBank in trust, Arthur will authorize transfer of title to Trillian, and ZBank will execute the document terminating its lien. The terms of the trust are that if ZBank receives all the money, the transfer authorization, and the termination statement by an agreed date, ZBank can "close" the transaction by filing the termination statement and the transfer authorization with the Department of Motor Vehicles and disbursing the $12,000 from its trust account to its operating account. If ZBank does not receive the money and the documents, ZBank must return what it did receive and the nonbreaching party may then seek appropriate legal remedies against the breaching party.

If Arthur doesn't have $2,000, he cannot close. He may then be in a position where he can neither make his payments on the car, nor sell it without ZBank's consent. If ZBank does not give consent, Arthur might need to seek relief in bankruptcy.

Of course, if Arthur owed less than the sale price of the car, he could have closed and walked away with some cash. For example, if he owed $12,000 and Trillian were buying for $14,000, the parties would still need the escrow arrangement to protect themselves, but the sale would go through and Arthur could get the $2,000 difference between the loan amount and the contract price.

Despite their contracts not to sell collateral without their secured party's consent, debtors often do so. Some even go a step further by collecting the purchase price and spending it without paying the secured loan. Many states have enacted statutes making such conduct criminal. For example, Illinois recently amended its version of U.C.C. §9-306 to add the section set forth below. Notice that this statute does not make every unauthorized sale a crime — only those in which the debtor ~~willfully and wrongfully fails to pay~~ the proceeds to the secured party.

Illinois Revised Statutes

ch. 26, para. 9-306.1 (1991)

It is unlawful for a debtor under the terms of a security agreement (a) who has no right of sale or other disposition of the collateral or (b) who has a right of sale or other disposition of the collateral and is to account to the secured party for the proceeds of any sale or other disposition of the collateral, to sell or otherwise dispose of the collateral and willfully and wrongfully to fail to pay the secured party the amount of said proceeds due under the security agreement. Failure to pay such proceeds to the secured party within 10 days after the sale or other disposition of the collateral is prima facie evidence of a willful and wanton failure to pay. [Such conduct is a Class 3 felony.]

New York goes a step further, making it a crime merely to sell collateral in violation of a security agreement that prohibits sale.

New York Penal Law

§185.05

A person is guilty of fraud involving a security interest when, having executed a security agreement creating a security interest in personal property securing a monetary obligation owed to a secured party, and . . . [h]aving under the security agreement no right of sale or other disposition of the property, he knowingly secretes, withholds or disposes of such property in violation of the security agreement. Fraud involving a security interest is a Class A misdemeanor.

Even if the security agreement expressly prohibits sale of the collateral, the debtor has the power under U.C.C. §9-401 to transfer ownership to a buyer. (The transfer will be a breach of the security agreement and perhaps even a crime.) To understand the effect of U.C.C. §9-401, you must read it together with U.C.C. §9-315(a)(1), which provides that a security interest "continues in collateral notwithstanding sale." The result is that after a sale that the secured party has not authorized to be free of the security interest, the buyer will own the collateral subject to the security interest. The buyer may or may not know of that interest. (In Assignment 36, we will examine U.C.C. §9-320(a), which protects buyers in the ordinary course of business against security interests created by their sellers, but for now you should assume that the sales we talk about are not in the ordinary course of business.)

Unless the secured party has authorized the debtor to sell the collateral free of the security interest, the security interest continues in the original collateral and also in the proceeds. U.C.C. §9-315(a). This is no mere tracing of the value of the collateral; it is potentially a multiplication of the value in favor of the secured creditor. Probably the rationale is that when the debtor sells without authorization, the secured creditor needs additional protection. The original collateral, the proceeds, or both are likely to be in jeopardy. Indeed, a common scenario is that the debtor sells the collateral to obtain cash, which it desperately needs to meet other obligations. By the time the secured party learns of the sale, the debtor has spent the money and the collateral itself is in the hands of a bona fide purchaser or somewhere the secured creditor cannot find it.

Nevertheless, the multiplication of collateral that can result from the rules of U.C.C. §§9-102(a)(12) and (64) and 9-315(a) is striking. Assume, for example, that ZBank has a security interest in Jack's cow. Without authorization from ZBank, Jack sells the cow to Barbara for $2,000. Zbank's security interest continues in the collateral (the cow) and also in the identifiable proceeds of that sale (the $2,000). If Jack then uses the $2,000 of proceeds to buy some beans, the beans will also be proceeds under U.C.C. §9-102(a)(64) (recall that the proceeds of proceeds are proceeds) and ZBank's security interest will continue in the beans under U.C.C. §9-315(a). ZBank can foreclose against the cow and the beans, and collect its money where it can. Whether Zbank can also collect from the cash in the hands of the bean seller is considered in the next section.

Now assume that before ZBank forecloses, Barbara resells the cow for $2,500. Under U.C.C. §9-315(a), ZBank's security interest continues in the cow despite the resale. (Notice that U.C.C. §9-315(a) does not say that the sale must be by the debtor.) The $2,500 Barbara received for the cow is also proceeds of ZBank's collateral because it was acquired upon disposition of the cow that was collateral. This example illustrates that unauthorized sales of collateral can cause it to multiply dramatically. Just as the monster in the old B-movie, *The Blob*, absorbed everything it came in contact with and grew constantly larger, the secured creditor's collateral absorbs everything for which it is exchanged and grows larger also.

Associated Industries v. Keystone General Inc. (In re Keystone General Inc.), 135 B.R. 275 (Bankr. S.D. Ohio 1991), gives an example of how collateral can proliferate through unauthorized disposition. Star Bank financed Keystone General's inventory under a security agreement that extended to after-acquired property. Keystone General bought $1.9 million dollars of inventory from Associated. Even though Keystone General never paid for the inventory, Star Bank's security interest attached to it. When Keystone General returned the inventory to Associated in exchange for a credit to Keystone's account, pursuant to U.C.C. §9-315(a), Star Bank's security interest continued in the inventory. Star Bank ended up with a security interest in electronic components that the debtor hadn't paid for, no longer owned, and didn't even possess. This result startles even jaded commercial law types.

Secured creditors who insist on security agreement provisions restricting the sale of their collateral often intend to enforce the restriction only if their relationship with the debtor sours. So long as the relationship remains good, they allow the debtor to sell portions of the collateral and ignore the restrictions. When the relationship later sours, these creditors often find that the courts will not enforce the restrictions. Instead, the courts may hold that the creditor waived the conditions on sale by its course of dealing with the debtor and that the sale to the third party was therefore impliedly authorized.

These waiver cases usually seem to arise in the context of sales of livestock, where sales by debtors are pretty much continuous and the buyers are not protected by U.C.C. §9-320(a). For example, in Gretna State Bank v. Cornbelt Livestock Co., 463 N.W.2d 975 (Neb. 1990), the security agreement prohibited sale of the dairy cows that served as collateral except with the express written permission of the Bank. The Bank knew, however, that the debtor had been selling cows without the Bank's express written permission in violation of the security agreement and had not objected. Later, when the Bank sued a livestock market that had participated in the sales, the Court directed a verdict against the Bank on the ground the Bank had waived the prohibition on sales.

4.   Limitations on the Secured Creditor's Ability to Trace Collateral

In *The Blob* it quickly became apparent to Steve McQueen that if his proceeds-like adversary went unchecked, it would eventually absorb everything. What keeps a secured creditor's collateral from doing the same? To answer this question completely, you will need some concepts that we do not discuss until Part Two of this book. But you should know that the protection is far from complete. The cereal you ate for breakfast this morning was probably covered with security interests. Yuck!

One limitation we can discuss here is that a security interest continues to encumber proceeds only so long as they remain "identifiable." See U.C.C. §9-315(a)(2). To figure out what this means, begin by distinguishing the concepts of *commingling* and *identifiability*. To commingle collateral is to put it together in one mass with identical noncollateral so that no one can tell which is *actually* which. When Farmer Brown puts her wheat in a storage silo in Oklahoma, the grain will become commingled with that of lots of other Okie farmers. No one could pick out which grains were Brown's. Nevertheless, such commingled grain may be legally identifiable: that is, the law may provide a rule that arbitrarily designates a particular part of the mass as the collateral. Such a tracing rule enables the court to tell which grain is *legally* which.

Tracing is most often required when the debtor commingles cash proceeds with other money in a bank account. The secured creditor may be quick on the debtor's heels but fail to arrive until after the debtor has written checks on the account disbursing some of the money to payees from whom it cannot be recovered. The secured creditor, of course, would like to claim that the money remaining in the account is its collateral and, if necessary, that the money paid out was someone else's. Other parties (typically other creditors and the bank in which the funds were deposited) will probably want to make the opposite claim: The secured creditors' collateral was used to make payments and the money remaining in the account is theirs. U.C.C. §9-315(b) provides that the secured party can prevail by identifying the funds remaining in the bank account as its collateral by "a method of tracing, including application of equitable principles" that is permitted under non-U.C.C. law with respect to the type of collateral. Comment 3 to that section refers to the "equitable principle" most commonly employed: the *lowest intermediate balance rule*. That rule provides that the amount of the secured creditor's collateral remaining in a bank account is equal to the lowest balance of all funds in the account between the time the collateral was deposited to the account and the time the rule is applied.

To return to an earlier example, assume that Arthur Dent sells his encumbered Ford Prefect for $12,000 and deposits the proceeds in his bank account, which already contains $3,000. At the end of the month, Arthur's bank statement reveals the following transactions:

Description	Deposits	Withdrawals	Balance
Opening balance			$ 3,000
Sale of Ford Prefect	$12,000		15,000
Tuition payment		$11,000	4,000
Student loan	6,000		10,000
Books		5,000	5,000

The amount of identifiable proceeds remaining in the account at the end of this sequence is the lowest intermediate balance between the deposit of $12,000 and the present balance of $5,000. The correct number? The $4,000 balance remaining after the tuition payment.

What about money emerging from the bank account? U.C.C. §9-332(b) provides that "a transferee of funds from a deposit account takes the funds free of a security interest in the deposit account unless the transferee acts in collusion with the debtor in violating the rights of the secured party." Even though the cash proceeds that the debtor transfers from the bank account are free of the security interest, anything the debtor purchased with that cash may nevertheless still be proceeds. Recall the example in which Jack sold the cow that served as collateral for $2,000, and used the $2,000 to buy beans. Provided the seller of the beans did not know that the cash it received was encumbered, Zbank could not recover the cash from the seller. But the beans are collateral as proceeds of the cash.

One limit on the ability of the security interest to follow the value of its collateral is that the secured creditor must be able to trace that value with specificity. The following case illustrates.

In re Oriental Rug Warehouse Club, Inc.

205 Bankr. 407 (Bankr. D. Minn. 1997)

NANCY C. DREHER, UNITED STATES BANKRUPTCY JUDGE.

1. The Debtor is a Minnesota corporation engaged in the business of selling oriental rugs and carpets at retail. On April 29, 1993, the Debtor and Yashar entered into a "consignment agreement," whereby Debtor took possession of several of Yashar's rugs for the purpose of reselling them in its business. Debtor agreed to pay Yashar a total consignment price of $106,073.00 for the rugs, and agreed to apply the proceeds received from resale to the outstanding amount owed to Yashar.

2. On May 7, 1993, Yashar filed a UCC-1 financing statement with the Secretary of State for the state of Minnesota to perfect its interest in the consigned rugs possessed by the Debtor.

3. Debtor sold a portion of the consigned rugs but failed to remit the proceeds from the sales to Yashar as provided by their agreement.

Instead, the Debtor invested the proceeds from the sale of Yashar's rugs into the purchase of replacement rug inventory or otherwise retained the proceeds. On or around May of 1995, the brother of the president of Yashar went to the Debtor's place of business and repossessed all of the consigned rugs which were still in the Debtor's possession and which had not yet been sold. Although the Debtor currently has rugs in its inventory, the Debtor no longer possesses rugs that were supplied by Yashar.

4. On April 15, 1996, Debtor filed a petition for relief under Chapter 11 of the United States Bankruptcy Code. On August 20, 1996, Yashar filed a proof of secured claim in the amount of $64,243.00, representing the outstanding amount still owed to Yashar for the rugs which had been sold by the Debtor without remitting the proceeds. Pursuant to 11 U.S.C. §502, the Debtor has objected to Yashar's secured claim.

CONCLUSIONS OF LAW

In this case, the objective characteristics of the agreement between the Debtor and Yashar indicate that the parties did not intend to create a true consignment, but instead intended to grant Yashar a security interest in the consigned rugs. . . . Therefore, instead of creating a true consignment relationship whereby the consignee acts as agent to sell the property of the consignor, the parties to the present case created a standard "floor plan" arrangement whereby Yashar agreed to finance the Debtor's inventory in exchange for a security interest in the consigned rugs. As a secured financing arrangement, therefore, the transaction between the Debtor and Yashar is governed by the provisions of Article 9 of the UCC.

II.   SECURITY INTERESTS IN PROCEEDS UNDER [U.C.C. §9-315(a)]

Although the originally consigned rugs no longer remain in the Debtor's possession, Yashar argues that the Debtor's current inventory constitutes "proceeds" from the Debtor's sale of the consigned rugs, and that Yashar is therefore entitled to a security interest in the Debtor's remaining inventory. Section [9-315] of the Uniform Commercial Code governs the continuation and perfection of a security interest in proceeds. Therefore, before addressing the merits of the arguments of counsel, it is appropriate to address the provisions of [§9-315] in some detail.

A.   Continuation of a Security Interest in Proceeds: §9-315(a)

Section [9-102(a)(64)] of the UCC defines the term "proceeds" to include "whatever is received upon the sale, exchange, collection or other disposition of collateral or proceeds." [U.C.C. §9-102(a)(64)]. Section [9-315(a)], in turn, provides that, upon the sale of collateral, a security interest in that collateral "continues in any *identifiable proceeds including collections received by the debtor.*" [U.C.C. §9-315(a)] (emphasis added). The secured party has the burden of establishing that something constitutes identifiable proceeds from the sale or disposition of the secured party's collateral. To do this, the secured party must "trace" the claimed proceeds back to the original collateral; in other words, the secured party must establish that the alleged proceeds "arose directly from the sale or other disposition of the collateral and that these alleged proceeds cannot have arisen from any other source." [C.O. Funk & Son v. Sullivan Equipment], 415 N.E.2d at 1313.

Special tracing problems arise where cash proceeds are commingled with other deposits in a single bank account. Because of the fungible nature of cash proceeds, there is some authority that cash proceeds are no longer identifiable once they are commingled with other funds. The majority of courts, however, have utilized equitable principles borrowed from the law of trusts to identify whether commingled funds constitute proceeds received from an earlier disposition of collateral. In particular, these courts have utilized the "intermediate balance rule," which creates a presumption that the proceeds of the disposition of collateral remain in a commingled account as long as the account balance is equal to or exceeds the amounts of the proceeds. Therefore, the intermediate balance rule presumes that a debtor who spends money from a commingled account spends first from his own funds. Once the balance of the commingled account drops below the amount of the deposited proceeds, then the secured creditor's interest in the proceeds abates accordingly. . . .

III. Yashar's Claim

In this case, Yashar alleges that the Debtor sold its collateral in exchange for cash proceeds, deposited the cash proceeds into the Debtor's general checking account, and then reinvested the cash proceeds to buy more rug inventory. Therefore, to succeed in its claim under the UCC, Yashar must show that: 1) the Debtor's current assets constitute "identifiable proceeds" arising from the disposition of its original collateral under [§9-315(a)]; and 2) the proceeds were properly perfected under [§9-315(c) and(d)]. Yashar has not argued that it can trace the Debtor's current rug inventory to the sale of its collateral, however. In fact, Yashar has conceded that "it is impossible to reconstruct exactly what the Debtor did with the proceeds of the sale of Yashar's consigned inventory." Instead, Yashar argues that, although a secured creditor claiming an interest in proceeds has the burden of tracing proceeds when it litigates against other secured creditors, a secured creditor should not bear the burden of tracing when it litigates against the debtor. In suits between a debtor and a secured creditor, Yashar asserts, it is unfair to place the burden of tracing proceeds on the secured creditor, who has no ability to control the debtor's books and record keeping procedures.

Yashar's argument simply has no support in either the case law or in the UCC. Although Yashar may think it unfair to place the burden of tracing proceeds squarely on the shoulders of the party claiming the security interest, both the case law and the leading commentaries are clear in this regard. Where a creditor wishes to claim a security interest in proceeds under [§9-315], the burden is on the party claiming the security interest to identify the proceeds. . . . In this situation, Yashar should have protected itself by carefully monitoring the Debtor's inventory and by requiring the Debtor to maintain segregated accounts for the deposit of proceeds. The Court declines to disregard the clear provisions of the UCC and holds that Yashar's argument is without merit. . . .

Accordingly, and for the reasons stated, it is hereby ordered that the secured claim of Yashar Rug Co., Inc. is disallowed in its entirety. Yashar has an unsecured, nonpriority claim in the amount of $64,243.00.

B. Other Value-Tracing Concepts

As we noted in our discussion of the U.C.C. §9-102(a)(64) definition of "proceeds," that term does not encompass all of the states the value of a secured creditor's collateral can assume. A secured party who wants to contract as nearly as possible for the value of its collateral, in whatever form it may take, will want to employ some additional value-tracing concepts.

The *product* of collateral is something the collateral produces. The term is most commonly used in the context of agriculture. It has been held that wool is the product of sheep, milk the product of cows (although, as you will see in the next assignment, not everyone agrees), and maple syrup the product of trees. These "products" may also be "proceeds" of the collateral named because they "aris[e] out of collateral," U.C.C. §9-102(a)(64), but that is not entirely clear.

Another value the secured creditor may take as collateral is the *profit* from other collateral. "Profit" is another term of art, but with more than one meaning. In a general sense, the word can be used to describe the excess of revenues of a business over the expenses where the business itself is the collateral. In the context of real property, "profit" may be short for *profit a prendre*: "a right exercised by one man in the soil of another, accompanied with participation in the profits of the soil thereof. A right to take a part of the soil or produce of the land. A right to take from the soil, such as by logging, mining, drilling, etc. The taking (profit) is the distinguishing characteristic from an easement." Black's Law Dictionary 1211 (6th ed. 1990). Note that even if U.C.C. §9-315 applied to real estate, a "profit" might not be "proceeds." The former is a right to remove; the latter typically is a thing received in exchange.

Two other value-tracing concepts are worthy of mention. *Rents* are money paid for the temporary use of collateral. The offspring of collateral is a term most often used with regard to animals. A calf is the offspring of a cow, although it may also be considered the product of a cow.

The concept described by each of these terms is to some degree a value-tracing concept, in that the value of the collateral and the value of the product, profit, rent, or offspring are the same value. For example, if the owner of property rents it, the value of the owner's remaining interest in the property will be approximately the value it had before it was rented, less the value of the rent to be paid. A portion of the value of a breeding animal is the offspring it is expected to produce. By including the rents or offspring as collateral, the secured creditor is, to some degree, not adding to the value of the collateral but merely anticipating a transformation of existing value.

Products, profits, rents, and offspring of collateral are all arguably "rights arising out of collateral." Thus they are arguably all proceeds. Assuming they are, adding these terms to a description of collateral in a security agreement adds nothing, at least according to Article 9. Even if a description of collateral does not mention proceeds, their inclusion is implied. See U.C.C. §9-203(f). But, as we shall see in the next assignment, bankruptcy law arguably employs a narrower definition of "proceeds" that leaves room for the concepts of products, profits, rents, and offspring to operate.

C. Non-Value-Tracing Concepts

Concepts such as "after-acquired property," "replacements," "additions," and "substitutions" in a description of collateral are non-value-tracing in that they can pick up property acquired by the debtor with value not derived from the previously existing collateral. The value in proceeds, product, offspring, rents, or profits arguably comes in whole or in part from previously existing collateral. The value in after-acquired property, replacements, additions, and substitutions can come entirely from some other source, such as unencumbered property of the debtor, a new loan, or a capital contribution by the debtors' owners.

To illustrate the difference between value-tracing concepts and non-value-tracing concepts, assume that Billie's Toy Shop has $100,000 worth of display equipment and that ZBank has a security interest in its "equipment, including after-acquired equipment." Billie's Toy Shop spends $6,000 to buy additional display cases. To know that ZBank's after-acquired property clause will reach the additional cases, we need only know that the cases are equipment and that Billie's owns them. We do not need to know the source of the $6,000.

Now assume instead that ZBank's security interest was in "equipment, not including after-acquired equipment, but including the proceeds of equipment." If Billie's spends $6,000 to buy the additional display cases, we can know if ZBank's security interest attaches to it only by knowing the source of the $6,000. If Billie's obtained the $6,000 by selling equipment that was already collateral, the $6,000 was proceeds, and the new equipment will be proceeds. If the $6,000 was neither collateral nor the proceeds of collateral, the new equipment will not be collateral either.

In the illustration where the $6,000 did not come from existing collateral, application of the after-acquired property clause increased the total value of ZBank's collateral. ZBank had $100,000 of collateral before the purchase and $106,000 afterward. In the illustration where the $6,000 did come from existing collateral, application of the proceeds doctrine did not change the total value of ZBank's collateral. ZBank had $100,000 of collateral in the debtor's possession before the purchase and $100,000 afterward.

The distinction between after-acquired property and proceeds is a fine one. In practice, the security agreement usually provides that the collateral includes both. When that occurs, it does not matter which is being applied and it becomes unnecessary to distinguish between the two.

Problem Set 10

10.1. Firstbank has a perfected security interest in all of the "equipment, inventory, and accounts" of Polly Arthur, who is doing business as Polly's Plumbing. The contract makes no mention of proceeds, products, offspring, substitutions, additions, or replacements. Are they included? U.C.C. §§9-102(64), 9-201(a), 9-203(f), 9-204(a).

10.2.   Which of the following are collateral of Firstbank under the security agreement described in Problem 10.1 and why? U.C.C. §§9-102(2) and (64), 9-315(a).

a.   The money now in Polly's bank account.

b.   A parrot that Polly took in payment of an overdue account.

c.   A new computer that Polly bought to replace the computer she owned at the time she granted the security interest to Firstbank.

d.   A Myna bird that Polly took from Robin Watts in payment for some plumbing work (Watts didn't have the money to pay for the plumbing work and arranged in advance to trade the bird for the work; Polly did the plumbing while Watts was at her own job; Watts gave Polly the Myna bird the following day and Polly kept it as a pet).

10.3.   A few months ago, Equipment Leasing Partners (ELP) financed the Lucky Partners Syndicate's acquisition of a thoroughbred race horse named Horace. ELP took a security interest in Horace and "all proceeds, products, and profits therefrom." Lucky Partners defaulted on the $750,000 loan. ELP repossessed Horace and sold him for $275,000. Shortly before the repossession, Horace won $50,000 in a race. Lucky Partners has demanded the purse, but the track has not yet paid it. ELP asks you whether they have a valid claim to the purse. What do you tell them? U.C.C. §9-102(64).

10.4.   Joey Teigh contracted to buy Billie's Toy Shop, including the leasehold, furniture, fixtures, equipment, goodwill, accounts receivable, and trademarks. Joey hired you to represent her in the closing. In preparing for the closing, you learned that Joey and Billie omitted the inventory from the sale because Firstbank had a security interest in it. You've looked at Firstbank's security agreement and the description of collateral is just "inventory." Is it possible that security interest encumbers some of the accounts receivable? The other property Joey is buying? (For now, don't worry about whether the security interest could be perfected; confine your inquiry to whether it could attach.)

10.5.   a. ELP consults you about a $35,000 loan to Golan Industries that was made for the express purpose of purchasing an XT-100 copier. Golan signed a security agreement granting ELP a security interest in the copier. (The entire description of collateral reads "XT-100 copier, serial number XEX3088372.") The copier was destroyed in a fire six months ago. Fortunately, the loss was insured. At this point, what is ELP's collateral? U.C.C. §§9-102(12)(A) and (64), 9-203(f).

b.   Unfortunately, ELP was not named as a loss payee on the policy, so the insurance company paid the $35,000 in insurance proceeds to Golan. Golan deposited the check to a little-used bank account that contained $5,000 at the time. At this point, what is ELP's collateral?

c.   From the account Golan wrote a check for $2,000 to rent another copier for the month it would take to replace the XT-100, leaving $38,000 in the account. At this point, what is ELP's collateral?

d.   Golan then wrote a check from the account for $32,000 to pay the IRS, leaving only $6,000 in the account. At this point, what is ELP's collateral? U.C.C. §§9-315, 9-332

10.6. Your investigation of the Golan account indicates that the $32,000 check that cleared the account was not to the IRS. Golan used the $32,000 to buy another XT-100 to replace the one that had been destroyed. (It seems the price of XT-100s had fallen a bit since the initial purchase.) The new XT-100 was delivered immediately and the debtor is operating it now. If this new information is correct, what is ELP's collateral?

Assignment 11: Tracing Collateral Value During Bankruptcy

Transformations of a debtor's property can continue to occur after the debtor is in bankruptcy. If the debtor or a trustee operates the business, inventory may be sold, accounts may be collected, and cows may produce calves or milk. These changes may result in increases or decreases in the categories of property originally described as collateral in the security agreement. In addition, the bankruptcy court may authorize the consumption of a secured creditor's collateral during bankruptcy, but, generally speaking, only if equal value is substituted for it.

A. Distinguishing Proceeds from After-Acquired Property

Article 9 permits a secured creditor to trace the value of its collateral through concepts such as proceeds or products and also to pick up additional collateral by means of an after-acquired property clause. Often, it is unnecessary to distinguish whether a creditor claims its security interest in property acquired after the security agreement was signed by proceeds or by an after-acquired property clause, so long as it is clear that at least one of the concepts would cover the property in question.

Once the debtor files for bankruptcy, however, the distinction becomes critical. Bankruptcy Code §552 permits the secured creditor to trace the value of its collateral, but it is narrower than Article 9 in two respects. First, once the debtor is in bankruptcy, the secured creditor can no longer pick up additional collateral by means of an after-acquired property clause. Bankr. Code §552(a). Second, Bankruptcy Code §552(b) limits value-tracing to five concepts: proceeds, product, offspring, rents, or profits.

The result is that the secured creditor generally can keep what collateral value it has as of the filing of the bankruptcy case, even if that collateral value is transformed, but cannot acquire additional collateral value during bankruptcy. The policy rationale is in keeping with general bankruptcy policies regarding the protection of secured creditors. Once bankruptcy stays creditors from exercising their state remedies, it must safeguard their entitlements. Bankruptcy law prohibits the debtor or trustee from favoring one creditor over another in its postpetition dealings. For example, the debtor cannot use property of the estate to pay one prepetition unsecured claim without paying other claims of the same kind pro rata. To permit an after-acquired property clause to operate postpetition would violate this basic principle of bankruptcy.

Consider this example. Tonia Wellfoot operates Wellfoot Electrical Service. She owes Sunshine Bank $10,000 on a loan giving the Bank a security interest in "all of Wellfoot Electrical's equipment, current and after acquired." At the time of the filing, the business owns only some power tools valued at $7,000. While she is in bankruptcy, Tonia has the opportunity to trade her collection of power tools for a compressor and several fittings that will permit her to do her work more easily. She makes the trade, and Sunshine's security interest attaches to the new tools as proceeds. U.C.C. §9-315(a); Bankr. Code §552(b). A little later, Tonia decides to use some of her income from the business to buy a computer system worth $3,000 to handle the billing and paperwork. In the absence of bankruptcy, Article 9 would have permitted the security interest to extend to the newly acquired computer, but bankruptcy law does not. Bankr. Code §552(a). Because Tonia is in bankruptcy, all her unencumbered assets, including the business's income, are property of the estate, equally available to all her creditors even though none of them can reach the assets while the automatic stay remains in place.

In effect, Bankruptcy Code §552 permits a secured creditor to trace collateral value from one form to another, but does not permit the secured creditor to enhance its position by claiming assets that would have been available equally to all the creditors. Without the security interest, Sunshine Bank had an allowed secured claim for $7,000 and an unsecured claim for $3,000. Assuming that Tonia's trade was for equal dollar value, Sunshine still had only a $7,000 secured claim afterward. The same is not true of the computer purchase. If Sunshine's security interest could attach to the computer, Sunshine's allowed secured claim would grow to $10,000, and Sunshine would receive payment in full on the underlying loan. The other unsecured creditors would get nothing in return for the $3,000 spent to enhance Sunshine's collateral.

To repeat: To permit debtors to use unencumbered property of the estate to buy property that would then be collateral for preexisting debts would enable debtors to apply the unencumbered values of their estates for the benefit of particular secured creditors and to thereby deprive their unsecured creditors of their expectancies in those unencumbered values. To prevent such applications, the Bankruptcy Code protects proceeds, products, offspring, rents, and profits for the secured creditors, but does not honor after-acquired property clauses.

In the following case, the court carries the value-tracing concept even further. Interpreting a provision in Bankruptcy Code §552 that permits orders based on the "equities of the case," the court holds that the equities require a tracing not in broad legal concepts, but with whatever mathematical precision can be brought to bear in the circumstances.

In re Delbridge

61 B.R. 484 (Bankr. E.D. Mich. 1986)

ARTHUR J. SPECTOR, U.S. BANKRUPTCY JUDGE

Question: Is the cup half full or half empty? Answer: yes.

The debtor in possession in this dairy farm Chapter 11 case strenuously argues that milk is not the product of a cow. Since about half of the published court opinions dealing with this logically preposterous proposition have adopted it, it must be conceded that the argument passes the straight-face test.[1] Of course, when this question is put to a lay-person, that is, someone not blinded or befuddled by excessive legal training, the response is blunt and distinctly to the contrary.

What has the learned folk so confounded — has, so to speak, caused them to throw up their hands in "udder" frustration — is the application of a federal statute to a common fact of economic life down on the dairy farm. Most dairy farmers who find their unfortunate way into the bankruptcy court come encumbered by liens on all bovine animals, their proceeds and their products (which, I suspect, even they would have conceded — until their first meeting with their bankruptcy lawyer — includes milk). . . .

[Production Credit Association of Mid-Michigan (P.C.A.)] is conceded to have a perfected prepetition lien on the debtor's cows and their milk. The debtor argues, however, that §552(a) limits that lien to the milk in being at the time the bankruptcy was filed, citing [five bankruptcy court cases]. P.C.A. counters by citing [five bankruptcy court cases] which hold to the contrary.

Since none of the relevant terms in §552(b) are defined in the Bankruptcy Code, reference should be made to state law or at least to a legal dictionary. In fact, §552(b) explicitly requires the court to look to "applicable non-bankruptcy law." Clearly, milk produced postpetition is neither

1. An argument passes the straight-face test if it is one which a competent and ethical lawyer can make while maintaining a straight face.

a "rent," a "profit" nor an "offspring"[2] of cow or of milk in being prepetition. U.C.C. [§9-102(a)(64)] states: " 'Proceeds' includes whatever is received upon the sale, exchange, collection or other disposition of collateral or proceeds." A "proceed" of milk or of a cow, is the cash or the account one receives after its disposition by sale or otherwise. The issue is thus whether milk which comes into existence postpetition is a "product" of a cow.

Most courts that have held that milk is indeed a product of a cow actually felt compelled to seek legal support for the proposition . . . and found it in U.C.C. §9-102(a)(34)(D), which defines farm products to include "products of livestock in their unmanufactured states (such as . . . milk)." Moreover, [Official Comment 4.a. to U.C.C. §9-102] states that:

> Products of crops or livestock, even though they remain in the possession of a person engaged in farming operation, lose their status as farm products if they are subjected to a manufacturing process. What is and what is not a manufacturing operation is not determined by this Article. At one end of the scale, some processes are so closely connected with farming — such as pasteurizing milk or boiling sap to produce maple syrup or maple sugar — that they would not rank as manufacturing. On the other hand an extensive canning operation would be manufacturing. The line is one for the courts to draw. After farm products have been subjected to a manufacturing operation, they become inventory if held for sale.

From this it is clear that the drafters intended that milk not lose its status as a farm product at least through delivery of the raw milk to the dairy, as is the case here. As Michigan has adopted that section of the UCC, one can confidently pronounce that, at least under Michigan law, milk is a farm product.

Some courts have taken the position that notwithstanding the UCC definition of farm products, something is a product of collateral "for purposes of §552(b)" only when the collateral is necessarily consumed or has its existence essentially and irrevocably altered during the manufacturing process. Thus they held that since a cow is neither consumed nor materially altered during the milking process, the milk is not a product. Some debtors take this hypothesis to its logical conclusion. In essence, this theory holds that a cow is a milk machine: the farmer puts feed in one end, waits awhile, and milk comes out the other. This process is no different, they argue, from the concept of work-in-process in fabricating plants. There, the lender typically has a security interest in equipment and inventory which consists of both raw material, such as steel, and work-in-process. If the debtor obtains new steel postpetition and shapes

2. "Rent" is "consideration paid for use or occupation of property." Black's Law Dictionary, 1166 (5th ed. 1979). A "profit" is "a right exercised by one man in the soil of another, accompanied with participation in the profits of the soil thereof. A right to take a part of the soil or produce of the land." Black's at 1090. According to my kindergarten teacher, a cow's offspring, i.e., a baby cow, is called a calf — not milk.

it into a product by use of its machinery, the lender's prepetition lien on this new work-in-process is cut off by §552(a) and not saved by §552(b). In the case of a dairy farmer, the feed is the steel and the cow is the machinery. They argue that milk is the product not of a cow — but of a farmer. Though this is an ingenious argument, it is its very genius which is its fatal flaw.

Courts ought not to use sophistry to turn what appears plain on its face into a conundrum. The argument that milk is a farm product for purposes of the UCC but is not a product for purposes of §552(b) is reminiscent of Humpty Dumpty's statement to Alice: "When [I] use a word . . . it means just what I choose it to mean — neither more nor less." L. Carroll, Through the Looking Glass, Chapter 6 (1872). "Definitions should not be too artificial. For example — 'dog' includes a cat is asking too much of the reader; 'animal' means a dog or a cat would be better." Memorandum on Drafting of Acts of Parliament and Subordinate Legislation (1951), Department of Justice, Ottawa, Canada, quoted in Ritchie, Alice Through the Statutes, 21 McGill L.J. 685 (1975). A common sense reading of the plain word "product" is all that ought to be necessary when applying a statute that simply is not ambiguous. Any ambiguity found by others is created only by going outside the statutory language for a peek at legislative history. But "[w]hen confronted with a statute which is plain and unambiguous on its face, we ordinarily do not look to legislative history as a guide to its meaning." Tennessee Valley Authority v. Hill, 437 U.S. 153, 184 n.29 (1978). The flaw in this theory, then, is that there is no need to consider the "purposes" of §552(b): courts need only read it and apply it.

I surmise that the real reason certain courts agonized over the meaning of this section is that they didn't like the result that would have occurred had they played the music the way it read. In their view, if the postpetition milk were indeed encumbered by the lender's prepetition lien, the farmer would be considerably less likely to successfully reorganize. However, policy-based decision making, if defensible at all, is even less so where it is unnecessary. In this context, policy ought to be irrelevant, since §552(b) itself contains ample room for the exercise of policy-anchored discretion.

Just as the answer to the question of whether the cup is half empty or half full is yes, the question of whether milk is produced by the cow or the farmer is yes. Neither is wrong. The cow can't make milk without being fed, cared for and milked. The farmer alone can't turn feed into milk any more than he can spin straw into gold. What any school child can see is that you need all of the above to produce milk for sale. That is not reason to say that milk is not a product of the cow; it's simply a reason to apply the "equities of the case" language found in §552(b). While I share the concern expressed by those courts which felt that it is unfair to let the creditor with a prepetition lien on milk walk away with the entire cash proceeds of milk produced largely as a result of the farmer's postpetition time, labor, and inputs, §552(b) allows the court leeway to fashion an appropriate equitable remedy, without the need to mangle the English language or cause judicial decision-making to become the object of derisive laughter. Indeed, legislative history is emphatic on this point:

> The provision allows the court to consider the equities in each case. In the course of such consideration the court may evaluate any expenditures by the estate relating to proceeds and any related improvement in position of the secured party. Although this section grants a secured party a security interest in proceeds, products, offspring, rents, or profits, the section is explicitly subject to other sections of title 11. For example, the trustee or debtor in possession may use, sell, or lease proceeds, products, offspring, rents, or profits under section 363.

124 Cong. Rec. H11,097-98 (daily ed. Sept. 28, 1978); S17,414 (daily ed. Oct. 6, 1978).

Although it has been stated, and I agree, that courts should not establish a hard and fast rule or formula when exercising their equitable powers under §552(b) it is often helpful if an easy-to-state and easy-to-apply rule can be formulated. The concepts of equity and mathematics are not necessarily mutually exclusive. . . . [A] rule based on sound economics is more desirable than one founded on nothing more than the judge's own policy predilections. With all due humility, I hereby announce what I hope is such a rule for application in this case and others like it.

"The purpose behind the 'equities of the case' rule of 11 U.S.C. §552(b) is, in a proper case, to enable those who contribute to the production of proceeds during Chapter 11 to share jointly with prepetition creditors secured by proceeds." In re Crouch, 51 B.R. 331, 332 (Bankr. D. Ore. 1985)). Since it is established that the farmer's labor, postpetition raw materials and the cow are all integral components of a commercial dairy farming operation, the owners of those commodities, are, in essence, joint venturers in the process of the commercial production and sale of milk. The mathematical equation which follows is intended to yield an equitable division of the products of that joint venture. The formula is as follows:

$$CC = \frac{D}{D+E+L} \times P$$

where: CC = "cash collateral," i.e.: the amount of the milk check which is encumbered by the lender's lien;

D = the average depreciation of the capital, i.e.: the cow;

E = the farmer's average direct expenses such
as for feed, supplement, and veterinary services;
L = the average market value of the farmer's or
his employees' labor (excluding labor in the
production of feed); and
P = the average dollar proceeds of the milk
sold.

The rule is easy to state. The lender is entitled to the same percentage of the proceeds of the postpetition milk as its capital contribution to the production of the milk bears to the total of the capital and direct operating expenses incurred in producing the milk. Because the parties are in a direct mathematical relationship, the rule should be easy to apply. Very simply, the larger is the lender's capital contribution to the venture, the larger its share of the proceeds ought to be. Conversely, if the farmer's input in the venture is great, the "equities of the case" compel that his share of the proceeds likewise be great.

Delbridge is an example of value-tracing made painfully explicit. Not all courts conduct their value-tracing so explicitly. In the following case, the court sets out a different formula for taking account of the debtor's and the secured creditor's respective contributions to postpetition revenues: First, the debtor is reimbursed for expenditures made to generate the postpetition revenue and whatever remains is collateral.

To understand the case, you must know a little history. Prior to the 1994 Amendments to the Bankruptcy Code referred to in the case, several courts had reached the somewhat surprising conclusion that the bill paid by customers of a hotel when they checked out was an "account" arising out of a sale of services, rather than "rent" for the use of a hotel room. These courts reasoned that (1) most of what the customer got was in fact services, such as check-in, check-out, room cleaning, bell-hop, food, telephone, ice-making, etc., and (2) rather than attempting to allocate the payment between services (earned by the debtor's expenditures of postpetition dollars) and rent (earned by use of the secured creditor's collateral), the courts should treat it as entirely what it was mostly: a payment for postpetition services. As such, it was not the proceeds of the secured creditor's collateral. Bankruptcy Code §552(a) prevented the secured creditor from claiming the postpetition revenues under the after-acquired property provision in its security agreement, leaving the revenues unencumbered.

Why this tortured reasoning? If secured creditors had been able to enforce their claims that postpetition revenues were proceeds and therefore cash collateral, debtors attempting reorganization would have been able to use them only by providing adequate protection. But where would debtors get the resources to provide adequate protection against loss of the revenues if all their revenues were collateral the moment they generated them? Had the secured creditors prevailed in their claims, bankruptcy reorganizations would have been impossible — not just in the hotel industry, but in other industries as well. Without the reorganizations that provide half the business of the bankruptcy courts, the jobs of the bankruptcy judges would have been in jeopardy. Hence the decisions. (The courts that made these decisions seemed not to notice their authority under §552(b) to except postpetition revenues from the secured creditors' collateral "based on the equities of the case.")

In 1994, Congress responded by amending Bankruptcy Code §552(b) to make clear that a security interest could extend to room revenues. In the following case, the Ninth Circuit casually sidesteps the amendment by interpreting it to mean only the *net* room revenues, after allowing the debtor to pay the expenses necessary to stay in business and complete the reorganization.

In re Hotel Sierra Vista Limited Partnership

112 F.3d 429 (9th Cir. 1997)

BEEZER, CIRCUIT JUDGE:

Hotel Sierra Vista Limited Partnership (HSVLP) built a 151-room hotel in Sierra Vista, Arizona, that opened for business in 1986 as a Ramada Inn franchise. Additional hotel facilities include a lounge, a restaurant, a ballroom, banquet rooms and meeting rooms.

HSVLP financed the hotel's construction by borrowing a total of $6,196,000 in two secured loans from [Chequers, a Texas-based investment group]. HSVLP defaulted on its loans in 1990. Chequers demanded payment in full from HSVLP and commenced foreclosure proceedings. HSVLP sought Chapter 11 protection in June 1993.

In August 1993, Chequers moved to sequester the hotel's post-petition room revenues. Chequers maintained that these revenues were "cash collateral" within the meaning of 11 U.S.C. §363(a). The bankruptcy court heard Chequers's motion in September 1993, but explicitly deferred deciding whether the room revenues were cash collateral. The court ordered HSVLP to sequester the room revenues and meet its operating expenses from those funds.

At the time of its initial filing, HSVLP's principal assets were the hotel itself, whose value the parties estimated and stipulated to be $2,200,000, together with $625,844 evidencing accumulated pre-petition revenues.

Between the time HSVLP filed its petition and the December 1994 plan confirmation, the hotel received an additional $812,425 in net revenues.

The bankruptcy court confirmed the plan over Chequers's objections by using the "cramdown" alternative of 11 U.S.C. §1129(b). In its order confirming the plan, the bankruptcy court concluded that the post-petition room revenues were cash collateral. The bankruptcy court nevertheless denied Chequers a secured interest in the post-petition hotel revenues. The bankruptcy court determined that Chequers had not met the burden of proving the "extent" of its interest as required by 11 U.S.C. §363(o)(2).

III

Sometimes yesterday's confusion resolves itself into today's easily-applied rule of law. Between the June 1994 confirmation hearing and the bankruptcy court's December 1994 order, Congress amended the statutory definition of cash collateral to clarify that the term "rents" included hotel room revenues. On this basis, the bankruptcy court concluded that the hotel's post-petition room revenues were cash collateral. This development places us in an unusual position, however, one where we must assess the actions undertaken by the parties and the bankruptcy court in this case in light of yesterday's confusion.

After its Chapter 11 filing and through the time of the bankruptcy court's order confirming its plan, HSVLP deposited all revenues received from the hotel, including those attributable to room occupancy, in a single money market account. Chequers contends that HSVLP's trustee violated 11 U.S.C. §363(c)(4) by so doing. That section provides that ". . . the trustee shall segregate and account for any cash collateral in the trustee's possession, custody, or control." 11 U.S.C. §363(c)(4).

IV

A party seeking to prove the "extent" of its interest under §363(o)(2) must do two things. First, as a preliminary matter, the party must prove that it holds a perfected security interest in post-petition revenues to which its liens still rightly attach. See Financial Security Assurance, Inc. v. Days California Limited Partnership, 27 F.3d 374, 377 (9th Cir. 1994) ("Days California"). Second, a party must prove the amount of money to which its liens attach. See 11 U.S.C. §363(o)(2). Our decision in *Days California* provides the formula for determining the amount of revenues to which liens may survive post-petition. In *Days California* we stated that

> Hotel methods of accounting will permit the identification of the revenues generated by the rooms and those generated by services. Determination of the net revenues will require allocation of direct and indirect expenses in proportion to each category of revenue.

Id. at 377. Thus, proving the extent of one's interest involves submitting evidence that enables the bankruptcy court to determine the sum to which the party asserting the security interest is entitled. See id.

Documentary evidence introduced at the confirmation hearing with respect to the extent of Chequers's post-petition security interest included both a copy of a valid security instrument and accounting statements reflecting post-petition gross room revenues. Because of the unusual timing of events in this case, neither the parties nor the bankruptcy court attempted to apply the *Days California* formula to the hotel's revenues and expenses. Equity requires that the court and the parties have the opportunity to allocate direct and indirect expenses to each category of revenues listed on the trustee's reports. This will result in a net diminution of gross room revenues to which Chequers's liens attach after petition, but will be consistent with effectuating the burden structure of 11 U.S.C. §363(o)(2) and our decision in *Days California*.

V

Days California requires Chequers to prove the exact amount of its interest in HSVLP's post-petition room revenues through application of the *Days California* formula. A new hearing in this case shall be conducted to apply that formula. We remand this case to the district court for proceedings consistent with this opinion.

Reversed and remanded.

If property is "proceeds" under Article 9 definition of that term, does that mean it is "proceeds" within the meaning of Bankruptcy Code §552(b)? The question is important because §9-102(a)(64)(C) arguably makes a dramatic expansion of the concept from what it was when Congress enacted Bankruptcy Code §552. In Financial Security Assurance, Inc. v. Tollman-Hundley Dalton, L.P., 74 F.3d 1120 (11th Cir. 1996), the court answered the question in the negative, noting that a positive answer would give state lawmakers control of the meaning of a word used in a federal statute:

> Contrary to the district court's determination, nothing in [the Supreme Court's opinion in] *Butner* suggests that state [law] defines the language of the federal Bankruptcy Code in general, or of §552 in particular. Neither does §552 dictate such a result. Section 552(b) provides that a prepetition security interest in derivative property may extend to post petition derivative property "to the extent provided by [the] security agreement and by applicable nonbankruptcy law." This reference to "nonbankruptcy law," or state law, is consistent with *Butner*: it prevents a creditor from using a debt-

or's bankruptcy to acquire rights to which he would not otherwise be entitled under state law. The reference to "nonbankruptcy law" does not suggest that state law defines the language of §552.

Thus, we hold that the district court erred in looking to Georgia law to define the language of §552, specifically, to define the term "rents" as used in §552(b). To construe this term, we look to the plain meaning of the statute.

The court noted that two other Circuits, the Fifth and the Ninth, had held to the contrary, but declined to follow them. The issue will almost certainly make its way to the Supreme Court.

Assuming that the Eleventh Circuit view prevails, what is the definition of "proceeds" as used in Bankruptcy Code §552? Probably most believe that, with regard to personal property, it is the definition of "proceeds" contained in the Official Text of Article 9 when the Bankruptcy Code was adopted in 1978:

U.C.C. §9-306(1) (1978). Proceeds includes whatever is received upon the sale, exchange, collection or other disposition of collateral or proceeds. Insurance payable by reason of loss or damage to the collateral is proceeds, except to the extent that it is payable to a person other than a party to the security agreement.

Thus, four views of the scope of the secured creditor's right to proceeds under Bankruptcy Code §552(b) are plausible. The secured creditor may be entitled to (1) "proceeds" as defined in U.C.C. §9-102(a)(64), (2) "proceeds" as defined under the 1978 Official Text of Article 9, (3) only that portion of proceeds that are collateral under the *Delbridge* test, or (4) only the net proceeds derived from use of the collateral as specified in *Hotel Sierra Vista*.

B.   "Cash Collateral" in Bankruptcy

As you have seen in earlier chapters, the debtor or trustee in a bankruptcy case is generally permitted to use the secured creditor's collateral. Bankr. Code §§363(c)(1) and (b)(1). Thus, if the secured creditor's collateral is a factory, the bankruptcy estate can operate the factory while it remains in bankruptcy. The debtor or trustee may also use highly liquid collateral, such as the money in a bank account or the rents that are paid by tenants of an apartment building. Such highly liquid collateral is referred to as *cash collateral*. Bankr. Code §363(a).

Regardless of whether collateral is cash collateral, the debtor or trustee who uses it must provide adequate protection to the secured creditor against its loss or decline in value. The debtor's or trustee's use of collateral such as a factory or apartment building ordinarily presents no immediate threat to the interests of the secured creditor. Significant decline in the value of the collateral is likely to occur only over a period of months or years; in the meantime, the secured creditor has access to the bankruptcy court to seek appropriate orders for adequate protection. Bankr. Code §361.

The debtor's or trustee's use of cash collateral presents a more immediate threat to the secured creditor. The typical use of cash collateral will be to pay expenses incurred by the estate during the bankruptcy case. This may be the wages and salaries of employees who operate the business, the utility bills, or the cost of other supplies. Once the cash collateral is used for such purposes, it may be permanently lost to the secured creditor. The typical solution in such a case is for the trustee or debtor to provide adequate protection in the form of a lien on other property of the estate. Often, that lien is against property which, although not "proceeds" under the definition of U.C.C. §9-102(a)(64), will come into existence only as a result of the cash expenditures. For example, when cash collateral is used to pay employees and for utilities and supplies, the ultimate result may be to produce factory inventory for sale. The value of such cash collateral becomes the inventory, but the relationship between the two is not tight enough for the inventory to qualify as proceeds of the cash within the definition in U.C.C. §9-102(a)(64). Because the inventory is not proceeds under U.C.C. §9-102(a)(64), the secured creditor is not entitled to it under Bankruptcy Code §552.

An order of the bankruptcy court permitting the use of cash collateral and granting a lien in the resulting inventory as adequate protection can bridge the gap left by U.C.C. §9-102(a)(64). In the example used here, it assures preservation of the value of the secured creditor's collateral as that value changes form. You should keep in mind, however, that adequate protection orders are not limited by the concept of value-tracing; the court can grant a substitute or replacement lien against property completely unrelated to the collateral the debtor or trustee uses. Recall from Assignment 6 that when Craddock-Terry Shoe Corporation had to provide adequate protection against the declining value of its $700,000 customer list, it did so by granting the creditor a security interest in all of its property, which was valued at $2,000,000.

Because a debtor or trustee can dissipate cash collateral almost instantly by using it, the Bankruptcy Code requires notice to the secured creditor and the opportunity for a hearing *before* the debtor or trustee can use cash collateral. Bankr. Code §363(c)(2). Nearly all assets of most debtors are fully encumbered by the time they file bankruptcy. Any expenditure of funds by such a debtor is an expen-

diture of cash collateral. It is a rare business that can go more than a
few days without paying anyone for anything. Thus, within a few
days of the filing of most bankruptcy reorganization cases, the debtor
has to obtain an order from the Bankruptcy Court authorizing the use
of cash collateral on an emergency basis. It is not unusual for such
hearings to be held by telephone, at the homes of judges, during
court recesses, or at uncivilized hours of the morning. Such hearings
are life-and-death matters for most debtors. If the debtor cannot find
a way to provide adequate protection so that it can use its cash collateral, it may also be unable to find a way to stay in business.

Problem Set 11

11.1.   On the facts of Problem 10.3, assume that some uncertainty
existed as to whether the $50,000 purse was ELP's collateral. Before
the matter could be resolved, Lucky Partners filed bankruptcy. Not
knowing of the filing, the track paid the purse to Lucky Partners a few
days later. The money is now in a trust account, awaiting the court's
decision. Is your claim to the purse stronger, weaker, or unchanged?
Bankr. Code §552.

11.2.   Polly Arthur, from Problem 10.2, filed bankruptcy but continued to run her business. A few days later, she worked for 28
straight hours repairing a dangerous leak at Golan Industries' power
plant and billed Golan at $65 an hour for a total of $1,820. When
Polly receives that money, will it be subject to Firstbank's security
interest? U.C.C. §9-102(64); Bankr. Code §552.

11.3.   You are still representing ELP against Golan Industries. After
the fire that destroyed the copier in Problem 10.5, but before the
insurance company paid the claim, Golan filed for bankruptcy under
Chapter 11. (The information ELP gave you earlier to the contrary
was wrong.) When Golan got the $35,000 in insurance proceeds, it
deposited them in its bank account and wrote the $2,000 and
$32,000 checks. Those checks have cleared the bank account, leaving
only $6,000 in the account. Today ELP got a call from Golan's attor-
neys notifying it of an emergency cash collateral hearing to be held
later this afternoon. What is ELP's collateral in the bankruptcy case?
U.C.C. §§9-315(a) and (b); Bankr. Code §§362(d), 552, 549(a),
363(c)(2).

11.4.   Your client, Globus Real Estate Investment Trust (Globus)
holds a security interest against Hotel Sierra Vista. The description of
collateral includes the real property, equipment, inventory, and "all
income, rents, royalties, revenues, issues, profits, fees, accounts, and
other proceeds (including without limitation, room sales and rev-

enues from sales of services, food and drink)." Hotel Sierra Vista filed for bankruptcy on October 14 and on that same day the court entered an order that the hotel segregate and account for any cash collateral in the hotel's possession, but also permitting the hotel to "meet its operating expenses from those funds." The value of all collateral for the loan is substantially less than the amount owing to Globus. In accord with the order, the hotel opened a new bank account, deposited all receipts in it, and paid all expenses from it. The hotel's attorney sent you the following list of revenues and expenses for the first 17 days after bankruptcy. Globus wants to know how much money you think should be segregated as cash collateral and why:

Revenues	Type	Amount
	Room charges	$510,000
	Food and drink	121,000
	Total	631,000
Expenses		
	Room-related	520,000
	Food and drink	100,000
	Total	620,000
Profit		11,000

Some of the food and drink is served in the bar and restaurant, some of it is served in the room.

a. If the court follows *Hotel Sierra Vista*, what is your answer?

b. If the court follows *Delbridge*, what is your answer? (Assume that the value of the hotel neither increased nor decreased during the 17- day period since the filing of bankruptcy.)

c. If the court applies Bankruptcy Code §552(b)(2) literally to the room revenues and declines to make an exception based on the equities of the case, what is your answer?

11.5. You also represent Globus in the reorganization of Pine Manor, a 360-unit apartment building that was in foreclosure for more than a year before it filed Chapter 11 yesterday. The apartment building is Pine Manor's only asset, Globus's mortgage is for $900,000, and the apartment building is worth only $700,000. The parties have no reason to believe that value will change during the bankruptcy case. Meredith Johnson, Pine Manor's attorney, filed a motion to use cash collateral along with the petition. The motion seeks use of whatever portion of the rents collected during the Chapter 11 case is necessary to pay the management company that will operate the building during the case and the other postpetition expenses of operation, such as maintenance, repairs, insurance, etc. The hearing is set for 7 A.M. tomorrow morning. Globus's mortgage extends to "rents and proceeds" of the apartment building and clearly was perfected prior to the filing of the petition. The parties expect $10,000 in rents each month. Globus wants you to get aggressive with Pine Manor because "it's our property and we are the ones losing money. Pine Manor doesn't even have an equity." Meredith wants you to sign a consent to the cash collateral order. "Every dime we propose to spend is going to benefit your collateral," she says. "There's no point in going to a 7 A.M. hearing when you don't even have an argument." Bankr. Code §§363(a), (c) and (e), 552(b). Working through the following may help you assess the situation.

a. What was the amount of Globus's secured claim at the time the petition was filed?

b. Was Globus entitled to accrue interest on that amount?

c. Will the $10,000 in rent received in the first month after filing be Globus's collateral?

d. If the court permits Pine Manor to use that $10,000, to what protection is Globus entitled? How will Pine Manor provide it?

Assignment 12: The Legal Limits on What May Be Collateral

Article 9 places no express limits on what may serve as collateral. Read only Article 9 and you might get the impression that a debtor can encumber anything that has value. Article 9 defines and expressly authorizes the use of broad categories, such as "equipment," U.C.C. §9-102(a)(33), and "general intangibles," U.C.C. §9-102(a)(44), in descriptions of collateral. The use of such categories makes it easy to take all-encompassing security interests. Article 9 makes such broad descriptions of collateral as "all personal property of the debtor" ineffective and this may at first glance seem to be a limit. But as we saw in Assignment 9, it is a limit in form, not in substance. Parties who intend a security agreement in all personal property can easily accomplish that intent by stringing together a list of categories expressly sanctioned by Article 9. For most businesses, "equipment, inventory, accounts, chattel paper, instruments, money, and general intangibles" will cover everything.

Transactions involving some kinds of collateral, such as real estate and insurance, are excluded from coverage under Article 9. U.C.C. §§9-109(d)(8) and (11). The intention of the drafters in making these exclusions was not to put limits on what can serve as collateral, but merely to yield to otherwise conflicting bodies of law that permit those categories of property to serve as collateral.

The one limit the U.C.C. places on what may serve as collateral is so broad as to be almost invisible. U.C.C. §1-201(37) defines "security interest" as an interest in "personal property or fixtures." State law defines "fixtures" such that only property can be fixtures. The effect is that items must be "property" or they cannot qualify as collateral. Yet, as you will see in this assignment, many things of significant monetary value are not "property." Toward the end of this assignment, we will explore the curious boundary between property and valuable nonproperty and the interesting problems in doctrinal metaphysics that result. But first we examine some limitations arising outside Article 9 that prevent even some items that are property from serving as collateral.

A.   Property That Cannot Be Collateral

1.   Property of a Personal Nature

During at least the past two decades, there has been a growing consensus that it is inappropriate for creditors to take and enforce *nonpossessory, nonpurchase-money security interests* in property that is
highly personal in nature and has little resale value. Lenders should
not be repossessing and reselling the debtor's false teeth, artificial
limbs, or personal clothing. The consensus weakens with distance
from the person's body, but still prevails as to furniture, appliances,
and household furnishings, so long as they are not of substantial
value.

Some might attribute this consensus to human sensibilities and
compassion. In testimony before Congress and the Federal Trade
Commission (FTC), critics of such repossession and resale focused on
the mean-spirited nature of the process. For example, secured creditors threatened to "clean out" their debtors' houses if the debtors did
not make payments. Such threats often emphasized those items of
collateral used by the children. Repossession was often not so much
an effort to collect the debt from the proceeds of the sale of collateral
as it was to make good on a threat to deprive the debtor of its use.
There was testimony about repossessors who wrenched collateral
from the hands of the impoverished debtor, only to take it directly to
the city dump.

But, as may already be apparent, the consensus against repossession of personal items has practical underpinnings as well. The
chances for conflict in such repossessions is high, making them difficult for the legal system to deal with. A case in which one of us served
as a Chapter 7 bankruptcy trustee will illustrate. The debtors were
husband and wife, and the husband was "head of the household."
Under the law of the state at that time, no property was exempt to a
person not the head of the household; everything not repurchased by
the debtor had to be surrendered to the trustee for resale. The wife,
who was entitled to no exemptions, owned a wedding ring that she
could not then afford to repurchase. When the author-trustee
requested possession of the ring, she explained its symbolic and emotional importance to her, and ended by looking him dead in the eye
and saying, "If you want my ring you are going to have to cut off my
finger." Months later, under threat of a contempt citation and in
response to the pleas of her own lawyer, she eventually surrendered
the ring. Months after that, she was successful in raising the money
to buy it back. In the interim, however, a lot of time, effort, and emo-
tions had been spent. (It may be merely coincidence that the author-
trustee left the practice of law shortly thereafter to go into teaching.)

In this illustration, the trustee sought to take possession of the ring on behalf of unsecured creditors. In most states, such a problem would not have occurred because the ring would have been exempt from execution under state law and from the estate under bankruptcy law. Centuries ago, exemption law recognized the problems involved in taking possession of personal items from debtors and accommodated to them. But, as you will recall from Assignment 1, these exemptions apply only to the collection efforts of unsecured creditors. The exemption laws themselves do not bar either the grant or foreclosure of security interests in debtors' homes, tools of trade, clothing, household goods, or wedding rings.

In this section, we discuss the existing limitations on the use of low-value personal items as collateral. As will be apparent, they afford debtors protection that is generally less extensive than the exemption laws. For example, most states have exemption laws protecting debtors' homes from execution by unsecured creditors, but only Texas has a law protecting debtors' homes from foreclosure by mortgagees. Even the Texas protection is limited.*

Taking nonpurchase-money security interests in personal items became a widespread practice only with the adoption of the U.C.C. in the 1960s. The fledgling consumer finance industry was just developing. Companies in the industry borrowed money from banks at low rates of interest and used it to make small loans to consumer debtors at higher rates. To protect themselves against a high rate of default by consumer debtors, the consumer finance companies took blanket security interests in their borrowers' household goods. When the debtors defaulted, the companies generally threatened to repossess the household goods, and in some cases actually did so. By the mid-1970s, problems with the practice were rampant. Congress sought to deal with them in §522(f) of the Bankruptcy Code it adopted in 1978.

Bankruptcy Code §522(f)(2) permits debtors who file bankruptcy to avoid nonpossessory, nonpurchase-money security interests in property listed in that section, if the security interest prevents the debtor from taking advantage of an exemption otherwise available. Bankruptcy Code §522(f)(2) was aimed squarely at the practices of the consumer finance companies.

Security interests in property in the possession of a secured creditor are excepted from §522(f) avoidance. A bank sometimes takes a security interest in jewelry, coin collections, or the like, and perfects by taking possession of the item and placing it in its vault. Because the bank already has possession of the collateral, repossession is not a problem. Purchase-money security interests in personal items also

---

*Article 16, §50 of the Texas constitution provides in part that "No mortgage, trust deed, or other lien on the homestead shall ever be valid, except for the purchase money therefor, or improvements made thereon. . . .

are excepted from §522(f) avoidance. Sears can and does take security interests in much of the property it sells, and it repossesses the property when the purchasers fail to pay for it. The rationale for the purchase-money exception may be that the repossessed items are more likely of value to a seller who is in the business of selling such items. But the rationale is not entirely convincing: If the property repossessed is clothing, even Sears may be taking it to the dump.

Bankruptcy Code §552(f) authorizes avoidance only of a lien that "impairs an exemption to which the debtor would have been entitled" were the lien not in existence. That restricts its protection to the categories of property exempt from the claims of unsecured creditors under state or federal law. But, as we noted above, the protection Bankruptcy Code §522(f)(2) provides against security interests is considerably narrower than the protection against unsecured creditors that exemption law provides. For a security interest to be avoidable under Bankruptcy Code §522(f), the property must be both exempt *and* of a type listed in Bankruptcy Code §522(f)(2).

Probably the most important difference between the two sets of protections are that the exemption laws typically protect both homes and automobiles, but §522(f)(2) protects neither. In addition, it applies only to liens against the property of debtors who are in bankruptcy. If a debtor is not in bankruptcy, the provision provides no protection. Bankruptcy Code §522(f) does not prohibit the taking of a security interest in the property listed or its enforcement against a debtor outside bankruptcy. In 1985, the FTC published regulations that prohibit both actions.

Federal Trade Commission, Trade Regulation Rules

16 C.F.R. 444

§444.1   DEFINITIONS

(a) *Lender.* A person who engages in the business of lending money to consumers within the jurisdiction of the Federal Trade Commission.

(b) *Retail installment seller.* A person who sells goods or services to consumers on a deferred payment basis or pursuant to a lease-purchase arrangement within the jurisdiction of the Federal Trade Commission.

(c) *Person.* An individual, corporation, or other business organization.

(d) *Consumer.* A natural person who seeks or acquires goods, services, or money for personal, family, or household use.

(e) *Obligation.* An agreement between a consumer and a lender or retail installment seller.

(f) *Creditor.* A lender or a retail installment seller.

(g) *Debt.* Money that is due or alleged to be due from one to another.

(h) *Earnings.* Compensation paid or payable to an individual or for his or her account for personal services rendered or to be rendered by him or her, whether denominated as wages, salary, commission, bonus, or otherwise, including periodic payments pursuant to a pension, retirement, or disability program.

(i) *Household goods.* Clothing, furniture, appliances, one radio and one television, linens, china, crockery, kitchenware, and personal effects (including wedding rings) of the consumer and his or her dependents, provided that the following are not included within the scope of the term "household goods":

(1) Works of art;

(2) Electronic entertainment equipment (except one television and one radio);

(3) Items acquired as antiques; and

(4) Jewelry (except wedding rings).

(j) *Antique.* Any item over one hundred years of age, including such items that have been repaired or renovated without changing their original form or character.

§444.2   UNFAIR CREDIT PRACTICES

(a) In connection with the extension of credit to consumers in or affecting commerce, as commerce is defined in the Federal Trade Commission Act, it is an unfair act or practice within the meaning of Section 5 of that Act for a lender or retail installment seller directly or indirectly to take or receive from a consumer an obligation that: . . .

(3) Constitutes or contains an assignment of wages or other earnings unless:

(i) The assignment by its terms is revocable at the will of the debtor, or

(ii) The assignment is a payroll deduction plan or preauthorized payment plan, commencing at the time of the transaction, in which the consumer authorizes a series of wage deductions as a method of making each payment, or

(iii) The assignment applies only to wages or other earnings already earned at the time of the assignment.

(4) Constitutes or contains a nonpossessory security interest in household goods other than a purchase money security interest.

The FTC can enforce these regulations by bringing actions for civil penalties or for cease and desist orders against violators. There is no private remedy under federal law, but most states have enacted "little

FTC statutes" that allow private actions against persons engaged in unfair trade practices. Remedies in private actions under these state laws include injunctions, actual damages, small civil penalties in the range of $50 to $300, and modest attorneys' fees.

Notice that the list of property in 16 C.F.R. §444.2 is similar to the list in Bankruptcy Code §522(f)(2), but it does not match it precisely. The FTC regulation is in some respects broader and in others narrower than the Bankruptcy Code provision. Both are vague and complex, and few consumer lenders are interested in litigating the outer boundaries. The practical effect has been to discourage generally the use of Article 9 security interests in consumer finance.

2. Future Income of Individuals

Perhaps the most valuable thing most debtors "own" is their ability to earn income in the future. A direct attempt to create a security interest in such income is referred to as an *assignment of wages*. Article 9 does not apply to such an attempt. U.C.C. §9-109(d)(3). The reason given for the exclusion is that "[t]hese assignments present important social issues that other law addresses." Comment 11 to U.C.C. §9-109. Non-U.C.C. law in most states restricts the assignment of wages as security or bars it altogether. When states permit some wage assignments, they frequently limit them using one or more of these devices: Assignments of wages cannot be made in consumer transactions, wages can be assigned only after they are earned, or assignments of wages cannot exceed a certain percentage of the debtor's income. You may have noticed that 16 C.F.R. §444.2(3), set forth in the preceding subsection of this assignment, prohibits the taking of security interests in future wages unless the assignment is revocable by the debtor or part of a payroll deduction or preauthorized payment plan.

State laws vary greatly on the extent to which they will permit wage assignments. Hostility to such assignments is usually based on the fear that a creditor's leverage over a debtor is so great in the case of a large wage assignment that the debtor is entirely in the creditor's sway. There is also concern that debtors with encumbered future incomes will have less incentive to work and tend to become public charges. Other state legislatures have seen the matter differently, concluding that debtors should decide what obligations to undertake and what to secure them with.

Once an individual debtor files bankruptcy, any encumbrance of his or her earnings from personal services performed after the commencement of the case is void and of no further effect. This principle was expressed by the Supreme Court in terms sufficiently broad and powerful that it is quoted and followed today, despite the lack of any specific governing provision in the 1978 Bankruptcy Code. The case also reminds us of the emotional underpinnings of wage assignment and the concern that a debtor emerge from bankruptcy with a fresh start:

> When a person assigns future wages, he, in effect, pledges his future earning power. The power of the individual to earn a living for himself and those dependent upon him is in the nature of a personal liberty quite as much if not more than it is a property right. To preserve its free exercise is of the utmost importance, not only because it is a fundamental private necessity, but because it is a matter of great public concern. From the viewpoint of the wage earner there is little difference between not earning at all and earning wholly for a creditor. Pauperism may be the necessary result of either. The amount of the indebtedness, or the proportion of wages assigned, may here be small, but the principle, once established, will equally apply where both are very great. The new opportunity in life and the clear field for future effort, which it is the purpose of the Bankruptcy Act to afford the emancipated debtor, would be of little value to the wage earner if he were obliged to face the necessity of devoting the whole or a considerable portion of his earnings for an indefinite time in the future to the payment of indebtedness incurred prior to his bankruptcy. Confining our determination to the case in hand, and leaving prospective liens upon other forms of acquisitions to be dealt with as they may arise, we reject the Illinois decisions as to the effect of an assignment of wages earned after bankruptcy as being destructive of the purpose and spirit of the Bankruptcy Act.

Local Loan Co. v. Hunt, 292 U.S. 234 (1934). Hence, even if it is possible to take a security interest in wages to be earned in the future, the debtor's bankruptcy will defeat it.

3. Pension Rights

People often save money toward their retirement. When they do so simply by putting cash in a savings account or buying stock, they have an asset that they can use or borrow against. Other people save for retirement either through an employer-sponsored retirement plan or by making payments to a specially designated retirement account such as an IRA. Such retirement plans, if they meet certain requirements, receive favorable tax treatment from the federal government.

As the following case also demonstrates, the requirements that make these plans eligible for these tax breaks also make the retirement funds ineligible to serve as collateral for a loan. The case involves a profit-sharing plan rather than a pension. But the particular plan was qualified under the Employee Retirement Income Security Act of 1974 (ERISA) so that its legal status as is relevant here was the same as a pension.

In re Green

115 B.R. 1001 (Bankr. W.D. Mo. 1990)

ARTHUR B. FEDERMAN, UNITED STATES BANKRUPTCY JUDGE. . . .

FINDINGS OF FACT

Debtors filed their Chapter 7 bankruptcy petition on July 27, 1989. [Debtor Howard C. Green has been employed as a store manager by Defendant Wal-Mart Stores, Inc. (Wal-Mart) for 16 years.] As of January 31, 1989, Wal-Mart operated 1,259 discount retail stores in 25 states, under the trade name "Wal-Mart Stores," and 105 additional stores in 21 states under the trade name "Sam's Wholesale Clubs." As of January 31, 1989, Wal-Mart employed over 200,000 persons on either a full-time or part-time basis.

Wal-Mart established the Wal-Mart Stores, Inc. Profit Sharing Plan and the Wal-Mart Stores, Inc. Trust (hereinafter referred to as either "Plan," "Trust," or "Wal-Mart Profit Sharing Plan and Trust") on September 1, 1971. . . . The Plan and Trust are apparently qualified under Section 401(a) of the Internal Revenue Code of 1986, as amended (the "Code"), and are subject to the Employee Retirement Income Security Act of 1974 ("ERISA"). . . . As of January 31, 1989, there were 124,780 participants in Wal-Mart Profit Sharing Plan and Trust. Plan assets, which include Wal-Mart common stock, totaled $649,000,000 as of January 31, 1989.

. . . [T]he Wal-Mart Profit Sharing Plan and Trust is intended to be a profit sharing stock bonus plan, investing primarily in Wal-Mart stock to enable Wal-Mart employees to share in the equity ownership of Wal-Mart. The Plan is entirely funded by contributions from Wal-Mart. . . . The annual contribution to the Plan is based on a formula as approved by the Executive Committee of the Board of Directors of Wal-Mart, and is a percentage of the annual eligible wages of the participants of the Plan, which percentage is based on the Wal-Mart's pretax profits. . . . A separate account is maintained for each participant in the Plan for accounting purposes, but [the assets] are not held as segregated funds.

Mr. Green . . . has participated in the Plan since 1978, and has been one hundred percent (100%) vested in his account balance since June, 1984. [The value of Mr. Green's interest is approximately $100,000.]

The amount of any distribution to a participant under the Plan is dependent upon the value of the participant's account balance (including the value of common stock of Wal-Mart) at the time of distribution.

The value of a participant's account balance in the Plan can increase or decrease from year to year depending upon the value of the Plan's assets, earnings on those assets, and contributions, if any, by Wal-Mart. Wal-Mart's contributions are allocated to participants' accounts at the end of each plan year.

Mr. Green is granted several powers and rights in the Wal-Mart Profit Sharing Plan and Trust. He is given the power to receive his interest upon termination of his employment. Upon notice, he also has the unrestricted right to vote the shares of Wal-Mart stock attributed to his account, and may also receive dividends from Wal-Mart stock. He also has the right to designate the beneficiary of certain benefits, and to elect the form of distributions from the profit sharing plan.

Defendant United Savings and Loan Association ("United Savings") is a Missouri state savings and loan association with its principal office located in Lebanon, Missouri. [During 1988, Mr. and Mrs. Green executed and delivered to United Savings for valuable consideration their promissory notes in principal amounts totaling $45,000.00. They also entered into security agreements with United Savings in order to secure the indebtedness represented by the notes with the grant of a security interest in their interests in the Wal-Mart Profit Sharing Plan.] On or about May 9, 1988, [the Debtors] executed, at the request of United Savings, a Wal-Mart Stores, Inc. Profit Sharing Trust Alternative Beneficiary Form for Married Participant, Form B, designating United Savings as beneficiary of [their] interest in the Wal-Mart Profit Sharing Trust.

. . . [The Debtors currently owe United Savings $44,776.50 on the promissory notes.]

The arguments of Wal-Mart . . . and debtors are similar to each other. They submit that the anti-alienation provisions [of ERISA, 29 U.S.C. §1056(d) (1993)] prohibit the assignment and alienation of debtors' interests. Therefore, a valid spendthrift trust has been created, thus preventing the attachment of United Savings' security interest. . . . Wal-Mart [also proposes] various policy arguments in support of their position. For example, they argue that ERISA requires all Plans, as a condition of their non-taxable status, to contain language prohibiting alienation of the interests of participants, that the effect of granting the Trustee's Complaint for Turnover would be to invalidate the anti-alienation provisions, and that the result would be that the entire Wal-Mart Plan and Trust would be stripped of its non-tax status. . . .

CONCLUSIONS OF LAW . . .

3. SECURITY INTERESTS OF UNITED SAVINGS

. . . It is clear that debtors and United Savings intended to create a security interest in debtors' profit sharing interests to serve as collateral for the debt owing to United Savings. At the time of the execution of the two promissory notes and security agreements, debtors were residents of the state of Missouri. Pursuant to the provisions of the Missouri version of the Uniform Commercial Code, United Savings had a perfected security interest in debtors' beneficial interest in the Wal-Mart Profit Sharing Plan and Trust, even though no financing statement was filed. Accordingly, but for the existence of the anti-alienation provisions, United Savings would have a valid security interest in the debtors' profit sharing plan interest.

The recent case of Guidry v. Sheet Metal Workers National Pension Fund, 493 U.S. 365, 110 S. Ct. 680, 107 L. Ed. 2d 782 (1990), is relevant. In *Guidry,* the Supreme Court protected the ERISA pension interests of a labor union official, who was not in bankruptcy, from the claims of the union which he had defrauded. In doing so, the Court said:

> Section 206(d) (29 U.S.C. §1056(d)(1)) reflects a considered congressional policy choice, a decision to safeguard a stream of income for pensioners . . . even if that decision prevents others from securing relief for the wrongs done them. If exceptions to this policy are to be made, it is for Congress to undertake that task. *Guidry,* 110 S. Ct. at 687-688.

The anti-alienation provisions prohibit the attachment of United Savings' security interest under the precedent established in *Guidry.* The court therefore holds that United Savings' security interest did not attach to the debtors' profit sharing interest due to the existence of the anti-alienation provisions included in the Wal-Mart Profit Sharing Plan. . . .

CONCLUSION AND ORDER

. . . ERISA was intended to allow workers to accumulate monies for retirement by not being taxed on savings until the funds are withdrawn for use. So that such funds would be available at retirement Congress required, as a prerequisite for such preferential tax treatment, that each Plan contain provisions prohibiting the participants from transferring or otherwise alienating their share of Plan assets, and shielding such assets from claims of their creditors until the funds are in fact withdrawn. When withdrawn, the creditors of course could gain access to such funds to satisfy their claims, even though they are the proceeds of an ERISA Plan with the required anti-alienation language.

The plan involved in *Green,* like many pension plans, had thousands of beneficiaries. Other pension plans, such as those set up by a doctor or lawyer sole practitioner to shelter part of his or her income from taxes, may have only one or two. While funds are in the pension plan, the beneficiary may be able, within certain bounds, to determine how the plan funds are invested. In order to qualify for favorable tax treatment, however, the plan must provide that the beneficiary cannot borrow against his or her interest.

Interestingly, the beneficiary ordinarily can withdraw all or part of the funds before retirement. To do so, the beneficiary must pay taxes on the money withdrawn plus a tax penalty equal to 10 percent of the amount withdrawn. Payment of the tax and penalty effectively becomes the price of borrowing against the beneficiary's interest in the plan.

The court in *Green* alludes to the policy Congress was implementing by restricting alienation of qualified retirement plans. The issues are similar to those raised by wage assignments. Some believe it is appropriate to limit the debtor's ability to use the pension as collateral for a loan. If the debtor fails to pay the loan, the debtor may lose the pension to foreclosure and be destitute at retirement. Others believe that use of the pension fund as collateral should be a matter of individual choice. Some debtors might have good reason to borrow, to pay for necessary medical care or to save the debtor's business from failing. The debtor may be unable to borrow at all without use of the pension fund as collateral. Allowing withdrawal of pension funds can be seen as a compromise between these two beliefs.

It is worthwhile to note an exception to the prohibition against the use of pension rights as collateral.

Assignment or Alienation of Plan Benefits

29 U.S.C.A. §1056(d) (West Supp. 1993)

(1) Each pension plan shall provide that benefits provided under the plan may not be assigned or alienated. . . .

(3) (A) Paragraph (1) shall apply to the creation, assignment, or recognition of a right to any benefit payable with respect to a participant pursuant to a domestic relations order, except that paragraph (1) shall not apply if the order is determined to be a qualified domestic relations order. Each pension plan shall provide for the payment of benefits in accordance with the applicable requirements of any qualified domestic relations order. [The section goes on to define a qualified domestic relations order at length.]

Not only do restrictions on alienation depend on the form they take (offering the pension plan as collateral rather than withdrawing money from the plan), but they also depend on the party who is attempting to reach the property in question (beneficiaries of qualified domestic relations orders rather than ordinary creditors). As this provision demonstrates, the policy explanations get more and more tangled as the restrictions on the use of property as collateral become more and more complex.

B. Future Property as Collateral

Under both the U.C.C. and real property law, a debtor can grant a security interest in property the debtor does not yet own (i.e., in after-acquired property). When the property comes into existence or into the hands of the debtor, the security interest attaches. An individual debtor ordinarily cannot effectively encumber his or her future earnings from personal services, but a business debtor, whether corporation or individual, can encumber future earnings of the business. The business debtor does this by encumbering accounts, including after-acquired accounts, chattel paper, money, and bank accounts — the income the business will receive over time. When customers later obtain services on credit or for cash, the security interest attaches to the accounts, chattel paper, money, or bank accounts thus created or augmented.

A business that has thus encumbered its future income can escape the encumbrance by filing bankruptcy. As we saw in the previous assignment, an after-acquired property clause ceases to be effective once the debtor files. Bankr. Code §552(a). The creditor is entitled only to the proceeds, product, offspring, rents, or profits of the collateral existing at the time of the filing.

C. Valuable Nonproperty as Collateral

Article 9 applies only to transactions "intended to create a security interest in personal property." If the subject of the transaction is not recognized as "property" for this purpose, the debtor and creditor cannot create a security interest in it. Policymakers often use this definitional ploy to place limits on what may be used as collateral. If they do not wish, as a policy matter, to see particular items of value encumbered, they make their point by classifying the items as "privileges," "mere expectancies," or some other term that implies they are not property.

Probably the most important category of nonproperty in the American economy is *licenses*. The federal government has issued television and radio broadcast licenses and airport landing rights that alone are probably worth hundreds of billions of dollars. State and local governments have issued liquor licenses and taxicab medallions each worth tens or even hundreds of thousands of dollars. Although they are routinely bought and sold, most of these licenses, rights, and medallions are by law nonproperty. The putative purpose of this classification is a government decision that the particular license, right, or medallion should exist only "for the public convenience" or some such purpose. The government theoretically prohibits transfer of the license, right, or medallion and retains the right to revoke it any time it ceases to be for the public convenience. Laws and regulations classify them as nonproperty to stress their fragile status. Cynics note that classifying these rights as revocable enables politicians to justify giving them away virtually free to their friends and supporters. The cynics also note that they are rarely revoked, the restrictions on their transfer are rarely enforced, and that they are routinely bought and sold for huge sums of money.

Some courts take the distinction between property and nonproperty seriously. In determining whether to enforce a security interest in a particular item, they limit their inquiry to whether the item is "property" under the law of the state. For example, in Jackson v. Miller, 93 B.R. 421 (Bankr. W.D. Pa. 1988), the court held a purported security interest in a liquor license to be void and of no effect. The court relied on a provision of state law that stated, "The license shall continue as a personal privilege granted by the board and nothing therein shall constitute the license as property." In the same opinion, the court acknowledged that any security interest taken in a liquor license after the repeal of that statute was valid.

Other courts look beyond classification as property or nonproperty and take a more policy-oriented approach. These courts examine the consequences of permitting or not permitting the taking of security interests in the particular items. They tend to permit the use of licenses as collateral, reasoning that the grant of the security interest in no way restricts the government's right and ability to cancel any license the existence of which no longer serves the public convenience. The secured creditor simply takes a security interest in something that might become valueless. The doctrinal explanation is that the license can be property between the licensee and the secured creditor without being property between the government and the licensee.

Contracts between private parties sometimes create valuable rights that are said not to be property and may not be assignable, but which are in practice routinely transferred. Probably the most common of

these are the rights of franchisees. In the typical franchise arrangement, the franchisee pays a substantial amount of money for franchise rights that are valuable but by contract are unassignable. When
the franchisee wants to assign the rights, the franchisee first finds an
interested buyer for the franchise business. The two enter into a contract for sale of all assets other than the franchise. The contract is
contingent on the franchisor's willingness to issue a new franchise to
the buyer upon surrender of the franchise currently owned by the
seller. If the franchisor is unwilling to issue the new franchise, the sale
is off and the seller continues as franchisee.

Even if the franchisor has no legal obligation to go along with the
deal, it ordinarily has two incentives for doing so. The first is that it
will be better off with a franchisee that wants to come into the business than with one who wants to get out. The second is that potential buyers of franchises from the franchisor will be willing to pay
more for them if they know that the company in fact will approve
their sale to an acceptable buyer. Legally, the franchisor has the right
to refuse to issue a new franchise to facilitate such a sale, but in practice most franchisors only use that right as a means of controlling the
quality of its franchisees. Although the parties agree that the franchise is not property and cannot be assigned, their understanding is
that the *value* of the franchise belongs to the franchisee. What is
unassignable in law becomes assignable in practice.

In the following case, the court wrestles with whether a security
interest in such a franchise should be enforceable and, if so, in what
manner.

In re SRJ Enterprises, Inc.

23 Bankr. Ct. Dec. 1630 (Bankr. N.D. Ill. 1993)

RONALD BARLIANT, UNITED STATES BANKRUPTCY JUDGE.

An automobile dealer financed the purchase and operation of its dealership with loan proceeds from two secured creditors. After filing a voluntary petition under chapter 11, the Debtor sold all of its dealership
assets to another automobile dealer. Included as part of the sales proceeds is $125,000 paid for the Debtor's voluntary termination of its fran-
chise agreement. The Debtor has filed a motion for summary judgment
to declare that the $125,000 is unencumbered. For the reasons stated
below, this Court will deny the Debtor's motion.

I.   BACKGROUND

In March, 1991, SRJ Enterprises, Inc. (the "Debtor") acquired a Nissan
franchise and entered into a floor planning financing arrangement with

NBD Park Ridge Bank ("NBD") to purchase new vehicle inventory for its dealership. Later that year, the Debtor obtained additional financing from Success National Bank of Lincolnshire ("Success"). A year after opening, the Debtor closed its doors. In March, 1992, the Debtor voluntarily filed for relief under chapter 11.

After filing the case, the Debtor sought a buyer for its dealership assets. In May, 1992, the Debtor filed a motion in this Court for an order approving the sale of the Debtor's assets to The Bob Rohrman Automobile Dealerships, n/k/a Rohr-Grove Motors, Inc. ("Rohrman"). . . . In June, 1992, this Court entered an order authorizing the sale to Rohrman. The order also indicated that the Debtor voluntarily would terminate its Nissan franchise upon the receipt of $125,000 from Rohrman. [The Debtor's motion] recited that the payment would be as "consideration of SRJ voluntarily terminating its Nissan Agreement in order that Rohrman may apply to obtain a new franchise agreement with Nissan." The order further provided that the sale to Rohrman was contingent upon Rohrman obtaining a Nissan franchise. Nissan later approved Rohrman as an authorized Nissan dealer at the Debtor's business location and the sale closed in September, 1992. . . .

II.   ANALYSIS

In order for the Debtor to prevail, the Termination Fee must be proceeds of newly created post-petition value or proceeds of unencumbered, pre-petition value. If the Termination Fee is proceeds of post-petition value, then section 552 of the Bankruptcy Code proscribes the reach of NBD's and Success' respective security interests. If, however, the Termination Fee is proceeds of pre-petition value, this Court must describe the pre-petition property interest and determine whether it is subject to a lien. . . .

[The court reviewed the descriptions of collateral in NBD's and Success's security agreements and concluded that the inclusion of "general intangibles" in the descriptions of collateral caused them to encumber all personal property owned by the Debtor.]

The proper inquiries then are whether the Termination Fee represents proceeds of pre-petition value and whether that value is encumbered. It is uncontested that Rohrman agreed to pay the Debtor the sum of $125,000 in consideration of the Debtor's voluntary termination of its Nissan franchise so that Rohrman might apply to obtain a new franchise agreement with Nissan. NBD claims that the Debtor held a valuable pre-petition right to terminate the franchise agreement, for which Rohrman paid $125,000. Success similarly urges that the termination right had value pre-petition because any subsequent franchisee could not acquire a new Nissan franchise before the Debtor terminated its franchise agreement. The Debtor, however, argues that the Termination Fee represents post-petition value, as it was paid to "exercise its rejection powers so as to free up the purchaser's right to operate a Nissan dealership in Debtor's primary market area." . . .

Though the Termination Fee may represent proceeds of some type of pre-petition value, the Debtor constructs a two-part argument to conclude that the Termination Fee is unencumbered. According to the Debtor, the Termination Fee cannot represent proceeds of the franchise because the Debtor did not assign the franchise agreement to Rohrman. Second, because the Debtor technically did not transfer the franchise agreement, the Termination Fee may be proceeds of something, but not proceeds of pre-petition collateral. Both arguments fail for essentially the same reason — Rohrman paid $125,000 to the Debtor to acquire a Nissan franchise in the Debtor's market area.

The Debtor's initial claim, that the Termination Fee is not proceeds of the Debtor's franchise, places form over substance. Rohrman was not obligated to purchase the Debtor's assets unless approved as a new Nissan franchisee. Nissan's grant of a new franchise to Rohrman was conditioned upon the Debtor's termination of its franchise agreement. So, the Debtor surrendered the franchise to Nissan. Then, Rohrman procured a new franchise from Nissan to operate in the Debtor's former market. Nissan did not buy the franchise from the Debtor and then sell the franchise to Rohrman. Nissan simply was the conduit through which the franchise rights passed. The value to Rohrman of obtaining the franchise, separate from the hard collateral, is the upper threshold of the price that Rohrman would be willing to pay for the termination of the Debtor's franchise agreement. Because this value previously belonged to the Debtor, as franchisee, the Termination Fee represents consideration paid for the "disposition" of the franchise, and therefore, either proceeds of NBD's lien on "contract rights" or "any other personal property," or Success' lien on "general intangibles." [U.C.C. §9-102(a)(64)] defines "proceeds" as "whatever is received upon the sale, exchange, collection or other disposition of collateral or proceeds . . . " (emphasis added). There is no requirement that the collateral be transferred or disposed of to anyone; rather, "proceeds" include any amount received for disposition of collateral, even if disposition is by termination.

Section 17.1 of the Debtor's franchise agreement, however, provides that the Debtor "shall not transfer or assign any right . . . under this Agreement without the prior written approval of [Nissan]. Any purported transfer, assignment or delegation made without the prior written approval of [Nissan] shall be null and void." It is unclear whether this prohibition encompasses security interests and, if so, whether it would be effective to avoid a consensual lien.

The problem faced by automobile dealership lenders arguably prohibited from taking security in a franchise agreement is closely analogous to that incurred by financiers of broadcast companies. Two recent bank-ruptcy cases have involved the interplay between the F.C.C. "no-lien" policy and a trustee's avoiding powers in bankruptcy. In both cases, In re Tak Communications, Inc., 138 Bankr. 568 (W.D. Wis. 1992) and In re Ridgely Communications, Inc., 139 Bankr. 374 (Bankr. D. Md. 1992), the secured lenders claimed perfected security interests in the proceeds from the sale of F.C.C. licenses. The *Tak* court adopted a deductive approach in declaring the license proceeds unencumbered. The lender could not lien the F.C.C. license by law; therefore, the proceeds were unencum-bered as proceeds of unencumbered collateral. The *Tak* court further rejected the creditors' argument that they held a "'limited' security inter-est in the proceeds from the sale of the license."

The *Ridgely* court took a more intuitive approach, notwithstanding the "no-lien" prohibition. "The right to transfer a license is a right between the F.C.C. and the licensee; the right to receive remuneration for the transfer is a right with respect to the two private parties." Reconciling its holding with the prohibition against liens on the license, the *Ridgely* court reasoned that the only lien right arising out of the lien on the license in that case "is the right of the creditor to claim proceeds received by the debtor licensee from a private buyer in exchange for the transfer of the license to that buyer." The *Ridgely* court acknowledged that the creditor was not entitled to foreclose on the license or to compel the transfer of the license, as "these are rights of the licensee vis-a-vis the F.C.C. and may not be abrogated by agreement."

If this Court adopted the *Tak* reasoning, proceeds from the termination of Debtor's franchise would be unencumbered because the Nissan fran-chise agreement arguably could not be subject to a lien. If this Court adopted the Ridgely analysis, the "no-lien" franchise agreement would be deemed ineffective to deprive either NBD or Success of a lien against proceeds from the sale to Rohrman. But these two approaches are not the exclusive means to resolve the problem presented by a "no-lien" franchise. This Court believes that a secured lender can protect itself by taking a lien either in the inherent value in the franchise or in general intangibles. See Freightliner Market Dev. v. Silver Wheel Freight, 823 F.2d 362, 369 (9th Cir. 1987) (transferability of license is irrelevant where creditor has a lien on general intangibles; "if the rights produce proceeds, those rights are in fact 'property'").

An automobile-floor planning financier may contemplate a bankruptcy filing by its borrower and take security in the inherent value of its borrow-er's market share. There is no reason why this value, or general intan-gibles such as goodwill and going concern value, cannot be deemed collateral separate from and derivative of the franchise. Obviously, a broader security interest in the automobile franchise would subsume these intangible interests and enable foreclosure of the dealership, but only if such security is available. But when the dealership is sold post-

petition and an independent security interest in the Debtor's market
share value is recognized, it becomes irrelevant whether the Nissan franchise itself could be subject to a lien.

For the contrary conclusion that the Termination Fee represents an
unencumbered "premium" paid for the Debtor's agreement to leave the
marketplace, the Debtor cites In re Oklahoma City Broadcasting Co., 112
Bankr. 425 (Bankr. W.D. Okla. 1990). In *Oklahoma City*, the debtor operated a television broadcasting company. The debtor granted its creditor
a lien on all of its assets, except its F.C.C. broadcasting license. The
secured creditor sought to determine the amount of its allowed secured
claim. As evidence of the value of the debtor's business, the creditor submitted an option contract showing a competing company's willingness
to pay $1,835,000 to buy the debtor's hard assets, plus $1,165,000 to
terminate the debtor's license and thereby reduce competition. Because
the creditor did not have a security interest in the F.C.C. license, the court
acknowledged that the only way the creditor could have a security interest in what it called the $1,165,000 "Bounty" is if "the Bounty or the
rights from which the Bounty arise are included within Debtor's general
intangibles." The court then summarily concluded that "where the
Bounty is being offered to take Debtor off the air, it is not a general
intangible."

It appears that the court in *Oklahoma City* was willing to recognize that
the "Bounty" could be viewed as collateral, or proceeds of collateral,
independent or derivative of the Debtor's unencumbered F.C.C. license.
To this extent, *Oklahoma City* is distinguishable from *Tak*. The problem
with *Oklahoma City*, however, is that it at once recognizes that certain
value exists but nevertheless concludes that the value is nondescript and
cannot be deemed a "general intangible." This Court disagrees. Indeed,
the very point of having a category of "general intangibles" subject to
encumbrance is to make available for financing purposes values not otherwise attributable to other categories of assets. To the extent that the
purchaser in *Oklahoma City* paid money to acquire market share, the
debtor gave up something of value, the type of miscellaneous intangible
property contemplated by the residual collateral category of "general
intangible." See [U.C.C. §9-102(a)(42)]. The contrary conclusion reached
in *Oklahoma City* means that certain types of valuable property vanish
into a black hole, unable to be financed or encumbered, only to emerge
unencumbered and transferable. Therefore, the reasoning of *Oklahoma
City* is unpersuasive — Rohrman paid $125,000 to induce the Debtor to
surrender valuable intangible rights evidenced by the franchise agreement, value that can be encumbered as an intangible property right.

This value, whether labelled "goodwill," "going concern value" or,
more aptly, "market share value," existed pre-petition at the time the
Debtor filed for relief. Indeed, this market share value represented by the
Nissan franchise became an asset of the estate much like the Nissan

automobiles. Recognizing the inherent market share value as pre-petition collateral comports with §552 of the Bankruptcy Code. Section 552 preserves to a great extent the status quo and protects state law property entitlements that existed as of the date of the filing. New, post-petition value is unencumbered. Old value is subject to perfected, pre-petition security interests in that value. Here, the Debtor's market share value constitutes pre-petition intangible property. The Rohrman purchase contract and the Termination Fee constitute proceeds of that intangible.

Judge Barliant takes an expansive view of property, pragmatically equating it with almost anything of value. Under his view, we can think of unencumberable property, such as franchises, licenses, and pension rights, as having the potential to produce property that can be encumbered. That potential is itself encumberable — a sort of "shadow property." We wonder whether the same might be true of other nonproperty, such as livers for transplant or babies for adoption.

D. Defeating the Limits on What May Be Collateral

Assume that debtors cannot create security interests in licenses and franchises. It nevertheless remains true that debtors can create security interests in (1) the proceeds that come into existence when debtors sell those licenses and franchises and (2) the revenues that debtors derive from the use of their licenses and franchises. Debtors can grant security interests in both kinds of collateral long before they come into existence. The sum of the value coming from the use and ultimate disposition of the licenses and franchises is necessarily equal to the value of the franchises and licenses themselves. It follows that the sale and use security interests one can take in relation to franchises and licenses are every bit as useful, valuable, and effective as are the direct security interests one cannot take because licenses and franchises are not "property." Judge Barliant understood this and we think it is the reason he was willing to recognize "market share" as an asset that can be used as collateral.

Of course, a security interest in the sale and use values of licenses and franchises does not protect the secured creditor from cancellation of the licenses or franchises by the governments or franchisors who created them. But that is a problem the secured creditor would

have even if the law permitted the secured creditor to take a direct
security interest in the licenses and franchises. An interest in the
value of a franchise is not quite as good as an interest in a franchise.
The former does not entitle the secured creditor to foreclose, take
over the franchise, and run the business itself to maximize the profits. But it is a lot better than nothing. Nor does it assure that a bankruptcy court will honor the security interest if the license or franchise
is exchanged for something else of value during bankruptcy.

When courts do honor the security interest upon exchange during
bankruptcy, the effect is to enable sophisticated creditors to take security interests in much of the value of licenses and franchises. What
appears at first to be a limit on what may serve as collateral is revealed
instead to be merely a limit on *how* creditors take their interests in
these kinds of value.

Problem Set 12

12.1.   Commodore National Bank is contemplating making a loan
in the amount of $20 million to superstation KROK-TV. Commodore
wants to make sure it has a security interest in each of the following
items. Can it get such an interest, and, if so, how should the security
agreement describe the collateral? U.C.C. §§9-102(2), (33), (42),
9-108(e)(1).
    a.   The electronic equipment used in broadcasting.
    b.   The station's "peacock" logo, which cost $15,000 to design and
test and which is protected by federal and state trademark registrations.
    c.   The station's broadcast license, which was issued by the Federal
Communications Commission (the lawyer and former member of
Congress who prepared the application for the license was paid fees
totaling $360,000). U.C.C. §9-408.
    d.   The station's reputation for accurate news reporting, which the
Wall Street Journal recently called "KROK-TV's greatest asset."
    e.   The station's cause of action for slander against a former
employee who told CNN that KROK had faked news footage of a
recent earthquake in Los Angeles.
    f.   The $7.3 million in advertising revenues that KROK-TV is
expected to earn from its operations in the remainder of the current
year (all but a few hundred dollars of it will be for advertising services
rendered before the advertiser pays for them).
    12.2.   After Commodore made the loan described in the previous
problem, KROK-TV defaulted, ceased broadcasting, and filed bankruptcy. The case was converted to Chapter 7 and Marietta Parker was
appointed trustee. At the time of filing, KROK owned nothing not on

the list in Problem 12.1. The balance owing on the loan clearly exceeds the present value of all of the items on that list. What steps do you take to realize on the loan? Bankr. Code §§362(a) and (d), 363(f) and 541(a)(1).

12.3. Our client, the Bank of Friend, plans to lend $125,000 to Saul Finkel to buy an establishment named Harry's Bar. Harry's Bar consists of furniture, fixtures (including the mounted head of an enormous rhino), and leasehold, but its most valuable asset is its liquor license. An employee of the Board of Liquor Control has told you this kind of license is worth about $80,000. The state law under which this liquor license was issued recites that "the license shall continue as a personal privilege granted by the board and nothing herein shall constitute the license as property." The law also provides a long list of grounds on which the license can be revoked. The Board's practice, however, has been to revoke licenses only in extreme circumstances or after numerous warnings against continuing violations of the liquor laws. Because licenses are "personal" and not "property," the Board maintains that they cannot be sold. But the Board nearly always issues a new license to a qualified person who buys a bar from an existing licensee. U.C.C. §9-408

a. What should the Bank of Friend take as security?

b. What can the Bank of Friend do to realize the value of this liquor license if the debtor does not repay the loan?

c. Would there be any advantage in requiring that Saul form a corporation to buy Harry's Bar?

12.4. Your client, Charles Desmond, is in serious financial difficulty. Takki Equipment, the creditor who will be the key to Desmond's financial recovery, is represented by your old law school classmate, Martin Short. Short turned down all of Desmond's workout proposals until he learned that Desmond had a vested interest in an ERISA pension plan valued at nearly $300,000. Short says that if you add a security interest in the pension plan to your earlier offer, he will recommend it to Takki. Desmond understands that his attempt to grant a security interest in the pension rights may have serious adverse tax consequences for him, but he says they won't be nearly as bad as his pending financial collapse — the only apparent alternative. Should you send Short the offer he asked for?

12.5. a. Zelda Pirosky has come to see you about her financial problems. She owes a considerable amount of money on charge cards, charge accounts, and personal loans. The creditor that is giving her the most trouble is Incredibly Friendly Finance (IFF). Zelda borrowed $2,500 from IFF two years ago. Even though her payments on the account seem to her substantial, interest is running at 36 percent per year (which is the maximum legally permissible rate in your state) and the balance is now over $3,000. The loan application Zelda made asked for a detailed listing of all the property she owned. Zelda listed clothing, furniture, appliances, her four-year-old Toyota automobile, and numerous other items. After IFF approved her application, they asked her to sign a security agreement granting them an interest in the following items: video game set (replacement cost $200), a collection of pictures drawn by her children (no market value), old family photographs dating back to the Civil War (market value unknown), her jewelry (replacement cost about $500), her Toyota automobile (market value $2,000), her portable computer (market value $500), and any "replacements or substitutions." Zelda signed because she wanted the loan. Has IFF done anything illegal? 16 C.F.R. 444.

b.   A few months ago, the video game set broke and Zelda replaced it with a new one, which she bought for $200. ("I know I shouldn't have bought it, but the kids were hassling me more than Bob White," Zelda says. Bob White is the IFF collection officer assigned to Zelda's account.) Does IFF have a security interest in the new video game set? U.C.C. §9-204(b)(1).

c.   During her last conversation with Mr. White, White reminded her of the terms of the security agreement and told her that if she did not get $200 to him by Monday, he very reluctantly would be forced to call the loan and take the collateral. Zelda is frantic. "I can't do without *any* of these things," she says, "but even if I paid Mr. White the $200, he'll just want more." What do you advise? Bankr. Code §522(f).

Chapter 4. Default: The Gateway to Remedies

Assignment 13: Default, Acceleration, and Cure Under State Law

A. Default

In the first five assignments of this book, we discussed the remedies available to creditors under state law. Creditors have access to those remedies if, and only if, the debtor is "in default." U.C.C. §9-601(a). Article 9 of the U.C.C. does not define default or make any effort to say when a debtor is in it. Defined most simply, *default* is the debtor's failure to pay the debt when due or otherwise perform the agreement between debtor and creditor.

Secured creditors may need to exercise their remedies as soon as a debtor goes into default. Yet, if they exercise their remedies under state law before the debtor goes into default, they act wrongfully and are liable for any damage they inflict. To clear the way for a speedy exercise of remedies, secured creditors generally prefer that the security agreement define precisely what acts or failures constitute default. Secured creditors also prefer that those acts or failures be expansively defined so that in any circumstance in which they may want remedies, remedies will be available to them.

Debtors typically share the secured creditors' preference for precise definition of the terms of default. Debtors, of course, want default defined narrowly and precisely so they can avoid it. The result is that most security agreements contain extensive definitions of default. As to the substance of the definition, the interests of secured creditors and their debtors are in conflict — it is in precisely those situations where secured creditors want to exercise remedies that debtors want contract protection against them. The conflict usually is resolved in favor of the secured creditor: Security agreements nearly always define default expansively. The reason may be that secured creditors are more concerned than debtors about default and more ready to contemplate it, or it may be that such terms merely reflect the relative bargaining power of the parties.

The default provisions that follow are typical of those included in well-drafted security agreements.

Standard Default Provisions

Howard Ruda, Asset Based Financing,
A Transactional Guide 3-285-86 (1997)

11.   EVENTS OF DEFAULT; ACCELERATION

. . . The following are events of default under this agreement . . . :

(a) Any of Debtor's obligations to Secured Party under any agreement with Secured Party is not paid promptly when due;

(b) Debtor breaches any warranty or provision hereof, or of any note or of any other instrument or agreement delivered by Debtor to Secured Party in connection with this or any other transaction;

(c) Debtor dies, becomes insolvent or ceases to do business as a going concern;

(d) it is determined that Debtor has given Secured Party materially misleading information regarding its financial condition;

(e) any of the collateral is lost or destroyed;

(f) a petition in bankruptcy or for arrangement or reorganization be filed by or against Debtor or Debtor admits its inability to pay its debts as they mature;

(g) property of Debtor be attached or a receiver be appointed for Debtor;

(h) Whenever Secured Party in good faith believes the prospect of payment or performance is impaired or in good faith believes the collateral is insecure;

(i) any guarantor, surety or endorser for Debtor defaults in any obligation or liability to Secured Party or any guaranty obtained in connection with this transaction is terminated or breached.

If debtor shall be in default hereunder, the indebtedness herein described and all other debts then owing by Debtor to Secured Party under this or any other present or future agreement shall, if Secured Party shall so elect, become immediately due any payable. . . .

13.   WAIVER OF DEFAULTS; AGREEMENT
INCLUSIVE

Secured Party may in its sole discretion waive a default, or cure, at Debtor's expense, a default. Any such waiver in a particular instance or of a particular default shall not be a waiver of other defaults or the same kind of default at another time. No modification or change in this Security Agreement or any related note, instrument or agreement shall bind

Secured Party unless in writing signed by Secured Party. No oral agreement shall be binding.

Under an agreement such as this, virtually any breach of contract by the debtor puts the debtor in default. In fact, the debtor may be in default even if the debtor has performed every obligation under its contract and done everything in its power to placate the secured creditor. In section D of this assignment, we explore the limits of the secured creditor's power under such expansive definitions of default. First, more basic matters beckon.

B.   When Is Payment Due?

Most defaults actually acted upon by secured creditors are defaults in payment. That is, the debtor failed to pay all or part of the loan by the deadline specified in the contract between the parties. To predict the likely legal consequences of failures in payment, it is helpful to understand the commercial contexts in which the particular failures occur. For that reason, we describe some of the more common arrangements for repayment. Keep in mind as you read about them that these arrangements are fixed by contract at the time the loans are made and are therefore subject to almost infinite variation.

1.   Installment Loans

A loan is an *installment loan* if the parties contemplate that the debtor will repay in a series of payments. Ordinarily, these payments will be at regular intervals. They may be due monthly, quarterly, or annually. The payments may vary in amount, but more often all the payments in the series are equal. Probably the most common kinds of installment loans are real estate mortgages and car loans, which usually specify repayment in equal monthly installments over a specified number of years. Installments are the typical form for repayment of a seller or lender who finances the debtor's purchase of a particular item of business equipment, such as an aircraft, a computer, or a drill press, or even an entire business. Even unsecured loans are often made on an installment basis. From the debtor's point of view, repayment in installments is preferable to many of the other repayment contracts discussed here, because it provides the debtor with maximum legal protection against arbitrary action by the lender. The debtor knows that if it makes each payment by the due date and otherwise complies with the loan agreement, it will not be in default or subject to creditor remedies. Installment payments also provide a form of enforced budgeting that is absent in single payment loans.

2. Single Payment Loans

Many secured loans are made payable on a particular day. Often this is because the parties expect that the debtor will have the money to pay on that date. For example, a loan secured by a large account receivable of the debtor may be payable on the date the account is due. In other instances, loans are made payable on a particular date, perhaps 60 days, 90 days, or a year later, with no expectation that the debtor will have the money to pay on that date. In such cases, the understanding is usually that if the debtor's financial circumstances remain satisfactory, the bank will renew the note for an additional period, without requiring actual payment. (This is referred to as *rolling the note* or a *rollover*.) The usual understanding is that the bank has no legally binding obligation to roll a note.

This combination of a legally binding document that says one thing and a nonlegally binding understanding that the document won't be strictly or arbitrarily enforced is even more apparent in the case of loans payable "on demand." The literal meaning of this term is that the debtor will pay the loan whenever the bank demands the money. (The making of such a demand is referred to as "calling" the loan.) Yet in most situations in which loans are made payable on demand, the parties know full well that if the bank calls the loan without warning, the debtor would not be able to pay and would go into default. One might expect that debtors would be reluctant to agree to repayment terms they know they cannot meet. That appears, however, not to be the case. Statistics issued by the Federal Reserve show that over 30 percent of the dollar amount of all loans by commercial banks is payable on demand. Whether the courts should give literal effect to repayment contracts such as these is considered in section D of this assignment.

3. Lines of Credit

A business's need for capital may vary widely over time. For example, a manufacturer of toys may need substantial amounts of capital to pay suppliers and payroll as it builds inventory in anticipation of the Christmas season. As it receives payment from sales of the Christmas inventory, its need for capital may decline. One way for this toy manufacturer to assure that it will have sufficient capital for the Christmas season would be to capitalize the business at its peak need and keep the money in a bank account or other liquid investment during the rest of the year. To illustrate, if the debtor assessed its peak capital need at $1 million, the debtor might attempt to raise about $1.1 million through the sale of stock in the company. Debtor would deposit the $1.1 million in a bank account and draw on those funds to meet its peak needs at Christmas. This way of dealing with the problem is rarely practical, because the toy manufacturer would have to pay a high rate of return for the stock investments, while for much of the year the funds would be in a bank account earning a much lower rate of return.

Probably most toy manufacturers prefer to borrow the money they need for the Christmas season and pay it back when the season is over. Our toy manufacturer could accomplish this in a crude fashion by estimating how much extra cash it will need at the peak of the season and borrowing a little more than that amount (in case the estimate is low) at the beginning of the season under a contract that calls for repayment on a date safely after the end of the season. By that means, the toy manufacturer could make sure it would have enough money to repay the loan when it was due and that it would not go into default. The problem with this approach is essentially the same as with the first. The toy manufacturer would be paying high interest rates to have money during times when it didn't need it and would be reinvesting the same money at much lower rates.

A *line of credit* is a more sophisticated application of the second approach. The bank contracts to lend up to a fixed amount of money (the line "limit") as the debtor needs it. Under most line arrangements, the debtor "borrows" the money simply by writing a check on its bank account. The bank covers all overdrafts up to the limit of the line of credit by drawing against the line, and charges the debtor interest on the money only from the time it pays the money out. As the debtor receives revenues from its operations, it uses the money to pay down on the line of credit obligation, thereby stopping the accrual of interest. A debtor operating under a line of credit may have no cash of its own; all payments may be made from the line and all revenues applied to the line. In some line of credit arrangements, the debtor does not even have a bank account. It pays bills by sending instruction to the bank; the bank writes and mails the checks, charging them to the debtor's loan account. When the debtor receives payments from customers, it forwards the payments to the bank, which logs them in as loan payments.

As we have described the line of credit thus far, the debtor is in the happy position of having to pay its debts only when it has the money to do so. Banks cannot be quite so accommodating. They must know there is some due date, so they can get out of the arrangement if they want. To make that possible, some require that the line debt fall due at a particular date during the debtor's off season. In the case of our toy manufacturer, that might be in January, when all of its Christmas revenues will be in and its cash needs will be at their lowest. A debtor who can pay the line to zero each year will not mind doing so. Many debtors, however, expect to have an outstanding balance on their line of credit during the entire year. Such a debtor's cash needs are for an indefinite time; yet banks do not make indefinite loans. Here again, the likely solution will be to set a date for repayment with the expectation of a rollover or to make the loan payable on demand with the expectation that the bank will be reasonable about calling it.

C. Acceleration and Cure

1. Acceleration

Assume that Debtor agrees to repay an interest-free loan in ten monthly installments of $10,000 each. Debtor makes the first payment when due and then misses the next two. Creditor sues. But for how much? Absent a contract provision to the contrary, the ten installments are treated as ten separate obligations. Debtor is in default only with regard to two payments, and Creditor is entitled to sue only for those two. Creditor will sue for $20,000.

From the creditor's point of view, this must seem entirely unreasonable. The creditor is put to a choice. It can sue now for only two payments and bring additional lawsuits when, as the creditor expects, the debtor misses more payments, or it can wait seven more months and then sue for all nine payments at the same time. (In the meantime, the debtor might dissipate its remaining assets or disappear altogether.)

Not surprisingly, most creditors require a provision in an installment loan agreement that opts out of the common law rule. Such provisions are referred to as *acceleration clauses*. Typically, they state that in the event of default by the debtor in any obligation under the repayment contract, the Creditor may, at its option, declare all of the payments immediately due and payable. (Such a provision appears at the end of paragraph 11 in section A of this assignment.) The creditor can then enforce the entire obligation in a single lawsuit.

The practical effect of acceleration is often to eliminate the debtor's ability to cure its default. Assume, for example, the typical case in which George finances the purchase of a $100,000 house by executing an $80,000 mortgage, payable in equal monthly installments, with interest at eight percent per year. The monthly payments on this mortgage are $587.02. George encounters temporary financial difficulties and falls three payments behind, for a total of $1,761.06. The creditor, Federal Savings, sends George a letter stating that George is in default and that if George does not "cure" the default by paying $1,761.06 within ten days, it will exercise its right to accelerate. If George pays the $1,761.06 arrearage before Federal Savings accelerates, the installment payment schedule continues in force and George can continue to pay $587.02 each month. If, however, George does not pay the arrearage within the ten-day period and Federal Savings sends George another letter electing to accelerate, the entire mortgage balance of approximately $80,000 becomes due and payable. George can no longer cure the default by paying $1,761.06. Of course, George still has the common law right to redeem the house by paying the entire balance of approximately $80,000. But it is a rare debtor who can't cure by paying the arrearage before acceleration, but can redeem by paying the entire balance after acceleration. So as a practical matter, acceleration usually ends the installment debtor's ability to retain the collateral and permits the creditor to get out of the installment lending arrangement.

2.   Limits on the Enforceability of Acceleration Clauses

A secured creditor can exercise its right to accelerate for even a tiny or fleeting default in payment, as the following case makes clear. But if the grounds for acceleration are merely that the secured creditor "deems itself insecure" (often called an *insecurity clause*), the creditor has the right to accelerate only if it in good faith believes the prospect of payment or performance is impaired. U.C.C. §1-208. 1-309

J.R. Hale Contracting Co. v. United New Mexico Bank at Albuquerque

799 P.2d 581 (N.M. 1990)

RANSOM, JUSTICE. . . .
    The company had been a customer of the bank for about eleven years prior to the circumstances that gave rise to this suit. During this period of time the company entered into numerous revolving credit notes with the bank in gradually increasing amounts. These notes routinely were renewed on or about the due date despite the fact that the company frequently was late a number of days or even weeks in making its payments. The bank seems not to have been troubled by the payments being past

due and took no action in each instance other than possibly contacting the company to request that the payments be brought up to date. The company would send a check or the bank simply would deduct the payment from one of the company's accounts at the bank and send a notice of advice regarding the transaction.

The note at issue in this case was executed in November 1982 in the amount of $400,000. This was double the amount of any previous note. The first and only interest payment on the note was due March 1, 1983, and the note itself was due on July 31, 1983. The note provided that:

> If ANY installment of principal and/or interest on this note is not paid when due . . . or if Bank in good faith deems itself insecure or believes that the prospect of receiving payment required by this note is impaired; thereupon, at the option of Bank, this note and any and all other indebtedness of Maker to Bank shall become and be due and payable forthwith without demand, notice of nonpayment, presentment, protest or notice of dishonor, all of which are hereby expressly waived by Maker. . . .

Toward the end of February 1983, J.R. and Bruce Hale, on behalf of the company, approached the bank to borrow additional funds to cover contracting expenses associated with construction at the Double Eagle II Airport in Albuquerque. The existing $400,000 line of credit was fully drawn. Beginning in the first week in March, the Hales met with the bankers several times a week hoping to arrange for additional financing. The company had not made the March 1 interest payment on the existing loan. J.R. and Bruce Hale stated that no one ever contacted them concerning the delinquent payment and the matter never came up during the March meetings. J.R. Hale carried a blank check to these meetings for the purpose of making the interest payment but stated that he forgot to do so. He stated that on one occasion he called the bank officer assigned to his account and asked the officer to remind him at the next meeting and he would make the payment, but the officer had not done so. Apparently, it was necessary for the bank to calculate the interest payment in order to know the specific amount to be paid.

At the same time that the company was seeking to secure additional financing, the bankers had become concerned about the existing $400,000 loan. The financial statements that the company periodically supplied the bank indicated that the company had lost approximately $800,000 during the last six to seven months. While the Hales were under the impression that additional financing was in the works (a loan application to this effect had been prepared and had been taken to the loan committee for discussion), the bank seriously was considering calling in the company's existing obligations. This possibility never was communicated to the Hales as the bank wished them to remain cooperative. After a meeting on March 22 the bank requested and received from the

Hales a list of customers for the undisclosed purpose of using it to collect directly the company's accounts.

The bank called a meeting on March 24 and presented the Hales with a letter stating that all amounts due on the $400,000 revolving line of credit were due and payable immediately. The grounds for the acceleration were stated to be that "The promissory note is in default due to your failure to pay the March 1, 1983 interest payment when due, and also due to the Bank's review of your financial situation which causes the Bank to believe that its prospect for receiving payment of the note is impaired." J.R. Hale produced a blank check and offered to pay the delinquent interest charges but the bank would not reconsider. The bank was able to collect the balance of the note with interest, $418,801.86, in about two weeks after exercising its right to set off the company's accounts at the bank and after receiving payments from the company's customers on their outstanding accounts. . . .

WAIVER, MODIFICATION, AND ESTOPPEL DISTINGUISHED

The company's arguments regarding waiver, modification, and estoppel are intertwined and rely upon the same root proposition: that the conduct of the bank negated the express default provision in the note. The distinctions to be made in the application of these concepts, especially in that of waiver and estoppel, have not always been clear in our cases and some discussion on the point is warranted. . . .

Generally, New Mexico cases have defined waiver as the intentional relinquishment or abandonment of a known right. Our decisions recognize that the intent to waive contractual obligations or conditions may be implied from a party's representations that fall short of an express declaration of waiver, or from his conduct. While not express, these types of "implied in fact" waivers still represent a voluntary act whose effect is intended.

In Ed Black's Chevrolet Center, Inc. v. Melichar, 81 N.M. 602, 471 P.2d 172 (1970), we stated that, based upon the honest belief of the other party that a waiver was intended, a waiver might be presumed or implied contrary to the intention of the party waiving certain rights. Following that decision a number of our opinions discussed a waiver "implied" from a course of conduct in terms of estoppel. These cases represent what we would term here as *waiver by estoppel.* To prove waiver by estoppel the party need only show that he was misled to his prejudice by the conduct of the other party into the honest and reasonable belief that such waiver was intended. The estoppel is justified because the estopped party reasonably could expect that his actions would induce the reliance of the other party. However, unlike the case of a voluntary waiver, either express or implied in fact, the waiver of the contractual obligation or condition and the effect of the conduct upon the opposite party may have been unintentional. . . .

NO ACTUAL WAIVER, EXPRESS OR IMPLIED
IN FACT

. . . We believe that the postagreement conduct of the bank does not suggest that the bank actually intended to waive its rights under the contract. When a party accepts a late payment on a contract without comment he waives the default that existed. With repetition his actions may suggest an intention to accept late payments generally. In this case, the overdue interest payment was the first payment due under the contract; the bank had not accepted any earlier late payments on that contract. The payment was overdue, the company did not request an extension, and after twenty-three days the bank declared a default. The parties agree that the matter of the overdue interest payment was not discussed during the series of meetings when the company sought to obtain additional financing. For good reasons, the fact that the bank would declare a default based upon the unpaid interest payment may have come as a surprise to the Hales, the bank's silence may have been misleading in the light of the earlier commercial behavior of the parties, but we do not believe that the bank's conduct during the month of March gives rise to a factual question that it was the bank's actual intention to relinquish any contractual rights. At most, the bank's conduct indicated an intention simply to ignore the delinquency for about three weeks.

NO MODIFICATION

Likewise, we agree with the trial court that the facts of this case do not raise an issue of contract modification. We have concluded in our discussion of the waiver issue that no factual question exists on whether the bank for its part actually intended to waive its right to declare a default based upon the past due interest payment. It follows that there can be no issue of whether the parties intended to substitute a new agreement for their earlier one, or whether the parties mutually agreed to amend the contractual provision concerning default and acceleration, and whether this agreement was supported by consideration. . . .

"WAIVER BY ESTOPPEL" PRESENTED AN ISSUE
OF FACT

The company's estoppel argument rests upon an important distinction from actual waiver. Here the previous course of dealings between the parties is relevant to show the meaning that the company reasonably might attribute to the bank's conduct in not mentioning the overdue interest payment. Implicit in [U.C.C. §1-205(1)] is the recognition that, as a practical matter, one party to a contract will use his past commercial dealings with another party as a basis for the interpretation of the other party's conduct. Thus it is to be expected that the company would interpret the bank's behavior during the month of March in light of their earlier dealings and we believe the bank should have been aware of this consideration. . . .

Some of the facts to which we refer can be regarded as silence on the bank's part in the face of an apparent false sense of security of the company. Silence may form the basis for estoppel if a party stands mute when he has a duty to speak. As we have discussed, the circumstances here suggest that the bank reasonably could expect that the company would rely on the bank's failure to request the interest payment. Under these circumstances we believe the bank had a duty to inform the company that the bank would enforce performance under the contract according to the letter of their agreement.

On the question of detrimental reliance we note that the company cannot be said to have been lulled by the postagreement conduct into missing the payment when it was first due on March 1. However, we believe the company reasonably might have been induced into not taking the initiative to correct the delinquency and waiting instead for the bank to request the payment or in some fashion draw the matter to the company's attention. Certainly to have the bank declare a default without warning and then accelerate all payments can be considered the detrimental result of the reliance on the impression that the bank's conduct reasonably might have conveyed.

"LACK OF GOOD FAITH" PRESENTED AN ISSUE OF FACT UNDER CLAUSE PROVIDING FOR ACCELERATION BECAUSE OF INSECURITY

At trial the bank moved for a directed verdict on a second ground, that the company failed to introduce sufficient evidence showing the bank lacked a good faith belief that its prospect for repayment was impaired. The company had the burden of proof on that issue. [U.C.C. §1-208]. The trial judge denied the bank's motion, stating that he believed there were facts in the record from which a jury could conclude that the bank lacked good faith. The bank asserts that the judge applied the wrong standard regarding "good faith" as used in an insecurity clause giving a secured party the power to accelerate payments.

[U.C.C. §1-208] governs the acceleration of notes. It provides that a party may accelerate payment or performance "only if he in good faith believes that the prospect of payment or performance is impaired." "Good faith" is defined by [U.C.C. §1-201(19)] as "honesty in fact in the conduct or transaction concerned.". . .

In essence, the requirement of honesty in fact is subjective and is concerned with the actual state of mind of the creditor. Nevertheless, the determination of ultimate fact, whether or not the bank lacked a good faith belief in the impairment of its prospect for repayment, should be based on the facts and circumstances surrounding the acceleration and not solely on the bank's testimony concerning its state of mind. Even under a subjective test of good faith the trier of fact may evaluate the credibility of a creditor's claim and in doing so may take into account the reasonableness of that claim. Thus, the conduct and credibility of the creditor may be tested by objective standards subject to proof and conducive to the application of reasonable expectations in commercial affairs.

We do not mean to suggest that dual elements of reasonableness and good faith are required. Put simply, in the absence of an objective basis upon which a reasonable person would have accelerated the note, the fact finder could infer that the creditor really did not perceive his prospect for repayment to be impaired. This inquiry necessarily will focus on the facts and circumstances that were known to the creditor. As Judge Sutin noted in [McKay v. Farmers & Stockmens Bank of Clayton, 585 P.2d 325, 329 (N.M. 1978)], expert testimony may be necessary to assist the trier of fact. 92 N.M. at 185, 585 P.2d at 329. . . .

CONCLUSION

For the reasons stated above, we reverse the district court's grant of a directed verdict in favor of the bank based on the interest default clause and hold that an issue of waiver by estoppel exists to be resolved by the jury. In addition, the company also must prove that the bank lacked a good faith belief that its prospect for repayment was impaired.

It is so ordered.

To most people, calling a loan when the debtor is current on the payments probably seems pretty outrageous. But the vast majority of security agreements contain laundry lists of provisions under which debtors can be in default even while current on the payments. The typical agreement permits the creditor to accelerate for any default, however small.

3. The Debtor's Right to Cure

As we noted above, a debtor has the right to cure a default by paying the amounts then due. If the debtor cures before the creditor accelerates, the necessary sum may be small. Some debtors, particularly those who get reminders from their creditors, make up the payments in time and get out of jeopardy. The following case illustrates the general rule that once acceleration has occurred, a debtor can cure, or, more accurately, redeem, only by paying the entire amount of the accelerated debt.

Old Republic Insurance Co. v. Lee

507 So. 2d 754 (Fla. Dist. Ct. App. 1987)

UPCHURCH, C.J.

Appellant, Old Republic Insurance Co., appeals an order granting a motion to reinstate a mortgage.

The promissory note that the second mortgage at issue secured provided for monthly payments of $387.85 each. On April 29, 1986, Old Republic declared the note in default because appellees, the Lees, had not made the payments due March and April 19th. The Lees were notified that the mortgage was being declared in default and the unpaid principal balance was being accelerated. On May 16, William Lee sent Old Republic a certified check for the payments due March, April and May 19. Old Republic returned the check and filed suit to foreclose. Lee filed an answer and a motion to reinstate the mortgage on the basis that the Lees had tendered payment and that the property was now for sale and Old Republic would be paid from the proceeds.

The court granted the motion to reinstate finding that there was substantial equity in the real estate subject to the mortgage, that the first mortgage, having a principal balance of approximately $47,000.00 was current, and that the second mortgage of Old Republic was to be paid out of the proceeds of a proposed sale.

We find that the reinstatement of the mortgage and the refusal of the court to order foreclosure was error and reverse. As a general rule of law, a mortgagor, prior to the election of a right to accelerate by the mortgage holder upon the occurrence of a default, may tender the arrears due and thereby prevent the mortgage holder from exercising his option to accelerate. However, once the mortgage holder has exercised his option to accelerate, the right of the mortgagor to tender only the arrears is terminated. . . .

REVERSED and REMANDED for further proceedings consistent with this opinion.

Statutes in some states permit cure and reinstatement of the original loan terms by payment of only the arrearages even after the secured creditor has exercised its contract right to accelerate.

Reinstatement

Ill. Rev. Stat. ch. 110, ¶5-1602 (1991)

In any foreclosure of a mortgage . . . which has become due prior to the maturity date fixed in the mortgage, or in any instrument or obligation secured by the mortgage, through acceleration because of a default under the mortgage, a mortgagor may reinstate the mortgage as provided herein. Reinstatement is effected by curing all defaults then existing, other than payment of such portion of the principal which would not have been due had no acceleration occurred, and by paying all costs and expenses required by the mortgage to be paid in the event of such defaults, provided that such cure and payment are made prior to the expiration of 90 days from the date the mortgagor [is served with summons or by publication in the foreclosure case or submits to the jurisdiction of the court]. . . . Upon such reinstatement of the mortgage, the foreclosure and any other proceedings for the collection or enforcement of the obligation secured by the mortgage shall be dismissed and the mortgage documents shall remain in full force and effect as if no acceleration or default had occurred. . . .

The state legislatures that enact provisions such as these usually limit their application to home mortgages, to consumer borrowers, or to some other circumstances that the legislators believe most require this form of regulation.

D. The Enforceability of Payment Terms

As we described in section B of this assignment, debtors and creditors often agree to payment terms the debtors have no real hope of satisfying. Given the severe consequences of a default, some courts have sought ways of softening those terms. If the facts of a particular case are capable of supporting a defense of waiver or estoppel, these courts may be amenable. (Recall the efforts of the court in J.R. Hale Contracting v. United New Mexico Bank.) But when lending institutions are careful in their administration of the loan, the courts are eventually forced to deal with the ultimate issues: Are harsh payment terms enforceable? Can debtors contract to be at the mercy of their secured creditors?

In a landmark case that helped establish the doctrine of "lender liability," the Sixth Circuit declined to enforce literally the contract between a bank and a borrower engaged in the wholesale and retail grocery business. KMC Co. v. Irving Trust Co., 757 F.2d 752 (6th Cir. 1985). In 1979, Irving and KMC entered into an agreement for a $3.5 million line of credit, secured by an interest in all of KMC's assets. The promissory note was payable on demand. In 1982, KMC sought to draw $800,000 on the line of credit, which would have increased the loan balance to just under the $3.5 million limit. Without prior notice, Irving refused to make the advance. At the time it sought the advance, KMC was attempting to sell its business. Irving's refusal of the advance killed the possibility of a sale and assured the collapse of KMC's business. Irving's defenses were that (1) KMC was already collapsing anyway, and (2) refusing to honor KMC's draw was no different from honoring the draw and immediately making a demand for the entire $3.5 million, which Irving had the right to do under the demand promissory note.

KMC sued Irving for breach of contract, arguing in part that Irving called the loan based on a "personality conflict" between a bank officer and KMC's president. The court instructed the jury that

> there is implied in every contract an obligation of good faith, that this obligation may have imposed on Irving a duty to give notice to KMC before refusing to advance funds under the agreement up to the $3.5 million limit; and that such notice would be required if necessary to the proper execution of the contract, unless Irving's decision to refuse to advance funds without prior notice was made in good faith and in the reasonable exercise of its discretion.

The jury found Irving liable and fixed damages at $7,500,000, the entire value of KMC's business. Irving appealed.

The Sixth Circuit upheld the verdict, saying:

> As part of the procedure established for the operation of the financing agreement, the parties agreed in a supplementary letter that all receipts of KMC would be deposited into a "blocked account" to which Irving would have sole access. Consequently, unless KMC obtained alternative financing, a refusal by Irving to advance funds would leave KMC without operating capital until it had paid down its loan. The record clearly established that a medium-sized company in the wholesale grocery business, such as KMC, could not operate without outside financing. Thus, the literal interpretation of the financing agreement urged upon us by Irving, as supplemented by the "blocked account" mechanism, would leave KMC's continued existence entirely at the whim or mercy of Irving, absent an obligation of good faith performance. Logically, at such time as Irving might wish to curtail financing KMC, as was its right under the agreement, this obligation to act in good faith would require a period of notice to KMC to allow it a reasonable opportunity to seek alternate financing, absent valid business reasons precluding Irving from doing so. . . .

Nor are we persuaded by Irving's reasoning with respect to the effect of the demand provision in the agreement. We agree with the Magistrate that just as Irving's discretion whether or not to advance funds is limited by an obligation of good faith performance, so too would be its power to demand repayment. The demand provision is a kind of acceleration clause, upon which the Uniform Commercial Code and the courts have imposed limitations of reasonableness and fairness. See U.C.C. §1-208. . . .

In the case that follows, the Seventh Circuit rejected the holding in *KMC.* While the case applies the equitable subordination doctrine from bankruptcy law, the case ultimately turns on the U.C.C. issue of good faith.

Kham & Nate's Shoes No. 2, Inc. v. First Bank of Whiting

908 F.2d 1351 (7th Cir. 1990)

EASTERBROOK, CIRCUIT JUDGE.

Kham & Nate's Shoes No. 2, Inc., ran four retail shoe stores In Chicago. . . . The Bank first extended credit to the Debtor in July 1981. This $50,000 loan was renewed in December 1981 and repaid in part in July 1982. The balance was rolled over until late 1983, when with interest it came to $42,000. . . . In late 1983 Debtor, experiencing serious cash-flow problems, asked for additional capital, which Bank agreed to provide if the loan could be made secure. . . . Debtor and Bank then signed their loan agreement, which opens a $300,000 line of credit. The contract provides for cancellation on five days' notice and adds for good measure that "nothing provided herein shall constitute a waiver of the right of the Bank to terminate financing at any time."

The parties signed the contract on January 23, 1984, and Debtor quickly took about $75,000. . . . On February 29 Bank mailed Debtor a letter stating that it would make no additional advances after March 7. Although the note underlying the line of credit required payment on demand, Bank did not make the demand. It continued honoring . . . draws. Debtor's ultimate indebtedness to Bank was approximately $164,000. . . .

Bankruptcy Judge Coar held an evidentiary hearing and concluded that Bank had behaved inequitably in terminating the line of credit. . . . [The remedy imposed by Judge Coar was to subordinate the bank's security interest to the interests of other creditors, essentially rendering it uncollectible.]

Cases subordinating the claims of creditors that dealt at arm's length with the debtor are few and far between. Benjamin v. Diamond, 563 F.2d

692 (5th Cir. 1977) (*Mobile Steel Co.*), suggests that subordination depends on a combination of inequitable conduct, unfair advantage to the creditor, and injury to other creditors. Debtor submits that conduct may be "unfair" and "inequitable" for this purpose even though the creditor complies with all contractual requirements, but we are not willing to embrace a rule that requires participants in commercial transactions not only to keep their contracts but also do "more" — just how much more resting in the discretion of a bankruptcy judge assessing the situation years later. Contracts specify the duties of the parties to each other, and each may exercise the privileges it obtained. Banks sometimes bind themselves to make loans (commitment letters and letters of credit have this effect) and sometimes reserve the right to terminate further advances. Courts may not convert one form of contract into the other after the fact, without raising the cost of credit or jeopardizing its availability. Unless pacts are enforced according to their terms, the institution of contract, with all the advantages private negotiation and agreement brings, is jeopardized.

"Inequitable conduct" in commercial life means breach plus some advantage-taking, such as the star who agrees to act in a motion picture and then, after $20 million has been spent, sulks in his dressing room until the contract has been renegotiated. Firms that have negotiated contracts are entitled to enforce them to the letter, even to the great discomfort of their trading partners, without being mulcted for lack of "good faith." Although courts often refer to the obligation of good faith that exists in every contractual relation, this is not an invitation to the court to decide whether one party ought to have exercised privileges expressly reserved in the document. "Good faith" is a compact reference to an implied undertaking not to take opportunistic advantage in a way that could not have been contemplated at the time of drafting, and which therefore was not resolved explicitly by the parties. When the contract is silent, principles of good faith — such as the UCC's standard of honesty in fact, U.C.C. §1-201(19), and the reasonable expectations of the trade, U.C.C. §2-103(b) (a principle applicable, however, only to "merchants", which Bank is not) — fill the gap. They do not block use of terms that actually appear in the contract.

We do not doubt the force of the proverb that the letter killeth, while the spirit giveth life. Literal implementation of unadorned language may destroy the essence of the venture. Few people pass out of childhood without learning fables about genies, whose wickedly literal interpretation of their "masters'" wishes always leads to calamity. Yet knowledge that literal enforcement means some mismatch between the parties' expectation and the outcome does not imply a general duty of "kindness" in performance, or of judicial oversight into whether a party had "good cause" to act as it did. Parties to a contract are not each others' fiduciaries; they are not bound to treat customers with the same consideration reserved for their families. Any attempt to add an overlay of "just cause" — as the bankruptcy judge effectively did — to the exercise of contractual privileges would reduce commercial certainty and breed costly litigation. The UCC's requirement of "honesty in fact" stops well short of the requirements the bankruptcy judge thought incident to contractual performance. "In commercial transactions it does not in the end promote justice to seek strained interpretations in aid of those who do not protect themselves." James Baird Co. v. Gimbel Bros., Inc., 64 F.2d 344, 346 (2d Cir. 1933) (L. Hand, J.).

Bank did not break a promise at a time Debtor was especially vulnerable, then use the costs and delay of obtaining legal enforcement of the contract as levers to a better deal. Debtor and Bank signed a contract expressly allowing the Bank to cease making further advances. The $300,000 was the maximum loan, not a guarantee. The Bank exercised its contractual privilege after loaning Debtor $75,000; it made a clean break and did not demand improved terms. It had the right to do this for any reason satisfactory to itself. See also U.C.C. §1-208 (official comment stating that the statutory obligation of good faith in accelerating a term note does not apply to a bank's decision to call demand notes). The principle is identical to that governing a contract for employment at will: the employer may sack its employee for any reason except one forbidden by law, and it need not show "good cause."

Although Bank's decision left Debtor scratching for other sources of credit, Bank did not create Debtor's need for funds, and it was not contractually obliged to satisfy its customer's desires. The Bank was entitled to advance its own interests, and it did not need to put the interests of Debtor and Debtor's other creditors first. To the extent KMC, Inc. v. Irving Trust Co., 757 F.2d 752, 759-763 (6th Cir. 1986), holds that a bank must loan more money or give more advance notice of termination than its contract requires, we respectfully disagree. First Bank of Whiting is not an eleemosynary institution. It need not throw good money after bad, even if other persons would catch the lucre.

Debtor stresses, and the bankruptcy judge found, that Bank would have been secure in making additional advances. Perhaps so, but the contract did not oblige Bank to make all advances for which it could be assured of payment. Ex post assessments of a lender's security are no basis on which to deny it the negotiated place in the queue. Risk must be assessed ex ante by lenders, rather than ex post by judges. If a loan seems secure at the time, lenders will put up the money; their own interests are served by making loans bound to be repaid. What is more, the bankruptcy judge's finding that Bank would have been secure in making additional advances is highly questionable. The judgment of the market vindicates Bank. If more credit would have enabled Debtor to flourish, then other lenders should have been willing to supply it. Yet no one else, not even the SBA, would advance additional money to Debtor. . . .

Although Debtor contends, and the bankruptcy judge found, that Bank's termination of advances frustrated Debtor's efforts to secure credit from other sources, and so propelled it down hill, this is legally irrelevant so long as Bank kept its promises. . . .

If there remained any doubt, Judge Easterbrook made clear his views about lender liability suits. When asked to comment on their rise, he said, "I have a five-word comment. Not in the Seventh Circuit." Speeches from the Federalist Society Fifth Annual Lawyers Convention: Individual Responsibility and the Law, 77 Cornell L. Rev. 955, 1111 (1992).

Ordinarily, contract law strives to fulfill the expectations of the parties. Easterbrook's rule would fit the law of contracts in a world where everyone expected it. But in the world we live in, expectations are far less clear. Undoubtedly, many debtors are willing to sign harsh contracts because they don't think the courts will enforce them. It is interesting to speculate on what the long-run effect of the absence of lender liability would be. Will the debtors who sign security agreements some day all realize that "what you contract for is what you get"? Or will some debtors continue to sign the kinds of agreements they sign today, on the assumption that if lenders act outrageously, equity will come to their rescue?

New Article 9 defines "good faith" as "honesty in fact and the observance of reasonable commercial standards of fair dealing." On its face, it seems to be taking the Sixth Circuit's side against the Seventh Circuit. But the revised Article 9 definition applies to "good faith" only when the term is used in revised Article 9. See U.C.C. 9-102(a). *KMC* and *Kham & Nates Shoes* are both cases construing the term "good faith" as used in Article 1. The current draft of proposed Article 1 would change the definition of "good faith" in that article to conform to Article 9, but at present that definition remains the same as it was when *KMC* and *Kham & Nates Shoes* were decided. See U.C.C. §1-201(19). 20

E. Procedures After Default

Once the debtor is in default, the secured creditor usually has a choice of remedies. As you saw in earlier assignments of this book, those remedies fall in two basic categories: (1) judicial remedies such as foreclosure and replevin, which are administered by the courts, and (2) self-help remedies such as repossession without judicial process, the notification of account debtors, or the refusal to make further advances to the debtor under a line of credit.

Figure 2. The Spider Ad. This ad ran full page in the *Wall Street Journal* just a few years after the bank was hit with a $105 million verdict for knocking off one of its customers, Port Bougainville of Key Largo, Florida. Should its implication that the bank will not act in an arbitrary manner in calling loans be considered part of the contract of a debtor who signs a demand note? Or should debtors know better than to believe this stuff?

The creditor's choice among these remedies is often based on the creditor's assessment of the likelihood that the debtor will resist, the creditor's appraisal of the strength of the debtor's defenses, if any, and the manner in which the sufficiency of those defenses will be determined in each remedial procedure. To illustrate the importance of the differences in procedures, consider the case of a bank that decides to call a loan secured by all the assets of a restaurant supply company, including equipment, inventory, and accounts receivable. Calling such a loan is almost certain to lead to the closing of the business. Probably the most aggressive approach the bank could take would be to notify the restaurant supply company's account debtors to make their payments directly to the bank. U.C.C. §9-607. The combination of the loss of the account revenues and the reputational damage to the debtor from the giving of notice are likely to destroy the restaurant supply company's business. If the bank has doubts about whether the debtor is really in default, or whether it (the bank) has the right to call the loan, it may be reluctant to employ so harsh a remedy. The bank could wind up on the wrong end of a lender liability action.

Judicial foreclosure would be a more cautious way to proceed. After declaring the debtor in default, the bank would file the foreclosure case. The bank's complaint would set forth the alleged nature of the default and the basis of its right to foreclose. To preserve its defenses — perhaps it wasn't in default, or, if it was, the default resulted from wrongful action by the bank — the restaurant supply company might have to raise them in its answer to the complaint or in a counterclaim. By pressing the foreclosure action to a conclusion, the bank could get a final judicial determination of the respective rights of itself and its debtor before taking irreversible action.

The weakness of foreclosure as a remedy is that it is slow. While the case makes its way through the courts, the debtor may be collecting the accounts, selling the inventory, and allowing the equipment to deteriorate. Replevin offers something of an intermediate course. Recall that in a replevin action the secured creditor can move for an order granting it temporary possession of the collateral. In most jurisdictions, the motion will be heard in the first month of the case. While the debtor is not under compulsion to raise its defenses in response to the motion or lose them, the debtor may choose to do so in an effort to retain possession of the collateral. That may give the secured creditor a basis for assessing the strength of the debtor's defenses.

Problem Set 13

13.1.   Pat Roskoi, a plumbing subcontractor, consults you about a problem she is having with Lincoln State Bank. Pat accidentally missed two $434 payments on her truck loan. Her contract with the bank says that missing two payments is a default and that "upon default, at the secured party's option, the entire balance of the loan shall become due and payable." She noticed her omission before she received any kind of notice from the bank and promptly sent a check for the two overdue payments.

a.   The bank mailed her check back to her with a note stating that the entire loan balance of $16,701 is due and payable. She called the Bank, but the person she talked with told her that there was no mistake, and she simply has to pay the entire balance of the loan. Pat says she doesn't have the money and that the loss of the truck would make it impossible for her to continue her business. Pat asks you, "can they get away with this?" What do you tell her? See U.C.C. §9-623, including the Comment.

b.   What would have been the effect if the Bank had accelerated the loan on their books before receiving the check? Instead of returning it, the bank deposited the check to the Bank's account, and promptly sent Pat a statement showing the entire balance, less the amount of the check, as due and payable. U.C.C. §9-601(a).

13.2.   Your friend, Art Leff, is experiencing what he calls "a temporary cash flow problem." He owes Lincoln State Savings a balance of about $127,000 on his house; his monthly payment is $860. He did not make his mortgage payment on the due date last week (October 1) and he is worried about what happens next. Of course, you refused to give any advice without first reading the agreement. The relevant provisions were as follows:

> *Default*. Upon the occurrence of any of the following events of default . . . (1) the Debtor shall have outstanding an amount exceeding one full payment which has remained unpaid for more than 10 days after the due dates . . . mortgagee shall have all of the rights and remedies for default provided by applicable law and this Agreement, including the right to declare the entire outstanding balance immediately due and payable.

Art wants to delay making his house payments as long as he can and would like you to tell him how long that will be.

a.   What will be the order of events? When is the last time he can make this and subsequent payments without serious repercussions? What are those repercussions?

b.   What difference would it make if Art's case were governed by the Illinois reinstatement statute?

13.3   You represent Harvey Macklin and his company, Macklin Mortgage. Two years ago, Macklin lent $60,000 to Lance's Landscaping, Inc. (LLI), repayable in equal monthly payments over seven years. The loan is secured by an interest in all of LLI's equipment; the default provisions of the agreement are those set forth in the standard default provisions in section A of this assignment. Harvey has come to see you today because he wants to call the LLI loan. When you asked why, Harvey told you it was because LLI had failed for two consecutive years to provide Macklin with proof of liability insurance, as required by the terms of the security agreement. But in response to your questions, Harvey admitted that LLI is a strong debtor that has made every payment on time and that the real reason he wants to call the loan is that Macklin itself is in financial difficulty and desperately needs the cash. ("When you need cash," Harvey explains, "you don't get it by calling your *bad* loans.") Harvey can't get his cash out by selling the loan, because the loan carries such a low rate of interest.

The last due date for proof of insurance was 23 days ago. Macklin doesn't know if LLI has the insurance or not. There has never been any discussion of the contract provision requiring it. "Do I or don't I have the right to call this loan?" Harvey asks. What is the answer to Harvey's question? If you were willing to continue representing Harvey, what would you advise? U.C.C. §§1-201(19), 1-203, 1-208, 9-102(43), and 9-601(a).

13.4. Teresa Revez, a personal friend of yours, recently resigned her position in a software development firm in order to start her own golf course supply business. She seeks your advice regarding a number of start-up concerns, including the acquisition of financing. She estimates her capital need (beyond the amount she can invest) at about $150,000 at the peak of the season in May and at about $75,000 at the minimum point in January. To hold her capital needs to that level, she will need to make extensive use of unsecured credit from suppliers, buy her inventory on credit, and perhaps pay the inventory suppliers a little slower than the 60 to 90 days the suppliers want. Teresa has tentatively arranged for a $150,000 line of credit loan from the Bank of Orange, through David Walker, another friend of hers who is a loan officer at the Bank.

a. Teresa was surprised to learn from David that the proposed line of credit would be payable "on demand." Once she is in business, she will have every dime of her money tied up in this business; if the Bank called the loan, she would have no way to meet the call. When she raised this point with David, he told her that line loans are all on demand and it was not something she should worry about. "Bank of Orange has been serving the community for 75 years and has a reputation to protect," he said. "We're not going to do anything unfair or unreasonable." Teresa believes that David is 100 percent sincere, but still wants your opinion as to whether she should enter into this arrangement. What do you advise? Are there any terms that might alleviate Teresa's concerns and be acceptable to the Bank?

b. Teresa was also bothered by David's statement that she would be signing a note for $150,000, but drawing only half that much money initially. David said that the Bank always has customers sign a note for the line limit, as a matter of convenience. "You don't want to be coming into the Bank every time you want a draw," he said. Should Teresa sign a note for $150,000 when she is only drawing $75,000? Would you in such circumstances?

13.5.   Arthur Oman, a loan officer at Second National Bank, has been given the unpleasant task of "pulling the plug" on one of the Bank's customers, Rebel Discount Drugs. Rebel owes $150,000 on a loan against inventory, equipment, and the debtor's interest under its lease. Rebel's note is payable "on demand." Arthur has come to see you, the Bank's lawyer, to discuss the possibility of giving 30 days' notice to Rebel before making the demand. "They won't find another lender in this market," he says, "but I feel like I owe it to Walt Rebel to let him try." In response to your questions, Arthur tells you that Rebel buys its inventory on credit from suppliers, floats them for about 90 to 120 days, and then pays them out of the $1,000 to $2,000 a day that comes in through the cash registers. (Arthur knows this because the agreement between Rebel and the Bank requires that Rebel keep its account at the Bank and deposit its cash register receipts to the account daily.) Once the Bank forecloses, the equipment is probably worth about $20,000 on the resale market and the inventory would probably bring in another $60,000. The lease might bring another $10,000 to $20,000 — if the Bank can find anyone who wants it. Arthur expects that the Bank will simply take a $50,000 loss on the balance. The Bank has always in the past met its obligations to Rebel and Walt Rebel has never had any complaints about the Bank's practices. Will you approve Arthur's proposal to give notice? If so, how much notice should the Bank give? If not, how should the Bank proceed?

13.6.   Assume that the facts are the same as in Problem 13.5, except that Arthur relates these additional facts: Six months ago Walt asked for an increase in his line of credit, and Arthur told him he "thought there would be no problem." The loan committee saw it differently and refused the increase. Walt then wrote an angry letter to the Bank, asserting that the Bank had "reneged on their commitment" and had also "given false information [about Rebel] on a credit reference." Arthur thinks the "false information" reference is to a conversation Arthur had with a loan officer from First National Bank shortly after the loan committee refused the increase. Rebel applied to First National for a line of credit and First National had, naturally, called Second National. "I didn't tell her anything that wasn't true," Arthur says. Would these facts change your advice?

Assignment 14: Default, Acceleration, and Cure Under Bankruptcy Law

As we saw in Assignment 13, state law generally enforces the contract between debtor and secured creditor regarding default, acceleration, and the possibility of cure. A contract for repayment of debt in installments usually gives the creditor, upon default, the option to accelerate the due dates of future payments. In some states, statutes intervene, permitting at least some debtors to cure their defaults and thereby reinstate their contracts for payment in installments. Generally speaking, however, once acceleration has occurred, it is irreversible. Without the ability to decelerate, most debtors in most situations cannot recover from their defaults.

To look at acceleration and cure only under state law, however, gives a false impression. To see the relationship between default, acceleration, and cure requires consideration of state and bankruptcy law together. Most of the creditor's rights are found in state law; most the debtor's rights are found in bankruptcy law. The two sets of laws combine to create a system in which the debtor who has the ability to cure a default and make the installment payments generally will have the opportunity to do so. There is a catch: To get that opportunity, the debtor must go into bankruptcy.

Bankruptcy protection of the debtor who has suffered an acceleration of installment debt occurs in two stages. In the first stage, which extends from the filing of the bankruptcy case until confirmation, the automatic stay protects the debtor from foreclosure while the debtor attempts to formulate a plan. In the second stage, confirmation of the debtor's plan reverses the acceleration, the debtor cures its default, and the installment payment contract between the debtor and creditor is reinstated.

A. Stage 1: Protection of the Defaulting Debtor Pending Reorganization

As we saw in Assignment 6, when a debtor files a bankruptcy petition an automatic stay against collection and foreclosure is instantly imposed by operation of law. Unless lifted pursuant to Bankruptcy Code §362(d), the stay of an act against property (e.g., foreclosure) continues until the property is no longer in the bankruptcy estate. The stay of any other act continues until the case is closed or dismissed, or the debtor is granted or denied discharge. Bankr. Code §362(c). Thus, in a successful case under either Chapter 11 or Chapter 13, the stay will remain in effect at least until a plan is confirmed.

A debtor who provides adequate protection to its secured creditor typically will be permitted to use the collateral while the case remains pending. Bankr. Code §§363(b)(2) and 363(c)(2). Thus, if the collateral is a house, the debtor can continue to live in it while seeking to cure and reinstate; if the collateral is a hotel, the debtor can continue to operate it. Keep in mind that the "adequate protection" the debtor is required to provide is only protection against decline in the value of the secured creditor's interest in the collateral. Use of the collateral does not itself trigger an obligation on the part of the debtor to make the installment payments that fall due during the bankruptcy case.

Whether the debtor will be required to make installment payments pending confirmation of a plan depends on the chapter under which the case is pending. Bankruptcy Rule 3015 requires Chapter 13 debtors to file plans within 15 days after the filing of the petition, a limit that the court can extend only for "cause shown." Bankruptcy Code §1326 requires that the debtor "commence making the payments proposed by the plan within 30 days after the plan is filed." If the plan proposes to reinstate a schedule for installment payments, the Chapter 13 debtor probably will have to resume making the installment payments no later than 45 days after filing the petition.

Chapter 11 is considerably more generous to debtors. Debtors need not begin making payments under the plan until the plan has been confirmed by the court. Empirical studies of Chapter 11 cases indicate that the median time to confirmation is about a year. In the interim, the debtor typically has the best of both worlds: It has the use of the collateral, but need not make the installment payments. (The Chapter 11 debtor may end up having to make some interim payments to the secured creditor if necessary to provide adequate protection. Such payments will be necessary only if the collateral is declining in value and the debtor cannot or does not want to furnish adequate protection in the form of additional collateral. The payments required to provide adequate protection may be more or less than the installment payments.)

B.   Stage 2: Reinstatement and Cure

Reinstatement and cure is a process accomplished through the confirmation of a plan of reorganization in either Chapter 13 or Chapter

11. To understand the legal requirements for accomplishing it, reinstatement and cure must be distinguished from *modification* of the rights of the secured creditor.

1. Modification Distinguished from Reinstatement and Cure

Modification is sometimes referred to as "rewriting the loan." You saw this technique used in *E.I. Parks* in Assignment 7. Like reinstatement and cure, modification is accomplished through confirmation of a plan that provides for it. The minimum amount the debtor must pay on a modified secured claim is determined in two steps: (1) Determine the amount of the allowed secured claim; and (2) formulate a schedule for payments that will have a value, as of the effective date of the plan, not less than the amount of the allowed secured claim. Under *E.I. Parks*, the accepted method for meeting that test is that the payments must be at least equal to the amount of the claim plus interest at the "market rate" from the effective date of the plan until the payments are made. In effect, when the debtor proposes to modify the rights of the holder of a secured claim, the debtor must propose to pay the full amount of the secured claim together with interest at the market rate. In cases under Chapter 11, payments can extend over any period of time that is "fair and equitable." Bankr. Code §1129(b)(1). It is not uncommon in cases involving real property for courts to approve periods as long as 20 or 30 years. In cases under Chapter 13, payments can extend only over the period of the plan. That period is usually three years, but the court can approve a period of up to five years for "cause" if the debtor proposes it. Bankr. Code §1322(d). Chapter 13 plans often provide for modification of loans against cars and other personal property, but few debtors can afford to pay their real estate loans over so short a period of time. Aside from the exception in Bankruptcy Code §1322(c)(2) for home mortgages with only a few years left to run, the Bankruptcy Code prohibits modification of principal-home mortgages altogether. Debtors are limited to modifying their car loans, mortgages on second homes, and similar kinds of obligations. Bankr. Code §1322(b)(2).

By contrast, reinstatement and cure is always a return to the repayment terms agreed to between the debtor and creditor. When a default is "cured" and terms for payment are "reinstated" the debtor takes on two obligations: Any payment that, by the contract between the parties, was due on a date after the reinstatement date remains payable on its original due date; any payment that, by the contract between the parties, is overdue as of the reinstatement date is part of the obligation to cure. As the requirements for cure differ from Chapter 11 to Chapter 13, we discuss them separately.

2.   Reinstatement and Cure Under Chapter 11

The Chapter 11 debtor's right to cure and reinstate is described in Bankruptcy Code §1124(2). That section provides that a class of claims (recall that each class of secured claims ordinarily contains only a single secured claim) is *unimpaired* if the debtor's proposed treatment of the class under its plan complies with four requirements:

(1) The debtor must cure any default that occurred before or after the commencement of the bankruptcy case. This provision does not state when the cure must be made, but the courts have generally held that cure must be in a lump sum at the effective date of the plan.

(2) The plan must reinstate the maturity of that part of the claim that remains outstanding after cure, as such maturity existed before such default. That is, future payments remain due at the times specified in the original contract.

(3) The debtor must compensate the holder of the secured claim for any damages incurred through reasonable reliance on the breached repayment contract.

(4) The plan must not otherwise alter the legal, equitable, or contractual rights to which the claim entitles its holder. For example, if the original contract between the parties provided that the debtor would pay the creditor's reasonable attorneys' fees for collection in the event of default, that term must continue to be applicable to the debtor's post-reinstatement obligations.

If a class of claims is unimpaired under a Chapter 11 plan, the holder of the claim in the class is conclusively presumed to have accepted the plan and is not entitled to vote on it. Bankr. Code §1126(f). If the plan meets the other requirements for confirmation, it can be imposed on the holder of the unimpaired claim over the holder's objection.

To illustrate the operation of these provisions, assume that Debtor borrowed $100,000 from Firstbank. By the terms of the agreement between them, the loan was repayable with interest at 8 percent per year in equal monthly installments over 25 years. The payment on such a loan is $771.82. The agreement provided that payments were due on the 26th day of each month. Debtor made the first 12 payments when due, missed the next three payments, and then filed under Chapter 11. After filing, Debtor continued to miss payments. Debtor then proposed a plan that specified an effective date ten days after confirmation, obligated Debtor to cure the default and to compensate Firstbank for resulting damages on the effective date of the plan, and thereupon reinstated the contract for repayment. Such a plan would meet the requirements of Bankruptcy Code §1124(2) and the court would impose it on Firstbank over Firstbank's objection. Bankr. Code §1129(a)(8).

Assuming that a year passed between the filing of the Chapter 11 case and confirmation of Debtor's plan on March 4, Debtor's payment obligations under the plan would be as follows. First, on March 14, Debtor would have to make up the 15 missed payments in a single payment of $11,577.30. As damages for its breach, Debtor probably would have to pay interest on the overdue sums and any attorneys' fees and expenses of collection provided for under the contract and incurred by Firstbank as a result of the breach. On March 26, and the 26th day of each month thereafter, Debtor would be required to make the originally scheduled payment of $771.82.

Why would Debtor have chosen to cure and reinstate this loan rather than modify the repayment schedule through cramdown under Bankruptcy Code §1129(b)(2)(A)(i)? If the loan was secured only by a mortgage against the principal residence of the debtor, modification was prohibited. See Bankr. Code §1123(b)(5). Otherwise, the likely answer is that Debtor wished to preserve some favorable term of the original contract for repayment that Debtor could not preserve in a cramdown. For example, assume that by the time Debtor proposed its plan, the market rate of interest on this kind of loan had increased to 12 percent per year. If Debtor had modified the secured claim through cramdown, Debtor would not have had to make a lump sum cure, but Debtor would have had to pay interest at 12 percent. See *E.I. Parks*, supra. By curing and reinstating the original terms of the loan, Debtor preserved the 8 percent interest rate specified in the original loan contract.

3.   Reinstatement and Cure Under Chapter 13

The Chapter 13 debtor's right to cure and reinstate is described in Bankruptcy Code §1322(b)(5). That section provides that a Chapter 13 plan may "provide for the curing of any default within a reasonable time and maintenance of payments while the case is pending on any . . . secured claim on which the last payment is due after the date on which the final payment under the plan is due." Although this provision is considerably shorter than §1124(2), its effect is to impose much the same four requirements:

(1)   The debtor must cure any default that occurred before or after the commencement of the bankruptcy case. But under Bankruptcy Code §1322, the debtor need only cure "within a rea-

sonable time." The courts have given a flexible meaning to this phrase and approved cures over periods of months or years. All seem to agree that the cure need not be in a lump sum at the effective date of the plan. But all seem also to agree that cure cannot extend beyond the period of the plan. Within that range, the courts consider the size of the arrearage and the debtor's ability to pay in determining whether a particular proposal is reasonable.

(2) Like a Chapter 11 plan, a Chapter 13 plan must reinstate the maturity of the claim as such maturity existed before such default. That is, future payments remain due at the times specified in the original contract.

(3) Chapter 13 does not expressly require compensation for damages incurred by the creditor as a result of the breach, but instead directs the courts to look to applicable nonbankruptcy law to determine the amount necessary to cure. Bankr. Code §1322(e). In some states, that law requires payment of interest on the overdue arrearages; in others it does not.

(4) Like a Chapter 11 plan, a Chapter 13 plan cannot otherwise alter the legal, equitable, or contractual rights to which the holder is entitled.

Debtors who file under Chapter 13 are far more likely to use reinstatement and cure than modification to deal with a long-term secured obligation because, as noted above, Chapter 13 requires full payment of modified claims within the period of the plan; most debtors cannot pay their long-term obligations in such a short time. Bankruptcy Code §1322(b)(2), like Bankruptcy Code §1123(b)(5), prohibits modification of the rights of the holder of a claim secured only by a security interest in real property that is the debtor's principal residence. Under either chapter, reinstatement is the only means available to save the family home once the lender has accelerated the debt. In Nobelman v. American Savings Bank, 508 U.S. 324 (1993), the Supreme Court gave this mortgagee protection provision an expansive reading. In that case, American Savings held a $71,000 purchase money mortgage against the Nobelmans' condominium, which was worth only $23,500. The Court held that the Nobelmans could not, in their Chapter 13 plan, modify even the unsecured portion of American Savings' claim. To save their $23,500 home, the Court ruled, the Nobelmans had to pay $71,000. Justice Thomas, writing for the Court, based his explanation solely on the language of Bankruptcy Code §1322(b)(2). Justice Stevens, concurring, explained the somewhat surprising result as follows:

> At first blush it seems somewhat strange that the Bankruptcy Code should provide less protection to an individual's interest in retaining possession of

his or her home than of other assets. The anomaly is, however, explained by the legislative history indicating that favorable treatment of residential mortgages was intended to encourage the flow of capital into the home lending market. It therefore seems quite clear that the Court's literal reading of the text of the statute is faithful to the intent of Congress.

508 U.S. 332.

Every secured debt other than a home mortgage can be modified. Evidently, either Congress was not so worried about the flow of capital into car loan markets or furniture loan markets or the lobbies for these consumer lenders were not so well organized.

4. When Is It Too Late to File Bankruptcy to Reinstate and Cure?

A debtor can reinstate and cure a default and acceleration even though the deadline for doing so under state law has passed before the debtor invokes bankruptcy procedure. Bankruptcy does not just preserve rights existing under state law, it recognizes rights that state law does not. But how far is bankruptcy willing to go in reversing what has already taken place under nonbankruptcy law? This case gives one view. It happens to involve a home mortgage, but that fact has no significant bearing on the portions of the opinion included here.

In re DeSeno

17 F.3d 642 (3d Cir. 1994)

ROTH, CIRCUIT JUDGE:

This appeal requires us to determine whether Chapter 11 of the Bankruptcy Code authorizes a debtor to cure or modify a foreclosure judgment obtained under New Jersey law. The bankruptcy court concluded that it does and thereby denied appellee Midlantic National Bank's motion requesting relief from the automatic stay. Midlantic appealed to the district court, which reversed the decision of the bankruptcy court. We will affirm the district court's decision insofar as it holds that a Chapter 11 debtor may not cure a default . . . following a foreclosure judgment in New Jersey. Because we agree with the bankruptcy court that Chapter 11 allows a debtor to modify such a foreclosure judgment, however, we will reverse the decision of the district court on that issue.

I

Midlantic holds a first purchase money mortgage, executed by the debtor Jean R. DeSeno and her ex-husband Stefano T. DeSeno and dated

November 19, 1979, on property owned by Ms. DeSeno. . . . On August 20, 1991, Midlantic obtained a foreclosure judgment in the Superior Court of New Jersey on the mortgage. Pursuant to the judgment, the court issued a writ of execution directing the Sheriff of Monmouth County to sell the property in order to satisfy the judgment. The Sheriff scheduled the sale for March 2, 1992; however, at the request of Ms. DeSeno the sale was postponed until March 30. On March 25, 1992, prior to the foreclosure sale, Ms. DeSeno filed her petition for protection under Chapter 11 of the Bankruptcy Code.

On September 9, 1992, Midlantic filed a motion for relief from the automatic stay, arguing, inter alia, that it was entitled to relief from the stay under this court's decisions in In re Roach, 824 F.2d 1370 (3d Cir. 1987), and First Natl. Fidelity Corp. v. Perry, 945 F.2d 61 (3d Cir. 1991). On October 19, 1992, the bankruptcy court entered an order denying Midlantic's motion on the basis of its conclusion that *Roach* and *Perry* do not apply in Chapter 11 cases.

Midlantic appealed this order to the district court. On April 5, 1993, the district court vacated the bankruptcy court's order, reasoning that *Roach* and *Perry* do apply in Chapter 11 cases, and remanded the case to that court. On May 3, 1993, Ms. DeSeno filed a timely appeal. The bankruptcy court has stayed all proceedings in the case pending the outcome of this appeal. . . .

                                III

Both Chapter 11 and Chapter 13 authorize a debtor's bankruptcy plan to provide for the "curing or waiving of any default." 11 U.S.C. §§1123(a)(5)(G) & 1322(b)(3). See also 11 U.S.C. §1322(b)(5). In *Roach*, 824 F.2d at 1376, this court observed that "[§]1123 of Chapter 11 and §1322 of Chapter 13 are parallel provisions, and we believe it very likely that Congress' understanding of the authorization to cure defaults in each was identical." Based on this understanding, we looked to the text and legislative history of 11 U.S.C. §§1123 & 1124 to guide our interpretation of the scope of the authorization to cure defaults in Chapter 13. . . . The Second Circuit has also concluded that the concept of "curing a default" has the same meaning in Chapters 7, 11, and 13. In re Taddeo, 685 F.2d 24, 28-29 (2d Cir. 1982).

In *Roach*, we held that "§1322(b) must be read in the context of state law and . . . its right to cure a default on a mortgage on a home located in New Jersey terminates upon entry of a foreclosure judgment." 824 F.2d at 1373. We reasoned that §1322(b)(5) authorized the curing of a default only in a contractual relationship, which, under New Jersey law, ceases to exist following a foreclosure judgment. Since the mortgage no longer exists, its default can no longer be cured, and the mortgagee's rights arise solely from the judgment. Moreover, we noted that the rights in the property created by a foreclosure judgment are of a different nature than those established by the mortgage in that the foreclosure judgment makes the entire amount of the debt immediately due and payable out of the proceeds of the sale of the property. Because we could find no "statutory language, legislative history, or a significant federal interest mandating federal interference with state foreclosure judgments," id. at 1378-1379, we held "that in New Jersey the right to cure a default on a home mortgage under §1322(b) does not extend beyond the entry of a foreclosure judgment." Id. at 1379.

We decline to reconsider our conclusions in *Roach* and we will specifically extend our holding in that case to Chapter 11. Neither the text of the statute, the legislative history, nor the policies animating the Bankruptcy Code suggest that the concept of "curing a default" should be ascribed any more than a single, consistent meaning throughout the Code. Thus, absent a change in New Jersey's law concerning foreclosure judgments, we will not reexamine our holding that entry of a foreclosure judgment on a New Jersey home mortgage terminates a debtor's right to cure a default on that mortgage. In this case, Midlantic has obtained a foreclosure judgment on Ms. DeSeno's mortgage. As a result, her right to cure her default on the mortgage has terminated, and Midlantic cannot be prevented from lifting the stay on this basis.

IV

We must next consider whether a Chapter 11 debtor has the authority to provide for modification of a foreclosure judgment as part of a plan of reorganization. The modification power is found in §1123(a), which provides in relevant part:

> Notwithstanding any otherwise applicable nonbankruptcy law, a plan shall . . .
>
>> (5) provide adequate means for the plan's implementation, such as . . .
>>
>>> (E) satisfaction or modification of any lien;
>>> (F) cancellation or modification of any indenture or similar instrument. . . .

The district court concluded that this provision does not give a debtor the authority to modify a foreclosure judgment created under New Jersey law. . . .

We believe the district court erred in reaching this conclusion . . . . The district court incorrectly characterized the foreclosure judgment as a judicial lien. In *Perry*, 945 F.2d at 64-65, we concluded that "a New Jersey home mortgage lender retains a security interest for the purposes of §1322(b)(2) following the entry of a foreclosure judgment." Id. at 65. We reasoned that a foreclosure judgment, since it is the product of the mortgage agreement, is created by this agreement, and thus is a "security interest" within the definition provided in 11 U.S.C. §101 [definition of "security interest"]. As such, it cannot also be a judicial lien.

Nevertheless, our analysis remains the same under the assumption that a foreclosure judgment is a security interest rather than a judicial lien. The Code's definition provides that a security interest is a "lien created by an agreement." 11 U.S.C. §101(51). Here again, the internal reference to the concept of "lien" compels the conclusion that the reference in §1123(a)(5)(E) to "any lien" includes rather than excludes security interests. . . .

V

For the foregoing reasons, the decision of the district court will be affirmed to the extent of its ruling that Ms. DeSeno is not authorized to cure her default on her home mortgage but will be reversed to the extent that it held that Ms. DeSeno may not modify Midlantic's foreclosure judgment in her Chapter 11 plan. The case will be remanded to the district court, for remand by it to the bankruptcy court, for further proceedings consistent with this opinion.

After *DeSeno* was decided, Congress adopted the Bankruptcy Reform Act of 1994 and in so doing amended Bankruptcy Code §1322 to add subsection (c). That subsection provides:

> Notwithstanding applicable nonbankruptcy law . . . a default with respect to, or that gave rise to, a lien on the debtor's principal residence may be cured . . . until such residence is sold at a foreclosure sale. . . .

This amendment would have no direct effect on *DeSeno*, because *DeSeno* was a case under Chapter 11. But it does cut away the logical roots of *DeSeno*: The court in *DeSeno* decided that entry of the final judgment of foreclosure should cut off the right to reinstate and cure in Chapter 11 because that was the rule in Chapter 13. Now the rule in Chapter 13 is that the debtor has until foreclosure to file and reinstate.

The fact that Congress amended Chapter 13 to deal with this problem but made no change in Chapter 11 is ambiguous. Perhaps Congress meant to give Chapter 13 debtors longer to file and for that reason amended only Chapter 13. Perhaps Congress thought that Chapter 11 debtors already had until the foreclosure sale to file, and therefore needed no change. It seems more plausible to us that Congress was lobbied for the change in Chapter 13 and restricted its attention to that chapter for that reason alone. In any event, we expect that the courts soon will be called upon to explain.

Ms. DeSeno apparently filed under Chapter 11 to save her home because, at the time of her case, debtors could modify mortgages against their principal residences in Chapter 11 but not in Chapter 13. The Bankruptcy Reform Act of 1994 amended Bankruptcy Code §1123(b)(5) to conform to Bankruptcy Code §1322(b)(2). Now debtors cannot modify mortgages against their principal residences under either chapter.

Thus the effect of the new legislation may have been to overturn both of the holdings of *DeSeno*. Under current law, it may well be that a debtor filing Chapter 11 after a final judgment of foreclosure but before the sale *can reinstate* a home mortgage but *cannot modify* it!

Consumer debtors are eligible to file under Chapter 11. Even after the 1994 amendments, Chapter 11 relief remains in some respects more favorable to the debtor than Chapter 13 relief. Why don't more consumer debtors take advantage of Chapter 11? Part of the answer is that Chapter 11 is a considerably more expensive procedure. For some debtors, the cost is not justified; the total cost of reinstatement and cure under Chapter 13 is lower than the total cost of modification under Chapter 11. Other debtors would be better off in Chapter 11, but simply can't raise the cash to get there.

How much money are we talking about? The filing fee for Chapter 13 is $130 as of this writing; the filing fee for Chapter 11 is $800. By our rough estimate, an inexpensive fee for taking a mortgage reinstatement case through Chapter 13 would be about $600; an inexpensive fee for taking a mortgage modification case through Chapter 11 would be about $2,500.

C. Binding Lenders in the Absence of a Fixed Schedule for Repayment

As we noted in Assignment 13, many lending relationships lack a fixed schedule for repayment. Probably the most common of these is the line of credit that is payable on demand. In that arrangement, borrowing and repayment are expected to occur at the convenience of the debtor — unless the secured creditor decides to call the loan. The debtor's right to cure and reinstate under bankruptcy law is of no avail to debtors in such relationships. Cure and reinstatement only restores to the debtor contract rights the debtor enjoyed before default. Debtors whose lines of credit were repayable on demand or at a specific time that has passed have no contract rights that bankruptcy could restore.

Such debtors are protected, if at all, only through their ability to modify the claim or to use the respite of reorganization proceedings to find a willing substitute lender. For modification to yield substantial benefits to the debtor, there must be a substantial loan outstanding at the time of bankruptcy. The automatic stay prevents secured creditors from trying to collect after a bankruptcy filing money they advanced to a debtor before the filing. But nothing in bankruptcy law or practice requires a lender to make advances during or after bankruptcy — even if the lenders have contracted to make those advances. See, e.g., Bankr. Code §365(c)(2). If, as is often the case, the line of credit lender simply waits until the debtor pays the line down and then precipitates the bankruptcy by refusing to make further advances, the lender has probably won the game.

Finding a substitute lender may not be out of the question. Many lenders actively seek relationships with borrowers who are in bankruptcy. Some demand a higher price. Some see a benefit to lending to debtors who are stripping away their other debt and have good collateral to offer.

Problem Set 14

14.1.   How does reading Assignment 14 change your response to the situation presented in Problem 13.5? What do you expect Rebel to do if Second National calls the loan without notice? Where is Second National going to come out on this? Bankr. Code §§362(a) and (d), 363(a) through (e), 1123(a)(5)(E), 1124.

14.2.   a. David Walker (from Problem 13.4) has come up with alternatives for Teresa Revez. He now says the Bank can lend Teresa the $150,000 she needs on either of two arrangements. The first is to lend her the money at prime plus 2 percent on a demand note. The second is to lend her the money at prime plus 3.25 percent on an arrangement that provides for 30 days' notice prior to call if she is not then in default. Teresa wants your advice on choosing between these options. Considering only these two, what do you recommend? Bankr. Code §§1123(a)(5)(E), 1124, and 1129(b)(2)(A)(i).

b.   Teresa's expression of concern about having the entire $150,000 outstanding at such a high rate of interest, even when she did not need it, prompted David Walker to sweeten the deal. Now the Bank is offering a line of credit for $150,000 on the same terms that they were offering to lend her $150,000 fixed. That is, she can choose between prime plus 2 percent on a demand note or prime plus 3.25 percent on a note with 30 days' notice before cancellation. Having this loan in the form of a line of credit entitles Teresa to pay back to the bank what she doesn't need, and draw it out again when she does need it. Under the options in part a of this problem, Teresa would have put the money she didn't need in a bank account at a relatively low rate of interest, so the savings offered by these line of credit options are substantial. Do you see any disadvantages? Which of the two line of credit arrangements seems more attractive?

14.3. Ever since the market for single-family houses collapsed in the town where you practice, you've had a steady stream of debtors looking for ways to save their homes. The circumstances of two of them are described below.

Willard Spivak bought his home three years ago from Rolling Green Developers for $100,000. He financed the home with a 30-year conventional mortgage from Gateway Savings and Loan. The mortgage provides for repayment in equal monthly installments with interest at 8 percent per year. The principal amount of the loan was $80,000. Willard made 29 monthly payments of $587.02 each, and then missed the 30th and all subsequent payments. As of yesterday, he is seven months in arrears, a total of $4,109.14. Willard shows you each of the communications he has received from Gateway since he went into default. The first was a "Friendly Reminder"; the second and third were titled "Notice of Delinquency." The fourth was a letter from a law firm detailing the status of the loan and stating that if Willard did not bring the loan current within ten days, the bank would declare a default and accelerate the due dates of all payments. The next letter was from the same law firm, dated 23 days later. It stated that Gateway declared the loan in default, that the entire balance of approximately $84,000 was immediately due and payable, and that if Willard did not pay it within ten days, Gateway would foreclose. The last document Willard shows you is the foreclosure complaint and summons served by the sheriff on Willard yesterday, one month after the last letter. Willard says he is back at work now and has the money to resume payments on the mortgage, but he doesn't know where he can get $4,109 to make up the arrearage. When Willard called the bank recently, an officer told him that even if he *does* tender the arrearage now, the bank won't accept it. "You have to pay the whole $84,000," the officer told him. One of the reasons Gateway wants to get rid of this loan is that rates have risen since Gateway made it. Gateway currently charges 11 percent for the same kind of loan. (At that rate, Willard's monthly payment would have been $761.86 on the same loan.) The home is probably worth only about the amount of the loan, but Willard wants to keep it.

a. What do you recommend? Bankr. Code §§1322(b)(5), 1322(c) and (d), 1123(a)(5), 1123(b)(5), 1124, 1129(b)(2)(A).

b. If Willard follows your recommendation, what is the minimum Willard must pay to keep the house and when will he have to pay it?

c. Winona Williams bought her home three years ago for $100,000. Thinking that interest rates would go down in a few years, she financed her purchase with an $80,000 purchase money mort-

gage from the seller, Marian Case. The terms are remarkably similar to
the terms of Willard Spivak's mortgage — the loan is amortized over
30 years with interest at 8 percent per year, for a monthly payment of
$587.02. The difference is that Winona's mortgage "balloons" at the
end of five years — just two years from now. (The term *balloon* means
that the entire balance becomes due.) Like Willard, Winona is seven
months in arrears, a total of $4,109, and Marian Case has accelerated
and commenced foreclosure. Winona's home is still worth $100,000
and she'd really like to hold on to it. What do you suggest? Bankr.
Code §§1123(a)(5), 1123(b)(5), 1124, 1129(a)(11), 1129(b)(2)(A),
1322(b)(2), 1322(b)(5), 1322(c)(2), 1325(a)(5), 1325(a)(6).

d.   Would it help if Winona were to move out of the house, rent
it to a tenant, and use that cash flow to rent another house for herself?

e.   Willard Spivak, from part a of this problem, felt he couldn't
afford your fees, so he didn't take your advice. Instead, he made a
deal with Gateway. Under the deal, the amount of his arrearage was
fixed at $6,000 ($4,109 plus Gateway's attorneys' fees) and Gateway
gave him six months to pay it. In return, Willard agreed to an
increase in the interest rate on the loan from 8 to 11 percent. Now
Willard's six months is almost up. He has been making the regular
monthly payments of $761.86 on the loan at the new interest rate,
but hasn't been able to save anything toward the $6,000 payment
that is about to come due. Realizing that he is about to default again,
Willard is back to see you. Is there anything you can do for him?
Bankr. Code §§1123(a)(5), 1123(b)(5), 1322(b).

14.4.   a.   In *Nobelman*, discussed in section B.3 of this Assignment,
American Savings held a mortgage in the amount of $71,000 against
the debtors' condominium, which had a value of only $23,500. The
Supreme Court held that the Nobelmans could not modify the unsecured portion of American Savings' claim. If you represented the
Nobelmans at this point, what would you advise with regard to this
condominium?

b.   If you represented American Savings, what would you advise
with regard to this condominium?

14.5.   On reading Justice Stevens' one-paragraph concurring opinion in *Nobelman* (set forth in section B of this chapter), Congresswoman Martha Pepper has an idea. If denying modification of home
mortgages can cause capital to flow into the home mortgage market,
why can't denying modification of auto loans cause capital to flow
into the auto market — and denying modification of business loans
cause capital to flow into the business markets? The congresswoman
is so excited by the whole idea that she is beside herself. "Maybe I've
found the key to the nation's economic problems," she says with her
characteristic modesty. Then she asks for your opinion. What do you
tell her?

Chapter 5.   The Prototypical Secured Transaction

Assignment 15: The Prototypical Secured Transaction

In Part One of this book, we have addressed various aspects of the relationship between a secured creditor and its debtor. In this assignment, we examine a specific example of such a relationship. The example we have chosen is a relationship between a boat dealer and its inventory lender. In preparing the description of this transaction, we were assisted by Deutsche Financial Services, a lender based in St. Louis, Missouri. The debtors, Bonnie Brezhnev and her corporation, Bonnie's Boat World, Inc., and their supplier, Shoreline Boats, are all fictional characters. But their relationships with Deutsche are not materially different from real relationships that others have with Deutsche and lenders like Deutsche.

While the relationships described in this assignment are typical of inventory lending, they are not typical of secured transactions generally. As you have already seen in earlier assignments, secured transactions come in a variety of forms. At one extreme, the secured transaction in which a consumer buys a color TV may be documented only by a half-page printed form signed when the debtor opens the charge account and a receipt issued for the particular sale. At the other extreme, the documentation for the financing of an office building or industrial plant may be hundreds or even thousands of pages in length. In its complexity, the transaction described in this assignment is perhaps about midway between those extremes.

We will discuss the strategies and motivations of both sides. The legal doctrine governing secured credit is best understood in relation to those strategies and motivations. But given the wide variety of circumstances in which creditors take security, it should come as no surprise that strategies and motivations differ from one kind of secured transaction to another and with the attitudes of different participants to the same kind of secured transaction. Thus, you should be cautious in attempting to generalize our prototype to other kinds of secured lending. To understand why a provision of Article 9 exists in the form it does, one must usually see how it operates in a variety of circumstances. At the same time, one must start somewhere, and we have chosen the context of inventory lending.

A.   The Parties

Deutsche Financial Services is among the largest commercial finance companies in the United States, with offices in 22 cities in the United States, Canada, and the United Kingdom. It lends against all kinds of business assets; a sister company is engaged in consumer finance. A substantial portion of its business is *floorplanning,* that is, financing the purchase of the inventory that is on a dealer's "showroom floor." The products financed by Deutsche's floorplanning program include computers, mobile homes, recreation vehicles, boats and motors, consumer electronics and appliances, keyboards and other musical instruments, industrial equipment, agricultural equipment, office machines, snowmobiles, and motorcycles.

Bonnie's Boat World, Inc. is a corporation invented by the authors of this book. Bonnie Brezhnev is a person invented along with the corporation to serve as its owner. She purchased Art's Boat World, Inc. about three months ago and changed the name to Bonnie's Boat World. The business is located on a commercial highway that passes within a few hundred feet of a lake. The boatyard, located on the narrow strip of land between the highway and the lake, consists of a small indoor showroom, sales offices, four acres of land surrounded by an eight-foot cyclone fence, a boat storage building, and a pier extending into the lake.

B.   Deutsche Approves Bonnie's Loan

Dissatisfied with the lender who has been financing her inventory, Bonnie makes her first contact with Deutsche. She visits the local Deutsche office and meets with Paul Kaplan, a Deutsche loan officer. They discuss the boat business, Bonnie's plans for the future, the terms on which Deutsche makes loans, and a number of other subjects. Generally pleased, Bonnie takes the blank form of a loan application with her when she leaves. The application seeks a variety of information about Bonnie and her business, including current balance sheets, income statements, and income tax returns for both herself and the corporation. Because Bonnie has to bring some of the accounting records up to date, it takes Bonnie and her bookkeeper a little over a week to complete the application.

When Paul Kaplan receives the application, he immediately orders a credit report from Dun and Bradstreet (D & B). D & B has not previously reported on Bonnie or Bonnie's Boat World, so they have no information on either at the time they receive Deutsche's request. To get the information they eventually include in their report, D & B searches several public records, interviews Bonnie, and checks with some of the credit references she gives them. Paul arranges for all of the information he has obtained about Bonnie's to be entered into Deutsche's Expert Credit System, a computer system that uses artificial intelligence to simulate the analytical approach of senior loan officers. Based on the computer analysis and Paul's independent review of the application and credit report, Paul decides to recommend authorization of the loan.

Paul presents the loan application to his branch manager a few days later. Based on the size of the requested credit line, the branch manager has sufficient credit authority to approve the account alone. Although the branch manager has some concerns about Bonnie's relative inexperience in the retail boat business, the application is otherwise strong and the branch manager approves it. Paul calls Bonnie that same afternoon to tell her that the loan has been approved and to set a time for closing the transaction.

C.   Deutsche and Bonnie's Document the Loan

Just a few days after her inventory loan was approved, Bonnie returns to the offices of Deutsche to complete the documentation for the loan. She has already seen and discussed with her own lawyers the Agreement for Wholesale Financing (Security Agreement — Arbitration) that she will have to sign. Prior to this meeting, Richard Feynman, a Deutsche employee, has searched the Article 9 filing system to verify the name and address of the bank that financed the boats already in Bonnie's possession. He has visited Bonnie's Boat World and made a list of all the boats currently in the company's possession. While there, Richard examined the books and records of the business to see how they are kept. Satisfied with what he had seen and been told, Richard advises Paul that the loan is ready for closing.

When Bonnie arrives in his office, Paul has all of the documents on his desk. Bonnie and Paul go through them one by one, discussing and signing them. Four of these documents, the security agreement, a sample form statement of transaction, the financing statement, and the personal guarantee are relevant to an understanding of the security aspect of the transaction.

1.   Security Agreement and Statement of Transaction

Subject to a few omissions indicated, this is the full text of the security agreement Bonnie signs at the closing:

AGREEMENT FOR WHOLESALE FINANCING
(SECURITY AGREEMENT — ARBITRATION)

This Agreement for Wholesale Financing ("Agreement") is made as of
January 24, 1999 between Deutsche Financial Services ("Deut-
sche") and Bonnie's Boat World, Inc., a SOLE PROPRIETOR-
SHIP, __ PARTNERSHIP, X CORPORATION (check applicable term)
("Dealer"), having a principal place of business located at

12376 HIGHWAY 441
BLUE MOON, MO 63131

1. Subject to the terms of this Agreement, Deutsche, in its sole discretion, may extend credit to Dealer from time to time to purchase inventory from Deutsche-approved vendors. Deutsche may combine all of
Deutsche's advances to Dealer or on Dealer's behalf, whether under this
Agreement or any other agreement, to make one debt owed by Dealer.
Deutsche's decision to advance funds on any inventory will not be binding until the funds are actually advanced. Dealer agrees that Deutsche
may, at any time and without notice to Dealer, elect not to finance any
inventory sold by particular vendors who are in default of their obligations to Deutsche, or with respect to which Deutsche reasonably feels
insecure.

2. Dealer and Deutsche agree that certain financial terms of any
advance made by Deutsche under this Agreement, whether regarding
finance charges, other fees, maturities, curtailments or other financial
terms, are not set forth herein because such terms depend, in part, upon
the availability from time to time of vendor discounts or other incentives,
prevailing economic conditions, Deutsche's floorplanning volume with
Dealer and with Dealer's vendors, and other economic factors which may
vary over time. Dealer and Deutsche further agree that it is therefore in
their mutual best interest to set forth in this Agreement only the general
terms of Dealer's financing arrangement with Deutsche. Upon agreeing
to finance a particular item of inventory for Dealer, Deutsche will send
Dealer a Statement of Transaction identifying such inventory and the
applicable financial terms. Unless Dealer notifies Deutsche in writing of
any objection within fifteen (15) days after a Statement of Transaction is
mailed to Dealer:

   (a) the amount shown on such Statement of Transaction will be an
       account stated;
   (b) Dealer will have agreed to all rates, charges and other terms
       shown on such Statement of Transaction;
   (c) Dealer will have agreed that the items of inventory referenced in

such Statement of Transaction are being financed by Deutsche at Dealer's request; and

(d) such Statement of Transaction will be incorporated herein by reference, will be made a part hereof as if originally set forth herein, and will constitute an addendum hereto.

If Dealer objects to the terms of any Statement of Transaction, Dealer agrees to pay Deutsche for such inventory in accordance with the most recent terms for similar inventory to which Dealer has not objected (or, if there are no prior terms, at the lesser of 16% per annum or at the maximum lawful contract rate of interest permitted under applicable law), but Dealer acknowledges that Deutsche may then elect to terminate Dealer's financing program pursuant to Section 12, and cease making additional advances to Dealer. Any termination for that reason, however, will not accelerate the maturities of advances previously made, unless Dealer shall otherwise be in default of this Agreement.

3. To secure payment of all Dealer's current and future debts to Deutsche, whether under this Agreement or any current or future guaranty or other agreement, Dealer grants Deutsche a security interest in all Dealer's inventory, equipment, fixtures, accounts, contract rights, chattel paper, instruments, reserves, documents and general intangibles, whether now owned or hereafter acquired, all attachments, accessories, accessions, substitutions and replacements thereto and all proceeds thereof. All such assets are as defined in the Uniform Commercial Code and referred to herein as the "Collateral." All Collateral financed by Deutsche, and all proceeds thereof, will be held in trust by Dealer for Deutsche, with such proceeds being payable in accordance with Section 7.

4. Dealer represents that all Collateral will be kept at Dealer's principal place of business listed above, and, if any, the following other locations:

Dealer will give Deutsche at least 30 days prior written notice of any change in Dealer's identity, name, form of business organization, ownership, principal place of business, Collateral locations or other business locations.

5. Dealer will:

(a) only exhibit and sell Collateral financed by Deutsche to buyers in the ordinary course of business;

(b) not rent, lease, demonstrate, transfer or use any Collateral financed by Deutsche without Deutsche's prior written consent;

(c) execute all documents Deutsche requests to perfect Deutsche's security interest in the Collateral;

(d) deliver to Deutsche immediately upon each request, and Deutsche may retain, each Certificate of Title or Statement of Origin issued for Collateral financed by Deutsche; and

(e) immediately provide Deutsche with copies of Dealer's annual financial statements upon their completion (which in no event shall exceed 120 days after the end of Dealer's fiscal year), and all other information regarding Dealer that Deutsche requests from time to time. All financial information Dealer delivers to Deutsche will accurately represent Dealer's financial condition either as of the date of delivery, or, if different, the date specified therein, and Dealer acknowledges Deutsche's reliance thereon.

6. Dealer will:

(a) pay all taxes and fees assessed against Dealer or the Collateral when due;

(b) immediately notify Deutsche of any loss, theft or damage to any Collateral;

(c) keep the Collateral insured for its full insurable value under a property insurance policy with a company acceptable to Deutsche, naming Deutsche as a loss-payee and containing standard lender's loss payable and termination provisions; and

(d) provide Deutsche with written evidence of such insurance coverage and loss-payee and lender's clauses.

If Dealer fails to pay any taxes, fees or other obligations which may impair Deutsche's interest in the Collateral, or fails to keep the Collateral insured, Deutsche may pay such taxes, fees or obligations and pay the cost to insure the Collateral, and the amounts paid will be: (i) an additional debt owed by Dealer to Deutsche; and (ii) due and payable immediately in full. Dealer grants Deutsche an irrevocable license to enter Dealer's business locations during normal business hours without notice to Dealer to:

(A) account for and inspect all Collateral;

(B) verify Dealer's compliance with this Agreement; and

(C) examine and copy Dealer's books and records related to the Collateral.

7. Dealer will immediately pay Deutsche the principal indebtedness owed Deutsche on each item of Collateral financed by Deutsche (as shown on the Statement of Transaction identifying such Collateral) on the earliest occurrence of any of the following events:

(a) when such Collateral is lost, stolen or damaged;

(b) for Collateral financed under Pay-As-Sold ("PAS") terms (as shown on the Statement of Transaction identifying such Collateral), when such Collateral is sold, transferred, rented, leased, otherwise disposed of or matured;

(c) in strict accordance with any curtailment schedule for such Collateral (as shown on the Statement of Transaction identifying such Collateral);

(d) for Collateral financed under Scheduled Payment Program ("SPP") terms (as shown on the Statement of Transaction identifying such Collateral), in strict accordance with the installment payment schedule; and

(e) when otherwise required under the terms of any financing program agreed to in writing by the parties.

Regardless of the SPP terms pertaining to any Collateral financed by Deutsche if Deutsche determines that the current outstanding debt owed by Dealer to Deutsche exceeds the aggregate wholesale invoice price of such Collateral in Dealer's possession, Dealer will immediately upon demand pay Deutsche the difference between such outstanding debt and the aggregate wholesale invoice price of such Collateral. If Dealer from time to time is required to make immediate payment to Deutsche of any past due obligation discovered during any Collateral audit, or at any other time, Dealer agrees that acceptance of such payment by Deutsche shall not be construed to have waived or amended the terms of its financing program. Dealer agrees that the proceeds of any Collateral received by Dealer shall be held by Dealer in trust for Deutsche's benefit, for application as provided in this Agreement. Dealer will send all payments to Deutsche's branch office(s) responsible for Dealer's account. Deutsche may apply:

(i) payments to reduce finance charges first and then principal, regardless of Dealer's instructions; and

(ii) principal payments to the oldest (earliest) invoice for Collateral financed by Deutsche, but, in any event, all principal payments will first be applied to such Collateral which is sold, lost, stolen, damaged, rented, leased, or otherwise disposed of or unaccounted for. . . .

8. Dealer will pay Deutsche finance charges on the outstanding principal debt Dealer owes Deutsche for each item of Collateral financed by Deutsche at the rate(s) shown on the Statement of Transaction identifying such Collateral, unless Dealer objects thereto as provided in Section 2. The finance charges attributable to the rate shown on the Statement of Transaction will:

(a) be computed based on a 360-day year;

(b) be calculated by multiplying the Daily Charge (as defined below) by the actual number of days in the applicable billing period; and

(c) accrue from the invoice date of the Collateral identified on such Statement of Transaction until Deutsche receives full payment of the principal debt Dealer owes Deutsche for each item of such Collateral.

The "Daily Charge" is the product of the Daily Rate (as defined below) multiplied by the Average Daily Balance (as defined below). The "Daily Rate" is the quotient of the annual rate shown on the Statement of Transaction divided by 360, or the monthly rate shown on the Statement of Transaction divided by 30. The "Average Daily Balance" is the quotient of

(i) the sum of the outstanding principal debt owed Deutsche on each day of a billing period for each item of Collateral identified on a Statement of Transaction, divided by

(ii) the actual number of days in such billing period.

Dealer will also pay Deutsche $100 for each check returned unpaid for insufficient funds (an "NSF check") (such $100 payment repays Deutsche's estimated administrative costs; it does not waive the default caused by the NSF check). Dealer acknowledges that Deutsche intends to strictly conform to the applicable usury laws governing this Agreement and understands that Dealer is not obligated to pay any finance charges billed to Dealer's account exceeding the amount allowed by such usury laws, and any such excess finance charges Dealer pays will be applied to reduce Dealer's principal debt owed to Deutsche. The annual percentage rate of the finance charges relating to any item of Collateral financed by Deutsche shall be calculated from the invoice date of such Collateral, regardless of any period during which any finance charge subsidy shall be paid or payable by any third party. Deutsche will send Dealer a monthly billing statement identifying all charges due on Dealer's account with Deutsche. The charges specified on each billing statement will be:

(A) due and payable in full immediately on receipt, and

(B) an account stated, unless Deutsche receives Dealer's written objection thereto within 15 days after it is mailed to Dealer.

If Deutsche does not receive, by the 25th day of any given month, payment of all charges accrued to Dealer's account with Deutsche during the immediately preceding month, Dealer will (to the extent allowed by law) pay Deutsche a late fee ("Late Fee") equal to the greater of $5 or 5% of the amount of such finance charges (such Late Fee repays Deutsche's estimated administrative costs; it does not waive the default caused by the late payment). Deutsche may adjust the billing statement at any time to conform to applicable law and this Agreement.

9. Dealer will be in default under this Agreement if:

   (a) Dealer breaches any terms, warranties or representations contained herein, in any Statement of Transaction to which Dealer has not objected as provided in Section 2, or in any other agreement between Deutsche and Dealer;

   (b) any guarantor of Dealer's debts to Deutsche breaches any terms, warranties or representations contained in any guaranty or other agreement between the guarantor and Deutsche;

   (c) any representation, statement, report or certificate made or delivered by Dealer or any guarantor to Deutsche is not accurate when made;

   (d) Dealer fails to pay any portion of Dealer's debts to Deutsche when due and payable hereunder or under any other agreement between Deutsche and Dealer;

   (e) Dealer abandons any Collateral;

   (f) Dealer or any guarantor is or becomes in default in the payment of any debt owed to any third party;

   (g) a money judgment issues against Dealer or any guarantor;

   (h) an attachment, sale or seizure issues or is executed against any assets of Dealer or of any guarantor;

   (i) the undersigned dies while Dealer's business is operated as a sole proprietorship or any general partner dies while Dealer's business is operated as a general or limited partnership;

   (j) any guarantor dies;

   (k) Dealer or any guarantor shall cease existence as a corporation, partnership or trust;

   (l) Dealer or any guarantor ceases or suspends business;

   (m) Dealer or any guarantor makes a general assignment for the benefit of creditors;

   (n) Dealer or any guarantor becomes insolvent or voluntarily or involuntarily becomes subject to the Federal Bankruptcy Code, any state insolvency law or any similar law;

   (o) any receiver is appointed for any of Dealer's or any guarantor's assets;

   (p) any guaranty of Dealer's debts to Deutsche is terminated;

   (q) Dealer loses any franchise, permission, license or right to sell or deal in any Collateral which Deutsche finances;

   (r) Dealer or any guarantor misrepresents Dealer's or such guarantor's financial condition or organizational structure; or

   (s) any of the Collateral becomes subject to any lien, claim, encumbrance or security interest prior or superior to Deutsche's.

In the event of a default

(i) Deutsche may at any time at Deutsche's election, without notice or demand to Dealer, do any one or more of the following: declare all or any part of the debt Dealer owes Deutsche immediately due and payable, together with all costs and expenses of Deutsche's collection activity, including, without limitation, all reasonable attorney's fees; exercise any or all rights under applicable law (including, without limitation, the right to possess, transfer and dispose of the Collateral); and/or cease extending any additional credit to Dealer (Deutsche's right to cease extending credit shall not be construed to limit the discretionary nature of this credit facility).

(ii) Dealer will segregate and keep the Collateral in trust for Deutsche, and in good order and repair, and will not exhibit, sell, rent, lease, further encumber, otherwise dispose of or use any Collateral.

(iii) Upon Deutsche's oral or written demand, Dealer will immediately deliver the Collateral to Deutsche, in good order and repair, at a place specified by Deutsche, together with all related documents; or Deutsche may, in Deutsche's sole discretion and without notice or demand to Dealer, take immediate possession of the Collateral together with all related documents.

(iv) Deutsche may, without notice, apply a default finance charge to Dealer's outstanding principal indebtedness equal to the default rate specified in Dealer's financing program with Deutsche, if any, or if there is none so specified, at the lesser of 3% per annum above the rate in effect immediately prior to the default, or the highest lawful contract rate of interest permitted under applicable law.

All Deutsche's rights and remedies are cumulative. Deutsche's failure to exercise any of Deutsche's rights or remedies hereunder will not waive any of Deutsche's rights or remedies as to any past, current or future default.

10. Dealer agrees that if Deutsche conducts a private sale of any Collateral by requesting bids from 10 or more dealers or distributors in that type of Collateral, any sale by Deutsche of such Collateral in bulk or in parcels within 120 days of

(a) Deutsche's taking possession and control of such Collateral; or
(b) when Deutsche is otherwise authorized to sell such Collateral;

whichever occurs last, to the bidder submitting the highest cash bid therefor, is a commercially reasonable sale of such Collateral under the Uniform Commercial Code. Dealer agrees that the purchase of any Collateral by a vendor, as provided in any agreement between Deutsche and the vendor, is a commercially reasonable disposition and private sale of such Collateral under the Uniform Commercial Code, and no request for bids shall be required. Dealer further agrees that 7 or more days prior written notice will be commercially reasonable notice of any public or private sale (including any sale to a vendor). If Deutsche disposes of any such Collateral other than as herein contemplated, the commercial reasonableness of such disposition will be determined in accordance with the laws of the state governing this Agreement.

11. Dealer grants Deutsche an irrevocable power of attorney to: execute or endorse on Dealer's behalf any checks, financing statements, instruments, Certificates of Title and Statements of Origin pertaining to the Collateral; supply any omitted information and correct errors in any documents between Deutsche and Dealer; do anything Dealer is obligated to do hereunder; initiate and settle any insurance claim pertaining to the Collateral; and do anything to preserve and protect the Collateral and Deutsche's rights and interest therein. Deutsche may provide to any third party any credit, financial or other information on Dealer that Deutsche may from time to time possess.

12. Time is of the essence. This Agreement is deemed to have been entered into at the Deutsche branch office executing this Agreement. Either party may terminate this Agreement at any time by written notice received by the other party. If Deutsche terminates this Agreement, Dealer agrees that if Dealer:

(a) is not in default hereunder, 30 days prior notice of termination is reasonable and sufficient (although this provision shall not be construed to mean that shorter periods may not, in particular circumstances, also be reasonable and sufficient); or

(b) is in default hereunder, no prior notice of termination is required.

Dealer will not be relieved from any obligation to Deutsche arising out of Deutsche's advances or commitments made before the effective termination date of this Agreement. Deutsche will retain all of its rights, interests and remedies hereunder until Dealer has paid all Dealer's debts to Deutsche. Dealer cannot assign Dealer's interest in this Agreement without Deutsche's prior written consent, although Deutsche may assign or participate Deutsche's interest, in whole or in part, without Dealer's consent. This Agreement will protect and bind Deutsche's and Dealer's respective heirs, representatives, successors and assigns. All agreements or commitments to extend or renew credit or refrain from enforcing payment of a debt must be in writing. Any oral or other amendment or waiver claimed to be made to this Agreement that is not evidenced by a written document executed by Deutsche and Dealer (except for each Statement of Transaction that Dealer does not object to in the manner stated in Section 2) will be null, void and have no force or effect whatsoever. If any provision of this Agreement or its application is invalid or unenforceable, the remainder of this Agreement will not be impaired or affected and will remain binding and enforceable. If Dealer previously executed any security agreement with Deutsche, this Agreement will only amend and supplement such agreement. If the terms hereof conflict with the terms of any such prior security agreement, the terms of this Agreement will govern. Dealer agrees to pay all of Deutsche's reasonable attorneys fees and expenses incurred by Deutsche in enforcing Deutsche's rights hereunder.

13. Binding arbitration. [Editor's note: The two-page arbitration clause was omitted for lack of space in this reproduction. That clause provided that the parties would submit all disputes between them to binding arbitration through the National Arbitration Forum or the American Arbitration Association.]. . . .

14. If Section 13 of this Agreement or its application is invalid or unenforceable, any legal proceeding with respect to any Dispute will be tried in a court of competent jurisdiction by a judge without a jury. Dealer and Deutsche waive any right to a jury trial in any such proceeding.

THIS CONTRACT CONTAINS BINDING ARBITRATION AND JURY WAIVER PROVISIONS.

Deutsche Financial
Services Corp.

Dealer's Name: Bonnie's
Boat World, Inc.

By: *Paul Kaplan*

By: *Bonnie Brezhnev*

Print Name: Paul Kaplan
Title: Loan Officer

Print Name: Bonnie Brezhnev
Title: President

[Editors' note: We have omitted the Dealer's certification that its Board of Directors adopted a specific resolution authorizing the corporation to enter into this financing arrangement with Deutsche.]

At the time she signs this agreement, Bonnie has not yet purchased any boats for Deutsche to finance. Deutsche disburses no money at this "closing" and there is no Statement of Transaction for Bonnie to approve. Paul shows Bonnie some information about the pricing of credit by Deutsche and a sample of a Statement of Transaction prepared on the basis of a hypothetical purchase (see Figure 3). The sequence of events that will occur when Bonnie buys some boats is discussed below.

```
RPT ID: H623A          40721                                              PAGE:     1
OFFICE: 01256015                    STATEMENT OF TRANSACTION           PRODUCT LINES
DEALER: 50580                                                            DLR  INV
                                                                         04   04

                                              INVOICE#:      0148291
                                              DATE OF NOTE:  07/13/1994


PLAN#    PLAN TITLE                   MFG#  MANUFACTURER NAME       DIST#  DISTRIBUTOR NAME
0216-01  EAGLE PROGRAM II - 30 DAY FFP   0523 SHORELINE BOAT MFG   1406   BONNIE'S BOAT WORLD, INC.

PRODUCT DESCRIPTION           MODEL #      SERIAL #         MFG# PRD UNIT-ID  QTY  UNIT PRICE     AMOUNT
                              SPP          1 PAY            0523 808 6089402   1   15,566.58    15,566.58

**** FINANCE TERMS: - SCHEDULED PAYMENT PLAN -

PLAN #   CHARGE TYPE       DAYS/DATE        RATE/AMOUNT       DESCRIPTION
0216-01  FINANCE:          31 -    90       PRIME- 1.00%      PER ANNUM OF ADB
                           91 -             2.4000 %         PER MONTH OF ADB
         FLAT:             31 -             .2500 %          OF BALANCE  EVERY   1  MONTH(S)
         LATE RATE:                         PRIME+ 5.50%      PER ANNUM OF ADB OF LATE PMT AMT
                                                             DAY 1 IS DATE OF INVOICE

"PRIME" MEANS THE HIGHEST PRIME RATE OR REFERENCE RATE OF INTEREST PUBLICLY ANNOUNCED FROM TIME TO TIME BY CHASE MANHATTAN
BANK, N.A., CHEMICAL BANK AND CITIBANK, N.A., AND SUCH RATE IN EFFECT ON THE LAST BUSINESS DAY OF ANY CALENDAR MONTH
WILL BE PRIME FOR THE FOLLOWING CALENDAR MONTH, SUBJECT TO ANY MINIMUM PRIME.

******************************
* PRINCIPAL PAYMENTS DUE:  *
******************************
08/10/1994    15,566.58

INVOICE TOTAL          15,566.58
TOTAL ITEM QUANTITY            1




BONNIE'S BOAT WORLD, INC.              OFFICE ADDRESS
12376 HIGHWAY 441                      DEUTSCHE FINANCIAL SERVICES
BLUE MOON, MO 63131                    P.O. BOX 502025
                                       ST. LOUIS      MO  63141 2025
```

CMF-2

Figure 3. Statement of Transaction

2. The Financing Statement

Bonnie also signs a financing statement for filing in the Uniform Commercial Code filing system of the state. The purpose of the financing statement is to give public notice that Deutsche claims a security interest in Bonnie's inventory (see Figure 4). We will discuss financing statements at greater length in Part Two of this book.

3. The Personal Guarantee

Although the loans contemplated by the agreement would be made to Bonnie's Boat World, Inc., Deutsche required that Bonnie personally guarantee repayment. Bonnie signed a one-page document to that effect at the closing.

Lenders such as Deutsche have at least two reasons for requiring personal guarantees from the owners of their corporate borrowers. First, if the borrower cannot repay the loan, the owners might. The guarantee gives the lender the right to obtain a judgment against the owners and proceed against their assets just as though the owners were the ones who had borrowed the money. In addition, personal guarantees can be, and sometimes are, secured by interests in property owned by the guarantors.

UCC FINANCING STATEMENT
FOLLOW INSTRUCTIONS (front and back) CAREFULLY

A. NAME & PHONE OF CONTACT AT FILER [optional]
PAUL KAPLAN   (314) 555-4875

B. SEND ACKNOWLEDGMENT TO: (Name and Address)

```
Deutsche Financial Services
655 Maryville Centre Drive
St. Louis, MO  63141
```

THE ABOVE SPACE IS FOR FILING OFFICE USE ONLY

1. DEBTOR'S EXACT FULL LEGAL NAME - insert only one debtor name (1a or 1b) - do not abbreviate or combine names

1a. ORGANIZATION'S NAME: Bonnie's Boat World, Inc.

1c. MAILING ADDRESS: 12376 Highway 441 | CITY: Blue Moon | STATE: MO | POSTAL CODE: 63131 | COUNTRY: USA

1d. TAX ID #: 57-12345 | 1e. TYPE OF ORGANIZATION: Corporation | 1f. JURISDICTION OF ORGANIZATION: Missouri | 1g. ORGANIZATIONAL ID #, if any: NONE

2. ADDITIONAL DEBTOR'S EXACT FULL LEGAL NAME - insert only one debtor name (2a or 2b) - do not abbreviate or combine names

3. SECURED PARTY'S NAME (or NAME of TOTAL ASSIGNEE of ASSIGNOR S/P) - insert only one secured party name (3a or 3b)

3a. ORGANIZATION'S NAME: Deutsche Financial Services

3c. MAILING ADDRESS: 655 Maryville Centre Drive | CITY: St. Louis | STATE: MO | POSTAL CODE: 63141 | COUNTRY: USA

4. This FINANCING STATEMENT covers the following collateral:

Inventory, equipment, general intangibles.

5. ALTERNATIVE DESIGNATION [if applicable]: LESSEE/LESSOR | CONSIGNEE/CONSIGNOR | BAILEE/BAILOR | SELLER/BUYER | AG. LIEN | NON-UCC FILING

FILING OFFICE COPY — NATIONAL UCC FINANCING STATEMENT (FORM UCC1) (REV. 04/23/98)

Figure 4. U.C.C.-1 Financing Statement

The second reason for a lender to take a personal guarantee is to assure, insofar as possible, that in the event of default, the lender will have the cooperation of the owners. When a corporate debtor becomes insolvent, the owners' interest in the business often becomes worthless. Unless the owners are personally liable for debts of the business, they may not care how much of the debt is repaid. Even if the owners have all of their wealth in the corporation and the corporation is hopelessly insolvent, if the owners are personally liable, they will continue to have an incentive to cooperate with the lender who holds the guarantee. Their incentive is to avoid or minimize the judgments that eventually might be taken against them. In the event of competition for the assets of the corporation, the owners are likely to be on the side of the creditor to whom they have given their personal guarantee. Even if the owners can discharge the personal guarantee through bankruptcy, the owners' desire to avoid the stigma of bankruptcy may also motivate them to repay.

D. Bonnie's Buys Some Boats

With her floorplan line of credit in place, Bonnie is ready to go shopping. She contacts Shoreline Boat Manufacturing Company and arranges to become a Shoreline authorized dealer. Her choice is in part motivated by the fact that Shoreline is one of the dozen or so boat manufacturers who have signed a Floorplan Agreement with Deutsche.

1. The Floorplan Agreement

The Floorplan Agreement provides that if Deutsche finances purchase of Shoreline Boats by dealers such as Bonnie's Boat World and then has to repossess those boats, Shoreline will buy them back at the full invoice price. These are the key terms of the Agreement:

FLOORPLAN AGREEMENT

To: Deutsche Financial Services
      655 Maryville Centre Drive
      St. Louis, Missouri 63141

We sell various products ("Merchandise") to dealers and/or distributors (collectively "Dealer") who may require financial assistance in order to make such purchases from us. To induce you to finance the acquisition of Merchandise by any Dealer and in consideration thereof, we agree that:
      1. Whenever a Dealer requests the shipment of Merchandise from us and that you finance such Merchandise, we may deliver to you an

invoice(s) describing the Merchandise. By delivery of an invoice we warrant the following:

   a. That we transfer to the Dealer all right, title and interest in and to the Merchandise so described contingent upon your approval to finance the transaction;

   b. That our title to the Merchandise is free and clear of all liens and encumbrances when transferred to the Dealer;

   c. That the Merchandise is in salable condition, free of any defects;

   d. That the Merchandise is the subject of a bona fide order by the Dealer placed with and accepted by us and that the Dealer has requested the transaction be financed by you; and

   e. That the Merchandise subject to the transaction has been shipped to the Dealer not more than 10 days prior to the invoice date.

If we breach any of the above-described warranties, we will immediately: (i) pay to you an amount equal to the total unpaid balance (being principal and finance charges) owed to you on all Merchandise directly or indirectly related to the breach; and (ii) reimburse you for all costs and expenses (including, but not limited to, attorney's fees) incurred by you as a direct or indirect result of the breach.

   2. You will only be bound to finance Merchandise which you have accepted to finance (which acceptances will be indicated by your issuance of an approval number or a draft or other instrument to us in payment of the invoice less the amount of your charges as agreed upon from time to time) and only if:

   (i) the Merchandise is delivered to the Dealer within 30 days following your acceptance;

   (ii) you have received our invoice for such Merchandise within 10 days from the date of delivery of the Merchandise to the Dealer; and

   (iii) you have not revoked your acceptance prior to the shipment of the Merchandise to the Dealer.

   3. Whenever you deem it necessary in your sole discretion to repossess or if you otherwise come into possession of any Merchandise, in which you have a security interest or other lien, we will purchase such Merchandise from you at the time of your repossession or other acquisition or possession in accordance with the following terms and conditions:

   a. We will purchase such Merchandise, regardless of its condition, at the point where you repossess it or where it otherwise comes into your possession;

      b. The purchase price that we will pay to you for such Merchandise will be due and payable immediately in full, and will be an amount equal to (i) the total unpaid balance (being principal and finance charges) owed to you with respect to such Merchandise or our original invoice price for such Merchandise, whichever is greater, and (ii) all costs and expenses (including, without limitation, reasonable attorney's fees) paid or incurred by you in connection with the repossession of such Merchandise; and

      c. We shall not assert or obtain any interest in or to any Merchandise acquired by us, until the purchase price, therefor is paid in full. . . .

5. You may extend the time of a Dealer in default to fulfill its obligations to you without notice to us and without altering our obligations hereunder. We waive any rights we may have to . . . require you to proceed against a Dealer or to pursue any other remedy in your power. Our liability to you is direct and unconditional and will not be affected by any change in the terms of payment or performance of any agreement between you and Dealer, or the release, settlement or compromise of or with any party liable for the payment or performance thereof, the release or non-perfection of any security thereunder, any change in Dealer's financial condition, or the interruption of business relations between you and Dealer.

6. We will pay all your expenses (including, without limitation, court costs and reasonable attorney fees) in the event you are required to enforce your rights against us. Your failure to exercise any rights granted hereunder shall not operate as a waiver of those rights. . . .

8. Either of us may terminate this Agreement by notice to the other in writing, the termination to be effective 30 days after receipt of the notice by the other party, but no termination of this Agreement will affect any of our liability with respect to any financial transactions entered into by you with any Dealer prior to the effective date of termination, including, without limitation, transactions that will not be completed until after the effective date of termination.

Dated: <u>August 29</u> , <u>1998</u>

ATTEST: <u>Shoreline Boat Company</u>

                              Alan R. Shoreline

                  By: <u>Alan R. Shoreline</u>

                         Title: <u>President</u>

Business Address:

Alachua, Florida

ACCEPTED:

Deutsche Financial Services

George Dobisky

By: George Dobisky

Title: Division President

The advantage to Deutsche of this agreement is obvious. If Deutsche has to repossess Shoreline Boats from Bonnie's Boat World, Shoreline has agreed to buy them back for at least their full original invoice price. The advantages to Shoreline are also significant. With the Floorplan Agreement in place, Shoreline can offer qualified dealers nationwide 100 percent financing on the boats they buy from Shoreline, making the boats more attractive to dealers. Shoreline has to be ready to take the boats back if Bonnie's defaults, but if Shoreline financed the boats itself, Shoreline would have to do that anyway. If Shoreline financed the boats itself, it would bear much of the risk of boats being lost, stolen, or detroyed through dealer fraud. Under the Floorplan Agreement, Deutsche bears these risks.

Bonnie gets three advantages from this agreement. Because the repurchase agreement reduces Deutsche's risk of loss on resale after repossession, Deutsche can offer Bonnie's a larger line of credit and finance a larger portion of each purchase than a bank typically could. Additionally, Bonnie's may benefit from time to time from subsidies offered by Shoreline to Deutsche to provide dealers such as Bonnie's with periods when little or no interest accrues.

2.   The Buy

Bonnie contacts Shoreline and selects the five boats she wants. The total price of the boats is $55,000. In accord with the Floorplan Agreement, Shoreline contacts Deutsche to obtain approval of the purchase. Deutsche verifies from its records that both Bonnie's and Shoreline are in compliance with their agreements with Deutsche and that the purchase will not overdraw Bonnie's line of credit. Satisfied that everything is in order, Deutsche gives Shoreline an approval number for the purchase. (This is essentially the same thing that happens when you use your Visa card to buy a pair of shoes at the mall.)

Shoreline ships the five boats to Bonnie and sends the invoice to Deutsche. Deutsche pays the $55,000 to Shoreline, recording it on their books as a loan to Bonnie's.

E.   Bonnie's Sells a Boat

The morning after the Shoreline boats arrive in Bonnie's yard, William and Gladys Homer come to Bonnie's looking for the boat of their dreams. It turns out to be one of the five Bonnie's has just purchased from Shoreline. Bonnie's invoice price from Shoreline is $15,566.58; its invoice price to the Homers is $20,000. Bonnie's will have a gross profit on the sale of $4,333.42.

Arthur Dent, the Bonnie's salesman who helps the Homers pick out the boat, also helps them arrange their financing. Bonnie's has an arrangement with First State Bank under which First State finances 90 percent of the purchase price of a boat for any Bonnie's customer who qualifies. The Homers qualify and First State approves their boat loan on the same day they pick out the boat. The Homers write Bonnie's a check for $2,000, sign a security agreement and financing statement for First State, load the boat on their trailer, and drive off into a sunset filled with monthly payment coupons. On receipt of the security agreement and financing statement, First State deposits $18,000 to Bonnie's bank account.

Recall that Bonnie's financed the purchase of these boats with Deutsche on a "pay-as-sold" basis. That is, ¶(7(b) of the Wholesale Financing Agreement provides that "Dealer will immediately pay Deutsche the principal indebtedness owed Deutsche on each item of Collateral financed by Deutsche (as shown on the Statement of Transaction identifying such Collateral) . . . when such Collateral is sold." In accord with this provision, Bonnie's sends Deutsche a check for $15,566.58 that same day. At the beginning of the next month, Deutsche will bill Bonnie's for the finance charges that accrued during the brief time this $15,566.58 loan was outstanding.

F.   Monitoring the Existence of the Collateral

If Bonnie's had used the $15,566.58 it received from the Homers to pay other bills instead of sending it to Deutsche and Deutsche had then foreclosed, Deutsche's collateral would have been about that much less than its loan. If Bonnie repeated this diversion of funds enough times, Deutsche would soon have no collateral at all. How would Deutsche have discovered this developing problem?

The answer is that Deutsche will send a person to Bonnie's Boat World once every 30 to 45 days to verify the continuing existence of the collateral and check its condition. For the first such inspection, Deutsche assigns its most experienced floorchecker, Richard Feynman. Feynman arrives at Bonnie's Boat World unannounced, introduces himself to Bonnie, and goes to work.

Feynman has with him a list of all of the boats Deutsche has financed for Bonnie's, except those for which Deutsche has already received payment. For each boat, Feynman's list shows the make, model, and serial number. Feynman begins at one end of the fenced-in property and works his way to the other. For each boat he reads the make, model, and serial number from a metal plate attached to the boat, finds that boat on his list, and checks it off. He also notes the condition of the boat alongside the check mark.

When Feynman is finished, there are still two boats on his list he has not seen. He asks Bonnie about them. One, Bonnie tells him, was sold yesterday and delivered to the customer earlier this morning. Bonnie tells Feynman that she has already mailed the check to Deutsche for this boat. Feynman does not take Bonnie's word for that. Instead, he examines Bonnie's check ledger and verifies that Bonnie has written the check. He notes the existence of the purported check on his list; when the check arrives at Deutsche's offices, he will check the postmark on it. The other boat, Bonnie tells him, is out on the lake on a demonstration. It will be back in an hour or so if Feynman wants to drop by after lunch to check it, Bonnie suggests. Feynman explains to Bonnie that would be contrary to the established procedure for a floor check: All of the boats must be checked at the same time. Bonnie radios the missing boat and makes arrangements to rendezvous with it. Bonnie and Feynman take a second boat out, meet with the missing boat, and check it off on Feynman's list.

Why couldn't Feynman just stop back after lunch to look at the missing boat? The answer is that the registration plates are not a foolproof method for identifying a boat. Given time to do so, a dishonest debtor could remove the registration plate from a boat Feynman has already checked and substitute a counterfeit plate bearing the make, model, and number of a boat the debtor no longer owns. Feynman checks the boats all at the same time so that he does not have to rely solely on the registration plates; to a large degree, he relies on the number of boats he can see on the premises all at the same time. In addition, the floor check serves as a simulated repossession. Deutsche wants to know how much collateral they would have recovered had this been a real repossession. If it had been, Bonnie might never have told them the location of the missing boat.

Problem Set 15

15.1.   As an attorney for Deutsche Financial Services, you have been asked to comment on the floor-checking procedures for a loan of $185 million against 160 million pounds of soybean oil stored in dozens of petroleum tanks in Bayonne, New Jersey. The procedure is as follows: the Deutsche floor checker shows up in Bayonne unannounced. With an employee of the debtor, Allied Crude Vegetable Oil Refining Corporation, the floor checker climbs the metal staircase that winds around the first tank. From any point along the circular walkway at the top of the tank, the floor checker can see (and taste) the oil. The checker sticks a 40-foot pole into the oil to test its depth. Then the floor checker and the employee move on to the next tank and do the same thing. The quantity of oil in each tank is determined by multiplying the depth of the oil by the surface area. Do you see any problems?

15.2.   If Bonnie Brezhnev had been up to the following tricks, how would Deutsche have discovered them?

a.   Bonnie sees that her business is about to go bankrupt. She holds a big sale, sells as many boats as possible over the period of a week, wires the proceeds to a bank account in the Bahamas, withdraws the money from that account, and disappears.

b.   Whenever Bonnie sells a boat, she offers to store it for the buyer. (Many boat buyers store their boats in the marinas where they purchased them. When they want to use the boat, the marina operator puts it in the water for them.) If the buyer doesn't use the boat much, Bonnie does not report the sale to Deutsche. When the floor checkers come around, these boats are there for Bonnie to show them.

15.3.   The law firm you work for is outside counsel to Archer Commercial Finance. For many years, Archer has insisted on personal guarantees from the individuals who own any closely held business they finance. Gordon Jamail, a department head at Archer, has proposed a change in policy. He reels off the names of four potential customers he says have gone to a competitor in the last month alone because by doing so they could avoid Archer's personal guarantee requirement. "The irony," Gordon says, "is that in nine out of ten cases, the judgment we might recover on a personal guarantee would be uncollectible. These people borrow from us because they've already put everything they have in the business." The president of Archer asks for your opinion. What do you tell her?

15.4. Three years after the events set forth in the reading, Bonnie Brezhnev comes to you for legal advice. For the past two years, the boat business has been lousy. During that time, she has put everything she has into the business, even to the extent of taking out a second mortgage on her home. Still short of working capital, she has been juggling boats, lying to the floor checker, and keeping phony records to back up her lies. On the floor check this morning she was five boats out of trust, a total of about $50,000. Deutsche has declared Bonnie's Boat World in default and demanded that she surrender the 20 Shoreline boats remaining in its possession. Over the past couple of weeks, Bonnie has come to the realization that the business cannot survive; what she wants now is to get out of the mess she is in.

a. Bonnie asks you whether Deutsche has the right to the boats. Do they? See the Agreement for Wholesale Financing ¶9(iii); Floorplan Agreement ¶3; U.C.C. §§9-601(a), 9-609.

b. If Bonnie surrenders the boats without a fight, what do you think will happen to her? U.C.C. §9-608(a)(4); 26 Ill. Stat. para. 9-306.01, set forth in section A.3. of Assignment 10.

c. Does Bonnie have the power to keep these boats? If so, how? For how long?

d. What advice do you give Bonnie? The Model Rules of Professional Conduct provide in relevant part:

> *Rule 4.4.* In representing a client, a lawyer shall not use means that have no substantial purpose other than to . . . delay or burden a third person.
>
> *Rule 1.2.* A lawyer shall not counsel a client to engage, or assist a client, in conduct that the lawyer knows is criminal or fraudulent . . . but a lawyer may discuss the legal consequences of any proposed course of conduct.
>
> *Rule 1.16.* A lawyer shall not represent a client . . . if the representation will result in violation of the rules of professional conduct or other law. . . .

15.5. As an arbitrator for the American Arbitration Association, you have been assigned a case in which Deutsche seeks to enforce provisions of the Agreement for Wholesale Financing against a dealer who signed it five years ago and has been borrowing under it since that time. The dealer's attorney argues that the contract is "void for lack of consideration" and "illusory" because nowhere in it does Deutsche agree to make a loan or necessarily do anything else. What do you think of this argument? See Agreement for Wholesale Financing ¶1.

15.6. Bonnie consults you prior to signing the agreement with Deutsche. What is your answer to each of the following questions?

a. What interest rate will Bonnie pay on her outstanding balance? See Wholesale Financing Agreement ¶2 and Statement of Transaction.

b.   Will Deutsche have a security interest in Bonnie's lease of the boatyard? In her bank accounts? Wholesale Financing Agreement ¶3; U.C.C. §§9-109(a) and (d)(11) and (d)(13), 9-604, 9-102(2) and (42), and 9-203(f).

c.   Would Bonnie violate her agreement with Deutsche by permitting an employee to take the boat for a demonstration ride? If she did, would that give Deutsche the right to call the loan? Wholesale Financing Agreement ¶¶5(b), 9; U.C.C. §§9-201(a), 9-601(a).

d.   Given that Shoreline has agreed, as part of the Floorplan Agreement, ¶3.b., to buy repossessed boats from Deutsche at the full amount owing on them, does that mean that Bonnie need not worry about a deficiency judgment on a repossessed boat? U.C.C. §§9-102(59) and (71), 9-618, and Wholesale Financing agreement ¶10.

15.7.   It has been a year since Deutsche entered into this financing arrangement with Bonnie's Boat World. Deutsche is not happy with the arrangement, in part because Bonnie has been difficult to deal with and in part because the boat business has been bad and Deutsche would like to get out of it altogether. Bonnie's, however, is not in breach. Can Deutsche get out of this deal? If so, how does Deutsche do it? Wholesale Financing Agreement ¶¶2, 9i, and 12. What will be the effect on Bonnie's?

Part Two
The Creditor-Third Party
Relationship

Chapter 6.   Perfection

Assignment 16: The Personal Property Filing Systems

A.   Competition for the Secured Creditor's Collateral

In Part One of this book, we examined the relationship between a secured creditor and its debtor. We focused on how the rights of secured creditors to collect from the debtor differed from those of unsecured creditors. We also examined the procedures by which creditors obtained secured status and the contracts that created those rights.

In Part Two, we shift our focus to the relationship between a secured creditor and others who may claim the same collateral. Our approach remains pragmatic. We ask what the secured creditor must do to prevail over these new adversaries, how effective the secured creditor's rights against them are likely to be, and how expensive these new rights will be to obtain and to enforce.

Debtors sometimes participate in the struggle between their secured creditors and third parties. Other times they have already given up in exhausted resignation and do not care who gets the collateral. The issue now is the rights of a secured creditor against others who also have rights superior to those of the debtor.

Just as debtors come in many different types — consumers and businesses, hard-working but unfortunate people, and sleazeballs, wealthy and poor — so do their creditors. An individual debtor in financial trouble is likely to owe money to 20 or 30 creditors, including a home mortgage lender, several credit card issuers, a finance company, the phone company, several local department stores, an auto lender, a cable company, the family doctor, and so on. A business debtor may owe money to hundreds or even thousands of creditors, including banks, commercial lenders, current employees, retired employees, lessors, suppliers, customers, utility companies, and taxing authorities. Some of these creditors may not have acquired their status voluntarily. The creditor of an individual debtor may be the victim of an automobile accident or a custodial parent with the right to payments for child support. The creditor of a business debtor may be a government agency that has spent money to remove toxic waste from the debtor's property, a competitor injured by the debtor's illegal business practices, or the Internal Revenue Service. To complicate matters further, the third party who claims the secured creditor's collateral may not be a creditor at all. It may be someone who bought the collateral from the debtor or someone who claims to remain the owner because the debtor never completed the transaction in which the debtor bought the collateral.

A particularly slippery, imaginative, or unfortunate debtor can create a vivid array of contestants for its limited assets. These competitors may see the secured creditor's collateral (or what the secured creditor thought was its collateral) as their only source of recovery or merely as the most convenient or cost-effective one.

The law treats many of the contests over rights to collateral as questions of *priority*. This assignment briefly addresses what it means for one creditor to have priority over another. It also begins a discussion of how creditors obtain priority over one another. The latter discussion extends through the remaining assignments of Part Two, Chapter 6.

In Chapter 7 we examine what creditors who have priority must do to keep it. We consider the effect of the passage of time; the filing of bankruptcy; changes in the identity, use, and location of collateral; and changes in the identity and location of the debtor.

In Chapter 8 we examine the concept of priority in more detail. We look at how priority is implemented in both state law and bankruptcy procedures, and then use that reality to give further definition to the concept.

In Chapter 9 we explore competitions between secured creditors and others over collateral. We begin with lien creditors. Then we consider trustees in bankruptcy, other secured creditors, those who sold the collateral to the debtor, those who bought the collateral from the debtor, statutory lienors, and finally the federal government as tax-lien holder. As we examine these contests one by one, you will see how the rules for resolving them fit together (sometimes well and sometimes badly) to form a single system of lien priority based for the most part on the principle, "first in time is first in right." Along the way, the policies underlying secured credit should become clearer.

B. What Is Priority?

In Part One of this book, we introduced the concept of a *lien*. A lien is a relationship between a debt and property that serves as collateral. If the debtor fails to pay the debt, the secured creditor can foreclose the lien, force a sale of the collateral, and have the proceeds of the sale applied to payment of the debt. We refer to this attribute of a lien as the secured creditor's *remedy*.

In Part Two, we will examine a second and perhaps even more important attribute of a lien: *priority*. If there is more than one lien against collateral, each will have a priority. Liens are commonly labeled "first," "second," "third," etc. (You may, for example, have heard of "second mortgages.") A lien with priority higher than another is referred to as the *senior* or *prior lien* and the other is referred to as the *subordinate* or *junior lien*. If the value of collateral is insufficient to pay all of the liens against an item of collateral, the junior liens yield to the senior ones.

To illustrate, assume that David owes Alice $7,000 and Betty $9,000. Each has a security interest (recall that a security interest is a type of lien) in David's BMW, which is worth $12,000. If Alice's lien has priority over Betty's lien and either is foreclosed, Alice will be entitled to $7,000 of the value of the BMW and Betty will be entitled to the remaining $5,000. Once the BMW has been liquidated and the proceeds distributed, Betty will be an unsecured creditor for the $4,000 balance owed to her.

(At this point, we pause to note the complexity of this scheme for resolving competition among creditors. Each creditor's lien is a relationship between an obligation and an item of collateral; priority is the relationship between these relationships. Don't be surprised if every implication of this complex scheme does not immediately spring to mind. It will come.)

While we usually think of priority as an attribute of a lien, priority can exist among creditors who do not have liens. For example, it is not uncommon for a large, publicly held company to raise some of its capital by borrowing from banks or insurance companies and some through the issue of unsecured bonds, or *debentures*. One term of the contract between the company and the purchasers of the bonds is that the bond debt is *subordinated* to the bank debt, which means that if the banks and the bondholders ever seek to satisfy their debts from assets of the debtor, the bondholders will take nothing until the banks have been paid in full. Even though the banks and the bondholders have contractually established priority between themselves, both remain unsecured.

Contracts establishing priority among unsecured creditors are relatively uncommon for the simple reason that debtors frequently encumber all of their assets with liens. Those liens have priority over all unsecured debts. When a debtor is in financial difficulty, even the most senior unsecured status is likely, in the metaphor popular among practitioners, to be "out of the money."

The system of lien priority is so fundamental a social and economic institution that many fail to realize that it is merely one of several ways that a legal system can resolve competition among creditors for the limited assets of a debtor. Some examples of other possible systems may help. First, such competitions could be resolved by allowing each competitor a pro rata share of the limited assets. Recall from Assignment 7 of this book that this is how competitions are resolved among unsecured creditors in bankruptcy. Second, competitions could be decided on the basis of the status of the competing creditors. Debts deemed more important, such as those owing to employees, taxing agencies, or widows and orphans, might be given higher priority, while less important ones, such as those owing to commercial creditors, might be assigned lower priority. Some of this kind of thinking is embodied in the distributional rules of Bankruptcy Code §§507(a) and 726(a) and in the statutory lien laws discussed in Assignment 37. Third, competitions over the value of a debtor's assets could be resolved by permitting competing creditors to trace and recover the value that each supplied to the debtor. But as the following case illustrates, the established legal system is comfortable with the idea that the winner takes all simply because it is secured, regardless of any competing social equities.

Peerless Packing Co. v. Malone & Hyde, Inc.

376 S.E.2d 161 (W. Va. 1988)

NEELY, JUSTICE.

Appellants are twelve companies that supply wholesale products to grocery stores. Appellee is also a wholesaler of grocery products, with operations covering the southeastern states. John Kizer was appellee's co-defendant below. This is an appeal from the trial court's award of a directed verdict for appellee.

Mr. Kizer . . . negotiated an agreement with appellee [to purchase the business of the former ADP store in Beckley]. Under this agreement, Mr. Kizer provided $50,000 for working capital that went into the purchase of inventory. Appellee allowed Mr. Kizer to use its trade name "PIC PAC," subleased the store to Mr. Kizer, sold him the store equipment for $200,000, and provided him with approximately $187,000 in additional inventory. In exchange, Mr. Kizer gave appellee a promissory note for approximately $387,000, plus interest, which was secured by a security interest in the present and after acquired inventory.

Appellee met all requirements of the Uniform Commercial Code (UCC) for perfecting its lien against the store's collateral and appellants do not challenge the technical validity of appellee's lien.

Mr. Kizer opened the store in November 1982. The store sold some goods in addition to those supplied by appellee. Many of these additional goods were supplied by the twelve appellant companies, who delivered the goods several times a week on open account credit extended to the store. None of appellants obtained purchase money security interests in the inventory supplied by them. Purchase money security interests could have given appellants priority over appellee's security interest in the inventory.

By March 1983, it was apparent to appellee that the store was not successful because it was meeting its obligations, in part, by reducing inventory. Also, one of Mr. Kizer's checks for the rent and note payments to appellee was returned for insufficient funds. Agents of appellee approached Mr. Kizer and told him that they were going to take the store back, and either he could voluntarily sign everything over to appellee, or "they would take everything he had." Mr. Kizer then signed a document presented by appellee called a Notice of Default and Transfer of Possession Agreement. This agreement transferred all of Mr. Kizer's rights in the store, equipment and inventory, and the balance of the store's bank account, about $64,000, to appellee. In return, appellee released Mr. Kizer from any liability, including personal liability for any deficiency, on the $387,000 note, the rent on the store and on an additional $54,000 [which was for groceries delivered by appellee and for which Kizer had not yet paid].

Appellee assumed ownership of the store and began operating it with Mr. Kizer as manager. Appellee sent a letter to the appellant vendors stating that appellee had realized on its security interest in the store's assets without assuming any liability to third parties, and would not pay any invoices for deliveries before 31 March 1988, the date appellee took ownership.

Appellants each sued Mr. Kizer for the unpaid accounts, and also sued appellee on a theory of unjust enrichment, with a claim for both compensatory and punitive damages. The cases were consolidated, and each appellant was granted default judgment before trial against Mr. Kizer, who discharged his obligation on the judgments in bankruptcy. At the close of appellants' case against appellee, appellee moved for a directed verdict, which the trial court granted.

I

. . . Appellants also contend that appellee was unjustly enriched by the transfer because appellee, knowing it was going to foreclose on the store, allowed appellants to continue to deliver goods for a week before appellee took over. . . .

. . . Appellee contends that a theory of unjust enrichment is not applicable in a case that is governed by the UCC. Appellee argues that it was entitled to keep the collateral and that it got no more than it was owed by Mr. Kizer. In fact, appellee insists that it "lost" about $130,000 through the transfer.

The trial court agreed with appellee that an unjust enrichment claim is not applicable in a UCC case, and stated in its final order, in part,

> First, the Court concludes as a matter of law that the plaintiffs cannot maintain this action, which is governed by Article 9 of the UCC, on a theory of recovery grounded upon the equitable doctrine of unjust enrichment. Evans Products Co. v. Jorgensen, 421 P.2d 978 (Oregon, 1966). The Court agrees with the rationale of the Oregon Supreme Court at p. 983 that "[T]he purpose and effectiveness of the UCC would be substantially impaired if interests created in compliance with UCC procedure could be defeated by application of the equitable doctrine of unjust enrichment."

We agree with the trial court's order and affirm his ruling with regard to appellants' equitable unjust enrichment claim. As the Oregon Supreme Court pointed out in *Jorgensen*, cited by the trial court in the quote above, although the result of disallowing an equitable unjust enrichment claim in such a case may appear harsh, the unsatisfied creditors, (appellants in the case before us), could have protected themselves either by demanding cash payment for their goods, or by taking a purchase money security interest in the goods they delivered.[4] . . .

In the beginning, there were 13 unsecured creditors. One took a security interest. When the business failed, that one got everything, including goods sold to the debtor by the other 12 creditors and for which those 12 were not paid. That is the meaning of priority.

C.   How Do Creditors Get Priority?

Central to the system of lien priority is the idea that liens rank in the chronological order in which they were created. There are a few exceptions to this rule, but they are in favor of liens such as property taxes that secure relatively small, predictable obligations. The ratio-

---

4. We do not hold that an equitable claim for relief never lies in a case controlled by the U.C.C. As appellants point out, [U.C.C. §1-203] requires that "[e]very contract or duty within this chapter imposes an obligation of good faith in its performance or enforcement." Some courts have held that equitable claims raised under this section can change priorities explicitly provided in Article 9. However, most of these cases involve situations of virtually fraudulent conduct. The U.C.C. provides justice in the long run in large part through the certainty and predictability of its provisions, which should not be set aside absent truly egregious circumstances verging on actual fraud. In the case before us, even allowing appellants every favorable inference from their evidence, we do not believe they have presented evidence of such circumstances sufficient to disturb the priorities set by the provisions of Article 9.

nale of the lien priority system depends heavily on the fact that once the priority of a lien is established, any lien created thereafter will be subordinate.

In a very general sense, priority by chronology makes it possible for a creditor to know, at the time it makes a loan, how it will fare in later competitions over the collateral. That is, it knows that it will rank behind liens already in existence and ahead of any liens created later. Because the liens it will rank behind are already in existence, the prospective lender can obtain information about them and, if necessary, contract with the holder regarding their disposition.

Of course, the mere fact that the prior liens exist does not itself assure that the prospective lender will be able to discover them or obtain needed information about them. There probably are liens against the inventory and fixtures in the grocery store where you shop, but to a person walking through the store, they are invisible. To assure that the prospective lender can discover a lien that will have priority over its own, the laws under which liens are created almost invariably condition the priority on the holder taking steps to make existence of the lien public and easily discoverable. The steps that must be taken differ with the type of lien, but nearly all include acts in one of four categories: (1) filing notice in a public records system established for that purpose, (2) taking possession of collateral, (3) taking control of collateral by means of the stake holder's agreement to hold for the secured creditor, or (4) posting notice on the property or where it will be seen by persons dealing with the property. The taking of whatever steps are required is generally referred to as *perfecting* the lien.

Secured parties usually choose to perfect their liens by public filing. But for particular kinds of property they may choose, or be required, to perfect by some other method. And recall from Assignment 1 that an unsecured creditor obtains an execution lien by reducing its claim to judgment, obtaining a writ of execution, and having the sheriff levy on the assets. Under the law of most states, the levy both creates the lien and perfects it by the sheriff's possession.

In the next four assignments we will discuss in more detail the actions that various kinds of creditors must take to perfect their liens in various kinds of collateral. For now, you can think of "perfection" as a series of steps that the holder of a lien must take to give public notice and thereby establish priority. Because priority is based on the time these steps were taken, it is important to document that time. To that end, the officers that receive notices for filing immediately stamp each with a date and time received. Similarly, the sheriff who seizes property pursuant to a writ of execution will immediately record the date and time of seizure. When disputes arise, the records of these officers can be used to prove these dates and times. Perfection sometimes can be accomplished in a manner that does not create a date-and-time-stamped public record. In that event, the secured creditor may have to prove the date and time by other evidence.

In the large majority of cases, the dates and times of perfection will determine the priorities of the liens. Notice that in the system thus created, the type of lien is unimportant. Except for the time of their perfection, one lien is the same as another. The assignment of dates and times of perfection makes it possible to quickly and simply determine the priorities among particular Article 9 security interests, mortgages, federal tax liens, execution liens, judgment liens, construction liens, and any others.

As you might guess from the number of pages in the remainder of this book, the model we present here is an oversimplification of the system for perfecting and prioritizing liens. In the real world, the steps for perfecting a lien may be complicated. It may be difficult even to know what they are. The rules that determine priority among liens are made by diverse legislative bodies, and they are not always consistent. Not all priority follows the rule of first in time, first in right. But for now, this simple model will do.

D. The Theory of the Filing System

As we noted above, the filing system is the principal means used to communicate the possible existence of a lien from a creditor who has one to a creditor who is thinking of acquiring one. The filing system gives constructive notice, but it is intended to do more than that. In theory, at least, it is supposed to give actual notice to the later creditor. The difficulty in transmitting notice from the holder of a lien to the creditor who seeks to acquire one is that neither of these creditors has any way of knowing who the other is until it is too late for the communication to do any good.

The solution to this problem is for each creditor who obtains a lien to leave a "to whom it may concern" message. For an Article 9 security interest, that message is in the form of a *financing statement*, also known by its form number, a "U.C.C.-1." Each year, the creditors who take security interests leave millions of these messages in the filing system. And before they take their liens, many of these filers search the records to see whether prior secured creditors left messages for them.

For such a system to work, prospective creditors must know that the system exists and that there may be messages waiting in it for them. Of course, banks and most lawyers will have this kind of knowledge. But many consumers and small business people are not aware this system exists. (Neither are some law students who opted not to take this course.) Unsophisticated lenders often fail to claim their priority by filing; the result is that even later lenders will come ahead of them. Unsophisticated lenders often fail to discover a lien that is on the public record before they obtain their own; the result is that the lien they take will be subordinate to the lien already recorded. Either consequence can be disastrous to a lender who does not expect it. The advantages of a filing system come at a considerable human and economic cost.

The theory of the filing system has suffered considerably in implementation. As we will see in this and the subsequent chapter, filing systems are highly imprecise and difficult and expensive to use. Filing is relatively easy and failure to file creates a significant risk that the creditor's lien will be avoided by a trustee in bankruptcy. Searching is relatively difficult, and failure to search leads to adverse consequences only if the debtor previously granted a security interest to a competing creditor and fails to mention that fact on the loan application. As a result, many creditors are lax in searching, and some do not search at all. The following exchange is between Professor Ronald Mann and Joe DeKunder, vice president of NationsBank of Texas, N.A.

Mann: When you do take a pledge of the receivables, even on these really small transactions, do you do a U.C.C. search before you disburse the money?

DeKunder: Yeah, we do a U.C.C. search, yes. Now, I want to qualify that somewhat. We do have situations where we feel that we want to make an exception, and it's a timing factor. Let's say we make a small loan and we do this on blanket receivables, and we want to close that loan tomorrow, let's say — for whatever reason. It's a working capital loan and we want to get it done, and we determine that the search is going to be too lengthy in time, we'll do a post-search. We've already funded the loan, you know. We'll do a search after the fact, just to determine where we are. And frankly, we do that fairly frequently. Now I know that doesn't sound like the prudent thing to do, but what happens in effect is we determine often, just like I mentioned earlier, there are liens that need to be released. We determine sometimes that, obviously, there is nothing there. Sometimes, we are surprised. But at any rate, the post-search is done occasionally. Usually, in those situations we are comfortable with the customer. We are comfortable with the fact that we would make this unsecured and probably we're just taking this as a matter of control.

Mann: But you've done that and gotten burned?

DeKunder: We've done it and gotten burned, yes. . . . Many small business owners, to a degree, don't really understand, sometimes, that someone's even filed . . . a U.C.C. on their collateral. They'll be surprised, they'll say "gosh, I didn't know they did that." Well, you know the obvious question is "you apparently signed the papers." "Well, I didn't know. They never mentioned it. They never said anything about taking a blanket on my . . . " Sometimes what happens is that the blanket is already in place by that bank, the customer pays their loan off, they come back and they take another pledge but don't refile the U.C.C., but it's still in effect.

Mann: It's still there.

DeKunder: It's still there . . . and the borrower didn't know it. He didn't know that they would continue with that. I've had situations where the borrower is quite upset. They will call that other financial institution and say "I didn't know you were gonna . . . " And a lot of times they'll just go ahead and release it. Some of those things are mechanical in nature; it's like well, they didn't know it, we didn't know it, but it can be resolved if we work it out.

E. The Multiplicity of Filing Systems

The task of a lender who would search for messages relating to the collateral, lend money, and leave a message of its own is vastly complicated by the fact that there is not just one message center, but many. With a few exceptions, each county in the United States maintains a real estate recording system in which not only real estate mortgages, but also Article 9 fixture filings are filed. See U.C.C. §9-501(a)(1). Many counties also maintain separate systems for property tax liens, local tax liens, and money judgments. All states except Georgia and Louisiana have state U.C.C. filing systems. See U.C.C. §501(a)(2). Georgia and Louisiana have local U.C.C. filing offices in each county, but the filings thus made can be searched through a statewide index. All states maintain certificate of title systems in which creditors can file notices of security interests in automobiles, and many states have separate certificate of title systems for boats and/or mobile homes. Some states maintain specialized systems for filing against particular kinds of collateral. For example, security interests in Florida liquor licenses are perfected by filing with the state agency that issues the licenses. The federal government maintains yet additional filing systems for patents, trademarks, copyrights, aircraft, and ship mortgages. International negotiations are under way for the creation of a world filing system for security interests in certain mobile property.

Although each of these systems is established by law and charged with keeping particular kinds of messages, the offices that keep the records have almost no communication with one another. If the secured creditor leaves its message in the wrong office, the message almost certainly will be ineffective. If the later lender searches only in the wrong office, it will miss whatever messages were left in the right office.

The statutes that create each of these systems specify, with differing degrees of clarity, the circumstances in which a message should be filed in that system. Usually the type of collateral is determinative. Thus, to decide which system is appropriate for a particular filing one might have to decide such weighty questions as whether particular collateral is a "ship" or a "boat," a "copyright receivable" or an "account," or a "motor vehicle" or "equipment." The definitions of controlling terms are often unexpected.

Bad as this situation is, it used to be worse. Former Article 9 permitted states to establish local filing systems (at the county level) for security interests in consumer goods and most farm-related property. Most states did so. In those states, filings against those kinds of property in the statewide filing systems were ineffective. In addition, former Article 9 permitted states to require two filings against collateral owned by any business that operated in only a single county in the state — one in the statewide U.C.C. filing system and the other in the county U.C.C. filings. Some states, including New York and Pennsylvania, required such dual filings. The Official Text of revised Article 9 provides for local filings only for real-estate-related collateral and only in the office designated for the filing or recording of real estate mortgages. But some states are likely to preserve their local U.C.C. filing systems for some period of time through non-uniform amendments.

Ideally, there would be one and only one correct system in which to file notice of a particular security interest. But with both the state and national governments defining the boundaries of the systems, uncertainties and overlaps are inevitable. The following case both illustrates and discusses the kinds of problems that occur. Because the case arose under a prior version of Article 9, the language quoted by the court does not precisely match the sections indicated in the new section numbers we have inserted in brackets.

National Peregrine, Inc. v. Capitol Federal Savings and Loan Association of Denver (In re Peregrine Entertainment, Ltd.)

116 B.R. 194 (C.D. Cal. 1990)

ALEX KOZINSKI, UNITED STATES CIRCUIT JUDGE. Sitting by designation pursuant to 28 U.S.C. §291(b) (1982).

This appeal from a decision of the bankruptcy court raises an issue never before confronted by a federal court in a published opinion: Is a security interest in a copyright perfected by an appropriate filing with the United States Copyright Office or by a UCC-1 financing statement filed with the relevant secretary of state?

I

National Peregrine, Inc. (NPI) is a Chapter 11 debtor in possession whose principal assets are a library of copyrights, distribution rights and licenses to approximately 145 films, and accounts receivable arising from the licensing of these films to various programmers. . . .

In June 1985, Capitol Federal Savings and Loan Association of Denver (Cap Fed) extended to [NPI] a six million dollar line of credit secured by . . . NPI's film library. Both the security agreement and the UCC-1 financing statements filed by Cap Fed describe the collateral as "[a]ll inventory consisting of films and all accounts, contract rights, chattel paper, general intangibles, instruments, equipment, and documents related to such inventory, now owned or hereafter acquired by the Debtor." Although Cap Fed filed its UCC-1 financing statements in California, Colorado and Utah, it did not record its security interest in the United States Copyright Office.

NPI filed a voluntary petition for bankruptcy on January 30, 1989. On April 6, 1989, NPI filed an amended complaint against Cap Fed, contending that the bank's security interest in the copyrights to the films in NPI's library and in the accounts receivable generated by their distribution were unperfected because Cap Fed failed to record its security interest with the Copyright Office. NPI claimed that, as a debtor in possession, it had a judicial lien on all assets in the bankruptcy estate, including the copyrights and receivables. Armed with this lien, it sought to avoid, recover and preserve Cap Fed's supposedly unperfected security interest for the benefit of the estate.

The parties filed cross-motions for partial summary judgment on the question of whether Cap Fed had a valid security interest in the NPI film library. The bankruptcy court held for Cap Fed. NPI appeals.

II

A.   WHERE TO FILE

The Copyright Act provides that "[a]ny transfer of copyright ownership or other document pertaining to a copyright" may be recorded in the United States Copyright Office. 17 U.S.C. §205(a). A "transfer" under the Act includes any "mortgage" or "hypothecation of a copyright," whether "in whole or in part" and "by any means of conveyance or by operation of law." 17 U.S.C. §§101, 201(d)(1). The terms "mortgage" and "hypothecation" include a pledge of property as security or collateral for a debt. In addition, the Copyright Office has defined a "document pertaining to a copyright" as one that "has a direct or indirect relationship to the existence, scope, duration, or identification of a copyright, or to the ownership, division, allocation, licensing, transfer, or exercise of rights under a copyright. That relationship may be past, present, future, or potential."

It is clear from the preceding that an agreement granting a creditor a security interest in a copyright may be recorded in the Copyright Office. Likewise, because a copyright entitles the holder to receive all income derived from the display of the creative work, see 17 U.S.C. §106, an agreement creating a security interest in the receivables generated by a copyright may also be recorded in the Copyright Office. Thus, Cap Fed's security interest could have been recorded in the Copyright Office; the parties seem to agree on this much. The question is, does the UCC provide a parallel method of perfecting a security interest in a copyright? One can answer this question by reference to either federal or state law; both inquiries lead to the same conclusion.

1. Even in the absence of express language, federal regulation will preempt state law if it is so pervasive as to indicate that "Congress left no room for supplementary state regulation," or if "the federal interest is so dominant that the federal system will be assumed to preclude enforcement of state laws on the same subject." Hillsborough County v. Automated Medical Laboratories, Inc., 471 U.S. 707, 713, 85 L. Ed. 2d 714, 105 S. Ct. 2371 (1985). Here, the comprehensive scope of the federal Copyright Act's recording provisions, along with the unique federal interests they implicate, support the view that federal law preempts state methods of perfecting security interests in copyrights and related accounts receivable.

The federal copyright laws ensure "predictability and certainty of copyright ownership," "promote national uniformity" and "avoid the practical difficulties of determining and enforcing an author's rights under the differing laws and in the separate courts of the various States." Community for Creative Non-Violence v. Reid, 490 U.S. 730, 109 S. Ct. 2166, 2177, 104 L. Ed. 2d 811 (1989). As discussed above, section 205(a) of the Copyright Act establishes a uniform method for recording security interests in copyrights. A secured creditor need only file in the Copyright Office in order to give "all persons constructive notice of the facts stated in the recorded document." 17 U.S.C. §205(c). Likewise, an interested third party need only search the indices maintained by the Copyright Office to determine whether a particular copyright is encumbered.

A recording system works by virtue of the fact that interested parties have a specific place to look in order to discover with certainty whether a particular interest has been transferred or encumbered. To the extent there are competing recordation schemes, this lessens the utility of each; when records are scattered in several filing units, potential creditors must conduct several searches before they can be sure that the property is not encumbered. It is for that reason that parallel recordation schemes for the same types of property are scarce as hen's teeth; the court is aware of no others, and the parties have cited none. No useful purposes would be served — indeed, much confusion would result — if creditors were permitted to perfect security interests by filing with either the Copyright Office or state offices.

If state methods of perfection were valid, a third party (such as a potential purchaser of the copyright) who wanted to learn of any encumbrances thereon would have to check not merely the indices of the U.S. Copyright Office, but also the indices of any relevant secretary of state. Because copyrights are incorporeal — they have no fixed situs — a number of state authorities could be relevant. Thus, interested third parties could never be entirely sure that all relevant jurisdictions have been searched. This possibility, together with the expense and delay of conducting searches in a variety of jurisdictions, could hinder the purchase and sale of copyrights, frustrating Congress's policy that copyrights be readily transferable in commerce.

This is the reasoning adopted by the Ninth Circuit in Danning v. Pacific Propeller. *Danning* held that 49 U.S.C. §1403(a), the Federal Aviation Act's provision for recording conveyances and the creation of liens and security interests in civil aircraft, preempts state filing provisions. 620 F.2d at 735-736.[8] According to *Danning,*

> [t]he predominant purpose of the statute was to provide one central place for the filing of [liens on aircraft] and thus eliminate the need, given the highly mobile nature of aircraft and their appurtenances, for the examination of State and County records.

---

8. Section 1403(a), which is similar in scope to section 205 of the Copyright Act, provides:

The Secretary of Transportation shall establish and maintain a system for the recording of each of each and all of the following:

(1)   Any conveyance which affects the title to, or any interest in, any civil aircraft of the United States;

(2)   Any lease, and any mortgage, equipment trust, contract of conditional sale, or other instrument executed for security purposes, which lease or other instrument affects the title to, or any interest in [certain engines and propellers];

(3)   Any lease, and any mortgage, equipment trust, contract of conditional sale, or other instrument executed for security purposes, which lease or other instrument affects the title to, or any interest in, any aircraft engines, propellers, or appliances maintained by or on behalf of an air carrier. . . .

49 U.S.C. §1403(a).

620 F.2d at 735-736. Copyrights, even more than aircraft, lack a clear situs; tangible, movable goods such as airplanes must always exist at some physical location; they may have a home base from which they operate or where they receive regular maintenance. The same cannot be said of intangibles. As noted above, this lack of an identifiable situs militates against individual state filings and in favor of a single, national registration scheme. . . .

The bankruptcy court below nevertheless concluded that security interests in copyrights could be perfected by filing either with the copyright office or with the secretary of state under the UCC, making a tongue-in-cheek analogy to the use of a belt and suspenders to hold up a pair of pants. According to the bankruptcy court, because either device is equally useful, one should be free to choose which one to wear. With all due respect, this court finds the analogy inapt. There is no legitimate reason why pants should be held up in only one particular manner: Individuals and public modesty are equally served by either device, or even by a safety pin or a piece of rope; all that really matters is that the job gets done. Registration schemes are different in that the way notice is given is precisely what matters. To the extent interested parties are confused as to which system is being employed, this increases the level of uncertainty and multiplies the risk of error, exposing creditors to the possibility that they might get caught with their pants down.

A recordation scheme best serves its purpose where interested parties can obtain notice of all encumbrances by referring to a single, precisely defined recordation system. The availability of parallel state recordation systems that could put parties on constructive notice as to encumbrances on copyrights would surely interfere with the effectiveness of the federal recordation scheme. Given the virtual absence of dual recordation schemes in our legal system, Congress cannot be presumed to have contemplated such a result. The court therefore concludes that any state recordation system pertaining to interests in copyrights would be preempted by the Copyright Act.

2. State law leads to the same conclusion. [Editors' note: We omit this section of the opinion because the revision of Article 9 made significant changes in language and perhaps in substance. In the omitted section, the court concluded that express provisions of Article 9 yielded to the Copyright filing system. The issue under new Article 9 would be slightly different: Did the filing provisions of the Copyright Act preempt the filing provisions of Article 9 with respect to copyrights? U.C.C. §9-109(c)(1).]

As discussed above, section 205(a) of the Copyright Act clearly does establish a national system for recording transfers of copyright interests, and it specifies a place of filing different from that provided in Article Nine. Recording in the Copyright Office gives nationwide, constructive notice to third parties of the recorded encumbrance. Except for the fact that the Copyright Office's indexes are organized on the basis of the title and registration number, rather than by reference to the identity of the debtor, this system is nearly identical to that which Article Nine generally provides on a statewide basis.[10] . . .

The court therefore concludes that the Copyright Act provides for national registration and "specifies a place of filing different from that specified in [Article Nine] for filing of the security interest." [U.C.C. §9-311(a)(1).] Recording in the U.S. Copyright Office, rather than filing a financing statement under Article Nine, is the proper method for perfecting a security interest in a copyright.

In reaching this conclusion, the court rejects City Bank & Trust Co. v. Otto Fabric, Inc., 83 Bankr. 780 (D. Kan. 1988), and In re Transportation Design & Technology Inc., 48 Bankr. 635 (Bankr. S.D. Cal. 1985), insofar as they are germane to the issues presented here. Both cases held that, under the UCC, security interests in patents need not be recorded in the U.S. Patent and Trademark Office to be perfected as against lien creditors because the federal statute governing patent assignments does not specifically provide for liens:

> Applications for patent, patents, or any interest therein, shall be assignable in law by an instrument in writing. The applicant, patentee, or his assigns or legal representatives may in like manner grant and convey an exclusive right under his application for patent, or patents, to the whole or any specified part of the United States . . . .
>
> An assignment, grant or conveyance shall be void as against any subsequent purchaser or mortgagee for a valuable consideration, without notice, unless it is recorded in the Patent and Trademark Office within three

---

10. Moreover, the mechanics of recording in the Copyright Office are analogous to filing under the U.C.C. In order to record a security interest in the Copyright Office, a creditor may file either the security agreement itself or a duplicate certified to be a true copy of the original, so long as either is sufficient to place third parties on notice that the copyright is encumbered. Accordingly, the Copyright Act requires that the file document "specifically identif[y] the work to which it pertains so that, after the document is indexed by the Register of Copyrights, it would be revealed by a reasonable search under the title or registration number of the work." 17 U.S.C. §205(c).

That having been said, it's worth noting that filing with the Copyright Office can be much less convenient than filing under the U.C.C. This is because U.C.C. filings are indexed by owner, while registration in the Copyright Office is by title or copyright registration number. See 17 U.S.C. §205(c). This means that the recording of a security interest in a film library such as that owned by NPI will involve dozens, sometimes hundreds, of individual filings. Moreover, as the contents of the film library changes, the lienholder will be required to make a separate filing for each work added to or deleted from the library. By contrast, a U.C.C.-1 filing can provide a continuing, floating lien on assets of a particular type owned by the debtor, without the need for periodic updates. See [U.C.C. §9-204].

This technical shortcoming of the copyright filing system does make it a less useful device for perfecting a security interest in copyright libraries. Nevertheless, this problem is not so serious as to make the system unworkable. In any event, this is the system Congress has established and the court is not in a position to order more adequate procedures. If the mechanics of filing turn out to pose a serious burden, it can be taken up by Congress during its oversight of the Copyright Office or, conceivably, the Copyright Office might be able to ameliorate the problem through exercise of its regulatory authority. See 17 U.S.C. §702.

months from its date or prior to the date of such subsequent purchase or mortgage.

35 U.S.C. §261.

According to *In re Transportation*, because section 261's priority scheme only provides for a "subsequent purchaser or mortgagee for valuable consideration," it does not require recording in the Patent and Trademark Office to perfect against lien creditors. See 48 Bankr. at 639. Likewise, *City Bank* held that "the failure of the statute to mention protection against lien creditors suggests that it is unnecessary to record an assignment or other conveyance with the Patent Office to protect the appellant's security interest against the trustee." 83 Bankr. at 782.

These cases misconstrue the plain language of [U.C.C. §9-109(c)(1)], which provides for the voluntary step back of Article Nine's provisions "to the extent [federal law] governs the rights of [the] parties." U.C.C. §[9-109(c)(1)]. Thus, when a federal statute provides for a national system of recordation or specifies a place of filing different from that in Article Nine, the methods of perfection specified in Article Nine are supplanted by that national system; compliance with a national system of recordation is equivalent to the filing of a financing statement under Article Nine. U.C.C. §[9-311(b)].

. . . Compliance with a national registration scheme is necessary for perfection regardless of whether federal law governs priorities.[13] Cap Fed's security interest in the copyrights of the films in NPI's library and the receivables they have generated therefore is unperfected.[14]

In the second paragraph of Part II.A. of his opinion, Judge Kozinski states that "because a copyright entitles the holder to receive all income derived from the display of the creative work . . . an agreement creating a security interest in the receivables generated by a

---

13. When a federal statute provides a system of national registration but fails to provide its own priority scheme, the priority scheme established by Article Nine . . . will generally govern the conflicting rights of creditors. Whether a creditor's interest is perfected, however, depends on whether the creditor recorded its interest in accordance with the federal statute. See U.C.C. §§[9-311(a) and (b)].

14. The court also finds two trademark cases, TR-3 Indus. v. Capital Bank (In re TR-3 Indus.), 41 Bankr. 128 (Bankr. C.D. Cal. 1984), and Roman Cleanser Co. v. National Acceptance Co. (In re Roman Cleanser Co.), 43 Bankr. 940 (Bankr. E.D. Mich. 1984), aff'd mem. (E.D. Mich. 1985), 802 F.2d 207 (6th Cir. 1986), to be distinguishable. Both cases held that security interests in trademarks need not be perfected by recording in the United States Patent and Trademark Office. However, unlike the Copyright Act, the Lanham Act's recordation provision refers only to "assignments" and contains no provisions for the registration, recordation or filing of instruments establishing security interests in trademarks. The Copyright Act authorizes the recordation of "transfers" in the Copyright Office, and defines transfers as including "mortgages," "hypothecations" and, thus, security interests in copyrights.

copyright may also be recorded in the Copyright Office." After all, what sense would it make to force secured creditors to file security interests in copyrights, but let them retain secret liens in the money produced by copyrights? None, as far as we can see. In what appears to us to be a dazzling disregard for system function, however, the Ninth Circuit held that an assignment of so much of the debtor's royalties as was necessary to pay certain debt was valid without being recorded in the Copyright Office, because it was not an assignment or mortgage of a copyright. Broadcast Music, Inc. v. Hirsch, 104 F.3d 1163 (9th Cir. 1997). Attempting to reconcile his opinion in *Broadcast Music* with *Peregrine*, Judge Schwarzer asserted that the assignment was absolute rather than in the nature of security. That argument, however, proves too much. Any mortgage of copyright receivables — or any other kind of receivables — can be described as an assignment absolute without changing its effect an iota. Taken literally, Judge Schwarzer's ruling would make recording against accounts receivable optional.

With regard to security interests in trademarks, Judge Kozinski states that a federal filing is not necessary to perfect; a state filing will do. In a more recent case, Joseph v. 1200 Valencia, Inc., 137 B.R. 778 (Bankr. C.D. Cal. 1992), the court held that a federal filing is not sufficient to perfect in a trademark. What makes the situation particularly interesting is that the Patent and Trademark Office accepts security agreements in trademarks for filing. There is obviously plenty of room for confusion here.

With modern computer technology, maintenance of thousands of isolated filing systems is no longer warranted. See LoPucki, Computerization of the Article 9 Filing System: Thoughts on Building the Electronic Highway, 55 Law & Contemp. Probs. 5 (1992), advocating a system in which every search covers all systems. By requiring filing against a corporation in the jurisdiction in which it is incorporated, new Article 9 has paved the way for joining the record of a U.C.C. filing against a corporation with the other records pertaining to that corporation. But the law has a tradition of staying behind the times, and we suspect that the consolidation across filing systems is still decades away.

F.   Methods and Costs of Searching

In many filing offices, only employees are permitted access to the records. In those systems, the lender or its lawyer must fill out a form precisely specifying the search requested and send it to the filing officer. In other filing offices a member of the public who knows how to do so can walk in and search the records or search them on the Internet. But most lenders and lawyers still choose not to deal directly with the filing office. Instead, they hire a "service company" to order or conduct the search for them.

The service companies are private businesses that serve as intermediaries between the lender or lawyer who needs a search and the filing office in which the search is conducted. Unlike many of the filing officers, who are government employees, the service companies will accept search requests by telephone and expedite them if necessary. If the service company has an office near the records to be searched, a company employee may go to the filing office and either conduct the search or order it "over the counter." If the service company does not have an office near the records, it may nevertheless provide the same service through a local correspondent. The local correspondent typically is an abstract company (known as a *title* or *escrow* company in some parts of the United States), a local U.C.C. search company, or an attorney.

The result is that, in most searches, the lender pays two fees: that of the filing officer and that of the service company. The filing officer's fee is usually specified by a state statute, and the service company's fee is determined by the service company or its correspondent. A typical fee for searching a single name would be about $50.* To search an additional name or a variation is likely to double the cost of the search. To search in an additional filing office is likely to double it again. About half the typical fee would go to the filing officer, the other half to the service company and its correspondent. If the search identifies relevant filings, the lender will usually wish to purchase copies. A typical search will turn up about ten pages of filings, although the actual number may vary from none to hundreds, depending on the complexity of the debtor's finances and distinctness of its name. Because filing officers typically charge about a dollar a page for making copies, the cost of copies can be considerable. Finally, many searches are conducted at remote locations on short notice, so the lender may also incur charges for overnight deliveries and the like.

Filing is usually a little cheaper than searching, but not much. The service company is likely to charge about $15 per filing and the filing officer may charge anywhere from about $5 to $25.

If the client is only an occasional user of the Article 9 filing system, the client will likely want the lawyer to arrange the necessary filings and searches. Involving even a relatively inexpensive lawyer (or an

---

* The authors wish to express their thanks to Ed Hand of U.C.C. Filing and Search Services in Tallahassee, Florida, for the estimates of typical costs in this section.

expensive one who delegates the task to a paralegal) can easily triple or quadruple the cost of filing or searching. On the other hand, a lender who deals with a particular filing office regularly may be familiar with the procedures of that office, have an account with the office, and perhaps even have the ability to search the records or make filings directly from a remote terminal. For such a lender, the cost of filing or searching in that particular office may be only a fraction of the cost the lender would incur working through a lawyer or a search company.

While the fees incurred by most filers and searchers may seem substantial to a student who is doing law school on $20 a day, they remain small in relation to the amounts of money involved in most commercial lending transactions. For this reason, a lawyer who is uncertain as to the filing office in which a particular search or filing should be made can often solve the problem by searching or filing in more than one system. The possibility has led some observers to advocate filing "everywhere," but that word tends to be used by people other than those paying the bills. We suggest that the issue of where to search and file is one that requires both a thorough knowledge of the law and the exercise of judgment in light of the likely cost and the amounts involved.

Problem Set 16

16.1.   Leonard Drapkowski's only valuable possession is his Pontiac Firebird (lemon yellow, five-speed transmission, named "Honey"). The car is fully paid for and worth about $10,000. Leonard owes about that same amount to Felicia Steinberg, his ex-wife, for child support and alimony arrearages. He also owes a number of other debts, including $12,000 to his business partner, Bernie Keller, for money he borrowed from Bernie over the past few years. Six months ago, Felicia hired you to collect the arrearages for her. You obtained a judgment on the debt, but because Leonard was making the current support payments, the judge declined to hold him in contempt. When Leonard ignored the judgment, Felicia authorized you to have the sheriff seize Honey. In investigating the title to the Firebird, you learned that just over three months ago, Leonard signed a security agreement granting Bernie Keller an interest in Honey to secure the $12,000 debt. Leonard and Bernie went together to the Department of Motor Vehicles and immediately recorded notice of Bernie's lien on the certificate of title for the Firebird.

a.   Now where does Felicia stand? Uniform Motor Vehicle Certificate of Title Act §20(b). U.C.C. §§9-102(a)(52), 9-317(a)(2), 9-323(b), and 9-311(b).

b.   Can you go ahead with the execution levy? If you can, should you? U.C.C. §9-401.

16.2.   Three Rivers Legal Services referred Sergio Morales to you. Sergio is a Salvadoran immigrant who has been in the United States a little over three years. For most of that time, he worked the graveyard shift at McDonald's, saving the money with which he hoped to start his own business. Five months ago, he found the opportunity he was looking for in an ad in a Spanish-language newspaper: a street vender cart with refrigeration for $2,000. Sergio paid the owner, Mark Winchell, $1,000 in cash, signed a promissory note for the balance, quit his job, and went into business for himself selling food and ice cream in the park. About two weeks ago, he received in quick succession (1) a notice that Winchell had filed for bankruptcy and (2) a letter from General Finance Company (GFC), demanding possession of the cart. Along with the GFC letter were copies of three documents. The first was Winchell's promissory note to GFC in the amount of $2,500. The second was a security agreement signed by Winchell more than a year ago granting GFC an interest in the cart to secure the note. The third was a financing statement bearing the date and time stamp of the Secretary of State U.C.C. division. U.C.C. §9-402.

In your check of the public records, you found that GFC had done everything necessary to perfect their security interest months before Sergio bought the cart. When you asked Sergio why he had not searched the U.C.C. records before buying the cart, he told you sheepishly that he did not know such a thing existed.

The partner you work for says that if you take Sergio's case on a pro bono basis, the firm will support you. You like Sergio and would like to help him keep his cart and his dreams. But another lawyer in the firm who does lots of Article 9 work says that Sergio is not protected as a buyer under U.C.C. §9-320(a) because he did not buy in the ordinary course of business, and you accept your colleague's expertise. (You will study this point in greater detail in Assignment 36.) When you asked whether there was any other provision of Article 9 that might provide a defense, she said "No, the whole point of Article 9 is that people are supposed to check the records." You remember a favorite law professor having said that if a sympathetic client has a just case and good facts there's always some legal theory "to hang your hat on," but you also remember that the professor did not teach any commercial subjects. Sergio will be in to talk with you in the morning. What do you plan to tell him? See U.C.C. §§1-103, 1-203, 9-201(a), and the footnote to the *Peerless Packing* case. If you discovered that GFC repossessed three vending carts in the past 12 months, each time from a defrauded buyer, would that help your case?

16.3.   As the most junior attorney in the Bank's legal department, you have been assigned to order U.C.C. filings and searches in anticipation of the Bank's lending against the collateral listed below. (The firm never mentioned this during their summer clerkship program.)

In what filing system or systems will you make the filings and conduct the searches?

a.   Keith Pipes, a auto mechanic, has applied to your client, ITT Services, for a consumer loan to be secured by $5,000 worth of tools, which Pipes bought and paid for a couple of years ago to use at the service station he and his wife own and operate. See U.C.C. §§9-102(a)(33) and (48), 9-109, and 9-501(a).

b.   Bernie Wolfson, an inventor who lives in San Diego, has applied to your client, a San Diego bank, for a $200,000 loan to be secured by a patent he obtained several years ago. See *National Peregrine* in this assignment, particularly the discussion of *Otto Fabric* and In re Transportation Design & Tech. Inc. U.C.C. §§9-311(a)(1), 9-109(c)(1).

c.   Your client is a New York bank that plans to lend $250,000 to famous author Nyl Ikcupol. The loan is to be secured by royalty payments Nyl receives from his New York publisher on the 119 books he has written. See U.C.C. §§9-102(2), 9-109(a) and (c), 9-501(a). Reread the first few paragraphs of section II.A. of *National Peregrine*. If the Copyright Office charges a $20 fee for filing the transfer of a copyright, what do you estimate will be the cost to the client of filing in the Copyright Office? See *National Peregrine*, note 10. Will you be needing some searches as well?

d.   Your client is an Indiana bank planning to make a $300,000 working capital loan to an Indiana dealer in rare automobiles. The collateral will include (1) the dealer's inventory of automobiles, (2) some automobiles that are not for sale, (3) accounts receivable from the sale of automobiles, (4) all of the dealer's rights to its "American Originals" trademark. U.C.C. §§9-311(a)(2) and (d), Comment 4 to U.C.C. §9-311, U.C.C. §§9-501(a), 9-109(a) and (b), 9-102(a)(2), (33), (42), and (48); UMVCTA §§3, 4(a), and 20(a) and (b); *National Peregrine*, note 14 (dealing with trademarks).

16.4.   The lawyer who assigned the Indiana bank case to you specializes in real property work and isn't familiar with the U.C.C. He explains that the bank is concerned that the debtor might encumber the property at any time, even as the debtor is negotiating with your client. The lawyer asks which should be done first, the U.C.C. searches or the filings? U.C.C. §§9-502(d), 9-523(c).

Assignment 17: Article 9 Financing Statements: The Debtor's Name

In Assignment 16, we used the metaphor of leaving messages to explain the function of a filing system. For the system to work, the filer must leave the message in the correct system and the searcher must know to look for it in the same system. In this assignment we examine a closely related problem. Even if a filer and searcher go to the same filing system, that may still not be sufficient to ensure that the message is received. A single statewide or nationwide filing system will typically contain millions of messages. For the message to be received, the filer must not only leave it in the right system, the filer must leave it in the right "place" in that system, in such form that the searcher who finds it can realize its relevance. In this section we explore how the Article 9 filing system is designed and "where" messages must be left so they can be found later.

A. The Components of a Filing System

Several states now permit the electronic filing of financing statements and other records. To accommodate these "paperless" filings, the provisions of revised Article 9 are "media neutral." That is, they are written to be applied to paper filings, electronic filings, or any other sort of filing the future may hold. Thus the new term "record" is defined as "information that is inscribed on a tangible medium or which is stored in an electronic or other medium and is retrievable in perceivable form. Accordingly, the filing officer does not "stamp" the file number on a financing statement, the filing officer "assigns" the file number to a financing statement.

A filing system consists not only of the filed records but also of subsystems for (1) adding new records, (2) searching among the records, and (3) removing obsolete records. The subsystems for adding new records are relatively simple. The clerk who receives a filing typically assigns a date and time of filing, makes a copy, and returns the original to the filer with a receipt. Later, someone else in the clerk's office will index the copy and add it to the body of prior filings. In many filing systems, subsystems for removing obsolete records do not exist at all: The store of records simply grows each year. The subsystem for removing obsolete records from Article 9 filing systems is discussed in Assignment 22. In this assignment, we focus primarily on the subsystems that search for relevant records in the filing system.

For reasons more related to technology than law, search methods differ widely from one filing system to another. The introduction of new technologies for processing, storing, and searching the records results in important changes in the ways these systems operate. Each new technology spawns a new set of legal problems. For this reason, we think it is useful to understand the system at a broad conceptual level — to understand what the system is designed to do and the basic strategies for accomplishing its goals. This kind of understanding transcends any particular filing system and the technologies in use at the time. But students also need to know how particular technologies have been implemented in particular systems, because it is only in the particularity of those implementations that the system generates problems that require the attention of a lawyer. Law functions almost entirely as a facilitator of the technology of its day.

1. Financing Statements

The Article 9 filing system was designed and implemented before the era of the photocopier. Early filers had to furnish carbon copies of their financing statements to filing officers who had no means of creating additional copies. Searches were conducted among the actual pieces of paper that were filed. As photocopying came into wide use in the 1960s, some systems began making copies of filed financing statements. But many of the systems went directly from using carbon copies to microfilm as the medium for storing and using financing statements. Microfilm later gave way to microfiche. In both micromedia, the filing officer films and stores the financing statements in the order in which they are received. In most systems even today, the searcher who needs to examine a financing statement must spin through a reel of microfilm or find the right page on a microfiche. The searcher who wants a copy prints it directly from the microfilm or microfiche.

In the past few years, a few of the larger Article 9 filing systems have switched from microfilm or microfiche to computer storage of financing statements. These offices photograph the financing statements using a camera digitizer. The image can be stored on a disk drive or tape, retrieved electronically, and viewed on a computer screen. An important limitation of this new medium is that while the computers can reproduce the image of a financing statement, most understand it only as a picture. The computers cannot "read" the words. Thus, whether the current system uses microfilm, microfiche, or digital storage, it is usually impossible to search the text of financing statements in the way that one can search the text of court opinions on LEXIS or Westlaw. The system can provide a reproduction of the financing statement, but it does not provide a way to search its text.

Some systems permit electronic filing. The filer, usually a financial institution that files frequently, sets up an account in advance with the filing officer. It transmits each record electronically, in text format. On receipt, the filing officer charges the filing fee to the filer's account. The entire text of these records could be word-searched, but a search of less than all filings in the system has little commercial value; one could never be sure that relevant filings did not lurk in the remainder.

2. The Index

When a financing statement is filed, the filing officer assigns it a unique number, usually referred to as the *file number* or, in some local systems, the *book and page number*. The system uses this number as a means of identifying, indexing, and retrieving the statement.

To find a particular financing statement on microfiche or in electronic graphic images, one must have its number. For any person who already has a copy of the filed financing statement, this presents no problem. So, for example, a filer who wants a copy of the financing statement to prove the date and time of its filing to a court might order a certified copy of "file number 92-183849."

The typical searcher is a lender who contemplates making a secured loan to the debtor and who wants to discover whether there are prior recorded interests in the debtor's property. This subsequent lender comes to the filing system without a file number. It seeks not a particular financing statement, but any and all financing statements that might encumber the prospective collateral. What the typical searcher knows is the name of the prospective debtor and the proposed collateral. The searcher will be able to find the messages about earlier filed interests only if they are indexed by description of the collateral or the identity of the debtor.

A few kinds of filing systems index by a description of the collateral. The description often includes a number to add distinctness and make searching easier. One example is the *tract index* employed in some real estate recording systems. (Real estate systems are often referred to as "recording" systems rather than filing systems, but, for convenience, we sometimes use the term *filing systems* to encompass real estate as well as personal property systems.) Each tract of land in the county is assigned a unique number, and these numbers are written on maps. Searchers find the numbers on the maps and then search the index under the tract number.

The motor vehicle certificate of title system is another that indexes filings by description of collateral. Each motor vehicle is assigned a Vehicle Identification Number (VIN) at the time of manufacture or importation and a registration number at the time it is licensed for operation on the highways. A searcher can use either number to locate the certificate. All filed liens appear on the face of the certificate.

Both the real estate and motor vehicle filing systems can index by collateral because the collateral they govern has a stable identity. Tracts of land are split or consolidated infrequently, and, even when they are, the land in question remains easy to trace. Similarly, a motor vehicle usually retains its identity throughout its useful life. The system assigns a unique identification number to each tract or vehicle, making it possible to search by number. But for most kinds of collateral governed by the Article 9 filing system — think of tubes of toothpaste on the supermarket shelf or oil in the hands of a refinery — the assignment of identification numbers is impractical. Nor would it be practical to index directly by the description of collateral. A searcher who intended to lend money against oil in the hands of a refinery might find thousands of filings under "oil" and have little means for knowing which relate to the oil it plans to take as collateral. The filer who financed the inventory of a supermarket would have to list each type of collateral separately, resulting in thousands of separate notations in the index ("toothpaste," "bread," "milk"). Problems such as these make the indexing of Article 9 financing statements by collateral impractical. Article 9 filing officers index financing statements only by the name of the debtor.

U.C.C. §9-519(c) requires that the filing office index financing statements according to the name of the debtor. The index thus prepared typically will include the address of the debtor. The address is often helpful to searchers in distinguishing the debtor who is the subject of their search from other debtors with the same or similar names. Some filing officers include additional information in the index, such as the name and address of the creditor, the date of filing, or even a brief description of the collateral. Of course, the file number must be part of the index entry; the searcher consults the index to obtain the number and then uses the number to retrieve the financing statement.

Today, nearly all filing systems use computerized data management systems to generate the debtor name index. Employees of the filing officer enter the information to be included in the index from the face of the financing statement to the computer. Keyboards are the usual means of entry, although scanners are in use in some systems. A few systems permit electronic filing, which eliminates the need to enter filings so made.

3. Search Systems

Some computer systems sort the index entries alphabetically and print hard (paper) copies of the index. In such a system, the searcher interested in Smith, John, begins by locating the entries that begin with "S" and goes on from there. Anyone who has made significant use of the telephone directory of a large city is in a position to appreciate the subtle problems inherent in such a search. A misspelling early in a name can throw a name to a distant part of the directory where only a psychic could find it. The position of even a correctly spelled name can be affected by arbitrary, difficult-to-discover rules for alphabetizing. See, for example, Chemical Bank v. Title Services, Inc., 708 F. Supp. 245 (D. Minn. 1989) (secretary of state's search under the true name "Boisclair" would not discover a filing erroneously made under name "Bois Clair" because "there were at least seven filings between Bois Clair and Boisclair [on the printout of the index] on the date of the search in question").

In other computer systems, the same search is conducted electronically. Here the searcher enters a name such as "Smith, John" and the computer returns a list of matching entries. Some systems would consider only a financing statement listing the debtor as "Smith, John" to be a match. But others are programmed to recognize as equivalents names such as "Smith, J.", "Smith, Jack," or even "Smyth, John." The rules that determine what the program will consider equivalent are referred to as the "search logic" of the program. As you will see later in this assignment, the search logic can play a critical role in determining not only the results of searches, but also the outcomes of disputes. Some systems inform users of the particular search logic employed, while in other systems only those who manage the system have that information.

Perhaps the most effective search logic is that employed on the Arizona Secretary of State's Web site, www.sosaz.com/scripts/ UCC_Search_engine.cgi. The searcher can enter as many letters of the debtor's name as the searcher chooses. If the debtor is an individual, the name is regarded as beginning with the debtor's last name. The program returns all filings against debtors whose names begin with the letters entered. The searcher can adjust the number of letters entered to return a manageable number of hits. You can discover other aspects of the Arizona Secretary of State's search logic by experimenting with that Web site.

Another important difference among filing systems is in who is permitted access to the records to search. In some systems, only an employee of the filing officer can execute a search. The user of this kind of system typically is required to submit in writing the exact name or names under which the search is to be conducted. The filing officer may respond to the search request only after a delay of several days or even weeks. The quality of the search results in such a system are likely to vary with the ability and experience of the employee conducting it.

In other systems, members of the public can conduct their own searches. The immediate feedback thus available enables the user to vary the search until the results are as expected. For example, if the searcher knows there will be financing statements on file against the debtor, but none shows up on the search, the searcher can guess that there is some variation of the debtor's name that the searcher has not yet tried.

The filing officer creates a record that bears the record and file numbers assigned to each financing statement filed and the date and time of its filing. The financing statement is effective as of that moment, even though it may take a few days, or even a few weeks, for the filing officer to make the index entry. Thus, at any given time, there will be financing statements on file and effective that are not yet discoverable in a search of the index. Because in many filing systems the not-yet-processed documents were kept in an in-basket on someone's desk, these unindexed and therefore undiscoverable records have come to be known as *the basket*. Filing officers running small systems sometimes conduct or permit hand-searching of the basket in connection with a search of the index. But in a large system, there may be no way to discover financing statements in the basket except to wait for the filing officer to enter them.

By now it should be apparent that the debtor name index is of critical importance to the functioning of an Article 9 filing system. The vast majority of searchers can find the financing statements they seek only through that index. Moreover, they may be able to find the entries for those financing statements in the debtor name index only if the debtor's name shown on the financing statement is sufficiently similar to the debtor's name as they know it that the computer will return a match, or, if the search is on a hard copy index, the searcher will find the debtor's name and recognize it. Debtors' names as they appear in the index are the searchers' link to the financing statements on file.

B.   Correct Names for Use on Financing Statements

U.C.C. §9-506(a) provides that "a financing statement substantially complying with the requirements of [part 5 of Article 9] is effective, even if it includes minor errors or omissions, unless the errors or omissions make the financing statement seriously misleading." In the next section, we consider what kinds of errors are considered seriously misleading, but first we address a preliminary question: What is the "correct" name of a debtor that *ideally* would appear on the financing statement? The answer to this question is surprisingly complex.

The analysis begins with the U.C.C. §9-503 safe harbor. That section provides that a financing statement sufficiently provides the name of a registered entity only if it provides the name of the debtor indicated on the public record of the debtor's jurisdiction of origin. As to an individual or partnership, the financing statement must provide the "individual or organizational name of the debtor." U.C.C. §9-503(a)(4). A financing statement is not rendered ineffective by the inclusion of the debtor's trade name and use of a trade name alone does not sufficiently provide the name of the debtor. U.C.C. §§9-503(b) and (c). We discuss each of these four types of names separately.

1.   Individual Names

The reference to "individual" names is to the names of human beings, as opposed to the names of other legal entities such as corporations, partnerships, or trusts. Unfortunately for all who deal with the filing system, our cultural and social practices are very tolerant of both variations and changes in individual names. An individual's birth certificate and college degree may indicate his name to be "Thomas Lawrence Smith," even though he never uses this form of his name on any other occasion. His friends may know him as "Bucky Smith," while his mother calls him "Tommy," but the line below his signature on documents is always "Thomas L. Smith," and his listing in the phone directory is under "T.L. Smith." If he wants to change any of these to "Tom Smith," most of us will consider that his prerogative and comply.

What is the legally correct name of this individual? Black letter law tells us that it is the name by which he is generally known, for nonfraudulent purposes, in the community. What community? Black letter law doesn't say, but the implication is that it might be a different community for different legal purposes. His birth certificate is not determinative. In other words, Tom has many names, but no single, unique identifier.

The naming problem is complicated by the fact that an individual can change his or her name by filing a court action for that purpose. Divorce courts commonly include desired name changes in their decrees. But an individual can change his or her name without legal action. All the individual need do is become generally known, for a nonfraudulent purpose, by a different name.

The implications for the Article 9 filing system are disconcerting. There may be no single version of an individual debtor's name that is "correct," and even if there is, it may be impossible to know for certain which version it is. To make matters even more complicated, more than one person may have precisely the same name. Together, these characteristics of individual names cause considerable confusion and uncertainty for both filer and searcher in the U.C.C. filing system. With regard to individual names, the indexing system is built on sand.

While the potential for chaos is great, we note one reassuring pattern in the reported cases on individual names: The courts have consistently favored the longer or more formal version of a name over shorter, more colloquial versions. For example, courts have rejected claims that debtors were known as Malcolm Hurt rather than the more formal John M. Hurt, Lee Anderson rather than the more formal James L. Anderson, and Jack Arnold rather than the more formal Herschel J. Arnold. United States v. Smith, 22 U.C.C. Rep. Serv. 502 (N.D. Miss. 1977); Central National Bank & Trust Co. of Enid v. Community Bank & Trustee Co. of Enid., 16 U.C.C. Rep. Serv. 2d 244 (Okla. 1974); In re Arnold, 21 U.C.C. Rep. Serv. 1479 (Bankr. W.D. Mich. 1977). These results suggest that a financing statement should ordinarily be filed in the full, formal name of the debtor as well as in the shorter versions by which the debtor is more commonly known. This largely solves the problem for filers, but not for searchers. The searcher must still contend with the fact that courts often accept shorter names as correct as well.

2.   Corporate Names

In the United States, corporations can be formed only by obtaining a *charter* or *certificate of incorporation* from the secretary of state of one of the 50 states. The federal government issues charters for a few kinds of corporations, such as national banks. The certificate will show the one and only legal name of the corporation. The corporation can change that name only by filing an amendment with the secretary of state. It follows that at any given time, a corporation has only a single correct name. By examining the certificate of incorporation on file with the Corporations division of the secretary of state, a searcher can discover the precise spelling of a corporate name, including the details of punctuation, hyphenation, and capitalization.

Two other characteristics of corporate names are of significance to the Article 9 filing system. First, in the large majority of states, the name must show that the entity is a corporation. It does that by including one of only a few permissible designators. The most common are "Corporation" or its abbreviation "Corp.," "Company" or its abbreviation "Co.," "Incorporated" or its abbreviation "Inc.," and "Limited Liability Company" or its abbreviation "L.L.C." If the corporation is formed for a particular purpose, such as to practice a licensed profession, alternative corporate designators may be required. For example, a corporation formed to practice law is a "Professional Association" or "P.A." under Florida law, a "Service Corporation" or "S.C." under Wisconsin law, and a "Profession Corporation" or "P.C." under California law. The primary significance of these rules for the Article 9 filing systems is that they make it possible to identify many names as not the names of corporations. For example, in the large majority of states, "McDonald's" cannot be a corporate name, but "McDonald's, Inc." can be. (California is an exception; it would permit the use of "McDonald's" as a corporate name.)

The other characteristic of the corporate naming system that is of significance to the Article 9 filing system is that no state will permit the formation of two corporations with the same name or confusingly similar names. (A name that differs from another only in its corporate designator is considered confusingly similar. If the state has already incorporated a McDonald's, Inc., it will refuse to incorporate a McDonald's Corporation.) Two corporations can have the same name only if they incorporate in different states. If one adds the state of incorporation to a corporate name, for example, "McDonald's, Inc., a Delaware Corporation," the result is a unique identifier. Together, these characteristics of corporate names make them more reliable and easier to use for filing and searching than individual names.

3. Partnership Names

A limited partnership is formed in much the same way as a corporation. The person causing it to be formed files papers with the secretary of state of one of the 50 states and the secretary issues a certificate. The certificate will contain the name of the limited partnership. The name generally must contain "Limited Partnership" or the abbreviations "Ltd." or "L.P." The secretary of state will not permit use of a name that is the same as, or confusingly similar to, that of a limited partnership already chartered by the state.

General partnerships are formed by contract, express or implied. No state registration is required or permitted. If there is a written partnership agreement, it may assign a name to the partnership. Regardless of the agreement among the partners, however, the legal name of a general partnership is the name by which it is generally known in the community. The name may, but need not, include some indication that the entity is a partnership. If Sally White and Grover Cleveland form a partnership, the name could be "White and Cleveland" (filed under "W"), "Sally White and Grover Cleveland" (filed under "S"), "White & Cleveland," "Realty Partners," or even "McDonald's."

Partnership names, like the names of individuals and corporations, can change over time. U.C.C. §9-507 contains rules dealing with the effects of these changes on filing and searching. Our discussion of the rules relating to name changes is in Assignment 23.

4. Trade Names

A "trade" or "fictitious" name is a name under which a person or entity conducts business that is not its legal name. For example, the purchaser of a McDonald's franchise may incorporate under a name like "McDonald's Restaurants of Atlanta, Incorporated." But if one visits the business premises, one sees only the name "McDonald's" in and about the golden arches. "McDonald's" is a trade name. Many trade names bear no resemblance to the name of the person or entity using them. For example, the Bernard Walker Corporation may do business as "Yellow Cab Company."

Trade names are the subject of several kinds of public record systems. The user of a trade name can register the name with a state or the federal government and thereby lodge a claim to exclusive ownership. Only a small portion of the trade names in use in the United States are so registered; most are simply adopted by a business without additional formality.

Most states have a "fictitious name" statute requiring that *every* person or entity doing business in a name other than its own file notice in a public record system provided for that purpose. Although the statutes typically make failure to file a misdemeanor, there are few prosecutions and no other effective penalties for not filing. Filing does nothing to preserve or to enhance the filer's claim to ownership of the trade name. As a result, most of these fictitious-name filing systems have fallen into disuse. Even large, publicly held companies that own and do business under many trade names do not file notices.

As a result, it can often be difficult to determine who or what is doing business under a particular trade name. The drafters of Article 9 deemed trade names too uncertain and too likely not to be known to the secured party or person searching the record to form the basis for a filing system. U.C.C. §§9-503(b) and (c) make clear that trade names are neither necessary nor sufficient to identify a debtor on a financing statement.

5. The Entity Problem

The difficulty of determining the correct name of a legal entity is easily confused with a much more basic question: Who, or what, can have a name? That is, in the contemplation of the law, who or what will be recognized as a separate entity, capable of being a debtor and therefore capable of being the subject of an Article 9 filing? For example, assume that your search assignment was to determine whether the personal property of the law school in which you are studying is encumbered. Would you search under the name of the law school? The university? The board of regents or trustees that operate the university?

The U.C.C.'s answer to this question begins with the definition of "debtor" in §9-102(a)(28). A debtor is a "person." "Person" is defined in U.C.C. §1-201(30) to include an individual or an organization. "Organization" is defined in §1-201(28) to include a variety of kinds of entities. The definition ends with the words "or any other legal or commercial entity." The apparent implication is that an entity might be a debtor under Article 9 and its name might show up on financing statements, even though it is not recognized as a *legal* entity for any other purpose.

C. Errors in the Debtors' Names on Financing Statements

Most searches are initiated by persons who intend to lend money to the debtor. They search to assure themselves that no one has perfected a prior security interest in the collateral. The search is conducted in the debtor name index and is for listings under the name of the debtor. If a search is conducted under the correct name of the debtor, it should discover any financing statement filed and indexed under that name. If the searcher has an incorrect name for the debtor, the search may fail to discover prior filings made and indexed under the correct name of the debtor. If the searcher lends money to the debtor pursuant to such a search, the searcher may later be surprised to find that its security interest is subordinate to undiscovered prior filings. If the searcher searches under the correct name of the debtor, but does not find the prior filing because the prior secured party listed an incorrect name for the debtor on its financing statement, the prior filing is ineffective. See U.C.C. §§9-503(a) and 9-506(a) and (c). Finally, if the search is made under the correct name of the debtor, but does not find prior filings made in the correct name of the debtor because the filing officer indexed the prior filings incorrectly, the prior filings are nevertheless effective. See U.C.C. §9-517. If the state has waived sovereign immunity for this purpose, the searchers have a cause of action against the filing officer.

Article 9 gives priority to the first creditor to file or perfect. Nothing in Article 9 requires that creditor to search for prior filings. A creditor that files its own financing statement second in time, an unsecured creditor who becomes a lien creditor after the prior creditor filed its financing statement, or a trustee appointed in the debtor's bankruptcy case can establish priority over the prior filer by demonstrating that the prior filing was "insufficient" because it did not "provide the name of the debtor." U.C.C. §§9-502(a) and 9-503. In fact, most cases in which the sufficiency of a financing statement is challenged are cases brought by trustees in bankruptcy or later lenders who did not search. When the sufficiency of the debtor's name as provided in the financing statement is challenged, the test is not whether the trustee or later lender *actually found* the financing statement, but whether a hypothetical search by the trustee or later lender under the correct name of the debtor *would have found* the financing statement. U.C.C. §9-506(c).

U.C.C. §9-506(c) tells us that this hypothetical search is conducted in the records of the filing office, under the debtor's correct name, using the filing office's standard search logic. Such a search might, for example, discover filings that a searcher could not discover using the search logic of LEXIS or Westlaw, or might fail to discover filings that a search could discover using the search logic of LEXIS or Westlaw. Because most filing offices do not disclose their search logic, the only way to know what their search logic would discover is to conduct the search in the filing office system; those who search on LEXIS, Westlaw, or alternative systems are at risk for the differences.

The following case was decided under former Article 9, but the court employed a hypothetical search test virtually identical to that

contained in U.C.C. §9-506. The case demonstrates that the hypothetical search test still leaves some questions unanswered.

Transamerica Commercial Finance Corp. v. General Electric Capital Corp. (In re Wardcorp, Inc.)

133 B.R. 210 (Bankr. S.D. Ind. 1990)

RICHARD D. VANDIVER, UNITED STATES BANKRUPTCY JUDGE. . . .

The issue in this case is whether a financing statement filed by Transamerica Commercial Finance Corporation ("Transamerica") was sufficiently accurate to perfect its security interest in the Debtor's assets. The
underlying facts are essentially undisputed.

On October 29, 1985, the Debtor entered into a security agreement
with Transamerica, then known as Borg-Warner Acceptance Corporation,
by which it gave Transamerica a security interest in its inventory, equipment, accounts receivable, contract rights and general intangibles. Transamerica filed a financing statement with the Secretary of State covering
this collateral on November 19, 1985. The Debtor's name was listed as
"Ward Corporation, Inc., DBA Wills Furniture and Appliances," and three
addresses were given. The legal name of the Debtor is "Wardcorp, Inc."

The Debtor filed for relief under Chapter 11 of the Bankruptcy Code,
and on December 13, 1988, Transamerica initiated this adversary proceeding by filing its Complaint to Determine Secured Status. Transamerica named as defendants the Debtor and other parties who may
assert an interest in the collateral in which Transamerica claims a security
interest.

The Debtor asserts that Transamerica's . . .filing under "Ward Corporation, Inc., DBA Wills Furniture and Appliances" did not give subsequent
creditors searching the files adequate notice of its security interest, and
thus its security interest was unperfected. . . . Transamerica contends that
its error in naming the Debtor was minor and not seriously misleading,
and that its . . . financing statement perfected its security interest.

There has apparently been much confusion over the Debtor's name.
The Debtor's name appears as Wardcorp, Inc., Ward Corporation, Inc.,
and Ward Corp, Inc. on various financing statements. Some of the Debt-
or's checks have its correct name, but others bear the name Ward Corp,
Inc., as does an insurance policy. A 1985 balance sheet names the Debtor
as Ward Corporation. The Debtor's name is shown as Ward Corporation,
Inc. at the beginning of its security agreement with Transamerica, but is
handwritten as WARDCORP, INC. in the signature block.

UCC filings and searches in the Secretary of State's office are conducted by a staff of eight. There are about four million items on file, with

about 300 new filings each day. The staff gets about 300 search requests a day. The financing statements are filed in an order similar to that of a phone book. Ward Corporation, Inc. would come before Wardcorp, Inc., with other names beginning with Ward and names beginning with Warda- and Wardb- between.

UCC searches under variations of the Debtor's name do not yield consistent results because the clerk in the Secretary of State's office has some discretion. A search for "Wardcorp, Inc.," properly executed by the clerk, will turn up all filings under that exact name, but will not necessarily disclose filings under Ward Corp, Inc. or Ward Corporation, Inc. The clerk may choose to note on the face of the request form that there are such filings, but is not required to do so. If a search is conducted for "Wills Furniture and Appliances," the clerk may or may not note filings under "Wills Furniture and Appliance" or "Wills Furniture and Appliances, Inc." Addresses play no official part of a search, but a clerk may consult them in the exercise of his or her discretion. Some abbreviations are recognized, such as Corp. for Corporation and Inc. for Incorporated. But the only certainty is that a party will get filings under the exact name and spelling given, assuming no error by the clerk.

When there are multiple debtors or DBA's listed on a financing statement, the Secretary of State's office makes copies of the filing and files one under each of the names. Thus, a financing statement with the debtor shown as "Ward Corporation, Inc., DBA Wills Furniture and Appliances" would be filed under both names and would turn up in a search of either name. A party requesting a search may make a special request for name and spelling variations and cross-references. The clerk will check all variations specifically given. If no specific variations are provided, the clerk would then search under reasonable variations of the name given, as determined by the clerk's discretion. A search request for Wardcorp, Inc. and unspecified variations may or may not turn up Ward Corporation, Inc. Not many search requests ask for name variations.

A party may conduct its own search of the files, with assistance from a clerk. About one party a day comes into the office to do such a search.

The Indiana Rules for Administration of the Uniform Commercial Code advise *"Because the debtor's name is the primary indexing tool, use of names other than the debtor's legal name may affect the validity of a filing and may create inconsistent files on the same debtor, lessening the accuracy of a future search. . . . [A] filing using a name other than the legal name may not be filed properly."* (emphasis in original). The booklet further advises that "it is the secured party's responsibility to check the accuracy of the name prior to filing. *The accuracy of corporate names may be verified by contacting the Secretary of State's Corporate Division."* (emphasis in original).

Prior to Transamerica's filing of its amended financing statement, at least one other creditor, CIT Group/Sales Financing, Inc., now AT&T

Credit Corporation ("AT&T"), searched the files under the name Ward-corp, Inc. (but not under Wills Furniture and Appliances), failed to find Transamerica's first financing statement, and extended financing to the Debtor, taking and perfecting a security interest in certain of its assets.

Transamerica concedes that it filed under the wrong name and that it had several documents in its files that showed the Debtor's correct name. But Transamerica argues that the names are so similar that the filing was not seriously misleading, and that a reasonably diligent searcher would have found the filing. It points to the fact the Debtor signed the security agreement with the name "Ward Corporation, Inc.," apparently not noticing the difference in the names, and that when Debtor's counsel requested the Secretary of State to reserve the name "Ward Corporation, Inc.," the request was refused because the name was too similar to "Wardcorp, Inc." Moreover, out of about fifteen creditors, about ten, including Transamerica, filed under the Debtor's trade name, either alone or with some variation of its legal name. A reasonably diligent searcher should be expected to use more than just a debtor's exact legal name and spelling. AT&T's search request did not request name variations or filings under the Debtor's trade name. If AT&T and other creditors had requested name and spelling variations, it may have found Transamerica's first filing, and if they had searched under Wills Furniture and Appliances, it would have found the first filing. Transamerica therefore argues that a creditor's search is not reasonable unless it takes advantage of the flexibility allowed by the Secretary of State's office, and that since a reasonably diligent searcher would have found Transamerica's first filing, its filing was not seriously misleading and was adequate to perfect its security interest.

CONCLUSIONS OF LAW

. . . The rule seems to be that an error in the debtor's name is seriously misleading if it would prevent the reasonably diligent searcher from discovering the financing statement. There are variances, however, in what is expected of a reasonably diligent searcher. . . .

The leading case in Indiana on errors in a debtor's legal name is Citizens National Bank v. Wedel, 489 N.E.2d 1203 (Ind. App. 1986), in which a bank's financing statement showing the debtor as "Post, Inc." rather than its legal name, "The Post, Inc.," was held sufficient. . . . [The court discussed the facts and reasoning in the *Wedel* case.]

To illustrate the bounds of minor errors, the Wedel court cited several cases finding other name variations to be minor. In Excel Stores, Inc., 341 F.2d 961 (2d Cir. 1965), the debtor was shown as Excel Department Stores rather than Excel Stores, Inc. In In re Southern Supply Co., 405 F. Supp. 20 (E.D. N.C. 1975), the debtor was shown as Southern Supply

Co. rather than Southern Supply Company of Greenville, N.C., Inc. In In re Nara Non Food Distributing, Inc., 66 Misc. 2d 779, 322 N.Y.S.2d 194 (1970), aff'd, 36 A.D.2d 796, 320 N.Y.S.2d 1014 (1971), the debtor was shown as Nara Dist. Inc. instead of Nara Non Food Distributing Inc. In Sales Finance Corp. v. McDermott Appliance Co., 340 Mass. 493, 165 N.E.2d 119 (1960), the debtor was shown as McDermott Appliance Co., Inc. rather than McDermott Appliance Company, Inc.

Under the Secretary of State's current rules (which may be different from those in place at the time of the search in *Wedel*), a search under those debtors' legal names alone would reliably turn up financing statements under the name variations in only the last of the four cited cases, "Co." being a generally recognized abbreviation for "Company" in the context in which it appears. In the other three cases, whether the existence of the financing statements filed under the name variations would be noted in a search under the legal name, or would turn up in a search with a special request for unspecified name variations, would be left to the discretion of the clerk conducting the search.

This Court has an advantage that the *Wedel* court did not — nonconflicting evidence of the manner in which financing statements are filed and searches are conducted by the Secretary of State. If the *Wedel* court had had the evidence before it that this Court has, it probably would have reached the same outcome, but it may have chosen different examples of other errors found to be minor. In *Southern Supply*, the evidence was that a search under the debtor's legal name had disclosed the filing under the variant name. In *Nara Non* and *Excel*, the courts assumed a subsequent searcher would have found the filings under the erroneous names. The *Wedel* court based its holding on the belief that the search under the debtor's correct legal name should have produced the bank's financing statement and that the Secretary of State's office erred in failing to produce it. The Court does not believe that the *Wedel* court would have found an error in a debtor's legal name to be minor and not seriously misleading if a properly conducted search under the debtor's correct legal name would not have revealed the financing statement.

The section excusing minor errors applies to all the contents of a financing statement, not just to the debtor's name. See [U.C.C. §9-506(a)]. It makes sense not to invalidate a financing statement if there is some small error, for instance, in the debtor's address or the secured party's name. A searcher finding such a financing statement is put on notice of a possible security interest and should have the duty of further inquiry. However, there can be less tolerance of errors in a debtor's name, since such errors may prevent a searcher from discovering the financing statement. If a searcher cannot find it, the searcher cannot be burdened with the duty of further inquiry. The Secretary of State's rules caution creditors that the debtor's name is the primary indexing tool and inaccuracies may compromise the validity of a filing, and direct creditors to a means of verifying corporate names. Any rule that would burden a searcher with guessing misspellings and misconfigurations of a legal name or that would make a searcher dependent on the discretion of the clerk conducting the search would not provide creditors with the certainty that is essential in these commercial transactions. Thus, the Court believes that under Indiana law, an error in a debtor's legal name is minor and not seriously misleading only if a properly executed search of the correct legal name by the Secretary of State's office would disclose the filing without depending on the discretion of the clerk conducting the search.

MISLEADING TEST

In this case, a search under the Debtor's correct legal name, Wardcorp, Inc., even with a special request for unspecified name variations, would not have reliably produced Transamerica's first filing under Ward Corporation, Inc. It would have been up to the discretion of the clerk finding the filing to note or produce it. Moreover, since it is not in close proximity to filings under the correct legal name, being separated from them by other filings under Ward and filings beginning with Warda- and Wardb-, the clerk may not have even run across it in searching under the correct legal name. Even if *Wedel* can be read as requiring a creditor to make special requests for searches under minor name variations (with and without the initial article in that case), a creditor in this case, dealing with Wardcorp, Inc., could not have been expected to specifically request a search under a name as different as Ward Corporation, Inc. The Court concludes that, even under a broad reading of *Wedel*, Transamerica's filing under Ward Corporation, Inc. was not a minor error, but was seriously misleading, and thus ineffective to perfect its security interest.

H

As we discussed in section A of this assignment, financing statements are stored and searched in a variety of ways. The searcher's difficulty in overcoming a particular error may depend more on the methods of storage and search employed than on the apparent magnitude of the error.

For example, in ITT Commercial Finance v. Bank of the West, 166 F.3d 295 (1999), the debtor's correct name was Compu-Centro, USA, Inc., but the secured creditor filed against Compucentro, USA, Inc. The court held the filing ineffective because a search under the correct name would not have retrieved the filing. (The search logic employed by the Texas Secretary of State treated the hyphen the same as a space. The search logic in most states ignores spaces, but the Texas search logic did not.)

Similarly, in In re Tyler, 23 B.R. 806 (Bankr. S.D. Fla 1982), the correct name of the debtor was Tri State Moulded Plastics, Inc. ("Moulded" spelled with a "u"), and the erroneous filing was against

"Tri State Molded Plastics, Inc." The Florida bankruptcy court that decided the case held the error to be seriously misleading, because in the Ohio statewide filing system, where the financing statement was filed, searches could be conducted only by computer. In that system at that time, the erroneous filing would not have been discovered by a computer search of the index under the correct name.

Had the search in *Tyler* been conducted using a hard copy printout of the index, the erroneous filing would almost certainly have been discovered. To understand why this is so, look for Tri State Moulded Plastics, Inc. in the business section of your local telephone directory. Although the "Tri State" listings may be separated from the "Tri-State" or "Tristate" listings by the particular method of alphabetization used, it would be difficult to look in the place where Tri State Moulded Plastics, Inc. would be without seeing the listing for Tri State Molded Plastics, Inc. Once the searcher lays eyes on the latter name, it is easy to conclude that the searcher *ought* to suspect that it is merely a misspelling of the former name.

In re Alexander, 39 B.R. 110 (Bankr. N.D. 1984), carried this kind of reasoning a step further. In that case, a secured creditor made an erroneous filing in the local records of Benson County, North Dakota. The debtors in that case were John Alexander and Larry Alexander. The creditor included those two names on the financing statement, but through the fault of the creditor, the financing statement appeared in the index only under the name "Alexander Farms." The court held the error not seriously misleading because "the court believes it reasonable that a creditor interested in the property of John and Larry Alexander within the largely rural county of Benson County, North Dakota, would examine all financing statements filed under the name Alexander."

Perhaps there were only a few financing statements under the name Alexander in the Benson County records; the opinion does not say. But how was the searcher supposed to know it was the searcher's duty to examine them? The answer must be by reading opinions like Alexander. The circularity of this reasoning should be apparent.

D. The Future of Article 9 Filing and Searching

Just as one can sometimes read the history of an ancient civilization in the layers of silt at an archeological site, one can read the history of the Article 9 filing systems in the layers of technology currently in use. In today's most primitive systems, the index is likely to be composed of 3 x 5 index cards in file drawers. Searchers pick through the cards. The financing statements may be literally kept in manila file folders. In a more advanced system, the index is likely to be on computer and the financing statements on microfiche. The searcher may be able to sit in the filing office and type in names to be searched. In the most advanced systems, graphic images of the financing statements are on the computer. Regular users of the most advanced systems can access the index by modem or even purchase a copy of the index for use in their own offices.

New technologies such as microfiche, computer data management, computer scanning, and electronic filing continue to sweep through the filing systems. As they do, the systems encounter new kinds of legal problems. With current technology, the debtor's name is central to the functioning of the system. But technology can change even something so basic as that. In the near future, the system may convert to social security numbers or to a combination of debtor's name and social security number. Over the longer run, full text word searches of financing statements may become possible, rendering the very concept of an index obsolete.

Problem Set 17

17.1.   Your client, Center Bank and Trust (CBT), plans to lend $2.5 million against equipment, inventory, and accounts receivable owned by McErny Leasing and Bob McErny, the owner of the company. How will you determine what names to search under? If Bob will be a source of information, what questions will you ask him? U.C.C. §§9-503, 9-102(70) and 9-506.

17.2.   The law firm for which you work is located in the state capitol, near the office of the Uniform Commercial Code Division of the Secretary of State. One of the partners has given you these three names and asked you to do U.C.C. searches: (1) Susan Alexander, (2) John Phillip ("Jack") Smith, and (3) Tessie's Tire City. You already know that in this particular filing office, members of the public have access to a hard copy printout of the index. You cannot computer search the index directly, but you can submit a written request to search a particular name or names. The financing statements are on microfiche in the same office. How will you do these searches? (Keep in mind the old adage that when a partner gives you instructions, the partner doesn't want you to do what the partner told you to do, the partner wants you to do what the partner needs done.)

17.3.   In response to your written search request for filings against "John Phillip Smith," the secretary of state sent you a list of 112 financing statements filed against persons with the first name John and the last name Smith. Of those filings, one is against John P.

Smith, three are against John Smith, one is against John Philip Smith, Jr., and the remaining 107 are against persons with middle initials other than P or middle names that don't begin with P. Which of the financing statements listed do you need to order and examine? U.C.C. §9-506(c).

17.4.   As the newest associate in the Office of the General Counsel of the Secretary of State, your first assignment is to make a recommendation regarding the search logic for a new computer program that will be used as the exclusive means of searching the U.C.C. filings. The computer consultants have asked two questions:

a.   When you get a request for "John Phillip Smith," which of the following should the computer program return? John P. Smith, J.P. Smith, J. P. Smith, John P. Smyth, John Phillip Smith, Jr., John Philip Smith, John Phillip Smith, Ltd.

b.   If the search is for a debtor at a particular address — for example, "John Phillip Smith, 333 Bush Street, San Francisco CA" — would it be helpful to report all filings against any debtors at that address? The consultants point out that such a system could overcome almost any error in the debtor's name, so long as the address is correct. U.C.C. §9-506(c).

17.5.   If the filing office receives an original financing statement on Wednesday, by what day must the filing office index it (and thereby render it searchable) to comply with U.C.C. §§9-519(a) and (h) and 9-523(c) and (e). If the filing office complies with these sections, on what day would the last search go out that did not include reference to this financing statement? What happens if the filing office does not comply with these sections? U.C.C. §§9-524, Comment 8 to U.C.C. §9-523.

17.6.   Isabelle Sterling, the partner you work for, unexpectedly had to travel to Hong Kong. She left you the Tang Aluminum Products file for your client, Global Bank. Global will be lending Tang $1.9 million for its purchase of all of the assets of Argon, Inc. and taking a security interest in those assets. The closing is set for 16 days from today. The contract for purchase and sale, signed a week ago, provides for transfer of Argon's assets free and clear of liens and payment of the purchase price in "cash at closing."

a.   Assuming that the secretary of state is in compliance with U.C.C. §9-523(e), what do you do, and in what order? Can you be ready by the scheduled closing date? U.C.C. §9-523(c).

b.   Assuming that the filing office takes two weeks to process incoming filings to the point that they will show up on a search, and that the filing office generally takes two business days to conduct a search and communicate the results, what do you do, and in what order? Can you be ready by the scheduled closing date?

17.7.   Sterling also asked you to run a U.C.C. search on John Phillip ("Jack") Smith. She thinks that Smith lives either in San Jose, California, or the San Jose suburb of Los Gatos. He also spends part of his time in Tucson or Golden Valley, Arizona. California U.C.C. filings are on LEXIS and Westlaw; Arizona filings are on the Internet at http://www.sosaz.com/scripts/UCC_Search_engine.cgi. Be sure your method of searching will find all versions of the debtor's name that are "not seriously misleading." (Do not restrict your search to filings against persons in the cities mentioned. As you will learn in later assignments, filings made under an address correct at the time generally remain effective after a change of address and filings bearing an incorrect address may nevertheless be effective.) U.C.C. §9-506(c).

17.8.   If the Tri-State Moulded Plastics case (discussed at the end of section C of this Assignment) arose in Arizona, what result? U.C.C. §§9-503(a)(1), 9-506(c). (Hint: Do the search yourself on the Arizona Secretary of State's Web site before you try to answer.)

Assignment 18: Article 9 Financing Statements: Other Information

A. Introduction

Financing statements typically are written documents prepared on pre-printed forms. U.C.C. §9-521 contains a standard form for filing and amending the financing statement in hard copy, but Article 9 does not require its use. The secured party can use its own form or even file a copy of the security agreement as a financing statement. In some states, some financing statements may exist solely in electronic form.

lower fee Most creditors prefer to file in hard copy on the official form. For one thing, most filing offices charge a lower filing fee when the *higher rate* secured party uses the official form. For another, when the secured *acceptance* party files on the official form, the filing office can refuse to accept the filing only for the limited reasons set forth in U.C.C. §9-516(b). Mandatory acceptance is no small advantage because filing officers historically have refused to accept a substantial percentage of all filings they have received.

U.C.C. §9-502(a) requires that three items of information be on an ordinary financing statement for the statement to be effective:

1. The name of the debtor
2. The name of the secured creditor
3. An indication of the collateral covered

Even if those items are on the financing statement, U.C.C. §520(a) requires the filing officer to refuse to accept it unless it contains these additional items:

4. The mailing address of the secured creditor. U.C.C. §9-516(b)(4).
5. The mailing address of the debtor. U.C.C. §9-516(b)(5)(A).
6. An indication of whether the debtor is an individual or a corporation. U.C.C. §9-516(5)(B).

If the debtor is an organization, U.C.C. §9-516(b)(5)(C) also requires rejection of the financing statement unless it contains three additional items of information:

354

7. The type of organization (corporation, limited liability company, etc.)
8. The debtor's jurisdiction of organization
9. The debtor's organizational identification number

If a financing statement lacks any of these nine pieces of information, the filing officer should refuse to accept it and communicate to the filer the reason for refusal and the date and time the record would have been filed. U.C.C. §9-520(b). The attempt at filing has accomplished nothing, but, notified of its failure, the filer has the opportunity to try again.

This does not mean that the filing officer should refuse filings that contain incorrect information — even if the incorrect information is implausible. The comment to U.C.C. §9-516 provides:

> Neither this section nor Section 9-520 requires or authorizes the filing office to determine, or even consider, the accuracy of information provided in a record. For example, the State A filing office may not reject under subsection (b)(5)(C) an initial financing statement indicating that the debtor is a State A corporation and providing a three-digit organization identification number, even if all State A organizational identification numbers contain at least five digits and two letters.

Generalizing on this example, it would seem that if the secured party fills in the key blanks on the financing statement, the filing officer must accept the filing almost irrespective of the content.

B. Filing Office Errors in Acceptance or Rejection

1. Wrongly Accepted Filings

The filing officer should not accept an initial financing statement that entirely omits any of items 4 through 9. (Completed but incorrect information presents a different problem, which is discussed below.) Notwithstanding the prohibition, filing officers make mistakes and sometimes accept filings that omit the required information. Although the filing officer's acceptance of such a financing statement is wrongful, the acceptance nevertheless renders the financing statement effective. U.C.C. §9-520(c) and Comment 3 to that section.

Why should a filing that the filing officers should have rejected have any effect at all? The answer can be derived from an understanding of how the system functions. First, while the omission might necessitate further inquiry, no one can be misled. The searcher who docs not have the required information, knows it does not have it. Second, if the filing officer had rejected the filing, that would have given the filer the opportunity to correct its error. Because the filing officer accepted it instead, the filer likely will remain unaware of its error until it is too late to correct it. Thus, the effectiveness of the filing saves the filer from its error without inflicting much harm on searchers. Here, as in other decisions they had to make, the drafters were forced to choose between inflicting a burden on filers or searchers, choosing in this case to leave it to the searchers to investigate further.   *Vc to searchers' benefit?*

2.   Wrongly Rejected Filings

If the filing officer should accept an initial financing statement, either because it is correct or because the manner in which it is incorrect does not warrant rejection under U.C.C. §9-516 but the filing officer rejects it instead, the financing statement will not appear on the public record. Instead, the filing officer will stamp it with the date and time of the attempt to file and return it to the filer. U.C.C. §9-520(b). The attempt to file nevertheless perfects the underlying security interest sufficiently to defeat lien creditors. U.C.C. §9-516(d). This is so even though subsequent searchers have no access to the filing and no means of knowing it was made. The explanation for this anomalous result is that the drafters of Article 9 believed (as a matter of faith, not empirical reality) that lien creditors do not search the filing system and therefore cannot be prejudiced by the failure of the financing statement to appear. The non-filing is ineffective against purchasers who are prejudiced by the absence of the record from the filing system. (Recall that, when used in the U.C.C., "purchasers" includes secured parties. U.C.C. §1-201(32) and (33).) As a result, the drafters reasoned, giving this limited perfected status to security interests for which no filing is on record injures no one.

We will refer to security interests such as these — which are effective against lien creditors, but not sufficient to give constructive notice to purchasers — as "lien-perfected." We will refer to security interests for which the filings are sufficient to give constructive notice — and therefore bind even purchasers — as "purchaser-perfected."

C.   Filer Errors in Accepted Filings

If a filer entirely omits a required piece of information from the financing statement, the filing officer can and should reject the filing.

U.C.C. §9-520(a). If the required piece of information is merely incorrect, however, that is insufficient reason for rejection. Filing officers are not required to read the filings and are specifically instructed not to evaluate the accuracy of any information contained therein. Properly accepted filings can, and frequently will, contain incorrect information. The effect of errors in the three pieces of information required for effectiveness is different from the effect of errors in the six pieces of information required only to qualify for filing.

1.   Information Necessary Only to Qualify for Filing

The items of information numbered 4 through 9 in section A of this assignment are not necessary to the sufficiency of a financing statement. U.C.C. §9-502(a). If the information furnished in response to any or all of these items is merely erroneous (as opposed to omitted entirely), the financing statement qualifies for filing. Such a financing statement, however, will be of limited effectiveness.

Article 9 lumps these limited-effectiveness filings together with wrongly rejected and fully effective filings in the category of "perfected" filings. See, for example, U.C.C. §9-338, referring to limited-effectiveness filings as "perfected." That section provides that filings with incorrect U.C.C. §9-516(b)(5) information will be effective against lien creditors, bankruptcy trustees, and others ("lien-perfected"), but not against purchasers who give value and act in reasonable reliance on the incorrect information ("purchaser-perfected"). U.C.C. §9-338. Whether the drafters intended the conclusions in this subsection to apply to errors in the address of the secured party is unclear. U.C.C. §9-502 does not require the address for sufficiency, but Comment 9 to U.C.C. §9-516 excludes them from the errors that merely invoke U.C.C. §9-338.

To illustrate, assume that Firstbank files a financing statement against Debtor Corporation. In filling out the financing statement, Firstbank's employee correctly states the name of the debtor, Firstbank's own name, and the description of collateral. But the employee gives an incorrect address for the debtor, wrongly states that the debtor is a limited partnership, gives the wrong state of incorporation, and lists the wrong identification number for Debtor Corporation. Even if the filing officer notices these errors, the filing officer is required to accept the filing. The filing is fully effective against lien creditors, including the trustee in any bankruptcy Debtor Corporation later files. Only a purchaser who read the financing statement and gave value in reasonable reliance on the incorrect information could defeat Firstbank's filing.

To understand how a purchaser might give value in reliance on these kinds of information one must consider how searchers use the information. For example, searchers use the debtor's address as a means of determining whether a financing statement relates to their debtor or another debtor with the same name. To illustrate, assume that a search for filings against John P. Smith returned 30 filings. If all of the filings show the same San Francisco address, a person named John P. Smith lives at that address, and the person who is the subject of the search lives in Los Angeles, the searcher who did not purchase and examine the financing statements would be justified. Further assume, however, that one of the 30 financing statements was against the John P. Smith who lived in Los Angeles. That financing statement nevertheless would not be effective against the John P. Smith who lived in Los Angeles.

2. Required Information

The items of information specified in items 1 to 3 on the above list are necessary to the effectiveness of the financing statement. If the financing statement substantially complies with the requirement to specify these items, the financing statement will be effective despite "minor errors or omissions unless the errors or omissions make the financing statement seriously misleading." U.C.C. §9-506(a).

In Assignment 17, we considered what errors in the debtor's name will render the financing statement ineffective. Here we consider only errors in the name of the secured party and the indication of collateral. Our theme will be the same as with errors in the debtor's name. Whether an error in a particular item of information is "seriously misleading" depends in part on the function that information serves (or is thought to serve) in the search process. To decide whether errors in financing statement information render the statement seriously misleading, one must first understand why the information is supposed to be there and what impact its omission or distortion can be expected to have on the search process.

a. *Name of the Secured Party*   Searchers may need the name of the secured party for two reasons. First, if terminations statements, releases of collateral, or subordination agreements are needed to modify or eliminate prior filings to pave the way for the new loan, the name of the secured party on the financing statement tells the searcher who can or must authenticate them. Second, the searcher may need information from the secured party; the secured party's name on the financing statement assures the searcher that it is inquiring of the right person.

This second reason requires some elaboration. The Article 9 filing system is frequently described as a "notice filing" system.

See Comment 2 to U.C.C. §9-502. That is, in contrast with the real estate recording system, where recording of the full text of the mortgage may be required, the Article 9 system requires only the recording of a notice of the existence of the security agreement. If the searcher wants to know the terms of the security agreement, the searcher is expected to inquire further outside the filing system. The searcher does that by requiring the debtor — typically a person who has applied to the searcher for a loan — to authorize the secured party to furnish information to the searcher. Unless otherwise agreed between the debtor and the secured party, a secured party has the right to respond to a request for credit information (as opposed to bank deposit information) from third parties, but no obligation to do so. The secured party ordinarily will do so, however, if the debtor so requests, either because of its ongoing business relationship with the debtor or because U.C.C. §9-210 requires the secured party to furnish certain information to the debtor on request. That is, if the secured party refuses to furnish information to the searcher, the debtor will make a formal request for it and the secured party will have to comply. Absent the name of the secured party on the financing statement, the searcher would be dependent on the debtor to tell the searcher of whom it should make these inquiries.

Once one understands that the function of the secured party's name on the financing statement is to unambiguously identify the holder of the security interest, one should realize that in some cases the secured party's address will be equally necessary. If the secured party's name is John P. Smith, without an address the debtor could steer searchers to any of the hundreds of John P. Smiths in the world. The debtor could easily defraud the searcher by steering the searcher to one who was not the secured party, but would claim to be.

b. *Description of Collateral*   The description of collateral in a financing statement is often identical to that in the security agreement, but that is not always so. For example, a secured creditor may contemplate lending money to the debtor to buy various items of equipment over a period of years. The secured creditor may file a financing statement indicating that the collateral is "equipment," and then, as the debtor buys each item of equipment, the secured creditor may require that the debtor authenticate a security agreement that describes the particular items of equipment. Under these circumstances, the secured creditor will have a perfected security interest in only the equipment described in the security agreements. See U.C.C.

§§9-308(b) and 9-203(b)(3)(A). Other equipment owned by the debtor may remain unencumbered.

Formally, the legal standard for adequacy of a description of collateral in a financing statement is the same as that for a security agreement — that it "reasonably identif[y] the collateral." See U.C.C. §§9-108, 9-504. But given that the description of collateral in a financing statement serves functions different from the description in a security agreement, it should not be surprising if the legal standard is applied differently to the two kinds of descriptions. The most obvious difference is the one expressly acknowledged in the statute: "Super-generic" descriptions such as "all assets" or "all personal property" are valid in financing statements but not in security agreements. (The drafters give no clue as to their reasons for invalidating super-generic descriptions in security agreements, but it probably was to protect debtors who otherwise might not realize that they were granting such a broad interest. We are skeptical. We fail to see why a page-long string of categories of property should be any clearer to a debtor than the phrase "all property." We can see many reasons to think it might be less clear.)

U.C.C. §9-108 approves of any description that renders the collateral "objectively determinable." To give content to that phrase requires two inquiries. First, what meaning should be assigned to words in the description? When we encountered this issue with regard to descriptions in security agreements in Assignment 9, we concluded that the words should mean whatever the parties intended them to mean. But in that context, the dispute over the description in the contract was a dispute among the parties to the contract. The function of the financing statement, by contrast, is to put third parties on notice of the identity of the collateral. Here, it would make sense to give words their common meaning and to require that they make sense to complete strangers. The second inquiry is how much work can the drafters of the financing statement require of the searcher to link the description to the collateral? In the *Schmidt* case, discussed briefly in Assignment 9, reference in the description to the ACSC records in another government office required that the searcher (1) know where to look for the ACSC records and (2) go there and look. The court upheld the description. In the *Ziluk* case, reference in the description to whether the item was purchased from the secured creditor department store required that the searcher (1) somehow obtain access to the records of the store and (2) examine those records. In the following case, the court expresses the traditional view that a filer's description can require a searcher to make inquiry of the secured creditor.

Deutsche Credit Corp. v. Lowe
(In re The Torgerson Co.)

114 B.R. 899 (Bankr. W.D. Tex. 1990)

RONALD B. KING, UNITED STATES BANKRUPTCY JUDGE. . . .

On May 21, 1986, Deutsche Credit Corporation ("Deutsche Credit") and The Torgerson Company ("Torgerson") entered into a Dealer Wholesale Inventory Financing Agreement. On June 10, 1986, Deutsche Credit filed its UCC-1 Financing Statement with the Secretary of State of Texas to perfect its interest in "all new equipment manufactured by Coyote Loader Sales, Inc. . . . now owned or hereafter acquired by debtor [Torgerson]." On December 16, 1987, Torgerson purchased a Coyote C72B loader for $144,943.00 from Coyote Loader Sales, Inc. This purchase was financed by Deutsche Credit under its floor plan agreement with Torgerson. In addition, the parties executed a Note and Supplemental Security Agreement dated December 16, 1987, which specifically described the loader.

On January 30, 1989, Miller Leasing Company ("Miller Leasing") [lent Torgerson $140,000.00 against the loader. The loan was repayable over 48 months at $3,896.30 per month. Shortly after the agreement was entered into, Miller Leasing filed its own UCC-1 financing statement with the Secretary of State of Texas]. Stephen Miller, president of Miller Leasing, testified that at no time prior to the [transaction] did he or anyone on his behalf search the Secretary of State's records to determine whether another UCC-1 financing statement was on file which included the loader either as inventory or equipment.

The Chapter 7 Trustee, John Patrick Lowe, is now the owner of whatever rights Torgerson had in the loader. The Trustee takes no position in this proceeding, and filed a stipulation stating that he will be bound by the Court's decision. The dispute is whether the Deutsche Credit lien or the Miller Leasing lease has priority with respect to the loader.

I.   ADEQUATE DESCRIPTION OF COLLATERAL

The first issue is whether Deutsche Credit adequately described the loader in its UCC-1. In its UCC-1 description, Deutsche Credit claimed a security interest in the following:

> All *new equipment manufactured by Coyote Loader Sales, Inc.,* attachments, accessories, and replacement parts therefor now owned or hereafter acquired by debtor, and all used equipment and attachments including trade-ins thereto, in which said debtor has granted to Deutsche Credit Corporation a security interest, and all proceeds of collateral including but not limited to cash accounts, instruments, documents, chattel paper, security agreements, and goods. [Emphasis added]

Miller Leasing contends that Deutsche Credit's UCC-1 description was fatally defective in two respects. First, Coyote Loader Sales, Inc. was not the actual "manufacturer" of the collateral. Second, Torgerson held the loader as inventory rather than "equipment."

A.   General Requirements of Notice Filing

Official Comment 2 to [U.C.C. §9-502] states that the Uniform Commercial Code adopts the system of "notice filing," which is not the filing of the security agreement itself, but only a simple notice which may be filed before or after the security interest attaches. The notice indicates merely that the secured party who filed the UCC-1 financing statement may have a security interest in the collateral described. Further inquiry from the parties involved is necessary to disclose the complete state of affairs.

The description of the property in the financing statement is required only to put a third party on notice that there may be a security interest in the debtor's property. It is not essential that the description be so specific that the property can be identified by it alone, if the description provides a method of inquiry or means of identification which, if pursued, will disclose the property that is covered. [The court set forth the text of the sections equivalent to U.C.C. §§9-108 and 9-506.] The critical inquiry, therefore, in assessing whether a security interest is perfected is whether a reasonably prudent creditor would have discovered the prior security interest.

B.   Adequacy of Description of Manufacturing or Brand

Miller Leasing argues that Deutsche Credit's reference to Coyote Loader Sales, Inc. as the manufacturer does not adequately describe the loader. Although Deutsche Credit's UCC-1 financing statement states that it covers goods manufactured by Coyote Loader Sales, Inc., all goods sold under the "Coyote" name in the United States are manufactured by Zettelmeyer Baumaschinen GmbH, a West German corporation. The equipment is embossed with the Coyote logo, however, and the accompanying literature refers only to Coyote Loader Sales, Inc.

Miller Leasing's president, Mr. Miller, stated in his deposition and at trial that he had [lent to Torgerson against] "Coyote equipment" on other occasions. The Miller [security agreement], the Miller UCC-1 financing statement and the Miller check to Torgerson clearly state that the [collateral was] a "Coyote C-72 loader." It appears that a reference on a UCC-1 financing statement to the loader in question as a Zettelmeyer Baumaschinen GmbH loader rather than a Coyote loader could be more misleading because these particular loaders are known exclusively as Coyote loaders in the United States. A reasonably prudent person who reviewed the UCC-1 filings would have discovered the prior security interest. The description of the manufacturer as Coyote, therefore, was adequate.

C.   ADEQUACY OF CLASSIFICATION OF COLLATERAL

The second issue relates to Deutsche Credit's classification of the Coyote loader as "equipment" in its UCC-1 description. [U.C.C. §9-102] sets forth the classifications of goods as consumer goods, equipment, farm products, and inventory. As stated above, the Deutsche Credit UCC-1 financing statement claimed an interest in "all new equipment manufactured by Coyote Loader Sales, Inc." Although the loader is a piece of equipment in its generic sense, it was actually held by Torgerson for sale or lease to a third party. As such, the loader would more correctly be classified as inventory rather than equipment because Torgerson was in the business of selling or leasing loaders and other types of machinery. Therefore, Miller Leasing maintains that Deutsche Credit's failure to properly classify the loader as inventory rather than equipment makes the UCC-1 description inadequate and ineffective.

The official comment to [U.C.C. §9-108] states that "the test of sufficiency of a description laid down by this Section is that the description do the job assigned to it — that it make possible the identification of the thing described." . . .

Regardless of whether the Coyote loader was classified as inventory or equipment, the UCC-1 financing statements for both types of goods would be located in the same file in the Secretary of State's office. If the UCC-1 filings were searched for a security interest in Coyote machinery under the name "Torgerson," the UCC-1 financing statement filed by Deutsche Credit would have appeared. "Equipment manufactured by Coyote Loader Sales, Inc." reasonably describes a Coyote loader held by Torgerson. A reasonably prudent person, after reading the UCC-1 description, would inquire as to the extent of the security interest identified in the UCC-1 financing statement if he had plans to finance or purchase a Coyote loader of Torgerson's. The description of the collateral, though not perfect, was sufficient to put an ordinarily prudent person on notice of the security interest claimed by Deutsche Credit. . . .

CONCLUSION

For the reasons stated, the Court finds that the Deutsche Credit UCC-1 financing statement contained a sufficient description of the collateral to perfect its prior security interest in the loader. . . . Deutsche Credit's perfected security interest, therefore, has priority over the perfected security interest of Miller Leasing.

The court in *Teel Construction, Inc. v. Lipper, Inc.,* 11 U.C.C. Rep. Serv. 2d 667 (Va. Cir. Ct. 1990), took an even more permissive approach to an error in the financing statement description of collateral than did the court in *Torgerson*. In *Teel*, the financing statement described the collateral as furniture and inventory at a certain address. The address given was nonexistent; the furniture and inventory intended were at another address. The court nevertheless held the financing statement effective, because the particular searcher "knew where Lipper was located and . . . is required to make further inquiry of the secured party in order to determine whether a particular asset is covered by a security agreement."

If our description of *Teel* leaves you wondering just what the function of the description in a financing statement might be, you are not alone. In a classic article, Professor Morris Shanker suggested that descriptions of collateral — in both financing statements and security agreements — should be optional. Shanker, A Proposal for a Simplified All-Embracing Security Interest, 14 U.C.C. L.J. 23, 25-29 (1981). Under Professor Shanker's proposal, if the parties did not include a description, the security interest would reach all property of the debtor rather than none of it, as under current law. Cases like *Torgerson* and *Teel* require the searcher to inquire beyond the description in the financing statement anyway. The searcher can learn what collateral is encumbered from the secured party's statement under U.C.C. §9-210.

We think financing statement descriptions of collateral could perform at least one valuable function: By making clear that particular collateral could not be covered, they might eliminate the necessity for a searcher interested only in that collateral to make further inquiry. Eliminating the further inquiry would also save the time the previous filer would spend responding to the inquiry. For this reason many filers limit their financing statement description of collateral to precisely their security agreement description of collateral.

For descriptions to perform this function, searchers would have to be confident that the courts would support their decision not to inquire further. In that regard, a decision like *Torgerson* might be a problem, and one like *Teel* certainly would. In any event, this is no argument against Professor Shanker's proposal; he would allow the parties to a financing statement to include a description of collateral if they so desired. He just would not require it.

D. Authorization to File a Financing Statement

The purpose of a financing statement is to advise later lenders of the existence of a prior security interest. If a prior interest exists, the later

lender may insist on different terms or decline to lend at all. Consequently, the presence of an incorrect or unauthorized financing statement in the filing system can interfere with the ability of the party
named as debtor to borrow money.

To illustrate, assume that a financing statement discovered by State
Bank in their search under "Teel, Inc.," showed "Alan Berkowitz" to
be the secured party. Teel insisted that Berkowitz was not its secured
creditor, but when State Bank contacted Berkowitz, he said he was.
Even if State Bank believed Teel, the Bank might not be willing to
make the loan, in the fear that its belief was wrong or that, even if it
wasn't, the loan might involve the Bank in litigation with Berkowitz.
Because of the uncertainty it creates, any filing that *might* encumber
particular property makes that property difficult to sell or use as collateral. The title to possibly encumbered property is referred to as
"clouded." Most lenders are reluctant to go forward until they can be
certain that the title can be "cleared" and the "cloud lifted."

Prior to the revision, Article 9 provided that a financing statement
was sufficient to perfect only if was signed by the debtor. Even with
that requirement in place, the filing of unauthorized financing statements was a significant problem. Prisoners, tax protestors, supporters
of the Republic of Texas, and other political protestors realized how
easy it was to cloud title to someone's property in the Article 9 filing
system — or other filing systems — and filed bogus financing statements to accomplish that. Of course, the victim of a bogus filing
could sue, prove the bogus nature of the filing, and have it declared
invalid. See, e.g., United States v. Greenstreet, 912 F. Supp. 224 (N.D.
Tex. 1996) (holding that the "political" filing of a financing statement
by a farmer was ineffective because the alleged debtors had not signed
it). But lawsuits are expensive and the victim cannot pass the cost on
to a judgment-proof prisoner or protestor. Recognizing the ineffec-
tiveness of the signature requirement in protecting public officials
and others from bogus liens, in 1997 Texas enacted legislation making it a felony to file or refuse to release a "fraudulent lien."

At about the same time, the drafters of Article 9 were deciding to
abandon the requirement of a signature on a financing statement.
The immediate impetus was to facilitate electronic filing of financing
statements by high-volume financial institutions. Electronic filings
could include the signature of the debtor only if those filings
included graphics. The U.C.C. filing offices were not up to that challenge.

The new system for the prevention of unauthorized filings is to
work as follows. Before filing a financing statement, the secured creditor must obtain authorization from the debtor in an authenticated
record. See U.C.C. §9-509(a)(1) ("A person may file [a] financing statement . . . only if the debtor authorizes the filing in an authenticated

record."). To make it easy for the secured creditor to obtain such authorization, U.C.C. §9-509(b) provides that "By authenticating a security agreement, a debtor authorizes the filing of [a] financing statement covering the collateral described in the security agreement." Thus, all the creditor need do to obtain the right to file a financing statement is what it already had to do to become a secured creditor: Get the debtor to authenticate a security agreement.

If the person filing a financing statement is not authorized, the financing statement is ineffective. See U.C.C. §9-510(a). That alone, however, will not lift the cloud on title, because the would-be lender still has no way to assure itself that its would-be debtor did not authorize the filing. U.C.C. §9-518 allows the victim of a bogus filing to file a "correction statement" that will show up on searches. But the correction statement does not lift the cloud on title either. The bogus filing was ineffective without the correction statement and remains ineffective after it is filed. U.C.C. §9-518(c). The problem is that the would-be lender has no way to know that the bogus filing is unauthorized and therefore ineffective other than to know and trust its borrower.

With these changes, the Article 9 filing system now stands in stark contrast to the real estate system. Real estate systems typically require not only that the debtor sign the mortgage, but that the signature be both witnessed and *acknowledged*. The witnesses themselves must sign the mortgage. Acknowledgment is before a notary public or other official licensed by the state for that purpose. The notary is supposed to determine the identity of the person making the signature and place the notary's seal on the statement of acknowledgment. If the new, signatureless system of Article 9 is successful, the real estate system will probably come under pressure to follow the same path.

Problem Set 18

18.1.   a. It's nearly 5:00 on Friday afternoon and you are working on an initial financing statement that *has* to be filed today. You know that the debtor is a Nevada corporation, but you just realized that you don't know its organizational identification number. You don't have time to get it. Would you be better off leaving the space for the number on the financing statement blank, or filling in the license plate number of your car? U.C.C. §§9-520(a) and 9-516(b)(5); Comment 3 to U.C.C. §9-516.

b.   You filled in the license number of your car and sent the financing statement to the filing office. The filing office sent the financing statement back to you with a notice of rejection and instructions for obtaining the correct number. If you don't do anything else, are you perfected? U.C.C. §§9-308(a), 9-310(a) and (b), 9-502(a), 9-516(b)(5) and (d), Comment 3 to U.C.C. §9-516.

c.   Contrary to the facts of b, the filing office accepted your financing statement with the incorrect organizational identification number. Are you perfected? Do you need to take any further action? U.C.C. §§9-520(a) and (c), 9-338.

18.2.   You represent Eric Bradford, a trustee in bankruptcy. One of the duties of a trustee is to examine the financing statements filed by secured creditors for irregularities. Bankruptcy Code §544(a) gives trustees the power to avoid security interests not sufficiently perfected to withstand attack by a lien creditor. That includes any that are unperfected and for which a required financing statement was not filed. See U.C.C. §9-317(a). In cases currently pending, Bradford noted the following irregularities in filed financing statements. Which would prevent a hypothetical searcher from making effective use of the financing statement? Which of the cases should the trustee pursue? Identify any additional information that would help in your evaluation. U.C.C. §§9-502(a), 9-516(b),(d), 9-520(c), and 9-506.

a.   The irregularity is the complete absence of any address for the secured party. The secured party's name is listed as "First National Bank of Wisconsin, N.A." The financing statement was filed in the Wisconsin statewide filing system. The secured party is a national bank with offices in several cities in Wisconsin. The debtor is a small business whose address is correctly stated on the financing statement. Comment 3 to U.C.C. §9-520.

b.   The irregularity is an incorrect mailing address for the debtor, Jeffrey Adams. The address listed is for a different Jeffrey Adams, who is unrelated to the transaction in which the security interest was given.

c.   The irregularity is the use of the secured creditor's trade name, Will's Furniture and Appliances, instead of its true name, Wardcorp, Inc. U.C.C. §§9-503(a), (b) and (c), Comment 2 to U.C.C. §9-506.

d.   The irregularity is that the secured creditor's name is listed as "Elizabeth Warren" instead of the correct name, "Lynn M. LoPucki." The paralegal who filled out the financing statement said, "I don't know why I wrote Elizabeth Warren; I really meant to write Lynn M. LoPucki."

e.   The irregularity is in the description of the collateral as "Pizza ovens, equipment, and fixtures located at 621 State Street, Madison, Wisconsin." The particular ovens, equipment, and fixtures covered by the security agreement have been at 514 East Washington Avenue, Madison, Wisconsin, at all relevant times. The debtor is Stoney's Pizza Parlour, Inc., a company that has operated stores at both locations at all relevant times. The creditor is Wisconsin State Bank. U.C.C. §§9-504, 9-108.

f.   The irregularity is the complete absence of a description of collateral. The debtor is "Holiday Inn of Westport, Inc." and the creditor is Missouri State Bank. Correct addresses were given for both.

18.3.   After three years of litigation, your client, Ron Smith, has won a judgment against his former employer, the Subterranean Circus, Inc. (SCI), in the amount of $26,000. SCI's lawyer says you might as well forget about collecting — the company has no unencumbered assets. Your U.C.C. search suggests otherwise. There are five financing statements, all showing Glacier Bank as the secured party. Each describes the collateral as "fixtures and equipment located at [a particular address]." The address of the SCI store on Trimble Avenue is not on any of the financing statements and there is no other public record showing any kind of lien against the fixtures and equipment located there. You know from talking with the landlord at the Trimble Avenue location that the fixtures and equipment were installed new and had never been used in any other store. Smith wants to levy on the Trimble Avenue store if the furniture and equipment there are not encumbered, but he is afraid of getting "bogged down in more litigation" if they are.

a.   If Glacier Bank's security agreement includes as collateral the fixtures and equipment located in the Trimble Avenue store, is it possible that Glacier is perfected against them?

b.   What's your next move?

18.4.   You represent Glacier Bank. You get a telephone call from a respectable law firm that represents Ron Smith, a creditor with a $26,000 judgment against SCI, one of Glacier's borrowers. Smith wants to know if Glacier's security interest encumbers the equipment and leasehold at SCI's Trimble Avenue store. In fact, Glacier was supposed to have a security interest in the Trimble assets, but someone did a poor job of drafting.

a.   What do you say to the lawyer?

b.   Would the situation be different if the law firm's client was another bank that had a loan application from SCI? U.C.C. §9-210.

18.5.   Walter's Department Store (from problem 9.4) has been taking security interests in everything purchased from them on the store's credit card accounts. Last week, Walter's lost two riding lawn mowers that were collateral under their security agreements to neighbors of Walter's bankrupt customers. Unaware of Walter's security interests, the neighbors had purchased the lawn mowers from the debtors prior to bankruptcy. See U.C.C. §9-320(b). When you mentioned to Susie that Walter's would have won the cases had it filed financing statements, Susie asked you to look into doing just that on every Walter's credit card account. Specifically, Susie has the following questions for you.

a.   Does Walter's need permission from each of the thousands of customers involved to file these financing statements? U.C.C. §§9-509(a), (b), 9-510(a).

b.   What should Walter's use for a description of collateral? U.C.C. §§9-504, 9-108.

c.   Can you think of any practical problems that are likely to arise?

Assignment 19: Exceptions to the Article 9 Filing Requirement

For most kinds of security interests, perfection is accomplished by a public record filing. If the filing is not made, the security interest remains unperfected. But there are a number of exceptions to the filing requirement. In this assignment we explore several ways a secured creditor might perfect a security interest without filing.

There are essentially three other ways to perfect. First, a secured party can perfect a security interest in many kinds of collateral by taking possession of it. Second, a secured creditor may enjoy automatic perfection by operation of law in some kinds of collateral. Third, the secured creditor may give notice to or through some person or organization that controls the collateral.

Problems involving exceptions to the filing requirement can be analyzed in much the same way as filing problems. Begin by categorizing the collateral. Determine whether perfection will be governed by Article 9, the real estate recording statutes, or other law. Finally, examine that law to determine what, if anything, it requires of the creditor to perfect the security interest.

A. Collateral in the Possession of the Secured Party

1. The Possession-Gives-Notice Theory

Both Article 9 and real estate recording statutes recognize *possession* of some kinds of collateral as a substitute for public notice filing. The Article 9 exception appears in U.C.C. §§9-310(b)(6) and 9-313. The latter section permits perfection by taking "possession" of the collateral if the collateral is ". . . goods, instruments, money, or tangible chattel paper."

In functional terms, this exception to the filing requirement is grounded on two assumptions. First, a person who buys or lends against certain kinds of collateral (we will refer to this person as the *searcher*) will look at the collateral before disbursing its money. Second, looking at collateral in the "possession" of a secured party will alert the searcher to the possible existence of a security interest. We will refer to these two assumptions as the *possession-gives-notice theory*.

Under the possession-gives-notice theory, to require filing with regard to collateral in the "possession" of the secured party would be redundant. Possession would give actual notice to the diligent searcher. In accord with this theory, both Article 9 and real estate recording laws assume that when a secured party is in possession of the collateral, searchers will or should realize that the secured party may have an interest in the property. Based on that assumption, they provide that possession constitutes constructive notice to the searcher and treat the searcher essentially as if the searcher had actual notice of the interest.

To illustrate both the theory and its shortcomings, assume that Thomas Olszynski borrows money from the Seminole Bank & Trust company, using his cast iron lawn dog* as collateral. Olszynski drags the lawn dog to the loan closing (on a cart specially made for that purpose). The banker gives Olszynski a check for the loan proceeds and Olszynski turns the lawn dog over to the banker. The banker drags the lawn dog into the Bank's vault, unloads it from the cart, and places it among the bags of money. There it will remain until the loan is repaid or the lien foreclosed by sale. Although the Bank does not file a financing statement, the Bank will be perfected so long as it retains possession. If Olszynski manages to sell the lawn dog or borrow from some other lender using the lawn dog as collateral while it remains in the Bank vault, the law will have no sympathy for that buyer or lender. Had the buyer or lender demanded to see the lawn dog before buying it or lending against it, the buyer or lender would have discovered that it was in the Bank vault. Had they known that, the theory goes, they should have been able to figure out that the Bank had a security interest in it.

By positing a situation in which the secured party was clearly, unmistakably in possession of the collateral, the lawn-dog-in-the-vault example probably makes the possession-gives-notice theory appear more reasonable than it is. Even so, the theory stumbles on application of the second assumption: Searchers should be able to guess the meaning of the bank's possession. A recently litigated (but unreported) case illustrates the ambiguity. In that case, the debtor solicited investments in a solid gold statue. At all relevant times, the bank held the statue in its vault. The debtor told the investors that the bank was holding the statue for safekeeping. Some of the investors viewed the statue. They did not ask whether the bank claimed a

---

* For a pithy history of the cast iron lawn dog in the teaching of secured transactions, see Ayer, An Unrepentant View of the Sale/Lease Distinction, 4 J. Bankr. L. & P. 291, 292 (1995).

security interest in the statue, and the bank did not tell them. Perhaps the particular employee who shepherded them into the room where they viewed the statue did not even know that the bank claimed an interest in it. The investors could see that the bank had immediate control of the statue, but that is hardly the equivalent of a sign that says, "This bank claims a security interest in this gold statue."

Because the investors in the gold statue case were relatively unsophisticated, possession did not make them actually aware of the bank's interest. But by operation of law, it constructively gave them notice. The bank prevailed in the case on the theory that the bank was perfected by possession of the statue. The case illustrates an important characteristic of the law governing secured transactions: It favors the relatively sophisticated parties who engage in these transactions repeatedly, at the expense of people who stumble occasionally into a system in which "everybody" knows things that they do not.

2. What Is Possession?

Possession is an ethereal concept. One dictionary defines it as the "control or occupancy of property without regard to ownership," Webster's Ninth New Collegiate Dictionary 918 (1991), while another defines it as "The detention and control, or the manual or ideal custody, of anything which may be the subject of property, for one's use and enjoyment, either as owner or as the proprietor of a qualified right in it, and either held personally or by another who exercises it in one's place and name. . . . That condition of facts under which one can exercise his power over a corporeal thing at his pleasure to the exclusion of all other persons." Black's Law Dictionary 1047 (5th ed. 1979). The definition in Black's adds a level of sophistication by recognizing that it is not mere custody of the thing possessed, but "ideal custody." We take that to be a recognition that possession is not merely an observable fact, but in many situations depends ultimately on the legal right of the would-be possessor.

To illustrate, assume that Oneida Schwin is a law student who lives alone in a rented apartment. At the moment, she is in class. Is she in possession of the television set she owns and that sits on a table in her apartment? We have no doubt that she is. We don't think it matters that Bonnie the Burglar is immediately outside the door of the apartment or that the door is unlocked. Right now, Bonnie can more easily exercise power over the television than Oneida, but Oneida remains in possession. Why? Because Oneida has the *right* to control the television, while Bonnie does not. Oneida has possession not solely from power, but in large part from legal right.

Oneida probably remains in possession of the television even after Bonnie enters the living room. A searcher who knocks on the door and is greeted by a smiling Bonnie would almost certainly conclude that Bonnie is in possession of the television, but the searcher would be wrong. The law looks to legal right, not just physical fact, to determine who is in possession, and once we recognize this we can see that the law's definition of "possession" is at least in part circular. We look to possession to see who has rights and we look to rights to see who has possession.

The legal *right* to control is not determinative of possession. At the moment Bonnie picks up the television, the observable fact of physical control so overwhelms the legal right to control that we think most courts would say that possession has passed to Bonnie. Some courts would refer to this as "naked" possession to illustrate that few of the attributes of ideal possession had passed to Bonnie. (The word "naked" also spices up otherwise dull legal opinions.)

A secured party can possess collateral through an agent. See U.C.C. §9-313(c). Like ownership, agency might be invisible to the searcher. A case one of us litigated will illustrate. The author represented a plaintiff oil company that won the right to possession of a gasoline service station. The order was entered on a Friday afternoon, after the sheriff's office had closed for the weekend. The debtor, another oil company, remained in "possession" and continued to sell the inventory and collect the money. Author and client went to the station and saw that an employee of the debtor oil company was the only person on the premises. The employee had the keys to the building and he sat behind the counter. Was he in possession? The answer is no. The debtor oil company was in possession through him as their agent. Yet, given that the signs on the premises disclosed only the brand of gasoline sold, not the name of the defendant oil company, the true possessor would have been invisible to a searcher who happened by at that moment.

The client introduced himself to the employee, showed him the court's order for possession, and asked if he would like a new job (very much like his current job). Undoubtedly seeing the limited future in the position he then held, the employee said yes. The two agreed on terms, one of which was that the new job started immediately. As author and client walked back to their car, every condition observable to a searcher who looked at the premises was identical to what it had been before. The same employee sat beneath the same sign, collecting money from the same customers in the same way. But assuming the validity of the new employment agreement, the client's oil company was now in possession. Here again, possession shows itself to be a legal construct, not the observable fact some theorists posit it to be.

3. Possession as a Means of Perfection

Depending on the type of collateral involved, possession may play any of three roles in the perfection of security interests. Possession is an alternative form of perfection for some types of collateral, an ineffective form for other types of collateral, and, as we discuss later in this section, the sole means of perfecting a security interest in money. U.C.C. §9-312(b)(3). If a debtor offers cash as collateral for a loan, the lender can perfect its security interest only by taking possession.

With regard to goods, instruments, tangible chattel paper, negotiable documents, and certificated securities, possession is an alternative to filing a financing statement. U.C.C. §§9-312(a), 9-313(a). Possession may appear to be *merely* an alternative means of perfecting. For goods, that is true, but for instruments, tangible chattel paper, negotiable documents, and certificated securities, perfection by possession is superior to perfection by filing. (One note before we go further: "Negotiable documents" include negotiable warehouse receipts, negotiable bills of lading, and similar documents, but the term does *not* include negotiable promissory notes. See U.C.C. §9-102(a)(30) and the definition of "document of title" in U.C.C. §1-201.)

Purchasers who subsequently take possession of these kinds of collateral generally take priority over secured creditors who previously perfected by filing. Possession and filing are both means of perfection, but perfection by possession trumps perfection by filing. U.C.C. §§9-328(1), 9-330(d), 9-331(a). Filing is, however, fully effective against lien creditors and trustees in bankruptcy.

With respect to goods, while the rule that either form of perfection is acceptable is good news for the secured creditor who may find one method easier or cheaper than the other in a particular set of circumstances, it is bad news for the searcher who is trying to discover the previous security interest. The effect of such liberalization of the perfection requirement is to impose an additional burden on the searcher. Whenever the collateral subject to a security interest includes goods of any kind or negotiable documents, the searcher must check both the filing system and the collateral itself.

For some kinds of collateral, perfection by possession is impossible. Security interests in accounts and general intangibles may be perfected only by filing or by some automatic perfection; they may not be perfected by possession. U.C.C. §9-313(a). At the most basic level, the rule may be explained by saying that these kinds of property are intangible and therefore incapable of being possessed, but the law can render intangible property tangible simply by recognizing some tangible object as the embodiment of the intangible rights. Thus the secured party who takes possession of a negotiable promissory note is regarded as having perfected in the right to payment it represents. U.C.C. §§9-313(a), 9-308(d). Similarly, the secured party who takes possession of a negotiable warehouse receipt or bill of lading is regarded as having perfected its interest in the goods in the warehouse or in the hands of the carrier. U.C.C. §9-312(c).

Notice the circular nature of this explanation: Because the law does not designate a particular document as the embodiment of the promise, the law does not recognize seizure of any document as perfecting the creditor's interest. It might seem that the law could easily resolve the problem by designating a particular document. For example, it might make the certificates issued by the state for liquor licenses or automobile titles the "physical embodiments" of liquor licenses and automobiles. Perfection could then be accomplished by taking possession of the certificates. In neither case would there be a competing document that might be seized by a competing creditor, yet in neither case has the law chosen to take this step.

The following passage offers an important clue as to what is going on:

> [To be suited to perfection by possession] collateral must have a physical embodiment recognizable as exclusively representing the right. Thus it follows that accounts and general intangibles cannot be perfected by possession. Even if the creditor collects ledger cards, journals, computer printouts, sales slips and any other items believed to represent receivables, he will not by those acts perfect a security interest in accounts. The exclusion of these items comports with the pre-Code common law and with the abstract nature of such property. For example, since no recognized embodiment of accounts exists, one creditor might seize ledger cards, another a computer print-out, and a third the sales slips. *When there is doubt in the business world about what if anything represents a property interest,* possession is not a reliable method of perfection.

White & Summers, Uniform Commercial Code: Student Edition §22-12 (3d ed. 1988) (emphasis added). That is, the law recognizes physical objects as embodying intangible rights when business people do. Business practice plays the tune and the law dances, not the other way around.

Ultimately, the impossibility of perfection by possession in accounts and general intangibles results from the lack of any commercial function to be served. Those who want to perfect by taking possession of their debtors' accounts can require their debtors to obtain promissory notes from the account debtors. The use of negotiable warehouse receipts and bills of lading saves time and effort for those who use them; nobody has yet figured out a way to save significant time and effort by making liquor licenses or copyrights negotiable. If someone did, we suspect there would be pressure to recognize certificates as "embodiments" of these otherwise intangible rights.

By excluding the possibility of perfection by filing, Article 9 protects those who accept money from the possibility that a prior security interest was perfected by filing. The intent is to encourage free negotiability of money, unhampered by the need to conduct searches in the Article 9 filing system. Both "money" and "instrument" are carefully defined in the U.C.C., and refer only to specialized kinds of property. U.C.C. §§1-201(24) and 9-102(a)(47).

U.C.C. §9-312(a) permits the perfection of security interests in both instruments and chattel paper by filing. Given that chattel paper often includes instruments, see U.C.C. §9-102(a)(11), permitting the perfection of security interests by filing in either of these types of collateral might seem to interfere with their negotiability. But U.C.C. §9-330 protects the "purchasers" who take possession of chattel paper or instruments from security interests perfected in them by filing. Because "purchaser" is defined to include those who take a security interest in the chattel paper or instruments as well as those who buy them, the effect is to give priority to those who perfect by taking possession over those who perfect by filing. What good is a security interest perfected by filing in these kinds of collateral? It is easy to take and it beats the trustee in bankruptcy — which was probably the whole point of these complex provisions.

Negotiability — essentially the ability to treat the holder of an instrument or money as the owner of it — is of declining commercial importance. Advances in communications and data storage make it progressively easier to identify the source and ownership of funds. Under the old technology, there were many legitimate reasons for transactions in cash, bearer bonds, or notes endorsed in blank. Today there are few, with the result that such transactions are suspect and often regulated.

B.   Collateral in the Control of the Secured Party

Article 9 recognizes "control" of some kinds of collateral as a substitute for filing. They include deposit accounts, electronic chattel paper, investment property, and letter of credit rights. U.C.C. §9-310(b)(8). Because the rules differ slightly from one of these four types of collateral to another and each is in itself a substantial topic, we focus here on deposit accounts.

A "deposit account" is the type of property generally referred to as a bank account. See U.C.C. §9-102(a)(29). However, that definition excludes instruments, a term whose definition includes one type of bank account — a bank account represented by a certificate of deposit that can be transferred by indorsement and delivery to the transferee.

U.C.C. §9-104 indicates three ways that a secured party can take "control" of a deposit account. First, the secured party can be the bank in which the account is maintained. Second, the debtor, the secured party, and the bank can authenticate a record instructing the bank to comply with the secured party's instructions with regard to the account. Third, the secured party can become the bank's "customer" by putting the account in the name of the secured party. See U.C.C. §4-104 (defining "customer").

The control required to perfect in a deposit account is undermined by U.C.C. §9-104(b), which provides that the secured party's "control" is not abrogated by permitting the debtor to retain "the right to direct the disposition of funds from the deposit account." That is, the secured party is in "control" of the account even though the debtor can write checks on the account and perhaps withdraw the entire amount. The "control" specified in U.C.C. §9-104 is potential control, not actual control.

What kind of notice does "control" of a bank account give? If the account is in the name of the bank, persons dealing with the debtor can hardly be misled. Anyone attempting to confirm the existence of the debtor's ownership of the account will discover the secured creditor's interest. If the secured party is the bank in which the debtor maintains the account, the drafters of Article 9 assert that "[n]o other form of public notice is necessary; all actual and potential creditors of the debtor are always on notice that the bank with which the debtor's deposit account is maintained may assert a claim against the deposit account." We doubt the drafters were naive enough to think that all or substantially all creditors actually know that a depositary bank can claim the account ahead of them. What they must mean is that they have declared the creditors to be on constructive notice of it.

Parties who wish to encumber a deposit account without putting other creditors on notice could do so by agreement. U.C.C. §9-104(a)(2) does not require that the agreement be filed or made public in any way. That section simply authorizes a secret lien.

C.   Purchase-Money Security Interests in Consumer Goods

U.C.C. §9-309(1) creates an exception to the filing requirement for most purchase-money security interests in consumer goods. Security interests that meet the terms of this exception are considered "automatically" perfected. To understand this exception to the filing requirement, one must understand the two concepts from which it is constructed: (1) purchase money security interest and (2) consumer goods. Each of these concepts is employed elsewhere in the law governing secured transactions, but this is as good a place to study them as any.

1.   Purchase-Money Security Interest (PMSI)

U.C.C. §9-103(b)(1) defines "purchase-money security interest." In essence, if the secured debt is for the purchase price of the collateral, the security interest is purchase money. Purchase-money security interests typically arise in two kinds of transactions. In the simplest transaction, Pauline Reed buys a piano from Sweigert's Pianos for an agreed price of $2,000. She pays $100 down and signs a note promising to pay the remaining $1,900 to Sweigert's. If the note is secured by a security interest in the piano, it is a purchase-money security interest.

In the second situation, Reed makes application to Friendly Finance for a loan that will enable her to buy the piano. She signs a promissory note for $1,900 and a security agreement listing the piano she is about to purchase as collateral. Friendly lends her the $1,900 and she uses that money, together with $100 of her savings, to buy the piano from Sweigert's. In the most common form of this transaction, Friendly pays the $1,900 loan proceeds directly to Sweigert's or makes a check out to Reed and Sweigert's jointly to make sure the money is "in fact so used." Notice that from Reed's point of view, this transaction reaches the same end point as the simpler one: Reed pays $100 to own the piano subject to a $1,900 security interest. The difference is that in the first transaction, the seller of the piano became the secured creditor; in the second, a third party who provided the financing for the purchase became the secured creditor.

A secured party can easily lose the purchase-money status of its interest. If, for example, Reed deposits the $1,900 loan proceeds from Friendly to her bank account and then writes a $2,000 check to Sweigert's Pianos, a question may arise as to whether the loan proceeds were in fact used to buy the piano. Assume, for example, that before she deposited the check to her account, the account already contained $2,100 from her income tax refund and her monthly paycheck. Did Reed pay for the piano with the loan proceeds, her tax refund, or her monthly paycheck? That depends on the always somewhat uncertain rules for tracing money through bank accounts. To avoid that uncertainty, and, not incidentally, to prevent Reed from spending the loan proceeds on something other than the collateral, lenders who finance a purchase usually pay the loan proceeds directly to the seller for credit against the purchase price.

We will return to the subject of purchase-money security interests in Assignment 34.

2. Consumer Goods

A purchase-money security interest is automatically perfected only in consumer goods. A PMSI in any other kind of goods must be perfected by the ordinary means required in the Code for the type of collateral. Thus, the classification as consumer goods becomes critical to determining whether perfection is automatic or whether the secured creditor needs to take some other steps.

U.C.C. §9-102(a)(23) tells us that "consumer goods" are "goods that are used or bought for use primarily for personal, family, or household purposes." It is not the nature of the goods but rather the use to which they are put or the purpose for which they are bought that determines their classification. The same computer might be "consumer goods" if the debtor uses it for family entertainment but "equipment" if the debtor uses it in business.

Courts and commentators all seem to agree that this exception from the filing requirement makes sense only when applied to consumer goods that are of relatively small value. Aside from those who finance the debtor's initial purchase of them, few lend against small-value consumer goods. Those who do rarely search in the filing system, because the amount of money at issue does not justify the expense. Given that filings against small-value consumer goods would be highly unlikely to achieve their purpose of alerting searchers to the existence of the prior lien, lawmakers have been reluctant to put purchase-money lenders to the expense of making them.

Unfortunately for the justification set forth in the preceding paragraph, there is nothing in the definition of "consumer goods" that assures that they will be of relatively small value. In the following case, the court confronted the problem that arises when the consumer goods are of substantial value and there has been no effective filing.

Gallatin National Bank v. Lockovich
(In re Lockovich)

124 B.R. 660 (W.D. Pa. 1991)

DONALD J. LEE UNITED STATES DISTRICT JUDGE. . . .

The facts at issue are not in dispute. On or about August 20, 1986, John J. Lockovich and Clara Lockovich, his wife (Debtors), purchased a 22-foot 1986 Chapparel Villian III boat from the Greene County Yacht Club for $32,500.00. Debtors paid $6,000.00 to Greene County Yacht Club and executed a "Security Agreement/Lien Contract" which set forth the purchase and finance terms. In the Contract, Debtors granted a security interest in the boat to the holder of the Contract. Gallatin paid to the Yacht Club the sum of $26,757.14 on Debtor's behalf, and the Contract was assigned to Gallatin.

Gallatin filed financing statements in the Greene County Prothonotary's Office and with the Secretary of the Commonwealth of Pennsylvania. Greene County was the county in which Gallatin was located, but Debtors were residents of Allegheny County. The filing of the financing statements, therefore, was ineffective to perfect the security interest in the boat.

The Debtors defaulted under the terms of the Security Agreement to Gallatin by failing to remit payments as required. Before the Gallatin could take action, Debtors filed for relief under Chapter 11 of the Bankruptcy Code. [The Bankruptcy Court held that Gallatin failed to perfect its security interest in the boat and therefore was an unsecured creditor in the Chapter 11 bankruptcy.]

The issue on appeal is whether Gallatin must file a financing statement to perfect its purchase money security interest in the boat. Gallatin's position is that the boat is a consumer good as defined by the [Uniform Commercial Code, Article 9]. Because the boat was a consumer good subject to a purchase money security interest, Gallatin contends it was not required to file a financing statement in order to perfect its security interest. For the reasons below stated, we reverse the decision of the Bankruptcy Court and find that Gallatin has a valid security interest in the boat.

To perfect a security interest in collateral under the Code, [U.C.C. §9-501], a secured party must file a financing statement in the offices of the Secretary of the Commonwealth and the Prothonotary of the county in which the debtor resides. Under [U.C.C. §9-309], the Code permits several exceptions to the general rule depending upon the type of collateral. [The court then set out the provisions of U.C.C. §9-309(1).]

There are three significant problems in determining automatic perfection of purchase money interests in consumer goods. First, what is a purchase money security interest? Second, what are "consumer goods"? Third, can massive and expensive items qualify as consumer goods?

. . . It is undisputed in the instant case that the security interest held by Gallatin was a purchase money security interest, [so] therefore the first hurdle has been cleared.

. . . "Goods" are defined as "consumer goods" if they are used or bought for use primary for personal, family or household purposes. The goods are not classified according to design or intrinsic nature, but according to the use to which the owner puts them. Debtors have never maintained that the boat was used for anything other than for their personal use.

The question remaining for this Court is whether a $32,500.00 watercraft can be properly classified as consumer goods under [U.C.C. §9-309(1)] . . . A Court of Common Pleas in Erie County, Pennsylvania, however, has held that a thirty-three (33) foot motor boat is not a consumer good. Union National Bank of Pittsburgh v. Northwest Marine, Inc., 27 U.C.C. Rep. Serv. 563, 62 Erie Co. L.J. 87 (1979). Though a lower court case is entitled to "some weight," it is not controlling.

It is apparent from the opinion of the Bankruptcy Court, and from the opinion of the court in *Northwest Marine*, that those courts perceive a void in the Code which does not address the problem of secret liens on valuable motorboats. The court in *Northwest Marine* stated that this void was "best filled by interstitial law-making by the court" until the Legislature acts to bridge the gap. Union National Bank of Pittsburgh v. Northwest Marine, Inc., 62 Erie Co. L.J. at 90.

We disagree. Determining what is a consumer good on an ad hoc basis leaves creditors with little or no guidelines for their conduct. Under the clear mandate of the Code, a consumer good subject to exception from the filing of financing statements is determined by the use or intended use of the good; design, size, weight, shape and cost are irrelevant. Should a millionaire decide to purchase the *Queen Mary* for his personal or family luxury on the high seas, under [U.C.C. §9-102(a)(23)] of the Code, the great Queen is nothing but a common consumer good. There need be no debate as to cost, size or life expectancy. Creditors must be confident that when they enter into a commercial transaction, they will play by the rules as written in the Code.

The Bankruptcy Court was also persuaded by Pennsylvania's history of disfavoring secret liens. It is undisputed that the Code's exemption of consumer goods from the burden of filing breeds the emergence of secret liens on such goods. Such secret liens, however, do not imperil the commercial world. Although the security interests described in [U.C.C. §9-309(1)] are perfected without filing, [U.C.C. §9-320(b)] provides that unless a financing statement is filed certain buyers may take free of a security interest even though perfected. [The court set forth the provisions of U.C.C. §9-320(b).]

This allows a secured party to file a financing statement, though one is not required for perfection, in order to insure that all buyers take subject to his security interest. At the same time, purchasers of consumer goods, who intend to maintain the characterization of such goods as consumer goods, are protected from hardships created by secret liens.

The Bankruptcy Court was also interested in protecting the reasonable expectations of subsequent creditors and purchasers. As above noted, a subsequent purchaser who intends to use the goods for personal, family or household purposes is protected by [U.C.C. §9-320(b)]. A subsequent purchaser with resale as its intent, such as the boat dealer in *Northwest Marine*, or a subsequent creditor, are, or should be, sophisticated in commercial dealings. They are charged with the knowledge of the contents of the Code, and should conduct themselves accordingly. A boat dealer is certainly aware when dealing with a consumer on the trade-in of a boat, that such boat could conceivably be subject to a purchase money security interest capable of perfection without filing. Likewise, a subsequent creditor is aware of the perils associated with accepting collateral which can clearly be subject to a secret lien.

Creditors, subsequent creditors and subsequent purchasers under the Code have options available to them that lend appropriate protection. To determine what protections are available to them "by interstitial lawmaking by the court" is more likely to defeat the intended simplification, clarification, and modernization of the law governing commercial transactions. . . .

There are two legislative solutions to the problem. One is to explicitly require the filing of security interests in motorboats.[2] The other approach, as done in some states, is to limit the value to which the exemption applies.[3] Durable, valuable "consumer goods" upon which a creditor is likely to rely for collateral, encompasses more than motorboats or mobile homes.[4] If motorboats or other expensive items are to be excluded from the dictates of [U.C.C. §9-309(1)], either via specific exemptions or a fixed ceiling price for consumer goods below which no financing statements are required, such determinations are necessarily for the Pennsylvania Legislature.

This Court, therefore, holds that Chapparel Villian III is a consumer good, and pursuant to [U.C.C. §9-309(1)] a financing statement was not required to be filed by Gallatin to perfect the security interest in the boat. Gallatin has a valid security interest in the boat. . . .

---

2. California requires a filing for a "boat required to be registered." See Cal. Com. Code §9-302(1)(d). Michigan requires a filing for a "vehicle, mobile home, or watercraft for which a certificate of title is required by the laws of this state." See Mich. Comp. Laws §440.9302(1)(d), Mich. Stat. Ann. §19.9302(1)(d).

3. Kansas ($1,000.00), Maryland ($1,500.00), Colorado ($250.00) and Wisconsin ($250.00) have imposed purchase price limitations above which automatic perfection is not allowed.

4. See Mayor's Jeweler's of Ft. Lauderdale, Inc. v. Levinson, 39 Ill. App. 3d 16, 349 N.E.2d 475 (1976) (a $10,000.00 diamond ring); Commercial Credit Equipment Co. v. Carter, 88 Wash. 2d 136, 516 P.2d 767 (1973) (a $24,000.00 airplane).

On appeal, the Third Circuit affirmed the decision in *Lockovich*, expressly endorsing Judge Lee's comment that "if motorboats or other expensive items are to be excluded from the dictates of §9-309(1), . . . such determinations are necessarily for the Pennsylvania Legislature." Gallatin National Bank v. Lockovich (In re Lockovich), 940 F.2d 916 (3d Cir. 1991).

What if goods are bought with one use in mind, then put to a different use? U.C.C. §9-102(a)(23) is ambiguous on the point. White and Summers would allow the intended use at the time of purchase to control. They reason that such a rule enables the creditor to procure the debtor's written statement about his intended use at the time the loan is made, and perfect (or assume perfection) on that basis. In fact, security agreements often contain such a representation by the debtor. But this relaxation of the requirements for perfection puts additional burdens on the searcher. Under the White and Summers rule, the searcher who contemplates taking a security interest in a computer that has been used only in business is expected to consider the possibility that the computer initially was bought for personal use and is encumbered by an automatically perfected purchase money security interest. The opposing view is that actual use should control classification of any goods put in use; the intent with which goods were bought should control only if the owner has not put them to use. Cases support each of these views. White & Summers, Uniform Commercial Code: Student Edition §22-12 (3d ed. 1988).

2 VIEWS

D.   Security Interests Not Governed by Article 9 or Another Filing Statute

Security interests in a variety of types of collateral are excluded from the coverage of Article 9. They include security interests in wage claims, U.C.C. §9-109(d)(3), insurance policies and claims, U.C.C. §9-109(d)(8), real estate interests, U.C.C. §9-109(d)(11), and non-commercial tort claims, U.C.C. §9-109(d)(12). The reasons for these exclusions vary. Security interests in wage claims, like other assignments of wages, are closely regulated in some states and prohibited in others. Security interests in insurance policies typically are "perfected" by notification to the insurance company and inclusion of the secured party as a "loss payee" on the policy itself. In the case of security interests in real estate interests, the purpose of the exclusion is to yield to an elaborate set of recording requirements found in real estate law. The drafters probably excluded non-commercial tort claims because granting security in them is controversial and their inclusion might have made adoption of revised Article 9 more difficult.

In the following case, the debtor owned a valuable lawsuit and several creditors sought to perfect liens against it. Ultimately all were successful, even the lawyers at Flynn & Stewart who filed an Article 9 financing statement to perfect a security interest that at the time was clearly not governed by Article 9. As you read the case, ask yourself what Flynn & Stewart ought to do next time they have to perfect in a non-commercial tort recovery.

Bluxome Street Associates v. Fireman's Fund Insurance Co.

206 Cal. App. 3d 1149, 254 Cal. Rptr. 198
(Cal. Ct. App. 1988)

Opinion by STRANKMAN J., with WHITE, P.J., and BARRY-DEAL, J. concurring. . . .

I. PROCEDURAL BACKGROUND AND ISSUES ON APPEAL

In March 1987, a settlement was reached in a legal malpractice action entitled Woods v. Neisar in the Superior Court of the City and County of San Francisco. The settlement provided in part for payment of the sum of $582,500 to Eric H. Woods. This sum was put into a trust account of the law firm of Hassard, Bonnington, Rogers & Huber (Hassard Bonnington), Woods's attorneys in Woods v. Neisar. Hassard Bonnington, appellant Haas & Najarian, appellant Fireman's Fund Insurance Company (Fireman's Fund), and respondent Flynn & Stewart, among others, each claimed a lien on the settlement proceeds.

On May 6, 1987, Woods filed a motion for order establishing lien priorities and allowing distribution of proceeds. Following extensive briefing by all lien claimants and two hearings, the trial court ordered the $582,500 in settlement proceeds to be disbursed as follows: (1) $352,562.14, plus interest, to Hassard Bonnington, pursuant to a retainer agreement which provided for a lien in favor of Hassard Bonnington on any judgment or proceeds recovered in the litigation; (2) $72,500 plus interest to Charles Schilling; (3) the remainder (approximately $150,000) to respondent Flynn & Stewart. [The court concluded that Haas & Najarian and Fireman's Fund held valid liens against the settlement proceeds, but the prior liens consumed the entire settlement, rendering them worthless.]

Appellants Haas & Najarian and Fireman's Fund do not challenge the priority of the liens of Hassard Bonnington or Charles Schilling. Rather, they contend that their liens have priority over the lien of respondent

Flynn & Stewart. . . . Flynn & Stewart contends that its lien was created prior in time to those of appellants and that, under the "first in time is first in right" rule, its lien takes priority. . . .

III.   VALIDITY OF LIENS

[California] Civil Code section 2881, subdivision 1, provides that liens may be created by contract: "A lien is created: 1. By contract of the parties; or, 2. By operation of law." The liens of Flynn & Stewart and Haas & Najarian were valid contractual liens under this section. . . . The security agreement provides that Woods "grants to Flynn & Stewart, . . . a security interest in any and all of the collateral," defined to include Woods's interest in Woods v. Neisar, to secure payment of a promissory note plus any additional amounts owing arising from the rendition of services by Flynn & Stewart to Woods. Such language describes a lien as defined by Civil Code section 2874. . . .

. . . That Flynn & Stewart is a law firm and the purpose of the lien is to secure payment of attorney fees is immaterial to the creation and enforceability of the lien under Civil Code section 2881, subdivision 1. The lien would be enforceable, barring other factors, even if Flynn & Stewart were not a law firm and the obligation secured were not payment of legal fees. . . .

Fireman's Fund as well as Haas & Najarian next contend that the Flynn & Stewart lien is invalid because the California Uniform Commercial Code (UCC) financing statement filed by Flynn & Stewart incident to the security agreement was void ab initio and did not constitute notice of or perfect the lien.

The security agreement reflects the attorneys' belief that their security interest came within the purview of [Article] 9 of the UCC in that it provides that a UCC financing statement is to be filed with the California Secretary of State to perfect the lien. A financing statement was in fact filed with the Secretary of State.

We agree with appellants that [Article] 9 of the UCC does not apply to the Flynn & Stewart security interest or lien. The security agreement grants to Flynn & Stewart a lien on Woods's interest in a cause of action based upon legal malpractice — a tort cause of action. [U.C.C. §9-109(d)(12)] specifically provides that such lien is not covered by [Article] 9. . . . Because [Article] 9 of the UCC did not apply to Flynn & Stewart's security agreement or lien created thereby, the filing of the UCC financing statement did not operate to provide notice of or "perfect" the lien under [U.C.C. §9-501].

However, although the Flynn & Stewart lien was not perfected under the UCC, and, accordingly, was not entitled to the benefits accorded to a perfected security interest, it nevertheless was valid and enforceable, as discussed ante, under Civil Code section 2881, subdivision 1. . . .

Appellants' next contention is that the Flynn & Stewart lien is unenforceable because there was no notice of the lien. Unlike appellants, who filed written notices of lien in Woods v. Neisar, Flynn & Stewart filed no such notice.

Providing notice of a lien is a statutory prerequisite to the creation or enforceability of certain types of liens. For example, as explained below, the creation of an attachment lien on a litigant's interest in an action is dependent upon the filing of notice of the lien in that action. A judgment lien on real property is created by the recording of an abstract of judgment with the county recorder, and a judgment lien on personal property is created by the filing of notice thereof with the Secretary of State. A mechanic's lien is enforceable only if the claimant first gives notice under Civil Code section 3097, and then records the claim of lien within certain time constrictions.

As to a contractual lien under Civil Code section 2881 on a litigant's interest in a tort claim, however, we find no authority, statute, or case law which requires notice to create such lien. . . .

We conclude that appellants' contentions relating to the validity and enforceability of the Flynn & Stewart contractual lien have no merit.

————————

The court decided that perfection of Flynn & Stewart's lien against Wood's lawsuit was not governed by Article 9 and no other California law established requirements for perfection. From there, the court could have reached any of three conclusions: (1) Flynn & Stewart were perfected because there was no law requiring them to do more than they did, (2) Flynn & Stewart were unperfected because there was no law specifying any means to perfect, or (3) the court could have established reasonable requirements for perfection, such as placing a notice of the lien in the court file. The court does not explain why it chose the first conclusion over the other two; other courts might choose differently.

D. What Became of the Notice Requirement?

In this assignment, we have examined a variety of kinds of security interests that are excepted from the filing requirement. In some cases, the diligent searcher can discover these security interests by viewing or investigating the collateral, examining the court file, or making inquiry with a stakeholder such as a bank or insurance company. But in other cases, security interests will be effective against later interests even though the most diligent search would not lead to their discovery. Our most recent addition to this latter category is the automatically perfected purchase-money interest in consumer goods.

In earlier assignments, we noted a number of other situations in which a security interest might be effective, even though it would not be discovered on a diligent search. In later assignments, we will note more.

Prevailing theory holds that the priority granted earlier created interests is justified in part by the fact that those who accepted later interests did so with knowledge of the earlier interests or after choosing not to acquire such knowledge. In many cases, however, the availability of such knowledge is a legal fiction. We offer an alternative justification of these rules: They are principally rules that allocate losses that lawmakers do not consider worth avoiding.

Problem Set 19

19.1. What are the permissible ways to perfect in each of these items of collateral? Be prepared to describe the physical processes.

a. The cash that comes into the debtor's cash register each day. U.C.C. §9-312(b)(3).

b. A negotiable promissory note. U.C.C. §§9-102(47), 9-312(a).

c. Money the debtor is keeping in a bank account. U.C.C. §§9-104, 9-312(b)(1), and 9-314(a) and (b).

d. Shares of stock in General Motors, for which a certificate has been issued. U.C.C. §§9-312(a), 9-102(49), 9-106(a), 8-102(a)(4), 8-106(b).

e. The obligations of customers of a used car lot to pay for the cars they purchased. The obligations are evidenced by promissory notes and security interests in the cars purchased. U.C.C. §§9-102(11), 9-312(a), 9-313(a).

19.2. Last year, Ruth and Gene Canard sold their Turkey Burger franchise to Watson Family Restaurants, Inc. They received part of the purchase price in the form of a document titled "Contract for Payment." In the document, Watson promised to pay $500,000 in yearly installments at a stated interest rate. Your client, Casa Grande, is about to lend $300,000 to the Canards, secured by what they have from Watson.

a. How should Casa Grande perfect? U.C.C. §§9-102(2), (42), (47), and (61), 9-310, 9-312(a), (b), 9-313(a), 9-330(d).

b. What if the document gives the Canards a security interest in the franchise and the Canards perfected that security interest properly at the time of the sale? U.C.C. §9-102(11).

19.3. Instead of the "Contract for Payment" the Canards received in the previous problem, the Canards received only a negotiable promissory note that was an "instrument" within the meaning of U.C.C. §9-102(47). The Canards tell Casa Grande that they cannot give Casa Grande possession of the instrument because Garp Associates is holding it. Garp has a first security interest in the instrument, securing a debt to them in the amount of $60,000. Casa Grande is willing to make their loan as a second security interest, but they are not willing to risk being unsecured. What do you suggest? U.C.C. §§9-312(a), 9-313, including Comments 3 and 4, 9-330(d).

19.4.   Chuck Kettering, former millionaire fallen on hard times, wants to borrow money from our client, Little Silverado Savings and Loan (LSSL). The loan officer is obviously uncomfortable with the loan and seems not to trust Kettering, but LSSL's president, Donald Paul, has been pressuring her to approve it. Paul argues that the appraisals show the collateral to be worth more than twice the amount of the loan, even at foreclosure prices. "If we get a clear U.C.C. search from both the county and the state, and we properly perfect our security interest in the collateral, and insure the collateral, what can go wrong?" The senior partner who advises the bank gave you the following list of proposed collateral and asked you to look into the possibility that there might be liens against the collateral that wouldn't show up on even a diligent search that included a viewing of the collateral. What do you advise? Are there other steps you might take to discover "automatically perfected" security interests? U.C.C. §§9-104, 9-309(1), 9-311(b), 9-313.

a.   *A $20,000 mobile home.* It is located in a remote corner of Kettering's estate. State law does not allow for the issuance of a certificate of title for a mobile home.

b.   *A rare book collection.* Valued at $1.5 million, the books are currently on display at the Library of Congress. If the Library were holding possession for someone who claimed a security interest in the books, would they have to tell the searcher?

c.   *A Mercedes-Benz automobile.* The certificate of title shows no liens.

d.   *A solid gold ingot and 20 unset diamonds.*

e.   *Computer equipment.* The equipment cost about $40,000 at retail and is in Kettering's office, where he uses it principally to review stock quotations.

f.   *A checking account.* The account is at Bank of the West and is in Kettering's name. The bank statements show no interest in favor of Bank of the West or anyone else.

19.5.   Janet Dakin is in financial trouble. The only bright spot in her financial dealings is that her lawsuit against her former financial adviser, Adam Hershey, goes to trial next week. Adam was on pain killers for most of the three years he managed Janet's investments and the performance of Janet's investment portfolio shows it. In several instances, Adam promised to make particular investments for her but did not. During the three years, $2.5 million turned into $450,000. Adam has offered Janet $800,000 in settlement, but she thinks she can win more. In the meantime, Janet wants to borrow $100,000 from her brother, Will Dakin, using the lawsuit as collateral. Will asks what he should do to perfect. What do you tell him? U.C.C. §§9-109(d)(12), 9-102(2),(42).

19.6   When your client Sally loaned her friend Joe $5,000, she took possession of Joe's Rolex watch and gold chain as security. She did not file a financing statement and kept the items in her apartment. Now Joe has filed bankruptcy. Joe's trustee is suspicious of the transaction with Sally because it is completely undocumented. One of his arguments for voiding Sally's security agreement is that Sally was out of town for two weeks on the date Joe filed bankruptcy. During that time, Joe's mother was staying in the apartment where the watch and chain were located. (Joe's mother says she didn't even know the items were there.) Sally wants to know if there is anything to the trustee's argument. Is there? U.C.C. §§9-203(b)(3)(B), 9-310(b)(6).

19.7.   Your client, Sabine Music Manufacturing (Sabine), wants to sell its electronic music tuning equipment to Jersey Music Associates (Jersey) for $84,000, payable over seven years with no money down, with the equipment to serve as security for payment of the purchase price. Jersey wants to put the equipment to use immediately, but insists that no financing statement be filed. "Our bank lender will see it on the credit report and go nuts," says Bill Jersey, president of Jersey. Is there any way Sabine can do the deal without taking the risk of Jersey's bankruptcy? Bill Jersey suggests that he can put the music tuning equipment in a separate room, sublease the room to Sabine, and agree that the manufacturing equipment is "at all times in Sabine's possession." Bill, "as Sabine's agent, will control access to the room on behalf of Sabine, permitting Jersey workers to enter the room and use the equipment only as authorized from time to time by Sabine." All this will be in large print, on a sign posted on the door of the room. Sabine wants to do the deal, unless you tell them it won't work. Will it? U.C.C. §9 313(a).

Assignment 20: The Land and Fixtures Recording Systems

A. Real Property Recording Systems

To be effective against third parties, notice of most security interests in personal property must be filed in the appropriate public records system. U.C.C. §9-310(a). The same is true of mortgages and deeds of trust in real property. If they are not *recorded* (the real estate equivalent of *filed*) in the appropriate set of public records, they are generally unenforceable against third parties.

The real property recording systems are generally older than, and physically separate from, the personal property filing systems you studied in Assignment 16. Each state in the United States is divided into counties,* and each county† maintains a real estate recording system. There are more than 3,000 counties and hence more than 3,000 real estate recording systems. The typical recording system is located in the county seat, either in the courthouse or in a county administration building, and has been in operation for hundreds of years.

Real estate recording systems resemble personal property filing systems in many respects. If you took a mortgage to the recording office, you would be greeted by a clerk (probably after waiting in a long line). You would pay a small fee for recording and the clerk would immediately stamp the date and time of recording on the face of the mortgage. As in the personal property filing systems, the clerk would place your now-recorded mortgage in the basket (literal or metaphoric) for photocopying and indexing. Later, someone in the recording office would add the reference to the mortgage at appropriate places in the indexes, place the mortgage copy in the records in chronological order, and mail the original back to you.

Real estate recording systems typically differ from personal property filing systems in other respects. First, the real estate recording system contains not only documents evidencing liens against real

---

* In Louisiana, the division is called a "parish."
† In some localities, the functions of the county, including the maintenance of the real property recording system, have been assumed by city governments.

estate, but also documents evidencing transfers of ownership — that is, deeds. Recall that bills of sale, the personal property equivalents of deeds, are not filed in the Article 9 filing system. Searchers in the Article 9 filing system may be able to determine who has a security interest in the collateral, but they definitely cannot determine who owns it. The inclusion of deeds in the real estate recording system, combined with more extensive indexing, enables users of the real estate system to determine who owns property as well as who has liens against it. We will explore the implications in later assignments.

Second, recording in the real estate system costs more than filing in the personal property system. The clerk who greeted you in the real estate recording office would not only charge you the modest filing fee, the clerk would also collect a transfer tax based on the value of the property or the amount of the mortgage. For example, when one of the authors recently sold a Wisconsin condominium for $102,000, the recording fees for the deed and mortgage were $48, while the *transfer fee* was $306. In larger transactions, the fees payable on recording can be considerable. For example, when Rockefeller Center Properties, Inc. recorded $1.25 billion in mortgages against the buildings by that name in New York City, it paid $34.5 million in recording taxes. By contrast, only a handful of states impose transfer fees on grants of security interests in personal property. Article 9 secured parties rarely decline to file a financing statement because of the expense, but real estate secured parties occasionally structure their transactions in ways designed to legally avoid or illegally evade the transfer fees. Rockefeller Center Properties left the above-mentioned $1.25 billion in mortgages unrecorded for years. Only when they discovered that their debtor was in financial trouble did they record the mortgage, and pay the recording taxes. Not all mortgagees who play these games are so fortunate; some fail to record in time and suffer avoidance of their unperfected mortgages in bankruptcy.

Third, real estate recording systems are not self-purging. When a document is filed, the clerk stamps it with identifying numbers. These are typically the number of the *book* in which it will be bound and the page at which it will appear in that book. It will remain permanently on the record and effective. (In many parts of the United States, the recording system still contains records from the seventeenth century.) The advantage of permanent retention is that the thorny issue of continuation does not arise. The disadvantage is that every filing represents a net increase in the number of documents that must be stored and searched.

For our purposes, perhaps the most important difference between the two types of systems is that the debtor's name problem is relatively insignificant in real estate recording systems. The principal reason is that the records reflect the chain of title to the property, up to and including the debtor. The creditor who searched in an incorrect name would not only fail to find prior mortgages against the property, it would fail to find any documents at all. The absence of documents showing title in the debtor would alert the searcher to its error. A second reason is that in most counties, real estate searches can be conducted not only by the names of the parties, but also by *tract* — the description of the property. Some counties maintain tract indexes to facilitate such searching. In many (if not most) counties, private firms known as *abstract* or *title companies* maintain sets of records that duplicate those of the county. That is, they photocopy every document as it is filed in the public records and conduct searches in their own copies. These private systems also enable searches by tract. When the search is conducted by tract, it will discover a mortgage that bears a correct tract number, even if the record name of the debtor bears no resemblance whatsoever to the correct name of the debtor.

The duplication of real estate public records by private firms has had a profound effect on the recording system in many parts of the United States. As the proportion of searches conducted in private systems has increased, the quality of indexing and the support for searching in the public systems has declined. The indexes in many public systems are replete with errors. Obtaining physical access to the dozens of documents relevant to a particular search may be impossibly time-consuming. In many counties, searching a real estate title in the public records is no longer feasible. Still, because so few searches are actually conducted in the public records, the effects of public indexing errors are relatively small and the indexes themselves relatively unimportant. For that reason, we do not discuss the problems of indexing and searching the real estate recording systems.

The real estate recording systems have also been spared another problem endemic to personal property recording systems. As you saw in Assignment 16, there is often uncertainty as to which personal property filing system is appropriate for a particular filing. Such uncertainty does not exist with regard to real property recording systems. A document that affects title to real estate in a particular county must be recorded in that county. A document that affects title to real estate in several counties must be recorded in each.

B. What Is Recorded?

In Assignment 8, we discussed the formalities for the creation of a mortgage against real property. They were, in essence: (1) a mortgage document (2) signed by the debtor and perhaps (3) containing a description of the debt secured and the collateral securing it. We say "perhaps" because there is a split of authority as to whether a mortgage that omits entirely the amount of the debt or expresses it in general terms is valid. And while the description of collateral in a mortgage may be so vague as to render it void, the general rule is that it does not so long as it is possible to identify the property by a rule of construction or through evidence extrinsic to the mortgage.

In the real estate system, the creditor must record the mortgage document, not merely a notice of its existence. The advantage is that the public record informs searchers not only of the existence of the mortgage but its terms. The disadvantage is that when collateral is added or deleted, or when other important terms change, an additional recording may be necessary.

Real estate law may impose and enforce additional formalities for recording. The most common are the requirements that the mortgage be signed in front of two witnesses and that it be *acknowledged* before a notary public or some such official, who authenticates the debtor's signature by affixing the official's own signature and seal. Some states, however, omit the requirement of two witnesses, the requirement of acknowledgement, or both.

C.   Fixtures

Even though buildings are constructed from personal property — bricks, mortar, lumber, nails, and the like — the law considers permanent buildings part of the land on which they are situated. Thus, a mortgage against Blackacre, like a deed to Blackacre, would include any permanent buildings located on it unless they were expressly excluded. Such a mortgage is perfected by filing only in the real estate system; a U.C.C. filing is unnecessary and ineffective. U.C.C. §9-109(d)(11).

Once you realize that "bricks and mortar" can be real property for recording purposes, it should be easy to see that the interface between the real estate and personal property recording systems will necessarily be either uncertain or complex. (In fact, it is both.) That a security interest in a building must be recorded in the real estate system suggests that security interests in everything that is part of the building must be recorded there as well, such as the built-in light fixtures, the light bulbs that screw into them, and maybe even the furniture.

The law requiring the recording of mortgages in real property came into existence long before the U.C.C. was drafted. That law, which was often inconsistent within a state and non-uniform from state to state, determined what property was so related to particular real estate that it would be treated as part of the real estate. Such property was referred to as *fixtures* because the property was usually physically affixed to the real estate.

1.   What Is a "Fixture"?

The drafters of the U.C.C. deferred to real estate law, and designed around it. They defined "goods" as being "fixtures" when they "have become so related to particular real property that an interest in them arises under real property law." U.C.C. §9-102(a)(41). White and Summers describe this provision as

> . . . merely an invitation to read the real estate statutes and the local case law on what is and what is not a fixture. What passes by deed in Minnesota may not pass in Wisconsin, and what is sufficiently related to a real estate interest in New York might not be sufficiently related in Georgia. Thus the general definition is no more than a cross-reference to state case law and state real estate statutes.

White & Summers, Uniform Commercial Code: Student Edition 26-8 (3d ed. 1988).

State law defining what is or is not a fixture is notoriously complex, confusing, and indeterminate. The big picture is captured by Professor Steve Knippenberg's definition: "You take the world, you shake it, and everything that doesn't fall off is [a fixture]." White and Summers add a second level of precision:

> Most courts start from the proposition that the status of goods as a fixture depends upon the intention of the parties. Of course, "objective manifestations of intention" are the windows through which we view actual intent. . . . Although the courts pay lip service to the proposition that they are merely determining the parties' intent, and although they will occasionally hoist one party on the petard of his written agreement which specifies that goods are or are not to be regarded as a fixture, for a majority of the courts the answer . . . ultimately depends on the manifestation of intent. For most courts intent is most clearly manifested by the firmness with which the goods are affixed to the real estate and the amount of sweat that removal would entail.

Id. The intention to which White and Summers refer is an intention to "permanently" affix the goods to the real property. See *Cliff's Ridge Skiing*, below. Lest you assume that you can determine whether goods are fixtures by how firmly they are affixed to the real estate:

> Many authorities take the position that any and all machinery essential to the proper functioning of a plant, mill, or similar manufacturing [sic] is a fixture, or is at least so presumed to be, irrespective of the manner in which it is annexed to the realty and *even though it is not attached thereto at all*. This view is sometimes referred to as the "integrated industrial plant" doctrine and represents the modern trend of decisions.

Commonwealth Edison Co. v. The City of Zion, 579 N.E.2d 1082 (Ill. Ct. App. 1991) (emphasis added).

In many situations, lawyers will find it impossible to predict whether the courts would consider particular property to be fixtures. In those situations, the best course is to attempt to protect the client regardless of what conclusion the court should later draw. Typically, that will require that searches and filings be made in both the real estate and the personal property filing systems.

2.   How Does a Secured Creditor Perfect in Fixtures?

Nothing in Article 9 prevents the creation or perfection of a security interest in fixtures under the real estate law of the state. U.C.C. §9-334(b). Thus, if some item of property could be encumbered by a real estate mortgage before the adoption of Article 9, it could be encumbered by one afterward as well.

In the case that follows, three creditors claimed perfected security interests in a ski lift. The court decided that the ski lift was a fixture and that all three creditors had perfected their interests in it. The case illustrates the variety of ways a secured creditor can perfect an interest in fixtures.

In re Cliff's Ridge Skiing Corp.

123 B.R. 753 (Bankr. W.D. Mich. 1991)

JAMES D. GREGG, UNITED STATES BANKRUPTCY JUDGE. . . .

On October 28, 1987, Cliff's Ridge Skiing Corporation, ("Debtor"), filed for bankruptcy. [The trustee sold a certain chairlift owned by the debtor for $22,500 in cash.]

Three creditors, First National Bank & Trust Company of Marquette ("First National"), Cliff's Ridge Development Co. ("Cliff's Ridge Dev."), and First of America Bank-Marquette, N.A., formerly known as Union National Bank & Trust Company of Marquette ("FOA"), each assert they are legally entitled to the escrowed proceeds and the interest earned therefrom. The chapter 7 trustee . . . now makes no claim to the chairlift proceeds. . . .

FACTS

On July 24, 1980, FOA loaned Cliff Ridge Dev. the sum of $300,000 pursuant to a note. Repayment of this indebtedness was secured by Cliff's Ridge Dev. executing a mortgage and a security agreement each dated July 24, 1980. The mortgage was properly perfected by recordation with the Marquette County Register of Deeds on August 1, 1980. The mortgage language granted FOA an interest in certain real property owned by Cliff's Ridge Dev. together with "all improvements now or hereafter created on the property . . . and all fixtures now or hereafter attached to the property, all of which, including replacements and additions thereto, shall be deemed to be and remain a part of the property covered by this mortgage." The security interest which granted FOA an interest in all tangible and intangible personal property of Cliff's Ridge Dev. was perfected by the filing of a financing statement with the State of Michigan, Secretary of State, U.C.C. Division, on July 29, 1980. No fixture filing was made with the Marquette County Register of Deeds. . . .

[The Debtor contracted to purchase all of Cliff's Ridge Dev.'s assets and began operating the ski area with the cooperation of one of Cliff's Ridge Dev.'s principals.] The Debtor determined it was advisable to purchase an additional chairlift and the purchase was discussed with a principal of Cliff's Ridge Dev. In April or May, 1982, the Debtor contacted Breckenridge Ski Area to purchase the chairlift on a cash-on-delivery basis. The price paid for the chairlift by the Debtor was $65,000. In addition, the Debtor paid $10,000 for shipping, $7,500 for engineering, and approximately $80,000 for erection of the chairlift. . . .

The chairlift was delivered and installed between August and December, 1982. . . .

. . . On November 22, 1982, Cliff's Ridge Dev. conveyed its ski hill real property to the Debtor pursuant to a warranty deed. The deed given to the Debtor was subject to the prior mortgage granted by Cliff's Ridge Dev. to FOA dated July 24, 1980. Also on November 22, 1982, the Debtor granted Cliff's Ridge Dev. a mortgage respecting the ski hill real property. The mortgage was properly perfected by recordation with the Marquette County Register of Deeds on November 23, 1982. . . . The mortgage does not contain any express language granting Cliff's Ridge Dev. an interest in the Debtor's fixtures, whether then owned or after acquired. Rather, the mortgage only grants an interest in the conveyed real property together "with the hereditaments and appurtenances thereunto belonging or in anywise appertaining." . . .

On December 13, 1982, the Debtor . . . and First National executed a Loan Agreement. . . . The Loan Agreement provides, inter alia, that (1) First National will loan $175,000 to [the Debtor] to be used to purchase the chairlift, (2) First National will receive a perfected security interest in the chairlift. . . . The agreement also includes a representation that the

Debtor has, or will obtain, good and marketable title to the chairlift except for liens disclosed to First National. At the time of this Loan Agreement, the parties apparently failed to recognize that Cliff's Ridge Dev. might claim an interest in the chairlift pursuant to its prior mortgage.

. . . At the time the [First National] loan documents were executed, the Debtor had a legal right or interest in the chairlift. The Debtor executed, and First National . . . filed, three financing statements regarding First National's . . . security interest in the chairlift collateral.

First, on December 14, 1982, a financing statement, intended as a fixture filing, was filed where mortgages are recorded with the Marquette County Register of Deeds. [First National] is listed as the secured party. . . . The real property description is attached to the financing statement. . . .

Second, on December 15, 1982, a financing statement, intended as a fixture filing, was filed with the Michigan Secretary of State, Uniform Commercial Code Section. This financing statement was identical to that filed with the Marquette County Register of Deeds. . . .

Third, on December 15, 1982, a financing statement, designated as a "Non-Fixture Statement", was filed with the Michigan Secretary of State, Uniform Commercial Code Section. The chairlift is identified on the financing statement.

DISCUSSION

Is the Chairlift a Fixture?

. . . In Michigan, whether personal property becomes a fixture and thereby part of realty is determined by a three-part test: (1) is the property annexed or attached to the realty, (2) is the attached property adapted or applied to the use of the realty, and (3) is it intended that the property will be permanently attached to the realty? The three-part test remains valid under current Michigan law. . . .

The chairlift was attached to the realty. Concrete pads were poured in the realty prior to the erection of the chairlift. Towers were then bolted to the concrete pads, cables were strung, and about 100 chairs were attached to the cables. The parties have stipulated that "chairlifts are part of ski hills but can be severed from the ski hills and sold." The court finds the chairlift was annexed or attached to the real property.

The parties have stipulated that the chairlift was engineered to be erected on the realty and the chairlift was specially modified to be attached to the realty. The court finds the chairlift was adapted to the ski hill real property for its use and purposes.

Very little testimony exists whether the parties intended to permanently affix the chairlift to the real estate. In the Project Plan, and other documents relating to the Debtor's request to obtain [the First National] financing, it is stated that the loan was intended to finance "construction" and "installation" of the chairlift "improvements" to the realty. Final approval of the requested financing was conditioned upon conveyance of the realty from Cliff's Ridge Dev. to the Debtor. In two financing statements dated December 14 and December 15, 1982, filed by First National, it is stated, "The goods are to become fixtures on 11-24-82." No other evidence regarding intent has been introduced by any party. Under Michigan law, attachments to realty to facilitate its use become part of the realty and, if done by the owner, are presumed to be permanent. Based upon the preponderance of the evidence, the court finds the Debtor intended to permanently affix the chairlift to the Realty.[3]

Under governing Michigan law, all requirements of the three-part test to determine whether personal property has become a fixture have been met. The court concludes that the chairlift in dispute is a fixture.

Creation and Perfection of an Interest in Fixtures

Under Michigan law, there are two methods by which a creditor may create and perfect an interest in fixtures. A creditor may utilize procedures under Michigan real estate law. Alternatively, a creditor may take a security interest in a fixture and perfect that interest under the Uniform Commercial Code as adopted in Michigan ("UCC").

Article 9 of the UCC allows the creation of an interest in fixtures pursuant to state real estate law. Prior to adoption of the UCC, Michigan law was well-settled that once a fixture is annexed or attached to realty, the fixture became part of the realty and title to the fixture is subject to a real estate mortgage.

As stated in Kent Storage Co. v. Grand Rapids Lumber Co., 239 Mich. 161, 164-165, 214 N.W. 111, 112-113 (1927): "It is a salutary rule that whatever is affixed to a building by an owner in complement, to facilitate its use and occupation in general, becomes a part of the realty, though capable of removal without injury to the building." When a fixture becomes complemental to real property, it becomes a permanent accession and becomes part of the realty; the fixture becomes part of the security with regard to any existing mortgage. A mortgage covers fixtures even when they are not expressly mentioned in the mortgage.

Once a mortgage creates an interest in fixtures under Michigan real estate law, the interest must be perfected. Perfection under state real

---

3. In making this finding, the court is cognizant of [Official Comment 3 to U.C.C. §9-334] which states:

> Since the determination in advance of judicial decision of the question whether goods have become fixtures is a difficult one, no inference may be drawn from a fixture filing that the secured party concedes that the goods are or will become fixtures. The fixture filing may be merely precautionary.

estate law is accomplished by recordation of the mortgage in the county where the real property is located.

The second method by which a security interest in fixtures may be created and perfected is under the UCC without reference to state real estate law. A "security interest" is defined very broadly to mean "an interest in personal property or *fixtures* which secures repayment of an obligation." [U.C.C. §1-201(37)]. (emphasis supplied.) Article 9 of the UCC applies "to any transaction (regardless of its form) which is intended to create a security interest in personal property or *fixtures*. . . ." [U.C.C. §9-109(a)(1)] (emphasis supplied.) . . .

To perfect a personal property interest in a fixture, and be accorded proper priority, a financing statement must be filed. [U.C.C. §9-310(a).] To be sufficient, a financing statement must: (1) state the names of the debtor and secured party, (2) be signed by the debtor, (3) provide the address of the secured party to allow inquiry about information regarding the security interest, (4) provide the mailing address of the debtor, and (5) contain a statement setting forth types or describing items of collateral. [U.C.C. §9-502(a)(3)]. In addition, a financing statement covering fixtures or goods to become fixtures must: (6) state that it covers this type of collateral; (7) recite it is to be recorded in the real estate records; (8) contain a description of the real estate where the fixtures are located or to be located, which is sufficient to provide constructive notice under state real estate mortgage law; and (9) if the debtor does not have an interest of record in the real estate, the owner of record must be disclosed. [U.C.C. §9-502(b)(4)].

The financing statement which covers fixtures, or goods to become fixtures, must be filed where a mortgage on the real estate would be recorded. [U.C.C. §9-501(a)(1)(B)]. In Michigan, an interest in real estate is properly recorded at the register of deeds in the county in which the real estate is located. When a sufficient financing statement is filed in the proper place, a "fixture filing" occurs. [U.C.C. §9-102(a)(40)]. After a proper fixture filing, a secured party has a perfected interest in the fixtures and may enforce its security interest against other persons according to designated priorities. [U.C.C. §§9-334(c)-(g)].

Under the UCC, a mortgage may be effective as a fixture filing from the date of its recordation provided four specified requirements are met, including that the mortgage describes the goods by "item or type." [UCC §9-502(c)]. An issue exists whether this UCC subsection mandates that a mortgage creating an interest in fixtures under state real estate law must contain a sufficient description of the fixtures, or the goods to become fixtures, by "item or type." At the hearing, some argument was made that if a mortgage fails to include such a description, no valid interest in fixtures can be created under state real estate law. The court has been unable to discover any reported case which addresses this issue.

As discussed above, an interest in fixtures, or goods which become fixtures, may be created under state real estate law, or under the UCC. State
real estate law creates real property interests in fixtures while the UCC
allows creation of personal property interests in fixtures. The UCC establishes priorities resolving conflict between these distinct legal creatures on
"turbulent waters . . . with difficulty." White & Summers, Uniform Commercial Code 1151 (3d ed. 1988).

A "sufficient" fixture filing requires a "statement indicating the types or
describing the items of collateral." [U.C.C. §9-502(a)(3),(b)]. A complying mortgage filed in lieu of a financing statement must also contain,
among other things, a description of goods "by item or type." [U.C.C.
§9-502(c)(1)]. The UCC requires, whether a fixture filing is accomplished
by filing a financing statement or recording a complying mortgage, the
information included must be the same. However, the UCC also permits
a valid security interest in fixtures to be created under state real estate
law. [U.C.C. §9-502(c)].

The UCC requirement that the type or items of collateral be adequately
described applies only to the creation and perfection of personal property
interests in fixtures under the UCC; this UCC requirement does not apply
to creation and perfection of real property interests in fixtures under state
real estate law. UCC law and state real estate law are separate and distinct
methods by which interests in fixtures are created and perfected. The
court therefore rejects any argument that the collateral must be explicitly
described by item or type in a mortgage which otherwise creates an
interest in fixtures under state real estate law.

Do the Creditors Hold a Valid Interest in the Chairlift and the Proceeds?

When a fixture becomes complemental to real property, it becomes a
permanent accession and the fixture becomes part of the security with
regard to any existing mortgage. The language [regarding after-acquired
fixtures] in FOA's prior recorded mortgage is sufficient to create and perfect its interest in the chairlift fixture under state real estate law. FOA
retained its interest in the proceeds pursuant to this court's order
whereby valid liens would attach to the proceeds of the sale. 11 U.S.C.
§§363(e); 361(2); [U.C.C. §9-315(a)(2)].

. . . Cliff's Ridge Dev.'s mortgage grants an interest in the real property
together "with the hereditaments and appurtenances thereunto belonging or in anywise appertaining." There is no language in the mortgage
relating to "fixtures". An "appurtenance" is an "article adapted to the use
of the property to which it is connected, and which was intended to be
a permanent accession to the freehold." Black's Law Dictionary 94 (5th
Ed. West Publishing Co. 1979). An "appurtenance" is equivalent to a
"fixture."

A mortgage covers fixtures even when they are not explicitly mentioned in the mortgage. If the chairlift became connected to the real property after the grant of Cliff's Ridge Dev.'s mortgage, Cliff's Ridge Dev. has an interest in the chairlift; the appurtenance or fixture becomes part of the security with regard to any existing mortgage. On the other hand, if the chairlift became connected to the real property before the grant of the mortgage, the chairlift would be covered by the subsequent mortgage without a special mention in the mortgage. Therefore, under state real estate law, Cliff's Ridge Dev. has an interest in the chairlift. Cliff's Ridge Dev. also has an interest in the proceeds from the chairlift sale in accordance with the court's prior order.

On December 14, 1982, a financing statement regarding the chairlift was filed [by First National] where mortgages are recorded with the Marquette County Register of Deeds. The form of the financing statement meets all the necessary requirements under the UCC. [U.C.C. §§9-502(a),(b)]. A sufficient financing statement regarding the chairlift fixture was filed in the proper place and a "fixture filing" occurred. [U.C.C. §§9-102(a)(40), 9-501(a)(1)(B)]. First National therefore holds a perfected personal property interest in the chairlift under the UCC. It now also holds an interest in the sale proceeds pursuant to this court's prior order. 11 U.S.C. §§363(e); 361(2); [U.C.C. §9-315(a)(2)].

We omitted the portion of the opinion that tells who won the case, because it deals with issues of priority among perfected, secured creditors that are reserved for the final chapter of this book. For those of you who can't bear not to know how the case came out, First National got the proceeds of sale and neither of the others got anything. But the reason will have to wait.

As *Cliff's Ridge* illustrates, there is more than one way to obtain and perfect a security interest in fixtures. The court mentions two, a mortgage and an Article 9 fixture filing. There is yet a third. By filing an ordinary financing statement in the U.C.C. personal property filing system, a secured creditor can perfect a security interest in goods that are fixtures. Such a filing does not qualify as a "fixture filing," U.C.C. §9-501(a), but there is nothing in Article 9 or elsewhere that says one must make a fixture filing to perfect in fixtures. U.C.C. §9-501 does not require filing in the real estate records to perfect in fixtures; it merely requires filing in the real estate records to perfect by means of a *fixture filing*. In Assignment 33, we will see that the perfection obtained in fixtures by a nonfixture filing is of very limited effect. For now, it is important to recognize that a personal property (nonfixture) filing is a "method permitted by this article" to perfect in property that is fixtures. See U.C.C. §§9-334(e)(2), (3).

3.   Perfecting in the Fixtures of a Transmitting Utility

Article 9 contains special rules for filing against the collateral, including fixtures, of a transmitting utility. The gist of the rules is to permit fixture filings against this type of debtor to be made in the office of the secretary of state rather than in county real estate filing systems. See U.C.C. §9-501(b). The paradigm cases that led to the adoption of this provision were railroads with tracks running through many counties and electric companies with power lines doing the same. Both the tracks and the lines might be fixtures, necessitating filings in all of the involved counties. To make such filings would be burdensome because the secured creditor would have to include in its fixture financing statements literally thousands of descriptions of parcels of land.

The transmitting utilities provisions of Article 9 may cause more problems than they solve. Read U.C.C. §9-102(a)(80). Under this definition, "transmitting utility" may include businesses such as radio and television stations that do not have lines or tracks running through numerous counties. Moreover, there is nothing in the transmitting utility rule that limits its effect to the special kinds of property that led to its adoption. Presumably, it would apply to the light fixtures in a railroad's headquarters building.

The effect of the rule is to require lenders to consider in every case the possibility that their borrowers qualify as transmitting utilities and, if so, to conduct additional searches in the offices of the secretaries of state. In most cases it will not be prudent for the lenders to dispense with the search of the real property records, because those records may contain mortgages on the railroad rights of way. The transmitting utility provisions are an excellent example of a characteristic of filing systems that we introduced earlier: Attempts to ease the burdens on filers tend to increase the burdens on searchers and vice versa.

Whatever mischief the transmitting utility rules are capable of causing seems at present largely inchoate. We have not been able to find a single reported opinion construing them.

D.   Personal Property Interests in Real Property

Direct ownership interests in land are real property, but many kinds of indirect ownership are not. For example, if Robin Finkelstein owns Blackacre in fee simple, her interest is real property and a security interest in that interest must be recorded in the real estate system. If she forms a corporation to own Blackacre for her (Robin Finkelstein,

Inc.), her interest, the stock of Robin Finkelstein, Inc., is personal property. If she grants a security interest in the stock, Article 9 governs that security interest. Similarly, the debtor's interest in a partnership or trust is personal property, even though the partnership or trust owns nothing but real estate. See, e.g., In re Cowsert, 14 B.R. 340 (Bankr. S.D. Fla. 1981) (a beneficial interest under an Illinois land trust is personal property and when given as collateral is classified as a general intangible). A secured creditor perfects its interest in the debtor's interest in the partnership or trust by filing in the Article 9 system.

The creation of a lease of real property is governed by real estate law. Most states require that if the lease is for a period longer than three years, it must be recorded to be effective against purchasers or encumbrancers of the real property. But there is a split of authority as to whether a *lessee's* grant of a security interest in its rights under the lease is governed by Article 9. See U.C.C. §9-109(d)(11); see, e.g., In re Associated Air Services, Inc., 42 B.R. 768 (Bankr. S.D. Fla. 1984) (U.C.C. applies to the use of a real property lease as collateral); In re Hodge Forest Industries, 59 B.R. 801 (Bankr. D. Idaho 1986) (a lease of real property may not be the subject of a security interest because it is excluded from Article 9 by §9-109(a)(1)).

A mortgagee can sell its interest in the mortgage or borrow against it. When the mortgagee does the latter, it usually gives a security interest in the mortgage. (Remember that the mortgagee does not own the land; it merely has a mortgage against the land.) How should such a security interest in a mortgage be perfected? By recording an assignment in the real property records or by filing a financing statement in the Article 9 filing system?

New Article 9 resolves a split of authority by deeming a security interest in a mortgage to be a security interest in a note — personal property — and thus covered under Article 9. It accomplishes that through two provisions. First, U.C.C. §9-109(b) provides that application of Article 9 to a security interest in a secured obligation (the mortgage note) is not affected by the fact that the note is secured by an interest (the mortgage) to which Article 9 does not apply. Having thus made clear that perfection in the note is under Article 9, the drafters extended coverage to the mortgage by providing in U.C.C. §9-203(g) that attachment of a security interest to a right of payment secured by a security interest in real property (the note) is also attachment of a security interest in the mortgage.

Problem Set 20

20.1.   Your client, Secured Lending Partners (SLP), specializes in high-risk secured lending to a class of clientele that, as SLP put it, "the banks won't touch." Billie Ochs, the managing partner of SLP, is negotiating to lend $1.5 million to an untouchable by the name of Pacific Interests. She has the following questions for you. Be prepared to cite to the governing law.

a. How should SLP perfect in Pacific Interests' one-third interest in a 160-acre tract of land known as Devil's Valley? Does the form in which title is held matter? U.C.C. §9-109(a) and (d)(11).

b. Billie also wants to make sure SLP is also perfected against the pine trees growing on Devil's Valley. The trees were planted 20 years ago in straight rows for easy harvesting. U.C.C. §§9-102(41) and (44), 9-334(a) and (b), 9-501(a), 9-502(b); Comment 12 to U.C.C. §9-334 and Comment 3 to U.C.C. §9-501.

c. How should SLP perfect in a parcel of land just west of Devil's Valley? The trees on this second parcel are virgin growth. They include some species that would be of considerable value as timber. (A single one of the walnut trees would be worth $10,000.) U.C.C. §§9-502(c), 9-102(41) and (44).

d. If SLP perfects by recording a mortgage against the second parcel, does the mortgage have to mention the trees?

e. Pacific Interests holds a mortgage and note from Mark VI Partners to Pacific Interests in the face amount of $200,000. The debt is for the purchase price of certain real property Pacific Interests sold to Mark VI. The note that evidences the promise to pay is physically incorporated into the purchase money mortgage. Pacific Interests recorded the mortgage and note in the real estate recording system; the original is now in the possession of Pacific Interests. SLP wants a security interest in the note and mortgage. How should SLP perfect it? U.C.C. §§9-102(2) and (47), 9-109(b), 9-203(g), 9-308(e), 9-310(a), 9-312(a), 9-313(a), 9-330(d).

f. Pacific Interests owns a corporate subsidiary, Pacific Broadcasting, Inc. (PBI). Billie tells you that PBI's only asset is a television broadcasting tower. Because SLP wants to make sure it gets a lien on everything, Billie wants to include a security interest in the tower itself. The steel tower is located on land owned by KRAT, Inc., the local ABC television network affiliate. PBI leases the tower to KRAT, Inc. under a lease that has five years left to run. The tower is 800 feet tall, is bolted to a concrete foundation, and is held in place by guy wires running from a high point on the tower to concrete pads located several hundred feet from the base of the tower. U.C.C. §§9-102(11), (41), (44), and (80), 9-501(b).

g. How should SLP perfect in a natural gas pipeline that runs through 119 counties in four states? In some counties the pipeline is buried; in others it runs above ground and is bolted to concrete pads. The pipeline is owned and operated by Pipes Holding, Inc. (Pipes), a wholly owned subsidiary of Pacific Interests. In some counties the pipeline runs on land owned by Pipes; in others it runs on easements granted by the landowners to Pipes. U.C.C. §§9-102(41), (44), (80), 9-334(a), 9-502(b).

h.   Pacific Interests also offers something they call "store fixtures" as collateral. These are items owned by Pacific Interests and used in a retail pet store known as Pet World, which is owned and operated by Pacific Interests and is located in a shopping center owned by Oaks Mall, Ltd. The "store fixtures" consist of shelving, counters, cages, cash registers, and similar items. Some are bolted to the building; some are freestanding. The lease between Oaks Mall, Ltd. and Pacific Interests gives Pet World, Inc. the right to remove the "store fixtures" at the expiration of the lease, provided that Pacific Interests is not then in default. U.C.C. §§9-102(41), 9-501(a), 9-502(b).

20.2.   Representing writer-adventurer Harold Philbrick has never been dull and today is no exception. Six months ago, Harold made a $1 million unsecured loan to Marland, Inc., a company owned by his friend, eccentric multimillionaire industrialist Arnold Edwards. Edwards has disappeared amid rumors of mismanagement and massive debt, leaving his companies in the hands of his estranged stepson, Robert. Harold shows you a napkin, printed with the logo of a bar called "One South" on which the following words have been handwritten:

> Marland, Inc. grants Harold Philbrick a security interest in the Marland manufacturing facility, Marland, Florida, to secure his loan to Marland, Inc.

The napkin bears what Harold says is the signature of Arnold Edwards, though it is difficult to tell because the napkin is torn and has some food stains on it. "I watched Arnold write it," Harold says. "Two other people were at the table when he did it."

The Marland manufacturing facility is a shoe factory located on ten acres of land. The land and building are worth at least $4 million; the machinery and other personal property on the premises, including unshipped inventory, are worth perhaps an additional $1 million. The only encumbrance of record is a real estate mortgage in the original amount of $1.5 million.

Harold wants to know what he should do about his million dollars and his napkin now that Edwards seems to be out of the picture. What do you tell him? U.C.C. §§9-203(b), 9-502(a) and (b), 9-509(a) and (b).

20.3.   Your client, Folds Mobile Homes, sells about 200 mobile homes a year at an average price of about $25,000. When Folds sells a home, it has the buyer execute a promissory note, security interest, and a standard U.C.C.-1 financing statement. In accord with the

advice of its former attorneys, Folds always describes the collateral as
"[brand] mobile home, [serial number]" and files the financing statement in the Office of the Secretary of State, U.C.C. Division, the place
specified in U.C.C. §9-501(a)(2). (The state does not permit perfection
in a mobile home by notation on a certificate of title.)

Folds repossesses from five to ten mobile homes a year. Until the
Bob Barker case, Folds had never had any legal problems with the
repossessions. Barker bought a mobile home from Folds about a year
ago. He put the home on a lot he owned about four miles outside the
city. After Barker disappeared, Folds was served with a summons and
complaint in a mortgage foreclosure brought by Pacific Security
Finance (PSF). It seems that PSF financed Barker's purchase of the lot
and Barker defaulted on his mortgage to them. PSF's complaint
alleges that the mobile home is a fixture and hence covered under
PSF's mortgage. It also alleges that Fold's security interest in the
mobile home is unperfected because it was not filed "in the office
where a mortgage on the real estate would be filed or recorded," citing U.C.C. §9-501(a), and "fails to comply with the requirements of"
U.C.C. §9-502(a) and (b).

a.   Allison Folds, the president of Folds, is very upset by the allegation that Folds' interest is unperfected and asks if the allegation is
correct. What do you tell him?

b.   Does Folds win or lose against PSF? U.C.C. §9-334(e)(1).

c.   Would Folds win or lose if the challenger was a trustee in bankruptcy? U.C.C. §9-334(e)(3).

d.   How should Folds perfect in the mobile homes it sells in the
future? U.C.C. §§9-102(41), 9-502(a) and (b).

20.4.   Sam Stoney, owner of Stoney's Pizza Parlour, is refinancing
his business with Western Commercial Bank and has asked you to
take a look at the documents. A portion of paragraph 20 of the real
property mortgage reads as follows:

> In addition, Borrower agrees to execute and deliver to Lender, upon
> Lender's request, any financing statements, as well as extensions,
> renewals and amendments thereof, and reproductions of this Instru-
> ment in such form as lender may require to perfect a security interest
> with respect to [the collateral]. Borrower shall pay all costs of filing such
> financing statements and any extensions, renewals, amendments and
> releases thereof, and shall pay all reasonable costs and expenses of any
> record searches for financing statements Lender may reasonably
> require.

A later provision in the mortgage defines "lender" as including the
Bank's "successors and assigns."

Sam says that when he read this paragraph in the Bank's form mortgage agreement, he was a little irritated. But considering the time and effort he has already put into this refinancing, he doesn't want to pull out and start over unless the clause presents a real and substantial problem. Does it?

Assignment 21: Characterizing Collateral for the Purpose of Perfection

In earlier assignments you have seen several situations in which the proper method of perfection depends on the type of collateral involved. If the collateral is a patent, perfection is by filing in the U.S. Patent and Trademark Office. If the collateral is real property or fixtures, perfection is by filing in the real estate records of the county where the real property is located. If it is consumer goods and the security interest is purchase money, no filing is required.

Article 9 makes numerous other distinctions among types of collateral. Most of these distinctions are made for the purpose of specifying the appropriate method for perfecting in the collateral. These distinctions can be broken down into two categories: those that relate to place of filing (federal, state, or local) and those that relate to method of perfection (filing, possession, control, notice to stakeholder, or automatic). In this assignment, we examine these distinctions among types of collateral in more detail.

A. Determining the Proper Place of Filing

There are more than four thousand filing systems in the United States. Filers cannot file in all of them, nor can searchers search in all of them. Article 9 and related law attempt to direct both filer and searcher to the single proper filing system in which their communication should take place.

For each filing system, the law specifies which filings are properly made in it. In doing so, the law necessarily *classifies* collateral. The classification may be based on the intrinsic nature of the collateral, such as when the law directs filing against a patent in the Patent Office. It may be based on the use to which the collateral is put. Filing may be required if the iMac computer that serves as collateral is equipment, but not if it is consumer goods. The law's instruction about where to file is sometimes based on complex classifications that depend on both the intrinsic nature of the collateral and the use to which it is put. For example, filing against a motor vehicle (intrinsic nature) that is inventory (use) is in the statewide filing system; filing against a motor vehicle that is used by the same debtor as equipment is by notation on the certificate of title. See U.C.C. §9-311(a)(2). In the subsections that follow, we examine the distinctions most important to determining the proper system in which to file.

1. Personal Property Distinguished from Real Property

In Assignment 20, we discussed the distinction between real and personal property and its impact on where filings should be made. The subject is, however, worthy of a quick review. Each county or the equivalent local government maintains a real estate filing system. That system is the proper place to file if the collateral is real estate or fixtures. U.C.C. §9-102(a)(41) defers to the real estate law of the state on the question of when goods are "so related to particular real estate" that filing should be in the real estate records, though the real estate law of the various states is often vague or confused on the point. Three factors are important in making the distinction between fixtures and nonfixtures: (1) the firmness with which the collateral is affixed to the real estate, (2) the intention of the parties as to whether the collateral is to become a permanent part of the real estate, and (3) the degree to which the collateral is essential to the proper functioning of the real estate. White and Summers warn that the distinction is highly indeterminate, and recommend filing and searching in both the real estate and personal property systems in a wide range of cases.

Although Article 9 defers to the real estate recording system as the proper place to file regarding a security interest in fixtures, Article 9 applies to the security interest (see U.C.C. §9-109(a)(1)) and specifies a form in which a proper fixture filing can be made in the real estate recording system (see U.C.C. §9-502(b)). Given that a fixture filing can be made against fixtures but not against "ordinary building materials incorporated into an improvement on land," the filer must also make that distinction to know whether it can perfect in those records by fixture filing or must file in the form of a mortgage. See U.C.C. §9-334(a).

2. Inventory Distinguished from Equipment

Security interests in inventory and equipment are both filed in the same filing system. See U.C.C. §9-501(a). Courts are called upon to distinguish the two principally in cases involving other issues. One such issue arises where the security agreement or financing statement describes the collateral as "inventory" or "equipment," but not both. Another is where the debtor sells the goods; buyers generally take free of a security interest in inventory, but not a security interest in equipment. There is, however, at least one instance in which classification of property as "inventory" or "equipment" controls the place of filing. We mentioned in section A that security interests in motor vehicles are perfected by notation on the certificate of title, but Article 9 creates an exception for motor vehicles "during any period in which [the vehicles] are inventory held for sale or lease" and the holder is "in the business of selling or leasing goods of that kind." U.C.C. §9-311(d). Perfection in motor vehicles held as inventory is by filing in the statewide Article 9 filing system. Comment 4 to U.C.C. §9-311.

U.C.C. §9-102(a)(48) tells us that goods are "inventory" when they are "held by a person for sale or lease or to be furnished under a contract for service." If goods are inventory, they are not equipment. U.C.C. §9-102(a)(33). Thus the distinction between inventory and equipment, like many other Article 9 distinctions between categories of collateral, depends not on the intrinsic nature of the goods but on the manner in which they are used.

Goods held for lease are explicitly included in the definition of inventory. Thus the videocassettes held by Blockbuster Video for rental are inventory even if copyright or contract restrictions make it impossible for Blockbuster ever to sell them. On the other hand, the computer system Blockbuster initially installed to keep track of the videocassettes will not be inventory, even if "it is the policy of [Blockbuster] to sell machinery when it becomes obsolete or worn." Implicit in the definition of "inventory" is that the debtor must be in the business of selling or leasing goods of the kind. See Comment 4 to U.C.C. §9-102.

3. Farm Products Distinguished from Inventory

A careful comparison between U.C.C. §§9-102(a)(34) and 9-102(a)(48) reveals that farm products are, in essence, the inventory of a farm. Several similarities are apparent on the face of the definitions. Goods are farm products if they are "used or produced" in farming operations. They are inventory if they are "raw materials [or] work in process . . . of a business." Similarly, goods are farm products if they are "supplies used . . . in farming operations" and inventory if they are "materials used or consumed in a business." The definition of "farm products" does not expressly require that the farmer hold them for sale, but it specifies as farm products the kinds of goods that farmers typically sell. If goods are farm products, they are not inventory. U.C.C. §9-102(a)(48).

Security interests in farm products and inventory are both perfected by filing in the statewide U.C.C. system. But for inventory it is
the statewide system of the state in which the debtor is located,
U.C.C. §9-301(1), while for farm products it is the state in which the
collateral is located. U.C.C. §9-302. (We realize these sections do not
exactly say that, but we ask you to trust us until we explain in Assignment 24.) Thus, to determine the proper place for filing against a person who holds goods for sale in the ordinary course of business, it is
necessary to determine first whether the debtor in possession of the
goods is "engaged in farming operations" and, if so, whether the
goods otherwise qualify as farm products. In Assignment 36, we will
introduce yet another need to distinguish farm products from inventory.

Here, again, focusing on the intrinsic nature of the goods is likely
to lead one to the wrong conclusion. Cattle are farm products in the
hands of a farmer, but inventory in the hands of a slaughterhouse.
Eggs are farm products in the hands of a farmer, but inventory in the
supermarket.

B. Determining the Proper Method of Perfection

Recall that there are essentially five ways that a security interest in
personal property can be perfected: (1) by filing, (2) by possession, (3)
by control, (4) by giving notice to the stakeholder (on non-UCC collateral such as insurance claims and tort actions), and (5) by doing
nothing (automatic perfection). For some kinds of collateral, more
than one of these methods will work. Determining which will work
in any particular instance depends on the type of collateral involved.
We will look at several distinctions made among types of collateral
for the purpose of determining what method or methods can be used
to perfect in each.

1. Instruments Distinguished from General Intangibles

In re Latin Investment Corp.
156 B.R. 102 (Bankr. D.C. 1993)

S. Martin Teel, Jr. United States Bankruptcy Judge

FACTS

In late 1988 and early 1989, the debtor, the bank, and Latin Credit Corporation entered into an arrangement for the financing of automobile

loans from the bank to minority buyers. For purposes of this decision, it is necessary to know only that the debtor pledged [a certificate of deposit (hereafter abbreviated "CD")] as security for Latin Credit Corporation's obligation to repurchase all defaulting automobile loans from the bank.

To effectuate the pledge, the bank issued the CD in the debtor's name in the amount of $200,000.00 after the debtor deposited $200,000.00 with the bank. The debtor and the bank then executed a hypothecation agreement giving the bank a security interest in the CD. Pursuant to the hypothecation agreement, the debtor delivered possession of the CD to the bank. Since then, the bank has continuously possessed the CD, but has not filed a financing statement covering the CD.

An involuntary chapter 7 petition was filed against the debtor on December 30, 1990. . . . [T]he trustee filed the instant adversary proceeding against the bank [alleging] that the bank failed to perfect its interest in the CD. Therefore, the trustee seeks to avoid the security interest in the CD by asserting his rights under §544. . . . In its summary judgment motion, the bank counters that its security interest in the CD is, and always has been, perfected by possession.

DISCUSSION

At issue is whether a writing purporting to be a CD but bearing on its face the legend "non-negotiable" and "non-transferable" is an "instrument" within the meaning of §9-102(a)(47) of Article 9 of the Uniform Commercial Code (UCC). If so, the bank's security interest is properly perfected by possession under U.C.C. §9-313(a). If the security interest is properly perfected, the trustee has no occasion to use his strong arm powers under Code §544(a)(1) to avoid the security interest. . . . Two cases appear to support the bank's contention that the writing is an Article 9 instrument. Jamison v. Society Natl. Bank, 66 Ohio St. 3d 201, 611 N.E.2d 307 (Ohio 1993) (CD bearing "non-transferable" and "non-negotiable" legend is Article 9 instrument); General Elec. Co. v. M & C Mfg., Inc., 671 S.W.2d 189 (Ark. 1984) (same).

If the writing is not an instrument, two other categories of collateral may apply. First, the writing may be a receipt evidencing a "deposit account" within the meaning of U.C.C. §9-102(a)(29). . . . Neither party espouses this position. Therefore, the court need not consider [it].

The other possibility is that the writing is a "general intangible" within the meaning of U.C.C. §9-102(a)(46). If so, the bank could perfect its security interest only by filing a financing statement in accordance with U.C.C. §9-310. This is the position taken by the trustee, who points to the fact that no financing statement was filed as grounds for avoiding the bank's security interest in the writing.

[The court then set out the definitions of "instrument" (U.C.C. §9-102(a)(47), "deposit account" (U.C.C. §9-102(a)(29), and "general intangibles" (U.C.C. §9-102(a)(44).]

Because "general intangibles" constitutes a catch-all category of collateral, the initial inquiry should be whether the writing at issue here escapes that catch-all category by being . . . an instrument. . . .

Neither party contends that the writing on its face is an Article 3 negotiable instrument or an Article 8 security. . . . In addition to Article 3 negotiable instruments and Article 8 securities, Article 9 instruments include the following:

> Any other writing which [1] evidences a right to the payment of money and [2] is not itself a security agreement or lease and [3] is of a type which is in ordinary course of business transferred by delivery with any necessary indorsement or assignment.

U.C.C. §9-102(a)(47). The first two requirements are met by the instant writing. Thus, the dispositive issue here is whether the writing "is of a type which is in ordinary course of business transferred by delivery with any necessary indorsement or assignment."

The trustee, focusing on the legend "non-transferable," maintains that the writing cannot be transferred by delivery in the ordinary course of business. (The trustee concedes that the legend "non-negotiable" does not preclude the instant writing from being an Article 9 instrument.) . . .

The court believes that the trustee is incorrect in his analysis. The language "of a type which is in ordinary course of business" indicates that the realities of the marketplace should control. The authorities the trustee relies on ignore this language. Instead, they take the particular writing before them at face value. They assume, without any basis for knowing the realities of the marketplace, that a CD labelled "nontransferable" simply cannot be transferred. . . .

This court believes that the test for transferability should be whether a particular type of writing customarily is transferred by delivery in the ordinary course of business. There is no basis in U.C.C. §9-102(a)(47) for allowing the legend on a writing to control its transferability. Instead, that section requires that actual business practices be consulted.

Moreover, if the business world regularly transfers writings bearing the legend "non-transferable," the court should give that practice legal effect unless doing so is inconsistent with the UCC. The UCC is not intended to thwart usual business practices but to effectuate them. Thus, the realities of business practice should control whether a particular writing meets the standard for transferability found in U.C.C. §9-102(a)(47). This is the approach advocated by the better reasoned authority. . . .

This court believes that the better view is that custom and usage in the marketplace should control whether the transferability requirement has been met. The court acknowledges that this view introduces an element of uncertainty into the classification of novel types of writings and into the perfection of security interests in them. But —

> The dividing line between instruments and pure intangibles — between writings, that is, which are and which are not "transferable by delivery" — appears to be a relatively stable one. Mutations do occur, and when they do they always move in one direction: intangibles become instruments, more or less negotiable. The mutations are infrequent and the market-place evidence that one has occurred usually becomes overwhelming in a short period of time. It seems unlikely that this theoretical problem will ever become a real source of trouble.

1 Gilmore, Security Interests §12.7, at 386. When faced with a novel writing, a prudent lender has ample means of protecting itself by perfecting both by possession and by filing. Accordingly, the court holds that for the transferability requirement to be met, it must be shown that a writing of a particular type, in this case, a CD bearing the legend "nontransferable," is generally recognized as being transferred by delivery in the ordinary course of business. In this respect, the court notes that the transferability requirement is satisfied where a particular type of writing is customarily transferred by a specific procedure for accomplishing delivery. The restrictive nature of such procedures does not defeat the writing's status of being an instrument.

In this case, there is insufficient evidence in the record to conclude as a matter of indisputable fact that the instant CD is customarily transferred by delivery in the ordinary course of business.[3] Therefore, this factual issue remains to be determined at trial or on further motion for summary judgment. . . .

An extraordinary amount of professional time (and consequently, money) must have gone into litigating the classification of this certificate of deposit. None of it would have been necessary if the bank's attorney at the time of the transaction had spent an extra $35 or so

3. At least one commentator, after surveying commercial lenders, has concluded that non-negotiable CD's (including "non-transferable" CD's) are transferable. Harris, Non-Negotiable CD's, 29 U.C.L.A. L. Rev. at 374-375; see also id. at 355 (expressly including "non-transferable" CD's among CD's that are the subject of the article). In addition, Federal Reserve Regulation D, governing reserve requirements for banks, allows a CD bearing the legend "non-transferable" to be transferred on a bank's books and also pledged without losing its non-transferable status. 12 C.F.R. §204.2(f)(1)(iv). The very existence of this regulation suggests that "non-transferable" CD's are in fact transferred. Nonetheless, the plaintiff did not present this as evidence and the court believes the trustee should be given the chance to show that "non-transferable" CD's are not customarily transferred by delivery in the ordinary course of business.

to file a financing statement. The hard part is to realize that the filing of a financing statement might be necessary.

2.   *True Leases Distinguished from Leases Intended as Security*

Article 9 applies to security interests in personal property but not to leases of personal property unless they are "intended as security." A lease intended as security is a sort of security interest in disguise; a lease not intended as security is referred to as a *true lease.*

Leases of personal property, even when "true," are similar in nature to security interests. Both are ways that someone with property or the money to buy it (the secured party or lessor) can make the property available to a user (the debtor or lessee) who will pay for the use over time. If the length of a lease and the payment schedule under a security agreement happen to be for exactly the useful life of the property, there may be no functional difference between the two.

Assume, for example, that Space Exploration Corporation wants to acquire some computer equipment, build it into a satellite, and send it into orbit around the earth as part of a five-year experiment. At the end of the five years, the satellite's orbit will skim the earth's atmosphere and, if those of us on the ground are lucky, the satellite will vaporize before striking the earth. Space Exploration might not care a bit whether the manufacturer of the equipment leased it to them for $99,000 per month on a five-year lease, or sold it to them for $500,000,000 payable with interest at 7 percent per annum in equal monthly payments (those payments would be $99,000 each). Either way, Space Exploration's tab is $99,000 a month and the company has nothing left at the end.

Despite the subtlety of the distinction between a true lease and a security interest in some circumstances, the distinction is crucial. If the transaction described in the previous paragraph is a true lease, under special tax rules addressed to the point, Space Exploration has a deduction equal to the monthly payment for federal income tax purposes; if the transaction is a security interest, Space Exploration has deductions for the annual depreciation and the interest instead. In some gross sense, the two may be about equal, but the only profits in some industries may lie in the difference. The lease-security distinction is also critical where a secured party, thinking the transaction is a true lease, does not file a financing statement. Once its debtor grants security to someone else or files bankruptcy, it is too late for the secured party to remedy its failure. U.C.C. §9-505 allows the financier that wants to be a true lessor, but isn't sure it has achieved that status, to file a financing statement just in case — without allowing the filing to be used as an admission by the "lessor" that the transaction is a security interest.

The label that the parties apply to their transaction will not be controlling; the law will search for its "true" nature. Many believe that the single issue most frequently litigated under Article 9 is whether a particular arrangement is a true lease or a security interest. The distinction between the two is supposedly an economic one and is set forth in U.C.C. §1-201(37). If, after reading that section, you know the difference, please write to tell us what it is.

3. Realty Paper

The term *realty paper* is sometimes used to refer to a promissory note secured by a mortgage or deed of trust. The issue of how one perfects in realty paper was dealth with in Assignment 20. Under U.C.C. §9-308(e), the proper method to perfect in realty paper is to perfect in the right to payment. In most instances, that note will be an "instrument" within the meaning of U.C.C. §9-102(a)(47). When it is, perfection can be accomplished by taking possession of the note, U.C.C. §9-313(a), or by filing, U.C.C. §9-312(a). But only perfection accomplished by possession will achieve priority over a later purchaser, U.C.C. §9-330(d), making perfection by possession preferable.

4. Chattel Paper and Instruments Distinguished from Accounts

The similarity between chattel paper and instruments and accounts is that all three involve a debt owed by a third party to the debtor. The debtor is using its right to that money as collateral to secured its own debt to the creditor. The principal difference among these three types of collateral is in the documentation of the debt from the third party to the debtor. If the documentation "evidence[s] both a monetary obligation and a security interest in specific goods, a security interest in specific goods and software used in the goods, or a lease of specific goods" the collateral is *chattel paper*, U.C.C. §9-102(a)(11), and perfection is by filing, U.C.C. §9-312(a)(1), or by taking possession, U.C.C. §9-313(a). If the documentation "evidences a right to the payment of a monetary obligation, is not itself a security agreement or lease, and is of a type that in ordinary course of business is transferred by delivery with any necessary endorsement or assignment," the collateral is an *instrument*, U.C.C. §9-102(a)(47), and, once again, perfection can be accomplished by filing or by taking possession, U.C.C. §9-313(a). If the debt is evidenced by neither, it is an *account or general intangible* (depending on the nature of the debt), U.C.C. §9-102(a)(2) and (42), and perfection is by filing.

To illustrate the use of chattel paper as security, assume that Bonnie's Boat World sells a boat to William and Gladys Homer for $20,000, "no money down." At the time of the sale, the Homers sign both a promissory note for $20,000 and a security agreement. Together, these two documents constitute chattel paper. As we saw in Assignment 15, when Bonnie's sells a boat, it must pay Deutsche Financial Services what it owes Deutsche on the boat. Bonnie's will get the cash by borrowing against or selling its chattel paper.

Whether Bonnie's borrows against or sells its chattel paper may seem like an important distinction. It is not. Either way, who bears the risk of default by the Homers will be determined by another term in the contract between Bonnie's and First State Bank. That term will provide that the transaction between Bonnie's and First State Bank is *with recourse* or *without recourse*. "With recourse" means that if the Homers default in payments under the note, First State Bank has "recourse" to Bonnie's. "Recourse" means that Bonnie's must buy the chattel paper back from the Bank and attempt to collect the debt itself. (Because this recourse transaction probably will be part of an ongoing relationship between Bonnie's and the Bank, Bonnie's will have to honor its agreement quickly and completely. Bonnie's does not get to play the debtor-creditor game with the Bank.) Once Bonnie's buys the chattel paper back from the Bank, Bonnie's will be in the same position as if it had never sold the chattel paper. That is, whether the transaction was a sale of chattel paper or a loan against chattel paper, it will have been reversed. Because sales of chattel paper and security interests in chattel paper are so similar in their effect, Article 9 applies to both and subjects them to the same rules. U.C.C. §9-109(a). Selling chattel paper and granting a security interest in chattel paper are, for our purposes, the same thing.

A security interest in chattel paper can be perfected either by filing or by taking possession. These two methods of perfection are not, however, equivalents. A purchaser of chattel paper who gives new value in the ordinary course of its business and who acts without knowledge of a security interest perfected by filing has priority over a security interest perfected earlier by filing. U.C.C. §9-330(b). Keep in mind that the definition of "purchaser" is broad enough to encompass both buyers and takers of security interests, including the bank lender in our example. U.C.C. §§1-201(32) and (33). Returning to that example, to buy or lend against Bonnie's chattel paper with assurance of a first security interest, First State Bank need not conduct a U.C.C. search. Even if there are earlier U.C.C. filings against the chattel paper, the Bank will have priority over them because the Bank will perfect by taking possession.

Then why does Article 9 permit perfection in chattel paper by filing? Permissive filing against chattel paper is part of an ongoing effort by the drafters of Article 9 to scale back the rights of trustees in bankruptcy and lien creditors. Notice that trustees in bankruptcy and lien creditors are not purchasers and thus are not entitled to the benefit of U.C.C §9-330 priority. By making the permissive U.C.C. filing, those who purchase chattel paper can gain an extra measure of protection. If they are careless with possession of the chattel paper they buy and some is still in the hands of the debtor when the bankruptcy is filed or the sheriff arrives, they can rely on their filing.

C. Multiple Items of Collateral

One can easily get so involved in determining the proper classification of collateral that one does not notice that more than one kind is involved. In the following case, the lawyers for one of the largest banks in the world failed to notice that their client had taken two items of collateral — the debtor's equipment and the debtor's right to payments from Plastimetrix under a lease of that equipment. To understand the nature of the Bank's error in filing, you need to know that, at the time of the case, a filing against goods had to be made in the state where the goods were located (New Jersey in the case) and a filing against chattel paper had to be made in the state where the debtor was located (New York in the case). (We discuss interstate filing problems in Assignment 24.)

In re Leasing Consultants, Inc.

486 F.2d 367 (2d Cir. 1973)

JAMESON, DISTRICT JUDGE.

Respondent-Appellant, First National City Bank (Bank), appeals from an order of the district court affirming, on a petition for review, the order of a referee in bankruptcy directing the Bank to turn over to the Petitioner-Appellee, George Feldman, Trustee in Bankruptcy (Trustee) of Leasing Consultants, Incorporated, (Leasing) the proceeds from the sale of equipment which had been leased by Leasing, located in New York, to Plastimetrix Corporation, located in New Jersey. The leases covering the equipment had been assigned to the Bank as security for a loan to Leasing.

The district court held, on the basis of stipulated facts, that the perfection by the Bank by filing and possession in New York of its security interest in the lease/chattel paper was not a perfection of the Bank's security interest in Leasing's reversionary interest in the leased property, located in New Jersey. Consequently, the Trustee's lien was held superior to the Bank's unperfected security interest in the leased equipment.

SUMMARY OF FACTS

In March and June of 1969 Leasing entered into eight leases with Plastimetrix covering heavy equipment. The leased equipment was at all relevant times located in New Jersey. Leasing filed financing statements with the Secretary of State of the State of New Jersey covering each transaction, each statement bearing the legend: "THIS FILING IS FOR INFORMATIONAL PURPOSES ONLY AS THIS IS A LEASE TRANSACTION."

On December 15, 1969 Leasing entered into a "Loan and Security Agreement" with the Bank for the financing of its business of purchasing and leasing equipment. The agreement provided in part for the assignment of "a continuing security interest in the (leases) and the property leased" as collateral security for advances and loans not to exceed 80% of aggregate unpaid rentals.

Pursuant to the security agreement Leasing borrowed money from the Bank in December, 1969 and February, 1970 and assigned as collateral security the eight Plastimetrix leases, each assignment covering all moneys due or to become due under the lease and the "relative equipment" described in the lease. The lease documents were delivered to the Bank.

On December 30 and 31, 1969 the Bank filed financing statements against Leasing with the Secretary of State of the State of New York and the Registrar of the City of New York, Queens County, where Leasing had its principal place of business.[1] No financing statements were filed by the Bank in New Jersey; nor did the Bank take possession of the leased equipment.

On October 14, 1970 Leasing was adjudicated bankrupt by the United States District Court for the Eastern District of New York. On October 30, 1970 Plastimetrix filed a petition under Chapter XI of the Bankruptcy Act in the United States District Court for the District of New Jersey.

The leases were in default and an offer was made to purchase the Bank's interest in the property for $60,000. On May 21, 1971 the Trustee, the Bank, and the purchaser entered into a stipulation providing for acceptance of the offer and execution of bills of sale by the Trustee

---

1. The financing statement covered "continuing security interest in leases and any and all rents due and to become due thereunder, including all related equipment described therein, chattel paper represented thereby, accounts receivable therewith and proceeds arising therefrom."

and Bank covering all "right, title and interest" in the property, and that the sum of $60,000 "be substituted for the Property" and the "respective rights of the Trustee and of the Bank . . . be impressed upon and relegated to said fund of $60,000 with the same priority and to the same extent as they now have against the Property."

The Trustee petitioned order directing the Bank to turn over to the Trustee the sum of $60,000. Under stipulated facts the Trustee and Bank agreed that the question presented was solely one of law — involving the construction of Article 9 of the Uniform Commercial Code — and that the precise issue was:

> Was the Bank required to file a financing statement against the Bankrupt with the Secretary of State of New Jersey in order to perfect a security interest in the leases assigned to it and the equipment leased thereunder by the Bankrupt to Plastimetrix?

The Referee answered in the affirmative and ordered the Bank to turn over the $60,000, with interest, to the Trustee. On review the district court affirmed.

DECISION OF DISTRICT COURT

As the district court recognized, the aim of Article 9 of the Uniform Commercial Code, relating to "Secured Transactions," is "to provide a simple and unified structure within which the immense variety of present-day secured financing transactions can go forward with less cost and with greater certainty." Uniform Commercial Code, §9-101, Official Comment. The drafters of this article eliminated many distinctions among security devices based on form alone. On the other hand, distinctions based on the type of property constituting the collateral were retained.

Based on the stipulation of counsel, the court assumed that the agreements between Leasing and Plastimetrix were "true leases" and not "conditional sales agreements" or devices intended to create only a security interest.[2] Accordingly the court found that the Bank acquired "a security interest in both the right to receive rental payments under the lease and in the reversionary interest in the underlying equipment."

The court held, and the parties agree, that the leases themselves were "chattel papers" [U.C.C. §9-102(a)(11)] and that the Bank's security interest in the chattel paper was perfected by filing financing statements in New York and taking possession of the leases. [U.C.C. §§9-312(a) and 9-313(a)].

---

2. Where a lease is intended as a security device the lessee usually becomes the owner or has the option to become the owner of the property at the end of the lease term. U.C.C. §1-201(37). The lessor holds merely a security interest and has no reversionary right in the leased property.

The court held further: "By contrast, the machines themselves constituted 'equipment' located in New Jersey and hence, for perfection purposes, came within the scope of the New Jersey requirements." The Bank having failed to perfect its interest in the reversion in New Jersey, the court concluded that the Trustee "— a lien creditor within the meaning of Uniform Commercial Code [§9-102(a)(52)] — has priority over an unperfected security interest under [§9-317(a)(2)]."

Emphasizing the distinction between rights under the chattel paper and the reversionary interest in the equipment, the court quoted from Professor Levie as follows:

> "In one situation the purchaser of a security agreement may have an advantage over the purchaser of a lease. Where [he] purchases equipment leases, he takes only an assignor's interest in the equipment lease itself. If [he] wishes to be secured by an interest in the goods as well, he must obtain a security interest [in the goods] and perfect it." Levie, Security Interests in Chattel Paper, 78 Yale L.J. 935, 940 (1969).[4]

The district court concluded:

> The distinction between the rights represented by the lease and those represented by the reversionary interest in the equipment is a real one, supported by logic and precedent. To ignore the distinction contributes neither to clarity nor uniformity under the Uniform Commercial Code. Moreover, it may mislead third party creditors. The simple solution for a bank in the situation of petitioner is to file notices as to its interest in the reversion in accordance with the law of the state where the equipment is located.

CONTENTIONS OF APPELLANT

Appellant Bank contends that (1) whether the leases be considered "true leases" or security devices, the filing of the security interest in New York (where lessor and the chattel paper were located) covered all of the les-

---

4. The court continued:

> Practical considerations support this conclusion. The property leased was heavy manufacturing equipment. A potential creditor observing these complicated and non-portable machines should be entitled to believe that he could discover all non-possessory interests by consulting the files in the state where the equipment is located. The equipment was obviously of great value; the New Jersey files revealed only that the lessee held it under a lease. Since the lease agreement required each piece of equipment to have a plate affixed indicating that it was the "property" of the lessor, judgment creditors of the lessor might assume that its reversionary interest in the equipment was of substantial value. Not being alerted to the diminution of value which would be effected by the creditor's security interest, they might then, for example, attach the lessor's interest, relying on an apparently unencumbered and valuable reversionary interest.

sor's rights in the rentals and related equipment wherever located, without a separate filing against the equipment; or (2) alternatively, if a distinction is recognized between a "true lease" and a security device, appellant is entitled to an evidentiary hearing to determine whether the instruments were "true leases" or security interests in the equipment through the device of a lease; and (3) in any event, Leasing in fact had no "reversionary" interest in the property leased to Plastimetrix.

FAILURE TO FILE FINANCING STATEMENT IN NEW JERSEY

In contending that the filing and physical possession of the lease instruments in New York were sufficient to cover the leased equipment located in New Jersey, appellant argues that the "reversionary interest" of Leasing is "an intangible interest, sited at Leasing's domicile in New York, and not in New Jersey." If the reversionary interest in the equipment were characterized as a "general intangible," the Bank's security interest in the equipment would have been perfected when it filed with the New York Department of State and in the county in which Leasing had a place of business.

The policies of the Code, however, militate against such an interpretation. We agree with the district court that the reversionary interest is an interest in "goods" rather than an interest in intangibles, and that to perfect the security interest in the reversionary interest in the equipment it was necessary to file a financing statement in New Jersey where the equipment was located.

Obviously the leased property itself is "goods." We conclude, as did the district court, that the future reversionary interest is likewise an interest in goods, whether it represents "equipment" or "inventory" collateral. The drafters of the Code classified collateral mainly according to the nature or use of the underlying entity, rather than the character of its ownership at any given time. Significantly, the examples of "general intangibles" given in [Official Comment 5 to §9-102] are all types of property that are inherently intangible. And several Code sections and comments suggest that a collateral interest in "goods" remains such even when the goods are leased. See [§9-102(48) and Official Comment 4(a)].

We conclude accordingly that if the instruments were "true leases," the security interest in the leased equipment was not perfected because of the failure of the Bank to file financing statements in New Jersey. . . .

[The court then considered whether the leases were true leases or leases intended as security. Finding the facts of record insufficient to make that determination, the court remanded the case for further proceedings.]

The parties who made the error in *Leasing Consultants* may have been confused not by Article 9 but by property law. If Leasing Consultants buys a photocopier and leases it to Plastimetrix for five years, what does Leasing Consultants own? The court held, consistent with the law generally, that it owned a photocopier and a lease. The incorrect conceptualization that may have caused the error in *Leasing Consultants* is that Leasing Consultants owned only its rights under the lease, and that those rights included both the right of reversion at the end of the lease and the right to repossess the photocopiers if Plastimetrix failed to make the payments.

The moral of this story is that in many cases there is a step the analyst must go through *before* trying to decide how the collateral should be classified within the scheme of Article 9. In that earlier step, the analyst must decide precisely what the collateral is and how that collateral is conceptualized and classified under the scheme of property law. You have already engaged in this process in earlier assignments. For example, in Problem 20.1.a, you had to determine whether the debtor's one-third interest in a parcel of real property was as a tenant in common (real estate) or an interest in a partnership (personal property) to determine the proper method of perfection.

Problem Set 21

21.1.   How should the secured party perfect a security interest in each of the following?

a.   *The lessee's interest under a lease of real property.* U.C.C. §§9-102(11) and (42), 9-109(d)(11), and Comment 10 to §9-109.

b.   *Wheat growing in the farmer-debtor's field.* U.C.C. §§9-102(a)(34) and (44), 9-109(d)(11); 9-334(a), and (i), 9-501(a); Comment 4.a. to U.C.C. §9-102 and Comment 12 to U.C.C. §9-334.

c.   *The franchise to operate a Burger King restaurant.* (The franchise agreement was signed yesterday. The franchisee has not yet contracted to purchase the land where the restaurant will be located.) The franchise is issued to the debtor and specifically states that it is nontransferable.

d.   *An electronic "book entry" certificate of deposit.* The certificate was issued by Citibank in the amount of $2 million to Kennedy Construction Company, but it is not now and never has been evidenced by anything on paper. U.C.C. §§9-102(a)(29), (42), and (47), 9-104, 9-312(a), 9-313(a), 9-314, 9-330(d).

e.   *Electronic chattel paper.* U.C.C. §§9-312(a), 9-314(a), and 9-105.

f.   *The software on a consumer debtor's personal computer, including software written by the debtor* U.C.C. §§9-102(a)(23), (44) and (75), 9-109(c)(1), 9-309(1), 9-310, 9-312(a), 9-313(a).

   g. *The documentation and manuals for that software.*

   21.2. You are working as a staff member for the National Conference of Commissioners on Uniform State Laws (NCCUSL), and you have been assigned the preparation of a preliminary assessment of a proposal by a NCCUSL member to amend Article 9. The proposal is to have only a single filing system in each state and require that if a debtor is located in the state, all security interests in personal property owned by the debtor be perfected by filing in that filing system. The effect would be to do away with nearly all distinctions among types of collateral except the distinction between "real" and "personal" property collateral. The proposal argues that if all of these distinctions could be eliminated, it would cut the text of Article 9 by one-third and with it the length of the Article 9 course in law schools. With some 15,000 students enrolled in Article 9 courses annually, the savings projected from this source alone might be as much as 315,000 person-hours. (The proposal also suggests that this time in law school be devoted to issues of professional responsibility or sports law.)

   NCCUSL does not want your assessment of whether the proposal would pass. They are principally interested in any possible side effects from the change. Are there good reasons for maintaining these separate filing systems and methods of perfection, and making all these distinctions among types of collateral? Restrict your consideration to perfection-related issues. Someone else will report on other uses made of these distinctions. Focus principally on the distinctions in the subheadings of sections A and B of this assignment.

   21.3. Monte Publishing Company has asked your client, Flexible Finance, to finance Monte's acquisition of a custom-built four-color printing press. The press will be manufactured by Thien Tool Company. The cost of the press will be $1.2 million. The parties have agreed that Monte will pay all closing costs and pay Flexible 10 percent interest on the amount of financing outstanding at any given time. Payment will be in equal monthly installments over seven years. Because of sizeable losses Flexible took as a secured creditor in two recent bankruptcy cases, Flexible insists that the transaction be structured as a lease. Flexible would like you to draft the lease and render an opinion that the transaction will be effective as a lease.

   Monte and Flexible agree that the expected useful life of the press is probably between five and 15 years, but no one can be sure how long it will in fact be useful and used because the technology is changing rapidly. Monte would like to use the press throughout its useful life; Flexible has no use for the press and does not want possession. If the press has to be resold, the commission on the sale probably would be about 25 percent of the value of the press at the time of sale. As its value approaches zero, brokers will be increasingly unwilling to undertake its sale.

Flexible understands that the lease might not give it exactly what it wants, but it would like you to come as close as possible. What wording do you recommend for the provisions of the lease controlling the lease term and the amount of rent payable? If you recommend that Flexible have a reversionary interest, how should Flexible deal with reversion? U.C.C. §1-201(37).

Chapter 7. Maintaining Perfection

Assignment 22: Maintaining Perfection Through Lapse and Bankruptcy

In the preceding chapter, we discussed what secured parties must do to perfect their security interests. In this chapter we discuss what they must do to maintain that perfection over time and how they terminate perfection when it has served its purpose. We begin with the problem of termination.

A. Removing Filings from the Public Record

From the time it is placed on the public record, a filing or recording serves as constructive notice to the world that a security interest may be outstanding against property of the debtor. The theory is that searchers will discover the existence of a prior holder's interest by examining the public record, and then contact the holder of the prior interest for more information. Ultimately, such searchers must either come to terms with the holder of the prior interest or accept a subordinate position. The prior interest encumbers the property and clouds title to it.

When the debt is paid, both debtor and creditor typically will want to "remove" the filing from the public record. The debtor will want the filing off the record to clear its title to the property. The creditor will want the filing off the record so it won't be bothered by inquiries about property in which it no longer has an interest.

We put "remove" in quotation marks because many filing systems do not permit the literal removal of documents at the request of the parties. All one can do is *add* a document stating that the earlier document is no longer in effect. Nearly all real estate recording systems operate in this manner. Not surprisingly, some systems are growing in physical size at alarming rates.

1. Satisfaction

We begin our discussion of removal of filings with the real property system because it is simpler. When a real estate mortgage is paid, the mortgagee executes a document called a *satisfaction of mortgage* for recording. The satisfaction identifies the mortgage and states that it has been satisfied. Both the mortgage and the satisfaction of mortgage remain permanently in the recording system. It is important to realize that even if the debtor has paid the mortgage debt, the mortgage will continue to cloud the debtor's title until a satisfaction is recorded. The satisfaction assures persons who deal with the property in the future that the mortgagee will not make claims against it.

To understand the role that the satisfaction plays in a real estate transaction, consider the following example. Seller owns a beach house that is subject to a mortgage in favor of Western Savings in the amount of $80,000. Seller has contracted to sell the beach house to Buyer, free and clear of the mortgage, for $100,000 in cash. Seller, like most of us, does not have $80,000 with which to satisfy the mortgage; she must use the proceeds of sale to pay it. Buyer, like most of us, does not have the $100,000 he will use to pay the purchase price. He will borrow the money from Eastern Savings, using the beach house as collateral. Eastern Savings will, of course, insist that the title to the beach house be free and clear of liens before they will disburse the loan proceeds. But Western Savings will not remove their mortgage from the title until they are paid the $80,000 owing to them. A stalemate looms.

The standard solution to this problem is to set a *closing* — a gathering of all the parties so that they can make a simultaneous exchange of documents and money. At the closing, Eastern will pay the mortgage to Western, using $80,000 of the loan proceeds, and Western will simultaneously deliver a satisfaction of the mortgage to Seller. Seller will deed the property to Buyer. Buyer will sign a new mortgage for the amount of the loan proceeds and Eastern will record it immediately. The satisfaction is Western's assurance to Eastern that Western will make no further claims under the mortgage. Unless Seller can obtain this satisfaction of the old mortgage, Buyer cannot get the new mortgage he needs to pay the purchase price. The transaction will not *close* and the sale will fall through.

Because of the importance of the satisfaction, statutes in most states provide for imposition of a penalty on a secured party who fails to give one to a debtor who has fully paid the mortgage debt. The following statutes are typical:

Arizona Revised Statutes Annotated

(1990)

§33-712   LIABILITY FOR FAILURE TO
ACKNOWLEDGE SATISFACTION

A. If any person receiving satisfaction of a mortgage or deed of trust shall, within thirty days, fail to record or cause to be recorded, with the recorder of the county in which the mortgage or deed of trust was recorded, a sufficient release, satisfaction of mortgage or deed of release or acknowledge satisfaction as provided in section 33-707, subsection C, he shall be liable to the mortgagor, trustor or current property owner for actual damages occasioned by the neglect or refusal.

B. If, after the expiration of the time provided in subsection A of this section, the person fails to record or cause to be recorded a sufficient release and continues to do so for more than thirty days after receiving a written request which identifies a certain mortgage or deed of trust by certified mail from the mortgagor, trustor, current property owner or his agent, he shall be liable to the mortgagor, trustor or current property owner for one thousand dollars, in addition to any actual damage occasioned by the neglect or refusal.

Florida Statutes Annotated

(West Supp. 1995)

§701.04   CANCELLATION OF MORTGAGES,
LIENS, AND JUDGMENTS

Whenever the amount of money due on any mortgage, lien, or judgment shall be fully paid to the person or party entitled to the payment thereof, the mortgagee, creditor, or assignee, or the attorney of record in the case of a judgment, to whom such payment shall have been made, shall execute in writing an instrument acknowledging satisfaction of said mortgage, lien, or judgment and have the same acknowledged, or proven, and duly entered of record in the book provided by law for such purposes in the proper county. Within 60 days of the date of receipt of the full payment of the mortgage, lien, or judgment, the person required to acknowledge satisfaction of the mortgage, lien, or judgment shall send or cause to be sent the recorded satisfaction to the person who has made the full payment. In the case of a civil action arising out of the provisions of this section, the prevailing party shall be entitled to attorney's fees and costs.

2. Release

Mortgages frequently encumber more than one parcel of real property. If such a mortgage has not been paid in full but the secured creditor is willing to release some of the property from the mortgage lien, the secured creditor accomplishes this by executing a *release* for recording. Most secured creditors release collateral only to the extent they are required to do so by contract. The debtor typically bargains for the secured creditor's contractual obligation to release collateral before the loan is made.

Provisions requiring the release of collateral on partial payment of the loan are customary in financing the development of real estate subdivisions. For example, assume that High Point Development Company intends to purchase Blackacre, divide it into 100 residential building lots, build a road through it, install utilities, and sell the lots to contractors. Fidelity Savings lends High Point $700,000 to buy and improve the property. High Point does so, and begins offering the improved lots for sale. Linda Easterbrook, a professional home builder, is High Point's first customer. Easterbrook agrees to buy one of the lots for $25,000.

Easterbrook will almost certainly demand that she receive the lot free and clear of Fidelity's mortgage. Only then can she use it as collateral for the mortgage she will take out to finance construction of her house. Neither she nor her new lender want the risk that High Point will later default in payment of its mortgage and Fidelity will foreclose against the Easterbrook lot along with the others. But where will that leave Fidelity? The $25,000 that High Point will receive from the sale to Easterbrook will fall far short of the amount necessary to satisfy Fidelity's mortgage.

The usual accommodation between parties like these is that Fidelity will release the Easterbrook lot in return for a partial payment of its mortgage (a *paydown*). Fidelity's mortgage will probably contain a provision requiring it to give the release, contingent on High Point's payment of the *release price*. If the release price for the Easterbrook lot is, for example, $12,000, High Point will use proceeds of the sale to Easterbrook to pay that amount to Fidelity, reducing the balance owing Fidelity to $688,000. In return, Fidelity will sign a release of the Easterbrook lot, reducing Fidelity's collateral to 99 lots. Easterbrook will see that the release is recorded.

Notice that Fidelity's collateral-to-loan ratio improves as a result of the sale to Easterbrook. Before the sale, Fidelity has 100 lots as collateral for a $700,000 balance outstanding, a ratio of one lot per $7,000 of debt. After the sale, Fidelity has 99 lots as collateral for a $688,000 balance outstanding, a ratio of one lot per $6,949 of debt. High Point's $12,000 paydown on each lot sold will pay the debt in full before High Point sells all the lots. With each successive sale, Fidelity will be better assured of payment of the remaining balance.

Absent a release provision in a mortgage, the mortgagee is under no obligation to release collateral on partial payment of the mortgage — even if the debtor offers a paydown that will improve the lender's collateral-to-loan ratio. The mortgagee's only obligation is to execute a satisfaction when the debtor pays the entire balance owing on the mortgage debt. The same rule applies to security interests under Article 9.

3. Article 9 Termination and Release

If the debtor has paid the secured obligation and the secured party is not required by contract to lend more money, the debtor can demand that the secured party file a *termination statement* within 20 days. U.C.C. §9-513(c)(1). If the secured party fails to do so, the secured party becomes liable for actual damages and, in addition, a civil penalty of $500. U.C.C. §§9-625(b) and (e)(4). Upon the filing of a termination statement, the financing statement to which it relates ceases to be effective. U.C.C. §9-513(d).

Release of collateral from the coverage of a financing statement is accomplished by amending the financing statement. U.C.C. §9-512(a). As under real estate law, the secured party is obligated to file a termination statement upon full payment of the secured debt, but is not obligated to file an amendment deleting collateral on partial payment unless the secured party has contracted to do so.

A termination statement or amendment must identify, by its file number, the initial financing statement to which it relates. In addition, a termination statement must indicate that the identified financing statement is no longer effective. U.C.C. §9-102(a)(79). A termination statement or amendment becomes part of the financing statement to which it relates. See U.C.C. §9-102(a)(39). As a consequence, it appears that minor errors or omissions in the termination statement would be subject to the "seriously misleading" test of U.C.C. §9-506. That is, such errors would not render the financing statement — including the termination statement or amendment — ineffective unless errors make the financing statement seriously misleading.

U.C.C. §9-512 requires that an amendment (including a termination statement) identify "by its file number, the initial financing statement to which the amendment relates." Could an erroneous file number in the termination statement or amendment be a minor error that did not render the financing statement seriously misleading? Imagine, for example, that an amendment bore the wrong file

number but contained the correct names and addresses of the debtor
and the secured party, and correctly indicated the date and time of
filing of the financing statement. If the filing officer noticed the problem at the time of filing, the filing officer could refuse to accept it
pursuant to U.C.C. §9-516(b)(3)(B) and send it back to the filer.
U.C.C. §9-520(b). The filer would correct the file number and refile.
The problem would be solved. But what if the filing officer did not
notice the problem, accepted the amendment for filing, created a
record, and indexed the filing under the wrong financing statement?
One possibility is that, although U.C.C. §9-506(c) would not literally
apply, the courts would apply it by analogy. If a search of the records
of the filing office under the debtor's correct name, using the filing
office's standard search logic, would disclose the amendment, the
erroneous number would not make the amendment seriously misleading. Another possibility is that this would be considered an
indexing error rendering the amendment effective regardless of
whether searchers could find it. U.C.C. §9-517. A third possibility is
that the hypothetical could not arise. Both the financing statement
and the amendment each contain both the file number and the debt-
or's name. See the official Amendment form in U.C.C. §9-521. By
programming their computers to reject a filing unless both the file
number and the name matched, the filing officer could prevent the
error, rendering the legal issue moot. The point is that, when available, physical systems (here, the programming) are capable of
addressing the same points addressed by law and will often provide
superior solutions.

B. "Self-Clearing" and Continuation in the Article 9 Filing System

As we mentioned above, the real estate recording system is committed to keeping your deed to Blackacre for eternity. Documents are
added to the system, but none are ever removed from it.

Perhaps cognizant of the record-storage problem confronting the
real estate recording systems, the drafters of Article 9 opted for what
they call a *self-clearing system*. Financing statements are effective for
only five years. (A few states have adopted non-uniform amendments
specifying longer periods.) Unless the secured party takes affirmative
action by filing a *continuation statement* during the last six months of
the five-year period, the financing statement "lapses." U.C.C.
§9-515(a) and (c). Only about 30 percent of financing statements are
terminated. Another 15 percent are continued. The remaining 55 per-

cent are cleared by lapse. 11 Clark's Secured Transactions Monthly 7 (Jan. 1996). One year after a financing statement lapses, the filing officer can remove it from the records and destroy it. U.C.C. §9-522(a). As a result, an Article 9 filing system may contain only the financing statements filed or continued in the past six years.

Not all Article 9 filing systems are set up to take advantage of this self-clearing feature. Local systems are often integrated with the real estate recording systems in such a way that lapsed financing statements cannot be thrown away. But they lapse just the same.

To understand how the self-clearing feature of the Article 9 filing system works, think of the filed financing statements as each standing vertically on a conveyor belt. At the place where the moving belt begins its horizontal trip, the filing officer places newly filed financing statements on it. The belt carries the filings for six years, at which time they drop off the end into a paper shredder. At four and a half years, the filing statements enter the six-months-long segment of the belt in which they can be continued. If a continuation statement is filed while the financing statement is in this continuation "window," the filing officer pulls the financing statement off the conveyor belt, attaches the continuation statement to it, takes it to the beginning point, and puts it back on the belt, just like a newly filed financing statement.

What about the statements that are not continued? One might think that the conveyor belt should arrive at the paper shredder five years from the point of beginning — that is, as soon as it is out of the continuation window. If the filing officer could process continuation statements immediately on receipt, it probably should. But sometimes the filing officer gets a bit behind in the work. Even though a filing officer receives a continuation statement (and, of course, notes the date and time of filing on it) while the financing statement is in the six-months continuation window, the financing statement may be past the window by the time the filing officer begins looking for it. The conveyor belt extends for a year beyond the continuation window so that the financing statement will not reach the shredder before the busy filing officer can snatch it off the belt.

U.C.C. §519(h) requires that the filing officer index records within two days of their receipt by the filing officer. Why, then, does §9-522 require that the filing officer maintain lapsed records for a year after lapse? Perhaps the reason is that the drafters did not really expect filing officers to comply with U.C.C. §519(h). Filing offices traditionally have been one or two weeks behind in indexing new filings and in extreme cases have been more than four months behind. When such delays occur, the filing officers invariably blame their legislatures for not appropriating sufficient funds for the filing offices to carry the workload. No one can prove the filing officer wrong and no penalty is imposed for violating U.C.C. §519(h) anyway, making that provision what some refer to euphemistically as "aspirational."

Provided that the secured party files a continuation statement each time its financing statement passes through the continuation window, the financing statement can ride the conveyor belt for decades. Each time it passes the window, the filing officer attaches a new continuation statement and it gets thicker and thicker.

The secured party who wants to maintain the priority of its initial filing must continue that filing rather than simply file a new financing statement. The reason for this requirement may seem obvious, but it is not. Exactly what harm would it cause if a secured party, rather than filing a continuation statement as its earlier financing statement passed through the continuation window, simply filed another financing statement? The second financing statement would be on the belt before the first one reached the shredder. Anyone who searched before taking an interest in the collateral could discover the secured party's interest.

What more does the continuation statement tell them? Only that the priority date of the existing interest is earlier than they might otherwise have supposed. To illustrate, assume that Firstbank filed a financing statement in 1991 and filed a continuation statement in 1995. A search in 1997 would discover the 1991 financing statement with the continuation statement attached. The searcher would know that Firstbank's priority date was in 1991. Had Firstbank filed a second financing statement in 1995 instead of a continuation statement, the 1997 search would discover only the 1995 financing statement; the 1991 financing statement would, by that time, have met the paper shredder. The searcher might have no way of knowing that the 1991 filing was ever made.

So long as new filers entering the system know their own priority, what difference does it make whether the filing system continues to show the initial priority dates of the earlier interests? Perhaps not much. So long as each filer keeps a certified copy of its own filing, the shredding of the filing officer's copy will not prevent the parties from reconstructing the situation. Perhaps the continuation system is designed to guard against the forgery of backdated financing statements after a dispute has arisen. Perhaps a later filer will want to know the order of priority between earlier filers and not trust what they say. Whatever the reasons, U.C.C. §9-515 distinguishes between a continuation statement and a later-filed financing statement, and the courts generally enforce the distinction with a vengeance.

Worthen Bank & Trust Co., N.A. v. Hilyard Drilling Co. (In re Hilyard Drilling Co.)

840 F.2d 596 (8th Cir. 1988)

WOLLMAN, CIRCUIT JUDGE . . .

I

On April 25, 1979, [Hilyard Drilling Co. (Hilyard)] granted [the National Bank of Commerce of El Dorado (NBC)] a security interest in all of its existing and future accounts receivable, and the proceeds thereof. This security interest was perfected by the filing of appropriate financing statements on April 26, 1979.

On April 28, 1983, Paul C. Watson, Jr., [a vice president of Worthen Bank & Trust Co., N.A. (Worthen)] wrote a letter to Hilyard, which stated in relevant part:

> Confirming our telephone conversation, our Loan Committee has approved a renewal of your $550,000 equipment line and your $500,000 short-term working capital line on the following conditions:
>
> 1. That Worthen take a second lien position on accounts receivable . . .
>
> I do not think that any of these items present a problem to you since we have previously discussed these. I understand that you need to talk with [NBC] regarding the receivables. We acknowledge their first lien and would be happy to do so in writing so that it is clear to everyone that our lien is junior to theirs.

NBC never requested a written acknowledgment. On June 14, 1983, Hilyard granted Worthen a security interest in the same accounts receivable. Neither Worthen's loan documents nor the financing statements it filed on June 14, 1983, stated that Worthen's security interest was subordinate to NBC's security interest.

On July 8, 1983, in connection with the reworking of Hilyard's loans, NBC filed a new financing statement giving notice of its security interest in Hilyard's accounts receivable. NBC did not file a continuation statement within six months preceding April 25, 1984, the expiration date of its 1979 financing statement, as required by [U.C.C. §9-515(d)].

On July 6, 1984, Eugene G. Sayre, Hilyard's attorney, wrote a letter to Steven C. Wade, a commercial loan officer at Worthen, which stated in relevant part:

> The only matter which I want to make absolutely sure is clarified deals with 4.(a) on accounts receivable. Though the Loan Agreement does not reflect

it, Hilyard Drilling Company, Inc., has previously made an assignment of its accounts receivable to the National Bank of Commerce of El Dorado, Arkansas. Thus, if the NBC in El Dorado has filed its financing statement and security agreement, Worthen Bank & Trust Company, N.A., would have a "second" position on these assets. As we have discussed, that was the intention of all parties concerned, as reflected in Paul Watson, Jr.'s letter to Ray Hilyard of April 28, 1983.

[Hilyard filed a Chapter 11 bankruptcy petition on January 25, 1985.] The schedule of assets filed in connection with Hilyard's Chapter 11 bankruptcy indicated that the debts to NBC and Worthen exceeded Hilyard's accounts receivable. Worthen filed a motion with the bankruptcy court for the determination of the priority of the security interests in Hilyard's accounts receivable. The bankruptcy court determined that Worthen's security interest was first in priority. On appeal, the district court affirmed the findings of the bankruptcy court. . . .

II

The effectiveness of a financing statement lapses five years from the date of filing, unless a continuation statement is filed prior to its lapse. [U.C.C. §§9-515(a), (c) and (d)]. Thus, unless NBC filed a continuation statement, its April 26, 1979, financing statement lapsed on April 25, 1984, prior to the filing of Hilyard's bankruptcy petition. NBC argues that its July 8, 1983, financing statement should be treated as a continuation statement under [U.C.C. §9-515(c)]. We disagree.

Under [U.C.C. §9-515(d)], a continuation statement must be filed within six months prior to the expiration of the original filing and "must be signed by the secured party, identify the original statement by file number and state that the original statement is still effective." [Editor's note: See U.C.C. §9-102(27).]

NBC admits that its July 8, 1983, financing statement does not satisfy the specific statutory requirements for a continuation statement because it "was not filed within six months of the expiration of the original financing statement, it does not refer to the file number of that financing statement, and it does not state that the original financing statement is still effective." NBC nonetheless argues that its July 8, 1983, financing statement should be treated as a continuation statement because its failure to fulfill the requirements of [U.C.C. §9-102(a)(27)] is "harmless error," comparable to that addressed in [U.C.C. §9-506(a)].

Without determining whether the harmless error concept applies to [U.C.C. §9-102(a)(27)],[6] the bankruptcy court found that NBC's July 8, 1983, financing statement did not substantially comply with the requirements for a continuation statement. This finding is not clearly erroneous.

Financing statements and continuation statements serve distinct and different purposes. A financing statement that does not refer to the original filing cannot suffice as a continuation statement. Bostwick-Braun Co. v. Owens, 634 F. Supp. 839, 841 (E.D. Wis. 1986). Compare In re Barnes, 15 U.C.C. Rep. Serv. 956, 962 (D. Me. 1974) (financing statement that specifically stated it was for "the purpose of continuing the Financing Statement filed with Town Clerk 5/1/67" provided the necessary linkage to original financing statement). NBC's failure to file a continuation statement cannot be considered harmless error, because the second financing statement gave no indication that it was filed for the purpose of continuing any other financing statement.

In addition, the fact that Worthen was aware of NBC's once-perfected security interest does not render harmless NBC's failure to file a proper continuation statement. "[S]ince the purpose of statutory filing requirements is, in most instances, to resolve notice disputes consistently and predictably by reference to constructive or statutory notice alone . . . consideration of a junior creditor's actual notice of a now lapsed prior filing by a competing senior creditor" is precluded. Bostwick-Braun Co., 634 F. Supp. at 841.

III

NBC argues that even if its July 8, 1983, financing statement is not considered a continuation statement, its security interest is first in priority because it was continuously perfected from April 26, 1979, pursuant to [U.C.C. §§9-308(c) and 9-322(a)(1)]. . . .

To interpret [U.C.C. §9-308(c)] as providing that a security interest can be continuously perfected by consecutively filed financing statements contradicts the express language of [U.C.C. §9-515(c)]. [U.C.C. §9-308(c)] is applicable to security interests that are originally perfected in one way and then subsequently perfected in some other way, without an intermediate unperfected period. NBC, which initially perfected by filing, subsequently perfected in the same way, by filing, as opposed to "in

---

6. The district court determined that "substantial compliance under [U.C.C. §9-506(a)] pertains to the formal requisites of a financing statement, not a continuation statement." In re Hilyard Drilling Co., 74 Bankr. at 128. Because we have determined that NBC did not substantially comply with the requirements of [U.C.C. §9-102(a)(27)], it is unnecessary for us to address this issue.

some other way" as required by the statute. [U.C.C. §9-308(c)] is inapplicable to NBC's security interest in Hilyard's accounts receivable. . . .

Worthen's security interest had first priority pursuant to [U.C.C. §9-322(a)(1)]. NBC's April 26, 1979, financing statement lapsed due to its failure to file a continuation statement, leaving the underlying security interest unperfected. [U.C.C. §9-515(c)]. Following the lapse, the other perfected security interests in Hilyard's accounts receivable advanced in priority. Of the remaining perfected security interests, Worthen's interest had priority because it was first in time of filing or perfection.

In an earlier case, In re Hays, 47 B.R. 546 (Bankr. N.D. Ohio 1985), Production Credit Association (PCA) perfected its security interest by filing a financing statement in 1976. In 1981, PCA filed a second financing statement instead of the continuation statement it should have filed. In 1982, the Farmer's Home Administration (FmHA) filed a financing statement against the same collateral. After PCA's original 1976 financing statement expired, the court held that PCA was unperfected and awarded priority to FmHA. The court reasoned that by attempting to substitute a financing statement for a continuation statement, PCA had "disregard[ed] a positive legislative enactment." That rendered the second financing statement a nullity and left PCA unperfected even though it had a facially correct financing statement on file at all relevant times. The court cited the predecessor of U.C.C. §9-515(c), which used almost the same language:

> The effectiveness of a filed financing statement lapses on the expiration of the five-year period. . . . Upon lapse the security interest becomes unperfected, unless it is perfected without filing.

While the result in *Hays* is consistent with the language of U.C.C. §9-515(c), we see no harm to the system that could have been caused by allowing PCA's second financing statement to operate as a financing statement rather than as a continuation statement, giving PCA a 1981 priority date.

The courts have generally been harsh in their treatment of errors in the filing of continuation statements. When creditors file continuation statements after their financing statements have lapsed, the courts uniformly hold the continuation statements ineffective, even if no one was prejudiced by the error. See U.C.C. §9-510(c) (providing that "[a] continuation statement that is not filed within the six-month period prescribed by Section 9-515(d) is ineffective"). Some explain it doctrinally, saying that upon lapse of the financing statement there was no longer a filing to be continued. The result also can be explained through the imagery of the filing system as conveyor belt: By the time the filing officer processes a late-filed continuation statement, the financing statement might already have met its fate in the paper shredder.

It is more difficult to explain why a continuation statement filed too early should be ineffective. That is, nevertheless, the law. See, e.g., U.C.C. §9-510(c), Lorain Music Co. v. Allied Inv. Credit Corp., 535 N.E.2d 345 (1987) (continuation statement filed seven months before expiration of five-year period was ineffective; creditor lost his status as first perfected security interest holder when original statement expired).

To explore the problems early filing might create, assume that Firstbank files its financing statement on April 1, 1991, and then files a premature continuation statement on April 1, 1993. If the continuation statement were held effective, it would continue the filing to March 31, 2001. U.C.C. §9-515(e). Thus, there will be a period of more than six years between the filing of the continuation statement and the lapse of the filing. If we employ the image of the conveyor belt leading to the paper shredder, interrupted only when the filer jogs the filing officer to action by filing another continuation statement, the possibility looms that both financing statement and continuation statement will have gone to the shredder before March 31, 2001, while the filing remains effective.

We can only speculate, however, on the degree to which the actual systems employed to purge lapsed filings resemble the conveyor belt image we invoke. Nothing need go to the shredder unless the filing officer sends it. Because so many filed financing statements are preserved on microfilm or microfiche, we doubt that many filing officers actually destroy their only copy in the few years following lapse. (Whether these lapsed filings will show up on a search is another matter. The typical search request is only for presently effective filings. U.C.C. §9-523(c).)

The American Bar Association's Article 9 Filing System Task Force recommended elimination of the six-month prelapse period for filing continuation statements, saying that modern record keeping practices are able to accommodate early continuation statements with delayed effective dates. The Article 9 Study Group that preceded the Drafting Committee recommended that the Drafting Committee "give attention to existing problems in the following areas: (xix) expansion or removal of the 6-month prelapse period for filing continuation statements." Recommendation 11. Ignoring both groups, the Drafting Committee retained the six-month window, presumably merely as a trap for the unwary. It seems to serve no other function.

Upon lapse, the security interest "becomes unperfected" and "is deemed never to have been perfected as against a purchaser of the collateral for value." U.C.C. §9-515(c). This retroactive loss of priority does not apply in favor of a lien creditor (or the trustee in bankruptcy). Provided that the security interest was perfected at the time the lien creditor levied (or at the filing of the bankruptcy petition), the secured creditor retains priority over the lien creditor or trustee. See Comment 3 to U.C.C. §9-515. The security interest will, however, be subordinate to a lien creditor that levies after lapse and to the trustee in a bankruptcy filed after lapse.

C. The Effect of Bankruptcy on Lapse and Continuation

Under earlier versions of Article 9, there was confusion over the effect of bankruptcy on lapse and continuation. The confusion has now been resolved. A secured party must file continuation statements at five-year intervals to avoid lapse. No exception is made simply because the debtor has filed bankruptcy. See U.C.C. §9-515(c). The filing of continuation statements during the pendency of the bankruptcy case does not violate the automatic stay. Bankruptcy Code §§362(b)(3), 546(b)(1)(B).

Problem Set 22

22.1. Your client, the Bank of East Palatka, perfected its $728,000 security interest in equipment owned by Horst Manufacturing by filing a financing statement on December 30, 1990. The bank filed a continuation statement on July 7, 1995. Today, March 22, 1999, Jan Swift, a loan officer from the bank, asks you the following questions:

a. Did the Bank file its prior continuation statement at the proper time? U.C.C. §9-515.

b. Swift wants to put on her calendar the time when she should file the next continuation statement for this filing. When will it be due?

c. A week after you answered those questions for Jan Swift, Horst Manufacturing filed a case under Chapter 11 of the Bankruptcy Code. Swift expects that the case will probably extend for about two years, but of course that time could vary. Swift would like to know if this changes your advice about the proper time for filing the Bank's next continuation statement. What do you tell her? Bankr. Code §362(b)(3); U.C.C. §9-515.

22.2. The discussion with Jan Swift reminded you that you did some U.C.C. closings in your early years of practice but hadn't yet realized the need to calendar your filings for continuation. You pulled the files and found that you filed one of the financing statements five years and two months ago on behalf of Juan Gomez. Gomez had sold his restaurant to The Cantina, Incorporated, and taken back a security interest in all of the restaurant equipment, including after-acquired property. The $60,000 note for the purchase price was amortized over 12 years, with a balloon payment at the end of six. A quick search in the filing system reveals that you're not the only one who didn't think about continuation; no continuation statement is on file for the financing statement you filed. What do you do now? U.C.C. §§9-102(39), 9-515, and §9-516(b)(7); 9-509(b).

22.3.   Two weeks ago, the Wriggling Brothers Circus (founded by the great escape artists) filed under Chapter 11. This was of some concern to you, because your client, Mark Ryerson, holds a $120,000 first security interest in most of the assets of the circus. Associates Financial Partners (Associates) also holds a security interest in the same property, securing their loan for over $1 million. Both interests were created at the same time, about nine years ago. Ryerson's financing statement was filed first; Associates' later the same day. Both creditors filed continuation statements in a timely fashion.

Associates is represented by Millie Parker. When you spoke to Parker this morning about the bankruptcy case, she tweaked you by casually referring to Ryerson's interest as a "second." When you pointed out that Ryerson filed before Associates, she said that wasn't controlling because Associates had possession of the circus assets on the day the two filings were made. You can't remember anything about possession of the circus assets nine years ago, and neither can Ryerson. Would it matter if Parker were right about possession of the circus nine years ago? U.C.C. §§9-515, 9-308(c), 9-322(a)(1).

22.4.   Philip Ghandi, a real estate broker, recently bought 16 lots in Brook Meadow, a residential subdivision, for $320,000. He financed the purchase with a $160,000 loan from Equity Investment Group (EIG) that is secured by a mortgage against the 16 lots. Ghandi has arranged to sell one of the lots for $30,000. When EIG learned about the sale, they told him that "of course, the entire proceeds of the sale must be applied against the mortgage." Ghandi says he can't do that, because there will be expenses of sale, including the fees of another broker involved in the deal that have to be paid. Ghandi would like you to "get tough with EIG, and free up some of this cash flow." What do you plan to say to EIG?

22.5.   a. You represent Firstbank. The bank's security agreement covers 12 fork lifts, a stamping machine, and all "replacements or additions." The bank initially lent $40,000 to the debtor, Beaver Manufacturing, and the loan balance currently stands at $21,174. Firstbank's financing statement covers "equipment." Now Beaver is trying to borrow money against its drill presses. It wants you to put a release in the filing system for the drill presses and office furniture, neither of which is covered by our security agreement. Firstbank does not want to give the release because it hopes to force Beaver to pay the loan off early or agree to a higher rate of interest. Your security agreement contains no provisions regarding release of collateral. Do you have to give Beaver the release? U.C.C. §§9-513, 9-512.

b. If you don't, will Beaver be able to assure another lender that it will have the first filed security agreement against the drill presses? Could Beaver solve its problem by demanding from you a written statement of collateral and showing it to the new lender? U.C.C. §§9-210, 9-401(b), 9-502(d), 9-322(a)(1).

22.6. Joe and Mary Suarez have contracted to sell their house and asked you to handle the closing. The first mortgage, originally given to First Florida Savings and Loan but now owned by Global Mortgage Service company of Newark, New Jersey, is to be paid in full at the closing.

Global has been very difficult to deal with. It was slow to respond to your request for an "estoppel letter" showing the balance owing on the mortgage. When Global did respond, its number, $42,678, was suspiciously high. After a laborious comparison of the mortgage amortization schedule and the Suarezes' payment record, you concluded that the correct balance was $40,711: Global was demanding $1,967 more than what was owed them. When you finally got someone from Global to talk to you on the phone, you discovered that Global had failed to credit the Suarezes for two payments they had actually made (Mrs. Suarez showed you cancelled checks) and had charged the Suarezes' account with "administrative fees" not authorized by the mortgage. The final blow was a $350 fee for recalculating the account and sending you the estoppel letter. Such a fee is neither customary, nor provided for in the mortgage. Despite your protests, the Global representative will not make any change in the estoppel letter.

The mortgage contract provides that in the event of default, the Suarezes will pay the secured creditor's attorneys' fees and costs, but does not provide for the secured creditor to pay the Suarezes' attorneys' fees under any circumstances. The closing is scheduled for 40 days from today. If you don't have a satisfaction of mortgage from Global, your clients won't be able to convey marketable title to the buyers and the deal may fall through. Mike Schwartz, attorney for the buyer, says his client won't disburse the purchase price unless "there's a satisfaction from Global on the table." The sale price is at about the market, but the Suarezes don't want to lose the sale because it may take a lot of time to find another buyer and they fear that this buyer might sue them. What is your advice? If this property is in Florida, is there any way that the Florida satisfaction of mortgage statute might be of help? Would the Suarezes be better off or worse off if the property was in Arizona?

22.7. Assume that the sale in the previous problem had been of the Suarezes' business equipment rather than their residence, and therefore governed by Article 9. Would they be in a stronger or a weaker position? U.C.C. §9-513.

22.8. Harry Montague, a senior partner in your firm, heard that you took an advanced course in secured transactions in law school and has invited you to lunch. The governor recently appointed Harry to the National Conference of Commissioners on Uniform State Laws. (Surely you remember that bunch that shares control of the official text of the U.C.C. and the other uniform and model acts.) NCCUSL is considering revisions to Article 9. Harry didn't take secured transactions in law school and cheerfully admits that he knows nothing about the subject. Nonetheless, a NCCUSL committee of which Harry is a member is about to vote on a proposed amendment to U.C.C. §9-515 that would permit the filers of financing statements to choose the length of time for which they would be effective. The options would be 5, 10, 15, or 20 years. After that time, the secured parties could still file continuation statements. Harry, whose background is in real estate, doesn't see why there ought to be any time limit on the effectiveness of filings at all. If they need a limit on regular filings, Harry says, how come they don't need one on mortgages that reach fixtures? U.C.C. §9-515(g). Harry asks your opinion. What do you tell him?

Assignment 23: Maintaining Perfection Through Changes of Name, Identity, and Use

Communication in real time is hard enough. As we saw in earlier assignments, a secured creditor who attempts to name its debtor or describe the collateral in which it claims an interest may have difficulty finding the right words. In this assignment, we discuss the additional complexity that arises because communication through the filing system does not occur in real time.

The filer's message may be in the filing system for years before the searcher looks for it. In the interim, the circumstances that shaped the message may have changed. The debtor who comes to the searcher for a loan may have changed her name and address since the filer put its financing statement on file. If the debtor does not reveal the debtor's old name and address to the searcher, the searcher may have difficulty finding the financing statement that is on file. Collateral described accurately on the financing statement may have changed so drastically in use and appearance that even if the searcher finds the old financing statement it will be unable to link the collateral it sees to the description on the statement. Remember that one of the changes collateral can undergo is exchange for proceeds. The proceeds may neither look nor be anything at all like the original collateral described in the financing statement. For example, the financing statement may describe the collateral as "beans," but by the time the debtor seeks a loan from the searcher, the debtor may have traded the beans for a circus elephant.

One way to deal with this problem is to hold the financing statement ineffective if it would not be effective as a new financing statement in the changed circumstances. That places responsibility on the filer to monitor the circumstances, discover changes, and make appropriate amendments to the financing statement.

Another way to deal with the problem is to hold that an initially effective financing statement remains effective even though circumstances change. That places responsibility on the searcher to discover the previous circumstances of the debtor and the collateral and then search for statements filed effectively under those circumstances. By thorough investigation, the searcher may be able to discover what changes have occurred and adjust its search to account for them.

The drafters of Article 9 chose to use a little of each approach, mixing them in a manner sufficiently complex to win them a place in both the law school curriculum and most state bar exams. In this assignment we explore that mix and raise questions about its impact: To what extent are both old filers *and* new searchers required to monitor the collateral, the debtor, or the public record to protect themselves? What is the cost of such monitoring? The cost of failing to monitor?

As you study the balance that has been struck between filer and searcher, you will be tempted to interpret each rule as placing an obligation on filers or searchers to do something. There is no harm in doing so, so long as you realize that in many situations real filers and searchers do not perform their obligations and can't realistically be expected to. These rules don't just tell filers and searchers what to do. In circumstances where losses are not worth the effort necessary to avoid them, the rules simply allocate those losses to the filers or searchers.

In this assignment, we focus on the three most important changes in circumstance: (1) changes of the debtor's name, (2) changes affecting the description of collateral, and (3) the conversion of the collateral into proceeds.

A.   Changes in the Debtor's Name

Individuals, corporations, and other entities can, and sometimes do, change their names. If a debtor changes names between the time a filing is made against the debtor and the time a search for that filing is made, the change may — or may not — cause the communication to fail. To illustrate, assume that Adams Corporation borrows money from Firstbank in 2001 and gives Firstbank a security interest in all of Adams's assets. Firstbank perfects by filing. In 2002, Adams Corporation changes its name to Baker Corporation. Firstbank does not learn of the change of name, so it does not amend its financing statement to reflect it. In 2003, the corporation applies to Secondbank for a loan and offers the same assets as collateral. Secondbank, who does not discover the change of name either, conducts its search only under the name "Baker Corporation." Of course, the search does not discover Firstbank's filing.

That is not to say that Secondbank *could not* have discovered Firstbank's filing through a search. A corporate debtor's change of name is a matter of public record. Even without the debtor's cooperation, Secondbank could have discovered it by (1) insisting that the debtor prove its incorporation under the laws of some state or country, (2) searching the records of that state or country for changes of the debtor's name, and (3) having discovered that the debtor was previously named Adams Corporation, conducting its search in that name as well as in Baker Corporation.

By going to some extra trouble, Firstbank could also have prevented this failure of communication. If Firstbank had been sensitive to changes in its borrower, it might have noticed the change on the debtor's letterhead, checks, or bank accounts. Even if the debtor did nothing to publicize the change, Firstbank could have discovered it by periodically checking the corporate records of the state in which the debtor was incorporated. When it discovered the change, Firstbank could have amended its financing statement to reflect it. By these methods, Firstbank could have minimized the time during which its financing statement was indexed only under an obsolete name, but it could not have entirely eliminated it. For example, even if Firstbank checked the corporate records for borrower changes of name every four months, its filings could be indexed under former names for up to four months plus the time it took Firstbank to amend its filing.

Were Adams an individual instead of a corporation, the banks might have found it more difficult to discover her change of name from Juanita Adams to Juanita Baker. Evidence of the change might be in the records of any of thousands of courts or not in any public record at all. Either bank might have discovered the change by checking the debtor's driver's license or other identification, but only if they checked both before and after the change. Although discovery of an individual name change is likely to be more difficult than discovery of a corporate name change, once the creditor discovers the former the analysis for determining what action is required is the same as for the latter.

U.C.C. §9-507(c) provides that even though a change in the debtor's name renders a filed financing statement seriously misleading, the financing statement remains effective with regard to (1) collateral owned by the debtor at the time of the name change and (2) collateral acquired by the debtor in the first four months after the change. The seriously misleading financing statement is not, however, effective to perfect a security interest in collateral acquired by the debtor more than four months after the change.

Under this rule, a secured party that financed the purchase of a specific item of collateral (such as a boat) has no reason to concern itself with later changes in the debtor's name. On the other hand, a secured party that is financing the debtor's inventory of boats on a continuing basis should concern itself with changes in the debtor's name. The secured party's filing will not be effective against inventory the debtor acquires more than four months after the debtor changes its name. An inventory financier who fails to notice the debtor's name change for a period of a year might find that its filing is no longer effective against anything of real value.

The name-change rule of U.C.C. §9-507(c) potentially affects every searcher. Even though a search in the current, correct name of the debtor discovers no filings against the collateral, there may be a filing in the debtor's former name that remains effective against the proposed collateral. Depending on the amount of money at stake and the degree to which the searcher trusts the debtor, the searcher may want to investigate the possibility of changes in the debtor's name.

It may have occurred to you in reading the preceding paragraphs that there is one person who could easily keep track of the debtor's name and make sure changes have been promptly memorialized in amendments to the relevant financing statements — the debtor. Although this is true, it is not very helpful. Most security agreements do in fact contain a promise by the debtor to notify the secured party of the debtor's change of name as well as the other kinds of changes that affect the effectiveness of filings. Most debtors, particularly those who have decided to borrow twice against the same collateral, fail to give notice nevertheless. Their failure constitutes a breach of contract, for which they will have civil liability, but that is of little concern to most debtors. If they pay their debts, their lenders won't care whether they gave notice. If they do not pay their debts, their liability for their failures to give notice of their changes of name adds nothing of consequence to their liability on the debts themselves.

The situation would be different if the failure to give notice subjected the debtor to criminal prosecution or even rendered the debt nondischargeable in bankruptcy. They do not. To impose such penalties on a debtor without proof of fraudulent intent is entirely out of keeping with legal tradition in the United States. We live in a nation founded in large part by people who did not pay their debts in the places from which they came. Our tolerance for debtor misbehavior is relatively high in relation to the tolerance shown in other cultures. In spite of this tolerance, or perhaps because of it, the U.S. economy has done relatively well. Neither the criminal nor the bankruptcy authorities are likely to get exercised about a debtor's failure to comply with a contractual obligation by giving notice of a change in circumstances.

For all these reasons, the systems created under the laws governing security in the United States are designed to function without the cooperation of the debtor. Lenders are expected to fend for themselves. B.T. Lazarus v. Christofides, 662 N.E.2d 41 (Ohio App. 1996) illustrates the kind of vigilance required. In that case, the creditor took a security interest in the assets of B.T.L. Inc. The creditor delayed the filing of its financing statement for nearly four months after the signing of the security agreement. In the period between the signing and the filing, B.T.L. Inc. changed its name to Alma Marketing, Inc. The court held the filing ineffective.

You should not conclude from our comments that filers or searchers now stalk their debtors for evidence of changes of name. Changes of name are somewhat uncommon. In most instances, either the filer or the searcher will discover them without much effort and take appropriate action. But at the same time, you should realize that the filing system has no fail-safe mechanism for dealing with name changes. Some debtors, particularly those who change their names for the purpose of defrauding their secured lenders, will succeed in borrowing from a second lender who searches, but who does not discover the first lender.

Even though the governing rules are similar, it is important to distinguish changes of name, which are covered by U.C.C. §9-507(c), from the transfer of collateral to a new debtor, which is covered by U.C.C. §9-507(a). To illustrate the potential for confusion, assume that while doing business as a sole proprietor, Teresa Williams borrowed money against the equipment of her business. If Teresa later incorporates the business under the name Williams Electronics, Inc., that is not a change of name. That is the formation of a new entity, probably followed by a transfer of the collateral from Teresa to the corporation. The governing law would be U.C.C. §9-507(a). The financing statement filed against Teresa would be effective against the collateral in the hands of Williams Electronics.

B.   Changes Affecting the Description of Collateral

If the collateral undergoes changes in its appearance, use, or location between the time a filing is made and a search for that filing is commenced, the changes may prevent the searcher from finding the filing or realizing its relevance. To understand these changes, begin by distinguishing two kinds.

Type 1 Changes. The first, which we will call a *type 1* change, is a change in circumstances that did not control the place of filing but that does make the collateral difficult for the searcher to identify as covered by the filing. For example, assume that Firstbank's security agreement correctly describes the collateral as "Coyote Loader, serial number 8203G45," that the debtor holds the loader as inventory at the time Firstbank files its financing statement, and that the financing statement describes the type of collateral as "inventory." Firstbank is perfected. Later, the debtor begins using the loader as equipment and seeks to borrow against it from Secondbank. Secondbank's search will discover Firstbank's financing statement, but Secondbank may not realize its significance. Secondbank is lending against equipment, and the filing they discover is only against inventory.

U.C.C. §9-507(b) addresses this example. That section provides that even if the change in circumstances has made the financing statement seriously misleading, the financing statement remains effective.

Type 2 Changes. A type 2 change in circumstances is one that is sufficient to affect the method of perfection that would have been appropriate for the initial filing. For example, assume that Dawson Lumber takes a security interest in lumber it sells to Michelle Pfeiffer and perfects by filing a financing statement in the office of the secretary of state. Later, Pfeiffer uses the lumber to build a hot tub that is attached to real property in such a manner that it becomes a fixture. U.C.C. §9-507(b) excuses the now-seriously-misleading description of collateral, but it does not excuse the failure to make a fixture filing. The same would be true of a financing statement that described automobiles on a dealer's lot as "inventory." If some of the automobiles are then used as equipment, U.C.C. §9-507(b) excuses the misdescription, but probably not the failure to require issuance of a certificate of title noting the security interest. U.C.C. §9-311(b).

C. Exchange of the Collateral

When a debtor exchanges collateral for either property or cash, the effect is to raise many of the same kinds of issues we discussed in the preceding section. Recall from Assignment 10 that on sale, exchange, collection, or other disposition of collateral, a security interest continues in identifiable proceeds. U.C.C. §§9-102(a)(64) and 9-315(a)(2). The holder of the security interest will want (1) the security interest to be perfected in the proceeds and (2) the perfection to be continuous from the creditor's initial filing. In this section, we examine what the secured creditor must do (if anything) to accomplish those two things.

1. Barter Transactions

Barter is the exchange of one commodity for another in a transaction in which no cash is involved. The rules in U.C.C. §9-315(d)(1) governing perfection in a barter exchange are different from the rules governing perfection in an exchange for cash that is then used to purchase the commodity. In this subsection we discuss only the barter transaction; the rules governing perfection in cash proceeds and proceeds acquired with cash proceeds are discussed in the next two sections.

To understand when secured parties must take action to perfect their interests in proceeds, distinguish three types of barters. We refer to them as *type 0, type 1, and type 2* so we can retain the numbering from the previous section. In a type 0 barter, the proceeds received by the debtor fall within the description of collateral in the already-filed financing statement. For example, assume that the security agreement described the collateral as "Coyote Loader, serial number 8203G45" and the financing statement, properly filed only in the office of the secretary of state, described the type of collateral as "loader." The debtor trades the Coyote loader for a Caterpillar loader. The security interest attaches to the Caterpillar loader as proceeds even without a statement to that effect in the security agreement. U.C.C. §9-203(f). The security interest is perfected in the Caterpillar loader because the description "loader" is broad enough to encompass it. (Recall that "A financing statement may be filed before a security agreement is made. . . ." U.C.C. §9-502(d).) After this type 0 barter, the secured creditor has a perfected security interest in the new collateral on the basis of the description; it need not rely on U.C.C. §9-315 at all.

A type 1 barter is an exchange of collateral for noncash proceeds where those proceeds are property not covered by the description in the financing statement but are property in which a security interest could be perfected by filing in the office where the secured creditor's financing statement is already on file. For example, the debtor's exchange of inventory for equipment would be a type 1 barter if the original financing statement covered only inventory. The equipment is not covered by the description in the financing statement, but the filing needed to perfect in equipment as original collateral would be made in the same filing office.

In a type 1 barter transaction, the secured party remains perfected without a new filing. The rule is contained in U.C.C. §9-315(d)(1). To illustrate, assume that the financing statement covers only inventory and the debtor trades inventory for a circus elephant that will not be inventory. The secured party remains perfected in the elephant without further action. Because this rule applies only to barter transactions, which are in themselves usually a bit odd, we refer to it as *the elephant rule*.

The elephant rule has potentially interesting implications for searchers. To illustrate, assume that Firstbank takes a security interest in the debtor's inventory and files a financing statement describing the collateral as "inventory." Later, the debtor trades some inventory for an elephant. Under the rule, Firstbank remains perfected against the elephant. When Secondbank conducts a search in preparation for lending against the elephant, which we assume is clearly and obviously not inventory, Secondbank finds only a filing against inventory. If, however, Secondbank is aware of the elephant rule, it will realize that Firstbank may be perfected in the elephant and know that it cannot be sure that it will have the first recorded interest in the elephant without exploring how the debtor came to own the elephant.

To generalize from this example, any time a debtor has swapped collateral, the financing statement may encumber property not described in it. Unless the searcher knows that the debtor did not acquire the collateral in question in a swap transaction, the searcher cannot rely on the description of collateral in any financing statement.

A type 2 barter is an exchange of collateral for noncash proceeds of a type in which filing is required in a filing office other than the one in which the original collateral was perfected by filing. For example, if a debtor traded a Coyote Loader that it used as equipment for an automobile and an aircraft, that would be a type 2 barter. Security interests in equipment are perfected by filing in the office of the secretary of state; security interests in automobiles are perfected by recordation on the certificate of title by the Department of Motor Vehicles; security interests in aircraft are perfected by filing with the Federal Aviation Administration in Oklahoma City.

Type 2 barters do not invoke the exception created by U.C.C. §9-315(d)(1) from the Article 9 filing requirement. To be perfected in these proceeds at all, the secured party must refile. In the case of the automobile, the new filing will be in the Department of Motor Vehicles, so that the security interest will be noted on the certificate of title. For the aircraft, the new filing will be with the FAA in Oklahoma City. To be *continuously* perfected in the two items so that it has one perfection dating from the time of the filing on the original collateral, the secured party must make these filings within 20 days from the time the debtor receives the proceeds. U.C.C. §9-315(d)(3).

The rules for type 2 barters require more vigilance on the part of the secured creditor, and, consequently, less on the part of the subsequent searcher. The secured creditor must discover the type 2 barter and perfect in the proceeds within 20 days of the debtor's receipt of them. Unless the filer is in a relationship that warrants close physical monitoring of the collateral, the filer may not learn of the exchange in time. The subsequent searcher need only realize that the debtor may have encumbered proceeds in its possession for as long as 20 days before anything shows up on the public records.

To the extent Article 9 governs, the secured party does not need any additional authorization to file the financing statement necessary to perfect in the proceeds of collateral. U.C.C. §9-509(b)(2). Were such authorization required, some debtors would refuse to give it, thereby preventing their creditors from perfecting in the proceeds. Not requiring further authorization relieves creditors of the fear that their debtors can block them from reaching the proceeds of their own collateral. It also makes it possible for aggressive secured creditors to file financing statements erroneously claiming collateral as proceeds.

The following case illustrates the effect of the opposite rule. In this case, the debtor who had given an Article 9 security interest exchanged the collateral for proceeds not governed by Article 9, producing unexpected consequences.

National Bank of Alaska v. Erickson (In re Seaway Express Corp.)

912 F.2d 1125 (9th Cir. 1990)

BEEZER, CIRCUIT JUDGE.

The National Bank of Alaska (NBA) appeals a decision of the Bankruptcy Appellate Panel (BAP), granting summary judgment to Erickson, trustee in the bankruptcy of Seaway Express Corp. (Seaway). NBA claims a priority interest in property owned by Seaway. The BAP rejected NBA's claim. We affirm.

I

During 1985-86, NBA provided a line of credit to Seaway secured by a credit agreement. Under the agreement, Seaway's credit line was set as a percentage of its inventory and "eligible" accounts receivable (accounts less than 90 days old). NBA eventually loaned Seaway over $9 million, of which at least $6 million remains owing. In exchange, Seaway granted NBA a security interest in all its inventory and accounts receivable, including any "proceeds" from the sale of either (outside the normal course of business). Seaway promised not to dispose of any of its secured assets without NBA's permission.

This dispute concerns an account receivable owed to Seaway by Anchorage Fairbanks Freight Service, Inc. (AFFS). By the end of 1985, AFFS owed Seaway in excess of $1 million. The account was over 90 days old and Seaway commenced legal action to collect it. In settlement, Seaway "sold" the account back to AFFS in exchange for a parcel of real property located in Auburn, Washington (the Auburn property). NBA was aware of the proposed settlement, but did not consent or object. After the transfer had been completed, NBA asked Seaway to record a deed of trust on the property in its favor. Seaway refused.

In February, 1986, Seaway declared bankruptcy under Chapter 11. It sold the Auburn property for approximately $1 million. The funds were placed in a segregated account. Seaway's bankruptcy was subsequently converted to Chapter 7, and Erickson was appointed the bankruptcy trustee.

NBA now claims it has a priority interest in the proceeds of the sale of the Auburn property . . . as "proceeds" from the sale of the AFFS account. . . .

II

A

NBA first argues that it had a perfected security interest in the Auburn property. We disagree.

Under its credit agreement with Seaway, NBA did have a perfected security interest in the AFFS account. Under the terms of the agreement and under the UCC, this interest continued in the "proceeds" of any unauthorized sale of the account. See [U.C.C. §9-315(a)]. NBA need only perfect its interest in the proceeds within [twenty] days of the sale. [U.C.C. §9-315(c),(d)(3)]. When perfection is impossible due to the actions of the debtor, such an interest may be deemed perfected.

NBA argues that under these principles, its interest in the Auburn property should be deemed perfected. It contends that the sale of the AFFS account was not authorized and that it attempted to perfect its interest in the Auburn property but was prevented by Seaway. We reject NBA's argument.

NBA concedes that by its terms the UCC does not extend to real property. See [U.C.C. §9-109(d)(11)]. NBA cites no case in which a perfected interest in UCC-covered goods has been extended to real property. Good reasons exist not to do so here. To "perfect" an interest in real property under Washington law, a party must record a deed signed by the grantor. An unrecorded interest in property is not binding on a subsequent purchaser in good faith. Such recording statutes are central to real property law.

We agree with the BAP that NBA's perfected security interest in the AFFS account did not extend to the Auburn property. . . .

AFFIRMED.

This case serves to remind secured creditors that while the Uniform Commercial Code gives them great protection by extending their security interests to proceeds, they nonetheless must make sure those security interests in proceeds are perfected. Here, the secured creditor's problem was that the law governing real estate recording did not contain a provision like U.C.C. §9-509(b)(2) allowing the secured creditor to perfect the security interest in the property into which it could trace its proceeds. The probable reason is that real estate financing is done parcel by parcel. When the debtor sells real estate, the secured party expects to be paid off or to remain secured by the same collateral in the hands of the buyer. It does not expect to leave its loan outstanding and trace the proceeds of its collateral. To put it another way, *National Bank of Alaska* does not result from legislative policy but from legislative neglect. If the designers of the real estate recording system had thought about it, they almost certainly would have adopted a provision like U.C.C. §9-509(b)(2).

2.   Collateral to Cash Proceeds to Noncash Proceeds

The debtor may exchange the original collateral for money, then use the money to buy collateral. Provided it can trace its value through both transactions, the creditor's security interest will reach the new property as proceeds of proceeds. U.C.C. §9-102(a)(12) and (64). In this section we consider the circumstances under which the original filing will give the secured creditor continuous perfection that extends to the new property.

In a type 0 change, the rule remains the same as it did in a barter transaction: The original filing remains effective to cover goods of the same description. To return to our earlier example, the security agreement described the collateral as "Coyote Loader, serial number 8203G45" and the financing statement, properly filed only in the office of the secretary of state, described the type of collateral as "loader." If the debtor sold the Coyote loader for cash and took that cash to buy a Caterpillar loader, the security interest would attach to the Caterpillar loader as proceeds and then would remain perfected because the description "loader" is broad enough to encompass it. U.C.C. §9-315(d)(3).

In a type 1 change, however, the exchange results in collateral that is no longer covered by the original description in the filing statement. Consider, again, the earlier example in which the security interest covered inventory and the debtor bartered the inventory for an elephant that would serve as the company's mascot. The creditor initially perfected in the inventory would remain continuously perfected in the elephant without taking any action. Now, assume instead that the debtor sold the inventory for cash and used the cash to buy the elephant. U.C.C. §9-315(d)(3) requires that the secured party file a financing statement to cover the new collateral. Unless the secured party accomplishes that within 20 days of the debtor's receipt of the new collateral, the perfection achieved by the filing is not continuous. If the second filing occurs within 20 days of the debtor's receipt of the new property, the second filing is effective as of the date of the first filing and perfection is continuous thereafter. If the second filing occurs after the end of the 20-day period, it dates only from the time it was made.

Type 2 changes are treated like type 1 changes. Recall that in a type 2 change the new property is of a type that requires filing in a different filing office. Here, also, the secured creditor must make the new filing within 20 days of the debtor's receipt of the collateral. To modify the earlier example, if a debtor sold its Coyote Loader for cash and used the cash to buy an automobile and an aircraft, a type 2 change has occurred. To be continuously perfected in the new property, the secured party must perfect on the certificates of title for the automobile and the aircraft within 20 days of the debtor's receipt of those items. See U.C.C. §9-315(d)(3).

3. Collateral to Cash Proceeds (No New Property)

The debtor may simply sell the original collateral and keep the cash. U.C.C. §9-315(d)(2) grants secured parties continuous, perpetual perfection in identifiable *cash proceeds*. To illustrate the application of that subsection, again assume that Firstbank has a perfected security interest in inventory. The debtor sells some of the inventory for cash and deposits the cash in its bank account at Thirdbank. The bank account is "cash proceeds." U.C.C. §9-102(a)(9). Under the rule of U.C.C. §9-315(d)(2), Firstbank will remain perfected in it even if the money sits in the bank account for months or even years.

Secured parties need not rely on perfection in proceeds under U.C.C. §9-315(d)(2). They can perfect in a deposit account as original collateral by taking "control" of the account. U.C.C. §9-314(a). "Control" is far less intrusive than the word suggests. Even if the debtor remains free to write checks on the account, the secured party is in control of the account for purposes of perfection if (1) the secured party is the bank with which the deposit account is maintained; (2) the debtor, secured party, and the bank have agreed in an authenticated record that the bank will honor instructions from the secured party without further consent from the debtor; or (3) the account is in the name of the secured party. The "control" of the secured party under any of these methods of perfection may be no more than the right to take control when it chooses to do so. We fail to see how this kind of control fulfills the notice function of perfection. See U.C.C.

§9-342, which provides that the bank need not even confirm the existence of the agreement to an inquiring searcher. But we've griped about this before.

Problem Set 23

23.1. Helen Monette is a compliance officer at Gargantuan Bank and Trust (GBT). Her job is to monitor the collateral securing loans outstanding from the Bank. Most of her work is devoted to verifying that collateral is physically in existence, but she occasionally encounters other problems. Currently, Monette is working with Bonnie Brezhnev, owner of Bonnie's Boat World Inc. (BBW). GBT finances BBW's inventory under a financing statement that describes the collateral as "inventory, accounts, and chattel paper." The agreement contains no restrictions on BBW's ability to finance equipment or real estate elsewhere. Today Monette called you with the following list of problems:

a. On a routine inspection of collateral, Monette discovered that, contrary to the provisions of the security agreement prohibiting the use of inventory, Bonnie kept one of the boats at her house and used it personally. Monette warned her not to do it again, but now wonders: Assuming no transfer of ownership to Bonnie personally, did the interlude have any effect on perfection of the bank's security interest? U.C.C. §§9-502(a)(1), 9-503(a)(1), 9-506(a), 9-507(b).

b. Assume that the facts in subpart a of this problem occurred in a jurisdiction that does not issue certificates of title for boats. If Bonnie transferred ownership of the boat from her corporation to herself before she took the boat home, what evidence would exist of that fact? If Bonnie did transfer ownership of the boat to herself, is GBT still perfected? U.C.C. §9-507(a).

c. BBW traded one of the boats for a forklift. BBW now uses the forklift to move the boats in and out of storage. Monette says she assumes the forklift is "ours" because BBW bought it with our collateral, but wonders whether we need to do anything about perfection. Do we? U.C.C. §9-315(a) and (d).

d. Would it make any difference if BBW bought the forklift in subpart c using cash it had received from a customer who bought a new boat? U.C.C. §§9-315(a) and (d).

e. About a month ago, two of the boats in inventory suffered severe storm damage. The security agreement provided that BBW would insure the boats against storm damage and required that GBT be named as a loss payee on the policy. BBW bought the insurance, but for some reason GBT was not named as a loss payee. Since the storm, BBW changed insurers and GBT is named as a loss payee on the new policy. Monette wonders whether GBT has a perfected security interest in the claim against the former insurer and, if not, what GBT needs to do to get one. U.C.C. §§9-109(d)(8), 9-102(64), 9-315(c) and (d), 9-203(f), 9-109(a).

23.2.   Recently, Monette has been monitoring GBT's inventory loan to South West Appliance Corporation. In a routine check of corporate records, Monette discovered for the first time that six months ago the debtor changed its corporate name to South West General, Inc. Does Monette need to do anything to make sure GBT remains perfected in all its collateral? U.C.C. §§9-502(a)(1), 9-503(a)(1), 9-512, 9-507(c), 9-506.

23.3.   Although GBT has never had formal procedures for discovering its debtors' name changes, GBT's recent loss of a name-change case has Monette thinking about adopting some procedures. She has three questions:

a.   How often would she have to check the corporate records to make sure she could amend GBT's financing statements in time to avoid loss of collateral? U.C.C. §9-507(c).

b.   Does a continuation statement have to include the new name of a debtor that changed its name since the original filing? U.C.C. §§9-102(27), 9-512(a), 9-516(3) and (5), form for Amendments in U.C.C. §9-521.

c.   In the investigation of a loan applicant, how old a change of name could be relevant? U.C.C. §9-515(e).

23.4.   GBT is about to lend $500,000 to Russell Lair Enterprises (RLE), which operates a small chain of army/navy surplus stores. The loan is to be secured by an interest in substantially all the debtor's assets. The U.C.C. search came back clean, except for a financing statement filed by Suti, a manufacturer of cast iron lawn dogs. The financing statement describes Suti's collateral as "lawn dogs manufactured by Suti." On Helen Monette's physical inspection of the proposed collateral, Monette found only $25,000 worth of Suti lawn dogs. GBT does not care whether the lawn dogs are included in their collateral. Unless you advise otherwise, Monette proposes to go ahead with the loan, without clearing the Suti interest or inquiring further about it. But, first, Monette wants to know: Is there any way the Suti filing could encumber more than the lawn dogs? Is there any way it could be for more than $25,000? U.C.C. §9-315.

23.5.   a. You represent October National Bank. ONB lent $1 million to Beaver Manufacturing, a local concern that produces and services commercial pumping equipment. The loan documents included a security agreement and financing statement, both of which describe the collateral as "equipment, inventory, accounts, chattel paper, general intangibles, fixtures, money, and bank accounts." You estimate the total value of all collateral at about $750,000. One of Beaver's assets is a bank account at Gargantuan Bank and Trust that contains $85,097. Does ONB have a security interest in the account? U.C.C. §§9-102(29) and (64), 9-109(d)(13), and 9-203(a) and (b); Comment 16 to U.C.C. §9-109.

b. If ONB has a security interest in the bank account, is it perfected? U.C.C. §§9-104, 9-312(b)(1), 9-314, and 9-315(d)(2).

c. Does it matter that some of the proceeds have been in the account for as long as 45 days? U.C.C. §§9-315(c) and (d).

d. Does it matter if Beaver commingled $100 of its own money into the GBT account? U.C.C. §9-315.

Assignment 24: Maintaining Perfection Through Relocation of Debtor or Collateral

In previous assignments, we implicitly assumed that every secured transaction occurred within the boundaries of a single state. In this assignment, we relax that assumption and address the problems inherent in using state-based filing systems to keep track of commerce that flows freely from state to state.

A. State-based Filing in a National Economy

In Assignment 16, we introduced a theory of the filing system. The filing system is a means for a secured creditor who takes a nonpossessory security interest in property of a debtor to communicate the existence of that security interest to others who may later consider extending credit to that debtor. We noted in that assignment that there is not one, but a multitude of filing systems. For a message left in a filing system to reach the later searchers for whom it is intended, the later searchers must be able to determine the correct filing system or systems in which to look. In Assignment 16, we examined how searchers made that determination as among state and federal filing systems specialized as to the type of collateral. In this assignment, we examine how searchers make that determination as among the state-wide filing systems of the 50 states and those of foreign countries.

The rules that specify where to file and search are found in U.C.C. §§9-301 to 9-307. Those rules are framed as conflicts rules that determine the law applicable to "perfection, the effect of perfection or nonperfection, and priority." If revised Article 9, like former Article 9, is adopted in all 50 states, the rules governing "the effect of perfection or nonperfection, and priority" will be the same in all 50 states. Generally speaking, it will not matter whether the law of New York or New Mexico applies, because for all practical purposes, both will be the same. In one important respect, however, the law of the two states will remain different. When the law of New York applies to require the filing of a financing statement in the Office of the Secretary of State, the reference will be to an office in Albany, New York. When the law of New Mexico applies, the reference will be to an office in Albuquerque, New Mexico. If revised Article 9 is adopted in all 50 states and all require filing with the secretary of state, the principal impact of the rules in U.C.C. §§9-301 to 9-307 will be to tell filers and searchers the state of the secretary of state's office in which they should file or search.

The rules in U.C.C. §§9-301 to 9-307 govern perfection by possession and perfection by control as well as perfection by filing. In exploring the impact of these sections, however, we deal almost exclusively with perfection by filing. Perfection by possession and perfection by control are likely to generate few interstate problems. When these kinds of perfection occur at all, they always occur in the right state.

Revised Article 9 was drafted "on the general assumption that all jurisdictions will have enacted substantially identical versions." See Comment to U.C.C. §9-701. Though it was submitted to state legislatures beginning in 1999, it carries a recommended effective date of July 1, 2001. U.C.C. §9-701. The purpose of the delay is to reduce the possibility that it will be enacted in some States and not others. The Comment to U.C.C. §9-701 continues: "While always important, uniformity is essential to the success of this Article. If former Article 9 is in effect in some jurisdictions, and this Article is in effect in others, horrendous complications may arise." What the drafters are gently hinting at is that the scheme of revised Article 9 is so complex that nobody knows what problems might result if it becomes effective in some major commercial states without becoming effective in all. Either all will reject revised Article 9 or enact it by July 1, 2001, and we will never have to find out. In the meantime, we ignore the possible problems of transition on the theory that this course should prepare students for a lifetime of commercial practice rather than the adrenalin rush of the year 2001 problem (Y2K1).

B.   Initial Perfection

1. At the Location of the Debtor

U.C.C. §9-301(1) states the general rule regarding the correct state in which to file a financing statement. While a debtor is located in a state, the local law of that state governs perfection of a nonpossessory security interest. (If the security interest is possessory, the more specific provision of U.C.C. §9-301(2) would override U.C.C. §9-301(1) and impose the law of the jurisdiction in which the collateral is located.) If the law of the state applies, §9-501(a)(2) will require filing in the statewide filing office of the state for non-real estate-related collateral.

U.C.C. §9-307 contains additional provisions specifying the locations of particular kinds of debtors. An individual debtor is deemed located at the individual's "principal residence." The term is not defined in the U.C.C. It is used in tax and bankruptcy law to refer to a building rather than a jurisdiction. One need not live in the building currently for it to qualify as one's principal residence.

Black's Law Dictionary defines "residence" as "Personal presence at some place of abode with no present intention of definite and early removal and with purpose to remain for undetermined period, not infrequently, but not necessarily combined with design to stay permanently." It states that "residence implies something more than mere physical presence and something less than domicile." Finally, Black's makes this distinction between residence and domicile: Residence means living in a particular locality, but domicile means living in that locality with the intent to make it a fixed and permanent home.

A "registered organization" is "an organization organized solely under the law of one State or the United States and as to which the State or the United States must maintain a public record showing the organization to have been organized." U.C.C. §9-102(a)(70). Virtually every corporation (profit or non-profit), limited partnership, limited liability company, service corporation, professional association, or limited liability partnership will qualify. The governments granting charters to such organizations are invariably required by law to maintain the necessary public record. While a few such organizations have managed to get charters from more than one government, that is extremely rare. If New York grants a corporate charter to "Acme Enterprises, Inc." and that corporation then applies for and obtains a charter in the same name from another state, the effect is to create a second corporation with the same name, not to obtain a second charter for the same corporation.

U.C.C. §9-307(e) provides that a registered organization that is organized under the law of a state is located in that state. (The provisions of U.C.C. §9-307(b) to the contrary expressly yield to the other provisions of U.C.C. §9-307.) Thus, for example, a Delaware corporation is located in the state of Delaware — even though it may have no offices or employees in that state, do no business in that state, and have all of its extensive operations in Texas. This feature of the new law is deliberate. Because the appropriate state in which to file depends solely on place of incorporation — a matter of public record — the proper place for filing and searching can be determined solely from the public record. Neither filer nor searcher need be concerned with the location of the debtor's collateral or operations.

Early in the Article 9 revision process, the drafters decided to adopt a system in which filing would be in the jurisdiction in which the corporate debtor had its headquarters (referred to as *debtor-based* filing). Filing at the corporate debtor's place of incorporation (*incorporation-based* filing) was initially proposed in the law review article that follows. Empirical data showing that the switch to filing at the debtor's place of incorporation would move only about $3 million a year in filing fees to Delaware from the other 49 states established the political viability of the proposal. But from a systems standpoint, the most important feature of filing at the place of incorporation was placing the U.C.C. filings against a corporate debtor in the same jurisdiction as the corporate records on that debtor. By joining the two sets of files, the secretary of state could make possible a dramatic reduction in filing errors.

Lynn M. LoPucki, Why the Debtor's State of Incorporation Should Be the Proper Place for Article 9 Filing: A Systems Analysis

79 Minn. L. Rev. 577 (1995)

Filers who desire a high level of certainty that their filing was in fact made and properly indexed often conduct a post-filing search to verify that fact. In a collateral-based system, that search will show the filer's financing statement and any effective filings made prior to it in the jurisdiction against the debtor. But that search will tell the filer little about whether the filing is in the right jurisdiction. A debtor-based system has a considerable advantage in this regard. Most filers have sufficient information about their debtors to form some sort of expectation as to how many filings there will be against them. In ordinary circumstances, all of those filings will be made in the same office. If the filer's post-filing search reveals substantially fewer or more filings than expected, the filer can decide whether to investigate further. For example, failure of a post-filing search against a debtor that should have many filings to discover many filings indicates that the filer has filed in the wrong office. I will refer to this system characteristic as the "echo effect."

An incorporation-based system can both provide a strong echo and "trap" some kinds of errors in filings. Because both the corporation records and the statewide UCC filing records would be under the control of the same Secretary of State, the Secretary could link them electronically. Each time a UCC filing would be made against a corporate debtor, the computer could match the name of the debtor to the names of the corporations formed under the laws of the state. If there were no match, the filing would be erroneous. The system could notify the filer of that fact. If there were a match, the system could display a list of filings against the debtor, the equivalent of the echo effect available in a debtor-based system.[1]

The feedback advantages of an incorporation-based system do not depend on the existence of an automatic computer link between the corporate and statewide UCC filing records. If no such link existed, the filer still could telephone the corporation division of the Secretary of State's office to make the verification.

As increasing numbers of filings are made electronically, error trapping can sharply reduce the number of errors entering the filing system. Although error trapping could not eliminate errors in which the filer mistakes one corporation for another, it could eliminate filings on which the name does not match the name of any corporation formed in the state.

Some organizations are not incorporated. They include general partnerships and a variety of associations, both for profit and not for profit. U.C.C. §9-307(b)(2) deems such a debtor located at its place of business if it has only one and U.C.C. §9-307(b)(3) deems such a debtor located at its chief executive office if it has more than one place of business. U.C.C. §9-307(a) defines "place of business" to mean "a place where a debtor conducts its affairs." Comment 2 to that section adds "Thus, every organization, even eleemosynary institutions and other organizations that do not conduct 'for profit' business activities, have a 'place of business.' "

Determining the location of an organization's "chief executive office" may not be as easy as it sounds. The concept has proven problematic in a number of other contexts, including (1) filing against mobile goods and intangible property under former Article 9, (2) locating corporations for purposes of diversity jurisdiction in the federal courts, and (3) determining proper venue for corporate bankruptcies. In those contexts, courts developed what came to be known as the "nerve center" test: the organization is located in the place from which it is managed — regardless of the location of its operations. The place from which it is managed is its "nerve center," the place from which commands originate.

That place might not be much else. To illustrate, assume that San Antonio Hotel Corporation (Hotel) owns and operates the San Anto-

---

1. The echo effect is stronger in an incorporation-based system because all effective filings against a debtor will be in the same system. In a debtor-based system, uncertainty about the location of the debtor will cause significant numbers of filers to make more than one filing, leading to the possibility of a false echo.

nio Hotel in Texas. Jose Sanchez, who owns 100 percent of the stock of the corporation, is the chief executive officer. He lives in Tennessee and manages the 100-room San Antonio Hotel from there. Sanchez keep the books and records on a personal computer in his home. He makes all major decisions for the business, including those regarding the hiring and firing of employees. He is in touch daily with Hector Williams, the on-site manager in Texas. On these facts, a court would be likely to hold that the chief executive office of Hotel is in Tennessee.

Finally, notice that "organization" is defined to include "two or more persons having a joint or common interest." Thus, if Alice Moore and Sara Wu are two farmers who share ownership of a tractor as tenants in common, they are an organization. As their organization has more than one place of business — their two separate farms — the proper place to perfect in the tractor is at their chief executive office. (They may be surprised to hear that they have one, but they do. See U.C.C. §9-307(b)(3).) The creditor is likely to solve the problem by filing at both places of business. U.C.C. §9-307(a).

2. At the Location of the Collateral

Recall that a fixture filing must be made in "the office designated for the filing or recording of a mortgage on the real property" to which the fixture is attached. U.C.C. §9-501(a)(1). The purpose of this rule is to keep all filings against a parcel of real property or the fixtures attached to it in the same set of records in the county where the land is located. The effect is that all filings and searches regarding a particular parcel of real property can be made in a single filing system — the real property records of the county in which the land is located.

The necessary effect is that those filings must sometimes be made in a state other than the state in which the debtor is located. For example, assume that Hotel Sierra Vista, Inc., a California corporation, is the owner of a free standing walk-in freezer. Regardless of where the freezer is located, non-fixture filings against it must be made in California. If the freezer is affixed to the Hotel property in Reno, Nevada, a fixture filing against the freezer must be made in the county real estate records in Reno.

U.C.C. §§9-304 to 9-306 specify the law applicable to the perfection and priority of security interests in deposit accounts, investment property, and letters of credit. Perfection in these kinds of property is by control of the collateral rather than by filing a financing statement. U.C.C. §9-314. As a consequence, these sections can never determine the proper states in which to file financing statements. The mostly simple and sometimes complex question of where an account, investment property, or letter of credit is located is beyond the scope of this book. Finally, the proper place to file against certificate of title property is reserved to Assignment 25.

C. Relocation of the Debtor

After the secured creditor has perfected its security interest in the collateral by filing in the state in which the debtor is located, the debtor may change its location to another state. An individual debtor would accomplish that by changing his or her *place of abode.* In most cases, such a change will be obvious: The debtor sells his or her house in the original state and a moving van takes the debtor's property to a new house in the destination state. Before the move, the debtor lived and worked in the original state; after the move, the debtor lives and works in the destination state. But many relocations will not be so tidy. Debtors may simultaneously have homes in two states and move back and forth between them. A debtor may own a home in one state but live in a rented home in another. Such a debtor may intend to return to the first state, may intend to remain permanently in the second, or may intend to move to a third. Although *principal residence* in a state requires that the debtor sometimes be physically present in the state, which of several states in which the debtor is sometimes physically present is the principal residence of the debtor is ultimately a matter of the debtor's intention — an intention that may be difficult to discern and that can change over time.

When an individual debtor changes his or her state of principal residence, the secured creditor who filed in the original state has four months in which to file in the destination state. U.C.C. §9-316(a)(2). If the secured creditor does not, the security interest becomes unperfected. U.C.C. §9-316(b). Security agreements under revised Article 9 will likely require that the debtors declare their jurisdictions of principal residence and notify the secured parties of any changes in them. Experience tells us that debtors will often fail to comply with the latter requirement — particularly debtors who are already in financial difficulty. To protect against loss of their perfection, secured creditors will have to discover changes of principal residence and respond.

No legal procedure exists to permit a registered organization to change the state in which it is organized. Lawyers have, however, developed strategies for accomplishing what amounts to the same thing. Those in control of an organization registered in Michigan can relocate the corporation to Florida by merging it into an organization registered in Florida. After the merger, all of the assets owned by the

Michigan organization will be owned by the surviving Florida organization. If, as is often the case, the Florida organization was incorporated for the specific purpose of the merger and owns no assets except those acquired through the merger, the owners of the Michigan organization can become the sole owners of the Florida organization. After the merger, the Florida organization will have precisely the same assets and the same owners that the Michigan organization had before the merger. The effect will be the same as if the Michigan organization had been permitted to change its state of incorporation to Florida.

Another strategy for accomplishing such a *reincorporation* is to register a new organization in the destination state and then transfer all of the assets of the existing organization to the new one. Both strategies — merger and sale of assets — reach precisely the same end. Which is employed will depend on the relative costs of the two transactions. Those costs are principally transfer taxes, attorneys' fees, and the costs of giving notice to interested parties.

If a debtor reincorporates by merger or sale of assets, U.C.C. §9-316(a)(3) will apply, giving the secured creditor one year in which to discover the merger and perfect in the destination state. The secured creditor's task in discovering the relocation by merger will usually be considerably easier than the secured creditor's task in discovering relocation by sale of assets or a debtor's change of principal residence. The merger will be a matter of public record, generally in both the original and the destination states. Because articles of merger must be filed in the states of incorporation of each of the merging entities, the secured creditor can discover a merger by monitoring the record of its debtor's incorporation in the original state.

If a debtor reincorporates by sale of assets, the transaction may be more difficult for the secured creditor to discover. Consider again the Michigan corporation that seeks to relocate to Florida. The Michigan corporation causes the formation of a new Florida corporation. The Michigan corporation then transfers all of its assets to the Florida corporation in return for all of the stock of the Florida corporation, and distributes the stock to its own shareholders. The Michigan corporation has no assets, but it may continue in existence. Nothing may occur on the corporate records of Michigan that would alert the monitoring secured creditor that the Michigan corporation no longer owns the collateral.

It is important to realize that reincorporation may be an entirely paper (or paperless) transaction. There may be no change whatsoever in the physical location of the assets or the conduct of the business. The new organization may do business under the same trade name in the same location, and even have the same name on its corporate charter. The only thing that necessarily has changed is the state of organization of the entity that owns the collateral.

An unregistered organization would move from one state to another by changing the location of its chief executive office. That might be an uprooting of an entire group of people, office machines, and records, and their transfer to a new address in another state. If it is, it will be easy to spot. But it may be nothing more than a move of the *chief executive officer* from one state to another. Today there are numerous examples of organizations being run by a chief executive officer who does not work in the same state as the officer's office staff. The drafters of revised Article 9 rejected location of the chief executive office as the place for filing against registered entities in part because of the ephemeral nature of the chief executive office in modern commerce. It remains the test for unregistered entities only for lack of a better alternative.

D.   Nation-based Filing in a World Economy

When Grant Gilmore, the original draftsman of Article 9, proposed in the 1940s that there be "one big filing system," he meant one in each state. More than a half-century later, revised Article 9 adopts his proposal by calling for the elimination of county U.C.C. filing systems (but not county real property filing systems). Gilmore's slogan of "one big filing system" has long since been adopted by others who mean by it a single filing system for the entire United States, perhaps operated by the federal government. They were not taken seriously in the drafting of revised Article 9 for precisely the reasons that Gilmore lost that battle in the 1940s — filing offices are already in place at the state level and both jobs and political power would be shifted in the move to "one big filing system." The political reality seems to be that this kind of change can occur only when the old system is so hopelessly and obviously out of date that it has become a political embarrassment.

In the meantime, secured transactions have moved from the national level to the international, and the events of the last 50 years have begun to repeat themselves with respect to countries of the world rather than states of the United States. Secured loans from institutions in one country to borrowers in another are becoming routine. Lawyers are attempting to accompany their clients as the clients go international, but lawyers in the destination countries are resisting and struggling to defend their turf. Both lawyers and policy makers have become concerned with the laws of other nations on the subject of secured transactions.

Virtually every country in the world recognizes at least some security devices. This should not be surprising, given that, as we saw in Assignment 2, security devices can be constructed from the devices of ownership, contract, and option. London attorney Philip R. Wood, who has written extensively on differences in world financial laws, identifies a group of

> about 80 English-based states [that allow] a universal monopolistic security over all the assets of the debtor which:
> [1] reaches future assets, including assets coming into existence after the bankruptcy of the debtor;
> [2] imposes few formalities;
> [3] imposes no limits on who may take the security;
> [4] permits the security to cover all future debt without stating a maximum amount; and
> [5] allows the secured creditor privately to appoint a possessory manager to run the business without selling and allows private sales.

Wood classifies the United States, except for Louisiana, and Canada, except for Quebec, as within this group. Wood classifies France as the major trading power most hostile to security; a large group of "Franco-Latin" countries as having "limited security"; and a small but important group lead by Germany, Japan, and Russia as having "moderate security." The anti-security groups "allow security over land, but make it more difficult to take security over goods, receivables, investments and contracts." Those jurisdictions do so

> by prohibiting non-possessory security and by:
> [a] imposing onerous initial formalities and unrealistic taxes;
> [b] excluding security for future debt or revolving credits;
> [c] insisting on a maximum amount [of debt to be specified in the security agreement];
> [d] downgrading the security below priority creditors so that no-one knows what it is worth; and
> [e] placing obstacles in the way of enforcement, such as judicial public auction, compulsory grace periods and freezes on enforcement.

Philip R. Wood, Maps of World Financial Law 24-25 (1997).

Requirements for public filing of notice of security interests are less common outside the United States. Where they exist, they are of all four major types: filing at the location of the collateral, filing at the location of the debtor, filing at the place of incorporation, and notation on the certificate of title.

The choice of law rule in U.C.C. §9-301(1) applies among nations as well as among states. Comment 3 to U.C.C. §9-307 gives the following example:

Example 1. Debtor is an English corporation with 7 offices in the United States and its chief executive office in London, England. Debtor creates a security interest in its accounts. Under subsection [9-307](b)(3), Debtor would be located in England. However, subsection (c) provides that subsection (b) applies only if English law conditions perfection on giving public notice. Otherwise, Debtor is located in the District of Columbia. Under Section 9-301(1), perfection, the effect of perfection, and priority are governed by the law of the jurisdiction of the debtor's location — here, England or the District of Columbia (depending on the content of English law).

While the reporters do not give an example going the other way, we submit the following:

Example 2. Debtor is a Delaware corporation with 7 offices in England and its chief executive office in New York. Debtor creates a security interest in its equipment, which is located in England. Under subsection 9-307(e), Debtor would be located in Delaware. Under Section 9-301(1), perfection, the effect of perfection, and priority are governed by the law of the jurisdiction of Debtor's location — here, Delaware.

Of course, England may have something to say about the equipment as well. English law provides for filing of financing statements in the corporate records, but we don't know whether that includes *foreign* corporate records. If it does, the result is a relatively smooth fit of the U.S. and English systems. Secured creditors file where the debtor is located regardless of where the collateral is located. A misfit would occur only where the "English" debtor — meaning a debtor having its chief executive office in England — happened to be incorporated in another country. If English law did not allow for filing against foreign corporations in the foreign filing systems, the misfit would be more severe and the resulting system more complex. The creditor in Example 2 would have to file in Delaware to satisfy U.S. law and in England to satisfy English law.

As international secured transactions become more common, we think the participants will become less tolerant of such misfits. They will demand international coordination that eliminates the necessity for multiple filings in a single transaction. When that occurs, the issue will be the basis for coordination. Two seem to us plausible. Requiring filing in the country where the collateral is located gives power over the form of filing to the country that already has power over the collateral, assuring that once the formalities are satisfied, the security can be enforced. Requiring filing in the country of the debtor's incorporation offers the different set of advantages described above. Ironically, the one project seeking international cooperation with regard to filing that seems likely to succeed in the near future, the Unidroit Convention Relating to the Recognition and Enforcement of Security Interests in Mobile Equipment, adopts neither of these approaches. Instead, it proposes to add yet another filing system devoted only to a narrow class of collateral.

Finally, it should be noted that revised Article 9 does not purport to reorder the world's filing systems. Although the text places no express limits on its application, Comment 3 to U.C.C. §9-307 notes:

> The foregoing discussion assumes that each transaction bears an appropriate relation to the forum State. In the absence of an appropriate relation, the forum State's entire UCC, including the choice-of-law provisions in Article 9 will not apply.

Problem Set 24

24.1. You have been assigned to file financing statements on behalf of your client, Firstbank, in connection with a loan in the amount of $250,000 to William Shatner, an inventor and professor of engineering. The collateral is the equipment, accounts, and inventory of Shatner Engineering, a small business located in Tucson, Arizona, that Shatner started before he began teaching. Shatner remains the sole owner of the business. Shatner's ex-wife, Louise Godfrey, runs the business on a day-to-day basis in return for a salary and a share of the profits, but Shatner himself makes all the big decisions. Shatner has a "permanent," tenured job at the University of Missouri in Kansas City. The school is in Missouri, three miles from the Kansas-Missouri state line. Shatner lives in an apartment on the Kansas side of the line, but is hunting for a house nearer the school — probably on the Missouri side of the line. During the summers, Shatner returns to the home he owns just outside of Tucson and spends his days working on the business. A friend of yours who knows Shatner well says Shatner intends to quit teaching in a few years, move to Hawaii, and operate the business from there. U.C.C. §§1-201(28), 9-102(28), 9-301, 9-307, 9-503(a)(4), 9-506(c), and Comment 2 to U.C.C. §9-307.

    a.   On the foregoing facts, in what states should you file?

    b.   What debtor names should be listed on each of the filings?

    c.   You just learned that three years ago Shatner formed a Nevada corporation under the name Shatner Engineering Products, Inc. Now where do you file?

d.   Contrary to the facts initially given you, the business is unincorporated and Louise owns a one-third interest as a tenant in common. In what states should you file? What names should be listed on each of the filings?

24.2.   a. What, if anything, should Firstbank do to monitor the location of these debtors?

b.   How would your answer change if the loan were for $25 million?

24.3.   Your client, Global Bank, is lending $1.9 million to Tang Aluminum Products to purchase the inventory, equipment, accounts, and general intangibles of Argon, Inc. The Bank will, of course, expect to receive a first security interest in those assets. You have been assigned to do the U.C.C. searches. What inquiries will you make? In what names will you search? In what filing systems? U.C.C. §§9-301(1), 9-307(a)-(e), 9-316(a), 9-507(a), and Comment 3 to U.C.C. §9-507.

24.4.   Assume that Afghanistan law gives priority to the first security interest created and that the country has no filing system. Firstbank loans $1 million to Afghan, Inc., an Afghanistan corporation whose headquarters and operations are all in New York. Where is Firstbank required to file a financing statement? U.C.C. §§9-301, 9-307(b), (c), and (e), and Comment 3 to U.C.C. §9-307.

24.5.   You are working for a politically connected firm in Wilmington, Delaware that does a lot of corporate work, including big bankruptcy cases that come from all over the United States. Carol Lynn Murphy, the youngest partner in the firm, explains that the firm got its start in the 1920s when Delaware replaced New Jersey as the jurisdiction of choice for the incorporation of large public companies. The firm got a big boost in the early 1990s when the Delaware Bankruptcy Court began attracting the bankruptcy reorganization cases of those same large public companies. Today, Delaware is the place of incorporation for somewhere over half of all large public companies and the venue for somewhere over half of the bankruptcies of large public companies. Now that Article 9 provides for filing at the place of incorporation, Murphy envisions a third wave of prosperity for Delaware and the firm. The new law will bring only about $3 million in new filing fees to the state and the private profits from the increase in filing and searching activity will mostly be captured by service companies. But Murphy thinks there may yet be a gold mine in revised Article 9.

a.   Murphy asks what you think would happen on the following facts. The other 49 states and the District of Columbia adopt revised Article 9 as proposed, but Delaware adopts revised Article 9 with a non-uniform amendment that excuses filing altogether. The Delaware law simply declares all security interests "perfected without filing." Cherokee, Inc., a Delaware corporation whose assets and operations are all located in New York, borrows money from a New York bank and grants the New York bank a security interest. The New York bank does not file a financing statement. A year later, Cherokee, Inc. files under Chapter 11 of the Bankruptcy Code in New York and seeks to avoid the New York bank's security interest as unperfected. U.C.C. §§9-301(1), 9-307.

   b.   Would a law that successfully excused some or all U.C.C. filings make Delaware a more or less attractive place for debtors to incorporate? Murphy notes a study by attorney Meredith Jackson, reported in Alces, Abolish the Article 9 Filing System, 79 Minn. L. Rev. 679, 690-691 (1995), indicating that the costs of filing and searching average about $25,000 for loans averaging in the range of $20 million to $70 million.

Assignment 25: Maintaining Perfection in Certificate of Title Systems

Each of the 50 states maintains a certificate of title system for motor vehicles. In each state, a motor vehicle certificate of title act enacted by the legislature governs that system. The most widely adopted certificate of title act is the Uniform Motor Vehicle Certificate of Title and Anti-theft Act (UMVCTA), which has been adopted in 11 states. In most states, a department with the name Department of Motor Vehicles, or something similar, operates the motor vehicle certificate of title system. We will refer to it as "the Department."

For the purpose of inclusion in this system, "motor vehicle" is defined as "a device in, upon, or by which a person or property is or may be transported or drawn upon a highway, except a device moved by human power or used exclusively upon stationary rails or tracks." UMVCTA §1(n). In other words, "motor vehicle" includes cars, trucks, buses, motorcycles, mobile homes, and the like. It does not include bicycles, trains, boats, or aircraft, even though some of these are vehicles that have motors.

For each motor vehicle in a system, the Department maintains a *certificate* that describes the vehicle and shows who owns it. When the system functions properly, there is one and only one certificate of title for any motor vehicle. A copy of a certificate appears later in this assignment. A certificate of title identifies the vehicle by Vehicle Identification Number (VIN), make, and model. It also identifies the owner and the holders of any liens against the vehicle by name and address. On the back of a certificate of title there is usually a form for transferring ownership of the vehicle.

Certificates of title are part of a complex system that serves a variety of purposes, most unrelated to secured credit. Certificates of title are part of the system by which the police identify the owner of a vehicle that is involved in an accident, lost, stolen, or used in the commission of a crime. Certificates of title are also used to transfer ownership of motor vehicles and to keep track of successive annual registrations and taxation of vehicles.

The reason we include an assignment dealing with certificates of title in this course is that for most kinds of property covered by a certificate of title, the face of the certificate is the proper place to record any security interest. (In certificate of title systems, security interests

Figure 5. Sample Certificate of Title (Front)

are referred to as *liens* and filing is referred to as *notation of the lien on the certificate of title*.) In all states, the certificate of title system is physically separate from the Uniform Commercial Code filing system. Several states also maintain a separate certificate of title system for motorboats and/or mobile homes but those that do keep the boat and mobile home systems physically separate from the motor vehicle system.

In the United States, security interests are perfected by notation on the certificate of title in all 50 states. In Canada, security interests in motor vehicles are filed in the personal property registration systems of the province (the equivalent of the Article 9 filing system in each state in the United States). There are no certificates of title for automobiles. In the late 1980s, New Zealand's Law Commission considered whether New Zealand should adopt a certificate of title system like that of the United States or permit perfection of security interests

MV-999 (7/96)

ANY CHANGE OR ERASURE WILL VOID THIS TITLE – ANY FALSE STATEMENT IS A MISDEMEANOR

SECTION I - Transfer by Owner

ODOMETER DISCLOSURE STATEMENT

Note: This vehicle cannot be registered or titled in the name of the new owner unless mileage is disclosed.

Federal and State Law require that you state the mileage of the vehicle described on this certificate when transferring ownership. Failure to do so, or providing a false statement, may result in fines and/or imprisonment.

☐ 1. I certify that, to the best of my knowledge, this odometer reading reflects the ACTUAL MILEAGE of the vehicle described on the front.

☐ 2. I certify that, to the best of my knowledge, this odometer reading "EXCEEDS MECHANICAL LIMITS."

☐ 3. I certify that, to the best of my knowledge, this odometer reading is "NOT THE ACTUAL MILEAGE. WARNING ODOMETER DISCREPANCY."

ODOMETER READING

(no tenths)

I or we transfer the vehicle, boat or manufactured home described on this certificate. At the time of transfer, this title is subject only to the liens or encumbrances listed on this certificate, if any. I also certify that this is the most recent title issued for this vehicle, boat or manufactured home.

Note: Application for a title must be made within 30 days of transfer.

I certify that, to the best of my knowledge, this vehicle ☐has ☐ has not been *(check one)* wrecked, destroyed or damaged to the extent that the total estimate or actual cost of parts and labor to rebuild or reconstruct the vehicle to its pre-accident condition, and for legal operation on the road or highways, exceeds 75% of the retail value of the vehicle at the time of loss.

Note: If the "has" box is checked, an anti-theft examination is required before registration. The title issued will have the brand "Rebuilt Salvage".

Seller's Signature		Seller's Name (Print in Full)			
Street Address	City	State	ZIP Code		Date of Statement
Buyer's Signature		Buyer's Name (Print in Full)			
Street Address	City	State	ZIP Code		Date of Statement

SECTION II - Reassignment by Manufactured Home Dealer or Registered Boat Dealer or Out-of-State Dealer

ODOMETER DISCLOSURE STATEMENT

Note: This vehicle cannot be registered or titled in the name of the new owner unless mileage is disclosed.

Federal and State Law require that you state the mileage of the vehicle described on this certificate when transferring ownership. Failure to do so, or providing a false statement, may result in fines and/or imprisonment.

☐ 1. I certify that, to the best of my knowledge, this odometer reading reflects the ACTUAL MILEAGE of the vehicle described on the front.

☐ 2. I certify that, to the best of my knowledge, this odometer reading "EXCEEDS MECHANICAL LIMITS."

☐ 3. I certify that, to the best of my knowledge, this odometer reading is "NOT THE ACTUAL MILEAGE. WARNING ODOMETER DISCREPANCY."

ODOMETER READING

(no tenths)

I or we transfer the vehicle, boat or manufactured home described on this certificate. At the time of transfer, this title is subject only to the liens or encumbrances listed on this certificate, if any. I also certify that this is the most recent title issued for this vehicle, boat or manufactured home.

Note: Application for a title must be made within 30 days of transfer.

Seller's Signature		Seller's Name (Print in Full)			
Street Address	City	State	ZIP Code		Date of Statement
Buyer's Signature		Buyer's Name (Print in Full)			
Street Address	City	State	ZIP Code		Date of Statement

CONTROL NUMBER

Boat Dealer's Facility #

Z 0615636

Figure 6. Sample Certificate of Title (Back)

in motor vehicles by filing financing statements in the personal property filing system, as is done in Canada. The Commission sent a delegation to study and compare the U.S. and Canadian systems firsthand. The following excerpt is from their report:

New Zealand Law Commission, Motor Vehicle Title Systems in the USA and Canada

Preliminary Paper No. 6 (1988)

We give as an example of a Certificate of Title jurisdiction, Illinois. In Illinois, which has had such a system since the 1920s, the motor vehicle title system is a substantial operation with a large computer entry and checking staff. This seemed to be bigger than the registry staff for the whole Personal Property Security Registry in Toronto. The volume of new titles was approximately three million per year and on the day of our visit 27,000 new titles were issued. Many of these were updates of old titles where a transfer of ownership or change in a security interest had occurred. We were informed that the registry had 65 to 70 people working in two shifts and at present was not able to produce a title until about 3-4 weeks after a request was made. During that time the vehicle was driven under a temporary permit. The motor vehicle certificate of title was printed on bank note paper which was difficult to counterfeit and a lamination strip which protects the vehicle information from being altered, allows changes to be detected under retro-reflective light and is of such a form that the removal of the lamination will destroy the information. Before these security features were introduced, several hundred counterfeit or altered titles were discovered each year in Illinois. Since June 1978 when the security features were introduced there has been a continual decrease in counterfeit and altered titles. In addition to Certificates of Title there are separate certificates for junking and salvage.

Vehicle information is processed through the National Crime Information Center and LEADS Hot Check to determine whether a vehicle has been reported stolen. This is not entered on the register itself. Thousands of stolen vehicles have been identified since the implementation of a computerized title system. Illinois has had a title system for motor vehicles since the 1920s.

In the Canadian provinces there are no title systems for motor vehicles. We understand that such a system was considered in Ontario in the 1950s but was rejected as a result of pressure from motor vehicle dealers who were worried about being unable to confer title in a sale effected at the weekend. We did not find this a very convincing reason for the rejection of a title system. The result of not having such a system means that all motor vehicle transactions come under the Ontario Act. In Ontario over 90 of all transactions recorded under the Ontario Act are concerned with motor vehicles or the financing of motor vehicles or dealers. We understand that a similar proportion would apply in the other provinces.

Compared with this a title system takes the pressure off the Article 9 system. In the Article 9 registry in Illinois 600-700 financing statements were filed daily. There were two people working full time entering particulars on the computer and dealing with searches. The system had been computerized in 1972.

There was little doubt to us that the title system seemed to work well in practice and ease the pressure off the Article 9 system, as well as providing prospective purchasers of motor vehicles with notice of security interests without the need to undertake a search. This was due to the degree of specialization involved and in keeping the bulk of motor vehicles transactions off the Article 9 registry. The Canadian provinces have to contend with motor vehicles and a variety of other transactions. There is at the same time also a greater degree of uncertainty regarding the title to motor vehicles in Canadian provinces. While the problems concerned with title are cut down by a Personal Property Security Act they are not eliminated, because, though security interests can be ascertained from the register, the identity of the owner is not itself recorded. However, the ability to obtain searches of motor vehicles by reference either to the debtor or the identification number of the vehicle reduces this shortcoming somewhat.

The optimal system seems to us to be to have a title system for motor vehicles separate from an Article 9 system.

In 1993, only about 2.5 million financing statements in total were filed in all the statewide Article 9 filing systems in the United States. Even allowing for the likelihood that most new titles were issued as a result of a change in ownership rather than to record a security interest in the car, it seems probable that the number of security interests granted against automobiles in the United States each year exceeds the total number of security interests granted in all other types of personal property combined.

Why then do certificate of title systems receive so little attention in law school courses in secured transactions? (As one of 40 assignments, a larger portion of this text than most others is devoted to certificates of title.) In part, it is because Article 9, as the product of an earlier generation of legal academics, has a certain cachet in legal academic circles. The motor vehicle certificate of title acts have far less lustrous histories. In part, certificate of title acts receive relatively little attention because the subject is narrow, the transactions routine, and the amounts of money in issue relatively modest. Although there is a small, steady flow of litigation emanating from the certificate of title system, the system has worked more smoothly than Article 9 and produced fewer problems.

Reference to this system as a "certificate of title" system implies that the certificate — the piece of paper issued by the state to the filer — has special importance such as that accorded negotiable instruments or documents. In a few states one can achieve some limited perfection merely by noting the lien on this piece of paper without sending the paper to the state. But with that minor exception, the implication is false. To perfect, the secured creditor must deliver to the Department its application for notation of its lien on the certificate of title.

The certificate for an automobile, motorboat, or mobile home does not control disputes over ownership of a vehicle. It is prima facie evidence of ownership, but if ownership is with a person other than the person shown on the certificate, the certificate is no impediment to proof of that fact. Owner liability statutes adopted in many states make the owner of a motor vehicle liable for the negligence of any person operating it with permission. But the "owner" for this purpose is the true owner, not the person whose name appears on the certificate of title as the owner. Thus, where A sells her car to B, turns over possession, but does not execute a transfer of the certificate of title so that the certificate remains in A's name, B is nevertheless generally treated as the owner.

The certificate has similarly little direct importance in granting and perfecting security interests in motor vehicles. A security interest can be granted by any writing; it need not be noted on the certificate of title to be valid. As will be discussed shortly, strictly speaking, perfection is accomplished not by notation on either the owner's or the Department's copy of the certificate, but by application to the Department of Motor Vehicles for such a notation. When an issued certificate of title differs from the Department's record of that certificate, the Department's record generally controls. The certificate of title system is best regarded as a filing system, closely analogous to the Article 9 filing system.

The certificate of title system has two principal advantages over the Article 9 system. First, the certificate of title system contains title as well as lien information. Searchers in the Article 9 system must determine from off-record sources who is the owner of the collateral they propose to finance. If they finance collateral not owned by their debtor, the true owner can reclaim it from them. This weakness in the Article 9 system is examined in Assignment 35, below. In a certificate of title system, as in a real estate system, the chain of title is on the public record. A searcher can trace the debtor's title back to its source.

Probably the most important advantage of the certificate of title system is that each item of collateral is identified by two numbers. Every vehicle registered in a state has a license plate number that is unique within the state. Every vehicle also has a VIN assigned at the time of manufacture and unique within the entire United States. Keep in mind that the ultimate purpose of nearly every search of a filing system is ultimately not to determine whether a particular *debtor* has filings against it, but to determine whether particular *collateral* has filings against it. In the Article 9 filing system, searches are conducted by the name of the debtor only because they cannot be conducted by an item of collateral. If an item of collateral has had more than one owner, the searcher must search under the name of each, with the result that multiple searches may be necessary to locate filings against a single item of collateral. The process of discovering former owners is imprecise, which means that Article 9 searching is imprecise as well. Conducting a search by a unique number assigned to the collateral, as can be done in a certificate of title system, eliminates the complexity and uncertainty of using the owner's (debtor's) name. Starting with the VIN number, the license number, *or* the name of the current owner, a searcher can immediately locate the certificate. On it will be every current piece of information in the system that relates to the particular vehicle.

Despite the powerful advantages of certificate of title systems, use is not likely to spread to very many kinds of collateral. To operate a certificate of title system, each item of collateral must be assigned a unique number. What made it worth doing this for motor vehicles was not the convenience of a smoothly operating filing system for security interests, but the vulnerability of motor vehicles to theft. Once the numbering system was adopted to control theft, the filing system simply took advantage of it.

The principal weakness of a certificate of title system is in its inability to deal with the addition of parts to, or the removal of parts from, the "whole" — that is, the object, such as the car or the boat, that is the subject of the system. This weakness restricts the use of certificate of title systems to objects, such as cars or boats, that are likely to remain essentially intact throughout their useful lives. The issues that arise when parts are added to or removed from collateral subject to a certificate of title are discussed in section B of this assignment.

A.   Perfection in a Certificate of Title System

Article 9 applies to transactions that create security interests, and to the security interests thus created, in automobiles, boats, mobile homes, and other property subject to certificate of title systems. U.C.C. §§9-109(a), (c) and (d). However, U.C.C. §§9-311(a)(2) and (3) provide that "the filing of a financing statement otherwise required by this Article is not necessary or effective to perfect a security interest in property subject to [listed certificate of title statutes of this state]" or "a certificate of title statute of another jurisdiction under the law of which indication of a security interest on the certificate is required as a condition of perfection."

The certificate of title act specifies what the secured party must do to perfect. While these acts vary somewhat in their requirements, most are similar to the UMVCTA. UMVCTA §20 provides:

> A security interest is perfected by the delivery to the Department of the existing certificate of title, if any, an application for a certificate of title containing the name and address of the lienholder and the date of his security

agreement and the required fee [and registration card]. It is perfected as of the time of its creation if the delivery is completed within ten (10) days thereafter, otherwise, as of the time of the delivery.

Notice that perfection occurs under this provision at the same moment it occurs under U.C.C. §§9-516(a) and 9-308(a), the moment when the filing officer receives the documents and the filing fee. UMVCTA §20 differs in two respects. First, the filing must include the existing certificate of title, if any. For the lien holder who anticipates the problem, unavailability of the certificate is not a serious problem. If the certificate is "lost, stolen, mutilated or destroyed or becomes illegible" the owner or legal representative of the owner is entitled to a replacement. Departments generally will accept both the application for a new title and the application for a lien on that title at the same time. Second, once made, the notation on the certificate of title relates back not just to the filing officer's receipt of the application but to the time of creation of the security interest. This second difference may soon disappear. The Legislative Note at the end of U.C.C. §9-311 advises that states with UMVCTA-type relation-back periods should amend their motor vehicle statutes to eliminate them.

When the Department issues a new certificate of title noting the existence of the lien, it mails the certificate to the secured party rather than to the debtor. UMVCTA §21(d). Until the lien is satisfied, only the secured party (whose name and address are shown on the face of the Department's copy of the certificate) has the right to apply for and obtain a duplicate certificate. UMVCTA §13. Ideally, this would make it impossible for a debtor to obtain release of the lien without the signature of the secured party. In fact, debtors or thieves sometimes manage to obtain "clean" certificates (that is, certificates showing no liens) from the Department where the lien is recorded or from the Department of another state. The erroneous issue of these certificates generates most of the litigation in this area.

Multiple liens against the same collateral pose a special problem in a certificate of title system. Assume that Ozzie Owner granted a security interest in his new Lexus to Firstbank. Later, Ozzie decides to grant a second interest to Larry Lender, who will loan him another $1,000. Larry's application for notation of his lien on the certificate must be accompanied by the existing certificate. But Ozzie, the person to whom he is lending the money, doesn't have the certificate. Firstbank has placed it in their vault for safekeeping. The solution is in UMVCTA §21(c). Larry makes application for notation of his lien on the certificate and gives it to Firstbank. Firstbank is then obligated to send the application and the certificate to the Department for processing. The Department issues a new certificate showing both liens and sends it to Firstbank, the holder of the first lien. UMVCTA §21(d).

The theoretical problems with such a system are numerous. First-bank might refuse to forward the application because it doubts the authenticity of Larry's lien. Firstbank might have no doubts about authenticity, but might just be slow in sending the certificate. First-bank might also go to the other extreme, releasing Larry's lien without Larry's authorization. Fortunately for the certificate of title system, such problems seldom arise in practice. Second and subsequent liens against motor vehicles are relatively uncommon. In fact, some states will record no more than two liens on the certificate because that is all that will fit on the form they use.

Searches can be requested by mail or, in most states, online. They can be by license number, VIN number, or owner's (debtor's) name. A few states prohibit name searches to prevent unwarranted invasions of privacy. Information on how to conduct searches in all 50 states is published by BRB Publications, Inc., in The MVR Book Motor Services Guide (1998).

B. Accessions and Removals

Just as personal property can be affixed to real property, creating a fixtures problem, one item of personal property can be affixed to another, creating an *accessions* problem. The accessions problem can occur with regard to property not covered by a certificate of title. For example, when the motor breaks on an industrial machine, the owner may repair the machine by installing a new motor. The new motor is an accession. The accessions problem causes the most difficulty, however, with regard to property covered by certificate of title systems. The certificate issued in a certificate of title system implicitly assumes that the collateral is a whole and is mortgaged as such; the certificate of title is not designed to deal with the possibility of mortgages against particular parts of that whole.

Examples of accessions to certificate of title property include radio equipment installed in an aircraft after it is sold by the manufacturer, the new tires installed on a car when the old ones wear out, or the camper top installed on the back of a pickup truck. In the typical accessions case, one creditor has lent against the accession while another has lent against the item to which it is affixed (referred to as the *whole*). The creditor secured by the accession, who may even be a purchase-money financier who perfected before the collateral was affixed, will expect to have priority in the accession over the creditor secured by the whole. In fact, *not* to give the accession-secured creditor priority would enable debtors to routinely defeat security interests just by affixing the collateral to a whole financed at some earlier time.

On the other hand, when a creditor secured by a car or truck repossesses its collateral, it does not expect accession-secured parties thereafter to strip the vehicle of its CB radio, let alone the tires, the engine, or the headlights. Yet in a system where accession lenders have priority, that might be a common occurrence. A repossessed car might look exactly like it did the day the secured creditor financed it, but the creditor's security interest might be subordinate to the suppliers of most of the parts. The creditor secured by the whole might well argue that this result too is absurd; a car lender cannot be expected to monitor repairs.

Just as with fixture problems, the courts that resolve accession problems divide affixed property into three categories: (1) that which is not sufficiently related to the whole to be considered part of it and therefore not an accession (e.g., a spare tire); (2) that which is so integrated into the whole that it is part of the whole for financing purposes (e.g., the mixer on the back of a cement truck); and (3) accessions, the property in between that is sufficiently affixed to be reached by a security interest in the whole, but not sufficiently integrated that it can no longer be the subject of separate financing (e.g., automobile tires).

Reexamine the certificate of title shown earlier in this assignment and you will see that it contemplates liens against the car but not against particular parts of the car. If secured parties are shown on the certificate, it is presumed that they have security interests in the entire car. There is no place for recording liens that cover only the radios, custom cabs, or motors. The accession-secured party can perfect its interest in the accession by filing in the Article 9 filing system, but probably only if it does so before the collateral becomes an accession. If perfection in an already-attached accession in the Article 9 system could defeat perfection in the whole in the certificate of title system, the creditor taking a security interest in property covered by a certificate of title statute would have to search in both systems. That may be why U.C.C. §9-311(a)(2) provides that "the filing of a financing statement . . . is not effective to perfect a security interest in property subject to [a certificate of title statute]."

U.C.C. §9-335(d) gives a security interest in the whole priority over a security interest in an accession to that whole — regardless of the order in which the two security interests were perfected and even though the security interest in the accession attached and became perfected before the accession was affixed and before the security interest in the whole was created. U.C.C. §9-335(e) bars the holder of the subordinate accessions interest from enforcing it, rendering it virtually worthless. To illustrate, assume that GMAC finances Dolly's purchase of a new automobile and perfects by notation on the certificate of title. After the warranty on the car expires, it becomes necessary to replace the engine. Joe's Garage sells Dolly a new engine on credit, takes a security interest in it, and perfects before installing the engine in the car. Under U.C.C. §9-335(d), GMAC has the first security interest in the car, including the new engine. Joe's Garage has a second security interest in the engine. If Dolly fails to pay Joe's Garage, Joe's Garage cannot foreclose against or repossess the car, because it does not have a security interest in it. Joe's Garage cannot foreclose against or repossess the engine, because it does not have "priority over the claims of every person having an interest in the whole." U.C.C. §9-335(e). On a literal reading of the statute, this would be true even if the car were of sufficient value to satisfy both liens. What *can* Joe's Garage do? It can hope that GMAC will eventually force a sale of the property. If GMAC does, Joe's Garage can then make a claim against any proceeds of sale in excess of the obligation owing GMAC. Alternatively, Joe's Garage can sue as an unsecured creditor. Presumably, the same result would obtain if Joe's Garage sold the engine to Dolly under a contract that prohibited installment in a whole.

U.C.C. §9-335 facilitates the financing of automobiles, aircraft, boats, and other certificate of title property as wholes, and effectively makes it impossible to finance accessions — such as radio equipment or custom cabs — separately. The effect will be to favor those who mass-produce and finance standard units at the expense of those who attempt to customize them. The biggest losers will be those who finance items not intended to be used as accessions, but that are. Under U.C.C. §9-335, any secured creditor whose non-certificate of title collateral is affixed to some other secured creditor's certificate of title collateral effectively loses its interest.

C.   In What State Should a Motor Vehicle Be Titled?

The manufacturer of each motor vehicle assigns it a unique VIN number. The manufacturer also issues a *certificate of origin* for the vehicle, which contains both the make and model of the vehicle and the VIN number. While the certificate of origin functions in some respects like a certificate of title, a security interest cannot be perfected by notation on the certificate of origin. Instead, while a motor vehicle is inventory in the hands of a manufacturer or dealer, the certificate of title statute is inapplicable. UMVCTA §2(a)(2). Perfection of a security interest in the inventory of a car dealer is accomplished by filing a financing statement, U.C.C. §9-311(d), in the state where the car dealer is incorporated, U.C.C. §§9-301(1), 9-307(e).

Upon sale of the motor vehicle to the first user, the dealer delivers the certificate of origin. That user makes application for the first certificate of title based on the certificate of origin. UMVCTA §4. Once the certificate of title is issued, liens against the motor vehicle can be perfected only by notation on the certificate of title, except while the vehicle is owned by a used car dealer.

In what state should the vehicle be titled? UMVCTA §4(a) answers with the statement that "every owner of a vehicle which is in this state and for which no certificate of title has been issued by [this state] shall make application . . . for a certificate of title of the vehicle." Obviously, this statute cannot be read literally, or it might require two applications when a resident of Texarkana goes out for a cup of coffee. UMVCTA §2(a)(3) may at first glance seem to require titling in a state only if the owner is a resident of the state, but that section protects nonresidents only with regard to vehicles "not required by law to be registered in this state." A combination of case and statutory law requires registration of the vehicles of nonresidents when the nonresidents acquire regular places of abode in the state or use the vehicles in connection with a business in the state for more than a period established by the state. Those periods range from about 30 to 90 days in various states. Merely because a motor vehicle is supposed to be registered in the state does not necessarily mean that it is supposed to be titled there, but it usually does mean that.

The case reporters are full of cases in which owners titled their vehicles in states that are clearly inappropriate. Often, the motivation is to pay registration fees or sales tax in a state that charges a lower rate. These owners may be subject to fines or penalties levied by the state in which they should have titled the car. But the fact that their certificate of title is from the wrong state does not prevent it from being the proper place for a creditor to note the existence of its lien. Perfection can be lost when an owner obtains a second title, but in no case has a security interest in an automobile been held unperfected because the owner obtained the only certificate from the wrong state. See U.C.C. §9-303(a).

The point is illustrated in Hoffman v. Associates Commercial Corp., 228 B.R. 70 (1998). That case involved a truck that was garaged in Connecticut and used for transport between Connecticut and New York. Connecticut law required that the owner obtain a Connecticut title. Instead, the owner obtained a Maine title. Maine law authorizes the issuance of titles for vehicles that have no relationship to the state, and charges reduced fees and taxes. Perhaps not surprisingly, it has become a truck-title haven. (Titling in Maine is undoubtedly the "contemporary business practice" referred to in Comment 2 to U.C.C. §9-303.) The secured creditor perfected by notation on the Maine title. The debtor filed bankruptcy and the trustee challenged the secured creditor's perfection. The court noted that "[a]n owner's failure to register a vehicle required to be registered in Connecticut is an infraction. An owner's illegal conduct — not registering to avoid paying fees and taxes in Connecticut — does not, however, unperfect a creditor's otherwise validly perfected lien."

D.   Motor Vehicle Registration

Each of the 50 states levies a license tax on automobiles. Except as otherwise provided in reciprocity agreements, within some period after becoming a resident of a state or bringing a car into the state as a nonresident, the owner is required to *register* the car in the state. The owner pays the tax, obtains license plates (tags) from the state, and displays them on the vehicle as proof of payment of the tax and to identify the vehicle.

The registration system in large part duplicates the function of the certificate of title system. A certificate of registration contains much the same information that appears on a certificate of title.

There are, however, some important differences between the two systems. First, liens cannot be perfected by notation on a certificate of registration. Second, the certificate of title system exists to keep track of ownership and liens, while the registration system exists to identify vehicles on the street and collect taxes. A vehicle should have only one certificate of title but may be required to have certificates of registration from every state in which the vehicle is operated. (Occasionally, you will see a semi-trailer truck on the highway displaying tiny license plates from as many as 20 states.) Third, not every movement of a motor vehicle that necessitates registration in the destination state also necessitates titling in the destination state. A motor vehicle can sometimes properly be titled in one state and registered in another. See UMVCTA §11.

WISCONSIN CERTIFICATE OF VEHICLE REGISTRATION		
Not Valid for Transfer of Ownership		
LICENSE NUMBER	VEHICLE IDENTIFICATION NUMBER	EXPIRES END OF Month Year
AUT PH5371 A	JN1HU11S8HT243470	JUL 91

YEAR	MAKE	Model	Body Style	Gross Wt.	VEHICLE TYPE	TITLE NUMBER	Fleet Number
87	NISAN		4DR		AUTO	9031706024-8	

AMOUNT RECEIVED $********.00

REGISTERED TO:

LOPUCKI LYNN M
975 BASCOM MALL
MADISON, WI 53706

Figure 7. Sample Vehicle Registration

E. Maintaining Perfection on Interstate Movement of Collateral

1. How It Is Supposed to Work

Marjorie Murphy, a resident of California who lives and works in California, owns a Toyota that is titled in that state. She still owes $10,000 on the car to the Upper Castro State Bank (UCSB). UCSB's lien is noted on the California certificate of title and the title is in the bank's vault. Murphy finds a better job in Georgia and makes the move, taking her car with her.

Georgia's version of the UMVCTA requires that Murphy make application to the Georgia Department of Motor Vehicles for a Georgia title and registration. UMVCTA §4(a). Murphy visits the local office of the Georgia Department and picks up the forms. UMVCTA §6(c)(1) requires that Murphy's Georgia application be accompanied by her California certificate of title. Because UCSB has possession of the certificate, Murphy calls the Bank to ask for its cooperation. Although there is no provision in the UMVCTA requiring UCSB to cooperate, the Bank agrees to do so. At the Bank's request, Murphy mails it the application and fee, and the Bank forwards it with the certificate of title to the Georgia Department. UCSB's cover letter asks the Georgia Department to reflect UCSB's lien on the new certificate and to send the certificate directly to the Bank.

Upon receipt of the completed application, the Georgia Department issues a Georgia certificate of title with UCSB's lien noted on it. UMVCTA §9(a)(3). They keep the old California certificate of title on file and mail the new Georgia certificate of title to UCSB. UMVCTA §10. They mail the license plate and certificate of registration directly to Murphy. Using a flat-head screwdriver, Murphy attaches the license plate to the rear of her Toyota (Georgia uses only one license plate), puts the certificate of registration in the glove compartment, and the process is complete.

2. Some Things That Can Go Wrong

If the certificate of title systems worked the way they are supposed to, there would be one and only one certificate of title for each motor vehicle. The searcher would need only examine the face of that certificate to determine who had liens and as of what date those liens were perfected.

There are, however, three kinds of problems that commonly occur. The first is when a lien-laden certificate from State *A* is surrendered to the Department in State B and the Department inadvertently issues a "clean" certificate. Given that the State B Department had the State *A* certificate in its possession in this scenario, issuance of the clean certificate was almost certainly an error, although the error might have been encouraged by fraud. The Department's failure to include the liens on the new certificate rendered them unperfected. Having made that error, the Department almost certainly would have made a second by failing to mail the certificate back to the first lien holder who surrendered it. UMVCTA §21(d) requires mailing to the first lien holder *named* in the certificate, and there is no one named on the new certificate. It would be up to each lien holder to notice that the first lien holder had not received the new certificate as it should have and complain.

An even more frequent problem is that a Department issues a new certificate without obtaining surrender of the old one. This might occur when the owner of the vehicle certifies that the original certificate of title has been lost, stolen, or destroyed. UMVCTA §13. It might also occur when the Department excuses surrender under UMVCTA §11. The result is that two certificates are in existence, each arguably covering the vehicle.

U.C.C. §9-303(b) takes the position that when a subsequent certificate of title to property is issued by any state, prior certificates cease to cover the property. The law of the state issuing the most recent (second) certificate for the property governs. Nevertheless, a security interest perfected by notation on the first certificate remains perfected permanently as against a lien creditor or a trustee in bankruptcy. See U.C.C. §9-316(d). But as against a purchaser for value — such as an Article 9 secured creditor — the security interest remains perfected for only four months after issuance of the second certificate. If the holder of the first lien fails to perfect on the second certificate during that four-month period, the first lien becomes unperfected as against that purchaser, whether the purchaser purchased before or after the end of the four-month period. See U.C.C. §9-316(e). (Remember that secured creditors are "purchasers," under Article 9. See U.C.C. §1-201(32), (33).) Thus, the trustee in a bankruptcy case commenced after issuance of the second certificate can be defeated by security interests noted on the first certificate before issuance of the second certificate and security interests noted on the second certificate.

UMVCTA §20(c)(2)(A) expresses a contrary view regarding the two-certificates problem. That section provides:

> (c) If a vehicle is subject to a security interest when brought into this state, the validity of the security interest is determined by the law of the jurisdiction where the vehicle was when the security interest attached subject to the following:
> (2) If the security interest was perfected under the law of the jurisdiction where the vehicle was when the security interest attached, the following rules apply:

(A) If the name of the lienholder is shown on an existing certificate of title issued by that jurisdiction, his security interest continues perfected in this state.

Because the first certificate still exists, the lien holder remains perfected, even when a second certificate is issued.

Another possible solution to the two-certificates problem is for the state to revoke the improperly issued one, leaving the properly issued certificate to govern. The statutory basis for this solution is UMVCTA §26(a), which authorizes the revocation of a certificate that was "fraudulently procured or erroneously issued." To illustrate, assume that Firstbank perfects by notation on the certificate issued in Illinois. The debtor fraudulently obtains a clean certificate from Alabama and Secondbank perfects by notation on that certificate. Firstbank uses UMVCTA §26(a) to persuade the Alabama Department to revoke the second certificate. Secondbank's security interest remains valid because the revocation does not "in itself, affect the validity of a security interest noted on [the revoked certificate]." But Firstbank's security interest is also arguably valid because after revocation it is on the only remaining certificate. Notice that this is a *strategic* solution to the problem. The lawyer must take action to change the facts before raising the issue and arguing the law.

Some states permit a creditor that loses its lien as a result of filing office negligence to sue the filing officer who committed the error. Recovery is usually from a bond or insurance policy and limited in amount. See, e.g., Va. Code Ann. §46.2-219 (1996).

3.   Movement of Goods Between Non-Certificate and Certificate Jurisdictions

Because all 50 states now have certificate of title systems for automobiles and trucks, the movement of automobiles and trucks between certificate and non-certificate jurisdictions has become far less a problem. Such movement remains a problem when automobiles and trucks are, for example, moved between the United States and Canada. In Canada, perfection of security interests in automobiles and trucks is accomplished by filing a financing statement. Because some states have certificate of title systems for boats and mobile homes, while others do not, the movement of boats and mobile homes between certificate and non-certificate states also remains a problem.

Certificate to non-certificate moves. Assume that Steve Harry, a resident of the state of Indiana, owns a boat. The boat is both registered and titled in Indiana. Firstbank has a lien against the boat perfected by notation on the Indiana certificate of title. The bank has possession of the certificate.

Harry changes his principal residence to Idaho, a state that issues certificates of registration for boats but not certificates of title on which a security interest can be perfected by notation. In Idaho, filing in the U.C.C. filing system is necessary to perfect a security interest in a boat. Harry takes his boat with him.

Does Firstbank's security interest remain perfected after the move? The starting point for analysis is to determine whether the boat is still covered by the Indiana certificate of title after it is out of Indiana. First, U.C.C. §9-303(a) assures us that the movement of the goods and Harry's severance of his connections with Indiana are not impediments to continued coverage by the Indiana certificate. U.C.C. §9-303(b) states the two circumstances in which goods cease to be covered by a certificate of title. The first is that the title "ceases to be effective under the law of the issuing jurisdiction" (Indiana). No provision of Article 9 or the UMVCTA suggests that has happened. The second is that "the goods become covered subsequently by a certificate of title issued by another jurisdiction." We conclude that the boat remains covered by the Indiana certificate. U.C.C. §9-316(d) and (e) do not apply, so Firstbank's security interest remains perfected indefinitely.

Non-certificate to certificate moves. Now assume that Harry's change in principal residence is in the other direction, from Idaho to Indiana, and that prior to the move, Firstbank was perfected in Idaho by the filing of a financing statement. Upon Harry's arrival in Indiana, U.C.C. §9-301(1) makes Indiana law applicable. Under Indiana law, the filing of a financing statement is neither necessary nor effective to perfect in a boat. See U.C.C. §9-311(a)(2). However, Indiana U.C.C. §9-316(a)(2) preserves Firstbank's perfection for four months. To remain continuously perfected, Firstbank must cause an application for an Indiana certificate noting its security interest to be filed within the four-month period.

If Firstbank does not perfect in Indiana within the four-month period, its interest will be defeated by a purchaser who buys or takes a security interest during or after the four-month period. U.C.C. §9-316(b). Firstbank's interest will not be defeated by a lien creditor who levies within the four-month period. That section is ambiguous on its face with regard to a lien creditor who levies after the four-month period, but a member of the Drafting Committee tells us that the intent was that the secured creditor prevail.

Problem Set 25

25.1.   a. Firstbank lends $65,000 to Kahled to purchase a teal blue Jaguar. Firstbank perfects by notation on Kahled's Wisconsin title and takes possession of the title. Kahled moves to Alabama and obtains a clean title from that state. One month after issuance of the new title, Kahled borrows $50,000 from Secondbank. Secondbank takes a security interest and perfects on the Alabama title. Six months after issuance of the new title, Kahled borrows $45,000 from Thirdbank. Thirdbank takes a security interest and perfects on the Alabama title. Seven months after issuance of the new title, Kahled files bankruptcy. Is Firstbank perfected?

b.   Change one fact: Firstbank learned of the issuance of the new title three months after issuance. Firstbank demanded that Secondbank apply for notation of Firstbank's lien on the Alabama certificate. See UMVCTA §21(c). Secondbank complied, and Firstbank's lien was noted on the Alabama certificate. As between Firstbank and Secondbank, who has priority? U.C.C. §9-316(d) and (e).

25.2.   Babs lives in Missouri and owns a Nissan sedan that is titled in Missouri. United Missouri Bank financed her purchase of the car. It applied for the title, had its lien noted on it, and has possession of the certificate. Babs recently moved to New York without notifying the Bank of her move.

a.   Four months have passed since her move and she has obtained neither a certificate of title nor a certificate of registration from New York. Is the Bank's security interest still perfected? If things continue as they are, how long will the Bank's security interest remain perfected? U.C.C. §§9-303, 9-316(d) and (e); UMVCTA §§20(c)(2), 2(a)(3), 4(a).

b.   Suppose that Babs registers the car in New York and gets New York license plates a week after she arrives. The Bank still has the Missouri certificate of title and New York does not issue a certificate of title. Is the Bank still perfected? If so, how long will it remain perfected?

c.   Suppose that Babs, rather than the Bank, is holding the Missouri certificate of title. A week after her arrival in New York, Babs applies for a New York certificate of title. She surrenders the Missouri title to the New York Department and tells them (falsely) that the Bank's lien has been satisfied. Ten days later, New York issues a clean certificate of title for the car. Is the Bank's lien still perfected? If so, how long will it remain perfected? U.C.C. §§9-303, 9-316(d) and (e); UMVCTA §§18(c), 20(c)(2), 26.

d.   Suppose instead that Babs, frustrated at the thought of trying to involve the Bank in her title application in New York, gave the New York Department her affidavit stating that she lost her Missouri certificate of title and that it had no liens on it. The clerk issued a clean New York certificate. Is the Bank's lien still perfected? If so, how long will it remain perfected? U.C.C. §§9-303, 9-316(d) and (e); UMVCTA §§20(c)(2) and 26.

25.3. Your client, Missouri River Bank, was newly incorporated just a few months ago. The Bank plans to finance about a thousand automobiles each year. The Bank's plan is to lend only to Missouri residents, require that the cars it finances be initially titled and registered in Missouri, make sure the certificate of title carries a notation of the Bank's lien, and retain possession of the certificate. The Bank asks you if perfection according to its plan will be adequate to maintain perfection against debtors who move out of the state. What is your answer? U.C.C. §§9-303, 9-316(d) and (e).

25.4. Shoreline Boats recently established Shoreline Credit Corporation (SCC) to finance the boats sold by Shoreline dealers at retail in 23 states.

a. SCC would like to know how it should perfect the purchase-money security interests it plans to take in the boats it sells. U.C.C. §§9-310(a) and (b), 9-311(a).

b. How should SCC protect itself against later movement or retitling of the boats? U.C.C. §§9-303, 9-309(1), 9-316(a), (b), (d) and (e). (In solving this problem, assume that the statute for titling boats is the same as UMVCTA.) Consider also the possibility that Shorelines's *debtors* may move out of state.

25.5. Missouri River Bank plans to lend $130,000 to Coldwell Construction Company against a bulldozer already owned by Coldwell. Coldwell's offices are in Illinois. Coldwell tells you that the bulldozer is used on various construction sites, all of which are in Missouri. Your client, the Bank, asks what it should do to perfect this interest. U.C.C. §§9-301, 9-303, 9-307, 9-311(a); UMVCTA §§1, 2, 4, and 5. What is your answer? If you need additional information, where will you get it?

25.6. Your client was recently injured in an automobile accident. The car that caused the accident was rendered inoperable. Before the police arrived, the driver removed the license plates from the car and fled the scene on foot. The accident report, which you obtained from the highway patrol, shows only the make and model of the car and the VIN. The police don't seem to be doing much to discover the name of the owner. Can you find it yourself, working only from the public records? Will your method discover the name of the owner if the car is from out of state? From Canada where no certificates of title are issued and the transfer of ownership of a motor vehicle is not recorded on any public record?

Chapter 8.   Priority

Assignment 26:   The Concept of Priority: State Law

This assignment explores in more depth what it means for a secured creditor to have priority. As should already be apparent, the order of priority among creditors can be crucial. Often, it spells the difference between effortless collection of the full amount of the debt and no possibility of collection at all. Reflecting the complexity and importance of priority, we devote the remainder of this book to it.

Because we often speak of priority as a right to be paid first, it may come as a surprise to realize that the "first" used here does not mean first in time. The holders of subordinate liens are often paid earlier in time than is the holder of the first lien. The actual meaning of priority is somewhat more difficult to describe. To say that one creditor has *priority* over another is to say that if the value of the collateral is sufficient to pay only one of them, the law requires that value be used to pay the one who has priority. The rules that award priority come into play whenever there is more than one interest in property. They include the rules governing foreclosure sales and the rules governing the rights of competing lien holders to possession of the property after default. We begin first with foreclosure sale procedure.

A.   Priority in Foreclosure

Two basic principles govern the timing of the enforcement of competing liens against the same collateral. First, absent an agreement to the contrary, any lien holder may foreclose while the debtor is in default to that lien holder. The existence of a prior lien generally does not block the exercise of rights under a subordinate one. Second, no lien holder is compelled to foreclose. Each has the option to extend the debtor's time for payment or simply to forebear from exercising its remedy. A creditor whose priority is sufficient to guarantee that the debt will be paid may see no advantage in foreclosing, even though its debt is in default. Such a creditor may prefer to wait for others to expend the effort and money necessary to resolve the debtor's financial problems. To give effect to these two principles, sale procedures must provide for the possibility that the holders of liens against particular collateral might foreclose in any order, and that some might choose to rely on their security without foreclosing at all.

Notice the specific recognition of these two principles in this statute governing foreclosure:

§667-3. *Proceeds, How Applied*   Mortgage creditors shall be entitled to payment according to the priority of their liens, and not pro rata; and judgments of foreclosure shall operate to extinguish the liens of subsequent
mortgages of the same property, without forcing prior mortgagees to their
right of recovery. The surplus after payment of the mortgage foreclosed,
shall be applied pro tanto to the next junior mortgage, and so on to the
payment, wholly or in part, of mortgages junior to the one assessed.

Hawaii Rev. Stat. §667-3 (1994).

The holder of virtually any type of lien may foreclose, but the procedure for doing so varies with the type of lien. For example, one
state statute may specify the procedure to foreclose a mortgage,
another state statute may specify the procedure to enforce a state
property tax lien, while a federal statute specifies the procedure for
enforcement of a federal tax lien. Even for a particular type of lien,
such as a mortgage on real property, the procedure may differ from
state to state, or a single state may offer more than one procedure.
Notwithstanding the many differences in detail, the general principles common to most foreclosure procedures can serve first as a
means of understanding the sale process in the abstract and then as a
frame of reference for understanding the sale process applicable to
particular kinds of sales in particular jurisdictions. The principles that
follow govern most judicial or foreclosure sales:

1. The sale discharges from the collateral the lien under which
    the sale is held and all subordinate liens. See U.C.C. §9-617(a).
    It does not discharge prior liens.
2. The sale transfers the debtor's interest in the collateral to the
    purchaser, subject to all prior liens. See U.C.C. §9-617(a).
    The holder of the prior lien cannot enforce the debt against the
    person who purchases at the foreclosure sale, because that per-
    son has not assumed the debt or agreed to pay it. But the
    holder of the prior lien can enforce the lien against the pur-
    chaser. Unless the debt underlying the prior lien is paid by the
    purchaser or someone else, the holder of the prior lien can
    foreclose.
3. The proceeds of sale are applied first to the expenses of sale,
    then to payment of the lien under which the sale was held,
    then to payment of subordinate liens in the order of their pri-
    ority. See U.C.C. §9-615(a). The remaining surplus, if any,
    is paid to the debtor. See U.C.C. §9-615(d)(1). Unsecured cred-

itors do not share in the distribution; their remedy is to levy on the surplus in the hands of the debtor.

4. The debt underlying each lien is reduced by the amount paid to the lien holder from the sale, but the balance remains owing. The lien holder is then entitled to a judgment against the debtor for the deficiency, unless there is a statute providing otherwise. See U.C.C. §9-615(d)(2).

To illustrate the operation of these rules, assume that a debtor's vacation home is subject to a first mortgage lien in the amount of $50,000 and a second mortgage lien in the amount of $30,000. Both mortgages are in default and it is the holder of the first mortgage that forces the sale. The value of the collateral is not yet specified, because it will be determined by bidding at the public auction sale. Sophisticated bidders at the sale would understand that:

1. The mortgage sale will discharge both liens so that the purchaser will own the vacation home free and clear of them.
2. The sheriff will use the first proceeds of sale to pay the expenses of sale.
3. The sheriff will pay the next $50,000 to the first mortgage holder.
4. The sheriff will pay the next $30,000 to the second mortgage holder.
5. The sheriff will pay any remaining balance to the debtor (ignoring the claims of unsecured creditors).

For example, if the amount bid at the sale was $100,000 and the costs of sale were $1,000, the sheriff would pay the costs of sale, pay both mortgage holders in full, and then pay the surplus of $19,000 to the debtor.

If instead the amount bid was $60,000 the sheriff would pay the costs of sale and the debt owing the first mortgagee in full, and pay the remaining $9,000 toward the debt owing the second mortgagee. The holder of the second mortgage could continue to pursue the debtor for the $21,000 deficiency, but the lien of the second mortgage would be discharged from the vacation home and the purchaser would take the home free and clear of both mortgages.

The result is different if it is the holder of the second mortgage that forces the sale. In that event:

1. The mortgage sale discharges only the second mortgage lien; the purchaser will take "subject to" the first mortgage.

2. The sheriff will use the first proceeds of sale to pay the expenses of sale.
3. The sheriff will not pay anything to the first mortgage holder, but will pay the next $30,000 to the second mortgage holder.
4. The sheriff will pay any remaining balance to the debtor.

A bidder who understands this difference will, of course, want to adjust for it. One likely adjustment is to stop bidding at $50,000 less than the bidder thinks the house is worth, reserving that amount to pay the first mortgage after the sale is complete. So, for example, if the bidder thought the home was worth $60,000 free and clear, it would bid only up to $10,000 at the sale. The sheriff would apply the $10,000 first to the expenses of sale and then to the second mortgage debt.

What happens if the purchaser at the foreclosure sale does not pay a mortgage to which it takes subject? Although the purchaser is not liable on the debt, the debtor is. But the debtor is not likely to pay a debt to avoid a foreclosure of a lien against someone else's property. If no one pays the first mortgage, the first mortgage holder can foreclose and almost certainly will do so. Purchasers usually choose to pay the mortgage debt.

Sophisticated bidders at a sale under a second mortgage sometimes arrange with the first mortgagee, before they bid, that if they buy the property they will assume the first mortgage. The deal might call for the bidder to cure any default in the first mortgage and then pay in accord with its original terms, or to pay on new terms negotiated between the parties. The actual terms are not governed by legal rules; they are negotiated in the shadow of what would happen in the absence of agreement. If no deal is struck, the prospective bidder might choose not to bid, or might bid and, if successful, pay the first mortgage.

Not surprisingly, not all bidders at judicial sales understand the rules of priority. Sometimes an unsophisticated bidder bids what he or she considers to be the value of the property, without deducting the amounts to cover the prior liens. To continue with the earlier example, a bidder who values the vacation home at $60,000 might bid the full $60,000, failing to account for the $50,000 mortgage outstanding, rather than bid only $10,000. Such a bid establishes the value of the property as $110,000 (a $60,000 bid for the debtor's interest in the property, subject to a $50,000 mortgage). This bidder is unlikely to learn of the first mortgage in time to correct the mistake. Once the sale is complete, it is unlikely that the purchaser can rescind on the basis of a unilateral mistake; judicial sales are one of the few places in the American economy where the rule of caveat emptor still applies. (See the discussion on the enforceability of judicial sales, even over bidder mistakes, back in Assignment 4.)

B. Reconciling Inconsistent Priorities

While the rules governing foreclosure sales and priority in proceeds discussed in the preceding section are typical of many, they are not universal. In some sale procedures the purchaser takes free of all liens against the property and proceeds of sale are distributed first (after payment of the expenses of sale) to the holder of the first lien. Such procedures are relatively rare for two reasons. First, they deprive the holders of senior liens of their option not to foreclose. In such a system, a small subordinate lien could force the liquidation of a large first mortgage. Second, a procedure that required payment of the first lien first would require some mechanism for identifying and giving notice to the holder of that lien so that the holder could protect its rights by bidding at the sale. That in turn would further complicate the foreclosure proceedings.

When legislatures create the procedures governing foreclosure and priority in the collateral, their attention is often focused on a particular type of creditor whom they wish to prefer or a dispute between two types of creditors that they wish to resolve. For example, many state legislative staffs have been called on to draft rules that resolve priority disputes between competing execution liens. But if the dispute is between execution liens and security interests, that subject is covered by the Uniform Commercial Code and therefore considered within the jurisdiction of the drafters of the Code. The legislature must eventually pass on the rule, but it will be in a different year, in the context of a bill proposing adoption of a set of amendments to the Uniform Commercial Code that cover many other subjects as well. Rules governing priority between execution liens or security interests and federal tax liens are beyond the power of the state legislature altogether, because those rules are enacted by Congress as part of the Internal Revenue Code. Priorities are granted in many other kinds of legislation. It should be obvious that in such a system, conflicting rules can be adopted. They often are.

Because all of these liens compete for the value of the same collateral, the conflicts eventually must be resolved. As the courts resolve them, they fuse diverse sets of state and federal statutes into a single system of priority. In the resulting system, all the schemes of foreclosure and distribution have one feature in common: Those creditors whose liens are discharged by the sale share in the proceeds of sale in the order in which their liens have priority. Without this feature, the system of lien priority would no longer be functional.

Mortgages usually have priority over judgment liens for the simple reason that when a debtor has judgment liens against his or her property, no one will make a mortgage loan to the debtor. Although the opinion does not explain how the mistake was made, in the following case Bank Leumi Trust made mortgage loans to Joseph Liggett even after his ex-wife Helen Liggett had perfected a judgment lien against his property. The mortgage was subordinate to Helen's lien, but senior to a lien later acquired by Cosden Oil. When Helen forced a sale of the property pursuant to her lien, Cosden Oil argued that even though Bank Leumi Trust's mortgage would be discharged, Bank Leumi Trust could not share in the proceeds of sale. Cosden's argument was supported by the clear language of the statute:

> §5236(g) *Disposition of Proceeds of Sale*   After deduction for and payment of fees, expenses and any taxes levied on the sale, transfer or delivery, the sheriff making a sale of real property pursuant to an execution shall, unless the court otherwise directs,
>   1.   distribute the proceeds to the judgment creditors who have delivered executions against the judgment debtor to the sheriff before the sale, which executions have not been returned, in the order in which their judgments have priority, and
>   2.   pay over any excess to the judgment debtor.

Had the court not decided that this was a situation in which it should "otherwise direct," Bank Leumi Trust's mortgages would have been discharged, but Bank Leumi Trust would not have been paid from the proceeds of sale. Their mortgages would have been worthless and the proceeds would have gone to Cosden Oil's subordinate lien. This was a possibility that the New York legislature did not address in drafting the statute. The court took the only reasonable course under the circumstances — it ordered otherwise.

Bank Leumi Trust Co. of New York
v. Liggett

496 N.Y.S.2d 14 (N.Y. App. Div. 1985)

MEMORANDUM DECISION.

. . . This case presents an issue of first impression, whether CPLR 5236(g) establishes priority of judgment creditors over mortgages which have been recorded prior to the judgments.

Joseph and Mylene Liggett purchased real property located at 6 Riverview Terrace in Manhattan in September 1974. The following year, the Liggetts transferred the property to Mylene individually. Joseph's first wife Helen Liggett subsequently prevailed in an action for moneys due under their 1970 separation agreement, and obtained a jury verdict of $388,472. In February 1980, Helen commenced a separate action to enforce her judgment in the matrimonial action by setting aside the conveyance of the Riverview Terrace property as fraudulent. She filed a notice of pendency against the property in conjunction with the second lawsuit. The following month a judgment ("the 1980 judgment") was entered in her favor for $508,129, including interest, against Joseph.

Between November 1980 and November 1981, petitioner Bank Leumi Trust Company of New York (Bank Leumi Trust) took successive mortgages on the Riverview Terrace property to secure the amounts of $550,000, $70,000 and $400,000. In February 1982, respondent Cosden Oil & Chemical Company (Cosden Oil) obtained and entered a $144,154 judgment against Joseph.

In September 1983, Helen won partial summary judgment in her action for fraudulent conveyance. By judgment resettled in February 1984, the sheriff was directed to sell the property and to make "distribution out of such proceeds to any judgment creditors in accordance with CPLR 5236(g) in the order of their statutory priority" ("the 1984 judgment"). This court denied petitioner's motion for a stay of the sheriff's sale and to intervene on that appeal. We affirmed the judgment (109 A.D.2d 642). Leave to appeal was denied by this court and the Court of Appeals.

Subsequent to the denial of the motion to intervene, Bank Leumi Trust commenced this proceeding pursuant to CPLR 5239. Only respondents Helen Liggett and Cosden Oil appeared in opposition. Special Term rejected petitioner's application to vacate the 1984 judgment. The court also denied and dismissed the remainder of the petition, which sought a declaration that Bank Leumi Trust had a right to share in the distribution of the proceeds of the sheriff's sale with judgment creditors in the order of priority of its recorded mortgages. Special Term held that CPLR 5326 did not contemplate participation by mortgagees since, on its face, it provides that only judgment creditors share in the distribution of proceeds. It relied upon the fact that petitioner bank's lien, which was junior to Helen's judgment, would be wiped out by the sale. It also interpreted the provision "unless the court otherwise directs" to require a showing of exceptional or unusual circumstances warranting departure from the statutory method of distribution. The dismissal was without prejudice to the petitioner's rights to share in any surplus remaining after distribution of the proceeds of the sheriff's sale to judgment creditors. On June 4, 1985, this court granted the petitioner a stay of the distribution of the proceeds of the sheriff's sale pending appeal, except as to respondents.

Bank Leumi appeals only from that portion of Special Term's order which denied its application insofar as it sought a declaration that its mortgages have priority in the distribution of proceeds from the sale over subsequently entered judgments. It concedes the validity of the 1984 judgment and the seniority of Helen Liggett's lien. We disagree with Special Term and reverse for the reasons set forth below.

Special Term misapprehended the issue presented here. This case is unusual since Cosden Oil's judgment is, like petitioner's mortgages, junior in time to the 1980 judgment. Both liens, not just the petitioner's, will be wiped out in the judicial sale. (CPLR 5203(a)(2).) Since there are other judgment creditors in addition to Cosden Oil, junior in time to petitioner, petitioner's mortgages cannot ride through this sale with the purchaser at the sale taking subject to the lien of its mortgages. Cosden Oil has refrained from executing on its judgment in hopes of utilizing the 1980 judgment to gain an advantage over Bank Leumi Trust. Therefore, the real issue is the right to share in the surplus proceeds between petitioner's 1980-1981 mortgages and Cosden Oil's 1982 judgment.

It has long been established that first-in-time priority obtains as between mortgages and judgments. CPLR 5203, not CPLR 5236, contains the substantive provisions concerning the priorities of competing judgment creditors with respect to realty. CPLR 5203 does not purport to determine all priorities among all categories of liens.

It is manifest from the legislative history and the language "unless the court otherwise directs" that CPLR 5236 simply establishes the procedural mechanism for the sale which converts realty into money to pay liens. The purpose of first enacting and later amending CPLR 5239, was, inter alia, to provide a procedural device by which lienors, other than judgment creditors, could stake their claims against the subject property, and have the validity and priority of all liens, including their own, judicially determined prior to a judicial sale. According to Professor Siegel, who recommended the amendment, which resulted from a study made at the request of the Committee to Advise and Consult with the Judicial Conference on the CPLR, the new language, "unless the court otherwise directs":

> recasts the subdivision to permit the court to "otherwise direct" the distribution of the proceeds of the sale when it appears to the court that someone other than those specified in the subdivision has an interest superior to the specified persons. Thus, whenever it appears that, e.g., a lien creditor (whether by way of judgment or mortgage or tax lien or mechanic's lien, etc.) has an interest superior to a judgment creditor (who would ordinarily share in the proceeds under present 5236(e) merely by issuing an execution), the court may apply the proceeds to the superior interest first. Siegel, The Sale of Real Property Pursuant to an Execution Under the CPLR, 10th NY Jud Conf Rep, pp.120, 148 [1965].

Respondent Cosden Oil contends that Bank Leumi is barred by CPLR 6501, which binds a person whose encumbrance is recorded after filing of a lis pendens in all proceedings taken in that action "to the same extent as if he were a party." This contention overlooks that in this respect Cosden Oil is in the same position as petitioner bank, both having liens junior to Helen Liggett's. The 1984 judgment should not be deemed final on the issue of priority as between Cosden Oil and Bank Leumi Trust, who were not parties to that action, where there was no opportunity to raise that issue as between these parties.

All concur.

How did the court know that this was a case in which it should disregard the distributions specified in the statute? The answer has to be that the court knew how the system was supposed to work, and knew it would not work that way if the court ordered the distributions specified.

C.   The Right to Possession Between Lien Holders

As we previously discussed, one of the basic principles underlying the system of priority is that any lien holder is free to foreclose at any time. But what happens if two lien holders decide to foreclose at the same time? Some courts require that junior lien holders surrender possession to senior lien holders, effectively giving seniors the right of way.

The Grocers Supply Co. v. Intercity Investment Properties, Inc.

795 S.W.2d 225 (Tex. Ct. App. 1990)

CANNON, J. . . .

The facts are undisputed. On February 3, 1989, Grocers Supply perfected a security interest exceeding $600,000 to secure its inventory financing of The Grocery Store, Inc. and Cedric Wise. On March 6, 1989, Intercity Investments obtained a judgment in the county court against The Grocery Store, Inc. and Cedric Wise for approximately $36,000 and on June 22, 1989, the county court issued a turnover order. Grocers Supply was not a party to that suit.

On July 12, 1989, the constable, accompanied by three attorneys for Intercity, levied writs of execution obtained by Intercity on The Grocery Store and took possession of the inventory of groceries, equipment, and other items described in the inventory to the writ of execution. The attorneys for Intercity were aware of the prior recorded security interest of Grocers Supply but did not contact Grocers Supply. Upon learning of the execution on The Grocery Store inventory, appellants filed this action on July 17, 1989, to determine their rights in the property, resulting in the judgment from which this appeal is taken. . . .

In its first cross-point, Intercity contends the trial court erred in awarding possession of the seized property to Grocers Supply. Intercity argues that both Tex. R. Civ. P. 643 and [U.C.C. §9-401] expressly authorize execution against collateral, the sale of which is subject to the existing encumbrance. Appellant argues that when confronted with facts almost identical to those in this case, a Florida court held that [U.C.C. §9-401] does not exempt collateral from execution and that it may be seized and sold by the judgment creditor, subject to the secured party's lien. Altec Lansing v. Friedman Sound, Inc., 204 So. 2d 740 (Fla. Dist. Ct. App. 1967). Intercity also cites First Natl. Bank of Glendale v. Sheriff of Milwaukee County, 34 Wis. 2d 535, 149 N.W.2d 548 (Wis. 1967), wherein the Wisconsin Supreme Court reached the same conclusion. Based upon these two cases, Intercity reasons this is the majority rule. We agree with Grocers Supply that the precedential effect of Altec Lansing is highly questionable because of the later case of Brescher v. Assoc. Fin. Serv. Co., 460 So. 2d 464 (Fla. Dist. Ct. App. 1984), in which the court made it clear that the "secured party, upon default by a debtor, may recover possession of a chattel by replevin from a sheriff who has taken possession thereof under execution." Id. at 465.

Texas' version of the Uniform Commercial Code provides that "unless otherwise agreed a secured party has on default the right to take possession of the collateral." [U.C.C. §9-609(a)]. It appears that, with the exception of Wisconsin, other states considering the issue have consistently held that the right of a prior perfected creditor to take possession of its collateral is superior to any right of a mere judgment creditor and that the prior perfected secured creditor may regain possession of the collateral from an officer who has levied on the property at the direction of a judgment creditor. We agree with this interpretation. To hold otherwise would be to take away from the perfected security interest holder the important right of repossession of the collateral.

The security agreement between Grocers Supply and The Grocery Store clearly provided that a judgment against the debtor, or the levy, seizure, or attachment of the collateral constituted a default, and upon the occurrence of any of those events, "the entire obligation becomes immediately due and payable at secured party's option without notice to debtor." We hold the right of Grocers Supply, as a prior secured creditor, to take possession of its collateral was superior to the right of Intercity, a mere judgment creditor, and that Grocers Supply could regain possession of the collateral from the constable who had levied on the property. . . .

In its second cross-point, Intercity contends the trial court erred in adjudging against it the transportation and storage costs incurred. Intercity argues that since such costs are not specifically authorized by rule or statute, and since they are not taxable as costs of court, adjudging those costs against Intercity was unauthorized and improper. We disagree. As stated above, the evidence shows that Intercity knew of Grocers Supply's security interest before it seized the collateral, yet they failed to notify appellant before taking action. Intercity's action caused Grocers Supply to incur the additional expense of $24,113.00 in order to recover its collateral. Since someone had to pay this expense, it is appropriate that the one causing the injury be ordered to pay. As pointed out by Grocers Supply, the Oregon Court of Appeals and the Utah Supreme Court have held that a secured creditor with a right of possession of the collateral after default may maintain an action for conversion against one who exercised unauthorized acts of dominion over the property to the exclusion of the creditor's rights. We believe these authorities are sound and support the court's award of the storage and transportation costs. . . .

We modify the judgment and order that The Grocers Supply Co., Inc. have judgment against Intercity Investment Properties, Inc. for $24,113.00, such sum being the amount which The Grocers Supply Co., Inc. paid to discharge the warehouseman's lien on the property seized under the writs of execution.

As modified, we affirm the judgment of the trial court.

Other courts have addressed the issues raised in *Grocers Supply*. As the court here noted, some have reached different conclusions. But *Grocers Supply* is not alone in holding that when junior and senior lien holders clash, the senior has the right of way. When the courts so conclude, where does this leave the junior creditor? If it cannot seize property of the debtor and force a sale merely because the holder of a senior lien whose debt is in default objects, what can it do to collect its debt? If the answer is that it cannot collect until the senior lets it, a junior lien is next to useless. The point has not gone unnoticed.

Frierson v. United Farm Agency, Inc.

868 F.2d 302 (8th Cir. 1988)

With respect to Merchants' and UFA's arguments under Article 9 of the Uniform Commercial Code, see [U.C.C. §9-101], et seq., we agree with the district court. As the district court stated:

> Most secured loans provide for numerous events which constitute default, many of which are technical in nature and are inserted in the loan documents to enable the lender to declare the note in default when even a relatively minor problem arises with the loan or the debtor. Thus, at any given time many secured loans are technically in default, but are never treated as such by secured creditors. In addition, a secured party will occasionally, as Merchants has done in this case, ignore a default which is more than just a technical default. If a secured creditor with a security interest over all the debtor's property is permitted to rely on a default, whether technical or not, to prevent another creditor from executing on the debtor's property, while treating the loan as not in default when dealing with the debtor and others, severe inequities would result. . . . Such an approach would be against both the spirit and the letter of the Uniform Commercial Code.

672 F. Supp. at 1276.

Merchants cannot refuse to exercise its rights under the security agreement, thereby maintaining UFA as a going concern, while it impairs the status of other creditors by preventing them from exercising valid liens. Allowing Merchants to do so would fly in the face of all Article 9, which is premised on the debtor's ability to exercise rights in the property. See [U.C.C. §9-401]. Regardless of whether the funds in question are viewed as collateral or as proceeds, Article 9 requires that Frierson take the remaining funds subject to Merchants' security interest if the bank refuses to exercise its remedies under the code. [U.C.C. §9-315(a)]. Merchants' security interest in the funds will continue, and Merchants can trace and recapture when it chooses to declare the loan in default and accelerate the debt.

U.C.C. §9-401 does not say that an unsecured creditor who has obtained a judgment against the debtor can levy on collateral encumbered by another creditor's security interest. It merely says that the issue "is governed by applicable law other than this article." The most obvious feature of that other law will be statutes authorizing judgment creditors to levy on the debtor's property. Those statutes make no exception for encumbered property.

We think there are at least two ways to reconcile *Grocers Supply* with U.C.C. §9-401. The first is the reasoning in *Frierson*: The right of the senior to possession is not the right to possession for the purpose of leaving the debtor in business and frustrating collection by junior lien holders. The senior lien holder must foreclose or stand aside so junior lien holders can do so. The second begins with the observation that *Grocers Supply* requires the junior lien holder to surrender possession to the senior, but it does not bar the junior from continuing with the sale. Under some sale procedures at least, property can be sold even though it is not physically present.

Problem Set 26

26.1. Your client, Katherine Kinski, has investigated an upcoming foreclosure sale for the purpose of bidding at it. The sale is being conducted by the sheriff under a final judgment of foreclosure in favor of John Gottleib on a debt in the amount of $10,000. The judgment specifically forecloses a subordinate mortgage in the amount of $29,000, but makes no mention of a senior mortgage in the amount of $17,000. Kinski has examined the property and concluded that she is willing to pay up to $25,000 to own the property free and clear of all liens. The sheriff's expenses in conducting the sale are $200. How much should Kinski bid at the sale? Compare U.C.C. §9-617(a).

26.2. A 1990 Rolls Royce automobile worth $75,000 was seized by the sheriff under a writ of execution on an $8,000 judgment. The car is subject to a first security interest in the amount of $60,000 and a second in the amount of $30,000. Both secured creditors are aware of the sale; neither has objected or demanded possession of the collateral. The expenses of conducting the sale are estimated at $200. If all bidders understand the sale procedure, what do you expect will be the highest bid at the sale? Compare U.C.C. §9-617(a).

26.3. You represent Diamond Head National Bank, which holds a first security interest against some mobile equipment owned by Henry Walker, securing a debt in the amount of $27,000. Walker is current on his payments. Diamond Head considers the loan very safe because, even at a sheriff's auction sale, the Bank is confident the equipment would bring at least $40,000. From friends at the Club, you have heard that Walker is in financial difficulty and the holder of some kind of second lien is forcing a sale of the equipment.

a. If this information is correct, is there any reason for Diamond Head to be concerned? U.C.C. §§9-611(c)(3), 9-617(b), 9-625(b).

b. Can Diamond Head protect its position by purchasing the equipment at the sale? U.C.C. §9-615(a).

c. Can Diamond Head prevent the sale? U.C.C. §§9-609(a), 9-401.

d. Assuming that the creditor forcing this sale was an Article 9 secured party, was Diamond Head entitled to receive notice of this sale? U.C.C. §9-611 and Comment 4 to that section.

26.4. You had never intended to get so intimately involved in debtor-creditor relations, but a friend needs to borrow $10,000 from you. She is willing to give you a second mortgage against the house she recently bought for $120,000. The house is subject to an $80,000 first mortgage and appears to be easily worth more than $90,000.

a. If your friend defaults on the $10,000 loan and you have to look to the house for repayment, what will you do?

b. Will taking that action assure recovery of your $10,000?

c. What will happen if your friend makes the payments on your mortgage, but defaults in payments under the first mortgage?

d. Can you protect yourself against default under the first mortgage by a provision in your loan or mortgage agreement?

26.5. After the decision in *Grocers Supply*, Bob Gorman, president of Intercity Investments, directed the sheriff to surrender possession of the Grocery Store inventory to Grocers Supply and paid Grocers Supply $24,000 in satisfaction of the judgment. Gorman discharged the attorneys who represented Intercity in the execution and came to you for advice on how to collect Intercity's $36,000 judgment against The Grocery Store and Cedric Wise. It appears that after its victory in court, Grocers Supply instructed the sheriff to return the inventory to The Grocery Store, the sheriff has done so, and The Grocery Store is back in business. Wiser from his earlier experience, Gorman contacted Grocers Supply and told them that he intended to execute on the inventory again to enforce his judgment. Grocers Supply objected, saying that they preferred that the inventory remain in place, and threatened that if Gorman executed "it will just be a repeat of the earlier case." Gorman thinks the inventory is worth more than enough to pay both liens, and Grocers Supply is only objecting in order to protect the Grocery Store. "If they can do this," Gorman says, "any debtor with a cooperative secured creditor can beat its judgment creditors." What do you tell Gorman?

26.6. Your firm has just picked up a new client, Fidelity Mortgage. Fidelity is an Alaska lender that frequently lends against real property, taking a first mortgage in the property. You review Fidelity's current standard loan documents and you notice they say nothing about property taxes, which may range anywhere from 1 to 3 percent of the value of the property each year. Alaska Stat. §29.45.300 has a provision of the type common in most U.S. jurisdictions: "Property taxes, together with penalty and interest, are a lien upon the property assessed, and the lien is prior and paramount to all other liens or encumbrances against the property." If they are not paid within two years, the state forecloses the property tax lien and the property is sold to the highest bidder at auction. The proceeds of sale are applied first to the tax and then to subordinate liens.

a.   If one of Fidelity's debtors fails to pay property taxes and the state forecloses, what is the effect on Fidelity's mortgage?

b.   If such a foreclosure is already under way against one of Fidelity's mortgagors, what can Fidelity do to protect itself?

c.   What suggestions do you have for reforming Fidelity's standard form contract?

26.7.   You represent Commercial Finance, a commercial lender. It holds a second mortgage in the amount of $2.3 million against an industrial plant. (That amount includes principal, interest, attorneys' fees, and the estimated costs of conducting the mortgage foreclosure sale.) The plant is the only asset of the debtor, Industrial Manufacturers, Inc. (Industrial). The principals of Industrial have personally guaranteed payment of the mortgage debt, but it is unclear whether any deficiency against them will be collectible. The foreclosure of Commercial's mortgage is complete and the sale is set for next week. The first mortgage in the amount of $4.1 million in favor of City State Bank is in default, but the bank has not yet begun to foreclose. Commercial has asked you to prepare the bidding strategy for the upcoming sale. It believes that if the property were marketed and sold privately, it would bring between $4.2 million and $5.6 million, with the most likely resale price being about $5 million. Commercial estimates its out-of-pocket costs of buying, holding, and reselling the plant at $200,000, and an additional $300,000 of interest and attorneys' fees will accrue on the first mortgage during the time it would take to resell the plant. How much should Commercial bid at the sale? Organize your answer by assuming a resale of the property for exactly $5 million, then explain how the numbers change if the property actually brings more or less.

Assignment 27: The Concept of Priority: Bankruptcy Law

As we discussed in Assignments 6 and 7, security interests and liens survive the filing of a bankruptcy case. Through confirmation of a plan in a case under Chapter 11, 12, or 13, bankruptcy can reduce the amount of the lien to an amount equal to the value of the collateral as determined by the court and extend the time for repayment. In addition, during bankruptcy, some kinds of liens can be *avoided* because they are unperfected (Assignment 30) or are preferences (Assignment 31). Except to the extent these things occur, security interests and liens survive the resolution of the bankruptcy case as well. Generally speaking, the liens of secured creditors and their order of priority are maintained both in and out of bankruptcy.

At the most fundamental level, "priority" means that when the value of collateral is sufficient to pay only one of two lien creditors, the law will seek to assure that the value is applied to payment of the one who has priority. In this sense, the meaning of "priority" does not change when the debtor goes into bankruptcy.

In other respects, the meaning of "priority" does change. Recall the two basic principles of priority with which we began Assignment 26. First, absent an agreement to the contrary, any lien holder may foreclose at any time after default. As we discussed in Assignment 6, the automatic stay contradicts that principle: The secured creditor cannot foreclose until the stay is terminated. Bankr. Code §362(a). Secured creditors can seek relief from the stay, but there is no assurance it will be granted. Bankr. Code §362(d). The second basic principle was that no lien holder could be compelled to foreclose. Although the debt might be in default, it remained the right of the secured creditor to choose the time to foreclose its own lien and to force a sale. As will be discussed in this assignment, the rules of bankruptcy procedure contradict that principle as well: The trustee or debtor in possession can sell the secured creditor's collateral "free and clear of liens," effectively foreclosing the secured creditor's lien on the trustee's or debtor's own timetable. Thus, while the debtor is in bankruptcy, the secured creditor continues to enjoy its priority, but the meaning of "priority" has been altered.

This transfer of control over the timing of foreclosure from the secured creditor to the trustee or debtor in possession signals an important difference in the focus of the state remedies and bankruptcy systems. In accord with the terms of the security agreement explicitly agreed to between the debtor and the secured creditor and implicitly agreed to by others who chose to become creditors knowing of the secured creditor's lien (or, when the others are unsecured creditors, knowing that the debtor could later grant a lien that would defeat them), the state remedies system puts the most senior secured creditor's interests first. The bankruptcy system gives less credence to these supposed agreements and focuses instead on maximizing the value of the bankruptcy estate for the benefit of all concerned. To accomplish that goal, it may compel secured creditors to leave their collateral in place so that the business of the estate can continue or so that the debtor can go on earning a living. This is not done for the benefit of the fully secured creditors: Most fully secured creditors could recover as much through foreclosure as they could through bankruptcy. Instead, the bankruptcy system holds fully secured creditors in place primarily for the benefit of the marginally secured or unsecured creditors and the debtor. This change in focus too can be thought of as a change in the meaning of "priority" as a case moves from the state remedies system to the bankruptcy system and perhaps back again if the bankruptcy case is dismissed.

In the remainder of this assignment, we take a closer look at three ways in which the priority rights of secured creditors are diminished in bankruptcy. The first is through the trustee or debtor in possession's ability to sell collateral free and clear of liens; the second is the trustee or debtor in possession's ability to grant liens senior to existing liens; and the third is the shift in focus from the protection of more senior creditors to the protection of more junior ones.

A.   Bankruptcy Sale Procedure

As we touched on briefly in Assignment 7, during a bankruptcy case the trustee or debtor in possession can sell collateral. These sales may be judicial sales, held pursuant to an order of the court and confirmed afterward by the court, or they may be nonjudicial sales held pursuant to the powers vested in the debtors in possession (DIPs) or trustees by statute. See Bankr. Code §§363(b)(1) and (c)(1).

As in foreclosure sales under state law, in bankruptcy sales the collateral may be sold subject to the liens of secured creditors. Once such a sale is complete, the collateral ceases to be "property of the [bank-ruptcy] estate," the automatic stay expires, and, if the debt is in default, the secured creditor will be free to foreclose. Bankr. Code §362(c). Again, as in a state law foreclosure action, purchasers in such a sale acquire only the debtor's equity in the property. Ordinarily they will deduct from their offers the additional amounts they expect to pay later to secured creditors to clear the title to the property. If the liens against collateral exceed its value, no one may be willing to buy it subject to the liens. The collateral is then con-sidered "burdensome" to the estate and the debtor or trustee can abandon it. Bankr. Code §554. Abandonment, like sale, removes the property from the estate, revests the property in the debtor, termi-nates the automatic stay, and opens the way for the lien holders to foreclose. Bankr. Code §362(c).

Unlike state law, bankruptcy law provides an alternative procedure under which a trustee or DIP can sell collateral "free and clear" of the liens of secured creditors. Bankr. Code §363(f). A sale free and clear of liens works much the same way as a foreclosure sale by the first lien holder in the absence of bankruptcy: The buyer takes unencumbered title to the property and presumably pays its full value as the pur-chase price. The liens are transferred to the proceeds of sale, with the ultimate effect that the proceeds are applied to the liens in the order of their priority.

In the absence of bankruptcy, a secured creditor can choose the time at which it will foreclose. Though another secured creditor with a prior lien can foreclose against it, neither the debtor nor secured creditors with subordinate liens can involuntarily dislodge the secured creditor from its position against the collateral by anything less than full payment. The ability to sell free and clear of liens in bankruptcy deprives the secured creditor of this control over the tim-ing of foreclosure. If the trustee or DIP can prove grounds for selling the collateral free and clear of liens, the trustee or DIP — *not* the secured creditor — chooses when to sell. The difference is critical to a lien holder who will recover nothing from an immediate sale free and clear of liens, but who might recover from a later sale if the property appreciated in value or was sold in a better market.

In the case that follows, a defaulting debtor won the right to sell a secured creditor's collateral over the secured creditor's vehement objection. According to a two-year-old appraisal, the collateral had been worth enough to cover nearly the entire amount of the creditor's $600,000 lien, but the court's decision authorizes its sale for an amount barely sufficient to pay the prior liens. The objecting creditor's $600,000 lien will be wiped out with only nominal payment.

In re Oneida Lake Development, Inc.

114 B.R. 352 (Bankr. N.D.N.Y. 1990)

STEPHEN D. GERLING, UNITED STATES BANKRUPTCY JUDGE. . . .

This contested matter comes before the Court on the motion of Oneida Lake Development, Inc., d/b/a Wood Pointe Marine ("Debtor") for an order pursuant to §363 of the Bankruptcy Code (11 U.S.C.A. §101-1330) (West 1989) ("Code"), permitting it to sell all of its real estate, together with all physical assets to Raymond H. Bloss ("Bloss") for the sum of $750,000.00 in accordance with the terms of a written purchase offer which is subject to the approval of this Court. . . .

At [a] hearing objections to the sale were interposed by Thomas K. Crowley ("Crowley") and Wood Pointe Venturers ("WPV"), both judgment creditors, while Merchants Bank & Trust Company of Syracuse ("Merchants"), conditionally objected to the sale seeking only to have its junior mortgage paid in full upon closing. . . .

FACTS

Debtor filed a voluntary petition pursuant to Chapter 11 of the Code on September 11, 1989. On November 11, 1989 Debtor entered into a contract for the sale of its real property designated as the Wood Pointe Marina at Oneida Lake, New York for the sum of $750,000.00. The contract also included all inventory and equipment, excepting boats subject to any floor plan agreement.

It does not appear that the contract was expressly contingent upon the approval of this Court, although it does contain a reference to "Bankruptcy proceedings." (See Offer to Purchase attached to Debtor's Motion Papers.)

As of the date of filing, it appears that the Debtor's real property was encumbered by three mortgages, three judgments and delinquent real estate taxes totaling in excess of 1.3 million dollars.

While there apparently is no dispute with regard to the validity of the three mortgages and the delinquent real property taxes, the Debtor has commenced an adversary proceeding to set aside two of the three judgments as preferences, and those proceedings are presently pending.

The third judgment in the sum of $600,000 is held by WPV and while the Debtor's moving papers suggest that it too will be either compromised or become the subject of a similar adversary proceeding, no such proceeding has as yet been commenced.

It is apparent that if all three judgments are set aside, a sale price of not less than $750,000.00 will be substantially in excess of the remaining liens. The Bloss offer, however, provides for the purchaser to assume the first and second mortgages and for the Debtor to take back a third mortgage securing $140,000.00, so that the Debtor will only receive $250,000.00 in cash at the time of closing.

Debtor has provided the Court with an appraisal of the real property prepared in 1987 reflecting the fair market value at 1.25 million dollars, however, a revision of that appraisal as of November 30, 1989 reflects a significant decrease in that value. . . .

ARGUMENTS

At the hearing held before the Court on December 19, 1989, both Crowley and WPV objected to the sale. However, in his Memorandum of Law filed January 2, 1990, Crowley purports to withdraw its objection based upon (1) improper notice, and (2) Code §363(f) and now urges the Court to approve the sale "upon the terms set forth both in the Debtor's motion and at the hearing."

WPV also faxed a Memorandum of Law to the Court on January 2, 1990 in support of their objection to the sale. WPV contends that a sale pursuant to Code §363(b) requires notice and a hearing, and that the hearing must be an evidentiary hearing. . . . WPV contends further that such a hearing is also necessary to determine the issues raised by Code §363(f). . . .

WPV also postures that Debtor cannot comply with Code §363(f) since there is no bona fide dispute as to its judgment (§363(f)(4)), that the sale will not produce a full money satisfaction of its judgment (§363(f)(5)), and that the remaining subsections of Code §363(f) are concededly inapplicable.

Crowley's Memorandum of Law argues that WPV's judgment is in bona fide dispute and that, in fact, Debtor's counsel has indicated its intent to commence an adversary proceeding challenging WPV's judgment as a preference, thus complying with the requirements of Code §363(f)(4). Crowley also contends that Debtor's sale may be approved pursuant to Code §363(f)(3) since a proper interpretation of that subsection requires the Court to value the secured creditor's lien at the actual value of the collateral subject to the lien, and not at the face amount of the lien, thus adequately protecting the lien which is all that a secured creditor is entitled to under the applicable provisions of the Code dealing with secured claims. . . .

DISCUSSION . . .

Turning to a consideration of Code §363(f), there appears to be no dispute that that section authorizes a debtor to sell its property free and clear of liens and encumbrances, so long as it can satisfy any one of the five subsections. It is equally clear that subsections (f)(1), (2) and (5) cannot be complied with by the Debtor. At issue then is whether the Debtor has established compliance with either subsection (3) or (4).

Subsection (f)(3) authorizes a sale by debtor free and clear of liens and encumbrances only where the sale price "is greater than the aggregate value of all liens on such property."

Both the Debtor and Crowley argue in their respective Memoranda of Law that the term "value" as utilized in Code §363(f)(3) must be defined by reference to Code §506(a) which defines secured status as extending only to "the value of such creditor's interest in the estate's interest in such property," thus negating the contention that value is determined by looking solely to the face amount of the lien in analyzing Code §363(f)(3).

Crowley cites the well-reasoned opinion of Bankruptcy Judge Howard Buschman, III, in In re Beker Industries Corp., 63 Bankr. 474 (Bankr. S.D.N.Y. 1986), which supports the concept that the value and not the amount of the liens is what the Court must look to in applying Code §363(f)(3).

Bankruptcy Judge Buschman suggests that the Code's statutory scheme authorizes a debtor to deal with its secured assets by insuring simply that the secured creditor receives only the value of its secured claim in debtor's property, even though that may be significantly less than the face amount of the claim by referencing Code §1129(b)(2)(A)(i) and §1129(b)(2)(A)(ii).

While Judge Buschman acknowledges that there is significant authority to the effect that *value* as used in Code §363(f)(3) is synonymous with *amount*, this Court believes that the *Beker* analysis comports with Congressional intent in utilizing the term "value" versus the term "amount" in the statute. *Beker* does point out, however, that the Court must conclude that the proposed sale price is the best price obtainable under the circumstances and further that it must find special circumstances justifying the sale for less than the amount of liens over the objection of a secured creditor.

Applying the rationale of *Beker* to the instant case, the Court concludes that, even without conducting an evidentiary hearing, which would only serve to significantly delay a sale of the marina property, the current appraisal submitted by Debtor in light of the bidding that occurred on December 19, 1989, is the best possible price that could be obtained for the property. That further both the status of the non-consenting creditor WPV as a non-consensual judgment lienor whose judgment is at least arguably subject to attack under Code §547 and the apparent rapid depreciation of the property provide special circumstances which suggest that the Debtor has met the requirements of Code §363(f)(3).

Turning to an analysis of Code §363(f)(4), both Debtor and Crowley contend that that subsection has been satisfied, since at a minimum, the lien of WPV, the objector, is in bona fide dispute, and should that lien be avoided, the [$750,000 offer] would easily exceed the sum of all of the other existing liens and leave significant equity for the Chapter 11 Debtor.

WPV postures that in order to satisfy the requirement of "bona fide dispute" the lien must be the subject of an adversary proceeding and there must be a high probability that the adversary proceeding will result in the avoidance of the lien. WPV points out that the validity of the judgment lien is not presently the subject of any adversary proceeding. . . .

Bankruptcy Judge A. Thomas Small's decision in In re Millerburg, 61 Bankr. at 125 (Bankr. E.D.N.C. 1986) is cited by both Crowley and WPV in support of their respective positions. However, the Court believes that WPV reads more into Judge Small's decision than its plain language will support.

WPV construes *Millerburg* as requiring that the facts must suggest that the debtor has a high probability of success in the adversary proceeding which seeks to avoid the lien in order for a bona fide dispute to exist within the meaning of Code §363(f)(4).

Bankruptcy Judge Small simply observed, however, that the facts in that particular case suggested that the debtor would have a high probability of success in avoiding the creditor's lien as a preference under Code §547, however, the debtor had not even commenced an adversary proceeding. The Court commented that "the potential preference action against GMAC would certainly qualify as a bona fide dispute for purposes of §363(f)(4)." Id. page 128. (emphasis added).

This Court reads *Millerburg* as supporting the position of Crowley and the Debtor, and it concludes that Code §363(f)(4) has been satisfied even though the Debtor has not as yet commenced the adversary proceeding versus WPV.

Under nonbankruptcy law, it probably would have been impossible for the debtor to sell WPV's collateral over its objection and free of its lien. Absent foreclosure by a senior lien, WPV could have sat tight, accrued interest, and waited for a better market or a better buyer. But the debtor's bankruptcy filing changed all that. If the value of the collateral rises back to $1.25 million, it will be the buyer, Bloss, not the mortgagee, WPV, who reaps the benefit.

One circumstance in which the bankruptcy power to sell free and clear of liens can achieve greater economic efficiency than the non-bankruptcy foreclosure sale procedure is where the amounts and priorities of competing liens against the collateral are in doubt and the collateral is depreciating in value. By selling free and clear of liens and transferring the liens, whatever their priority and amount, to the proceeds of sale, the debtor or trustee can prevent further losses.

Consider, for example, the case of two creditors who hold mortgages against a shopping center that is under construction. The debtor is in financial difficulty and has defaulted in payments under both mortgages. Work on the property has ceased and the building now sits idle. Assume that the two mortgage holders are unsure which mortgage is entitled to priority.

In the absence of bankruptcy, one of the creditors would file a foreclosure action, alleging that the other was subordinate. The court would determine the priority of the mortgages before entering final judgment of foreclosure. Only then could the sale be held. The litigation might go on for years, while interest accrued and the property remained vacant.

In a bankruptcy case, the debtor or trustee could effect a sale free and clear of the two mortgages. Bankr. Code §363(f)(4). The buyer could resume construction immediately while the proceeds of sale earned interest in a bank account under the control of the bankruptcy court. The court could then determine the priority of the two mortgages at its leisure.

Just as in a nonbankruptcy foreclosure sale, secured creditors in a bankruptcy sale free and clear of liens are protected by their right to "bid in" the amounts of their liens. Bankr. Code §363(k). But in this regard, the major strength of the sale free and clear of liens is also its great weakness. The secured creditor who is unsure of the amount and priority of its lien may face a difficult problem in determining how much to bid.

B. The Power to Grant Senior Liens

As we discussed in the preceding section, a trustee or DIP can elect to sell encumbered collateral. Alternatively, the trustee or DIP can keep the property and offer it as collateral for postpetition loans. In the latter case, the trustee or DIP may be able to alter the priority of pre-existing liens in ways not possible at state law.

Under state law, liens generally rank in priority in the order in which they are created and perfected. As we saw in earlier assignments, the usual procedure for lending against collateral is to inspect the collateral and search the public records to determine what liens currently encumber it. Thus, the lender can know before making the loan what priority its security interest initially will have. Moreover, because *liens rank in priority in the order in which they are created*, the lender can also know that its initial priority will not change. That is, if there are no liens against the collateral at the time a creditor lends and perfects its security interest, the lender's security interest will become a first lien. Once it becomes first, it will remain first; competing liens will be subordinate because they were created at a later time. The value of the lender's security interest may still fluctuate with the value of the collateral, but the lender can rest assured that whatever that value may be, the lender has the first claim to it.

Even under state law, there may be exceptions to the rule that the first lien created and perfected has first priority. But the exceptions are rare and generally of a manageable nature. The example we have used before is that, under the statutes of most states, property taxes assessed against collateral constitute a lien prior to all others, including first mortgages. To maintain their first position, first mortgage lenders generally seek to compel their debtors to pay the property taxes as they accrue. If their debtors do not, the secured creditors pay the property taxes and foreclose. This approach is feasible because property taxes accrue at predictable times and in predictable amounts that are generally small in relation to the amount of the first mortgage. Property taxes are not the only exception. In a few states, the lien of a person who repairs collateral, such as a mechanic, will have priority over preexisting security interests. Here, too, the creditor's strategy is likely to be to pay such liens as they accrue in order to maintain a first position.

Once a debtor is in bankruptcy, this seemingly fundamental tenet of security — that the lien first created and perfected has first priority — no longer holds. In limited circumstances, the trustee or DIP can borrow additional money from a *postpetition lender*, secured by a lien prior to existing liens. Bankr. Code §364(d). Before doing so, the trustee or DIP must notify the holder of the first lien of its intention. If the holder objects (which it almost certainly will), the court must hold a hearing to determine that the Code prerequisites to such borrowing have been satisfied. The prerequisites are that (1) the estate is unable to borrow the money without granting a prior lien and (2) there is adequate protection of the interest of the secured creditor whose lien is being displaced.

The Bankruptcy Code permits the granting of prior liens on the theory that additional, postpetition financing is often essential to the successful operations of the business. If it is not forthcoming, the business may fail and its future income be lost. If the senior lender is adequately protected from loss, it presumably will suffer no loss from its demotion in priority. By permitting the debtor to do what is necessary to keep the business running, the debtor may be able to protect the junior creditors (and, not incidentally, itself) against loss without harming anyone.

Why, then, are secured creditors usually so unhappy about this supposedly win-win strategy? First, the secured creditor typically gains nothing from the transaction. It was already secured, and probably would have come out just fine in a foreclosure. Second, the adequate protection dispensed by the bankruptcy courts is no guarantee against loss. To illustrate, assume that the DIP seeks to borrow from Newlender and grant Newlender a first mortgage against property already encumbered by Oldlender's mortgage. On the DIP's motion, the bankruptcy court decides that the value of the collateral is well in excess of both mortgages and that the excess (the "cushion of equity") will provide Oldlender with adequate protection. Further assume that the court's decision proves to be wrong, either because the property was never worth as much as the judge thought or because it later declined in value. The DIP then sells the property, free and clear of liens, for less than enough to pay both mortgages. The DIP pays Newlender in full and applies any excess to Oldlender's mortgage debt. What happens to the unpaid balance of Oldlender's mortgage debt? If you guessed that the judge pays it out of the judge's salary, you were wrong. In fact, it becomes an unsecured claim. Although it has priority over virtually all other kinds of unsecured claims, Bankr. Code §507(b), it may not be paid because the estate has insufficient assets. Although this scenario occurs with some frequency, neither of the authors has ever known a judge or a debtor even to apologize.

Granting senior liens to postpetition lenders is not a common occurrence, but the effect of permitting it is nevertheless profound. In essence, it transforms priority from the right of the secured creditor to be paid first to the mere right to adequate protection against nonpayment. Oldlender in the above illustration can be likened to a mountain hiker who, having arrived first on a dangerous ledge, positions herself as far from the edge as possible. As other hikers arrive behind her, they ask that she move a little closer to the edge to make room for them against the mountainside. When she protests, they tell her she'll still be safe, because the distance between her and the edge will still be adequate. Probably her best retort is that if it's so safe out there, why don't *they* stand there and let *her* stay against the mountainside? To understand the somewhat disingenuous position of the Bankruptcy Code on this point, consider that the trustee must prove two things to make Oldlender stand closer to the edge: (1) it's safe out there and (2) the debtor couldn't find anyone else who would stand out there.

At the inception of the following case, John Hancock Insurance Company held a $4 million first mortgage on the debtor's building, which was worth only $2.2 million. By a feat virtually the legal equivalent of alchemy, the debtor used Bankruptcy Code §364(d) to borrow even more money against the building — and put the new lender ahead of John Hancock.

In re 495 Central Park Avenue Corp.

136 B.R. 626 (Bankr. S.D.N.Y. 1992)

HOWARD SCHWARTZBERG, UNITED STATES BANKRUPTCY JUDGE

DECISION ON APPLICATION FOR AN ORDER
AUTHORIZING SENIOR SECURED CREDIT UNDER
SECTION 364(d)

495 Central Avenue Corp. ("495 Central Avenue"), the debtor in this
Chapter 11 case, has moved pursuant to 11 U.S.C. §364(d) for an order
authorizing it to borrow funds from either Leon Silverman ("Silverman")
and Tom Borek ("Borek"), shareholders of the debtor, or from third-party
lenders supported by the personal guaranties of Silverman and Borek and
permitting the lender to obtain a security interest senior to all existing
security interests. John Hancock Mutual Life Insurance Company ("Hancock"), a secured creditor which holds a first mortgage on the debtor's
property, opposes the debtor's motion. Hancock contends that the
debtor has failed to meet the requirements of 11 U.S.C. §364(d) asserting that the debtor has not demonstrated that it has been unable to
obtain credit by any other means and that the debtor has failed to show
that Hancock's position is adequately protected. . . .

FINDINGS OF FACT

1. The debtor, 495 Central Avenue, filed with this court on September
5, 1991, a voluntary petition for reorganizational relief under Chapter 11
of the Bankruptcy Code. The debtor thereafter continued in possession
and control of its assets as a debtor in possession in accordance with 11
U.S.C. §§1107 and 1108.
2. The debtor's primary asset is real property and a building located at
495 Central Avenue, Scarsdale, New York. The debtor leases space in the
building to various commercial tenants.
3. The debtor acquired the premises at 495 Central Avenue from Viewpoint Realty Corporation ("Viewpoint") in April, 1991. The debtor took
the property subject to an existing mortgage held by Hancock. In addition, the debtor paid Viewpoint $202,500.00 in cash and executed a
purchase money mortgage in the amount of $200,000.00 payable to
Viewpoint over five years in six-month installments. The purchase money
mortgage is subordinate to Hancock's secured position.
4. Hancock holds a mortgage on the property in the principal
amount of $3,950,000.00. In October, 1988, Viewpoint executed a
promissory note and a mortgage to Hancock secured by the premises.

Hancock duly recorded the mortgage. Under the terms of the security agreement, principal and interest are payable in monthly installments over a period of five years and the entire amount of unpaid principal is due on November 1, 1993. In the event of default, Hancock has the right to accelerate the entire debt. The agreement also requires real estate taxes to be placed in an escrow account on a monthly basis.

5. Under the security agreement, $35,418.34 is the monthly amount presently payable to Hancock on the mortgage and $12,954.64 must be escrowed for real estate tax liability each month. Because the debtor purchased the property at 495 Central Avenue subject to Hancock's mortgage, the debtor must make required payments to avoid foreclosure. While the debtor only purchased the property subject to Hancock's mortgage, the debtor did not assume the promissory note that Viewpoint had executed in favor of Hancock. Therefore, Viewpoint remains obligated on the mortgage note held by Hancock. Thus, Viewpoint, the former owner of the property, will be liable for any mortgage deficiency in the event of a foreclosure.

6. The debtor violated the terms and provisions of the mortgage held by Hancock by failing to make the required monthly mortgage payments on July 1, 1991. Following the default, Hancock accelerated the entire debt which totaled $3,937,993.25 and, in August, 1991, commenced a foreclosure action in New York State Supreme Court, Westchester County. That action was stayed upon the debtor's filing of the bankruptcy petition pursuant to 11 U.S.C. §362(a).

7. The debtor has moved in this court for an order permitting it to obtain credit under 11 U.S.C. §364(d), either from its shareholders, Silverman and Borek, or from a third-party lender, which would prime the secured positions of Hancock and Viewpoint. The debtor asks the court to grant its motion on the grounds that it has met the requirements imposed by 11 U.S.C. §364(d). First, the debtor contends that it has shown through its appraiser that Hancock's secured position is adequately protected. The debtor also argues it has established, through the testimony of Silverman as well as an independent expert witness, that alternate financing could not be obtained. Hancock opposes the debtor's motion arguing that the debtor has failed to demonstrate that the requirements of 11 U.S.C. §364(d) have been met. Hancock further argues that the motion should be denied because subordination of its position would violate 11 U.S.C. §1129(b), which provides that secured claims are entitled to priority over junior claims. Viewpoint, the second mortgagee, does not oppose the debtor's motion.

8. Silverman, the president of the debtor, explained that the debtor needed to borrow money to enable it to make structural changes in the building at 495 Central Avenue to attract new tenants. [The court discussed Silverman's negotiations with prospective tenants and the kinds of renovations the prospective tenants wanted.]

14. The debtor needs money to renovate the building in order to enter into a lease agreement with Leather Center. Silverman testified that he has diligently sought to borrow funds on behalf of the debtor from various financial institutions. He stated that every bank has refused to lend the debtor money despite his and Borek's offers to guarantee the debt personally.

15. Henry Farrand ("Farrand"), a Commercial Loan Officer at Hudson Valley National Bank, is a commercial loan specialist and was certified as an expert in this case in commercial lending practices under Federal Rule of Evidence 702. Farrand testified that, in his opinion, all legitimate financial institutions would refuse to lend the debtor money because such a loan would be junior to Hancock's secured position. He explained that banks ordinarily demand a first position on commercial real estate loans and that a junior lien or an administrative priority simply will not suffice.

16. Roger Miller ("Miller"), the debtor's real estate appraiser, valued the building at 495 Central Avenue at $2,250,000.00. Miller utilized the income approach in making his valuation, basing his appraisal on the net income that the property is presently capable of producing. According to Miller, the income approach is the method typically used by appraisers to value income producing property such as the debtor's building.

17. Miller testified that additional rental revenue would enhance the building's market value. In his opinion, if the debtor invested $625,000.00 in renovating the property in question, its value would immediately increase to $3,500,000.00 because, after the infusion of capital, the building would be capable of producing higher rental income. Miller explained that this figure is based upon the current discounted value of the cash flow which he predicted the building would generate during the next seven years. According to his cash flow projections, Miller estimated that the building would be worth $4,000,000.00 in three years and $5,000,000.00 in five years.

18. Steven Levine ("Levine"), Hancock's appraiser, employing the income approach to valuation, concluded that the debtor's building is presently worth $2,200,000.00. Levine testified that the market value of the property would rise if its ability to produce rental income increased. He testified that after the proposed renovations, the building would be worth approximately $2,800,000.00.

19. Both experts agree if improvements of the property are made with the proposed borrowed funds, the property will increase in value. They differ, however, as to the extent of the increase in value. It is no surprise that Hancock's expert appears to be extremely conservative in calculating the expected increase in value, whereas the debtor's expert is overly optimistic in his view. The court finds that the proposed improvements will probably cause the property to increase in value to approximately $3,000,000.00. This amounts to an increase of $800,000.00 over the $2,200,000.00 appraised value expressed by Hancock's appraiser.

20. In light of the fact that the projected property improvements to be made with the requested credit will exceed the $650,000.00 loan, it follows that Hancock's secured interest will be adequately protected after the approval of the proposed $650,000.00 senior loan.

Discussion

The procedure by which a debtor may obtain credit is set forth in 11 U.S.C. §364. 11 U.S.C. §364(d)(1) enables a debtor to obtain financing secured by a lien senior to all other interests. . . . A debtor in possession has the rights, powers, and duties of a trustee pursuant to 11 U.S.C. §1107(a). Therefore, 495 Central Avenue, as a debtor in possession, may utilize 11 U.S.C. §364(d) to obtain credit. The debtor has the burden of proving that the requirements of 11 U.S.C. §364(d) have been met. In this case, the debtor has presented substantial evidence that both prongs of 11 U.S.C. §364(d) have been satisfied.

Inability to Obtain Alternate Financing

The first prong of 11 U.S.C. §364(d) requires the debtor to show that alternate financing is unavailable. Because superpriority financing displaces liens on which creditors have relied in extending credit, the debtor must demonstrate to the court that it cannot obtain financing by other means. The Bankruptcy Code permits a debtor to borrow money in various ways less onerous to secured creditors. 11 U.S.C. §364. A debtor, pursuant to 11 U.S.C. §364(b), may incur unsecured debt as an administrative expense with first priority status under 11 U.S.C. §507(a)(1). If the debtor cannot obtain credit as an administrative expense, it may acquire a loan that is either unsecured but senior to all administrative expense claims, secured by a lien on property that is not secured, or secured by a junior lien on property already secured. 11 U.S.C. §364(c). If the debtor cannot obtain financing by any of these means, the debtor may invoke 11 U.S.C. §364(d) and obtain credit secured by a lien on property senior or equal to a prior lien.

In this case, it is clear that apart from 11 U.S.C. §364(d), the debtor cannot obtain credit. Section 364(d)(1) does not require the debtor to seek alternate financing from every possible lender. However, the debtor must make an effort to obtain credit without priming a senior lien. Silverman, on behalf of the debtor, has repeatedly tried to procure financing from various banks and lending institutions. Nevertheless, he testified that he was unable to receive financing in exchange for an unsecured position. No one was willing to lend the debtor money as an administrative expense or as an expense senior to all administrative claims.

Silverman also could not obtain credit secured by a lien junior to Hancock's secured position despite his diligent efforts. He stated that the banks were simply not interested in lending to the debtor. Farrand, a specialist in commercial lending practices, substantiated Silverman's testimony and explained that most banks lend money only in return for a senior secured position. The debtor cannot obtain financing secured by a lien on unencumbered property pursuant to 11 U.S.C. §363(c)(2) because there is no property in the estate which is not already subject to a lien. The debtor's property is encumbered by Hancock's lien which exceeds its appraised value.

Adequate Protection

The second prong of 11 U.S.C. §364(d) requires the debtor to show that the interests of the holder of an existing lien on the property are adequately protected. The Bankruptcy Code does not expressly define adequate protection. However, 11 U.S.C. §361 sets forth examples of this concept. Although 11 U.S.C. §361 presents some specific illustrations of adequate protection, the statute is not exclusive. Rather, it suggests a broad and flexible definition providing in pertinent part as follows:

> When adequate protection is required under section . . . 364 of this title of an interest of an entity in property, such adequate protection may be provided by . . .
>
>   (3) granting such other relief, other than entitling such entity to compensation allowable under section 503(b)(1) of this title as an administrative expense, as will result in the realization by such entity of the indubitable equivalent of such entity's interest in such property.

11 U.S.C. §361.

The statute confers upon "the parties and the courts flexibility by allowing such other relief as will result in the realization by the protected entity of the value of its in the property involved." House Report No. 95-595, 95th Cong., 1st Sess. (1978), reprinted in 1978 U.S. Code Cong. & Admin. News 5787, 6296. The goal of adequate protection is to safeguard the secured creditor from diminution in the value of its interest during the chapter 11 reorganization.

In the instant case, to determine whether Hancock is adequately protected, the court must consider whether the value of the debtor's property will increase as a result of the renovations funded by the proposed financing. Although appraisers for both sides disagree as to what the value of the building would be following the infusion of approximately $600,000.00, there is no question that the property would be improved by the proposed renovations and that an increase in value will result. In effect, a substitution occurs in that the money spent for improvements will be transferred into value. This value will serve as adequate protection for Hancock's secured claim. . . .

CONCLUSIONS OF LAW . . .

2. The debtor's motion to obtain senior priority financing under 11 U.S.C. §364(d) is granted because the statutory requirements have been satisfied. The debtor has shown that it could not incur debt by less onerous means. The debtor has also established that Hancock's secured position is adequately protected because the infusion of capital into the building will increase the value of the property.

3. The debtor may borrow money from Silverman and Borek, shareholders of the debtor, as a senior priority loan under 11 U.S.C. §364(d) because the statute does not prohibit such a loan.

SETTLE ORDER ON NOTICE

Some readers may have trouble with the court's finding that spending $650,000 on improvements to this $2,200,000 building will increase its value to $3,000,000. If the building plus the $650,000 are worth $3,000,000, why isn't the building worth $2,350,000 as it is? The explanation is that the court is not talking about market value, at least not in the sense that economists use the term. Rather, the court is saying that it thinks the investment is likely to be a productive one that will yield a good return.

Notice also that the court in *495 Central Park Avenue Corp.* adopts some of the colorful language of the bankruptcy lawyers. The court speaks of the proposed postpetition mortgage that will "prime" the first mortgage — meaning that it will have priority over it. It also talks of a "super priority," a phrase used to refer to the priority the court can grant to a new lender under Bankruptcy Code §364(d). (The same terminology is more commonly used to refer to the priority under Bankruptcy Code §507(b) of an adequately protected creditor whose protection proved inadequate.)

C. Protection of Subordinate Creditors

As noted earlier in this assignment, nonbankruptcy law emphasizes the protection of senior lien holders. Once the debtor is in default, a senior lien holder controls the timing of its own foreclosure, even though that foreclosure may have severe adverse effects on the positions of other lien holders and unsecured creditors. The power of the senior creditor to foreclose will be felt by all subordinate creditors, even as the subordinate creditors cannot force the senior to take any action.

Bankruptcy policy shifts the emphasis, positing essentially that the collection efforts of senior lien holders should be stayed if (1) the senior lien holders are adequately protected against loss (that is, the bankruptcy court does not think they are being asked to stand too close to the edge) and (2) the stay is likely to facilitate the collection efforts of subordinate creditors.

Bankruptcy policy can be thought of as analogous to the concept of triage in medicine. When resources are scarce, the injured are divided into three groups: (1) those who cannot benefit greatly from care because their injuries are relatively minor (they are told to wait), (2) those who cannot benefit greatly from care because their injuries are so severe they will die anyway, and (3) those who can benefit most from care because their injuries constitute a serious but probably not fatal threat. The scarce resources are expended on the third group. Bankruptcy policy can be viewed as dividing creditors into three analogous groups. In the first are adequately protected secured creditors who are likely to recover the full amounts of their claims regardless of what happens in the bankruptcy case (the automatic stay compels them to wait). In the second group are the holders of debts and liens so subordinate that they are unlikely ever to be paid, regardless of what happens in the bankruptcy case. Bankruptcy lawyers and judges talk about them as no longer having a real interest in the case. As with triage in medicine, bankruptcy policy focuses its attention and resources on the plight of the third group of creditors: those whose priority is sufficiently high that they may be able to be paid through an efficient and effective liquidation or reorganization, but not so high that they will be paid in any event.

To those versed solely in nonbankruptcy law, this emphasis on the rights of creditors of intermediate priority may seem contrary to the concept of priority itself. But it is important to keep in mind that the large majority of lenders consider the effects of both state law and bankruptcy law in determining what loans they will make and the terms upon which they will make them. As we noted at the outset, the concept of priority is defined not by state law, but by state law and bankruptcy law together.

Problem Set 27

27.1.   Katherine Kinski (from Problem 26.1) is back in your office. The foreclosure sale she investigated was never held. About an hour before the sale was to take place, the debtor filed under Chapter 7 of the Bankruptcy Code and the sheriff concluded that continuation of the sale was barred by the automatic stay. Kinski contacted the Chapter 7 trustee, who told her that in two weeks he would sell the property at auction sale free and clear of liens. How much should Kinski bid at the auction? Bankr. Code §§363(b)(1), (f), (k), and (m).

27.2.   You represent the Sicilian State Bank (SSB), which holds an $800,000 second security interest in railroad cars. In the current depressed market, the cars are worth only about $1 million. The first security interest in the amount of $1.1 million is held by Citibank. SSB made the loan two years ago when the market for railroad cars was at its peak and the collateral was worth $3 million. SSB thinks that within a year or two the market will come back and the cars will again have that value.

The debtor who owns the cars has filed for a Chapter 11 bankruptcy and proposes to sell the cars, free and clear of liens, for their current market value. If the cars are sold for $1 million, who will get what? Is there anything SSB can do to prevent the sale? Bankr. Code §§363(b), (f), and (k).

27.3.   Toi San Development is the owner of an office complex currently under construction. Liens against the property total $5 million. The first is in favor of American Bank, the construction lender, in the amount of $4 million. The remainder are mechanic's liens filed by suppliers and subcontractors who have not been paid. If the complex is sold in its present state of completion, it will bring only about $2 million. The cost of completing it will be about $1.5 million. Even then, it will be worth only about $4 million, still less than the amount of the liens.

Although Toi San Development is not in bankruptcy, it is out of cash and in financial trouble. The office complex is its only significant asset. Wendy Toi San, the owner of Toi San Development, has asked for your help in borrowing the money necessary to finish the project. American is preparing papers for foreclosure and says there is no way the Bank is putting another dime in this project. What are your ideas for getting financing to complete the construction? What legal obstacles will you face? Bankr. Code §§364, 506(a).

27.4.   Despite your attorney's advice to the contrary, you made the $10,000 loan to the friend described in Problem 26.4 and took a second mortgage against the house. Just as the attorney predicted, your friend defaulted on both mortgages and the first mortgage holder has filed for judicial foreclosure of its $80,000 mortgage loan. The house still appears to be worth as much as $120,000, but housing sales are slow and there are no buyers on the horizon. Even if there were, your friend is not yet ready to sell. You are not in bad shape financially, but as a first-year associate in a medium-size firm, there is no way you can raise $80,000 to pay off the first mortgage. What do you think will happen if the foreclosure sale is held? Where do you stand if your friend files for bankruptcy? Bankr. Code §§362(a) and (d), 363(b) and (f), 506(a).

Chapter 9. Competitions for Collateral

Assignment 28: Lien Creditors Against Secured Creditors: The Basics

In Assignment 16, we introduced a crude model of priority among liens. That model ranked liens chronologically in the order in which they were perfected. In Assignment 26, we refined the model by noting that the rules governing priority among the various kinds of liens are contained in diverse bodies of law. To list just a few, Congress determines the priority of tax liens, a complex superstructure of organizations controls the priority rules contained in the U.C.C., and state legislatures control priority among judgment liens. The courts are left to deal with the resulting inconsistencies. In this series of assignments, we examine these rules as they were written, one competition at a time.

Along the way, we will consider the effects of two circumstances that have spawned their own special rules of priority: future advances and purchase-money status. As to future advances, the principal issue is whether the priority date of a later advance should be the date of that advance or the date of the earlier transaction in which the future advance was contemplated. As to purchase-money status, the principal issue is what steps a later purchase-money lender must take to have priority over competing liens perfected earlier. We will see that the rules governing future advances and purchase-money lending, like the rules governing priority generally, differ from one competition to another.

In this assignment, we discuss three competitions, all involving lien creditors. They are (1) lien creditor against lien creditor, (2) lien creditor against Article 9 secured party, and (3) lien creditor against real estate secured party.

A. How Creditors Become "Lien Creditors"

The prototypical lien creditor is an unsecured creditor who won a judgment against the debtor, obtained a writ of execution, and then obtained a lien by levying on specific property of the debtor. U.C.C.

§9-102(a)(52) defines "lien creditor" somewhat more broadly as including any "creditor who has acquired a lien on the property involved by attachment, levy or the like."

Like execution, *attachment* is a legal process in which the plaintiff in litigation obtains a writ and delivers it to a sheriff, marshal, or other law enforcement officer, who then levies on property of the debtor. In a few jurisdictions, "attachment" is virtually a synonym for "execution." But in most, the distinction between attachment and execution is that an attachment occurs before judgment is entered, while execution occurs afterward. As you might expect, property seized pursuant to attachment is not immediately sold; it is held by the sheriff pending the outcome of the litigation.

Two other procedures by which an unsecured creditor may obtain lien creditor status are worthy of mention. *Garnishment* is the process by which a judgment creditor in most states reaches debts owing from a third party to the debtor or property of the debtor that is in the hands of a third party. The garnishing creditor becomes a lien creditor at the moment the writ of garnishment is served on the third party. In many jurisdictions, an unsecured creditor can garnish before obtaining a judgment in certain kinds of cases, subject to numerous statutory and constitutional restrictions. However, garnishment of wages held by an employer is prohibited prior to judgment in all states and even after judgment in a few.

The second procedure worth mentioning is the recordation of a judgment for money damages. In nearly all states, recordation of a money judgment in the real property recording system creates and perfects a lien against all real property owned by the debtor within the county. The judgment lien thus created will also reach any such property that the debtor later acquires while the judgment lien remains perfected.

Also, in a small but growing minority of states, a judgment creditor can record its judgment — or a notice of it — in the Uniform Commercial Code filing system and thereby create and perfect a lien against personal property of the debtor.

Judgment Liens on Real and Personal Property

Cal. Civ. Proc. Code (West 1994)

§697.310

(a) Except as otherwise provided by statute, a judgment lien on real property is created under this section by recording an abstract of a money judgment with the county recorder.

§697.510

(a) A judgment lien on personal property described in Section 697.530 is created by filing a notice of judgment lien in the office of the Secretary of State pursuant to this article.

§697.530

(a) A judgment lien on personal property is a lien on all interests in the following personal property that are subject to enforcement [of a money judgment] at the time the lien is created if a security interest in the property could be perfected under the Commercial Code by filing a financing statement at that time with the Secretary of State:

(1)   accounts receivable
(2)   chattel paper
(3)   equipment
(4)   farm products
(5)   inventory
(6)   negotiable documents of title

The filing officer indexes the notice of judgment lien thus filed in the same system with financing statements. A search of the Article 9 filing system will disclose the existence of the judgment.

Last, but certainly not least, a trustee in bankruptcy, including a debtor in possession under Chapter 11, has the rights of an hypothetical ideal lien creditor — essentially a lien creditor with no debilitating history or knowledge — who obtained a lien on all property of the debtor on the date of the filing of the bankruptcy case. For example, even if none of the debtor's creditors could prevail over an unrecorded mortgage because all knew about it, the debtor's trustee, as an ideal lien creditor, could prevail over it. See Bankr. Code §544(a). The trustee's rights as an ideal lien creditor are the subject of a later assignment in this book. We alert you to their existence now, because they lend added significance to the subject of this assignment. You must first know the rights of a lien creditor to calculate the rights of a trustee in bankruptcy.

B.   Priority Among Lien Creditors

The rules governing priority among competing lien creditors are generally found in state statutes. They set up a first-come, first-served system. That is, the first creditor to take the legally designated crucial step has the first lien, the second to take that step has the second lien, and so forth. The laws generally award a lien priority as of one of four dates; we list them roughly in their frequency of use.

1. *Date of levy.* The reference here is to the date on which the sheriff or other officer took possession of particular property. Some states honor only actual physical possession by the sheriff; others consider various kinds of constructive or symbolic possession adequate. In some jurisdictions, the sheriff actually hauls moveable property back to a warehouse maintained for the purpose of holding property subject to a lien. In others, it may be adequate for the sheriff to post a notice on or about the property stating that the property is in the sheriff's possession.

2. *Date of delivery of the writ.* A writ of execution, attachment, or garnishment typically is issued by the clerk of the court on the request of a creditor who is entitled to it. The creditor then delivers the writ to the sheriff. In a large minority of states, including Illinois and Florida, writs of execution rank in the order in which they are delivered to the sheriff with instructions for levy on the property in issue. In some of these states, the lien comes into existence only on levy and may then be said to "relate back" to the date of delivery to the sheriff. This means that if two executions are delivered to the sheriff but only one is levied, then only the one levied is a lien. If and when the other execution is levied, it will have priority as of the date the creditor delivered the writ to the sheriff.

3. *Date of service of a writ of garnishment.* Service is the delivery of the writ by the sheriff to the garnishee, which is typically a bank or an employer.

4. *Date of recordation of judgment.* The date will be the date the judgment is delivered to the filing or recording officer. (In the large majority of states, this rule gives liens only in real estate.)

In a competition between writs of execution, the majority rule gives priority to the first to levy on the particular property. For example, in California, "A levy on property under a writ of execution creates an execution lien on the property from the time of levy. . . ." Cal. Civ. Proc. Code §697.710 (West 1994). Recall that a *levy* occurs when the sheriff takes possession of property pursuant to a writ of execution or attachment.

Under the minority rule, priority depends on the order in which the writs were delivered to the sheriff. While the New York statute that follows employs a combination of the minority and majority rules, the minority rule is predominant.

Priority Among Execution Creditors

N.Y. Civ. Proc. Law & Rules §5234(b)
(McKinney Supp. 1995)

Where two or more executions or orders of attachment are issued against the same judgment debtor and delivered to the same enforcement officer, they shall be satisfied out of the proceeds of personal property or debt levied upon by the officer in the order in which they were delivered. Where two or more executions or orders of attachment are issued against the same judgment debtor and delivered to different enforcement officers, and personal property or debt is levied upon within the jurisdiction of all of the officers, the proceeds shall be first applied in satisfaction of the execution or order of attachment delivered to the officer who levied, and thereafter shall be applied in satisfaction of the executions or orders of attachment delivered to those of the other officers who, before the proceeds are distributed, make a demand upon the officer who levied, in the order of such demands.

It is important to keep in mind that the priority rules for lien creditors are the creatures of state legislatures, and that diversity is great. To answer any particular question, it is nearly always necessary to consult the applicable statute.

C.   Priority Between Lien Creditors and Secured Creditors

Priority between a lien creditor and a nonpurchase-money Article 9 secured creditor depends on whether the lien creditor "becomes a lien creditor" before the secured creditor does either of two things: (1) perfects its security interest or (2) files a financing statement and complies with U.C.C. §9-203(b)(3).

Article 9 defines "perfection" in a highly technical manner. U.C.C. §9-308(a). A security interest is perfected only after it has attached and the "applicable steps required for perfection" have been taken. If, for example, the step taken to perfect is to file a financing statement, perfection will occur at the time of attachment or of filing, whichever is later. The important thing to notice here is that filing and perfection are not the same thing; they may or may not occur simultaneously.

It is, of course, possible that a lien creditor and a secured creditor will take the steps to assure their priority in a piece of collateral at about the same time. In fact, however, most competitions in priority between these two parties involve no race to the courthouse or the filing office and no close measurement of which party completed the necessary tasks first. Instead, most U.C.C. §9-317(a)(2) cases will involve either a trustee in bankruptcy or a creditor who took the steps necessary to become a lien creditor against the property. (Recall that every bankruptcy filing immediately gives the trustee the rights of an ideal lien creditor that levied at the moment of the filing of the petition.) After becoming a lien creditor, that person asserts that the apparently prior secured creditor failed to properly perfect its interest. The claim is often based on a defect in the secured creditor's filing. The issue is not when the secured creditor perfected, but whether the secured creditor perfected at all.

D. Purchase-Money Priority

As we mentioned previously, the fundamental principle underlying the system of priority among liens is that liens rank in the order in which they become public. Because the liens that will have priority are already public, one who contemplates taking a lien can evaluate the priority it will have before accepting it.

When a second-in-time interest takes precedence over an earlier interest, the cognoscenti describe the second secured creditor as "priming" the first. One of the most frequent events of priming occurs with *purchase-money security interests* (PMSIs), which may be granted and perfected long after the competing liens they prime. PMSIs are an exception to the fundamental principle of first in time is first in right, but the exception is not nearly so broad as it at first appears. In the context of competition between security interests and lien creditors the exception is brief and unlikely to cause difficulty for the holders of earlier interests. Under the rule stated in U.C.C. §9-317(e), a PMSI can prime a lien creditor's interest only if the PMSI comes into existence and attaches to the collateral before the creditor obtains its lien against that collateral. If the PMSI attaches first, the holder of the PMSI has a 20-day grace period in which it can perfect and thereby defeat a lien that came into existence between the dates of attachment and perfection of the PMSI. This means that if a debtor buys property on credit and the lien creditor levies before the secured creditor perfects its interest, the lien creditor will prevail unless the secured creditor perfects its interest within 20 days of the time the debtor received delivery of the property. The effect is that a purchase-money secured creditor that went public later can defeat a lien creditor who went public up to 20 days earlier.

The reason for allowing a 20-day grace period is to facilitate sales of personal property on secured credit. The grace period makes it possible for the seller to give immediate delivery to the buyer, without first filing its financing statement. Absent the grace period, purchase-money secured sellers might feel the need to file before delivery. The result might be to delay sale transactions.

The benefits of the grace period do not come without cost to the system. Relation back of the PMSI might surprise and disappoint the lien creditor who levied on the debtor's new property after running a U.C.C. search and finding them apparently free and clear. But the injury is likely to be relatively minor. Through its unsuccessful levy on the property, the lien creditor may have suffered additional expense and delay, but no lien creditor is likely to advance additional funds to the debtor on the basis of the deceptively clear title. Lien creditors who are concerned about the possibility of secret purchase-money liens might choose to delay their levies for 20 days after the debtor acquires new property to see if a PMSI shows up on the public record. But we don't think that will happen often. Lien creditors are usually in a hurry to establish their priority. Probably most will levy and wait to see if a purchase-money secured party files later.

Problem Set 28

28.1.   The local credit bureau reported today the entry of a judgment in the amount of $125,000 in favor of Sheng Electronics, an unsecured creditor of Conda Copper. Conda Copper also owes a $50,000 unsecured obligation to one of your clients, RFT Enterprises. Billy Williams, the owner of RFT, is concerned that by the entry of this judgment, Sheng will obtain priority in Conda's assets. "I have been patient with Conda, and they haven't," says Williams. "Why should my account be subordinated to theirs?" Can you think of a way that Williams could get priority over Sheng? U.C.C. §§9-317(a) and 9-323(b).

28.2.   Melinda Hu is in financial difficulty. Her friend, Phyllis Goldman, decides to lend her $20,000, which is to be secured by scaffolding and construction equipment owned by Melinda and located in Melinda's construction yard. On March 7, Melinda signs a financing statement, security agreement, and promissory note, but Phyllis does not disburse the money. Phyllis files the financing statement that same day and orders a search. On March 10, the sheriff levies on the equipment pursuant to a writ of execution in favor of Star Plastering. On March 11 Phyllis receives from the filing officer the report of her expedited search showing Phyllis's interest to the first filed against the equipment.

[handwritten marginal note: See Growers Supply — sellout-on party right as absolute to possess.]

a.   As matters now stand, is Phyllis perfected? U.C.C. §§9-308(a), 9-203(b).

b.   If Phyllis makes the $20,000 loan despite the levy, will she have priority over Star in the equipment? U.C.C. §9-317(a).

28.3.   Your client, National Business Credit (National), specializes in asset-based lending to small businesses that are in financial distress. All of National's loans are nonpurchase-money loans secured by tangible personal property. All are made in a state with clear precedent that a creditor "becomes a lien creditor" only when the sheriff takes actual physical possession of the property levied on. Because many of its debtors are high-risk, National wants to make sure its procedures are perfect. Ned Williams, head of the loan department, explains the theory under which National operates: "First, we get our own financing statement on file. Then we search to make sure no one filed ahead of us and we check the collateral to make sure it's in the possession of the debtor. Typically, we disburse within two weeks of the time we file and within a few days after we receive the search report." Ned wonders if, aside from an error in the search or physical verification, "there's any way an execution creditor could come ahead of us." What do you tell him? U.C.C. §§9-317(a)(2), 9-308(a). If there is a problem, what should he do about it?

28.4.   Assume that the state in which National lends adopts statutes identical to California Code of Civil Procedure §§697.510 and 697.530 (set forth in section A of this assignment), but its law otherwise remains the same. Should National change its loan procedure? U.C.C. §9-317(a)(2).

28.5.   Assume that the state in which National lends adopts a statute identical to New York Civil Procedure Law and Rules §5234(b) (set forth in section B of this assignment), but its law otherwise remains the same. Should National change its loan procedure? U.C.C. §9-317(a)(2).

28.6.   Bonnie Brezhnev, who recently purchased Bonnie's Boat World (BBW), calls to ask your advice. Earlier in the day, BBW sold a $35,000 Bayliner Boat to Edith Jones. BBW ran an "instant" credit check, which missed the fact that Edith's former husband, Orville, held an unrecorded judgment against her in the amount of $22,000 for unpaid alimony and child support. Edith paid $3,500 of the purchase price of the boat by check and signed a promissory note for the balance. Along with the note she signed a security agreement and a financing statement in favor of BBW. Edith immediately took possession of the boat and the documents landed in the in-basket of BBW's bookkeeper for processing.

As a result of some good detective work, Orville and a sheriff's deputy were waiting a block away when Edith rolled out of BBW's yard with the boat in tow. Orville and the sheriff followed her to the marina. As soon as she stopped, the sheriff levied on the boat and took possession of it.

Bonnie has two questions. First, can she get the boat back from the sheriff today? (The security agreement Edith signed provides that any levy on the collateral constitutes a default.) Second, is there anything else Bonnie should do? See The Grocers Supply Co. v. Intercity Investment Properties, Inc., in Assignment 26. See also U.C.C. §§9-102(23), 9-308(a), 9-309(1), 9-317(a) and (e), 9-609.

28.7.   Bonnie Brezhnev calls back with some bad news and some good news. The bad news is that she checked the documents after her earlier conversation with you. Edith signed the financing statement but not the security agreement. The space for the signature on the security agreement is blank. The good news is that Edith is at this very moment sitting in Bonnie's office, willing to sign the security agreement if you say it is okay. "I'd rather you got the boat than that #@$%&*," Edith tells Bonnie. What do you tell Bonnie? U.C.C. §9-317(e).

28.8.   You are a member of the U.C.C. Drafting Committee. The committee is considering a proposal to incorporate provisions permitting judgment creditors to obtain liens by filing their judgments in the statewide U.C.C. filing systems. The provisions are similar to California Civil Procedure Code §§697.310 and 607.530 set forth in section A. Do you think such provisions are in the public interest? Why or why not?

Assignment 29: Lien Creditors Against Secured Creditors: Future Advances

A. Priority of Future Advances: Personal Property

As we discussed in Assignment 9 of this book, secured creditors often continue to disburse money to their debtors after the initial loan transaction. For example, the secured party with an interest in the debtor's inventory and accounts receivable may advance additional funds each time the debtor acquires additional inventory or accounts. Similarly, the lender who finances construction of a building may make advances (referred to as *draws*) as the building reaches particular stages of completion.

Of course, most of the secured parties who make these advances would be unwilling to do so if their interest securing them might be subordinate to a lien creditor who levied on the collateral before the secured creditor made the advance. Such a secured party theoretically could protect itself against that possibility by repeating its search for lien creditors before making each new advance and refusing to make the advance if one has intervened. That would, however, be expensive. Instead, U.C.C. §9-323(b) gives future advances priority over the lien, provided the creditor making the advance does not have knowledge of the lien. The rule enables a secured creditor to conduct one search at the time it begins its lending relationship with the debtor and make future advances without fear of lien creditors of whom the secured creditors do not have actual knowledge.

But the exception for future advances made without knowledge of the lien creditor's levy is not the only exception in U.C.C. §9-323(b) in favor of secured parties who continue to make advances after a levy. The section provides two other exceptions. First, every secured advance made within 45 days after the levy is entitled to priority over the lien, even if the secured creditor making the advance knows of the lien's existence. Second, every advance made "pursuant to commitment entered into without knowledge of the lien" is similarly protected. U.C.C. §9-323(b)(2). Knowledge at the time of the advance, even if the advance is more than 45 days after the levy, does not prevent the lender making the advance from having priority, provided the advance is made pursuant to a commitment made when the creditor did not have knowledge of the lien.

The reason for giving priority to advances made by the secured party with actual knowledge of the levy during the 45 days after the levy is technical. As Comment 4 to U.C.C. §9-323 makes a weak attempt to explain, only by giving unconditional priority over lien creditors to secured creditors' future advances made during the 45-day period could the drafters qualify those future advances for the maximum priority over IRS tax liens available under the Tax Lien Act, 26 U.S.C. §§6321 et seq. Keep in mind, however, that the provision enables secured creditors to prevail over lien creditors in these circumstances; it is not restricted just to beating out the IRS.

The exception in favor of advances made "pursuant to a commitment entered into without knowledge of the lien" is considerably more difficult to justify. The secured creditor who makes advances pursuant to commitment can do so knowing of the lien and secure in the knowledge that its security interest will prevail over the lien. To illustrate the justifications for the exception and give you the opportunity to evaluate the arguments, we present our discussion in the form of a debate between a bank and a lien creditor.

Bank: The same reasons that warrant a priority for advances we make without knowledge of the lien also warrant a priority for advances we *commit* to make without knowledge of the lien. The appropriate time to consider our state of knowledge is when we commit; at the time of the advance, we have no choice.

Lien Creditor: That is simply not true. Suffering a judgment lien is nearly always a default under the bank's security agreement, so once you know of a lien, you are not obligated to make further advances. Yet U.C.C. §9-102(a)(68) defines "pursuant to commitment" such that these optional advances are pursuant to commitment. In nearly every instance where you make an advance "pursuant to commitment" with knowledge of the lien, you had the right to refuse it.

Bank: But for us to refuse to make advances pursuant to commitment because you became a lien creditor in the interim, we would have to know you did. Without the "pursuant to commitment" exception, we would have to search before making each advance.

Lien Creditor: Not so. You could lend without searching even if the "pursuant to commitment" exception did not exist. The "without knowledge" exception in U.C.C. §9-323(b) would still protect you against liens you did not know about. The "pursuant to commitment" exception only comes into play when you know of the lien and make advances anyway.

Bank: But you can easily destroy our protection under the exception, merely by notifying us of your levy. We'd have to stop making future advances and the debtor's business would be history.

Lien Creditor: What's wrong with that?

Bank: Many of these businesses can be saved if we continue to make advances.

Lien Creditor: You're not the right ones to make that decision. You have priority in the debtor's assets for the amounts you already advanced. In most cases, you are going to get paid whether or not the debtor's business survives. It is more likely our money than yours that is at risk in the decision on whether to continue the business. We are the ones with the right incentives to make the decision whether the business should continue or not — but the law gives you the power to decide.

Bank: Who has the right incentives will vary from case to case. But we are the ones with the big money at stake. A lone tort creditor or supplier shouldn't be able to sabotage a multimillion dollar lending relationship.

Lien Creditor: If you can make discretionary advances against any property we lien and take it from us, how are we *ever* supposed to get paid?

Bank: Who said you were supposed to get paid?

B.   Priority of Nonadvances: Personal Property

Most security agreements provide that in the event of default, the debtor will pay the secured creditor's reasonable costs of collection, including attorneys' fees. In complex transactions, the debtor often agrees to pay many other kinds of expenses that may be incurred by the secured creditor before or after default. Do these *nonadvances* qualify for priority over lien creditors under U.C.C. §9-323(b)? In the following case, the court addresses that question.

Uni Imports, Inc. v. Exchange National Bank of Chicago

978 F.2d 984 (7th Cir. 1991)

CRABB, DISTRICT JUDGE. . . .

FACTS

On August 12, 1987, Exchange National Bank and Aparacor, Inc. executed a document entitled "Security Agreement," which granted

Exchange a security interest in Aparacor's assets at Exchange. On October 9, 1987, the two executed a note due April 30, 1988, which incorporated the security agreement and established a revolving line of credit of up to $7.2 million for Aparacor and related entities. After the note expired, Exchange continued to make advances of funds without an additional written agreement.

On November 18, 1988, UNI obtained a $66,000 judgment against Aparacor in the United States District Court for the Central District of California. UNI registered the judgment in the United States District Court for the Northern District of Illinois. On January 12, 1989, UNI tried to enforce the judgment against Aparacor's assets at Exchange by delivering a writ of execution to the United States Marshals Service. The marshals service served the writ on Exchange the following day, but Exchange refused to turn over any of Aparacor's assets, contending that it had priority status.

Exchange continued to advance money to Aparacor. . . . By February 26, 1989 (45 days after Exchange had been served with the writ), the principal balance of Aparacor's loan had grown to approximately $2.8 million from a balance of approximately $780,000 as of January 12, 1989. Between February 26, 1989 and March 2, 1989, Exchange advanced an additional $274,000 to Aparacor. . . . Between March 2 and May 31, 1989, Exchange made additional payments of over $2 million as follows:

Advances to Assignee	$ 636.595
Payment of Sales Commissions	419,080
Payment of Real Estate Taxes	728,753
Payment of Interest under Modification Note to Mar. 2	27,056
Payment of Mechanics' Lien	2,200
Payment of Legal Fees	30,708
Letter of Credit Draws	277,716
Miscellaneous	19,326
TOTAL	$2,141,438

After . . . March 2, 1989, Exchange credited to Aparacor's outstanding balance the following: credit collections from accounts receivable, $2,584,638.21; proceeds from the sale of real estate and equipment, $1,414,287.30; and proceeds from the application of a certificate of deposit, $51,203.00, for a total of $4,050,128.51.

On September 27, 1990, UNI petitioned the district court for turnover of Aparacor's assets in the possession of Exchange. The court granted the petition and this appeal followed. UNI's $66,000 judgment has not been satisfied. Aparacor still owes $938,553.78 to Exchange. . . .

OPINION

When a person in need of money borrows a lump sum secured by specific collateral, such as real estate, the question of priorities between the lender and any subsequent person who obtains a judgment against the borrower is relatively straightforward: the judgment creditor's interest is subordinate to the lender's, so long as the lender has obtained and perfected a security interest in the borrower's realty before the lien attaches. This straightforward situation becomes complicated when the borrower wants a line of credit rather than a lump sum loan and when the collateral is a constantly changing one in the form of inventory or accounts receivables. Scholars and practitioners have debated whether the lender's security interest in the collateral attaches from the outset, that is, from the first advance under the line of credit (the "unitary" theory), or whether each advance gives rise to a new security interest, each of which arises no earlier than the time the creditor extends value (the "multiple" theory). . . .

[U.C.C. §9-323(b)] rests on the assumption that the multiple theory is operative for future advances, that is, each advance gives rise to a new security interest, which arises when the creditor extends value. See Dick Warner Cargo Handling Corp. v. Aetna Business Credit, 746 F.2d at 133:

> Sections [9-323(b) and (d)] generally accepted Coogan's conclusion that security interests relating to advances created subsequent to the intervention of a third party as lien creditor or purchaser should be subordinated to the interest of the third party.

Section [9-323(b)] applies to situations in which there is a "perfected" security interest in existence when the judgment lien attaches. (Perfection occurs when a debtor signs a security agreement containing a description of the collateral, value has been given and the debtor has rights in the collateral. [U.C.C. §9-203(b)(2)].) Under [§9-323(b)], future advances are protected (1) in all cases for 45 days following attachment of the lien; (2) beyond 45 days if the secured party makes the advance without knowledge of the lien; and (3) beyond 45 days if the secured party is committed to make advances, provided the commitment was entered into without knowledge of the lien. . . .

Left unanswered by the drafters of [§9-323(b)] was the question of the treatment of the other parts of a secured obligation such as interest and collection expenses. Were these different parts of the obligation subsumed by the term "advances" (and treated identically) or did they give rise to their own security interests and, if so, did those security interests arise when value was given or at the outset when the obligation was entered into? In the only case to address this issue, Dick Warner Cargo

Handling Corp. v. Aetna Business Credit, 746 F.2d 126 (2d Cir. 1984), the Court of Appeals for the Second Circuit concluded that the separate parts of the obligation were not intended to be treated as advances. Although the court did not say so explicitly, in effect it treated such obligations as giving rise to their own security interests, at least some of which arose with the execution of the financing agreement. . . .

In *Dick Warner*, [the secured party, Aetna Business Credit and its borrower, Best Banana, entered into a security agreement that obligated Best Banana to indemnify Aetna for various expenses that Aetna might have to incur in connection with the loan and to reimburse Aetna for its expenses in enforcing or protecting its security interest or its other rights in the transaction. Best Banana defaulted under the agreement, Dick Warner obtained an execution lien against the collateral, and then Aetna incurred expenses that Best Banana was obligated under the security agreement to reimburse].

The Second Circuit held that Aetna's interest in the [collateral] had priority over Dick Warner's lien, based on Best Banana's undertaking in the original financing agreement to reimburse Aetna for attorneys' fees and other expenses it might incur in defending against suits such as Dick Warner's. According to the court, the drafters of [§9-323(b)] did not intend to include such expenditures by the lender in the term "advances" because the lender's obligation to advance funds to the borrower differs from the lender's obligation for expenses in connection with the loan, such as attorneys' fees. Expenditures in the latter category

> do not constitute "advances" as that term is commonly used; in the ordinary meaning of language, "advances" are sums put at the disposal of the borrower — not expenditures made by the lender for his own benefit.

Id. at 130. The Second Circuit suggested use of the term "nonadvances" for the debtor's obligation to pay interest and indemnify the lender for various expenses it has incurred. The court held that a lender that perfects its security interest with respect to such obligations is entitled to protection against a subsequent lien creditor. In other words, the lender is entitled to priority reimbursement insofar as a prior-perfected security interest

> secures a nonadvance obligation relating to a transaction prior to the levy, like that of the debtor to pay interest or even to reimburse the creditor for attorneys' fees incurred reasonably and in good faith with respect to loans made prior to the imposition of the lien or otherwise protected by it.

Id. at 134. The court took the view that the drafters of [§9-323(b)] never intended to include nonadvance obligations under this section. Thus, although for the purpose of the section, advances were treated as multiple (giving rise to a new security interest with each new advance), the treatment of future "nonadvance" obligations was not affected by the new [§9-323(b)]. Such obligations retained their unitary character, relating back to the original agreement. They continued to have priority over a later judicial lien if they had been undertaken before the lien attached, even if they did not mature until after attachment. The court acknowledged that a straightforward reading of [§9-323(b)] would not support such an interpretation, but concluded that it was what the drafters must have meant and that any other result "would be so plainly unreasonable and inconsistent with commercial practice that such an interpretation must be avoided." *Dick Warner*, 746 F.2d at 134.

The result reached in *Dick Warner* is not wholly convincing. As a general rule, security interests under Article 9 do not arise until value is extended. The court does not explain satisfactorily why it should be different for "nonadvances." Although protecting nonadvances benefits revolving credit lenders and thus, presumably improves debtors' chances of obtaining such loans, it does so at the cost of squeezing out lien creditors. One can reasonably ask whether it is fair or commercially useful to strike the balance in favor of the financier. After all, the lender in these situations has a close and continuing relationship with the debtor, enabling him to supervise and control all of the debtor's transactions, whereas the judgment lien creditor may well be an involuntary creditor of the debtor. See Grant Gilmore, The Good Faith Purchase Idea and the Uniform Commercial Code: Confessions of a Repentant Draftsman, 15 Ga. L. Rev. 605, 627 (1981) ("The financing assignee, who serves a useful function in providing working-capital loans is not an ignorant stranger. . . . He does not need to be insulated, as a matter of law, from the risks of the transactions in which [his borrowers] engage. Because he can investigate, supervise, and control, he should be encouraged to do so and penalized if he has not done so.") The drafters of the 1972 amendment noted this unfairness with respect to future advances:

> It seems unfair to make it possible for a debtor and secured party with knowledge of the judgment lien to squeeze out a judgment creditor who has successfully levied on a valuable equity subject to a security interest, by permitting later enlargement of the security interest, by an additional advance, unless that advance was committed in advance without such knowledge. [Footnote omitted.]

U.C.C. §9-312 (1972) Reasons for 1972 Change. Ironically, the possibility of squeeze-out posed by future advances is less than for nonadvance value. Future advances have the positive value of enlarging the estate; reimbursing the secured creditor for nonadvance value only depletes the estate. In *Dick Warner*, for example, Best Banana was obligated to pay

Aetna a $7500 minimum monthly charge. Aetna had no incentive and no apparent obligation to stop the running of the charge, other than the declining [value of the collateral].

Nonetheless, the *Dick Warner* result is endorsed by the Permanent Editorial Board for the Uniform Commercial Code. . . . In light of [the Board's] commentary and the holding of the Second Circuit, we conclude that the Illinois courts would hold [nonadvances not to be advances for purposes of §9-323(b)]. This conclusion is not the end of the inquiry in this case, however. It remains to be determined just which nonadvance payments and expenditures have priority under UNI's lien. Neither *Dick Warner* nor the Permanent Editorial Board's commentary can be read as giving priority to every expense claimed by a secured creditor, whenever incurred and for whatever purpose. [The court went on to distinguish nonadvances relating to advances made before the levy (which have the priority of the first advance) from nonadvances relating to advances made after the levy (which have only the priority of the future advance).]

After the case, the drafters reworded U.C.C. §9-323(b) to endorse *UNI Imports'* holding on the principal issue in the case. Comment 4 to U.C.C. §9-323. The rewording does not address the issue of nonadvances relating to advances made after the lien.

As *UNI Imports* demonstrates, a lien creditor's position can deteriorate even if the secured creditor does not add another dollar to the debtor's estate. Interest, attorneys' fees, and costs accruing on the prior liens will eat away the lien creditor's potential for recovery. The case for the priority of nonadvances is stronger than the case for the priority of future advances. The secured creditor often has no way to avoid making nonadvances. The secured creditor has to incur attorneys' fees and costs to foreclose, and interest will accrue while the secured creditor forecloses regardless of how diligent the secured creditor may be. Yet it is also worth noting that the accruing nonadvances have priority even when the nonadvances do not contribute value to the debtor's estate and the secured creditor forebears from foreclosure until the debtor has predictably dissipated all value from which junior creditors might have recovered.

C.   Priority of Future Advances and Nonadvances: Real Property

The law governing real estate transactions is even more tolerant of future advances made after a lien creditor perfects an interest in the collateral. In the following case, the Supreme Court of Mississippi explains what is generally considered the modern view, and compares it with U.C.C. §9-323(b).

Shutze v. Credithrift of America, Inc.

607 So. 2d 55 (Miss. 1992)

ROBERTSON, J.

I

This is a lien priority case. The holder of a second deed of trust securing future advances made such an advance after a junior creditor had enrolled his judgment and perfected his lien. The Chancery Court enforced the future advance clause and assigned its lien a priority relating back to the recording of the original deed of trust, priming the judgment lien.

We affirm on this issue. . . .

II

In the early 1980s, Hobart W. Gentry, Jr., and Georgia C. Gentry owned Lot 53 of Rosewood Heights Subdivision to the City of Hattiesburg, Mississippi, commonly known by street number as the residence at 1105 North 34th Avenue. At all times relevant hereto, this property has been subject to the lien of a deed of trust, the beneficiary of which was Deposit Guaranty Mortgage Company and its predecessors in interest. The Deposit Guaranty lien was a conventional, residential first mortgage.

The first of today's combatants is Credithrift of America, Inc. On April 8, 1981, the Gentrys negotiated a second mortgage, home equity loan with Credithrift, borrowing the sum of $23,679.36. The Gentrys executed and delivered a second deed of trust conveying a security interest in the 34th Avenue property to Ben Hendrix, trustee for the benefit of Credithrift, and this deed of trust was duly recorded in the land records of Forrest County, Mississippi. Of considerable consequence, this deed of trust contains a future advance clause, in legal colloquia sometimes a "dragnet clause," which reads as follows:

> In addition to the indebtedness specifically mentioned above and any and all extensions or renewals of the same or any part thereof, this conveyance shall also cover such future and additional advances as may be made to the Grantor, or either of them, by the beneficiary. . . .

The clause went on to provide that the conveyance in trust secured

> any and all debts, obligations, or liabilities, direct or contingent, of the grantor herein, or either of them, to the beneficiary, whether now existing or hereafter arising at any time before actual cancellation of this instrument on the public records of mortgages and deeds of trust, whether the same be evidenced by note, open account, overdraft, endorsement, guaranty or otherwise.

Nothing in any of the papers obligated Credithrift to make any future advances. . . .

Enter Thomas E. Shutze, our other combatant. Shutze resides in Lamar County, Mississippi, and apparently had business dealings with the Gentrys, the nature of which is not disclosed in the record, nor is it important, except that on September 20, 1984, the County Court of Forrest County entered a judgment in favor of Shutze and against Hobart W. Gentry, Jr., in the original principal sum of $4,541.78. This judgment was duly enrolled in Forrest County on October 23, 1984, and its lien thereupon acquired the powers our law provides.

Re-enter Credithrift — eleven months later. By this time, the Gentrys had reduced their indebtedness to Credithrift to $11,215.13. On August 23, 1985, the Gentrys again refinanced — "renewed" — their loan with Credithrift and executed a new note in the principal sum of $14,150.26, repayable in installments at interest. The future advance — "the new money" — the Gentrys received was $2,784.13. Credithrift again regarded the renewal and advance as within the dragnet clause of the 1981 deed of trust which it in no way canceled or released, although it did take the precaution of a new deed of trust.

Over the next several years, the Gentrys struggled financially. It appears they made their payments to Credithrift through the Spring of 1988. At some point thereafter, they abandoned all and left for the West Coast and are believed in Reseda, California. Their creditors immediately resorted to the 34th Avenue residence to satisfy their respective debts.

No one questions that Deposit Guaranty Mortgage Company held a good, valid and perfected first lien and security interest by virtue of its 1978 deed of trust. Second mortgage holder Credithrift and judgment lien creditor Shutze, however, litigated below regarding their respective rights, and particularly the priority thereof with regard to Credithrift's future advance of $2,784.13 made after Shutze perfected his judgment lien. . . .

III

Future advance clauses are enforceable according to their tenor. Accepting their creative and constructive role in a credit economy and, as well, freedom of contract, we have upheld such clauses for more than a century. The point has been repeatedly litigated since, and we have repeatedly ruled, incident to a secured transaction, the debtor and secured party may contract that the lien or security interest created thereby shall secure other and future debts which the debtor may come to owe the secured party. Such clauses are treated like any other provisions in a contract and will be enforced at law subject only to conventional contract defenses, e.g., fraud, duress, and the like, none of which are present here.

We noted the practical rationale for such clauses in Newton County Bank v. Jones, 299 So. 2d 215 (Miss. 1974).

> When inserted in a deed of trust, such a clause operates as a convenience and an accommodation to [borrowers]. It makes available additional funds without [their] having to execute additional security documents, thereby saving time, travel, loan closing costs, costs of extra legal services, recording fees, et cetera.

Newton County Bank, 299 So. 2d at 218. And so Whiteway Finance Co., Inc. v. Green, 434 So. 2d 1351 (Miss. 1983), but repeats the obvious when it says matter-of-factly, as between the parties, "'dragnet clauses' are valid and enforceable in Mississippi."[1]

There can be no question but that, vis-à-vis the Gentrys, the lien or security interest Credithrift held in the 34th Avenue residence secured all sums the Gentrys owed Credithrift through and including the 1985 refinancing, renewal and new advance.

IV

A

Shutze accepts all of this but argues, instead, it proves little regarding the conflicting priorities issue he tenders. More specifically, Shutze concedes the 1981 deed of trust established Credithrift's priority the moment it was recorded, regarding of like priority the 1983 renewal and refinancing and any other indebtedness within the dragnet's reach, up until October of 1984. Shutze's point is that on October 23, 1984, he enrolled his judgment to the tune of some $4,541.78 plus interest and that, from and after that date, he held by law a lien on all of Gentry's property in the county. He argues further that his judgment lien is entitled to priority as of the date of enrollment, and in this he is correct. Credithrift does not dispute this. Indeed, our question is not which lien came first. All admit

---

1. The term "dragnet clause" connotes breadth of reach and is thought something much more than a conventional future advance clause. Future advances are one sort of debt included within dragnet clauses. All such clauses are enforced by reference to their language and law and not their label.

that the lien of Credithrift's April 8, 1981, deed of trust has priority over Shutze's October 23, 1984, judgment lien. . . .

The more difficult question concerns the 1985 future advance of $2,784.13. Witczinski v. Everman, 541 Miss. 841, 846 (1876), though decided a good while back, speaks perceptively to the point.

> A mortgage to secure future advances, which on its face gives information as to the extent and purpose of the contract, so that a purchaser or junior creditor may, by an inspection of the record, and by ordinary diligence and common prudence, ascertain the extent of the encumbrance, will prevail over the supervening claim of such purchaser or creditor as to all advances made by the mortgagee within the terms of such mortgage, whether made *before or after* the claim of such purchaser or creditor arose. [Emphasis supplied.]

The *Witczinski* future advance clause was far less elaborate than Credithrift's but was nevertheless held "enough to show a contract that . . . is to stand as a security . . . for such indebtedness as may arise from future dealings between the parties," by reason of which the Court held it "sufficient to put a purchaser or encumbrancer on inquiry. . . ." *Witczinski*, 51 Miss. at 846. . . .

[F]or priority purposes, the lien securing the future advance takes its date from the recording of the original deed of trust and by operation of law reaches forward to secure the advance made after intervening rights became perfected. The reason we permit this is the same we found in *Witczinski* . . . almost 120 years ago. . . . Third parties dealing with the debtor — . . . Thomas E. Shutze in today's case — are given notice by the public record that the recorded lien secures any future advances. Those third parties are charged at their peril to inquire of the debtor and prior secured creditors. The device of a subordination agreement or notice to terminate may be available but, failing some legally effective contract or notice rearranging rank, third parties cannot be heard to complain when the original secured creditor's future advances are accorded the priority its publicly recorded instrument imports.

Nothing said here turns on the fact that in 1985, at the time of its last advance to the Gentrys, Credithrift had no actual knowledge of Shutze's judgment nor the lien thereof. We quite agree with the point Shutze stresses on appeal, that the Circuit Court erred when it held Credithrift prevailed by reason of its lack of actual knowledge. Shutze's enrolled judgment became notice to the world from and after October 23, 1984, and the fact that Credithrift did not know of it in no way affects Shutze's rights. Where Shutze fails is in his inability to see that Credithrift's lien was perfected three-and-a-half years prior to his judgment lien and, by reason of the dragnet clause, Credithrift's lien reaches forward and secures the 1985 renewal and advance. Credithrift's dragnet clause had been a matter of public record since 1981, and under *Witczinski* and progeny would-be creditors such as Shutze were charged with knowledge thereof and with a duty of diligent inquiry regarding further details, before doing business with Gentry whether on open account or otherwise.

All of this makes perfectly good sense in today's world. Our citizens and their secured creditors need the flexibility dragnet clauses provide. The demands of our agricultural credit economy are as great as in the days of *Witczinski*. . . . Draws on construction loans and disbursements under lines of credit are other common examples of future advances businessmen need and secured lenders make. Second mortgage home equity loans are a more recent area of need. Many Mississippians need to borrow substantial sums with which to educate their off-spring and to borrow by the semester as tuition payments become due. They and their lenders need the security of the knowledge that their priority position will remain fixed to the date of the original deed of trust or security agreement, so that they can save "time, travel, loan closing costs, costs of extra legal services, recording fees, et cetera," as in Newton County Bank v. Jones, 299 So. 2d at 218. There is no reason our law should demand new title searches incident to each advance. Any other view could imperil the student's education in mid-stream. The same may be said for opportunities our citizens pursue in many other areas of social and economic life. The public records system each county maintains affords third parties full opportunity for knowledge which, if pursued with diligence, protects such third parties from being blind-sided. And because they will know we mean what we say, creditors do not have to record a new deed of trust every time a future advance is made which, if nothing else, avoids cluttering up the land records.

B

There is another dimension. The Uniform Commercial Code as originally enacted in Mississippi treated the priority of liens securing future advances the same as our cases noted above. Effective July 1, 1986, we amended our law to limit the lien's priority (though not its enforceability) to future advances made within forty-five days of perfection of an intervening lien or without actual knowledge of the new lien. [U.C.C. §9-323(b)]. This enactment does not directly reach real estate secured transactions. [U.C.C. §§9-109(a) and 9-109(d)(11)]. It does, however, pronounce the public policy in an area on its face indistinguishable in principle from real estate secured transactions. Dragnet clauses legally identical to Credithrift's abound in personal property security agreements across this state. We perceive no good reason why this legal language should have one meaning and effect where the security is personalty and an altogether different meaning and effect where the security is realty. We sharpen the point when we see dragnet clauses in mixed security agreements, where the collateral is a combination of real and personal property and a single dragnet clause says all collateral stands to secure all future advances.

If we imported [U.C.C. §9-323(b)] into our law of real estate secured transactions, we would cut back the reach of the dragnet clause. We need not take that step today, for Credithrift prevails even under the UCC. The Chancery Court found as a fact that, at the time of its 1985 refinancing and advance, Credithrift "had no actual notice of [Shutze's] judgment." . . . The point for the moment is, given the findings of fact, Credithrift prevails even under amended [U.C.C. §9-323(b)] if we enforced it by analogy.

Obtaining a judicial lien against personal property is generally a more intrusive process than obtaining one against real property. The usual means of obtaining a judicial lien against personal property is for the sheriff to take possession of the property by levy. Both the debtor and the lien creditor are likely to know that the lien has been created and there is a good chance the secured creditor will find out as well. The usual means of obtaining a judicial lien against real estate is for the creditor to record its judgment in the real estate records. Unless the lien creditor thereafter conducts a search, it will not know whether its lien attached to any property of the debtor. While the debtor typically will know that the judgment was entered, it is unlikely to discover that the judgment was recorded until it tries to sell or borrow against the property. It is thus perhaps more understandable that the real estate system should give absolute protection to the prior mortgagee, while the personal property system gives only limited protection to the holder of the prior security interest.

Even with regard to real property, not all jurisdictions follow the *Shutze* view. The *Shutze* court gave Credithrift's future advance priority over the earlier judgment, even though Credithrift was not obligated to make it. Surely that court would reach the same result with regard to a future advance the mortgagee was obligated to make. Other jurisdictions refuse priority to such optional advances made by the mortgagee with knowledge of a subsequent lien, but give priority to *obligatory* advances. This distinction between "optional" and "obligatory" advances is similar to the U.C.C. distinction between advances made "pursuant to commitment" and those that are not.

Problem Set 29

29.1.   Mortgagor borrows $50,000 from Mortgagee, and executes a note and mortgage that state that future advances up to an additional

$25,000 may be made by Mortgagee in the future. However, Mortgagee has no obligation to make such advances. The mortgage also states that it secures interest at 10 percent per annum and Mortgagee's attorneys' fees in any collection action. Thereafter *J* obtains a judgment for $100,000 against Mortgagor and properly records it so as to impose a lien on Mortgagor's real estate. Mortgagee has actual knowledge of this lien. Then Mortgagee lends and Mortgagor accepts an additional $25,000 advance. Mortgagor defaults on the loan, owing the full balance and $10,000 in interest. After default, Mortgagee incurs $5,000 of attorneys' fees that are recoverable against Mortgagor under the terms of the mortgage. As between Mortgagee and *J*, who has priority in the real property?

29.2. Debtor borrows $50,000 from Secured Party and executes a note and security agreement that state that future advances up to an additional $25,000 may be made by Secured Party in the future. However, Secured Party has no obligation to make such advances. The security agreement also states that it secures interest at 10 percent per annum and Secured Party's attorneys' fees in any collection action. Thereafter, *J* obtains a judgment for $100,000 against Debtor and becomes a lien creditor by levying on the collateral. Secured Party has actual knowledge of the lien. Sixty days after the levy, Secured Party lends and Debtor accepts an additional $25,000 advance. Debtor defaults on the loan, owing the full balance and $10,000 in interest. Secured Party incurs $5,000 of attorneys' fees that are recoverable against Debtor under the terms of the security agreement. As between Secured Party and *J*, who has priority in the personal property? U.C.C. §9-323(b).

29.3. A year ago, Carol Dearing lent $1,000 to her friend, Bob Muzzetti. Bob gave her a security interest in his 32-foot Bayliner boat, and saw that her financing statement was duly filed. Business Credit Associates (BCA) recently recovered a judgment against Muzzetti in the amount of $45,000. Yesterday, March 1, they levied on the boat. It now sits in the Sheriff's compound, behind an eight-foot cyclone fence that is topped with concertina wire.

Now Bob is back to ask another favor of Carol. What Bob wants is an additional advance of $31,000. Bob's lawyer, John Sung, says that the advance will protect the boat from judicial sale. "Even if they go through with the sale, they won't get anything," he says. Carol, who has been your client for years, asks whether this will work. What do you tell her? U.C.C. §9-323(b).

29.4. Assume that instead of representing Carol Dearing, you represent BCA in its attempt to collect the $45,000 judgment. You assess the value of the boat at $32,000. The sheriff's sale is set for March 29, just a few days from now. In preparation for bidding at the sale, you conducted a U.C.C. search and discovered Carol Dearing's financing statement. Because you believe that a deficiency judgment against Muzzetti may be collectible, you don't want to bid higher than the value of Muzzetti's equity in the boat. But to know how much that is you need know the amount secured by Dearing's interest.

When you called Dearing, she said she would have to consult her attorney before giving you that information. Although she said she would call you back, you have not heard from her.

a.   How do you plan to get the information? U.C.C. §9-210.

b.   If you can't get the information, what will be your bidding strategy at the sale? U.C.C. §9-323(b).

29.5.   You represent Sheng Electronics (from Problem 28.1). In preparing to levy, you ran a U.C.C. search on Conda Copper, the judgment debtor. Your search turned up three financing statements filed a little over three months ago. Each names a different secured party and describes the collateral as "all of the assets of Conda Copper." From your discovery earlier in the case, you know that at the time of those filings Conda Copper was in such bad financial condition that you doubt anyone would have been stupid enough to lend them money unsecured. In that discovery, you asked whether Conda Copper had granted any security interests and Conda answered, "no."

a.   What do you think is going on? U.C.C. §§9-317(a) and 9-323(b).

b.   What should you do?

Assignment 30: Trustees in Bankruptcy Against Secured Creditors: The Strong Arm Clause

Back in Assignment 7 we discussed the fact that security interests generally retain their priority when the debtor goes into bankruptcy. That is not true, however, as to *unperfected* security interests. Under Bankruptcy Code §544(a), sometimes referred to as the *strong arm clause*, a bankruptcy trustee or debtor in possession has the power to avoid most kinds of security interests that remain unperfected as of the time of filing of the bankruptcy case. If the trustee or debtor in possession avoids a security interest, the once-secured creditor loses the benefit of it and is thereafter treated as an unsecured creditor. Because perfection of a security interest is so likely to be challenged in bankruptcy, bankruptcy is often referred to as the acid test of the perfection of a security interest.

A. The Purpose of Bankruptcy Code §544(a)

Courts often attribute Bankruptcy Code §544(a) to a policy against *secret liens*. They see §544 as reinforcing the requirements of Article 9 that creditors give public notice of their security interests whenever feasible. The creditors can do that by filing notice of the security interest in an appropriate public record or by taking possession of tangible collateral. Generally speaking, if secured creditors have perfected their liens in the manner required by law prior to the filing of the bankruptcy case, the policy is considered satisfied. If secured creditors have not, their security interests are considered secret liens and the trustees or debtors in possession can avoid some of them.

Courts and commentators frequently speak of bankruptcy trustees as "policing" compliance with Article 9 perfection requirements. Trustees do so by inspecting security documents, checking the secured creditors' compliance with filing requirements, and bringing actions in bankruptcy court to avoid the security interests they discover are unperfected. Although we know of no empirical data on the point, most commentators assume that the large majority of legal attacks on the perfection of security interests are brought by bankruptcy trustees. Attacks by other secured creditors or buyers are far less common.

If the trustee is successful in avoiding a security interest, the interest is "preserved for the benefit of the estate." Bankr. Code §551. The trustee, in effect, steps into the shoes of the unperfected secured creditor and enforces the security interest for the benefit of the estate and, indirectly, the unsecured creditors.

B.   The Text of Bankruptcy Code §544(a)

If, instead of writing what they did, the drafters of Bankruptcy Code §544(a) had written that "the trustee can avoid unperfected security interests and liens," they would have accomplished essentially the same thing. Law students and lawyers alike would have been spared a great deal of suffering and anguish. Relating the complex language of Bankruptcy Code §544(a) to its simple effect is one of the most difficult tasks facing students of secured credit.

Probably the reason that the drafters did not simply authorize the avoidance of "unperfected security interests and liens" is that Bankruptcy Code §544(a) was intended to apply to a wide variety of statutory and judicial liens authorized under the laws of each of the 50 states. The statutes under which those liens arise do not all use the word "perfection." And, as you have already seen, liens may be sufficiently "perfected" to prevail against one kind of competitor at a time when they are not sufficiently perfected to prevail against another. Simply authorizing the avoidance of unperfected security interests and liens would have left the courts with the job of interpreting hundreds of statutes to determine the moment of perfection in numerous scenarios against varieties of competitors. Instead, the drafters tried to speak with greater precision by establishing a standard for lien avoidance that the courts could apply without regard to the type of competing lien involved or the statutory language authorizing that competing lien.

The technique the drafters came up with was to invent three hypothetical persons who might compete with those holding less than perfect liens in debtors' property. They gave the trustee the right to step into the shoes of the one who would have the greatest rights against the particular competitor and defeat any liens that hypothetical person could defeat. Federal law determines the characteristics of the three hypothetical persons. Aside from the characteristics specified, the trustee has the freedom to imagine the characteristics of the most powerful creditor possible, the *ideal lien creditor,* and to assume the rights of a lien creditor with those characteristics. Federal law leaves it to state law, however, to determine what rights these ideal lien creditors have against others. Because the outcomes of contests between the trustee as "ideal lien creditor" and competing creditors depend upon state law, those outcomes differ from state to state. The result is that the impact of §544 differs from state to state.

Bankruptcy Code §544(a) gives the trustee the power to avoid "any transfer" that could be avoided by one of the three hypothetical persons. Recall that the Bankruptcy Code §101 definition of "transfer" is broad enough to encompass the voluntary grant of a security interest or the involuntary suffering of a judicial or statutory lien. It also includes other kinds of transfers, but in this book we restrict our consideration to the trustee's ability to avoid grants of security interests and liens.

1. The Judicial Lien Creditor of §544(a)(1)

Under Bankruptcy Code §544(a)(1), the trustee can step into the shoes of a hypothetical "creditor that extends credit to the debtor at the time of the commencement of the case, and that obtains, at such time and with respect to such credit, a judicial lien on all property on which a creditor on a simple contract could have obtained such a judicial lien." For a real creditor to have these characteristics is impossible. Even if a real creditor extended credit at the time of the commencement of the bankruptcy case, that creditor could not obtain a judicial lien at the same moment.

Why did the drafters choose this contortionist as their hypothetical lien creditor? They wanted to test perfection as of the filing of the bankruptcy case. Giving the hypothetical lien creditor its lien only as of the commencement of the bankruptcy case prevents the trustee from challenging a security interest for being unperfected at some earlier time. Allowing the hypothetical lien creditor to be other than a simple contract creditor would have created the same problem, because other kinds of creditors are sometimes accorded rights that relate back to some earlier time. The following statute, for example, gives tort victims a lien that dates not from the date the tort victim becomes a lien creditor, but from the date of the accident:

Lien on Motor Vehicle for Damages

S. C. Code Ann. §29-15-20 (Law. Co-op. 1976)

When a motor vehicle is operated in violation of the provisions of law or negligently, carelessly, recklessly, willfully or wantonly and any person receives personal injury or property is damaged thereby or a cause of action for wrongful death arises therefrom, damages recoverable therefor shall be and constitute a lien next in priority to the lien for State and county taxes upon such motor vehicle . . . and the person sustaining such damages . . . may attach such motor vehicle in the manner provided by law for attachments in this State. But this lien shall not exist if the motor vehicle was stolen by the breaking of a building under a secure lock or when the vehicle is securely locked.

If a bankruptcy trustee were permitted to imagine a creditor like the tort creditor in the statute and step into that creditor's shoes, the trustee could defeat virtually any competitor. The limitation that the hypothetical lien creditor must extend credit only at the time of the commencement of the case is also explained by examples such as this South Carolina tort creditor.

In cases where the interest under attack is a lien or security interest, the only characteristics of the hypothetical lien creditor that seem to make any difference are (1) that the hypothetical lien creditor obtains its rights through the exercise of judicial remedies such as execution, attachment, garnishment, levy, and the like, and (2) that the hypothetical lien creditor obtains its rights at the moment of the filing of the case. To describe the effect of §544(a)(1) another way, it is as though the trustee were a judgment creditor who exercised every remedy available to unsecured creditors under state law against all of the debtor's property at the moment of the filing of the bankruptcy case. The trustee will win any competition that such a judgment creditor would win under state law. What competitions would such a judgment creditor win under state law? When the competing claim is a security interest, the applicable state law will be U.C.C. §§9-317(a)(2) and 9-323(b). Under it, ideal lien creditors defeat unperfected security interest for which no effective financing statements exist, but lose to other security interests.

2.   The Creditor with an Execution Returned Unsatisfied

Under Bankruptcy Code §544(a)(2), the trustee can choose to step into the shoes of a hypothetical "creditor that extends credit to the debtor at the time of the commencement of the case, and obtains, at such time and with respect to such credit, an execution against the debtor that is returned unsatisfied at such time." The original purpose of this provision was to remedy a shortcoming in §544(a)(1). Under §544(a)(1) the trustee could not avoid some fraudulent transfers that occurred prior to bankruptcy. Only a creditor with an execution returned unsatisfied was eligible for the remedies that would reach the fraudulently transferred property in the hands of the third party. Because the subject of fraudulent transfers is beyond the scope of this book, so too is §544(a)(2).

3.   The Bona Fide Purchaser of Real Property

If the property in dispute is real property other than fixtures, the trustee can step into the shoes of a hypothetical bona fide purchaser who bought and paid for the property (that is, "perfected such transfer") at the time of the commencement of the bankruptcy case. The bona fide purchaser must, however, be one "against whom applicable law permits such transfer (the lien under attack) to be perfected." To put it another way, the trustee gets the rights of a bona fide purchaser only in circumstances where the competing transfer was capable of perfection. While the language used in Bankruptcy Code §544(a)(3) is as foggy as any in the Code, courts are fairly consistent in interpreting it. They allow the trustee to prevail only where (1) the competing creditor was supposed to do something to perfect its lien (that is, "applicable law . . . permits . . . perfect[ion]" against a later bona fide purchaser) and (2) the competing creditor failed to do it. If the competing creditor was supposed to perfect and did, the competing creditor prevails over the trustee because the competing creditor would prevail over a bona fide purchaser who bought the collateral after the competing creditor perfected.

Bankruptcy Code §544(a)(3) does not give the trustee the rights of a hypothetical bona fide purchaser in a fight over fixtures. With regard to fixtures, the trustee has only the lesser rights of a hypothetical judicial lien creditor.

In a case involving real estate, the trustee can use his or her rights as a hypothetical lien creditor or as a hypothetical bona fide purchaser. But, as the following case illustrates, the rights of a bona fide purchaser of real property are generally greater than those of a lien creditor.

Midlantic National Bank v. Bridge
18 F.3d 195 (3d Cir. 1994)

BECKER, CIRCUIT JUDGE.

This is an appeal from an order of the district court affirming an order of the bankruptcy court. Both courts rejected the claim of appellant Midlantic National Bank ("Midlantic") that, notwithstanding Midlantic's failure to record a refinanced real estate mortgage prior to the bankruptcy of the mortgagor, it must prevail over the bankruptcy trustee because Midlantic's unrecorded mortgage stands in the shoes of its prior recorded mortgage under the doctrine of equitable subrogation. We conclude that under New Jersey law, which we find applicable to the controversy, the trustee's "strong arm" powers as a hypothetical bona fide purchaser, see 11 U.S.C. §544(a)(3), entitle the trustee to avoid the equitable lien of the unrecorded mortgage, and hence we will affirm.

I

The underlying facts are not in dispute. On March 31, 1987, the debtor, Frank Bridge, obtained a $260,000 mortgage loan from Midlantic to finance the construction of improvements on his property at 94 South Main Street in Ocean Grove, Monmouth County, New Jersey. The mortgage was recorded on April 3, 1987, in the Monmouth County Clerk's Office. In 1988, Bridge and Midlantic agreed to refinance the loan and, on October 18, 1988, Bridge secured another mortgage on the Ocean Grove property for $260,000. Bridge used the proceeds from the note underlying this mortgage to discharge the debt from the original mortgage.

Throughout these transactions with Midlantic, Bridge was represented by counsel who also acted as the settlement agent for the October 18, 1988 transaction, and, as such, was required by Midlantic to record the new mortgage. Bridge's counsel subsequently certified that the mortgage had been sent for filing and was now the primary lien on the Ocean Grove property. Unbeknownst to Midlantic and Bridge, however, the October 18, 1988 mortgage was not recorded, although on July 13, 1990, the original mortgage was marked satisfied. . . .

On August 15, 1990, Bridge filed a voluntary petition under Chapter 7 of the Bankruptcy Code in the Bankruptcy Court for the District of New Jersey. As of this time, the new mortgage was unrecorded and remained so until September 12, 1990, when Midlantic ultimately recorded it.

In December of 1991, Midlantic initiated an adversary proceeding in the bankruptcy court. Although It conceded that in view of the failure to record the mortgage, the New Jersey recording statute appeared to favor the trustee, see N.J.S.A. 46:22-1 (1989),[1] Midlantic argued that it

1. Title 46, section 22-1 of the New Jersey recording statute provides:

Every deed or instrument of the nature or description set forth in section 46:16-1 of this title shall, until duly recorded or lodged for record in the office of the county recording officer in which the affected real estate or other property is situated, be void and of no effect against subsequent judgment creditors without notice, and against all bona fide purchasers and mortgagees for valuable consideration, not having notice thereof, whose deed shall have been first duly recorded or whose mortgage shall have been first duly recorded or registered; but any such deed or

retained an equitable lien on the Ocean Grove property, which was superior to all other interests in the property because the doctrine of equitable
subrogation operated to place it in the position of its discharged first
mortgage. [The bankruptcy court granted summary judgment against
Midlantic and the district court affirmed.]

II

Section 544(a) of the Bankruptcy Code [provides that] as of the date of
the petition's filing, §544(a)(1) confers upon the trustee the rights of a
hypothetical judgment lien creditor; §544(a)(2) confers upon the trustee
the rights of a hypothetical unsatisfied execution creditor; and §544(a)(3)
confers upon the trustee the rights of a bona fide purchaser when, as in
this case, real property is at issue. . . .

It is thus clear from the legislative history of the 1978 Act and from case
law that although the trustee's strong arm powers arise under federal law,
the scope of these avoidance powers vis-à-vis third parties is governed
entirely by the substantive law of the state in which the property in question is located as of the bankruptcy petition's filing. The trustee's avoidance powers do not supplant state law; rather the trustee's powers under
§544(a) are subject to the law of the locus of the property. The incorporation of state law in this regard establishes that "wherever under the
applicable law such a creditor or bona fide purchaser might prevail over
prior transfers, liens, encumbrances or the like, the trustee will also prevail." 4 Collier at §544.01, 544-3.

Accordingly, we apply New Jersey law to determine: (1) whether Midlantic possesses an equitable lien on the Ocean Grove property; and (2)
if so, whether the doctrine of equitable subrogation operates to place
Midlantic in the priority position as mortgagee of the first recorded
(though extinguished) mortgage, and thus defeat the trustee's strong
arm powers.

III

A

. . . On October 18, 1988, Bridge executed a written agreement that
pledged the Ocean Grove property as security for the funds advanced to

---

instrument shall be valid and operative, although not recorded, except as against
such subsequent judgment creditors, purchasers and mortgagees.

N.J.S.A. 46:22-1 (1989). As New Jersey's recording statute is of the race-notice variety, "in
order for a subsequent purchaser to have a priority she must achieve a dual status: she must
not only take without notice of the prior interest, but she must also put her interest on the
record before the holder of the prior interest is able to do so." 6A Richard R. Powell, The
Law of Real Property ¶905[1][iii] (1993).

him by Midlantic in the refinancing transaction. While the resulting mortgage was unrecorded, it resulted in an equitable lien on the Ocean Grove property. . . . As the New Jersey Chancery Court stated in Rutherford Natl. Bank v. H.R. Bogle & Co.:

> The whole doctrine of equitable liens or mortgages is founded upon that cardinal maxim of equity which regards as done that which has been agreed to be, and ought to have been, done. To dedicate property, or to agree to do so, to a particular purpose or debt is regarded in equity as creating an equitable lien thereon in favor of him for whom such dedication is made. . . .
>
> The form which an agreement shall take in order to create an equitable lien or mortgage is quite immaterial, for equity looks at the final intent and purpose rather than at the form. If an intent to give, charge or pledge property, real or personal, as security for an obligation appears, and the property or thing intended to be given, charged or pledged is sufficiently described or identified, then the equitable lien or mortgage will follow as of course.

169 A. 180, 182 (N.J. Ch. 1933).

Therefore, notwithstanding its unrecorded status, the mortgage agreement between Midlantic and Bridge evidences that Midlantic retains an equitable lien on the Ocean Grove property by operation of New Jersey law. Accordingly, we now must examine whether the doctrine of equitable subrogation enables Midlantic's unrecorded equitable lien to trump the strong arm powers of the trustee.

B

Generally, when a creditor advances funds to a debtor to pay an existing debt and takes a new mortgage to secure the loan there is no subrogation because the new security manifests the creditor's intent to rely upon it, rather than upon the old security, which was discharged. Sometimes, however, a creditor's new security may prove to be defective due to fraud or some kind of mistake. In such cases, the doctrine of equitable subrogation can operate to subrogate the new creditor to the position of the lender whose lien was discharged and permits the new creditor to assert its right to priority against subsequent claimants.

New Jersey courts widely recognize the doctrine of equitable subrogation. The rationale for the doctrine rests on the overarching tenet that "the principle of subrogation is one of equity merely, and it will accordingly be applied only in the exercise of equitable discretion, and always with a due regard to the legal and equitable rights of others." Gaskill v. Wales, 36 N.J. Eq. 527, 533 (E&A 1883).

New Jersey courts have implemented the doctrine in situations in which "a state of facts fraudulently concealed from the lender, or of which he was ignorant, impaired the lien of the new mortgage." [Home Owners' Loan Corp. v. Collins, 184 A. 621, 623 (N.J. Eq. 1936.)] In such instances, New Jersey courts have permitted an equitable lienholder to defeat the intervening interests of lien creditors and levying execution creditors. Since the rights of transferees of real property are at issue in this case, however, we concern ourselves with the trustee's status as a hypothetical bona fide purchaser under §544(a)(3) and the interrelationship of the rights of such a bona fide purchaser and an equitable lienholder under New Jersey law.

Midlantic asserts that, according to the doctrine of equitable subrogation, the interest of an equitable lienholder is superior to the trustee's interest as a bona fide purchaser. Thus, Midlantic argues, it should be subrogated to the position of its first discharged mortgage on the Ocean Grove property and escape the trustee's strong arm powers under §544(a)(3). Midlantic offers no direct precedent for its position, but argues that Kaplan v. Walker, 164 N.J. Super. 130, 395 A.2d 897 (N.J. Super. Ct. App. Div. 1978), mandates this result.

In *Kaplan*, a motor vehicle was encumbered by a properly perfected lien in favor of Newton Trust Company, but the loan fell into default and the owner of the motor vehicle sought and attained a second loan from Commercial Trust Company to satisfy the original debt. The Newton Trust Company lien was discharged of record, but Commercial Trust neglected to record its lien as required by New Jersey Motor Vehicle Law. The owner later became insolvent and a receiver was appointed.

In an action to determine the validity of the lien, the trial court held that Commercial Trust's unperfected security interest was subordinate to the receiver's interest as a lien creditor without knowledge under [§9-317] of the New Jersey Uniform Commercial Code. See [U.C.C. §9-317]. The Appellate Division reversed, noting that, while [§9-317] "yields a facial result favoring the receiver in this case," the Uniform Commercial Code has not displaced the doctrine of equitable subrogation. The court proceeded to apply the doctrine and held that Commercial Trust, despite its negligence, would be subrogated to the position of Newton Trust's discharged lien due to "the absence of supervening equities" and the lack of "prejudice to or justified reliance by a party in adverse interest.". . .

[The court then discussed the *Gaskill* case, where bona fide purchasers of real property prevailed over the holder of an equitable lien.] Even in title disputes when parties have not sought equitable subrogation, the New Jersey courts have espoused *Gaskill's* holding that a bona fide purchaser of real property for value without actual or constructive notice, takes title to the property free from unrecorded equitable liens. See Howard v. Diolosa, 241 N.J. Super. 222, 574 A.2d 995, 1000 (N.J. Super. Ct. App. Div. 1990) ("A purchaser or mortgagee for value without notice, actual or constructive, acquires a title or lien interest free from all latent equities existing in favor of third persons.").

C

. . . As a hypothetical bona fide purchaser, the trustee is deemed to have paid value for the Ocean Grove property and is deemed to have perfected (i.e., recorded) his interest as legal title holder in the subject property as of the date of the bankruptcy petition's filing. The trustee has the status of a hypothetical bona fide purchaser who is deemed to have searched the title of the Ocean Grove property as of the petition's filing.

In the face of *Gaskill*, we find Midlantic's reliance on Kaplan inapposite. First, *Kaplan* concerned personal property; thus the court there examined the applicability of the doctrine of equitable subrogation within the framework of the New Jersey Uniform Commercial Code, which specifically mandates the incorporation of equitable principles, see N.J.S.A. 12A:1-103 (1962). In contrast, realty was the subject property in *Gaskill*, and the New Jersey Court of Errors and Appeals concerned itself with the applicability of the doctrine within the confines of New Jersey common law. In the instant case, therefore, we must apply the principles of *Gaskill* as the controlling common law precedent.

Second, although the state of the title in *Kaplan* similarly furnished the receiver, as hypothetical lien creditor, with no actual or constructive notice of the second unrecorded lien on the motor vehicle, the competing interests of the two lien creditors were in equipoise, i.e., lien creditor versus lien creditor. In *Gaskill*, however, as in the case sub judice, the disparity between the competing interests is clear: the mortgagee is defending his equitable lien against the bona fide purchaser's interest as legal title holder of the real property. In such a contest, the bona fide purchaser, as supervening legal title holder, prevails.

The trustee here took title on August 15, 1990, at the time the bankruptcy petition was filed. The first mortgage was marked satisfied on July 13, 1990; but the second mortgage was not recorded until September 12, 1990, hence when the trustee took title, there was no recorded mortgage. The short of it is that, since a bona fide purchaser acquiring title under such circumstances would have taken clear of the mortgages, the trustee must also take clear of the mortgages. We therefore conclude that, under New Jersey law, the rights of the trustee, as a hypothetical bona fide purchaser of real property for value without notice, prevail over the rights of Midlantic, as the holder of an unrecorded equitable lien, and prevent the operation of equitable subrogation in this case.

The order of the district court will be affirmed.

Proposals have recently been made to extend the rights of the trustee in bankruptcy to those of a bona fide purchaser in all cases —whether the collateral is real estate or personalty. In most cases, the shift would not change the result. The trustee will beat the holder of an unperfected, unfiled security interest under either rule. But *Midlantic* demonstrates that the change would make a difference in at least some cases.

C.   The Implementation of Bankruptcy Code §544(a)

Bankruptcy Code §544(a) makes certain transfers avoidable, but it does not *require* the trustee to avoid them. When a transfer is avoidable, the trustee has the discretion to avoid it or not, as may be in the interests of the estate. In Chapter 7 cases, the discretion is almost invariably exercised in favor of avoidance. In Chapter 11 cases, the debtor in possession usually wields the trustee's discretion with regard to avoidable transfers. Bankr. Code §1107(a). The debtor in possession often has reason not to avoid transfers that it could avoid. To understand the reasons for this difference, it is helpful to understand the different contexts in which trustees and debtors in possession operate.

1.   *Exercise of Bankruptcy Code §544(a) Discretion by Chapter 7 Trustees*

As we mentioned in Assignment 6, Chapter 7 trustees are professional persons, usually lawyers, appointed by the U.S. trustee to administer the bankruptcy estates of strangers. They are paid for their work from the estate. Their claims for compensation are subordinate to the rights of secured creditors, equal in priority to other expenses of administration, and senior to virtually every other kind of claim. They are required to perform extensive duties in every case, Bankruptcy Code §704, but they are paid reasonable compensation only in cases where there are sufficient funds in the estate to pay them.

More than 99 percent of Chapter 7 cases are filed by the debtor. Most debtors either have no non-exempt assets to begin with. Most others liquidate their own estates before filing, by paying creditors, granting security interests, or converting assets into property that will be exempt from the estate. In about 95 percent of all Chapter 7 cases, all assets of the estate are fully encumbered by security interests and liens at the time of filing. In those cases, the trustee receives $60 from the filing fee paid by the debtor. The remainder of the trustee's fees go unpaid. See Bankr. Code §330(b).

If the trustee manages to avoid one or more security interests or liens against property of the debtor, that property becomes property of the estate. Bankr. Code §§541(a)(3) and (4). The proceeds of its sale are available to pay the expenses of administration, including the fees of the trustee for administering the estate. If the trustee cannot avoid some security interest or lien and the case is otherwise a no-asset case, the trustee gets only the $60. Lawyers use the phrase "eat what you kill" to describe one of the ways revenues can be divided among the lawyers in a firm; the system for compensating Chapter 7 trustees elevates the concept to an entirely new level.

In addition to the risk they take as trustees, trustees who are lawyers usually retain themselves to do the estate's legal work, including filing actions for avoidance. The avoiding actions represent additional legal work for the attorney-trustees, which they are delighted to have if they will be paid for it. In a large percentage of cases, it works out that the fees of the trustee and the attorney for the trustee will be paid only if they are successful in avoiding someone's security interest or lien. Working in this incentive system makes trustees particularly vociferous advocates. Their zeal often prompts the more genteel breed of lawyer who defends banks and finance companies in avoidance actions to refer to the trustee as a "pit bull" or "junkyard dog." In any event, the result of this compensation system is that in Chapter 7 cases, policing of the perfection requirements of Article 9 and other lien statutes is stringent.

Secured creditors can file proofs of claim in bankruptcy cases, but they are not required to do so. In Dewsnup v. Timm, 502 U.S. 410 (1992), the Court held that unless someone sues them and serves them with process, secured creditors have the right to ignore their debtors' bankruptcies. If they ignore the bankruptcy and nobody comes after them, secured creditors' liens "pass through bankruptcy unaffected." The debtor's obligation to pay the underlying debt is discharged, but the secured creditor can still foreclose the lien.

If a secured creditor chooses to file a proof of claim, the secured creditor must attach the evidence of its security interest. The trustee is likely to examine that evidence carefully and perhaps even conduct a search of the public records to verify that the financing statement was filed. If the secured creditor does not file a proof of claim, the trustee is nevertheless likely to demand that the secured creditor informally furnish proof of the validity and perfection of the security interest. Either way, once the trustee has the documentation, the trustee is likely to examine it carefully for errors, such as a misspelled name or an incorrect place of filing that might render the lien unperfected and therefore vulnerable to avoidance. The trustee can bring an action under Bankruptcy Code §544(a) whether or not the secured creditor has filed a proof of claim in the Chapter 7 case. Under Bankruptcy Code §546(a), the trustee has up to two years from the time of his or her appointment in which to bring the action.

2. Exercise of §544(a) Discretion by Chapter 11 Debtors in Possession

Trustees are rarely appointed in Chapter 11 cases. Ordinarily, the debtor serves as debtor in possession (DIP) and in that capacity exercises its discretion to bring or not bring avoiding actions. If a DIP is successful in avoiding a secured creditor's lien, the effect is to change that creditor's status from secured to unsecured. That, in turn, will generally reduce the formerly secured creditor's leverage in the negotiation of a plan. But even an unsecured creditor is entitled to absolute priority over shareholders. If, as is usually the case, the persons in control of the debtor are shareholders, they may have little to gain by avoiding the security interest. The secured creditor will have lost its priority over the other creditors, but the total amount of debt will remain the same and the shareholders will remain subordinate to all of it. Moreover, DIPs and their owner-managers often have reasons *not* to avoid transfers made by the debtor in the period prior to the bankruptcy filing. For example, the transfer of a security interest may be to the owner-managers themselves, to their friends or relatives, or to persons with whom they have ongoing business relationships. If, for example, the DIP voids the defectively perfected lien of a key supplier, the supplier may refuse to make sales in the future. That may increase the DIP's costs or disrupt its operations if the supplier is the only available source.

The DIP is a fiduciary and is bound to act in the interests of the estate. If the DIP abuses its discretion by failing to bring an avoiding action that clearly should be brought, some bankruptcy courts permit the unsecured creditor's committee to sue in place of the DIP. In extreme cases, failure to bring the avoiding action may be grounds for the appointment of a trustee.

Most Chapter 11 cases eventually are converted to Chapter 7. When that occurs, a Chapter 7 trustee is appointed. As you might expect, the appointment of the Chapter 7 trustee often results in an abrupt change of policy toward the avoidance of unperfected security interests. So long as the conversion and appointment occur within two years of the commencement of the Chapter 11 case, a newly appointed Chapter 7 trustee will have sufficient opportunity to examine the secured creditors' documentation and file avoiding actions against secured parties who were not perfected at the time the Chapter 11 case was filed. Bankr. Code §546(a).

D. Recognition of Grace Periods

Many of the state statutes that require public filing to perfect a lien also provide the creditor with a grace period within which to make the filing. If the creditor files within the grace period, it will have priority over anyone who becomes a lien creditor in the interim. An example is U.C.C. §9-317(e), which gives the holder of a purchase-money security interest 20 days from the debtor's receipt of possession of the collateral in which to file. If the holder files within that time, it has priority over a lien creditor who becomes such between the time the security interest attaches and the time of filing. Another example of such a grace period is found in U.C.C. §9-324(e), which governs the rights of the holder of a purchase-money security interest in collateral other than inventory against the holder of a competing security interest. Yet a third example are construction (mechanic's) lien laws, which typically require recording of a claim of lien within 90 days of the lien holder's completion of work. If the holder records in a timely fashion, the lien relates back to some earlier date, usually the date construction commenced on the job or the date the lien holder commenced construction on the job.

What happens when the debtor goes into bankruptcy during such a grace period and before the secured creditor has perfected? For example, assume that Sandra Smith buys a new car from Big Motors, grants Big Motors a security interest, signs the application for a certificate of title showing the lien to Big Motors, and takes the car home. Two days later, while the application is still sitting in a basket in Big Motors' offices and Big Motors therefore remains unperfected, Smith files bankruptcy. In these circumstances, Big Motors can still perfect by delivery of its application to the Department of Motor Vehicles within the ten-day grace period of UMVCTA §20(b). If it does so, Big Motors' rights will be superior to those of the trustee in bankruptcy.

This result flows from the combination of three provisions of the Bankruptcy Code: Bankruptcy Code §362(a)(4) automatically stays "any act to . . . perfect . . . any lien against property of the estate"; Bankruptcy Code §362(b)(3) creates an exception from the stay to permit perfection "to the extent that the trustee's rights and powers are subject to . . . perfection under section 546(b)"; Bankruptcy Code

§546(b) makes "the rights and powers of a trustee . . . subject to any generally applicable law that permits perfection of an interest in property to be effective against an entity that acquires rights in such property before the date of perfection." UMVCTA §20(b) and U.C.C. §9-317(e) both meet this test because they permit perfection of a security interest to be effective against a person who became a lien creditor before the date of perfection of the security interest.

E.   Resistance to Bankruptcy Code §544(a)

In a provocative article published in 1993, Professor James J. White, one of the leading commentators on Article 9, proposed the repeal of U.C.C. §9-317(a)(2). His proposal raised fundamental issues about the role of bankruptcy trustees in policing compliance with Article 9.

James J. White, Revising Article 9 to Reduce Wasteful Litigation

26 Loy. L.A. L. Rev. 823 (1993)

II.   THE PROPOSAL AND ITS LEGAL EFFECT

I propose that the drafters of Article 9 repeal section [9-317(a)(2)]. . . . To one unfamiliar with Article 9 of the UCC, the consequences of such revision will not be obvious. To begin to understand those consequences, consider the first sentence of section 9-201:

> Except as otherwise provided by this Act a security agreement is effective according to its terms between the parties, against purchasers of the collateral and against creditors.

Section 9-201 makes even an unperfected security interest king of the hill "[e]xcept as otherwise provided by this Act." Unless some other rule contained in Article 9 deposes an unperfected security interest, it is king. Section [9-317(a)(2)] does subordinate unperfected security interests to the rights of lien creditors. If that subsection were removed, the priority would be reversed and an unperfected security interest would be superior to a lien creditor's claim.

The direct and most obvious effect of the repeal of section [9-317(a)(2)] would be to subordinate a creditor who had procured a judicial lien — usually after judgment and levy — to an unperfected secured creditor who had a security interest in the personal property on which the lien creditor levied. Because creditors with judicial liens on personal property are more scarce than wise men in President Clinton's Cabinet, this consequence would be unimportant. I predict that subordination of the judicial lien creditor's claim to an unperfected secured creditor's claim in Article 9 and outside of bankruptcy would go almost unnoticed by lawyers and courts.

Because trustees in bankruptcy are as ubiquitous as judicial lienors are scarce, the principal effect of the repeal of section [9-317(a)(2)] would be in bankruptcy. . . .

Section 544(a)(1) rides on state law; it gives the federally created trustee in bankruptcy only the rights that a lien creditor has under state law. Therefore, a repeal of section [9-317(a)(2)], that subordinates the lien creditor to the unperfected secured creditor in state law, also subordinates the trustee in bankruptcy. Nothing in §544(a) or in any other section of the Bankruptcy Code gives the trustee in bankruptcy an independent right under federal law to strike down an unperfected security interest.

Before one considers the arguments for and against my proposal, understand how limited its effect is. Mostly it will impose the same priority on unsecured creditors in bankruptcy that would apply to them outside bankruptcy. Section 9-201 now grants priority to unperfected secured creditors over unsecured creditors unless the former procure a lien. Only a minuscule part of all unsecured creditors in and out of bankruptcy ever procure judicial liens. Therefore, my proposal would merely put these unsecured creditors in bankruptcy in the same status that they would suffer outside of bankruptcy, namely, a status subordinate to the unperfected secured creditors. . . .

Understand what the repeal of section [9-317(a)(2)] would not do. It would not give an unperfected secured creditor priority over a perfected secured creditor under section [9-322]. Thus, if secured creditors wished to have protection against other secured creditors, they would still have to perfect their security interest, usually by a filing. For that reason, many secured creditors would file financing statements even under the regime I propose.

The basic argument for my proposal is straightforward — to eliminate waste. This waste is the cost of unnecessary filings and needless litigation over the efficacy of secured creditors' perfection. I also argue that fairness supports my proposal; on that question I would expect reasonable people to differ. Consider the arguments.

III.   FAIRNESS

. . . Fundamentally, section 9-201 rests upon the empirical judgment that few if any general creditors rely on the filing records when they lend.

Neither the plumber, carpenter, accountant, Commonwealth Edison nor any other thousands of general creditors check the files to determine who has a financing statement on file before it decides whether it will extend unsecured credit in the form of the sale of goods or services. In the words of the trade, these are "non-reliance creditors" and are not entitled to protection of a lack of filing because they would not rely on it in any case.

It is exactly these people — the dross of Article 9 subordinated by section 9-201 — whom the trustee transforms into the precious persons entitled to section 9-317(a)(2)'s priority even though none of them has ever procured a lien. . . .

If one ignores bankruptcy and focuses on state law competition between unperfected secured creditors and lien creditors, what is fair? Some potential lien creditors might act or fail to act in reliance upon the state of the filing record. For example, a prospective lien creditor might levy on a particular asset and fail to levy on another because the UCC filings appear to show that there is no security interest on either and because the first was more valuable or easily liquidated than the second. If a secured creditor has an undisclosed but superior security interest in the first asset, the lien creditor might be injured, at least to the extent of the cost of the levy. If the second asset were sold to a bona fide purchaser or subjected to a superior claim by the time our creditor turns to it, the creditor's loss would be greater. Conceivably, too, the potential lien creditor could rest upon existing rights and not pursue lien rights upon default if the record were devoid of filing and he or she was so lulled into the belief that there were many assets available. Of course, once it became known that unfiled security interests were superior to judicial liens, neither of these forms of reliance would be reasonable.

In an elaborate article dealing with lien creditors' claims on real property, Professor Schechter has argued that unfiled claims should be subordinate to lien creditors' claims. Part of his argument is based on cases that illustrate the reliance of potential lien creditors. Ignoring for the moment the differences between personal property and real property and the differences in reliance that might attend a lien creditor's claim on one versus the other, I do not find Professor Schechter's citations persuasive. The illustrations in his footnote 95 of "number of cases" that show reliance are three. One is from 1965, one from 1931, and the third is from 1928.

That real estate law routinely grants priority to unrecorded transferees over subsequent lien creditors suggests that at least some believe it to be the fairest outcome. In real property law, it is common for an unrecorded real estate transfer to be subordinate to the rights of a subsequent bona fide purchaser, but superior to the rights of a subsequent lien creditor. Presumably, these decisions are based on ad hoc judgments about lien creditors' reliance and about the fairness of their subordination. Some courts openly question the injury suffered by the subordination of a lien creditor in these circumstances. I do not believe that fairness dictates victory for the lien creditor over an unperfected secured creditor. The potential injury inflicted by a failure to file is so problematic and inconsequential that I see no unfairness in asking a lien creditor to suffer that hypothetical injury.

But treating the conflict as one between an unperfected secured creditor and a lien creditor misses the point. Because the real competitor for the unperfected secured creditor is not a lien creditor under state law but an unsecured creditor whose debtor is in bankruptcy, I think it ultimately unnecessary to argue the morality of an unperfected secured creditor's supremacy over a lien creditor. In summary, the real fairness argument — that an unsecured general creditor without a lien has a moral claim to superiority over the rights of an unperfected secured creditor — was properly rejected by the drafters of section 9-201. It has been resurrected only by the alchemy of §544(a) and section 9-317(a)(2).

IV.   WASTE

My basic argument for the superiority of an unperfected security interest depends not on fairness; it depends on efficiency. My proposal could eliminate waste in two ways. First, the proposal would render certain filings by secured creditors unnecessary. Those who seek priority only over the trustee in bankruptcy and not over other perfected secured creditors or bona fide purchasers would not need to file. Second, and more importantly, my proposal would eliminate a significant percentage of all of the litigation under Article 9, namely, litigation on the question of whether a particular security interest is perfected. First consider the cost of filing itself. One must decide where to file, prepare the documents for filing, present them for filing, pay the fee, and later check whether one's own filing has been properly made. Undoubtedly, some accomplish these through clerical personnel; however, others engage an expensive lawyer to ensure the filing is properly performed. If the creditor's only interest is in defeating a trustee in bankruptcy and the creditor is unconcerned about other competitors, the creditor can save the entire cost of preparing, filing, searching and the like.

The greater cost of the current system arises from litigation over perfection. Here lawyers will be involved on both sides and both (one directly and the other indirectly) will be paid by the creditors. Because this litigation arises mostly in bankruptcy, the secured creditor will pay its lawyer directly, and the unsecured creditors, who are the beneficiaries of the insolvent bankruptcy estate, will pay the trustee and the trustee's lawyer indirectly.

With the help of a research assistant and LEXIS, I have tried to find all of the cases in bankruptcy between the beginning of 1980 and the end of 1990 in which the issue before the court was the perfection of a security interest in personal property. These are cases in which the trustee used §544(a) to challenge the perfection of the secured creditor's security interest. . . . Ultimately, I found 343 reported cases in which the perfection issue would never have been litigated under my proposed regime. In all of them the trustee in bankruptcy would have been subordinate and the secured creditor would have taken the asset or been treated as a perfected secured creditor within the Bankruptcy Code.

Finding 343 cases is only the beginning of wisdom. How should one evaluate the savings in lawyers' and trustees' fees that could have been enjoyed had none of these issues been litigated? First, how much on average do these cost? The most direct costs are lawyers' fees, second are trustees' fees and the time of the court system. In addition, of course, there is the time and cost of various witnesses and experts, investigation and the like. The estimation is further complicated by the fact that some of the cases went all the way to the court of appeals, an expensive proposition, whereas many were settled on motion before the bankruptcy court.

But there are still more uncertainties. How many reported decisions were not captured by the research? Worst of all, how many decisions are unreported? Should one assume that for every mouse seen, forty go undetected? Or is the ratio only one for one or five for one? I have no way of knowing, but surely not all of the opinions were reported, and I suspect that my reported opinions are a small minority of the total. In my judgment, society's total expenditure on these cases — all saved under my proposal — could not be less than millions per year, and it might be as high as tens of millions.

Clearly the elimination of many filings and much litigation about the legal effect of such filings will produce a large efficiency dividend. The money that would otherwise be spent in filing, checking files and litigating over such filings will be available to the players in the credit market — secured and unsecured creditors and debtors. . . .

The "dross of Article 9" whom Professor White objects to having transformed into "precious persons" are tort victims, trade creditors, public utilities, alimony recipients, credit card companies, defrauded investors, environmental damage claimants, unpaid employees, and other creditors who for one reason or another didn't get a security interest. For the argument that many of the dross should have priority over Professor White's precious banks, commercial lenders, and finance companies, see Lynn M. LoPucki, The Unsecured Creditor's Bargain, 80 Va. L. Rev. 1887 (1994), part of which is reproduced in Assignment 40.

The drafters of revised Article 9 did not adopt White's proposal as a whole. But they did make a series of changes that permit defectively filed security interests to prevail over lien creditors. Among them are U.C.C. §§9-338 and 9-520(c), which allow security interests perfected by the filing of incorrect financing statements to prevail over lien creditors, and U.C.C. §9-515(c), which allows a security interest that is no longer perfected because the financing statement has lapsed to prevail over a creditor that became a lien creditor while the security interest was perfected.

Problem Set 30

30.1. You are employed as attorney for the trustee in the Chapter 7 bankruptcy of Gargantuan Industries, Inc. Gargantuan filed under Chapter 11 of the Bankruptcy Code on April 15, and the case was converted to Chapter 7 on October 15. The trustee, a political appointee who is new to this kind of work, asks you which of the following she can avoid under Bankruptcy Code §544(a).

a. Wyandotte State Bank financed Gargantuan's acquisition of new machinery in the year preceding the bankruptcy filing. At the closing, one of the attorneys handed the signed financing statement to a paralegal and instructed her to "file it." The paralegal did — she put it in the "Wyandotte State Bank loan to Gargantuan Industries, Inc." file in the attorney's office. The Bank's attorney discovered the error after Gargantuan filed its Chapter 11 case. The attorney filed the financing statement on April 22. Bankr. Code §§544(a), 301, 348(a), 362(a)(4) and (b)(3), 546(b); U.C.C. §9-317(a)(2).

b. Same facts as above, but the Bank discovered its error and properly filed its financing statement on April 14, one day before Gargantuan filed under Chapter 11.

c. Torgeson, a creditor secured by an interest in some front-loaders, listed the debtor as "Gargantuan Industries" on the financing statement, but omitted all of the information required by U.C.C. §9-516(b)(5). As a result, the filing still shows up on a search under the correct name of the debtor, but it is impossible to tell that the filing is against Gargantuan Industries, Inc., rather than a business using Gargantuan Industries as a trade name. U.C.C. §§9-338, 9-506(a), 9-520, and Comment 3 to §9-520.

d. Glasco, Inc., a creditor secured by an interest in other equipment of Garguantuan, filed a financing statement five years prior to July 15. Glasco has not filed a continuation statement. U.C.C. §§9-317(a)(2), 9-515(c), Comment 3 to U.C.C. §9-515, and Bankr. Code §9-362(b)(3).

e. Florida National Bank made a "secured" loan to Gargantuan about two years before the filing of the Chapter 11 case. Gargantuan signed a promissory note, a security agreement, and a financing statement, but the description of the collateral in the security agreement was left entirely blank. The trustee learned of that fact from a young attorney named Grace Washington who had been an associate with the firm that represented the Bank. A partner in the firm instructed Grace to fill in the blank and "maintain client confidentiality." Instead, Grace resigned her position with the law firm that represented the Bank and eventually told the trustee what had happened. ("I cannot tell a lie," she said later in her deposition.) On April 24, after Grace had resigned but before she spoke with the trustee, Benny Arnold, another young associate with the same firm, filled in the description of collateral with words identical to those on the filed financing statement. On the following day, both the Bank and Gargantuan acknowledged in writing that the completion correctly expressed their original intention. U.C.C. §§9-203(b), 9-308, 9-317(a)(2) and 9-323(b); Bankr. Code §§362(a)(4), 544(a). What happens to Grace and Benny? See Model Rules of Professional Conduct set forth in Problem 8.4, above.

f. On April 6, nine days before it filed under Chapter 11, Gargantuan bought a new Lexus automobile for use by its executives. Gargantuan signed a security agreement in favor of Union Bank, which financed the purchase, but as of the time of filing of the petition, Union Bank's application for a certificate of title showing its lien was still sitting on someone's desk at the Bank. As soon as Union Bank learned of the Chapter 11 filing on April 25, an employee of the Bank hand-delivered the application to the Department of Motor Vehicles. Bankr. Code §§544(a), 362(a)(4) and (b)(3), 546(b); U.C.C. §§9-317, 9-311(a) and (b); UMVCTA §20(b); Comment 8 to U.C.C. §9-317. Did Union Bank's delivery of the application violate the automatic stay?

g. On April 8, one week before Gargantuan filed its petition, the Yarn Shop, Inc. delivered its writ of execution to a New York sheriff along with instructions to levy on an automobile owned by Gargantuan. Two days after the filing of the Chapter 11 case, the sheriff, who was unaware of the filing, levied on the automobile in her own county and took possession of it. Bankr. Code §544(a); U.C.C. §9-317; N.Y. Civ. Prac. L. & R. 5234(b), reproduced in Assignment 28.

30.2. A senior partner in your firm has asked you to review and comment on the firm's procedures for closing on sales of businesses. She describes one of the problems as follow:

> At the time of closing, we often receive all of the transfer documents and purchase price in trust for the parties. Once we have all of the documents and all of the money, we are authorized to record and disburse. The person entitled to the money usually wants it at the earliest possible moment. If

that person is our client, we want to give it to them as soon as we can do so without unreasonable risk on our part. We never disburse until we have sent all financing statements and certificate of title applications to the appropriate offices, but in some cases we disburse before those documents are received by those offices. We don't always represent the lenders, but we always undertake to perfect their interests. Is our practice of early disbursement safe? In particular, what happens if we have already disbursed the proceeds of sale and the purchaser files bankruptcy before the documents are received and recorded by the filing offices?

What is your answer? Bankr. Code §§362(a)(4) and (b)(3), 544(a), and 546(b); U.C.C. §§9-311 and 9-317; UMVCTA §20(b).

30.3. You represent Gargantuan Industries in its case under Chapter 11. The company's massive size is fueled by even larger debts. The company has assets worth about $10 million and secured debt of about $8 million, nearly all of which is owing to its line-of-credit lender, Oriental State Bank. Gargantuan also has unsecured debt in excess of $20 million. Oriental has indicated its opposition to any plan of reorganization and is attempting to withdraw from its relationship with the company. Other lenders are willing to come in, but none will extend $8 million in credit against a mere $10 million in assets.

Earlier today, you got your first break in the case. You discovered that the financing statement Oriental filed three years ago misspelled Gargantuan's name in a manner that causes it not to show up in a search.

a. What is the legal effect of this defect? Bankr. Code §544(a); U.C.C. §§9-317(a)(2) and 9-506.

b. To how much money is Oriental State Bank entitled under the Chapter 11 plan?

c. To how much money are the unsecured creditors entitled under the Chapter 11 plan?

d. To how much money are the shareholders entitled under the Chapter 11 plan?

e. Assume Gargantuan proposes the following plan of reorganization: Oriental State Bank's claim will be reduced to $5 million and will remain secured. The unsecured creditors will receive a second security interest for $2 million and will be entitled to an additional $2 million, for a total of $4 million. The shareholders will retain ownership of Gargantuan, which is estimated to have a value of $1 million. Should Oriental accept this plan?

f. Should the unsecured creditors accept this plan?

30.4. a. Debtor grants a real estate mortgage to *M*, who does not record. *C* levies on the real estate. As between *M* and *C*, who has priority? (Hint: You will find the applicable rule in the White excerpt.)

b.   Assume the facts are the same as in b, except that the collateral is personal property and Article 9 governs. As between *M* and *C*, who has priority? U.C.C. §9-317(a).

30.5.   a. If the property in Midlantic v. Bridge had been personal property rather than real estate, would that have changed the outcome?

b.   Should there be different rules in Bankruptcy Code §544(a) for real property and personal property? If not, what should the uniform rule be?

30.6.   Professor White's proposal has been adopted and U.C.C. §9-317(a)(2) repealed. Just as he predicted, Congress has made no changes in Bankruptcy Code §544(a). Unperfected secured creditors have priority over both lien creditors and the trustee in bankruptcy. Advise each of the following:

a.   Electronic Ideas, a vendor of personal computers, printers, and peripheral devices, has been taking security interests in each of the thousands of personal computer systems it sells each year and filing financing statements. They wonder if they can now continue taking the security interests but cease filing the financing statements and eliminate the expense. Bankr. Code §544(a); U.C.C. §§9-317, 9-324(e), and 9-322(a).

b.   Grocer's Supply distributes a variety of grocery products to grocery stores. It does not take security interests because most grocery stores borrow from inventory lenders whose loan agreements bar any competing liens against the collateral. At a trade association meeting the credit manager for Grocer's Supply heard that under the new law such bars would no longer be enforceable. The credit manager asks you why that would follow merely from the repeal of U.C.C. §9-317(a)(2). How should Grocer's Supply respond to the change?

c.   Grocer's Supply aggressively pursues buyers who do not pay. They obtain judgments and then look at credit reports to try to decide what assets to levy on. Should they change their policies with regard to making these levies? Bankr. Code §544(a); U.C.C. §§9-317(a), 9-322(a).

d.   Professor White's proposal is before Congress, and the National Association of Bankruptcy Trustees (NAB) has retained you to argue against it. NABT realizes that they will be vulnerable in this debate — the reply will be that the bankruptcy trustees are just defending their own fees. That will, of course, be true, but not necessarily the whole story. How do you plan to argue the case?

Assignment 31: Trustees in Bankruptcy Against Secured Creditors: Preferences

A. Priority Among Unsecured Creditors

1. Priority Under State Law: A Review

In Assignment 28, we looked briefly at the competition among unsecured creditors for assets of the debtor. We saw that state law gives priority among unsecured creditors based on the order in which they take particular legal steps to collect their debts. The critical step was nearly always one of four: (1) levy on the asset, (2) deliver a writ of attachment or execution to the sheriff with instructions to levy on the asset, (3) record a judgment in the appropriate public record, or (4) serve a writ of garnishment on a third party who owes money to the debtor or holds property of the debtor. Taking the critical step was said to create a *judicial lien* on the particular property, which was simply a way of saying that the creditor had established a priority in it. By giving priority to the unsecured creditor who acts first to collect its debt, state law potentially gives each unsecured creditor an incentive to act. By fostering this "race of diligence" among creditors, as it is sometimes called, state law seeks to bring early attention to the fact that a debtor is not paying its obligations as they become due.

In Assignment 28 we also saw another way for an unsecured creditor to win the race of diligence. That was to obtain and perfect a security interest in the property before competitors established their judicial liens. The grant of a security interest to a previously unsecured creditor is valid and enforceable even if the creditor who receives the grant furnishes no new consideration. U.C.C. §§9-203(b)(1) and 1-201(44)(b); U.F.T.A. §3(a). The effect can be to prefer one creditor over others similarly situated. (Recall, for example, *Peerless Packing* in Assignment 16, where the debtor granted a security interest to one of its 12 unsecured suppliers, enabling that creditor to be the only one eventually paid.) The justification for such preferential security interests under state law is simple. Debtors have the right to pay one creditor in preference to another. In fact, they do so every time they write a check to one creditor without writing a check to all. If the debtor can pay creditor C outright, the argument goes, the debtor should be able to take the intermediate step of assuring payment to *C* by a grant of security.

The effect, however, of this seemingly reasonable justification is disconcerting. If a debtor is unable to pay all of its creditors, the debtor can decide which it will pay. In some circumstances, this discretion can translate into power in the hands of the debtor. An example would be where the debtor lets a particular creditor know that if the creditor presses too hard for a payment owed the creditor, the debtor will prefer other creditors.

2.   *Priority Under Bankruptcy Law: A Review*

Recall from Assignment 6 that the moment a debtor files for bankruptcy, the automatic stay bars unsecured creditors from further collection efforts. Unsecured creditors are expected to file claims against the estate. Some unsecured creditors, such as wage claimants and taxing authorities, will be entitled to priority over general unsecured creditors. See Bankr. Code §§507(a) and 726(a). But, to the extent that general unsecured creditors are paid at all, they are paid pro rata, in proportion to their claims. Treating all general unsecured creditors alike is a basic tenet of bankruptcy policy. It follows that once the debtor is in bankruptcy, neither the debtor nor the trustee can take any action to prefer one prepetition unsecured creditor over another. (To the extent this policy is expressed in the Bankruptcy Code, it is in §549(a), which restricts postpetition transfers.) A bankruptcy estate can grant a security interest, but only for new value furnished to the estate at the time of the grant. Bankr. Code §§364(c) and (d).

3.   *Reconciling the State and Bankruptcy Policies*

State policy encourages unsecured creditors to seek priority over others of their same class; bankruptcy policy discourages it. The policies do not come into direct conflict only because once a bankruptcy petition is filed by or against a debtor, bankruptcy policy supersedes state policy.

Bankruptcy law also goes a step further. It imposes its policy of equal treatment of general unsecured creditors retroactively for a period of one year against creditors who are "insiders" of the debtor and for 90 days against those who are not. We will refer to these periods of one year and 90 days by the commonly used term, the *preference period*. Bankruptcy Code §547 authorizes the trustee or debtor in possession to "avoid" any transfer made during the preference period that would have the effect of preferring one unsecured creditor over others.

Bankruptcy law does not prohibit a debtor from granting preferences in the period before bankruptcy. Indeed, the parties to a prebankruptcy transaction may have no way of knowing when or whether a bankruptcy case will be filed, so they may have no way of knowing whether their transaction is within the preference period. Preference law authorizes avoidance of transactions that were legal and proper when done, but that are seen retrospectively to violate the preference policy of bankruptcy law.

The explanation of preference law we find most persuasive is that it prevents debtors from defeating the bankruptcy policy of pro rata distribution by liquidating their own estates on the eve of a bankruptcy. If there were no law authorizing avoidance of security interests granted on the eve of bankruptcy, debtors could spend that last evening granting security interests in all their assets to their favorite creditors, thereby depriving the remaining creditors of any chance of recovery. Preference law permits the avoidance of such security interests.

B. What Security Interests Can Be Avoided as Preferential?

1. Generally

Bankruptcy Code §547(b) states which "transfers" can be avoided as preferences. To be avoidable, a transfer must satisfy each element of that subsection. Even if it does, it may nevertheless be excepted from avoidance by Bankruptcy Code §547(c). The elements of Bankruptcy Code §547(b) are the following:

a. *§547(b). Transfer.* Only a "transfer of an interest of the debtor in property" can be avoided as a preference under §547(b). Bankruptcy Code §101 sets forth a broad definition of "transfer." It includes "every mode, direct or indirect, absolute or conditional, voluntary or involuntary, of disposing of or parting with property or with an interest in property. . . ." The transfers trustees most commonly seek to avoid are payments. But the creation and perfection of a security interest is clearly a transfer within the meaning of this section. In this assignment, we focus on the avoidance of security interests and leave the avoidance of other transfers, including payments, for the course on bankruptcy.

b. *§547(b)(1), to or for the benefit of a creditor, and §547(b)(2), for or on account of an antecedent debt.* The transfer must have been to a party who, at the time of receipt, was already a creditor. Bankr. Code §§547(b)(1) and (2). The principal effect of this limitation is to shelter from avoidance interests securing loans that were secured from the time they were made. To illustrate, Firstbank agrees to lend $100,000 to Debtor on a secured basis. Debtor executes a security agreement and financing statement. Firstbank files the financing statement and then makes the $100,000 advance. Debtor files bankruptcy the next day. The transfer of this security interest is not avoidable as a preference. It was not made "for or on account of an *antecedent* debt" because no debt was owing from Debtor to Firstbank until the transfer of the security interest was complete. To continue with the same example, suppose that Debtor's trustee in bankruptcy could prove that at the closing of this $100,000 loan, Firstbank's representative gave Debtor the check before Debtor signed the security agreement and financing statement and transferred the security interest to Firstbank. The existence of the debt preceded the existence of the security interest, making the transfer of the security interest arguably "for or on account of the [the $100,000] debt." Prior to 1979, trustees sometimes made arguments such as this. To silence these arguments, Congress enacted the exception in Bankruptcy Code §547(c)(1) that prohibits avoidance of a transfer that was intended to be a contemporaneous exchange for new value and that was in fact a substantially contemporaneous exchange.

c. §547(b)(3). Insolvency. If the debtor is solvent at the time of the transfer, the transfer is not avoidable as a preference for that reason alone. See Bankr. Code §547(b)(3). The rationale is that when a debtor is solvent, it has assets sufficient to satisfy all of its creditors. Paying or securing one creditor does not harm others because the debtor still has sufficient assets to pay or secure the others. If they choose to remain unsecured creditors, they choose to assume the risk that the debtor might no longer have sufficient assets when they finally try to collect — even if the insufficiency develops a few days or a few weeks later. This perfectly reasonable-sounding rationale does not look quite so good when you see the insolvency requirement in operation. Debtors who are hopelessly insolvent at the time of their bankruptcies may maintain that they were solvent 60 days earlier when they made the transfers they now seek to avoid. They may really have been so, or the debtors may just be relying on the difficulty their creditors will have proving it. The facts underlying a debtor's solvency or insolvency are complex and often uniquely within the knowledge and control of the debtor. To compensate for this tilt of the playing field, Bankruptcy Code §547(f) arms the trustee trying to set aside the transaction with a presumption of the debtor's insolvency that extends 90 days before the filing. The creditor must affirmatively prove solvency to escape the application of this provision.

d. §547(b)(4). The Preference Period. To be avoidable, the transfer must have occurred within the preference period. Bankr. Code §547(b)(4). Nearly all security interests have the effect of preferring the secured creditor in a later bankruptcy distribution; that is one of the principal purposes for taking one. Only those security interests transferred during the preference period are avoidable. Once again, the preference period is 90 days for most creditors and one year for insider creditors.

e. §547(b)(5). The Improvement Test. To be avoidable, the transfer must have improved the creditor's position. That means the transfer must have enabled the creditor who received it to recover more than the creditor would have if the debtor had been liquidated under Chapter 7 without making the transfer. The purpose of preference law is to achieve a pro rata distribution; if the transfer did not result in the creditor's getting more than its pro rata share, there is no reason to avoid it. Nearly any transfer of a security interest that meets the other requirements for avoidance will meet this one. Secured claims are paid in full up to the value of collateral in bankruptcy and unsecured claims are rarely paid in full. The secured creditor who gets such a transfer without paying new value for it almost certainly comes out ahead. If the debtor could be liquidated in the hypothetical Chapter 7 for enough to pay all creditors in full, the prebankruptcy transfer of a security interest to one creditor does not improve that creditor's position in the sense discussed here. But such a transfer would be from a solvent debtor and would be unavoidable as a preference for that reason alone.

2. When Does the "Transfer" of a Security Interest Occur?

The highly technical nature of preference law is nowhere more evident than on the issue of when the transfer of a security interest occurs. The precise time of the transfer is important for two reasons. First, the transfer can be avoided only if it occurs within the preference period. Second, both state law and Bankruptcy Code §547 permit transfers of security interests that occur within certain grace periods to relate back to earlier dates. If the earlier date is at or about the time the transferee first became a creditor, the transfer is no longer "for or on account of an antecedent debt" and becomes unavoidable even though it occurred within the preference period.

The basic rule, which can be derived from Bankruptcy Code §547(e), is that the transfer of a security interest is made when it is perfected. To illustrate, Firstbank takes a security interest and advances funds to Debtor on April 1. Firstbank does not perfect the security interest until June 1. On August 1, Debtor files bankruptcy. Even though this security interest attached and became enforceable under U.C.C. §§9-203(a) and (b) on April 1, the transfer of this security interest for purposes of Bankruptcy Code §547 did not occur until June 1, within the preference period. If the other elements of §547 are satisfied, the security interest is avoidable.

To determine when a security interest is perfected, Bankruptcy Code §547(e)(1) refers to state law. That subsection establishes different rules for real and personal property. A security interest in real property is perfected when it is too late for a bona fide purchaser to acquire a superior interest; a security interest in fixtures or personal property is perfected when it is too late for a lien creditor to acquire a superior interest. U.C.C. §§9-317(a)(2) and 9-323(b) tell us when it is too late for a lien creditor to acquire a superior interest: when the security interest is "perfected" within the Article 9 meaning of the term or at such earlier time that a security agreement is executed and a financing statement is filed. It follows that some security interests are perfected under bankruptcy law when they are not perfected under Article 9: security interests for which financing statements have been filed but that have not yet attached because value has not been given.

Some of the implications of U.C.C. §§9-317(a)(2) and 9-323(b) are not obvious. To illustrate, Firstbank takes a security interest in Debtor's "equipment, including after-acquired equipment" and advances funds to Debtor on April 1. On that same day, Firstbank files a financing statement describing the type of collateral as "equipment." Firstbank perfects in the collateral existing on that day. If Debtor files bankruptcy on August 1, the transfer of this security interest to Firstbank is not avoidable both because it was made outside the preference period and because it was not made on account of an antecedent debt. Now assume that on June 1, Debtor acquires a new, computerized chicken scratcher for use as equipment. Pursuant to the after-acquired property clause in Firstbank's security agreement description of collateral, Firstbank's security interest attaches to the scratcher on June 1. U.C.C. §§9-203(a) and (b). The "transfer" was the transfer of a security interest in the chicken scratcher to Firstbank. It became too late for a creditor of Debtor on a simple contract to acquire an interest in the scratcher that is superior to Firstbank's at the moment Debtor acquired ownership. Therefore, the transfer of the security interest in the scratcher did not occur until June 1, a date within the preference period. Bankr. Code §547(e)(2). To make this point perfectly clear, even in cases not governed by the U.C.C., Bankruptcy Code §547(e)(3) states it more directly: "For the purposes of this section, a transfer is not made until the debtor has acquired rights in the property transferred."

3. The §547(c)(5) Exception for Accounts Receivable and Inventory

The rule of Bankruptcy Code §547(e)(3) that the transfer of a security interest in after-acquired property is not made until the debtor has acquired rights in that property is potentially devastating to accounts and inventory lenders. Debtors are constantly selling their inventory, collecting their accounts receivable, and replacing them with newly acquired inventory and accounts. When a debtor who borrows against accounts receivable and inventory files bankruptcy, it is not at all unusual to find that most of the secured creditor's collateral was acquired by the debtor during the preference period. Under the rule of §547(e)(3) the transfer of the security interest in that collateral would also have occurred during the preference period, possibly rendering the security interest vulnerable to avoidance.

Yet, if the relationship between the debtor and such an accounts receivable and inventory lender is viewed as a whole, it may not run afoul of bankruptcy policy. If, for example, there was $60,000 worth of collateral serving as security for a $100,000 loan during the entire preference period, the secured creditor has not improved its position during the period even if most of the items of collateral existing on the date of the bankruptcy filing were first acquired during the period. The secured creditor's gains in collateral have been offset by losses; any payments the secured creditor received have been offset by new advances. In recognition of these facts, Bankruptcy Code §547(c)(5) creates a safe harbor for security interests in accounts receivable and inventory. Instead of treating the acquisition of each new item of after-acquired collateral as a transfer to the secured creditor to be tested and possibly avoided as a preference, §547(c)(5) treats the receivables and inventory as a single item of collateral. Only increases in the value of the receivables and inventory as a whole that exceed the accompanying increases, if any, in the amount of the secured creditor's claim are left vulnerable to preference avoidance. On the facts of the example in the preceding paragraph, the security interest would be within the safe harbor of §547(c)(5) and the trustee could avoid no part of it.

Because it is measuring aggregate changes in the value of the collateral and the amount of the debt rather than individual transactions, §547(c)(5) employs what is referred to as a *two-point test* of whether the receivables and inventory lender has improved its position. In re Ebbler, Furniture and Appliances, Inc., 804 F.2d 87 (7th Cir. 1986), gives the following particularly succinct, clear explanation of the two-point test:

The first step in applying section 547(c)(5) is to determine the amount of the loan outstanding 90 days prior to filing and the "value" of the collateral on that day. The difference between these figures is then computed. Next, the same determinations are made as of the date of filing the petition. A comparison is made, and, if there is a reduction during the 90-day period of the amount by which the initially existing debt exceeded the security, then a preference for section 547(c)(5) purposes exists. The effect of 547(c)(5) is to make the security interest voidable [only] to the extent of the preference. Of course, if the creditor is fully secured 90 days before the filing of the petition, then that creditor will never be subject to a preference attack.

Ebbler at 89-90.

4. Relation-Back Rules

Determining when the transfer of a security interest was made is complicated by the existence of rules in both state and federal law that permit perfection, once made, to relate back to an earlier date. Bankruptcy Code §547(e)(2), for example, provides that if a secured creditor perfects its security interest within ten days after the interest takes effect between debtor and secured creditor (that is, within ten days after attachment), the interest is deemed perfected as of the time it took effect between debtor and secured creditor. To illustrate, assume a debtor and its secured creditor create a security interest that attaches to the collateral on March 1. The secured creditor perfects that interest on March 10. Bankruptcy Code §547(e)(2)(A) deems the transfer made on March 1. To put it another way, the perfection that occurred March 10 relates back to March 1.

Bankruptcy Code §547(e)(2)(A) is probably the broadest of these relation-back rules, but it is not the only one. Bankruptcy Code §547(c)(3) exempts a purchase-money security interest from preference avoidance provided that the secured creditor disburses the loan proceeds at or after the signing of the security agreement and perfects the interest within 20 days after the debtor receives possession of the collateral. Recall that U.C.C. §9-317(e) created a sort of grace period for perfection of a purchase-money security interest. The secured creditor who perfected within that grace period defeated a lien creditor who levied during it. Bankruptcy Code §547(c)(3) extends to that same secured creditor protection against preference avoidance.

Can a state extend a longer grace period for perfecting than is available under the Bankruptcy Code? Some courts held that a state could. Those courts reasoned that if a creditor-car dealer delivered possession of a car on April 1 and delivered its application to note its security interest on the title to the Department on April 30 and state law deemed perfection of that interest to occur on April 1, then April 1 was both the first date "a creditor on a simple contract could not acquire a judicial lien superior to the interest of the [secured creditor]" and the date of perfection for purposes of Bankruptcy Code §547(e)(2). Because the transfer was perfected within ten days of the day it took effect between the debtor and the secured creditor, Bankruptcy Code §547(e)(2)(A) also deemed it made on the day it took effect between the debtor and the secured creditor. In the following case, the Supreme Court rejected that reasoning.

Fidelity Financial Services, Inc. v. Fink

522 U.S. 211 (1998)

<small>Syllabus:</small> Diane Beasley purchased a new car and gave petitioner, Fidelity Financial Services, Inc., a promissory note for the purchase price, secured by the car. Twenty-one days later, Fidelity mailed the application necessary to perfect its security interest under Missouri law. Beasley later filed for bankruptcy, and the trustee of her bankruptcy estate, respondent Fink, moved to set aside Fidelity's security interest on the ground that the lien was a voidable preference under 11 U.S.C. §547(b). Section 547(c)(3)(B) prohibits the avoidance of a security interest for a loan used to acquire property if, among other things, the security interest is "perfected on or before 20 days after the debtor receives possession of such property." Fink argued that this "enabling loan" exception was inapposite because Fidelity had not perfected its interest within the 20-day period. Fidelity responded that Missouri law treats a motor vehicle lien as having been "perfected" on the date of its creation (in this case, within the 20-day period), if the creditor files the necessary documents within 30 days after the debtor takes possession. The Bankruptcy Court set aside the lien as a voidable preference, holding that Missouri's relation-back provision could not extend §547(c)(3)(B)'s 20-day perfection period. The District Court affirmed on substantially the same grounds, as did the Eighth Circuit, holding a transfer to be perfected when the transferee takes the last step required by state law to perfect its security interest.

Held: A transfer of a security interest is "perfected" under §547(c)(3)(B) on the date that the secured party has completed the steps necessary to perfect its interest, so that a creditor may invoke the enabling loan exception only by satisfying state law perfection requirements within the 20-day period provided by the federal statute. Section 547(e)(1)(B) provides that "a transfer of . . . property . . . is perfected when a creditor on a simple contract cannot acquire a judicial lien that is superior to the interest of the transferee." This definition implies that a transfer is "perfected" only when the secured party has done all the acts required to perfect its interest, not at the moment as of which state law may retroactively deem that perfection effective. A variety of considerations support this conclusion, including §546, which raises a negative implication that Congress did not intend state relation-back provisions or grace periods to control a trustee's power to avoid preferences, and the fact that, under Fidelity's reading, the net effect of the 1994 amendment extending the §547(c)(3)(B) perfection period from 10 to 20 days would be merely to benefit a class of creditors in only ten jurisdictions. Indeed, the broader statutory history of the preference provisions persuasively suggests that Congress intended §547(c)(3)(B) to establish a uniform federal perfection period immune to alteration by state laws permitting relation back. Thus, the statutory text, structure, and history lead to the understanding that a creditor may invoke the enabling loan exception only by acting to perfect its security interest within 20 days after the debtor takes possession of its property.

It seems to us that after *Fidelity Financial Services*, it no longer matters for purposes of preference avoidance what grace period a state gives the holders of purchase-money security interests in which to perfect. If state law gives less than the 20 days given by Bankruptcy Code §547(c)(3), the security interest is saved from avoidance by that section. If state law gives more than the 20 days given by Bankruptcy Code §547(c)(3), the extension is ineffective under the precedent of *Fidelity Financial Services*. Consistent with this observation, the Legislative Note at the end of U.C.C. §9-311 recommends repeal of grace period provisions contained in certificate of title laws.

C.   Strategic Implications of Preference Avoidance

When applied to debtors who are forced into bankruptcy with little warning, preference law probably has the effect its drafters intended. Creditors who were promoted from unsecured to secured status on the eve of bankruptcy are demoted to their former status. Debtors are discouraged from making such transfers because they won't stick.

Many debtors, however, are able to choose when they will file bankruptcy. These debtors can make the preferential transfers they wish, wait until the preference period expires, and then file. The reported cases are full of debtors who exercised this strategy. The transfers remain unavoidable because they are not within the preference period.

Savvy unsecured creditors usually can overcome this strategy. Because the transfer of a security interest is made only when it is perfected, the event that starts the preference period running is a public one. Unsecured creditors often monitor the public records for grants of security. When one appears, they demand an explanation of the debtor. If the debtor cannot or will not justify the transfer to their satisfaction, the unsecured creditors petition for involuntary bankruptcy before the preference period expires. The petition stops the preference period from expiring and renders the transfer avoidable if the other elements of §547(b) are present.

Ironically, the unsecured creditor that monitors, discovers the preferential transfer, files the involuntary petition, and thereby enables the trustee to avoid the transfer, receives only its pro rata share of the recovery after the expenses of the litigation (possibly including payment of the unsecured creditors' attorneys' fees incurred in bringing the petition) have been paid. The watchdog gets no special reward.

As a result, the most sophisticated watchdogs don't bark. They approach the debtor privately, point out their ability to file an involuntary petition and thereby upset the transfer, and cut a deal. They may themselves get preferential treatment directly from the debtor (in which case another red flag might go on the public record) or the creditor already preferred may agree to share its bounty with them. In either event, preference law fails to accomplish its purpose. All it does is to shift wealth from the less sophisticated to the more sophisticated players.

Even if the debtor is in bankruptcy, the mere fact that a transfer is avoidable as a preference does not assure that it will be avoided. Bankruptcy Code §547(b) says that the trustee *may* avoid the transfer, not that the trustee *must*. In a Chapter 7 case, the trustee will be a disinterested member of the panel of trustees, a lawyer or member of another profession, who makes his or her living from administering the estates of strangers. For these trustees, preference avoidance is a major source of income and expense money. Most of these trustees are like hungry pit bulls. They are likely to avoid whatever prepetition transfers they can.

In a Chapter 11 case, the debtor in possession administers the estate and, at least initially, exercises the discretion to avoid or not avoid avoidable preferences. The debtor in possession is unlikely to avoid a preference, often for the same reason it made the preference in the first place. The transferee may be a friend, a business associate, or a supplier whose cooperation is necessary to the continued operation of the business. Even if the transferee is a person with no other leverage against the debtor, the debtor may strike an agreement, express or implied, by which the transfer remains undisturbed and the transferee votes in favor of the debtor's plan.

In recent years, when debtors in possession have abused their discretion to avoid preferences, unsecured creditors' committees have sometimes sought to exercise the discretion themselves. They have petitioned the bankruptcy court to allow them to bring the preference avoidance action that the debtor will not. Particularly in egregious circumstances, the bankruptcy courts have tended to allow creditors' committees to bring these preference avoidance actions in the name of the estate.

Problem Set 31

31.1.   As the newest associate at a glamorous, big-city bankruptcy firm, you have been assigned the Gargantuan Industries bankruptcy. Gargantuan filed under Chapter 11 of the Bankruptcy Code on September 1. On December 30, the case was converted to Chapter 7 and a partner in your firm was appointed trustee. Bankr. Code §348(a). He asks you to review the following transactions for possible avoidance as preferences:

a.   On August 15, Gargantuan borrowed $300,000 from Firstbank. Gargantuan executed the loan documents that day. They included a security agreement and financing statement, both covering certain equipment owned by Gargantuan. Firstbank filed the financing statement the following morning. Bankr. Code §§547(b), (c)(1), and (e).

b.   On February 7, Gargantuan borrowed $300,000 from Secondbank on an unsecured one-year note. On July 11, Gargantuan signed a security agreement that granted Secondbank a security interest in certain equipment. Secondbank immediately perfected the security interest by filing a financing statement. Bankr. Code §§547(b), (c), and (e).

c.   On February 7, Gargantuan borrowed $300,000 from Thirdbank on a secured one-year note. Gargantuan signed a financing statement and Thirdbank attempted to file it, but it was lost in the mail. Six months later, a Postal Service employee found the envelope stuck to the inside of a mail sack by a piece of carelessly disposed-of chewing gum. On July 11, the U.C.C. filing office received the still-sticky envelope and accepted the filing. Bankr. Code §547(e); U.C.C. §9-317(a)(2).

d.   On July 21, Gargantuan purchased network software and hardware from the Electronic Machine Shop (EMS). Gargantuan financed the purchase with a $30,000 loan from Fourthbank. Gargantuan signed a promissory note for the $30,000, a security agreement granting Fourthbank a security interest in the network, and a financing statement. Fourthbank issued the $30,000 check to EMS on July 21. EMS delivered the network to Gargantuan the following day. EMS mailed the financing statement to the office of the Secretary of State, where it was received and accepted for filing on July 30. U.C.C. §§9-103(a) and (b), 9-317(e); Bankr. Code §§547(c)(1), (c)(3), and (e).

e.   Would the result be different if, on the facts of d, Fourthbank had issued the check to Gargantuan and Gargantuan had used other funds to purchase the network?

f.   On March 9, Gargantuan did not have the money to make its payroll. It solved the problem by borrowing $300,000 that day from Elsa Cohen, the wife of Gargantuan CEO, president, and 30 percent shareholder, Michael Cohen. Mike promised Elsa that the loan would be secured, but he didn't get the papers over to her for signing until April 9. The financing statement was filed late on the afternoon of April 9. Elsa has never been involved in the management of Gargantuan. Bankr. Code §§547(b)(4), (e), and §101 (definitions of "insider" and "relative"). What do you advise?

31.2.   Over a year ago, you filed suit against Mofo Cycles, Inc., on behalf of your client, Soichi Dysan. The suit is on an unsecured promissory note. The case was tried more than two months ago, and you won a verdict in the amount of $547,000. On the day after the verdict, four other creditors of Mofo Cycles filed U.C.C. financing statements and recorded real estate mortgages against Mofo. Eleven days ago, the court entered judgment on your verdict. Yesterday, the judgment became final, and you became entitled to writs of execution or garnishment against Mofo's property. Mofo is still selling motorcycles from its spacious showroom on a major highway. What is your next move? Bankr. Code §§303(a) and (b), 547(b), 706(a), 1107(a).

31.3.   Swissbank holds a perfected security interest in the inventory of Gift of Love. On June 1, the outstanding balance on the loan was $250,000 and the value of the inventory was $120,000. By August 29, when Gift of Love was petitioned into Chapter 7, the loan balance had been reduced to $150,000 and the inventory to $70,000. Every item in inventory at the time of bankruptcy was acquired by Gift of Love on unsecured credit after June 1. Does the trustee have any rights against Swissbank? Bankr. Code §§547(b), (c)(5). Does it matter that all $70,000 of the inventory remaining at the time of the filing of the petition was purchased by Gift of Love less than 90 days before the petition was filed? Bankr. Code §547(e)(3).

31.4.   Your new boss, Congresswoman Patricia Wright, asks your opinion of Professor James W. Bowers's proposal to abolish preference law. Bowers maintains that there is nothing wrong with letting debtors liquidate their own estates on the eve of bankruptcy so long as they are paying or securing bona fide creditors. (If they try to give the money to someone who isn't a bona fide creditor, they will run afoul of fraudulent transfer law, which Bowers does not propose to abolish.) The distribution that will result from a market interaction between the debtor and its creditors will be better than the pro rata distribution preference law seeks to promote, because the creditors who need the money the most will fight the hardest for it. In any event, preference law doesn't really prevent preferences; it just delays bankruptcy filings. What do you tell the congresswoman?

Assignment 32: Secured Creditors Against Secured Creditors: The Basics

In this assignment we examine the rules governing priority among Article 9 security interests. These rules appear in U.C.C. §9-322. As we discuss them, keep in mind that they do not apply to competitions between Article 9 security interests and other kinds of liens except agricultural liens. If the competitor is a lien creditor, a real estate mortgagee, or a tax lien, to give but three examples, you must look to rules other than those in U.C.C. §9-322. Because the rules governing priority among different kinds of liens are spread among several bodies of law, priority is a subject that must be learned one competition at a time.

A. The Basic Rule: First to File or Perfect

The basic rule governing priority among security interests is in U.C.C. §9-322(a)(1). Between the holders of two security interests in the same collateral, the first to file or perfect has priority. In other words, the priority date of a security interest is the earlier of the dates on which the secured party filed with respect to the interest or perfected it. As between two security interests, the one with the earlier priority date has priority. The holder who gains priority by first filing or perfecting retains it so long as the holder remains continuously filed or perfected. U.C.C §9-322(a)(1).

To illustrate the basic rule, assume that on December 1, Bank1 files a financing statement against collateral the debtor already owns, but neither lends money nor enters into a security agreement with the debtor. So far, Bank1 remains unperfected, because its security interest has not attached. U.C.C. §9-308(a). On December 5, Bank2 files a financing statement against the same collateral and perfects by entering into a security agreement with the debtor and lending money. On December 10, Bank1 perfects by entering into a security agreement with the debtor and lending money. Bank1 has priority, because Bank1 filed *or* perfected (it filed on December 1) before Bank2 filed or perfected (it filed and perfected on December 5).

The explanation for this complex rule is itself complex, and not entirely satisfactory. The drafters sought by this rule to "[protect] the filing system." The concept is explained in Comment 5 to U.C.C. §9-322. Given the rule, a secured party could file a financing statement before either lending or agreeing to lend, U.C.C. §9-502(d), search the filing system at its leisure (or perhaps, more to the point, at the leisure of the filing officer) to make sure its financing statement was the first on file, and then lend without worrying that a competing security interest had been perfected in the interim.

The trouble with this explanation is that it justifies a "first to file" rule rather than the "first to file or perfect" rule of U.C.C. §9-322(1)(a). The reference to "perfection" was probably added as an afterthought to deal with the situation in which one of the competitors perfected without filing — that is, automatically or by taking possession. In all probability, the drafters acted without malice in adopting the "first to file or perfect" language — they just wanted to cover all cases with a single pronouncement.

To illustrate the operation of the rule, assume that US Bank and Trust (USBT) contemplates lending against assets already owned by, and in the possession of, Davis Industries. USBT files a financing statement on September 1. USBT waits for the Secretary of State to process all filings through September 1, which the Secretary of State manages to do by September 15. Knowing that its priority date against competing security interests will be the date of its September 1 filing, USBT also knows that any filing with priority over its own is now in the index and discoverable. USBT orders its search for filings against Davis Industries. The search report it receives on September 22 shows its filing to be the only one on record against Davis as of the effective date of the search, September 1.

Because the rule is first to file or *perfect*, USBT must also view the collateral to make sure it is not in the possession of the holder of a competing security interest. The ideal time to conduct this inspection would be at the moment USBT files on September 1. That inspection would ensure absolutely that no competing creditor had priority over USBT by virtue of filing or perfection by possession.

If USBT conducts the visual inspection on September 7, there is the possibility that the competing creditor was perfected by possession until September 6 and relinquished possession on that day only after filing a financing statement. The competing creditor would be continuously perfected, U.C.C. §9-308(c), but its financing statement would not show up on USBT's search because the search would only cover the period through September 1. Neither secured creditors nor their lawyers are likely to lose much sleep over such a possibility — unless a *very* large amount of money is at issue.

Notice that U.C.C. §9-322(a) assigns priority without reference to either creditor's state of mind. The drafters intend that the first to file or perfect have priority even if the first knows that the debtor intended that another creditor have priority and even if the first believed itself to be subordinate at the time it filed or perfected. White and Summers explain:

> Note that [§9-322(a)] is a "pure race" statute. That is, the one who wins the "race" to the court house to file is superior without regard to the state of his knowledge. The section nowhere requires that the victor be without knowledge of its competitor's claim. [Example 1 in comment 4 to §9-322] illustrates the irrelevance of knowledge under the subsection. One justification for that rule is the certainty it affords. Under [§9-322(a)] no disappointed secured creditor can trump up facts from which a compassionate court might find knowledge on the part of the competitor. If the competitor filed or perfected first, as the case may be, that's the end of it; this party wins even if it knew of the other party's prior but unperfected claim.

James J. White & Robert S. Summers, Uniform Commercial Code §24-4 (4th ed. 1995).

U.C.C. §9-325 sets forth an important exception to the rule of first to file or perfect. That section subordinates security interests perfected against a transferee to those perfected against the transferor To illustrate, assume that Firstbank takes a security interest against all equipment of Debtor2, including after-acquired property, and perfects by filing a financing statement on March 1. On April 1, Secondbank takes a security interest in all of the assets of Debtor1 and perfects by filing a financing statement. On May 1, Debtor1 sells an item of equipment — an automated chicken scratcher — to Debtor2. Because Secondbank did not authorize the sale free and clear of its security interest, the interest continues to encumber the chicken scratcher in the hands of Debtor2. Firstbank's security interest attaches to the chicken scratcher pursuant to the after-acquired property clause. Firstbank is perfected in the chicken scratcher because its financing statement is sufficiently broad to cover it.

Which of the two banks has priority? Simply applying the rule of U.C.C. §9-322(a)(1), it would seem that Firstbank has priority: It filed against the chicken scratcher before Secondbank did. But U.C.C. §9-325 gives priority to Secondbank, because Secondbank perfected in the chicken scratcher before Debtor1 sold it to Debtor2.

Even without U.C.C. §9-325, someone who understood how the Article 9 system of priority functioned would have realized the necessity for the §9-325 exception. Security interests rank in order of perfection so that lenders can discover the security interests to which they will be subordinate. If a lender to Debtor 1 could be subordinate to a security interest filed earlier against Debtor2, that lender's search could not discover prior competing interests. The lender could not search for filings against Debtor2 because even Debtor1 may not yet have identified Debtor 2 as a potential transferee.

B.   Priority of Future Advances

In competitions between Article 9 secured creditors, the rule regarding future advances is essentially the rule you saw applied between a mortgage holder and a lien creditor in Shutze v. Credithrift of America in Assignment 29. Provided only that the secured creditor's financing statement "covers the collateral," all advances made by the secured creditor to the debtor have priority as of the filing of the financing statement. This rule is implicit in U.C.C. §9-322(a)(1).

To illustrate, reconsider the scenario in which Bank1 files a financing statement against collateral owned by the debtor, Bank2 files and perfects in the same collateral, and Bank1 then perfects by taking a security interest in the collateral and making an advance against it. We concluded that Bank1's interest had priority over Bank2's interest because Bank1 was the first to file or perfect. If Bank1 later makes additional advances against the collateral, those advances will have the same priority as the first. They will have priority over Bank2's security interest.

The justification for this priority under Article 9 is the same given for the priority of future advances in real estate law. Bank1's filing put Bank2 on notice of the possible existence of a security interest that might secure future advances, so Bank2 should not be heard to complain if such advances are made. An important function of an Article 9 financing statement is to put searchers on notice of present and future interests that may prime the one they intend to take. So long as searchers understand the rule regarding priority of future advances, the financing statement will in fact convey notice to searchers. The understanding is that one who takes a second security interest agrees to take subject to the amount outstanding under the first filing and any future advances the holder of the first may later make.

This justification is less persuasive under Article 9 than under real estate law. Under real estate law, the future-advance clause must appear in the mortgage and the mortgage must be recorded. To gain actual notice of the possibility of future advances, one need only know how to search and how to read. Under Article 9, only the financing statement need be on the public record. Rarely will it mention the existence of the future-advance clause in the security agreement. In fact, the security agreement containing the future-advance clause need not yet be in existence. To realize the possibility of future advances under Article 9, one must know a little law as well as how to search and read.

An important function of the future-advance rule under Article 9 is to relieve the lender who will make future advances from the necessity to file and search in conjunction with each advance. The same is true in the real estate system. In both systems, once the lender achieves priority with regard to its security interest, it can make future advances secure in the knowledge that they will have that priority.

Who would take a second security interest in a system in which the first can increase without limit? The takers fall essentially into three categories: (1) lenders who do not understand the future-advance rule, (2) creditors who hope to benefit from their second interest but do not advance funds in reliance on it, and (3) lenders who protect themselves against future advances by contract with the holder of the first interest. U.C.C. §9-339.

Subsection (a) of U.C.C. §9-322 refers to the priority of a "security interest." Ironically, the security interest whose priority date is fixed by filing may not yet be in existence at the time. The filing has the effect of reserving priority for whatever security interest the debtor later grants in favor of the filer — limited, of course, by the description of collateral in the financing statement.

Can a single financing statement secure more than one such interest? To illustrate the problem, assume that the debtor gives the bank a security interest in the debtor's inventory of auto parts. The parties file a financing statement describing the type of collateral as "inventory" and the bank advances funds under the first promissory note and security agreement. Later, the debtor gives the bank a security interest in the debtor's inventory of automobiles and the bank advances funds under a second promissory note and security agreement. The parties do not file a second financing statement. On these facts, both advances have priority as of the filing of the financing statement. See U.C.C. §§9-322(a) and 9-502(d). A single financing statement is adequate to perfect any number of security interests, to the limits of the description of collateral in the financing statement.

C.   Priority in After-Acquired Property

Recall from Assignment 9 that Article 9 permits the grant of a security interest in property the debtor does not yet own. The security agreement can describe the collateral to be acquired specifically ("John Deere tractor bearing serial number 5843F877Y99") or in general terms ("any inventory or equipment the debtor acquires in the future"). Debtors who grant security interests in after-acquired property often do not even contemplate acquiring any property of the kind described. If the debtor later acquires property that fits the description in the security agreement, the security interest attaches. U.C.C. §9-203(b).

If the description of collateral is broad enough to cover the after-acquired property, the filing covers it. As against other Article 9 secured creditors of the debtor, the after-acquired lender's priority dates from the time of its filing. U.C.C. §9-322(a)(1). To put it another way, a security interest has the same priority with respect to after-acquired property that it has with respect to the original collateral.

To illustrate, assume that Bank1 files a financing statement on April 1 against the equipment of Davis Industries and Bank2 files such a financing statement on April 5. On April 11, Davis Industries signs a security agreement granting a security interest in equipment, including after-acquired equipment, to Bank2. Bank2 makes an advance. On April 15, Davis Industries signs such a security agreement in favor of Bank1 and Bank1 makes an advance. On April 10, Davis Industries acquires its first and only item of equipment, a Giant Mashing Machine. On these facts, Bank1 has priority over Bank2 in the Giant Mashing Machine. Under U.C.C. §9-322(a)(1), Bank1's priority dates from the filing of its financing statement.

The most common commercial use of after-acquired property clauses is in inventory-secured financing. The typical debtor is continually selling inventory and replacing it with new inventory. If an inventory-secured lender's interest did not reach property acquired after the initial loan transaction, in a few days or a few weeks little collateral would remain. The debtor and creditor could solve this problem without the use of an after-acquired property clause: They could simply enter into a new security agreement every time a new shipment of inventory arrived. That would be cumbersome. Instead, nearly all inventory loan agreements provide that after-acquired inventory will serve as collateral for all amounts outstanding under the loan. The lender perfects its interest in both currently owned and after-acquired inventory by the filing of a single financing statement.

Many regard the validation of after-acquired property clauses as the most important innovation in Article 9. They argue that modern-day inventory lending could not exist without the use of after-acquired property clauses and that without such lending, the overall level of economic activity would be considerably lower. To understand the factual assertions on which their argument is based, consider the example of Sally Raj, who is planning to open a stereo store in a small shopping center. Sally estimates the cost of the inventory the store will need to open at $100,000. She has $100,000 that she has raised through savings and unsecured borrowing from friends, but she will have to use nearly all of that money to rent and furnish store space, hire employees, and get the business under way. How will she buy the inventory she needs? Most suppliers of inventory for stereo stores are themselves short of working capital. They will sell their products on credit, even unsecured credit, but they are unwilling to "carry" a debtor for more than 30 to 60 days after the sale. They want to be paid quickly so they can reinvest the money in their own business. If all of Sally's suppliers would sell on 30 to 60 days' credit, if they would sell her enough to adequately stock the store, and if Sally could sell all of that inventory for cash quickly enough to pay her suppliers when due, Sally would not need inventory financing. But that is a lot of "ifs."

Most people in Sally's situation find it necessary to seek an inventory loan from a bank or finance company. We discussed inventory lending at some length in Assignment 15. The lender will take a security interest in the debtor's inventory (which may be nothing at the time the loan is closed), including after-acquired inventory. A common arrangement would be for the bank to lend 60 percent of the cost of the inventory. The bank chooses this particular level of financing because it is the level at which the bank feels "secure" — that is, the bank estimates that in the event of default on the loan, they could take possession of the inventory, sell it, and net about 60 percent of its cost.

Each time a new shipment of inventory arrives, Sally sends proof of its arrival to the bank and the bank deposits 60 percent of the invoice amount to Sally's bank account. Each day the business is open, Sally deposits all of the proceeds from sale of inventory to the same bank account, and the bank takes an amount equal to what they lent against the items of collateral that have been sold. From time to time, an employee of the bank might stop by the stereo store to make sure there is as much inventory there as the bank thinks there is. So long as Sally's revenues are sufficient to pay her debts as they fall due, the bank is always fully secured, Sally has sufficient inventory, and the suppliers get paid on time. If her revenues are insufficient, the bank can make itself whole by selling the inventory and Sally and the suppliers will have to take the hit. That is the very meaning of priority.

D.   Priority of Purchase-Money
Security Interests

1.   Purchase-Money Security Interests Generally

Under U.C.C. §9-324(e), a purchase-money security interest in collateral other than inventory has priority over a conflicting security interest in the same collateral if the purchase-money security interest is perfected not later than 20 days after the debtor receives possession of the collateral. To illustrate, assume Bank1 files its financing statement against the equipment of Davis Industries on February 1. On July 1, Preferred Micro Sales, Inc. (PMSI) sells a computer to Davis Industries, delivers possession, and retains a purchase-money security interest. On July 20, PMSI perfects by filing a financing statement. Under U.C.C. §9-324(e), PMSI has priority over Bank1 with regard to the computer.

The rules regarding the priority of purchase-money security interests on their face may seem to violate the principle of first in time, first in right. The after-acquired lender files before, and attaches simultaneously with, the purchase-money lender, yet the purchase-money lender gets priority.

But the purchase-money lender is "first" in another important sense: It either supplied the collateral or made advances "to enable the debtor to acquire . . . the collateral." U.C.C. §§9-103(a) and (b). The purchase-money lender could have made its interest first by insisting that a straw man take title to the collateral and grant a perfected purchase-money interest, before the collateral was transferred to the debtor. The debtor then would have taken title subject to an already perfected purchase-money security interest, the after-acquired lender's security interest would have attached only at that time, and we would not have thought of the after-acquired lender as having been "first in time." See U.C.C. §9-325(a). Purchase-money priority can be understood as recognizing that, in the sense described here, the purchase-money lender has a relationship with the collateral before the after-acquired lender does. The purchase-money priority rule merely excuses the purchase-money lender from going through a straw man transaction to prove it.

The priority of purchase-money security interests is often justified on another basis. It enables companies like Preferred Micro Sales to sell and deliver immediately without having to check the public record. Provided that Preferred Micro Sales files within 20 days of the day the debtor receives possession, it will have priority over any earlier filings against the debtor that might exist.

As you have seen in other contexts, any easing of the burden on filers is likely to increase the burden on searchers. The 20-day grace period in U.C.C. §9-324(e) is no exception. Because it exists, anyone lending against noninventory collateral in the possession of the debtor must consider the possibility that (1) the debtor obtained possession of the collateral in the past 20 days and (2) the holder of one or more purchase-money security interests in the collateral has not yet filed a financing statement, but will do so before the end of that 20 days. One way for the searcher to remedy this problem is to verify the debtor's possession of the collateral and then wait 20 days beyond the basket period before searching.

Commentators on Article 9 have advanced yet another justification for the rules establishing purchase-money priority:

> A more modern justification for purchase money priority may be found in a desire to protect the *debtor* from the initial secured creditor's overreaching. If the security agreement with the first creditor contained a blanket description of the debtor's assets, including after acquired collateral and a broad definition of debt, the debtor would become virtually indentured to the initial secured creditor. If that creditor refused to lend more money and also refused to grant a subordination agreement, the debtor would be unable to borrow to finance the purchase of a new asset from a second creditor willing to lend only against a security interest in that very asset having priority over the first creditor. The purchase money priority rule in effect frees the debtor from the reach of the first security agreement.

Speidel, White & Summers, Secured Transactions Teaching Materials, 205 (West 1987).

We disagree. Many, if not most, debtors *are* virtually indentured to their initial secured creditor. The security agreement they signed makes anything they buy collateral and makes the attachment of any other lien to the collateral a default, whether it is a purchase-money lien or not. Default at the option of the secured party generally leads to catastrophe for the debtor. Thus a properly indentured debtor cannot take advantage of purchase-money financing over the objection of his or her master.

We think the rule permitting purchase-money priority is better explained as a default rule that governs only if the parties make no agreement to the contrary. Not every secured party chooses to indenture its borrowers and not every secured party who indentures its borrowers chooses to enforce the indenture. A secured party may be willing to tolerate the debtor's acquisition of additional collateral through purchase-money financing because it increases the aggregate value of the secured party's collateral. That is, without having to advance additional funds, the secured party gets a second security interest in new collateral the debtor might not otherwise have been able to acquire. To the extent that the new property is used to produce income for the debtor, it also increases the likelihood that the first secured creditor will eventually be repaid.

More than one creditor may have a valid purchase-money security interest in the same collateral. For example, Mary Parker wants to buy some well-drilling equipment for $10,000. The seller is willing to sell the equipment for $2,000 cash-down and accept a promissory note secured by a purchase-money security interest for the $8,000 balance. But Mary does not have $2,000. She borrows the $2,000 down payment from Firstbank, giving Firstbank a security interest in the well-drilling equipment. Provided that Mary uses the $2,000 to make the down payment, both Firstbank and the seller have security interests that qualify for purchase-money priority. Both their interests would have priority over any non-purchase-money security interest Mary granted in the same collateral.

U.C.C. §9-324(g)(1) gives the seller's purchase-money security interest priority over cash-lender Firstbank's purchase-money security interest. The rationale for this priority is stated in Comment 13 to U.C.C. §9-324. "[T]he law is more sympathetic to the vendor's hazard of losing [well-drilling equipment] previously owned than to the third party lender's risk of being unable to collect from an interest in the [well-drilling equipment] that never previously belonged to it." (Not much of a rationale, is it?)

Had both competing purchase-money security interests been in favor of lenders rather than sellers, U.C.C. §9-324(g)(2) would have referred the issue of priority to be determined under U.C.C. §9-322(a). That section gives priority to the first to file or perfect — which may come as a surprise to a PMSI lender that thinks it has a 20-day "grace period" in which to file and assure itself complete priority.

2. Purchase-Money Security Interests in Inventory

The 20-day grace period for the filing of a PMSI in U.C.C. §9-324(e) does not apply when the property sold will be inventory in the hands of the buyer. This exception is designed to accommodate the customs and practices in inventory financing. Most inventory financing is extended on the understanding that the inventory-secured lender's lien will be the only lien against inventory owned by the debtor. Within days, or even hours, of the arrival of a new shipment of inventory, the inventory-secured lender will make advances against it. The inventory-secured lender will do so on proof that the debtor is in possession of the inventory, without investigating whether the debtor has paid for it. (In fact, the understanding is usually that the debtor will *not* have paid for the inventory at the time it borrows against the inventory.) The inventory-secured lender may or may not require the debtor to use the loan proceeds to pay for the inventory, but the understanding is that the debtor will grant no PMSIs in it.

If these understandings applied to all inventory financing, a flat prohibition on PMSIs in inventory would have been appropriate. But some inventory lenders are willing to allow their debtors to take advantage of some purchase-money secured financing. Even these more tolerant lenders must, of course, have some way of knowing that others are financing some of the debtor's inventory. Inventory-secured lenders do not want to lend in reliance on collateral that is fully encumbered by a prior interest.

To protect against such double borrowing, it is not enough that the inventory lender learn of the purchase-money secured financing. The inventory lender must learn of the financing before disbursing against the collateral. If a purchase-money secured lender against inventory could, like its noninventory counterpart, obtain priority by filing a financing statement 20 days after delivery, the debtor would have (and spend) its double financing long before the inventory lender learned of the conflict.

These special needs of inventory financiers are reflected in the special rules in U.C.C. §9-324(a). These rules permit purchase-money priority in inventory only on these conditions:

1. The purchase-money financier must perfect no later than the time the debtor receives possession of the collateral, and
2. The purchase-money financier must give advance notice to the inventory lender that it expects to acquire a purchase-money security interest in inventory. To give this notice the purchase-money lender first searches the filing system for the names and addresses of all secured parties with a filing against inventory of the type it plans to sell. The lender then sends the notice, typically by certified mail, to each of the inventory lenders. Like a financing statement, the notice expires at the end of five years. The purchase-money supplier can avoid expiration by repeating the notice at intervals of less than five years.

As Comment 3 to U.C.C. §9-324 explains,

> The notification requirement protects the inventory financier [against attempts by the debtor to borrow from both inventory financier and supplier against the same collateral]: If he has received notification, he will presumably not make an advance; if he has not received notification . . . any advance he may make will have priority.

Most important, the protection comes without necessity for the inventory lender to search the filing system before making each advance.

If the security agreement prohibits liens against inventory other than the lien of the inventory lender, a notification pursuant to U.C.C. §9-324(a) is a notification to the inventory lender that the debtor is about to go into default. To avoid that, debtors typically refuse to grant purchase-money security interests to their suppliers. The suppliers typically have little choice but to sell on unsecured credit and hope that the debtor pays.

E. Purchase-Money Priority in Proceeds

Assume that a seller manages to acquire purchase-money priority in property of the debtor. What happens when the debtor exchanges the collateral for proceeds? Of course, the seller must take whatever action is required under U.C.C. §9-315(d) to continue its perfection in the proceeds. But will it have purchase-money priority over a competing security interest perfected by an earlier filing against the debtor naming those proceeds as original collateral?

Generally speaking, the answer is yes. Purchase-money priority under U.C.C. §9-324(e) extends to the "collateral or its proceeds." To illustrate the operation of this rule, assume that Bank1 has perfected a security interest in the equipment of Davis Industries and Bank2 has perfected a security interest in the accounts of Davis Industries. Seller sells a piece of equipment to Davis Industries, retaining a PMSI. Seller perfects within the 20-day grace period of U.C.C. §9-324(e), thereby obtaining priority over Bank1. Davis later sells the piece of equipment to Buyer, resulting in an account owing from Buyer to Davis that is proceeds of the equipment. Seller has a security interest in the account as proceeds of the sale of its collateral. U.C.C. §9-315(a)(2). In addition, Seller's purchase-money priority flows through to the account, giving Seller priority over Bank2's earlier filing against "accounts." U.C.C. §9-324(e).

The rule that purchase-money status flows through into proceeds is subject to an important exception. The exception, found in U.C.C. §9-324(a), is that purchase-money status in inventory flows only into chattel paper, instruments, and cash proceeds. The limitation prevents purchase-money status from flowing into other kinds of proceeds, most notably accounts.

The reason for the exception was to facilitate account financing. To understand the perceived necessity for the exception, assume that Davis Industries had no financing statements on file against it when it approached Bank1 for a loan against its accounts receivable. Absent the exception, the unencumbered accounts would not have been adequate collateral for a loan in any amount. Bank1's fear would be that after it perfected its security interest and advanced funds against the accounts, Bank2 would make a purchase-money loan against inventory. As Davis Industries converted the inventory to accounts through sales, Bank2's purchase-money priority would flow through into the accounts, priming Bank1's lien. By limiting Bank2's purchase-money status in the proceeds of inventory to just the chattel paper, instruments, and cash proceeds, the exception arguably makes it possible for Bank1 to lend against Davis's accounts.

A later purchase-money inventory lender can protect itself against the possibility that such an account lender exists. The inventory lender would know of the account lender from the outset, because the account lender would have filed a financing statement before the inventory lender entered the picture. (If the inventory lender filed first, it could have filed against both the inventory and the accounts, and would have had priority over the later account lender on that basis.) The inventory lender can refuse to lend unless the debtor arranges to pay the inventory lender upon sale of the inventory. The obvious source of that payment is the advance made by the account lender each time a new account comes into existence. The arrangement can provide for the account lender to pay an appropriate portion of each advance directly to the inventory lender.

F.   Priority in Commingled Collateral

Collateral is *commingled* when it is mixed with other property. Commingling may occur when the debtor deposits cash collateral to a bank account that also contains funds that are not proceeds. It may occur when a debtor mixes corn purchased from one supplier with corn purchased from another, or it may occur when a debtor manufactures a car using steel purchased from one supplier and aluminum purchased from another.

The commingling of funds in a bank account was discussed in Assignments 10 and 11. Here we discuss the commingling of goods. Distinguish two situations. The first is where the identity of the collateral is lost by commingling as the collateral becomes part of a product or mass. The effect is that the security interest "continues in the product or mass." U.C.C. §9-336(c). For example, assume that Firstbank holds a security interest in a shipment of potassium nitrate that the debtor combines with other chemicals to manufacture fertilizer. Under U.C.C. §9-336(c), Firstbank's security interest continues in the resulting shipment of fertilizer even though the potassium nitrate constitutes only a small part of the fertilizer.

The second is where the identity is not lost, as where a replacement part is installed in a machine. (The identity of the replacement part is not lost because we can still see the part and perhaps take it back out of the machine.) As we saw in Assignment 25, such a replacement part is an *accession*. If the secured party has taken a security interest in only the replacement part, U.C.C. §9-335 will apply. The secured party's interest will continue to be perfected, and will have priority over later-perfected interests in the whole. But the accession-secured party's remedies may be severely impaired by U.C.C. §9-335(e). Under that section, any secured party with priority over the accession-secured party is entitled to prevent removal of the accession from the whole. For example, assume that Firstbank has a security interest in a generator that is perfected by filing against the debtor and that the debtor installs the generator in a machine. Firstbank continues perfected in the generator. If Secondbank perfects in the machine after installation of the generator, Firstbank's interest has priority over Secondbank's. U.C.C. §§9-335(c), 9-322(a). What if Secondbank perfected its interest in the machine before Firstbank perfected in the generator? Again, U.C.C. §9-335(c) refers us to other provisions of Part 3 of Article 9. Firstbank will have priority in the generator if its security interest is purchase-money, see U.C.C. §9-324(e); otherwise Secondbank will have priority, see U.C.C. §9-322(a)(1).

If more than one security interest attaches to a product or mass as a result of commingling, the interests rank equally and share in the proportion that the cost of each party's contribution bears to the total cost of the product or mass. For example, assume that Farmer Green sells wheat to Processing Co. for $20,000 and Farmer Brown sells wheat to Processing Co. for $80,000. Processing Co. commingles the two shipments. Further assume that Farmer Green's wheat is subject to a security interest in favor of PCA in the amount of $20,000 and Farmer Brown's wheat is subject to a security interest in favor of WestBank in the amount of $20,000. PCA and WestBank have equal priority in the commingled wheat and are entitled to a pro rata distribution of the proceeds of its sale. PCA will be entitled to 20 percent of any proceeds from the sale of the commingled wheat; WestBank will be entitled to 80 percent. If Processor sells the commingled wheat for $10,000, PCA will be entitled to $2,000 and WestBank will be entitled to $8,000.

Problem Set 32

32.1.   In late July, Dawgs & More (Dawgs) applied to Bank One for a loan against its inventory of lawn dogs. Without committing to make the loan, on August 1 Bank One filed a financing statement against Dawgs showing the lawn dogs as collateral. Also in late July, Dawgs applied for a similar loan from Bank Two. On August 5, Bank Two approved the loan and filed a financing statement against Dawgs showing the inventory of lawn dogs as collateral. Bank Two and Dawgs signed a security agreement on August 5 and Bank Two advanced funds to Debtor. On August 7 C-Dogs, a supplier and judgment creditor of Dawgs, became a lien creditor by levying on the inventory of lawn dogs. On August 10, Bank One received the report of their U.C.C. search showing their financing statement to be in first position. They approved the loan to Dawgs. Bank One and Dawgs signed a security agreement, and Bank One advanced funds against the lawn dogs. As soon as the check from Bank One cleared, the owner of Dawgs wired the Bank One loan proceeds to Freeport in the Bahamas, where they paused only long enough to join the proceeds from the Bank Two loan, and then continued on to places unknown. Who has priority in the inventory of the lawn dogs? U.C.C. §§9-203(b), 9-308(a), 9-317(a), 9-323(b), 9-322(a)(1).

32.2.   A year ago, Centurion National Bank loaned Flight Analysis, Inc. $250,000, took a security interest in "flight simulation equipment" and filed a financing statement using those words as the description of collateral. Centurion filed its financing statement on September 21. A few days ago, Centurion learned for the first time that First National Bank had filed a financing statement against the same collateral on July 21 of the same year. Centurion's chief loan officer, Harley Davidson, sees what is coming and is scrambling for a way out. He recalls that Centurion filed a financing statement on March 21 of last year against Pilots Unlimited that employed the same description of collateral. Harley now proposes to get Flight Analysis to sell the flight simulation equipment to Pilots Unlimited. Harley figures that once Pilots Unlimited owns the collateral, "Centurion will be first because we will have the earliest financing statement on file that covers the collateral." Will this work? U.C.C. §§9-322(a)(1), 9-325, and 9-507.

32.3.   A year ago, George Sol Estes borrowed $7,500 from Octopus National Bank (ONB) to purchase a computer for his dry cleaning business. The security agreement he signed at that time provided that the collateral would consist of the computer and any "substitutions, replacements or accessions." The security agreement contained no provision regarding future advances, because none was contemplated at the time. ONB filed a financing statement indicating that the collateral was "equipment."

ONB has just approved a $40,000 line of credit for George, to be secured by the dry cleaning equipment in his shop. Molly Parker, the loan officer at ONB, tells you that she knows she must prepare a new security agreement, but wonders if she must also file a new financing statement. U.C.C. §§9-322(a)(1), 9-502(d).

32.4.   a. A year ago, Carol Dearing lent $1,000 to her friend, Bob Muzzetti. Bob gave her a security interest in his 32-foot Bayliner boat and saw that her financing statement was properly filed in accord with the law of the state. About a month later, Business Credit Associates (BCA) lent Muzzetti $45,000, taking a security interest in several items of collateral, including the boat. BCA also filed an effective financing statement. Muzzetti fell behind in his payments to BCA and yesterday, March 1, BCA repossessed the boat. The boat now sits in the repo agent's compound, behind an eight-foot cyclone fence that is topped with concertina wire.

Now Bob is back to ask another favor of Carol. What Bob wants is an additional advance of $31,000 "to protect the boat from sale by BCA and prevent BCA from collecting." Carol, who has been your client for years, asks whether this will work. What do you tell her? U.C.C. §§9-322(a)(1), 9-609(a).

b.   Assume that Carol had filed a financing statement against Bob before BCA repossessed, but Bob had not authorized a security agreement and Carol had not lent any money. Would the scheme work under these circumstances? Comment 4 to U.C.C. §9-322.

32.5.   On the heels of its bad experience with Bob Muzzetti, your client, BCA, has sensed the need for a change in the way it does business. While its high-risk lending remains profitable overall, BCA does not want to continue being victimized by the likes of Bob Muzzetti and Carol Dearing. Restricting its loans to first security interests is not a practical solution because nearly all of BCA's borrowers have given security interests in their collateral and the creditors who have taken them want to retain their current priority until they are paid. Is there anything else you can suggest? U.C.C. §9-339.

32.6.   Harley Davidson is under a lot of pressure in his job at Centurion National Bank. Davidson's freewheeling lending policies have generated a number of "nonproducing assets." (To put it as politely as possible.) "One more," Harley says, "and I may no longer be viable in my current position."

Harley tells you this in the context of a discussion of the Paul Grumman loan. Until yesterday, Grumman's deteriorating financial condition looked like it would be the bale of straw that broke the camel's back. Centurion's loan to Grumman is in the amount of $150,000 and is unsecured. The financial statements Grumman has given Centurion from time to time have always shown Centurion's principal competitor, First National Bank, as the holder of a $1.5 million security interest in all of Grumman's assets (principally equipment, inventory, and accounts). In the event of liquidation, Harley is sure the assets will yield less than $1.5 million. Two weeks ago, desperate for ideas, Harley ran a U.C.C. search under Grumman's name.

Yesterday, a miracle happened. Harley received the Secretary of State's search report in the mail. The certificate, which Harley has laid gently on the desk in front of you, shows no filings against Paul Grumman. Harley says he is sure that the assets are in Grumman's possession and that "Paul Grumman" is the correct name of the debtor — sure enough to bet his career on it.

To seize his opportunity, Harley has tentatively cut a deal with Grumman. Centurion is to advance an additional $100,000 to Grumman. In return, Grumman will grant a security interest in favor of Centurion that will secure both the $150,000 advance already outstanding and the new $100,000 loan. "The way I figure," Harley says, "that will leave us with a $250,000 first on almost a million five in collateral."

The bankruptcy expert in your firm tells you that the old $150,000 advance will remain vulnerable as a preference for 90 days, but the new $100,000 advance will not. From her point of view, Centurion has something to gain and nothing to lose by making the new loan — *provided that Centurion will have priority over First National.* Harley would like you to give your opinion that Centurion will have priority. If Harley loses his job, you worry that the firm may not be able to hang onto Centurion's business, perhaps putting your job in jeopardy as well.

a.   In there any way that First National could have an effective financing statement that doesn't show up on an official search in the state in which Grumman's business is located? U.C.C. §§9-316(a) and (b), 9-338, 9-502(d), 9-506(c), 9-515(c), 9-516(d), 9-517.

b.   How can you find out if such a financing statement exists, without shooting yourself in the foot? U.C.C. §9-322(a)(1) and Comment 4 to that section. For example, what if you search under "Gruman" (an incorrect spelling) and find First National's filing?

c.   What should you do?

d.   Is there an ethical issue here?

32.7.   Sara Wisnewski has been manufacturing high-quality speakers for audio systems since 1979. Her speakers are among the best available and her prices are reasonable. For the past few years, orders have been running in excess of her manufacturing capacity and she has been unable to fill all she receives from dealers.

At the same time, she has been losing a considerable amount of money on bad debts. In your initial conference, she told you about a case in which she sold $15,000 worth of speakers to a dealer, who promptly filed bankruptcy. The dealer still had most of her speakers in stock when it closed its doors, but the bankruptcy court gave them to the inventory lender. Sara literally ended up having to buy her own speakers back from the bank to fill other orders. Her attorney in the bankruptcy case explained to her that "the bank got the speakers because they had the first security interest."

    a.   Sara thinks she should have the first security interest and she'd like you to tell her what she needs to do to get it. What do you tell her? U.C.C. §§9-102(a)(48), 9-324(a) and (b).

    b.   What problems do you foresee? What can Sara do about them?

    32.8.   Harley Davidson, who is still hanging on at Centurion National Bank, has made an appointment with you to discuss a letter he received from Mark Kauffman, attorney for Weil's Feed and Seed (WFS). For years, WFS has been the only feed supplier to Harley's borrower, the now-defunct Murray Cattle Company. Now WFS has surprised the bank by claiming a security interest "of equal priority with the bank" in Murray's cattle and its inventory of manure, and a prior security interest in the feed on hand. WFS has a financing statement on file against Murray, but WFS filed it two years after Centurion's. Harley says he is sure that WFS never served a §9-324 notification on the bank.

    Kauffman's letter contains copies of WFS's security agreement and financing statement. His argument is that when the cattle ate the feed, WFS's collateral became part of the "mass" (the cow) and, some time later, part of the collateral became the "product" (the manure). Kauffman cites U.C.C. §9-336. Harley wants to know if he should take the Kauffman letter seriously or whether "it's just a bunch of bull****." What do you tell him? U.C.C. §§9-102(a)(34) and (48), 9-324.

    32.9.   Your new client, the Equitable Lending Group (ELG), specializes in high-risk, high-profit lending. It lends to debtors in possession under Chapter 11 and buys nonperforming loans from other institutions and restructures them. ELG is now interested in a new lending concept and would like your opinion on it. Harley Davidson, who recently moved to ELG from his position at Centurion and brought ELG to you, explains a typical case.

    Silicon Microchip (SM) is a manufacturer of computer components. Its business is fundamentally sound, but the company is overburdened with debt. First National Bank has a perfected security interest in its inventory and accounts, worth about $600,000, securing First National's loan in the amount of $825,000. The SM-First National relationship is currently in a holding pattern while the parties attempt to renegotiate. While they are doing that, ELG wants to finance SM's acquisition of new inventory and have purchase-money priority over First National in both the inventory and the accounts that arise when that inventory is sold. Harley says he can handle the problem of monitoring the collateral, but wants you to tell him whether ELG can get the priority its seeks without agreement from First National. Harley says the folks at First National will be "mad as hell" when they see what ELG is doing, but "they're so conservative they'll still be having meetings about it six months from now. In the meantime, we'll be making six points over prime. As long as we've got first priority, it's zero risk." Can ELG get priority? U.C.C. §§9-324, 9-401(b).

Assignment 33: Secured Creditors Against Secured Creditors: Land and Fixtures

In this assignment, we explore the law governing priority among the holders of liens on real property. In section A, we begin with the paradigm case of competition among mortgages. In section B we consider the priority of mortgages in the special circumstance of a building that is under construction. There we introduce a new kind of competitor, a form of statutory lien known as a *construction* or *mechanic's lien*. In section C we return to Article 9 of the Uniform Commercial Code to consider competitions among mortgages and Article 9 fixtures filings. In the final section, we consider some special circumstances in which ordinary, nonfixture filings can give secured creditors priority in goods that are fixtures under real estate law.

A. Mortgage Against Mortgage

As you read about the rules governing priority among real estate mortgages, keep in mind that they are merely *default* rules that apply in the absence of an agreement among the parties. In most cases, a mortgagee contracts with the debtor for its priority. That is, the mortgage signed by debtor and mortgagee provides that it is a first, second, or fifth mortgage. So long as the debtor has such an agreement with all of the mortgagees and the agreements are consistent, the agreements determine priority among the mortgages. Only when there is some kind of slipup or ambiguity in the contracting do the rules discussed in this section determine priority.

The rules governing priority among real estate mortgages are similar to those governing priority among security interests. As under Article 9, unperfected security interests in real property are binding on the debtor who grants them. The real estate rules give somewhat wider effect to these unperfected mortgages and deeds of trust, but the general rule is that real estate mortgages, like security interests in personal property, rank in the order in which they are perfected. Like an Article 9 security interest, a mortgage can secure future advances.

It can reach after-acquired property, but it will be subordinate to a purchase-money mortgage in the same property provided that the purchase-money mortgage is recorded timely.

1.   Recording Statutes: The Rules of Priority

Most of the rules of priority among interests in real estate are embedded in the statutes that govern recording and specify its effect. One that is not is the rule governing priority among unrecorded mortgages. Recall that under U.C.C. §9-322(a)(3), unperfected security interests rank in the order in which they attach.

Example 1.   Debtor grants an Article 9 security interest to *A*; then Debtor grants an Article 9 security interest to *B*. Neither *A* nor *B* perfects. *A*'s security interest has priority over *B*'s.

Under Article 9, this rule had almost no practical importance, because the holder of the later-created interest nearly always could alter the priority by filing. The rule governing priority among unperfected mortgages is the same as the rule illustrated in Example 1.

In the mortgage context, however, the rule has a much wider effect, because the priority thus gained is not so easily upset by the recording of one of the mortgages. The protection available to one who records a mortgage under some real estate recording statutes is narrower than the protection available to one who records an Article 9 financing statement.

While the protection available to Article 9 filers is essentially the same throughout the United States, the protection available to real estate recorders varies significantly from state to state. To understand the differences among recording regimes, begin by distinguishing three archetypes: *race, notice,* and *race-notice* regimes. (Actual recording statutes are highly varied and seldom match any of these archetypes, but understanding the archetypes will help you know what to look for when you study an actual recording statute.) Under a pure race statute, the first mortgage recorded has priority, regardless of the mortgagee's state of mind.

Example 2:   Debtor grants a mortgage to *A*; then debtor grants a mortgage to *B*. At the time B acquires its mortgage, *B* knows of the mortgage to *A*. *B* records, then A records. *B* has priority.

U.C.C. §9-322(a) is often characterized as a "race" statute because under Article 9, "a filing secured creditor prevails even over those unrecorded security interests of which he was aware." Langley v. Federal Deposit Ins. Corp., 484 U.S. 86 (1987). Here is an example of a real estate recording statute that is generally characterized as a race statute:

Race Statute

North Carolina General Statutes §47-20(a) (1991)

No deed of trust or mortgage of real or personal property, or of a leasehold interest or other chattel real, or conditional sales contract of personal property in which the title is retained by the vendor, shall be valid to pass any property as against lien creditors or purchasers for a valuable consideration from the grantor, mortgagor or conditional sales vendee, but from the time of registration thereof. . . .

Under a pure "notice" statute, the order in which competing mortgages are recorded does not matter at all. The statute provides, in essence, that if a second mortgagee acquires an interest in the property without notice of the first, the second prevails. The holder of the first mortgage can prevent that from happening by recording its mortgage immediately upon receiving it; recording will constitute constructive notice to later takers. Thus, the statute gives an incentive to record promptly. But the outcome of the case will never depend on which mortgagee recorded first.

Example 3: Debtor grants a mortgage to *A*; then debtor grants a mortgage to B. At the time *B* acquires its mortgage, *B* knows of the mortgage to *A*. B records. *A* has priority.

The following statute is generally considered a "notice" statute:

Notice Statute

Massachusetts General Laws ch. 183, §4 (1986)

A conveyance of an estate in fee simple . . . shall not be valid as against any person, except the grantor, . . . his heirs and devisees and persons having actual notice of it, unless it . . . is recorded in the registry of deeds for the county or district in which the land to which it relates lies.

While the statute is not clear on the point, the intention apparently is that *A*'s recording is effective only against *B*s who receive mortgages after the recording. Those later *B*s have constructive notice of *A*'s mortgage. Provided that *B* took prior to *A*'s recording, *B* would prevail over *A*, without regard to whether *B* even recorded at all.

The most common kind of real estate recording statute is a blend of the race and the notice statutes. Its catchy name is *notice-race statute* (or, for those of us who grew up in another part of the country, *race-notice*). A notice-race statute provides, in essence, that if the recipient of the second conveyance takes the conveyance without notice *and* records before the holder of the first conveyance does so, the second conveyance has priority.

Example 4: Debtor grants a mortgage to *A*; then debtor grants a mortgage to *B*. At the time *B* acquires its mortgage, *B* does not know of the mortgage to *A*. *B* records. Then *A* records. *B* has priority.

Notice-Race Statute

New York Real Property Laws §291 (McKinney 1984)

A conveyance of real property . . . may be recorded in the office of the clerk of the county where such real property is situated. . . . Every such conveyance not so recorded is void as against any person who subsequently purchases or acquires by exchange or contracts to purchase or acquire by exchange, the same real property or any portion thereof . . . in good faith and for a valuable consideration, from the same vendor or assignor, his distributees or devisees, and whose conveyance, contract or assignment is first duly recorded. . . .

B can lose in two different ways under a notice-race statute. If *B* knows of the mortgage to *A* at the time *B* acquires its mortgage or if *B* loses the race to the courthouse, *B* will not have priority under the statute. *A* will prevail under the general common law rule that the first conveyance has priority over the second. The "notice" portion of notice-race rules is based on knowledge at the time of the conveyance. Subsequent notice is irrelevant. Thus, if *B* takes its mortgage without notice of *A*'s prior mortgage, learns of it, and then hustles in to record before *A* does, *B* will prevail.

A notice-race statute gives both *A* and *B* incentives to record promptly upon receiving their mortgages. By recording, *A* can prevent later transferees from gaining priority; a later-created mortgage can defeat an earlier one only by winning the race to the courthouse. If *B* takes without notice of the prior mortgage to *A*, *B* too has an incentive to record promptly. If *B* records before *A*, *B* will have satisfied both requirements and will have priority over A. If A records first, A wins because A was, by definition, without knowledge of the transfer to B at the time of the transfer to A (it hadn't happened yet), and A recorded first.

2. Who Is a Good Faith Purchaser for Value?

Most recording statutes protect only good faith purchasers for value. Few specify who is a good faith purchaser for value, but there is much law on the subject. "Value" or "valuable consideration" generally must be more than just a nominal consideration. (Compare U.C.C. §1-201(44), which takes a contrary view.) A $20,000 mortgage given in return for a peppercorn would not be entitled to the protection of the recording statute. On the other hand, a mortgagee should not be denied the protection of the recording statute merely because it made a good deal in an arm's length exchange. That the $20,000 mortgage was exchanged for goods worth only $15,000 does not mean that it was not given for value.

Often, a mortgage is given to secure a preexisting debt. In those situations, the question may arise whether the mortgage is given for value.

Example 5.   On February 1, O borrows $25,000 from A on an unsecured basis. On July 1, O grants A a mortgage against Blackacre. Whether A acquires its mortgage "for value" depends on what, if anything, A gave in exchange for the July mortgage. The majority view distinguishes mortgages granted with the hope of winning forbearance from the grantee from mortgages explicitly exchanged for a legally binding extension of the due date for payment. Only the latter constitutes "value."

As is discussed in section B, below, those who acquire liens against the collateral by legal proceedings are not "purchasers." To be a purchaser, one must take in a voluntary transaction.

3. Purchase-Money Mortgages

Most states recognize some kind of priority for purchase-money mortgages. The California statute set forth below, like U.C.C. §9-317(e), gives a purchase-money mortgage priority over some liens created and perfected before the purchase-money mortgage comes into existence. In contrast, Pennsylvania's statute appears to leave the purchase-money mortgage subordinate to liens perfected before the purchase-money mortgage is delivered.

Purchase-Money Mortgages

California Civil Code §2898(a) (West 1994)

A mortgage or deed of trust given for the price of real property, at the time of its conveyance, has priority over all other liens created against the purchaser, subject to the operation of the recording laws.

Purchase-Money Mortgages

42 Pennsylvania Consolidated Statutes §8141 (1978)

Liens against real property shall have priority over each other on the following basis:

(1) Purchase money mortgages, from the time they are delivered to the mortgagee, if they are recorded within ten days after their date; otherwise, from the time they are left for record. A mortgage is a "purchase money mortgage" to the extent that it is:

(i) taken by the seller of the mortgaged property to secure the payment of all or part of the purchase price; or

(ii) taken by a mortgagee other than the seller to secure the repayment of money actually advanced by such person to or on behalf of the mortgagor at the time the mortgagor acquires title to the property and used by the mortgagor at that time to pay all or part of the purchase price, except that a mortgage other than to the seller of the property shall not be a purchase money mortgage within the meaning of this section unless expressly stated so to be.

(2) Other mortgages and defeasible deeds in the nature of mortgages, from the time they are left for record. . . .

We elaborate on a point we made earlier: Archetypes are useful in learning how the system works, but real property law is highly variable from state to state on nonfunctional detail and, occasionally, even on more basic matters.

B.   Judgment Liens Against Mortgages

In nearly all states, an unsecured creditor can obtain a lien against the debtor's real property by suing the debtor, obtaining a judgment against the debtor, and recording the judgment in the real estate recording system of the county where the real property is located. The judgment will constitute a lien against real property owned by the debtor at the time of recording and real property the debtor later acquires. (This right to later property should seem familiar; it is the equivalent of an after-acquired property clause in an Article 9 security agreement.)

The rules governing priority between a judgment lien and a mortgage are similar to those governing priority between mortgages. The recording of the judgment both creates and perfects the judgment lien. Unless the recording statute changes the result, priority between a judgment lien and a mortgage depends on which was first created. In some states, the holder of a judgment lien is entitled to the benefit of the recording statutes. Notice, for example, that the North Carolina Statute in section A of this assignment provides that an unrecorded mortgage is not valid to pass title as against a "lien creditor." The holder of a judgment lien is such a lien creditor. Thus, if the judgment lien is recorded in North Carolina before the competing mortgage, the judgment lien has priority even if the mortgage was created first.

In many states, however, the recording statutes do not protect judgment lien or other lien creditors. The New York recording statute set forth earlier in this assignment is an illustration: It protects only "purchasers." (A mortgagee under real property law, like a secured party under the U.C.C., is a "purchaser." See U.C.C. §§1-201(32) and (33) defining "purchaser" as including only those who take in voluntary transactions.) Thus, in New York, an unrecorded mortgage has priority over a recorded judgment, provided that the mortgage was created before the judgment was recorded.

C.   Construction Liens Against Construction Mortgages

Perhaps the mortgagee's most common competitor for priority is the *construction lien*. Although these liens are often referred to as *mechanics' liens*, we refer to them by their other common name in order to avoid confusion. (In many, if not most, states, the mechanic who fixes your car gets an *artisan's lien*, while the nonmechanic who supplies labor or materials in the construction of a building gets a *mechanic's lien*.) Construction liens are "statutory" liens — that is, they arise by operation of law pursuant to the statute creating them. All 50 states have such statutes. The purpose of these liens is to protect those who supply labor or material incorporated into the construction of a building. The protection comes in the form of a lien against the real property into which the labor or material was incorporated.

To understand the competition between construction liens and mortgages, one must start with an understanding of the context in which construction liens arise.

1. A Prototypical Construction Financing Transaction

Sick of apartment living, Ozzie Owner has decided to build the house of his dreams. After an extensive search, he finds the perfect lot in a subdivision owned by Valerie Vendor. Ozzie enters into a contract to buy the lot from Valerie for $20,000. The contract is contingent upon Ozzie obtaining acquisition and construction financing acceptable to him. With the help of architect-homebuilder Conrad Contractor, Ozzie comes up with a design for the house. Conrad and Ozzie then enter into a contract whereby Conrad agrees to build the house on Ozzie's lot and Ozzie agrees to pay $80,000 for it. This contract too is contingent upon Ozzie obtaining acquisition and construction financing acceptable to him. Ozzie's last stop is at the Beaufort Bank, where he applies for and is offered acquisition and construction financing in the necessary amount of $100,000. The loan closing and the commencement of construction are scheduled for April 1.

The construction loan agreement between Ozzie and the Bank provides for disbursement in five *draws* of $20,000 each. The Bank will pay the first $20,000 draw when Ozzie obtains clear title to the lot on which the house is to be built. The next three draws will be payable at particular stages of construction. The second draw will be paid when the concrete slab has been poured. The third will be paid when the roof is on. The fourth will be paid when the house is "weathered in" — that is, when windows and walls are in place so that wind and rain are excluded. The fifth and last $20,000 draw is payable only after construction is complete in accord with the plans. This arrangement is designed to suit the interests of both Ozzie and the Bank. Ozzie needs money to buy the land and to pay Conrad, subcontractors, suppliers, and laborers while the house is under construction. But the Bank does not want to lend Ozzie money before he has a use for it (cash tends to disappear) or in amounts that exceed the value of the collateral. The further construction has progressed, the more the partially completed house will be worth. Hence the five-draw disbursement. The Bank will lend for each stage of construction only when that stage is complete.

It is easy enough to see how Ozzie will earn the first draw. He need only arrange for a closing at which Valerie will deed the lot to him and be paid with the first draw check from the Bank. But if Ozzie has no cash of his own, how will he advance construction to the pouring of the slab when he will be entitled to the next draw? Typically, the answer is that Conrad Contractor does the construction on credit, looking to the draw for payment. Conrad Contractor does not put his own money in the project either. Instead, he chooses subcontractors who will do the work on credit. One of them is Randy Rock, the concrete subcontractor who will pour the slab. Randy, who lives in the country and has seven dogs who sleep under the porch, is no financier either; he is counting on Sandy's Sand and Gravel for supplies and on John Williams to drive the truck and do the pouring and leveling. Randy will pay them when he gets the draw. Ultimately, it is John (the laborer) and Sandy (the materialman) who are going to finance this construction.

But how do John and Sandy — and everyone else in the chain — know that when the bank pays the draw, the money will filter down to them? For example, what if Bank pays the first draw check to Ozzie, Ozzie pays Conrad, and Conrad uses the money to pay his alimony payment and a couple of subcontractors that worked on a house he built a few months ago? (A sizeable number of contractors use their draw checks in these ways.) Theoretically, the Bank could contract to pay everybody directly, but that rarely is practical. Hundreds of people may work on or supply materials to even a small construction job; the Bank has no way of knowing their identity, let alone their arrangements for compensation. Neither does Ozzie, or even Conrad. Each subcontractor contracts to do its work; it is up to the subcontractor to decide how to get it done and who participates. Last-minute changes in the construction team are common; even the plumbing subcontractor may not know the name of the person who is out on the site hooking up the pipe.

Construction lien laws address this problem in two ways. First, they require that each person in the construction chain hold the draw money they receive *in trust* and use the trust funds only to make *proper payments*. Proper payments are payments that go only to subcontractors, laborers, and materialmen who work under the payor, until all of those people have been paid in full. Only the balance remaining is the payor's and available for payment of the payor's alimony. The statutes typically provide that the making of improper payments from construction draw money is embezzlement and subject the persons making them to criminal penalties. This aspect of construction lien law protection does not rely on the concept of security and for that reason is outside the scope of this book.

The second manner in which the construction lien law seeks to assure payment to everyone who supplies labor or materials to a construction site is by entitling all such persons to construction liens. To claim its lien, a contractor, subcontractor, materialman, or supplier must record a *claim of lien* in the real estate recording system by a deadline that typically is 90 or 120 days after the claimant completes its work on the building. (Yes, there are often tales of would-be lien holders going back to the site to put in a light bulb and thereby arguably reviving an expired deadline.)

To illustrate, when Rock finishes pouring the slab, he will expect payment from Conrad within a few weeks. If the payment is not forthcoming, Rock will prepare a claim of lien against Ozzie's property and file it in the real estate recording system. Rock will then have a construction lien against the land and the partially completed house on it.

When the draws from a construction loan are sufficient and applied to proper payments, everyone who works on the job will be paid on time. No one will have reason to file a claim of lien. When claims of lien do appear on the public record, they signal that something has gone wrong. Once a construction project is in financial difficulty, subcontractors, suppliers, and laborers may refuse to extend further credit, thereby bringing construction to a halt. Resumption of construction may be difficult to achieve because those asked to supply labor and materials on credit fear not being paid. The rescheduling of their work may put the work in conflict with other jobs they are doing. During the inevitable delays, the physical condition of a partially completed building may deteriorate from exposure to the elements. All these factors tend to cause the value of the partially completed building to decline. The rule of thumb is that when liens are filed, the work stops, and everybody is in trouble.

The capacity of a claim of lien to doom a construction project is both its strength and its weakness. Owners and contractors may pay the lienor who threatens to record a claim of lien because they fear the consequences. But in the strange world of debtor and creditor, the weakness of defaulting owners and contractors may also be their strength. Such owners and contractors often argue to their unpaid lienors that by filing claims of lien, they would be cutting their own throats. Filing of the lien will stop construction and prevent the owners and contractors from reaching the only possible source of payment: the next draw.

What if the recording of a claim of lien does not result in payment? The answer is that the lienor must bring an action for judicial foreclosure. In most states, the statute of limitations for an action on a construction lien is one year and runs from the filing of the claim of lien. If the action is not filed by the end of the year, the lien expires and the debt becomes unsecured. If lienor and owner wish to extend payments over a longer period of time, they will usually wish to substitute a mortgage for the construction lien.

2. Who Is Entitled to a Construction Lien?

While construction liens are usually associated with the construction
of buildings, the statutes of many states provide for liens in favor of
virtually anyone who participates in the making of any improvement
to real property. The New York Lien Law is illustrative. (We have
reversed the order of the two sections for easier reading.)

New York Lien Law

(McKinney 1993)

§3. MECHANIC'S LIEN ON REAL PROPERTY

A contractor, subcontractor, laborer, materialman, landscape gardener,
[or] nurseryman . . . who performs labor or furnishes materials for the
improvement of real property with the consent or at the request of the
owner thereof, or of his agent, contractor or subcontractor . . . shall have
a lien for the . . . value, or the agreed price, of such labor . . . or materials upon the real property improved or to be improved and upon such
improvement, from the time of filing a notice of such lien as prescribed
in this chapter. . . .

§2. DEFINITIONS. . . .

2. *Real property.* The term "real property," when used in this chapter,
includes real estate, lands, tenements and hereditaments, corporeal and
incorporeal, [and] fixtures. . . .

3. *Owner.* The term "owner," when used in this chapter, includes the
owner in fee of real property, or of a lesser estate therein, a lessee for a
term of years, a vendee in possession under a contract for the purchase
of such real property, and all persons having any right, title or interest in
such real property, which may be sold under an execution in pursuance
of the provisions of statutes relating to the enforcement of liens of judgment. . . .

4. *Improvement.* The term "improvement," when used in this chapter,
includes the demolition, erection, alteration or repair of any structure
upon, connected with, or beneath the surface of, any real property and
any work done upon such property or materials furnished for its permanent improvement, . . . and shall also include the drawing by any architect or engineer or surveyor, of any plans or specifications or survey,
which are prepared for or used in connection with such improvement
and shall also include the value of materials actually manufactured for but
not delivered to the real property. . . .

9. *Contractor.* The term "contractor," when used in this chapter, means
a person who enters into a contract with the owner of real property for
the improvement thereof. . . .

10. *Subcontractor.* The term "subcontractor" when used in this chapter, means a person who enters into a contract with a contractor and/or with a subcontractor for the improvement of such real property . . . or with a person who has contracted with or through such contractor for the performance of his contract or any part thereof.

11. *Laborer.* The term "laborer," when used in this chapter, means any person who performs labor or services upon such improvement.

12. *Materialman.* The term "materialman" when used in this chapter, means any person who furnishes material or the use of machinery, tools, or equipment . . . either to an owner, contractor or subcontractor, for, or in the prosecution of such improvement. . . .

20. *Persons.* The term "persons" when used in this chapter, includes an individual, partnership, association, trust or corporation.

---

3.   Priority of Construction Liens

Statutes that fix the priority of construction liens usually distinguish the obvious construction of buildings from the not-so-obvious casual alteration or repair of a building. A lien for an alteration or repair, such as the installation of a new furnace in an existing building, takes priority as of the recording of the claim of lien. By contrast, liens that arise out of the construction of a building typically all take priority as of the same date. In most states, that date is the date of the commencement of construction.

In re Skyline Properties, Inc.

134 B.R. 830 (Bankr. W.D. Pa. 1992)

A mechanics' lien for services which constitute alterations and repairs takes effect and has priority as of the date the mechanics' lien claim is filed. In the case of erection and construction, the lien of a claim takes effect and has priority "as of the date of the visible commencement upon the ground of the work of erecting or constructing the improvement." 49 Pa. Cons. Stat. Ann. §1508(a) (Purdon 1965). . . .

The within matter involves the following relevant dates: Visible commencement of construction: April 20, 1987; Bank's mortgage: June 5, 1987; Mealy Claim filed: September 23, 1987.

Thus, if Mealy's work is erection and construction, Mealy's Claim has priority over the Bank; if the work is an alteration or repair, the Bank's mortgage takes priority.

Section 1201(10) of the Mechanics' Lien Law defines "erection and construction" as follows:

"Erection and construction" means the erection and construction of a new improvement or of a substantial addition to an existing improvement or any adaptation of an existing improvement rendering the same fit for a new or distinct use and effecting a material change in the interior or exterior thereof.

49 Pa. Cons. Stat. Ann. §1202 (Purdon 1965).

The Bank asserts that no buildings were erected nor constructed in conjunction with Mealy's work and Mealy's lien is for alterations and repairs. Thus, the Bank asserts that Mealy's lien takes priority as of the date of filing of the Claim and not the date of visible commencement of the work. . . .

The concern in determining whether the work is "erection and construction" or "alterations or repairs" is whether a substantial change to the existing structure has occurred such that any third party, such as the Bank, would be on notice that potential liens could exist. A change in the appearance or use of a building is sufficient to give such notice.

If there is a construction lender in the picture, the project is probably "erection or construction." The liens will date from the commencement of construction. The construction lender will want its mortgage to have priority over any construction liens eventually filed. The simplest, most direct way of accomplishing that is to record the construction mortgage before the commencement of construction. Draws paid after creation and recording of the mortgage will be *future advances* that will in nearly all circumstances have priority over liens arising out of the construction. But how can the construction lender be sure at the time it records its mortgage that construction has not yet begun? The usual method is for someone from the bank to examine the property to make sure there are no signs of recent construction and to prepare dated photographs so the bank will later be able to prove that in court. Is the lack of any sign of construction on the site a sufficient basis for concluding that construction has not yet begun? The court faced that issue in the case that follows.

Ketchum, Konkel, Barrett, Nickel & Austin v. Heritage Mountain Development Co.

784 P.2d 1217 (Utah Ct. App. 1989)

Judith M. Billings, Judge:

Appellants . . ., among other lien holders, filed actions to foreclose their mechanics' liens recorded against property being developed as a ski resort in Utah County. The construction lender, Guaranty Savings and Loan Association ("Guaranty"), moved for partial summary judgment claiming its trust deed had priority over all mechanics' liens on the property. The lien holders opposed the motion and filed cross-motions for partial summary judgment on the priority issue. The trial court ruled in favor of Guaranty. . . .

. . . In October 1972, . . . Heritage Mountain Development Co. ("Heritage"), began the planning and development of a ski resort. The master plan for the ski resort contemplated the common development of three contiguous parcels of property in Utah County: 110 acres owned in fee simple ("Fee Property"); 41 acres leased from the State of Utah ("Leased Property"); and 4500 acres of federal land under a special use permit ("Permit Property"). . . .

Beginning in April of 1983, an engineering firm surveyed and staked the boundaries of the property. In June 1983, Heritage obtained a predevelopment loan from Guaranty. To secure the loan, Heritage executed a trust deed on the property. Guaranty recorded the trust deed on September 15, 1983. At the time of this loan, Guaranty knew that appellants had performed extensive design work on the project. Between June and September of 1983, appellants and others resumed design work on the project.

The long-term financing for the ski development fell through and no additional on-site construction took place. Heritage abandoned the project by the summer of 1984 and left appellants and other contractors unpaid. The lien holders, including appellants, sued to foreclose their mechanics' liens and Guaranty opposed the suits by asserting its trust deed had priority over all mechanics' liens. . . .

I.   EFFECT OF OFF-SITE ARCHITECTURAL WORK ON MECHANICS' LIENS PRIORITY

Appellants claim that, under Utah Code Ann. §§38-1-5 and -10 (1988), their . . . pre-trust deed, off-site design work on the project gives their mechanics' liens priority over Guaranty's trust deed. We disagree.

Under Utah law, architects' services are lienable. Utah Code Ann. §38-1-3 (1981) expressly provides for liens for architectural services:

> [L]icensed architects and engineers and artisans who have furnished designs, plats, plans, maps, specifications, drawings, estimates of cost, surveys or superintendence, or who have rendered other like professional service, or bestowed labor, shall have a lien upon the property upon or concerning which they have rendered service, performed labor, or furnished or rented materials. . . .

Guaranty does not challenge the validity of the appellants' liens, but claims its trust deed has priority over all valid mechanics' liens under the statutory scheme. Priority of mechanics' liens, including architectural liens, are governed by Utah Code Ann. §38-1-5 (1988), which provides:

> The liens herein provided for shall relate back to, and take effect as of, the time of the commencement to do work or furnish materials on the ground for the structure or improvement, and shall have priority over any lien, mortgage or other encumbrance which may have attached subsequently to the time when the building, improvement or structure was commenced, work begun, or first material furnished on the ground. . . .

Lien statutes are construed broadly in order to achieve their protective purpose. . . . Further, the phrase "commencement to do work" is construed in favor of the lien claimant.

The precise statutory construction issue presented is the meaning of the language "commencement to do work or furnish materials on the ground for the structure or improvement" in section 38-1-5. The district court construed this section to require the commencement of visible, on-site improvements without regard to whether a subsequent lender had actual notice of prior off-site lienable work such as appellants'. . . .

This issue has never been squarely dealt with by Utah courts. However, Utah case law discussing priority under section 38-1-5 has emphasized visible work performed on the property or the presence of materials, giving notice that work has commenced on the property. In Calder Bros. Co. v. Anderson, 652 P.2d 922 (Utah 1982), the court rejected the lien claimant's claim of priority because "[a]t no point up to and including the time [the lender's] mortgage was recorded, was it evident from the inspection of the premises that an improvement had been commenced." The court stated that "visible evidence of work performed provides notice to any interested party that work has commenced." . . .

The majority of other jurisdictions which have considered the issue of whether off-site services of architects and engineers constitute the commencement of work for purposes of the priority of mechanics' liens have answered in the negative. Although each statutory scheme is unique, the decisions are in harmony that physical notice of work on the property must be present before mechanics' liens have priority over other third parties, especially lenders. . . .

If this court were to allow architects' work to establish the "commencement" of the project, not just architects' liens but all other liens would relate back to the date of the architectural work. Under Utah Code Ann. §38-1-10 (1988), all mechanics' liens are on equal footing for purposes of priority. Accordingly, a trust deed recorded after attachment of a mechanics' lien is inferior in priority to that lien and all other mechanics' liens filed on the property. . . .

We believe the predictability sought by the mechanics' lien statutory scheme would be undermined if actual notice of architectural work by a third party claiming priority qualified this off-site design work as "commencement to do work" for priority purposes under section 38-1-5. First, it would multiply litigation over the issue of whether the third party had actual notice. Second, all mechanics' liens for work performed on the project, not just the work of the architect, would suddenly take priority over a secured lender with the consequent adverse impact on construction financing. Finally, and most importantly, had the legislature intended priority under section 38-1-5 to be affected by actual notice, it could have so stated but did not.

We are persuaded that the policy of giving third parties notice of possible mechanics' liens requires visible, on-site construction to qualify for "commencement of work" under section 38-1-5. Thus, the off-site work of architects does not constitute commencement of work under section 38-1-5. . . .

IV.   . . . PRE-TRUST DEED, ON-SITE IMPROVEMENTS

Appellants finally contend that their liens can relate back to surveying, staking, and soil core sampling work performed on the Leased Property . . . prior to the recording of the trust deed. Once again, appellants contend that because the work is "lienable," it automatically constitutes "commencement of work" under section 38-1-5. However, the "mere fact that work was a proper subject of a lien cannot establish priority where it does not give notice of commencement." Clark v. General Elec. Co., 243 Ark. 399, 420 S.W.2d 830, 834 (1967).

This court has previously considered the issue of whether surveying work is sufficient to establish relation back under section 38-1-5. In Tripp v. Vaughn, 747 P.2d 1051 (Utah Ct. App. 1987), the court concluded that the staking, which was the only visible manifestations of the surveyor's work, was not "sufficiently noticeable or related to actual construction to impart notice to a prudent lender." . . .

Utah's position is consistent with the majority of jurisdictions which have ruled that preparing the soil, leveling the ground, placing survey stakes, and taking soil samples do not constitute "visible" on-site improvements required to establish priority under mechanics' liens statutes. . . .

Based on the authority discussed, we conclude there was no . . . pre-trust deed work sufficient to qualify for commencement of work because surveying, staking, and soil testing do not constitute a visible on-site improvement as required by Utah law for relation back under sections 38-1-5 and -10.

D. The Priority of Article 9 Fixture Filings

In Assignment 20, we discussed the fact that an Article 9 security interest can exist in goods that are fixtures under real estate law. Article 9 authorizes the perfection of such an interest by a "fixture filing" in the real estate recording system. U.C.C. §§9-102(b), 9-501(a)(1)(B), and 9-502(b)). The priority achieved by fixture filings is governed by the rules stated in U.C.C. §9-334.

1. Priority in Fixtures Incorporated During Construction

The distinction between a fixture filing made during construction and a construction lien that arises during the same period is important. The following examples may help to make that distinction:

Example 1.   Debtor, Inc. is building a 200-unit apartment building on its property. During construction, Debtor, Inc. buys 200 water heaters from the H_2OT Co. If H_2OT Co. delivers the water heaters to the construction site, H_2OT Co. has a construction lien against the land and building that it can perfect by recording a claim of lien. H_2OT Co. will have this lien even though the parties did not sign a security agreement.

Example 2.   Now assume that, on the same facts, Debtor, Inc. and H_2OT Co. executed an agreement granting H_2OT Co. an Article 9 security agreement in the water heaters. Because the hot water heaters will become fixtures, H_2OT Co. should perfect this interest by a fixture filing in the real estate records. H_2OT Co. might also wish to file its claim of lien at the same time, but Debtor, Inc. might find the latter filing distressing.

Notice that the construction lien in Example 1 encumbers the entire apartment building property, while the fixture filing in Example 2 encumbers only the fixtures described in it, the water heaters. If H_2OT Co. forecloses the security interest in the water heaters, only the water heaters will be sold. Because the construction mortgage has priority over H_2OT Co.'s security interest, the holder of the construction mortgage can prevent H_2OT Co. from removing the water heaters. U.C.C. §9-604(c).

These two liens may also differ in their priority against the construction mortgage. The construction lien will have priority as of the commencement of construction, which may be months before Debtor, Inc. purchased the water heaters. But it will have priority over the construction mortgage only if construction commenced before Firstbank recorded the mortgage — an unlikely possibility. The Article 9 security interest will have priority as of the time the fixture filing is made. Accordingly, the fixture filing will have priority over the construction mortgage only if H_2OT Co. made the fixture filing before Firstbank recorded the mortgage. See U.C.C. §9-334(h). In practice, the construction lender will virtually always record first, thereby giving it priority over both the construction lien and the Article 9 security interest.

Notice that H_2OT Co.'s security interest is subordinate to Firstbank's construction mortgage even if H_2OT Co.'s security interest is a purchase-money security interest and Firstbank's construction mortgage is not a purchase-money mortgage. See U.C.C. §§9-334(h) and 9-334(d). If H_2OT Co. sells hot water heaters to Debtor, Inc. after recording of the construction mortgage, H_2OT Co. has no way to obtain priority over Firstbank.

2.   Priority in Fixtures Incorporated Without Construction

Again, the basic rule is that Article 9 fixture filings and mortgages rank in the order in which they are recorded in the real estate recording system. U.C.C. §§9-334(c) and 9-334(e)(1). In the typical case, the mortgage will have been recorded during the construction of the building or some other time long before the fixture is purchased and incorporated into the building. Generally, the nonpurchase-money fixture financier will be subordinate to whatever mortgages exist at the time of fixture filing. If this result is unacceptable to the fixture financier, the fixture financier may wish to seek the mortgagee's consent to the security interest. U.C.C. §9-334(f)(1).

There are two important exceptions to the basic rule. First, the fixture filing will have priority over the mortgages if the debtor has the right under the mortgages to remove the fixtures. Second, the fixture filing will have priority over the mortgages if the security interest is a purchase-money security interest in goods affixed after the mortgage is in place and the fixture filing is made not later than 20 days after the goods become fixtures. U.C.C. §9-334(d). To illustrate, assume that after Firstbank's mortgage is recorded against Debtor, Inc. and construction of the apartment building is completed, Debtor Inc. finds it necessary to replace all the hot water heaters in the building. If H_2OT Co. sells the water heaters to Debtor, Inc., retains a purchase-money security interest in them, and makes a fixture filing before they are installed or within 20 days after they are installed, H_2OT Co.'s security interest will have priority over Firstbank's mortgage in the hot water heaters.

As is true of security interests and liens generally, the priority of a fixture filing is important not just for its effect on the distribution of proceeds from a sale of collateral. The priority of a fixture filing also determines the secured party's right to possession after default. The fixture-secured party has the right to remove the fixture from the real property if the security interest in the fixture has priority over the owners and encumbrancers of the real estate. U.C.C. §604(c). Otherwise, the secured party can only wait in the hope that someone else will liquidate the collateral.

E. Priority in Real Property Based on Personal Property Filing

Recall our mysterious reference in Assignment 20 to the possibility of perfecting in fixtures by a nonfixture filing. (We hope the reference hasn't been causing you sleepless nights.) Here, at last, is the answer. There are two levels of perfection a secured party can achieve in fixtures — one by fixture filing and one by nonfixture filing. The supposedly "right" place to perfect in fixtures is in the real property recording system and the supposedly "right" way to do it is by fixture filing. Nevertheless, an ordinary nonfixture filing in the U.C.C. filing system, as opposed to a fixture filing in the real estate recording system, is sufficient to perfect a security interest in the goods. Such a filing may seem to have been made in the wrong place and by the wrong method, but U.C.C. §9-501(a)(2) specifically authorizes it.

This seemingly wrong but technically acceptable filing perfects the security interest in fixtures. The catch is that the perfection thus attained is relatively ineffective. Those who purchase interests in the real estate are expected to search in the real estate records. They probably will not search in the U.C.C. filing system and probably will not find the ordinary U.C.C. filing. Consistent with this expectation, the ordinary U.C.C. filing is ineffective against a later mortgagee or fixture filer who perfects by filing in the real estate recording system. U.C.C. §9-334(e)(1).

What good, then, does such a filing do for the creditor who made it? First, it is sufficient to give the filer priority over lien creditors, including the trustee in bankruptcy. See U.C.C. §9-334(e)(3) and Comment 4c. The drafters of the U.C.C. attempt to justify their grant of priority based on a filing that no one is likely to find with the assertion that "generally, a judgment creditor is not a reliance creditor who would have searched the records." We doubt the accuracy of this assertion; unsecured creditors commonly monitor U.C.C. filings against their debtors through various reporting services, and many judgment creditors search the U.C.C. records before they levy. More to the point, the fact that most members of a group do not search does not warrant the enforcement of unfindable filings against members who do search and are misled. Comment 4c explains what the drafters of Article 9 were up to: They wanted to protect U.C.C. filings in fixtures against the secured creditors' nemesis, the trustee in bankruptcy, even if the secured creditor had failed to realize that a fixture filing was appropriate and instead filed in the "wrong" office.

The second important effect of a nonfixture filing against property that is fixtures is that such a filing is fully effective against certain kinds of fixtures. Recall that, in general, the U.C.C. leaves the defining of "fixtures" — and therefore the determination of which filing system governs — to the real estate law of the state. U.C.C. §9-102(a)(41). Real estate law makers have in some ways abused the privilege by defining "fixtures" so broadly as to include property such as the machinery in a factory or the freestanding appliances in a house. The drafters of the U.C.C. struck back in U.C.C. §9-334(e)(2). That section does not challenge real estate law's characterization of such property as fixtures or prevent encumbrance of the property through recordings in the real estate system, but it does permit earlier filings in the U.C.C. personal property system to defeat mortgages and fixture filings later recorded in the real estate system. The result is that, in essence, there are two alternative ways to perfect in this kind of property. You may recall that in the *National Peregrine* case in Assignment 16, Judge Kozinski assured us that such "parallel" filing systems did not exist. The reason he gave is that such a system necessitates a search of both sets of records to determine whether the collateral is encumbered. But by this time, you should not be bothered by one more example of a situation in which the poor design and coordination of these systems necessitates multiple searches. Even without U.C.C. §9-334(e)(2), a sophisticated secured creditor who sought to encumber the kinds of property described in that section usually would be uncertain whether the property was fixtures or personal property and would be dealing with the uncertainty by conducting multiple searches.

Problem Set 33

33.1.   Fifteen years ago, Wanda Fish recovered a judgment against her ex-husband, Marshall, for $35,000 in lump-sum alimony. Marshall resolved never to pay it, and moved to California. Five years ago, Wanda tracked him down, established her judgment in California, and recorded it in the county where Marshall lived. Because Marshall had no assets at the time, she did not pursue the matter further. Later, Marshall prospered. On March 1 of this year, Marshall paid $100,000 in cash to buy a house: $20,000 of that was from his savings, the other $80,000 was a loan from Security Finance. The mortgage to Security Finance was a purchase-money mortgage and that fact was recited in it. As a result of the sudden death of an office employee, Security Finance did not record their mortgage until March 10. As between Wanda and Security Finance, who will have priority in Marshall's home? The California statute regarding priority of a purchase-money mortgage is set forth in this assignment. Assume that the California recording statute is the same as New York Real Property Laws §291, also set forth in this assignment.

33.2.   Add these facts to those of the preceding problem: Marshall discovered Security Finance's delay in recording, and he borrowed $50,000 from Pacific State Bank on March 8 (Marshall moves quickly). Pacific State recorded on the same day. Marshall used part of the loan proceeds to purchase airfare to the Bahamas and has not been seen since.

a.   As between Security Finance and Pacific State, who has priority in Marshall's house?

b.   As between Wanda and Pacific State, who has priority in Marshall's house? See Cal. Civ. Code §697.510(a) in Assignment 28.

c.   If all three end up in court together, who will win?

33.3.   George Onasis, the trustee in bankruptcy for William Miller, has retained you to advise on avoidance matters. Eighteen months before filing bankruptcy, Miller bought a mobile home on credit from Folds Mobile Home Sales (Folds). Folds took a security interest in the mobile home, and filed a non-fixture financing statement in the office of the Secretary of State. The state in which this took place does not issue certificates of title for mobile homes. Under its laws, the mobile home was a fixture even before Folds filed its financing statement. Onasis asks your opinion as to whether the estate has priority over Folds. U.C.C. §§9-102(40), (41), and (52); 9-317(a) and 9-334(e)(3) and (4); 9-501(a). Comment 4 to U.C.C. §9-501(4).

33.4.   a. Two months ago your client, Sound City, Inc., sold a sound system to Jake's Bar and Restaurant during Jake's remodeling. The installer spent three days on the site, running wiring from the stage to the control booth and from there to speakers throughout the premises. Most of the wiring is above the drop ceiling, but some was fished through the conduits used in the electrical wiring of the building. Speakers are bolted to walls and ceiling beams; some of the control panels are built in. Jake was supposed to pay for the sound system as soon as it was installed. Instead, he complained about the quality of the sound and had the installer back every few days. Now the installer says that Jake's complaints are bogus and "he's just stalling for time." Sound City has neither promissory note nor security agreement. What do you recommend?

b.   You discovered that the reason Jake was stalling for time was that he was in the process of refinancing the bar and restaurant. Before you could do anything, the new lender, Mercantile Bank, recorded their mortgage. Assuming that the Bank acted in good faith and without knowledge that Sound City had installed the sound system, where does this leave you?

33.5.   Sound City has contracted for another installation. The job is similar to the one they did for Jake's Bar and Restaurant, except this time the customer is Dub's Lounge. No remodeling will be done, and the customer will pay in installments over a period of 18 months after installation. Bill Sauls, the owner of Sound City, says he wants at least the right to "rip everything back out if they don't pay for it." In response to your questions, he says he doesn't know whether Dub's owns the place where the installation will be done or whether they rent it. Nor does he know whether there are mortgages outstanding against the property.

a.   Assume Sound City installs a sound system on Dub's authority and Dub's doesn't pay for it. Will Sound City be entitled to a construction lien? If it is, will that be an adequate remedy?

b.   Assume Sound City decides to make a fixture filing. Whose authorization does Sound City need? U.C.C. §§9-102(28), 9-203(b), 9-502(b)(4), 9-509, 9-604(c), and 9-334(f). For example, if it turns out that Dub's has the premises under a long-term lease from Realty Partners Ltd., do you have to have a contract with Realty Partners, or can Sound City do the deal on Dub's signature alone? U.C.C. §§9-334, 9-502(b)(4).

c.   Does your answer to part b. change if Sound City is installing a sound system in a new building that is under construction? U.C.C. §§9-334(d), (e), and (h). In the construction scenario, would Dub's consent in writing to removal of the sound system in the event of default be of help? U.C.C. §9-334(f).

33.7.   Three years ago, your client, Barney Wells, loaned $75,000 to his brother Wilbur to help Wilbur buy a small apartment building in New York. Wilbur executed a mortgage against the property to Barney at the time, but Barney did not record it because he thought recording might offend Wilbur. Since then, Wilbur's financial condition and Barney's relationship with him have grown progressively worse. Concerned about rumors of profligacy and financial ruin, Barney finally recorded his mortgage two weeks ago and purchased a title and encumbrance search. The search shows four encumbrances against the property:

1. A mortgage in favor of Walter Weyrauch in the amount of $45,000 recorded four years ago (the mortgage is actually on a different piece of property owned by Wilbur; it shows up on your search because the mortgage contains an after-acquired property clause).
2. A judgment for $38,000 in favor of Talbot Financial Services, Inc., recorded two years ago.
3. A mortgage in favor of Allie Toklas, recorded one year ago in the amount of $60,000.
4. The mortgage to Barney Wells.

Each of the three documents is regular on its face. Barney says Toklas is a close friend of Wilbur; he does not recognize the other two names. Barney estimates that the property is worth about the amount of his mortgage. Barney acknowledges that he "screwed up" by not bringing this matter to you at the time of the loan, but he wants to know if there is anything you can do for him now. Is there? Can you imagine any facts consistent with what Barney has told you that would make his mortgage valuable? Or is he, as Wilbur told him yesterday, "dead in the water"? New York Real Property Laws §291. Assume that New York defines "purchase-money mortgage" in accord with 42 Pennsylvania Consolidated Statutes §8141 and gives it priority in accord with California Civil Code §2898 (all three sections are reproduced in this assignment).

Assignment 34: Competitions Involving Cross-Collateralization and Marshaling Assets

You may have noticed already that more than one item of collateral can secure a single debt. The formal term for this is *cross-collateralization*. To determine whether a particular debt is cross-collateralized, one need only read the security agreement. If it provides that multiple items of collateral are security for a single debt, they are. If it does not, they aren't. In the first part of this assignment we will examine the effect of cross-collateralization and explore why parties might make this kind of arrangement.

A. Cross-Collateralization Provisions in Security Agreements

To set the stage for the analysis that follows we begin with a story. Assume that South Bank lends $50,000 to Michael Williams, secured by Red Mars, Williams's racehorse. The horse is worth $70,000. As you saw in the early assignments of this book, in the event of default South Bank could foreclose by selling the horse and pay itself from the proceeds. If Red Mars were lame at the time of foreclosure and sold for only $1,000, South Bank would get the $1,000 and be entitled to a judgment against Williams for the $49,000 deficiency. U.C.C. §9-615(d)(2). The deficiency judgment would be unsecured, and South Bank would be back in Assignment 1 trying to collect.

Now assume that prior to his default, South Bank lent Williams an additional $50,000 to acquire Green Mars, another horse also worth $70,000. South Bank could have treated this second loan as entirely separate from the first. That is, it could have prepared a second note and security agreement, securing the second $50,000 loan by a security interest in Green Mars. Each horse then would have been collateral for only the corresponding loan. Williams would have been personally liable for any deficiency on either loan.

Continuing with this scenario, if Williams had defaulted on both loans and South Bank foreclosed, the separateness of the two loans might have put South Bank at a disadvantage. For example, if Red Mars had sold for $1,000 and Green Mars had sold for $70,000, the result would have been a $49,000 deficiency judgment against Williams on the first loan and a $20,000 surplus in favor of Williams on the second. South Bank would have had the right to enforce its $49,000 deficiency judgment against Williams's interest in the surplus, but in doing so, South Bank could have employed only the remedies available to an unsecured creditor. South Bank would have been subject to any exemptions Williams might have had under state law and subordinate to any junior liens then existing against Green Mars. If Williams got his hands on the $20,000 surplus before South Bank could enforce against it, Williams might have spent the money or used it to pay other creditors.

A secured creditor may have no way of knowing at the time of the loan which particular items of collateral will be most valuable at the time of foreclosure. In our first illustration, Green Mars was the valuable one. But it might have been Red Mars that sold for $70,000 and Green Mars that sold for only $1,000. The risk of collateralizing each loan separately is that South Bank could have a deficiency on one loan at the same time that it had a surplus on the other. Indeed, if Red Mars had turned out to be worth enough to satisfy both loans, with separate collateralization, South Bank might still be facing a $49,000 deficiency on its loan against Green Mars. Williams's other creditors might be able to beat South Bank to the $50,000 surplus from the sale of Red Mars.

Cross-collateralization is the usual method for solving this problem. When South Bank makes the second loan to Williams, it requires him to sign a security agreement stating that both horses are collateral for the entire balance of each loan. The effect is that, in the event of default on either loan, South Bank would be entitled to foreclose against either horse or both horses, and apply the proceeds to the two loans in any manner South Bank chose. If Red Mars were lame at the time of the sale and were to bring only $1,000, but Green Mars were to sell for $70,000, South Bank would get both the $1,000 and the $70,000 in its capacity as a secured creditor. As a secured creditor, South Bank would not be subject to any exemptions to which Williams might be entitled. Security interests created and perfected after that of South Bank would be subordinate. South Bank could lose money only if the total value of the two horses were less than the total amount owing on the two loans.

In the above example, South Bank did not anticipate making a second loan to Williams against a second horse. If it had, South Bank could easily have provided for both security interests in a single set of documents. You are already familiar with the necessary contract provisions. The security agreement would secure all obligations owing from Williams to South Bank, including future advances (a future-advance clause). It would provide for a security interest in Red Mars "and all racehorses hereafter acquired by the debtor" or some such language (an after-acquired property clause). Perhaps the only document Williams would sign at the time of the second loan would be a promissory note for the additional $50,000.

When a loan is secured by more than one item of collateral, we refer to the loan as *cross-collateralized*. Cross-collateralization occurs almost any time an after-acquired property clause reaches an additional item of collateral. You have been working with cross-collateralization since early in this book.

In this assignment, we consider two new aspects of cross-collateralization. The first is the right of the holder of a cross-collateralized security interest to choose when, in what order, and by what remedy it will proceed against its various items of collateral. Whatever flexibility the cross-collateralized creditor is given may come at the expense of other creditors. Junior lienors or unsecured creditors may be unable to determine whether there is any equity for them in Green Mars until they know which horse South Bank will choose first to enforce its security interest against. Their ability to limit the cross-collateralized creditors' choice is described in a doctrine called *marshaling of assets*. We discuss marshaling in section C. The second new aspect of cross-collateralization we will consider relates to purchase-money status. We will explain it in section D.

B.   The Secured Creditor's Right to Choose Its Remedy

As we saw in Assignment 26, a secured creditor generally has the right to choose when it will foreclose. We now add the rule that a creditor secured by more than one item of collateral generally has the right to choose when it will foreclose against each. To illustrate, consider again the situation where South Bank has lent $100,000 and secured the loan with a security interest in both horses. Upon default, South Bank would have the right to foreclose against Green Mars, see how much it could recover at the sale, and then decide when and whether to foreclose against Red Mars. If Green Mars sold for enough to pay the entire debt, South Bank might be saved the time and trouble of trying to squeeze money out of a lame horse. If South Bank collected only $70,000 from the sale of Green Mars, it need not immediately proceed against Red Mars. It could wait and see what Williams did about paying the remaining balance.

Under this general rule, a creditor secured by multiple items of collateral might have numerous strategic options. A secured creditor that wanted to force its debtor into bankruptcy reorganization with minimum effort (perhaps to get court supervision of the debtor's payouts) might file an action for replevin of just a single item of collateral — but one without which the debtor could not continue in business. The creditor's intent would not be to take possession of the item and sell it, but to leave the debtor no practical option other than to "voluntarily" file for bankruptcy reorganization.

The general rule we have just discussed may seem too generous to the cross-collateralized creditor. But the opposite rule — a secured creditor must foreclose against all of its collateral or none — would be completely unworkable. A secured creditor's collateral might be scattered through dozens of jurisdictions, necessitating the simultaneous filing of actions in all of them. The cross-collateralized creditor might have to bring several forms of action and join numerous owners. Some of the collateral might be of such little value that the creditor would prefer to abandon it, but to make that determination might require extensive investigation. In most circumstances, these problems do not arise because the applicable rule permits the creditor to foreclose against part of the collateral without waiving or abandoning its rights against the rest.

1. Debtor-Enforceable Limits on the Secured Creditor's Right to Choose Its Remedy

Limits in favor of a debtor on a secured creditor's right to choose the sequence in which it will proceed against its various items of collateral are rare. Yet some exist. A secured party might bring so many separate foreclosure actions against a debtor that the court would bar further actions as a nuisance. A few states (most notably California) have "single action" rules. The California version states that "[t]here can be only one action to enforce payment on a debt secured by a mortgage on real property." A creditor in one of these states who forecloses against one parcel of real estate omitting another may find that it has lost the omitted parcel as collateral. These single action rules do not apply to personal property. U.C.C. §9-604(a)(1) specifically authorizes secured creditors to sever the foreclosure against personal property collateral from their foreclosure of the same security interest against real estate collateral, and foreclosure against one piece of personalty does not, in ordinary circumstances, bar later foreclosure against another.

2. Release of Collateral

A corollary of the secured creditor's right to choose what collateral it will proceed against is that all collateral remains encumbered until the debt is paid in full. To illustrate, assume that South Bank has made a $100,000 loan to Williams secured by the $140,000 value of the two horses. William finds a buyer who will pay $70,000 in cash for Green Mars. He wants to make the sale. The buyer, of course, insists on receiving clear title. If this sale were in the ordinary course of Williams's business, that would be no problem. As will be discussed in Assignment 36, under U.C.C. §9-320(a), a buyer in the ordinary course of business would take free of the security interest of South Bank. But Williams is not in the business of selling horses, so the buyer will not take free of the security interest. See U.C.C. §9-323(d).

How can Williams clear South Bank's security interest from the title? One way would be for Williams to pay his debt to South Bank and insist that South Bank file a termination statement under U.C.C. §9-513(c). Provided that South Bank has no obligation to make further advances to him, the Bank will be obliged to comply. But to trigger his right to a termination statement under U.C.C. §9-513(c), Williams must pay the entire $100,000 debt. That he cannot afford to do, because he is receiving only $70,000 for Green Mars and he doesn't have the other $30,000 he needs.

Hat in hand, Williams goes to South Bank to ask that the Bank *release* — that is, voluntarily surrender, its right to Green Mars as collateral. Williams explains his predicament to the loan officer. He proposes that the loan officer attend the closing on his sale of the horse. In return for a release of Green Mars from South Bank's security interest, Williams offers to apply $50,000 of the proceeds of sale to South Bank's loan — that is, the buyers will pay $50,000 to South Bank and $20,000 to Williams. South Bank will then have a $50,000 loan outstanding secured by Green Mars, which is alone worth $70,000. South Bank will still be oversecured and, Williams argues, have no significant risk of loss. After a brief review of the file, the loan officer advises Williams that his proposal is not acceptable to South Bank and that it will be necessary for Williams to pay the full balance of the loan at closing. Williams thinks about that for a few minutes and decides to increase his offer.

"How about if I just pay you the full $70,000 I am getting for Green Mars?" Williams asks. "The $30,000 balance on your loan will then be secured by a horse worth $70,000."

"I'm sorry," says the loan officer, "but in cases like this it is the bank's policy to insist upon full payment at closing."

At this point, Williams is more than just a little annoyed. "You have no *reason* to insist on full payment at closing. You're getting every penny from the sale. You'll be better off as a result of this sale.

Now you have collateral worth 140 percent of the loan; after the sale I've arranged, you'll have collateral worth 233 percent of the loan."

"I'm sorry," the loan officer says, repeating himself, "but in cases like this it is the bank's policy to insist upon full payment at closing."

Now Williams is really agitated. "You're *preventing* me from repaying this loan," he says. "I can't sell both horses at the same time and expect to get full value for them. I've arranged a sale that is entirely for your benefit, and you are making it impossible for me to do it. What you're doing is illegal."

At the sound of the word "illegal," the loan officer perks up. He begins speaking slowly and deliberately. "This bank is not *preventing* you from doing anything. You signed the security agreement and we are just insisting on our rights under it. You *say* that at $70,000 you are getting full value for Green Mars, but we have no way of knowing that. You *say* that Red Mars is worth $70,000 and so we'll be oversecured, but for all we know, the horse could be lame. It's not our job to figure out all this stuff every time you want to sell some of the collateral. We don't know anything about horses; we're a *bank*." Now the loan officer is just as agitated as Williams. "If it's such a great deal to have Red Mars as collateral for a $30,000 loan, why don't you borrow the $30,000 from somebody else and pay us off?"

"How am I going to get some other bank to make the loan when you've already made it and are trying to weasel out of it? You might as well have called my loan!" Williams was on his feet, storming out of the loan officer's office.

"We just want our rights under the contract," the loan officer yells at the retreating debtor. "The contract you *signed*."

The loan officer in this story was not being entirely honest with Williams. His real reason for insisting on the bank's rights under the contract was that state bank examiners were pressing the bank to reduce the size of its outstanding loan portfolio. Insisting on their rights under their contracts is one of the few legal ways a bank can do that. But then Williams was not being entirely honest with the loan officer. He stormed out in such a hurry because he had to meet with the veterinarian who had just taken her second look at the problem with Red Mars's leg.

In other circumstances, the bank might have been willing to negotiate for the release of Green Mars. South Bank might have had the horses appraised and, if they did, certainly would have required that Williams pay for the appraisals. They might also have taken this opportunity to cure any perceived defects in the loan documents by having Williams sign new ones, or to request that Williams give additional collateral. South Bank might have required a paydown of the loan in an amount more or less than the full $70,000 Williams was getting for the sale of Green Mars.

Sophisticated debtors often negotiate release clauses as part of the initial loan agreement. For example, assume that Williams antici- pated this problem with South Bank. Before acquiring the second horse, he might have negotiated for the right to a release of either horse upon payment of a specified portion of the loan. South Bank would probably have required a paydown of more than half the loan to obtain a release of one of the two horses. Alternatively, South Bank might have required that Williams give advance notice of the release request and pay for South Bank to appraise the horses immediately prior to release. That would have enabled them to use a percentage paydown formula that assured they would be more secure after the release than before.

Debtors do not need release clauses for collateral that is inventory. U.C.C. §9-320(a) sets as the default rule that a sale of inventory auto- matically releases the property sold from any security interest created by the seller. The rule can be varied by agreement, and some inven- tory loan agreements do require that the debtor obtain the consent of the secured party to the sale of each item of inventory. (This method typically is used for "big ticket" items such as aircraft or industrial machinery, where a single transaction is big enough to warrant this kind of attention.) The most common response, however, is to leave the default rule in effect and provide in the security agreement for payoff of particular portions of the loan upon sale of particular por- tions of the collateral. To illustrate, if the collateral for the loan is two horses of equal value, the agreement might provide that immediately upon sale of either horse the debtor must repay 65 percent of the loan.

C. Marshaling Assets

An oversecured creditor's election to proceed against one item of col- lateral rather than another can determine the fate of other unpaid creditors. Consider again our previous example in which Red Mars and Green Mars are each worth $70,000, and South Bank has a first security interest in both horses for $100,000. Add to the facts that Williams has given Becky Sansei a second security interest in Green Mars, securing her loan to Williams in the amount of $40,000. Later, Williams defaults on his payments to South Bank and the Bank fore- closes. If the Bank repossesses Green Mars and sells it, the sale will discharge Sansei's security interest. U.C.C. §9-617(a)(3). The bank will be entitled to all of the sale proceeds. U.C.C. §9-615(a). Sansei will then have nothing but an unsecured claim. Sansei will be left to compete as an unsecured creditor for Williams's equity in Red Mars or his other nonexempt assets.

Notice that if, instead of repossessing Green Mars first, South Bank had repossessed Red Mars first and sold it for $70,000, Sansei would have been assured a full recovery. Application of the $70,000 in proceeds of the Red Mars sale to South Bank's loan would have reduced the balance to $30,000. If South Bank later sold Green Mars for $70,000, South Bank would have been entitled to only the first $30,000, leaving just enough to pay the $40,000 balance owing to Sansei under her second security interest. The point of this example is that South Bank's decision to pursue Red Mars or Green Mars first determines whether Sansei can recover from her collateral at all.

1. Marshaling as a Limit on the Secured Creditor's Choice

Marshaling assets is an equitable doctrine developed to limit the senior secured creditor's choice of which collateral to pursue. When the doctrine applies, it requires that a creditor such as South Bank look for its recovery to the asset not encumbered by junior liens, so that the holders of the junior liens, such as Becky Sansei, can recover from the only collateral available to them. As the following case illustrates, when this doctrine operates to the benefit of junior lienors, it is usually to the detriment of the debtor's unsecured creditors.

In re Robert E. Derecktor of Rhode Island, Inc.

150 B.R. 296 (Bankr. D.R.I. 1993)

ARTHUR N. VOTOLATO, UNITED STATES BANKRUPTCY JUDGE

Robert E. Derecktor Of Rhode Island, Inc., which for approximately 13 years had conducted a ship building and repair facility in Portsmouth, Rhode Island, filed a Chapter 11 petition on January 3, 1992. Since the filing the debtor has operated in varying but limited fashion, and is presently in the final stages of total liquidation, with no future operations contemplated.

Before us is the Rhode Island Port Authority's Motion . . . wherein it asks this Court to order marshaling as to Federal Deposit Insurance Corporation's (FDIC) interest in the Debtor's assets. Several unsecured creditors oppose the relief sought by the Port Authority on the ground that to allow marshaling would diminish or wipe out any dividend they might otherwise receive. . . .

FACTS

The relevant facts, as they appear below, are not in dispute: On April 13, 1979, the Port Authority loaned Derecktor $6,500,000 for the acquisition of facilities and equipment to be used in its ship building and repair business. As collateral for the loan the Port Authority retained a security interest in all of Derecktor's then owned and after acquired fixtures, furniture, furnishings, equipment, machinery, inventory, and other tangible personal property. As of February 15, 1992, the Debtor owed $4,975,000 to the Port Authority on the original obligation.

On October 23, 1987, to purchase a 20,000-ton floating dry dock (Dry Dock III), Derecktor borrowed $6.5 million from, and executed a purchase money security mortgage to Bank of New England-Old Colony. As additional collateral, Derecktor granted the bank a security interest in all of its presently owned and after acquired machinery, docks, equipment, inventory, personal property, and general intangibles. As of February 6, 1992, approximately $5.8 million was due on this loan.

On December 21, 1988, Bank of New England loaned Derecktor $2,500,000 more, and received a security interest in Debtor's accounts, contracts, contract rights, inventory, and equipment. This security interest also covered the balance due on the original $6.5 million loan. As of February 6, 1992, approximately $1.2 million remained due on the December 1988 loan. When Bank of New England was deemed insolvent, FDIC became its successor-in-interest, entitling it to payment under Derecktor's obligations to Bank of New England.

As is evident, both FDIC and the Port Authority have a security interest in some of the same collateral, namely the equipment, inventory, machinery, and Dry Dock III. FDIC has the senior secured position on Dry Dock III, and it has the only security interest in the Debtor's intangibles, accounts, contracts, and contract rights. The Debtor's major assets include: (1) Dry Dock III; (2) an assignable tug boat contract (the Assignment); (3) a claim against Insurance Company of North America (INA Settlement); and (4) equipment, machinery, and inventory. The parties have agreed to liquidate the assets in the most efficient manner, and to defer the resolution of the marshaling issue pending the disposition of the assets.

Dry Dock III, the first asset liquidated, was sold in July, 1992 for $6.6 million. The Tug Assignment and the INA Settlement were both approved on September 25, 1992, producing approximately $2.1 million from the Assignment, and $650,000 from the INA Settlement. The equipment, machinery, and inventory were sold in January, 1993, and proceeds were approximately $1.0 million.

In the normal course, i.e. without marshaling, because Dry Dock III was the first asset liquidated, FDIC would apply the entire $6.6 million against its $7.0 million secured claim. The balance of its claim would then be satisfied from the proceeds of the Tug Assignment, and thereafter the funds remaining from the Assignment and INA Settlement would be used to pay junior secured creditors, and finally unsecured creditors. Again, without marshaling, the Port Authority's security interest would extend only (after the Dry Dock III proceeds go to FDIC) to the equipment, machinery, and inventory and therefore, it would recover, at best, $1.0 million of its $5.0 million claim. Through marshaling however, the Port Authority can realize the benefit of its second secured position on Dry Dock III, with FDIC looking first to the INA Settlement and the Assignment for payment, and thereafter to Dry Dock III, leaving a surplus for junior lienors.

DISCUSSION . . .

The remainder of the present dispute concerns the propriety of applying the doctrine of marshaling to the facts before us. Marshaling is an equitable doctrine which "rests upon the principle that a creditor having two funds to satisfy his debt may not, by his application of them to his demand, defeat another creditor, who may resort to only one of the funds." Sowell v. Federal Reserve Bank, 268 U.S. 449, 457, 69 L. Ed. 1041, 45 S. Ct. 528 (1925). The purpose of the doctrine is to "prevent the arbitrary action of a senior lienor from destroying the rights of a junior lienor or a creditor having less security." Meyer v. United States, 375 U.S. 233, 237, 11 L. Ed. 2d 293, 84 S. Ct. 318 (1963). Equity requires the senior creditor to look first to property which cannot be reached by the junior creditor, but only if the senior creditor or third parties are not prejudiced. . . .

To apply the marshaling doctrine, three elements must be present: (1) the existence of two creditors of the Debtor; (2) the existence of two funds owned by the Debtor; and (3) the ability of one creditor to satisfy its claim from either or both of the funds, while the other creditor can only look to one of the funds.

The instant controversy falls squarely within these requirements: (1) FDIC and the Port Authority are two creditors of the Debtor; (2) there are (more than) two funds of the Debtor available for these creditors, i.e. sale proceeds from Dry Dock III, the Assignment, the INA Settlement, and the equipment, machinery, and inventory; and (3) FDIC can satisfy its claim from all of the Debtor's funds, while the Port Authority can only look to Dry Dock III and the equipment, machinery, and inventory for payment.

The unsecured creditors object to the application of the doctrine on the ground of prejudice, in that marshaling will give the Port Authority more security than it originally bargained for. The FDIC's claim is roughly $7.0 million, which would be almost entirely satisfied from the proceeds of the Dry Dock III sale. If FDIC were paid these proceeds, the Port

Authority's recovery on its $5.0 million claim would be limited to approximately $1.0 million from the sale of the equipment and machinery, and the balance of its claim would be rendered unsecured. However, if FDIC is required to look first to the proceeds from the Assignment and the INA Settlement before looking to Dry Dock III, the Port Authority will receive an additional $2.0 million on its secured claim. While it is clear that marshaling in this manner will deplete the fund otherwise available to unsecured creditors, we do not find such a result to constitute legal prejudice, in the marshaling context.

The history and intended purpose of the doctrine, as well as a review of the more recent cases addressing the issue, supports this conclusion. Historically, marshaling has been applied for the benefit of the junior secured creditor by preserving its collateral through a court established order of distribution of secured assets. This is accomplished by requiring the senior secured creditor to look first to its single interest collateral, i.e. property that the junior secured creditor cannot reach, before looking to the shared collateral to satisfy its claim, and this of course invariably results in a diminution of the funds available for unsecured creditors. If we were to accept the unsecured creditors' argument regarding prejudice, the doctrine of marshaling would rarely, if ever, be utilized in bankruptcy because its application almost always results in diminished assets for the unsecured creditors. . . .

The Port Authority bargained for security on its loan, whereas the unsecured creditors did not, and this allows the junior secured creditor to realize the benefit of its bargain. The caveat against causing harm or prejudice to others applies only to parties having equity equal to the party seeking to invoke marshaling. As the Supreme Court in *Meyer* stated,

> [Marshaling] deals with the rights of all who have an interest in the property involved and is applied only when it can be equitably fashioned as to all of the parties. Thus, state courts have refused to apply it . . . where the rights of third parties having equal equity would be prejudiced.

Here, the parties do not stand on equal footing — the Port Authority's rights as a secured creditor are legally superior to those of the unsecured creditors, and accordingly the "prejudice" argument does not apply in this instance.

Accordingly, based upon all of the foregoing, the Port Authority's Motion . . . requesting FDIC to marshal its interest in Debtor's assets, is GRANTED. . . .

The doctrine of marshaling assets is subject to several limitations on its applicability. Notice, for example, Judge Votolato's comment in passing that the doctrine of marshaling assets can be applied "only if the senior creditor [is] not prejudiced." In Matter of Woolf Printing Corp., 87 B.R. 692 (Bankr. M.D. Fla. 1988), the senior creditor, Mac Papers, had a security interest in the proceeds of a life insurance policy and also in the debtor's personal property, including furniture, fixtures, equipment, inventory, and accounts receivable. The junior creditor, NCNB, had a security interest only in the proceeds of the life insurance policy. The insured was dead, and the proceeds of the life insurance were in the hands of the court. The court refused to require Mac Papers to recover from the personal property, thereby denying NCNB any recovery from its lien at all. The court explained its decision in terms of "equity."

> NCNB argues Mac Papers should satisfy its debt by first looking to the Debtor's personal property. In order to accomplish this satisfaction, Mac Papers would have to have relief from the automatic stay, then sell the property to satisfy the debt with the sale proceeds. There is no evidence to show the time frame within which the property could be sold. On the other hand, if Mac Papers were not compelled to marshal, it would be able to look to the insurance proceeds first. This is ready cash which would be immediately available. Upon a review of the characteristics of the two funds it is clear that compelling Mac Papers to look to the Debtor's personal property prior to the insurance proceeds would cause undue delay in satisfying the debt. Since marshaling would injuriously affect the secured interests of Mac Papers, this Court declines to compel the requested equitable relief.

While the *Woolf Printing* court's idea of equity (NCNB should not recover at all rather than put Mac Papers through the delay of personal property foreclosure) is probably not widely shared, the case stands as a good reminder that marshaling assets is available only when the court thinks it ought to be.

Another limitation on the doctrine of marshaling assets is that it generally cannot be used to compel the senior creditor to foreclose against homestead property. If the senior creditor has both homestead and nonhomestead property to which it can look for recovery, a creditor with a junior lien on only the nonhomestead property cannot force the senior creditor to foreclose against the homestead.

Finally, marshaling cannot be used by one junior lienor where the effect would be to prevent recovery by another junior lienor. To illustrate, again assume that Sansei holds a $40,000 second security interest in Green Mars and Rodriguez holds a $50,000 second security interest in Red Mars. On these facts, it is no more "equitable" to require the holder of the first security interest, South Bank, to look to Red Mars for its recovery in a suit brought by Sansei than it is to require South Bank to look to Green Mars for its recovery in a suit brought by Rodriguez. Neither Sansei nor Rodriguez can use marshaling assets to force the bank's choice of a remedy. The effect is to allow the bank to determine, by its choice of remedy, whether Rodriguez or Sansei will suffer the loss.

2.   Equitable Assignment as an Alternative to Marshaling

As you read the description of *Woolf Printing* you may have wondered what would have happened if NCNB had offered to eliminate the prejudice to Mac Papers by paying the expenses Mac Papers would incur in foreclosing and making cash immediately available to Mac Papers in the form of an interest-free loan secured by Mac Paper's interest in the debtor's personal property. Mac Papers would have suffered no prejudice and NCNB would have been able to recover. The same result could be reached another way: Let Mac Papers recover from the insurance policy, but give NCNB Mac Papers's rights against the personal property. Faced with situations like *Woolf Printing*, where the prejudice to the senior creditor from marshaling assets was merely procedural, some courts have done precisely that. That is, they deny marshaling and let the senior creditor recover from the most convenient source. But as a condition of doing so, they require the senior creditor to assign its security interest in the unforeclosed collateral to the junior creditor. The effect is like marshaling, but the risks and procedural burdens have been transferred to the junior creditor.

The case of Janke v. Chace illustrates this *equitable assignment* remedy. Jack Chace owned 280 acres of land, subject to a mortgage in favor of Farm Credit Bank of Omaha. At the time of the dispute, this mortgage had been paid down to $19,000. Chace sold two of the 280 acres to his son, James Chace. James was married to Diana Janke. The couple borrowed $116,000 from Diana Janke's parents (the Jankes) to build a house on the two acres and gave the Jankes a mortgage on the house and two acres. James and Diana defaulted in payments on this mortgage and the Jankes foreclosed. At that time, the house and two acres were worth less than the $116,000 owing against them. After the foreclosure judgment was entered, the Jankes requested that the court "marshal the assets" by requiring Farm Credit to look to the remaining 278 acres for payment of its $19,000 and letting the Jankes have all the proceeds from the house and two acres.

The court concluded that the doctrine of marshaling assets was inapplicable because the requirement of a "common debtor" was not met. (Jack Chace was debtor to Farm Credit; James Chace and Diana Janke were debtors to the Jankes. Nobody owed both loans.) For that reason, the court denied marshaling and allowed Farm Credit to recover its $19,000 from the proceeds of the sale of the house and two acres. The court concluded, nevertheless, that "equitable principles" required a remedy for the Jankes. It ordered that the $19,000 be treated not as a payment of the mortgage to Farm Credit but as a purchase of it. That is, upon receiving the $19,000 from the foreclosure of the house and two acres, Farm Credit had to assign to the Jankes all of its right, title, and interest in the $19,000 note and mortgage. Farm Credit would have its $19,000 from the house and two acres, but the Jankes could then recoup their loss by recovering $19,000 from the 278 acres owned by Jack Chace.

3. Can Unsecured Creditors Marshal?

In *Derecktor*, Judge Votolato permitted marshaling assets *against* unsecured creditors. That is, he forced the senior creditor to look for recovery to the only assets from which the unsecured creditors could hope to recover. There are cases that hold to the contrary when the debtor has filed bankruptcy. Doctrinally, the argument for this minority view goes as follows. Bankruptcy Code §544(a) gives the trustee or debtor in possession the rights of an ideal lien creditor. Thus, any attempt to marshal against a bankruptcy estate is an attempt to marshal against a junior lienor. As we noted above, the doctrine of marshaling assets cannot be used by one junior lienor to the detriment of another.

Acceptance of this argument protects the bankruptcy trustee and, through the bankruptcy trustee, the unsecured creditors, from the attempts of other lienors to marshal against them. But it provides only a limited ability for the bankruptcy trustee to marshal against others. Marshaling doesn't produce additional assets; it merely shifts assets from one application to another. Marshaling is always *for* someone's interest and *against* someone else's. A bankruptcy trustee cannot marshal against other lien holders for reasons already stated; it cannot marshal against unsecured creditors because it already represents all of the unsecured creditors; it cannot marshal against the debtor because the debtor has no interests separate from the estate (all of the debtor's interests in property have already become property of the estate pursuant to Bankruptcy Code §541(a)(1)). The only circumstance in which a bankruptcy trustee can marshal at all is where some of the collateral is owned by a person other than the debtor. Only a minority of courts permit marshaling in that circumstance.

4. Marshaling Against Property Owned by Third Parties

It is not unusual for a creditor to take a security interest in property that does not belong to its debtor. To illustrate, assume that Mark

Aman has decided to open a clothing store in the local shopping mall. He forms a corporation, Aman Corporation, that will own the business. The Corporation then applies to Power Bank for a loan to be secured by its fixtures, equipment, and inventory. Power Bank agrees to make the loan to the Corporation, but only on the condition that Mark further secure the loan with a mortgage against a beach house he owns personally. Mark does so.

Assume Janus, an unsecured creditor of the Corporation, obtains a judgment, levies on the fixtures, equipment, and inventory, and seeks marshaling to compel Power Bank to look to the beach house for its recovery. Assuming further that Mark's beach house has no liens against it that are junior to Power Bank's, the Bank's recovery from it will not injure other lienors. Provided Mark Aman is solvent, marshaling will injure no one but him.

Nevertheless, the courts split on cases like this where a lienor seeks to compel marshaling against the assets of a third party. The objection is expressed in the *common debtor* requirement. Most courts read that requirement to have two parts. The marshaling must be between two or more creditors of the same debtor *and the funds or assets must be in the hands of that common debtor.* Here the marshaling is between two creditors of the Corporation, but the assets subject to marshaling (the beach house and the assets of Aman Corporation) are owned by different debtors. Janus's attempt to marshal against Power Bank fails the second part of the common debtor requirement.

Other courts impose only the first part of the common debtor test. There need be only a debtor who owes money to both creditors — here Aman Corporation — and the common debtor requirement is met regardless of who owns the encumbered property. In those courts, Janus could marshal against Power Bank.

Now assume that instead of Janus becoming a lien creditor, the Corporation had gone into bankruptcy; a trustee had been appointed to represent the interests of the unsecured creditors of the Corporation; and the trustee, asserting his status as a lien creditor, tried to use marshaling to force Power Bank to look to the beach house. Given that the trustee has the rights of a lien creditor, it should not surprise you that the analysis is the same as when Janus attempted to marshal. The trustee loses in the majority of courts, and wins only in those that employ a one-part common debtor test. As we discussed in the preceding section, if the trustee cannot use marshaling to force a secured creditor to look to property owned by a third party, there remains no situation in which a trustee can use marshaling.

D.   The Effect of Cross-Collateralization on Purchase-Money Status

We introduced the concept of a purchase-money security interest in Assignment 19 and developed it further in Assignments 28 and 32. Purchase-money status is an important attribute of a security interest, in part because it enables a security interest that is second in time to prevail over liens and security interests perfected earlier. The knowledge that its interest will be first in priority even if it is not first in time enables the purchase-money lender to extend credit without conducting a search of the filing system.

Historically, a security interest has been considered purchase money only to the extent that the collateral secures an obligation that is the purchase price of the collateral. This rule survives the drafting of new Article 9 with regard to collateral other than inventory. U.C.C. §§9-103(a) and (b)(1). But to determine the extent to which collateral secures only its purchase price can be difficult both as a matter of fact and of theory. Two types of problems contribute to the difficulty.

First, the secured creditor may not keep a separate account for the purchase-money obligation. For example, Becky Sansei sells Green Mars to Williams for $40,000 and takes a security interest for the purchase price. At the closing on this sale, the parties cancel Williams's promissory note to Sansei in the amount of $300,000 and Williams signs a new one in the amount of $340,000. At this point, $40,000 of the $340,000 obligation is the purchase price of Green Mars. Even if the entire $340,000 is secured by the security interest in Green Mars, that does not prevent $40,000 of the security interest from being purchase money. U.C.C. §9-103(f)(1). This is the so-called dual status rule: A security interest may be part purchase money and part non-purchase money. Nor would the purchase-money status of the $40,000 be lost merely because the entire $340,000 were secured by other collateral in addition to Green Mars.

The purchase-money status of the security interest in Green Mars becomes less clear when $3,000 of interest accrues on the note and then Williams pays $10,000. The new balance is $333,000, but how much of that is the purchase price of Green Mars?

U.C.C. §9-103(f) addresses the problem by placing the burden of establishing what part of the balance is the purchase price of Green Mars on the secured creditor. Sansei must provide the court with evidence showing what payments or accrual were made. U.C.C. §9-103(e) tells Sansei how to apply the payments she receives. If the parties have agreed to a method, she must follow it. If they have not, Williams can direct the application of the payments as he makes them. If he fails to do so, Sansei must apply the payments to obligations that are unsecured before applying them to payments that are secured. Among secured obligations, she must apply them first to the oldest.

The second type of problem in determining the extent to which security interests are purchase money is the problem of aggregating "collateral." To understand the problem, assume that Sansei sells both Green Mars and Red Mars to Williams and takes $80,000 of the purchase price in the form of a promissory note secured by Green Mars and Red Mars. That is, the security interest is cross-collateralized. Is this a single purchase-money security interest in which the two horses are the purchase-money collateral and the $80,000 is the purchase-money obligation? Or are there two purchase-money security interests, each to the extent of $40,000 and each encumbering only one horse?

To illustrate why it matters, assume that after the loan is made, Sansei releases Red Mars for a payment of $10,000 because the horse is lame. Is the remaining $70,000 obligation an obligation "incurred as . . . the price of the collateral"? Though U.C.C. §9-103 does not address the point, some authorities take the position that "the collateral" is whatever is sold in the transaction in which the purchase-money obligation arose. That is, a security interest can be purchase-money even though cross-collateralized, provided that the entire purchase-money obligation arises on a single occasion. Under that rule, Sansei could have a $70,000 purchase-money obligation in a horse that never alone had a price nearly so high.

U.C.C. §9-103(b)(2) sets forth an even more liberal rule for purchase-money security interests in inventory. If the two horses would be inventory in the hands of Williams and the security interest is cross-collateralized, the entire $80,000 can be a purchase-money security interest in each of the horses, even though they were not purchased at the same time. As the following illustration from Comment 4 to U.C.C. §9-103 shows, an inventory lender can have a purchase-money security interest in an item of inventory that secures an obligation that is not even arguably the purchase price of that item.

Seller (S) sells an item of inventory (Item-1) to Debtor (D), retaining a security interest in Item-1 to secure Item 1's price and all other obligations, existing and future, of D to S. S then sells another item of inventory to D (Item-2), again retaining a security interest in Item-2 to secure Item-2's price as well as all other obligations of D to S. D then pays to S Item-1's purchase price. D then sells Item-2 to a buyer in ordinary course of business, who takes Item-2 free of S's security interest.

The Comment explains:

> Under subsection (b)(2), S's security interest in Item-1 securing Item-2's unpaid price would be a purchase-money security interest. This is so because S has a purchase-money security interest in Item-1, Item-1 secures the price of (a "purchase-money obligation incurred with respect to") Item-2 ("other inventory"), and Item-2 itself was subject to a purchase-money security interest.

Although this rule plays fast and loose with the English language, it is directed against a serious practical problem. Absent the rule, an inventory lender that advanced money against successive deliveries of collateral as they arrived would have not a single purchase-money security interest in the debtor's inventory but a series of purchase-money security interests each in the collateral delivered on a particular occasion. Such a secured party could meet its obligation of establishing the extent of its purchase-money security interest in particular items of collateral, U.C.C. §9-103(g), only by keeping track of which items of inventory were sold. That might be a simple matter with regard to automobiles or other such collateral where the parties are already keeping track on a serial number basis, but it would impose an additional and perhaps extensive record-keeping burden with regard to groceries in the hands of a restaurant supply house or a grocery store.

Problem Set 34

34.1. Your client, Paula Jones, holds a second mortgage on a house owned by Rupert Waldoch. Waldoch apparently has defaulted in payments under the first mortgage and the mortgage holder, Watson Federal Savings, has filed a complaint for foreclosure. The complaint recites that the amount outstanding on the first mortgage is $220,000; your investigation indicates the house to be worth not more than about $200,000.

a. If no additional relevant facts come to light, what do you expect to recover?

b. What additional facts might yet entitle Paula to recover by virtue of her second mortgage?

34.2. When David Paul filed for bankruptcy, he owned only two nonexempt assets, a 22-unit apartment building and a yacht. The first mortgage on the apartment building was in the amount of $450,000 and was held by University City Bank. The first security interest in the yacht was in the amount of $400,000 and was held by Capital Equities. The $400,000 note to Capital Equities was also secured by a second mortgage against the apartment building. Paul's lawyer, William Hurst, held a second security interest in the yacht securing payment of $25,000 in legal work done by Hurst more than a year before the bankruptcy filing. By consent of all parties, the Chapter 7 trustee sold the two assets free and clear of liens and the liens were transferred to the proceeds of sale.

a.   The apartment building sold for $660,000; the yacht for $250,000. The three lien holders and the trustee all claim the proceeds of sale. Who is entitled to them?

b.   If the yacht had sold for only $200,000, who would have been entitled to the money?

34.3.   About six months ago, you obtained a judgment in the amount of $10,000 on behalf of your client, Miller's Feed and Seed, against Estelle LeNotre. At that time you recorded the judgment in the real property records of the county. Under the majority rule and local law, by recording, the judgment became a lien against real property owned by the debtor in the county. Your investigation since that time reveals the following additional facts. LeNotre owes a balance of $44,000 to Production Credit Association (PCA). The loan is secured by a first security interest in her farm machinery and by a second mortgage against her farm. The first mortgage on the farm is held by National City Bank and is in the amount of $35,000. LeNotre owes $54,000 to the Small Business Administration (SBA). That loan is secured by a first mortgage against her home and a second against her farm machinery. Your best estimates of value are that the farm machinery is worth $55,000, the farm is worth $60,000, and the home is worth $63,000. The home appears to be an exempt homestead under the debtor-creditor laws of the state. If your estimates of value are correct and LeNotre owns no other property, is your judgment collectible? What problems do you foresee and how do you plan to deal with them?

34.4.   Willard Kurtz, a friend of yours from college, asks that you take a look at a contract for him before he signs. For several years, Willard has been looking for a five-acre tract of wooded land on a river at a reasonable price — not an easy bill to fill — and he has finally found it. The document he shows you is titled "Contract for Deed." The contract provides for a sale price of $30,000, payable with interest at 9 percent in equal monthly installments of $380.03 over a period of ten years. Upon payment of the full purchase price, the owner, Rancho Mirage Development, Inc., will transfer the property by deed, free and clear of all encumbrances. The contract gives Willard the right to prepay the outstanding balance at any time and to receive his deed at the time of payment. The title search you ordered on the property shows a mortgage in the original face amount of $940,000. The mortgage is signed by Rancho Mirage Development,

Inc. and is in favor of Robert L. Henderson, the former owner of the property. It encumbers not only the tract Willard is buying, but also about 60 other five-acre parcels. Based on your knowledge of real estate in the area, you estimate that all 60 tracts together are probably worth more than $2 million.

    a.   What are your concerns as you advise Willard whether to buy under this contract?

    b.   Would it change your mind if Rancho Mirage had already sold over half the tracts in this development and was receiving monthly payments from purchasers that were well in excess of the payment Rancho Mirage must make each month to Henderson?

    34.5.   In a parallel universe, you represent Rancho Mirage in the scenario described in the previous problem. Willard Kurtz has just refused to close and Mr. Mirage is worried about whether he can sell *any* of his tracts. What do you recommend?

    34.6.   On October 1, Becky Sansei sells a Sansei submersible robot to Michael Williams for $70,000. Williams pays $20,000 in cash and signs a promissory note for the remaining $50,000. Williams also signs a security agreement granting Sansei a security interest in "all Sansei equipment" to secure "all obligations owing from Williams to Sansei." The security agreement makes no mention of purchase-money status and provides no rules for applying payments. The robot will be equipment in the hands of Williams.

    a.   Is Sansei's security interest purchase money? If so, to what extent? U.C.C. §§9-103(a) and (b).

    b.   On November 1, Sansei sells a Sansei miniature submarine to Michael Williams for $60,000. Williams pays $20,000 in cash and signs a promissory note for the remaining $40,000. The submarine will be equipment in the hands of Williams. In what amount is the submarine encumbered?

    c.   Is Sansei's security interest in the submarine purchase money? If so, to what extent?

    d.   Assume that no interest is accruing on either obligation. On November 2, Williams pays Sansei $1,000. Sansei deposits Williams's check and credits $1,000 against the $90,000 shown owing on Sansei's books. Now what is the extent of Sansei's purchase-money security interest in the submarine? U.C.C. §9-103(e). Comment 7 to U.C.C. §9-103.

    e.   Would your answers to part c. be different if the collateral were inventory in the hands of Williams? U.C.C. §§9-103(a) and (b). Comment 4 to U.C.C. §9-103.

    34.7.   On May 31, Bonnie's Boat World, Inc. purchases two Coyote Loaders for $90,000. Coyote takes a security interest for $50,000 of the purchase price. Bonnie's borrows another $40,000 from Firstbank against the loaders, without mentioning Coyote's lien. Firstbank takes a security interest in the loaders, disburses the loan proceeds directly to Coyote, and perfects by filing a financing statement on June 1. Coyote perfects by filing a financing statement on June 2, and delivers the loaders to Bonnie's on June 3. Bonnie's bought and uses the loaders as equipment.

    a.   Who has priority in the loaders? U.C.C. §§9-324(a) and (g).

    b.   What should the losing party have done to avoid this unexpected setback?

    34.8.   Deutsche Financial Services plans to finance an inventory of boats that Bart's Boat World will purchase from Shoreline Boats. In accord with their usual practice, Deutsche filed a financing statement covering "inventory" and conducted a search for other filings against Bart's. The search discovered a financing statement filed by Firstbank covering "inventory." Bart tells Deutsche that Firstbank is financing only Bart's inventory of Bayliner boats. Deutsche wonders whether they need a subordination agreement with Firstbank or whether they can simply give notice as required by U.C.C. §§9-324(b) and (c) and begin lending. They ask you to consider the following possible scenario: Firstbank lends Bart's $100 to help make the down payment on a Shoreline boat and Bart's uses the money for that purpose. The description of collateral in Firstbank's security agreement is sufficiently broad to cover a Shoreline boat.

    a.   On these facts, would Firstbank have a purchase-money security interest in the Shoreline boat? U.C.C. §§9-103(a) and (b).

    b.   If so, for how much money? U.C.C. §9-103(b)(2).

    c.   Between Firstbank and Deutsche, who would have priority in the Shoreline boat? U.C.C. §§9-324(b), (c), and (g).

    d.   Would your answer to c. be different if Deutsche filed and began lending first, Firstbank gave notice to Deutsche under U.C.C. §§9-324(b) and (c), and then Firstbank lent Bart's $100 to help make the down payment on a Shoreline boat and Bart's used the money for that purpose?

Assignment 35: Sellers Against Secured Creditors

After-acquired property may seem to spring from nowhere, but it does not. In most instances, someone sells it to the debtor. If the debtor buys from the true owner of the property, does so honestly, and pays the purchase price, the transaction is unlikely to present legal issues of significance. The secured creditor who obtains its interest from the buyer can have a security interest only in what the buyer purchased. The disputes arise in two kinds of cases. The first is where the debtor buys from someone who has less than full ownership of the collateral. The second is where the debtor induces the sale through questionable conduct, such as fraud, misrepresentation, or payment by worthless check, and then fails to pay for the collateral. In either kind of case, the secured creditor may have rights to the collateral even greater than its debtor-transferor.

We begin this assignment by examining the limits on what a debtor who does not have full ownership of the collateral can transfer to its secured lender. Then we turn to the rights of those who own what they sell to recover the property from their debtor's secured lender. In that regard, we consider various protections available to sellers, including purchase-money security interests, rights of reclamation, and actions against secured creditors for unjust enrichment.

A. Limits of the After-Acquired Property Clause

U.C.C. §9-203(b)(2) does not require that the debtor be the owner of collateral to grant a valid security interest in it. The debtor need only have "rights in the collateral." The usual rule is that a debtor's grant of a security interest in collateral in which the debtor holds only a limited interest conveys only a security interest in the limited interest. For example, assume that Debtor leased a computer from LeaseCo under a one-year lease. Debtor grants Bank a secured interest in the computer. Bank probably will be held to acquire only a security interest in Debtor's leasehold. It is not true, however, that the transferee of a security interest can never obtain greater rights than those of its debtor-transferor. To understand why and in what circumstances the secured creditor can obtain greater rights, it is first necessary to understand the basic rules governing title to personal property.

1.   Rules Governing Title to Personal Property

In 1990, a thief stole a car belonging to a Philadelphia man. Some months later, the man found the car again by an odd coincidence. A taxicab pulled up in front of the man while he was standing beside a city street. Despite the markings of the cab company, the man recognized the cab as the car he had lost. (His clue was a piece of tape he had placed on the car before it was stolen.) He called the police. They tracked the cab down and verified that it was indeed the car previously stolen from the man. The cab company, however, was not the thief; it had purchased the car for value, in good faith, from a used car dealer. As between the man and the cab company, who gets the car?

The answer is that, because the car was stolen, the man (the "true owner") prevails over the cab company (the "good faith purchaser for value"). The rule of law that yields this result is generally referred to as the *void title rule*. An outright thief obtains no title (a "void" title) to the property he or she steals. Thus the purchaser from the thief (in this case the used car dealer) obtains no title, and thus can convey no title to the taxicab company. This reasoning is grounded, of course, in the even more basic assumption that one who does not have title cannot convey title. That assumption is often expressed in Latin, *nemo dat qui non habet* (or just *"nemo dat"* to be *very* cool).

It is easy to take a rule like *nemo dat* too seriously. A title is merely a legal construct. It exists only because the law says it does. There are no physical limitations on what a title can do. A title can spring into existence from nowhere if a court of sufficient authority solemnly so declares. It can disappear just as suddenly. The rule of *nemo dat* does not cause the result in the taxicab case or necessitate the void title rule. What the rule of *nemo dat* does is to provide a convenient metaphor for keeping track of and explaining the outcomes in the variety of cases that can arise. In short, if a thief steals the property from the true owner, the true owner can recover the property regardless of who the competing party is or how that party acquired its interest. The rule can apply even against the shopper who buys a piano from a retail store in a shopping mall.

A key policy behind the rule is to discourage theft. Theft is most profitable when the stolen goods can be reintroduced into the stream of commerce and ultimately sold to good faith purchasers for their full value. The rule of *nemo dat* makes that difficult. A good faith purchaser who is not careful about the source of the goods it buys always runs the risk that a true owner will appear and reclaim them. If Edith buys her piano from a reputable store and it turns out to be stolen, she will lose the piano, but she will have a cause of action against the store. The store in turn will have an action against its seller. Assuming that all sellers in the chain are financially responsible, the loss will fall on the person who dealt with the thief.

The equities change if the true owner also dealt with the thief; appropriately, the result changes as well. To illustrate, if the true owner of the Philadelphia taxicab lost his car not to a thief who snatched it off the street at night but to a car dealer who agreed to repair it for the true owner but sold it instead, the true owner could not have recovered it from the taxicab company. See U.C.C. §§2-403(2) and (3). Notice that this result violates the rule of *nemo dat*. A car dealer to whom a car is entrusted for repair does not have title to the car, but under U.C.C. §2-403(2) can pass good title to a buyer in the ordinary course of business. In this illustration, the owner who selected the garage had a better opportunity to avoid the loss. As between the owner and the subsequent buyer, the owner must bear the loss.

The taxicab company would also win over a true owner who lost the car in a *transaction of purchase*, even if the true owner was defrauded in the transaction. This would be the case, for example, if a con artist bought the car from the true owner with a check drawn on a nonexistent bank account. The true owner would be able to void the transaction as against the con artist for fraud, but if the taxicab company bought the car from the con artist in good faith for value before the true owner caught up with it, the taxicab company would prevail. U.C.C. §2-403(1). That provision deals with the *nemo dat* argument by saying that the con artist obtains a voidable title through his or her fraud, and that the holder of a voidable title has the power to transfer a good title to a good faith purchaser for value.

2.   Rules Governing Security Interests in Personal Property

One of the great favorites of American law is the good faith purchaser for value. The drafters of the U.C.C. applied considerable skill and cunning to cast secured creditors in that role. They defined "purchaser" as a person who takes by purchase, and defined "purchase" as including taking by "mortgage, pledge . . . or any other voluntary transaction creating an interest in property." U.C.C. §§1-201(32), (33). When a creditor acquires a security interest in collateral, the creditor is a purchaser of the collateral and eligible for whatever protection purchasers have elsewhere in law. This result is unaltered even when the creditor's interest in a particular piece of property is obtained by virtue of an after-acquired property clause, long after the creditor has made any loans to the debtor, and without any showing that the creditor relied on the security interest's covering the new collateral.

The drafters of the U.C.C. also played fast and loose with the other two elements necessary to become a good faith purchaser for value. They defined "good faith" as meaning only "honesty in fact in the conduct or transaction concerned." U.C.C. §1-201(19). Thus, a secured creditor can be in good faith even if it does not observe "reasonable commercial standards of fair dealing in the trade." (The definition of "good faith" in U.C.C. §2-103(1)(b) ordinarily will not apply in the crucial context of U.C.C. §2-403 because the secured creditor will not be a "merchant" with respect to the goods. See U.C.C. §2-104. The definition of "good faith" in U.C.C. §9-102(a)(43) will not apply in that context because it applies only to "good faith" as used in Article 9. U.C.C. §9-102(a).) The only requirement is that the secured creditor not lie.

The drafters also defined "value" such that "any consideration sufficient to support a simple contract" would qualify. U.C.C. §1-201(44). Thus, a secured creditor can be a purchaser for value when it takes an interest in property of far more value than the loan it makes. Similarly, when the secured creditor obtains an interest in property simply as part of its after-acquired collateral clause, without advancing any additional money, the Code drafters ensured that this transaction was nonetheless for "value." Adding all this together, a secured creditor can be a good faith purchaser of collateral for value even though the secured creditor does not purchase the collateral in the ordinary sense of the word, has bad intentions, and pays nothing for it.

Among the rights that a secured creditor obtains through these remarkable feats of definition are the rights of a good faith purchaser under U.C.C. §2-403. The secured creditor can prevail over the true owner of goods even if the title of its transferor, the debtor, was avoidable because the debtor procured it through fraud.

There have been some famous cases that have played this rule out to its extreme. Perhaps the most lively is In re Samuels, 526 F.2d 1238 (5th Cir.), *cert. denied*, 429 U.S. 834 (1976). In that case, CIT had financed the inventory of Samuels's slaughterhouse. Samuels bought cattle from Stowers over an 11-day period and paid for the purchases by check. On the twelfth day, Samuels filed bankruptcy. The checks bounced, and Stowers wanted his cattle back. CIT claimed the cattle under the after-acquired property clause in its security agreement. CIT ultimately prevailed in a hotly contested case that twice made its way to the Fifth Circuit Court of Appeals. The court reasoned that CIT was a good faith purchaser for value. Even though Samuels never acquired good title to the cattle, he had the power under U.C.C. §2-403(1) to transfer good title to CIT simply by bringing the cattle within the scope of CIT's after-acquired property clause.

Correctly perceiving how outrageous it is for Article 9 secured creditors to steal sellers' property in this manner, but mistakenly thinking that the problem was unique to livestock, Congress granted the sellers of livestock in such "cash sales" priority over inventory lenders, but not without first taking a shot at the drafters of Article 9:

> It is hereby found that a burden on and obstruction to commerce in livestock is caused by financing arrangements under which packers . . . give lenders security interests in . . . livestock purchased by packers in cash sales . . . when payment is not made for the livestock and that such arrangements are contrary to the public interest. 7 U.S.C. §196.

The drafters have not responded to this comment on the quality of their work.

3. The Filing System as an Exception to Nemo Dat

It is worth noting that the concept of a filing system is also inconsistent with the rule of *nemo dat*. Assume that *O* is the true owner of Blackacre. *O* executes and delivers a deed to *A*. Despite *A*'s failure to record, *A* is now the true owner. *O*, who no longer has title, executes and delivers a deed to *B* for value. If *B* records without knowledge that *A* is the true owner, *B* becomes the true owner. The title "springs" from *A* to *B*, enabling *O* to transfer what *O* did not have.

B. Suppliers Against Inventory-Secured Lenders

Recall from Assignment 32 the example in which Sally Raj used inventory secured lending to set up a stereo store on a shoestring. Sally bought $100,000 worth of inventory, but the bank lent only $60,000 against it. Where did Sally get the other $40,000? The answer is that she got it from her suppliers in the form of a *float*. In the week before Sally opened her store, she bought her $100,000 of inventory on unsecured credit from the suppliers. The invoices for that inventory came due 30 to 60 days later. By then, Sally had not only the $60,000 from her inventory financier, but also another $40,000 from sales of inventory. She then paid for the original $100,000 of inventory, purchased more on credit to replace what she sold, and borrowed 60 percent of the cost of the replacements. As these bills came in, she repeated the cycle. Provided that Sally could turn over at least $40,000 of inventory every 30 to 60 days, she would always have had at least that much in unsecured credit from her suppliers.

After a few months of operation, Sally discovers that her cash flow is insufficient to pay her bills as they become due. She might deal with the situation by using some of her sales revenues to pay creditors other than the bank instead of depositing it all to her bank account, as her contract requires. If she does, she is in breach. The bank might not discover her breach; it might think the low amount she deposited represents the entire proceeds of her sales. (If so, the bank would think the remaining inventory that serves as its collateral is larger than it actually is.) If the bank does discover Sally's breach, it probably will call the loan, and Sally will be in a full-fledged financial crisis.

Sally will probably elect to deal with the situation by disappointing some of her suppliers instead of the bank. If she waits an average of 90 days rather than 45 to pay her invoices, she will have an additional $40,000 of float. Her "slow pay" should be a warning sign to the suppliers that Sally may be in financial trouble. If the suppliers are making substantial profits on their sales to Sally, they might be willing to accept the additional risk. If they are not, they will stop selling inventory to Sally, and perhaps even sue her for the outstanding balance. But they will do so as unsecured creditors, assuring that the remedy will be slow and probably ineffective. Remember Assignment 1.

If Sally's business closes, the bank will have the right to take possession of the inventory and sell it. U.C.C. §9-609(a). As a secured creditor, it will have priority over the suppliers in the inventory. The result is somewhat ironic. The supplier who sold Sally 25 compact disc changers just two weeks ago (and has not been paid for them) stands by helplessly while the bank sells the changers and pockets the proceeds. Proponents of the broad scope of the Article 9 "floating lien" against after-acquired property argue that there is no unfairness here. The bank that made the inventory loan put suppliers on notice of its security interest when it filed its financing statement. Even if the supplier did not check the records or learn of the bank's interest through a credit report, the supplier should have anticipated — and probably did — that its buyer would grant a security interest to an inventory financier. If the supplier wanted the ability to reclaim its products in the event Sally did not pay for them, the supplier should have insisted that Sally grant the supplier a security interest. Such a security interest would have been a purchase-money security interest with priority over the bank. U.C.C. §9-324(a). By failing to take such an interest, the supplier agreed to take the risk of unsecured status and perhaps even extracted compensation for that risk in the form of higher interest on the account or a higher price for the product it sold.

Opponents of the broad scope of the Article 9 floating lien on after-acquired property argue that while the carefully calculating supplier of the proponent's argument may be common, it is far from universal. In many applications, the concept of after-acquired property is deceptive. If suppliers often don't understand the system and therefore don't charge adequately for the risks they assume, it is no answer to say that they *ought to*. Even if they do understand, they may be unable to extract competing security interests because other financiers with more leverage, such as banks and commercial lenders, insist on having the only interest in the inventory.

C. Sellers' Weapons Against the After-Acquired Property Clause

Many sellers are shocked to discover how helpless they are when the debtor fails to pay the purchase price and the secured creditor claims the property sold as its collateral. They naturally search for legal devices that will enable them to repossess what they sold if the debtor does not pay for it.

1. Purchase-Money Security Interests

Theoretically, sellers have the option to timely comply with the purchase-money requirements of Article 9 and thereby obtain priority in the property they sell. But recall that many lenders bar their debtors from granting purchase-money security interests. To grant such an interest is a breach of the security agreement that will entitle the inventory lender to call the loan. As a result, many sellers are unable to retain security interests in what they sell.

2. Retention of Title

A seller's first reaction to the treatment of sellers under Article 9 is often to decide not to sell on credit. The seller has that option, and it is an effective protection. Some sellers, however, will fall into the trap of *contracting* to sell, with title to pass to the buyer only when the buyer pays for the goods. For example, *S*, the owner of goods, might give possession of goods to *B* pursuant to an agreement that says (1) the goods are in *B*'s possession merely on loan and *S* remains the owner, and (2) B has an option to buy the goods for $3,000 in cash. As you have already seen in earlier assignments, such a contract is treated as an immediate sale, with the seller retaining a security interest. If the seller did not anticipate this treatment, the seller probably will not have filed a financing statement or given the notice necessary to retain a purchase-money security interest entitled to priority. As a result, the seller's security interest will be subordinate to that of the inventory secured lender.

3.   Consignment

Consignment is an arrangement in which a manufacturer or wholesaler of goods entrusts the goods to an agent or bailee (the *consignee*) for sale. When the agent or consignor sells the goods, title passes directly from the consignor to the buyer. The consignee remits a portion of the sale proceeds to the consignor and keeps the rest as a sort of fee for selling the goods. By the consignment contract, unsold goods remain the property of the consignor and the consignee ultimately returns them to the consignor.

Consignment is a common arrangement in particular industries, most notably retail clothing. Seen in operation, its true nature is easily apparent. The consignee is an independently owned and operated retail store, just like any other retail store. The fees of the consignee are what other retail stores log in as *gross profit* — simply the difference between the wholesale and retail prices of the goods. The only real difference between the relationship of consignor and consignee and that of a seller that gives its buyer 100 percent financing is that the consignor freely accepts return of unsold goods. But that is a minor difference; many financing sellers accept returns. From the perspective of competing creditors of a consignee, consignment is no different from a retain-title contract. That is, consignment is a sale subject to a security interest for the entire purchase price — dressed up to look like something else.

Revised Article 9 governs consignments. U.C.C. §9-109(a)(4). U.C.C. §9-319(a) deems the consignee to have full "rights and title to the goods" and U.C.C. §1-201(37) deems a consignment, even if it is a "true" consignment, to be a security interest. U.C.C. §9-103(d) states that "the security interest of a consignor in goods that are the subject of a consignment is a purchase-money security interest in inventory." As a result, the consignor will have priority over the inventory lender only if the consignor complies with the perfection and notice requirements of U.C.C. §9-324(b).

4.   The Seller's U.C.C. §2-702 Right of Reclamation

In certain narrow circumstances, U.C.C. §2-702(2) grants unpaid sellers the right to reclaim goods they have sold. The buyer must have received the goods while insolvent and the seller must make a demand for reclamation within ten days of the receipt. (The ten-day limit does not apply if the debtor misrepresented its solvency to the seller in writing within three months before delivery of the goods.) This looks like slim (but at least some) protection for the financing seller.

U.C.C. §2-702(3) effectively nullifies the seller's right of reclamation. That section makes the right "subject to the rights of a buyer in the ordinary course of business or other good faith purchaser under this Article (Section 2-403)." The courts have uniformly held the seller's right of reclamation under U.C.C. §2-702 to be subject to the security interest of the debtor's inventory lender. Because the large majority of all commercial buyers have granted a security interest in their inventory, including after-acquired property, and that security interest attaches as soon as the debtor-buyer obtains "rights in the collateral," the right of reclamation will be subject to the rights of an inventory secured lender in the large majority of cases.

Bankruptcy Code §546(c) recognizes the seller's right of reclamation as superior to the rights and avoiding powers of the bankruptcy trustee. But in the process of recognizing the right of reclamation, the Bankruptcy Code narrows it even further. First, §546(c) expressly provides that the demand for reclamation must be written. Second, it provides that the demand must be made within ten days after receipt of the goods by the debtor even in cases where the debtor misrepresented its solvency to the seller in writing within three months before delivery of the goods. Third, it permits the Bankruptcy Court to substitute an administrative expense priority or a lien for the right to reclaim the particular goods.

In the following case, tobacco companies that sold inventory to the debtor on credit just a few days earlier tried to reclaim what they sold. Not only had the inventory lender not supplied a penny of the purchase price of that inventory, but the inventory lender had literally lain in wait for the new inventory to arrive. Nevertheless, the court held that the inventory lender was a "good faith" purchaser entitled to priority over the tobacco companies' right to reclaim.

In re M. Paolella & Sons, Inc.

161 Bankr. 107 (E.D. Pa. 1993)

RAYMOND J. BRODERICK, UNITED STATES DISTRICT JUDGE

Since this Court has determined that the findings made by the Bankruptcy Court are not "clearly erroneous," we summarize the relevant facts as found by the Bankruptcy Judge as follows:

The debtor, M. Paolella & Sons, Inc., was the largest wholesale distributor of tobacco products in the Delaware Valley. On January 26, 1982, the debtor and MNC entered into a financing agreement that provided a line of credit secured by virtually all of the debtor's assets, i.e., receivables, inventory, and equipment. These security interests were perfected by filings pursuant to the Uniform Commercial Code ("UCC"). Initially of two-year duration, the agreement was renewed and was in effect up to January 26, 1986. The financing agreement was asset-based in that it provided the debtor with a line of credit determined by a formula whereby the debtor could borrow against 85% of eligible accounts receivable and 60% of eligible inventory.

In October 1982, the debtor requested and MNC permitted an increase in credit to enable the debtor to participate in a special buying program offered by the tobacco companies. Thereafter, the debtor's loan was always out of formula. That is, after October 1982, the amount advanced by MNC always exceeded the sum of 85% of eligible receivables plus 60% of eligible inventory. Although MNC attempted repeatedly to bring the loan within formula, MNC agreed on several occasions to increase the amount of the overadvance to enable the debtor to participate in the tobacco companies' special buying programs; the debtor participated in these programs regularly.

As a consequence of the loan being out of formula, MNC, pursuant to the financing agreement, exercised considerable control of the debtor's business operations. Each business day the debtor would submit a report disclosing daily information as to receivables and weekly data as to the inventory. In addition, the debtor submitted weekly reports denoting invoices received. The financing agreement also gave MNC reasonable access to the debtor's premises during regular business hours and at other reasonable times, in order to conduct audits of its collateral. Pursuant to the agreement, MNC conducted frequent audits of the debtor's operations. MNC used all of this information to calculate the value of its collateral, the daily loan balance, and the additional loan sums then available to the debtor. . . .

By the early part of 1984, MNC became concerned about the debtor's ability to repay its loan. At this time, MNC classified the loan in the "watch" category and further reduced the classification to "substandard" by October 1985. . . .

In May 1985, the debtor and MNC discussed plans to liquidate debtor's assets and repay all of the debtor's creditors. Robert Stewart [MNC's president] was aware of the liquidation plan, which was expected to be complete within three-five months with a "target date" of January 1, 1986. A condition of the plan was the debtor's reduction of the overadvance by $50,000 per week.

In September 1985, the debtor started to sell its assets. [From the proceeds of sales of debtor's subsidiaries, debtor paid MNC $3,217,300 and provided MNC with $560,000 in promissory notes as additional collateral.]

In the latter part of 1985, MNC decided to inventory the debtor's goods and sent Mr. Baldwin, MNC executive vice-president, to physically count all tobacco products. . . . Mr. Baldwin conducted three audits in the early-morning hours of January 8, 15, and 21, 1986. The inventories were conducted while the debtor was closed for business, and there was no one in the warehouse except the audit team and the debtor's representative. . . .

In expectation of an orderly liquidation, Michael Paolella began informing certain tobacco companies that he would not be renewing personal loan guarantees. He did not inform these companies, however, of his liquidation plans.

American Tobacco had previously obtained a letter of credit in the amount of $120,000 from the debtor secured by Maryland National Bank. The letter allowed American Tobacco to draw upon the letter if payment from the debtor was more than thirty days overdue. The letter required that American Tobacco be given . . . notice if the letter was to be canceled or not renewed. On January 3, 1986, twenty-two days before the deadline for notification, Maryland National Bank sent notice to American Tobacco that the letter of credit would not be renewed [with respect to invoices issued after January 10, 1986].

American Tobacco was aware that the letter of credit would not be renewed by January 9, 1986, when its employee, Frank Gallagher, contacted Michael Paolella regarding the notice of non-renewal. Gallagher wanted to ascertain whether the decision not to renew had been made by the debtor or by the bank. Gallagher was not entirely satisfied with Paolella's explanation that the non-renewal was the debtor's decision. Accordingly, he called Maryland National Bank and was referred to Cromwell at MNC. Gallagher called Cromwell on Wednesday, January 15, 1986, and Cromwell confirmed that the decision not to renew the letter of credit was the debtor's. It appears, however, that the decision not to renew the letter of credit was MNC's.

In the interim, American Tobacco, despite Gallagher's dissatisfaction with Michael Paolella's explanation regarding the letter of credit, continued to sell tobacco inventory to the debtor after January 10, 1986 and during the period when the letter of credit had expired.

[Through special buying programs announced by the tobacco plaintiffs in December 1985, the debtor purchased $1.9 million more inventory than usual in January 1986.]

On Tuesday, January 28, 1986, MNC decided not to advance the funds to honor the debtor's checks presented the previous day; Paolella was informed of this decision on Wednesday, January 29, 1986. Paolella told Cromwell that MNC should take over and operate the debtor. On Thursday, January 30, 1986, MNC notified the debtor that the loan was in default and requested immediate repayment of the entire balance and possession of all collateral securing the loan. In addition, Rick Sell, MNC's audit manager, took possession of the debtor's assets and secured the warehouse. . . .

Also on January 30, 1986, credit collection managers from several tobacco companies came to the debtor's business in Philadelphia after their companies learned that the debtor's checks had been dishonored by Maryland National Bank. On Friday, January 31, 1986, despite entreaties by Paolella that the debtor be given until Monday, February 3, 1986 to liquidate its assets, the tobacco company plaintiffs filed an involuntary bankruptcy petition against the debtor. . . .

[A trustee appointed by the Bankruptcy Court liquidated the debtor's assets, selling the inventory for $4.5 million, 75% of debtor's cost.] As a result of the trustee's liquidation of the estate, MNC received a distribution totaling $6,606,678.37. . . .

The five tobacco Company plaintiffs filed proofs of claim as follows: American Cigar — $23,923.40; American Tobacco — $283,671.51; Lorillard — $759,636.04; Philip Morris — $1,712,608.13; and Reynolds — $1,181,585.70. . . .

VI.   RECLAMATION UNDER THE UNIFORM COMMERCIAL CODE §2-702

[T]he five tobacco companies delivered reclamation notices to the debtor pursuant to [U.C.C. §2-702(2)], which states in pertinent part that "where seller discovers that the buyer has received goods on credit while insolvent he may reclaim the goods upon demand made within ten days after the receipt." However, [U.C.C. §2-702(3)] makes the seller's reclamation "subject to the rights of a buyer in ordinary course or other good faith purchaser under [U.C.C. §2-403]."

In this case, the parties agree that the debtor received the goods while insolvent and that the tobacco companies made demand to reclaim within ten days after receipt of the goods. Thus, the only issue remaining is whether MNC is a "good faith purchaser" for purposes of [U.C.C. §2-702(3)].

[The Court quoted Creeger Brick v. Mid-State Bank, 385 Pa. Super. 30, 560 A.2d 151 (Pa. Super. Ct. 1989):]

It seems reasonably clear from the decided cases that a lending institution does not violate a separate duty of good faith by adhering to its agreement with the borrower or by enforcing its legal and contractual rights as a creditor. The duty of good faith imposed upon contracting parties does not compel a lender to surrender rights which it has been given by statute or by the terms of its contract. . . . Similarly, Judge Easterbrook reasoned in Kham & Nate's Shoes:

> Firms that have negotiated contracts are entitled to enforce them to the let-ter, even to the great discomfort of their trading partners, without being mulcted for lack of "good faith." Although courts often refer to the obligation of good faith that exists in every contractual relation, this is not an invitation to the court to decide whether one party ought to have exercised privileges expressly reserved in the document. "Good faith" is a compact reference to an implied undertaking not to take opportunistic advantage in a way that could not have been contemplated at the time of drafting, and which there-fore was not resolved explicitly by the parties. When the contract is silent, principles of good faith — such as the UCC's §1-201(19) . . . fill the gap. They do not block use of terms that actually appear in the contract.

Kham & Nate's Shoes, 908 at 1357 (citations omitted). Thus, it is plain that under Pennsylvania law, a creditor that enforces a financing agree-ment in a manner consistent with the clear terms of the agreement and the expectations of the parties acts in "good faith."

In this case, the contract that must be examined to determine whether MNC acted in "good faith" is the financing agreement between MNC and the debtor. The Bankruptcy Judge found that MNC's overall plan, i.e., to gather information without alerting the other creditors of its future plan to cease funding the debtor when the warehouse was full, consti-tuted inequitable conduct that deprived MNC of its status as a "good faith purchaser" under [U.C.C. §2-702(2)]. Notably, the Bankruptcy Judge did not find that any of these actions were outside the scope of the financing agreement. It is clear from the Bankruptcy Judge's exhaustive ninety-three page opinion that MNC did not overstep its rights under the financing agreement. . . . [The court reversed the Bankruptcy Judge and denied reclamation.]

Today, it is a rare debtor whose inventory is not encumbered. The interpretation of U.C.C. §2-702(3) that recognizes the inventory secured lender as a good faith purchaser to whom the seller's right of reclamation is subject practically eviscerates the right of reclamation granted in U.C.C. §2-702(2). Inventory can no longer be reclaimed the moment the inventory security interest attaches.

5. Express or Implied Agreement with the Secured Creditor

The most direct means for a seller to protect itself against the buyer's inventory secured lender is by agreement with the secured lender. Inventory secured lenders often sincerely intend that the money they advance to the debtor be used to pay those who supply the inventory. If approached by the seller and debtor together with a request to do so, many inventory secured lenders will disburse loan proceeds directly to the seller to pay for the debtor's purchases. Some inventory secured lenders insist on doing so. An agreement by the inventory secured lender to pay for the goods is enforceable by action against the lender.

Ordinarily, however, the debtor does not want the secured lender to pay suppliers directly. Recall that when Sally Raj decided to open her stereo store, she could only do so if she could get a $40,000 float from her suppliers. Direct payment would eliminate the float. Suppliers are reluctant to insist on direct payment from the inventory secured lender if such payment is not customary in the industry. Such a request may imply to the inventory secured lender that the debtor is in financial difficulty. Rather than join in such a request, the debtor may take its business to a competing supplier.

Inventory secured lenders have another motive for not wanting to make direct payment. As you saw in *Paoella*, when a collapsing debtor manages to buy additional inventory on credit, the purchase can directly benefit the lender. To illustrate, assume that the liquidation value of the inventory of Sally's Stereo Store is $55,000 and the amount owing on the inventory loan is $60,000. If Sally can buy an additional $5,000 worth of inventory on unsecured credit, the new inventory will "feed the [bank's] lien" — that is, it will increase the amount of the collateral without increasing the amount of the debt. If the bank waits for the new inventory to arrive and then calls the loan without disbursing against it, the bank has shifted $5,000 of value from the supplier to themselves. To the extent that the bank agrees in advance to pay suppliers directly, it has eliminated the possibility that purchases such as these will feed its lien. The bank will be able to obtain additional collateral only by paying for it.

6. Equitable Subordination

The doctrine of equitable subordination exists under both state and bankruptcy law, but only the bankruptcy courts seem to have taken to it. The following excerpt is from the same opinion presented earlier in this assignment on reclamation. In it, the court makes clear its opinion that there is nothing inequitable about feeding a lien.

In re M. Paolella & Sons, Inc.
161 Bankr. 107 (E.D. Pa. 1993)

It is a long-standing principle that bankruptcy courts, sitting as courts of equity, have the authority to subordinate claims on equitable grounds. See, e.g., Pepper v. Litton, 308 U.S. 295, 60 S. Ct. 238, 245-46, 84 L. Ed. 281 (1939) (holding that bankruptcy courts have the equitable power "to sift the circumstances surrounding any claim to see that injustice is not done in the administration of the bankrupt estate"). Nevertheless, equitable subordination is an extraordinary departure from the "usual principles of equality of distribution and preference for secured creditors." In re Osborne, 42 Bankr. at 992.

Section 510(c) of the Bankruptcy Code codified pre-existing case law allowing bankruptcy courts to adjust the status of claims on equitable grounds. . . . Because of Congress' clear intent that §510 codify then-existing principles of equitable subordination, most courts applying the doctrine have adopted the three-prong test articulated by the United States Court of Appeals for the Fifth Circuit on the eve of the Bankruptcy Code's enactment:

> (i) The claimant must have engaged in some type of inequitable conduct.
> (ii) The misconduct must have resulted in injury to the creditors of the bankrupt or conferred an unfair advantage on the claimant.
> (iii) Equitable subordination of the claim must not be inconsistent with the provisions of the Bankruptcy Act.

In re Mobile Steel Co., 563 F.2d 692, 700 (5th Cir. 1977).

Although there is general acceptance of the Mobile Steel three-part test, courts have struggled to define the precise conduct that constitutes grounds for equitable subordination. Generally, there are three categories of conduct that satisfy the first prong of the three-part test: (1) fraud, illegality, or breach of fiduciary duties; (2) undercapitalization; and (3) claimant's use of the debtor as a mere instrumentality or alter ego.

Further, in applying equitable subordination principles, the courts differentiate between insider and non-insider claimants. As stated in In re Teltronics Servs., Inc., 29 Bankr. 139, 169 (Bankr. E.D.N.Y. 1983):

> The primary distinctions between subordinating the claims of insiders versus those of non-insiders lie in the severity of misconduct required to be shown, and the degree to which the court will scrutinize the claimant's actions toward the debtor or its creditors.

. . . Whether a claimant is an insider is a question of fact and subject to review under the "clearly erroneous" standard. Although "insider" is defined by the Bankruptcy Code at 11 U.S.C. §101(31), courts applying the doctrine of equitable subordination look beyond the statutory definition and examine whether the party has attained fiduciary status by exercising control of the debtor. Thus, courts have found that control over the debtor may render non-insiders "fiduciaries" for purposes of equitable subordination; however, such control must be "virtually complete." In re Osborne, 42 Bankr. at 997. In *Teltronics*, the court summarized the "control" required to find that a creditor is a fiduciary of the debtor:

> The cases cited above strongly suggest that a non-insider creditor will be held to a fiduciary standard only where his ability to command the debtor's obedience to his policy directives is so overwhelming that there has been, to some extent, a merger of identity. Unless the creditor has become the alter ego of the debtor, he will not be held to an ethical duty in excess of the morals of the marketplace.

Teltronics, 29 Bankr. at 171 (citing Rader v. Boyd, 252 F.2d 585, 587 (10th Cir. 1958)).

In this case, the Bankruptcy Judge found that MNC did not participate in the debtor's management, determine its operating decisions, or have any presence on its board. It was Michael Paolella who controlled the debtor, who decided that the debtor would participate in tobacco company purchase programs, and who decided that the debtor would expand and then later liquidate. We agree with the Bankruptcy Court's finding that MNC is neither an insider nor a fiduciary of the debtor. . . .

Equitable subordination has seldom been invoked, much less successfully so, in cases involving non-insiders and/or non-fiduciaries. As Judge Easterbrook pointed out in Kham & Nate's Shoes No. 2, Inc. v. First Bank, 908 F.2d 1351, 1356 (7th Cir. 1990), "cases subordinating the claims of creditors that dealt at arm's length with the debtor are few and far between." The dearth of cases subordinating the claims of non-insiders is readily explained by the high threshold of misconduct that must be established by the objectant in non-insider cases. In In re Osborne, 42 Bankr. 988, 996 (W.D. Wis. 1984), the court discussed the conduct required for equitable subordination in non-insider cases:

> [The degree of misconduct] has been variously described as "very substantial" misconduct involving "moral turpitude or some breach of duty or some misrepresentation whereby other creditors were deceived to their damage" or as gross misconduct amounting to fraud, overreaching or spoliation.

Although courts have struggled to articulate the misconduct that must be established to subordinate non-insider claims, it is clear that the non-insider's misconduct must be "gross or egregious.". . .

V.   THE BANKRUPTCY COURT'S CONCLUSIONS
OF LAW REGARDING EQUITABLE SUBORDINATION

... For purposes of the doctrine of equitable subordination, it is not inequitable for a non-insider creditor to monitor a debtor closely, pursuant to a valid financing agreement, for the purpose of choosing the most advantageous time to foreclose on a loan that has been out of formula for several years. Not only is it not inequitable conduct, but MNC would have been derelict in its duty to its own stockholders and depositors, if it had failed to obtain additional information so as to exercise its contractual right not to lend at a propitious time relative to tobacco company creditors. This principle has even more force in cases such as this one, where the Bankruptcy Judge found that all creditors were aware of the debtor's precarious financial position. Accordingly, there was no reliance by any creditor that MNC would continue funding; nor was there an explicit or implicit promise by MNC to continue funding. Indeed, the Bankruptcy Judge found that the tobacco plaintiffs knew that the debtor was overleveraged and knew that there was a risk that MNC might declare the loan in default or refuse to advance additional loan funds or make available to the debtor the proceeds of its receivables. Yet, knowing for some time of the substantial risk of nonpayment of their outstanding invoices, these tobacco companies continued making unsecured loans to the debtor. Within this context, MNC's conduct hardly can be considered inequitable under the doctrine of equitable subordination. As discussed by the Fifth Circuit Court of Appeals in In re Clark Pipe, 870 F.2d 1022, 1024 (5th Cir. 1989), withdrawn by 893 F.2d 693 (5th Cir. 1990), it is not gross or egregious misconduct warranting equitable subordination of a lender's claim to monitor the debtor closely; to extend sufficient funds so as to improve the lender's position at the expense of the other creditors; and to refuse to supply further funds at a propitious moment on a loan that is in default. Banks are not "eleemosynary institutions" required to "throw good money after bad." Kham & Nate's Shoes, 908 F.2d at 1358 (Easterbrook, J.).

---

7.   Unjust Enrichment

Recall that the unsecured creditors who fed the secured creditors' lien in Peerless Packing Co., Inc. v. Malone & Hyde, Inc. in Assignment 16 sued for unjust enrichment. The court denied recovery, stating that "an unjust enrichment claim is not applicable in a U.C.C. case because "the purpose and effectiveness of the U.C.C. would be substantially impaired if interests created in compliance with U.C.C. procedure could be defeated by application of the equitable doctrine of unjust enrichment."

Since *Peerless*, the courts have become more receptive to unjust enrichment claims, but only slightly. In what is perhaps the leading case today, the Supreme Court of Colorado said:

> The central issue in this case is whether a creditor that holds a perfected security interest in collateral can be held liable to an unsecured creditor based on a theory of unjust enrichment for benefits that enhance the value of the collateral. We conclude that this question cannot be answered categorically. Such a dispute involves tension between the priority system established in Article 9 of the Uniform Commercial Code (UCC or the Code) and equitable principles of unjust enrichment. Although the policies underlying the UCC support a uniform, reliable system of priorities among creditors, we are unwilling to hold that alteration of that hierarchy of priorities is never necessary to implement the equitable principles on which the doctrine of unjust enrichment is based. There is obvious tension between the doctrine of unjust enrichment and the priority system established by Article 9. When an unsecured creditor confers a benefit upon a secured creditor by adding to or enhancing the creditor's collateral and a claim for unjust enrichment against the secured creditor is recognized, the secured creditor in effect loses its priority status despite its compliance with the procedures set forth in Article 9. We have recognized in other settings, however, that the scope of the remedy under the doctrine of unjust enrichment "is broad, cutting across both contract and tort law, with its application guided by the underlying principle of avoiding the unjust enrichment of one party at the expense of another." [Cablevision of Breckenridge v. Tannhauser Condominium Assn., 649 P.2d 1093, 1096-1097 (Colo. 1982)]. . . .
>
> The UCC priority system thus reflects the legislative judgment that the value of a predictable system of priorities ordinarily outweighs the disadvantage of the system's occasional inequities. At the same time, however, the Code recognizes that equitable principles may require alteration of the priority system in particular circumstances.
>
> In a situation where a secured creditor initiates or encourages transactions between the debtor and suppliers of goods or services, and benefits from the goods or services supplied to produce such debts, equitable principles require that the secured creditor compensate even an unsecured creditor to avoid being unjustly enriched. The equitable claim is at its strongest when the goods or services are necessary to preserve the security, as in *Producers Cotton Oil*. A secured creditor can protect itself from unjust enrichment claims by remaining uninvolved or by informing the proper parties of its intent not to pay for debts incurred in maintaining, enhancing, or making additions to secured collateral.

Ninth District Production Credit Association v. Ed. Duggan, Inc., 821 P.2d 788 (Colo. 1991).

Problem Set 35

35.1. a. The Faith Diamond was stolen from the Faith Family Museum. The thief sold it to Borges, a professional fence. Borges sold it to Madame Downs, an English baroness who claims not to have known Borges's true profession at the time. Her story is made somewhat more credible by the fact that she paid the reasonable value of the diamond, not the reduced price that a stolen diamond would be expected to bring. If a representative of the Faith Family Museum claims the diamond from Madame Downs, who wins?

b. Add some facts. The representative didn't find the diamond that quickly. Instead, Madame Downs took the diamond to Fairchild and Sons, a retail jewelry store, and selected a setting for a diamond ring. The proprietor suggested that Madame Downs stop back in a week to pick up her ring. During the week, Fairchild and Sons sold the diamond to Curtis Whittington, a customer who visited Fairchild's store in the Flamingo Mall. Whittington grossly overpaid for the diamond and had no suspicion of its tortured history. Fairchild and Sons filed for bankruptcy. When Whittington made a gift of the ring to the Guru Maraji during his U.S. tour, the story hit the newspapers. The Museum, Madame Downs, the trustee in bankruptcy for Fairchild and Sons, Curtis Whittington, and the Guru all claim the diamond. Now who prevails?

35.2. You represent Foster Musical Manufacturing, a small company that manufactures musical instruments and sells them directly to retail stores. In the past two years, it has suffered a number of losses when customers have gone out of business or filed for bankruptcy. Each time, an inventory secured lender has taken possession of some of Foster's products and sold them. Frances Foster, the owner of Foster Musical Manufacturing, wants to do something about it. "Don't tell me to raise our prices to cover these losses," Frances tells you. "We can't. Our good customers will just go elsewhere; they don't want to pay for our bad customers."

a. Would selling on consignment do any good? U.C.C. §§1-201(37), 9-103(d) 9-109(a), 9-319(a), 9-324(b).

b. Could Frances use her right of reclamation to protect herself? U.C.C. §2-703, Bankruptcy Code §546(c).

c. Can you think of anything else that might help?

35.3. When the customer pictured in the cartoon on the following page sues the airline to whom his luggage was sold, who wins? United States airlines sell more than 73,000 pieces of luggage each year to dealers in lost luggage. The dealers operate stores, principally in Scottsboro, Alabama, through which they sell individual items to the public. The airline in the cartoon is likely to have one or more

"BECAUSE OF FINANCIAL DIFFICULTIES, WE SOLD YOUR LUGGAGE TO ANOTHER AIRLINE."

Reprinted with special permission of North American Syndicate.

employees who specialize in selling the lost luggage. U.C.C. §§1-201(9), 2-104(1), and 2-403.

35.4. Your client is Willis Trillian, a novelist of considerable repute. Willis has asked you to take a look at the contract he is about to sign with Big Brown Publishing for publication of his latest book. The contract provides that:

1) The Author hereby grants and assigns to the Publisher . . . the sole and exclusive right to publish, cause to be published, sell, and license others to sell, in book form or in any other form, in the United States of America and elsewhere, in the English language and in any other language, the work tentatively entitled "Blood, Sex, and Secured Credit."

2) The Publisher agrees to pay to the author, his representatives or assigns a royalty of 15 percent of the amount charged by the Publisher for copies of said Work, less returns.

3) The Publisher shall register the copyright in said work in the name of the Author and the Author shall remain the owner absolute of such copyright.

Big Brown was recently acquired by Paramount Communications. The rumors are that Big Brown was heavily leveraged in the transaction, but you cannot confirm those rumors because Big Brown is privately held and does not disclose financial information. Willis wonders what would happen to him if Big Brown went belly up. At your last meeting he pointed out that "if worse came to worse, at least I'd still have the copyright, wouldn't I?" Would he? What will happen to Willis if Big Brown goes belly up? If Big Brown won't change the deal, what is your advice? U.C.C. §9-109(a)(1).

35.5. Harley Davidson (your old friend and client from Assignment 32) is back. After a short stint in the unemployment lines, Harley is now a loan officer for SwissBank, Ltd. SwissBank ("Not really a bank," Harley tells you, "but they've got a lot of money and they make a lot of loans") has some nasty exposure on a chain of gift shops called Gift of Love. Gift of Love is "headed for the tank," Harley says. A balance outstanding of $950,000 is on a demand note, secured by inventory worth not more than $400,000. Accounts receivable are also covered, but they are minimal because most customers use charge cards and the debits are processed very quickly. Harley's manager has authorized him to call the loan, but Harley has what he thinks is a better idea. In four months, the Christmas season will begin. By then, Gift of Love will have drawn down the remaining $50,000 on its $1 million line of credit. Then, in a period of about two months, their inventory will increase to $700,000. "We wait for the additional inventory to arrive and then we call the loan," Harley tells you. "Unless the folks at Gift of Love are real idiots, they file Chapter 11, we get adequate protection on a secured claim of $700,000, and we finish the Christmas season hand in hand. We lose $300,000 instead of $550,000." What do you tell Harley? U.C.C. §§2-702, 9-322(a)(1), 9-324(b); Bankr. Code §§506(a) and 510(c).

Assignment 36: Buyers Against Secured Creditors

A. Introduction

In the preceding chapter we discussed property that came in the debtor's door and fell under the spell of the secured creditor's earlier security interest. In this assignment we look at property that goes out the debtor's door and may or may not fall out of that spell.

Secured creditors have a variety of expectations about possible sale of their collateral by the debtor. The bank that lends against the inventory of a retail store typically expects the debtor to sell the collateral and apply the proceeds to payment of the debt or the purchase of new inventory that will serve as collateral. The insurance company that provides financing for an apartment building may expect the debtor to sell the building without paying off the loan, but, if so, the insurance company expects that its mortgage will continue to encumber the building in the hands of its new owner. The finance company that makes a car loan may expect the debtor to repay the loan in full as a condition of selling the car. All these scenarios share two characteristics. First, the secured creditor recognizes that the debtor has the right to sell the collateral. Security does not interfere with the free alienability of property. See U.C.C. §9-401. Second, the secured creditor expects to be protected as to the *value* of its interest. The protection may be in the form of a lien on the proceeds the debtor receives from the buyer, a continuing lien on the collateral in the hands of the buyer, payment of the loan, or some combination of these protections.

Buyers have a variety of expectations as to what, if anything, they must do to make sure they get good title to what they buy. The consumer who buys a refrigerator from a store in the mall does not expect to search the public records, but does expect to be protected against preexisting security interests. This expectation of protection without search is not limited to consumers: After all, Sears doesn't search the U.C.C. records when it buys refrigerators from a manufacturer or wholesaler either. But buyers of real estate have a very different set of expectations. Even the young couple buying their first home are likely to be aware of the expectation that there must be a search of the real estate records and, if there is not, they may find that the property they buy could be saddled with mortgages that others were supposed to pay. The buyer of a negotiable instrument does not expect to search public records, but probably knows that it must take possession of the instrument at the time it buys or risk taking subject to a security interest in favor of the person who does have possession.

It is possible to view these expectations as the product of law. When doing that, we might say, for example, that the buyer of real estate must search because the law subjects its title to mortgages of record, including those of which the buyer is not aware. But it may be more useful to view the law as the product of these expectations. When doing that, we might say that the law subjects the buyer's title to mortgages of record because the custom of searching is so strong that the buyer *should* know of them.

B. Buyers of Real Property

The general rule resolves the competition between buyer and mortgagee on the basis of first in time. That is, if the mortgage was created before the debtor sold the property to the buyer, the buyer takes subject to the mortgage. If the sale takes place first, it will be free of a later mortgage granted by the debtor-seller. A recording statute may reverse either of these results. One who buys in good faith, for value, without notice of an unrecorded mortgage may take free of it under the recording statute. Similarly, one who takes a mortgage in good faith, for value, without notice of an unrecorded deed may have priority over the rights of the buyer pursuant to the recording statute. If a mortgage is recorded before the debtor sells the property, its priority over the rights of the purchaser is pretty much absolute. All purchasers of real property are expected to search the public record, are deemed to have notice (*constructive notice*) of duly recorded mortgages, and take subject to them. No exceptions are recognized for sales in the ordinary course of business or even sales to consumers.

To illustrate, assume that Bob Mason sees a magazine ad for five-acre tracts of land in the Rocky Mountains. He calls the Mountain Development offices in Denver and they send a salesman to Bob's home in New York. In good faith, Bob pays the salesman $20,000 in return for a deed that recites conveyance of lot 237 "free and clear of all liens and encumbrances." Unknown to Bob, American Finance holds a first mortgage against Mountain's entire inventory of lots, including lot 237, to secure a $1.2 million loan American made to

Mountain Development. American recorded their mortgage in Colorado before Bob purchased the lot. Bob is a bona fide purchaser for value, but he nevertheless takes lot 237 subject to the $1.2 million mortgage. Although Bob did not search the public record and therefore did not know of the mortgage before paying his money, the law regards that as his fault, not his virtue. Consumer Bob, like every other purchaser of real property, is expected to search, and takes with constructive notice of all duly recorded mortgages.

If the mortgage exists but remains unrecorded at the time Bob buys lot 237, the recording statute of the state will govern the validity of the mortgage against Bob. Recording statutes, which we discussed in Assignment 20, apply to conveyances by deed to purchasers, as well as conveyances to lenders by mortgage.

The applicable statute may be a pure *race statute*, such as the North Carolina statute reproduced in Assignment 33. It may be a *notice-race statute*, such as the New York statute also reproduced in Assignment 33. In either case, Bob will prevail so long as he records his deed before American records its mortgage. If the statute is a pure *notice statute*, such as the Massachusetts statute also reproduced in Assignment 33, Bob will prevail even if American records after Bob buys but before Bob files. (Remember, this is a buyer against an unperfected security interest.) Thus, in general, a bona fide purchaser of real estate for value will take free of a prior unrecorded mortgage if that purchaser records before the mortgage holder.

Had Bob contacted a lawyer, the lawyer would have recommended a search of the public records before Bob paid for the land. The search would have discovered the mortgage. It then would have been up to the debtor, Mountain Development, to obtain a release of lot 237 from American's mortgage. Bob would simply have refused to pay the purchase price until the record title to lot 237 was clear.

The importance of searching title has become so much a part of real estate purchases and sales that in every state some group — usually lawyers or title companies — routinely handles sales, checking all the paperwork to make certain that liens have been properly cleared from the property before the purchase money is released to the seller. Title searches also explain why it takes so much longer to buy a home than it takes to buy a car or a stereo, even when the latter sales are financed and the goods are valuable.

C. Buyers of Personal Property

The general rule governing sales of encumbered personal property is essentially the same as the general rule governing sales of real estate:

Buyers take subject to encumbrances of record. The personal property rule is reflected in U.C.C. §§9-201 and 9-315(a). The former section provides that "a security agreement is effective . . . against [subsequent] purchasers." The latter provides that even in the absence of a provision to that effect, "a security interest continues in collateral notwithstanding sale." The personal property rule is, however, subject to considerably more exceptions than is the corresponding rule of real property law.

1. The Authorized Disposition Exception: U.C.C. §9-315(a)(1)

The *authorized disposition exception* appears in U.C.C. §9-315(a)(2). The security interest does not continue in the collateral if "the secured party authorized the disposition free of the security interest."

This exception is broader than may at first appear. First, the exception does not depend for its operation on equities in favor of the buyer. It can apply in favor of a buyer who did or did not search the public record. It can apply in favor of a buyer who knows or does not know of the security interest or the secured creditor's authorization to sell.

Second, the authorization to sell need not be express. In numerous cases, the courts have held that a secured creditor who knew that the debtor was making sales of collateral in violation of provisions of the security agreement thereby waived the provisions and "authorized" the sale so that the buyer took free of the security interest. For example, in Gretna State Bank v. Cornbelt Livestock Co., 463 N.W.2d 795 (Neb. 1990), the bank held a security interest in the debtor's cows and hogs, which were farm products under U.C.C. §9-102(a)(34). The security agreement expressly prohibited sale of the collateral without the prior written consent of the bank. The debtor sold some of the cattle without written consent and the bank sued the buyer. The court held that the bank's security interest did not continue in the cattle after their sale because the sale was "authorized" within the meaning of U.C.C. §9-315(a)(1). The court relied on the fact that the debtor previously had sold cattle and hogs without the bank's written consent on numerous occasions, the bank knew about many of those sales, and the bank had not objected to them or rebuked the debtor for having made them. The court concluded that the bank had thereby waived the security agreement provision requiring its consent to sales and authorized such later sales as the debtor might make. This problem would rarely arise with regard to inventory, for reasons presented in the next section.

For the authorized disposition exception to apply under revised Article 9, the authorization must be to dispose of the collateral free of the security interest. This element of the authorization also can be express or implied.

But revised Article 9 leaves unresolved a split of authority as to conditional authorizations. To illustrate, assume that Gretna State Bank holds a security interest in cattle owned by Cornbelt Livestock Co. Gretna authorizes Cornbelt to sell 30 head of cattle free of Gretna's security interest, but only on the condition that Cornbelt immediately pay the proceeds of sale to Gretna as a payment on the loan. Cornbelt sells the cattle to Butler, receives the proceeds from Butler, but does not pay them to Gretna. In an action by Gretna to enforce its security interest in the cattle now owned by Butler, the courts split. Some treat the disposition as authorized; others do not. The courts are more likely to treat the disposition as authorized if Butler knows of the condition, but that factor is not determinative.

2.   The Buyer-in-the-Ordinary-Course Exception: U.C.C. §9-320(a)

Every purchaser of real estate is expected to search the public records before paying the purchase price and is deemed to have notice of what it would have found. The same is not true for buyers of most kinds of personal property. An obvious example is the shopper at a grocery store. To charge such a buyer with constructive notice of what the buyer would have found on a search of the public records under the name of the grocery store would be absurd. One might think that the distinction in what the law expects of a real estate shopper and a personal property shopper results from the difference in the amounts of money involved. Perhaps the amounts typically involved in the two kinds of transactions contributed to the decision to make the real/personal distinction. But we think the distinction is principally an accident of history perpetuated by custom. Some real estate purchases involve only a few hundred dollars, but the system expects a search; some personal property purchases involve millions of dollars, but the system does not. In addition, a search is expected for some kinds of personal property, including automobiles, aircraft, and intellectual property. Whatever the reason, the system does not require those who buy and sell most kinds of personal property in the ordinary course of business to play the search-and-file game.

The ordinary course of whose business? Under U.C.C. §9-320(a), a buyer in the ordinary course of business can take free of a security interest created by its seller. "Buyer in the ordinary course of business" is defined in revised U.C.C. §1-201(9). "Buying" is "in the ordinary course" only if it is "from a person in the business of selling goods of that kind." Thus, the buy must be in the ordinary course of the *seller's* business, not the *buyer's* business. To illustrate, assume that Linda Westerbrook buys and sells used traffic lights. State Street Bank holds a perfected security interest in her inventory. When she sells a traffic light to Peter Kollander (who knows nothing about how Linda finances her business) and installs it in his living room, the sale is in the ordinary course of Linda's business, U.C.C. §9-320(a) applies, and Peter takes free of State Street's security interest. When Linda buys a used traffic light from Disney World, U.C.C. §9-320(a) does not apply. This buy is in the ordinary course of Linda's business. Selling traffic lights is not in the ordinary course of Disney World's business, although it may sell a traffic light from time to time. Linda would not take free of a security interest granted by Disney World to its bank.

In the foregoing example, it was a consumer buyer who took free of a security interest granted by his seller. U.C.C. §9-320(a) is not limited to consumer buyers. If Linda sold one of her traffic lights to Neiman Marcus, for display or for resale, Neiman Marcus would be a buyer in the ordinary course of Linda's business, and they would take free of the State Street Bank security interest.

The buyer's knowledge. U.C.C. §9-320(a) protects a buyer in the ordinary course of business "even though the buyer knows of [the security interest's] existence." U.C.C. §1-201(9) limits "buyer in the ordinary course of business" in a manner that may at first seem to contradict U.C.C. §9-320(a). One cannot be a buyer in the ordinary course if one knows "that the sale to him is in violation of the . . . security interest of a third party." Comment 3 to U.C.C. §9-320 explains: "Reading the definition together with the rule of law results in the buyer's taking free if the buyer merely knows that a security interest covers the goods but taking subject if the buyer knows, in addition, that the sale violates a term in an agreement with the secured party." In other words, merely knowing that Neiman Marcus has granted a security interest in its inventory should not prevent shopper Edith Parker from taking free of the security interest under U.C.C. §9-320(a). Many, if not most, businesses that sell goods from inventory have granted security interests in their inventories. Those security agreements almost invariably authorize the debtors to sell the collateral free and clear of the security interests. U.C.C. §9-320(a) entitles Edith to assume that is true of every merchant's inventory security agreement until she learns otherwise.

As we noted above, some inventory security agreements impose conditions on the sale of collateral. For example, a bank that finances the inventory of a yacht dealer may want to be involved in and scrutinize every sale. The security agreement employed in such a relationship may prohibit sales of yachts from inventory except with the express written consent of the bank for sale to the particular buyer. A customer who knows that this dealer has inventory financing will not be bound by this sale condition if it does not know of it, but will be bound if it does. If the customer knowingly buys in violation of the condition, the customer takes subject to the bank's security interest.

"Created by his seller." Assume that First National Bank holds a security interest in all personal property owned by Disney World, including its single traffic light, to secure a loan in the amount of $90 million. Disney World sells the traffic light to Linda in a sale that is not in the ordinary course of Disney World business. As previously noted, Linda takes subject to First National's security interest. Not realizing that the traffic light is encumbered, Linda sells it to Neiman Marcus. Does Neiman Marcus take free of First National's security interest under U.C.C. §9-320(a)? The answer is no. Although Neiman Marcus is a buyer in the ordinary course of business, under U.C.C. §9-320(a), it only takes free of "a security interest created by [its] seller," Linda Westerbrook. It does not take free of security interests created by her predecessors in title.

The effects of this limitation of U.C.C. §9-320(a) become even more surprising when Neiman Marcus decides to sell vintage traffic lights as a Christmas special from their store in the Galleria Mall. When Christmas shopper Edith Parker buys one as a gift for her husband George, both may be in for a surprise. The traffic light inside their gift-wrapped package may have a $90 million perfected security interest firmly attached to it. Should Disney World default on its debt to First National, the Bank may hunt George down and repossess the traffic light. (One of us heard a GMAC representative refer to this as "going knocking on doors.")

The farm products exception. U.C.C. §9-320(a) affords no protection to those who buy farm products. But the federal Food Security Act provides parallel protection. That law provides:

> Except as provided in subsection (e) and notwithstanding any other provision of Federal, State, or local law, a buyer who in the ordinary course of business buys a farm product from a seller engaged in farming operations shall take free of a security interest created by the seller, even though the security interest is perfected; and the buyer knows of the existence of such interest.

7 U.S.C. §1631(d) (1994). The exceptions in subsection (e) of §1631 provide farm lenders with various ways of notifying prospective buyers of their security interests. The security interests of lenders who do give notice continue in the collateral notwithstanding sale. The result is that farm lenders can preserve their security interests somewhat more easily than nonfarm lenders. The details of the Food Security Act system are, however, outside the scope of this book. For our purposes it is sufficient to see that the farm products exception of U.C.C. §9-320(a) may not be much of an exception at all.

When does a buyer become a buyer? At the moment a bankruptcy petition is filed or the moment that a secured creditor takes possession of its collateral, there typically will be persons who have contracted to buy some of the collateral but who have not yet completed their transactions. If such a person is a "buyer" within the meaning of U.C.C. §9-320(a), the person will take free of the inventory lender's security agreement and be able to keep what was bought. If the person has paid part of the purchase price, the person will get credit for that part, and owe the balance. If the person is not yet a "buyer," the person is merely an unsecured creditor of the seller for any part of the purchase price paid and for the benefit of the bargain the person has lost. Particularly if the person has paid part of the purchase price in advance, the moment when the person becomes a "buyer" within the meaning of U.C.C. §9-320(a) can be of tremendous importance. As the following case illustrates, there are many permutations of this problem and much remaining uncertainty.

Daniel v. Bank of Hayward

425 N.W.2d 416 (Wis. 1988)

SHIRLEY S. ABRAHAMSON, J. . . .

This case presents the following issue: When does a retail purchaser who makes a down payment on a motor vehicle but does not take title to the vehicle become a "buyer in ordinary course of business" under [U.C.C. §1-201(9)] and [U.C.C. §9-320(a)] to prevail over the security interest of the motor vehicle dealer's floor plan financier? . . .

In Chrysler Corp. v. Adamatic, 59 Wis.2d 219, 208 N.W.2d 97 (1972), this court concluded that a purchaser becomes a buyer in ordinary course of business when he or she takes title to the goods. . . . We conclude that the purchasers in this case became buyers in ordinary course of business when the vehicle was identified to the contract. To the extent that our decision in the *Chrysler* case is inconsistent with our decision in this case, we overrule the *Chrysler* case.

The facts in the record are undisputed. Joseph and Marijane Daniel, the purchasers, entered into a motor vehicle purchase contract in May 1983 with Don Hofstadter, Inc., a motor vehicle dealership in the City of Hayward. The purchasers agreed to purchase a 1984 Chevrolet van which had not yet been manufactured and to trade in the older motor home. According to the contract, the cash price of the vehicle was $12,077.55; the trade-in allowance was $8,675.55; and the amount the purchasers owed on delivery was $3,402.00. The contract described the motor vehicle and its various accessories but did not set forth the vehicle identification number because the vehicle had not been manufactured when the contract was signed.

The purchasers signed over title to their existing motor home and delivered the home to the dealership. The dealership sold the motor home on or about June 6, 1983. The record does not reflect how much the dealership received on the sale of the motor home, and it is not clear whether the Bank received any of the proceeds.

The dealership did its financing, including floor plan financing on new vehicles, with defendant Bank of Hayward (Bank). The floor plan financing operated as follows: There was a master note in the original sum of $150,000 dated April 19, 1982. When the dealership would order a new vehicle from General Motors, the Bank would receive a copy of that order. Prior to GM's delivery of the new vehicle to the dealership, GM would send the Bank a sight draft which included the vehicle identification number. The Bank would then prepare an individual floor plan note in the amount of the draft and the dealership would sign it. When the individual note was signed by the dealership, the Bank would pay GM. GM would then send the Manufacturer's Statement of Origin (MSO) to the Bank which retained the MSO. Because the MSO is necessary to obtain title to the motor vehicle, the Bank effectively controlled delivery of title to the retail purchaser and ensured itself of being paid. This procedure was unusual. Ordinarily, GM would send the MSO directly to the dealership. The Bank used the unusual procedure in this case because it was concerned about the financial status of the dealership.

On September 30, 1983, the Bank received a sight draft from General Motors for the van the purchasers had ordered. The dealership executed a floor plan note in the amount of $9,905.22 to pay General Motors for a 1984 Chevrolet van, I.D. No. 1GCGG35M6E7105325. The parties agree that the van bearing this identification number is the vehicle the purchasers ordered. The Floor Plan Note conveyed a security interest in the van to the Bank on September 30, 1983.

Sometime on Friday, October 21, 1983, the Chevrolet van was delivered to the dealership. On Saturday, October 22, 1983, the Bank discovered that its debtor, the dealership, was removing used vehicles from the lots. Because these used vehicles were collateral for the Bank's loans, the Bank called all loans and secured the lot so that no vehicles could be removed. The purchasers' Chevrolet van was among the new vehicles on the lot when the Bank took possession of the dealership's premises.

On October 24, 1983, the purchasers went to the dealership to complete the purchase of the van. . . .

The Bank was willing to release the van only if the purchasers paid in full the Bank's interest in the van pursuant to the Floor Plan Note, namely, $9,905.22. According to their contract with the dealership, the purchasers did not owe the dealership $9,905.22. By virtue of the trade-in, the purchasers owed the dealership only $3,402.00. Because the purchasers needed the van to go to Florida, they [paid] $9,905.22 . . . and they then took title to and possession of the van. They brought this action against the Bank to recover damages "to the extent of the over-payment together with consequential damages including interest on the monies that plaintiff had to borrow to meet the extorted demands of the bank, actual attorney's fees incurred and a great inconvenience all to their damage in the sum of $15,000."

As we stated previously, the sole question in this case is: When do purchasers who make a down payment under a contract for sale and have not taken title to the vehicle achieve the status of buyer in ordinary course of business? If the purchasers in this case became buyers in ordinary course of business prior to the Bank's seizing the van, their interest in the van takes priority over the Bank's perfected security interest.

We examine first the relevant provisions of the Wisconsin Uniform Commercial Code. [U.C.C. Article 9] establishes a priority system for determining the rights of parties who claim competing interests in secured property. As a general rule, the holder of a perfected security interest has an interest in the secured property which is superior to the interests of the debtor, unsecured creditors of the debtor and subsequent purchasers of the secured property. [U.C.C. §9-201] thus protects the secured creditor. The Code provides, however, exceptions to the rule that the secured creditor has priority over purchasers of the collateral. A principal exception to the rule is found in [U.C.C. §9-320(a)], captioned "protection of buyers of goods," which permits a buyer in ordinary course of business as defined in [U.C.C. §1-201(9)] to take free of a security interest created by the seller. The Code thus recognizes a potential conflict between the buyer in ordinary course of business and the seller's secured creditor and attempts to seek a fair accommodation between the two. [The court set forth the provisions of U.C.C. §9-320(a).] [U.C.C. §9-320(a)] severs the inventory lender's security interest in favor of the buyer in ordinary course of business. In order to prevail over the Bank's perfected security interest, the purchasers in this case must qualify as buyers in ordinary course of business, as that term is defined in [U.C.C. §1-201(9)]. [The court set forth the provisions of U.C.C. §1-201(9).] The exception for a buyer in ordinary course of business accommodates the interests of all parties. Buyers desire to be free of the lender's interest after they have committed themselves to paying for the goods. A buyer cannot easily determine how the seller finances its inventory, nor can the buyer afford to negotiate subordination agreements with the seller's lenders for each purchase made. Secured creditors at some point expect to surrender their security interest in the goods and look to the proceeds of a sale for repayment of the loan. The secured creditor thus depends on the goods being sold. The secured lender expects a constant flow of inventory in and out of the seller's possession; it is usually in the business of lending funds and is in a better position to take precautions against the loss of its security.

Although the Code protects the buyer in ordinary course of business, the Code provides no explicit guidance to the question presented in this case, namely when does a purchaser under a contract for sale achieve the status of buyer in ordinary course of business. There are at least five possible dates on which a purchaser may be viewed as having achieved the status of buyer in ordinary course of business: (1) the date of initial contract; (2) the date the goods are identified; (3) the date title passes to the purchaser; (4) the date the purchaser gets delivery; and (5) the date the purchaser accepts the goods.[1]

Relying on Chrysler Corp. v. Adamatic, 59 Wis.2d 219, 208 N.W.2d 97 (1973), the Bank maintains that the purchasers can not become buyers in ordinary course of business who take free of the seller's secured creditor until the purchasers take title or delivery of the van. Because the purchasers in this case did not take title or delivery, the Bank contends that the purchasers do not take free of its interest as the dealership's secured creditor. . . .

We have reconsidered our analysis in *Chrysler* and are persuaded by the reasoning of the commentators and courts which have, since our decision in Chrysler Corp. v. Adamatic, addressed the issue presented in this case. The commentators and courts have, for the most part, opted for an earlier date than the date that title passed as the time when a purchaser achieves the status of a buyer in ordinary course of business.

We conclude that we erred in relying on the date of transfer of title as the date on which a purchaser becomes a buyer in ordinary course of business. Reliance on the concept of title is contrary to the thrust of the Uniform Commercial Code and the commentary. The drafters of the Uniform Commercial Code tried to avoid giving technical rules of title a central role in furthering the policies of the Uniform Commercial Code. See [U.C.C. §§2-401, 9-202]. Although title questions may be of significance in determining some issues under the Code, we conclude that reliance on title to interpret [U.C.C. §9-320(a)] is an unduly narrow and technical interpretation. . . .

Courts have overwhelmingly rejected a definition of buyer in ordinary course that focuses on whether title has passed. These courts reason that the inventory financier is better able to guard against the risks inherent in this type of financing than is the average retail buyer because the financier is more knowledgeable and has the resources to guard against the risks. These courts conclude that placing the burden on the buyer would inhibit retail sales.

Furthermore, focusing on the words "in ordinary course," these courts reason that a court must consider the substance of the transaction; a court must look to the customary manner in which sales are made in the seller's business and to the expectations of the buyer under the contract. The language "in ordinary course" indicates deference to commercial

1. In similar but not precisely the same fact situations, several courts have adopted dates ranging from initial contract through identification.

practice and is consistent with the purposes and policies underlying the Code "[t]o permit the continued expansion of commercial practices through custom, usage and agreement of the parties." [U.C.C. §1-102(2)(b)]. If it is customary in the seller's business to sell goods in a particular manner (e.g., seller and purchaser enter into a contract for sale and purchaser makes a down payment), then the court may find that the purchaser who makes a down payment without taking title is a "buyer in ordinary course of business."

The purchasers in this case ask the court to reject the title or delivery date in this case and adopt an "identification" date as the date on which they became buyers in ordinary course of business. The purchasers rely on [U.C.C. §2-501(1)], which provides that a buyer obtains a special property interest on identification. [U.C.C. §2-501(1)] provides:

> The buyer obtains a special property and an insurable interest in goods by identification of existing goods to which the contract refers even though the goods so identified are nonconforming and he has an option to return or reject them. Such identification can be made at any time and in any manner explicitly agreed to by the parties. In the absence of explicit agreement identification occurs:
> (a) When the contract is made if it is for the sale of goods already existing and identified;
> (b) If the contract is for the sale of future goods . . . when goods are shipped, marked or otherwise designated by the seller as goods to which the contract refers. . . .

The purchasers argue that adoption of the identification date strikes a fair balance between the interests of the buyer in ordinary course and the secured party. The purchasers argue that once the goods have been identified they have an insurable interest in the goods and can maintain an action against a third party who has injured them through his or her dealings with the goods. The purchasers reason that their interest at identification justifies considering them buyers in ordinary course at that time.

The purchasers conclude that they became buyers in ordinary course of business when the van became identified to the contract, that is, when it was produced or when GM sent the Bank the sight draft including the vehicle identification number. We need not decide in this case which is the appropriate date of identification. Whichever date, the purchaser would prevail over the Bank. Because the purchasers do not ask this court to adopt the date of contract as the triggering date for transforming the purchasers to buyers in ordinary course, we need not decide this issue.

We merely hold today that the purchasers became buyers in ordinary course of business when the goods became identified to the contract. We rest our decision on the circumstances surrounding the transaction in this case and the manner in which sales are made in this industry.

This case presents the situation that [U.C.C. §9-320(a)] was designed to address. The purchasers were ordinary retail consumers purchasing a vehicle from a dealership, an entity in the business of selling vehicles. The purchasers made a down payment and signed a contract. The Bank as financier of the inventory authorized the sale of the inventory. It was only through the sale of the inventory that the Bank would receive cash from the dealership to repay the loan. The Bank knew of the purchasers. The Bank knew of the purchase order and paid the manufacturer for the vehicle in question on September 30, 1983.

In its amicus brief the Wisconsin Bankers Association states that protecting the purchasers in this case will make a security interest in inventory an unworkable concept. The position we adopt today is the position most courts have adopted, concluding that the floor plan financier can guard against the risks. The Bank was in a better position than the purchasers to guard against the risk of loss. Most retail purchasers probably have never heard of the Uniform Commercial Code and would not know how to go about protecting their interest. The Bank, on the other hand, is in the business of lending money and has access to information about how to protect itself, as best it can, against risk of loss. Accordingly, under the facts of this case, we hold that the purchasers were buyers in ordinary course of business upon identification of the merchandise to the contract. The purchasers assert that the van had been identified to the contract before the Bank took over the dealership's premises and that their interest prevails over the Bank's. Because it is unclear whether the Bank disputes the date of identification, this issue may have to be resolved in remand. . . .

The Judgment of the circuit court is reversed and the cause remanded.

After *Daniel*, the drafters revised U.C.C. §1-201(9) to add that "[o]nly a buyer that takes possession of the goods or has a right to recover the goods from the seller under Article 2 may be a buyer in ordinary course of business." The Comment to that section identifies U.C.C. §§2-502 and 2-716 as the law identifying the buyers who do not take possession but still can qualify as buyers in ordinary course of business.

Sales of goods in the possession of the secured party. Daniel v. Bank of Hayward illustrates that a buyer in the ordinary course of business can defeat the inventory lender's security interest without taking possession of the goods. In that case, the seller-debtor, Don Hofstadter, Inc., had possession. What if, instead, the Bank of Hayward had possession of the vehicle at the time the Daniels purchased it? Could the Daniels still have bought the vehicle in the ordinary course of business and taken free of the Bank's now doubly perfected security inter-

est? If so, it would seem to be virtually impossible for a secured
creditor to prevent its debtor from selling collateral free of the creditor's security interest. Even collateral resting in the bank's vault
would not be safe. On the other hand, the Wisconsin Supreme Court
determined that the Daniels were buyers in the ordinary course of
business even though they had never seen the van they bought. For
all the Daniels knew, their van might have been in the Bank's vault.

Tanbro Fabrics Corp. v. Deering Milliken, Inc., 350 N.E.2d 590
(N.Y. 1976), illustrates both the problem and the solution. The
secured creditor, Deering, had possession of 267,000 yards of a certain
fabric as security for an account owing from Mill Fabrics, the debtor,
to Deering. Mill Fabrics sold the fabric to Tanbro. Tanbro was familiar
with the industry practice of leaving goods in the possession of the
seller's seller as security and hence did not find it unusual to be buying fabric the seller did not possess. Tanbro paid the purchase price to
Mill Fabrics. Mill Fabrics promptly went belly-up without paying
Deering. Deering refused to give the fabric to Tanbro and Tanbro
sued. The court held that Tanbro was a buyer in the ordinary course
of Mill Fabric's business and that Tanbro therefore took free of Deering's security interest.

Some of the early drafters of Article 9 were apoplectic over *Tanbro
Fabrics*. Although they never managed to overturn that decision, the
drafters of revised Article 9 have. U.C.C. §9-320(e) provides somewhat
mysteriously that "Subsections (a) and (b) do not affect a security
interest in goods in possession of the secured party under Section
9-313." Comment 8 explains that U.C.C. §9-320(e) "rejects the holding of *Tanbro Fabrics Corp. v. Deering Milliken* . . . and, together with
Section 9-317(b), prevents a buyer of collateral from taking free of a
security interest if the collateral is in the possession of the secured
party." The Comment makes explicit reference to the fact that under
U.C.C. §9-313, a secured party may be in possession of collateral that
is in the physical possession of a third party.

3. The Buyer-Not-in-the-Ordinary-Course Exception: U.C.C. §§9-323(d) and (e) and 9-317(b)

Those who buy goods outside the ordinary course of business have no
exemption from the search-and-file game. They are expected to
search the U.C.C. records and are charged with constructive notice of
the filings they would have found. The result is that in a sale not
authorized by the secured creditor, the buyer not in the ordinary
course takes subject to any security interest that is perfected, but has
priority over unperfected ones. This hierarchy of interests is reflected
in U.C.C. §§9-323(d) and (e) and 9-317(b).

To illustrate, assume that Thomas Redding plans to open a frozen yogurt store. He needs a walk-in cooler to refrigerate the yogurt mix. He spots one for $2,000 in the newspaper want ads. The owner, Peter's Pizzas, used the cooler to store food and drinks in connection with its pizza business, but the business closed a few weeks ago. Because Peter's is not in the business of selling coolers, the sale of this cooler to Redding will not be a sale in the ordinary course. Redding will take subject to any perfected security interest in the cooler. U.C.C. §§9-323(d) and (e). For that reason, Redding is well advised to search the public record before paying the $2,000 purchase price.

If, instead, Redding bought his cooler from Paul's Restaurant Supply, a company that sells, among other things, used coolers, he would not have been expected to search the public record. He would have taken free of any security interest given by Paul's Restaurant Supply. U.C.C. §9-320(a).

4.   The Consumer-to-Consumer-Sale Exception: U.C.C. §9-320(b)

When a sale is outside the ordinary course of business, even consumer buyers are expected to play the search-and-file game. Assume, for example, that Peter Waldoch offers to sell his riding lawn mower to Thomas Redding for $600. If Sears holds a security interest in the lawn mower that is perfected by filing and Sears has not authorized the sale, Redding will take subject to it. Redding is not protected by U.C.C. §9-320(a) because Waldoch does not deal in lawn mowers. See U.C.C. §1-201(9). Redding is not protected by U.C.C. §9-320(b) because of the exception in that section in favor of secured parties who have filed a financing statement. Ordinary people would consider it absurd that Redding be expected to search the public record before buying a lawn mower in a garage sale. But you should realize by now that the drafters of Article 9 were not ordinary people.

We refer to the exception in U.C.C. §9-320(b) as the consumer-to-consumer-sale exception* because the exception applies only if the goods are consumer goods in the hands of the seller before the sale and consumer goods in the hands of the buyer after the sale. The requirement that the goods be held for personal, family, or household purposes of the seller prior to the sale is contained in the main part of section (b); the requirement that they be held for personal, family, or household purposes of the buyer after the sale is contained in subsection (b)(3). The buyer in a consumer-to-consumer sale is protected from an automatically perfected purchase-money security interest

---

* Some think it is better remembered as the garage sale exception.

(PMSI) in consumer goods. Thus, if Sears had not filed a financing statement in the illustration given in the previous paragraph, but instead relied on its PMSI protection from U.C.C. §9-309(1), the consumer-to-consumer-sale exception of U.C.C. §9-320(b) would apply to permit Redding to take free of Sears' perfected security interest. Given that consumers such as Redding are not going to search the U.C.C. records, we can think of no reason for letting them take free of automatically perfected interests, but not interests perfected by filing. But that is how the rule reads.

Problem Set 36

36.1.   Davis Department Store sold a combination TV-stereo-VCR-popcorn popper to Beavis on credit for $1,925. Beavis paid no money down, but signed a promissory note, security agreement, and financing statement. Davis filed the financing statement in the statewide U.C.C. records. The security agreement provided that Beavis "agrees not to sell the collateral." Six months later, Beavis lost his job at the meat processing plant and moved to Tennessee. Before leaving, he held a garage sale at which he sold the entertainment unit to his friend Butthead for $960. Butthead didn't know about the security agreement with Davis Department Store and (wouldn't you know it?) made the mistake of paying by check. Davis identified Butthead as the buyer from Beavis's checking account records. Davis asks whether it is entitled to repossess the entertainment unit from Butthead. If so, do they have to refund his $960? U.C.C. §§1-201 (9), 9-315(a), 9-320, 9-401(b).

36.2.   Your client, University City Bank (UCB), has a security interest in the inventory of Sound City, Inc. Sound City sells sound systems at retail to consumers and businesses. The security agreement between UCB and Sound City authorized sales only in the ordinary course of business, prohibited sales on credit, and required that "Debtor deposit all proceeds of sales of collateral to Debtor's account #937284 at University City Bank." UCB perfected the security interest by filing a financing statement. On October 20, Sound City, Inc. filed under Chapter 7 of the Bankruptcy Code. The trustee abandoned the inventory, the debtor surrendered it to UCB, and UCB sold it and applied the proceeds to the inventory loan. A deficiency of $36,000 remains owing to UCB on the Sound City loan. Through discovery, you learned of the following transactions that took place before the filing of the bankruptcy petition:

a.   Sound City sold a sound system to Rhonda Fried for $12,000. Rhonda paid $2,000 in cash and signed a negotiable promissory note for the remaining $10,000. There is no evidence that she knew of the restrictive provisions of the security agreement. Sound City deposited Rhonda's check to an account with a bank other than UCB and used the money to pay a utility bill. About a month later, Sound City sold the Rhonda note for $9,200. UCB has been unable to determine what Sound City did with the proceeds. Is UCB entitled to repossess the sound system from Rhonda? U.C.C. §§9-315(a); 9-320, 9-323(d) and (e); 1-201(9).

b. George Paulos is a lawyer who has been representing Sound City for several years. As of July 17, Sound City owed George $16,458 for legal services rendered in two employment discrimination suits. George agreed to accept a $14,000 sound system as partial payment and Sound City installed it in his home. Is UCB entitled to repossess the sound system from George? U.C.C. §§1-201(9), 9-315, 9-320, 9-323(d) and (e).

36.3. Alecia Card bought a used 1992 "Lindy Delux Housecar" (the Lindy) from the used car lot of Sunrise R.V. She paid for the recreational vehicle with a $23,000 cashier's check and drove it home. The salesman at Sunrise assured her that she would receive title to the Lindy directly from the Division of Motor Vehicles within two weeks. When the title did not arrive as promised, Alecia complained to Sunrise.

Eventually she learned the history of the Lindy. A man named Kenneth Eddy purchased it from All Seasons R.V. over a year ago. Eddy granted All Seasons a security interest in the Lindy to secure a part of the purchase price. In the security agreement, Eddy agreed "not to transfer any interest in the vehicle." A few weeks ago, Eddy violated the security agreement by trading the Lindy to Sunrise R.V. (Sunrise) for another recreational vehicle. At the time he sold the Lindy to Sunrise, Eddy still owed All Seasons $17,000 of the purchase price. Sunrise bought the Lindy subject to that lien and agreed to pay it. Instead, Sunrise deposited Alecia's $23,000 to its operating account and spent the money on rent and other expenses. Alecia also learned that Eddy did not notify All Seasons that he was selling to Sunrise and did not obtain All Seasons' permission to sell.

a. Alecia wants to sue to remove All Seasons' lien from the title to the Lindy. How good is her case? U.C.C. §§9-315(a), 9-320(a).

b. If Alecia had insisted on seeing the certificate of title for the Lindy before she paid her $23,000, what would she have learned? See U.C.C. §9-311(d) and Comment 4 to that section; form for motor vehicle certificate of title in Assignment 25.

36.4. Alecia Card is back to see you for the fourth time since you represented her in the *All Seasons* case. Although she is a bright, energetic, friendly person, she has been asking questions that seem . . . well, a little too basic. Even before today, you had been suspecting that Alecia might be showing signs of paranoia. In your meeting this morning, Alecia explained that she has been shopping for a piano, has found a reconditioned one she likes for $5,000 at American Piano Company in the Galleria Mall, and would like you to "represent her at the closing." Covering your surprise, you told her that most people who buy things in the mall just represent themselves. "Yes," she replied matter-of-factly, "but they haven't been through what you and I have." You told her you'd think about it and give her a call this afternoon.

a. Is there anything to her fears? U.C.C. §9-320(a).

b. Can the problem be dealt with by a thorough search of the public records? U.C.C. §9-507(a), including Comment 3.

c. Should you recommend a psychiatrist or try to deal with this yourself? If you try to deal with it yourself, what will you say to Alecia and what will you do to get ready for the "closing"?

d. Is this a problem that is unique to used goods, or could it occur with respect to new goods as well?

36.5. Would the Daniels still prevail over Bank of Hayward under the new penultimate sentence of U.C.C. §1-201(9)? That is, would the Daniels have "a right to recover [the van] from the seller under Article 2"? See Comment 9 to U.C.C. §1-201.

36.6. Charles Hayward, president of the Bank of Hayward, was really angry about the Bank's loss in the *Daniel* case. Fresh from a meeting of bankers in which they all grumbled about "the end of inventory financing," he would like your advice on damage control. The Bank finances several motor vehicle dealerships. Before the *Daniel* case, the Bank sent inspectors out at unpredictable times to physically inspect the inventory. Each inspector carried a list of vehicle ID numbers for the vehicles against which the Bank had lent money. As the inspector found each vehicle on the lot, the inspector checked it off on the list. If a dealer could not satisfactorily account for all of the vehicles on the list, the Bank would consider calling the loan.

a. "After *Daniel*," Charles says, "the presence of a vehicle on the lot means nothing. The dealer could already have sold it and been paid for it. The lot could be full of vehicles, but every one of them sold to a prepaying buyer." Do you agree?

b. "Under *Chrysler*," Charles says, "we controlled delivery of the title to the retail purchaser by holding the MSO. Now the buyer doesn't need title; they can just sue us for it." Is he right?

c. The *Daniel* court said that "The bank . . . is in the business of lending money and has access to information about how to protect itself, as best it can, against risk of loss." Charles wants to know how the Bank can protect itself. What do you suggest?

36.7. Charles Hayward, president of the Bank of Hayward is back. He would like your opinion of "a great new scheme" he just heard about at a meeting of bankers. The bills of lading for new vehicles will provide that from the moment of identification of a new vehicle to a dealer's contract for sale until the vehicle actually arrives on the dealer's lot, the manufacturer and the carriers will hold possession of the vehicle as agents for the bank that finances the dealer's inventory. That way, Hayward says, buyers like the Daniels won't be entitled to vehicles on which they have made down payments unless those vehicles actually arrive on the dealers' lots before repossession.

    a. Is Hayward right? U.C.C. §§9-313(a), 9-315(a), 9-317(b), 9-320(a) and (e).

    b. Is there any way the Bank can use U.C.C. §9-320(e) to prevail even as to vehicles actually delivered to the dealer's lot?

    c. What advice would you give to people like the Daniels who want a car custom-made for them, but are faced with the inevitable demand from the dealer for a substantial down payment?

    36.8. Robert and Edward Sherrock are partners in Sherrock Brothers, a Toyota dealership. Ed tried to call you early this afternoon, but you were in a meeting and he was unable to get through. Your secretary took a lengthy message and now relates it to you. Ed called from Dover Motors, the Toyota dealership in a nearby city. He bought two cars from Dover and made arrangements to pay for them by transfer of funds later this afternoon. Dover agreed to keep the cars for a few days until Sherrock Brothers could send a couple of drivers to move them. After he left Dover's lot, Ed had second thoughts. He had heard some rumors that Dover was in financial difficulty, so he called you to find out if it's okay to leave the cars there till he gets back from Chicago in two days. Actually, you were on your way out of town as well. Does this have to be dealt with now? U.C.C. §§9-320, 1-201(19), 2-103(1)(b), 2-102, 2-403(2) and (3). Consider two possibilities:

    a. Dover sells the two cars to buyers in the ordinary course of business and then files bankruptcy.

    b. Dover files bankruptcy and Dover's inventory lender claims the cars.

    36.9. Frances Foster (from Problem 35.2) is back again. She has been thinking about what you told her, and has an idea. She has never really enjoyed the marketing end of the business. For some time, she has been considering a deal with Greg Drake, a marketing whiz, under which she would finance him and he would sell her products. "Instead of making Greg a marketing rep," she says, "I will sell my products to him on a nonrecourse basis with a hundred percent financing, and take back one of those purchase-money security interests you keep talking about. I'll file a financing statement against Greg, and authorize him to resell the products only subject to my security interests. When he does, my security interest will remain with the product and the customer will assume the debt. The customer will of course be aware that I have a security interest, but neither I nor Greg will have to file a financing statement against the customer or send the U.C.C. §9-324(a) notice to the customer's bank. The inventory will be encumbered, but there won't be anything on the public record in the name of the customer and the customer's inventory-secured lender will be none the wiser unless it does a search under Greg's name. If the customer doesn't pay, I'll have priority over the customer's inventory secured lender, won't I?" What do you tell Frances? U.C.C. §§1-102(3), 9-315(a), 9-320(a), 9-322(a), 9-324(b), 9-325, 9-507(a), 9-602.

Assignment 37: Statutory Lien Creditors Against Secured Creditors

The discussion of construction liens against real property in Assignment 33 introduced the concept of a *statutory lien*. When the term is used in its narrow sense, as it is in the Bankruptcy Code, it means a lien that arises by operation of a statute. But the term is also used in a broader sense to include any lien that arises by operation of law, which includes liens that arise under common law or equity as well as those that arise by operation of a statute.

A statutory lien, used in this broader sense, is one of the three major categories of liens. The other two are *consensual liens* and *judicial liens*, which we have been working with throughout the course. Consensual liens arise by contract between debtor and creditor. This category includes security interests, mortgages, and deeds of trust. Judicial liens arise as the result of some act taken during litigation. This category includes execution, attachment, and garnishment liens, as well as judgment liens that arise against real property upon the recording of a money judgment in the real property recording system. Statutory liens differ from consensual liens in that the debtor need not give consent for the lien to arise; they differ from judicial liens in that the creditor need not engage in litigation to acquire the lien.

Although most kinds of statutory liens arise without any action on the part of the lien holder, some kinds of statutory lien holders must take steps to perfect. For example, in Assignment 33, we noted that the construction lien holder typically has to record a Claim of Lien in the real property recording system within 90 days of the last date on which the lien holder furnished labor or materials, or it loses its lien. The laws of many states require that the holder of a lien for improvements or repairs to personal property retain possession of the property for the lien to remain in effect, a requirement that has much the same functional effect as perfection by possession.

A. The Variety of Statutory Liens in Personal Property

We have discussed statutory liens as they arise in the real estate context, but here we take up statutory liens against personal property.

The subject is broad. Most states recognize dozens of different types of statutory liens; among the 50 states there are well over a thousand statutes granting liens to particular kinds of creditors. Federal law also creates dozens of types of statutory liens, with the federal tax lien as the one with greatest economic importance. In this section, we reproduce examples of these statutes, which, taken together, illustrate the nature and variety of this kind of legislation.

1. Artisans' Liens

Black's Law Dictionary defines "artisan" as a person skilled in some kind of trade, craft, or art requiring manual dexterity, such as a carpenter, plumber, tailor, or mechanic. At common law, artisans had a lien against personal property they improved or repaired. Persons successfully claiming artisans' liens have included jewelers, laundry operators, garage mechanics, and accountants. To retain its lien at common law, the artisan had to retain possession of the property; if the artisan surrendered possession of the property, the lien was lost.

Most state legislatures have codified the artisan's lien. Some have done so in general terms that essentially track the common law. Others have created separate lien rights for particular kinds of artisans. California is an example of a state that has done both. Its general artisan's lien law provides:

Personal Property Lien for Services, Manufacture, or Repair

Cal. Civ. Code §3051 (West 1994 Supp.)

Every person who, while lawfully in possession of an article of personal property, renders any service to the owner thereof, by labor or skill, employed for the protection, improvement, safekeeping, or carriage thereof, has a special lien thereon, dependent on possession, for the compensation, if any, which is due to him from the owner for such service; a person who makes, alters, or repairs any article of personal property, at the request of the owner, or legal possessor of the property, has a lien on the same for his reasonable charges for the balance due for such work done and materials furnished, and may retain possession of the same until the charges are paid. . . .

This section shall have no application to any vessel, as defined in Section 21 of the Harbors and Navigation Code, to any vehicle, as defined in Section 670 of the Vehicle Code, which is subject to registration pursuant to that code, to any manufactured home, as defined in Section 18007 of the Health and Safety Code, to any mobile home, as defined in Section

18008 of the Health and Safety Code, or to any commercial coach, as defined in Section 18001.8 of the Health and Safety Code, whether or not the manufactured home, mobile home, or commercial coach is subject to registration under the Health and Safety Code.

This California statute expressly excepts motor vehicles from coverage because California, like many states, has a more specific statute that covers them.

2. Garage Keepers' Liens

Persons who repair motor vehicles are in most states entitled to common law artisans' liens, but a substantial minority of states have enacted a statute specifically entitling garage keepers and mechanics to liens. (Although the liens awarded by these statutes are commonly referred to as *mechanics' liens*, in most states "mechanics' liens" are liens in favor of persons who supply labor or materials for building construction. The liens of garage mechanics in those states may be referred to as *artisans' liens* or the statute may give them another name.) The following is the garage keeper's lien law in Maine:

Garage Keeper's Lien
10 Me. Rev. Stat. Ann. (West 1991)

§3801   VEHICLES, AIRCRAFT AND PARACHUTES

Whoever performs labor by himself or his employees in manufacturing or repairing the ironwork or woodwork of wagons, carts, sleighs and other vehicles, aircraft or component parts thereof, and parachutes, or so performing labor furnishes materials therefor or provides storage therefor by direction or consent of the owner thereof, shall have a lien on such vehicle, aircraft or component parts thereof, and parachutes for his reasonable charges for said labor, and for materials used in performing said labor, and for said storage, which takes precedence of all other claims and encumbrances on said vehicles, aircraft or component parts thereof, and parachutes not made to secure a similar lien, and may be enforced by attachment at any time within 90 days after such labor is performed or such materials or storage furnished and not afterwards, provided a claim for such lien is duly filed as required in section 3802. Said lien shall be dissolved if said property has actually changed ownership prior to such filing.

§3802   FILING IN OFFICE OF SECRETARY OF STATE

The liens mentioned in section 3801 are dissolved unless the claimant within 90 days after the labor is performed, or storage furnished, files in the office of the Secretary of State a true statement of the amount due the claimant for the labor and materials or for storage, with all just credits given, together with a description of the vehicle manufactured or repaired sufficiently accurate to identify it and the name of the owner, if known, which must be subscribed and sworn to by the person claiming the lien or by someone in that person's behalf, and recorded by the Secretary of State. . . .

The Maine statute is unusual in requiring that the garage keeper file notice of its lien with the Secretary of State. In most states, the garage keeper perfects its lien by retaining possession of the vehicle and loses the lien if it surrenders possession of the vehicle.

3.   Attorneys' Charging and Retaining Liens

Under the law of every state, attorneys are granted statutory liens to secure the payment of at least some kinds of fees. These liens are of two general types. A "charging lien" is a lien that attaches to the client's recovery in an action against a third person. A "retaining lien" is a lien that attaches to documents and records that the client has delivered to the lawyer for use in connection with the representation. The following statute is narrower than some in that it grants only a charging lien. It is broader than some in that the charging lien attaches upon the case being "placed in [the attorney's] hands"; some attach only upon the attorney filing a lawsuit on behalf of the client.

Attorneys' Lien

Ill. Rev. Stat. ch. 770, §5/1 (West 1991)

Sec. 1. Attorneys at law shall have a lien upon all claims, demands and causes of action, including all claims for unliquidated damages, which may be placed in their hands by their clients for suit or collection, or upon which suit or action has been instituted, for the amount of any fee which may have been agreed upon by and between such attorneys and their clients, or, in the absence of such agreement, for a reasonable fee, for the services of such suits, claims, demands or causes of action, plus costs and expenses. To enforce such lien, such attorneys shall serve notice in writing, which service may be made by registered or certified mail, upon the party against whom their clients may have such suits, claims or causes of action, claiming such lien and stating therein the interest they have in such suits, claims, demands or causes of action. Such lien shall attach to any verdict, judgment or order entered and to any money or property which may be recovered, on account of such suits, claims, demands or causes of action, from and after the time of service of the notice. On petition filed by such attorneys or their clients any court of competent jurisdiction shall, on not less than five days' notice to the adverse party, adjudicate the rights of the parties and enforce the lien.

4.   Hospital Liens

Persons who are hospitalized as the result of an injury often receive medical services on credit. Those same persons often have causes of action against someone for the negligence that caused the accident. Many states have enacted statutes giving the hospital that renders treatment on credit a lien against the recovery in the negligence action. The following is such a statute:

Hospital Lien

Tex. Prop. Code Ann. §55.002 (West 1953)

(a) A hospital has a lien on a cause of action or claim of an individual who receives hospital services for injuries caused by an accident that is attributed to the negligence of another person. For the lien to attach, the individual must be admitted to a hospital not later than 72 hours after the accident.

(b) The lien extends to both the admitting hospital and a hospital to which the individual is transferred for treatment of the same injury.

5.   Landlord's Lien

Although landlord's liens have in recent decades fallen into disfavor, the large majority of states recognizes a landlord's lien in at least some landlord-tenant contexts. The most common context is between a landlord and a tenant-farmer who is growing crops on the property. Many states recognize the lien in commercial contexts such as shopping center leases and some even recognize it in the residential context. In most states, the landlord's lien is against personal property of the tenant that remains on the leased premises, but in a few, it is against all personal property of the debtor. While no statute is typical, the following provides an example:

Landlord's Lien

Or. Rev. Stat. Ann. (1981)

§87.146. PRIORITIES OF LIENS

(1) Except as provided in subsection (2) of this section: (a) Liens created by ORS . . . 87.162 have priority over all other liens, security interests and encumbrances on the chattel subject to the lien, except that taxes and duly perfected security interests existing before chattels sought to be subjected to a lien created by ORS 87.162 are brought upon the leased premises have priority over that lien.

§87.162. LANDLORD'S LIEN

(1) [A] landlord has a lien on all chattels, except wearing apparel as defined in ORS 23.160 (1), owned by a tenant or occupant legally responsible for rent, brought upon the leased premises, to secure the payment of rent and such advances as are made on behalf of the tenant. The landlord may retain the chattels until the amount of rent and advances is paid.

---

6. Dry Cleaners' and Launderers' Liens

Some states specifically provide liens in favor of cleaners and launderers. In most other states, cleaners and launderers are entitled to liens under the general artisan's lien law. If you don't pay for the clothes they clean for you, the cleaners or launderers can sell them.

Dry Cleaners' and Launderers' Lien

Ariz. Rev. Stat. §33-1021.01(A) (1990)

When any garment, wearing apparel or other article is cleaned, pressed or washed by any dry cleaner or launderer, the dry cleaner or launderer has a lien on the garment, apparel or article for the labor and may retain possession of the garment, apparel or article until the amount due is fully paid.

This statute, like many other lien laws, addresses a type of property that typically has little dollar value. Although such laws may be worded essentially the same as laws that address types of property typically of larger dollar value, they function very differently. Given the cost of litigation, few people are going to litigate over their laundry. The principal impact of a small-value lien law is to determine the right to possession. The law tells the police at the local station not to help you retrieve your laundry unless you have paid for it. The principal impact of a high-value lien law is to determine the priority between competing claimants to the property. The priority of statutory liens is covered later in this assignment.

7.   Agricultural Liens

Agricultural lien laws are perhaps the most numerous and chaotic of the lien laws of the various states. In 1991, a report of the American Bar Association's Agricultural Lien Task Force listed hundreds of state agricultural lien laws. For each of 11 major farming states, the report listed an average of 11 separate statutes. A law review version of that report stated:

> [E]ach state has its own unique set of agricultural liens that reflects each state's own agricultural history. Many of these liens, on their face, reflect an agricultural history and past agricultural needs that seem quaint and old-fashioned, or possibly even anachronistic and detrimental when compared to today's agricultural realities. Just to hear the names of such agricultural liens makes one recall the times in which these agricultural lines arose: thresher's liens, horseshoer's liens, livery stable liens, moss gatherer's liens. Yet these liens cannot be easily dismissed as outmoded and unneeded. Naming other agricultural liens immediately makes their modern relevance clear: landlord's liens, seed supplier liens, fertilizer supplier liens, veterinarian's liens. Even an old-fashioned sounding lien, such as a thresher's lien, covers the modern practice of custom combining. Hence, each state has its own set of agricultural liens that may or may not be completely responsive to the needs of modern agriculture.

Steven C. Turner et al., Agricultural Liens and the UCC: A Report on Present Status and Proposals for Change, 44 Okla. L. Rev. 9, 12-13 (1991). The report noted that in several states these liens are scattered throughout the statutes, making them difficult to find. Procedures for enforcement are often included in the statutes, and differ from one statute to another even within the same state.

Revised Article 9 applies to agricultural liens. U.C.C. §9-109(a)(2). Who is entitled to an agricultural lien continues to be governed by the patchwork of statutes described above. The liens continue to come into existence by operation of the statutes granting them. But in some respects, the inclusion of agricultural liens within the scope of Article 9 has made the procedures for perfection and enforcement of agricultural liens more uniform.

Before Article 9 was revised, most agricultural liens were automatically perfected; the lien holder did not have to file a financing statement or take any other action as a condition of perfection. Revised Article 9 requires that the holders of agricultural liens file financing statements as a condition of perfection. U.C.C. §9-310(a). This requirement has likely come as a shock in the hinterlands, where sellers of feed and seed, crop dusters, and farmers who rent a little land to a neighbor have been accustomed to the benefits of agricultural liens without having to file financing statements. As we read revised Article 9, agricultural lien holders who fail to file will be unperfected and subordinate to perfected secured creditors, lien creditors, trustees in bankruptcy, and buyers. U.C.C. §§9-308(b), 9-310(a), and 9-322(a).

The agricultural lien holder who does manage to file a financing statement will enjoy priority as of the filing. See U.C.C. §9-322(a). For most, that will mean subordination to the security interests of banks and other farm lenders who will have filed financing statements in earlier seasons and continued them. If the statute that creates the agricultural lien expressly gives it priority over other security interests, U.C.C. §9-322(a) yields to that statute. U.C.C. §9-322(g). But if the priority derives from case law or is untested in the courts, revised Article 9 reverses it.

The interplay between secured lenders and agricultural lien creditors illustrates a dynamic tension in the law. As secured lenders win revisions of Article 9 that enable them to lock up their debtors' assets with perfected security interests, the unsecured creditors who supply goods and services to farms have less asset value they can reach when those debtors fail. These unsecured lenders ask the legislature for relief, and sometimes get it in the form of agricultural liens that prime the secured lenders. Under former Article 9, such priming was effective. In revised Article 9, the secured lenders strike back with two new requirements for priming. First, the agricultural lien holder must file a financing statement as a condition of perfection and thus priority. U.C.C. §9-310(a). Second, revised Article 9 strips priority from all agricultural liens that have priority from a source other than "the statute creating the agricultural lien." U.C.C. §9-322(g). We wonder if the creditors with the political power to get statutory liens will escalate the fight, getting legislatures to amend the agricultural lien enabling statutes to avoid the revised Article 9 provisions that would demote them.

The holders of agricultural liens are not entitled to purchase-money status under U.C.C. §9-103, regardless of the kind of contribution they make to the debtor's estate. States are invited, however, to enact the Model Provisions for Production-Money Priority to grant analogous protection. U.C.C. §§9-103A and 9-324A. To obtain protection under that law, the agricultural lienor would have to obtain a security interest in addition to filing a financing statement.

In addition to the state agricultural liens discussed above, the federal Perishable Agricultural Commodities Act (PACA) imposes a "statutory trust" that gives sellers and suppliers of perishable agricultural commodities — including farmers — priority in payment even over secured creditors of the buyers. Although the federal statute does not use the word "lien," the effect is to grant one. This lien applies only against the creditors of "commission merchants, dealers, or brokers" who purchase the commodities. But, as the follow case illustrates, that may extend the lien all the way to the restaurants that serve those "commodities" to hungry patrons.

Royal Foods Co. v. L.R. Holdings, Inc.

1999 U.S. Dist. LEXIS 18010 (N.D. Cal. 1999)

WILLIAM ALSUP, U.S. DISTRICT JUDGE

Perishable agricultural commodities must be sold and distributed quickly or not at all, often across great distances. To facilitate the rapid sale and distribution of perishable produce, Congress amended the Perishable Agricultural Commodities Act in 1984 to impress a "statutory trust" on the chain of distribution of such products, a trust that grants to sellers and suppliers a priority in payment over even secured lenders. . . . The statute itself reflects the same intent expressed in the legislative history:

> It is hereby found that a burden on commerce in perishable agricultural commodities is caused by financing arrangements under which commission merchants, dealers, or brokers, who have not made payment for perishable agricultural commodities purchased, contracted to be purchased, or otherwise handled by them on behalf of another person, encumber or give lenders a security interest in, such commodities, or on inventories of food or other products derived from such commodities, and any receivables or proceeds from the sale of such commodities or products, and that such arrangements are contrary to the public interest. This subsection is

intended to remedy such burden on commerce in perishable agricultural commodities and to protect the public interest.

7 U.S.C. §499e(c)(1).

Lyon's Restaurants, Inc. operates a large chain of restaurants. Prior to filing for bankruptcy, Lyon's had purchased $1,220,024.91 worth of produce from Royal Foods Co. Royal delivered the produce, but Lyon's did not pay for it. Royal sent invoices to Lyon's that contained the wording required by the Act to preserve its trust rights. . . .

The Act's trust is impressed on sales of perishable agricultural commodities to "commission merchants, dealers or brokers." 7 U.S.C. §499e(c). A "dealer" is defined by the statute as:

> any person engaged in the business of buying or selling in wholesale or jobbing quantities, any perishable agricultural commodity in interstate or foreign commerce. . . .

7 U.S.C. §499a(6). . . . At issue is whether the Act's definition of "dealer" excludes restaurants, like the Lyon's chain, that buy perishable goods in wholesale or jobbing quantities. The bankruptcy court concluded that restaurants were not dealers under the Act, and that therefore the trust provision did not apply to Royal's sale of perishable goods to Lyon's. On this pure issue of law, reviewed de novo, this Court disagrees with the bankruptcy court's conclusion and therefore REVERSES the bankruptcy court's order. . . .

Appellee, real party in interest U.S. Bank National Association, argues that the Act's definition of dealer is at best ambiguous. According to U.S. Bank, the phrase "in the business of" suggests that "dealer" includes only those businesses in which the buying or selling of produce in large volume is the primary business. U.S. Bank argues that restaurants are excluded from the definition because buying wholesale quantities of perishable goods is only an adjunct function to restaurants' real business — preparing and selling meals. The Court disagrees. In a recent decision, Judge Levi of the Eastern District of California persuasively rejected a similar argument:

> Paragon provides no authority for its argument that by "dealers" the statute intends only to describe those who resell products in unaltered form. In fact, the statute implies exactly the opposite; one of the three exceptions [to the definition of "dealer"] enumerated in the statute makes it clear that processors of food are generally to be considered "dealers" unless they process food only in the state where grown: "(C) no person buying any commodity . . . for canning and/or processing within the State where grown shall be considered a 'dealer' whether or not the canned or processed product is to be shipped in the interstate or foreign commerce. . . ." See 7 U.S.C. §499(a)(6)(C). Moreover, the trust provisions at issue here

apply not only to produce, but also to products derived therefrom, and to the revenue derived from sales of produce and produce-derived products, which plainly encompasses menu items, such as those sold in Paragon's restaurants, and revenues derived therefrom.

J. C. Produce, Inc. v. Paragon Steakhouse Restaurants, Inc., 1999 U.S. Dist. LEXIS 17216, No. 99-1473 slip op. at 5-6 (E.D. Cal. Oct. 19, 1999). As noted by Judge Levi, the trust provisions contemplate that covered businesses will transform perishable goods into "food or other products derived from perishable agricultural commodities." 7 U.S.C. §499e(c)(2). . . .

Moreover, the purpose of the Act's trust provisions, as expressed in the statute itself, supports that the proceeds from the perishable goods sold from Royal to Lyon's should be held in trust for payment to Royal. The trust provisions identify as a burden on commerce those purchasers of perishable agricultural goods who would "encumber or give a security interest in such commodities, or on inventories of food or other products derived from such commodities" such that the perishable goods seller would not receive payment for the goods. The aim of the Act was to protect the flow of perishable products from the field to the last link in the chain purchasing at wholesale levels. A restaurant that purchases in wholesale quantities is clearly in that chain.

Despite the fit of the plain language of the "dealer" definition and the purpose of the trust provisions to the instant facts, however, this is not an easy case. U.S. Bank raises two more arguments, both of which other courts have found persuasive. . . . Second, U.S. Bank raises that the United States Department of Agriculture has consistently acted in such a way as to suggest that it does not consider restaurants to be dealers under the Act. In In re Magic Restaurants, Inc., No. 97-300 (D. Del. Jan. 6, 1999) (unpublished memorandum) (D. Del. 1999), the District Court for the District of Delaware reversed the published ruling of a bankruptcy court and held that restaurants are not dealers. The court based its decision on the actions of the Department of Agriculture. There, the court reasoned that [Chevron v. Natural Resources Defense Council, 467 U.S. 837 (1984)] mandated deference to the Department of Agriculture's interpretation of the Act.

The Court agrees that the indications from the Department of Agriculture on this issue are troubling. In 70 years of administering the Act, the Department has never licensed restaurants, regardless of what quantities of perishable goods they buy, even though the Act states that "no person shall at any time carry on the business of a commission merchant, dealer, or broker without a license valid and effective at such time." 7 U.S.C. §499c(a). . . . U.S. Bank has convincingly shown a long-standing failure by the Department of Agriculture to apply the Act to restaurants. . . .

. . . The purpose of the trust provisions, as expressed in the 1984 amendment, applies as naturally to restaurant chains as it does to supermarkets. In the Court's view, the Department of Agriculture should then have formally re-evaluated its benign neglect of restaurant chains. The plain language and purpose of the Act call out for inclusion of restaurants that buy in large wholesale quantities.

The order of the bankruptcy court granting summary judgment in favor of debtor and U.S. Bank National Association and against Royal Foods Co. is REVERSED. This matter is REMANDED to the bankruptcy court to resolve whether Lyon's purchased perishable agricultural commodities in wholesale or jobbing quantities.

The trouble with a lien on perishables is that they are likely to perish before the lien holder can obtain a remedy. For that reason, as *Royal Foods* indicates, the lien extends to proceeds. The statute provides: "The seller of these commodities retains a trust claim over these commodities, all inventories of food or other products derived from these commodities, and any receivables or proceeds from the sale of these commodities until full payment is received." That the seller's right is in the nature of a trust affords additional remedies. A trustee who knowingly misapplies trust funds is liable to the extent of the resulting loss to the beneficiary. Under PACA, this may include personal liability on the particular owner or officer who directs the misapplication.

B. Statutory Liens in Bankruptcy

The bankruptcy system generally recognizes and gives effect to liens and priorities that creditors perfected under nonbankruptcy law prior to the filing of the bankruptcy case. In general, bankruptcy law gives effect to statutory liens as well.

There are, however, three types of statutory liens that the trustee in bankruptcy can avoid. See Bankr. Code §545. The first is a lien that becomes effective not when the debt arises but only after the debtor is in financial difficulty. See Bankr. Code §545(1). Given that provision, legislatures have no reason to create such liens. By their terms, such liens are ineffective before the debtor is in bankruptcy; by §545(1), they are ineffective afterward. Not surprisingly, legislatures seldom bother enacting such statutes — which probably suits Congress just fine.

Under §545(2), the trustee can avoid a statutory lien that, at the time of the filing of the bankruptcy case, was not sufficiently perfected to be effective in the absence of bankruptcy against a hypothetical bona fide purchaser. To illustrate, some statutory lien laws require that the lien holder make a public filing or give notice to a stakeholder to perfect the lien. If failure to perfect would make the lien ineffective against a bona fide purchaser — or if even a properly perfected lien of the type would be ineffective against a bona fide purchaser — the trustee can avoid the statutory lien. Bankruptcy takes a statutory lien seriously only if state law takes it seriously.

Under §§545(3) and (4), the trustee can avoid statutory liens for rent and liens of distress for rent. "Distress for rent" was a self-help remedy available to landlords at common law. Without notice to the debtor or the opportunity for a hearing, the unpaid landlord could have the help of the sheriff in seizing property of the tenant. The remedy was declared unconstitutional in its most common form, but still survives in some others. Because the procedure for obtaining a distress lien includes filing a lawsuit, distress liens are arguably judicial liens. The drafters of Bankruptcy Code §545 probably mentioned them separately to make sure that a distress lien could not survive avoidance of the underlying lien for rent.

Prior to enactment of the Bankruptcy Code in 1978, not only were landlord's liens fully effective in bankruptcy cases, but the Bankruptcy Act gave priority to unsecured claims for rent. The legislative history gives no clue as to why, with hundreds of kinds of statutory liens to choose from, Congress chose to nail the landlords. At that time, the procedure of distress for rent was intimately tied to the landlord's lien for rent. The most common forms of distress had been declared unconstitutional as a result of the *Fuentes* line of cases, perhaps throwing landlord's liens into general disrepute. In any case, the event stands as testimony to the arbitrary (or perhaps it would be more accurate to say political) nature of statutory liens and creditor priorities in general.

When the trustee avoids a statutory lien in bankruptcy, the lien is "preserved for the benefit of the estate." Bankr. Code §551. That is, the trustee has the rights of the holder of the avoided lien, including the right to the lien's priority. To illustrate, assume that the debtor owns property worth $10,000 that is subject to a first statutory lien in the amount of $7,000 and a subordinate security interest in the amount of $20,000. If the trustee avoids the statutory lien, the trustee will then be entitled to the first $7,000 of value in the property and the holder of the security interest will be entitled to the remaining $3,000. The secured creditor in second position neither benefits nor loses from the trustee's avoidance of the first lien.

C. The Priority of Statutory Liens

A statutory lien has the priority specified in the law that creates it. The statutory provisions addressing priority are often complex, giving priority in some circumstances and withholding it in others. Overall, statutory liens probably have priority over security interests more often than not.

There are three types of rules governing priority between statutory liens and security interests. One type gives priority to the lien or to the security interest based on which is first in time. A second type gives priority to the statutory lien regardless of the order in which the two arose. The third gives priority to the security interest regardless of the order in which the two arose. If the statute gives priority on the basis of first in time, it will probably, but not necessarily, specify what the holder of the lien or security interest must do first in order to prevail. Security interests are usually dated as of perfection. Statutory liens may be dated as of the time the lien holder gives value, contracts to give value, files a claim of lien, or takes some other action.

To illustrate the various approaches to priority in the context of garage keeper's liens, assume that GMAC advances $10,000 to Mildred Washington to buy a new car and secures the loan with a purchase-money security interest. GMAC perfects the lien by having it noted on the certificate of title by the Department of Motor Vehicles. After the one-year warranty on the car expires, the car develops mechanical problems and Mildred takes the car to Central Auto Repair for repair. The repairs, all of which are authorized by Mildred, cost $3,000. Mildred is unable to pay for them. Under the most commonly applied rule, Central Auto Repair's lien has priority over GMAC's security interest. Under the other two rules, GMAC's lien has priority.

Most security interests in automobiles are purchase-money security interests taken at the time the debtor acquires the automobile. In the context of garage keepers' liens, a rule based on which lien is first in time nearly always gives priority to the security interest. As a consequence, we sometimes think of the rules as coming in only two categories: those that give priority to the garage keeper and those that give priority to the secured creditor. There are more statutes of the former type than of the latter.

The context in which landlords' liens arise is different. The debtor that operates a store in a shopping center may sign a lease that, with renewal options, runs for 30 years or more. In most jurisdictions, the landlord's lien is held to arise upon the signing of the lease and to attach to personal property when it is first brought upon the premises. Under the rule of first in time, such a landlord's lien is likely to be subordinate to the security interest of the bank that finances the debtor's initial purchase of fixtures, equipment, and inventory. But during the term of such a long lease, the debtor may refinance the equipment and inventory several times. The landlord's lien will prevail over these later lenders. In the context of landlord's liens, the rule of first in time, first in right will sometimes give priority to the landlord and other times to the secured party.

Most states follow the rule of first in time, first in right with regard to landlord's liens, but some states give priority to the landlord regardless of when the competing liens arise, and some states give priority to the secured party regardless of when the competing liens arise.

Since 1979, the rules determining priority between landlord and secured party have declined sharply in importance. In that year, the new Bankruptcy Code took effect. It included §§545(3) and (4), which authorized avoidance of landlord's liens in bankruptcy. Considering the high likelihood that a failing debtor will pass through bankruptcy on its way out of existence, a lien that can be avoided in bankruptcy does not provide very much security. Since 1979, commercial lessors have increasingly included in their leases provisions granting themselves Article 9 security interests in their debtor's property then on the premises or later brought onto it. The effect of such provisions is to create a consensual "landlord's lien," that trustees in bankruptcy have no power to avoid.

U.C.C. §9-333 addresses the issue of priority between security interests and liens arising by operation of law. That section grants no lien and determines the relative priority of a statutory lien only if the statute or rule of law creating the lien does not. U.C.C. §9-333 provides as the default rule of priority that a lien by operation of law has priority over even an earlier perfected Article 9 security interest. The liens to which this default rule applies are narrowly defined. The lien must be (1) in favor of a person who furnishes services or materials in the ordinary course of his or her business, (2) for the purchase price of the services and materials, (3) on goods in the possession of the lien holder. The lien holder must have furnished the services or materials "with respect to [the] goods against which the lien holder claims. Essentially, the liens described are possessory artisan's liens. Landlord's liens are not affected by U.C.C. §9-333; they are excluded from the coverage of Article 9. See U.C.C. §9-109(d)(1).

In situations to which U.C.C. §9-333 applies, it reverses a presumption in case law that statutory liens are subordinate to mortgages and security interests unless the statute creating the lien clearly specifies to the contrary.

In the following case, the court construes a California lien statute to determine whether it gives the lienors priority over previously recorded security interests. The facts of the case illustrate the potential importance of such liens in the context of a failing business. Those in control of such a business may help themselves, their friends, and (in this case) their attorneys to whatever assets remain by granting security interests. Absent a statutory lien, "outsiders" such as employees, tort creditors, and occasional suppliers will be out of luck.

Myzer v. Emark Corporation

45 Cal. App. 4th 884, 53 Cal. Rptr. 2d 60
(Cal. App. 1996)

Huffman, J.

Jeff Myzer brought this class action on behalf of employees of Emark Corporation (Emark) who had been denied wages and benefits due. The court denied his motion to determine priority of claims and granted the cross-motions of defendants Pat Keig, Mike Rummel and Rieck and Crotty, P.C. (Rieck & Crotty), Emark's secured creditors. Myzer appeals the denial of his motion and the ensuing judgment, contending the employees' claims are entitled to priority under Code of Civil Procedure section 1205. We agree.

FACTUAL AND PROCEDURAL BACKGROUND

Rieck & Crotty's Claim

Rieck & Crotty were Emark's corporate counsel until around March 1993. On April 29, 1992, Emark executed a $170,000 promissory note and an agreement granting Rieck & Crotty a perfected security interest in accounts, general intangibles, inventory, equipment, cash and records. On July 1, 1993, after Emark defaulted, Rieck & Crotty agreed not to seek immediate enforcement in exchange for a $229,260.62 note secured by the same collateral.

After Emark again defaulted, Rieck & Crotty foreclosed and acquired the collateral through a $170,000 credit bid at the November 11, 1993, foreclosure sale, subject to prior secured claims of the Bank of Southern California (BSC) and Alliance Financial of California, Inc. (Alliance). On November 22, 1993, Rieck & Crotty sold the collateral to Sorrento Electronics, Inc. (Sorrento) for $350,000. . . .

Keig and Rummel's Claim

Keig was a director of Emark and Rummel was its chief financial officer. On January 1 and 2, 1992, Emark executed a $74,549.73 note in favor of

Rummel, notes totaling $591,668.41 in favor of Keig, and agreements granting them perfected security interests in certain property. On April 29, 1992, Emark executed a $50,000 note in favor of Keig. On July 1, 1993, after Emark defaulted, Keig and Rummel agreed not to seek immediate enforcement and Emark executed a $129,210 secured note in favor of Rummel and a $772,993.14 secured note in favor of Keig. On September 2, 1993, Keig and Rummel recorded a "UCC-1" financing statement. Emark again defaulted.

The Employees' Lawsuit

In late 1993, the paychecks of all Emark employees were held and the employees were told they would be paid as part of the closing costs of the sale to Sorrento. After the sale was finalized, Emark's creditors told the employees they would be offered a percentage of their wages and benefits because there was not enough money for everyone. Apparently, no employees were paid after August 30, 1993.

On October 25, 1993, Myzer filed the complaint to recover wages and benefits and for damages, an accounting, and declaratory and injunctive relief. . . . [A]pproximately 45 Emark employees seek recovery of unpaid wages and benefits earned between August 30 and October 21, 1993. . . .

Discussion

Myzer contends section 1205 gives Emark's employees' claims priority over the claims of Emark's secured creditors Keig, Rummel and Rieck & Crotty.

Section 1205 states:

Upon the sale or transfer of any business or the stock in trade, in bulk, or a substantial part thereof, not in the ordinary and regular course of business or trade, unpaid wages of employees of the seller or transferor earned within ninety (90) days prior to the sale, transfer, or opening of an escrow for the sale thereof, shall constitute preferred claims and liens thereon as between creditors of the seller or transferor and must be paid first from the proceeds of the sale or transfer.

There appears to be no case law interpreting §1205. . . . [T]he statute here accords wage claimants a lien, not merely a preferred claim, and moreover sets forth no exclusions or limitations. . . . We conclude §1205 accorded Emark's employees' claims priority over those of Emark's secured creditors Keig, Rummel and Rieck & Crotty.

D. Statutory Liens as a Challenge to the First-in-Time Rule

The fundamental rule of priority under Article 9 is the rule of first in time, first in right. The putative advantage of that rule is that, when used in combination with an effective filing system, it lets lenders know where they will stand if they lend to the debtor. That is, if First-bank is considering making a loan to Mildred Washington against her car, Firstbank can search the certificate of title records and determine what prior liens exist. If there are none, Firstbank can lend with the assurance that they will have the first lien, and that it will remain the first lien.

To the extent that statutory lien laws permit the taking of liens that prime prior perfected liens, they arguably upset this expectation. Central Auto Repair can later acquire a garage keeper's lien that primes the security interest taken by Firstbank. Knowing its security interest can be primed by a later lien may deter Firstbank from lending Mildred Washington any money in the first place.

Arguments for giving priority to later statutory liens focus on the value contributed by the lienor. Assume, for example, that Mildred Washington owes GMAC $7,000 against her car, which on Tuesday is worth exactly that amount. On Wednesday, the engine overheats, requiring a $3,000 repair, which Central Auto Repair performs on credit on Thursday. On Friday, the car is running again, and is again worth $7,000. But now the car is in the possession of Central Auto Repair and Central has both a $3,000 lien and the right to retain the car until paid. Because Mildred can't pay for the repair, Central Auto Repair eventually sells the car for $7,000. In a state that gives priority to the garage keeper's lien, Central takes $3,000 from the proceeds for the repair bill, and remits the $4,000 balance to GMAC. Defenders of statutory lien priority would argue that GMAC was not injured by this deviation from first in time, first in right. Immediately prior to the repair, the car must have been worth only $4,000. If the law did not give Central Auto Repair priority, Central would not have made the repair and Firstbank would have recovered only $4,000 anyway.

There are several weaknesses in this value-added justification for statutory lien priority. First, nearly all debts result from the creditor furnishing new value. If that were enough to justify priority over an earlier lien holder, the result would be a system in which the last in time was generally the first in right. It might be difficult to persuade anyone to make the first loan in such a system. Second, many statutory lien laws award liens to persons who do not even arguably add value to the collateral. They include some kinds of tax liens, the lien for towing a vehicle from a place where it is safely but illegally parked, the attorney's retaining lien, and many others. Third, even when a statutory lien is of a type for which the lienor *gives* value, that does not mean that the debtor *gets* value. The debtor may be exercising poor judgment in deciding to have the car repaired. A repair for which the lien holder appropriately charges $3,000 will not necessarily increase the value of the car by $3,000.

Ideally, statutory lien holders would get priority in any case where the statutory lien holder gave value *and* the secured creditor got value. That, however, is the view expressed in the doctrine of unjust enrichment. The courts have generally rejected unjust enrichment as a justification for upsetting the priority granted to secured creditors under Article 9. Recall that this argument was raised in *PCA v. Duggan* in Assignment 35. The fear is that a fair rule would be too difficult to administer.

Instead, the priority of particular statutory liens differs from state to state. In some instances, the system gives secured creditors priority on the theory that letting each creditor know where it stands at the time it makes its loan will result in more credit being available in total. In other instances, the system gives statutory lien holders priority on the presumption that the value they give will not exceed the value added to the collateral.

E. Secured Creditor Responses to Statutory Lien Priority

On close examination, most laws giving statutory lien holders priority over earlier perfected secured creditors turn out to provide limited protection against the secured creditors. Secured creditors can and do take steps to protect themselves. Among the means that secured creditors can use are the following:

1. *Covenants*. Most secured lenders require, as a condition of the loan, that the debtor agree not to do anything that would give rise to a statutory lien. Such covenants are relatively ineffective. They do not bind statutory lien holders who are not party to them. The covenant will be in the security agreement, and most garage keepers, for example, will not see that document before they perform a repair. While the debtor will be liable for breach of the covenant, a debtor who incurs a statutory lien and fails to discharge it by payment is

almost certainly insolvent. Any judgment the creditor recovers against such a debtor for breach of this covenant is likely to be uncollectible. Besides, the damages are likely to be measured by the unpaid balance of the loan that was not satisfied from the collateral. Thus, the action for breach of the covenant adds nothing but an alternative, unneeded basis for the entry of an unsecured judgment for the amount of the debt.

2. *Payment.* Most statutory liens that have priority over earlier perfected security interests are relatively small and predictable in amount. Real property taxes are a good example. Every state levies an annual tax on real property. The tax varies in amount from about 1 percent to about 3 percent of the total value of the property. Mortgages against real property are typically in an original amount between about 50 percent and 100 percent of the total value of the property. The tax is thus small in relation to the mortgage. Mortgages typically provide that the debtor will make timely payment of the property tax. Default in payment of the tax is a default under the mortgage, giving the mortgagee the right to foreclose. Because the tax debt is relatively small, the mortgagee can prevent the taxing authority from foreclosing by paying the taxes. Most mortgages give the mortgagee the right to do that and add the amount so paid to the amount due under the mortgage. While the mortgagee might lose an amount equal to a year's taxes because of the debtor's failure to pay them, it cannot lose its collateral to foreclosure. Many mortgages require that the debtor pay the taxes to the mortgagee in advance, so that the mortgagee can pay them to the taxing authority.

3. *Waiver.* Some statutory lien laws permit the lien holder to waive its rights. If the debtor has sufficient leverage with the lien holder to extract such a waiver, the secured creditor may, as a condition of its loan, require that the debtor obtain the waiver. For example, in some states it is customary for those who supply labor or materials in the construction of a building to waive their liens in advance. The debtor simply refuses to hire any subcontractor or supplier that will not waive its statutory lien. The debtor does this because construction lenders will not lend to debtors who do not obtain waivers. In these jurisdictions, construction lien holders and construction lenders are permitted to and do contract out of the statutory rule giving priority to the construction lien holders.

4. *Monitoring.* Statutory liens that prime prior perfected mortgages and security interests can arise in substantial amounts in favor of creditors who have no reason to give waivers. For example, statutes in three states give the state's environmental cleanup lien priority over earlier perfected security interests and mortgages. One such statute is that of the environmentally active (pun intended) state of New Jersey:

Cleanup and Removal of Hazardous Substances

N.J. Rev. Stat. §58:10-23.11f (West 1994)

a. (1) Whenever any hazardous substance is discharged, the department may, in its discretion, act to clean up and remove or arrange for the cleanup and removal of such discharge. . . .

f. Any expenditures made by the administrator pursuant to this act shall constitute, in each instance, a debt of the discharger to the fund. The debt shall constitute a lien on all property owned by the discharger when a notice of lien, incorporating a description of the property of the discharger subject to the cleanup and removal and an identification of the amount of cleanup, removal and related costs expended from the fund, is duly filed with the clerk of the Superior Court. . . .

The notice of lien filed pursuant to this subsection which affects the property of a discharger subject to the cleanup and removal of a discharge shall create a lien with priority over all other claims or liens which are or have been filed against the property, except if the property comprises six dwelling units or less and is used exclusively for residential purposes, this notice of lien shall not affect any valid lien, right or interest in the property filed in accordance with established procedure prior to the filing of this notice of lien. The notice of lien filed pursuant to this subsection which affects any property of a discharger, other than the property subject to the cleanup and removal, shall have priority from the day of the filing of the notice of the lien over all other claims and liens filed against the property, but shall not affect any valid lien, right, or interest in the property filed in accordance with established procedure prior to the filing of a notice of lien pursuant to this subsection.

An environmental cleanup lien can easily exceed the entire market value of the property, rendering the prior perfected security interests worthless. Faced with a statute such as this, the secured lender's best response may be to monitor its debtor's activities to make sure that the need for a cleanup does not arise. Such monitoring begins at the time the loan is made. Through its own employees or a subcontractor, the secured lender will inspect the property for environmental contamination that might later require cleanup. If such contamination is present, the secured creditor can refuse to lend until the debtor has cleaned the property and paid the bills. Because even a later contamination can give rise to a prior lien, the secured creditor must continue to monitor the debtor's activities after the loan is made.

Statutory lien laws that force secured lenders to monitor the activities of their debtors are highly controversial. They have the potential to provide a social benefit by preventing environmental contamination, pension underfunding, nonpayment of taxes, and numerous other social ills. But in accomplishing that, they require lenders to involve themselves in activities outside their traditional role and make lending more costly.

Problem Set 37

37.1.   a. Debtor owns an original painting by Vincent Van Gogh, which is subject to a duly perfected security interest in favor of First-bank. The painting was damaged in an attempted burglary and Debtor takes it to Elisa Morse, a specialist, for repair. Morse repairs the painting. When Debtor proves unable to pay for the cleaning, Morse retains possession. Pressed by this and other financial problems, Debtor files bankruptcy. As between Morse, Firstbank, and the Chapter 7 trustee, who has priority? Bankr. Code §§101 (definition of "statutory lien"), 545, 547(c)(6); U.C.C. §§9-333, 9-109(d)(2). Assume that California law applies and that no provisions other than the U.C.C. and California Civil Code §3051, set forth in section A of this assignment, are relevant.

b.   Norman Farms sold 400 bushels of California tomatoes to American Produce, a licensed dealer in perishable agricultural commodities. Norman failed to take a security interest in what it sold, but it did include in its invoice the statement that "The perishable agricultural commodities listed on this invoice are sold subject to the statutory trust authorized by section 5(c) of the Perishable Agricultural Commodities Act." American paid by check. American sold half the tomatoes to Star Markets, a regional grocer in Massachusetts and the other half to Haunt's Cannery in Mississippi. Both Star and Haunt's paid American by electronic cash transfer. Star sold their Norman tomatoes to retail customers over the next five days. Haunt's canned their half of the Norman tomatoes and sold them to Publix, a regional grocer in Florida. Publix has not yet paid the purchase price to Haunt's, but has received delivery of the cans in its Jacksonville warehouse. American's check to Norman Farms bounced, and it now appears that American is deeply insolvent. Norman asks you whether there are sources other than American Produce from which they might recover. Are there?

37.2.   Jean Widdington bought a car for $8,000. GMAC lent Widdington $7,000 of the purchase price and secured the loan with a purchase-money security interest. GMAC had its lien noted on the certificate of title. When the engine overheated, Widdington took it to Central Auto Repair. Although Widdington's contract with GMAC required that she notify GMAC and obtain their permission before contracting for any repair costing more than $2,500, she did neither. The repair cost $3,000. Central Auto Repair asserted a lien under the following Wisconsin statute, gave proper notice under Wisconsin Statute §779.48, and eventually sold the car at auction for $5,000.

Mechanic's Liens

Wis. Stat. Ann. (West 1994)

§779.41

(1) Every mechanic and every keeper of a garage or shop, and every employer of a mechanic who transports, makes, alters, repairs or does any work on personal property at the request of the owner or legal possessor of the personal property, has a lien on the personal property for the just and reasonable charges therefor, including any parts, accessories, materials or supplies furnished in connection therewith and may retain possession of the personal property until the charges are paid. The lien provided by this section is subject to the lien of any security interest in the property which is perfected as provided by law prior to the commencement of the work for which a lien is claimed unless the work was done with the express consent of the holder of the security interest, but only for charges in excess of $1,000 except if the personal property is:

    (a)   A trailer or semitrailer designed for use with a road tractor, for charges in excess of $3,000.

    (b)   Road machinery, including mobile cranes and trench hoes, farm tractors, machines of husbandry, or off-highway construction vehicles and equipment, for charges in excess of $5,000. . . .

§779.48   HOW SUCH LIENS ENFORCED . . .

(2) Every person given a lien by §779.41   may in case the claim remains unpaid for two months after the debt is incurred enforce such lien by sale of the property substantially in conformity with [U.C.C. §§9-601 to 9-628] and the lien claimant shall have the rights and duties of a secured party thereunder. . . .

---

    a. Does Central have a lien?

    b. If so, with what priority in relation to GMAC? U.C.C. §9-333.

    c. Is the buyer's title free and clear of GMAC's security interest? U.C.C. §9-617.

d.   Who is entitled to the $5,000? U.C.C. §9-615.

e.   What would the result be under Maine law? See 10 Maine Statutes §§3801-3802, set forth in section A of this assignment.

37.3.   a. You represent Oaks Mall, Ltd., a shopping center whose business is located in Oregon. Buffy Oaks, the CEO of Oaks Mall, consults you regarding Powder Puff, Inc. For 12 years, Powder Puff's sole place of business has been a store in the Oaks Mall. Powder Puff is now six months in arrears in the payment of rent for a total of $42,000, and has just closed the store. Does Oaks have a lien against any of the following assets: equipment (estimated value $25,000, inventory (estimated value $25,000), and fixtures (estimated value $25,000) remaining in the store, equipment that Power Puff recently removed from the store (estimated value $5,000), and accounts receivable for sales made from the store's Web site (estimated value $10,000)? See Oregon Statutes §§87.146, 87.162 in section A of this assignment. U.C.C. §§9-333, 9-109(d)(1) and (2).

b.   Five years ago, Powder Puff obtained a loan from Secondbank. Secondbank perfected a security interest in all of Powder Puff's "fixtures, equipment, and inventory." The amount currently owing on that debt is $80,000. All of the fixtures and equipment were in the store before Secondbank made its loan. Powder Puff acquired the inventory presently on hand with funds supplied by Secondbank. Secondbank complied with the requirements of U.C.C. §9-324(b) for obtaining purchase-money status in the inventory. Between Secondbank and Oaks Mall, who has priority? U.C.C. §§9-203(a) and (b).

c.   In addition to the creditors mentioned above, Powder Puff has $100,000 in unsecured debt owing to 25 creditors. Powder Puff makes a restructuring proposal that calls for sale of Powder Puff's assets and the collection of its accounts receivable. From the proceeds, Powder Puff will pay $21,000 to Oaks, $45,000 to Secondbank, and the remaining $24,000 will be divided pro rata among the unsecured creditors, including the unpaid portion of Secondbank's debt. Power Puff says that unless Oaks and Secondbank agree to its proposal, Powder Puff will file under Chapter 11 and liquidate under the protection of the Bankruptcy Court. Buffy wants to know what you think of this offer. Bankr. Code §§545, 547(c)(6), 551.

37.4.   One of your first clients after you set up in solo practice was John Gage, who owns a local restaurant. Gage gave you a will his former lawyer prepared for him seven years ago and instructions for preparing a new will. Drafting the new will required sophisticated tax research and Gage agreed to pay for it. After you had invested about 15 hours in the project, Gage instructed you to stop work because he had decided not to change wills. A week ago, you sent Gage a bill for $1,800 (reduced from your regular billing rate because the job had been canceled). Gage has not paid the bill, but he is now in your office seeking return of the original will. When you asked about payment of your bill, Gage said that you should "send me another copy." You have the distinct feeling that if you give Gage the original will, he will never pay you. What do you do now? See §770 of Illinois Statute 5/1, set forth in section A of this assignment.

Rule 1.16 of the Model Rules of Professional Conduct provides:

> (d) Upon termination of representation, a lawyer shall take steps to the extent reasonably practicable to protect a client's interests, such as giving reasonable notice to the client, allowing time for employment of other counsel, surrendering papers and property to which the client is entitled and refunding any advance payment of fee that has not been earned. The lawyer may retain papers relating to the client to the extent permitted by other law.

37.5. Governor Margaret Delgado was elected in large part on the basis of her promise to "put the environment first." As a legal aide to the Governor, you have been assigned to evaluate a proposed change in the priority of the state's lien for environmental cleanup. Under current law, the state has a lien for its expenditures made to clean up contaminated property. The lien is subordinate to earlier perfected mortgages. The state frequently cleans up a property only to find that its lien is worthless. Earlier mortgages absorb the entire value of the property. The Governor would specifically like to know how well environmental cleanup lien priority is working in New Jersey, Massachusetts, and Connecticut. What questions would you ask to find out, and of whom would you ask them?

Assignment 38: Competitions Involving Federal Tax Liens: The Basics

The U.S. government is one of the principal competitors for debtors' assets. It competes on the basis of hundreds of kinds of obligations, including taxes, criminal fines, small business loans, student loans, accidental overpayments of Social Security benefits, and many others. In this assignment, we examine the government's rights with regard to the most frequent of these obligations, the debt for unpaid taxes. The government's receipts from taxes now exceed $1 trillion per year. At any given time, delinquent taxes total some $30 billion owed by about 4.5 million taxpayers.

Debtors owe many kinds of taxes to the U.S. government. Probably the largest amounts owing at any given time are for income taxes. Although they account for many tax delinquencies, income taxes are not the principal source of tax losses for the U.S. government. The threat of criminal prosecution and large civil penalties is generally sufficient to cause debtors who have money to pay their income taxes. Tax losses are usually incurred on taxes owing from debtors with business losses; they often do not have the money to pay. A debtor with business losses will tend not to owe income tax. Income tax delinquencies sometimes result in federal tax liens, but only a small percentage of federal tax liens arise from income taxes.

By far the most common source of federal tax liens is payroll taxes, in the form of federal withholding taxes and Social Security contributions owed by employers to the U.S. government. Provisions of the Internal Revenue Code (IRC) require that every employer "deduct" from every employee's pay the estimated income tax the employee will owe to the government at the end of the year and pay that money directly to the Internal Revenue Service (IRS). (We put "deduct" in quotes because the word implies that the employer takes money from a fund when in fact the employer may never have had the money it "deducts.") The Federal Insurance Contributions Act (FICA) divides the Social Security tax levy, imposing half on employers and half on employees. FICA requires that the employer "deduct" the employee's half of the tax from the employee's pay and pay both halves directly to the IRS. If the payroll is small, the employer is required to forward the money for these taxes to the IRS quarterly; if larger, the employer is required to forward the money more frequently.

For many businesses, payroll taxes are a substantial portion of cash flow. Considering that most payroll taxes are deducted from the pay of employees, it might seem that employers should have little trouble paying them. But the "deduction" is a legal fiction; the employer may never have had the "deducted" funds in the first place. To illustrate, assume that Rhonda is an employer who has agreed to pay her only employee, Ernie, $1,000 a week. Based on current tax rates and Ernie's personal circumstances, Rhonda is required to withhold $250 a week for Ernie's income taxes and an additional $80 for Social Security. At the end of the week, she pays Ernie $670. Rhonda's half of the Social Security is an additional $80, for a total of $410 that Rhonda is supposed to pay the IRS. Because Rhonda's payroll is small, she need only pay the IRS four times a year. For now, she keeps the $410. At the end of the 13-week quarter, she will make a single payment to the IRS in the amount of $5,330.

If Rhonda is in financial difficulty and unable to pay all of her bills as they become due, things may not work so smoothly. As Rhonda decides which bills to pay and which to leave for later, those bills the nonpayment of which will immediately bring her business to a close are likely to be highest on her list. That probably will include Ernie's $670 paycheck each week, because if Ernie doesn't get paid, he will quit. It probably will include the utility company if it is about to turn off the lights, and it will include payments to suppliers whose products are needed and who will deliver them only for cash. What about the payroll taxes owing to the IRS? Their nonpayment represents no threat to Rhonda's business — at least until they become due. When they do, Rhonda may not have the money, having spent it on later payroll, utility bills, and suppliers. Or Rhonda may never have had the money in the first place. What happens if she doesn't pay the taxes? Immediately, not much. In all likelihood, it will take the IRS weeks to discover that Rhonda did not make the payment. Penalties will accrue in the interim. Tax law designates the money collected for these taxes as held in a "trust fund" even in the absence of any separate account for these receipts, and it imposes penalties for nonpayment from the day these "trust funds" are due. Rhonda may be well aware that her knowing and intentional failure to pay these "trust funds" to the IRS is a crime and that the resulting liability will be nondischargeable in bankruptcy. But frightening as they may be in the long run, in the short run they pale beside the problems of a person whose business is failing. Persons like Rhonda pay what they must to keep their businesses and their hopes alive. While the IRS sleeps on its rights, people like Rhonda lie awake at night worrying about their mounting liabilities to that sleeping giant.

Eventually, the sleeping giant will awaken. When it does, it will not charge Rhonda with the crime she committed by embezzling the "trust funds" she used to pay the light bill; too many employers have done the same thing to attempt to prosecute them all. Instead, the IRS will assess the amount of payroll tax due and then, within a matter of weeks or months, file a Notice of Tax Lien against Rhonda. When it files the Notice, the U.S. government enters the competition that has been the subject of the second half of this book. The IRS files about 1.5 million Notices of Tax Lien each year.

A. The Creation and Perfection of Federal Tax Liens

1. Creation

I.R.C. §§6321 and 6322 govern the creation of a federal tax lien. When the IRS determines that tax is owing, it *assesses* the tax by recording the amount on its own records. When it notifies the taxpayer of the assessment, that notice constitutes the *demand* described in I.R.C. §6321 and the tax lien comes into existence and relates back to the date and time of assessment.

The lien attaches to "all property and rights to property, whether real or personal, belonging to" the taxpayer. I.R.C. §6321. This is the ultimate floating lien; it reaches all property the debtor owns. But like a security interest that has attached under U.C.C. §9-203 but not yet been perfected under §9-308(a), this unperfected tax lien will be effective against the debtor, but not against third parties who acquire liens against or purchase the property.

2. Perfection

The Federal Tax Lien Act does not use the word "perfection." Instead, it deems the federal tax lien not "valid" until the IRS files notice of its lien. I.R.C. §6323(a). I.R.C. §6323(f) defers to state law as to the system in which the IRS must file the notice. In response to that section, each state has enacted a law specifying the appropriate public record system. The following statute is typical:

New York Lien Law

(McKinney 1994)

§240. PLACE OF FILING NOTICES OF LIENS
AND CERTIFICATES AND NOTICES AFFECTING
SUCH LIENS

1. Notices of liens upon real property for taxes payable to the United States of America or otherwise created by federal law in favor of the United States of America or one or more of its instrumentalities, hereafter in this article referred to as "federal liens" and certificates and notices affecting such liens shall be filed in the office of the clerk of the county in which real property subject to any such lien is situated, except that if real property subject to any such lien is situated in the county of Kings, the county of Queens, the county of New York or the county of Bronx they shall be filed in the office of the city register of the city of New York in such county. If such property be situated in two or more counties, such notice or certificate shall be filed in the office of the clerk or the city register, as the case may be, in each of such counties.

2. Notices of federal liens upon tangible or intangible personal property and certificates and notices affecting such liens shall be filed as follows:

(a) If the person against whose interest the lien applies is a corporation or a partnership, as defined in the internal revenue laws of the United States, in the office of the secretary of state;

(b) In all other cases, in the office of the clerk of the county where the lienee, if a resident of the state, resides at the time of filing of the notice of lien, except that if such lienee resides at such time in the county of Kings, the county of Queens, the county of New York or the county of Bronx, the place for filing such liens shall be in the office of the city register of the city of New York in such county. . . .

Although the Federal Tax Lien Act (FTLA) does not use the term "perfected," the filing of a Notice of Tax Lien has essentially that effect. If a Notice of Tax Lien has not yet been filed when a debtor sells its property, grants a security interest in it, or loses possession to a sheriff under a writ of execution, the tax lien will not be valid against that competitor. If a Notice of Tax Lien has been filed before any of those events occur, the tax lien will be valid against that competitor. The

Federal Tax Lien Act does not use the term "priority" either. Instead, it deems the tax lien "not valid" against a particular competing interest until notice of the lien is filed. Read literally, this language probably would not have integrated the federal tax lien into the state law system of priorities, but, fortunately, it has not been read literally. The admonition in §6323(a) that "the lien . . . shall not be valid against" certain competitors "until notice . . . has been filed" has been read to mean that the lien is subordinate to those competitors if those competitors perfect before the notice of tax lien is filed.

The big picture here is that with regard to tax liens, the U.S. government participates in the perfection and priority game along with everybody else. Its tax liens prevail over the liens of others if the IRS files first, and loses to them if it does not. The IRS plays this game badly. It usually is slow to discover that taxes are owing and slow to file its Notice of Tax Lien when it does. But what is most interesting is that the IRS plays at all. The U.S. government could have enacted a statute giving federal tax liens priority over all other liens against the debtor's property. This is in fact what state governments have done with regard to property taxes. When a state property tax lien comes into existence under state law, it primes mortgages and other liens against the property.

Why didn't the federal government do the same for its tax liens? The answer to this question has two parts. First, the principal reason for not putting federal tax liens ahead of security interests and mortgages was a fear that doing so would deter needed commercial lending. State property taxes are relatively small in relation to the value of the property, and both the time of assessment and the amount of the taxes are fairly predictable. When such a lien arises and primes the mortgage lender, the mortgage lender can deal with it by paying the tax and adding it to the balance owing on the mortgage loan. Federal tax liens for payroll taxes are often large in relation to the value of the property and they can accumulate quickly and unpredictably. To give them priority irrespective of when they arise would pose a problem of an entirely different magnitude for secured lenders.

The second part of the answer is that the U.S. government may yet reconsider its decision to play in the perfection/priority game. Canada recently adopted a statute giving payroll taxes priority over creditors secured by accounts receivables. The practical effect has been to force accounts receivable lenders to monitor their debtors' operations to make sure payroll taxes are paid when due and do not accumulate. While Canadian circumstances differ from those in the United States, if the Canadian experiment succeeds, it may prompt reconsideration of the priority of tax liens here.

While the U.S. government plays in the perfection/priority game essentially as it is defined by state law, the government brings its own set of rules. Those rules, most of which are contained in I.R.C. §6323, reconceptualize much of state law in ways disconcerting to those already familiar with Article 9. For example, I.R.C. §6323(h)(1) defines a security interest as existing only if it is perfected and only to the extent that the holder has "parted with money or money's worth." Thus, security interests that have attached and become enforceable under U.C.C. §§9-203(a) and (b) may not yet exist for purposes of the Federal Tax Lien Act. (We deal with this reconceptualization at length in the next assignment.) For now, the best way to deal with this and other inconsistencies in the perfection/priority system is what we call the "finger" method. When you are solving a problem, make sure your finger is on the governing rule (and, of course, that you read what your finger is on).

3. Remedies for Enforcement

The Federal Tax Lien Act provides the remedy for enforcement of federal tax liens. If the taxpayer does not pay the tax within ten days after notice and demand, the IRS can levy on the taxpayer's property. (The notice is notice that a levy is forthcoming, not merely a Notice of Tax Lien.) The IRS is not required to use the services of a sheriff or marshal to levy; IRS employees can perform the levy and, if necessary, sell the assets. The IRS can levy in either of two ways. The first is physically to seize property of the debtor. The second is to serve a notice of levy on a bank at which the debtor has an account or on some other third party who is in possession of the debtor's property. The third party must then remit the bank account or other property to the IRS or be liable for its value. Serving a notice of levy is easier and less complicated, which probably accounts for the fact that the IRS serves about 3.5 million notices of levy on third parties each year, but makes only about 11,000 physical seizures of property.

State exemption laws do not apply against the IRS; the Federal Tax Lien Act contains a set of exemptions from federal tax levies that are less favorable to debtors than the exemption laws of most states. (Here, too, the government brings its own rules to the game.) As soon as practicable after seizure, the IRS sells the property to the highest bidder by public auction or by public sale under sealed bids and applies the proceeds of sale to the tax debt. As you would expect, the tax sale is subject to prior liens, which often include security interests and mortgages. The buyer at the tax sale takes free of subordinate liens, which are discharged by the sale.

4. Maintaining Perfection of a Tax Lien

I.R.C. §6323(g) establishes a "required refiling period" for a Notice of Tax Lien. The period is the one-year period ending 30 days after the expiration of ten years after the date of assessment of the tax. If the IRS fails to refile during the required refiling period, the effect is that the lien lapses. The IRS may be able to revive the lien by refiling after lapse, but the lien will then be subordinate to competing liens perfected against the collateral before the refiling. If the IRS does refile within the required periods, it can maintain the lien perpetually.* All of this should seem familiar; it is essentially the scheme of Article 9 with regard to continuation and lapse, but with different time periods.

The Federal Tax Lien Act contains no provision analogous to U.C.C. §9-507 regarding name changes and sales of collateral. But, as you can see from the following case, these issues occasionally arise.

United States v. LMS Holding Co.

161 B.R. 1020 (N.D. Okla. 1993)

THOMAS R. BRETT, DISTRICT JUDGE

Now before the Court is the United States of America's appeal of a decision by the United States Bankruptcy Court for the Northern District of Oklahoma. The Bankruptcy Court found that Appellees could avoid a lien by the Internal Revenue Service ("IRS") pursuant to 11 U.S.C. §544(a)(1). The result of that decision left the IRS with an unsecured claim against Debtors.

I. THE FACTS

In January 25, 1988, the IRS filed a perfected Notice of Tax Lien against property held by MAKO, Inc.[1] MAKO filed bankruptcy and filed a plan that listed the IRS claim as a "Disputed Secured Claim." Subsequently, Retail Marketing Corporation ("RMC") acquired the property that was subject to the tax lien. The IRS had notice of the MAKO bankruptcy and was aware of the formulation and confirmation of the plan, which included the terms of the sale of the MAKO property to RMC. The MAKO plan was confirmed in August of 1989.

The IRS did not file a Notice of Tax Lien against RMC or any other type of filing in the name of RMC or the other debtors, alerting others of its tax lien on the property. RMC later filed for bankruptcy. . . .

[T]he Bankruptcy Court held that the IRS, pursuant to 26 U.S.C. §6323, was required to file a new notice of tax lien against RMC. Since it failed

---

* It is important to distinguish the tax lien from the underlying tax debt. If the statute of limitations runs on the underlying tax debt, the lien becomes ineffective even if the lien has not itself expired. The IRS may prevent the statute of limitations from running by taking certain actions, or the debtor may have taken some action that will toll the statute.

1. The IRS claimed that MAKO owed it some $350,000 in delinquent taxes and interest.

to do so, the Bankruptcy Court found that the RMC was entitled to avoid the lien pursuant to 11 U.S.C. §544(a)(1). That decision left the IRS with an unsecured claim against RMC.

II.   LEGAL ANALYSIS

The issue is whether the Bankruptcy Court erred as a matter of law in finding that the IRS was required to file a second Notice of Tax Lien under 26 U.S.C. §6323 against RMC to retain their status as a judgment lien creditor. Section 6321 states that the IRS can file a lien against delinquent taxpayers. But §6323(a) states:

> The lien imposed by section 6321 shall not be valid as against any purchaser, holder of a security interest, mechanic's lienor, or judgment lien creditor until notice thereof which meets the requirements of subsection (f) has been filed by the Secretary.

No mandatory precedent on this specific issue was found, but a close analogy exists between the facts here and cases involving a taxpayer's name change. For example, in Davis v. United States, 705 F. Supp. 446 (C.D. Ill. 1989), the IRS filed a notice of tax lien against the property of "Gillian Renslow" for delinquent taxes. Gillian Renslow, however, was divorced in 1981 and changed her name to "Gillian Rongey" in 1982 when she remarried. The IRS did not file a second tax lien against Gillian Rongey. Rongey then sold the property in 1986. The IRS started foreclosure proceedings [against the person who bought the property from Rongey], asserting that it did not have to refile notice of a tax lien when a taxpayer has changed her name. The court rejected that argument:

> The entire statutory scheme under which the IRS is granted the duty and authority to file notices of tax liens compels a finding of a duty to refile under such circumstances. The sine qua non of Section 6323 is notice to subsequent takers of the existence of the IRS lien.

The court held that "where the IRS has notice that a delinquent taxpayer has changed his or her name, and where the notice of tax lien was filed under the taxpayer's original name, the IRS is under an affirmative duty to refile the notice of tax lien to show the taxpayer's new name." Another court, facing a similar issue, concluded:

> The remarriage of Carolyn Clark (of which the Internal Revenue Service received notice) resulted in a situation where there was no reasonable opportunity for a prudent person dealing with the delinquent taxpayer to ascertain the existence of a federal tax lien. A "reasonable inspection" would not reveal the lien.

United States v. Clark, 81-1 U.S.T.C. P 9406 (S.D. Fla. 1981).

While the facts in the *Davis* and *Clark* cases differ from the instant case, the issues are similar. Here, the IRS filed a tax lien against property belonging to MAKO. The property changes hands, and the IRS — which knew about the RMC acquisition — failed to file a new lien in the name of RMC.

The IRS attempts to distinguish the instant case from Davis and Clark because no "name change" took place (i.e. MAKO did not become RMC). Yet, as the Bankruptcy Court pointed out, RMC's acquiring of MAKO property through bankruptcy is much more complex than a simple name change. If the IRS must file a new notice of a tax lien against taxpayers who merely change their name, the same result should ensue when an entirely new entity is involved. Otherwise, how would a reasonable inspection reveal that property owned by RMC is the subject of a federal tax lien that was filed originally against MAKO? In addition, the problem could have been eliminated had IRS simply followed the statute.

In essence, the IRS — which fails to provide persuasive or mandatory legal authority on point — asks the Court to ignore the requirements of §6323. That should not be done.[2] A valid lien under §6321 against judgment lien creditors must follow the requirements set forth in §6323(f). By not filing a new notice in the name of RMC, despite having knowledge of the RMC's acquisition of the MAKO property, the IRS erred. As a result of that error, the Bankruptcy Court found that the IRS now has an unsecured claim. That decision was not an error as a matter of law. As a result, the decision is AFFIRMED.

By imposing an obligation on the IRS to refile Notices of Tax Lien that could not be discovered on a search, cases like *LMS Holding Company* raise more questions than they answer. Article 9 contains several provisions that in essence give secured creditors four months or one year to react to a change in circumstances by refiling. The Federal Tax Lien Act contains no analogous provisions, leaving the courts to decide

---

2. Part of the IRS' argument appears to be that, once the IRS files a federal tax lien, it must do no more. See United States v. Cache Valley Bank, 866 F.2d 1242, 1244 (10th Cir. 1989) ("The federal tax lien arises when unpaid taxes are assessed and continues until the resulting liability is either satisfied or becomes unenforceable through lapse of time."). It is true that once a lien has attached in property, the lien cannot be extinguished (if it has been properly filed) by a transfer or conveyance of the interest. See, generally, United States v. Rodgers, 461 U.S. 677, 103 S. Ct 2132, 2141, fn.16, 76 L. Ed. 2d 236. But if no proper filing has taken place, the priority of the lien can be affected. See Title Guaranty Company v. Internal Revenue Service, 667 F. Supp. 767, 769 (D. Wyo. 1987) ("Failure to refile the lien does not necessarily affect the validity of the lien, but affects . . . the priority of the lien."). In the instant case, the Bankruptcy Court did not extinguish the lien. It merely concluded that, due to the IRS' failure to follow §6323, the IRS had only an unsecured claim.

what circumstances should trigger refiling and how long the IRS should have to refile.

Also notice the difference between *LMS Holding Company* and Article 9 with regard to the burden of discovering the change in circumstance. The refiling periods under Article 9 are periods in which the secured creditor must *discover* the change. *LMS Holding Company* imposed a duty to refile only because the IRS *knew of* the change. To our knowledge, no courts impose a duty on the IRS to *discover* changes, only to react to them when the IRS knows of them.

We earlier examined numerous obligations Article 9 places on secured parties to discover changes and make filings based on those discoveries. The penalty for failure was loss of perfection. Given that the priority system functions without placing any obligation on the IRS to discover and react to changes in the circumstances that controlled the filing of the federal tax lien, we wonder about the necessity for all those obligations under Article 9.

B. Competitions Involving Federal Tax Liens

The basic rule governing competition between federal tax liens and the rights of third parties is in I.R.C. §6323(a). That section provides that the tax lien "shall not be valid as against any purchaser, holder of a security interest, mechanic's lienor, or judgment lien creditor" until the IRS files a Notice of Tax Lien. The section is poorly drafted. Read literally, §6323(a) could yield a system in which tax liens had priority over nearly every other third-party interest. To illustrate the dangerous reading, assume that Debtor is the owner of Blackwidget and owes taxes, but the IRS has not yet filed a Notice of Tax Lien. Debtor borrows $60,000 from Firstbank and grants a security interest. Firstbank perfects by filing. Charles Creditor, an unsecured creditor of Debtor, obtains a judgment and levies on Blackwidget. Debtor then sells Blackwidget to Bess Buyer for $40,000. She pays the purchase price and takes possession without knowledge of Debtor's problems with the IRS. The IRS then files a Notice of Tax Lien. Reading §6323(a) literally, the tax lien was not "valid" against Firstbank, Creditor, or Buyer *until* the IRS filed the Notice of Tax Lien. The clear implication is that the tax lien is valid against those competitors *after* it is filed. You already know, however, that interpretation is incorrect. To get the right answer from I.R.C. §6323(a), one must read into it something it does not say: Tax liens and third-party interests rank in the order in which they became "valid" within the meaning of the Federal Tax Lien Act. The idea of "first in time, first in right" is so basic that the drafters of I.R.C. §6323 did not even consider it necessary to mention.

What is it that each of these competitors must do for their interests to be valid within the meaning of the Federal Tax Lien Act? To put the question another way, what is it that the holder of the competing interest must do before the IRS files its Notice of Tax Lien to be valid and prevail over the tax lien?

1. Security Interest

With regard to security interests, the answer to this question is in I.R.C. §6323(h)(1), which defines "security interest." That section provides that a security interest "exists" only when (A) the property is in existence and the interest has become protected against a judgment lien under local law and (B) the holder has parted with the money or other value, the repayment of which is secured. In essence, an Article 9 security interest will satisfy this test when it is perfected with respect to the particular advance. The security interest will prevail over the tax lien if the security interest satisfies that test before the government files the Notice of Tax Lien. (The validity of the Article 9 security interest as to advances not made until after the filing of the Notice of Tax Lien is a subject dealt with in the next assignment.) With regard to a mortgage, the rule of §6323(h)(1) has a somewhat less definite meaning. As to advances already made, a mortgage certainly has priority over competing judgment liens from the moment the mortgage is recorded. But, as we saw in Assignment 33, even an unrecorded mortgage might in some circumstances prevail over a recorded judgment lien. In those circumstances, it might prevail over the tax lien.

2. Purchaser

To prevail over a tax lien, a purchaser must acquire its status as such before the government files notice of the tax lien. I.R.C. §6323(a). I.R.C. §6323(h)(6) defines "purchaser" as a person who, "for adequate and full consideration in money or money's worth," acquires an interest valid under local law (that is, state law) against a subsequent purchaser without actual notice of the interest. Thus, a purchase can prevail over the tax lien if, before the government files notice of the tax lien, the purchaser does whatever it must to prevail over a second, later purchaser of the same property who buys without actual notice of the would-be purchaser's interest. A first purchaser of real estate ordinarily will prevail over later purchasers if the first purchaser records its deed before the second purchaser contracts to purchase and pays value. It follows that a purchaser of real estate prevails over a federal tax lien if the purchaser records its deed before the IRS records its Notice of Tax Lien.

In some states, a purchaser of real estate that goes into possession but does not record prevails over a later purchaser who does not have actual notice of the sale. Thus, it has been held that "possession alone gives actual notice under Florida law, sufficient to defeat a subsequent federal tax lien." United States v. Pledger, 158 F. Supp. 612, 614 (N.D. Fla. 1958); Waldorff Insurance and Bonding, Inc. v. Elgin National Bank, 453 So. 2d 1383, 1385 (Fla. Dist. Ct. App. 1984).

In the opinion that follows, the court appears to have decided that the same rule should not apply to the purchase of an automobile.

Mayer-Dupree v. Internal Revenue Service

1993 U.S. App. LEXIS 24639 (10th Cir. 1993)

DEANELL REECE TACHA, CIRCUIT JUDGE.

Appellant challenges the dismissal on motion for summary judgment of her wrongful levy action under 26 U.S.C. §7426. The government seized a vehicle in 1991 in satisfaction of federal tax liens that accrued in 1985 and were noticed in 1988 and 1990. Appellant alleges that she purchased the vehicle from the delinquent taxpayer in 1986. Although she alleges that she received the certificate of title at that time, she did not register the title until after the government seized the vehicle. The district court dismissed her action. We . . . affirm. . .

Under 26 U.S.C. §6323(a), a federal tax lien is not valid against a purchaser until the government files proper notice of the lien. Section 6323(h)(6) defines a purchaser as one who "acquires an interest (other than a lien or security interest) in property which is valid under local law against subsequent purchases without actual notice." We agree with the district court that appellant was not a purchaser because, under Colorado law, her failure to register the certificate of title as required by Colo. Rev. Stat. §42-6-109 (1984) rendered her interest in the vehicle invalid against a subsequent purchaser without notice.

Because appellant was not a purchaser, §6323(a) affords her no relief. We therefore AFFIRM for substantially the reasons given by the district court. The mandate shall issue forthwith.

As *Mayer-Dupree* illustrates, if local law requires the filing or recording of transfers of the particular type of personal property, the filing or recording is likely to be the act that protects the transferee against a tax lien later filed against the transferor. This will be true for sales of automobiles, aircraft, patents, trademarks, copyrights, accounts receivable, and chattel paper (remember U.C.C. §9-109(a)(3)). For most kinds of personal property, such filing or recording is not required. For them, the purchase is likely to be effective against later purchasers as soon as it is effective against the debtor. A purchase generally will be effective against the seller-debtor when the contract so provides. See U.C.C. §2-401(1) ("Subject to these provisions and to the provisions of [Article 9], title to goods passes from the seller to the buyer in any manner and on any conditions explicitly agreed to between the parties."). U.C.C. §2-403(2) is, however, an important exception. Under that section, a purchaser who leaves the property purchased with a seller who deals in goods of the kind loses to a later buyer in the ordinary course of business. This purchaser could well lose to a later filed tax lien.

3. Judgment Lien Creditor

The Federal Tax Lien Act does not define "judgment lien creditor" or say when one comes into existence for purposes of I.R.C. §6323(a). The Supreme Court has, however, developed extensive case law on the issue.

United States v. McDermott

507 U.S. 447 (1993)

JUSTICE SCALIA delivered the opinion of the Court.

We granted certiorari to resolve the competing priorities of a federal tax lien and a private creditor's judgment lien as to a delinquent taxpayer's after-acquired real property.

I

On December 9, 1986 the United States assessed Mr. and Mrs. McDermott for unpaid federal taxes due for the tax years 1977 through 1981. Upon that assessment, the law created a lien in favor of the United States on all real and personal property belonging to the McDermotts, 26 U.S.C. §§6321 and 6322, including after-acquired property. Pursuant to 26 U.S.C. §6323(a), however, that lien could "not be valid as against any purchaser, holder of a security interest, mechanic's lienor, or *judgment lien creditor* until notice thereof . . . has been filed." (Emphasis added). The United States did not file this lien in the Salt Lake County Recorder's Office until September 9, 1987. Before that occurred, however — specifically, on July 6, 1987 — Zions First National Bank, N. A., docketed with the Salt Lake County Clerk a state-court judgment it had won against the McDermotts. Under Utah law, that created a judgment lien on all of the McDermotts' real property in Salt Lake County, "owned . . . at the time or . . . thereafter acquired during the existence of said lien." Utah Code Ann. §78-22-1 (1953).

On September 23, 1987 the McDermotts acquired title to certain real property in Salt Lake County. To facilitate later sale of that property, the parties entered into an escrow agreement whereby the United States and the Bank released their claims to the real property itself but reserved their rights to the cash proceeds of the sale, based on their priorities in the property as of September 23, 1987. Pursuant to the escrow agreement, the McDermotts brought this interpleader. . . .

II

Federal tax liens do not automatically have priority over all other liens. Absent provision to the contrary, priority for purposes of federal law is governed by the common-law principle that "the first in time is the first in right." United States v. New Britain, 347 U.S. 81, 85 (1954). For purposes of applying that doctrine in the present case — in which the competing state lien (that of a judgment creditor) benefits from the provision of §6323(a) that the federal lien shall "not be valid . . . until notice thereof . . . has been filed" — we must deem the United States' lien to have commenced no sooner than the filing of notice. As for the Bank's lien: our cases deem a competing state lien to be in existence for "first in time" purposes only when it has been "perfected" in the sense that "the identity of the lienor, *the property subject to the lien*, and the amount of the lien are established." United States v. New Britain, 347 U.S., at 84 (emphasis added).

The first question we must answer, then, is whether the Bank's judgment lien was perfected in this sense before the United States filed its tax lien on September 9, 1987. If so, that is the end of the matter; the Bank's lien prevails. The Court of Appeals was of the view that this question was answered (or rendered irrelevant) by our decision in United States v. Vermont, 377 U.S. 351 (1964), which it took to "stand for the proposition that a non-contingent . . . lien on all of a person's real property, perfected prior to the federal tax lien, will take priority over the federal lien, regardless of whether after-acquired property is involved." That is too expansive a reading. Our opinion in *Vermont* gives no indication that the property at issue had become subject to the state lien only by application of an after-acquired-property clause to property that the debtor acquired after the federal lien arose. To the contrary, the opinion says that the state lien met (presumably at the critical time when the federal lien arose) "the test laid down in *New Britain* that . . . 'the property subject to the lien [be]

established.' " 377 U.S., at 358 (citation omitted). The argument of the
United States that we rejected in *Vermont* was the contention that a state
lien is not perfected within the meaning of New Britain if it "attaches to
all of the taxpayer's property," rather than "to specifically identified portions of that property." 377 U.S., at 355 (emphasis added). We did not
consider, and the facts as recited did not implicate, the quite different
argument made by the United States in the present case: that a lien in
after-acquired property is not "perfected" as to property yet to be
acquired.

The Bank argues that, as of July 6, 1987, the date it docketed its judgment lien, the lien was "perfected as to all real property then and thereafter owned by" the McDermotts, since "nothing further was required of
[the Bank] to attach the non-contingent lien on after-acquired property."
That reflects an unusual notion of what it takes to "perfect" a lien. Under
the Uniform Commercial Code, for example, a security interest in after-
acquired property is generally not considered perfected when the financing statement is filed, but only when the security interest has attached to
particular property upon the debtor's acquisition of that property. [U.C.C.
§§9-203(a) and (b), 9-308(a)]. And attachment to particular property was
also an element of what we meant by "perfection" in *New Britain*. See
347 U.S., at 84 ("when . . . the property subject to the lien [is] established"); id., at 86 ("the priority of each statutory lien contested here
must depend on the time it attached to the property in question and
became [no longer inchoate]"). The Bank concedes that its lien did not
actually attach to the property at issue here until the McDermotts
acquired rights in that property. Since that occurred after filing of the
federal tax lien, the state lien was not first in time.

But that does not complete our inquiry: Though the state lien was not
first in time, the federal tax lien was not necessarily first in time either.
Like the state lien, it applied to the property at issue here by virtue of a
(judicially inferred) after-acquired-property provision, which means that it
did not attach until the same instant the state lien attached, viz., when
the McDermotts acquired the property; and, like the state lien, it did not
become "perfected" until that time. We think, however, that under the
language of §6323(a) ("shall not be valid as against any . . . judgment
lien creditor until notice . . . has been filed"), the filing of notice renders
the federal tax lien extant for "first in time" priority purposes regardless
of whether it has yet attached to identifiable property. That result is also
indicated by the provision, two subsections later, which accords priority,
even against filed federal tax liens, to security interests arising out of certain agreements, including "commercial transactions financing agreements," entered into before filing of the tax lien. 26 U.S.C. §6323(c)(1).
That provision protects certain security interests that, like the after-
acquired-property judgment lien here, will have been recorded before
the filing of the tax lien, and will attach to the encumbered property after

the filing of the tax lien, and simultaneously with the attachment of the tax lien (i.e., upon the debtor's acquisition of the subject property). According special priority to certain state security interests in these circumstances obviously presumes that otherwise the federal tax lien would prevail — i.e., that the federal tax lien is ordinarily dated, for purposes of "first in time" priority against §6323(a) competing interests, from the time of its filing, regardless of when it attaches to the subject property.

The Bank argues that "by common law, the first lien of record against a debtor's property has priority over those subsequently filed unless a lien-creating statute clearly shows or declares an intention to cause the statutory lien to override." Such a strong "first-to-record" presumption may be appropriate for simultaneously-perfected liens under ordinary statutes creating private liens, which ordinarily arise out of voluntary transactions. When two private lenders both exact from the same debtor security agreements with after-acquired-property clauses, the second lender knows, by reason of the earlier recording, that category of property will be subject to another claim, and if the remaining security is inadequate he may avoid the difficulty by declining to extend credit. The Government, by contrast, cannot indulge the luxury of declining to hold the taxpayer liable for his taxes; notice of a previously filed security agreement covering after-acquired property does not enable the Government to protect itself. A strong "first-to-record" presumption is particularly out of place under the present tax-lien statute, whose general rule is that the tax collector prevails even if he has not recorded at all. 26 U.S.C. §§6321 and 6322. Thus, while we would hardly proclaim the statutory meaning we have discerned in this opinion to be "clear," it is evident enough for the purpose at hand. The federal tax lien must be given priority.

The judgment of the Court of Appeals is reversed, and the case is remanded for further proceedings consistent with this opinion.

[JUSTICES THOMAS, STEVENS AND O'CONNOR dissented.]

In this assignment, we have examined the race between the IRS and the holders of competing interests in situations where the first to come into existence will prevail. In the next assignment, we continue our examination of competitions involving federal tax liens by examining a number of interests that prevail over earlier filed tax liens.

Problem Set 38

38.1. Ronald Cheek was the hottest real estate developer in town, until it came to light how he was doing it. Ronald was selling multiple "first" mortgages on each of his properties, and forging title insurance policies to cover it up. Your law firm was the first to recover a money judgment against Cheek. The associate who worked the file before you recorded the $250,000 judgment in favor of Major Construction Company on May 5, 1994. The IRS filed a tax lien against Cheek on August 23, 1994, in the amount of $953,000. The IRS levied on three parcels of real property owned by Cheek on December 24, 1994. Cheek filed bankruptcy three days later. Subsequent investigation shows that the three parcels are the only property owned by Cheek that have value in excess of the mortgages against him. Cheek bought the Adams parcel in 1993; he bought the Baker parcel in June of 1994; and he inherited the Charlie parcel from his mother, who died in November 1994. Each of the parcels is worth between $30,000 and $50,000 more than the mortgages. Who is entitled to that value? I.R.C. §6323(a); United States v. McDermott.

38.2. Two years ago, Sally Deng opened a pretzel shop in a local mall, which she operates as a sole proprietorship. The business got off to a slow start; only in the past few months have revenues been sufficient to pay the bills. Even though Sally has been taking no salary from the business, she estimates that it lost $15,000 the first year and about $5,000 the second. She hopes that the flow of cash will reverse in the coming year and she will finally be able to get something for her efforts. In the meantime, Sally has been supporting both herself and her business with money from her divorce settlement and loans from friends and relatives. For the past three quarters, Sally has been filing payroll tax returns, but not sending the money. "I simply didn't have it," she says. She owes a total of $14,923. She received one notice of assessment about three months ago and another just a few days ago, but as yet has not received notice of the filing of a tax lien. Yesterday, there was a message on her answering machine from a Mr. Dobbins at the local office of the IRS. Sally has not yet returned the call. Sally (who is very well organized) has written the following list of questions for you:

a. Does the IRS have a lien against her business? Her home (which is exempt from execution under state law)? Her two myna birds, which have a value of approximately $5,000? I.R.C. §§6321, 6322.

b. What can the IRS do? What are they likely to do?

c. Sally wants to sell one of the birds to her friend George for $2,500 to raise money to keep the business going. If George pays her the $2,500 and she gives him possession of the bird, the IRS can't take it back, can it? Does it matter whether George knows about the unpaid payroll taxes? I.R.C. §§6323(a) and (h)(6).

d. Sally's mother, June, lent Sally $2,500 to make the payroll and pay some key suppliers two weeks ago. Sally told June that the other myna bird would serve as collateral for the loan. Sally wants to know how to arrange that and whether, once it is done, the IRS will be able to undo it. U.C.C. §§1-201(44), 9-203(a), (b), 9-310(a), 9-317(a), 9-313(a); I.R.C. §§6323(a) and (h)(1).

38.3. Sally, from Problem 38.2, lives in Wyoming County, New York, and her business is in neighboring Niagara County, New York. The only real estate she owns is her home in Wyoming County.

a. Where should the IRS file their Notice of Tax Lien against Sally?

b. Assume that instead of running her business as a sole proprietorship, Sally had incorporated it as "Sally Deng, Inc." The corporation owned the pretzel shop in Niagara County and also a second one in Erie, Pennsylvania, but owned no real property at either location. Sally ran the business from her office in the back of the Niagara County store. Under these circumstances, where should the IRS file their Notice of Tax Lien? I.R.C. §6323(f); New York Lien Law §240 (reproduced above in this assignment). You may assume for purposes of this problem that Pennsylvania has a statute identical in all relevant respects.

38.4. Dan's only asset is a lunch wagon worth about $18,000. Dan grants a security interest in the wagon to Firstbank to secure a loan in the amount of $10,000. The IRS files a $9,000 tax lien against Dan. Dan sells the wagon to a buyer who does not check the records and does not have actual knowledge of either encumbrance. Eighteen months later, the buyer files under Chapter 7 and you are appointed trustee. What do you do? U.C.C. §9-507; I.R.C. §6323(a); Bankr. Code §544(a); United States v. LMS Holding Co., 50 F.3d 1526 (10th Cir. 1995).

Assignment 39: Competitions Involving Federal Tax Liens: Advanced Problems

In this assignment, we continue our examination of competitions involving federal tax liens. We focus on I.R.C. §6323(b), which contains a number of exceptions to the general rule of first in time, first in right. These are all exceptions that cut against the government; they apply to situations where the government has filed its tax lien first, and yet the Federal Tax Lien Act (FTLA) grants priority to a competitor whose interest arises later.

Nearly all of these exceptions seem to flow from a single motivation: the protection of commerce. (Well, okay, there is a bit of evidence that they are the direct result of lobbying by the interests involved.) The drafters have assumed that debtors will in many instances continue to run their business and manage their financial affairs without letting third parties they deal with know that the Notice of Tax Lien has been filed. The drafters certainly have not set out to prevent debtors from doing that. Often, those operations and dealings will contribute to the debtor's ability to pay the taxes that are outstanding and therefore be in the interest of the government as a creditor.

Although the Notice of Tax Lien is on the public record, many of the third parties who deal with these debtors will not actually know of the tax lien. To realize the extent of third-party ignorance, just consider how often you have dealt with people without first checking the public record to determine whether they had Notices of Tax Liens filed against them. One effect is that the government profits from the "errors" of those who do business without keeping an eye on the public record.

A. The Strange Metaphysics of the Internal Revenue Code

The provisions of the Federal Tax Lien Act may at the same time seem both strange and familiar. What is strange is the language and some of the concepts employed. Terms such as "security interest" and "purchaser" are assigned meanings slightly askew from those assigned in Article 9. The familiar concepts of "attachment" and "perfection" — or at least those words — are nowhere to be seen. Despite the differences in language and conceptualization, the Federal Tax Lien Act creates a world with familiar characters: the buyer in the ordinary course of business, the accounts and inventory financier, the construction lender, the mechanic's lien holder, and the holder of a property tax lien. There is a remarkable similarity in the level of clout these characters exercised in the other competitions we have studied and the level they exercise here against a federal tax lien.

This is probably no accident. As the 500-pound gorilla in the debtor-creditor game, the U.S. government insisted on describing the rules of that game in language of its own choosing and in a statutory scheme it has full power to amend. But that cannot change the fact that the menagerie of security interests, statutory liens, and judicial liens with which federal tax liens must compete exists and competes among themselves independent of the Federal Tax Lien Act. The United States can choose to insert its lien with any priority it likes, but it is beyond the federal government's power to alter the existing priorities among the other players or to make third parties do business without protection against unacceptable risks. If the Federal Tax Lien Act failed to recognize the existing hierarchy it would generate circular priorities and tangle up the system. Instead, the Federal Tax Lien Act reflects the system of perfection and priority that existed before the Act was adopted in 1966 and specifies the tax lien's priority in it.

While this preexisting system of perfection and priority based on the principle of "first in time, first in right" is in most respects consistent and coherent, it is not entirely so. As earlier assignments have indicated, the rules governing this system are made by different governing bodies and typically regulate competitions one by one. That is, they do not tell us the priority of A in relation to other liens. Instead, one rule tells us that A has priority over B and another, perhaps written and enacted by different bodies at different times, may tell us that B has priority over C. It is not safe to assume from these two rules that A will have priority over C: The rules may simply be inconsistent. The precision required of a lawyer called on to give advice, who virtually always is dealing in the particular, necessitates considering these competitions one at a time.

The rules governing priority between a federal tax lien and an ordinary Article 9 security interest provide an excellent example. These rules can be derived from I.R.C. §§6323(a), (d), and (h). The federal tax lien has priority if the IRS files a Notice of Tax Lien before the security interest comes into existence; otherwise, the security interest has priority over the federal tax lien.

I.R.C. §6323(h)(1) provides that a security interest comes into existence when it is protected by local law against a subsequent judgment lien, but it only comes into existence to the extent that the secured creditor has parted with money or money's worth. The first part of this test is a reference to U.C.C. §§9-317(a) and 323(b), the sections that govern priority between a security interest and a judgment lien. In essence, a security interest is protected against a subsequent judgment lien under U.C.C. §§9-317(a) and 323(b) when it is filed or perfected.

The second part of the I.R.C. §6323(h)(1) test as to when a security interest comes into existence differs from the U.C.C. test in an important respect. The value requirement of U.C.C. §9-203(b)(1) is met when the secured creditor parts with *anything*. Thus, a security interest can be perfected under Article 9 before the secured creditor has made the loan. The second part of the I.R.C. §6323(h)(1) test requires more: The security interest "exists" under that section only to the extent that the secured creditor has made the loan.

With such different metaphysics at work, one might assume that these two bodies of law were headed for inconsistent results — that, for example, a FTLA-designed security interest would be less powerful in competition with a tax lien than a U.C.C.-designed security interest would be in competition with a judgment lien. In fact, as you will see in the next section, they reach remarkably similar results. We are unable to discern the purpose for which the drafters of the Federal Tax Lien Act redefined and reconceptualized the Article 9 security interest. Maybe it was a slow day in the drafting department.

B. Protection of Those Who Lend After the Tax Lien Is Filed

1. The General Provision Regarding Future Advances, I.R.C. §6323(d)

The virtual insignificance of the Federal Tax Lien Act redefinition and reconceptualization of the Article 9 security interest is illustrated in the rule protecting future advances made by secured creditors against federal tax liens. Assume that Firstbank takes a security interest in Debtor's Widgematic, files a financing statement, but makes no advance. At this point in time, Article 9 characterizes Firstbank's security interest very differently than does the Federal Tax Lien Act. Under Article 9, Firstbank's security interest may be both attached and perfected (if Firstbank has given "consideration sufficient to support a simple contract"). Under the Federal Tax Lien Act, Firstbank has no security interest at all. Article 9 encourages us to think of this security interest as having priority over one who might become a lien creditor; the Federal Tax Lien Act encourages us to think of this security interest as completely ineffective against a federal tax lien that might be filed. But, in reality, what either law says about this unfunded security interest makes no difference; a security interest can't compete with anyone until it is funded. As soon as this security interest is funded, the metaphysical differences between Article 9 and the Federal Tax Lien Act disappear.

To continue with the illustration, assume that the IRS files a Notice of Tax Lien and 30 days later Firstbank, unaware of the Notice, makes a $1,000 advance. Now the FTLA-defined security interest "exists." Despite the security interest's late arrival on the scene, I.R.C. §6323(d) gives it priority over the tax lien. It does so only to the extent that the security interest would be "protected under local law against a judgment lien arising, as of the time of tax lien filing, out of an unsecured obligation." Under these circumstances that would be to the full extent of the $1,000; U.C.C. §9-323(b) would fully protect this security interest against a lien creditor who levied at the time of the filing of the tax lien. (The fact that U.C.C. §9-323(b)'s 45-day protection is coextensive with that provided the holder of a security interest under §6323(d) is no coincidence. The drafters of the U.C.C. designed §9-323(b) specifically to give secured creditors the full advantage available against tax liens under I.R.C. §6323(d). See Comment 4 to U.C.C. §9-323.) Thus, once the FTLA-defined security interest is funded, it performs just as well against the tax lien as the U.C.C.-defined security interest performed against the lien creditor. The difference in how this security interest was conceptualized under the U.C.C. and the FTLA ends up making no difference in outcome.

2. Commercial Transactions Financing Agreements

I.R.C. §6323(c) offers somewhat incomplete protection to lenders secured by Article 9 floating liens against the sudden effects of tax lien filings. The protection I.R.C. §6323(c) offers, like the protection I.R.C. §6323(d) offers with regard to future advances, extends only to transactions occurring within 45 days after the tax lien filing. The 45-day period is, in essence, an opportunity for the lender to learn of the tax lien filing and react to it.

Much of the protection afforded secured creditors under I.R.C. §6323(c) would be available under I.R.C. §6323(d) anyway. Both give advances made by the lender within 45 days after the filing of the tax lien priority over the tax lien. But I.R.C. §6323(c) is both broader and narrower than I.R.C. §6323(d). The I.R.C. §6323(c) protection is narrower than I.R.C. §6323(d) in that the former applies only with respect to advances to be secured by "commercial financing security": accounts, inventory, chattel paper, and mortgage paper. I.R.C. §§6323(c)(2)(A) and (C). Subsection (d), by contrast, contains no limit as to the type of collateral involved.

Subsection (d) is narrower than (c) in that (d) protects only future advances; it does not protect the secured creditor's interest in after-acquired collateral. The subsection (c) protection of commercial transactions financing extends to collateral acquired by the debtor during the 45 days after the tax lien filing — apparently even to collateral the debtor acquires after the secured creditor learns of the tax lien filing. (Note the absence of an "actual notice or knowledge" limitation in I.R.C. §6323(c)(2)(B).) The need for protection of a security interest right in after-acquired property results from the Federal Tax Lien Act view that security interests exist only when "the property is in existence," I.R.C. §6323(h)(1), by which the drafters mean that the debtor has acquired it. This view, which you also saw reflected in *McDermott* in the previous assignment, is frequently referred to as the *choateness doctrine*.

How will the commercial financing lender learn of the tax lien in time to react? The Fifth Circuit addressed the issue in Texas Oil & Gas Corp. v. United States, 466 F.2d 1040 (5th Cir. 1972):

> Of course we realize that [§6323(c)] does not afford the protection that commercial lenders who deal with after-acquired property might prefer. As the law appears to stand, the commercial lender must check the applicable records every 45 days or else seriously jeopardize his security under the varying degrees of rigor promulgated by the choateness doctrine. Even that 45-day grace period is probably of minimal efficacy. Commercial lenders might often be lulled into a false sense of security with debtors who are doing badly, for it might appear to the lender that such a debtor is unlikely to have any income to tax. Yet it is precisely in these circumstances that back taxes are likely to accrue. In addition, the lender would most likely not have the entire 45-day period in which to act unless he were lucky enough to discover the tax lien filing almost immediately after it was filed. Finally, there is often not a great deal that the lender can do to protect his advances even after he discovers the tax lien in time. Of course, he has little control over the actual receipt of after-acquired property by the taxpayer-debtor, which is usually subject to contracts and contingencies entirely within the authority of the taxpayer-debtor, and various third-parties. The lender can attempt to substitute other existing collateral for his interest in after-acquired property if the taxpayer-debtor has any substitutable assets and if there is sufficient time. . . . But the whole genesis and historicity of section 6323(c) appears to have been to give only a slight handicap (45 days) to a private lien holder.

3. Real Property Construction or Improvement Financing

I.R.C. §6323(c) protects construction lenders against a tax lien filed during construction. Subsection (c) requires that the construction lender have entered into a contract to finance the construction prior to the filing of the tax lien. The protection afforded against the tax lien extends only to the real property improved.

The protection is not limited to advances made within 45 days of the filing of the tax lien. The only condition of protection is that the construction lender's priority must be protected under local law against a judgment lien arising as of the time of tax lien filing, out of an unsecured obligation. I.R.C. §6323(c)(1)(B). Protection extends to advances made more than 45 days after the filing of the tax lien and to those made after the construction lender knows of the tax lien. The rationale is that construction lenders cannot, as a practical matter, withdraw from a partially completed project. If they do, construction stops. The army of subcontractors, laborers, and suppliers painstakingly assembled by the contractor disperses, the property begins to deteriorate, legal claims are made that deter others from resuming construction, and the project gets a bad reputation that may carry through to its sale or leasing. Presumably, everyone with an interest in the construction project, including the IRS, will be better off if the construction lender continues to fund construction. While an argument like this can be made on behalf of one who makes advances to any business debtor after the filing of the tax lien, in the context of construction lending, the factual basis for the argument seems to be particularly widely accepted.

4. Obligatory Disbursement Agreements

I.R.C. §6323(c)(4) protects lenders who have agreed before the tax lien is filed to make disbursements that the lenders then make after the lien is filed. This is not, however, a general protection of such disbursements analogous to Article 9's protection of advances made "pursuant to commitment." As the tax regulations explain:

> (b) *Obligatory disbursement agreement.* For purposes of this section the term "obligatory disbursement agreement" means a written agreement, entered into by a person in the course of his trade or business, to make disbursements. An agreement is treated as an obligatory disbursement agreement only with respect to disbursements which are required to be made by reason of the intervention of the rights of a person other than the taxpayer. The obligation to pay must be conditioned upon an event beyond the control of the obligor. For example, the provisions of this section are applicable

where an issuing bank obligates itself to honor drafts or other demands for payment on a letter of credit and a bank, in good faith, relies upon that letter of credit in making advances. The provisions of this section are also applicable, for example, where a bonding company obligates itself to make payments to indemnify against loss or liability and, under the terms of the bond, makes a payment with respect to a loss.

26 C.F.R. 301.6323(c)-3. The vast majority of advances made pursuant to commitment are not pursuant to obligatory disbursement agreements. It is nearly always the case that the loan commitment provides that when a tax lien is filed, the creditor is excused from making the promised advances. The unusual security agreements that do qualify as obligatory disbursement agreements are outside the scope of this assignment.

5.   Statutory Liens

Statutory liens, you will recall, are liens that arise against specific property by operation of a statute. Statutes typically provide such liens for activities of a nature that they at least arguably tend to improve the value of the property against which the lien is granted.
      I.R.C. §6323(b) grants some statutory liens priority over the federal tax lien, even when those statutory liens arise after the federal tax lien is filed. Among those granted priority are artisans' liens in favor of those who make repairs or improvements to personal property and retain possession of the property as security for their claims ((b)(5)), real property tax and special assessment liens ((b)(6)), mechanics' liens for improvements made to real property (although the Act limits them sharply to liens against the debtor's personal residence and to contracts not in excess of $1,000, (b)(7)), and attorneys' liens for fees against a judgment or settlement amount obtained by the attorney on behalf of a client ((b)(8)). Numerous other kinds of statutory liens are not recognized in I.R.C. §6323(b) and hence are subordinate to federal tax liens filed before they arise.

6.   Purchase-Money Security Interests

Notice that there is no provision in I.R.C. §6323(b) protecting purchase-money security interests against earlier-filed tax liens. This was undoubtedly a mistake in drafting. The courts quickly read such a provision into I.R.C. §6323(b) and the IRS acquiesced. In the case that follows, the court explores the limits of the resulting protection.

The following case applied the definition of "purchase-money security interest" from former Article 9, but the key words of that definition are the same in revised Article 9.

First Interstate Bank of Utah, N.A.
v. Internal Revenue Service

930 F.2d 1521 (10th Cir. 1991)

ALDISERT, CIRCUIT JUDGE.

This appeal . . . requires us to interpret [U.C.C. §§9-103(a) and (b)], which provides that:

> A security interest is a purchase money security interest to the extent that it is . . . taken by a person who by making advances or incurring an obligation gives value to enable the debtor to acquire rights in or the use of collateral if such value is in fact so used.

First Interstate Bank of Utah, N.A., the appellant, argues that it obtained a purchase money security interest in certain accounts receivable when it advanced funds to Olympus Glass Company . . . enabling the debtor to complete performance of specified obligations. This question of statutory construction is a legal issue of first impression before this court. At issue here is whether the statute affords purchase money priority to First Interstate to preempt a tax lien previously asserted by the federal Government. . . .

I

At a time when the debtor's assets were subject to a federal tax lien, First Interstate and Olympus Glass entered into a financing arrangement whereby the bank agreed to fund Olympus' performance of six glazing contracts. The bank paid the material and labor cost incurred by Olympus. After Olympus went into bankruptcy the question arose as to whether the tax lien was to be afforded the normal consequences of a lien filed prior in time to the extension of credit. While recognizing the existence of orthodox rules of lien priority, First Interstate relies upon a competing legal precept that a purchase money security interest has priority over a previously filed tax lien.

The general proposition is that a security interest based on the extension of purchase money defeats a previously filed federal tax lien. Slodov v. United States, 436 U.S. 238, 56 L. Ed.2d 251, 98 S. Ct. 1778 (1978) ("The [Internal Revenue] Code and established decisional principles subordinate the tax lien, to certain perfected security interests in . . . collateral which is subject to a purchase-money mortgage regardless of whether the agreement was entered into before or after the filing of the tax lien."). Although a statement of this priority is not found in the express language of the Code, "the purchase-money mortgage priority is based upon recognition that the mortgagee's interest merely reflects his contribution of property to the taxpayer's estate and therefore does not prejudice creditors who are prior in time." Id. at 258 n.23.

The parties before us urge diametrically opposed interpretations of the U.C.C. provision defining a purchase money security interest. First Interstate argues that the phrase, "a person who by making advances . . . to enable the debtor to acquire rights in or the use of collateral" brings it within the statutory definition when it extended money secured by accounts receivable. The Internal Revenue Service (IRS) contends that the money was extended to perform pre-existing contracts of the debtor and did not represent funds advanced to acquire property or rights in property.

The facts are not in dispute. The bankruptcy court's conclusions of law affirmed by the district court are subject to de novo review.

II

Olympus is a glazing contractor and wholesale supplier of glass. On January 23, 1984, First Interstate extended to Olympus a $500,000 line of credit. Pursuant to this line of credit, Olympus drew down the entire amount. The line was secured by an Accounts Receivable and Inventory Security and Loan Agreement by which Olympus conveyed to First Interstate a security interest in all of Olympus' accounts (as defined in the agreement) "now existing or hereafter existing" and "all the proceeds of . . . the foregoing." The bank filed the U.C.C.-1 financing statement with the Utah Secretary of State, thereby perfecting its security interest in the debtor's accounts and proceeds. On August 1, 1985, the IRS filed a Notice of Federal Tax Lien against the debtor in the amount of $57,147.94 for unpaid taxes withheld from the wages of the debtor's employees.

Several months later, First Interstate agreed to extend to the debtor a secured line of credit in the amount of $200,000, known as "[a] revolving loan." Pursuant to the agreement, signed on November 27, 1985, the loan was to be "secured by specifically assigned contracts." Borrowing was limited to the "amounts necessary for payment of direct labor expense and materials" and in no event was to "exceed 75% of the face value of the assigned contract." These advances were to be based on invoices for materials and appropriate records of labor expended on the contract, "with such invoices and records subject to Bank approval prior to disbursal of each advance." First Interstate signed a promissory note for the loan.

First Interstate did not file a U.C.C.-1 financing statement in conjunction with the November Security Agreement; instead it relied on the financing statement accompanying the previous loan that it had filed on January 23, 1984, some twenty months earlier. The prior financing statement covered "all present and future accounts" of the debtor. . . . Olympus used no source of financing other than the advances from First Interstate to perform the contracts.

On July 2, 1986, Olympus filed a voluntary Chapter 11 petition. . . . In the bankruptcy court, as before us, First Interstate argued that its lending arrangement with the debtor falls squarely within the definition of a purchase money security interest: It advanced approximately $193,000 to fund the performance of specific, identified glazing contracts by issuing cashier's checks directly to third party suppliers of materials and labor. Accordingly, the bank argued, it is a "person" who "by making advances," gave "value to enable the debtor to acquire rights in . . . the . . . collateral," i.e., the accounts receivable that arose by virtue of performance of the glazing contracts. It conceded that the federal tax lien attached to the debtor's "contingent rights to payments under the Glazing Contracts," but argued that its funds enabled the debtor "to convert the contingent rights into matured rights."

The IRS responded, and the bankruptcy court agreed, that within the concept of purchase money security rights a fundamental difference exists between those funds advanced to purchase or acquire contracts and any accompanying accounts receivable, and those funds advanced to perform contracts which were already in existence at the time the tax lien had attached. The IRS emphasized that the rights to the accounts represented by the glazing contracts were already in existence at the time the lien was filed; all that remained was to perform the preexisting contracts; the debtor has already "acquire[d] rights in or the use of collateral." Reduced to its essence, the IRS argument before the bankruptcy court, and repeated before us, is that First Interstate did nothing more than fund the debtor's performance of its contracts in its ordinary business operations; it did not enable the debtor to acquire a discrete new asset.

The bankruptcy court held for the IRS, ruling that "unless the funds loaned to a debtor are used for the purpose of purchasing accounts directly, the lending creditor would not obtain a purchase money security interest in those accounts." According to the bankruptcy court, "First Interstate did not obtain a purchase money security interest in accounts because the funds loaned to the debtor did not enable the debtor to acquire accounts, but rather enabled the debtor to generate accounts." The court reasoned that a "contrary ruling would elevate any loan to a purchase money status if the loan enabled the borrower to conduct its business and generate a profit," and ruled that the Government had a prior lien against the proceeds of the contracts.

First Interstate appealed to the District Court from that part of the bankruptcy court's judgment that held it did not possess a security interest to trump the previous IRS lien. The District Court affirmed the bankruptcy court determination. First Interstate has appealed.

III

As was the task of the bankruptcy and district courts, our responsibility is to construe the security interest provision of [U.C.C. §§9-103(a) and (b)]. Under the U.C.C. and the Utah legislature's adoption of its key provisions, this purchase money security interest is generally manifested when taken or retained by the seller of collateral to secure all or part of its price. But such a security interest also may be created when a person gives value to enable a debtor to acquire rights in, or the use of collateral; this is the species of security interest asserted by First National Bank in these proceedings. New value may be given either in the form of advances or the incurring of an obligation. Such value must be used for this purpose in order to form the basis of this type of priority.

By definition, purchase money security interests are available to lenders as well as sellers. A lender may acquire it in collateral to be purchased with a loan provided the proceeds are in fact so used. This special category of security interest is entitled to special priority because it is considered an exception to the first-to-file rule of priority. Accordingly, such an interest takes priority over any pre-existing lien on the theory that because the lender has augmented the capital assets of the borrower, previous creditors are not prejudiced.

It is undisputed that First Interstate agreed to, and did, lend money to the debtor to fund the performance of specific, identified contracts. It is also undisputed that the U.C.C. priority in question is given not only to lenders who permit a borrower to "acquire" collateral, but is conferred whenever the lender enables the borrower to "acquire rights in collateral." The debtor here already had acquired the collateral — the executory contracts — and thus the right to perform the contracts, and accordingly, the federal tax lien attached to these executory contracts. First Interstate anchors its claim on the basis that it advanced the funds that enabled the debtor to "acquire rights in [this] collateral" by converting contingent rights into matured rights. . . .

IV

We return then to our task of statutory construction. Professor Grant Gilmore, a primary drafter of the U.C.C., has written that the purchase money security interest provision was narrowly constructed and that such an interest in intangibles would be the extraordinary situation. In describing what could or could not qualify under the statute, he stated:

> Farm products which are grown or raised by the debtor (such as crops or the increase of a herd of livestock) cannot become the subject matter of a purchase money security interest, since the secured party's loan does not go directly into their purchase price. *Nor could such intangibles as accounts, contract rights,* chattel paper, or instruments normally be acquired by the debtor in a purchase money transaction.

Gilmore, The Purchase Money Priority, 76 Harv. L. Rev. 1333, 1385 (1963) (emphasis added).

A

It is clear that the drafters of the purchase money security interest provision in the U.C.C. used precise and narrow language. First, the lender must have given "value" by making advances or incurring an obligation. Second, the value must have been "to enable the debtor to acquire rights in or the use of collateral." Third, such value must have been "in fact so used." [Comment 3 to U.C.C. §9-103] tells us that this requirement excludes "any security interest taken as security for or in satisfaction of a pre-existing claim or antecedent debt."

Given this narrow construction, we must determine whether the interest in the case before us fits within these three requirements.

B

Clearly, the lender, First Interstate, gave value. The problem is with the second prong that requires that the value must have been given "to enable the debtor to acquire rights in or the use of collateral." Without surmounting this second requirement we cannot reach the third. We are assisted in our task by previous court decisions that have discussed whether contract rights qualify as "collateral" under this U.C.C. provision.

In Northwestern Natl. Bank Southwest v. Lectro Systems, Inc., 262 N.W.2d 678 (Minn. 1977), the court faced the question of whether a "contract right" could be "collateral" under the second requirement. In *Lectro System*, the lender advanced money to subcontractors to enable them to complete their contract and took back a security interest in their contract right to payment. The lender claimed priority as a purchase money lender over a bank which had a prior perfected security interest in the contract right.

In rejecting the lender's claim, the court held that the loaned funds must be intended, and actually used, for the purchase of an identifiable asset and that "performance of a contract" is not such an asset. . . .

C

At the risk of being guilty of *ad terrorem* discourse, we believe that First Interstate's argument proves too much. If accepted, it would make virtually any loan incurred in the course of fulfilling pre-existing business obligations a purchase money loan if it enabled the debtor to operate its business and generate a profit. The conceptual underpinning of our commercial purchase money security tradition with its concomitant priority attributes is that the extension of such funds reflects a contribution of property to the borrower's estate; accordingly, this extension does not prejudice creditors who are prior in time.

An important distinction exists between funds extended for asset acquisition and those extended for the ordinary operation of business. A bright-line demarcation must always exist between these two purposes. To accept the lender's contention in this case would be to blur, if not eliminate, that line.

V

Court precedent, comments of the Code drafters, and dictates of public policy concerning financing support the principle that the line of demarcation be respected. We see no reason to cross it here. Accordingly, we conclude that the right to perform the pre-existing executory contract in this case is not "collateral" or the "rights in collateral" within the requirements of the U.C.C.

VI

. . . We have considered all of the contentions of the appellant and find them to be without merit. The judgment of the district court is AFFIRMED.

The Court says that "[a]n important distinction exists between funds extended for asset acquisition and those extended for the ordinary operation of business." We don't find this distinction as important as the court does. Lending the debtor money to make its payroll enables the debtors to acquire an asset — it is just not quite as tangible an asset. The court continues that "[t]he conceptual underpinning of our commercial purchase money security tradition with its concomitant priority attributes is that the extension of such funds reflects a contribution of property to the borrower's estate; accordingly, this extension does not prejudice creditors who are prior in time." But doesn't providing money for "ordinary operation" do the same? For example, if a lender advances funds that a manufacturer uses to pay employees to turn raw materials into finished inventory, the advances may contribute value to the estate without prejudicing prior creditors. Unless the new money is *wasted* in operations, it should increase the value of the estate just as surely as money used to buy raw material. Funds extended for operations can disappear when operations are unprofitable. But so can funds extended for asset acquisition. For example, a retail store may buy inventory that does not appeal to its customers and find that it is ultimately of little or no value.

The decline does not detract from the argument in favor of purchase-money priority because the value of the priority shrinks with the value of the collateral. But neither does it detract from the argument in favor of purchase-money priority for contributions to "ordinary operations." If the debtor accepted First Interstate's loan proceeds, but did not manage to complete the contracts and thereby convert them to accounts, the value of First Interstate's purchase-money priority would shrink. If the debtor managed to complete the contracts using First Interstate's money, First Interstate contributed to the estate and, it seems to us, ought to have a purchase-money priority.

The distinction between lending to purchase the collateral and lending to keep the business going is made under Article 9 as well. Purchase-money protection under U.C.C. §9-324(e) is afforded to the lender who assists with the purchase of asset; there is no corresponding protection of the lender who assists by financing continuing operations. We confess to much discomfort with the distinction.

Bankruptcy law resolves the same issue differently. If Olympus were in Chapter 11 and Olympus and First Interstate came to the court, hats in hands, to ask for permission to do specifically the deal they did in this case, the Bankruptcy Court would almost certainly approve the loan under Bankruptcy Code §364(d). The court would probably justify this priority in something like the same words the court used to justify the purchase-money priority in *First Interstate Bank*: "such funds reflect a contribution of property to the borrower's estate; accordingly, this extension does not prejudice creditors who are prior in time." This greater flexibility is one more advantage that the bankruptcy system can offer the struggling debtor who is in need of an infusion of new capital.

C. Nonadvances

In Assignment 9 we introduced the concept of *nonadvances*, the interest, attorneys' fees, and other expenses that may be incurred by a secured creditor in protecting and recovering its collateral and collecting the amount owing from the debtor. Nonadvances are analogous to future advances. The difference is that future advances result from a decision on the part of the lender; nonadvances just grow of their own accord. Nonadvances are a great favorite of both the U.C.C. and the Bankruptcy Code, perhaps because they usually have in them a healthy component of attorneys' fees and it is attorneys who design these systems. At least if they are provided for in the security agreement and are reasonable, nonadvances under a security agreement are equal in priority to the first advance. That enables these late-created charges to prevail over the intervening interests of secured creditors, lien creditors, and trustees in bankruptcy.

I.R.C. §6323(e) gives nonadvances equivalent protection against intervening tax liens. To illustrate, assume that on March 1, Firstbank lends $80,000 to Debtor, secured by an interest in Debtor's summer cottage, which is worth $100,000. The mortgage provides that in the event of default, Debtor will pay a higher "default rate" of interest, will pay Firstbank's reasonable attorneys' fees incurred as a result of the default, will pay all expenses of insuring and preserving the property, and will pay any property tax liens or assessments levied against the property. On April 1, the IRS files a tax lien against Debtor for payroll taxes in the amount of $20,000. Having received no payments on the loan, Firstbank commences foreclosure against Debtor on May 1. On June 1, the city levies a $5,000 assessment against the property for emergency sewer repairs. Under local law, the assessment has priority over Firstbank's mortgage, so Firstbank pays the assessment to maintain its first position. On December 1, Firstbank completes the foreclosure and sells the property for $100,000. Firstbank pays its attorney $6,000 for the foreclosure and pays expenses of $3,000 for insurance, maintenance of the property, and other expenses of the legal proceeding and sale. As it is entitled to do under its contract with Debtor, Firstbank adds this $14,000 of expenditures to the amount of its mortgage, which has also increased by $2,000 as a result of accruing interest. The amount outstanding under the mortgage is now $96,000. Even though this $16,000 increase in Firstbank's mortgage occurred after the filing of the tax lien, it has priority over the tax lien. Firstbank gets $96,000 of the proceeds of the sale; the IRS gets only $4,000. To be a nonadvance is good.

Problem Set 39

39.1. In late July, Dawgs and More Dawgs (DAMD) applied to Bank One for a loan against its inventory of lawn dogs. Without committing to make the loan, on August 1, Bank One filed a financing statement against DAMD showing the lawn dogs as collateral. Also, in late July, DAMD applied for a similar loan from Bank Two. On August 5, Bank two approved the loan and filed a financing statement against DAMD showing the lawn dogs as collateral. Bank Two and DAMD signed a security agreement on August 5 and Bank Two advanced funds to Debtor. The IRS filed a Notice of Tax Lien against DAMD on August 7 in the county records, the place specified by state law for the filing of tax liens. On August 10, Bank One receive the report of their U.C.C. search showing their financing statement to be in first position. They approved the loan to DAMD. Bank One and DAMD signed a security agreement, and Bank One advanced funds against the lawn dogs. As soon as the check from Bank One cleared, the owner of DAMD wired the Bank One loan proceeds to Freeport in the Bahamas, where they paused only long enough to join the proceeds from the Bank Two loan, and then continued on to places unknown. What are the relative priorities among Bank One, Bank Two, and the IRS in the lawn dogs? I.R.C. §§6321, 6322, 6323(a), (d), (h)(1); U.C.C. §§9-317(a) and 9-323(b), 9-322(a). We suggest you solve the problem by breaking it into three parts: (1) priority between Bank One and the IRS, (2) priority between Bank Two and the IRS, and (3) priority between Bank One and Bank Two.

39.2.   Tony Redding is the owner and operator of The Perfect Pet, a two-store chain that sells everything from kitty cats to boa constrictors. A variety of "non-recurring business setbacks" (as Tony calls them) have caused him to fall behind in his payroll tax deposits. Although he has been working with the IRS to make up the deficit, it has been going pretty slowly. The agent told him yesterday that the IRS will be filing a tax lien against Redding within a few days. Redding still believes in the business and wants to keep operating. "I've put my life into this business, and I'm going to fight it if there's any way I can." Redding is concerned about these situations:

a.   Will customers who buy pets from the store's inventory after the Notice is filed take free and clear of the IRS lien? I.R.C. §6323(b)(3).

b.   Tony needs to install a new fish tank that will cost $5,000. The seller of the tank will provide 100 percent financing and Tony will make payments over five years. For a number of reasons, Tony sees no way to get the deal done before the tax lien is filed. The seller will file a U.C.C.-1, but probably won't do a search of the public record. I.R.C. §§6323(a) and (b); *First Interstate Bank*, supra.

c.   Tony is worried about his employees. If he pays them with money on which the IRS has a lien, can the IRS take the money back? If the IRS levies on the day before payday, where do the employees stand?

d.   The business is financed with an inventory and accounts receivable loan from Glengary State Bank. Glengary lends 65 percent of the cost of inventory as The Perfect Pet receives it. The security interest contains the usual provisions regarding future advances and after-acquired property. Tony believes Glengary will work with him if the Bank can. "They don't have much choice," he says. "I have $175,000 outstanding on the loan. In continued operations the collateral is worth that amount, but if this business closes, Glengary won't get $50,000 out of it." Can Glengary work with him without losing its priority over the tax lien? I.R.C. §§6323(c) and (d); *First Interstate Bank*, supra.

e.   Can Tony keep going after the tax lien is filed?

39.3.   Your client, Wilmington State Bank (WSB), does a substantial amount of inventory and accounts receivable financing. Its contract with the debtor requires that the debtor notify WSB of any tax lien that arises. Not only do the Bank's debtors not give the required notice, most of them actively conceal their failure to pay payroll taxes. WSB was recently burned in a situation where the tax lien was filed and 45 days went by without WSB learning of it. WSB continued to fund the loan and eventually lost nearly all of the remaining collateral to the tax lien. WSB asks what they should be doing to avoid recurrence of the problem in the future. What do you tell them? I.R.C. §6323(f); *Texas Oil & Gas Corp.*, supra.

39.4.   Alecia Card (the client you were thinking of referring to a psychiatrist in Assignment 36) is back to see you. You know from reading the newspapers that she is now active in the local chapter of HALT, an antilawyer organization (the acronym stands for "Help Abolish Legal Tyranny"). "I'm not mad at you," she says "but we have to stop what lawyers and courts are doing to this country." Alecia has been researching tax liens and has a couple of questions. She has concluded that if she buys something at retail — a dress, a car, or a piano — she must never leave it in the possession of the seller for even a minute. "If there is a Notice of Tax Lien outstanding against the store, it will have priority over my purchase, *even if I paid for what I bought.*" In fact, Alecia won't let the store clerk wrap her packages after they ring up the sale; she grabs the items and stuffs them in the sack herself. Is Alecia right on the law? U.C.C. §§2-403(2) and (3); I.R.C. §§6323(a), (b)(2), (b)(3), (b)(4), and (h)(6). Is she right to be upset?

39.5.   Alecia has another question. She shows you the following quotes from Davis v. Internal Revenue Service, 705 F. Supp. 446 (C.D. Ill. 1989):

Under [§6323], as illustrated by its history, it is clear that Congress intended the IRS notice of tax lien to serve as notice to subsequent purchasers wherever possible. . . . The sine qua non of §6323 is notice to subsequent takers of the existence of the IRS lien.

"Hypocrisy!" Alecia exclaims. "If I see a want ad for a used sailboat in the newspaper and want to buy it for the $3,000 the owner is asking, how am I supposed to know whether the owner has a tax lien against him?" Assume that the applicable tax lien filing statute is the same as the New York statute reproduced in Assignment 38 and that sailboats of the type Alecia is buying are covered by a certificate of title act. Explain to Alecia how this is transaction is "supposed" to work in a world where there are tax liens. I.R.C. §§6323(a), 6323(b)(3), 6323(b)(4), 6323(f), 6323(h)(6).

Assignment 40: Why Secured Credit?

The idea that a debtor should be able to grant a security interest in property while retaining possession and use did not come easily to American law. In the earliest cases, such transfers were held to be a fraud on other creditors. For example, see Clow v. Woods, 5 Sergeant & Rawle 275, 9 Am. Dec. 346 (Sup. Ct. Pa. 1819). Even after the basic concept of security was accepted, grants of security interests in after-acquired property continued to be controversial. But with the widespread adoption of the Uniform Commercial Code in the 1960s, both concepts gained virtually full acceptance. The battle temporarily abated while the U.C.C. was lauded as one of the greatest legislative accomplishments in history. If there were opponents of Article 9 during the 1970s, they left no written record.

The controversy reignited in the 1980s with the publication of an article by Professors Jackson and Kronman. Ironically, they were merely attempting to explain in passing what no one in their generation of scholars questioned.

Thomas H. Jackson and Anthony Kronman, Secured Financing and Priorities Among Creditors

88 Yale L.J. 1143, 1147-1148 (1979)

At first blush, it may seem unfair that a debtor should be allowed to make a private contract with one creditor that demotes the claims of other creditors from an initial position of parity to one of subordination. This thought may in turn suggest that debtors should be denied the power to prefer some creditors over others, and that all creditors should instead be required to share equally in the event of their common debtor's insolvency, each receiving a pro rata portion of his claim. The idea that all creditors should be treated equally, regardless of the private arrangements they may have made with their debtor, has played an important role in the evolution of the federal bankruptcy system. Reported case law is replete with references to the bankruptcy "principle" that "equality is equity."

Despite its apparent appeal, however, the principle of equal treatment has never succeeded in supplanting, even in the Bankruptcy Act itself, a basic recognition of the debtor's contractual power to prefer one creditor over another. When a debtor grants a security interest to one of his creditors, he increases the riskiness of other creditors' claims by reducing their expected value in bankruptcy. It is a fair assumption, however, that these other creditors will be aware of this risk and will insist on a premium for lending on an unsecured basis, will demand collateral (or some other form of protection) to secure their own claims, or will search for another borrower whose enterprise is less risky. In general, whatever level of risk he faces, if his transaction with the debtor is a voluntary one, a creditor may be expected to adjust his interest rate accordingly and to take whatever risk-reducing precautions he deems appropriate. Since creditors remain free to select their own debtors and to set the terms on which they will lend, there is no compelling argument based upon considerations of fairness for adopting one legal rule (debtors can rank creditor claims in whatever way they see fit) rather than another (all creditors must share equally in the event of bankruptcy).

Other scholars questioned Jackson and Kronman's explanation for the acceptance of secured credit and put forth their own. The following excerpt describes the early years of debate over what became known as the "puzzle of secured debt."

Robert E. Scott, A Relational Theory of Secured Financing

86 Colum. L. Rev. 901, 904-911 (1986)

A.   THE SECURITY PUZZLE RECONSIDERED: THE COMPETING HYPOTHESES

1. The Zero-Sum Hypothesis — The conventional vision of secured credit assumes that security expands debtors' access to credit markets. This conception rests on the premise that security offers financing opportunities to high-risk debtors who would not otherwise qualify for credit. However, the insights of modern finance theory have seriously undermined the conventional wisdom.

Finance theory offers two complementary visions of the capital structure of the firm. The most provocative hypothesis traces its lineage to the Modigliani-Miller Irrelevance Theorem. Modigliani and Miller demonstrated that, under certain carefully specified assumptions, the value of a firm is independent of its capital structure. In essence, the Irrelevance

Theorem holds that in perfectly functioning capital markets, absent taxes or bankruptcy costs, the particular mix of debt or equity held by a firm has no effect on the firm's value. Recently, legal scholars have begun to apply the insights of the Irrelevance Theorem to the debate over the function of secured debt. Alan Schwartz has shown that with homogeneous, risk-neutral creditors possessed of perfect information, a system of security operates as a zero sum game. Under these conditions, the benefits to one creditor by taking security are exactly offset by the increased cost imposed on an unsecured creditor whose claim to the debtor's asset pool has been correspondingly diminished. The "zero sum hypothesis" implies that the existing system of secured credit may operate as a net loss to debtors. Security interests are costly to create and administer. Moreover, if creditors are generally informed about credit risks, the reduction in interest charges that secured creditors are able to offer the debtor will be offset by more or less equivalent increases in interest charges by unsecured creditors. Thus, the debtor's total credit bill may well be larger under a system which permits security interests than in a world in which security is banned.

The zero-sum hypothesis searches for an explanation of secured financing through the systematic relaxation of its carefully articulated assumptions. Theorists have attempted explanations based on differing risk preferences of creditors or imperfections in the credit markets themselves. Thus, for example, in the real world of costly information, security may function as a means of signaling other creditors of the debtor's creditworthiness or, in the alternative, as a means of screening for eligible debtors. These explanations, however, are incomplete. They do not show convincingly why security is a preferable means of overcoming such informational barriers as compared to alternatives such as financial audits, the development of commercial reputation, or long term financial relationships.

Underlining the inadequacy of signaling or screening explanations is the possibility that information asymmetries explain the persistent use of secured credit. Assume that poorly informed creditors do not respond to the increased risk when others take security. In this case, security may persist not because of its socially beneficial effects, but because it permits informed creditors to capture wealth at the expense of other, uninformed creditors. Thus, firms may issue secured debt to protect themselves against informed creditors who expect it and to exploit uninformed creditors who neither expect it nor react to it. But such distributional explanations are inconsistent with the observed characteristics of credit markets. Specifically, distributional explanations predict that "firms will issue as much secured debt as possible; yet firms often borrow without security . . . many unsecured creditors appear well informed." As viewed through the lens of the zero sum hypothesis, therefore, the puzzle of security remains unresolved.

2. The Costly Contracting Hypothesis — The . . . "costly contracting hypothesis" asserts that contractual mechanisms that control inevitable debtor-creditor conflicts can, in fact, increase the value of the firm.

Several legal theorists working in this tradition have attempted to explain secured credit as a means of controlling the risk of "asset substitutions." Thus, for example, after the credit contract is negotiated, a debtor may gamble with the creditor's money by substituting riskier business projects for the more conservative investments originally planned. Presumably, some creditors are better able to monitor the debtor for such misbehavior than are others. Jackson and Kronman have used a monitoring advantage theory to suggest that poorer monitors take security to focus their efforts at controlling asset substitutions, while the better monitors are able to lend unsecured and exploit their comparative monitoring advantage.

The Jackson and Kronman theory is an important and original contribution. However, the argument yields the counterintuitive conclusion that those creditors who are typically unsecured, such as trade creditors and employees, are better at monitoring against debtor misbehavior than are those typical secured parties such as banks and financial institutions. Moreover, the Jackson-Kronman model fails to account for the signaling effects of security. If some creditors take security to reduce the risks of misbehavior, it is because they regard monitoring the collateral as a good proxy for continued supervision of the entire enterprise. To the extent that a debtor's efforts to increase business risks — or otherwise to cheat on the agreement — require it to convert assets, a secured creditor who merely guards against substitution of its collateral has a monitoring advantage over the unsecured creditor who presumably must continue to police the debtor's activities more expansively. But if the continued viability of the collateral provides a signal to the secured creditor, it presumably provides a signal to other creditors as well. Saul Levmore has suggested, therefore, that unsecured creditors would simply follow the secured creditor's signal and thus free ride on the monitoring efforts of security holders. Since under the Jackson-Kronman regime secured creditors are the less able monitors, the free-rider problem implies that a system of secured credit would generate unnecessarily high monitoring costs for the creditors as a group.

As an alternative explanation, Levmore suggests that the disequilibrium produced by the tendency of unsecured creditors to free ride on the monitoring efforts of secured creditors would cause the better monitors to take security as compensation for their efforts in reducing monitoring costs for the less capable creditors. This free-rider analysis resolves some of the empirical problems encountered by Jackson and Kronman. Most importantly, it is compatible with the intuition that banks and finance companies — parties that are typically secured — are better at monitoring the debtor than are employees and trade creditors.

On reflection, however, several problems remain unresolved. In what way does granting secured creditors priority produce a more efficient level of monitoring than would otherwise occur? And why is taking security superior to substitute methods of controlling debtor-creditor conflicts? The costly contracting hypothesis is a powerful analytic tool. But lacking a coherent theory for predicting when security is the optimal contractual mechanism for controlling conflict, current explanations only partially illuminate the patterns of secured and unsecured credit.

A security agreement is merely a contract between a debtor and a creditor. In Assignment 8, however, we noted that U.C.C. §9-201 imbues that contract with an amazing attribute. A security agreement is binding on purchasers of the collateral and creditors — even though they neither sign the contract nor know of its existence. Security is a contract between *A* and *B* that *C* take nothing.

In the following excerpt, professors Harris and Mooney respond with the argument that security belongs not so much to the world of contract as to the world of property. In the world of property, that attribute is unremarkable.

Steven L. Harris and Charles W. Mooney, Jr., A Property Based Theory of Security Interests: Taking Debtor's Choices Seriously

80 Va. L. Rev. 2021, 2021-2023, 2047-2053 (1994)

INTRODUCTION

In embarking upon the revision of what many consider the most successful commercial statute ever, we take as our "first principle" that Uniform Commercial Code Article 9 should facilitate the creation of security interests. Stated otherwise, we think the transfer of an effective security interest ought to be as easy, inexpensive, and reliable as possible. For the most part, the current version of Article 9 reflects our position: The law should not impair the ability of debtors to secure as much or as little of their debts with as much or as little of their existing and future property as they deem appropriate.

Our position has been controversial. The nineteenth and early twentieth century saw many secured transactions struck down on the ground that they were at least potentially injurious to unsecured creditors. A good deal of the perceived injury stemmed from the distributional consequences of security: property subject to a security interest would be unavailable for distribution to unsecured creditors. If the debtor became insolvent, allocation of particular property to secured creditors would unjustly interfere with, and perhaps eliminate, the recovery by unsecured creditors. Even the original drafters of Article 9, who expressly validated future-advance and after-acquired property clauses, did so with some reluctance, apparently experiencing a discomfort with "all assets" financing that we (the authors) do not share.

Despite widespread familiarity with Article 9 and the passage of more than three decades, this discomfort persists. Contemporary commentators have continued the tradition of expressing diffuse suspicion about the "favored" treatment the law affords to security interests. . . .

Our normative theory of security interests is grounded upon the normative theories that justify the institution of private property. The right to own private property is the bedrock of capitalism and an essential component of a market economy. . . .

We embrace the baseline principles that underlie current law insofar as it generally respects the free and effective alienation of property rights and the ability of parties to enter into enforceable contracts. We believe that these principles reflect widely shared normative views that favor party autonomy concerning both property and contract. We need not undertake, here, a defense of these principles. Instead, we accept them as sound and consider their implications for the law of secured transactions.

It seems clear enough that security interests, under Article 9 and real estate law alike, are interests in property.[1] The legal regime for security interests reflects property law functionally as well as doctrinally. We believe it follows that the law should honor the transfer or retention of security interests on the same normative grounds on which it respects the alienation of property generally. Because security interests are property, any general theory of the law of secured transactions must emanate from theories of property law. . . . We explained in Part I that, insofar as any distributive effects of wealth transfers and any adverse effects on existing and future unsecured creditors are concerned, the transfer of a security interest does not differ fundamentally from other transfers of a property interest in exchange for equivalent value. Thus, to carry the day, those who question secured transactions must attack the generally applicable treatment of party autonomy in property and contract law or must explain why secured transactions differ from other transactions that the law respects.

---

1. See, e.g., U.C.C. §1-201(37) (" 'Security interest' means an interest in personal property. . . ."). But see Lynn M. LoPucki & Elizabeth Warren, Secured Credit: A [Systems] Approach ([1995]). . . . Professors LoPucki and Warren scrupulously eschew any acknowledgment that security interests are property interests. This approach is likely to obscure both the doctrine imbedded in current law and many of the functions of security.

The debate over the appropriate division of assets between secured and unsecured creditors was an abstract affair, pitting archtypical "secured creditors" against archetypal "unsecured creditors." But, as virtually every discussion in this book has demonstrated, neither of those groups is monolithic. The category of "unsecured creditor" includes big banks who decided to make unsecured loans, trade creditors who made credit decisions that were part and parcel of their sales decisions, and utility companies that extended service at prices fixed without regard to creditworthiness, to mention but a few. They differ widely in their opportunity and ability to compete for priority. Some of those who end up with unsecured claims against a failing debtor never had the opportunity to refuse to extend credit. Tort victims cannot ask for financial references before they are injured. Environmental claimants, both governmental and civil, must advance funds to clean up toxic waste regardless of the balance sheet of the polluting company. The government cannot make an economically in-informed decision to withhold services from businesses who are not good credit risks.

Beginning in the mid-1980s, a number of commentators reached the conclusion that creditors who had no opportunity to bargain with the debtor for their status — including most kinds of tort creditors — should have priority over secured creditors. The following excerpt explains the economic rationale.

Lynn M. LoPucki, The Unsecured Creditor's Bargain

80 Va. L. Rev. 1887, 1896-1899, 1907-1914 (1994)

To reach the conclusion that involuntary creditors, including most kinds of tort creditors, should have priority over secured creditors on efficiency grounds we need only assume that the economy operates more efficiently when involuntary creditors are paid than when they are not. To understand why this is so, assume that a debtor has two creditors, one involuntary and one secured, and that the debtor's wealth is sufficient to pay either, but not both of them. If we view the competition between these two creditors ex post, that is, after both have extended credit, it appears not to matter which is paid. The aggregate loss to the economy is the same.

But if we view the competition ex ante, from the perspective of the two creditors before they extend credit, the superiority of the rule granting priority to involuntary creditors becomes apparent. In a world where involuntary creditors have priority, the secured creditor who can anticipate the priority contest can react to it by declining to extend credit beyond the debtor's ability to pay. On the facts assumed in the preceding paragraph, the secured creditor would not extend any credit, the involuntary creditor would be paid, and the aggregate loss to the economy would be zero.

In a world where secured creditors have priority, both these creditors would extend credit. The involuntary creditor would extend it because the involuntary creditor has no choice. The secured creditor would extend credit for the simple reason that it would be repaid. Because the debtor's wealth was assumed sufficient to pay only one creditor, the involuntary creditor would not be paid. The involuntary creditor's loss would be an aggregate loss to the economy.

In a very thoughtful, well-written article, Professor Shupack makes a variant of this argument. He notes that in a world where tort creditors had priority over secured creditors, secured creditors would condition their loans on the debtor's payment of a premium sufficient to compensate the secured creditors for their additional risk. He concludes, as I have, that the secured creditor suffers no loss.

He asserts, however, that the tort creditors will not necessarily be better off in the world where they have priority. His argument is one that others have made less formally, to justify the preferred status of secured creditors. It is that in the world where secured debt comes first and tort creditors take their leavings, entrepreneurs can borrow more money, there is more economic activity, the society is wealthier, and perhaps even the tort creditors themselves are better off.

To understand why neither tort creditors, nor the economy as a whole, are better off under current law than they would be in a tort-first regime, consider the following proof:

W = The wealth created by economic activity that will occur in a world where tort debt comes first

A = The added wealth created by activity that would not occur in a world where tort debt comes first but will occur in a world where secured debt comes first

T = The added uncompensated torts that would not occur in a world where tort debt comes first but will occur in a world where secured debt come first

I assert that:

$$W > = W + A - T$$

The left side of this inequality is total wealth in the tort-first world; the right side is total wealth in the secured-first world. The right side of this equation can be greater only if A is greater than T, that is, as Shupack asserts, the added activity A is greater than the tort loss resulting from that activity T. For A to be greater than T for the economy as a whole, A must be greater than T for at least some person in the economy. That is, there must be some person who would increase his or her wealth through expanded economic activity in the secured-first world over what it would have been in the tort-first world and whose increased wealth is greater than the expanded tort liability that results from the expanded economic activity. The existence of many such people seems unlikely. They would all be people who could have expanded their activity in the tort-first world, paid the tort liability with their added wealth, and had some left over.

In his comment, Professor Knippenberg notes that giving involuntary creditors priority over secured creditors may compel secured creditors "to become managers with or close monitors of" their borrowers. He would instead allow lenders to focus narrowly on being repaid and leave debtors to worry about the tort liability. The difficulty with such a division of labor is that there is no reliable way to bring it about. When a debtor operates with substantial equity in a tort-first system, the secured creditor's risk is minimal and its incentive to monitor small. As the amount of equity the debtor has in the business declines, the secured creditor's risk and incentive to monitor increase. That is as it should be. Unless the secured creditor's incentive to monitor increases as the debtor's decreases, the total level of monitoring will be inappropriately low. In our current, secured-first system, this point is illustrated each time the fully encumbered truck of an insolvent toxic waste disposal company hits the road.

The tort-first regime I propose is grounded in the premise that whoever supplies the capital that enables a business to operate should be legally responsible for its torts, at least to the extent of the supplier's investment. Whether the capitalist should control that liability by monitoring, involving itself in management, lending only to those whom it trusts, or delegating the task to an insurance company, is left to the capitalist to decide. But if civil liability is to provide the necessary incentives to hold tort risk to economically optimal levels, the liability must be placed on participants who have something to lose.

This proposal for a "tort first" system was not without precedent. In the world of admiralty, wage and tort claims have long primed ship mortgages. The seemingly topsy-turvy nature of the system of priorities in admiralty suggests the narrowness of the contemporary view that the world will come to an end if the priority of Article 9 secured creditors is disturbed in any minute respect.

Donald B. Dowart, Memorandum: Priorities of Maritime Lien and Preferred Ship Mortgages

February 9, 1993

There is no universal statutory law regarding the ranking of maritime liens; instead, the courts have formulated a common law ranking scheme based on equitable considerations and traditions of admiralty law. The priority-of-liens analysis has two parts. First, the different classes of the liens must be ranked. Next, a determination must be made of which liens come first within each class.

Although the case law is not completely uniform, assuming that all liens are of equal age, the ranking of maritime liens is generally as follows:

1. Expenses of justice while the vessel is in custodia legis.
2. Seaman's and master's liens for wages, maintenance and cure.
3. Salvage and general average liens.
4. Liens for maritime torts.
5. A maritime contract lien arising before the filing of a preferred mortgage.
6. Preferred ship mortgages.
7. Maritime contract liens.
8. State created liens of a maritime nature.
9. Liens for penalties and forfeiture.
10. Government tax liens.
11. Perfected non-maritime liens.

Within each class of lien, the "inverse order rule" applies. Under this rule, liens which arise later in time outrank liens which occur earlier in time. This rule of priority is unique to admiralty, and has been justified in a variety of ways. Perhaps the two best rationales for the inverse order rule are that, (i) a lienholder who fails to assert his liens risks subordination to subsequent liens, and (ii) so long as the inverse order rule is in place, a creditor dealing with a vessel can be assured of a relatively high lien priority. . . .

[T]he priority of a preferred ship mortgage against competing preferred ship mortgages is controlled by filing date. 46 U.S.C. §31321 (1992). Concerning other issues, a court will honor an agreement among lien claimants as to the priority of their liens that was executed prior to the sale of the vessel. . . .

As one scholar has suggested, a claimant should not hesitate to challenge the general priority scheme, as it applies to his or her specific claim dispute, if it duly limits the vessel's creditworthiness or works undue hardship or inequity. In some cases, a claimant may prevail on a priority claim, the basis of which is seemingly contrary to the general priority scheme.

For example, some courts have found that, although tort liens generally outrank contract liens, a contract claim arising on a voyage subsequent to the voyage on which the tort occurred will prime such lien. In another example, some courts have held that, where fault of the crew is involved, collision claims will prime other tort, salvage and wage liens.

When an early draft of Article 9 was considered by the Council of the American Law Institute, there was discussion of the treatment of unsecured creditors. Institute Director Geoffrey Hazard instructed Professor Elizabeth Warren, the strongest advocate for reconsideration of the position of unsecured creditors, to draft a proposal.

Elizabeth Warren, Article 9 Set Aside for Unsecured Creditors

Memorandum to the Council of the American Law
Institute April 25, 1996

[Text of proposal:] *A person who becomes a lien creditor and levies while a security interest is perfected shall be entitled on account of such person's inferior judicial lien to receive from the proceeds of the collateral subject to such protected security interest an amount no greater than 20 percent of the value of the property subject to the levy which is also subject to the security interest, if and only if*

(a)   *the lien creditor gives notice of the intent to satisfy the lien to the person holding the perfected security interest at least ten days prior to the disposition of the property;*
(b)   *the property levied upon is not consumer goods; and*
(c)   *the person holding the perfected security interest is unable to protect the property subject to the security interest by compelling the lien creditor to marshal.*

The thrust of this proposal is to permit a judgment lien creditor to attach up to twenty percent of the value of a debtor's assets without regard to outstanding security interests. The proposal permits secured creditors to marshal so that the lien creditor can be forced to satisfy itself first from unencumbered assets. If unencumbered assets are not available, however, the lien creditor can execute on property subject to a security interest and recover up to twenty percent of the value of the proceeds from the judicial sale. In order to avoid the problems of financing purchase money consumer sales, the proposal is limited to commercial loans. There is little evidence that the problem that prompts consideration of this proposal occurs in consumer settings.

During the past fifty years, Article 9 has shifted in practice from a statute that assured commercial creditors that they could reliably encumber some of the debtor's assets to a statute that permits secured creditors to take a first lien on virtually all of the debtor's assets. When the secured creditors encumber everything a debtor owns, the debtor's other creditors — particularly the trade creditors, the tort victims, employees, and the environmental claimants — are unable to reach the debtor's assets even when they can win a judgment against a debtor. The careful secured creditor with an interest in all the debtor's property is in the enviable position of not only creating a monopoly lending arrangement with the debtor, but also participating in the debtor's success (through continued interest payments) without suffering losses if the debtor fails (by taking all the hard assets of the business). This proposal requires that trade creditors, tort victims, employees, and other unsecured creditors who also contribute to the life of a business have some access to the assets of that business if it is unable or refuses to pay its debts.

The idea that there should be a limit to the reaches of secured credit is not new. Professor Grant Gilmore, the eminent Yale (and University of Chicago) professor who was the principal draftsman of the original Article 9, observed in his treatise:

> Considerations of policy and common sense suggest that there must be a limiting point somewhere. Borrowers should not be encouraged or allowed to hypothecate all that they may ever own in the indefinite future in favor of a creditor who is willing to make a risky loan now. . . . And ways should be found to penalize a lender who, after allowing his borrower to pile up an intolerable weight of debt, then claims all the assets of the insolvent estate, leaving nothing to satisfy other claims. [footnotes omitted]

1 Gilmore §7.12 at 248. Professor Gilmore used the approach of limiting the property to which the secured creditor would have access. Through the years, the restrictions on the kinds of property that could become collateral were eased. The current proposed revision of Article 9 eliminates most of the remaining limits.

The trend in the law of security interests toward encumbering all the property of the debtor caused Professor Gilmore to entitle his last law review article "Confessions of a Repentant Draftsman." He decried what had happened to Article 9: "[D]oes it make any sense to award everything to a secured party who stands idly by while a doomed enterprise goes down the slippery slope into bankruptcy?" 15 Ga. L. Rev. 605, 627 (1981). This proposal restores a balance among creditors by making a systematic set aside for unsecured creditors.

A set aside for unsecured creditors discourages asset-based lending to 100% value of the collateral. Would it therefore constrict commercial lending? That is a difficult question to answer. To the extent that much commercial lending is not based on the liquidation value of the assets, but is based instead on the ability to tie the debtor up and fence it off from other competing lenders, there would be no change in lending activity. To the extent that much commercial lending does not rely on the full liquidation value, but is based on significantly lower loan-to-value ratios, this proposal would not cause changes. To the extent that markets are rational, any constriction in the rights of secured creditors should be felt in offsetting benefits to unsecured creditors and might therefore be expected to produce more unsecured commercial debt as well as lower-cost trade debt.

But the proposal would have some important effects. If a business is viable only because the creditor can lend to 100% loan-to-value, thereby externalizing the risks of unpaid debt to the trade and tort creditors, this proposal would cause a constriction in credit. Even for creditors who currently lend on 90% or even 80% loan-to-value ratios, a proposal that permits unsecured creditors to take some collateral value might cause such creditors to re-adjust their percentages downward. In effect, this proposal would encourage some de-leveraging of American businesses, particularly of high-risk businesses.

The carve-out proposal was met by a storm of protest. Secured creditor advocates branded the attempt to limit priority "radical." The most frequently repeated argument was that without full priority for secured creditors, the total amount of credit available in the economy would decline sharply, injuring all businesses. Professor Warren responded:

Elizabeth Warren, Making Policy with Imperfect Information: The Article 9 Full Priority Debates

82 Cornell L. Rev. 101 (1997)

While there may be no way to test the credit-constriction assertion directly or to measure either the magnitude or the direction of the changes that would occur with partial priority, it is interesting to note how the assertion is treated as a debate-stopper. If credit is reduced, the assumption runs, both commercial lenders and their borrowers will be hurt, their potential trade creditors will be hurt, and even a robust economy will be threatened.

The argument proves too much. If the only test of any part of a commercial law system were whether it promoted or constricted credit, then our system would look very different. Why not return to the days of debt servitude? There were efficiency concerns about servitude, but the bottom line was that servitude made credit available to people who otherwise could not obtain it. Nonetheless, it was gone by the mid-1700s.

If the goal of a commercial law system is expansion of credit, then perhaps the revisions of Article 9 should reflect changes in medical technology since the 1960s. Why not permit security interests in body parts? Any debtor who promised her liver or her heart would surely have strong incentives to perform on the loan. It would be possible to restrict security interests to body parts that leave the debtor diminished but alive, such as offering a kidney, skin for a graft, a womb, or a cornea as collateral. It appears that the expansion of credit notion has not been embraced fully.

The idea here is not to give the current Article 9 drafters new ideas. Instead, the point is to note that even if a security device promotes lending, there may be reasons not to support it. Some of the reasons may be grounded in efficiency arguments. Some may be naked applications of paternalism. Some of the arguments may refer to community sensibilities and fairness that are hard to quantify in an equation full of sigmas and betas, but that have to do with our collective confidence in the commercial law system.

Even when the discussion is about nothing but money, the argument that full priority is justified whenever it promotes more lending still proves too much. . . . The incursions on priority in tax law, in statutory liens, and in bankruptcy make clear that fostering as much lending as possible is not the only goal of any commercial law system. The question is always one of balance. Taxing authorities get priorities in part because of a judgment that a business that cannot meet its tax obligations should not be operating. Cattle feed suppliers get a priority in part because they add value in a way that makes it virtually impossible for them to take a protected interest through any other method. Employees may take priority because they are poor risk spreaders. And so on. Bankruptcy law takes precedence over contractual agreements in part because the rights of third parties to pro rata distribution at liquidation cannot be negotiated away without the consent of the losing parties.

The ultimate question is not whether a partial priority scheme might cause some constriction in lending. The empirical question remains open, although there are strong arguments both to refute and to support the idea that total credit available would remain the same. The real question is how the efficiency arguments, even if they were unambiguously true, stack up against other considerations.

Despite some popularity among academics and the adoption of a somewhat similar proposal in Germany and other countries, the "carve out" proposal, as it came to be called, failed to win favor either with practicing lawyers or members of the Article 9 Drafting Committee. As Professor Mooney has described it, the carve out proposal "died for lack of a first" in the Drafting Committee.

While the debate over the appropriateness of the rules governing the priority of secured debt continues, commercial practices continue to evolve. In the article excerpted below, Professor LoPucki argues that with computerization of business practices and the increasingly strategic nature of legal practice, secured credit threatens to engulf the entire system of civil liability.

Lynn M. LoPucki, The Death of Liability

106 Yale L.J. 1 (1996)

The liability system works solely through the entry and enforcement of money judgments. Debtors can defeat it by rendering themselves judgment proof. Judgment-proofing strategies are of four basic types: secured debt, third-party ownership, exemption, and foreign haven.

Secured debt strategies are the most complex and the most common of the judgment-proofing strategies. They are employed primarily by small, relatively uncreditworthy businesses, whose lenders insist on security interests. . . . The debtor becomes judgment proof by incurring secured debts in amounts exceeding the liquidation values of the debtor's properties. Money judgments thereafter enforced against the debtor's properties are subordinate to the secured debt. Enforcement is by liquidation of the debtor's property. Pursuant to the principle of subordination, the proceeds of liquidation go first to pay the secured creditors. Because the proceeds are less than the secured debt, no balance remains to be paid to the holder of the money judgment. It follows that the holder of the money judgment cannot obtain full or even partial payment by exercising its legal remedies. The buyer at the sale of fully encumbered collateral will own the property and the judgment creditor will receive nothing.

Because it is costly and risky for a judgment creditor to liquidate the assets of its debtor and the judgment creditor recovers nothing anyway, judgment creditors who understand the system often give up without liquidating their debtors. They simply write off the debt. When judgment creditors and potential judgment creditors behave in this manner, their debtors can continue in business indefinitely without paying their debts.

Some judgment creditors will attempt to liquidate their debtors. Those debtors can still prevail by any of three strategies. First, the debtor who has the cooperation of a strategically placed secured creditor can enlist the secured creditor's help in blocking the judgment creditor's levy. In recent years, several courts have held that a secured creditor whose own debt is in default has the right to possession of its collateral and that the right primes even the right of a sheriff who would seize the property under a judgment creditor's writ of execution.

Second, the debtor may allow the sale to take place, but in some indirect manner become a purchaser at the sale. Sale of the property will move ownership to a new legal entity, leaving the debt behind in the old. For this strategy to succeed, the debtor must find a surrogate to purchase the property for it and must prevent the judgment creditor from purchasing at the sale. In the most common circumstance, where the debtor is itself a corporation, the surrogate may be another corporation created specifically for that purpose and owned by the owners of the debtor or its managers. The surrogate can then permit the debtor to continue using the property, as a gift or in return for periodic payment of rent. . . .

In many circumstances, the strategy of stripping judgment liens from property through state court sales will not work. The sheriffs who conduct the sales may insist on interfering with the debtor's possession of the property and operation of the business between the time of the levy and the time the state court confirms the sale.

In those circumstances, debtors can employ a third and even more powerful strategy for defeating subordinate lien creditors. Under the principle of productive use, the bankruptcy court will permit a debtor to operate its business while attempting to sell it. Thus protected, the debtor can propose a plan of reorganization that provides for the sale of the property to the new entity owned by the insiders, for an amount modestly below market value.[2] Provided that value is less than the amount of the prior liens, pursuant to the principle of subordination, the judgment creditor recovers nothing from the bankruptcy proceeding. Thus, Chapter 11 enables the debtor to strip from its property liabilities in excess of the property's value, even without the formality of a sale. It permits the debtor to do directly what it could do indirectly under state court or bankruptcy liquidation procedures. By confirmation of a Chapter 11 plan, the debtor can reduce its total debt to the value of its property and reschedule that debt for future payment. The owner-managers of a debtor corporation ordinarily can retain ownership and control through Chapter 11.

A debtor that enters Chapter 11 with secured debt exceeding the liquidation value of its collateral is likely to emerge with secured debt approximately equal to the value of that collateral. The effect is that the

---

2. See, e.g., In re Met-L-Wood Corp., 861 F.2d 1012, 1019 (7th Cir. 1988) (refusing to invalidate sale in which owner of debtor corporation purchased property through agent who did not disclose that owner was purchaser, because owner outbid at least one disinterested competitor).

emerging debtor is also judgment proof. If it incurs post-bankruptcy liabilities, it can file another Chapter 11 case, and strip those liabilities from the assets. This judgment-proof structure can operate perpetually.

The secured debt strategy is a relatively recent phenomenon. It is effective only in a system that permits debtors to encumber all, or substantially all, of their assets. . . .

In the parent-subsidiary strategy, the debtor isolates the most valuable assets of the business in an entity other than the one that conducts the liability-producing business activity. For example, assume that a large company (Operations, Inc.) sells its products on credit and then borrows from banks against its accounts receivable. To employ a secured debt strategy, the company would grant the banks a security interest in the accounts. To employ the parent-subsidiary strategy, the company incorporates a subsidiary (Finance, Inc.), and retains ownership of all the stock. As Operations sells its products, it creates accounts receivable. Operations sells the accounts to Finance, and distributes any proceeds beyond its immediate cash needs to its shareholders. Under the principle of transferability, both transfers become final as they occur, leaving Operations with minimal assets. Finance pays for the accounts by borrowing on an unsecured basis from a bank. If Operations sells defective products and incurs liability, its creditors eventually will obtain judgments against Operations. They can force the liquidation of Operations's assets, including its shares of stock in Finance. But in the ensuing liquidation of Finance, the bank will have priority over the judgment creditors. The bank claims the assets of Finance as an unsecured creditor while the judgment creditors claim them as a shareholder. Unsecured creditors are entitled to absolute priority over shareholders, so by the principle of subordination the bank prevails and the judgment creditors take nothing.

If the bank makes sure that Finance engages in no liability-generating activities, but is merely a borrower and a repository of accounts receivable, the bank assures itself of priority over any liability the business generates. That is precisely the result obtained through use of the secured debt strategy. But the parent-subsidiary strategy is an ownership strategy rather than a secured debt strategy because the bank defeats the judgment creditors by proving ownership by a separate entity rather than subordination to secured debt.

This parent-subsidiary ownership strategy is in wide use among the largest companies in America. Most large companies consist of numerous corporate entities. Limiting liability — that is, defeating part of it — is the principal reason for creating those entities.[3] But the parent-subsidiary

---

3. For example, the Eighth Circuit has written:

The doctrine of limited liability is intended precisely to protect a parent corporation whose subsidiary goes broke. That is the whole purpose of the doctrine, and those who have the right to decide such questions, that is, legislatures, believe that the

strategy itself rarely renders companies entirely judgment proof. Alone, it defeats only liability in excess of the value of the assets of the operating company. Nevertheless, the parent-subsidiary strategy has had a major effect in the bankruptcy reorganizations of large, publicly held companies. Its use in combination with a secured debt strategy can defeat a company's liability entirely.

The parent-subsidiary strategy is vulnerable to legal attack. In theory, at least, courts can disregard a corporate entity if it is being used too aggressively to defeat liability. But the rhetoric of entity disregard far outstrips the reality. . . . Overall, disregard of the entities that compose a corporate group remains very much the exception.[4]

Not everyone agrees. Professor Ronald Mann argues that the same macro changes in the commercial environment referred to by Professor LoPucki are eroding the use of secured credit and thereby solving the problem of secured credit.

Ronald J. Mann, The Role of Secured Credit in Small-Business Lending

86 Geo. L.J. 1 (1997)

[O]ne of the most prominent bank lending programs of the last few years is Wells Fargo's BusinessLine program, which offers unsecured debt to small businesses nationwide. Relying on publicly available credit information analogous to the information credit-card issuers use in pre-approving potential credit-card customers, Wells Fargo identifies large numbers of small businesses that are potential loan customers. It then sends unsolicited mailings to those businesses offering a hassle-free unsecured line of credit, ranging from $5,000 to $75,000, requiring only a one-page mail-in application. Because the borrower's signature on the application includes a promise to repay funds advanced under the line and a personal guaranty of that obligation, the signature on the application completes the documentation process. There are no separate promissory notes, guaranties, loan agreements, or financing statements.

---

doctrine, on the whole, is socially reasonable and useful. We think that the doctrine would largely be destroyed if a parent corporation could be held liable simply on the basis of errors in business judgment.

Radaszewski v. Telecom Corp., 981 F.2d 305, 311 (8th Cir. 1992).

4. See, e.g., NLRB v. Fullerton Transfer & Storage Ltd., 910 F.2d 331, 336-39 (6th Cir. 1990) (upholding division of single business among three corporations — one to hire truck drivers, one to own trucks, and one to own real estate — and refusing to enforce NLRB back-pay order, obtained against corporation that hired drivers, against corporations that owned assets).

Those mailings have enabled the program to create a large portfolio that gives Wells Fargo a nationwide presence for its small-business lending program. Competing lenders (many of whom do require collateral) doubt Wells Fargo's ability to cut into their market share significantly, and are quick to point out that Wells Fargo's loans are significantly more expensive than more conventional, individually priced, small-business loans. However true those arguments may be, Wells Fargo clearly has tapped into a significant preference of many small-business owners. That program brought Wells Fargo substantially more than a billion dollars in new loans in 1995 and has brought its total portfolio of unsecured small-business loans up to about $4 billion. The fact is, many small-business owners are happy to pay more for money that comes with fewer strings attached.

Nor is it easy to dismiss Wells Fargo's program as an odd fad that will pass when cooler heads prevail. On the contrary, other major players recognizing the desire of borrowers for hassle-free lending are beginning to follow suit. Most prominently, two of the largest lenders in my sample — BankAmerica and Chase Manhattan — have altered their small-business lending programs to eliminate the use of collateral from large segments of that program. Most crucially, the borrowers eligible for those unsecured loans are selected not because they are the safest or most creditworthy borrowers in the portfolio. Rather, those programs extend unsecured loans to all borrowers in the portfolio whose loans are under $100,000. If that sounds like a small segment of the market, consider that it is more than half of BankAmerica's business banking portfolio, more than a billion dollars at that institution alone. Finally, even banks that typically take collateral on small business loans do make a substantial number of those loans without taking a lien. . . .

The pattern of secured credit revealed by the evidence in Parts II and III is not a simple one. Some banks' small-business loans are entirely or predominately secured. Other banks' small-business loans are entirely or predominately unsecured (at least for loans below $100,000). Still other banks have a mix of the two. One interpretation of the evidence would be a static one, that the relevant considerations are so closely balanced that there is little or nothing to choose between secured and unsecured transactions. Under that view, the choice between secured and unsecured credit matters so little that the choice of a particular bank can end up resting on the "philosophy" of that particular institution, with neither choice leading to a significant competitive disadvantage.

That interpretation, however, seems to me to ignore the dynamic character of the market. The small-business lending market is not some sleepy corner of the economy in which lending transactions are structured "the way we've always done it." This is an arena into which the largest financial institutions in our economy are throwing tremendous resources, motivated by the perception that technology provides an opportunity for profitable lending opportunities in areas banks historically have left underserved.

. . . Two of the most powerful factors proffered in part III to justify the use of unsecured credit — declining constraints on future borrowing and advances in information technology — are factors that have changed dramatically during the last few decades and significantly during the last few years alone. Consider first the ability of secured credit to constrain future borrowing. The main source of funding that is defeating that use of secured credit is the credit card. Twenty-five years ago the credit-card market was in its infancy. Few individuals operating small businesses could have used credit cards to fund businesses with the tens of thousands of dollars of credit-card borrowing that has been thrust on any reasonably solvent individual during the last few years.

The story of information technology is the same. Twenty-five years ago it would have been completely impractical for banks to develop standardized scoring criteria for evaluating small-business loan applications. Only in the last few years have computers developed to the point where it is cost-effective for lenders to use credit-scoring and early-warning systems effectively. Indeed, even now it is clear that the costs of those technologies give the largest institutions a considerable advantage in their use. It takes a massive small-business portfolio to support a completely cutting-edge credit-scoring and early-warning system. Thus, although hundreds of banks are using credit scoring in some manner, only a handful of our banks have developed systems that reflect their own loan experience; the others rely on a standardized third-party scorecard developed from a sampling of several bank's portfolios. Similarly, I do not think it is a coincidence that the only institutions I interviewed with proprietary early-warning systems were Home Savings of America (the largest savings bank in the United States) and Chase Manhattan Corporation (perennially one of the largest banks in the United States).

Based on the rapid development of those factors, I prefer a dynamic interpretation of the mixed pattern of secured and unsecured credit. As I see it, only in the last few years has the comparative advantage passed from secured credit to unsecured credit. Under that perspective, the small-business bank lending market is in the middle of a shift of institutions, with secured credit quickly becoming the way of the past and unsecured credit quickly coming to dominance.

———————

Although we have presented a skeptical view of secured credit in this book, revised Article 9 constitutes a ringing endorsement of the concept. As of this writing, the attack on secured credit in the academic literature seems to have had little effect. Revised Article 9 was promulgated virtually without opposition in the ALI or NCCUSL and the first states have already adopted it. One effect of adoption will be to increase the rights of secured creditors and with them the significance of the concept of security in commerce. Secured credit is not only alive and well, it is expanding.

Problem Set 40

40.1.   Your long-time client and friend, Harley Davidson, is back. Harley now works for Steady Hand, a venture capital firm that makes both loans and equity investments in high tech start-up businesses. His client, Robert Alvin, is a geneticist who specializes in marketing "biological solutions" to diseases in plants, animals, and human beings. He identifies products developed in other countries and brings them to the United States for production and sales. (Alvin was the highest bidder on the rights to distribute the French abortion pill in the United States, but the developer of the drug preferred an already-established company.)

Alvin seeks $4 million in financing for three products he seeks to introduce. Because the safety of these products is unproven, liability insurance is unavailable. No established company will manufacture the products for Alvin, or even lease him a plant in which to do so. One million dollars of the financing he seeks will be invested in a plant, another million will go into inventory and equipment, a third will be paid to developers of the product for licensing fees (they want their money in advance), and the last $1 million will go for "soft costs" such as labor, start-up costs, advertising, etc. Each of the three products is alone capable of generating billions of dollars in profits (or in liability). The deal tentatively struck is that Steady Hand will receive 15 percent interest on the $4 million dollars while it remains outstanding and half the profits on these three products. Both parties are willing to talk about other structures, "so long as the bottom line stays about the same."

Harley asks your advice on structuring the investment to minimize the risk to Steady Hand if one of the products should "blow up on us" — without, of course, limiting the profit potential. For the purpose of structuring the discussion, Harley posits the following prospects for the business: It does three projects, two of which make a billion dollars each in profits and the third of which results in $3 billion dollars in liabilities. What do you tell Harley?

40.2.   In a parallel universe, you represent Alecia Card, who was severely injured by microbes released from the premises of Continental Magnatech Corporation, a corporation owned by Robert Alvin with financing from Steady Hand in accord with the scheme you came up with in Problem 40.1. Liability is clear. The doctors predict an extended agony followed by a horrible death, so the damages will likely be huge. Alecia is only the first of what are likely to be many victims of the microbe release over many years. How will you proceed? For example, against whom will you initially file suit? How will you discover the names and roles of entities other than Continental Magnatach that are part of the scheme?

> Federal Rules of Civil Procedure, Rule 11. The signature of an attorney or party constitutes a certificate by the signer that the signer has read the pleading . . . ; that to the best of the signer's knowledge, information, and belief formed after reasonable inquiry it is well grounded in fact and is warranted by existing law or a good faith argument for the extension, modification, or reversal of existing law, and that it is not interposed for any improper purpose, such as to harass or to cause unnecessary delay or needless increase in the cost of litigation.

> Federal Rules of Civil Procedure Rule 26(b)(1). In General. Parties may obtain discovery regarding any matter, not privileged, which is relevant to the subject matter involved in the pending action, whether it relates to the claim or defense of the party seeking discovery or to the claim or defense of any other party, including the existence, description, nature, custody, condition, and location of any books, documents, or other tangible things and the identity and location of persons having knowledge of any discoverable matter. The information sought need not be admissible at the trial if the information sought appears reasonably calculated to lead to the discovery of admissible evidence.

40.3. For the past 14 years a member of your law firm, Shelley Kramer, has been doing the intellectual property work for Sigmet Electronics, a manufacturer of avionic components. Shelly bills Sigmet monthly. At any given time, Sigmet is indebted to the firm for about $20,000 to $50,000 worth of work in the form of hours not yet billed or bills not yet paid. This morning, while scanning recent U.C.C. filings for another matter, you noticed a U.C.C. filing against Sigmet as debtor and in favor of Portage State Bank. The filing is against "equipment, inventory, and accounts receivable." What are the implications of this filing for the firm? Are you relieved because Portage will now assist you in monitoring the debtor? Concerned? If so, what should you do? Should you be monitoring for U.C.C. filings against all the firm's clients?

40.4. As chair of the recently appointed National Secured Credit Review Commission, your job is to decide whether to recommend federal legislation to replace Article 9 and, if so, what that legislation should provide. How do you rank the following options going in and how do you respond to the arguments noted?

a. *Retain Article 9 in basically its current state.* If you choose this option, how do you respond to the arguments that (1) secured credit encourages excessive lending by making it possible to finance even bad businesses; (2) secured credit facilitates judgment proofing, which eventually will destroy the liability system; and (3) secured credit is unfair to trade creditors and buyers of collateral because it is fundamentally deceptive.

b.   *Give nonconsensual tort creditors and/or small wage claims priority over secured creditors under federal law.* If you choose this option, how do you respond to the argument that every secured lender will be at the mercy of runaway juries in tort cases, leading them to cut back on the amounts they lend, and ultimately leading to a slowing of the economy.

c.   *Adopt the Warren carve-out proposal, in its current form or some closely related form, under federal law.* If you choose this option, how do you respond to the arguments that (1) granting a security interest harms unsecured creditors no more than selling property or paying one creditor in preference to another; (2) lenders will cut back on the amounts they lend, leading to a slowing of the economy; and (3) the 20 percent carve-out won't benefit general unsecured creditors significantly because most of the money will go to bankruptcy lawyers and other creditors with priority under Bankruptcy Code §507(a)?

d.   *Adopt solution 2 or 3, above, but do it through uniform state law, rather than federal law.* If you choose this option, how do you deal with the problem of particular states giving absolute priority to secured creditors in order to attract business?

Table of Cases

Italics indicate principal cases.

Adamatic; Chrysler v., 680, 683
Aetna Bus. Credit; Dick Warner Cargo
  Handling Corp. v., 540, 541
Airco, Inc.; Marine Nat'l Bank v., 62
Alexander, In re, 349
Allen, In re, 169
Allied Inv. Credit Corp.; Lorain Music
  Co. v., 439
Alma Realty Co.; Maher v., 32
Altec Lansing v. Friedman Sound, Inc.,
  502
American Restaurant Supply Co. v. Wil-
  son, 182
American Sav. Bank; Nobleman v., 276
Amex-Protein Dev. Corp., In re, 163
Anderson; Calder Bros. Co. v., 622
Anderson; Straus v., 74
Apex Oil Co., In re, 137
Acacia Mut. Life Ins. Co.; Chew v., 74
Armstrong v. Csurilla, 71
Arnold, In re, 340
Associated Air Servs., Inc., In re, 403
Associated Commercial Corp.; Hoffman
  v., 484
Associated Indus. v. Keystone Gen., Inc.,
  200
Associates Fin. Serv. Co.; Brescher v., 502
Automated Med. Labs., Inc.;
  Hillsborough County v., 323

Baker Indus. Corp., In re, 513
Balcain Equip. Co., In re, 185
Baldi v. Chicago Title v. Trust Co., 81
Bank Leumi Trust Co. of N.Y. v. Liggett,
  498
Bank of Hayward; Daniel v., 680, 685
Bank of the W.; ITT Commercial Fin. v.,
  349
Basile v. Erhal Holding Corp., 30
Benjamin v. Diamond, 262
Black's Chevrolet Co., Inc. v. Melichar,
  255
Blundell, In re, 169
*Bluxome St. Assocs. v. Fireman's Fund Ins.
  Co.*, 384
Bob Schwermer & Assoc., Inc., In re, 179
Bollinger Corp., In re, 163
Bostwick-Braun Co. v. Owens, 437
Boyd; Rader v., 667
Braxtan; Home Owners' Loan Corp. v.,
  74
Brescher v. Associates Fin. Serv. Co., 502
Bridge; Midlantic Nat'l Bank v., 556

Broadcast Music, Inc. v. Hirsch, 328
Bruett; Norwest Bank of Des Moines,
  N.A. v., 46
B.T. Lazarus v. Christofides, 447

Cablevision of Breckenridge v.
  Tannhaiser Condominium Ass'n, 669
Cache Valley Bank; United States v., 726
Calder Bros. Co. v. Anderson, 622
Capital Bank; TR-3 Indus. v., 327
Capital Fed. Sav. & Loan Ass'n of Den-
  ver; National Peregrine, Inc. v. (In re
  Peregrine Entertainment, Ltd.), 321
*Carpenter Cook, Inc.; Del's Big Saver Foods,
  Inc. v.*, 49
Carter; Commercial Credit Equip. Co. v.,
  382
Central Nat'l Bank & Trust Co. of Enid v.
  Community Bank & Trustee Co. of
  Enid, 340
Chavers v. Frazier, 98
Chemical Bank v. Title Servs., Inc., 337
Chevron v. Natural Resources Defense
  Council, 703
Chew v. Acacia Mut. Life Ins. Co., 74
Chicago Pneumatic Tool Co.; Siboney
  Corp. v., 96
Chicago Title v. Trust Co.; Baldi v., 81
Christofides; B.T. Lazarus v., 447
Chrysler v. Adamatic, 680, 683
Chrysler Credit Corp.; Wallace v., 59
Citicorp Nat'l Servs., Inc.; Robinson v.,
  55
Citizens Nat'l Bank v. Wedel, 347
City Bank & Trust Co. v. Otto Fabric,
  Inc., 326
City of, *see* specific city by name
Clark v. General Elec. Co., 623
Clark; United States v., 726
Clark Pipe, In re, 668
Clow v. Woods, 754
C.O. Funk & Son v. Sullivan Equip., 204
Collins; Home Owners' Loan Corp. v.,
  560
*Colorado Cent. Credit Union; Salisbury
  Livestock Co. v.*, 55
Commercial Credit Equip. Co. v. Carter,
  382
Commonwealth Edison Co. v. The City
  of Zion, 395
Community Bank & Trustee Co. of Enid;
  Central Nat'l Bank & Trust Co. of Enid
  v., 340

Community for Creative Non-Violence v.
Reid, 323
Condon; Winkle Chevy-Olds-Pontiac,
Inc. v., 5
Connecticut; Griswold v., 12
Cornbelt Livestock Co.; Gretna State
Bank v., 200, 676
Cottam v. Heppner, 56
Couch, In re, 169
Covey v. First Nat'l Bank (In re Balcain
Equip. Co.), 185
Cowsert, In re, 403
Creditthrift of Am, Inc.; Schultz v., 544
Creeger Brick v. Mid-State Bank, 663
Crocker Equip. Leasing, Inc.; Hall v., 96
Crouch, In re, 215
Csurilla; Armstrong v., 71

Daley-Hodkin Corp.; Global Castings,
Etc. v., 60
Daniel v. Bank of Hayward, 680, 685
Daniels; Smith v., 98
Danning v. Pacific Propeller, 324
Davis; Peugh v., 31
Davis v. United States, 725
Day Cal. Ltd. Partnership; Financial Sec.
Assurance, Inc. v., 218
Deering Milliken, Inc.; Tanbro Fabrics
Corp. v., 686
*Del's Big Saver Foods, Inc. v. Carpenter
Cook, Inc.*, 49
*Deutsche Credit Corp. v. Lowe (In re The
Torgerson Co.)*, 361
Dewsnup v. Timm, 563
Diamond; Benjamin v., 262
Di-Chem, Inc.; North Ga. Finishing, Inc.
v., 50, 51
Dick Warner Cargo Handling Corp. v.
Aetna Bus. Credit, 540, 541
Diolosa; Howard v., 560
Doud; United States v., 150

Ebbler Furniture and Appliances, Inc., In
re, 581
Ed Duggan, Inc.; Ninth Dist. Prod. Credit
Ass'n v., 669
Elgin Nat'l Bank; Waldorf Ins. and Bond-
ing, Inc. v., 729
Elsen; State Bank of La Crosse v., 178
Emark Corp.; Myzer v., 708
Erhal Holding Corp.; Basile v., 30
Erickson; National Bank of Alaska v. (In
re Seaway Express Corp.), 452
Evans v. Everett, 163
Evans Prods. Co. v. Jorgensen, 316
Everett; Evans v., 163
Excel Stores, Inc., In re, 347

*Exchange Nat'l Bank of Chicago; Uni
Imports, Inc. v.*, 538

Family Fin. Corp.; Sniadach v., 50
Farm Credit of St. Paul v. Stedman, 35
FDIC; Langley v., 609
FDIC v. Lanier, 95
Federal Reserve Bank; Sowell v., 640
Fidelity Fin. Servs., Inc. v. Fink, 583
Financial Sec. Assurance, Inc. v. Day Cal.
Ltd. Partnership, 218
Financial Sec. Assurance, Inc. v. Tollman-
Hundley Dalton, L.P., 219
Fink; Fidelity Fin. Servs., Inc. v., 583
*Fireman's Fund Ins. Co.; Bluxome St.
Assocs. v.*, 384
*First Bank of Whiting; Kham & Nate's
Shoes No. 2, Inc. v.*, 262, 667, 668
First Interstate Bank of Utah, N.A. v. IRS,
743
First Nat'l Bank; Covey v. (In re Balcain
Equip. Co.), 185
First Nat'l Bank & Trust Co. of Ravenna,
Ohio; Morris v., 58
First Nat'l Bank of Glendale v. Sheriff of
Milwaukee County, 502
First Nat'l Fidelity Corp. v. Perry, 278
Ford Motor Credit Co.; K.B. Oil Co. v.,
60
Ford Motor Credit Co.; Wade v., 60
Ford Motor Credit Co.; Williams v., 60
Frazier; Chavers v., 98
Freightliner Mkt. Div. v. Silver Wheel
Freight, 241
Friedman Sound, Inc.; Altec Lansing v.,
502
Frierson v. United Farm Agency, Inc.,
504
Fuentes v. Shevin, 51, 53
Fullerton Transfer & Storage Ltd.; NLRB
v., 771

Gagnon; Pawtucket Inst. for Sav. v., 188
Gallatin Nat'l Bank v. Lockovich, 380, 383
Gaskill v. Wales, 559
General Elec. Capital Corp.;
Transamerica Commercial Fin. Corp. v.
(In re Wardcorp, Inc.), 345
General Elec. Co.; Clark v., 623
General Elec. Co. v. M&C Mfg., Inc., 412
Genuario, In re, 179
Giese; Suring State Bank v., 74
Gimbel Bros, Inc.; Janes Baird Co. v., 264
Global Castings, Etc. v. Daley-Hodkin
Corp., 60
Grand Rapids Lumber Co.; Kent Storage
Co. v., 398

Green; Whiteway Fin. Co. v., 546
Greenstreet; United States v., 365
Gretna State Bank v. Cornbelt Livestock
  Co., 200, 676
Grieves, In re, 125
Griswold v. Connecticut, 12
Grocers Supply Co. v. Intercity Inv. Proper-
  ties, Inc., 501
Guidry v. Sheet Metal Workers Nat'l Pen-
  sion Fund, 234

Hall v. Crocker Equip. Leasing, Inc., 96
Hays, In re, 438
Heppner; Cottam v., 56
Heritage Mountain Dev. Corp.; Ketchum,
  Konkel, Barrett, Nickel & Austin v., 620
Hewn, In re, 169
Hill; Tennessee Valley Auth. v., 214
Hillsborough County v. Automated Med.
  Labs., Inc., 323
Hilyard Drilling Co.; Worthen Bank & Trust
  Co., N.A. v., 435, 437
Hirsch; Broadcast Music, Inc. v., 328
Hodge Forest Indus., In re, 403
Hoffman v. Associated Commercial
  Corp., 484
Home Owners' Loan Corp. v. Braxtan, 74
Home Owners' Loan Corp. v. Collins,
  560
Horicon State Bank v. Kant Lumber Co.,
  82
Hotel Cal., Inc.; Vitale v., 6
Howard v. Diolosa, 560
H.R. Bigle & Co.; Rutherford Nat'l Bank
  v., 559
Hunt; Local Loan Co. v., 231

In re, *see* name of party
Intercity Inv. Properties, Inc.; Grocers Supply
  Co. v., 501
IRS; First Interstate Bank of Utah, N.A. v.,
  743
IRS; Mayer-Dupree v., 729
IRS; Title Guaranty Co. v., 726
Irving Trust Co.; KMC Co. v., 261, 264
ITT Commercial Fin. v. Bank of the W.,
  349

Jackson v. Miller, 237
Jamison v. Society Nat'l Bank, 412
Janes Baird Co. v. Gimbel Bros., Inc., 264
J.B. Hale Contracting Co. v. United N.M.
  Bank at Albuquerque, 253
J.C. Produce, Inc. v. Paragon Steakhouse
  Restaurants, Inc., 703
Jones; Newton County Bank v., 546, 548

Jorgensen; Evans Prods. Co. v., 316
Joseph v. 1200 Valencia, Inc., 328

Kant Lumber Co.; Horicon State Bank v.,
  82
Kaplan v. Walker, 560
K.B. Oil Co. v. Ford Motor Credit Co., 60
Kent Storage Co. v. Grand Rapids Lum-
  ber Co., 398
Ketchum, Konkel, Barrett, Nickel & Austin
  v. Heritage Mountain Dev. Corp., 620
Keystone Gen., Inc.; Associated Indus. v.,
  200
Kham & Nate's Shoes No. 2, Inc. v. First
  Bank of Whiting, 262, 667, 668
Killmnick; Stoumbos v., 185
KMC Co. v. Irving Trust Co., 261, 264

Langley v. FDIC, 609
Lanier; FDIC v., 95
Las Vegas Ry. & Power v. Trust Co. of St.
  Louis County, 73
Laurel Coal Co. v. Walter E. Heller &
  Co., 59
Lectro Sys., Inc.; Northwestern Nat'l
  Bank Southwest v., 747
Lee; Old Republic Ins. Co. v., 259
Levinson; Mayor's Jewelers of Ft. Lauder-
  dale, Inc. v., 382
Liggett; Bank Leumi Trust Co. of N.Y. v.,
  498
Lipper, Inc.; Teel Constr., Inc. v., 364
Litton; Pepper v., 666
LMS Holding Co.; United States v., 724
Local Loan Co. v. Hunt, 231
Lockovich; Gallatin Nat'l Bank v., 380, 383
Longtree, Ltd. v. Resource Control Int'l,
  165
Lorain Music Co. v. Allied Inv. Credit
  Corp., 439
Lowe; Deutsche Credit Corp. v. (In re The
  Torgerson Co.), 361
L.R. Holdings, Inc.; Royal Foods Co. v., 701

Magic Restaurants, Inc., In re, 703
Maher v. Alma Realty Co., 32
Malone & Hyde, Inc.; Peerless Packing
  Co. v., 314, 668
M&C Mfg., Inc.; General Elec. Co. v.,
  412
Marine Nat'l Bank v. Airco, Inc., 62
Marino v. United Bank of Ill, N.A., 79
Mayer-Dupree v. IRS, 729
Mayor's Jewelers of Ft. Lauderdale, Inc. v.
  Levinson, 382
McDermott; United States v., 730

McDermott Appliance Co.; Sales Fin. Corp. v., 348

McKay v. Stockman's Bank of Clayton, 258

McLemore, Trustee v. Mid-South Agi-Chemical Corp., 194

Melichar; Black's Chevrolet Ctr., Inc. v., 255

Met-L-Wood Corp., In re, 769

Meyer v. United States, 640

Midlantic Nat'l Bank v. Bridge, 556

Mid-South Agi-Chemical Corp.; McLemore, Trustee v., 194

Mid-State Bank; Creeger Brick v., 663

Miller; Jackson v., 237

Millerburg, In re, 514

Mitchell v. W.T. Grant Co., 51

Mobile Steel Co., In re, 666

Monnier; Prudential Ins. Co. v. (In re Monnier Bros.), 150

Morris v. First Nat'l Bank & Trust Co. of Ravenna, Ohio, 58

Moss; United Okla. Bank v., 187

Myzer v. Emark Corp., 708

Nara Non Food Distrib., Inc., In re, 348

National Acceptance Co.; Roman Cleanser Co. v., 327

National Bank of Alaska v. Erickson (In re Seaway Express Corp.), 452

National Peregrine, Inc. v. Capital Fed. Sav. & Loan Ass'n of Denver (In re Peregrine Entertainment, Ltd.), 321

Natural Resources Defense Council; Chevron v., 703

Neal Pharmacal Co.; United States v., 150

New Britain; United States v., 731

Newton County Bank v. Jones, 546, 548

Ninth Dist. Prod.Credit Ass'n v. Ed Duggan, Inc., 669

NLRB v. Fullerton Transfer & Storage Ltd., 771

Nobleman v. American Sav. Bank, 276

North Ga. Finishing, Inc. v. Di-Chem, Inc., 50, 51

Northwestern Nat'l Bank Southwest v. Lectro Sys., Inc., 747

Northwest Marine, Inc.; Union Nat'l Bank of Pittsburgh v., 381

Norwest Bank of Des Moines, N.A. v. Bruett, 46

Oklahoma City Broadcasting Co., In re, 242

Old Republic Ins. Co. v. Lee, 259

Osborne, In re, 666, 667

Otto Fabric, Inc.; City Bank & Trust Co. v., 326

Owens; Bostwick-Braun Co. v., 437

Owensboro Canning Co., In re, 165

Pacific Propeller; Danning v., 324

Paragon Steakhouse Restaurants, Inc.; J.C. Produce, Inc. v., 703

Pawtucket Inst. for Sav. v. Gagnon, 188

Peerless Packing Co. v. Malone & Hyde, Inc., 314, 668

Pepper v. Litton, 666

Peregrine Entertainment, Ltd., In re, 321

Perry, In re, 279

Perry; First Nat'l Fidelity Corp. v., 278

Peugh v. Davis, 31

Pledger; United States v., 729

Prudential Ins. Co. v. Monnier (In re Monnier Bros.), 150

Radaszewski v. Telcom Corp., 771

Rader v. Boyd, 667

Rainwater v. Rx Med. Servs. Corp., 61

Ram Mfg., Inc., In re, 124

Reid; Community for Creative Non-Violence v., 323

Resource Control Int'l; Longtree, Ltd. v., 165

Ridgely Communications, Inc., In re, 241

Roach, In re, 278

Robinson v. Citicorp Nat'l Servs., Inc., 55

Rockafellar; White v., 13

Rodgers; United States v., 726

Roman Cleanser Co. v. National Acceptance Co., 327

Royal Foods Co. v. L.R. Holdings, Inc., 701

Rutherford Nat'l Bank v. H.R. Bigle & Co., 559

Rx Med. Servs. Corp.; Rainwater v., 61

Sales Fin. Corp. v. McDermott Appliance Co., 348

Salisbury Livestock Co. v. Colorado Cent. Credit Union, 55

Samuels, In re, 655

S&J Holding Corp. v. Shazamm Enters. Ltd., 183

Schmidt, In re, 182

Schultz v. Creditthrift of Am, Inc., 544

Schumacher; Wolf v., 173

Seaway Express Corp., In re, 452

Shazamm Enters. Ltd.; S&J Holding Corp. v., 183

Sheet Metal Workers Nat'l Pension Fund; Guidry v., 234

Sheriff of Milwaukee County; First Nat'l

Bank of Glendale v., 502
Shevin; Fuentes v., 51, 53
Shockley Forest Indus., Inc., In re, 123
Siboney Corp. v. Chicago Pneumatic
Tool Co., 96
Silver Wheel Freight; Freightliner Mkt.
Div. v., 241
Slodov v. United States, 743
Smith v. Daniels, 98
Smith; United States v., 340
Sniadach v. Family Fin. Corp., 50
Society Nat'l Bank; Jamison v., 412
Southern Supply Co., In re, 347
Sowell v. Federal Reserve Bank, 640
Spiegel v. Taylor, 12
State Bank of La Crosse v. Elsen, 178
Stedman; Farm Credit of St. Paul v., 35
Stockman's Bank of Clayton; McKay v.,
258
Stoumbos v. Killmnick, 185
Straus v. Anderson, 74
Sullivan Equip.; C.O. Funk & Son v., 204
Suring State Bank v. Giese, 74

Taddeo, In re, 278
Tak Communications, Inc., In re, 241
Tanbro Fabrics Corp. v. Deering Milliken,
Inc., 686
Tannhaiser Condominium Ass'n;
Cablevision of Breckenridge v., 669
Taylor; Spiegel v., 12
Teel Constr., Inc. v. Lipper, Inc., 364
Telcom Corp.; Radaszewski v., 771
Teltronics Servs., Inc., In re, 666
Tennessee Valley Auth. v. Hill, 214
Texas Oil & Gas Corp. v. United States,
740
Timm; Dewsnup v., 563
Title Guaranty Co. v. IRS, 726
Title Servs., Inc.; Chemical Bank v., 337
Tollman-Hundley Dalton, L.P.; Financial
Sec. Assurance, Inc. v., 219
Torgerson Co., In re, 361
TR-3 Indus. v. Capital Bank, 327
Transamerica Commercial Fin. Corp. v.
General Elec. Capital Corp. (In re
Wardcorp, Inc.), 345
Transportation Design & Tech., Inc., In
re, 326
Tripp v. Vaughn, 623
Trust Co. of St. Louis County; Las Vegas
Ry. & Power v., 73
1200 Valencia, Inc.; Joseph v., 328
26 Trumbull St., In re, 118

Tyler, In re, 349

*Uni Imports, Inc. v. Exchange Nat'l Bank of
Chicago*, 538
Union Nat'l Bank of Pittsburgh v. North-
west Marine, Inc., 381
United Bank of Ill, N.A.; Marino v., 79
United Farm Agency, Inc.; Frierson v.,
504
*United N.M. Bank at Albuquerque; J.B. Hale
Contracting Co. v.*, 253
United Okla. Bank v. Moss, 187
United States v., *see* name of opposing
party

Vaughn; Tripp v., 623
Vermont; United States v., 731
Vitale v. Hotel Cal., Inc., 6

Wade v. Ford Motor Credit Co., 60
Waldorf Ins. and Bonding, Inc. v. Elgin
Nat'l Bank, 729
Wales; Gaskill v., 559
Walker; Kaplan v., 560
Walker v. Walthall, 58
Wallace v. Chrysler Credit Corp., 59
Walter E. Heller & Co.; Laurel Coal Co.
v., 59
Walthall; Walker v., 58
Wardcorp, Inc., In re, 345
Wedel; Citizens Nat'l Bank v., 347
White v. Rockafellar, 13
Whiteway Fin. Co. v. Green, 546
Williams v. Ford Motor Credit Co., 60
Wilson; American Restaurant Supply Co.
v., 182
Winkle Chevy-Olds-Pontiac, Inc. v.
Condon, 5
Winslow Ctr. Assoc., In re, 124
Wolf v. Schumacher, 173
Woods; Clow v., 754
Woolf Printing Corp., In re, 642
*Worthen Bank & Trust Co., N.A. v. Hilyard
Drilling Co.*, 435, 437
W.T. Grant Co.; Mitchell v., 51

Ziluck, In re, 183
Zion, City of; Commonwealth Edison
Co. v., 395
Zurline, In re, 165

Table of Statutes

Bankruptcy Code

§101	24, 280, 554, 577
§101(5)	133
§101(12)	133
§101(31)	667
§101(37)	133
§101(51)	133, 280
§330(b)	563
§361	118, 124, 221, 522
§361(2)	400, 401
§361(a)	111
§362	124
§362(a)	115, 120–22, 126, 508, 519
§362(a)(4)	565
§362(b)(1)	115
§362(b)(2)	118, 272
§362(b)(3)	440, 565
§362(b)(4)	115
§362(c)	116, 510
§362(c)(1)	142
§362(c)(2)	272
§362(d)	117, 119, 122, 124, 272, 508
§362(d)(1)	118, 119, 122, 123
§362(d)(2)	119, 122, 123
§362(e)	127
§362(h)	115
§363(a)	217, 220
§363(b)	512
§363(b)(1)	220, 509
§363(c)(1)	220, 509
§363(c)(2)	221, 522
§363(c)(4)	218
§363(e)	400, 401
§363(f)	143, 510, 512
§363(f)(3)	512, 513
§363(f)(4)	512–15
§363(f)(5)	512
§363(k)	515
§363(o)(2)	218, 219
§364	521, 522
§364(b)	521
§364(c)	521, 576
§364(d)	516–19, 521–23, 576, 749
§364(d)(1)	521
§365(c)(2)	282
§501(a)	135
§502	203
§502(a)	135, 140
§502(b)	133, 134, 137
§502(b)(1)	135, 137
§502(b)(2)	137
§502(c)	136
§506	124
§506(a)	124, 140, 148, 513
§506(b)	141
§506(c)	144
§507(a)	136, 576
§507(a)(1)	521
§507(b)	517, 523
§510	666
§510(c)	666
§522(b)	112
§522(d)	112
§524(a)(2)	132
§541(a)	111, 142
§541(a)(1)	644
§541(a)(3)	563
§541(a)(4)	563
§544	554
§544(a)	529, 552–54, 558, 562, 564, 567, 569, 570, 644
§544(a)(1)	412, 554, 555, 558, 567, 724, 725
§544(a)(2)	555, 556, 558
§544(a)(3)	556–58, 560
§545	704, 705
§545(1)	704
§545(2)	705
§545(3)	705
§545(4)	705
§546	584
§546(a)	564
§546(b)	565, 566
§546(b)(1)(B)	440
§546(c)	660
§547	513, 514, 576, 579, 580
§547(b)	577, 583, 585
§547(b)(1)	577
§547(b)(2)	577
§547(b)(3)	578
§547(b)(4)	578, 579
§547(b)(5)	579
§547(c)	577
§547(c)(1)	578
§547(c)(3)	582, 584
§547(c)(3)(B)	583, 584
§547(c)(5)	581, 582
§547(e)	579
§547(e)(1)	580
§547(e)(1)(B)	583
§547(e)(2)	580, 582, 583
§547(e)(2)(A)	582, 583
§547(e)(3)	580, 581
§547(f)	578
§549(a)	576
§551	705
§552	210–12, 219–21, 239, 243
§552(a)	187, 210–12, 214, 216, 236
§552(b)	210–15, 217, 219, 220
§552(f)	227, 228
§552(f)(2)	227, 228, 230
§558	136
§704	112, 562
§726(a)	142, 576
§727(a)(1)	113
§1104(a)	112
§1107	518
§1107(a)	562

§1108   518
§1111(a)   135
§1123   278
§1123(a)   279
§1123(a)(5)(E)   280
§1123(a)(5)(G)   278
§1123(b)(5)   275, 276, 281
§1124   278
§1124(2)   274, 275
§1126(f)   274
§1129(a)(7)   113
§1129(a)(8)   275
§1129(b)   218, 519
§1129(b)(1)   273
§1129(b)(2)(A)   146
§1129(b)(2)(A)(i)   275, 513
§1129(b)(2)(A)(i)(I)   146
§1129(b)(2)(A)(i)(II)   149
§1129(b)(2)(A)(ii)   513
§1141(d)(1)(A)   146
§1302   113
§1322   275, 278, 280
§1322(b)   278, 279
§1322(b)(2)   273, 276, 279, 281
§1322(b)(3)   278
§1322(b)(5)   275, 278
§1322(c)(2)   273
§1322(d)   273
§1322(e)   276
§1325(a)(5)   113, 146
§1325(b)   113
§1326   272
§1328   113
§1328(a)   146

Code of Federal Regulations
12 C.F.R. §204.2(f)(1)(iv)   414
16 C.F.R. §444   228
16 C.F.R. §444.1   228
16 C.F.R. §444.2   229, 230
16 C.F.R. §444.2(3)   230
26 C.F.R. §301.6323(c)-3   742

Internal Revenue Code
§6321   537, 720, 725, 726, 730, 733
§6322   720, 730, 733
§6323   725–27
§6323(a)   720, 722, 725, 727–33, 737
§6323(b)   736, 742
§6323(b)(5)   742
§6323(b)(6)   742
§6323(b)(7)   742
§6323(b)(8)   742
§6323(c)   739–41
§6323(c)(1)   732
§6323(c)(1)(B)   741
§6323(c)(2)(A)   740
§6323(c)(2)(B)   740
§6323(c)(2)(C)   740

§6323(c)(4)   741
§6323(d)   737–40
§6323(e)   750
§6323(f)   720, 726
§6323(g)   723
§6323(h)   737
§6323(h)(1)   24, 133, 723, 728, 738, 740
§6323(h)(6)   728, 729
§7426   729

Uniform Commercial Code (U.C.C.)
§1-102(2)(b)   684
§1-102(37)   225
§1-201   374
§1-201(3)   178
§1-201(9)   677, 678, 680, 682, 685, 687
§1-201(19)   258, 263, 265, 655
§1-201(24)   376
§1-201(28)   343
§1-201(30)   343
§1-201(32)   356, 417, 487, 614
§1-201(33)   356, 417, 487
§1-201(37)   399, 416, 420, 659, 759
§1-201(44)   170, 612, 655
§1-201(44)(b)   170, 575
§1-203   316
§1-203(31)   654
§1-205   178
§1-205(1)   257
§1-208   257, 262
§1-210(19)   664
§2-103(1)(b)   655
§2-103(b)   263
§2-104   655
§2-401   683
§2-401(1)   730
§2-403   172, 655, 660, 663
§2-403(1)   654, 656
§2-403(2)   654, 730
§2-403(3)   654
§2-501(1)   684
§2-502   685
§2-702   660, 663
§2-702(2)   660, 663, 664
§2-702(3)   663, 664
§2-716   685
§4-104   377
§9-101   420, 504
§9-102   363
§9-102, Comment 4   410
§9-102, Comment 4a   213
§9-102, Comment 5   421
§9-102(a)   265, 655
§9-102(a)(2)   61, 178, 179, 220, 417
§9-102(a)(7)   160
§9-102(a)(9)   455
§9-102(a)(11)   376, 416, 420
§9-102(a)(12)   195, 199, 454
§9-102(a)(23)   178, 379, 381, 383
§9-102(a)(27)   436, 437

§9-102(a)(28)	343
§9-102(a)(29)	377, 412, 413
§9-102(a)(30)	374
§9-102(a)(33)	178, 179, 225, 410
§9-102(a)(34)	410, 676
§9-102(a)(34)(D)	213
§9-102(a)(39)	431
§9-102(a)(40)	399, 401
§9-102(a)(41)	394, 409, 627
§9-102(a)(42)	178, 242, 417
§9-102(a)(43)	655
§9-102(a)(44)	225, 413
§9-102(a)(46)	412
§9-102(a)(47)	178, 376, 412, 413, 416
§9-102(a)(48)	178, 410
§9-102(a)(52)	133, 421, 528
§9-102(a)(55)	133
§9-102(a)(64)	193, 194, 199, 203–5, 213, 220, 221, 240, 449, 454
§9-102(a)(64)(C)	194, 219
§9-102(a)(68)	537
§9-102(a)(70)	461
§9-102(a)(73)	177
§9-102(a)(79)	431
§9-102(a)(80)	402
§9-102(b)	624
§9-103	647, 701
§9-103, Comment 3	747
§9-103, Comment 4	647
§9-103(a)	596, 646, 743, 746
§9-103(b)	596, 743, 746
§9-103(b)(1)	378, 646
§9-103(b)(2)	647
§9-103(d)	659
§9-103(e)	646
§9-103(f)	646
§9-103(f)(1)	646
§9-103(g)	648
§9-103A	701
§9-104	377
§9-104(a)(2)	377
§9-104(b)	377
§9-108	360, 362, 363
§9-108(a)	183
§9-108(c)	183
§9-109, Comment 11	230
§9-109(a)	417, 479, 548
§9-109(a)(1)	32, 33, 399, 403, 409
§9-109(a)(1), Comment 2	32
§9-109(a)(2)	700
§9-109(a)(3)	730
§9-109(a)(4)	659
§9-109(b)	403
§9-109(c)	479
§9-109(c)(1)	325, 327
§9-109(d)	479
§9-109(d)(1)	707
§9-109(d)(3)	230, 383
§9-109(d)(8)	225, 383
§9-109(d)(11)	225, 383, 393, 403, 453, 548
§9-109(d)(12)	383, 385
§9-201	566–69, 676, 682, 758
§9-201(a)	178
§9-202	683
§9-203	165, 180, 720
§9-203, Comment 3	167
§9-203, Comment 6	171
§9-203(a)	159, 579, 580, 723, 732
§9-203(b)	159, 162, 163, 579, 580, 594, 723, 732
§9-203(b)(1)	170, 575, 738
§9-203(b)(2)	171, 540, 652
§9-203(b)(3)	160, 169, 531
§9-203(b)(3)(A)	160, 164, 165, 169, 182, 360
§9-203(f)	195, 206, 450
§9-203(g)	403
§9-204	326
§9-204(a)	184
§9-204(c)	188
§9-210	359, 364
§9-301 to 9-307	459, 460
§9-301(1)	411, 460, 469, 483, 489
§9-301(2)	460
§9-302	411
§9-303, Comment 2	484
§9-303(a)	484, 489
§9-303(b)	487, 489
§9-304 to 9-306	464
§9-306(1)	220
§9-307	461, 469, 470
§9-307(a)	463, 464
§9-307(b)	461
§9-307(b)(2)	463
§9-307(b)(3)	463, 464, 469
§9-307(e)	461, 469, 483
§9-308(a)	162, 182, 480, 531, 589, 720, 732
§9-308(b)	360, 700
§9-308(c)	437, 438, 590
§9-308(d)	375
§9-308(e)	416
§9-309	380
§9-309(1)	378, 380–83, 688
§9-310	412
§9-310(a)	162, 390, 399, 700
§9-310(b)(6)	370
§9-310(b)(8)	377
§9-311	480, 584
§9-311, Comment 4	410
§9-311(a)	327
§9-311(a)(1)	326
§9-311(a)(2)	409, 479, 482, 489
§9-311(a)(3)	479
§9-311(b)	327, 449
§9-311(d)	410, 483
§9-312	542

§9-312(a)	162, 374, 376, 416, 420
§9-312(a)(1)	416
§9-312(b)	162
§9-312(b)(3)	374
§9-312(c)	375
§9-313	370, 686
§9-313(a)	162, 374, 375, 409, 412, 416, 417, 420
§9-313(c)	373
§9-314	464
§9-314(a)	455
§9-315	203, 205, 206, 450
§9-315(a)	195, 199, 200, 203, 204, 211, 453, 504, 676
§9-315(a)(1)	196, 198, 676
§9-315(a)(2)	201, 400, 401, 449, 600, 676
§9-315(b)	201
§9-315(c)	204, 453
§9-315(d)	204, 600
§9-315(d)(1)	449, 450, 451
§9-315(d)(3)	451, 453–55
§9-316(a)(2)	465, 489
§9-316(a)(3)	466
§9-316(b)	465, 489
§9-316(d)	487, 489
§9-316(e)	487, 489
§9-317	560
§9-317(a)	738
§9-317(a)(2)	421, 532, 555, 566–69, 580
§9-317(b)	686
§9-317(e)	532, 565, 566, 582, 612
§9-319(a)	659
§9-320, Comment 3	678
§9-320(a)	199, 200, 635, 637, 677–80, 682, 683, 685, 687
§9-320(b)	381, 382, 687, 688
§9-320(e)	686
§9-320(e), Comment 8	686
§9-322	567, 589, 593
§9-322, Comment 5	590
§9-322(a)	591, 593, 598, 602, 609, 700
§9-322(a)(1)	437, 438, 589, 590, 591, 592, 594, 602
§9-322(a)(3)	609
§9-322(g)	700, 701
§9-323	537, 543, 739
§9-323(b)	536, 537, 540–44, 548, 549, 555, 580, 738, 739
§9-323(b)(2)	536
§9-323(d)	635, 686, 687
§9-323(e)	687
§9-324	598, 599
§9-324(a)	599, 600, 658
§9-324(b)	660
§9-324(e)	565, 596, 597, 600, 602, 749
§9-324(g)(1)	598
§9-324(g)(2)	598
§9-324A	701
§9-325	591
§9-325(a)	596
§9-328(1)	374
§9-330	376, 418
§9-330(b)	417
§9-330(d)	374, 416
§9-331(a)	374
§9-332(b)	202
§9-333	707
§9-334	624
§9-334(a)	409
§9-334(b)	395
§9-334(c) to 9-334(g)	399
§9-334(c)	625
§9-334(d)	625
§9-334(e)(1)	625, 626
§9-334(e)(2)	401, 627
§9-334(e)(3)	401
§9-334(e)(3), Comment 4c	626
§9-334(f)(1)	625
§9-334(h)	625
§9-335	483, 602
§9-335(c)	602
§9-335(d)	482, 483
§9-335(e)	482, 483, 602
§9-336(c)	601
§9-338	357, 571
§9-339	593
§9-342	456
§9-401	198, 502, 504, 505, 673
§9-406(a)	62
§9-501	162, 380, 385, 401
§9-501(a)	409
§9-501(a)(1)	320, 464
§9-501(a)(1)(B)	399, 401, 624
§9-501(a)(2)	320, 461, 626
§9-501(b)	402
§9-502	162, 357
§9-502, Comment 2	359, 362
§9-502(a)	344, 354, 357, 401
§9-502(a)(3)	399, 400
§9-502(b)	400, 401, 409, 624
§9-502(b)(4)	399
§9-502(c)	399, 400
§9-502(c)(1)	400
§9-502(d)	450, 590, 593
§9-503	339, 344
§9-503(a)	344
§9-503(a)(4)	339
§9-503(b)	339, 343
§9-503(c)	339, 343
§9-504	360
§9-505	415
§9-506	345, 362, 431
§9-506(a)	339, 344, 348, 358, 436, 437
§9-506(c)	344, 432
§9-507	342, 724
§9-507(a)	448
§9-507(b)	449
§9-507(c)	446–48

§9-509(a)(1)	365	§9-615(d)(2)	495, 631
§9-509(b)	366	§9-617	95
§9-509(b)(2)	452, 454	§9-617(a)	39, 494
§9-510(a)	366	§9-617(a)(3)	637
§9-510(c)	438, 439	§9-617(b)	93
§9-512	431	§9-620	91
§9-512(a)	431	§9-620(a)	92
§9-513(c)	635	§9-620(a)(2)	92
§9-513(c)(1)	431	§9-620(a)(4)	92
§9-513(d)	431	§9-620(c)	92
§9-515	434, 440	§9-620(c)(2)	91
§9-515(a)	432, 436	§9-620(e)	92
§9-515(c)	432, 436–38, 440, 571	§9-623	39, 41, 93
§9-515(d)	435, 436, 438	§9-624(b)	92
§9-515(e)	439	§9-625(b)	431
§9-516	355, 356	§9-625(c)(2)	93
§9-516, Comment 9	357	§9-625(e)(4)	431
§9-516(a)	480	§9-626(a)	95
§9-516(b)	354	§9-626(a)(3)	103, 107
§9-516(b)(3)(B)	432	§9-627(a)	98
§9-516(b)(4)	354	§9-701	460
§9-516(b)(5)	357		
§9-516(b)(5)(A)	354	**Uniform Fraudulent Transfers Act**	
§9-516(b)(5)(B)	354	§3(a)	575
§9-516(b)(5)(C)	354		
§9-516(d)	356	**Uniform Motor Vehicle Certificate**	
§9-517	344, 432	**of Title Act**	
§9-518	366	§2(a)(2)	483
§9-518(c)	366	§2(a)(3)	484
§9-519(c)	336	§4	484
§9-519(h)	433, 434	§4(a)	484, 486
§9-520	354	§9(a)(3)	486
§9-520(a)	357	§10	486
§9-520(b)	355, 432	§11	485, 487
§9-520(b)(5)(C)	355	§13	480, 487
§9-520(c)	355, 571	§20	479, 480
§9-521	157, 354, 432	§20(b)	565, 566
§9-522	433	§20(c)(2)(A)	487
§9-522(a)	433	§21(c)	480
§9-523(c)	439	§21(d)	480, 487
§9-601(a)	247	§26(a)	488
§9-601(a)(1)	68		
§9-602(10)	91		
§9-604(a)(1)	634	**United States Code**	
§9-604(c)	624, 626	7 U.S.C. §196	656
§9-607	62, 267	7 U.S.C. §499a(6)	702
§9-609	48–50, 52–54, 56, 58	7 U.S.C. §499(a)(6)(C)	702
§9-609(a)	502, 657	7 U.S.C. §499c(a)	703
§9-609(a)(2)	55	7 U.S.C. §499e(c)	702
§9-609(b)(2)	55	7 U.S.C. §499e(c)(1)	702
§9-610	48, 92	7 U.S.C. §499e(c)(2)	703
§9-610(a)	39, 68, 94	7 U.S.C. §1631	679
§9-610(b)	68, 92, 95, 97	7 U.S.C. §1631(d)	679
§9-611	95	15 U.S.C. §1671	19
§9-611(c)(1)	93	17 U.S.C. §101	323
§9-612	96	17 U.S.C. §106	323
§9-613	96	17 U.S.C. §201(d)(1)	323
§9-613(1)(E)	96	17 U.S.C. §204	326
§9-615(a)	95, 494, 637	17 U.S.C. §205	324
§9-615(d)(1)	494	17 U.S.C. §205(a)	322, 325

17 U.S.C. §205(c)   323   42 U.S.C. §1983   50
17 U.S.C. §702   326   46 U.S.C. §31321   763
26 U.S.C. §206(d)   234   49 U.S.C. §1403(a)   324
28 U.S.C. §291(b)   321
29 U.S.C. §1056(d)   233, 235   **United States Constitution**
29 U.S.C. §1056(d)(1)   234   Art. I, §8   109

Index

Alphabetization is letter-by-letter (e.g., Subordinated precedes Subordinate liens). References are to page numbers.

Abstract company, 329, 392
Acceleration, 252-58, 271
Acceleration clauses, 252
Accessions, 481-83, 602
Account, 417
Accounts as collateral, 61-63
Acknowledgement, 366, 393
Additions, 206
Adequate protection, 118, 119
Advertising, 76, 77
After-acquired property
    article 9 secured creditors, 593-95
    limits, 652-56
    non-value tracing concept, as, 206
    overview, 183-87
    proceeds, distinguished, 210-20
After-acquired title, 187
Agricultural liens, 699-704
Amending the financing statement, 431, 432
Antideficiency statutes, 84, 85
Arizona Secretary of State's search logic, 337, 338
Article 9 financing statement. *See* Financing statements
Article 9 sale, 39, 91-107
    commercially reasonable sale, 97-103
    failure to sell collateral, 94
    functional analysis, 104, 105
    notice of sale, 95-97
    sale procedure, 92-94
    strict foreclosure, 91, 92
Article 9 security interests. *See* Security interests
Article 9 termination and release, 431, 432
Artisans' liens, 694, 695
Assignment of rents, 47
Assignment of wages, 230
Attachment, 528
Attorneys' liens, 696, 697
Authenticated security agreement, 160-69
Authorized disposition exception, 676, 677
Automobiles. *See* Certificate of title systems

Bankruptcy, 109-54
    abandonment of property, 143
    amount of secured claims, 140-42
    amount of unsecured claim, 137-39
    automatic stay, 114-16
    cash collateral, 220-22

chapter 7, 113, 139
chapter 11. *See* Chapter 11 bankruptcy
chapter 12, 113
chapter 13. *See* Chapter 13 bankruptcy
claims process, 134-37
cramdown, 146
default, 271-84
discharge, 132
future payments, 147-52
lapse/continuation, and, 440
lifting the stay, 116-27
overview, 111-14
payment of unsecured claims, 139, 140
perfection, and, 552, 553
preferences, 575-88. *See also* Preferences
priority, 508-25
proceeds, 220
purchase money security interests, 749
sale procedure, 509-15
selling the collateral, 142, 143
senior liens, power to grant, 515-23
state collection system, contrasted, 109
statutory liens, 704, 705
stay, 114-29
stay violations, 114, 115
strong arm clause, 552-74. *See also* Strong arm clause
subordinate creditors, protection of, 523, 524
supremacy doctrine, 110
terminology, 132-34
tracing, 210-24
triage analogy, 524
trustee's expenses, 143
unsecured creditors, 114-16, 137-40
Bankruptcy purposes, 118
Bankruptcy sale, 509-15
Barter transactions, 449-54
Basket, 338
Black widow spider ad, 266
Blob, The, 199, 200
Boats. *See* Certificate of title systems
Bona fide purchaser of real property, 556-62
Bonds, 313
Book and page number, 335
Breach of the peace, 55-61
Buyer-in-ordinary-course exception, 677-86
Buyer-not-in-ordinary-course exception, 686, 687

Buyers against secured creditors, 673-92.
    See also Sellers against secured
    creditors
  authorized disposition exception, 676,
    677
  buyer-in-ordinary-course exception,
    677-86
  buyer-not-in-ordinary-course excep-
    tion, 686, 687
  buyers of personal property, 675-88
  buyers of real property, 674, 675
  consumer-to-consumer-sale exception,
    687, 688
  farm products exception, 679
  garage sale exception, 687n
  when does buyer become buyer, 680-
    85

Calling the loan, 250
Cars. *See* Certificate of title systems
Carve-out proposal, 764-68
Cash collateral, 220-22
Certificate of incorporation, 340
Certificate of origin, 483
Certificate of title systems, 473-91
  accessions, 481-83
  certificate of origin, 483
  certificate to non-certificate moves,
    488, 489
  certificate, affect of, 477, 478
  interstate movement of chattel, 486-
    89
  non-certificate to certificate moves,
    489
  perfection, 479-81
  registration system, 485
  two-certificates problem, 487, 488
  weakness, 479
  where should vehicle be titled, 483-85
Changes in debtor's name, 445-48
Changes in description of collateral, 448,
    449
Chapter 7 bankruptcy, 113, 139, 562-64
Chapter 11 bankruptcy, 113, 145-47
  claims process, 135
  cramdown, 146
  filing fee, 281
  installment payments, 272
  reinstatement and cure, 274, 275
  statistical study, 140
  strong arm clause, 564, 565
Chapter 12 bankruptcy, 113
Chapter 13 bankruptcy, 113, 145-47
  cramdown, 146
  filing fee, 281
  installment payments, 272
  reinstatement and cure, 275-77
  statistical study, 139, 140
Charging lien, 696

Charter, 340
Chattel paper, 416-18
Choateness doctrine, 740
Choice of remedy, 633-37
Claim, 133
Claims process, 134-37
Cleaners' and launderers' liens, 698, 699
Closing, 428
Collateral
  account (general intangible), 417
  accounts as, 61-63
  cash, 220-22
  characterizing, for purpose of perfec-
    tion, 408-32
  chattel paper, 416-18
  competitions for. *See* Competitions for
    collateral
  description of. *See* Description of col-
    lateral
  exchange of, 449-56
  farm products, 410, 411
  fixtures, 409
  franchises, 238-44
  future income of individuals, 230, 231
  future property as, 236
  instrument, 416
  inventory, 409, 410
  lease, 403, 415, 416
  licenses, 237-44
  multiple items of, 418
  pension rights, 231-36
  personal property, 409
  property of personal nature, 226-30
  realty paper, 416
  repossession of. *See* Repossession of
    collateral
  valuable nonproperty as, 236-44
  what is it, 225-46
Commercial transactions financing
    agreements, 739, 740
Commercially reasonable sale, 97-103
Commingling, 201, 601, 602
Common debtor requirement, 645
Competitions for collateral, 527-775. *See
    also* Priority
  buyers against secured creditors, 673-
    92. *See also* Seller against secured
    creditors
  cross-collateralization, 631-33, 646-48
  federal tax liens, 718-53. *See also* Fed-
    eral tax liens
  future advances. *See* Future advances
  lien creditors versus secured creditors,
    527-51
  marshaling assets, 633-45
  preferences, 575-88. *See also* Prefer-
    ences
  purchase money status. *See* Purchase
    money status
  secured creditors versus secured credi-

Competitions for collateral *(Continued)*
    tors, 589-630. *See also* Secured
    creditors versus secured creditors
  sellers against secured creditors, 652-
    72. *See also* Sellers against secured
    creditors
  statutory liens, 693-717. *See also* Statu-
    tory liens
  strong arm clause, 552-74. *See also*
    Strong arm clause
  trustees in bankruptcy versus secured
    creditors, 552-88
Composite document rule, 165, 166
Consignment, 659
Construction liens, 614-23
Consumer goods, 379
Consumer-to-consumer-sale exception,
    687, 688
Continuation statement, 432-40
Contract for deed, 69
Control, 376, 377, 455
Conversion, 5
Corporate names, 340, 341
Correction statement, 366
Costly contracting hypothesis, 757
Covenants, 711
Cramdown, 146
Credit bidding (foreclosure sale), 85-87
Cross-collateralization, 631-33, 646-48
Cushion of equity, 119, 120

Debentures, 313
Debt, 132
Debt adjustment, 109
Debtor, 343
Debtor-based filing, 462
Debtor's name
  changes in, 445-48
  corporate names, 340, 341
  entity problem, 343
  errors, 343-50
  individual names, 339, 340
  partnership names, 341, 342
  trade name, 339, 342, 343
Deed in lieu of foreclosure, 37
Deed of trust, 38, 133
Default, 247-84
  acceleration, 252-58, 271
  bankruptcy, 271-84
  defined, 247
  enforceability of payment terms, 260-
    65
  procedures after, 265-67
  reinstatement and cure, 258-60,
    272-81
  standard provisions, 248
  state law, 247-70
Default rate, 138
Deficiency, 35

Deposit account, 377
Description of collateral
  changes, 448, 449
  errors, 359, 360
  filing system index, as, 335, 336
  mortgages, 187, 188
  security agreement, 160, 169, 179-83
Deutsche Financial Services, 285, 286
DIP, 509, 564
Discharged debt, 132
Doctrine of equitable mortgages, 169
Doctrine of lender liability, 260
Domicile, 461
Draws, 536
Dry cleaners' and launderers' lien, 698,
    699
Dual filings, 321

Early continuation statements, 439
Echo effect, 463
Effective date of the plan, 147
Elephant rule, 450
Enforceability of payment terms, 260-65
Entity problem, 343
Environmental cleanup lien, 712-14
Equitable assignment, 643, 644
Equitable mortgages, 169
Equitable subordination, 262, 665-68
Errors
  amendment, 432
  continuation statement, 438
  debtor's name, 343-50
  description of collateral, 359, 360
  limited effectiveness filings, 357, 358
  name of secured party, 358, 359
  wrongly accepted filings, 355, 356
  wrongly rejected filings, 356
Escrow company, 329
Examples
  certificate of title, 474, 475
  default provisions, 248
  floorplan agreement, 299-302
  prototypical secured transaction, 285-
    307
  security agreement, 288-96
  vehicle registration, 485
Exceptions to filing requirement, 370-
    89. *See also* Perfection
Exchange of collateral, 449-56
Execution, 528
Execution creditors, 530, 531
Exemption statutes, 17-19
Extension, 109

Farm products, 410, 411
Farm products exception, 679
Federal tax liens, 718-53
  commercial transactions financing

Federal tax liens *(Continued)*
    agreements, and, 739, 740
    construction lenders, and, 741
    creation, 720
    exceptions to general rule, 736-53
    future advances, and, 738, 739
    improvement financing, and, 741
    judgment lien creditors, and, 730-33
    maintaining perfection, 723-27
    nonadvances, and, 749, 750
    obligatory disbursement agreements,
        and, 741, 742
    perfection, 720-23
    purchase money security interests,
        and, 742-49
    purchasers, and, 728-30
    remedies for enforcement, 723
    security interests, and, 728, 737, 738
    statutory liens, and, 742
Fictitious name statute, 342
Field warehousing, 160
File number, 335
Filing systems. *See also* Perfection
    components, 333-38
    costs/fees, 329, 330
    history, 334
    index, 335-37
    motor vehicles. *See* Certificate of title
        systems
    multiplicity, 320-28
    nation-based filing (world economy),
        467-70
    removing filings, 427-32
    search logic, 337, 338
    searching, 319, 328-30, 343
    self-clearing system, 432, 433
    state-based filing, 459, 460
    subsystems, 333
    theory of, 318-20
    where to file, 460-65
Fill-in-the-blanks-later problem, 169
Final judgment of foreclosure, 34
Financing statements, 318
    amendment, 431, 432
    challenges to sufficiency, 344
    continuation statement, 432-40
    debtor's name, 339-43. *See also* Debt-
        or's name
    errors. *See* Errors
    lapse, 432, 433, 439, 440
    other information, 354, 355
    required information, 354
    unauthorized, 364-66
    when effective, 338
First in time is first in right, 312, 318
First to file or perfect, 589-92
Fisherman's pier, 156-58
Fixtures, 393-402
    bankruptcy (bona fide purchaser), 556
    defined, 394, 395, 409

perfection, 395-402
priority issues, 624-27
state law definition, 225
transmitting utilities, 402
Floating lien, 186, 656-58
Floorplan agreement, 299-302
Floorplanning, 286
Foreclosures
    defined, 33
    judicial, 33-38. *See also* Judicial sale
    possession pending, 43-54. *See also*
        Repossession of collateral
    power of sale, 38
    priority, 493-97
    U.C.C. foreclosure, 39. *See also* Article
        9 sale
    weakness as remedy, 267
Franchises, 238-44
Future-advance clauses, 188, 189
Future advances, 188
    article 9 secured creditors, 592, 593
    lien creditors versus secured creditors,
        536-51
    personal property, 536-38
    principal issue, 527
    real property, 543-49
    tax liens, and, 738, 739
Future income of individuals, 230, 231
Future payments (bankruptcy), 147-52
Future property as collateral, 236

Garage keepers' liens, 695, 696
Garage sale exception, 687n
Garnishment, 528
General creditors. *See* Unsecured credi-
    tors
General intangible, 417
General partnerships, 342
Gilmore, Grant, 467
Good faith, 262-65
Good faith purchaser for value, 612,
    652-54
Grace periods, 532, 533, 565, 566

Homestead exemption, 19
Hospital liens, 697

Ideal lien creditor, 554
Illustrations. *See* Examples
Improvement test, 579
Incorporation-based filing, 462
Indentifiability, 201
Index, 335-37
Individual names, 339, 340
Insecurity clause, 253
Inspection, 77, 78
Installment land contract, 68

Installment loans, 249, 250
Instrument, 416
Intended as security doctrine, 30-32
Interpretation of categories of collateral, 178, 179
Inventory, 409, 410
Inventory-secured financing, 594
IRS. *See* Federal tax liens

Judgment creditors, 4, 15, 498. *See also* Lien creditors, Unsecured creditors
Judicial liens, 24
Judicial sale, 33-38, 68-90
  action to set aside sale, 71-76
  advertising, 76, 77
  antideficiency statutes, 84, 85
  caveat emptor, 79
  credit bidding, 85-87
  functional analysis, 87, 88
  hostile situation, 82, 83
  inadequate sale prices, 76-84
  inspection, 77, 78
  notice of sale, 77, 78
  principles, 494-96
  procedure, 69-71
  redemption, 70, 83
  strict foreclosure, 68, 69
  title/condition, 79-82
  weakness as remedy, 267
Junior liens, 313, 501-05, 523, 524

Landlord's lien, 697, 698
Lapse, 432, 433, 439, 440
Launderers' liens, 698, 699
Lease, 403, 415, 416
Lease-security distinction, 415, 416
Lender liability suits, 260-65
Licenses, 237-44
Lien creditors
  future advances. *See* Future advances
  how to become one, 527-29
  ideal, 554
  priority among, 529-31
  secured creditors, versus, 531, 532, 536-51
  tax liens, and, 730-33
Liens
  date when effective, 530
  defined, 24, 312
  federal tax, 718-53. *See also* Federal tax liens
  floating, 186, 656-58
  junior, 313, 501-05, 523, 524
  maritime, 763
  senior, 313, 501-05, 515-23
  statutory. *See* Statutory liens
Limited partnership, 341
Line of credit, 250-52, 281, 282

Lowest intermediate balance rule, 201

Maintaining perfection, 427-91
  bankruptcy, 440
  changes in debtor's names, 445-48
  changes in description of collateral, 448, 449
  continuation statement, 432-40
  exchange of collateral, 449-56
  release, 430, 431
  relocation of debtor, 465-67
  removing filings, 427-32
  satisfaction, 427-29
  tax liens, 723-27
  where to file, 460-65
Maritime liens, 763
Market rate of interest, 148
Marshaling assets, 633-45
Mechanics' liens, 614, 695
Microfiche, 334
Microfilm, 334
Mobile homes. *See* Certificate of title systems
Model Provisions for Production-Money Priority, 701
Modification, 273, 282
Mortgages
  buyers, and, 674, 675
  description of property, 187, 188
  formalities, 172, 173
  future-advance clauses, 188, 189
  judgment liens, and, 498, 613, 614
  nonadvance provisions, 189
  paydown, 430, 431
  priority issues, 498, 608-23
  purchase money, 612, 613
  release, 430, 431
  satisfaction, 428
  security interest, 403
Motor vehicle filing systems, 336. *See also* Certificate of title systems
Motor vehicle registration, 485

Naked possession, 373
Names. *See* Debtor's name
Nation-based filing (world economy), 467-70
Negotiable documents, 374
Nemo dat qui non habet, 171, 653, 656
Nerve centre test, 463
Non-value-tracing concepts, 206, 207
Nonadvance provisions, 189
Nonadvances, 189, 538-43, 749, 750
Nonpurchase-money security interests, 226-30
Nonrecourse secured debt, 133
Nonrecourse unsecured debt, 132
Not-yet-processed documents, 338

Notation of the lien on the certificate of title, 474
Notice of foreclosure sale
  article 9 sale, 95-97
  judicial sale, 77, 78
Notice-race statute, 611
Notice statute, 610

Obligatory advances, 549
Obligatory disbursement agreements, and, 741, 742
Offspring, 206
Optional advances, 549
Ordinary course of business, 677, 678
Ordinary creditors. *See* Unsecured creditors
Out of the money, 313
Owner liability statutes, 478

Partnership names, 341, 342
Pawnshops, 159
Payable on demand, 250
Paydown, 430, 431
Payroll taxes, 718, 719. *See also* Federal tax liens
Pension rights, 231-36
Perfecting the lien, 317
Perfection, 317, 408
  article 9 definition, 531
  bankruptcy, and, 552, 553
  certificate of title system, 479-81
  control, 376, 377
  federal tax liens, 720-23
  filing. *See* Filing systems, Financing statements
  fixtures, 395-401
  maintaining. *See* Maintaining perfection
  method of, 411-18
  motor vehicles, 410
  multi-state transactions, 459-72
  personal property, 411
  place of filing, 408-11
  possession, 370-76
  purchaser-money security interests in consumer goods, 378-83
  security interest in mortgage, 403
Perishable Agricultural Commodities Act (PACA), 701, 704
Personal nature, property of, 226-30
Personal property
  foreclosure. *See* Article 9 sale
  future advances, 536-38
  interests in real property, 402, 403
  nonadvances, 538-43
  perfection, 411
  real property, distinguishable, 409
  repossession of collateral, 47-54

security interests, 654-56
statutory liens, 693-704
title to, 653, 654
Personal property filing systems. *See* Filing systems
Place of filing, 408-11
PMSI, 378, 379, 532, 533
Policy arguments, 754-75
Possession
  competing lienholders, 501-05
  defined, 372, 373
  means of perfections, as, 374-76
  naked, 372
  pending foreclosure, 43-54
  repossession. *See* Repossession of collateral
Possession-gives-notice theory, 370-72
Power of sale foreclosure, 38
Preference, 17
Preference period, 576, 578, 579
Preferences, 575-88
  accounts receivable and inventory, 581, 582
  improvement test, 579
  insolvency, 578
  preference period, 578, 579
  relation-back rules, 582-84
  strategic implementations, 584-86
  when does transfer occur, 579, 580
Preferred ship mortgage, 763
Present value, 147
Priming, 532
Priority, 312-16. *See also* Competitions for collateral
  article 9 security interests. *See* Secured creditors versus secured creditors
  bankruptcy, 508-25
  chronological order, 316-18
  defined, 493
  execution creditors, 530, 531
  foreclosure, 493-97
  inconsistent, 497, 498
  lien creditors, 529, 530
  state law, 493-507
  statutory liens, 706-10
Proceeds
  bankruptcy, 220
  defined, 193-95
  maintaining perfection, 454-56
  purchase money priority, 600, 601
  tracing, 193-205
Product, 205
Profit, 205, 206
Profit a prendre, 205
Proof of claim, 135
Property
  after-acquired. *See* After-acquired property
  personal nature, of, 226-30

Prototypical secured transaction, 155-59, 285-307
Pseudo history (invention of security), 27-29
Purchase money mortgages, 612, 613
Purchase-money security interest (PMSI), 378, 379, 532, 533
Purchase-money security interests in consumer goods, 378-83
Purchase money status
  article 9 secured creditors, 596-601
  automatic perfection (PMSI in consumer goods), 378-83
  bankruptcy, 749
  cross-collateralization, 646-48
  grace period, 532, 533
  inventory, 598-600
  priming, 532
  principal issue, 527
  proceeds, 600, 601
  sellers versus secured creditors, 658
  tax liens, 742-49
Pure notice statute, 610
Pure race statute, 609
Puzzle of secured debt, 755

Race statute, 609
Real estate mortgages. See Mortgages
Real property recording systems, 336, 390-94
Realty paper, 416
Receiver, 45, 46
Reclamation, 660-64
Record, 333
Record-storage problem, 427, 432
Recordation of money judgment, 528
Recourse, 417
Redemption, 70, 83
Registered organization, 461
Reincorporation, 466
Reinstatement and cure, 258-60, 272-81
Relation-back rules, 582-84
Release, 430, 431, 635-37
Relocation of debtor, 465-67
Remedy, 312
Removing filings, 427-32
Rents, 206
Replacements, 206
Replevin action, 48-53, 267
Repossession of collateral, 43-67
  accounts, 61-63
  assignment of rents, 47
  breach of the peace, 55-61
  personal property, 47-54
  possession pending foreclosure, 43-47
  receivers, 45, 46
  replevin action, 48-53
  self-help repossession, 54-63
Residence, 461
Retaining lien, 696
Rewriting the loan, 273

Right to choose remedy, 633-37
Rolling the note, 250
Rollover, 250

Samples. See Examples
Satisfaction, 427-29
Satisfaction of mortgage, 428
Search logic, 337, 338
Searching, 319, 328-30, 343
Secured creditors versus secured creditors, 589-630
  after-acquired property, 593-95
  basic rule (first to file or perfect), 589-92
  commingled collateral, 601, 602
  construction liens, 614-23
  fixtures, 624-27
  future advances, 592, 593
  mortgage against mortgage, 608-23
  purchase money mortgages, 612, 613
  purchase money priority, 596-601
Security, 24-33
Security agreement, 160, 177-79
  description of collateral, 179-83
  example, 288-96
  interpretation of categories of collateral, 178, 179
  nonadvance provisions, 189
  third parties, and, 178
Security interests
  debtor's rights in collateral, 171, 172
  defined, 24, 25
  excluded from coverage of Article 9, 383, 384
  formalities, 159
  lease, 403, 415, 416
  mortgage, 403
  personal property, 654-56
  possession, 159
  tax liens, and, 728, 737, 738
  value, 170, 171
  writing, 160-69
Self-clearing system, 432, 433
Self-help repossession, 54-63
Sellers against secured creditors, 652-72. See also Buyers against secured creditors
  agreement with secured creditor, 665
  consignment, 659
  equitable subordination, 665-68
  purchase-money secured interests, 658
  reclamation, 660-64
  retention of title, 658, 659
  security interests in personal property, 654-56
  seller protections, 658-69
  suppliers against inventory-secured lenders, 656-58
  title to personal property, 653, 654
  unjust enrichment, 668, 669
Senior liens, 313, 501-05, 515-23

Service company, 328, 329
Single action rules, 634
Single payment loans, 250
Spider ad, 266
State-based filing, 459, 460
Statute of Frauds, 166, 167
Statutory liens, 693-717
    agricultural liens, 699-704
    artisans' liens, 694, 695
    attorneys' liens, 696, 697
    bankruptcy, 704, 705
    construction liens, 614-23
    dry cleaners' and launderers' lien, 698, 699
    environmental cleanup lien, 712-14
    garage keepers' liens, 695, 696
    hospital liens, 697
    landlord's lien, 697, 698
    priority, 706-10
    secured creditor protections, 711-14
    tax liens, and, 742
Stay
    automatic, 114-16
    lifting, 116-27
    senior lienholders, 524
    strategic uses, 127-29
Strict foreclosure
    article 9 sale, 91, 92
    judicial sale, 68, 69
Strong arm clause, 552-74
    bona fide purchaser of real property, 556-62
    chapter 7 trustees, 562-64
    chapter 11 debtors in possession, 564, 565
    complexity of language, 553
    creditor with execution returned unsatisfied, 555
    grace periods, 565, 566
    hypothetical persons, 553
    ideal lien creditor, 554
    judicial lien creditor, 554, 555
    perfection and bankruptcy, 552, 553
    resistance to, 566-71
Subordinate liens, 313, 501-05, 523, 524
Substitute lender, 282
Substitutions, 206
Supremacy doctrine, 110

Tax liens. See Federal tax liens
Termination statement, 431
Theoretical agreements, 754-75
Time value of money, 147
Title company, 329, 392
Tort first system, 760-62
Tracing, 192
    bankruptcy, 210-24
    commingling, 201
    indentifiability, 201
    lowest intermediate balance rule, 201

non-value-tracing concepts, 206, 207
    offspring, 206
    proceeds, 193-205
    product, 205
    profit, 205, 206
    rents, 206
    unauthorized sale, 196-200
Tract index, 335, 336
Trade name, 339, 342, 343
Transformations in value. See Tracing
Transmitting utilities, 402
Triage analogy, 524
True lease, 415, 416
Two-certificates problem, 487, 488

U.C.C. foreclosure, 39. See also Article 9 sale
U.C.C.-1. See Financing statements
Unauthorized financing statements, 364-66
Unauthorized sale, 196-200
Uniform Motor Vehicle Certificate of Title and Anti-theft Act (UMVCTA). See Certificate of title systems
Unjust enrichment, 668, 669
Unsecured creditors
    bankruptcy, and, 114-16, 137-40
    compelling payment, 5-19
    defined, 3-5
    limitations, 15-19
    marshaling, 644
    rights, 25
    why one assumes the role, 25

Valuable nonproperty as collateral, 236-44
Value, 170, 171
Value of security, 177
Value-tracing concepts, 192-206. See also Tracing
Void title rule, 653

Waiver
    sales of livestock, 200
    statutory liens, 712
Whole, 481
With recourse, 417
Wood, Philip R., 468
World filing systems, 467-70
Writ of assistance, 35
Writ of possession, 35
Writing requirement (security interests), 160-69
Wrongful sale, 38
Wrongly accepted filings, 355, 356
Wrongly rejected filings, 356

Zero-sum hypothesis, 755, 756